AF516214

DIRECTORY OF PUBLISHERS AND BOOKSELLERS IN INDIA

Third Edition
Revised, Updated and Enlarged

Compiled by
K.R. Gupta

Published by

ATLANTIC

PUBLISHERS & DISTRIBUTORS (P) LTD

7/22, Ansari Road, Darya Ganj,
New Delhi-110002
Phones : +91-11-23273880, 23275880, 23280451
Fax : +91-11-23285873
Web : www.atlanticbooks.com
E-mail : info@atlanticbooks.com

Branch Office
5, Nallathambi Street, Wallajah Road,
Chennai-600002
Phones : +91-44-64611085, 32413319
E-mail : chennai@atlanticbooks.com

ISBN 978-81-269-1071-7

Printed in India at Nice Printing Press, A-33/3A, Site-IV,
Industrial Area, Sahibabad, Ghaziabad, U.P.

PREFACE

I have great pleasure to place in the hands of the readers revised, updated and enlarged edition of the *Directory of Publishers and Booksellers in India*. The revised edition contains much larger number of addresses of publishers and booksellers. Moreover, much more information has been provided about them and their field of operation.

It is hoped that the *Directory* in its present form would be highly useful to publishers and booksellers in mailing their publicity material. The *Directory* would also be useful to librarians for getting information about publishers and booksellers in India for the procurement of books.

Apart from the publishers and booksellers, the *Directory* would be useful to companies dealing in products and services used by the publishing & book selling industry, for example, paper-manufacturers & distributors, computers—software & hardware; packaging machinery & materials; printers & binders; EPABX-manufacturers & distributors; office furniture and equipment; photocopy machines and supplies; slotted angle racks, etc.

The compilation of such a voluminous directory is a time consuming job and in the course of time some changes take place and therefore some information in this *Directory* may not be up-to-date.

While every possible care has been taken to avoid mistakes, neither the publishers of this *Directory*, nor I accept responsibility for any mistakes which may still have crept in.

I will be grateful if any mistakes in the *Directory* are brought to my notice and the same would be corrected in the next edition.

K.R. GUPTA

CONTENTS

ABBREVIATIONS

Academic	Acad.
Agriculture	Agri.
Architecture	Arch.
Behavioural	Beh.
Bio-science	Bio.Sci.
Bookseller	B.S.
Branch Manager	Br.Man.
Branches	Br.
Business Interest	Bus.Intt.
Chief Executive	Ch.Exe.
Commerce	Comm.
Computers	Comp.
Director	Dir.
Distributors	Dist.
Economics	Eco.
Education	Edu.
E-mail	@
Engineering	Engg.
English Literature	Eng.Litt.
Environment	Env.
Established	Estd.
Export Division	Exp.Div.
Exporter	Exp.
General	Gen.
Geography	Geo.
Head of Organisation	Hd.Org.
History	Hist.
Importer	Imp.
Institutional Suppliers	Insti.Sup.
Library Supplier	L.S.
Management	Mang.
Marketing	Mkt.
Mathematics	Math.
Medical, Medicine	Med.
Mobile	▮
Partners	Prt.
Personnel	Hd.Org.
Philosophy	Phil.
Phones	✆
Political Science	Pol.Sci.
President	Pres.
Proprietor	Prop.
Psychology	Psych.
Publisher/s	Pub.
Publisher's Representative	Pub.'s Rep.
Registered Office	Rgd.Off.
Religion	Rel.
Retailer	Rt.
Road	Rd.
Sciences	Sci.
Scientific	Sci.
Secretary	Secy.
Showroom	Sh.
Social Sciences	Soc.Sci.
Sociology	Sol.
Specialisation	Spl.
Street	St.
Subjects	Sub.
Subscription Agent	Sub.Ag.
Technical, Technology	Tech.
Website	e
Wholesaler	WS

PEACOCK BOOKS

AN IMPRINT OF ATLANTIC PUBLISHERS & DISTRIBUTORS (P) LTD.

PEACOCK BOOKS, an imprint of Atlantic Publishers & Distributors brings to you the works of great writers of the world like Shakespeare, Daniel Defoe, Charles Dickens, Thomas Hardy, Jane Austen, D.H. Lawrence, Joseph Conrad, Virginia Woolf, Henry James and a host of other masters. The books are beautifully produced as per the international standards, with glossy covers and at prices that every one can afford. Complete, unabridged and authentic versions have been reproduced in size and style of type designed for easy reading, beautiful looks and are suitable for lasting collection. The chosen classics in this series have eternal value and would continue to be of interest for the present and future generations.

BRAM STOKER

...... Dracula 80.00

CHARLES DARWIN

...... The Origin of Species 85.00

CHARLES AND MARY LAMB

...... Tales from Shakespeare 75.00

CHARLES DICKENS

...... Great Expectations 90.00
...... Hard Times 65.00
...... Oliver Twist 85.00
...... A Tale of Two Cities 85.00

CHARLOTTE BRONTË

...... Jane Eyre 85.00

D.H. LAWRENCE

...... Lady Chatterley's Lover 80.00
...... The Rainbow 85.00
...... Sons and Lovers 85.00
...... Women in Love 85.00

DANIEL DEFOE

...... Moll Flanders 60.00
...... Robinson Crusoe 75.00

EDITH WHARTON

...... The Age of Innocence 75.00

EMILY BRONTË

...... Wuthering Heights 85.00

F. SCOTT FITZGERALD

...... The Great Gatsby 60.00

GEORGE ELIOT

...... Adam Bede 85.00
...... The Mill on The Floss 95.00
...... Silas Marner 60.00

GUSTAVE FLAUBERT

...... Madame Bovary 85.00

H.G. WELLS

...... The Invisible Man 60.00
...... The Time Machine 60.00

...... Joseph Andrews 75.00

HENRY JAMES

...... The Ambassadors 85.00
...... The Portrait of a Lady 85.00

JAMES JOYCE

...... Dubliners 60.00
...... A Portrait of the Artist as a Young Man 75.00

JANE AUSTEN

...... Emma 90.00
...... Mansfield Park 80.00
...... Northanger Abbey 60.00
...... Persuasion 70.00
...... Pride and Prejudice 75.00
...... Sense and Sensibility 75.00

JONATHAN SWIFT

...... Gulliver's Travels 90.00

A. MUKHERJEE & CO. (P) LTD.
2, Bankim Chatterjee St., Kolkata-700073 (West Bengal)

A. SAGAR BOOK HOUSE
H-60, St. No. 3, Laxmi Nagar, Delhi-110092
✆ (O) 22427658, 22469169 (R) 23281065
✉ asagarbh@yahoo.com
Estd.: 1988; **Prt.:** Vinod Verma, Ajay Verma; **Bus.Intt.:** Pub., WS, L.S. & Rt.; **Spl.:** Acad., Beh.Sci., Soc.Sci., Comm., Sci., Tech., Fiction & Rare

A. THREE BOOK CENTRE
4, Sharavati Buildings, Balmatta, Mangalore-575001 (Karnataka)

A&A PERIODICAL SUBSCRIPTION AGENCY (P) LTD.
4735/32, 2nd Floor, Prakash Deep Building (Near Punjab National Bank), Ansari Road, Darya Ganj, New Delhi-110002
✆ 23240257, Fax: 91-11-23240273
✉ aasub.delb.vsnl.net.in
Estd.: 1980; **Hd.Org.:** Arvind Kumar Jain; **Bus.Intt.:** Sub.Ag. (Indian & Foreign Journals); **Spl.:** Sci. & Tech., Med.

A.A. BOOK GALLERY
1241-A, Sri Amman Complex, Only Vimal Building, Big Bazaar St., Coimbatore-641001 (Tamil Nadu)
✆ 2304650, 5358713 ▮ 9842277764, 9842222764, 9842207764,
✉ aabookshop@rediffmail.com
Hd.Org.: M. Prabu; **Bus.Intt.:** WS, L.S.

A.A. HUSSAIN & CO.
5-8-551, Arastu Trust Building, Abid Rd., Hyderabad (Andhra Pradesh)
✆ 23202724, Fax: 040-23203724
Estd.: 1929; **Prt.:** Asif Husan Arastu, Mannan Hussain; **Bus.Intt.:** Rt. of Gen. & Trade, Greeting Cards and Children Books (Indian & Foreign Books)

A.B. BOOK AGENCY
31/1, 4th Cross, Malleswaram, Bangalore-560003 (Karnataka)
✆ 3317189, Fax: 3348390
✉ abba@bgl.vsnl.net.in
Prop.: N. Balaji; **Bus.Intt.:** L.S.; **Spl.:** Humanities & Soc.Sci., Sci., Engg. & Tech., Med.Sci.

A.B.C. BOOK COMPANY
32, Venus Apartment, Inder Enclave, Near Pira Garhi Chowk, New Delhi-110087
✆ (R) 25257063 ▮ 9811006273
Estd.: 1999; **Prop.:** Anil Moolchandani; **Bus.Intt.:** Rt., WS, Pub.'s Rep. & L.S.; **Spl.:** Beh.Sci., Comm., Tech. & Fiction Books

A.B.C. PUBLISHERS & DISTRIBUTORS
4226/1, Bhargava Lane, Ansari Road, Darya Ganj, New Delhi-110002
✆ 23278399, Fax: 91-11-23283380
✉ abcpd@rediffmail.com
Hd.Org.: P.D. Arora; **Bus.Intt.** Dist.; **Spl.:** General Books, Dictionaries, Encyclopaedias, Reference Books, Fiction, Books on Cookery, Self-improvement, etc.

A.B.C. PUBLISHING HOUSE
72-A, Shankar Market, Connaught Circus, New Delhi-110001
✆ 23314900
Estd.: 1971; **Prop.:** C.P. Choudhri; **Bus.Intt.:** Pub.; **Spl.:** Pol. & Military Sci.

A.B.C. SERVICES
409/410, Brigade Towers, Brigade Rd., Bangalore-560025 (Karnataka)
✆ 2277892/93, Fax: 2217894

A.B.D. PUBLISHERS & OXFORD BOOK CO.
B-46, Natraj Nagar, Imliwala Phatak, Jaipur-302015 (Rajasthan)
✆ (O) 2594705 (R) 2762072, Fax: 2597527
Prop.: G.K. Agarwal; **Bus.Intt.:** Pub., L.S., WS; **Spl.:** Humanities & Soc.Sci., Mang. & Comm., Sci., Fiction & Gen.

A.B.M. (ASSAM BUSINESS MACHINES) CO.
Guwahati Club, Guwahati-781001 (Assam)
Estd.: 1968; **Prop.:** S.K. Barkataki; **Bus.Intt.:** Pub.; **Spl.:** School Text and Children Books in Assamese & English

A.B.P. (P) LTD.
Third Floor, Express Building, 9-10 Bahadur Shah Zafar Marg, New Delhi-110002
✆ 23702170-79, Fax: 91-11-23702061
www.businessworld.in
Hd.Org.: D. Puskayastha; **Bus.Intt.:** Pub.; **Spl.:** **Business World** Magazine

A.B.R. ENTERPRISE
4, Daya Ram Naskar Lane, Post Ghvsuri, Howrah-7 (West Bengal)
Estd.: 1993; **Prop.:** R. Basu; **Bus.Intt.:** L.S.; **Spl.:** All Sub.

A.B.S. BOOK DISTRIBUTORS
60/15, Ramjas Rd., Karol Bagh, New Delhi-110005

A.B.S. PUBLICATIONS
27, First Floor, Modern Market, M.G. Rd., Jalandhar City-144001 (Punjab)

✆ 181-2221104, 2220425
Estd.: 1984; **Prt.:** Rajeev Kohli; **Bus.Intt.:** Pub. & L.S.; **Spl.:** Eng.Litt., Hist. & Pol. Sci. Books in English only

A.B.V.T. PUBLICATIONS (ANANDA BUDDHA VIHARA TRUST)
Sainagar, Tukaram Gate, North Lallaguda, Secunderabad-500017 (Andhra Pradesh)
✆ 27732421, Fax: 040-2842477
Hd.Org.: Sangharakshita Mahathera

A.C. BROTHERS
181, Ravi Sadan Civil Lines, Etawah-206001 (Uttar Pradesh)
Bus.Intt.: B.S. & Pub.

A.C. CHAWLA & SONS
4787/23, Ansari Rd., Darya Ganj, New Delhi-110002

A.C.E. PUBLICATIONS
14, Goabagan St., Kolkata-700006 (West Bengal)
✆ 033-23502532
Bus. Intt.: Pub.; **Spl.:** Fictions from Indian and Foreign and also Children's books in Bengali

A.C.E. PUBLISHING HOUSE
B-1/41, Phase-II, Ashok Vihar, New Delhi-110052

A.D. PUBLICATIONS
8/3, Roop Nagar, Delhi-110007

A.D.R. PUBLICATIONS
G-51, Saket, New Delhi-110017

A.H. WHEELER & CO. LTD.
15, Lal Bahadur Shastri Marg, Allahabad-200001 (Uttar Pradesh)
✆ 23312629, 23318357 (R) 26858306, Fax: 23724798
✉ wheelerbooks@mantraonline.com
www.wheelerbooks.com
Estd.: 1958; **Pres.:** Alok Banerjee
Br.: 6, Averest House, Plot No. 13, Sector-1, Nural, Navi Mumbai-400076 ✆ 27708969
• 18, Netaji Subhash Rd. Kolkata-700001 ✆ 22204945, 22481564, Fax: 22481564
Bus.Intt.: Pub., WS, L.S. & Rt., Imp., Exp.; **Spl.:** Humanities & Soc. Sci., Sci. & Tech., Med., Gen. & Fiction etc.

A.I.E.TS.COM. PVT. LTD.
B-32, Basement, Shivalik Rd., Shivalik, Malviya Nagar, New Delhi-110017
✆ 26691021, 26691713
✉ aiets@rediffmail.com
Ch.Exe.: Mr. Avinash Agarwal; **Bus.Intt.:** Pub.; **Spl.:** MBA-CAT, MCA, Med. LTP CBSE-PMT, CPMT, DPMY, AIIMS, P.PMT, Mahe, UP.PMT, K-CET etc., Engg.: CBSE-PET, CRACK-JEE, IIT-Mains, DCE, UP Set, K-Set

AITBS PUBLISHERS INDIA
J5/6, Krishan Nagar, Delhi-110051
✆ 22549313, Fax: 91-11-22543416
✉ aitbs@vsnal.com
Hd.Org.: Virender Kumar Arya
Bus.Intt.: Pub.; **Spl.:** Textbooks on Economics, Management, Medicine, Dentistry, Nursing, Litt., Mathematics

A.K. AGENCIES
Shop No. 11, Bhanumati Society, P.O. Bangur Nagar, Goregaon (W), Mumbai-400090 (Maharashtra)
✆ (O) 28737347 (R) 28661249
✉ agrawalajay@indya.com
Estd.: 1974 **Bus.Intt.:** B.S.; **Spl.:** Adv. Books for Lib., Gen. Books, Indology

A.K. BOOKS
6, Bankim Chatterjee St., Kolkata-700073 (West Bengal)

A.K. BOOK DISTRIBUTORS
18, Jain Bhawan. Opp. N.B.C., Shantinagar, Jaipur-302006 (Rajasthan)
✆ 2220590
Estd.: 1987; **Prop.:** A.K. Jain; **Bus.Intt.:** B.S.; **Spl.:** Adv. Books for Lib. and Gen. Books

A.K. EXPORTS
Mumbai (Maharashtra)
✆ 26327007
✉ akexports@rediffmail.com

A.K. MISHRA AGENCIES
Banka Bazar, Cuttack-753002 (Orissa)

A.K. SARCAR PUBLICATIONS PVT. LTD.
1/1A, Bankim Chatterjee St., Kolkata-700073 (West Bengal)

A.M. BOOK STALL
Stall No. 9, College St., Kolkata-700073 (West Bengal)

A. 'N' B. PUBLISHERS PVT. LTD.
O-11, Lajpat Nagar-II, New Delhi-110024

A.P. PUBLISHERS
19, Books Market, Chowk Adda Tanda, Jalandhar-144008 (Punjab)
✆ (O) 2404352, 2405855 (R) 2211102
Estd.: 1980; **Hd.Org.:** Ashok Kumar Kalra
Br.: 1936/10, Chuna Mandi, Paharganj, New Delhi ✆ 23559376
Bus.Intt.: Pub.; **Spl.:** Comp., Health, Phy., Edu., Sports

A.P.C. BOOKS
1569/30, Naiwala, Karol Bagh, New Delhi-110005

✆ 28752604, Fax: 91-11-28756921
✉ apcmedicalbooks@yahoo.co.in
Hd.Org.: S.P. Gupta
Bus.Intt.: Pub.; **Spl.:** School Textbooks

A.P.C. PUBLICATIONS (P) LTD.
8798/7, Rani Jhansi Rd., Karol Bagh,
PB No. 2679, New Delhi-110005
✆ 23517879, 23624945, Fax: 23513456
✉ apc@apcbooks.com
Dir.: S.K. Dulta; **Bus.Intt.:** Pub., Dist. and Insti.Sup.; **Spl.:** Agri., Forestry, Phil. Books in Eng. & Hindi

A.P.H. PUBLISHING CORPORATION
4435-36/7, Ansari Road, Darya Ganj,
Delhi-110002
✆ 23285807, Fax: 23274050
✉ aphbooks@vsnl.net
www.aphbooksindia.com
Hd.Org.: S.B. Nangia

A.P.M. PUBLICATION
F-160, Mangal Bazar, Laxmi Nagar,
Delhi-110092
✆ 22445052
Estd.: 1972; **Hd.Org.:** R.K. Goyal

A.R. BOOK AGENCY
K-371, Kangra Niketan, Vikas Puri,
New Delhi-110018
✆ 25524515, Fax: 25506207
Estd.: 1989; **Hd.Org.:** Anil Sood, **Bus.Intt.:** WS, L.S. & Rt.

A.S. BOOKS DISTRIBUTORS
4230/1, Ansari Rd., Darya Ganj,
New Delhi-110002
✆ (O) 35986686 (R) 27515113, Fax: 23280028
Estd.: 2001; **Prop.:** Lalit Joshi
Br.: B/403, Rohini Awantika Sector 1st,
New Delhi-110085
Bus.Intt.: B.S., L.S.; **Spl.:** Comp., Mang., Law

A.S. PRAKASHAN
D-106, Saket, Meerut-250004 (Uttar Pradesh)
✆ 0121-2654661, 2663838, Fax: 0121-2663838
Estd.: 1964; **Prt.:** A.K. Mittal, S.K. Mittal;
Bus.Intt.: Pub.; **Spl.:** Sci. & Tech.

A TO Z BOOKS
5/1864, IIIrd Floor, Mahalaxmi Market,
Bhaghirath Place, Chandni Chowk,
Delhi-110006
✆ 23869513
✉ rkdc@mantraonline.com
Prt.: R.R. Kand Pal, Uma Kant Bansal;
Bus.Intt.: Rt.; **Spl.:** Tech. Books

A.V.I. BOOKS
Guwahati (Assam)
✉ avibooks2003@rediffmail.com

A.V.I. BOOKS (P) LTD.
7/28, (Basement), Mahavir Gali, Ansari Rd.,
Darya Ganj, New Delhi-110002
✆ (O) 23271887, 23259151 (R) 26484854
▮ 9811325467, Fax: 23262021
✉ avibooks@rediffmail.com
Estd.: 2000; **Hd.Org.:** Sheela Jagasia, Kamal Jagasia; **Bus.Intt.:** Rt., WS, Pub., Sub.Ag., Pub.'s Rep., L.S.; **Spl.:** Tech. & Sci., Journals and Magazines

A-1 BOOK CENTRE
Station Rd., Secunderabad-500003
(Andhra Pradesh)
✆ 27703533, 23532663

AACHARYA SHRI ENTERPRISES
Vivekanand Hospital, Patparganj Rd., Khureji,
Delhi-110051
✆ 31042570, Fax: 22424057
✉ acharyashri@bol.net.in
www.mudrasforhealing.com
Hd.Org.: Acharya Vikramaditya; **Bus.Intt.:** Pub.; **Spl.:** Indian occult Sci. and Traditions, as well as on Astrology and Yoga

AADHAR PRAKASHAN PRIVATE LIMITED
SCF-267, Sector 16,
Panchkula-134113 (Haryana)
✆ 2566952, 5048541, Fax: 91-172-2570725
✉ aadhar_prakashan@yahoo.com
www.aadharprakashan.com
Hd.Org.: Puja Sardana
Bus.Intt.: Pub.; **Spl.:** Hindi Language Books on Contemporary Indian Litt., Soc.Sci. and History

AADHUNIK PUSTAK UDYOG
WZ-61, Shadipur Main Bazar,
New Delhi-110008
Bus.Intt.: Pub. & Dist.

AAKAR BOOKS
28-E, Pocket IV, Mayur Vihar, Phase-I,
Delhi-110091
✆ (O) 22795505 (R) 22716654,
Fax: 91-11-22795641
✉ aakarbooks@gmail.com
www.aakarbooks.com
Estd.: 1991; **Prop.:** Mrs. Anupam Saxena, Mr. K.K. Saxena
Sh.: 49, Shiv Mandir Lane, Pratap Nagar, Mayur Vihar, Phase-I, Delhi-110091
Bus.Intt.: Pub., L.S., Mail order & Exp.;
Spl.: Soc.Sci., Mang., Humanities, Art, Archaeology, Com.Sc. & Tech. Gen. & Reference Books

AAKAR IMPEX
Sharda Chambers No. 2-206, Keshvaji Naik
Rd. No. 27A, Masjid Bunder (W),
Mumbai-400009 (Maharashtra)

✆ 23773006, Fax: 91-22-23773005
Hd.Org.: Suresh Shiudkar; **Spl.:** Rel. Books, Stationery Articles

AAKARSHAN COMPUTER SYSTEMS PVT. LTD.
B-56, Lajpat Nagar-I,
New Delhi-110024
✆ 26840453, 26827005,
Fax: 91-11-26839133
✉ acs_b56@hotmail.com
Ch.Exe.: R. Srinivasan; Spl.: Edu. CDs, Stickers, Comp. Books etc.

AAKASH PUBLISHERS
MU-61D, Vishakha Enclave,
Pitampura, Delhi-110034
Hd.Org.: V.K. Sharma; **Bus.Intt.:** Pub.; **Spl.:** Novels, Stories, Criticisms, etc.

AAKIF BOOK DEPOT
3243, Kucha Tara Chand, Darya Ganj,
New Delhi-110002
✆ 23257189, Fax: 23265480
✉ aakif@del3.vsnl.net.in
www.aakif.com
Estd.: 1985; **Prop.:** S.M. Zafar Ali;
Bus.Intt.: Pub., WS, L.S. & Rt., Imp., Exp.;
Spl.: Humanities & Soc.Sci., Gen. & Fiction, Law

AAKRITI PRAKASHAN
C-5/S-2, East Jyoti Nagar, Durgapuri Chowk,
Shahdara, Delhi-110032
✆ 22110879
Hd.Org.: Arun Maheshwari; **Bus.Intt.:** Pub.;
Spl.: Books in Hindi and English

AALEKH PRAKASHAN
V-8, Navin Shahdara, Delhi-110032
✆ 22277625, 22290582, Fax: 22290582
✉ alekh@mantraonline.com
Hd/Org.: Umesh Chandra Agarwal;
Bus.Intt.: Pub.; **Spl.:** Hindi Language Books on Language, Journalism, Dictionaries, etc.

AAMIR KITAAB GHAR
2075, Masjid Nahar Khan, Kucha Chelan,
Darya Ganj, New Delhi-110002
✆ 23283494, Fax: 26987191
Hd.Org.: Syed Asad Hussain; **Bus.Intt.:** Pub.; **Spl.:** Indian Language Books, Med. and Unani

AAPKI SAMASYA HAMARA SAMADHAN
Delhi
✆ 23278761, 22170794
✉ arihant-int@vsnl.com

AAR ESS PUBLISHING HOUSE
Barbar Shah, Srinagar, Kashmir-190001
(Jammu and Kashmir)
✆ 278049
Estd.: 1982; **Prop.:** Yehya Rafiqi;
Bus.Intt.: WS, L.S. & Rt.

AAR PEE BOOK SERVICE
B-19, Vardhman Jamuna Plaza, C-Block
Commercial Complex, Yamuna Vihar,
Delhi-110053

AARATI BOOK CENTRE
Super Market, Shop No. 5, Aurangpura,
Aurangabad-431001 (Maharashtra)
✆ 0240-3233366
Estd.: 1989; **Prop.:** P.S. Swami
Br.: Aarati Prakashan, 9, Jai Hind Colony,
Aurangabad-431001 ✆ 3239611; **Estd.:** 1991
Bus.Intt.: Pub., Rt.; **Spl.:** Edu. Help Books in Marathi and English

AARATI GENERAL STORES
Beldari Chak, Masaurhi, Patna-804452 (Bihar)
Bus.Intt.: Pub. and B.S.

AARTI PRAKASHAN
C-14, First Floor, Amar Colony Market,
Lajpat Nagar-IV, New Delhi-110024
✆ 26441516, 26485210, Fax: 91-11-26418721
✉ aartiprakashan@hotmail.com
Hd.Org.: M.L. Chowdhary; **Bus.Intt.:** Pub.;
Spl.: Children's textbooks in English and Hindi

AARATI PUBLICATIONS
M-39-D, 7th Cross St., Basant Nagar,
Chennai-600009 (Tamil Nadu)

AARATI PUBLISHERS
248, Hans House, Between 16 & 17 Cross,
Sampige Rd., Malleswaram,
Bangalore-560003 (Karnataka)
✆ 080-2362777, 2364488
Estd.: 1989; **Hd.Org.:** Dr. Nirupama;
Bus.Intt.: Pub.; **Spl.:** Children Books, Novels, Short Stories and Translation Works

AARTU BOOK SHOP
Zangsti Rd., Leh. (Jammu and Kashmir)

AASHI BOOKS INTERNATIONAL
K-67, Laxmi Nagar, Delhi-110092
✆ (O) 91-11-55258984 (R) 22513962
9871758717
Hd.Org.: Ajay Sharma; **Bus.Intt.:** L.S.

AARUSHI BOOKS
4, Super Bazar Subway, Connaught Circus,
New Delhi-110001
✆ 9118085090, Fax: 91-11-23326744
✉ aarushibooks@hotmail.com
Hd.Org.: Sanjeev Ohri; **Bus.Intt.:** Pub. & Dist.; **Spl.:** Indian Art, Culture, Fiction Spiritualism

AATHMEEYA YATHRA PUBLICATIONS
Manjady, Thiruvalla-689105 (Kerala)

AAVISHKAR PUBLISHERS & DISTRIBUTORS
807, Vyas Building, Chaura Rasta,
Jaipur-302003 (Rajasthan)

✆ 2578159, Fax: 91-141-2568159
✉ aavishkarbooks@hotmail.com
www.pointerpublishers.com
Hd.Org.: Prem Chand Bakliwal; **Bus.Intt.**: Pub. and Dist.; **Spl.**: Eng. Books on Art, Sci. and Comm.

ABANI BOOK STALL
10/C/H/10, Upendra Banerjee Lane,
Kolkata-700054 (West Bengal)

ABEE BOOKS
V-61, West Patel Nagar, New Delhi-110008
✆ (R) 25405329
Prop.: Sanjay Dhawan; **Bus.Intt.**: L.S. & Rt.;
Spl.: Sci., Med., Tech.

ABHAY PUSTAK BHANDAR
Bhore Complex, Mahavir Chowk,
Nanded-431601 (Maharashtra)
✆ 02462-240265 ▮ 9822192490
Hd.Org.: Abhay Kotalwar

ABHIBYANJANA PRAKASHAN
B-70-72, DSIDC Complex, Lawrence Rd.,
Delhi-110035
✆ 27180701, 25191287
Prop.: Jaideep Singh; **Bus.Intt.**: Pub.;
Spl.: Litt., Sol., Hist., Gen. Knowledge and Current Affairs

ABHIJAT PRAKASHAN
251, Subhash Rd., Jaisinghpur, Distt.
Kolhapur-416114 (Maharashtra)

ABHIJEET PUBLICATIONS
2/46, Tukhmeerpur Extension,
Delhi-110094
✆ 65698474
✉ abhijeetpublication@gmail.com
Hd.Org.: J.K. Singh
Bus.Intt.: Pub.; **Spl.**: Academic and Reference Books on Soc.Sci. and Humanities

ABHIMANI PUBLICATIONS
No. 2/4, Dr. Rajkumar Rd., Rajajinagar,
Bangalore-560010 (Karnataka)
✉ abhimani@bgl.vsnl.net.in
Bus.Intt.: Pub. and B.S.

ABHIMANYU PRAKASHAN
C-19, C.C. Colony, Opp. Rana Paratap Bagh,
Delhi-110007
✆ 27119316, 27466476
Hd.Org.: Abhimanyu Kumar Gupta
Bus.Intt.: Dist. and L.S.; **Spl.**: Books to Schools, Colleges and Other Educational Institutions

ABHINANDANA PUBLICATIONS
28-24, Jaleel St., Karl Marx Rd.,
Vijayawada-520002 (Andhra Pradesh)
✆ (R) 0886-264011
Estd.: 1990; **Prop.**: B. Babjee
Bus.Intt.: Pub.; **Spl.**: Fiction, Non-Fiction and Edu. Books in Telugu

ABHINAV BHARATI PRAKASHAN
C/o Dr. G.M. Parikh, 19, Atmajyoti Society,
Subhanpura, Baroda-390007 (Gujarat)

ABHINAV PRAKASHAN
1st Floor, 56, Kutchery Rd.,
Ajmer-305001 (Rajasthan)
✆ (O) 2431158 (R) 2421687
Estd.: 1976; **Hd.Org.**: Anil Goyal;
Bus.Intt.: Pub. and B.S.; **Spl.**: Fiction, Non-fiction, Reference, Comp., Children, Embroidery, Drawing & Painting, Quiz, Dictionary, Encyclopedia, etc.

ABHINAV PRAKASHAN
4424, Guru Nanak Market, Nai Sarak,
New Delhi-110006
✆ 22931801
Prop.: Abhinav Thakur; **Bus.Intt.**: Pub.;
Spl.: Gen. Books in Hindi

ABHINAV PRAKASHAN
Keshav Niketan, 50, Arunanagar,
Etah-207001 (Uttar Pradesh)
✆ 91-5742-234887, 234495
Hd.Org.: Krishna Prabhakar Upadhyaya;
Bus.Intt.: Pub.; **Spl.**: Research Theses and Select Litt. in Hindi

ABHINAV PUBLICATIONS
E-37, Hauz Khas, New Delhi-110016
✆ (O) 26566387, 26562784, 26524658
(R) 26560932, 26866112, Fax: 26857009
✉ shakti@nde.vsnl.net.in
www.abhinavexports.com
Estd.: 1972; **Hd.Org.**: Shakti Malik;
Bus.Intt.: Pub.; **Spl.**: Eng. Language Books on Art, Archaeology, Dance, Soc.Sci., etc.

ABHIRAMI PUBLISHERS & BOOKSELLERS
307, Lingi Chetty St., Chennai-600001
(Tamil Nadu)

ABHIRUCHI PRAKASHAN
3/114, Karan Gali, Biswasnagar,
Shahdara, Delhi-110032
✆ 22200199
Hd.Org.: Shrikrishan

ABHIRUCHI SAHITYA PRASAR KENDRA
Kolhatkar Natyagriha, Civil Lines,
Khamgaon Buldhana Distt.-444303
(Maharashtra)

ABHISHEK BHARATI
Near R. Mitra School, Nagra Kothi,
Baidyanath-Deoghar-814112 (Bihar)
Bus.Intt.: Pub. and B.S.

ABHISHEK PRAKASHAN
5818/7, New Chandrawal, Jawahar Nagar, Delhi-110007
✆ 65640278
✉ abhpub@hotmail.com
Hd.Org.: Ramesh Kumar Chaudhry
Bus.Intt.: Pub. and Dist.; **Spl.:** Books in Hindi and Sanskrit

---

ABHISHEK PUBLICATIONS
S.C.O. 57-59, Sector-17C, Chandigarh-160017
✆ 5003768, Fax: 91-172-2707562
✉ abhpub@yahoo.com
www.abhishekpublications.net
Hd.Org.: Bharat Bhushan
Bus.Intt.: Pub.; **Spl.:** Books on Textile Technology, Performing Arts, Education and Soc.Sci.

ABHISHEK PUBLICATIONS
B-1A/40A, Janak Puri, New Delhi-110058
✆ 25599327, Fax: 91-11-25549327
Hd.Org.: Deepak Bajaj; **Bus.Intt.:** Pub.; **Spl.:** Children Books, Table Mats and Wall Charts, Products like Educational Audio Tapes, ACD's, CD Rom and VCD's

---

ABHIYAN PRAKASHAN
29/61, Gali No. 11, Biswas Nagar, Delhi-110032
Hd.Org.: Ram Anand

ABHOY PUBLICATIONS
36, College Row, Kolkata-700009 (West Bengal)
Hd.Org.: Abhoy Kumar Ghosh

ABINASH LIBRARY
Palassy, Tangra Bazar, Nadia (West Bengal)

ABIRAM PRAKASHAN
29/62, Gali No. 11, Biswas Nagar, Delhi-110032
✆ 22205703
Hd.Org.: Ramesh Sharma

ABISHEK PRAKASHAN
ISH Kipa Kuter, Near Balika Dasa School, Ghoka Rd. Gangasher, Bikaner (Rajasthan)
✆ 2542156

ABIVYAKTI PRAKASHAN
26/61, Gali No. 11, Vishwas Nagar, Delhi-110019
✆ 22228285
Hd.Org.: Harsh Kumar Sharma

ACADEMIA BOOKS
Kharagpur
✆ 03222-779254
✉ acad173@netscape.net

ACADEMIC AND LAW SERIALS
F-22B/3, Laxmi Nagar, Delhi-110092
✆ 22413394, Fax: 22223543
Estd.: 1991; **Bus.Intt.:** Exp.; **Spl.:** Journals, Books, Magazines and Newspapers

---

ACADEMIC BOOK (STALL) CENTRE
43, Shamsul Huda Rd., Kolkata-700017 (West Bengal)

ACADEMIC BOOK CENTRE
10, Walkeshwar Ambawadi, Ahmedabad-380015 (Gujarat)
✆ 2425808
Estd.: 1971; **Hd.Org.:** Ratilal N. Shah; **Bus.Intt.:** Pub., Imp., Exp.; **Spl.:** Humanities & Soc.Sci., Sci. & Tech.

ACADEMIC BOOK CENTRE
Ambedkar Circle, Bikaner-334001 (Rajasthan)
✆ 0151-2526898, Fax: 2209388
✉ yash_pub@yahoo.com
Estd.: 1990; **Hd.Org.:** Arun Verma
Br.: Pearl Books, 20, Saraswati Nagar, Udaipur (Rajasthan) ✆ 2584425
Bus.Intt.: Pub., WS, L.S. & Rt.; **Spl.:** Humanities & Soc.Sci., Sci. & Tech., Med.

ACADEMIC BOOK CORPORATION
C-1491, Rajaji Puram, Lucknow-226017 (Uttar Pradesh)

ACADEMIC BOOK HOUSE
Press Rd., Pulimoodu, Thiruvananthapuram-695001 (Kerala)
✆ 2333349, 2331850, 2331878, Fax: 2331879
Estd.: 1979; **Prop.:** Mrs. Radha Gopinath
Br. XL-817, Chittoor Rd., South Junction, Ernakulam-682016 (Kerala) ✆ 0484-2376613
Bus.Intt.: Pub., WS, L.S. & Rt., Exp.; **Spl.:** Humanities & Soc.Sci., Sci. & Tech., Med., Juvenile/Children, Gen. & Fiction etc.

ACADEMIC BOOK HOUSE
No. 11, Nirmala Nivas, 209-C, Dr. Ambedkar Rd., Matunga (G.R.) Mumbai-400019 (Maharashtra)
✆ 24142587
✉ kg_krishan@vsnl.net

ACADEMIC BOOK SELLERS
1103/A/13, Shivajinagar, Venu Apartment, Opp. Vidya Bhavan School, Pune-411016 (Maharashtra)
✆ (R) 0212-2454028
Hd.Org.: Ulhas K. Joshi

ACADEMIC BOOKS DIVISION (STERLING PUBLISHERS PVT. LTD.)
A-59, Okhla Industrial Area, Phase-II, New Delhi-110020
✆ 26387070/7071, Fax: 91-11-26383788
✉ ghai@ned.vsnl.net.in
Man.Dir.: S.K. Ghai; **Bus.Intt.:** Pub.;
Spl.: Acad. Books on a Wide Range of Sub.

ACADEMIC BOOKS INTERNATIONAL
Jaipur (Rajasthan)
✉ abishukla@yahoo.com

ACADEMIC BOOKS & PERODICALS
106-B, St. No. 2, Govind Puri, Kalkaji, New Delhi-110019
✆ 26487655 ▮ 9811143335
✉ abpsunil@yahoo.co.in
Prop.: Mr. Sunil Sharma; **Bus.Intt.:** Sub. Ag. & L.S.; **Spl.:** Academic, Beh. Sci., Comm., Sci., Med. & Tech. Books

---

ACADEMIC BOOKS SERVICE
B-Block, Gali No. 12, Opp. Govt. Boys Senior Secondary School, Tomar Colony, Burari, Delhi
✆ (O) 31072589 (R) 27619489
Estd.: 1996; **Prop.:** Aditya Kumar Bajpai;
Bus.Intt.: L.S.; **Spl.:** Humanities & Soc.Sci., Sci. & Tech., Comp., Mang., Arts & Arch., Bio.Sci., Children & General

---

ACADEMIC EXCELLENCE
42, Ekta Apartments, Geeta Colony, Delhi-110031
✆ 22445526, 22453953
✉ books@indianacademicpublisher.com
🌐 www.indianacademicpublishers.com
Hd.Org.: Raj Kumar Gupta
Bus.Intt.: Pub. and Dist.; **Spl.:** Books on Education, Soc.Sci. and Humanities in English and Hindi

---

ACADEMIC FOUNDATION
24-A, Sriram Rd., Civil Lines, Delhi-110054
✆ 2232966, 23981502, 2233730, Fax: 011-22911852
Estd.: 1990; **Hd.Org.:** Sanju (Mkt. Incharge);
Bus.Intt.: Pub.; **Spl.:** Soc.Sci., Humanities, Informative Books in English

---

ACADEMIC FOUNDATION
AF House, B-5, Chandra Nagar (Opp. Vivek Vihar) (Delhi-U.P. Border), Ghaziabad-201011
✆ 42621793, 42611015, Fax: 4611016
✉ academic@vsnl.com
Hd.Org.: Raj Kapila; **Bus.Intt.:** Pub.;
Spl.: Journals and CD-ROMs on Humanities and Soc.Sci. in English

---

ACADEMIC FOUNDATION
4772/23, Bharat Ram Rd. (23 Ansari Rd.), Darya Ganj, New Delhi-110002
✆ 23245001-04, Fax: 23245005
✉ academic@vsnl.com
🌐 www.academicfoundation.com
Hd.Org.: Raj Kapila; **Bus.Intt.:** Pub.;
Spl.: Books, Journals, CD-ROMs on Soc.Sci., Humanities with specialisation in Indian Economy, Banking and Finance

---

ACADEMIC (INDIA) PUBLISHERS (REGD.)
B-9, Rattan Jyoti, 18, Rajendra Place, New Delhi-110008
✆ (O) 25742171, 25812181 (R) 25764880, Fax: 25722671
✉ angelaip@del3.vsnl.net.in
🌐 www.chowdhryexporthouse.com
Estd.: 1984; **Prop.:** Ambar Raj Chowdhary;
Bus.Intt.: Pub.; **Spl.:** Academic

ACADEMIC PRESS (THE)
887/5, Patel Nagar, Gurgaon
✆ 2322779, 2322005, Fax: 91-2324782
✉ ind-doc-sea@satyam.net.in, academic@hotmail.com
Estd.: 1969; **Bus.Intt.:** Pub. and B.S.;
Spl.: Humanities, Law, Gen. Books

ACADEMIC PUBLICATIONS
Rasta Sanghiji, S.M.S. Highway, Jaipur-302003 (Rajasthan)

ACADEMIC PUBLICATIONS INTERNATIONAL
PB No. 418, 007/Sovereign Park, 56-58, K.R. Rd., Basavanagudi, Bangalore-560004 (Karnataka)
✆ 26604730, Grams: APIbang
Estd.: 1967; **Ch.Exe.:** A.M. Desai; **Bus.Intt.:** Pub., B.S. and L.S.; **Spl.:** Sci., Tech., Med., Edu.

ACADEMIC PUBLISHERS
12/1A, Bankim Chatterjee St., Kolkata-700073 (West Bengal)
✆ (O) 22414857 (R) 23500559, Fax: 22413702
✉ acabooks@cal.vsnl.net.in
Estd.: 1958; **Hd.Org.:** B.K. Dhur;
Bus.Intt.: Pub.; **Spl.:** Med., Mang. and Tech. Books

ACADEMIC PUBLISHERS
5A, Bhawani Dutta Lane, Kolkata-700073 (West Bengal)
✆ 22571071, Fax: 91-33-22413702
✉ info@acabooks.net
🌐 www.acabooks.net
Estd.: 1958; **Hd.Org.:** Bimal Kumar Dhur;
Bus.Intt.: Pub.; **Spl.:** Med., Mang. and Tech. Books

ACADEMIC PUBLISHING LTD.
E-252/4, West Vinod Nagar, Delhi-110092
Fax: 22249614
✉ pkgupta@giasdlw.vsnl.net.in

Estd.: 1997; **Man.Dir.**: Suresh Pandey; **Bus.Intt.**: Pub., L.S., Sub.Ag.; **Spl.**: Comp., Med., Engg. books in English & Hindi

ACADEMY OF BUSINESS STUDY
24/4866, Sheeltara House, Ansari Rd., New Delhi-110002
✆ 23281314

ACADEMY OF INDIAN NUMISMATICS AND SIGILLOGRAPHY
115, Kailash Park, Manoramaganj, Indore-452001 (Madhya Pradesh)
✆ 2493931, Fax: 2532796
✉ skaca_numisigind@indiatimes.com
Hd.Org.: S.K. Bhatt; **Bus.Intt.**: Pub.; **Spl.**: Research papers on Numismatics, Epigraphy, Archaeology, etc.

ACADEMY OF LAW & RELIGION
B-114, SFS Sheikh Sarai-I, New Delhi-110017

ACCURATE PUBLISHERS & SUPPLIERS
Auqaf Complex, Budshah Chowk, Srinagar-190001 (Jammu and Kashmir)
✆ 2798223 (PP), Cable: Accurate
Estd.: 1994; **Prop.**: Tahir J. Salati; **Bus.Intt.**: Pub., WS, L.S.

ACCUPRESSURE HEALTH CARE SYSTEMS
A-163-169, Nehru Vihar, Near Timarpur, Delhi-110054
✆ 23991804
✉ acs_syscm@yahoo.com
Ch.Exe.: Mr. Babulal Choudhary
Br.: Accupressure Health Care System, India, A-13, DC, Kamla Nehru Nagar, Jodhpur (Rajasthan) ✆ 2635852, Fax: 2759042
✉ info@acupressureindia.com
www.acupressureindia.com
Bus.Intt.: Pub.; **Spl.**: Health Care and Alternate Medicare and lifestyle books and products related to Accupressure, Magnetic Therapy, Feng Shui, Vastu etc.

ACHARYA PRAKASHAN
190-B/10, Rajrooppur, Dhumalganj, Allahabad-211004 (Uttar Pradesh)
✆ 2430698
Hd.Org.: Sarvesh Shukla
Bus.Intt.: Pub. and B.S.; **Spl.**: Rel. & Phil.

ACHARYA PRAKASHAN
35, 6th Main Chamarajapet, Bangalore-18 (Karnataka)
✆ 080-2620641
Hd.Org.: A. Hanumantachar; **Bus.Intt.**: Pub.; **Spl.**: Fiction and Collections books in Kannada

ACHARYA SHREE ENTERPRISES
Vivekanand Yogash Ram Hospital, Patpar Ganj Rd., Delhi-110051
✆ 2202142, Fax: 011-2210663
Estd.: 1967; **Prop.**: Acharya Kishan Dev Ji; **Bus.Intt.**: Pub.; **Spl.**: Occult Sci. & Yoga Books in English & Hindi

ACME BOOKS PRIVATE LIMITED
104, Nirmal Tower, 26, Barakhamba Rd., New Delhi-110001
✆ (O) 23315398, 23264180, 23279113 (R) 257244581, Fax: 91-11-23260538
Hd.Org.: Sunny Malik; **Bus.Intt.**: WS, L.S. & Imp.

ACOUSTICS ENGINEERS
Pune (Maharashtra)
✆ 25534693, Fax: 25533453
✉ acen@vsnl.com
Spl.: Cassettes and CD's

ADABI DUNIYA
510, Matia Mahal, Delhi-110006
Estd.: 1958; **Hd.Org.**: Sultan Ahmed; **Bus.Intt.**: Pub., WS, L.S., Exp.

ADAM PUBLISHERS & DISTRIBUTORS
1542, Pataudi House, Darya Ganj, New Delhi-110002
✆ 23284740, 23282550, Fax: 23267510
✉ apd@bol.net.in
Hd.Org.: Syed Sajid Ali; **Bus.Intt.**: Pub.; **Spl.**: Books on Islam, Soc.Sci. and Humanities in English

ADARSHA PUSTAKALAYA
G.S. Majirgram, Nadia (West Bengal)

ADARSH ENTERPRISES
E-22-C, Jawahar Park, Laxmi Nagar, Delhi-110092
Estd.: 1994; **Prop.**: Nirmal Kumar Karan; **Bus.Intt.**: Pub., WS; **Spl.**: Humanities & Soc.Sci., Gen. & Fiction, etc.

ADARSH ENTERPRISES
4393/4, Tulsi Dass St., Ansari Rd., Darya Ganj, New Delhi-110002
✆ 23246131, 23246132, Fax: 23246130
✉ adarshbooks@vsnl.com
www.adarshbooks.com
Estd.: 1993; **Hd.Org.**: Nirmal Kumar Karan; **Bus.Intt.**: Pub. & Dist.; **Spl.**: Rel., Phil., Craft, Reference, etc.

ADARSH GRANTHA
Adarsha Grandha Mandir, Museum Rd., Vijayawada-520002 (Andhra Pradesh)
✆ 0866-2434118
Prop.: G.V.K. Sinha; **Bus.Intt.**: Pub.;

Spl.: Children's Litt., Sci., Short Stories, Fiction, Hist. & Biographies in Telugu

ADARSH PRAKASHAN MANDIR
Daoji Rd., Bikaner-334001 (Rajasthan)
Hd.Org.: Kedarnath Vyas

ADARSH PRAKASHAN
Opp. Jamma Masjid, Gandhi Rd., Ahmedabad-380001 (Gujarat)
✆ 079-2357934

ADARSH PRAKASHAN
Khazanchi Rd., Patna-800004 (Bihar)
Bus.Intt.: Pub. and B.S.

ADARSH PUSTAK BHANDAR
Ramna Rd., Patna-800004 (Bihar)
Bus.Intt.: Pub. and B.S.

ADARSH PUSTAK BHAWAN
Nawada Bazar, Bhagalpur (Bihar)
Bus.Intt.: Pub. and B.S.

ADARSH SAHITYA SANGH
Anuvrat Bhawan, 210,
Deen Dayal Upadhyaya Marg,
New Delhi-110002
✆ 23234641, 23238480
Hd.Org.: R.M. Bhandari; **Bus.Intt.:** Pub.; **Spl.:** Regional Language Books on Spiritualism, Rel., Yoga, Meditation and Moral Sci.

ADARSH STATIONERIES MART
7/1, Baibhav Chamber Jagdale, Indore (Madhya Pradesh)
✆ (O) 2478290 (R) 2479298

ADARSHA PUBLICATIONS
"Sreeranga", 5th Cross, Nrupathunga Ext.
Jayanagara East, Shettyhally Main Rd.,
Tumkur-572102 (Karnataka)
✆ 0816-2292777
Estd.: 1991; **Man.Dir.:** R.K. Murthy; **Bus.Intt.:** Pub., **Spl.:** Gen. Books

AD-DARUL QAYYIMAH
Bhiwandi, Thana-421204 (Maharashtra)
Bus.Intt.: Exp.

ADDISON-WESLEY PUBLISHING CO.
C/o Narosa Book Distributors, 6,
Community Centre, Panchsheel Park,
New Delhi-110017

ADHAAR PRAKASHAN PVT. LTD.
S.C.F. 267, Sector-16, Panchkula-134113 (Haryana)
✆ 2566952, 2567004, Fax: 91-172-2570725
✉ adhaar@sancharnet.in
Hd.Org.: Puja Sardana; **Bus.Intt.:** Pub. & Dist.; **Spl.:** Contemporary Hindi Litt. and WS, L.S. & Rt., Imp., Exp.

ADHINAV PRAKASHAN
Bachh Raj Bhavan, Purani Mandi,
Ajmer-305001 (Rajasthan)

ADHUNIK PRAKASHAK
197-B, Muktaram Babu St., Kolkata-700073 (West Bengal)

ADHUNIK PRAKASHAN GRIHA
Alopibagh, Allahabad (Uttar Pradesh)
✆ 2662935
Hd.Org.: Arvind Kumar Pandey

ADHYATAM VIGYAN SATSANG KENDRA
160, Gulab Niwas, 11th Choposani,
PB No. 41, Jodhpur (Rajasthan)

ADHYATMA VIJNANA PRAKASHAN
1552/Sector-6, Bahadurgarh-124507 (Haryana)
✆ 91-1276-243646, 243656,
Fax: 91-1276-210344
✉ adhyatmavijnana@rediffmail.com
Hd.Org.: Prem Sagar; **Bus.Intt.:** Pub.; **Spl.:** Spiritualism, Rel. and Phil.

ADHYAYAN PUBLISHERS AND DISTRIBUTORS
4378/4B, 105 JMD House,
Murari Lal Street, Ansari Road,
Darya Ganj, New Delhi-110002
✆ 23263018, 23277156
Fax: 91-11-23280028
✉ adhyayanpublishers@yahoo.com
Hd.Org.: Harish Chandra Yadav
Bus.Intt.: Pub.; **Spl.:** Books on Soc.Sci., Pol.Sci., Litt., Tourism, L.S., Women Studies, Mathematics, Environment and Encyclopaedias

ADI DHAKESWARY LIBRARY
18-B, Shyama Charan Dey St., Kolkata-700073 (West Bengal)

ADI PAUL BROTHERS
48, K.K. Mitra Rd., Barasat, 24-Parganas North-743201 (West Bengal)
✆ 25523634

ADISHAKTI PRAKASHANA
Rajashree Hosamani Publisher,
No. 42, Manjushri Nilaya, 2nd Stage,
2nd Cross, Vinobanagar, Shimoga-577204 (Karnataka)
✆ 08182-249790
Estd.: 2004; **Bus.Intt.:** Pub.; **Spl.:** Humanities & Soc.Sci., Others in Kannada

ADITI BOOK DISTRIBUTORS
43, Parnami Mandir, Govind Marg,
Adarsh Nagar, Jaipur-302004 (Rajasthan)

ADITI LIBRARY SERVICE
Dispur Cast Gate, Basistha Rd.,
Guwahati-700006 (Assam)

ADITI PUSTAK BHAWAN
27/B, Sri Gopal Mallick Lane, Kolkata-700012 (West Bengal)
✆ 22417396

ADITYA BOOKS PVT. LTD.
119, Vinoba Puri, Lajpat Nagar-II, New Delhi-110024
✆ (O) 51724129-30, 29841409, 29849132 (R) 26922991 ▮ 9810773223, Fax: 51724167, 29841116
abooks@vsnl.net.in
www.aditya-books.com
Estd.: 1987; **Man.Dir.:** Kailash Balani
Br.: 2/37, Sant Vihar Gali, Ansari Rd., Darya Ganj, New Delhi-110002
✆ 23268655, 23285677 ▮ 9811052180, Fax: 23268655
lawmanindia@vsnl.net
www.lawman-books.com
• **Man.:** Sanjeev Dogra; Shree Ram Centre, Block-B, 1st Floor, 3 Abdul Hamid St., Kolkata-700069 ✆ 22483797 ▮ 9830169097, Fax: 22107948 abooks@cal3.vsnl.net.in
• **Sales Man.:** Gautam Mukherjee; 390/4566/5A, Tagore Nagar, Vikroli (East), Mumbai-400083 ✆ 25743371,
Resident Rep.: Aspi Khan • Sir Puttanna Chetty Complex, 3rd Floor, 32/9 & 10, Bull Temple Rd., Basavanghudi, Bangalore-560004
✆ 6609050, 6609053 ▮ 9886208446
abooks@vsnl.net
Bus.Intt.: Pub., WS, L.S., Rt., Imp., Exp., Sub.Ag.; **Spl.:** Humanities & Soc.Sci., Sci. & Tech., Med., Law, Gen., Fiction, etc.

ADITYA MEDICAL BOOK DISTRIBUTORS
2/4, Anadh Complex 5, Cant Rd., Lucknow-226001 (Uttar Pradesh)
✆ 2231724, 2233416, Fax: 2229164
adityamedical@msm.com
Estd.: 1993; **Prop.:** Sunil Talwar; **Bus.Intt.:** Pub., WS, L.S. & Rt.

ADITYA MEDICAL PUBLISHERS
2/7, Ansari Rd., Darya Ganj, New Delhi-110002
✆ 23243088, Fax: 91-522-2629164
adityamedical@msn.com
www.medicalbookseller.com
Hd.Org.: Sunil Talwar; **Bus.Intt.:** Pub. and Dist.; **Spl.:** Med. Books

ADITYA PRAKASHALAYA
2, Shyama Charan Dey St., Kolkata-700073 (West Bengal)

ADITYA PRAKASHAN
78, Patrakar Colony, Bandra (East), Mumbai-400051 (Maharashtra)

ADITYA PRAKASHAN
F-14/65, Model Town-II, Delhi-110009
✆ 27245584, 27420564, Fax: 23282047
bibimpex@giasd101.vsnl.net.in
Prop.: Pradeep K. Goel; **Bus.Intt.:** Pub.; **Spl.:** Indology, Buddhism and Lib.Sci. in English and Tibetan

ADITYA PUBLISHERS
Jogeshwari Mata Complex, Pathak Ward, Bina-470113 (Madhya Pradesh)
✆ (O) 221372 (R) 220644
Hd.Org.: Madhav Dhamecha; **Bus.Intt.:** Pub. and L.S.

ADVAITA ASHRAMA
5, Delhi Entally Road, Kolkata-700014 (West Bengal)
✆ 22164000
mail@advaitaasharma.org
www.advaitaashrama.org
Hd.Org.: Swami Bodhasarananda; **Bus.Intt.:** Pub.; **Spl.:** Books on the Lives and Teachings of Sri Ramakrishna, Swami Vivekananda, besides Vedantic Litt. and the *Upanishads*

ADVANCED MANAGEMENT SERVICES
19, Nariman Bhawan, Nariman Point, Mumbai-400021 (Maharashtra)
✆ 20223256, Fax: 20223256, Telefax: 118 5132 HRVD IN

ADVANCED PUBLICATIONS
61/4, Belgachia Rd., Kolkata-700037 (West Bengal)

ADVANCE STUDY CENTRE
Motilal Nehru Rd., Opp. Pan Baza Girls H.S. School, Guwahati-781009 (Assam)
✆ 2546533, 2525736, Fax: 0361-2660291
lahkar1@sify.com
Estd.: 1994; **Prop.:** H.K. Lahkar; **Bus.Intt.:** WS, L.S. & Rt.; **Spl.:** Humanities & Soc.Sci., Mang. & Comm., Sci. Engg. & Tech.

ADVENT BOOKS
V-227, Rajouri Garden, New Delhi-110027
✆ (O) 011-55450290 (R) 25455731, Fax: 011-25161868
advent_books@hotmail.com
Estd.: 2001; **Hd.Org.:** Naresh Malik; **Bus.Intt.:** Pub., Exp.; **Spl.:** Books for Children

ADYAR LIBRARY AND RESEARCH CENTRE THEOSOPHICAL SOCIETY
Adyar, Chennai-600020 (Tamil Nadu)

AERO EXPORTS
3756, Churiwalan, Delhi-110006
✆ 23274339, 26222766, Fax: 23263567
✉ gagans@vsnl.com,
sgagans@nde.vsnl.net.in
Estd.: 1977; **Prop.:** Mrs. Shubita Sachdev;
Bus.Intt.: Pub., Exp.; **Spl.:** Humanities & Soc. Sci., Islam, Islamic Religious Books

AERO TRADERS
15, Shankarnagar Society, Mahavirnagar,
Himmatnagar-383001 (Gujarat)

AFFILIATED EAST-WEST PRESS (P) LTD.
105, Nirmal Tower, 26, Barakhamba Rd.,
Connaught Place, New Delhi-110001
✆ 23315398, Fax: 23260538
✉ affiliat@vsnl.com, affiliat@nda.vsnl.net.in
www.eastwestpress.com
Estd.: 1962; **Man.Dir.:** Kamal Malik, Sunny Malik, Karan Malik
Br.: G-1/16, Ansari Rd., Darya Ganj,
New Delhi-110002
✆ (O) 23279113, 23264180
(R) 25724581, Fax: 23260538
✉ affiliat@vsnl.com
www.aewpress.com
Bus.Intt.: Pub. and Imp.; **Spl.:** Sci., Engg. & Tech. & Med.

AFRO-ASIAN BOOK COUNCIL
4835/24, Ansari Road, Darya Ganj,
New Delhi-110002
✆ 23258865, Fax: 91-11-23267437
✉ afro@aabcouncil.org
www.aabcouncil.org
Hd.Org.: Sukumar Das; **Bus.Intt.:** Pub. and Promoter; **Spl.:** Books in English from Afro-Asian Countries

AFTAB BOOK DEPOT
Sabzibagh, Patna-800004 (Bihar)
Bus.Intt.: Pub. and B.S.

AGAM KALA PRAKASHAN
34, Central Market, Ashok Vihar,
Delhi-110052
✆ 27212195, 27401485-6,
Fax: 27401485, 27242427
Hd.Org.: Agam Prasad; **Bus.Intt.:** Pub.;
Spl.: Indology, Hist., Art, Culture, Arch., Tourism, Buddhism, Humanities and Soc. Sci.

AGARAWAL BOOK DEPOT
Jamhore, Aurangabad-824121 (Bihar)
Bus.Intt.: Pub. and B.S.

AGARAWAL PUSTAK BHANDAR
Kahalgaon (Colgong),
Bhagalpur-813203 (Bihar)
Bus.Intt.: Pub. and B.S.

AGARWAL & SONS
6-F Kamala Nagar, Delhi-110007
✆ 22913891

AGARWAL BOOK CENTRE
Itarsi Rd., Pratap Nagar, Rasulia,
Hoshangabad-461001 (Madhya Pradesh)
✆ 07574-255073, Fax: 07574-252954
Estd.: 1986; **Hd.Org.:** Pankaj Kumar Agarwal;
Bus.Intt.: WS and L.S. & Rt.; **Spl.:** Sci. & Tech., Med., Comm. & Mang., Humanities, Law, Gen. Books

AGARWAL BOOK DISTRIBUTORS
B-41, Natraj Nagar,
Emliwala Pathak Tank Rd.,
Jaipur-302015 (Rajasthan)
✆ 2513611
Hd.Org.: V.K. Gupta

AGARWAL BOOK STORE
Patnipura Marg, Indore (Madhya Pradesh)

AGARWAL PRAKASHAN
S.C.F.-8, Vikas Vihar, Ambala City-134003 (Haryana)
✆ (O) 2444407 (R) 2440408
Hd.Org.: Ramesh Kumar Singla

AGARWAL PUSTAK BHANDAR
Chowk, Patna City, Patna-800008 (Bihar)
Bus.Intt.: Pub. and B.S.

AGGARWAL BOOK CENTRE
19, DDA, A-I Market, Mayapuri,
New Delhi-110064
✆ 25410225, 2534430, Fax: 25403100
Bus.Intt.: Exp.; **Spl.:** Edu. Books

AGRAWAL BOOK CENTRE
Hanuman Nagar, Rasuliya,
Hoshangabad-461001 (Madhya Pradesh)
✆ 07574-255480, 255073, Fax: 252954
Estd.: 1986; **Hd.Org.:** Pankaj Kumar Agrawal
Br.: Pratap Nagar, Rasuliya, Hoshangabad, (Madhya Pradesh)
• A.B.C. Book Distributors, Opp. MPEB Gate, Rasuliya, Hoshangabad (Madhya Pradesh)
Bus.Intt.: Pub. WS, L.S. & Rt.; **Spl.:** School, Graduate, Adv. Books for Lib., Gen. Books, Engg., Med., Sci. & Tech., Comm. & Mang., Humanities, Law etc.

AGARWAL BOOK STORE
J-Road, Pratap Tower, Bistupur,
Jamshedpur-831001 (Bihar)
✆ 439906, Fax: 424849
✉ abs@tatanagar.com
Estd.: 1958; **Prop.:** S.K. Agarwal;
Bus.Intt.: L.S., Rt., WS; **Spl.:** Humanities

& Soc.Sci., Mang. & Comm., Sci., Engg. & Tech., Med. Sci., Journals, Magazines & Periodicals Fiction & Gen.

AGRADUTA
Banka Bazar, Cuttack-753002 (Orissa)
✆ (R) 0671-2401109 (BBSR)
Estd.: 1973; **Hd.Org.**: Arati Mohanti; **Bus.Intt.**: Pub. & B.S.; **Spl.**: Short Stories, Novels, Criticisms and Popular Sci. in Oriya

AGRICOLE PUBLISHING ACADEMY
208, Shopping Complex, Defence Colony Flyover, New Delhi-110024

AGRICULTURAL & FORESTRY PUBLICATIONS
Information Centre, 345, Sector 15-A, Hissar-125001 (Haryana)

AGRICULTURAL RESEARCH INFORMATION CENTRE
49, Priti Nagar, Hissar-125001 (Haryana)

AGROBIOS (INDIA)
Behind Nasarani Cinema, Chopasani Road, Jodhpur-342002 (Rajasthan)
✆ 2643993, Fax: 91-291-2642319
agrobios@sify.com
www.agrobiosindia.com
Hd.Org.: Updesh Purohit
Bus.Intt.: Pub.; **Spl.**: Books on Science and Technology Including Agriculture and Biological Sciences

AGRO BOTANICAL PUBLISHERS
4E-176, J.N. Vyas Nagar, Bikaner-334003 (Rajasthan)
✆ 2522523, Fax: 0151-2526756
agrobios@sify.com
Hd.Org.: Smt. Saraswati Purohit

AGRO SCIENCES BOOK CENTRE
Rd. No. 11-D, (Behind Telephone Exch.), Rajendra Nagar, Patna-800016 (Bihar)

AGROSCIENCES BOOK CENTRE
4634-4636, 19B, Ansari Rd., Darya Ganj, New Delhi-110002
✆ 23242905, 23243058 ▮ 9810003188, Fax: 23243058
abc_jain@123india.com
Estd.: 1978; **Prop.**: Surinder Kumar Jain; **Bus.Intt.**: WS, Sub.Ag. & L.S.; **Spl.**: Acad., Beh. Sci., Tech., Sci. & Journals & Magazines

AGROTECH PUBLISHING ACADEMY
1-G-24, Sector-5, Hiran Magri (Gayatri Nagar), Udaipur-313001 (Rajasthan)
✆ 0294-2465635
agrotechbooks@rediffmail.com

AHAM AHINSA-SAMATA EVAM
Prakritik Sansthan, Padmani Marg, Sundervas, Udaipur (Rajasthan)

AHANAYAN
B-125, Gariahat CMC Market, Kolkata-700019 (West Bengal)
✆ (O) 24600330 (R) 24158372
Estd.: 1986; **Bus.Intt.**: B.S.; **Spl.**: Adv. Books for Lib., Gen. Books and Rare & Folk

AHLUWALIA BOOK DEPOT
9988, New Rohtak Road, Sarai Rohilla, Gali No. 6, New Delhi-110005
✆ 91-11-28715142
Estd.: 1954; **Prop.**: Rakesh Ahluwalia; **Bus.Intt.**: Pub., WS, L.S. & Rt.; **Spl.**: Gen. & Fiction etc.

AHMADDIYYA MUSLIM MISSION
No. 3, Ist Main Rd., U.I. Colony, Kodam Bakkam, Chennai-600034 (Tamil Nadu)
✆ 28278538
Pres.: Mohamed Ahmad; **Bus.Intt.**: B.S.; **Spl.**: Islam Litt. Particularly; the Holy Quran in different *Languages* of the world

AHMADIYYA MUSLIM JAMA'AT
53, Institutional Area, Tughlakabad, Near Batra Hospital, New Delhi-110062
✆ 26059094, Fax: 29958055
www.alislam.org
Hd.Org.: Iradat Ahmad; **Bus.Intt.**: Pub.; **Spl.**: Litt. and Translations of the *Quran*

AHUJA BOOK COMPANY
K1/101, C.R. Park, New Delhi-110019
✆ 26438673, 26232071 ▮ 9810048119
Estd.: 1971; **Prop.**: Suresh Ahuja; **Bus.Intt.**: Rt.; **Spl.**: Law

AHUJA BOOK COMPANY PVT. LTD.
4348/4C, Ansari Road, Darya Ganj, New Delhi-110002
✆ 23276564, 23245859
Fax: 91-11-23281514
info@ahujabooks.com
www.ahujabooks.com
Estd.: 1981; **Hd.Org.**: R.N. Ahuja

AHZAZ PUBLISHING HOUSE
Kucha Nahar Khan, Darya Ganj, New Delhi-110002

AIJAZ PUBLISHING HOUSE
2861, Kucha Chelan, Darya Ganj, Delhi-110002
✆ 23253268, Fax: 91-11-26987191
Hd.Org.: Syed Azhar Hussain; **Bus.Intt.**: Pub. and B.S.; **Spl.**: Unani and Tibbi Med. Books in Urdu Language and Urdu Litt.

AINTHINAI PATHIPPAGAM
279, Pycrofts Rd., Triplicane,
Chennai-600005 (Tamil Nadu)
✆ 28549410
Prop.: Kuzhakathiresan; **Bus.Intt.:** Pub.;
Spl.: Children's Books and Audio Cassettes in Tamil, Janakiraman's Novels, Short Stories etc.

AIRAVAT PRAKASHAN
230/9C, Mandawali, Fazilpur, Railway Colony,
Delhi-110092

AIRPORT BOOK SHOP
H.A.L. Cooperative Society, Bangalore Airport,
Bangalore (Karnataka)

AIRPORT BOOK SHOP
Santacruz Airport, Mumbai-400029 (Maharashtra)

AIRPORT BOOK SHOP
Meenambakkam Airport, Chennai (Tamil Nadu)

AIWAN-E-ADAB
2936, Kalan Masjid, Bazar Turkman Gate,
Delhi-110006
✆ 23232714, 23230453, Fax: 23232714
Hd.Org.: Nasir Dehlvi; **Bus.Intt.:** Pub. and Exp.; **Spl.:** Urdu Books on Poetry, Short Stories and Novels

AJAB PUSTAKALAYA
321-B, Bhausingji Rd., Bhavani Mandap,
Kolhapur-416012 (Maharashtra)
✆ (O) 2546710 (R) 2653180
Estd.: 1965; **Prop.:** Ulhas D. Mehta;
Bus.Intt.: Pub., B.S., L.S., WS; **Spl.:** All Sub. in English, Hindi, Marathi

AJAI BOOK DISTRIBUTORS
1882, Jagram Mandir Marg,
Kotla Mubarakpur, Near H-58-59,
South Extension-I, New Delhi-110003
✆ 24646404, 24615224, Fax: 24615224
✉ abddelhi49@yahoo.co.in
Hd.Org.: Ajai Singh; **Bus.Intt.:** Dist.;
Spl.: Tourism, Art, Culture, Textiles, Cookery and Books for Children

AJANTA BOOK DEPOT
Gandhi Chowk, Madhupur,
Deoghar-815353 (Bihar)
Bus.Intt.: Pub. and B.S.

AJANTA BOOK DISTRIBUTORS
Vazhappully, Beach Rd., Edmuttam,
Trichar Distt.-680568 (Kerala)

AJANTA BOOK DISTRIBUTORS
No. 19/1, 8th Cross, Sampangiramanagar,
Bangalore-560027 (Karnataka)

AJANTA BOOKS INTERNATIONAL (PUNJABI)
I, U.B. Jawahar Nagar, Bungalow Rd.,
Delhi-110007
✆ (O) 23926182 (R) 27415016,
Fax: 91-11-27415016
✉ ajandabi@ndf.vsnl.net.in
www.ajantabooks.com
Estd.: 1975; **Ch.Exe.:** S. Balwant;
Bus.Intt.: Pub.; **Spl.:** Punjabi Litt. and Books

AJANTA BOOK STORE
Masaurhi, Patna-804452 (Bihar)
Bus.Intt.: Pub. and B.S.

AJANTA PRAKASHAN
D.N. Singh Rd., Bhagalpur-812002 (Bihar)
Bus.Intt.: Pub. and B.S.

AJANTA PRAKASHAN
Khazanchi Rd., Patna-800004 (Bihar)
Bus.Intt.: Pub. and B.S.

AJANTA PUBLICATIONS (INDIA)
S-417, Greater Kailash, New Delhi-110048
✆ 26414870
Estd.: 1978; **Prop.:** Harish Arora;
Bus.Intt.: Pub.; **Spl.:** School Textbooks in English, Hindi and Oriya

AJANTA STUDIO
Obra, Aurangabad-824202 (Bihar)
Bus.Intt.: Pub. and B.S.

AJANTHA BOOK CENTRE
83, First Agraharam, Salem-636001
(Tamil Nadu)
✆ 265655
Estd.: 1961; **Man.Prt.:** Y.N. Ramanujam;
Bus.Intt.: Pub., WS, L.S. & Rt.

AJAY BOOK DEPOT
110/1, Plot No. 11 B.H.U. Hyd Gate,
Vishwanthpuri, Varanasi-221005
(Uttar Pradesh)

AJAY BOOK DEPOT
G.D. College Rd., Begusarai-851101 (Bihar)
Bus.Intt.: Pub. and B.S.

AJAY BOOK DISTRIBUTORS
19, Edward Line, Kingsway Camp,
Delhi-110009
✆ 22043229, Fax: 91-11-22043229
✉ abd_books@yahoo.co.in
Hd.Org.: B.R. Sadana
Bus.Intt.: Pub. and Dist.; **Spl.:** Books on Soc.Sci., Humanities, Management and Education

AJAY BOOK SERVICE PUBLISHERS & DISTRIBUTORS
4215/1 (Basement), Ansari Road, Darya Ganj,
New Delhi-110002
✆ 23287655
Fax: 91-11-23279443
✉ info@ajaybookservice.com
www.ajaybookservice.com

Estd.: 1977; **Hd.Org.**: Nand Lal Verma
Br.: H-60, St. No. 3, Laxmi Nagar, Delhi
✆ 22469169, 22427658
Bus.Intt.: Pub., WS, L.S. & Rt., Imp., Exp.; **Spl.**: Humanities & Soc.Sci., Juvenile/Children, Gen. & Fiction etc.

AJAY BOOK STORE
Naubatpur, Patna-801109 (Bihar)
Bus.Intt.: Pub. and B.S.

AJAY LAW AGENCIES
S.C.O. No. 4-5, IInd Floor,
Above S.B.I., Sector 17-B,
Chandigarh-160017
✆ 2710762
Estd.: 1992; **Prop.**: Ajay K. Sharma;
Bus.Intt.: L.S. and B.S.; **Spl.**: Law Books in English

AJAY PARMAR & CO.
Ist Floor, Arun House, 2/25, Ansari Rd.,
New Delhi-110002
✆ 23284894, Fax: 23281819
✉ aparmar@vsnl.com
Estd.: 1985; **Hd.Org.**: Ajay Parmar;
Bus.Intt.: Pub.; **Spl.**: Gen. & Fiction etc.

AJAY PRINTERS & PUBLISHERS
Roorkee (Uttarakhand)
✆ 273140, 274740
✉ mehta@ndb.vsnl.net.in
Bus.Intt.: Pub.'s Rep. and Pub.

AJAY PUBLISHERS & DISTRIBUTORS
House No. 6, First Floor,
Behind Moti Masjid, Bhopal-462001
(Madhya Pradesh)
✆ 2542556, 5240574
Estd.: 1984; **Prop.**: Arun Gupta; **Bus.Intt.**: Pub., B.S. and L.S.; **Spl.**: Humanities & Soc.Sci., Sci. & Tech., Gen. & Fiction, etc.

AJAY PUSTAK BHANDAR
Obra, Aurangabad-824124 (Bihar)
Bus.Intt.: Pub. and B.S.

AJAY PUSTAK BHANDAR
Samookhiyamore, Bhagalpur-814164
(Bihar)
Bus.Intt.: Pub. and B.S.

AJAY PUSTAK BHANDAR
Sheikhpura, Patna-800014 (Bihar)
Bus.Intt.: Pub. and B.S.

AJAZ BOOK DEEPO
Exchange Rd., Madina Chowk,
Gow Kadal, Srinagar-190001
(Jammu and Kashmir)
Estd.: 2003; **Hd.Org.**: Ajaz Ahmad Wani;
Bus.Intt.: Pub., WS, L.S. & Rt.;
Spl.: Humanities & Soc.Sci, Gen. & Fiction, etc.

AJAZ BOOKSELLER & STATIONERY DEALERS
Jadeed Link Rd., Baramulla, Kashmir
(Jammu & Kashmir)
✆ 235242
Estd.: 1996; **Hd.Org.**: Ajaz Ahmad Chalkoo;
Bus.Intt.: L.S. & Rt.; **Spl.**: Humanities & Soc.Sci., Sci. & Tech., Juvenile/Children books, Gen. & Fiction, etc.

AJINKYA PRAKASHAN
331, Vadgopalpet, Satara-415002
(Maharashtra)

AJIT LAW BOOK DEPOT
31, Budhwar Peth, Behind Suvarna,
Sahakari Bank, Pune-411002
(Maharashtra)
✆ 2451546
Bus.Intt.: B.S. and Pub.; **Spl.**: Law

AJITH BOOK STALL
GSS Shopping Complex, Near Public Library,
Convent Rd., Cochin-682035 (Kerala)
Hd.Org.: N.S. Shibu and C.N. Ajith;
Bus.Intt.: L.S.

AJITH PUBLICATIONS
College Rd., Sasthamcotta,
Kollam-690521 (Kerala)
Estd.: 1969; **Bus.Intt.**: Pub.

AJOY BOOK STALL
15, Bankim Chatterjee St., Kolkata-73
(West Bengal)

AKADEMIC BOOK CENTRE
10, Valkeshwar Society, Ahdawadi,
Ahmedabad-380015 (Gujarat)
✆ 079-2403495

AKALANK PUBLICATIONS
3622, Mori Gate, Post Box No. 1029,
Delhi-110006
✆ (O) 23915064, 32215064 (R) 23976292,
Cable: Actrules, Fax: 23986793
✉ info@akalank.com
www.akalank.com
Estd.: 1972; **Prop.**: Narendar Kumar Jain;
Bus.Intt.: Pub., WS, L.S. & Rt.; **Spl.**: Law, Comm., Civil Engg. & Service Matters Books

AKALANKA PRAKASHANA
8-1-64B, Sudheendra Teertha Marg,
Udupi-576102 (Karnataka)
Hd.Org.: K.V. Subbanna; **Bus.Intt.**: Pub.;
Spl.: Fiction, Collections, Poems, Dramas and Gen. Books in Kannada and English

AKALWADI BOOK DEPOT
Vijaya Road, Dharwad-580001 (Karnataka)
✆ (S) 2211324 (R) 2211323
Founder: Ramanna Akalwadi; **Bus.Intt.**: Pub., B.S.; **Spl.**: Educational Kannada Law Books

AKANSHA PUBLISHING HOUSE
4649-B/21, Ansari Road, Darya Ganj,
New Delhi -110002
✆ 23263193, Fax: 91-11-23263193
✉ ektabooks@yahoo.com
Estd.: 1994; **Hd.Org.:** M.P. Misra;
Bus.Intt.: Pub.; **Spl.:** English Language Books on Soc.Sci., Humanities and North-east

---

AKANT BOOKS CENTER
BS-63, Paschimi Shalimar Bagh,
New Delhi-110088
✆ 91-11-65152825
Hd.Org.: Anita; **Bus.Intt.:** Pub.;
Spl.: Fiction, Non-fiction, Children's Books, Reference Books, etc.

AKARSH BOOK DEPOT
Tower Chowk, Darbhanga (Bihar)
✆ (O) 06272-222123, 231891 (R) 224792,
Fax: 06272-222123
Estd.: 1998, **Bus.Intt.:** B.S.; **Spl.:** School, Graduate, Adv. Books for Lib. and Gen. Books

---

AKASH BHARTI COMPUTECH
C-9/5, Sector-8, Rohini, New Delhi-110085
✆ 27949224 ▮ 9891463330
✉ professorfunny@yahoo.com
Hd.Org.: Akash Gupta; **Bus.Intt.:** Pub.;
Spl.: Comp. Books, COS, Institute ADD

AKASHDEEP PRINTERS
20, Ansari Rd., Darya Ganj, New Delhi-110002
✆ 23271561, 23275854, Fax: 011-23280287,
Telex: 31-62573
Bus.Intt.: Exp.

AKBARALI H. JETHA
Hasambhoy Jetha Bldg., FF. Opp. Byculla Goods Dept., Dr. B.R. Ambedkar Rd.,
Mumbai-400027 (Maharashtra)
✆ (O) 23710426/7 (R) 23868990, 23871581,
Fax: 23878712
Prop.: A.H. Jetha; **Bus.Intt.:** Exp.

AKHAND JYOTI SANSTHAN/GAYATRI PARIVAR
Ghiya Mandi, Mathura (Uttar Pradesh)
✆ 2403940, Fax: 2412273
✉ ajsansthan@awgp.org
Hd.Org.: Shriram Sharma Acharya
Bus.Intt.: Pub.; **Spl.:** Books in Hindi Language

AKHHAR
C/o Caxton Printers, East of B.K. Girls School, Krishnanagar, P.O. Agartala, Tripura
(West Bengal) ✆ 0381-2224500
Bus.Intt.: Pub.; **Spl.:** North East India's in Bengali Language

---

AKHIL BHARATI
3014, Charkhewalan, Delhi-110006
✆ 23947589
Hd.Org.: Kalpana Sharma
Bus.Intt.: Pub.; **Spl.:** Hindi Litt.

AKHIL BHARATIYA HINDI PRAKASHAK SANGH
139, Purani Anarkali, Gali No. 4, Delhi-110051
✆ 22519398
Hd.Org.: Krishan Dev Sharma; **Bus.Intt.:** Pub. and Promoter; **Spl.:** Hindi Litt.

AKHIL BHARATIYA MARATHI PRAKASHAK SANGH
C/o Mehta Publishing House,
1941, Sadashiv Peth, Madiwala Colony,
Pune-411030 (Maharashtra)
✆ 91-20-25654949
✉ jyotsnaprakashan@vsnl.com
Hd.Org.: Vishwas R. Dastane
Bus.Intt.: Promoter; **Spl.:** Marathi Language and Litt.

AKHIL KARNATAKA PUSTAK VYAPARIGAL SANGH
Hangaraki Enterprises, Vidyanagar,
Hubli-580021 (Karnataka)
✆ 2375989, 2374035
Hd.Org.: S.S. Hangaraki; **Bus.Intt.:** Pub.;
Spl.: Edu. Books and Bulletin *Pushthaka Waratha*

AKHIL STORES
Pritinagar, Distt. Nadia (West Bengal)
Hd.Org.: Atul Ghosh

AKHIL VISHWA GAYATRI PARIWAR
220/6, J.K. Colony, Jajmau, Kanpur-10
(Uttar Pradesh)
✆ 91-512-2461754, Fax: 91-512-2409163
✉ vishwagayatri@rediffmail.com
www.gayatripariwar.com
Hd.Org.: Manoj Sengar; **Bus.Intt.:** Pub.;
Spl.: Books on Self-improvement, Meditation etc.

AKSHAR BHARATI
5, Raj Gulab, Opp. N.K. Chambers,
Vaniyawad, Bhuj-370001 (Gujarat)

AKSHAR DHAM
Front D.C. Niwas, Karnal Rd., Kaithal-136027
(Haryana)
Hd.Org.: Suresh Jangid

AKSHAR PRAKASHAN PVT. LTD.
2/36, Ansari Rd., Darya Ganj,
New Delhi-110002
✆ 23270377, 23250047
Hd.Org.: Rajendra Yadav; **Bus.Intt.:** Pub.;
Spl.: Hindi Monthly *Hans*

AKSHAR PUBLICATIONS
Sanjib Villa, Jagannathbari Road,
Agartala, Tripura (West)-700001
✆ 2307500, Fax: 91-381-2323468
✉ rana-agt@yahoo.co.in
Hd.Org.: Subhabrata Deb; **Bus.Intt.:** Pub.

AKSHARA
8-2-273, Pavani Estate, Rd. No. 2,
Banjara Hill, Hyderabad (Andhra Pradesh)
✆ 040-23543906, 23540568
✉ akshara@hd2.dot.net.in
Estd.: 1997; **Hd.Org.:** Ms. M. Lakshmi;
Bus.Intt.: L.S. & Rt.; **Spl.:** Gen. and Trade, Acad. Professional, Electronic Products, Greeting Cards, Stationery, Music & Children Books (Indian & Foreign Books)

AKSHARA BOOK CENTRE
Municipal Library Building, T.B. Rd.,
Tirur-676101 (Kerala)
✆ 2422465
Estd.: 1991; **Man.Prt.:** P.P. Abdul Rahman;
Bus.Intt.: B.S.

AKSAYAVAT PRAKASHAN
26, Balrampur House, Allahabad-211003
(Uttar Pradesh)
Hd.Org.: Satyabrata Mishra

AKSHAT PUBLICATIONS
B-250, Ashok Vihar Phase-I,
Delhi-110052
✆ (O) 27240483/3234, 27114425 (R) 27231293, 27132411, Fax: 27254734, 27218836
Hd.Org.: Roopa Vohra; **Bus.Intt.:** Pub.

AKSHAY LIBRARY
Nazirpur, Nadia (West Bengal)

AKSHAY MALANCHA
B-5, College St. Market, Kolkata-7
(West Bengal)

AKS-O-AAWAZ
2724/16, First Floor, Metropole Building,
Behind Moti Mahal Restaurant,
Darya Ganj, New Delhi-110002
▮ 9899478610
✉ aksoaawaz@yahoo.com
Hd.Org.: Aizaz Hasan
Bus.Intt.: Pub.; **Spl.:** Books on Islam

AKUL BOOK CENTRE
C-371/A, Shaheed Nagar, U.P. Border,
Ghaziabad (Uttar Pradesh)

AKUL BOOK CENTRE
39, DDA Flats, New Seemapuri,
Delhi-110095
✆ 28627887
Prop.: Murli Jha; **Bus.Intt.:** Rt., WS, L.S.

ALAKANANDA PRACHURANALU
59-6-15, Kanchukota Street,
Opp. Maris Stella College, Vijayawada-520008
(Andhra Pradesh)
✆ 2476966, Fax: 91-866-2476652
✉ viwabooks@vsnl.in
Hd.Org.: D. Ashok Kumar

ALAMGEER TRADING CORPORATION
4142, Urdu Bazar, Jama Masjid, Delhi-110006
✆ (O) 23266422, 26266067 (R) 23266439,
Fax: 91-11-23266067
Bus.Intt.: Exp.; **Spl.:** Experts of the Holy *Quran* and Islamic Books Manufacturers of Books

---

ALANKAR BOOK HOUSE
1/9929, West Gorkh Park, Gali No. 3H,
Shahdara, Delhi-110032
✆ 22821465 ▮ 9810429755
Estd.: 2000; **Prop.:** Rajesh Kumar Tandon;
Bus.Intt.: L.S.

ALANKAR PRAKASHAN
3611, Netaji Subhash Marg, Darya Ganj,
New Delhi-110002
✆ 23265691, 23274470, 23289818
Hd.Org.: Mahesh Chand Jain; **Bus.Intt.:** Pub.;
Spl.: Hindi Books on Yoga and Meditation

AL-BALAGH PUBLICATIONS
10, Azami Apartment, N-1,
Abul Fazl Enclave, Jamia Nagar,
New Delhi-110025
✆ 26914592
✉ abpublications@gmail.com
Hd.Org.: Abu Talha; **Bus.Intt.:** Pub.;
Spl.: Islamic Litt., Hist. and Biographies in Urdu

AL DARUSSALAFIAH
6/8, Hazart Terrace, Sankli St., Byculla
Bridge, Mumbai-400008
(Maharashtra)
✆ 23088989, 23082737, Cable: Alsalafiah,
Fax: 23065710
✉ salafiah@hotmail.com
Estd.: 1976; **Prt.:** Akram Mukhtar
Br.: (Belasis Rd.), 242, J.B.B. Marg,
Nagpada, Mumbai-400008
✆ 23082737, 23088989, Fax: 23065710
Bus.Intt.: Pub. & Exp.; **Spl.:** Rel.

ALEKH PRAKASHAN
27/109A/3, Pandav Road,
Opp. Shankar Gali, Jwala Nagar,
Shahdara, Delhi-110032
✆ 22381582, 32911582
Fax: 91-11-223811582
✉ alekhprakashan@gmail.com
Hd.Org.: Umesh Chand Aggarwal;
Bus.Intt.: Pub. & Dist.; **Spl.:** Hindi Litt. including Children Books

---

ALEKH SAMVAD
V-8, Navin Shahdara,
Delhi-110032
✆ 32911582, Fax: 91-11-22382582
✉ alekhsamvad@gmail.com
🌐 www.alakhsamvad.com
Hd.Org.: Umesh Chand Aggarwal

Bus.Intt.: Pub. **Spl.:** Monthly Magazine *Alekh Samvad* on Hindi Litt.

ALEKH PRAKASHAN
V-8, Naveen Shahdara, Delhi-110032
✆ (O) 22290582, 31062289 (R) 22293196
alekh@mantraonline.com
Hd.Org.: V.C. Aggarwal; **Bus.Intt.:** Pub. & Dist.; **Spl.:** Hindi Litt. including Children Books

AL-FASSY PUBLICATIONS
151, Alagappa Naicket St., P.B. No. 1750, Chennai-600001 (Tamil Nadu)

AL-HASANT BOOKS (P) LTD.
3004/2, Sir Syed Ahmed Road, Darya Ganj, New Delhi-110002
✆ 23271845, Fax: 91-11-41563256
m_alhasanat@rediffmail.com
www.alhasanatbooks.com
Hd.Org.: A.M. Faheem
Bus.Intt.: Pub. and Exporter; **Spl.:** Books on Islam, Litt., Unani Medicine, Children's Books, etc.

AL-KAUSER PUBLISHERS
H.No. 11-4-714, Opp. Cancer Hospital, Red Hills, Hyderabad-500029 (Andhra Pradesh)

AL-KITAB PUBLISHERS & DISTRIBUTORS
A-110, Mayur Kushal's, Abids, Hyderabad-500001 (Andhra Pradesh)

AL-RISALA
C-29, Nizamuddin West, New Delhi-110013

AL-SHEED PUBLICATIONS
"Shiraz", 3-6-22, Himayatnagar, Hyderabad-500029 (Andhra Pradesh)

AL ULA PUBLICATIONS
P.O. Box 1, New Delhi-110025
Fax: 91-11-26828646
Bus.Intt.: Pub., L.S.; **Spl.:** Islamic Books in Indian and Foreign Languages and Religious Stationery and Indian Origin Arabic Books

AL VARD GRACIA SPANISH NATIONAL
C/o Dilip Kumar, D-28/123, Pandey Haveli, Varanasi-221001 (Uttar Pradesh)

ALFA PUBLISHERS
4398/5, Ansari Road, Darya Ganj, New Delhi-110002
✆ 91-11-23275092
alfapublications@yahoo.co.in
Hd.Org.: Atul Goel
Bus.Intt.: Pub.; **Spl.:** Books on Education, Tourism, Pol.Sci., Humanities, Soc.Sci.

ALFA PUBLISHERS & DISTRIBUTORS
Amar Kala Niketan, Near Major Pooran Singh Circle, Hospital Rd., Bikaner-334001 (Rajasthan)

ALFALAH PUBLICATIONS
E-20, Abul Fazl Enclave, Jamia Nagar, New Delhi-110025

ALFALAND
12/2, Jaganathan Rd., Nungambakkam, Chennai-600034 (Tamil Nadu)

ALGORITHM PUBLICATIONS
16, V.D.A. Commercial Complex, Opp. Tulsi Manas Mandir, Varanasi-221005 (Uttar Pradesh)

ALI MOHAMMAD & SONS
1, Budshan Hotel Building, Lal Chowk, Srinagar, Kashmir-190001 (Jammu & Kashmir)

ALI MOHAMAD & SONS
2652, Kucha Chelan, Darya Ganj, New Delhi-110002
✆ 23251329

ALKA PRAKASHAN
Khazanchi Rd., Patna-800004 (Bihar)
Bus.Intt.: Pub. and B.S.

ALKA PUBLICATIONS
Shop No. 2, Sai Sadan, 76/78, Mody St., Fort Mumbai-400001 (Maharashtra)
✆ 22624439, Fax: 91-22-22632585
manojlakhani@vsnl.net
Hd.Org.: Prabhudas Lakhani; **Bus.Intt.:** Pub.; **Spl.:** Activity Books as well as Puzzles and Storybooks for Children

ALL INDIA CONFEDERATION OF THE BLIND
Sector-5, Rohini, New Delhi-110085
✆ 27054082, Fax: 91-11-27050915
aicbdelhi@yahoo.com
www.aicb.org.in
Hd.Org.: J.L. Kaul
Bus.Intt.: Printer and Seller; **Spl.:** Books for the Visually Impaired

ALL INDIA EDUCATIONAL SUPPLY COMPANY
17, Shri Ram Building, Jawahar Nagar, (New Delhi-110007)
✆ 22914448, 22517476
Estd.: 1944; **Hd.Org.:** R.D. Agarwal;
Bus.Intt.: Pub., L.S. & Rt., Exp.

ALL INDIA INSTITUTE OF LOCAL SELF GOVT.
Sthanikraj Bhavan, C.D. Barfiwala Marg, Andheri (West), Mumbai-400058 (Maharashtra)

ALL INDIA MANAGEMENT ASSOCIATION
Management House, 14, Institutional Area, Lodhi Rd., New Delhi-110003
✆ 24634026, Fax: 24626689
adcms@aima-ind.org

Hd.Org.: D.N. Khurana; **Bus.Intt.:** Dealer; **Spl.:** VCDs, Video Cassettes and Printed Material on Mang. and Related Sub.

ALL INDIA NATURE CURE FEDERATION
BM-7, (West) Shalimar Bagh,
Delhi-110088
✆ 27482211, 27481710, Fax: 27477576
✉ bb_goel@indiatimes.com
Estd.: 1993; **Hd.Org.:** Dr. B.B. Goyal; **Bus.Intt.:** Pub. & B.S.; **Spl.:** Naturopathy & Yoga

ALL INDIA POULTRY BUSINESS DIRECTORY
5A-104, Shastri Nagar,
Ghaziabad-201001 (Uttar Pradesh)

ALL INDIA PUBLISHERS & DISTRIBUTORS (REGD.)
113, Poonamallee, High Rd.,
(Peryar) E.V.R., Salai, Chennai-600084
(Tamil Nadu)
✆ 28233004, 55250321 Fax: 28204911
✉ aipdraj@vsnl.com,
aipdrajdelhi@vsnl.net
www.aipdraj.com
Estd.: 1987; **Prop.:** Rajender K. Arya
Br.: B-4/9, Krishna Nagar, Delhi-110051
✆ 55250321, Fax: 22467613
• 4380/4B, No. 6, Kaushalya Building,
Ansari Rd., Darya Ganj, New Delhi-110002
✆ 31033253
Bus.Intt.: Pub., Imp., Exp.; **Spl.:** Med., Mang., Gen. & Fiction

ALL INDIA REPORTER LTD.
Congress Nagar, Nagpur-400012
(Maharashtra)
Bus.Intt.: Exp.

ALL INDIA SOCIETY FOR ELECTRONICS & COMPUTER TECHNOLOGY
NH-12, Hoshangabad Road, Bhaironpur,
Bhopal-462016 (Madhya Pradesh)
✆ 3293214, Fax: 91-755-2429096
✉ aisect_bpl@sancharnet.in
www.aisect.org
Hd.Org.: Santosh Chaube; **Bus.Intt.:** Pub.; **Spl.:** Technological Books in Hindi, English, and Regional Languages

ALL INDIA TRAVELLER BOOKSELLER (REGD. A.I.T.B.S.)
J-5/6, Krishan Nagar, Near Hans Raj School,
Delhi-110051
✆ 22549313, 22460494, 22054798,
Fax: 22543416, 22218401
✉ aitbs@ndf.vsnl.net.in
www.aitbs.com
Estd.: 1978; **Prop. & Pub.:** Virender Kumar Arya; **Bus.Intt.:** Pub., B.S.; **Spl.:** Humanities & Soc.Sci., Sci. & Tech., Med., Mang. & Eco., Dental, Comm., Eco., Comp., Math. & Gen.

ALL INDIA TRAVELLERS BOOKSELLERS (REGD.)
920, Poonamallee High Rd.,
Chennai-84 (Tamil Nadu)
✆ 26411911

ALL INDIA URDU PUBLISHERS & BOOKSELLERS ASSOCIATION
3243, Kucha Tara Chand, Darya Ganj,
New Delhi-110002
✆ 23257189, Fax: 91-11-23265480
✉ aakif@del3.vsnl.net.in
Hd.Org.: Khaliq Anjum

ALL KERALA PUBLISHERS AND BOOKSELLERS ASSOCIATION
D.C. Kizhakemuri Edam, Good Shepherd St.,
Kottayam-686001 (Kerala)
✆ 2563114, Fax: 2564758
Hd.Org.: E.N. Nandakumar; **Bus.Intt.:** Pub. and B.S.

ALLAHABAD LAW AGENCY
387, Sector 16-A, Faridabad
(Haryana)
✆ 2295647, 2295768, 2220965,
Pager: 9810070229, Fax: 0129-2280099
Hd.Org.: Rajen Narula; **Bus.Intt.:** Pub.; **Spl.:** Standard Law Books of Students Text Books, etc. for Over Four Decades

ALLI NILAYAM
19, Muthu Mudali Rd., Veporty P.O.,
Chennai-600007 (Tamil Nadu)

ALLIANCE BOOK SUPPLIERS (PVT.) LTD.
B-721/602, MIG Flats, East of Loni Rd.,
Delhi-110093
✆ 22811856, 22288583, 22817533,
Fax: 22812619
✉ abspl@vsnl.com, sdhar@nde.vsnl.net.in
www.abspl.com
Estd.: 1988; **Man.Dr.:** Subrata Dhar; **Bus.Intt.:** Sub.Ag.; **Spl.:** Humanities & Soc.Sci., Sci. & Tech., Med., Law, Juvenile/ Children

ALLIANCE FRANÇAISE DE DELHI
72, Lodi Estate, New Delhi-110003
✆ 91-11-43500200,
Fax: 91-11-43500228, 43500229
✉ front_desk@afdelhi.org
Hd.Org.: R.N. Rai; **Bus.Intt.:** Promoter; **Spl.:** Directory

ALLIANCE PUBLISHERS
A-121, Sector 63, Noida (Uttar Pradesh)
✆ (O) 2539073, 2401752, 2401753, 2580920
(R) 2430068, 2430314,
Fax: 2584159, 2663699
✉ alliancepublishers@aisnoida.com,
info@alliancepublishers.com
www.alliancepublishers.com

Estd.: 1999; **Hd.Org.**: Sanjeev Malhotra; **Bus.Intt.**: Pub.; **Spl.**: School Textbooks and Software Developer

ALLIBHOY SHARAFALLY & CO. P. LTD.
Mohamadi Building Gunpowder Rd., Mazgoan, Mumbai-400010 (Maharashtra)
Bus.Intt.: Exp.

ALLIED BOOK AGENCY
18/1, Shyamcharan Dey St., Kolkata-700073 (West Bengal)
Hd.Org.: Biren Sarkar

ALLIED BOOK CENTRE
9/5, Rajpur Rd., 1st Floor, Dehradun-248001 (Uttarakhand)
✆ (O) 09837066875 (R) 0135-2650945, Fax: 0135-2656554
✉ abc_rediffmail.com
Estd.: 1995; **Prop.**: Mohit Gahlot; **Bus.Intt.**: Pub., L.S.; **Spl.**: Sci. & Tech., Bio.

ALLIED BOOK DISTRIBUTORS
Bhangagarh, Guwahati-781014 (Assam)

ALLIED BOOKS CENTRE
Behind Nasarani Cinema, Chopasani Rd., Jodhpur-342002 (Rajasthan)
✆ 2643993
✉ agrabios@vsnl.com
Estd.: 2001; **Prop.**: Dr. S.S. Purohit; **Bus.Intt.**: WS; **Spl.**: Sci. & Tech.

ALLIED CHAMBERS (INDIA) LTD.
1/13-14, Asaf Ali Rd., New Delhi-110002
✆ 23239001, 23233001, Fax: 23235967
✉ aplnd@del2.vsnl.net.in
Hd.Org.: Sunil Sachdev; **Bus.Intt.**: Pub.; **Spl.**: Dictionaries and Reference Books in Eng.

ALLIED PUBLISHERS LIMITED
15, J.N. Heredia Marg, Ballard Estate, Mumbai-400038 (Maharashtra)
✆ 22626476, 22617926, 22617924, Fax: 22617926
✉ alliedpl@bom4.vsnl.com
🌐 www.alliedpublishers.com
Estd.: 1934; **Man.Dr.**: S.M. Sachdev
Br.: 1-13/14, Asaf Ali Rd., New Delhi-110002 ✆ (O) 23234269, 23233002, 23233004 (R) 24698751, Fax: 23235967 ✉ aplnd@del2.vsnl.net.in, allied.delhi@vsnl.com • 17, Chittaranjan Avenue, Kolkata-700072 ✆ 22257023, 22252514, Fax: 22361158 ✉ alliedcal@vsnl.com • 751, Anna Salai Chennai-600002 ✆ 28523938-84-58 (R) 26254691, Fax: 28520649; ✉ aplchn@vsnl.net, **Project Man.**: S. Ramasubban • 5th Main Rd., Gandhinagar, Bangalore-560009 (Karnataka) ✆ 22262081, 2253234, Fax: 22265064 ✉ aplbngl@bgl.vsnl.net.in • 3-2-844/6&7 Kachiguda Station Rd., Hyderabad-500027 (Andhra Pradesh) ✆ 24619079, 24619081, Fax: 24619079 ✉ alliedhd@hd2.dot.net.in • Prarthna Flats, 2nd Floor, Navrangpura, Ahmedabad-380009 ✆ 26465916, 26630079, Fax: 26465916 ✉ alliedad@ad1.vsnl.net.in • 16A, Ashok Marg, Patiala House, Lucknow-226001 ✆ 2214253, 2287312, Fax: 2214253 ✉ apptdlko@sify.com • 81-Hill Rd., Ramnagar, Nagpur-440010 ✆ 2521122, 2542625, Fax: 2542625 ✉ alliedng@nagpur.dot.net.in
Bus.Intt.: Pub., WS, L.S. & Rt., Imp., Exp., Sub.Ag.; **Spl.**: Sci., Tech. & Med., Humanities & Soc.Sci., Juvenile/Children Books

ALLIED PUBLISHERS PVT. LTD.
1/13-14, Asaf Ali Road, New Delhi-110002
✆ (O) 23239001, 23233002 (R) 24358751, Fax: 91-11-23235967 ▮ 9810054233
✉ alliedpublishers@eth.net
🌐 www.alliedpublishers.com
Hd.Org.: Sunil Sachdev
Bus.Intt.: Pub., Wholesaler, L.S.

ALLIED PUBLISHING SYNDICATE
61, Mahatma Gandhi Rd., Kolkata-9 (West Bengal)

ALMOE DIGITAL SOLUTIONS (P) LTD.
S-705, Manipal Centre, 47 Dickenson Road, Bangalore-560042 (Karnataka)
✆ 40468686, Fax: 91-80-40468687
✉ sumeet@almoe.com
🌐 www.almoe.com
Hd.Org.: Rajiv Johar, Sumeet Marwah, Anand Sunny

ALMORA BOOK DEPOT PUBLICATIONS DIVISION
A-2/71-B, Lawarance Rd., Delhi-110052
✆ 27100104

ALOFT SOFTWARE
416, Flat 34-B, Block E-5, Sector-61, Noida (Uttar Pradesh)
▮ 9810342216
Hd.Org.: Devinder Singh; **Bus.Intt.**: Dealer; **Spl.**: Software and Books

ALOK BOOK CENTRE
Near Harlert School, Gali No. 5, Maujpur, Delhi-110053
✆ 22857116
Man.Dir.: K.B. Shrivastva; **Estd.**: 1982
Br.: 8, Gandhi Nagar, Agra-282003 (Uttar Pradesh)
Bus.Intt.: L.S.; **Spl.**: Humanities & Soc.Sci., Sci. & Tech., Comp., Med., Mang., Bio.Sci.

ALOK BOOK STORE
Masaurhi, Patna-804452 (Bihar)
Bus.Intt.: Pub. and B.S.

ALOK PRAKASHAN
2607-B, Nai Sarak, Delhi-110006
✆ 23281532
Estd.: 1976; **Hd.Org.:** Vijay Kumar Aggarwal; **Bus.Intt.:** Pub.; **Spl.:** Rel. Books in Hindi

ALOK PRAKASHAN
New Extension Area Sadar, Nagpur-440001 (Maharashtra)

ALOKPARVA PRAKASHAN
1/6588, Poorvi Rohtas Nagar, Shahdara, Delhi-110032
✆ 22578142
Hd.Org.: Urmila Sharma; **Bus.Intt.:** Pub. and Dist.; **Spl.:** Novels Satires, Criticisms, Litt. and Books on Env., Travel, etc. in Hindi

ALOKPRIYA STORES
Station Rd., Mokameh, Patna-803302 (Bihar)
Bus.Intt.: Pub. and B.S.

ALPANA
19, Ramakant Sen Lane, Kolkata-700067 (West Bengal)

ALPANA BOOK DEPOT
Saroj Market, Kankerbagh, Patna-800020 (Bihar)
Bus.Intt.: Pub. and B.S.

ALPESH BOOK STORES
5, Gundawadi Chose, Rajkot-360001 (Gujarat)

ALPHA BOOK CENTRE
Dwarakanagar, Visakhapatnam-530016 (Andhra Pradesh)
✆ 0891-2501513, Fax: 2554122
Estd.: 1987; **Man.:** Finny Samuel; **Bus.Intt.:** Rt. & L.S.; **Spl.:** Gen. & Trade, Rel., Professional, Children Books, Greeting Cards & Toys (Indian & Foreign Books)

ALPHA BOOK DISTRIBUTORS
No. 32, (G.F.) Anna Plaza, Anna Nagar, Chennai-600040 (Tamil Nadu)

ALPHA BOOK STALL
Kozhikode-673001 (Kerala)

ALPHA LAND BOOKS PVT. LTD.
12/2, Jaganathan Rd., Nugambakkam, Chennai-600034 (Tamil Nadu)
✆ 28277090, Fax: 28250621
Estd.: 1996; **Hd.Org.:** N.V. Raghavan, N.R. Pradip (Dir.); **Bus.Intt.:** Dist.; **Spl.:** All Kind of Books in Tamil Nadu, Kerala & Pondicherry

ALPHA PUBLICATION
2640, Roshanpura, Nai Sarak, Delhi-110006
✆ 23268053, 23275468
Hd.Org.: Amrit Lal Jain; **Bus.Intt.:** Pub.; **Spl.:** Astrology, Edu., Engg., etc. in English and Hindi

ALPINE BOOKS PVT. LTD.
H-1536, Chittaranjan Park, New Delhi-110019
✆ 26478332
Prop.: Tapesh Chowdhury; **Bus.Intt.:** Rt., L.S.; **Spl.:** Acad., Comm. Technical, Beh.Sci., Sci., Soc.Sci., Med., Law

ALTAMONT PUBLICATIONS
11-E/23, Central Market, Lajpat Nagar-II, New Delhi-110024

ALTER MEDIA
Thrissur (Kerala)
✆ 0487-2422974
✉ altmedia@md4.vsnl.net.in

ALTERNATIVE BOOK PUBLISHER COLLECTIVE
142, Maitri Apartments, Plot No. 28, Parparganj, Delhi-110092
✆ 22432054

ALVINA PUBLISHING HOUSE
10452, East Park Rd., New Delhi-110005
✆ (O) 27776565, 27228303 (R) 26414087, Fax: 91-11-27776565
Estd.: 1980; **Prt.:** S.K. Ranade; **Bus.Intt.:** Pub.; **Spl.:** Edu. & Cultural Books in English & Hindi

AMAN BOOK STALL
Gatury Building, Ist Floor, New Bus Stand, Kozhikode-673004 (Kerala)

AMAN ISHARA
394, Delhi Gate Bazar, Darya Ganj, New Delhi-110002
✆ 23265371, Fax: 91-11-23286630
✉ amanishara@yahoo.com
Hd.Org.: Man Mohan Lal

AMAN PRAKASHAN
1041, Urban Estate-II, Hissar-125005 (Haryana)
✆ 245251
Hd.Org.: Bimla Devi; **Bus.Intt.:** Pub.; **Spl.:** Hindi Satires and Litt.

AMAN PRAKASHAN
W.Z.-1322, Rani Bagh, Delhi-110034
✆ 27015013, 27018426
✉ amanprakashan87@mantraonline.com
Hd.Org.: Sukhbir Singh; **Bus.Intt.:** Pub.; **Spl.:** Children's Books and Edu. Books in English, Hindi and Punjabi

AMAN PRAKASHAN
104-A/118, Rambagh, Kanpur-208012 (Uttar Pradesh)
Hd.Org.: Arvind Kumar Bajpai

AMAN PUBLISHING HOUSE
4319, Madhu Market,
Budhana Gate, Meerut-250002
(Uttar Pradesh)
✆ 2529501, 2528753
Estd.: 1972; **Bus.Intt.:** Pub. and B.S.;
Spl.: Agri. Books in School & Graduate Level

AMAR BHARATI
8/C, Tamer Lane, Kolkata-9 (West Bengal)

AMAR BOOK CENTRE
P66/4, Mayru Market, Officers Colony,
Bathinda Cantt-151004 (Punjab)
Bus.Intt.: L.S.; **Spl.:** Approved Army & MES

AMAR BOOK SELLERS
Stall No. 16, Between Statesman House and
New Delhi House, Barakhamba Rd.,
Connaught Place, New Delhi-110001
✆ 23324142, 23324153, Fax: 22434436
✉ amarbook@satyam.net.in
Bus.Intt.: B.S., L.S. and Pub.

AMAR BOOK STORE
Masaurhi, Patna-804452 (Bihar)
Bus.Intt.: Pub. and B.S.

AMAR GRANTH PUBLICATIONS
8/25, Vijay Nagar, Delhi-110009
✆ 27252362, Fax: 27252362
✉ amargp@ndf.vsnl.net.in
Hd.Org.: Inder Raj; **Bus.Intt.:** Pub., B.S. and
Dist.; **Spl.:** Indology in Sanskirit

AMAR HIND BOOK DEPOT
4073, Nai Sarak, Delhi-110006
✆ 22918382
Bus.Intt.: Retail B.S.; **Spl.:** School and College
Text and Help Books

AMAR JYOTI BOOK STALL
15/1, Abinash Ghosh Lane,
Kolkata-700006 (West Bengal)

AMAR PRAKASHAN
A-1/139B, Lawrence Rd., Delhi-110035
✆ 27183182
Estd.: 1982; **Hd.Org.:** Maheep Singh Juneja;
Bus.Intt.: Pub.

AMAR PUSTAKALAYA
Bankim Chatterjee St., Block No. 6,
Stall No. 8, Kolkata-700073
(West Bengal)

AMAR PUSTAK BHANDAR
Vijayhat, Bhagalpur (Bihar)
Bus.Intt.: Pub. and B.S.

AMARJEET SINGH PARAMJIT PUBLICATIONS
V. Jandiali P.O. Jamsher, Distt.
Jalandhar-144020 (Punjab)
Estd.: 1993; **Man.:** Amarjeet Singh
Paramjit; **Bus.Intt.:** Pub.; **Spl.:** Rel., Soc. &
Gen. in Punjabi, English & Hindi

AMARJI PUBLICATION
New Delhi-110049

AMARSATYA PRAKASHAN
109, Block-B, Preet Vihar, Delhi-110092
✆ 22050766
✉ amarsatya-prk@yahoo.com
Bus.Intt.: Pub.; **Spl.:** Books in Hindi Language

AMAZAN BOOKS
G-4, Akarshan Bhawan, 23 Ansari Road,
Darya Ganj, New Delhi-110002
✆ 23245111
Fax: 91-11-23245444
✉ uniqueselar@hotmail.com
Hd.Org.: Gurmeet Singh Pooji

AMAZON HOUSE OF BOOK & MUSIC
Aurangabad (Maharashtra)
✆ 0240-722928, 335220
✉ sharayuamazon@ip.eth.net
Bus.Intt.: B.S., Rt.

AMBALIKA PUBLISHERS
Bengali Tala, Laterisaria-846001 (Bihar)

AMBANI BOOK DISTRIBUTORS
26/44, Prahlad Plot, Rajkot-360001 (Gujarat)
▮ 9824511244,
Fax: 0281-2221254
✉ ambanibooks@yahoo.co.in
Hd.Org.: Shirish Ambani

AMBAR PRAKASHAN
888, East Park Rd., Karol Bagh,
New Delhi-110005
✆ 23625528, 23522997, 23670067,
Cable: Ambar, Fax: 23676058
✉ pitambar@bol.net.in
Estd.: 1977; **Prt.:** Ved Bhushan; **Bus.Intt.:** Pub.,
L.S. & Rt.

AMBEDKAR FOUNDATION (DR.)
25, Ashoka Rd., New Delhi-110001

AMBEDKAR PUBLICATIONS
Dr. Ambedkar Bhavan, Peermade P.O.,
Idukki-685531 (Kerala)
✆ 223387, 223254, 226138, 234290
Estd.: 1948; **Prop.:** K.B. Aboobacker Hajee;
Bus.Intt.: Pub. and B.S

AMBIKA BOOK AGENCY
A-312, Indra Verma Colony,
Nahri Ka Naka, Shastri Nagar, Jaipur-302016
(Rajasthan)
✆ 0141-2304921
✉ vikram.agri1@usa.net
Estd.: 1979; **Sales Officer:** Vikram
Sharma; **Bus.Intt.:** L.S.; **Spl.:** Fisheries,
Agri.

AMBIKA PUBLICATIONS
8949/14B, Shidipura, East Park Rd., Karol Bagh, New Delhi-110005
✆ 27522837
Estd.: 1992; **Prop.:** Dr. K.L. Taneja; **Bus.Intt.:** Pub.; **Spl.:** Math. for Primary in English & Hindi

AMERICAN BOOK CO.
8/3, Anna Salai, Chennai-600002 (Tamil Nadu)

AMERICAN INFN. RESOURCE CENTRE
24, Kasturba Gandhi Marg, Connaught Place, New Delhi-110001
✆ 23316841, Fax: 23329499
✉ libdel@pd.state.gov
Bus.Intt.: Pub. and Imp.

AMERICAN MATHEMATICAL SOCIETY
C-62, Inderpuri, New Delhi-110012

AMERICAN STUDIES RESEARCH CENTRE
Osmania University Campus, Hyderabad-500007 (Andhra Pradesh)

AMERIND PUBLISHING CO. PVT. LTD.
66, Janpath, 2nd Floor, New Delhi-110001
Bus.Intt.: Exp.

AMEYA PRAKASHAN
474-B Sadashiv Peth, Tilak Rd., Opp. New English School, Pune-411030 (Maharashtra)

AMICUS BOOKS
NIGIEE R.E.C. Rd., Hazratbal, Srinagar, Kashmir-190006 (Jammu & Kashmir)
✆ 2427227, 2420493, 2426457
Fax: 0194-2427227
✉ amicusbooks@yahoo.com
Estd.: 1990; **Hd.Org.:** Mir Abdul Rashid
Br.: #40, Suderabal, Srinagar
✆ 2420493 Fax: 2427227
Bus.Intt.: Pub., WS, L.S. & Rt.; **Spl.:** Sci. & Tech.

AMINA BOOK STALL
Post Office Rd., Thrissur (Kerala)

AMINA BOOK STALL
1, Bankim Chatterjee St., Kolkata-73 (West Bengal)

AMISH PUBLICATIONS
137, Patiala House, New Delhi-110001

AMIT BOOK DEPOT
Ashok Rajpath, Opp. Patna College, Patna-800004 (Bihar)
✆ 2656601, 2671819

AMIT BOOK DISTRIBUTOR
D-14/73, Sector-8, Rohini, New Delhi-110085
✆ 65164316, Fax: 91-11-27062968
✉ amit_abd@yahoo.com
Hd.Org.: Amit Kumar Mittal

AMIT BOOKS
1, U.B. Jawahar Nagar, Bungalow Rd., Delhi-110007
✆ 23926182, Fax: 27415016
Ch.Exe.: Mr. S. Balwant; **Bus.Intt.:** Dealer; **Spl.:** Hindi Books on Various Sub.

AMIT BOOKS/AMIT PRAKASHAN
C-29, Amar Colony Market, Lajpat Nagar-IV, New Delhi-110024
✆ 26452255, 26489507, Fax: 26478458
✉ amitprakashan@yahoo.co.in
Hd.Org.: A.D. Chowdhary; **Bus.Intt.:** Pub.; **Spl.:** Textbooks for Children

AMIT PRAKASHAN
K.B. 97, Kavi Nagar, Ghaziabad-201002 (Uttar Pradesh)
✆ 2753902, 2782835
Hd.Org.: Mahendra Sharma; **Bus.Intt.:** Pub. and L.S.

AMIT PUBLISHERS & DISTRIBUTORS
206, Vardaan House, Second Floor, 7/28, Ansari Road, Darya Ganj, New Delhi-110002
✆ 65396510, 43560006
Fax: 91-11-23281136
✉ sb_amitpub@yahoo.com
Hd.Org.: Amit Bansal

AMITY PUBLICATIONS
Vyapar Vikas Kendra, Shanti Sadan Estate, Mirzapur Rd., Ahmedabad (Gujarat)

AMNESTY INTERNATIONAL (INDIA) FOUNDATION/ DAANISH
C-1/22, First Floor, Safdarjung Enclave, New Delhi-110016
✆ 26854763, Fax: 91-11-26510202
✉ mukul1961@yahoo.co.in
🌐 www.amnesty.org.in
Hd.Org.: Mukul Sharma

AMRIT BOOKS
K-45, Jangpura Extension, New Delhi-110014
✆ 51611861-65, Fax: 91-11-51611866
✉ sales@diamondpublications.com
🌐 www.diamondpocketbook.com
Hd.Org.: Ankur Verma; **Bus.Intt.:** Pub.; **Spl.:** Children's Books in Hindi, English, Bengali, Marathi and Gujarati

AMRIT BOOKS & GENERAL STORES
Nanmuhiyan, Patna-800006 (Bihar)
Bus.Intt.: Pub. & B.S.

AMRITA DHARA
8, Patuatola Lane, Kolkata-700009
(West Bengal)

AMRITA SAHITYA MANDIR
16/1, Shyama Charan Dey St., Kolkata-700073
(West Bengal)

AMRITLOK SAHITYA PARISHAD PUBLISHERS & BOOKSELLERS
Dak Bungalow Rd., Midnapore,
P.O. Midnapore-721101 (Bihar)

AMUDHA NILAYAM LIMITED
No. 7, Sripuram Second St., Royapettah,
Chennai-600014 (Tamil Nadu)
✆ 28261343, 28261790, Fax: 28257158
✉ japonica@rediffmail.com
Chairperson: V. Kalyane; **Bus.Intt.:** Pub.;
Spl.: Literary and Religious Books in Tamil
Laser Printing and Offset Printing Providing
Telecom Services

ANADA PRAKASHAN PVT. LTD.
'Granthsetu' 1756, Gandhi Rd., NR Bala
Hanuman, Ahmedabad-380001 (Gujarat)
✆ (O) 22139900, 22169956 (R) 25464118,
25468235, Fax: 91-79-22139900
✉ anadaadi@sancharnet.in
www.anada.com
Estd.: 1937; **Hd.Org.:** B.R. Anada;
Bus.Intt.: Pub., Exp.; **Spl.:** Edu. & Children's
Books, Dictionaries, etc.

ANAMAYA PUBLISHERS
F-154/2, Lado Sarai, New Delhi-110030
✆ 29523205, Fax: 91-11-29523205
✉ anamayapub@vsnl.net
Hd.Org.: Manish Sejwal

ANAMIKA BOOK STALL
Bethuadahari, Nadia (West Bengal)

ANAMIKA PUBLISHERS & DISTRS.
129 A, Pocket-D, Deep Enclave,
Ashok Vihar-III, Delhi-110052

ANAMIKA PUBLISHERS & DISTRIBUTORS (P) LTD./ ANAMIKA PRAKASHAN
4697/3, 21-A, Ansari Rd., Darya Ganj,
New Delhi-110002
✆ 23281655
Hd.Org.: Pankaj Sharma, Anil Sharma;
Bus.Intt.: Pub.; **Spl.:** Humanities and
Soc.Sci. in English and Hindi

ANAND ASHRAM
P.O. Anand Ashrama, Kanhangad-671531
(Kerala)

ANAND ASSOCIATES
1068, Sector B, Pocket-I,
Vasant Kunj, New Delhi-110070
✆ 26123365, Fax: 91-11-22723067
✉ thrupti@vsnl.com
www.myown.org
Hd.Org.: Jayaram Hegde; **Bus.Intt.:** Dist.;
Spl.: World Bank and IMF Publications

ANAND ASSOCIATES
1219, Stock Exchange Towers, 12th Floor,
Dalal St., Mumbai-400023
(Maharashtra)
✆ 22723065-66, Fax: 22723067
✉ thrupti@vsnl.com
www.myown.org
Hd.Org.: Jayram Hegde; **Bus.Intt.:** Dist.;
Spl.: World Bank and IMF Publications

ANAND BHAWAN
Khazanchi Rd., Patna-800004 (Bihar)
Bus.Intt.: Pub. and B.S.

ANAND BOOK DEPOT
Anand Pustak Nagar P.O. Junction,
Muvattupuzha-686661 (Kerala)
✆ (O) 04858-233112 (R) 233031
Estd.: 1985; **Prop.:** D.R. Nair; **Bus.Intt.:** Pub.
& B.S.

ANAND BOOK DISTRIBUTORS
29-A, Krishan Kunj Extn. Part II,
Near Bank Enclave, Laxmi Nagar,
New Delhi-110092
✆ 22456072, 23218146
Hd.Org.: Rajiv Anand; **Bus.Intt.:** Dist.;
Spl.: Children's Books, Dictionaries, Edu.
Cassettes and Videos

ANAND BOOK HOUSE
Q-20, 3rd Floor, West Patel Nagar,
New Delhi-110008
✆ (O) 25725274 (R) 23735353 ▮ 9868092922
Prt.: R.K. Gupta, Mrs. Santosh Kumari;
Bus.Intt.: Pub.'s Rep., L.S.; **Spl.:** Acad., Beh.
Sci., Soc.Sci., Comm., Sci., Med, Tech. & Law

ANAND BOOK STORE
Bakhtiarpur, Patna-803212 (Bihar)
Bus.Intt.: Pub. & B.S.

ANAND EDUCATIONAL AIDS
10, Nehru Nagar Market, New Delhi-110065
✆ 26316301
Hd.Org.: S.K. Anand; **Bus.Intt.:** Dist.,
Imp.; **Spl.:** Books for Children

ANAND PAPERBACKS
Madrasa Rd., Kashmeri Gate,
New Delhi-110006

ANAND PRAKASHAN
Rameswaranm, 1-L-1, Dadavari Spl, Kota
(Rajasthan)
Hd.Org.: Dr. Kshama Chaturvedi

ANAND PUBLICATIONS
C/o Mrs. S.U. Jadhav, 430,
Shalaka-Sangh, Co-op. Housing Society,
Queen's Barracks, Karve Rd.,
Mumbai-400021 (Maharashtra)

ANAND PUBLICATIONS
Khazanchi Rd., Patna-800004 (Bihar)
Bus.Intt.: Pub. and B.S.

ANAND PUSTAK BHANDAR
Chiraiya, Bhagalpur-813127 (Bihar)
Bus.Intt.: Pub. & B.S.

ANAND PUSTAK BHANDAR
Naubatpur, Patna-801109 (Bihar)
Bus.Intt.: Pub. & B.S.

ANAND SAHITYA BHANDAR
Mithapur, Patna-800001 (Bihar)
Bus.Intt.: Pub. & B.S.

ANAND SAHITYA SADAN
Sidhartha Marg, Cantonment-20,
Aligarh-202001 (Uttar Pradesh)
Prop.: A.R. Akela; **Spl.:** Litt. on Dr. Ambedkar and related Dalit affairs etc. in Hindi

ANAND T. HINGORANI
C-18/D, Munirka, New Delhi-110067

ANANDA BALA PRACHURANALU
3-16-1, Pattabhipuram, Guntur-522006
(Andhra Pradesh)

ANANDA BAZAR PATRIKA LTD.
6, Beniatola Lane, Kolkata-700009
(West Bengal)
Bus.Intt.: Pub. & Exp.

ANANDA NIKETAN TRUST
Jyoti Ashram, 68, Lulla Nagar, Pune-411040
(Maharashtra)
✆ 020-26832632
Estd.: 1961; **Bus.Intt.:** Pub.;
Spl.: Spiritual, Gen. Books

ANANDA PUBLISHERS PVT. LTD.
45, Beniatola Lane, Kolkata-700009
(West Bengal)
✆ 224214352, 224213417, Fax: 22193856
ananda@cal3.vsnl.net.in
www.anandapub.com
Estd.: 1957; **Ch.Exe.:** Mr. Subir Mitra;
Bus.Intt.: Pub.; **Spl.:** Bengali Novels, Short Stories, Poems, Travelogues, Eco., Autobiography and Rel. Books

ANANDA SANGHA
DLF Phase 1, B 10/8, Gurgaon-122002
(Haryana)
✆ 0124-5059550
ananda@anandaindia.org
www.anandaindia.org
Hd.Org.: William Swanner
Br.: Crystal Clarity Publishers, (Office) 16, Ansari Rd., New Delhi-110002
9899247247

ANANDAM
19, Shyama Charan Dey St., Kolkata-700073
(West Bengal)
Bus.Intt.: Pub.; **Spl.:** Illustrated Children's Books in Bengali

ANANG PRAKASHAN
B-202, Gali No.1, Mandirwali,
North Ghonda, Delhi-110053
✆ 22199683
Hd.Org.: Anangpal Singh Chauhan;
Bus.Intt.: Pub.; **Spl.:** Criticisms, Poetry, Novels, etc. in Hindi

ANANT PRAKASHAN
149, Hanivarpeth, Pune-411080 (Maharashtra)
✆ (O) 0212-2454893 (R) 2412658
Estd.: 1989; **Prop.:** A.S. Puranik;
Bus.Intt.: Dist.; **Spl.:** School Library Books for 1st to 12th Study in Marathi

ANANTA BOOK STALL
Mahishbathan, Nadia (West Bengal)

ANANTHANANTHA PRAKASHAN
Canara Bank Rd., Tq. & Distt. Hassan,
Gorur-573120 (Karnataka)

ANANYA PRAKASHAN
C-6/128C, Lawrence Rd., Delhi-110035

ANANYA PROKASHAN
College St. (1st Floor), Kolkata-700073
(West Bengal)
✆ 033-22414348

ANDHRA BRAHMA SAMAJ
303, Mahesh Apartments, Yellareddy Guda,
Hyderabad-500073 (Andhra Pradesh)

ANDHRA JYOTI PRINTERS LTD.
P.B. No. 712, Vijayawada-520010
(Andhra Pradesh)

ANDHRA PRADESH BOOK DISTRIBUTION
Eluru Rd., Vijayawada-522002 (Andhra Pradesh)
✆ 0866-267498
Estd.: 1989; **Prop.:** D. Vijaya Kumar;
Bus.Intt.: Pub.; **Spl.:** Novels, Sci. Dictionaries, Gen. Books, Adult Edu., Children Books etc. in Telugu

ANDHRA PRADESH JUDICIAL ACADEMY
S.P. Rd., Secunderabad-500003
(Andhra Pradesh)

ANDHRA UNIVERSITY PRESS & PUBLICATION
Visakhapatnam-530003
(Andhra Pradesh)

ANDREAS-PUNNOOSE FOUNDATION
Kunnuparambil Building, Kurichy, Kottayam-686549 (Kerala)
✆ 2430470, Fax: 91-481-2320041
✉ kppunnoose@gmail.com
Hd.Org.: K.P. Punnoose

ANE BOOKS
4821, Parwana Bhawan, 1st Floor, 24, Ansari Rd., Darya Ganj, New Delhi-110002
✆ (O) 23276843-44 (R) 27011631, Fax: 011-23276863
✉ anebooks@vsnl.com
www.anebooks.com
Estd.: 1997; **Hd.Org.:** Sunil Saxena, J.R. Kapoor
Br.: Avantika Niwas, 19, Dorai Swami Rd., T. Nagar, Chennai-600017
✆ 28141554, 28141209
• Flat No. 16-A, 220, Vivekanand Rd., Manicktala, Kolkata-700006
✆ 23547119
Bus.Intt.: Pub., WS; **Spl.:** Acad., Beh., Sci., Soc.Sci., Comm., Sci., Tech. & Med.

ANEES ENTERPRISES
1741, Rodhgran (Lalkuan), Delhi-110006
✆ 27532732
Hd.Org.: Mohd. Anees

ANEKANT BHARTI PRAKASHAN
E/1/2, Charyl, Near Sahjanand College, Dr. Sarvapalli Radhakrishnan Marg, Ambawadi, Ahmedabad-380015 (Gujarat)

ANGEL PUBLISHING HOUSE
4C/9, Basement, Old Rajinder Nagar, New Delhi-110060
✆ 25772171, 25742171
✉ angelaip@del3.vsnl.net.in
Estd.: 1997; **Hd.Org.:** A.R. Chowdhary; **Bus.Intt.:** Pub.; **Spl.:** Children Picture & Story Books

ANGEL'S PUBLISHERS, BOOKSELLERS & DISTRIBUTORS
Mandi Bal, Nowshera, Srinagar (Jammu & Kashmir)
Estd.: 1992; **Prop.:** M.S. Mir; **Bus.Intt.:** Pub., WS, L.S.

ANGELS PUBLISHING CORPN.
19, British Indian St., Kolkata-700069 (West Bengal)
✆ 91-33-22485370/9357, Fax: 91-33-22485370
Hd.Org.: S. Lodha; **Bus.Intt.:** Pub.; **Spl.:** Gen. Books and New Year Diaries

ANGILA BOOKS
69, Chowringhee, Kolkata-700013 (West Bengal)

ANGKOR PUBLISHER
B-62/10, Naraina Industrial Area, Phase II, New Delhi-110028

ANGOOR PRAKASHAN
C-709, Third Floor, Ganesh Nagar-II, Shakarpur, Delhi-110092
✆ 91-11-65426615
✉ angoorprakashan@yahoo.in
Hd.Org.: Padmini Gupta, Harish Chand Gupta; **Bus.Intt.:** Pub. and Dist.; **Spl.:** Novels, Plays, Criticisms, Poetry and Books for Children in English and Hindi

ANIL BOOK AGENCY
Tanksale Complex, Sitabuldi, Nagpur-440012 (Maharashtra)
✆ 2546149
Estd.: 1977; **Prop.:** A.D. Tanksale; **Bus.Intt.:** Pub., Dist., L.S.; **Spl.:** Hist., Novel and Shortstories in Marathi

ANIL BOOK CORNER
H-Block, Plaza Cinema Building, Connaught Circus, New Delhi-110001
✆ 23713223
✉ abcplaza@yahoo.com
Hd.Org.: Anil Kumar; **Bus.Intt.:** Dist.; **Spl.:** Mang., Photography, Fashion, Furniture, Travel, etc.

ANIL BOOK DEPOT
Sector Six A Market, Bhilai Distt.-490006 (Madhya Pradesh)
✆ 2355067, 2355267
Estd.: 1975; **Hd.Org.:** Anil Jain; **Bus.Intt.:** Pub., WS, L.S. & Rt.

ANIL BOOK SERVICE
270/2, Patpar Ganj, Opp. Anand Sab Lok Society, Mayur Vihar, Phase-I, Delhi-110091
▮ 9810648580
Prop.: Rajendra Prasad; **Bus.Intt.:** L.S.; **Spl.:** Arts, Archaeology, Hist., Pol., Sol.

ANIL BOOKS
Parippally, Kottayam-691574 (Kerala)
✆ 22179
Estd.: 1989; **Hd.Org.:** P.S. Anil; **Bus.Intt.:** B.S.

ANIL BROTHERS
Khajuri Bazar, Indore-452002 (Madhya Pradesh)
✆ 2450042

ANIL PRAKASHAN
2619-20 New Market, Nai Sarak, Delhi-110006
✆ 23286781, 27211659
Hd.Org.: Anil Kumar Gupta

ANIL PUSTAK BHANDAR
Obra, Aurangabad-824124 (Bihar)
Bus.Intt.: Pub. & B.S.

ANIMA PRAKASHANI
141, Keshab Chandra Sen St.,
Kolkata-700009 (West Bengal)
✆ 033-23507913
Bus.Intt.: Pub.; **Spl.:** Juvenile Litt., Biographies, Novels, Short Stories Fictions, Essays Sports, Music and Law in Bengali

ANINDITA PUSTAKALAYA
P-36, Babu Bagan Lane, Dhakuria,
Kolkata-700031 (West Bengal)

ANIRUDH SAHITYA
1493-C, Sadashivpet, Tilak Rd., Pune-411002 (Maharashtra)

ANITA PRAKASHAN
8-11-301, Jyoti Colony, Behind KEB,
Bidar-585401 (Karnataka)

ANITA PUBLISHING HOUSE
A-93, Azad Enclave, Pooja Colony, Loni,
Ghaziabad-201102 (Uttar Pradesh)
9810326389
Hd.Org.: Santosh Srivastava

ANJALI
P.B. No. 340, 20.10.8, N.R. Naidu St.,
Suryaraopet, Vijayawada-520002
(Andhra Pradesh)

ANJALI BOOK STALL
Stall-43, Manton Syoer & Mkt.,
Kolkata-700034 (West Bengal)

ANJALI PUBLISHING HOUSE
1511, Sadashivpet, Pune-411030
(Maharashtra)

ANJANA BOOK DISTRIBUTORS
19/1, 8th Cross, Sampangirama Nagar,
Bangalore-560027 (Karnataka)
✆ 22271380
Estd.: 1987; **Bus.Intt.:** L.S., Rt., Imp.

ANJANI PRAKASHAN
B-16/8, Indranagar, Pune-411037
(Maharashtra)
Estd.: 1989; **Prop.:** Anjana Burte;
Bus.Intt.: Pub. & B.S.; **Spl.:** Children's Books in Marathi

ANJANI PUSTAK BHANDAR
Chiraiya, Bhagalpur-813127 (Bihar)
Bus.Intt.: Pub. & B.S.

ANJU BOOK STALL
B.P.S.C. Gate, Bailey Rd., Patna-800001
(Bihar)
Bus.Intt.: Pub. & B.S.

ANJUMAN TARAQQI URDU (HIND)
Urdu Ghar, 212, Rouse Avenue,
New Delhi-110002
✆ 23237210, 23236299, Fax: 23239547
✉ urduadabndli@bol.net.in
Hd.Org.: Khaliq Anjum; **Bus.Intt.:** Pub., Dist. and B.S.; **Spl.:** Encyclopaedias and Dictionaries in Urdu and Hindi

ANJUMAN TARAQUI URDU (BIHAR)
IInd Floor, Urdu Bhavan, Chohatta
Patna-800004 (Bihar)

ANKIT INFORMATICS (P) LTD.
818, Vikas Deep, 18,
Lakshmi Nagar District Centre,
New Delhi-110092
✆ (O) 22468417, 22019574 (R) 22457606,
Fax: 22019574
✉ ankinfo@yahoo.com
Hd.Org.: Vikas Morarka, **Bus.Intt.:** Pub. & B.S.

ANKUR BOOKS
308, Pocket 5, Sector-2, Rohini, Delhi-110058
Bus.Intt.: Pub.; **Spl.:** Edu. books

ANKUR PRAKASHAN
H-1536, Chittaranjan Park, New Delhi-110019

ANKUR PRAKASHAN
G-17, Jagat Puri, Delhi-110051
✆ 22505852
Hd.Org.: Rakhi Maheshwari; **Bus.Intt.:** Pub.;
Spl.: Literary Books by Eminent Authors in Hindi

ANKUR PRAKASHAN
13, Pipaleshwar Mahadeb St., Naiyon Kee Talai, Udaipur-313001 (Rajasthan)
✆ 2414871
Hd.Org.: Rajender Kumar Paneri

ANKUR PRAKASHAN
A-31C, New Gupta Colony,
Delhi-110009
✆ 91-11-27247827
Hd.Org.: Arun Kumar Gupta

ANKUR PUBLICATIONS
30/20, Shakti Nagar, Delhi-110007
✆ 27242795
Hd.Org.: Omprakash Sharma

ANKUR PUBLISHING HOUSE
Uphaar Cinema Building, Green Park Extn.,
New Delhi-110016

ANKUR PUSTAKALAYA
31B, College Row, Kolkata-700009
(West Bengal)

ANMOL PRAKASHAN
Appa Balwant Square, Pune-411052
(Maharashtra)

ANMOL PUBLICATIONS PVT. LTD.
4374/4B, Ansari Rd., Darya Ganj,
New Delhi-110002
✆ 23261597, 23255577, 23278000,

Fax: 23280289
anmolpublications@vsnl.com
www.anmolpublications.com
Estd.: 1985; **Man.Dr.:** Jawahar Lal Kumar
Br.: 7/25, Ansari Rd., Darya Ganj, New Delhi-110002 23286871, 23286874, 23286875 anmolpublications@vsnl.com
• V. Srinivasa Murthy, No. 166, 'Bellichukki', New Bank Colony, Konankunte, Bangalore-560062 9845518763 (R) 26322490
Bus.Intt.: Pub., WS, L.S. & Rt., Exp.;
Spl.: Encyclopaedias, Multi-volume Reference Books, Dictionaries, Mang. Studies, Hist., Pol.Sci., Eco., Sol., Geology & Geo., Language & Literature, Env.Studies, Women Studies, Journalism, Tourism, Physics, Chemistry, Botany, Zoology, Math. etc.

ANNAI NILAYAM
Sivakasi (Tamil Nadu)
04562-20683
annai_nm@angelfire.com
Bus.Intt.: Pub.

ANNAM (P) LTD.
No. 2, Sivam Koil South St., Sivaganga-623560 (Tamil Nadu)
Man.Dr.: K. Kathir; **Bus.Intt.:** Pub.;
Spl.: Tamil Litt.

ANNAPURNA STORES
Barwbandu Banagraaj, Purulia (West Bengal)

ANNEY PRAKASHAN
C-6/128C, Lawrence Rd., Delhi-110035
27184727, 27185092, Fax: 23252174
Hd.Org.: Umesh Mehta

ANNIS ENTERPRISES
1741/42, Rodgran, Delhi-110006

ANOOP BOOK AGENCY
Near Telangpura Akhada, Indira Market Rd., Wardha-442001 (Maharashtra)

ANSHU PRAKASHAN
152/3, Jacob Pura, Gurgaon-122001 (Haryana)

ANSHU PRAKASHAN
1143/31, Old Katra, Allahabad-211002 (Uttar Pradesh)
2609370
Hd.Org.: Shri Ashutosh Mishra

ANTARCTICA GRAPHICS PVT. LTD.
1A, Vidyasagar St., Kolkata-700009 (West Bengal)
23502173, 23510564, Fax: 23507658
anta.graphic@gems.vsnl.net.in
Bus.Intt.: Exp.

ANTHRASHTRA PUSTHOKAL SAVA SAMITHI
P.B. No. 1883, Kaloor Towers, Kaloor, Kochi-682017 (Kerala)

ANTHROPOLOGICAL SOCIETY OF INDIA (THE)
27, Jawaharlal Nehru Rd., Kolkata-16 (West Bengal)
033-22498731/3
Gen.Dr.: R.K. Bhattacharya
Bus.Intt.: Pub.; **Spl.:** Anthropological Survey is a Govt. Org. engaged on the Anthropological Research in Eng.

ANTIQUE PUBLICATIONS
80-M, Sector-4, Pushap Vihar, New Delhi-110017

ANTIQUITIES PRESERVATION & SERVICES
C/3/L, Verma Colony, 35, Laurence St., Uttarpara, Hooghly-712258 (West Bengal)

ANTIKA PRAKASHAN
C-56/UGF-4, Shalimar Garden, Ghaziabad-201005 (Uttar Pradesh)
91-120-6475212
aantika1999@yahoo.co.in
Hd.Org.: Gourinath

ANU BOOKS PUBLISHERS & DISTRIBUTORS
Shivaji Rd., Meerut-250001 (Uttar Pradesh)
Bus.Intt.: Pub. & Dist.

ANUBHAV BOOK DISTRIBUTORS
618/95/38, Sarvodaya Nagar, Allapur, Allahabad-211006 (Uttar Pradesh)
2501620
Estd.: 1990; **Prop.:** Lalji Maurya;
Bus.Intt.: L.S. & Rt.

ANUBHAV PRAKASHAN
13-B, Sanchar Lok Appt, Parparganj Depot, I.P. Ent., Delhi-110092
22203396

ANUBHAV PRAKASHAN
E-28, Lajpat Nagar, Sahibabad, Ghaziabad-201005 (Uttar Pradesh)
2630699, 2635277
anubhavprakashan@gmail.com
Hd.Org.: Anubhav Kaushik
Bus.Intt.: Pub.; **Spl.:** Fiction, Poetry, Plays Memoirs, etc. in Hindi

ANUBHAV PRAKASHAN
146, Gyankhand-3, Indirapuram, Ghaziabad (Uttar Pradesh)
9811701935, 9811271465, Fax: 91-11-23270889
Hd.Org.: Ranvijay; **Bus.Intt.:** Pub.;
Spl.: Hindi Litt., Sci., Novels, Criticisms and Books for Children

ANUBHUTI PRAKASHAN
53-Karanpur, Near Prayag Station, Allahabad-211002 (Uttar Pradesh)
✆ (O) 0532-2466870, 3152109 (R) 2466870
✉ am26j@rediffmail.com
Estd.: 1988; **Hd.Org.:** Ashutosh Mitra; **Bus.Intt.:** Pub., L.S.; **Spl.:** Hindi Litt., Children & General in Hindi

ANUPAM INTERNATIONAL
B-265, Mangolpuri Ind. Area, Phase-1, New Delhi-110083
✆ 27913709/10/7913425, Fax: 91-11-27910216
Hd.Org.: Anil Kumar; **Bus.Intt.:** Pub.

ANUPAM PRAKASHAN
Banjari Chowk, Raipur (Madhya Pradesh)

ANUPAM PRAKASHAN
T.K. Ghosh (Near Academy School), Patna-800004 (Bihar)
✆ 250449
Hd.Org.: Bheem Sen

ANUPAM PRAKASHANI
18-J, Tamer Lane, Kolkata-700009 (West Bengal)

ANUPAMA
Banagram, Court Rd., Distt. 24-Parganas (North) (West Bengal)
Hd.Org.: Biman Behari Mukherjee

ANUPAMA PUBLICATIONS
20, New Layalpur Extn., Delhi-110051
Bus.Intt.: Pub. & B.S.

ANUPRIYA PUBLISHING HOUSE
C-263, Hans Marg, Malviya Nagar, Jaipur-302017 (Rajashtan)
✆ (0141) 2521627, 2524039
✉ mmgoyalg@satyam.net.in, anupriya_pub@yahoo.com
Estd.: 1992; **Bus.Intt.:** Pub. and B.S.; **Spl.:** Sci. and Tech., Med., Comm. and Mang., Humanities, Law, Gen. Books, Env.

ANURADHA PRAKASHANI
49, Milan Park, P.O. Garia, Kolkata-700084 (West Bengal)

ANURADHA PUBLICATIONS
G-68, Kamakodi Flats, 20, Rameswaram Road, T. Nagar, Chennai-600017 (Tamil Nadu)
✆ 24360134, Fax: 91-44-24357410
✉ anuradhaags@vsnl.net
Hd.Org.: Sethuraaman

ANURAG PRAKASHAN
131, Sant Ravidas Marg, Purana Behrana, Allahabad-211003 (Uttar Pradesh)
✆ 2610169 (PP)
Hd.Org.: Lakshminarayan Singh

ANURAG PRAKASHAN
1/1073 D, Mehrauli, New Delhi-110030
✆ 26511833, 26516773
Hd.Org.: Parveen Kumar Gupta

ANURAG PRAKASHAN
B-110-D, DDA, Munirka, New Delhi-110067
✆ 26103581, 26178668
Hd.Org.: Rashmi Malhotra

ANURAG TRUST
D-68, Nirala Nagar, Lucknow-226010 (Utttar Pradesh)
✆ 91-522-2786782, 91-11-26895809
✉ anurag_trust@rediffmail.com
Hd.Org.: Kamla Pandey; **Bus.Intt.:** Pub.; **Spl.:** Picture Books, Cartoon Books and Gen. reading material for Children in Hindi

ANUSTUP
2B, Nabin Kundu Lane, Kolkata-700009 (West Bengal)
✆ 033-23507613
Bus.Intt. Pub.; **Spl.:** Books in Bengali

ANWESHA
M.C. Rd., Barowari, Guwahati-781003 (Assam)
✆ 2664662
✉ anweshaguwa@sify.com
Hd.Org.: Dudulmoni Sarmah; **Bus.Intt.** Promoter; **Spl.:** Asamiya, English, Hindi and Bengali and Organiser of Seminars and Book Fairs

APARNA BOOK DISTRIBUTORS
73, M.G. Rd., Kolkata-700009 (West Bengal)

APARNA BOOKS & PERIODICALS
2799/1A, 8th Cross, Adipampa, Rd., V.V. Mohalla, Mysore-570002 (Karnataka)
✆ 0821-2412258
✉ aparnabooks@vsnl.com
🌐 www.aparnabooks.com
Estd.: 1990; **Prop.:** Lalita S. Murthy, Samba Murthy N.
Sh.: 3, SLN Temple Complex, Kalidasa Rd., V.V. Mohalla, Mysore-570002 ✆ 0821-2510011
Bus.Intt.: Pub., WS, L.S. & Rt.; **Spl.:** Humanities & Soc.Sci., Sci. & Tech., Juvenile/Children, Gen. & Fiction etc.

APEKSHA BOOK DEPOT
Near Peakup Stand, Bodeli Tq. Sankheda, Distt. Vadodara-391135 (Gujarat)

APEX PUBLISING HOUSE
11109, Karol Bagh, Doriwalan, East Park Rd., New Delhi-110005

✆ 23512722, 31068948, Fax: 23622726
✉ apexhouse@rediffmail.com
Hd.Org.: Vipin Arora; **Bus.Intt.:** Pub.;
Spl.: Children's Edu. Books in English and Hindi

APNA PUSTAK BHANDAR
Barahat, Bhagalpur-813103 (Bihar)
Bus.Intt.: Pub. & B.S.

APNA PUSTAK MAHAL
Majhaul, Begusarai-851127 (Bihar)
Bus.Intt.: Pub. & B.S.

APNA STORE
Kankerbagh, Near Central School,
Patna-800020 (Bihar)
Bus.Intt.: Pub. & B.S.

APOORVA PUBLIC PVT. LTD.
Shree Shilya, Raghukul Society, Karvenagar,
Pune-411052 (Maharashtra)

APPLE BOOKS
7/28, Vardaan House, Mahavir St., Ansari Rd.,
Darya Ganj, New Delhi-110002
✆ (O) 23289282 (R) 27125707 ▮ 9811010262
✉ applebooks@now-india.net.in
Prop.: Sanjay Gandhi; **Bus.Intt.:** L.S., Rt.;
Spl.: Med. and Life Sci., Agri.

APPLE PUBLISHING INTERNATIONAL PVT LTD
V-5, 4th Main Road, Anna Nagar,
Chennai-600040 (Tamil Nadu)
✆ 26224690, Fax: 91-44-26211085
✉ infor@applebooks.org
www.applebooks.org
Hd.Org.: R. Manokaran; **Bus.Intt.:** Pub.;
Spl.: Children's Books and Reference Titles in English

APPLIED MEDIA
206, Ashoka Apartment, Ranjit Nagar,
Commercial Complex, New Delhi-110008
✆ 25707820, 25708940 ▮ 9868157782,
Fax: 25707820
✉ appliedmedia@vsnl.com
Estd.: 1991; **Prop.:** Sudhir Kumar Bansal;
Bus.Intt.: Pub.'s Rep. and Literary Agent;
Spl.: Sci., Tech., Humanities, Soc.Sci.,
Reference and Electronics

APPLIED MEDIA
196, Pruthi Building, Prabhat Colony,
Opp. Yoga Institute, Santa Cruz,
East Mumbai-400055 (Maharashtra)
✆ 22-26100406, Fax: 26115237
✉ applied@nda.vsnl.net.in

APRITAM PRAKASHAN
B-201, Sadatpur, Delhi-110094
✆ (O) 22266349 (R) 25162587
Hd.Org.: Maheswar Dutt Pandey

AQIB BOOK CENTRE
Opp. University Gate, Sudrabal Rd.,
Hazratbal, Srinagar-190006
(Jammu and Kashmir)
✆ 2410251
Estd.: 2003; **Prop.:** Mehrajuddin Wani;
Spl.: Humanities & Soc.Sci., Mang. & Comm.,
Sci., Med.Sci., Engg. & Tech., Law, Fiction &
Gen.

AR-RAHMAN PUBLICATIONS
550, Churiwalan, Gali Hakimwali,
Jama Maszid, Delhi-110006
✆ 23266198 ▮ 9899031430, Fax: 23257196
✉ triveni@ndf.vsnl.net.in
Hd.Org.: Sayaid Muzibur Rahman;
Bus.Intt.: Pub. and Pub.'s Rep.

ARADHNA BROTHERS
124/152-C, Govind Nagar, Kanpur-208012
(Uttar Pradesh)
Hd.Org.: Krishanchand Shukla

ARASARKADAVIL BOOKS
Pathirappally, Alappuzha-688521 (Kerala)
Estd.: 1991; **Man.Dr.:** Unni Joseph;
Bus.Intt.: Pub.

ARATLLI BOOKS
P.O. Box 33, Central Junction,
Kanjirappally-686507 (Kerala)
✆ 23002
Estd.: 1984; **Prop.:** T.T. Thomas;
Bus.Intt.: Pub. & B.S.

ARAVALI BOOKS INTERNATIONAL (P) LTD.
W-30, Okhla Industrial Area, Phase II,
New Delhi-110020
✆ 26388830-32, 26389736-38, Fax: 26388829
✉ aravali@nde.vsnl.net.in
www.aravalibooks.com
Dr.: Subhash Goel; **Bus.Intt.:** Pub.; **Spl.:** Gen.
& Reference books on Soc.Sci., Comm., Sci.,
Medical, Rare, Journals

ARAVAZHI PUBLICATIONS
New No. 13, III St., Lakshmipuram Extn. II
Tambaram (W), Chennai-600045
(Tamil Nadu)
✆ 22261713
Estd.: 1981; **Bus.Intt.:** Pub.; **Spl.:** Novels

ARCHAEOLOGICAL SURVEY OF INDIA
Janpath, New Delhi-110011
✆ 23019108, 23015283, Fax: 23010953
✉ asi@del3.vsnl.net.in
Hd.Org.: Amarendra Nath; **Bus.Intt.:** Pub.;
Spl.: Postcards and Guides on Archaeology,
Art, Indology and Monuments

ARCHANA PUBLICATIONS
38/A, Lakshmi Nagar, Delhi-110032

▮ 9968037542
Hd.Org.: Surya Prakash

ARCHANA PUBLICATIONS (P) LTD.
CB-349, Ring Rd., Naraina,
New Delhi-110028
✆ 25698295, 25742276, 25767516
✉ booksforall@bookhiveindia.com
Hd.Org.: Manmohan Nanda; **Bus.Intt.:** Pub.; **Spl.:** Books for Children

ARCHIES LTD.
C-113, Naraina Industrial Area,
Phase-I, New Delhi-110028
✆ 41410000, Fax: 91-11-41410060
✉ cb@archiesonline.com
www.archiesonline.com
Hd.Org.: Anil Moolchandani; **Bus.Intt.:** Pub.; **Spl.:** Greeting cards, Quotation Books Educational Charts, Posters, Activity Books for Children, etc.

ARCHIES INTERNATIONAL
28/C, Alipur Rd., Delhi-110054
Bus.Intt.: Exp.

ARCHNA PUBLICATIONS
Jr. LIG 88, I, Drug Pattern Kotra, Sultanabad, Bhopal (Madhya Pradesh)

AREEB PUBLICATIONS
1542, Pataudi House, Darya Ganj,
New Delhi-110002
✆ 23282550, 23284740,
Fax: 91-11-23267510
✉ apd@bol.net.in
adambooks.com
Hd.Org.: Syed Sajid Ali

ARESS SYNDICATE
148/9, N.S.C. Bose Rd., Rani Kuthi,
Kolkata-700040 (West Bengal)
Bus.Intt.: Exp.

ARGUS BOOK SERVICE
107, 4832/24 Ansari Rd., Darya Ganj,
New Delhi-110002
✆ 23285856, 23270309 ▮ 9810162182,
Fax: 011-23270309
Estd.: 1991; **Prop.:** Ashwani Sharma;
Bus.Intt.: WS, L.S., Exp.; **Spl.:** Soc.Sci., Humanities Mang., Comm., Energy Env., Eng.Litt., Fiction, Journal, Magazines, Arts & Arch.

ARIANA PUBLISHERS & DISTRIBUTORS
F-198, Vishnu Garden, New Delhi-110018
✆ 25461409
Estd.: 1988; **Prop.:** H.S. Sethi
Br.: B.O. Raj Bagh Ext., Srinagar (Jammu & Kashmir)
Bus.Intt.: Pub., B.S., L.S.; **Spl.:** Humanities & Soc.Sci., Sci. & Tech., Bio.

ARIDHI HI-TECH INDUSTRIES LTD.
Mumbai (Maharashtra)
✆ 22873257, 22844117, Fax: 22870330
✉ aridhi@vsnl.com
Bus.Intt.: Pub.

ARIES BOOKS INTERNATIONAL
12/7, Crescent Park, First St., Gandhi Nagar, Adyar, Chennai-600020 (Tamil Nadu)
✆ 24952605
✉ aries@md3.vsnl.in
Prop.: V. Sankar; **Bus.Intt.:** Pub., L.S.

ARIHANT INTERNATIONAL
239, Gali Kunjas, Dariba Kalan, Delhi-110006

ARIHANT PRAKASHAN
Kalindi, Transport Nagar, Meerut-250002 (Uttar Pradesh)
✆ 2401479, 2512970, Fax: 91-121-2401648
✉ info@arihantprakashan.com
www.arihantprakashan.com
Hd.Org.: Deepesh Jain; **Bus.Intt.:** Pub.; **Spl.:** Edu., Engg., Med. and Competition

ARIHANT PUBLISHERS
Opp. Rajasthan University, Jawaharlal Nehru Marg, Jaipur-302004 (Rajasthan)

ARIJIT PRAKASHAN
15A, Tamer Lane, Kolkata-700009
(West Bengal)

ARIVU NILAYAM
60/1, Bharathi Salai, Triplicane,
Chennai-600005 (Tamil Nadu)
Prop.: L. Vasantha; **Bus.Intt.:** Pub.; **Spl.:** Children Books, Novels, Med., Astrology and Self Improvement Books

ARJUN BOOKS
Alankar, Kozhikode-673032 (Kerala)
✆ 256832, 250455, 263248
Estd.: 1985; **Hd.Org.:** P.S. Ramachandran; **Bus.Intt.:** Pub.

ARNAYAK PRAKASHAN
Madhoo Press Building, 242, Old Behrana,
Allahabad-211003 (Uttar Pradesh)
✆ (O) 2604635 (R) 2872330
Hd.Org.: Rahul Sahay; **Bus.Intt.:** Pub.; **Spl.:** Hindi Books

ARNOLD ASSOCIATES
B-58, May Fair Garden, New Delhi-110016
✆ (O) & (R) 26861466, Fax: 26877571
Man.Dr.: Gulab Vazirani
Br.: 33-A, Imperial Court, Cunningham Rd., Bangalore-560001 (Karnataka)
• 113A/1C, S.C. Banerjee Rd.,
Kolkata-10 (West Bengal)
Bus.Intt.: Pub., Exp. and Allied Trades

ARNOLD PUBLISHERS
4262/3, Lower Ground Floor, Ansari Rd., New Delhi-110002
✆ 23270718, Fax: 23267224
✉ arnoldind@mantraonline.com
Hd.Org.: Andrew White; **Bus.Intt.:** Dist.; **Spl.:** Med., Nursing, Env., Psych., Statistics, etc.

AROGYADHAM RASTRIYA PARIVARIK SAWASTHYA PATRIKA
Arya Samaj Rd., Muzaffar Nagar-251001 (Uttar Pradesh)
✆ 2408226, 2401031, Fax: 2420476
✉ arogyadham@vsnl.com

AROMA BOOKS & STATIONERY
2A/3, Jai-Sarai, Near IIT, Hauz Khas, New Delhi-110016
✆ 26527443, 26534552
Prop.: Vinay Kumar Sharma
Bus.Intt.: Rt., WS
Spl.: Humanities & Soc.Sci., Mang. & Comm., Sci., Med.Sci., Engg. & Tech., Journals, Magazines & Periodicals, Fiction & Gen.

AROO PUBLICATIONS PVT. LTD.
9, Darya Ganj, New Delhi-110002
✆ 64140001, Fax: 91-11-23245011
✉ aroopublications@hotmail.com
Hd.Org.: Atul Gupta

ARORA BOOK COMPANY
109, Prakash Mahal, Near Delhi Medical Association, Ansari Rd., Darya Ganj, New Delhi-110002
✆ 23257092, 23257964, Fax: 23257964
✉ sumit311@hotmail.com
Estd.: 1975; **Ch.Exe.:** P.D. Arora
Bus.Intt.: Pub.; **Spl.:** Children Stories, Reference, Dictionaries, Edu., Cross-stitch and Embroidery

ARORA BOOKS HOUSE
Near Satyam Complex Civil Lines, Link Rd., Bilaspur (Madhya Pradesh)

ARORA PUBLISHERS
PB. No. 701, Sector No. 19-B, Chandigarh (Punjab)

ARPANA ASHRAM
P.O. Madhuban, Dist. Karnal-132037 (Haryana)
✆ 2380801-03, Fax: 2380810
✉ at@arpana.org
www.arpana.org
Hd.Org.: R.M. Sabharwal; **Bus.Intt.:** Pub.; **Spl.:** Litt. on Spiritualism

ARPIT BOOK SERVICE
1/11053, West Subhash Park, Shahdara, Delhi-110032
✆ 22823347
Estd.: 2002; **Prop.:** Rajesh Gupta
Bus.Intt.: L.S.; **Spl.:** Fiction

ARPIT PUBLICATIONS
11/C, Kalaji Goraji, Udaipur-313004 (Rajasthan)
✆ 2415305, 2528024, Fax: 91-294-2415305
Hd.Org.: Mohan Bohra

ARSEE PUBLISHERS
12-B, Pleasure Garden Market, Chandni Chowk, Delhi-110006
✆ 91-11-65966481, 23280657
✉ arseepublishers@rediffmail.com
Hd.Org.: Gurbachan Singh; **Bus.Intt.:** Pub.; **Spl.:** Punjabi Authors in Punjabi

ARSH SAHITYA PRACHAR TRUST
455, Khari Baoli, Delhi-110006
✆ 23953112, 23958360, Fax: 23926672
Hd.Org.: Dharmpal Arya; **Bus.Intt.:** Pub.; **Spl.:** Books in Hindi

ARSHAD BROTHERS
3095, Kucha Tarachand, Darya Ganj, New Delhi-110002 ✆ 23276879

ART BOOK CENTER
Madalpur, Near Jain Temple, Ellis Bridge, Ahmedabad-380006 (Gujarat)
✆ (O) 26582130 (R) 26750361, Fax: 79-26306376
✉ artbookcenter_2000@yahoo.com
Estd.: 1995; **Prop.:** Smt. Vasantben M. Patel; **Bus.Intt.:** L.S. & Rt.; **Spl.:** Indian Art, Arch. & Textile Design

ART BUZZ
3948/29, R.P. Padam Singh Rd., Karol Bagh, New Delhi-110005
✆ 25747235
Hd.Org.: Rekha Anand; **Bus.Intt.:** Pub.; **Spl.:** Art Books

ART HERITAGE
Triveni Kala Sangam, 205, Tansen Marg, New Delhi-110001
✆ 23719470, 23726226, Fax: 23353812
Estd.: 1976; **Dr.:** Mrs. R. Alkazi; **Bus.Intt.:** Pub.; **Spl.:** Books and Journals on Art of Contemporary and Medieval Periods in English

ART UNION PRINTING WORKS PVT. LTD.
165, Sri Aurobinda Sarani, Kolkata-700006 (West Bengal)
Bus.Intt.: Exp.

ARTS INDIA PUBLICATIONS
85, Muktaram Banu St., Kolkata-700007 (West Bengal)

ARULMIGU AMMAN PATHIPPAGAM
8, Gangai Amman Koil St., Opp. Ajantha Hotel, Royapettah, Chennai-600014 (Tamil Nadu)
✆ 28233470
Estd.: 1978; **Prop.:** Amman H. Sathiyanathan; **Bus.Intt.:** Pub.; **Spl.:** Titles on Spiritual, Yoga, Austrology, Cooking and also Sci., Children, Drama etc. Some Books Translated in English

ARUN BOOK SERVICE
315, Guru Ram Das Nagar, Gali No. 4, Laxmi Nagar, Delhi-110092
✆ 22426897
Prop.: K.R. Nanda; **Bus.Intt.:** L.S., Rt., WS

ARUN BOOK STORE
Bakhtiarpur, Patna-803212 (Bihar)
Bus.Intt.: Pub. & B.S.

ARUN BROTHERS
Mumbai (Maharashtra)
@ arunbros@vsnl.com
Bus.Intt.: Exp.

ARUN PRAKASH COLLEGE
Hostel Rd., Panbazar, Guwahati-781001 (Assam)

ARUN PRAKASHAN
A-47, Amar Colony, Lajpat Nagar, New Delhi-110024
✆ 26486121, 22205935
Hd.Org.: Arun Kumar Sharma

ARUN PRAKASHAN
613, Khajuri Bazar, Indore-452002 (Madhya Pradesh)
✆ 2254448

ARUN PRAKASHAN
High Court Rd., Gwalior-474009 (Madhya Pradesh)
✆ 224271
Hd.Org.: Arun Kumar Gupta

ARUN PUBLISHING HOUSE (P) LTD.
S.C.O. 49-51, Basement, P.B. No. 52, Sector 17-C, Chandigarh-160017 (Punjab)
✆ 2702318, Fax: 2702189
@ arunpublishing@hotmail.com, nebaaph@sancharnet.in
Hd.Org.: Anil Sharma; **Bus.Intt.:** Pub.; **Spl.:** Reference, Gen. and Textbooks in English

ARUN PUSTAK BHANDAR
Ishipur, Barahat, Bhagalpur-813206 (Bihar)
Bus.Intt.: Pub. & B.S.

ARUNA BOOK MART
50, Vadamalai Pillai St., Purasawakkam, Chennai-600001 (Tamil Nadu)

ARUNA PUBLISHERS
Mayfair Marine Lines, Mumbai (Maharashtra)

ARUNA PUBLISHING HOUSE
Eluru Rd., Vijayawada-520002 (Andhra Pradesh)
✆ 0866-2431181
Estd.: 1972; **Prop.:** B. Basu Rao; **Bus.Intt.:** Pub.; **Spl.:** Novels and Plays in Telugu

ARUNODAYA PRAKASHAN
21-A, Ansari Road, Darya Ganj, New Delhi-110002
✆ 91-11-23275710
@ vaniprakashan@gmail.com
Hd.Org.: Arun Maheshwari; **Bus.Intt.:** Pub.; **Spl.:** Literary and Other Books in Hindi

ARUNOTHAYAM
3, Gowidia Mutt Rd., Royapettah, Chennai-600014 (Tamil Nadu)
✆ 28267553, 28269887
Estd.: 1952; **Prop.:** L. Arunachalam; **Bus.Intt.:** Pub.; **Spl.:** Children Books in Tamil, Telugu, Marathi, Hindi, English

ARUSHI PRAKASHAN
F-48, Green Park (Main), New Delhi-110016

ARVIND BOOK DISTRIBUTORS
D-1/18, Rajouri Garden, New Delhi-110027
✆ (O) 25107455, 25107456 (R) 25190992
Fax: 91-11-25467782
@ arvindm@vsnl.net.in
Estd.: 1989; **Prop.:** Arvind Malhotra; **Bus.Intt.:** Dist.; **Spl.:** Tech. Comp.

ARVIND BOOKS DISTRIBUTORS AGENCY
Aravind Ashram, Pondicherry-605002 (Tamil Nadu)
Hd.Org.: A. Podhdar

ARVIND NIKETAN
Charthawal, Muzaffarnagar (Uttar Pradesh)

ARVIND PRAKASHAN
15, Durga Nursery Road, Ashok Nagar, Main Road, Udaipur-313001 (Rajasthan)
✆ 2412758, Fax: 91-294-2413563
@ arvindprakashan@hotmail.com
Estd.: 1982; **Hd. Org.:** Anil Kumar Somani; **Bus.Intt.:** Pub., WS, L.S. & Rt.; **Spl.:** Humanities & Soc.Sci., Sci. & Tech., Med., Gen. & Fiction etc.

ARVIND PRAKASHAN PVT. LTD.
H-2, Vijay Chowk, Laxmi Nagar, Delhi-110092
✆ 22217364

Br.: 9-8, Lalit Nagar, Dissukh Nagar, Hyderabad-60 (Andhra Pradesh)
✆ 040-24064063

ARVIND PRAKASHAN PVT. LTD.
Sports Complex Enclave, Delhi Rd., Meerut-250002 (Uttar Pradesh)
✆ 2520263, 2533607, Fax: 91-121-2521607
✉ arvind@surevin.net
Hd.Org.: C.K. Mittal; **Bus.Intt.:** Pub.; **Spl.:** School Textbooks in English, Hindi, Sanskrit, Urdu and Punjabi

ARVIND VIVEK PRAKASHAN
Dr. Rangav Ragjav Marg, Agra-282002 (Uttar Pradesh)
✆ (O) 2261923 (R) 2357923
Hd.Org.: Govind Agarwal

ARYA BOOK DEPOT
30, Naiwala, Karol Bagh, New Delhi-110005
✆ 28751221/23, Fax: 91-11-28756324
✉ aryabookdepot@yahoo.com
Estd.: 1943; **Hd.Org.:** Man Singh Gupta; **Bus.Intt.:** Pub., L.S.; **Spl.:** School & College Text Books, Children Litt., Hindi fiction & Litt., Arts/Comm./Sci., CBSE & ICSE Based Text Books

ARYA (MEDI) PUBLISHING HOUSE
4805/24, Bharat Ram Rd., Darya Ganj, New Delhi-110002
✆ 23274004, 23277444 ▮ 9810195696
✉ amph@mantraonline.com
🌐 www.aryamedipublishing.com
Estd.: 1996; **Hd.Org.:** Sudhir Kumar Arya; **Bus.Intt.:** Pub., WS; **Spl.:** Books on Med., especially Dentistry

ARYA PRAKASHAN
814, Khundewalan, Ajmere Gate, Delhi-110006
✆ 91-11-23233280
✉ sanjeevaryaprakashan@rediffmail.com
Hd.Org.: Tilak Raj Arya; **Bus.Intt.:** Pub. and Dist.; **Spl.:** *Vedas, Upanishads* and Vedic Litt.

ARYA PRAKASHAN MANDAL
IX/221, Saraswati Bhandar, Gandhi Nagar, Delhi-110031
✆ 22072602
Hd.Org.: Amarlata Sharma; **Bus.Intt.:** Pub.; **Spl.:** Hindi Language books on Culture, Biographies, Gen. Knowledge, Self-improvement and Books for Children

ARYA PUBLICATIONS
1569/30, Naiwala, Karol Bagh, New Delhi-110005
✆ 28755383, 28752745, Fax: 91-11-28756921
Hd.Org.: Deepak Gupta; **Bus.Intt.:** Pub.; **Spl.:** Textbooks covering Sub. like Math., Soc.Studies, Sci. EVS and Gen. Knowledge for Primary, Middle and Plus Two Level

ARYA PUBLICATIONS
7, Industrial Area, Trilokpur Rd., Dist. Sirmour, Kala-Amb-173030 (Himachal Pradesh)
✆ 238832, Fax: 238832
Ch.Exe.: Mr. Praveen Gupta; **Bus.Intt.:** Pub.; **Spl.:** Textbooks covering Sub. like Math., Soc.Studies, Sci. EVS and Gen. Knowledge for Primary, Middle and Plus Two Level

ARYA PUBLISHING HOUSE
30, Naiwala, Karol Bagh, New Delhi-110005
✆ (O) 25767012 (R) 25766144, 25751410, Fax: 25716921
✉ aryabookdepot@yahoo.com
Estd.: 1980; **Hd.Org.:** Naveen Gupta; **Bus.Intt.:** Pub.; **Spl.:** Textbooks for CBSE and ICSE Board Examination in Hindi and English

ARYA PUSTAK BHANDAR
Daniyawan, Patna-803201 (Bihar)
Bus.Intt.: Pub. & B.S.

ARYA VAIDYA SALA PUBLICATIONS
Kottakkal, Malapuram-676503 (Kerala)
✆ 2742210, 2742216, 2742219, 2742561, 2742564, 2742571, 2742573
Estd.: 1902; **Man.Dr.:** Dr. P.K. Warrier; **Bus.Intt.:** Pub.

ARYAN BOOKS INTERNATIONAL
Pooja Aptts., 4-B Ansari Rd., Darya Ganj, New Delhi-110002
✆ 23287589, 23255799, Fax: 23270385
✉ aryanbooks@vsnl.com
Estd.: 1992; **Prop.:** Vikas Arya; **Bus.Intt.:** Pub., Exp.; **Spl.:** Art, Archaeology, Arch., Indology, History, Culture, as also Dictionaries and Encyclopaedias

ARYAN PRAKASHAN
1/11873, Vidhanpur, Naveen Shahdara, Delhi-110032

ARYAN PUBLISHING CO. (P) LTD.
76, Bepin Behari Ganguly St., Kolkata-700012 (West Bengal)
✆ (91-033) 22375278, 22121690; Fax: 22120278
✉ aryan2@cal3.vsnl.net.in
🌐 www.aakif.com
Estd.: 1954; **Prop.:** Narendranath Dey
Br.: 9A, Santosh Mitra Square, Kolkata-700012 ✆ 2270261
Bus.Intt.: L.S. & Rt.; **Spl.:** Humanities & Soc.Sci., Sci. & Tech.

ARYANA PUBLISHING HOUSE
EG 132, Indrapuri, New Delhi-110005

ARYAS' BOOK CENTRE
Hospital Rd., Udaipur-313001 (Rajasthan)
✆ (O) 2526060 (R) 2584669, Fax: 2523086
✉ aryabooks@datainfosys.net
Estd.: 1977; **Prop.:** B.D. Arya
Br.: Himanshu Publications, 464, Sector No. 11, Hiranmagri, Udaipur-313002
✆ 2424659, Fax: 2523086;
✉ aryabook@datainfosys.net
• Suresh Book Service, Hospital Rd., Udaipur-313001 ✆ 2523086
• Aryas' Book Centre, 4379/4B, Prakash House, Ansari Rd., Darya Ganj, New Delhi-110002 ✆ 23255920
✉ aryabook@datainfosys.net
• Unique Classes, Krishna Plaza Complex, Court Chouraha, Udaipur-313001
✆ 2424959
Bus.Intt.: Pub., WS, L.S. & Rt., Imp., Exp., Sub.Ag.; **Spl.:** Humanities & Soc.Sci., Sci. & Tech., Med., Law, Juvenile/Children, Gen. & Fiction etc.

ASAD BOOK STALL
Thodupuzha-685584 (Kerala)

ASAMATA PRAKASHAN
14-7-262, Churi Bazar, Hyderabad-500012 (Andhra Pradesh)

ASCENT PUBLICATIONS
21/29, Shakti Nagar, Delhi-110007
✆ 91-11-23847953
✉ ascentlawpub@yahoo.com
Hd.Org.: Ashok K. Jain; **Bus.Intt.:** Pub.; **Spl.:** Books on Law

ASHA BOOK AGENCY
8A, College Row, Kolkata-700009 (West Bengal)

ASHA POLYMERS PVT. LTD.
'Asha House', 3rd Floor, 808-C, Dr. B.A. Rd., Dadar TT, Mumbai-400014 (Maharashtra)
Bus.Intt.: Exp.

ASHA PRAKASHAN
Gargoti Distt. Kolhapur, Mumbai (Maharashtra)

ASHA PRAKASHAN GRAHA
30, Nai Wala, Karol Bagh, New Delhi-110005
✆ 28750159, Fax: 91-11-28756324
✉ aryabookdepot@yahoo.com
Hd.Org.: Man Singh; **Bus.Intt.:** Pub.; **Spl.:** School Textbooks, Hindi Litt. and Books for Children and Adults

ASHA PUBLISHING HOUSE
S-228, Greater Kailash-II, New Delhi-110048
✆ 26415434, 26445420
Prop.: Asha Rani Lakhotia; **Bus.Intt.:** Pub.; **Spl.:** Income Tax and other Sub. in English

ASHA PUBLISHING HOUSE
Chaura Rasta, Jaipur-302003 (Rajasthan)

ASHA SAHITYA PRAKASHAN
32, Bhashyam Circle, Sadashivanagar, Bangalore-560080 (Karnataka)
✆ 080-2364476
Hd.Org.: A.V. Shanbhag; **Bus.Intt.:** Pub. & Dist.

ASHARFI BOOK DEPOT
Deoband, Saharanpur-247554 (Uttar Pradesh)
Bus.Intt.: Pub., Exp., Printers & B.S.

ASHBHA BOOK HOUSE
Unit-12, Inderprastha, Building, E-109, Pandav Nagar, Near Petrol Pump, Delhi-110092
✆ 22445595, 22713103, Fax: 22713103
✉ ashbhabooks2002@yahoo.com
www.aakif.com
Estd.: 1989; **Prop.:** Ashok Vaid; **Bus.Intt.:** Pub., L.S. & Rt.; **Spl.:** Humanities & Soc.Sci., Sci. & Tech.

ASHIANA
Bullock Rd., Bandstand, Bandra, Mumbai-400050 (Maharashtra)

ASHIMA PRAKASHANI
Sreebas Angan, Shyampore, Howrah (West Bengal)

ASHIMA PUSTAKALAYA
43, Sitaram Ghosh St., Kolkata-700073 (West Bengal)

ASHIR PRAKASHAN
Ramjiwan Nagar, Chilkana Rd., Saharanpur-247001 (Uttar Pradesh)
✆ 2743877
Hd.Org.: Devendra Sharma

ASHISH ALOK PRAKASHAN
Chainpur Kothi, Gangzala, Ward-12, Saharsa, Distt. Saharsa, North (Bihar)

ASHISH BOOKS MARKETING SERVICES
257-B, Pocket-N, Sarita Vihar, New Delhi-110044
✆ 26944293 ▮ 9818975698, Fax: 26954200
✉ bisht_abms@rediffmail.com
Estd.: 2000; **Prop.:** Shivcharan Singh;

Bus.Intt.: L.S.; **Spl.:** Power Engg. & Tech., Cement & Concrete Tech., Fire & Safety Engg., Petroleum, Petrochemical, Polymers, Enery & Env.Engg.

ASHISH PRAKASHAN
B-88, Gali No. 8, Kranti Nagar Bistaar, Delhi-110051
✆ 22210950 (PP)
Hd.Org.: Sabaraj Mishr

ASHISH PUSTAK BHANDAR
Sunderganj, Aurangabad (Bihar)
Bus.Intt.: Pub. & B.S.

ASHOK BOOK AGENCY
36B, College Row, Kolkata-700009 (West Bengal)

ASHOK BOOK CENTRE
Opp. Maris Stella College, Vijayawada-520008 (Andhra Pradesh)
✆ 0866-2476966, 2472096, Fax: 2476652, Telex: 0475-339
✉ abcbooks@md3.vsnl.net.in
Estd.: 1982; **Prop.:** Ashok Kumar D.
Br.: 13-1-C, St. Anthony's Church Compound, Apsara Rd., Visakhapatnam-530002 (Andhra Pradesh) ✆ 2565995; **Estd.:** 1991
Bus.Intt.: WS, L.S. & Rt., Exp.

ASHOK BROTHERS
7/315, Lalita Park, Laxmi Nagar, Delhi-110092

ASHOK DILWALI
22, Jorbagh, New Delhi-110003
✆ 23324446, Fax: 23328731
✉ kinsey@del2.vsnl.net.in
Hd.Org.: Ashok Dilwali; **Bus.Intt.:** Pub.; **Spl.:** Pictorial Litt. on Himalayas and Nature

ASHOK GENERAL STORES
Lakhna, Punpun, Patna-804456 (Bihar)
Bus.Intt.: Pub. & B.S.

ASHOK PRAKASHAN
2615, Nai Sarak, Delhi-110006
Hd.Org.: Jagdish Gupta

ASHOK PRAKASHAN
JG-33, Khirki Extension, Malviya Nagar, New Delhi-110017
✆ 26676609, Fax: 26235255
Hd.Org.: Akhil Bansal; **Bus.Intt.:** Pub.; **Spl.:** Hindi Litt. and Children's Books

ASHOK PRAKASHAN
21, Vishwa Shanti Society, Quarry Rd., Vazeer Compound, Malad East, Mumbai-400064 (Maharashtra)
Hd.Org.: Hans Yagnik

ASHOK PRAKASHAN
A-61-62, College St. Market, Kolkata-700007 (West Bengal)
Hd.Org.: Dhananjay Pramanik

ASHOK PRAKASHAN MANDIR
39-B, Chahchand, Allahabad-211003 (Uttar Pradesh)
Hd.Org.: Ashok Kumar Agarwal

ASHOK PUSTAK BHANDAR
Maulviganj, Pothu, Aurangabad (Bihar)
Bus.Intt.: Pub. & B.S.

ASHOK PUSTAK BHANDAR
Banika, Bhagalpur-813102 (Bihar)
Bus.Intt.: Pub. & B.S.

ASHOK PUSTAK BHANDAR
New Market, Begusarai-851101 (Bihar)
Bus.Intt.: Pub. & B.S.

ASHOK PUSTAK BHANDAR
Barh, Patna-803203 (Bihar)
Bus.Intt.: Pub. & B.S.

ASHOK PUSTAK SADAN
Punpun Bazar, Punpun, Patna-804453 (Bihar)
Bus.Intt.: Pub. & B.S.

ASHOKA BOOK DEPOT
Shop No. 127, Plot No. 26, Vikas Royal Arcade, Pitam Pura, Rd. No. 44, Delhi-110034
✆ 27032416, 23288391
✉ ashoka@indianbookfair.com
Hd.Org.: Ashok Kumar Sehgal; **Bus.Intt.:** Pub.; **Spl.:** Drawing, Physical Edu., Health, etc.

ASHOKA BOOKS
Opp. Govt. College, Hoshiarpur-146001 (Punjab)

ASHOKA PRESS
Shekhpur, Patna-800014 (Bihar)
Hd.Org.: Udeyraj Singh

ASHOKA PUBLICATIONS
C-3/64A, Keshav Puram, (Lawrence Rd.), Delhi-110035
✆ (O) 27193256 (R) 27106381
Estd.: 1986; **Prop.:** Ashok Vij; **Bus.Intt.:** Pub.; **Spl.:** Edu. Books in English & Hindi

ASHOKA PUBLISHING HOUSE
'Om Shree', Shop No. 25, C.S.C. 13, DDA Market, Opp. D-3 Pkt., Sector-16, Rohini, Delhi-110089
✆ 27858255, Fax: 91-11-27858355

mail@goldenseriesbooks.com
www.goldenseriesbooks.com
Hd.Org.: Satish Kumar Sehgal;
Bus.Intt.: Pub., B.S.; **Spl.:** Gen. Books and Children's Books in English and Hindi

ASHRAF BOOK CENTRE
Red Cross Rd., Srinagar, Kashmir-190001 (Jammu & Kashmir)
✆ 2482371
Estd.: 1972; **Hd.Org.:** Mohd. Ashraf Quri
Br.: Kabir Sons Plaza, Budshah Bridge, Sri Nagar, Kashmir ✆ 2450350
Bus.Intt.: Pub., WS, L.S. & Rt.; **Spl.:** Juvenile/ Children Books

ASHRAVAT PRAKASHAN
26, Balrampur House, Allahabad-211002 (Gujarat)
✆ 2641846
Hd.Org.: Satyavrat Misra

ASHU PRAKASHAN
FF-56, Kutchery Rd., Saharanpur-247001 (Uttar Pradesh)
Hd.Org.: Abhay Mishra

ASHU PRAKASHAN
1143/31, Purana Katra, Allahabad-211002 (Uttar Pradesh)
Hd.Org.: Ashutosh Mishra

ASHUTOSH BOOK STALL
90, B.S.P. Mukherjee Rd., Kolkata-26 (West Bengal)

ASHUTOSH LIBRARY
Chakdah Rathtola, Nadia (West Bengal)

ASHUTOSH TECHNICAL BOOKS
C-3/327, Yamuna Vihar, Delhi-110053
✆ (O) & (R) 22915762
Estd.: 1997; **Prop.:** Smt. Purnima Bansal;
Bus.Intt.: WS & Rt., B.S., L.S.

ASHWANI PRAKASHAN
Gyanbapi, Varanasi-221001 (Uttar Pradesh)
✆ 2321742, 2331624
Hd.Org.: Shivkumar Agarwal

ASHWANI PUBLISHERS
176, Lalitha Nagar, Hyderabad-500044 (Andhra Pradesh)

ASIA BOOK HOUSE
26, Naya Bazar, Jabalpur-482002 (Madhya Pradesh)

ASIA LAW HOUSE
Shop No. 10, Aiyangar Plaza, Reside UTI, Bank St., Koti, Hyderabad-500095 (Andhra Pradesh)
✆ (O) 24742324, 24608000 (R) 23540517
Fax: 24564007
asialaw@satyam.net.in
www.asialawhouse.com
Estd.: 1965; **Prop.:** S.P. Gogia
Br.: Opp. High Court, Hyderabad-500002 (Andhra Pradesh) ✆ 24526212, 24520276
Bus.Intt.: Pub., B.S., L.S., WS; **Spl.:** Law, Gen. Books

ASIA NEWS AGENCY
Classic Publications, B-483, Meera Bagh, New Delhi-110063

ASIA PACIFIC BUSINESS PRESS
106-E, Kamla Nagar, New Delhi-110007
✆ 23923955, Fax: 91-11-23941561

ASIA PUBLISHER'S
A-36, Chetak Apartments, Plot No. 27/2, Sector-9 Rohini, Delhi-110085
✆ 27261823
Hd.Org.: Smt. Ratika Chopra

ASIA PUBLISHING COMPANY
A-132-133, College St. Mkt., Kolkata-700007 (West Bengal)
✆ 033-22412386
Estd.: 1954; **Hd.Org.:** Mrinal Dutta;
Bus.Intt.: Pub.; **Spl.:** Textbooks in Bengali

ASIAN BOOK CENTRE
24, DDA Shopping Complex, Ber Sarai (Opp. JNU), New Delhi-110016
✆ (O) 26518359 (R) 26189402
Fax: 011-26961034
rameshsondhi@yahoo.com
Estd.: 1986; **Prop.:** Ramesh Pal Sondhi;
Bus.Intt.: Rt., L.S.; **Spl.:** Soc.Sci., Mang. and Comp., Comm. & Acad. books

ASIAN BOOK CIRCUIT
Stall-56, College Sqr. (West), Kolkata-700073 (West Bengal)

ASIAN BOOK HOUSE
Narwara Ahad Zargar Rd., Srinagar, Kashmir-190002 (Jammu & Kashmir)
✆ 0194-2426989, 2428235 (R) 2427595
abh32@rediffmail.com
Man.Dir.: Ishtiyaq Mushtaq Mir;
Bus.Intt.: Rt. & B.S.

ASIAN BOOKS PVT. LTD.
7/28, Mahavir Lane, Vardan House, Ansari Rd., Darya Ganj, New Delhi-110002
✆ 23282098, 23271887, 23287577, 23259151-71-81, Fax: 23262021
rtaneja@asianbooksindia.com
www.asianbookindia.com

Estd.: 1988; **Gen.Manager.**: R. Taneja
Br.: 103, Swiss Complex No. 33, Race Course Rd., Bangalore-560001 ✆ 22200438, Fax: 22256583; ✉ asianblr@blr.vsnl.net.in
• Palani Murugan Bldg., New No. 21 West Cott Rd. Royapettah, Chennai-600014
✆ 28486927, 28 ✉ asianmds@vsnl.net
• 5, Himalaya House, 79, Palton Rd., Mumbai-400001 ✆ 22619322, 22623572, Fax: 22623137 ✉ asianbk@bom3.vsnl.net.in
• 3/5, 1101/1/B 2nd Floor, Opp. Blood Bank, Narayanguda, Hyderabad-500029
✆ 24754941, 24750951, Fax: 24751152
✉ hydasian@hd2.vsnl.net.in
• 10-A, Hospital St., Kolkata-700072
✆ 22363040, Fax: 22369899
✉ calasian@cal.vsnl.net.in
• Anandaram Barua Rd., Pan Bazar, Opp. Don Bosco Church, Guwahati, Assam-781001
✆ 2513020, 2635729
✉ asianghy@sancharnet.in
Bus.Intt.: Imp., Dist., Pub., Sub.Ag.; **Spl.**: Sci. & Tech., Med., Soc. & Beh. Sci., Mang., Acad., Comm.

ASIAN COMMERCIAL CORPORATION
Khalmulla (Ahmedabad) Alustang, Shrinagar-190006 (Jammu & Kashmir)
✆ 0194-2262300
Estd.: 1998; **Prop.** M.G. Ahmed; **Bus.Intt.**: B.S. and L.S.; **Spl.**: Sci. & Tech., Med., Comm. and Mang., Humanities, Law, Art Gen. Books, etc.

ASIAN DISTRIBUTORS SERVICES (THE)
456, Double Storey, New Rajinder Nagar, New Delhi-110060
✆ (O) 23243050 (R) 26466179, Fax: 23246975
Hd.Org.: Mrs. Pinky Subharwal;
Bus.Intt.: Pub. & Dist.; **Spl.**: Picture Post-cards, CD-ROMs, etc.

ASIAN EDUCATIONAL SERVICES
31, Hauz Khas Village, New Delhi-110016
✆ (O) 26560187, 26568594
(R) 26480728, Fax: 26852805, 26855499
✉ asian37@vsnl.com
www.asianeds.com
Estd.: 1972; **Hd.Org.**: Jagdish Lall Jetley
Br.: 5, Sripuram 1st St., Royapettah, Chennai-600014 (Tamil Nadu)
✆ 28115040, Fax: 28111291
✉ asianeds@md3.vsnl.net.in
Bus.Intt.: Pub. and Dist.; **Spl.**: Travel, Rel., Art, Hist., Phil.

ASIAN EDUCATIONAL SERVICES
6A, Shahpur Jat, New Delhi-110049
✆ 26491586, Fax: 91-11-26494946
✉ aes@aes.ind.in
www.aes.ind.in
Estd.: 1972; **Hd.Org.**: Gautam Jetley
Br.: 5, Sripuram 1st St., Royapettah, Chennai-600014 (Tamil Nadu)
✆ 28115040, Fax: 28111291
✉ asianeds@md3.vsnl.net.in
Bus.Intt.: Pub. and Dist.; **Spl.**: Travel, Rel., Art, Hist., Phil.

ASIAN FISHERIES SOCIETY
C/o College of Fisheries, University of Agriculture Science, Mangalore-575002 (Karnataka)
✆ 0824-2439322, Fax: 0824-2438366
Estd.: 1986; **Bus.Intt.**: Pub. and B.S.;
Spl.: Fisheries and Gen. Books

ASIAN PUBLICATION SERVICES
243, Defence Colony, Flyover Market, New Delhi-110024

ASIAN PUBLISHERS
3911, Roshanpura, Nai Sarak, Delhi-110006
✆ 23915650, 23941531, Fax: 91-11-23915650
Hd.Org.: Salil Mehta

ASIAN PUBLISHING COMPANY
E-159, Greater Kailash, Part-I, New Delhi-110048

ASIAN RECORDER & PUBLICATIONS (P) LTD.
C-2, Gulmohar Park, Journalists Colony, New Delhi-110049
Bus.Intt.: Exp.

ASIAN TRADING CORPORATION
58, 2nd Cross, Dacosta Layout, St. Mary's Town, Bangalore-560084 (Karnataka)
✆ 548744, 5490444, Fax: 5479444
✉ mail@atcbook.net
Estd.: 1946; **Hd.Org.**: Nigel Fernandes
Br.: Mallikatte Kadri, Mangalore-575002
✆ 2212646, 2216944
Bus.Intt.: Pub., WS, L.S. & Rt., Imp., Exp., Sub.Ag.; **Spl.**: Humanities & Soc.Sci., Rel. & Phil.

ASIATECH PUBLISHERS INC.
E-20, Arya Nagar Apartments, Plot No. 91, I.P. Extn., Patpar Ganj, Delhi-110092
✆ (O) 91-11-22724601
✉ asiatech@pb.com
Hd.Org.: N.K. Murleedharan
Bus.Intt.: Pub.; **Spl.**: Academic, Bio-Science, Soc.Sci. and Technical

ASM PRESS/NELSON THORNES
New No. 8, Old No. 32, Second Main Rd., CIT Nagar, East, Chennai-600035 (Tamil Nadu)
✆ 24346244, 24346266, Fax: 24346529
✉ itpsesha@giasmd01.vsnl.net.in

Hd.Org.: R. Seshadri; **Bus.Intt.:** Pub.; **Spl.:** Microbiology and Med. Microbiology in English

ASOMI PRAKASHAN
Ananda Ram Baruah Rd., Pan Bazar, Guwahati-781001 (Assam)

ASSAM BOOK DEPOT
M.L. Nehru Rd., Pan Bazar, Guwahati-781001 (Assam)
✆ 2543896, 2543701
Estd.: 1933; **Man.Prt.:** K.K. Guha; **Bus.Intt.:** Pub. & Dist.; **Spl.:** School/ College Books, Dictionaries etc. in Assemese, English, Bengali

ASSAM BOOK DEPOT
21, Patuatola Lane, Kolkata-700009 (West Bengal)

ASSAM CHILDREN'S LITERATURE TRUST
Bamuni Maidan, Guwahati-781021 (Assam)

ASSAM PUBLISHING CO.
42, Beniatola Lane, Kolkata-700009 (West Bengal)

ASSAM PUBLISHING CO.
College Hostel Rd., Pan Bazar, Guwahati-781001 (Assam)

ASSAM SAHITYA SABHA
Pan Bazar, Guwahati-781001 (Assam)

ASSISSI PRINTING AND PUBLISHING HOUSE
P.B. No. 12, Changanacherry, Kottayam Dist.-686101 (Kerala)
✆ 2420188, 2429188, Fax: 04824-2420466
✉ assissi@giasmd01.vsnl.net.in, scaria@assissipublishers.com
🌐 www.assissipublisher.com
Estd.: 1943; **Man.Dr.:** K.J. Joseph; **Bus.Intt.:** Pub.

ASSISTANT SECRETARY
Publication Board Assam, Bamunimaidan, Guwahati-781021 (Assam)

ASSOCIATE PUBLISHING HOUSE AND THE CENTRE FOR ADMINISTRATIVE CHANGE
E-22, Preet Vihar, Vikas Marg, New Delhi-110092
✆ 22429392
Hd.Org.: R.K. Paul; **Bus.Intt.:** Pub.; **Spl.:** Journal-*Administrative Change* and Books on Soc.Sci, Eng.Litt., Hist., Public Administration & Mang.

ASSOCIATED BOOK AGENCY
Ashok Rajpath, Patna-800006 (Bihar)
Bus.Intt.: Pub. & B.S.

ASSOCIATED BOOK CENTRE
72-A, Shankar Market, Connaught Place, New Delhi-110001
✆ (O) 23314900 (R) 2615093
Prop.: C.P. Chodhary; **Bus.Intt.:** Pub. & Rt.

ASSOCIATED BOOKSELLERS
Block-77, Sanjay Place, Agra-282002 (Uttar Pradesh)
✆ 9897877556, Fax: 91-562-4008061
✉ vikram_jain2000@yahoo.com
Hd.Org.: H.K. Jain; **Bus.Intt.:** L.S.; **Spl.:** Classified Books and Journal on all Sub.

ASSOCIATED SUBSCRIPTION AND INFORMATION SERVICES (INDIA) PVT. LTD.
P.O. Box. No. 8649, "Shivani", Block II-F4, (4th Floor), 40, East Coast Rd., Thiruvanmiyur, Chennai-600041 (Tamil Nadu)
✆ (O) 24454500, 24421229 (R) 24413792
▮ 3135921, Fax: 044-24910910, 24918747
✉ asissb@md3.vsnl.net.in
Estd.: 1984; **Man.Dr.:** N. Lakxmikanth
Br.: 75/95, 4th Main Rd., Bapuji Nagar, Bangalore, ✆ 080-26747006
Bus.Intt.: L.S. & Rt., Imp., Sub.Ag.; **Spl.:** Sci. & Tech., Med.

ASSOCIATION OF INDIAN UNIVERSITIES
AIU House, 16 Comrade Indrajit Gupta Marg, New Delhi-110002
✆ 23230059, Fax: 91-11-23232131
✉ publicationsales@aiuweb.org
🌐 www.aiuweb.org
Hd.Org.: Dayanand Dongaonkar; **Bus.Intt.:** Pub.; **Spl.:** Edu. Books for Higher Edu.

ASTER EDUCATIONAL PUBLISHERS (P) LTD.
11298, Doriwalan, East Park Rd., Karol Bagh, New Delhi-110005
✆ 23620108, 23947108, 23610108, Fax: 91-11-23620108
Hd.Org.: Anurag Anand; **Bus.Intt.:** Pub.; **Spl.:** Children Books

ASTHA PRAKASHAN
346/K.G.-1, Vikaspuri, New Delhi-110018
Hd.Org.: Sandipika Sapra

ASTHALAKSHMI BOOK STALL
Vinoba Rd., 6th Cross, Subash Nagar, Mandya-571401 (Karnataka)
Estd.: 1989; **Prop.:** S. Nagaraja

ASTRA MARKETING
22/3rd Floor, Hasan Bldg., N.M. Joshi Marg, Lower Parel, Mumbai-400013 (Maharashtra)

ASWAMEDH PRAKASHAN
Nivargee Bldg., Phadke Rd., Dombivali East, Thane-421201 (Maharashtra)

ATEQAD PUBLISHING HOUSE (REGD.)
1561, Kotana St., Suiwalan,
New Delhi-110002
✆ 23276879
Bus.Intt.: Pub., Printers & Exp.; **Spl.:** Holy *Qur'an* and Islamic Books in Arabic, Urdu, English & Hindi

ATHULYA BOOKS
M.G. Rd., Thalasserry-670101
(Kerala)
✆ (O) 0490-2324099 (R) 2321053
Prop.: T. Sasidharan
Br.: V.K. Complex, Fort Rd., Kannur-670001
✆ 0497-2709294, 2702846
Bus.Intt.: B.S. and L.S.

ATLANTIC EXPORTS WORLDWIDE
7/22, Ansari Rd., Darya Ganj,
New Delhi-110002
✆ 23273880, 23275880, 23280451
Fax: 23285873
Prop.: Manish Kumar Gupta
Bus.Intt.: Exp.; **Spl.:** Humanities & Soc.Sci., Tech., Med., Mang.

ATLANTIC PUBLISHERS & DISTRIBUTORS (P) LTD.
Sal.Off.: 7/22, Ansari Rd.,
Darya Ganj, New Delhi-110002
✆ 23273880, 23275880, 23280451
Fax: 91-11-23285873
✉ info@atlanticbooks.com;
manish@atlanticbooks.com
www.atlanticbooks.com
Estd.: 1977; **Man.Dir.:** Manish K. Gupta
Dir.: Ashish Kumar
Br.: 5, Nallathambi Street, Wallajah Road, Chennai-600002 (Tamil Nadu)
✆ 91-44-64611085, 32413319
✉ chennai@atlanticbooks.com
Bus.Intt.: Pub., WS, L.S., Rt., Exp. & Imp.; **Spl.:** Eng.Litt., Arts, Med., Tech., Humanities, Soc.Sci., Sci., Comp., Multimedia CD-Roms

ATLAS BOOK STALL
Opp. N.S.S. Boys High School,
M.C. Rd., Pandalam-689501
(Kerala)
Estd.: 1987; **Man.Dr.:** T.I. Zachariah;
Bus.Intt.: B.S.

ATLAS BOOKS & PERIODICALS
24, Pocket D-2, Sector-11, Rohini,
Delhi-110085
✆ (O) 27154313 (R) 27040781
✉ atlasbooks@yahoo.com
Prop.: Anil Kumar Jain; **Bus.Intt.:** L.S.; **Spl.:** Acad., Biological Sci. Agri., Env., Horticulture, Botany, Forestry, Bio., Animal Sci., Zoology & Related Sub.

ATLAS BOOKS & PERIODICALS
37-B, Vidya Nagar, E.B.S. Rd., Hissar (Haryana)

ATMA RAM & SONS
1376, Kashmere Gate, P.B. No. 1429,
Delhi-110006
✆ 91-11-23946466, 23973082
✉ atmarambooks@hotmail.com
Hd.Org.: Sushil Puri
Br.: 17, Ashok Marg, Lucknow-226001 (Uttar Pradesh) ✆ 2244915
Bus.Intt.: Pub. & B.S.; **Spl.:** Primarily in Hindi

ATMA RAM & SONS
57, University Campus, Chandigarh-160014
✆ 2541406
Estd.: 1909; **Prop.:** Dipak Puri, Karan Puri;
Bus.Intt.: Pub., WS, L.S. & Rt.

ATMONNATI PRAKASHAN
28/B, Chatham Lines, Ranipur,
Allahabad-211002 (Uttar Pradesh)
✆ 2645716, 2645757, Fax: 2645757
✉ atmonnati@hotmail.com
Hd.Org.: Carmel Kizh; **Bus.Intt.:** Pub.;
Spl.: Self-improvement, Human Relationship, Value Edu., Fiction, etc. in Hindi

ATUL ALOK PRAKASHAN
3543, Jatwada, Darya Ganj, New Delhi-110002
✆ 22240935
Hd.Org.: Alok Chowdhary

ATUL PRAKASHAN
1493-C, Sadashiv Peela Bangla, Pune-411030 (Maharashtra)

ATUL PRAKASHAN
3/1, Batuk Krishan Banerjee Marg,
Naya Katra, Allahabad-211002
(Uttar Pradesh)
✆ 2640948, 2641594, Fax: 0532-2609843
Hd.Org.: Ramesh Tiwari, Atul Bhargav

AUDIO & VIDEO CASSETTES
37A, Guru Nanak Marg, Kewal Park Extn., Azadpur, Delhi-110033

AUGUSTAN PUBLISHERS & DISTRIBUTORS
601/9, Som Dutt, Chamber-II,
Bhikaji Cama Place, New Delhi-110066
✆ 26193514, 26169374, 26175481,
Fax: 26184046
✉ basi@del3.vsnl.net.in
Prt.: Manjeet Singh Basi, Lovekesh Wadhwa, Surinder Gill (Ms.); **Bus.Intt.:** Rt., Pub., L.S.; **Spl.:** Arch. & Interior, Fashion, Design &

Textiles, Graphic & Photographics, Glass, Furniture & Jewellery, Art and Craft, Mang. etc.

AUM SHANTI 'CANCER NIDAN' SANSTHAN
Chandan Mahal Apartment, (Jagdeo Path), Balley Rd., Patna-800014 (Bihar)
✆ 2598175

AURAN MAHAL
2853, Bulbuli Khana, Turkman Gate, Delhi-110006
✆ 23268819, 23230152, 23235571, Fax: 91-11-23237985
Hd.Org.: Asif Iqbals; **Bus.Intt.:** Pub.; **Spl.:** Islamic Books

AURANGABAD BOOK DEPOT
Jethalia Towers, Gulmandi, Aurangabad-431001 (Maharashtra)
✆ 2353116, 2323244
Estd.: 1996; **Prop.:** Sharad T. Shah; **Bus.Intt.:** B.S.; **Spl.:** Newspapers & Perodicals, Greeting Cards and Gifts

AUREOLE PUBLISHING PVT. LTD.
B-38, Second Floor, Sector 5, Noida-201301 (Uttar Pradesh)
✆ 4346022, Fax: 91-120-4346025
✉ customerservice@aureole.com
🌐 www.aureole.com
Hd.Org.: Jaycee Menon; **Bus.Intt.:** Pub. and Rep.; **Spl.:** Foreign Books, Magazines and CD-ROMs

AUREOLE PUBLISHING PVT. LTD.
K-26, Sector-11, Noida-201301 (Uttar Pradesh)
✆ 91-120-2531807, 2534301, 2440053, Fax: 91-120-2531807
✉ vineet@aureole.co.in, aureole_pub@vsnl.net
🌐 www.aureole.co.in
Dir.: Vineet Sharma; **Bus.Intt.:** Pub. and Rep.; **Spl.:** Foreign Books, Magazines and CD-ROMs

AUTHORSPRESS
E-35, Jawahar Park, Laxmi Nagar, Delhi-110092
✆ 22436299, 22460145, 26851905, Fax: 22460145
✉ authorspress@yahoo.com
Hd.Org.: K.N. Sudarshan; **Bus.Intt.:** Pub.; **Spl.:** Soc.Sci. and Humanities

AUTOMOBILE ASSOCIATION OF EASTERN INDIA
13, Pramothesh Barva Sarai, Kolkata-19 (West Bengal)

AUTOMOBILE ASSOCIATION OF UPPER INDIA
14-F, Connaught Place, New Delhi-110001

AUVAYAR PUSTAKASALA
Collectorate, P.O., Kottayam-686002 (Kerala) ✆ 2561694
Estd.: 1992; **Hd.Org.:** Anita Titus; **Bus.Intt.:** Pub. .

AVADESH PUSTAK BHANDAR
Sadar Bazar, Dinapore, Patna-801503 (Bihar)
Bus.Intt.: Pub. & B.S.

AVANTGARDE PRESS
Kolkata (West Bengal)
✆ 4664094, 4100500
✉ ipslind@cal2.vsnl.net.in
Bus.Intt.: B.S.

AVANTY PUBLICATIONS
Tribeni Complex, T.B. Rd., Kottayam-686001 (Kerala)
✆ 2560649
Estd.: 1985; **Hd.Org.:** T.A. Mathews; **Bus.Intt.:** Pub.

AVI BOOKS PVT. LTD.
7/28, Mahavir Lane (Basement), Vardan House, Ansari Road, Darya Ganj, New Delhi-110002
✆ 23287577, Fax: 91-11-23262021
✉ avibooks@rediffmail.com
Hd.Org.: Avinash Jagasia

AVICHAL PUBLISHING COMPANY
1569/30, Naiwala, Karol Bagh, New Delhi-110005
✆ 28752745, 28755383, Fax: 91-11-28756921
✉ aryabookdepot@yahoo.com
Estd.: 1998; **Hd.Org.:** Dr. Vipin Gupta
Br.: 7 & 8, HPSIDC Industrial Area, Trilokpur Rd., Kala Amb Distt., Sirmour-173030 (Himachal Pradesh)
✆ 01702-238688
Bus.Intt.: Pub.; **Spl.:** Acad. Comm., Sci., Pure & Applied, Soc.Sci. & Med. books

AVIN BOOKS DISTRIBUTOR
32/13, B.S. Colony Gali No. 7, Vishwas Nagar, Shahdara (Delhi)
✆ 22303965, 55292065
Hd.Org.: Arjun Lal Dua; **Bus.Intt.:** Dist.; **Spl.:** Children Books Fiction Reference, Coloring Books, Encyclopedia etc.

AVIRAM PRAKASHAN
29/62, Gali No. 11, Vishwas Nagar, Delhi-110032
✆ 22205703
Hd.Org.: Madan Lal Sharma, Ramesh Sharma;
Bus.Intt.: Pub.; **Spl.:** Regional Languages as also Dictionaries and Sanskrit Literature

AVON PUBLICATIONS
D-288/10, Wadhwa Complex,
Laxmi Nagar, Delhi-110092
✆ (O) 22504668 (R) 95120-2776711
Estd.: 1988; **Prop.:** Abdul Wahed Malik; **Bus.Intt.:** L.S.

AVON PUBLISHERS
Shop No. 4, Convenient Shopping Centre, Pradhan Marg, 'C' Block Malaviya Nagar, Jaipur-302017 (Rajasthan)

AWASMI BOOK DEPOT
5, J.M. Rd., Rishikesh-249201
(Uttar Pradesh)

AWASTHI ASSOCIATES
40, Bai Ka Bagh, Allahabad-211003
(Uttar Pradesh)

AYAN PRAKASHAN
1619/6-B, Ulanganpur, Naveen Shahdara, Delhi-110032
✆ 26960604
Hd.Org.: Bhopal Sud

AYIM KHAN
Bikram, Patna-801104 (Bihar)
Bus.Intt.: Pub. & B.S.

AYURVED SANSKRIT HINDI PUSTAK BHANDAR
Jhalanio Ka Rasta, Kishanpoal Bazar,
Jaipur-302001 (Rajasthan)
✆ 2312974
Hd.Org.: Ganga Sahai Joshi; **Bus.Intt.:** Pub. and B.S.; **Spl.:** *Vastushastra, Vedas*, Phil., Astrology, etc.

AYURVED-VIKAS
Dabur India Ltd., Dabur Tower, Kaushambi, Sahibabad, Ghaziabad-201010
(Uttar Pradesh)
✆ 24777901-925 (Ext. 2108), Fax: 24777935
✉ shastrias@dabur.com
Hd.Org.: Ashwini Shastri; **Bus.Intt.:** B.S. and Pub.; **Spl.:** Hindi monthly *Ayurved-Vikas*

AZAD BACHAO ANDOLAN PRAKASHAN
Gandhi Bhavan, Allahabad-211002
(Uttar Pradesh)

AZAD BOOK CENTRE
Sultanganj, Mahendru, Patna-800006
(Bihar)
Bus.Intt.: Pub. and B.S.

AZAD KITAB GHAR
Sakchi Bazar, Jamshedpur-831001
(Jharkhand)
Hd.Org.: Abdul Sattar Khan

AZAD PUSTAK BHANDAR
Baunsi, Bhagalpur-813104 (Bihar)
Bus.Intt.: Pub. and B.S.

AZAD STORES
Naubatpur Lok, Naubatpur,
Patna-801109 (Bihar)
Bus.Intt.: Pub. and B.S.

■ ■ ■

B. ADINARAYANA SHETTY & SONS
Devaraj Market Complex, Mysore-570001 (Karnataka)
Bus.Intt.: B.S. and Pub.; **Spl.:** Kannada Language

B. BOOK HOUSE
134, Dhakka, Guru Tegh Bahadur Nagar, Delhi-110009
✆ 27441804
Hd.Org.: Veena Sharma; **Bus.Intt.:** Pub., **Spl.:** Books in English and Hindi

B. BROS. & CO.
13-A, Nirmal Chandra St., P.B. No. 7866, Bowbazar P.O., Kolkata-700012 (West Bengal)
✉ bbrothersco@yahoo.com

B. CHAND & SONS
9/4, Patuatola Lane, Kolkata-700009 (West Bengal)

B. CHATTAR SINGH JIWAN SINGH
Bazar Mai Sewan, Near Golden Temple, Amritsar (Punjab)
✆ 2542346, 2547974, 2557973
Fax: 91-183-2542346
✉ contact@csjs.com, csjssales@hotmail.com
www.csjs.com
Estd.: 1875; **Bus.Intt.:** Pub., B.S., Exp. and Printers

B. JAIN PUBLISHERS PVT. LTD.
1921/10, Chuna Mandi, Pahar Ganj, New Delhi-110055
✆ 23580800, 51698991,
Fax: 91-11-23580471, 51698993
✉ info@bjain.com
www.bjain.com
Estd.: 1976; **Hd.Org.:** Kuldeep Jain
Bus.Intt.: Pub., L.S. & Rt., Exp.; **Spl.:** Sci., Tech. & Medicine

B. SARKAR & CO.
15, College Sqr. (B.S. St.), Kolkata-700073 (West Bengal)
Hd.Org.: Sanjib Sarkar

B. SARKAR & SONS
67/1, M.G. Rd., Kolkata-700009 (West Bengal)

B. & B. EXPORTS
8, Community Centre, Basant Lok, Vasant Vihar, New Delhi-110057
Bus.Intt.: Exp.

B.B. AGENCY
Rishi Bazar, Thakurbari Rd., Kadamkuan, Patna-800003 (Bihar)
Bus.Intt.: Pub. and B.S.

B.B. BROTHERS & CO.
16/1, Shyamacharan Dey St., Kolkata-700009 (West Bengal)
✆ 033-22412095
Estd.: 1948; **Bus.Intt.:** Pub.

B.B. KUNDU & SONS
79/2, Mahatma Gandhi Rd., Kolkata-9 (West Bengal)

B.B.P. PUBLICATIONS PVT. LTD.
Bharati Bhawan, Western Kutchery Rd., Meerut-250001 (Uttar Pradesh)
✆ 0121-2663699, 2667799,
Fax: 2663699, 2667799
✉ bbpmrt@vsnl.net
Estd.: 2000; **Hd.Org.:** Namendra Agarwal; **Bus.Intt.:** Pub.; **Spl.:** Engg., Polytechnic, Competition Books

B.C. EXPORTS (INDIA)/BUTALA PUBLICATIONS
16/194, Gali No. 7, Faiz Rd., Karol Bagh, New Delhi-110005
✆ 23626782, 23527048, Fax: 23626782
✉ bcexpo@vsnl.net
Hd.Org.: B.C. Butala; **Bus.Intt.:** Pub., Exp.; **Spl.:** Rel., Indology, Ayurveda, Yoga, etc. in English and Regional Languages

B.C.I. PUBLICATIONS
No. 50, 1st Floor, Mohan Towers, P.B. No. 25014, Residency Rd., Bangalore-560025 (Karnataka)
✆ 22219184, 25084623, 25716993,
Telex: 08452696,
Fax: 91-080-25084632/5712077
✉ bcipub@vsnl.com
Estd.: 1992; **Bus.Intt.:** Imp., Sub.Ag.; **Spl.:** Humanities & Soc.Sci., Sci. & Tech., Med., Law, Juvenile/Children, Gen. & Fiction etc.

B.D.P. EDUCATIONAL BOOKS PVT. LTD.
103/C-7, Sector-8, Rohini, Delhi-110085
✆ 27947795, Fax: 27944625
✉ bdpc@yahoo.com
Hd.Org.: Anand Garg; **Bus.Intt.:** Pub.; **Spl.:** Edu. and Law Books on CD-ROMs

B.I. CHURCHILL LIBINGSTONE
54, Janpath, New Delhi-110001
✆ 23325313-17, Fax: 23323138
✉ bigroup@del3.vsnl.net.in
Hd.Org.: Y.R. Chadha; **Bus.Intt.:** Pub.; **Spl.:** Med., Sci. and Tech.

B.I. PUBLICATIONS PVT. LTD.
54, Janpath, New Delhi-110001
✆ 23325313 (4-5-6-7), Fax: 23323138

📧 bigroup@del3.vsnl.net.in
Estd.: 1949; **Hd.Org.:** Y.R. Chadha
Br.: 147, Infantry Rd., Bangalore-560001 (Karnataka) ✆ 080-22204652, Fax: 22205696 📧 bipbang@satyam.net.in • Lansdowne House, 18, Landsdowne Rd. Mumbai-400039 (Maharashtra) ✆ 022-22021766, 22022396, Fax: 22046778 📧 bipmu@vsnl.com • 9/10, Agurchand Mansions, 1st Floor, 150 Mount Rd., Chennai-600002 (Tamil Nadu) ✆ 044-28460861, 28461287, 28461289, Fax: 28460361 📧 bipm_2000@satyam.net.in • 13, Darya Ganj, New Delhi-110002 ✆ 23274443, 23259352, 23255118, Fax: 23261290 📧 bidel@ndb.vsnl.net.in • 13/IA, Govt. Place East, Kolkata-700069 (West Bengal) ✆ 033-22488742, 22201351, Fax: 22488743 📧 bipcal@satyam.net.in • Aishwarya Apartments, 9-B, Kumkum Society, Near Sardar Patel Statue, Stadium Rd., Ahmedabad-380014 (Gujarat) ✆ 079-6420247, Fax: 6401303 📧 bipahd@icenet.in • Direct Mail Division 61-63, Lakshmi Bldg. 4th Floor, Sir P.M. Rd., Mumbai-400001 ✆ 022-22660230, Fax: 022-22672537 📧 bipdmd@vsnl.com • 28/2776, Geetanjali, Chettikulangara, Thiruvananthapuram-695001 (Kerala) ✆ 0471-2472013, Fax: 0471-2472073 📧 biptvpm@satyam.net.in
Bus.Intt.: Pub., Imp., Exp., Dist.; **Spl.:** Med., Tech., Gen. Books

B.K. BOOK AGENCY
Madaripur Pally, P.O. Rahara-743186, Distt. North, 24 Parganas, (West Bengal)
✆ 25681274, 22486604, Fax: 91-33-22486604, 22481620
📧 bkba@vsnl.net
Estd.: 1990; **Prt.:** R. Bhattacharya;
Bus.Intt.: Pub. and B.S.; **Spl.:** Humanities

B.K. CHAKRAVERTY BOOKSELLERS
Banamalipur, Near Central Jail, Agartala-799001 (Tripura)

B.K. ENTERPRISE
61, Mahatma Gandhi Rd., Kolkata-700009 (West Bengal)

B.K. PRAKASHANI
6, R.G. Kar Rd., Kolkata-700004 (West Bengal)

B.K. PUSTAK BHANDAR
Punpun, Patna-804453 (Bihar)
Bus.Intt.: Pub. and B.S.

B.K.S. PUBLISHERS DISTRIBUTORS
100, Tilak Khand, Giri Nagar, Kalkaji, New Delhi-110019
✆ 26225623
Prop.: Mrs. Sushma Saini; **Bus.Intt.:** WS, Sub.Ag., Pub., Rep., L.S.; **Spl.:** Acad., Beh. Sci., Soc.Sci., Comm., Sci., Pure & Applied, Med., Tech. Rare, Journals & Magazines

B.L. BOOK STALL
14, Bankim Chatterjee St., Kolkata-700073 (West Bengal)

BHARATI BOOK STALL
6-B, Ramanath Majumder St., Kolkata-700009 (West Bengal)
✆ 2241-26382/28089
📧 bmpl@cal3.vsnl.net.in
Hd.Org.: Ashoke Kumar Barik; **Bus.Intt.:** Pub.

B.M.W. EXPORTS
B-41, Sawan Park, Delhi-110052

B.P.B. MULTIMEDIA
201, Manish Plaza, Ansari Rd., Darya Ganj, New Delhi-110002
✆ 23267741, 23325760, Fax: 23262008
📧 bpb@vsnl.net
Hd.Org.: Manish Jain; **Bus.Intt.:** Pub. and Dist.; **Spl.:** Edu. Games, CD-ROMs and Softwares

B.P.B. PUBLICATIONS (P) LTD.
20, Munish Plaza, Ansari Rd., Darya Ganj, New Delhi-110002
✆ (O) 23325760, 23723393, 23254990-91 (R) 23969355, Fax: 23266427
📧 bpb@vsnl.com
🌐 www.bpbonline.com
Prt.: Manish Jain, Mrs. Rippan Jain, Mrs. S. Rani Jain
Br.: B-14, Connaught Place, New Delhi-110001 ✆ 23325760, 23723393, Fax: 23351856 • B.P.B. Book Centre, 376, Old Lajpat Rai Market, Delhi-110006 ✆ 22961747 • Business Promotion Bureau, 8/1, Ritchie St., Mount Rd., Chennai-600002 ✆ 2834796 • Computer Book Centre, 12, Shrungar Shopping Centre, M.G. Rd., Bangalore-560001 ✆ 25587923, 25584641 • Business Promotion Bureau, 4-3-268-C, Giriraj Lane, Bank St., Hyderabad-500195 ✆ 2512280 • Computer Book Centre, SCF-65, Sector-6, Panchkula-134109 ✆ 2561613 • Computer Book Centre, Shanti Niketan Building, 8, Camac St., Kolkata; **Bus.Intt.:** Pub., WS, Imp., Exp.; **Spl.:** Sci. & Tech.

B.P.I. (INDIA) PVT. LTD.
229-A, 2nd Floor, Kranti Veer, Raj Guru Marg, Girgaon, Mumbai-400004 (Maharashtra)
✆ 23808817, 23808819, Fax: 23872625
📧 bpipl@vsnl.com
Estd.: 1997; **Man.Dir.:** Jai Saxena
Br.: 3, Ch. Tara Bhawan, F-344/1, Old M.B. Rd., Lado Sarai, New Delhi-110030

© 51665005-6, Fax: 51665736
✉ help@bpiindia.com
🌐 www.bpiindia.com
Bus.Intt.: Pub.; **Spl.:** Edu. and Professional Books in English Language

B.R. INTERNATIONAL PUBLISHERS / B.R. WORLD OF BOOKS
1036, Raghubar Pura No. 1, Gandhi Nagar, Delhi-110031
© 22212894, 22227885
✉ br_intel@rediffmail.com
Hd.Org.: Anand Sharma; **Bus.Intt.:** Pub.; **Spl.:** Physical Edu., Health and Information Tech.

B.R. PAPERBACK/B.R. PUBLISHING CORPORATION
4737, A/23, Ansari Rd., Darya Ganj, New Delhi-110002
© 23259196, Fax: 91-11-23263035
✉ brpc@vsnl.com
Hd.Org.: Neeraj Mittal; **Bus.Intt.:** Pub.; **Spl.:** Soc.Sci. and Humanities in English, *Vastu*, Litt. and Sai Baba in Hindi

B.R. RHYTHMS
425, Nimri Colony, Ashok Vihar, Phase-IV, Delhi-110052
© 27432112
✉ info@brbhythms.com
Prop.: Neeraj Mittal; **Spl.:** Books on Music, Dance Drama & Theatre

B.R. WORLD OF BOOKS
4737, A/23, Main Ansari Road, Darya Ganj, New Delhi-110002
© 23259648, Fax: 91-11-23263035
✉ brpc@bsnl.com
Hd.Org.: Praveen Mittal

B.S. PUBLICATIONS
4-4-309, Giriraj Lane, Sultan Bazar, Hydrabad-500095 (Andhra Pradesh)
© 23445600-1, Fax: 91-11-23445611
✉ contactus@bspublications.net
🌐 www.bspublications.net
Hd.Org.: Nikhil Nandan C. Shah

B.S. SHARMA & BROTHERS PUBLISHER & DISTRIBUTORS
F-10, H.I. Complex, Surya Nagar, M.G. Rd., Agra-2 (Uttar Pradesh)
© 0562-3104192, 2526779
✉ bssharmapublishers@rediffmail.com
Hd.Org.: B.S. Sharma; **Bus.Intt.:** Pub., Dist.; **Spl.:** University Level Text, Reference Books on all Sub. by Indian and Foreign Publishers

B.S.B. INFO CENTRE PVT. LTD.
A-68, South Extension Part-I, New Delhi-110049
© 24611991, 24634222, 51646667, Fax: 24627172
✉ standard@del3.vsnl.net.in, bsb@nda.vsnl.net.in
🌐 www.standardsindia.com
Estd.: 1998; **Dir.:** C. Krishnan, Ms. Valsamma Thomas; **Bus.Intt.:** Pub.'s Rep.; **Spl.:** Tech.

B.V. ENTERPRISES
Unit No. A1/A-18, New Empire Indl. Estate, Kondivite Rd., J.B. Nagar, Andheri (E) Mumbai-400059 (Maharashtra)
Bus.Intt.: Exp.

B.X. FURTADO & SONS
Jer Mahal, Dhobitalao, Mumbai-400002 (Maharashtra)
© 22080759, 22013163, 22051068, Cable: ORCHESTRA, Fax: 22058750
Estd.: 1865; **Prop.:** John A. Gomes
Br.: B.X. Furtado & Sons, 14, Grace Estate, Margao, Gao © 2222997, 2221340
• L.M. Furtado & Company, 540-544, Kalbadevi Rd., Mumbai-400002
© 22013105, 22012756, 22013656, Cable: ORCHESTRA, Fax: 22058750
Bus.Intt.: Imp., Exp.; **Spl.:** Gen. & Fiction etc., Music

BABA ENTERPRISES (REGD.)
Dignity Sales, Lal Chowk, Srinagar-190001 (Jammu & Kashmir)
© 2474500, Fax: 2475929
✉ imraubaba1@yahoo.com
Estd.: 1993; **Hd.Org.:** Imran Ashraf Baba
Br.: 153, Gole Market, Karan Nagar, Srinagar-190010 (Jammu & Kashmir)
© 2474197, Fax: 2475929
Bus.Intt.: L.S., Rt., Imp., Exp.; **Spl.:** Sci. & Tech.

BABA POCKET BOOKS
D-14/73, Sector-8, Rohini, New Delhi-110085
© 65164316, Fax: 91-11-27062968
✉ amit_abd@yahoo.com
Hd.Org.: Amit Kumar Mittal

BABBAR PUBLICATIONS PVT. LTD.
A 8-9, Ansal Building Behind Batra Cinema, Dr. Mukherji Nagar, Delhi-110009
© 27651938, 27258475, Fax: 27651453
Mkt.Man.: B.S. Kapoor

BABLOO BOOK AGENCY
Pribahore, Patna-800004 (Bihar)
Bus.Intt.: Pub. and B.S.

BADAGARA CO-OPERATIVE PRINTING & (PAPCOS)
Convent Rd., Badagara-673101 (Kerala)
Estd.: 1974; **Hd.Org.:** Co-Operative Society; **Bus.Intt.:** Pub. and B.S.

BADALTE SAMIKARAN
G-1/1165-A, Mansarovar Park, Shahdara, Delhi-110032
✆ 91-11-64614501
Hd.Org.: Suresh Chand Kaushik;
Bus.Intt.: Pub.; **Spl.:** Hindi Journal *Badalte Samikaran*

BADSHA AND COMPANY
2, Kailash Bose St., Kolkata-700009 (West Bengal)

BADSHAH BOOK SALES
L.G. 15, City Centre, M.G. Rd., Indore-452001 (Madhya Pradesh)
✆ (O) 2531384 (R) 2470693
Estd.: 1983; **Bus.Intt.:** B.S.; **Spl.:** Gen. Books

BAGCHEE ASSOCIATES
523, Kalyan Nagar, Pansila-743180 (West Bengal)

BAGCHI & BAGCHI
Nagpur
✆ 22265244, Fax: 22266240
bagchis@nagpur.dot.net.in
Bus.Intt.: B.S., L.S. & Exp.

BAHAI PUBLISHING TRUST OF INDIA
F3/6, Okhla Industrial Area, Phase-I, New Delhi-110020
✆ 26819391, 26818990, Cable: BAHAI FAITH
Fax: 26812703
bptindia@del3.vsnl.net.in
www.bahaibooksindia.com
Estd.: 1954; **Man.:** Jiten Mishra; **Bus.Intt.:** Pub. & Exp.

BAHRI BROTHERS
742, Lajpat Rai Market, P.O. Box No. 2032, Delhi-110006
✆ 23861740, 23866291
Fax: 23868488
bahribrs@ndb.vsnl.net.in
www.bahribrothers.com
Prt.: Devendra Malhotra, Sanjiv Malhotra; **Bus.Intt.:** Pub., Dist. and Rt., Dist., Imp., Exp.; **Spl.:** Service & Labour Laws

BAHRI PUBLICATIONS
997/A/9 Gobind Puri, P.O. Box-4453, Kalkaji, New Delhi-110019
✆ 26445710, 26448606
Fax: 26448606
bahrius@del6.vsnl.net.in, bahrius@vsnl.com
www.bahripublications.org
Estd.: 1973; **Prop.:** U.S. Bahri, Deepinder Bahri (Man.); **Bus.Intt.:** Pub., WS, L.S. & Rt., Imp., Exp., Sub.Ag.; **Spl.:** Humanities & Soc.Sci., Gen. & Fiction etc.

BAHRI SONS (BOOKSELLERS & STATIONERS)
Opp. Main Gate, Khan Market, New Delhi-110003
✆ (O) 24694855, 24694610 (R) 26196234, 26101053, Fax: 24618637
bahrisons@vsnl.com
www.booksatbahri.com
Estd.: 1953; **Prt.:** Balraj Malhotra, Anuj Bahri Malhotra; **Bus.Intt.:** Imp., L.S. and Exp.;
Spl.: Acad. & Soc.Sci.

BAHUJAN BOOKS
31/735, Velliparamba, Calicut, P.B. No. 236, Kozhikode-673001 (Kerala)
✆ 0495-2359363

BAHUJAN DIVERSITY MISSION
Gupta Apartment B-1, 149/9, Kishangarh, Vasant Kunj, New Delhi-110070
✆ 91-11-65948667
diversitymission@yahoo.com
Hd.Org.: Kavish Kumar

BAHUMUKHI
New Market, Patna-800004 (Bihar)
✆ 256682; **Bus.Intt.:** Pub. and B.S.

BAIKUNTHA BOOK HOUSE
183, Bidhan Sarani, Kolkata-700006 (West Bengal)

BAIPARA PUBLICATIONS
18A, Gobinda Mandal Rd., Kolkata-700002 (West Bengal)

BAIPATRA
8-B, College Row, Kolkata-700009 (West Bengal)

BAIT-AL-HIKMAH TRUST
165, Zakir Bagh, New Delhi-110025

BAJRANG PRAKASHAN
RZ/E-5, Gandhi Market, West Sagarpur (Pankha Rd.), New Delhi-110046
✆ 25398187, 25392086
Hd.Org.: Sanjay Kumar Gupta; **Bus.Intt.:** Pub. & B.S.; **Spl.:** Hindi Litt., Children's Litt., Sci., Religious, Gen. and Children's Books

BAKA BOOK STALL
9, S.C. Dey St., Kolkata-700073 (West Bengal)

BAKSHILPA
17C, Telepara Lane, Kolkata-700031 (West Bengal)

BAKTIVEDANTA BOOK TRUST
T.C. 24/1073, Hospital Rd., Thycaud, Thiruvananthapuram-695014 (Kerala)
✆ 2368197
Estd.: 1966; **Man.Trustee:** A.C. Bhaktivedanta, Swamy Prathupada; **Bus.Intt.:** Pub.

BAL BHARATI PRAKASHAN
30, Old Allapur, Allahabad-211006 (Uttar Pradesh)
✆ 2500255
Hd.Org.: Nagendra Shukla

BAL HANS
5-E, Jhalana Institutional Area, Jawaharlal Nehru Marg, Jaipur-302004 (Rajasthan)
✆ 2510535, Fax: 2516615
Hd.Org.: Gulab Kothari; **Bus.Intt.:** Pub.; **Spl.:** Children's Magazine *Bal Hans* in Hindi

BAL SAHITYA MANDIR
1312/1131, Katra, Allahabad-211002 (Uttar Pradesh)
Hd.Org.: Kanak Bhargava

BAL SAHITYA SHODH SANSTHAN
1-120, Kirti Nagar, New Delhi-110015

BAL UPYOGI PRAKASHAN
Khazanchi Rd., Patna-800004 (Bihar)
Bus.Intt.: Pub. and B.S.

BAL VIKAS PRAKASHAN PVT. LTD.
1/6611, East Rohtas Nagar, Shahdara, Delhi-110032
Bus.Intt.: Pub.; **Spl.:** Edu. books

BALAJI BOOK DISTRIBUTORS
Faridabad (Haryana)
✆ 0129-5278504
✉ balajibooks@sify.com
Bus.Intt.: B.S., L.S.

BALAJI BOOKS
FF-12, Mangal Bazar Rd., Laxmi Nagar, Delhi-110092
✆ 22012532 ▮ 9868421290
Prop.: Mrs. Chandra Raman; **Bus.Intt.:** Rt.; **Spl.:** Acad., Beh. Sci., Comm., Sci., Pure & Applied, Tech. Books

BALAJI PUBLICATIONS
103, Pyscrofts Rd., Chennai-600014 (Tamil Nadu)
✆ 24340205
Prop.: C. Viswananthan; **Bus.Intt.:** Pub.; **Spl.:** National Integration Languages series English Vernacular. Books for Learners of Most Indian Languages

BALAKA PRAKASHAN
18-A, Nabin Kundu Lane, Kolkata-700009 (West Bengal)

BALANI INFOTECH PVT LTD
121-122, Vinoba Puri, Lajpat Nagar-II, New Delhi-110024
✆ 46573379, Fax: 91-11-41724167
✉ balani@vsnl.net
🌐 www.balaniinfotech.com
Hd.Org.: Kailash Balani; **Bus.Intt.:** Dist.; **Spl.:** Tech., Sci., Med., Tech., Journals & Magazines, Law

BALGOVIND KUBERDASANI CO.
Fernandis Bridge, Gandhi Rd., Ahmedabad-380001 (Gujarat)

BALGOVIND PRAKASHAN
Bala Hanuman, Gandhi Rd., Ahmedabad-380001 (Gujarat)

BALIT PUBLICATIONS PVT. LTD.
34/1 Yusuf Sarai, Green Park, New Delhi-110016
✆ (O) 26529459, 26511459
(R) 95124-2324263, Fax: 26855465
✉ kanuj@vsnl.com
Estd.: 1997; **Man.Dir.:** Anil Kharbanda, Deepak Kharbanda (Dir.); **Bus.Intt.:** Pub. and B.S.; **Spl.:** Tech. & Industrial Books

BALKRISHNA LAXMAN NALAVADE
3, Rakhi Apts. Plot No. 31, Rambagh Colony Paud Rd., Opp. Anand Nagar, Kothrud, Pune-411038 (Maharashtra)

BALMEX LAWRIE & CO. LTD
32-33, Ground Floor, Kushal Bazar, Nehru Place, New Delhi-110019
✆ 26463628, Fax: 91-11-26467383
✉ srivastava@balmexlawrie.net
🌐 www.balmexlawrie.com
Hd.Org.: Niraj Gupta

BALSAHITYALAYA
Public Trust, F-838, 1015, Sadashiv Peth, Pune-411030 (Maharashtra)

BANALATA
H.O.: New Market, Dibrugarh-1
Estd.: 1972; **Prop.:** Ananta Hazarika
Br.: Jaswant Rd., Panbazar, Guwahati-781001 (Assam)
✆ 2522070, 2600876 ▮ 9864026668
Bus.Intt.: Pub.; **Spl.:** Children & Gen., Novels, Poems, Translation works etc.

BANAPHOOL PRAKASHANI PVT. LTD.
28/3A, Convent Rd., 2nd Floor, Kolkata-700014 (West Bengal)
✆ 22450400, 22446504,
Fax: 91-33-22446504, 22424330
Hd.Org.: Lattu Bhattacharya; **Bus.Intt.:** Pub., WS, Exp.; **Spl.:** Gen. Books and Articles etc.

BANARAS HINDU UNIVERSITY
Publication Cell, Banaras Hindu University, Varanasi-221005 (Uttar Pradesh)
✆ 2368598, Fax: 91-542-2368598
✉ pppcellbhu@gmail.com
🌐 www.bhu.ac.in

Hd.Org.: Prof. Panjab Singh; **Bus.Intt.:** Pub.; **Spl.:** Indian Phil., Sanskrit, Sci., Med., Ancient Hist., Culture, Oriental Learning, Doctoral Theses Translations, Biographies, etc.

BANARAS MERCANTILE CO.
109, Mahatma Gandhi Rd., Kolkata-700007 (West Bengal)
✆ 033-22193608
Estd.: 1952; **Bus.Intt.:** Pub. and B.S.; **Spl.:** Indological, Religious, Oriental Books

BANASTHALI BOOK CENTRE
Banasthali Vidyapith-304022, Distt. Tonk (Rajasthan)
✆ (O) 01438-228377 (R) 01438-222227
✉ navjeewannew@yahoo.com
Prop.: Paras Mal Jain; **Bus.Intt.:** Pub., B.S., L.S.

BANERJEE BOOK STALL
B.C. St., Stall No. 72/1, Kolkata-700073 (West Bengal)

BANERJEE BROTHERS
54, Biren Roy Rd., (West) Kolkata-700061 (West Bengal)

BANERJEE LIBRARY
Majdia, Nadia (West Bengal)

BANERJEE PUBLISHERS
5/1A, College Row, Kolkata-700009 (West Bengal)
Hd.Org.: Surya Banerjee

BANERJEE PUSTAKALAYA
Santaldi, Purulia (Bihar)

BANGABANI PRAKASHAN
56, Surja Sen St., Kolkata-700009 (West Bengal)

BANGALORE BOOK BUREAU
M.G. Rd., Bangalore-560001 (Karnataka)

BANGALORE BOOK CENTRE
No. 4, Rangaswamy Temple St., Bangalore-560002 (Karnataka)
✆ (O) 22264123 (R) 26620114
Estd.: 1969; **Prop.:** C. Venkataswamy; **Bus.Intt.:** Pub. & WS; **Spl.:** Children Books, School Text Books in English and Hindi

BANGALORE BOOK HOUSE
POB-007-Sovereign Park, 56-58, K.R. Rd., Basavanagudi, Bangalore-560004 (Karnataka)
✆ 2604730, Cable: APIBANG
Estd.: 1967; **Prop.:** A.M. Desai; **Bus.Intt.:** Pub., L.S. and Rt., Imp., Sub.Ag.

BANGALORE PRINTING AND PUBLISHING CO. LTD.
P.B. No. 1807, 88, Mysore Rd., Bangalore-560018 (Karnataka)
Bus.Intt.: Exp.

BANGASREE LIBRARY
Kamalpur, Chakdan, Nadia (West Bengal)

BANI LIBRARY
54/7, College St., Kolkata-700009 (West Bengal)

BANI MANDIR
Post Nalhati, Distt. Birbhum (West Bengal)
Hd.Org.: Amiya Kumar Chatterjee

BANI MANDIR
New Market, Dibrugarh-786001 (Assam)
✆ 036-122513
Estd.: 1949; **Prop.:** C.K. Hazarika
Br.: Ranivari, Panbazar, Guwahati-1 (Assam)
✆ 036-1520241, 1564488

BANI MANDIR PUBLISHERS (P) LTD.
197-B, Muktarambabu St., Kolkata-7 (West Bengal)

BANI PRAKASH PVT. LTD.
Panbazar, Guwahati-781001 (Assam)
✆ 545030, Fax: 454751
✉ devchoudurygp@rediffmail.com
Bus.Intt.: Pub.

BANI PRAKASH
A-129, College St. Market, Kolkata-700073 (West Bengal)
Hd.Org.: Akhar Hossain

BANI PRAKASHAN
7, Nabin Kundu Lane, Kolkata-700009 (West Bengal)

BANI PROKASANI
College Hostel Rd., Panbazar, Guwahati-781001 (Assam)

BANISHILPA
14A, Tamer Lane, Kolkata-700009 (West Bengal)
Bus.Intt.: Pub.; **Spl.:** Cinema and Allied Arts, Serious Litt. and Edu. Topics in Bengali

BANISON INDIA
107, Unique Industrial Estate, Chakla Rd., Andheri (East), Mumbai-400099 (Maharashtra)
Bus.Intt.: Exp.

BANKERS COLLEGE
I-47, Kirti Nagar, New Delhi-110015

BANKIPORE GENERAL STORES
B.G.H. School Compound, Near Golghar, Patna-800001 (Bihar)
Bus.Intt.: Pub. and B.S.

BANSAL BROTHERS
Dispensary Rd., Dehra Dun-248001 (Uttarakhand)
✆ (O) 2654615 (R) 2520703 ▮ 9897351136, Fax: 2659316
✉ bansalbrothers1@rediffmail.com

Estd.: 1960; **Prop.:** Anurag Bansal; **Bus.Intt.:** Pub., L.S. & B.S.; **Spl.:** School and College Books

BANSAL PUBLICATIONS
Hospital Rd., Agra (Uttar Pradesh)
Bus.Intt.: Pub.; **Spl.:** Hindi Books

BANU PATHIPPAGAM
Periyarpathai, Chennai-600026 (Tamil Nadu)
✆ 044-24839722
Hd.Org.: Dr. Valampuri Johm

BANWARILAL JAIN
Motikatra, Agra-282003 (Uttar Pradesh)
✆ 2361320, Cable: RAREBOOKS, Agra
Estd.: 1948; **Hd.Org.:** Banwarilal Jain; **Bus.Intt.:** Pub., L.S., Rt., Imp., Sub.Ag.

BANYAN TREE BOOKS PVT LTD.
7/31, Ansari Road, Darya Ganj,
New Delhi-110002
✆ 23274463, 23288769, Fax: 91-11-23278144
✉ info@banyantreebooks.com
www.banyantreebooks.com
Hd.Org.: Ashok K. Maheshwari

BAPPCO PUBLICATIONS
Bangalore Press, 88, Mysore Rd.,
Bangalore-560018 (Karnataka)
✆ (O) 2601638, 2609279 (R) 23341306, 23311067
Hd.Org.: H.R. Anantha; **Bus.Intt.:** Pub.; **Spl.:** Fiction, Gen., Edu. Books, Diaries and Calendars in English and Kannada

BARAJ PUSTAK BHANDAR
Garhpura, Begusarai-848204 (Bihar)
Bus.Intt.: Pub. and B.S.

BARISHA GRANTHALAYA
P-506, Diamond Harbour Rd., Kolkata-700008 (West Bengal)

BARKAKOTI CO.
A.T. Rd., Jorhat (Assam)

BARAL & CO.
104/12, Narkeldanga North Rd.,
Kolkata-700011 (West Bengal)
Bus.Intt.: Exp.

BARNALI
73, Mahatma Gandhi Rd., Kolkata-700009 (West Bengal)
Estd.: 1964; **Bus.Intt.:** Pub.; **Spl.:** Literary Criticism, Biography, Social Culture and also P.A.D. Papers in English and Bengali

BARODA BOOK CENTRE
28, Shop No. Stop Plaza, Optal Tower
Premsar, Alkapari, Baroda (Gujarat)

BARODA BOOK CORPORATION
20, Stop-n-shop Plaza, R.C. Dutt Rd., Alkapuri, Baroda-390007 (Gujarat)
✆ 2358736, Fax: 91-265-334920
✉ bbcorp@satyam.net.in
Bus.Intt.: B.S.; **Spl.:** Library Books in All Sub. except Law

BARODA PRODUCTIVITY COUNCIL BOOKS DIVISION
Productivity House, Productivity Rd.,
Baroda-390005 (Gujarat)
✆ 2322431, 2322433, Cable: UTPADAKTA, Baroda, Telex: 0175-6338 BPC IN
Estd.: 1959; **Hd.Org.:** D.I. Patel, D.K. Patel

BAROWALIA PUBLICATIONS
Khalini, Shimla-171002 (Himachal Pradesh)

BARTHCAKUR BOOK STALL
Station Charati, Sibsagar (Assam)

BARUA AGENCY
Dighali Pukhuri Par, Guwahati-781001 (Assam)

BARUA CHOWDHURY & CO.
26, College St., Kolkata-700073 (West Bengal)

BARWARA BOOK HOUSE
Jaipur (Rajasthan)
Fax: 2223042
✉ sudharamchandani@hotmail.com
Bus.Intt.: B.S.

BASA BOOK DEPOT
Majhaul, Begusarai-851127 (Bihar)
Bus.Intt.: Pub. and B.S.

BASAK BOOK STORE
4, Shyama Charan Dey St., Kolkata-700009 (West Bengal)

BASANTI PUBLICATION
Ramanand Path, New Balbhadrapur,
Laheriasarai, Darbhanga-846001 (Bihar)

BASEELIYA BOOKS
Devalokam, Kottayam-686038 (Kerala)
Estd.: 1991; **Man.Prt.:** Paul Ciniraj; **Bus.Intt.:** Pub.

BASHARATH PUBLISHERS
No. 83, New # 171, Angappa Naick St.,
Chennai-600001
✆ 25225028, Fax: 91-44-25230687
Bus.Intt.: Pub., Dist. & Exp.; **Spl.:** Holy *Quran* and Islamic Books

BASIL BOOKS
Municipal Office Buildings, Ankamali (Kerala)
Estd.: 1982; **Prop.:** Achamma Peter; **Bus.Intt.:** B.S.

BASU BOOK STALL
B.C. St. Stall No. 72/1, Kolkata-700073 (West Bengal)

BASUDEO PRASAD GUPTA
Khusrupur, Patna-803202 (Bihar)
Bus.Intt.: B.S.

BATRA BOOK SERVICE
1/5, Bhagat Singh Lane, Gole Market, New Delhi-110001
✆ (O) 23360129, 23365374 (R) 23545654, Fax: 091-11-23638484
✉ batrabooks@mantramail.com
Estd.: 1980; **Prop.:** J.C. Batra; **Bus.Intt.:** Pub. & Dist.; **Spl.:** Military Books

BATRA DIARIES
B-23, Mayapuri Indl. Area, Phase-II, New Delhi-110064
✆ 25404532, 25145035
Hd.Org.: J.C. Batra; **Spl.:** Diaries, Calendars, Telephone Indexes, Organisors

BATRA PUBLISHERS & DISTRIBUTORS
Ram Niwas, Bairagpura, Dawauli, Lashkar, Gwalior-1 (Madhya Pradesh)

BAUDDHABHARATI
'Panchsheel', S10/6, A-2A Magbhool Alam Road, Varanasi-221002 (Uttar Pradesh)
✆ 91-542-3298044
✉ bauddhabhrti@satyam.net.in
Hd.Org.: Swami Dwarika Das Shastry; **Bus.Intt.:** B.S.; **Spl.:** Buddhism in Sanskrit, Hindi and Pali

BAULMON PRAKASHAK
28, Ballygunge Gardens, Kolkata-700019 (West Bengal)

BAZME KHIZRE RAH
80, Intazar Lodge, Ghaffar Manzil Extn., Jamia Nagar, Delhi-110025
✆ 26844816
Estd.: 1988; **Hd.Org.:** Khush Hal Zaidi

BEACON BOOKS
203, Shivam Tower, Community Centre, Paschim Vihar, New Delhi-110063
✆ (O) 25584782, 25584771 (R) 25588306, Fax: 25575492
Estd.: 1993; **Man.Dir.:** Rajeev Sethi; **Bus.Intt.:** Pub.

BEAULA PUSTAK BHANDAR
Chaigaon, Kamrup (Assam)

BEENA PUBLISHING HOUSE
41, Deb Lane, Engtally, Kolkata-700014 (West Bengal)

BELIAGHATA VARIETY STORES
134, R.R.L.M. Rd., Kolkata-700085 (West Bengal)

BENGAL BOOK AGENCY
1, Shyama Charan Dey St., Kolkata-700073 (West Bengal)

BENGAL LAW HOUSE
Ashok Rajpath, Patna-800004 (Bihar)
Bus.Intt.: Pub. and B.S.

BENGAL PUBLISHERS PVT. LTD.
14, Bankim Chatterjee St., Kolkata-700073 (West Bengal)
✆ 033-2313207
Bus.Intt.: Pub.; **Spl.:** Bengali Language

BENNETT COLEMAN & CO. LTD
9-10, Times Annex, Indian Express Building, 2nd Floor, Bahadur Shah Zafar Marg, New Delhi-110002
✆ 91-11-42512162
✉ jaideep.chakravorty@timesgroup.com
Hd.Org.: Jaideep Chakravorty

BENU BOOK STALL
15, College Square, Kolkata-700073 (West Bengal)

BENU BOOK SUPPLY AGENCY
10/1, Ramanath Majumder St., Kolkata-700007 (West Bengal)

BEST BOOK CO.
6373/2, First Floor, Block-7, Dev Nagar, Karol Bagh, New Delhi-110005
✆ 25862162
Hd.Org.: R.R. Karn; **Bus.Intt.:** Pub.; **Spl.:** Children's Books, Dictionaries, Encyclopaedia, Biographies, Litt., Sports, *Vaastu*, etc.

BEST BOOK COMPANY
S.M.S. Highway, Jaipur-313001 (Rajasthan)
Prop.: R.K. Gupta
Br.: Shop No. 1, 2 & 3, Rajashtan University Campus, Jaipur-302004
✆ 2705773, Fax: 2512193
Bus.Intt.: WS, L.S. & Rt., Imp., Sub.Ag.; **Spl.:** Humanities & Soc.Sci.

BEST BOOKS (THE)
1A, College Row, P.B. No. 10830, Kolkata-700009 (West Bengal)
✆ 2841-20634
Ch.Exe.: Sribindu Bhattacharya; **Bus.Intt.:** Pub.; **Spl.:** Wide range of Books and Thought Provoking Sub.

BEST (I) EXPORTS
Oshiwara Ind. Centre, Wing 219, New Link Rd., Goregaon, Opp. Goregaon Bus Depot, Mumbai-400104 (Maharashtra)
✆ 28754546, 28749636, Fax: 28749636
Hd.Org.: P.R. Sampath; **Bus.Intt.:** Exp.; **Spl.:** Books, Newspapers

BEST SELLERS
D-13, Kailash Colony, New Delhi-110048

✆ (O) 26411419 (R) 26424690
Hd.Org.: O.P. Agarwal; **Bus.Intt.:** Imp. & WS

BETHANY BOOKS
Pazhavangadi Ranny, Pathanamthitta-689673 (Kerala)
Estd.: 1972; **Prop.:** J.C. Dev; **Bus.Intt.:** Pub. and B.S.

BETHANY PUBLICATIONS
Bethany Ashram Generalate, Vadavathoor, Kottayam-686010 (Kerala)
✆ 0481-2571515, 2578494, Fax: 0481-2571057
✉ bethanyg@vsnl.com
Estd.: 1980; **Hd.Org.:** Mathai Kadavil OIC; **Bus.Intt.:** Pub. and B.S.; **Spl.:** Soc. and Rel.

BETHESDA COMMUNICATIONS (P) LTD.
L-16, South Extn.-II, New Delhi-110049

BETTER BOOK SERVICE PUBLISHERS & DISTRIBUTORS
B-65A, Indira Gandhi Marg, East Vinod Nagar, Near Mayur Vihar, Phase-II, Delhi-110091
✆ 22775630, 22773282, 35602800, 35801198, Fax: 22773282
✉ dks@nda.vsnl.net.in
Hd.Org.: D.K. Sharma; **Bus.Intt.:** Pub., Dist. and B.S.; **Spl.:** Sci., Agri., Med., Mang., Edu.

BETTER BOOKS
P.O. Box 1020, Palton, Thiruvananthapuram-695002 (Kerala)

BETTER YOURSELF BOOKS
58/23rd Rd. TPS-III, P.B. 9814, Bandra (W), Mumbai-400050 (Maharashtra)
✆ 26510023, 26408557, 26403312, Fax: 26510925, 26454425
✉ marketing@stpaulbyb.com
🌐 www.stpaulsbyb.com
Hd.Org.: Larry Toms; **Bus.Intt.:** Pub. and Dist.; **Spl.:** Books and Audio-visuals that promote Human values and Gen. knowledge, Magazines (*The Teenager and Inspirational Quote*)

BHAGALPUR PUSTAK BHANDAR
M.P. Dwivedi Rd., Bhagalpur-812002 (Bihar)
Bus.Intt.: Pub. and B.S.

BHAGAT PUSTAK BHANDAR
Kenduar, Amarpur, Bhagalpur-812006 (Bihar)
Bus.Intt.: Pub. & B.S.

BHAGAT STORES
Khazanchi Rd., Patna-800004 (Bihar)
Bus.Intt.: Pub. and B.S.

BHAGAT VANI PRAKASHAN
Stya Mandir B1116/2, Indira Nagar, Lucknow (Uttar Pradesh)
✆ 343083

BHAGAVATI PRAKASHAN
H-1/2, Model Town, Delhi-110009

BHAGIRATH SEWA SANSTHAN
3, LF, Todarmal Sq. Bengali Market, New Delhi-110001
✆ 2719521
Hd.Org.: Kusamakar Sukal

BHAGIRATH SEVA SANSTHAN
R-10/144, Rajnagar, Ghaziabad-201002 (Uttar Pradesh)
✆ 2719521, 2726193, Cable: BHAGIRATH
Prop.: Dharanidhar; **Bus.Intt.:** Pub. in Hindi

BHAGVATI DISTRIBUTION SERVICES
2563-64, Chuna Mandi, St. No. 10, (1st Floor), Pahar Ganj, New Delhi-110055
✆ (O) 51698737 (R) 23583783 ▮ 9891326056
Hd.Org.: Jayesh Kumar, Ghanshyam Bhai; **Bus.Intt.:** WS, Order Supplier; **Spl.:** Imported and Indian Children Books

BHAGWADVANI PRAKASHAN
Satya Mandir, B-116/2, Indira Nagar, Lucknow-226016 (Uttar Pradesh)
✆ 0522-26340923
✉ thesatyamandir@yahoo.com
🌐 www.geocities.com/thesatyamandir
Estd.: 1977; **Prop.:** Smt. Kusum Asthana; **Bus.Intt.:** Pub.; **Spl.:** Books on Devima Kusumji

BHAGWAN BOOK STORES
Diwan Deodi, Aurangabad-431001 (Maharashtra)
✆ 2320430
Estd.: 1968; **Prt.:** Bhagwandas Bhukandas Daulatabadker; **Bus.Intt.:** Pub. and B.S.; **Spl.:** Adv. Books for Lib. and Gen. Books

BHAI MEHAR SINGH & SONS
Bazar Mai Sewan, Amritsar (Punjab)

BHAI VIR SINGH SAHITYA SADAN
Bhai Vir Singh Marg, Gole Market, New Delhi-110001
Hd.Org.: P.B. Singh

BHAIRAB GRANTHALAYA
45, Manickj Bose Ghat St., Kolkata-6 (West Bengal)

BHAIYA STORES
166, Khazuri Bazar, Indore-452002 (Madhya Pradesh)
✆ (O) 2531207, 2540166 (R) 2410401, 2412984

Br.: Bhaiya Sotres, 626, Khajuri, Bazar, Indore (Madhya Pradesh) ✆ 2431314
• Bhaiya's, Navneet Tower, Old Palasia, Indore (Madhya Pradesh) ✆ 2564307
• Pen Arts Kothari Market, Indore (Madhya Pradesh) ✆ 2536248
Bus.Intt.: Stationer and Order Suppliers

BHAKTIVEDANTA INSTITUTE
RC/8, Raghunathpur, Manasi Manjil Building, 4th Floor, VIP Road, Kolkata-700059 (West Bengal)
✆ 25009018, Fax: 91-33-25009018
info@binstitute.org
www.binstitute.org
Hd.Org.: K. Vasudeva Rao

BHAKT MANDLI NAI DILLI
C-159, Naraina Industrial Area, Phase-I, New Delhi-110028
✆ 56223494 9868026219, Fax: 91-11-25587139
newkoncepts@yahoo.com
Hd.Org.: Pub.; **Spl.**: Phil., Spiritualism and Rel. in Hindi

BHALANI BOOK DEPOT
21, Hind Rajasthan Bldg., Dadasaheb Phalke Rd., Near Dadar (C. Rly.) Station, Mumbai-400014 (Maharashtra)
✆ 24148941, 24150803, Fax: 022-24145846
bhalani@bom3.vsnl.net.in
Estd.: 1976; **Prt.**: Shashimant C. Bhalani, Rajesh C. Bhalani, Kirit C. Bhalani

BHALANI MEDICAL BOOK HOUSE
Near Dhanasutar's Pole, Opp. Bank of India, Relief Rd., Ahmedabad (Gujarat)
✆ 2384248

BHALANI MEDICAL BOOK HOUSE
11, Mavawala Building, Opp. K.E.M. Hospital Parel, Mumbai-400012 (Maharashtra)
✆ 022-24137650, 24171660 (R) 24145027, Fax: 24138041
bhalani@vsnl.com
www.bhalani.com
Estd.: 1969; **Hd.Org.**: Hemant S. Bhalani
Br.: The Medical Book Corporation, 446, Nana Peth, Laxmi Rd., Poona-411002
Bus.Intt.: Pub. & B.S.; **Spl.**: Med. Sci.

BHALANI PERIODICALS AGENCY
21-Hind Rajashthan Building, Dadasaheb Phalke Rd., Dadar, Mumbai-400014 (Maharashtra)
✆ 24131569, 24180481, Fax: 24131569
hetal@bom3.vsnl.net.in
Prop.: Kirit Bhalani
Br.: 3, Palav Sadan, Jer Bai Wadia Rd. Parel, Mumbai-400012 ✆ 24180481, 24131569, Fax: 24131569
hetal@bom3.vsnl.net.in
Bus.Intt.: Pub., WS, L.S., Rt., Imp.;
Spl.: Med., Sci., Tech.

BHARASA STORES
97, Dr. Giruindra Sekhar Bose Rd., Kolkata-39 (West Bengal)

BHARAT BHARATHI
Hindi Unit, Ruikar Path, Nagpur-484002 (Maharashtra)

BHARAT BHARATI
G-3/520, Gulmohar, E-8, Bhopal-462016 (Madhya Pradesh) ✆ 2570981
Hd.Org.: Dr. Ramlal Suri

BHARAT BHARATI PRAKASHAN
1, Bhai Ka Bagh, Allahabad (Uttar Pradesh)
✆ 2605672
Hd.Org.: Rajeswarnath Bhargava

BHARAT BHAWAN
Nayatola, Patna-800004 (Bihar)
✆ 250592
Bus.Intt.: Pub. and B.S.

BHARAT BOOK AGENCY
206, Bidhan Sarani, Kolkata-700006 (West Bengal)
✆ (O) 033-22412746 (R) 26602261
Estd.: 1963; **Prop.**: Mohit Basu; **Bus.Intt.**: Pub.; **Spl.**: Acad. Books, Engg. Text Books and Books on Foreign Exchange Concept in Bengali

BHARAT BOOK AGENCY
Nathnagar, Bhagalpur-812006 (Bihar)
Bus.Intt.: Pub. and B.S.

BHARAT BOOK AGENCY
Nayatola, Patna-800004 (Bihar)
Bus.Intt.: Pub. and B.S.

BHARAT BOOK BUREAU
207, Hermes Atrium, Plot No. 57, P.B. No. 54, Sector 11, C.B.D. Belapur, New Mumbai-400614 (Maharashtra)
Phone-cum-Fax: (00-91-22) 27579131/27578668
Chettiar@.giasbm01.vsnl.net.in, info@bharatbook.com
www.bharatbook.com
Estd.: 1989; **Ch.Exe.**: M.K. Chettiar;
Bus.Intt.: Rt., WS, L.S., Imp., Exp.; **Spl.**: Sci. & Tech.

BHARAT BOOK CENTRE
17, Ashok Marg, (Behind Citi Bank), Lucknow-226001 (Uttar Pradesh)
✆ 91-522-2230381, 2200959
bharatbookcentre@yahoo.com
Hd.Org.: V.K. Bahri; **Estd.**: 1980;

Bus.Intt.: Pub. and B.S.; **Spl.**: Humanities, Law, Gen. Books

BHARAT BOOK CENTRE
305, Triplicane High Rd., 8-B, Ist Floor, Triplicane, Chennai-600005 (Tamil Nadu)
✆ (O) 28549787 (PP) (R) 2404701
Hd.Org.: Mr. A. Raman, N. Ravi Chandran

BHARAT BOOK CO.
36A, Shanker Market, Connaught Circus, New Delhi-110001 ✆ 23315764

BHARAT BOOK DEPOT
Ashok Rajpath, Patna-800004 (Bihar)
✆ 251030
Bus.Intt.: Pub. and B.S.

BHARAT BOOK DEPOT
Sujaganj, Bhagalpur-812002 (Bihar)
✆ 2420429
bbbdbooks@sancharnet.in
Bus.Intt.: Pub. and B.S. and Order Suppliers

BHARAT BOOK STORE
Masaurhi, Patna-804452 (Bihar)
Bus.Intt.: Pub. and B.S.

BHARAT EDUCATIONAL STORES/BHARAT GRAPHICS
Flat No. 1-A, First Floor, Prehlad Market, Karol Bagh, New Delhi-110005
✆ 25723493, 25767576, 32363597, Fax: 91-121-2654212
hk8000@yahoo.com
bharatednstores.com
Hd.Org.: P.S. Chadha; **Bus.Intt.**: Imp., Exp., Pub.; **Spl.**: 3D Maps, Charts, Models, Globes

BHARAT EDUCATIONAL STORES/PIONEER EDUCATIONAL AIDS
1E/17, Jhandewalan Extn. Near Metro Station, New Delhi-110055
✆ 23543179, Fax: 91-121-4002776
hk8000@yahoo.com
www.bharatednstores.com
Hd.Org.: Prithipal Singh Chadha; **Bus.Intt.**: Imp., Exp., Pub.; **Spl.**: 3D Maps, Charts, Models, Globes

BHARAT ENTERPRISES
307, N.C. Kelkar Rd., Mumbai-400028 (Maharashtra)
Bus.Intt.: Exp.

BHARAT GRAPHICS
194, Industrial Area, Phase-II, Chandigarh-110002

BHARAT GYAN VIGYAN SAMITHI
Basement of YWA Building, Hostel No. 2, Block-G, Saket, New Delhi-110017
✆ 26569943, Fax: 91-11-26569773
bgvs_delhi@yahoo.co.in
www.bgvs.org
Hd.Org.: Kuldeep Singh Tanwar; **Bus.Intt.**: Agency for Literacy and Health Movements as also for creating Sci. and Tech. awareness

BHARAT ITIHAS SAMSHODHAK MANDAL
1321, Sadashiv, Pune-411030 (Maharashtra)

BHARAT KRANTI PRAKASHAN
R-4/17, Raj Nagar, Ghaziabad (Uttar Pradesh)
✆ 91-9350728743
Hd.Org.: Satyendra Yadav

BHARAT LAW HOUSE
Opp. Golcha Cinema, Chaura Rasta, Jaipur-302003 (Rajasthan)
✆ 236388, 2362216
bharatlawhouse@yahoo.com
Estd.: 1989; **Prt.**: V.S. Wadawa; **Bus.Intt.**: Pub., WS; **Spl.**: Humanities & Soc. Sci., Mang. & Comm., Journals, Magazines & Periodicals, Law

BHARAT LAW HOUSE (P) LTD.
T-1/95, Mangolpuri Industrial Area, Phase I, New Delhi-110083
✆ (O) 27910001, 27910002, 27910003 (R) 27012323, 27016884, Fax: 011-27910004
blh@nda.vsnl.net.in
www.bharatlawhouse.com
Estd.: 1988; **Man.Dir.**: D.C. Puliani, **Dir.**: Ashok Puliani, Ravi Pulani & Mahesh Puliani; **Bus.Intt.**: Pub., L.S.; **Spl.**: Law, Acad., Journals & Magazines

BHARAT LITHOGRAPHING CO.
98/4, S.N. Banerjee Rd., Kolkata-700014 (West Bengal)
Bus.Intt.: Exp.

BHARAT NATIONAL AGENCY
Sadar Bazar, Raipur-492001 (Chhattisgarh)
✆ 2535105
Estd.: 1949; **Bus.Intt.**: B.S.; **Spl.**: Graduate, Adv. Books for Lib. and Gen. Books, Engg., Tech. and Comp.

BHARAT PRAKASHAN MANDIR
142, Vijay Nagar, W.K. Rd., Meerut (Uttar Pradesh)
✆ (O) 0121-2642123, 2656446 (R) 2762165, 2762089, Fax: 2656446
Estd.:1970; **Hd.Org.**: Chandra Pal Sharma

BHARAT PRAKASHAN TRUST
Kommuvar St., Satyanarayanapuram, Vijayawada-520002 (Andhra Pradesh)
✆ 0866-2434112
Estd.: 1991; **Hd.Org.**: K. Uma Maheswaradu; **Bus.Intt.**: Pub.; **Spl.**: Indian Culture and Fine Art in Telugu

BHARAT PUBLISHING HOUSE
123, Durga Chambers, Desh Bandhu Gupta Rd., Karol Bagh, New Delhi-110005
✆ (O) 25757081, 23670067 (R) 25817796, Fax: 91-11-23676058
✉ pitambar@bol.net.in
Estd.:1986; **Hd.Org.**: Jaideep Aggarwal; **Bus.Intt.**: Pub.; **Spl.**: Edu. and Reference Books for Children in Various Languages

BHARAT PUBLISHING HOUSE
222, Tarun Enclave, Pitampura, Delhi-110034
Bus.Intt.: Pub.

BHARAT PUSTAK BHANDAR
E1/265, Sonia Vihar, Delhi-110094
✆ 91-11-22967960
Hd.Org.: Tilak Raj Sharma

BHARAT SCIENTIFIC SYNDICATE
17, Buddha Apartments, C.C. Colony, Opp. R.P. Bagh, Delhi-110009
✆ (O) 27454322 (R) 9810215495
✉ bhanu262@rediffmail.com
Estd.: 1999; **Prop.**: Mrs. Archana Bhanu, P.C. Bhanu (Man.Dir.)
Br.: G-8, Abhiyanva Nagar, Ashiyana Nagar, Patna (Bihar)
Bus.Intt.: Rt., Pub., Sub.Ag., Pub.'s Rep. & L.S.; **Spl.**: Acad., Beh. Sci., Soc.Sci., Comm., Sci., Med., Tech. & Law Books

BHARAT SECURITIES
New Delhi ✆ 25163321
✉ bharatsecurities@hotmail.com

BHARATHI PATHIPPAGAM
108, Usman Rd., T. Nagar, Chennai-600017 (Tamil Nadu)
✆ 044-4340205
Ch.Exe.: C.T. Rajenderan; **Bus.Intt.**: L.S. Rt. and Pub.

BHARATI
Bara Bazar, Baidyanath, Deoghar-814112 (Bihar)
Bus.Intt.: Pub. and B.S.

BHARATI BHANDAR
Main Rd., Begusarai-851101 (Bihar)
Bus.Intt.: Pub. and B.S.

BHARATI BHANDAR
Rajendra Prasad Rd., Bhagalpur-812002 (Bihar)
Bus.Intt.: Pub. and B.S.

BHARATI BHASHA PRAKASHAN
518/6/B Vishwas Nagar, Shahdara, Delhi-110032
✆ 22204524
Hd.Org.: Harish Kumar Sharma

BHARATI BHAWAN
4271/3, Ansari Road, Darya Ganj, New Delhi-110002
✆ 91-11-23286557
✉ bbpddel@airtelbroadband.net
Hd.Org.: Tarit Kumar Bose

BHARATI BHAWAN
Barauni, Begusarai-851112 (Bihar)
Bus.Intt.: Pub. & B.S.

BHARATI BHAWAN
Terhi Nath Mandir Chowk, Begusarai-851101 (Bihar)
Bus.Intt.: Pub. and B.S.

BHARATI BHAWAN
Bihat, Begusarai-851135 (Bihar)
Bus.Intt.: Pub. and B.S.

BHARATI BHAWAN AGENCY
Rajendra Prasad Rd., Bhagalpur-812002 (Bihar)
Bus.Intt.: Pub. and B.S.

BHARATI BHAWAN (PUBLISHERS & DISTRIBUTORS)
Thakurbari Rd., Kadam Kuan, Patna-800003 (Bihar)
✆ 2670325, 2689717, 2671356, Fax: 2670010
✉ bbpdpat@vsnl.net.in, bbpdpat@sancharnet.in
Estd.: 1942; **Prt.**: Tarit Kumar Bose
Br.: I-15, Sector-9, G-B-Nagar, Noida-201301, ✆ 2548672, 2541755, Fax: 2549648
✉ bbpddel@mantraonline.com
• 30, Jadunath Dev Rd., Kolkata-700012
✆ 22258836, Fax: 22155315
✉ bbpdcal@vsnl.com
• Shankara Building, 1st Floor, 36, Avenue Rd., Bangalore-560002
✆ 22212783, Fax: 22212793
✉ bbpdblr@vsnl.com
• 20, Jail Rd., East Tharpakhna, Ranchi-834001 ✆ 2208613, Fax: 2316185 • Parao Pokhar, Amgola, Muzaffarpur-842002
✆ 2246193, 2242651, Fax: 2242651
• 4271/3, Ansari Rd., Darya Ganj, New Delhi-110002 ✆ 23290162, 23290161, Fax: 23290161
✉ bbpddel@mantraonline.com
Bus.Intt.: Pub., WS, Imp.
Spl.: Humanities & Soc.Sci., Sci. & Tech., Juvenile/Children

BHARATI BOOK DEPOT
Khazanchi Rd., Patna-800004 (Bihar)
Bus.Intt.: Pub. and B.S.

BHARATI BOOK ORGANISATION
C-1/177, Nand Nagari, Delhi-110093
✆ 22125784 ▮ 011-35381084
Prop.: Shyam Bihari Bharti; **Bus.Intt.**: L.S.

BHARATI BOOK STALL
5/2, Ramanath Majumdar St., Kolkata-700009 (West Bengal)
✆ 22416382, 22190260, Fax: 22418089
Ch.Exe.: Ashoke Kumar Barik
Bus.Intt.: B.S.; **Spl.:** Company Stocks Books for Children and Gen. Reading

BHARATI BOOK STORES
Gandhi Chowk, Madhupur, Deoghar-815353 (Bihar)
Bus.Intt.: Pub. and B.S.

BHARATI PRAKASHAN
F-6/1, Shahpur Jat, New Delhi-110049
Hd.Org.: Shankar Vinayak

BHARATI PUSTAK BHANDAR
Haspura, Aurangabad-824120 (Bihar)
Bus.Intt.: Pub. and B.S.

BHARATI PUSTAK BHANDAR
Madanpur, Aurangabad-824208 (Bihar)
Bus.Intt.: Pub. and B.S.

BHARATI PUSTAK BHANDAR
Court Rd., Baidyanath, Deoghar-814112 (Bihar)
Bus.Intt.: Pub. and B.S.

BHARATI PUSTAK BHANDAR
Rajaun, Bhagalpur-813107 (Bihar)
Bus.Intt.: Pub. and B.S.

BHARATI PUSTAK BHANDAR
Bhikhanpur, Bhagalpur-812002 (Bihar)
Bus.Intt.: Pub. and B.S.

BHARATI PUSTAK BHANDAR
Barauni, Begusarai-851112 (Bihar)
Bus.Intt.: Pub. & B.S.

BHARATI PUSTAK BHANDAR
Chauriya Bariyarpur, Begusarai (Bihar)
Bus.Intt.: Pub. and B.S.

BHARATI PUSTAK BHANDAR
Opp. Khuda Baksh Library, Ashok Rajpath, Patna-800004 (Bihar)
Bus.Intt.: Pub. and B.S.

BHARATI PUSTAK BHAWAN
New Market, Patna-800001 (Bihar)
Bus.Intt.: Pub. and B.S.

BHARATI PUSTAK MANDIR
Anisabad, Patna-800002 (Bihar)
Bus.Intt.: Pub. and B.S.

BHARATI PUSTAK SADAN
Khazanchi Rd., Patna-800004 (Bihar)
Bus.Intt.: Pub. and B.S.

BHARATI PUSTAK SADAN
New Market, Patna-800001 (Bihar)
Bus.Intt.: Pub. and B.S.

BHARATI SADAN
Main Rd., Mokameh, Patna-803302 (Bihar)
Bus.Intt.: Pub. & B.S.

BHARATI STATIONERY STORE
Tilakmanjhi, Bhagalpur-812002 (Bihar)
Bus.Intt.: Pub. and B.S.

BHARATIYA ANUVAD PARISHAD
203, Ashadeep, 9 Heli Rd., New Delhi-110001
✆ 23327202, 23352278, 23714838, Fax: 26823217
Hd.Org.: Gargi Gupt

BHARATIYA AURVISHYAN ANUSANDHAN PARISHAD
Ansari Nagar, New Delhi-110066

BHARATIYA BHANDAR PUSTAKALAYA
K-45, Jangpura Extn., New Delhi-110014
✆ 51611861-65, Fax: 51611866
✉ sales@diamondpublications.com
🌐 www.diamondpocketbooks.com
Hd.Org.: Ankur Verma; **Bus.Intt.:** Pub.; **Spl.:** Astrology, Rel., Health, Indology, Vedic Sci., etc. in English and Hindi

BHARATIYA BHASHA PEETH
LIG/85, Kotra Sultanabad, Bhopal-462003 (Madhya Pradesh)
Hd.Org.: B.P. Pandey

BHARATIYA BHAWAN
Barh R.S. Patna-803214 (Bihar)
Bus.Intt.: Pub. and B.S.

BHARATIYA BOOK CORPORATION
I.U.B. Bungalow Rd., Jawahar Nagar, Delhi-110007

BHARATIYA GRANTH NIKETAN
2713, Kucha Chelan, Darya Ganj, New Delhi-110002
✆ (O) 23276234 (R) 26833991
Hd.Org.: Yashpal Mahajan

BHARATIYA JNANPITH
18, Institutional Area, Lodhi Rd., New Delhi-110003
✆ 24626467, Fax: 91-11-24654197
✉ sales@jnanpith.net
🌐 www.jnanpith.net
Hd.Org.: N.C. Jain
Br.: Bharatiya Jnanpith Vikray Kendra, 10, Darya Ganj (Times of India Old Building), New Delhi-110002 ✆ 23241614, Fax: 23241619
✉ jnanpith@satyam.net.in
Bus.Intt.: Pub.; **Spl.:** Award-winning Novels, Plays, Poetry, Short Stories, Autobiographies, etc. in Hindi.

BHARATIYA KALA PRAKASHAN
3421-A, Second Floor, Narang Colony, Tri Nagar, Delhi-110035
✆ 32967505, Fax: 91-11-27393083

✉ bkp3421@yahoo.co.in
Hd.Org.: C.P. Gautam; **Bus.Intt.:** Pub.; **Spl.:** Indology, Art, Archaeology, Rel. and Phil. in English

BHARATIYA PRACHYA TATVA PRAKASHAN SAMITI
C/o Shah Ramanlal Lal Chand, 135/137, Zaberu Bazar, Mumbai-400002 (Maharashtra)

BHARATIYA PRAKASHAN
Bharatiya Prakashan Bhavan, 136, Vivekanand Marg, Allahabad-211003 (Uttar Pradesh)

BHARATIYA PRAKASHAN
Kazipur, Nayatola, Patna-803214 (Bihar)
Bus.Intt.: Pub. and B.S.

BHARATIYA SAHITYA BHANDAR
Kabraji Bazar, Bijapura-586101 (Karnataka)
✆ 08352-220248
Hd.Org.: Siru Sangamesh
Bus.Intt.: Pub.; **Spl.:** Children's Books, Engaged in its Promotion

BHARATIYA SAHITYA BHAVANA
4382/4B, Ansari Rd., Darya Ganj, New Delhi-110002
✆ (O) 23280585 (R) 25102109
▮ 981113639, 9868178633
✉ pragati1@ndf.vsnl.net.in
Estd.: 1952; **Hd.Org.:** Vinod Kapoor
Bus.Intt.: L.S. & Imp.; **Spl.:** Eng.Litt., Soc.Sci., Phil., Humanities and Library Sci. & Comm. Books

BHARATIYA SAHITYA PRAKASHAN
286, Chankyapuri, Sadan, Meerut-250001 (Uttar Pradesh) ✆ 2540338
Hd.Org.: Parmatma Sharan

BHARATIYA SANSKRITI VIDYAPEETA
29, Ist Main Chamarajapet, Bangalore-560018 (Karnataka)
✆ 080-2602562
Hd.Org.: Dr. K. Nagesh Hathwar;
Bus.Intt.: Pub.; **Spl.:** Gen. Books of Edu. value in Kannada, Sanskrit and Hindi

BHARATIYA VIDYA BHAVAN
Kasturba Gandhi Marg, New Delhi-110001
✆ 23387595, Fax: 91-11-23382003
✉ bhavidya@del2.vsnl.net.in
🌐 www.bhavans.info
Hd.Org.: H.N. Dastur; **Bus.Intt.:** Pub.;
Spl.: Propagating Indian Culture by Various Activities

BHARATIYA VIDYA BHAVAN
37/39, East Mada St., Mylapore, Chennai-600004 (Tamil Nadu)
✆ 24940811, 24943550, 24943420, Fax: 24941045
Dir.: T.K. Parameswaran; **Bus.Intt.:** Pub.; **Spl.:** Propagating Indian Culture by Various Activities

BHARATIYA VIDYA BHAVAN
Kulapati K.M. Munshi Marg, Chowpatty, Mumbai-400007 (Maharashtra)
✆ 24950916, 24968466, Fax: 23630058
✉ brbhavan@bom7.vsnl.net.in
🌐 www.bhavans.info
Hd.Org.: Dhiru S. Mehta; **Bus.Intt.:** Pub.; **Spl.:** Art, Litt., Culture, Hist., etc. and Two Periodicals

BHARATIYA VIDYA PRAKASHAN
1-U.B., Jawahar Nagar, Bungalow Rd., Delhi-110007
✆ 91-11-23851570, 23850944
✉ bvpbooks@hotmail.com
Hd.Org.: Kishore Chander Jain;
Bus.Intt.: Pub. and B.S.; **Spl.:** Indology, Sanskrit, *Tantra*, Phil., Astrology, etc.

BHARATODEY PRAKASHAN
204-A, West end Rd., Sadar, Meerut-250001 (Uttar Pradesh)
✆ 2510353
Hd.Org.: Vijay Bhushan

BHARATVARSHIYA ANEKANT
Viduat Parishad, Gulab Vatika, Loni Rd., District Ghaziabad (Uttar Pradesh)

BHARAVI
13/1, Bankim Chatterjee St., Kolkata-700073 (West Bengal)

BHARDWAJ BOOK CENTRE
155, Jhakuria Sadan, Arya Nagar, Almora-301001 (Rajasthan)

BHARGAV AND COMPANY
4, Bhai Ka Bagh, Allahabad, (Uttar Pradesh)
Hd.Org.: Arvind Bhargava

BHARGAV BOOK DEPOT
Chowk, Varanasi-221001 (Uttar Pradesh)
Hd.Org.: S. Bhargav

BHARGAVA BOOK HOUSE
13, Lakh Chand Market, Raja Mandi, Agra-282002 (Uttar Pradesh)
✆ 2364926, 2350113
Estd.: 1947; **Prop.:** Dr. Mahesh Bhargava

BHARTI BOOK ORGANISATION
C-1/177, Nand Nagri, Delhi-110093
✆ 91-11-22125784 ▮ 9312543205
Hd.Org.: Shyam Bihari Bharti
Bus.Intt.: L.S.

BHARTIYA PRAKASHAN SANSTHAN
24, Ansari Rd., Darya Ganj, New Delhi-110002
✆ 22246695

Ch.Exe.: Mr. Ritu Sharma; **Bus.Intt.:** Pub.; **Spl.:** Novels, Stories, Drama, Poems, Biography & Children Litt., Gen. Sci. in Hindi

BHASHA BHAVAN
Halanganj, Mathura-281001 (Uttar Pradesh)

BHASHA EVAM SANSKRITI VIBHAG
S.D.A. Complex, Block No. 39, Kusumpati, Simla-171009 (Himachal Pradesh)
✆ 2226616, Fax: 2226616
Hd.Org.: K.R. Bharti; **Bus.Intt.:** Pub. and Promoter; **Spl.:** Hist. Litt., Archaeology and Culture of Himachal Pradesh

BHASKAR BOOK DEPOT
G.D. College Rd., Begusarai-851101 (Bihar)
Bus.Intt.: Pub. and B.S.

BHASKAR BOOKS PVT. LTD.
302, Avenue Rd., Bangalore-560002 (Karnataka)
Bus.Intt.: Exp.

BHASWATI
103-C, Sitaram Ghosh St., Kolkata-700009 (West Bengal)

BHATKAL BOOK INTERNATIONAL
35-C, Pt. Madan Mohan, Malviya Marg, Opp. Roche', Tardeo, Mumbai-400034 (Maharashtra)
✆ 24941656, Fax: 022-24938049
@ bhatkal.sen@axcess.net.in
Bus.Intt.: Library Association Publishing

BHATKAL BOOKS INTERNATIONAL
4648/1, Ansari Rd., 21, Darya Ganj, New Delhi-110002
✆ 23265245, 23280068, 2630381, Fax: 23279203
@ vansdel@nda.vsnl.net.in
Prt.: R.G. Bhatkal, H.R. Bhatkal; **Bus.Intt.:** WS, Rt. and L.S.

BHATRI SANGHA
Subhash Rd., Distt. Bankura (West Bengal)
Hd.Org.: Ashish Mukherjee

BHATT BOOKS DISTRIBUTORS
Shanti Nagar, Sector-2, C-19/11 Mira Rd. (East) Mumbai-401107 (Maharashtra)
✆ 28116435
@ bhattbooks@usa.net
Bus.Intt.: Dist. & B.S.

BHATT BROTHERS
3/17, Barahat, Uttar Kashi, Uttarakhand-249193 (Uttaranchal)
✆ 01374-274232, 223977 ▮ 9412077677
@ madhubhatt@sancharnet.in, bhattsrikrishna@yahoo.in

Prop.: S.K. Bhatt; **Bus.Intt.:** B.S. & L.S.; **Spl.:** Humanities, Soc.Sci., Sci. & Tech., Med., Mang., Law, Arts & Arch., Bio., Children & Gen.

BHATTACHARJEE BOOK HOUSE
75/1/1, Mahatma Gandhi Rd., Kolkata-700009 (West Bengal)

BHAVANA BOOKS
Angamali-683572 (Kerala)

BHAVANA BOOKS & PRINTS
101, AVG Bhawan, M-3, Connaught Circus, New Delhi-110001
✆ 23415198, 23415205, Fax: 51517091
@ rajanarya@vsnl.com
Estd.: 1984; **Ch.Exe.:** Rajan Arya; **Bus.Intt.:** Pub.; **Spl.:** Humanities & Soc.Sci.

BHAVANA BOOKS & PRINTS
A-38/2 Mayapuri Phase-I, New Delhi-110064

BHAVANA EDITION
Thiruvananthapuram (Kerala)
✆ 2467157
@ bhavana_ed@rediffmail.com
Bus.Intt.: B.S.

BHAVANA PRAKASHAN
109-A, Patparganj, Delhi-110091
✆ 22756734, 22754663
@ bhavna_pub@rediffmail.com
Hd.Org.: Satish Chandra Mittal; **Bus.Intt.:** Pub.; **Spl.:** Hist., Pol.Sci., Eco., Criticisms and Children's Litt. in Hindi and Regional Languages

BHAVANI PRAKASHANA
103, 15th Cross Malleswaram, Bangalore-560003 (Karnataka)
✆ 080-2341361
Hd.Org.: Smt. Padma Seetaram; **Bus.Intt.:** Pub.; **Spl.:** Own Books and Collection of Poems in Kannada

BHAVDIY PRAKASHAN
Shingarhaat Ayodhya, Faizabad (Uttar Pradesh)
✆ 232115, 232720
Hd.Org.: Mishrilal Verma

BHAVI BOOKS
Convent Rd., Ernakulam, Cochin-682035 (Kerala)
✆ 2369911
Estd.: 1985; **Prop.:** K.P. Ravindran; **Bus.Intt.:** B.S.

BHAVSAR BOOK DEPOT
Khajuri Bazar, Indore-452002 (Madhya Pradesh)
✆ 2452260

BHOLA PUSTAK BHANDAR
Bikram, Patna-801104 (Bihar)
Bus.Intt.: Pub. and B.S.

BHOLANATH PRAKASHANI
37/11, Beniatola Lane, Kolkata-700009 (West Bengal)
Hd.Org.: Pub. and B.S.

BHOPAL BOOK HOUSE
Budhwara, Bhopal (Madhya Pradesh)
Estd.: 1967; **Hd.Org.:** Ahdul Baut Khan

BHOWMIK & CORPORATIONS
1B-28 Mauriya Complex, Subhash Chowk, Laxmi Nagar, Delhi-110090
✆ 22228097
Hd.Org.: Sisir Kumar Bhowmik; **Bus.Intt.:** L.S.

BHOWMIK BOOK TRADERS
B-3, Pankaj Tower, Near Ahlcon Public School, Mayur Vihar, Phase-I, Delhi-110091
Prop.: Piyush Bhowmik; **Bus.Intt.:** Rt., Sub.Ag., Pub.' Rep., L.S.; **Spl.:** Acad., Med., Tech., Journals & Magazines, Law

BHUDEV PUSTAK BHANDAR
Banka, Bhagalpur-813102 (Bihar)
Bus.Intt.: Pub. and B.S.

BHUMIKA PRAKASHAN
G-17, Jagatpuri, Delhi-110051
✆ 22505852
Hd.Org.: Rakhi Maheshwari; **Bus.Intt.:** Pub.; **Spl.:** Eminent and Upcoming Hindi Writers and Children's Litt.

BHUVANA VIJAYAM PUBLICATIONS
Somdarya Lahari Kespavani St., Governorpet, Vijayawada-522002 (Andhra Pradesh)

BIBILIOCLUB.COM
New Delhi
✉ info@bibilioclub.com

BIBLE SOCIETY OF INDIA
Post Box 502, Park Town, Chennai-600003 (Tamil Nadu)
✆ 2563631, Cable: TESTAMENTS, Chennai
Estd.: 1811, **Ch.Exe.:** Rev. Dr. Thejus, Auxiliary Secretary; **Central Off.:** 206, Mahatma Gandhi Rd., Bangalore-560001
✆ 25584877, Cable: TESTAMENTS, Bangalore
Fax: 080-25584701

BIBLIA IMPEX PVT. LTD.
2/18, Ansari Rd., Darya Ganj, New Delhi-110002
✆ 23262515, 23278034, Fax: 23282047
✉ bibimpex@nda.vsnl.net.in
Estd.: 1980; **Hd.Org.:** Pradeep Kumar Goel; **Bus.Intt.:** Exp. and Pub.; **Spl.:** Humanities and Soc.Sci.

BIBLIA PUBLICATIONS
Bible Commission, B.L.M. Aloor, Thrissur-680683 (Kerala)
Estd.: 1992; **Man.Dir.:** Jose Maniparampil; **Bus.Intt.:** Pub.

BIBLIOMATICS
P.O. Box 177, Main Rd., Manipal
✆ 2572186, Fax: 2573062
✉ embese@sanchrnet.in
Estd.: 1988; **Bus.Intt.:** WS, L.S. & Rt., Sub.Ag.; **Spl.:** Med.

BIBLIOPHILE SOUTH ASIA/PROMILLA & CO PUBLISHERS
C-127, Sarvodaya Enclave, New Delhi-110017
✆ 65284748, Fax: 91-11-26961462
✉ ashokbutani@gmail.com
www.biblioasia.com
Hd.Org.: Ashok Butani; **Bus.Intt.:** Pub. & Dist.; **Spl.:** Soc.Sci. and Humanities

BIBLO INFORMATION SERVICES
407, 6th Main, 6th Phase, Ist Stage, Basaves Waranagar, Bangalore-560044 (Karnataka)

BICHINTA BHABAN
37/5, Beniatola Lane, Kolkata-700009 (West Bengal)

BICHINTA PRAKASHAN
9/7B, Ramanath Majumder St., Kolkata-700009 (West Bengal)

BICHITRA
64/1, K.K. Roy Chowdhury Rd., Barisha, Kolkata-700008 (West Bengal)

BIDHAN BHARATI
B.D. Local Centre Bidhan Nagar, Kolkata-700064 (West Bengal)

BIDISHA
31, Narasingha Dutta Rd., Distt. Howrah-1 (West Bengal)
Hd.Org.: Samarendra Sen

BIGHT MEDIA IMPEX (P) LTD.
2769, Kucha Chellan, Darya Ganj, New Delhi-110002
✆ 23282226

BIHAR BOOK DEPOT
Banka, Bhagalpur-813102 (Bihar)
Bus.Intt.: Pub. and B.S.

BIHAR BOOK DEPOT
Khazanchi Rd., Patna-800004 (Bihar)
Bus.Intt.: Pub. and B.S.

BIHAR HINDI GRANTH ACADEMY
Premchand Marg, Rajendra Nagar, Patna-800016 (Bihar)

✆ 91-542-2671432
Hd.Org.: Vrashin Patel; **Spl.:** University-level Text-Books in Hindi

BIHAR RASHTRA BHASHA PARISHAD
Uchch Shiksha Vibhag Govt. of Bihar, Aacharya Shivbhushan Sahay Marg, Saidpur, Patna-800004 (Bihar)
✆ 91-612-2672336
Dir.: Ram Bhujawal Singh

BIHAR SCHOOL OF YOGA
Ganga Darshan, Munger-181201 (Bihar)

BIHAR STORES
Narayan Market, Langertoli, Bari Path, Patna-800004 (Bihar)
✆ 251410
Bus.Intt.: Pub. and B.S.

BIJOLI BOOK HOUSE
6/D, Ramanath Majumder St., Kolkata-700009 (West Bengal)

BIJOY BOOK STORE
Barracks, Berhampur (GM) (Orissa)

BIJOY PUSTAK BHANDAR
226, Rabindra Sarani, Kolkata-700007 (West Bengal)

BIJOYGARH BOOK HOUSE
2/1, Bijoygarh Katra, Kolkata-700092 (West Bengal)

BIKASH GRANTHA BHAWAN
79/1B, M.G. Rd., Kolkata-700009 (West Bengal)

BIMAL PRAKASHAN
C/2/78, Mukund C.H. Society, LVS Rd., Ghatkopar (West), Mumbai-400086 (Maharashtra)

BIMLA BOOK DEPOT
Khazanchi Rd., Patna-800004 (Bihar)
Bus.Intt.: Pub. and B.S.

BINA LIBRARY
College Hostel Rd., Panbazar, Guwahati-781001 (Assam)

BINDOO BOOK DEPOT
Rao Pura, Baroda (Gujarat)

BINDU PRAKASHAN
Sri Janardhan Mandir, Sarafa Bazar, Ujjain (Madhya Pradesh)

BINGSHA SATABDI
75/C, Park St., Kolkata-700016 (West Bengal)

BINNY PUBLISHING HOUSE
1691, Nai Sarak, Delhi-110006
✆ 23250635
✉ kaushalgoyal@yahoo.com
🌐 www.generalbooks.com
Hd.Org.: Minaxi Goyal; **Bus.Intt.:** Pub. & Dist.; **Spl.:** School Textbooks, Gen. Mang., Fiction, Dictionaries

BIO GARD PRIVATE LTD.
640, 10-A Cross, West of Chord R.D., 2nd Stage, Bangalore-560086 (Karnataka)
✆ 2320037, Fax: 2320037, Cable: BIOGARD
Estd.: 1983; **Dir.:** P.V.V. Krishnanan;
Bus.Intt.: Pub.

BIOTECH BOOKS
4762-63/23, Ansari Rd., Darya Ganj, New Delhi-110002
✆ (O) 23245578, 23244987 (R) 27382765, Fax: 27382329
✉ biotechbooks@yahoo.co.in
🌐 www.dayabooks.com
Estd.: 1997; **Man.Dir.:** Sunil Mittal;
Bus.Intt.: Pub. and Dist.; **Spl.:** Agri., Botany, Soc.Sci., etc. in English

BIOTEK BOOK COMPANY
3923/18, Kanhaiya Nagar, Tri Nagar, Delhi-110035
✆ 27385809
✉ biotek@ndb.vsnl.net.in
Hd.Org.: Avtar Walia; **Bus.Intt.:** L.S. & Rt.;
Spl.: Sci., Bio.Sci., Chemistry, Comp.Sci. and Phy.

BIOVED RESEARCH SOCIETY
252A/4A Om Gayatri Nagar, P.O. Teliagaj, Allahabad-211004 (Uttar Pradesh)

BIO-VISUAL PRODUCTS
310, (3rd Floor) Oasis Plaza, Tilak Road, Abods, Hyderabad-500001 (Andhra Pradesh)
✆ 24760088, 65524946, Fax: 040-24760077
📱 9391231100
✉ info@bio-visual.com, biovisual@satyam.net.in
🌐 www.bio-visual.com
Br.: IE/17, Jhandewallan Extension, (Near Jhandewallan Metro Railway Station), New Delhi-110055
✆ 23537644, Fax: 91-11-23537644
📱 9319320015; **Hd.Org.:** M.S. Chadha;
Bus.Intt.: Edu. Aids; **Spl.:** Sci.

BIPANEE
Ramlal Bazar, Kolkata-700078 (West Bengal)

BIPUL PUSTAK BHANDAR
Madanpur, Aurangabad-824208 (Bihar)
Bus.Intt.: Pub. and B.S.

BIRJOO BOOK DEPOT
Sanjat, Begusarai (Bihar)
Bus.Intt.: Pub. and B.S.

BIRLA PUBLICATIONS PVT. LTD.
1/9185, Street No. 5, West Rohtash Nagar, Shahdara, Delhi-110032
✆ 91-11-22323254
Hd.Org.: B.S. Kohli

BIRKHAEUSER-VERLAG
C/o Springer Books (India), 6, Community Centre, Panchsheel Park, New Delhi-110017

BISHALAXMI PRAKASHAN
16, Nabin Kundu Lane, Kolkata-700009 (West Bengal)

BISHAN CHAND AND SONS
25/114, Gali No. 6, Mahavir Block, Bholanath Nagar, Shahdara, Delhi-110032
✆ (O) 22303184, 56058032 (R) 22203524, Fax: 22155926
Hd.Org.: S.K. Sharma; **Bus.Intt.:** Pub.;
Spl.: Hindi Books on Sci., Litt., and Adult Edu.

BISHEN SINGH MAHENDRA PAL SINGH
23-A, Connaught Place, Dehra Dun-248001 (Uttarakhand)
✆ 2655748, Fax: 0135-2650107
bsmps@vsnl.net.in, smps@del2.vsnl.net.in
www.bishensinghbooks.com
Estd.: 1976; **Prt.:** Gajendra Singh Gahlot; **Bus.Intt.:** Pub., WS, L.S. & Rt., Imp., Exp.; **Spl.:** Sci. & Tech., Med.

BISHNU BOOK STALL
10A, Bankim Chatterjee St., Stall 16, Kolkata-700073 (West Bengal)

BISHWANATH PRAKASHAN
New Market, P.O. Dibrugarh, Distt. Dibrugarh, (Assam)

BISMOI PRAKASHAN
Hedayetpur, Guwahati-781003 (Assam)

BISWA BANGIYA PRAKASHAN
1/9, Marcus Square, Barnaporichoy (Formerly B-9, College St. Market), Kolkata-700007 (West Bengal)
9830012947, Fax: 91-33-22906591
bbp_cal@indiatimes.com
Hd.Org. Kazi Md. Mohasin

BISWA BHARATI
Dolmukh, Sibsagar (Assam)

BISWA BIKSHA PRAKASHAN
33A, Beniatola Lane, Kolkata-700009 (West Bengal)

BISWAKOSH
Dolmukh, Sibsagar (Assam)

BISWANATH BOOK HOUSE
Rameshwar Patna, Bhubaneshwar-751001 (Orissa)

BISWAS BOOK STALL
80, Mahatma Gandhi Rd., Kolkata-700007 (West Bengal)
Prt.: Phani Bhusan Biswas

BISWAS PUBLISHING HOUSE
5/1A, College Row, Kolkata-700009 (West Bengal)

BLACK ROSE PUBLICATIONS
229, Bhola Nath Nagar, Shahdara, Delhi-110032
✆ 91-11-65271509
vinodkalia@hotmail.com
www.blackrosepublications.com
Hd.Org.: Vinod Kalia; **Bus.Intt.:** Pub.; **Spl.:** Childrens Books

BLACKIE & SON (CALCUTTA) PVT. LTD.
Ravindra Mansion, Ram Nagar, New Delhi-110055
✆ 23672082, Fax: 91-11-23677446
schand@vsnl.com, schandco@giasd101.vsnl.net.in
www.schandgroup.com
Hd.Org.: Ravindra Kumar Gupta; **Bus.Intt.:** Pub.; **Spl.:** School-level Text-books on Sci. and Tech.

BLACKIE BOOKS
Bharat Building, 93, Anna Salai, Chennai-600002 (Tamil Nadu)
✆ 2840225
Hd.Org.: S.V. Parthasarathy; **Bus.Intt.:** Dist. and Pub.; **Spl.:** School, College Text and Gen. Books

BLACKWELL PUBLISHING LTD.
B-10, First Floor, Kailash Colony, New Delhi-110048
✆ 26293624, 26293841, Fax: 011-26477033
bslsesha@giasdl01.vsnl.net.in
Hd.Org.: R. Sessadri; **Bus.Intt.:** Pub.

BLACKWELL SCIENCE LTD.
New No. 8, Old No. 32, Second Main Rd., CIT Nagar (E), Chennai-600035 (Tamil Nadu)
✆ 24346244, 24346266, Fax: 24346529
itpsesha@giasmd01.vsnl.net.in
Hd.Org.: R. Seshadri; **Bus.Intt.:** Pub.; **Spl.:** Soc. Sci., Humanities and Sci. & Tech. in English

B.L.R. LOGISTICS
(A division of BLR India Pvt Ltd)
351/1, Main Road, Bijwasan, (Opp. Golok Dham Mandir), New Delhi-110061
✆ 91-11-28062446
Hd.Org.: Gautam Suri & Mansingh Jaswal

BLUEMOON BOOKS
S-201, Essel Mansion, 2286-87, Arya Samaj Rd., Karol Bagh, New Delhi-110005
✆ 25725844, Fax: 91-11-25762230

Hd.Org.: Suman; **Bus.Intt.**: Pub.; **Spl.**: Soc.Sci., Humanities, Buddhism and Dalits

BOARD OF ISLAMIC PUBLICATIONS
C/o Radiance News-weekly, Dawat Nagar, Abul Fazl Enclave, Jamia Nagar, New Delhi-110025
✆ 26311423, Fax: 26820975
✉ radiance@del3.vsnl.net.in

BOBBY EXPORTERS
4/3B, Golden Valley, Opp. Canara Bank, Kalina, Mumbai-400098 (Maharashtra)
Bus.Intt.: Exp.

BODHI BOOKS
Court Rd., Kozhikode-673001 (Kerala)
✆ (O) 0495-2365874 (R) 0495-2374051
✉ bodhibooks@hotmail.com
Estd.: 1984; **Bus.Intt.**: Pub. and B.S.; **Spl.**: Law, Litt.

BODHI PUBLISHING HOUSE
Court Rd., Near Link Rly. Gate, Kozhikode-673001 (Kerala)
Estd.: 1986; **Hd.Org.**: Joy Mathew; **Bus.Intt.**: Pub. and B.S.

BODHITARU
260, DG-III, Vikaspuri, New Delhi-110018

BODHITARU
C-5/B-23C, Janak Puri, New Delhi-110058
✆ 25540952

BOHRA PRAKASHAN
Bagde Bhawan, No. 1, Chaura Rasta, Jaipur-302003 (Rajasthan)
✆ (O) 2572589 (R) 2323064
Hd.Org.: Sushil Kumar Jain

BOMBAY BOOK BUREAU
109, Arenja Arcade, Ist Floor, Plot No. 4, Sector-17, Vashinavi, Mumbai-400703 (Maharashtra)

BOMBAY BOOKS & PERIODICALS SERVICES
Khaushe House, 1st Floor, 237/1/12, 20th Rd., Khar (W) Mumbai-400052 (Maharashtra)
✆ 26460649, Fax: 26059265
Hd.Org.: Suresh Salian

BOOK & STATIONERY HOUSE
82/30, M.N.K. Rd., Barahanagar, Kolkata-700036 (West Bengal)

BOOK BANK
10-A/M.I.G. Kankerbagh, Patna-800020 (Bihar)
Bus.Intt.: Pub. and B.S.

BOOK BIRD
Shop No. 1 to 4, Police Guest House, Opposite Head Post Office, Hanamkonda-506001 (Andhra Pradesh)
✆ 279785

BOOK CENTRE
J-I/160, Main Market, Rajouri Garden, New Delhi-110027
✆ (O) 25434336 (R) 2537560
Hd.Org.: Balbir Bajaj; **Bus.Intt.**: Pub., Rt.; **Spl.**: Gen. Paperbacks, Gifts & Cards

BOOK CENTRE
Gur-Banga Complex, 47-15-4 Dwaraka Nagar, Visakhapatnam-530016 (Andhra Pradesh)
✆ 0891-2562684, 2747759
✉ bookcentre@eth.net
Estd.: 1956; **Hd.Org.**: M. Gurunath; **Bus.Intt.**: L.S. & Rt.; **Spl.**: Gen. and Trade, Acad., Children Books, Greeting Cards and Toys (Indian and Foreign Books)

BOOK CENTRE
Opp. B.E.M.P. High School, Tellicherry-670101 (Kerala)

BOOK CENTRE
76, Bowbazar St., Kolkata-700012 (West Bengal)
Bus.Intt.: Exp.

BOOK CENTRE
Haspura, Aurangabad-824113 (Bihar)
Bus.Intt.: Pub. and B.S.

BOOK CENTRE
Sarai, Bhagalpur-812007 (Bihar)
Bus.Intt.: Pub. and B.S.

BOOK CENTRE
West Nada, Guruvayoor (Kerala)
✆ 2556438
Estd.: 1964; **Hd.Org.**: M.M. Varghese; **Bus.Intt.**: B.S.

BOOK CENTRE
Y.M.C.A. Rd., Kottayam-686001 (Kerala)
✆ 2567392, 2566992
Estd.: 1988; **Hd.Org.**: D. Vijaya Kumar; **Bus.Intt.**: B.S.

BOOK CENTRE
Barh, Patna-803213 (Bihar)
Bus.Intt.: Pub. and B.S.

BOOK CHANNEL
21, Rajgir Chambers 12/14, Shahid Bhagat Singh Rd., Opp. Old Customs House, Mumbai-400023 (Maharashtra)
✆ 22663337, 22662328, Fax: 22-22663281
✉ bookchannel@vsnl.com

BOOK CIRCLE
Rajendra Mansion, 19-A, Ansari Rd., Darya Ganj, New Delhi-110002
✆ 23264444, Fax: 91-11-23263050
✉ heritage@nad.vsnl.net.in
🌐 www.meditechbooks.com
Estd.: 2001; **Hd.Org.**: Himanshu Chawla;

Bus.Intt.: Imp. and Dist.; **Spl.:** Art, Arch., Cookery, Fashion, Mang., Photography, Acad., Soc.Sci., Med., Tech., Law

BOOK CLUB
3, Middleton Row, Flat H-10, Kolkata-700071 (West Bengal)

BOOK CORNER
M.I. Rd., Jaipur-302001 (Rajasthan)
✆ 2366323, 2371910

BOOK CORNER
12, Burla Market, P.O. Burla Distt., Sambalpur (Orissa)

BOOK CORNER
Gujari Bazari, Patna City, Patna-800008 (Bihar)
Bus.Intt.: Pub. and B.S.

BOOK CORNER
Patna Market, Muradpur, Patna-800004 (Bihar)
Bus.Intt.: Pub. and B.S.

BOOK CORNER (THE)
Block 77, Sanjay Place, Agra-282002 (Uttar Pradesh)
✆ (O) 2353506 (R) 2260384, 2261091
Estd.: 1987; **Prop.:** Dilip Kumar Jain; **Bus.Intt.:** B.S.; **Spl.:** All Sub.

BOOK CORPORATION OF INDIA
B-162, Fateh Nagar, New Delhi-110018

BOOK DEPOT
Main Rd., Kollam-691001 (Kerala)
✆ 278272
Estd.: 1952; **Hd.Org.:** P. Madhavan Pillai
Bus.Intt.: Pub. and B.S.

BOOK DISTRIBUTORS (I) PVT. LTD.
107/108, Arcadia, 195, Nariman Point, Mumbai-400021 (Maharashtra)
Prop.: K. Jagwani

BOOK EMPORIUM
Nathnagar, Bhagalpur-812006 (Bihar)
Bus.Intt.: Pub. and B.S.

BOOK EMPORIUM
Sabzibagh, Patna-800004 (Bihar)
Bus.Intt.: Pub. and B.S.

BOOK ENCLAVE
Jain Bhavan, Opp. N.E.I., Shanti Nagar, Jaipur-302006 (Rajasthan)
✆ 2220590, 2221456
Estd.: 1993; **Hd.Org.:** S.K. Jain; **Bus.Intt.:** Pub. and Dist.; **Spl.:** Humanities, Soc.Sci., Eco., Mang., etc. in English

BOOK FAITH INDIA
9, Netaji Subhash Marg, (IInd Floor) Darya Ganj, New Delhi-110002
✆ 23285722, Telefax: 23285081
✉ pilgrim@del2.vsnl.net.in
🌐 www.pilgrimsbooks.com
Estd.: 1992; **Hd.Org.:** Ramanand Tiwari, Krishna Nand Tiwari; **Bus.Intt.:** Pub. and Dist., Imp. & Exp.; **Spl.:** Juvenile/Children's Books, Rel., Phil., Fiction etc.

BOOK FORT
106-E, First Floor, Kamla Nagar, Delhi-110007

BOOK FRIEND
8/1B, S.C. Dey St., Kolkata-73 (West Bengal)

BOOK FROM SYRIA
C/o Embassy of the Syrian, 28, Vasant Marg, New Delhi-110057

BOOK FRONT PUBLICATIONS FORUM
AJ-162, Sector 11, Bidhannagar, Kolkata-700091 (West Bengal)

BOOK GALLERY
887/5, Street No. 6, Patel Nagar, Gurgaon-122001 (Haryana)
✆ 2324782, Fax: 91-124-2324782
✉ bookgallery@gmail.com
Hd.Org.: Satya Prakash

BOOK GUILD (THE)
H.No. 37, Village & P.O. Pitampura, Delhi-110034

BOOK HEAVEN
10, G.D. Complex Marhatal, Jabalpur-482002 (Madhya Pradesh)
✆ 2406919, 2411127
Estd.: 1988; **Prt.:** Arun Surana, Vineet Surana; **Bus.Intt.:** L.S. & Rt.; **Spl.:** Humanities & Soc.Sci., Sci. & Tech.

BOOK HILL (INDIA)
2047/6, Chuna Mandi, Paharganj, New Delhi-110055
✆ 23585291, 23582785, Fax: 011-23587922
✉ bookhillindia@rediffmail.com, bookhill@indiatimes.com
🌐 www.bookhillindia.com
Hd.Org.: Rajeev Sharma; **Bus.Intt.:** Pub.; **Spl.:** Edu. & Com. Books for Children

BOOK HOME
32, College Row, Kolkata-700009 (West Bengal)
Hd.Org.: Satyajit Majumder

BOOK HOUSE
Poramatola, Nabadwip, Nadia (West Bengal)

BOOK HOUSE
Perunnai, Changanacherry-686102 (Kerala)

✆ 222584
Estd.: 1989; **Prop.:** Babu Thomas
Bus.Intt.: Pub. and B.S.

BOOK INDIA PUBLISHING CO.
68-C, LIG DDA Flats, Rampura, Delhi-110035
✆ 27100135
Estd.: 1987; **Prop.:** V.R. Sharma
Bus.Intt.: Pub., Rep. and L.S.; **Spl.:** Arts & Acrh.

BOOK INTERNATIONAL
No. 281/D, 10th Main 4th Cross, 5th Block, Jayanagar, Bangalore-560041 (Karnataka)
Bus.Intt.: L.S.

BOOK INTERNATIONAL
P.O. Kharba, Muzzaffarpur-842001 (Bihar)

BOOK LAND
58, U.B. Banglow Rd., Jawahar Nagar, Delhi-110007
✆ 23912210 (R) 22154208, Fax: 011-23919045
worldview@vsnl.com
Estd.:1995; **Prop.:** Rakesh Rastogi;
Bus.Intt.: Rt., WS, Pub.; **Spl.:** Acad., Beh. Sci., Soc.Sci., Comm., Sci. Pure & Applied & Fiction

BOOK LAND
7, 9, Shantidoot, Opp. Muktangam English School, Pravati Darshan, Pune-411007 (Maharashtra)
✆ 2521043
Bus.Intt.: B.S.; **Spl.:** Sci., Mang. and Gen. Hobby Books

BOOK LAND
Gandhari Amman Coil Rd., Thiruvananthapuram-695001 (Kerala)
Estd.: 1984; **Hd.Org.:** A. Manikantan Nair;
Bus.Intt.: B.S.

BOOK LAND
Pan Bazar, Guwahati-781001 (Assam)
✆ 2520617, 2637772
bookland@satyam.net.in
Hd.Org.: Deepankar Roy; **Bus.Intt.:** B.S. and Pub.

BOOK LAND INTERNATIONAL (P) LTD.
12, Jansukh Niwas, Kasturba Road, Kandivli (West), Mumbai-400067 (Maharashtra)
✆ 28643640, 28643674
Fax: 91-22-28619394
bookland@vsnl.com
www.bookland.co.in
Bus.Intt.: Pub., B.S.

BOOK LAND (P) LTD.
1, Sankar Ghosh Lane, Kolkata-700070 (West Bengal)
Hd.Org.: Subhankar Bose

BOOK LINE (THE)
106, 1st Floor, 4787/23, Ansari Rd., Darya Ganj, New Delhi-110002
✆ (O) 56056760 (R) 25283394
9810691567
Telefax: 23242009
sales@thebooklineonline.com, tb18@hotmail.com
Prop.: R.L. Bhanot; **Bus.Intt.:** Dist.;
Spl.: Books and Journals on Petroleum and related Areas, Engg., Mang. etc.

BOOK LINKS (INDIA)
Flat No. 15, Block C, Pocket No. 4, Sector 5, Rohini, Delhi-110085
Estd.: 1990; **Prop.:** Brij Bhusan
Bus.Intt.: L.S. & Rt., Sub.Ag.
Spl.: Humanities & Soc.Sci., Sci. & Tech., Med., Tech., Law, Juvenile/Children, Gen. & Fiction etc.

BOOK LINKS CORPORATION
3-4-423/5 & 6, Narayanguda, Hyderabad-500029 (Andhra Pradesh)
✆ 27567068, 27611582, Cable: BOOKLINK
books@booklinkscorp.com
booklinks@usa.net
www.booklinkscorp.com
Estd.: 1965; **Prop.:** K.B. Satyanarayana;
Bus.Intt.: Pub., L.S. & Rt., Imp., Exp.;
Spl.: Humanities & Soc.Sci.

BOOK LOVERS' CONTACT
Shop No. 60, Satya Niketan, Moti Bagh II, P.O. Box No. 5272, New Delhi-110021
✆ (R) 24623021 (PP)
Prop.: O.P. Chowdhry; **Bus.Intt.:** Rt., Mail Order Suppliers and L.S.

BOOK LOVER RETREAT
Hall Bazar, Amritsar (Punjab)
Bus.Intt.: Rt., B.S.

BOOK MAN
41-B, Sawan Park, Delhi-110052
✆ (R): 7235239, 7456025
Prop.: Atma Ram Dogra; **Bus.Intt.:** Rt.

BOOK MAN
A-10, College St. Market, Kolkata-700009 (West Bengal)

BOOK MARK
#32, Vyalikaval Main Rd., Bangalore-560003 (Karnataka)
✆ 2346444, 23446445
Estd.: 1979; **Hd.Org.:** Hirel K. Singha;
Bus.Intt.: L.S., WS; **Spl.:** Humanities & Soc.Sci., Mang. & Comm., Engg. & Tech., Fiction & Gen.

BOOK MARK DISTRIBUTORS
32-B, Pleasure Garden Market, Chandni Chowk, Delhi-110006
✆ 23278392
Estd.: 1994; **Prop.:** Hardev Singh; **Bus.Intt.:** L.S.; **Spl.:** Sol., Eco., Pol.Sci. Books

BOOK MARKETING & CONSULTANCY P. LTD.
6, Ananda Puram, Mylapore, Chennai-600004 (Tamil Nadu)
✆ 24997129, Fax: 044-24991360
Estd.: 1991; **Dir.:** C. Janaki Raman; **Bus.Intt.:** Pub.

BOOK MARKETING SERVICES (INDIA) PVT. LTD.
2A, Ramaniyam Building, 216-217, Peters Rd., Chennai-600014 (Tamil Nadu)
✆ 28480220, Fax: 28480222
jai@xlweb.com
www.bookmarketing.org
Estd.: 1987; **Dir.:** S. Janaki Raman; **Bus.Intt.:** Pub.'s Rep.; **Spl.:** Sci., Tech. & Medicine, Humanities & Soc.Sci.

BOOK MARY (THE)
New Delhi
debashisnandy@rediffmail.com
Bus.Intt.: L.S.

BOOKMATE AGENCY
RZ-H-14A, Gali No. 10, Gurdwara Road, Mahavir Enchalve, Part-1, New Delhi-110045
98185-34566, Fax-011-25054188
bookmate_agency@rediffmail.com
Estd.: 2000; **Prop.:** Shri Jagan Nath Singh; **Bus.Intt.:** Bookseller, Library Supplier; **Spl.:** Humanities & Social Science, Sc & Tech; Law, Bio, Sc.

BOOK MEDIA
Dalgate, Srinagar-190001 (Jammu and Kashmir)
✆ 278218
Estd.: 1993; **Bus.Intt.:** Pub., WS, L.S. and Rt.

BOOK MEDIA INTERNATIONAL
Swarna 314th Cross, Malleswaram, Bangalore-560003 (Karnataka)
✆ 23449470
Estd.: 1996; **Prop.:** T.R. Raghunath; **Bus.Intt.:** L.S.; **Spl.:** Sci., Engg. & Tech., Institution Pub.

BOOK-N-BOOK
Opp. Kumar Book Depot, Near Raja Park, Adarsh Nagar, Jaipur (Rajasthan)

BOOK N CD
54, Arihant, 5/A Rd., Sardarpura, Jodhpur-342002 (Rajasthan)
✆ 9414131894, Fax: 91-291-2441964
info@bookncd.com
www.bookncd.com
Hd.Org.: B.K. Chandak; **Bus.Intt.:** Dist.; **Spl.:** Edu. Books and CDs

BOOK N CDS SYNDICATE
WZ-97, Market Wali Gali, 1st Floor, Jawala Heri, Paschim Vihar, New Delhi-110063
✆ 35340557, 32361740
booksncds@yahoo.co.in
Hd.Org.: Ms. Shradha Kaushal; **Spl.:** Children's Books, Edu. CD's, Work Sheets for Jr. School, Encourging Picture Books from USA, Mang. & Self-Improvement Books

BOOK NEST
Govind Mitra Rd., Patna-800004 (Bihar)
Bus.Intt.: Pub. and B.S.

BOOK PALACE
4598/12-B, Gola Cottage, Darya Ganj, New Delhi-110002
✆ 23277655, 23287586, 23257494, Fax: 91-11-23276646
bookpalacepublishers@yahoo.com
www.bookpalaceindia.com
Estd.: 1989; **Hd.Org.:** Geeta Sachdeva
Br.: E-391, Ramesh Nagar, New Delhi-110015
Bus.Intt.: Pub.; **Spl.:** Juvenile/Children

BOOK PALACE
S.B. College Rd., Aurangpura, Aurangabad-831001 (Bihar)
✆ 2333545, Fax: 2351297
Prop.: Somnath Dongopure; **Bus.Intt.:** Rt.; **Spl.:** School Level Books and Stationers in English and Marathi

BOOK PALACE
Opp. Patna College, Ashok Raj Path, Patna, (Bihar)

BOOK PARADISE
No. 751, 8th E Main, N.I.I.T. Towers, Near 4th Block Post Office, Jayanagar, Bangalore-11 (Karnataka)
✆ 26637466, Fax: 226639954
jai@blr.vsnl.net.in
Bus.Intt.: Rt. & B.S.

BOOK PARADISE
7, K.K. Plaza, Zone II, M.P. Nagar, Bhopal-462011 (Madhya Pradesh)
✆ (O) 0755-5272247 (R) 2578950
Estd.: 1999; **Prop.:** D.K. Jain; **Bus.Intt.:** B.S., L.S.; **Spl.:** Sci. & Tech., Comp., Bio.

BOOK PARADISE (THE)
13/11, Subhash Nagar, Old Rly. Rd., P.O. Box-50, Gurgaon-122001 (Haryana)
✆ 2322330, 2327543, Fax: 2327543

📧 bookparadise@hotmail.com
Estd.: 1994; **Prop.:** T.R. Sachdeva; **Bus.Intt.:** Dist.; **Spl.:** Gen. & Fiction etc.

BOOK PLANET
7/22, Ansari Rd., Darya Ganj, New Delhi-110002
✆ (O) 23273880 (R) 27458666, Fax: 23285873
Prop.: Mrs. Ameeta Gupta; **Bus.Intt.:** B.S., L.S.

BOOK PLAZA
Sun House Basement, Opp. Navrangpura Tele.Ex., below Raymond Shop, C.G. Rd., Ahmedabad-380006 (Gujarat)
✆ 079-6430386, Telefax: 079-6440763
📧 bookplaza1@sanchanrnet.in, bookplaza@yahoo.co.in
Hd.Org.: Nitin Doshi; **Bus.Intt.:** B.S.

BOOK RESORT
Plot No. 18, D. No. 50-48-23/A, P. & T. Colony, Seethammadhara, Visakhapatnam-530013 (Andhra Pradesh)
✆ 252732
Prop.: P.K. Reddy

BOOK REVIEW LITERARY TRUST (THE)
35A/1, Shahpur Jat, 3rd Floor, New Delhi-110049
✆ 26492031, Fax: 2355500
📧 thebookreview@hotmail.com, prchari@vsnl.net
🌐 www.thebookreviewindia.org
Estd.: 1976; **Hd.Org.:** Mrs. Chandra Chary; **Bus.Intt.:** Pub.; **Spl.:** Journal and English Translations of Indian Classics

BOOK ROUTE
Chamber No. V, 88, Bangla Sahib Marg, Gole Market, New Delhi-110001
✆ 22751804 ▮ 9811331694
📧 abidi7@now-india.net.in
Estd.: 2001; **Prop.:** Shakil Abidi Deeba Abidi; **Bus.Intt.:** Rt., L.S.; **Spl.:** Acad., Fiction, Soc.Sci.

BOOK SALES
Examiner Press Building, Second Floor, 35, Dalal St., Fort, Mumbai-400023 (Maharashtra)
✆ 22671801, 22671367
Estd.: 1982; **Prop.:** Samir Shah
Br.: 16, State Bank St., 2nd Floor, Mount Rd., Chennai-600002 (Tamil Nadu) ✆ 28570594
Bus.Intt.: WS, Imp.; **Spl.:** Humanities & Soc.Sci., Juvenile/Children, Gen. & Fiction

BOOK SALES COMPANY
4327/3 Ansari Rd., Darya Ganj, New Delhi-110002
✆ 23264619, Fax: 91-11-25783229
Prt.: Navin Anand; **Bus.Intt.:** Imp., WS, Dist.; **Spl.:** Children, Art, Reference, Gen., Edu. & Soc.Sci. books

BOOK SCAN
Shop No. 8, 1st Floor, Shah-e-Jahan Complex, Madina Chowk, Gow Kadal, Srinagar-190001 (Jammu & Kashmir)
Estd.: 2003; **Hd.Org.:** M.G. Ahmed; **Bus.Intt.:** L.S.; **Spl.:** Humanities & Soc.Sci., Mang. & Comm.

BOOK SEA
Shop No. 4-5-48, Beside Andhra Bank, Women's College Rd., Kothi, Hyderabad-500095 (Andhra Pradesh)
✆ 24757526
📧 bookseay@yahoo.com
Hd.Org.: S.A. Sohaib; **Bus.Intt.:** B.S., L.S.; **Spl.:** Polytechnic, Engg., Arts, Sci., Comm., Agri. & Veterinary, Comp.Engg., Med., Pharmacy, Nursing, Arch. and Competitive Books etc.

BOOK SEARCH
G-81, LGF, Lajpat Nagar-II, New Delhi-110024
✆ 29813206, 32334772, Fax: 29813206
📧 ifusion@bol.net.in
Hd.Org.: Ashish Gupta, Jatin Mehta; **Bus.Intt.:** Pub., Rt. and WS; **Spl.:** Children's Books and CD-ROMs

BOOK SELECTION
Shop No. 14, Sector 17-C, Chandigarh-160017
✆ 2774976
Estd.: 1998; **Hd.Org.:** Shailendra Pandey; **Bus.Intt.:** B.S. and L.S.; **Spl.:** Comp. and Text Books up to M.A. in English & Hindi

BOOK SELECTION CENTRE
Arya Samaj Mandir, 1st Floor, Sultan Bazar, Hyderabad-500195 (Andhra Pradesh)
✆ 24750909, 24753218, Fax: 24752054
📧 bschyd@hd2.dot.net.in
Estd.: 1966; **Prt.:** N.D. Parekh
Sh.: No. 1-7-281, Opp. Kamat Hotel, S.D. Rd., Secunderabad ✆ 27843221, Fax: 27897067
• 3-5-121/E/1/2, Ramkote, Hyderabad-500001 ✆ 24750624, 24752053, Fax: 24752054
📧 6 schyd@ad2.dot.net.en
• Shree Book Square, Vysya Hostel Bldg., Kachiguda, Hyderabad-500027 ✆ 27566820
Bus.Intt.: WS, L.S. & Rt., Imp., Exp., Sub.Ag.; **Spl.:** Humanities & Soc.Sci., Sci. & Tech., Med., Gen. & Fiction

BOOK SELL (INDIA) COMPANY (P) LTD.
H-295, Naraina Vihar, New Delhi-110028
✆ (O) 25797815 (R) 25797576, Fax: 2579554, 25791111
Hd.Org.: Shivnidhi Wasan; **Bus.Intt.:** Pub., L.S.

BOOK SERVICE SYNDICATE
No. 83, Vysya Bank Colony, Ist Main, Ist Cross,

Bannerghatta Rd., Bangalore-560076 (Karnataka)
✆ 26686532, Fax: 26686286
✉ haren_bss@vsnl.com, haren@bgl.vsnl.net.in
Estd.: 1995; **Bus.Intt.:** Rt., WS, L.S.; **Spl.:** Mang., Computing other Tech. and Gen.

BOOK SHELF
16, City Centre, Near Swastic, Char Rasta, C.G. Rd., Navrangpura, Ahmedabad-380009 (Gujarat)
✆ 079-26441826, 26563707
✉ bookshelf@wilnetonline.net
Estd.: 1993; **Hd.Org.:** Haresh Shah; **Bus.Intt.:** Rt.; **Spl.:** Gen. and Trade, Acad., Professional and Children Books (Indian and Foreign)

BOOK SHELF
Shop No. 15, Ground Floor, Haveli Complex, Opp. Zilla Parishad, Chandrapur-442401 (Maharashtra)
✆ (O) 07172-252437 (R) 255001, Fax: 256702
Estd.: 1997; **Hd.Org.:** Prashant Potdukhes; **Bus.Intt.:** B.S. and L.S.; **Spl.:** College and University

BOOK SHOP (THE)
14 A, Khan Market, New Delhi-110003
✆ 24697102, 2697102
Estd.: 1980; **Ch.Exe.:** K.D. Singh
Br.: 13/7, Jorbagh Market, New Delhi-3
✆ 24611008
Bus.Intt.: Rt. and Mail Order and L.S.; **Spl.:** Gen. and Trade Books, Professional, Children, Electronic and Products Books (Indian & Foreign)

BOOK SHOP (THE)
Ludhiana (Punjab)
✆ 2404728, 2407142, Fax: 2403856
✉ shawls@shingora.net
Bus.Intt.: Business & Rt.

BOOK SHOP (THE)
S.R. 7, Ashoka Market, Station Square, Unit-II, Bhubaneshwar-751009 (Orissa)
✆ (O) 2531568, 9861028585 (R) 0674-2575071, Fax: 2544090
✉ thebooks@sify.com
Estd.: 1982; **Hd.Org.:** Sanjay Dhir; **Bus.Intt.:** B.S., Rt., L.S., WS; **Spl.:** Mang., Law

BOOK SOCIETY
College Rd. (Dt. Darjeeling), Siliguri-734401 (Assam)

BOOK SOCIETY OF INDIA LTD.
2, Bankim Chatterjee St., Kolkata-73 (West Bengal)
✆ (O) 033-2314053 (R) 2420291
Estd.: 1994; **Ch.Exe.:** K.S. Banerjee; **Bus.Intt.:** Pub.; **Spl.:** Fiction, Edu. Value and Allied Sub., Text Books for Schools, Colleges and Tech. Institutions in Bengali

BOOK SOCIETY
Ashok Rajpath, Patna-800004 (Bihar)
Bus.Intt.: Pub. and B.S.

BOOK SPACE
593/94, Ganesh Peth, Kondhre Wade, Pune-2 (Maharashtra)

BOOK SQUARE
36149, (3rd Floor), Netaji Subhash Marg, Darya Ganj, New Delhi-110002
✆ (O) 23274959 (R) 27118949

BOOK SUPPLY BUERAU
A-68, South Extension, Part-I, New Delhi-110049
✆ 24611991, 24634222, Fax: 91-11-24627172
✉ standard@del3.vsnl.net.in, bsb@nda.vsnl.net.in
🌐 www.standardindia.com
Hd.Org.: C. Krishnan
Bus.Intt.: Dist.

BOOK SYNDICATE (THE)
Opp. Central Bank, Bank St., 4-3-378, Old Deveka Mahal, Hyderabad-500095 (Andhra Pradesh)
✆ 24755951, 24756722, Fax: 24756271
✉ booksynd@hd2.dot.net.in
🌐 www.thebooksyndicate.com
Estd.: 1961; **Prop.:** Sushila C. Shah; **Bus.Intt.:** B.S. & Sub.Ag.; **Spl.:** Sci. & Tech.

BOOK SYNDICATE PVT. LTD.
2, Ramnath Biswas Lane, Kolkata-700009 (West Bengal)
✆ (O) 23543123, 23500549, 2241092223507158 (R) 24661854, 23349648, Fax: 23503881
✉ bs_pl@sify.com
Man.Dir.: Biplab Bhowal; **Bus.Intt.:** Pub.

BOOK TEMPLE
C-7/84, Yamuna Vihar, New Delhi-110053
✆ 22910377
✉ booktemple@rediffmail.com
Dir.: Deepak; **Bus.Intt.:** B.S.

BOOK TEMPLE
Ashok Rajpath, Patna-800001 (Bihar)
Bus.Intt.: Pub. and B.S.

BOOK TRACK
Renushree, 4-12/12, Near Mahalingeshwara High School, Suratkal, Mangalore-574158 (Karnataka)
✆ (O) 0824-2475628 (R) 2476431 (PP)

BOOK TRADERS
Kothi, Hyderabad-500196 (Andhra Pradesh)
✆ 2594185, 2512835
Hd.Org.: Syed Mubashiruddin

BOOK VENTURE PUBLISHERS
23, Thanikachalam Rd., T. Nagar, Chennai-600017 (Tamil Nadu)
✆ 044-24344519, Fax: 044-24342009
✉ k.k.cheenu@ppl.sprintrpg.ems.vsnl.net.in ksm@md2.vsnl.net.in
Dir.: S. Bhuvaneshwari; **Bus.Intt.:** Pub.; **Spl.:** Organic Farming, Env. Issues, Productivity Tech.

BOOK VISION
B-1, First Floor, Auquaf Shopping Complex, Opp. University Gate, Srinagar-190006 (Jammu & Kashmir)
✆ 2424282, 2423208 Fax: 91-194-2424282
✉ bookvision@rediffmail.com
www.bookvision.8k.com
Estd.: 1999; **Hd.Org.:** Shabir Ahmad Bhat; **Bus.Intt.:** Pub., WS, L.S. & Rt., Sub.Ag.; **Spl.:** Humanities, Soc.Sci., Mang. & Comm., Sci., Med.Sci., Engg. & Tech., Journals, Magazines & Periodicals, Fiction & Gen.

BOOK WALA
Near P.N.B., Azad Rd. Amroha-244221 (Uttar Pradesh)
✆ 05922-250277, 259167 ▮ 9837028782
✉ amrohaeducation@mickyonline.com
Hd.Org.: Shailesh Agarwal
Br.: ABD Group of Publications, 393, Swami Para, Meerut • Kanika Publications, 393, Swami Para, Meerut
Bus.Intt.: Dealers; **Spl.:** All kinds of School Books. Self-improvement, Eng. Books, Personality Development, General Mang., Word Power & All Types of Dictionaries, Mang. and Eng. Spoken Books etc.

BOOK WAVE
T.B. Rd., Changanacherry, Kottayam-686101 (Kerala)
Estd.: 1984; **Prop.:** T.P. Georgekutty; **Bus.Intt.:** Pub. and B.S.

BOOK WORLD
Rajasthan University Campus, Jaipur-302004 (Rajasthan)
✆ (S) 0141-2705773 (R) 2592384
▮ 9829145519
Hd.Org.: Rajnish Kr. Choudhary

BOOK WORLD
7, Palika Bazar, New Delhi-110001
✆ 23320128, 23353223, Fax: 23721188
✉ fln@del2.vsnl.net.in
Estd.: 1978; **Prop.:** Deepan Jain; **Bus.Intt.:** Rt.; **Spl.:** Indian Art, Arch., Travel & Fictions

BOOK WORLD
No. 10, Sri Ramakrishna Apartments, Vidyaranyapura Main Rd., Doddabommasandra, Bangalore-560097 (Karnataka)
Bus.Intt.: L.S.

BOOK WORLD
10-A, Astley Hal, Dehradun-248001 (Uttarakhand)
✆ 2655845 ▮ 6836051914, Fax: 2652111
Hd.Org.: Sukhdev Arora; **Bus.Intt.:** Rt., WS, and Pub.; **Spl.:** Military, Administration and Co-operatives in English Language

BOOK WORLD
Panaji (Goa)
✆ 0832-2421857, Fax: 5643606
✉ books@goatelecom.com

BOOK WORLD DISTRIBUTORS
41, Tripolia Zero Rd., Allahabad (Uttar Pradesh)

BOOK WORLD ENTERPRISES
9, Dr. M.B. Velkar St., Kalbadevi Rd., Mumbai-400002 (Maharashtra)
✆ 22015331, 22068538, Fax: 22059934
✉ bookworld@vsnl.com, bookworl@bom.7.vsnl.net.in
Hd.Org.: Satish Shah; **Bus.Intt.:** Dist.; **Spl.:** Tech., Arch., Mang., Interiors and Comp. Sub. and Foreign Publications

BOOK WORLD INDIA
111 & 115, Munish Plaza, 20, Ansari Rd., Darya Ganj, New Delhi-110002
✆ 23258766, 23258774, Tele Fax: 23258774
✉ bwindia@vsnl.com
Man.Dir.: Nishant Saxena; **Bus.Intt.:** L.S.; **Spl.:** Soc.Sci., Comm., Comp., Sci., Pure & Applied, Tech., Law

BOOK WORLD PUBLISHERS & DISTRIBUTORS
102, Rd. No. 2, Rajendra Nagar, Patna-800016 (Bihar)
✆ 2674260, 2687759
Estd.: 1993; **Prop.:** Atul Jaiswal
Bus.Intt.: L.S. & Rt.; **Spl.:** Humanities & Soc Sci., Sci. & Tech.

BOOK WORM (THE)
B-29, Connaught Place, New Delhi-110001
✆ 23322260, 23311140, Fax: 23723440
✉ bookworm@del2.vsnl.net.in, bookworm@ vsnl.com
Estd.: 1977; **Hd.Org.:** Anil Arora
Br.: Bookworm Computer Co., D-22, Defence Colony, New Delhi-110024

© 23322260, 24601757, 24640844, Fax: 23723440, 24640844
Bus.Intt.: Rt.; **Spl.:** Fiction, Soc.Sci., Indology Litt., Phil. (Indian & Foreign)

BOOK WORM
Kerala Catholic Trust Building, Kanjikuzhy
K.K. Rd., Kottayam-686004 (Kerala)
© 2570992
Estd.: 1982; **Hd.Org.:** Kiran J. Kallivayalil; **Bus.Intt.:** Book Lending Library

BOOK WORM
Panjim (Goa)
✉ confident@sancharnet.in
Bus.Intt.: B.S.

BOOK ZONE—THE ASSISSI
Kottayam (Kerala)
© 2429188, 2420188, Fax: 2420466
✉ suman@assissipublishers.com
Bus.Intt.: B.S. & Rt.

BOOKHIVE (INDIA)
CB-349, Ring Rd., Naraina, New Delhi-110028
© 25778295, 6582518, ▮ 9811700512
✉ bookhire@yahoo.com
Hd.Org.: Sudhir Sakhuja; **Bus.Intt.:** Pub.; **Spl.:** Competition Guides and GK Books

BOOKIES THE BOOK SHOP
106, Prakashan St., P.S. Park, Erode-638001 (Kerala)
© 0424-273414; **Hd.Org.:** R.B. Anbu

BOOKIONICS
3-5-11, 14/7, Kachiguda Cross Rd.,
Opp. Hotel Traveller, Hyderabad-500027 (Andhra Pradesh)
© 24753654, 25751134, Fax: 24756271
✉ bookionics@yahoo.com
🌐 www.bookionics.com
Estd.: 1985; **Prop.:** Chandrakant P. Shaw; **Bus.Intt.:** WS, L.S. & Rt.; **Spl.:** Sci. & Tech.

BOOKLINE
7, Tottee Lane, Kolkata-700016
© 22440903, 22454238,
Fax: 91-33-22454238
✉ bookline@cal3.vsnl.net.in
Hd.Org.: Brijesh Tiwari

BOOKMAN ASSOCIATES
Dimapur
© 230364, 233565, Fax: 233216
✉ bookmanassociates_dmr@rediffmail.com
Bus.Intt.: B.S.

BOOKMAN INDIA
151/1A, South Civil Lines,
Muzaffarnagar-251001 (Uttar Pradesh)
© 2407870, 2400954, Fax: 2404925
✉ bmipph@hotmail.com
🌐 www.bookmanindia.com
Hd.Org.: R.C. Gupta; **Bus.Intt.:** Pub.; **Spl.:** Children's Books

BOOKMART PUBLISHERS
New Delhi
✉ bookmart@vsnl.com
Bus.Intt.: Pub.

BOOKMATE AGENCY
N-23, Hari Nagar, Gali No. 1, Sorabh Vihar,
Near Amar Market, Badarpur,
New Delhi-110044
© 23351267 ▮ 9818904249
Estd.: 2000; **Prop.:** J.N. Singh; **Bus.Intt.:** B.S., L.S.; **Spl.:** Acad., Beh., Soc.Sci., Comm., Med., Tech., Juveniles, Law

BOOKMATE AGENCY
RZ-H-14A, Street No. 10, Gurudwara Road,
Mahavir Enclave Part-1, New Delhi-110045
© Fax: 25054188, ▮ 9818534566
Estd.: 2000; **Prop.:** J.N. Singh;
Bus.Intt.: B.S., L.S.; **Spl.:** Acad., Beh., Soc.Sci., Comm., Med., Tech., Juveniles, Law

BOOKMATRIX
203-4 & 7, Mohan Complex
H-Block Market, Ashok Vihar, Delhi-110052
© 47091404, Fax: 91-11-47091473
✉ info@bookmatrix.com
🌐 www.bookmatrix.com
Hd.Org.: Sandeep Kaushik

BOOKMEN ASSOCIATES
9, Opp. Rajasthan University, Jawaharlal Nehru Marg, Jaipur-302004 (Rajasthan)
© 2515192, 2519808
Estd.: 1984; **Hd.Org.:** Arihant Jain; **Bus.Intt.:** Pub. and Dist.; **Spl.:** Sci., Humanities, Soc.Sci.

BOOKPOINT (INDIA) LTD.
Indian Mercantile Chambers, Ground Floor,
R. Kamani Marg, Mumbai-400001 (Maharashtra)
© 022-22611972
Estd.: 1980; **Hd.Org.:** Osborne Almeida
Br.: D. No. 3-6-272, Himayatnagar,
Hyderabad-500029 (Andhra Pradesh)
© 23222138, Fax: 23222900
✉ bookpoint01@yahoo.co.in
Estd.: 1985; **Hd.Org.:** Sunder Thomas
Bus.Intt.: L.S., Rt., B.S.; **Spl.:** Gen. and Trade, Acad. Professional, Children Books, Greeting Cards, Audio and Video Cassettes, Magazines, Jigsaw, Puzzles (Indian and Foreign)

BOOKPOINT (INDIA) LTD. (THE)
160, Anna Salai, Chennai-600002
(Tamil Nadu)

© 28523019
Estd.: 1997; **Hd.Org.**: S. Sundar Kumar; **Bus.Intt.**: Rt. and L.S.; **Spl.**: Gen. and Trade, Acad., Professional, Children Books and Greeting Cards (Indian and Foreign)

BOOKS & ALLIED
P-82, C.I.T. Rd., Kolkata-700014 (West Bengal)
© 2245-20858, 22284-2719
Hd.Org.: Kalyan Shah

BOOKS & BOOKS
601, D.H. Rd., Kolkata-700034 (West Bengal)

BOOKS & BOOKS
903, Kirti Shikhar, 11, Janakpuri Distt. Centre, New Delhi-110058
© (O) 25593426 (R) 2551252
Hd.Org.: Indramohan Sharma; **Bus.Intt.**: Pub.

BOOKS & BOOKS
5, Taj Point, Nawal Kishore Rd., Lucknow-1 (Uttar Pradesh)
© & Fax: 281417
Hd.Org.: Abis Naqvi; **Bus.Intt.**: WS

BOOKS & BYTES INDIA PVT. LTD.
N-16, Malviya Nagar, New Delhi-110017
© (O) 26672163, 26689383 (R) 29543849, Fax: 26689562
@ books_bytes@mantraonline.com, books_bytes@hotmail.com
Estd.: 1998; **Dir.**: D.P. Sapru, Amit Sood; **Bus.Intt.**: Pub., Dist., Rt., Sub.Ag. & L.S.; **Spl.**: Sci. & Tech., Social & Beh. Sci., Mang. & Comp. Sci., Reference & Gen.

BOOKS & GIFTS SHOPPERS PARADISE
S.C. Goswami Rd., Pan Bazar, (Near Hari Sabha), Guwahati-781001 (Assam)
©/Fax: 2633860
@ jainmanojp_in@yahoo.com
Estd.: 1997, **Prop.**: Jain Manoj; **Bus.Intt.**: B.S. & Rt.

BOOKS & PERIODICALS
10, Ramanath Majumder St., Kolkata-700009 (West Bengal)
Hd.Org.: Ashoke Ghosh

BOOKS & PERIODICALS AGENCY
B-1, Inder Puri, New Delhi-110012
© 25786046, 25755096, Cable: BACKVOLUME
@ bpage@del2.vsnl.net.in
Bus.Intt.: Exp.; **Spl.**: Edu. and Journals Books

BOOKS & PERIODICALS CORPORATION (INDIA)
C-8, Safdarjung, Development Area, Opp. I.I.T. Gate, New Delhi-110016
© 23264039, 26863145, Fax: 23282623
Prop.: A.S. Gujral; **Bus.Intt.**: Rt., WS, L.S. & Sub.Ag.; **Spl.**: Biological Sci., Engg. Pure & Applied, Mang., Med., Journals & Periodicals

BOOKS & PERIODICALS CORPORATIONS
Rasta Singhi Ji, S.M.S. Highway, Jaipur-302003 (Rajasthan)
Hd.Org.: Suresh Runthla; **Bus.Intt.**: Pub., WS, L.S., Rt., Exp.

BOOKS' BAR
D-19/220, Nandanvan Aptt., Navavadej, Ahmedabad (Gujarat)
Prop.: Tej Pal Singh

BOOKS-DEN
86, Hamidia Rd., Bhopal-1 (Madhya Pradesh)
© (O) 2538564 (R) 2766520
@ vikasjaitley@usa.net
Estd.: 1970; **Bus.Intt.**: Pub. & B.S.; **Spl.**: Sports

BOOKS-EN-AMEE
Boring Rd., Patna-800001 (Bihar)
© 0612-2232888
Estd.: 1982; **Prop.**: Atmanand Das; **Bus.Intt.**: Pub. and B.S., L.S.; **Spl.**: Gen., Electronic Products, Children Indian and Foreign Books and Greeting Cards

BOOKS4U.IN
Oswal House, 1/11, Sahitya Kunj, M.G. Road, Agra-282002 (Uttar Pradesh)
© 2856550, Fax: 91-562-2854582
@ contact@books4u.in
www.books4uin
Hd.Org.: Prashant Jain

BOOKS FOR ALL
A-6, Nimri Community Centre, Near Ashok Vihar, Phase-IV, Delhi-110052
© 27401672, Fax: 23264368
@ ipp@nde.vsnl.net.in
Bus.Intt.: B.S.

BOOKS FOR CHANGE
139, Richmond Rd., Bangalore-560025 (Karnataka)
© 25321747, 25580346, Fax: 25586284
@ bfc@actionaidindia.org
www.booksforchange.in
Estd.: 1997; **Hd.Org.**: Shoba Ramachandran; **Bus.Intt.**: Pub. and Dist.; **Spl.**: Soc. Sub. in English and Regional Languages

BOOKS INDIA
P.K. House, Behind M.J. Library, Ellis Bridge, Ahmedabad-380006 (Gujarat)
© 29575542, Fax: 079-26577349
Estd.: 1973; **Hd.Org.**: Kanak J. Dalal; **Bus.Intt.**: Rt.; **Spl.**: Gen. & Trade, Acad. Professional Books (Indian & Foreign)

BOOKS INDIA CORPORATION
B-1328, Shastri Nagar, Delhi-110052
✆ 23554141 ▮ 9810055408, Fax: 27538448
Man.Dir.: O.N. Kalia; **Bus.Intt.:** Pub.; **Spl.:** Govt. Agent, Parliament

BOOKS INN
Kanth Manzil, Mirza Bagh, Nagin, Srinagar (Jammu & Kashmir)
✆ (O) 0194-2481364 (R) 2424673
Hd.Org.: Imtiyaz Ahmed; **Bus.Intt.:** L.S.; **Spl.:** Humanities & Soc.Sci., Mang., Law, Children & Gen.

BOOKS INTERNATIONAL
42-A, Nilgiri Apartment, Alakhnanda, New Delhi-110019
✆ 42143438, Fax: 91-11-42143438
✉ lalwani_books@yahoo.com
Hd.Org.: G.C. Lalwani, Nitin Lalwani; **Bus.Intt.:** Dealer; **Spl.:** Art, Arch., Interior Designing, Furniture, etc.

BOOKS INTERNATIONAL
Shop No. 11, Aliganj Shopping Complex, Sector-B, Kapoorthala Rd., Lucknow-226024 (Uttar Pradesh)
✆ 2376960, 2335846
✉ bookinter1@satyam.net.in
Estd.: 1979; **Prop.:** A.K. Shukla; **Bus.Intt.:** L.S. & Rt., Imp., Sub.Ag.; **Spl.:** Sci. & Tech., Arch. Books, Juvenile/Children Books, Comp., Mang., Competition Books

BOOKS INTERNATIONAL
Bangalore (Karnataka)
✆ 080-6642273
✉ bookinti@bgl.vsnl.net.in

BOOKS-N-BITIS
M-601, Mahima Apts., Civil Lines, Nagpur-1 (Maharashtra)
✆ 2552516
Bus.Intt.: Rt., B.S.

BOOKS 'N' BOOKS
C-403, Som Vihar, Sangam Theatre Rd., New Delhi-110022
✆ 26876209, 26876206, 2679065
Hd.Org.: B.K. Bhandari

BOOKS N CDS SYNDICATE
A2/11A, Adarsh Apartment, Paschim Vihar, Delhi-110063
✆ 25285278, 25272401, Fax: 25276386, 25265397
✉ booksncds@yahoo.co.in
Hd.Org.: Shradha Kaushal; **Bus.Intt.:** Pub., Dealer; **Spl.:** Children's Books

BOOKS SUPPLY BUREAU
A-68, South Extension-1, New Delhi-110049
✆ 24611991, 24628182, 24634222, Fax: 011-24627172
✉ standard@del3.vsnl.net.in, bsb@nda.vsnl.net.in
🌐 www.standardsindia.com
Estd.: 1972; **Prt.:** C. Krishnan
Br.: 628, 1st Main Rd., 1st Stage, Indira Nagar, Bangalore-560038
✆ 25250374, 25253511, Fax: 25250662
✉ bsb@bgl.vsnl.net.in
• 503, 5th Floor Thacker Tower Plot No. 86, Sector-17, Vashi, New Mumbai-400705
✆ 27801805, Fax: 27801806
✉ bsbstaand@vsnl.com
Bus.Intt.: Dist.; **Spl.:** National & International Standards *viz.* ASTM, ASME, BSI, ISO, IEC, DIN, JIS, etc.

BOOKS TODAY
1A, Hamilton House, Connaught Place, New Delhi-110001
✆ 23352233, Fax: 23712998
✉ ashoke@indiatodaybookclub.com
🌐 www.indiatodaybookclub.com
Estd.: 1999

BOOKS TREASURE
Sojati Gate, Jodhpur-342001 (Rajasthan)
✆ 2342001
Estd.: 1990; **Prop.:** Mrs. K. Singhri; **Bus.Intt.:** Pub. and Dist.

BOOKS WORLD
33, Bhod Bhoda Rd., TT Nagar, Bhopal-462003 (Madhya Pradesh)
✆ (O) 2554061 (R) 2776541
▮ 9827020455
Estd.: 1969; **Prop.:** A.K. Jain;
Br.: M.I.G. 6, MLA Quarters, Rang Mahal, Bhopal (Madhya Pradesh)
Bus.Intt.: B.S., L.S., WS; **Spl.:** Humanities & Soc.Sci., Sci. & Tech., Comp., Mang., Law, Children & General, Arts & Arch., Bio.Sci.

BOOKS' WORLD
607, Chira Bazar, Opp. Wadia Fire Temple Mumbai-400002 (Maharashtra)
✆ 22073178, 22333465, Fax: 91-22-22051072
Hd.Org.: Manoj Jain

BOOKSELL AGENCIES
Nadiadwala Building, Room No. 7, 1st Floor, S.V. Rd., Next to P.O., Opp. Paaneri Savroad, Near Andheri Station (W), Mumbai-400058 (Maharashtra)
✆ 26281138, Fax: 26211658
✉ booksellagencies@hotmail.com
Estd.: 1962; **Bus.Intt.:** Rt.; **Spl.:** Sci. & Tech.

BOOKSHOP (THE)
769, Anna Salai, Spencer Plaza, Chennai, (Tamil Nadu)
✆ 28524419
Estd.: 1994; **Hd.Org.:** V.N. Seetharam; **Bus.Intt.:** Rt.; **Spl.:** Gen. and Trade, Acad. and Children Books (Indian and Foreign)

BOOKSLINE
Sagar 46/1590, Subhash Nagar, Chembur, Mumbai-400071 (Maharashtra)
✆ 25213976
✉ ashokan66@yahoo.co.uk, booksline@vsnl.net
Estd.: 2000; **Prop.:** Ashokan Manickam; **Bus.Intt.:** B.S. & L.S.; **Spl.:** Humanities & Soc.Sci., Mang., Children and Gen.

BOOKSLINE
Hyderabad (Andhra Pradesh)
✆ 55578506
✉ supriyabha@indiatimes.com

BOOKSTOP AT CHARNOCK CITY
KB-26, Salt Lake, Sector II, Kolkata-700064 (West Bengal)
✆ 23581086, Fax: 033-23349908
✉ bright@gist1giasc101.vsnl.net.in
Estd.: 1997; **Man.:** Ronodab Paul; **Bus.Intt.:** Rt. & Mail Order; **Spl.:** Gen., Trade, Children Books (Indian & Foreign) and Electronic Products

BOOKWELL
2/72, Nirankari Colony, Delhi-110009
✆ 27251283, Fax: 91-11-23281315
✉ bkwell@nde.vsnl.net.in
Estd.: 1974; **Prt.:** M.S. Khurana
Sales Off.: 24/4800, Ansari Rd., Darya Ganj, New Delhi-110002
✆ 23268786, 23257264, Fax: 23281315
✉ bookwell@vsnl.net
Bus.Intt.: Pub., WS, L.S. & Rt., Imp., Exp., Sub.Ag.; **Spl.:** Govt. of India Publication, Humanities & Soc.Sci.

BOOKWELL PUBLICATIONS
24/4800, Ansari Rd., Darya Ganj, New Delhi-110002
✆ 23268786, Fax: 91-11-23281315
✉ bookwell@vsnl.net
Hd.Org.: Surjeet S. Khurana

BOTANICAL SURVEY OF INDIA
CGO Complex, 3rd MSO Building, Block F (5th Floor), DF Block, Sector 1, Salt Lake City, Kolkata-700064 (West Bengal)
✆23584240, Fax: 91-33-23346040
✉ bsipubl@yahoo.com
🌐 www.bsi.gov.in
Dir.: M. Sanjappa; **Bus.Intt.:** Engaged in Research and Pub.; **Spl.:** Flora, Forestry, Conservation of Wildlife and Endangered Species

BOUDHBHARATI
J-13/93, A-5, Cotton Mill Colony, Varanasi-221002 (Uttar Pradesh)
✆ 2210094
✉ bauddhabhrti@satyam.net.in
Hd.Org.: Swami Dwarikadas Shastri; **Bus.Intt.:** B.S.; **Spl.:** Buddhism in Sanskrit, Hindi and Pali

BRAHASPATI PUBLICATIONS
D/4-C DDA, Flats Munirka, New Delhi-110067

BRAHMA KUMARIS ISHWARIYA VISHWAVIDYALAYA
19/17, Shakti Nagar, Delhi-110007

BRAIN MAPPING ACADEMY
16-11-16/1-B, Saleem Nagar, Makalpet, Hyderabad-500036 (Andhra Pradesh)
✆ 66135169, Fax: 91-11-24542215
✉ bmahyd@rediffmail.com
🌐 www.bmatalent.com
Hd.Org.: Kalluri Srinivas

BRAIN TREE
Hyderabad (Andhra Pradesh)
✆ 27644110
✉ braintreeindia@rediff.com

BRAJINDRA BOOK CO.
21, Chhoti Market, Model Town, Karnal-132001 (Haryana) ✆ 91-184-2266637
Hd.Org.: Kuldip Singh Kalra

BRAND VISION (INDIA) PVT. LTD.
103, Mittal Chambers, Nariman Point, Mumbai-400021 (Maharashtra)
✆ 56366662-63, 56314454 ▮ 9892192706, Fax: 22837214
✉ sniklje@usp-age.com
Circulation Man.: Shankar M. Nikalje

BRASPATI PUBLICATIONS
Sahitya Sangeet Sangam, D/4-C, DDA Flats, Munirka, New Delhi-110067

BRAZARK INFORMATION SYSTEM (P) LTD.
112, Humayunpur (Near NCC Office), Safdarjung Enclave, New Delhi-110029
✆ 26882366, Fax: 23269227
Hd.Org.: Prabhat Pandey, Bina Pandey; **Bus.Intt.:** Rt., L.S.

BREPO SYSTEM INDIA PVT. LTD.
10, Community Centre, 3rd Floor, Ashok Vihar, Phase-II, Delhi-110052
✆ 27432104, 27432629, Fax: 27451555
✉ brepo@vsnl.com
Ch.Exe.: Mr. Sanjeev Bhasin; **Bus.Intt.:** Pub.;

Spl.: Edu. Software which cover the syllabus of NCERT, CBSE, ICSE as well as All State Board

BRIGHT BOOK BUREAU
M-17-18, Shri Balaji Market, 2605, Nai Sarak, Delhi-110006
✆ 23273681, 55253169, Fax: 23273681
Prop.: Alok Bedi; **Bus.Intt.:** Rt., WS, L.S.; **Spl.:** Acad., Beh. Sci., Sci.-Pure & Applied, Med., Tech., Journal & Magazines

BRIGHT BOOK CO.
5-5, Chameliwala Market, M.I. Rd., Jaipur (Rajasthan)

BRIGHT BOOK SERVICE
C-41/17, Gali No. 1, Gamari Ext., Delhi-110053
✆ 22943390 ▮ 9818245758
Prt.: S.K. Sharma, J.K. Sharma; **Bus.Intt.:** L.S.; **Spl.:** Beh. Sci., Soc.Sci., Comm., Sci., Pure & Applied, Tech., Law

BRIGHT EDUCATIONALS
No. 10, Mohan Marg, Kewal Park, Azadpur, Delhi-110033
✆ 27231675, 27246022
Hd.Org.: Rajiv Kumar; **Spl.:** Innovative Teaching Aids, Pictorial Teaching Boards, Wooden Block Games, Children Books

BRIGHT GROUP OF PUBLICATIONS
4739/23, UGF, Ansari Road, Darya Ganj, New Delhi-110002
✆ 23283226, 23282226
Fax: 91-11-23269227
✉ editorial@brightpublications.com, sales@brightpublications.com
🌐 www.brightcareers.com
Estd.: 1968; **Hd.Org.:** P.S. Bright; **Bus.Intt.:** Pub.; **Spl.:** Competitions Refresher, Junior Sci. Refresher, Gen. Knowledge Refesher & Careers' Books

BRIGHT SPORTS
IVth Floor, Parkashdeep Building, 7th Tolstoy Marg, New Delhi-110001
✆ 55303278, Fax: 23327884
✉ tildelhi@vsnl.net
Bus.Intt.: B.S.

BRIJBASI ART PRESS LTD.
A-81, Sector-5, Noida-201301 (Uttar Pradesh)
✆ 2423846-48, Fax: 91-120-2420324
✉ brijbasi@airtelbroadband.in
🌐 www.brijbasiartpress.com
Bus.Intt: Pub. & B.S.

BRIJBASI PRINTERS PVT. LTD.
E-46/11, Okhla Indl. Area, Phase II, New Delhi-110020
✆ 26841897, 26314115
Fax: 91-11-26824230
Hd.Org.: M.L. Garg

BRIJESHWARI PRAKASHAN
B-51, Phase-II, Vivek Vihar-II, Delhi-110095
✆ 91-11-22381344
Hd.Org.: Rameshwari Devi

BRILLIANT EDUCATIONAL AIDS
D-25, Green Park, New Delhi-110016
✆ 26611073 ▮ 9811092425
✉ umaparikh24@hotmail.com
Hd.Org.: Uma Parikh; **Bus.Intt.:** Pub.; **Spl.:** Edu. Books and Material for Children

BRILLIANT SCIENCE ACADEMY
E-14/16, Vasant Vihar, New Delhi-110057

BRITISH BOOK DEPOT
Hazratganj, Lucknow (Uttar Pradesh)

BRITISH COUNCIL DIVISION
17, Kasturba Gandhi Marg, New Delhi-110001
✆ 23711401, Fax: 23710717
✉ info@in.britishcouncil.org
Hd.Org.: A.N. Sanderson
Br.: British Deputy High Commission, 737, Anna Salai, Chennai-600002 (Tamil Nadu)
✆ 28525005, Fax: 9144-28523234
✉ rootbodm.iitm.ernet.in
Bus.Intt.: Library and Information Services

BRITISH LIBRARY
Hyderabad (Andhra Pradesh)
✆ 23230774, Fax: 23298273
✉ bl.hyderabad@in.britishcouncil.org

BRITISH MEDICAL JOURNAL
C/o S.K. Medical Distributors, L-9, Sunder Singh Bldg., Mahipalpur, New Delhi-110037

BROWSER: THE BOOKSHOP
Chandigarh
✆ 607680
✉ thebrowser@glide.net.in

BUILDING BOOK SHOP
101-D, Kitchlu Nagar, Post Bag No. 1001, Ludhiana-141001 (Punjab)
✆ 2471771, 2670913, 2673928, 2676993
Estd.: 1968; **Hd.Org.:** Vidyasagar; **Bus.Intt.:** L.S. and Rt.; **Spl.:** Arch., Building and Quality Surveying in Hindi and English (Indian and Foreign Publications)

BULBUL PRAKASHAN
18-L, Tamer Lane, Kolkata-700009 (West Bengal)

BULSAR BOOK STORE
6/7, Gulmohar Aptt., Opp. Riddhi & Siddhi Aptt., Vasant Talkies, Valsad-396001 (Gujarat)

✆ (O) 254077, 222377 (R) 241027, 253909
✉ bbs_valsad@yahoo.com
Estd.: 1960; **Prt.:** Ashok Shah, Prateek Shah
Br.: C-2, Maheshwari Aptt., Opp. Maakhan Bhog, Timalyawad, Surat-395001
Bus.Intt.: B.S., L.S.; **Spl.:** Humanities, Soc. Sci., Tech., Mang., Art & Arch., Children & Gen.

BULUSU VENKATESHARALA
822-14 Gandhi Nagar, Kakinanda-533004 (Andhra Pradesh)

BURAPANI BOOK STALL
B. Chareli, Sonitpur (Assam)

BURAPANI BOOK STALL
Boarding Rd., Sibsagar (Assam)

BURAPANI BOOK STALL
Patsala, Barpeta (Assam)

BURDA INDIA AGENCY
B-5/132 Safdarjung Enclave, New Delhi-110029

BURDWAN SISKHAK SANSAD
4, After Avenue, Burdwan (West Bengal)

BUREAU FOR PROMOTION OF URDU
West Block 8, R.K. Puram-1, New Delhi-110006
✆ 2609746
Hd.Org.: Ms. Fehmida Begum; **Bus.Intt.:** Pub.; **Spl.:** All Sub. including Glossary in Urdu Encyclopedia and runs Calligraphy centres in the country

BURGUNDY INFOTECH
23, Sundernagar Market, New Delhi-110003
✆ 24354513/617, Fax: 24356489
✉ info@burgundyinfotech, sales@burgundyinfotech.com
Ch.Exe.: Dhruv Choudhrie; **Bus.Intt.:** Enterprise and Edu. Institution Software Solution

BUSINESS BOOK PUBLISHING HOUSE
13, Lakshmi, 17th Rd., Chembur, Mumbai-400071 (Maharashtra)

BUSINESS EXPLORER
6/17, Rajinder Nagar, Sector-2, Sahibabad-201005 (Uttar Pradesh)
✆ 2633137
Prop.: T.D. Bhalla

BUSINESS HORIZONS
G-59, Masjid Moth, Greater Kailash-II, New Delhi-110048
📱 9212061554, Fax: 91-11-41637296
✉ info@businesshorizons.com
🌐 www.businesshorizons.com
Hd.Org.: J.P.S. Kohli

BUTALA PUBLICATIONS
Opp. Surya Narayan Baugh, Raopura Rd., Baroda-390001 (Gujarat)
✆ 0265-2541820, Fax: 0265-2851963
Prop.: B.C. Butala; **Bus.Intt.:** Pub. and Exp.; **Spl.:** Indology in English

BUTALA PUBLICATIONS
New Delhi
✆ 23515310, Fax: 23514825
✉ butala@del.3.vsnl.net.in
Bus.Intt.: Exp.

BUTTERWORTH-HEINEMANN
G-2, Vardaan House, 7/28, Ansari Rd. Darya Ganj, New Delhi-110002
✆ 23282580, 23279256, Fax: 23282650
✉ bh_india@id.eth.net, bh_india@satyam.net.in
Hd.Org.: Ravindra Saxena; **Bus.Intt.:** Pub.; **Spl.:** Med., Engg., Tech. and Mang. in English

BUTTERWORTHS INDIA
14th, Floor Vijaya Building, 17, Bara Khamba Rd., New Delhi-110001
✆ 23739614, 23739616, 23326454
Fax: 23326456
✉ info@bworthsindia.com
🌐 www.butterworth_india.com
Estd.: 1997; **Gen.Man.:** Sudarshan Sharma; **Bus.Intt.:** Pub.; **Spl.:** Law

BUZME KHIZRE RAH
80, Ghaffar Manzil, St. No. 8, Jamia Nagar, New Delhi-110025
✆ 26844816, Fax: 26822414
✉ abbaszaidi84@rediffmail.com
Estd.: 1965; **Man.Dir.:** Dr. Khushal Zaidi; **Bus.intt.:** Pub.; **Spl.:** Urdu Language books for Children

BYWORD EDITORIAL CONSULTANTS
A-217, Somdatt Chambers I, Bhikaji Cama Place, New Delhi-110066
✆ 26180427, 51658883
Fax: 51658456
✉ byword@vsnl.com
Hd.Org.: Bandana Malhotra; **Bus.Intt.:** Editorial and Publishing Consultants; **Spl.:** Areas of Med. and Sci.

■ ■ ■

C. MALAGATTI
94, Sadashivanagar, "Shiva Chethana", 5th Cross, Belagavi (Karnataka)
Hd.Org.: C. Malagatti; **Bus.Intt.:** Pub.; **Spl.:** Gen. Books in Kannada

C. RAMAMURTHY
54/20, Viswanathan Rd., Sivakasi-626123 (Tamil Nadu)
✆ (O) & (R) 279567
Estd.: 1978; **Bus.Intt.:** Pub. and B.S.; **Spl.:** Grammar of Thoughts

C.B.H. PUBLICATIONS
51/4, Sri Ganesh North Amman Kovil Street, Kamraj Nagar, Nagercoil-629003 (Tamil Nadu)
91-4652-222813
Hd.Org.: M. Easwaran

C.B.S. PUBLISHERS & DISTRIBUTORS
4596/11A, 11, Darya Ganj, New Delhi-110002
✆ (O) 23271632, 23289259 (R) 22303431, 22517735 ▮ 9810310858, Telefax: 91-11-23276712
✉ cbspubs@del3.vsnl.net.in
🌐 www.cbspd.com
Estd.: 1983; **Prt.:** Satish Kumar Jain, Smt. Shanti Devi, Smt. Saroj Jain, Smt. Manju Jain
Sh.: 4819/XI, Prahlad St., 24, Ansari Rd., Darya Ganj, New Delhi-110002
✆ (O) 23289259, 23266861, 23266867, 23266838 (R) 22308078, Fax: 23271632
Bus.Intt.: Pub., WS, L.S. & Rt., Imp., Exp.; **Spl.:** Engg. and Tech., Sci., Med., Humanities, Soc.Sci., Gen. and Reference

C.B.T. BOOK SHOP
G-14, Kamalalaya Centre, 156-A, Lenin Sarani, Kolkata-700013 (West Bengal)
✆ 2265094

C.B.T. BOOK SHOP
18C, Rayala Towers, 781 Mount Rd., Chennai-600002 (Tamil Nadu)
✆ 28521850

C.C.H. (A WOLTERS KLUWER BUSINESS)
202, Second Floor, Unit No. 4, Plot No. 7 & 8, Vardhman Trade Centre, Nehru Place, New Delhi-110019
✆ 46530300, Fax: 91-11-46530399
✉ vinay.singh@wolterskluwer.com
🌐 www.cchindia.co.in
Hd.Org.: Jonathan Seifman

C.D. POINT
B-126, Sadatpur, Karawal Nagar Road, Delhi-110094
Hd.Org.: Sunil Jha

C.D. ROM
17A/53, Gurudwara Rd., Karol Bagh, New Delhi-110005
✆ 41040428, Fax: 91-11-28755446
✉ sales@cdrom.india.com
🌐 www.cdrom-india.com
Hd.Org.: Gaurav Gupta; **Bus.Intt.:** Pub. and Dist.; **Spl.:** CD-ROMs on Rel.

C.I.C.C. BOOK HOUSE
Press Club Rd., Ernakulam, Cochin-682001 (Kerala)
✆ (O) 2353557, 2355658 (R) 2315295
Estd.: 1962; **Prop.:** V. Parameswaran; **Bus.Intt.:** Pub. and B.S.; **Spl.:** Gen. Books and Translation

C.L.E.O. MARKETING NETWORK
H-8, IDPL Apts., Rd. No. 44, Pitampura, New Delhi-110034

C.L.S.
M.C. Rd., Opp. College Ground, Ernakulam, Kochi-682011 (Kerala)

C.L.S. BOOK SHOP
Cross Junction, M.C. Rd., Thiruvalla-689101 (Kerala)

C.L.S. BOOK SHOP
Pulimood, M.G. Rd., Thiruvananthapuram-695001 (Kerala)
Estd.: 1984; **Hd.Org.:** Christian Litt. Society Chennai; **Bus.Intt.:** Pub. and B.S.

C.M. PUBLISHERS & DISTRIBUTORS
56A/1, Circular Rd., Shahdara, Delhi-110032

C.M.S. COLLEGE (PUB. DIVISION)
Kottayam-686001 (Kerala)

C.P.I. (M) PUBLICATIONS
New Delhi
✆ 23711870
✉ cpim@vsnl.com
Bus.Intt.: Pub.

C.P.M. DISTRIBUTORS
Navjivan Complex, Lamington Rd., Mumbai-400008 (Maharashtra)
✆ 23092282, 23094386, Fax: 23098587
✉ meetac@giasbma.vsnl.net.in

C.P.R. ENVIRONMENTAL EDUCATION CENTRE
1, Eldams Rd., Alwarpet, Chennai-600018 (Tamil Nadu)

C.P.R.I. BOOK STORE
Central Potato Research Institute, Shimla-171001 (Himachal Pradesh)
✆ 2624830, Fax: 2624460
✉ library@cpri.hp.nic.in
Estd.: 1982; **Incharge**: S.R. Yadava; **Bus.Intt.:** Pub., WS, L.S. & Rt., Imp., Sub.Ag.; **Spl.:** Sci. & Tech.

C.R. BOOK DEPOT
2709, Bank St., Karol Bagh, New Delhi-110005
✆ 25728959
Bus.Intt.: B.S.; **Spl.:** Gen. Children and Text Books

C.R. COMPETITION REFRESHER (P) LTD.
2767, Bright House, Darya Ganj, New Delhi-110002
✆ 23282226/27, Fax: 23269227
✉ psbright@ndb.vsnl.net.in
Bus.Intt.: Pub.

C.R.C. PRESS
New No. 8, Old No. 32, Second Main Rd., CIT Nagar, East, Chennai-600035 (Tamil Nadu)
✆ 24346244, 24346266, Fax: 24346529
✉ itpsesha@giasmd01.vsnl.net.in
Hd.Org.: R. Seshadri; **Bus.Intt.:** Pub.; **Spl.:** Sci. and Tech. in English

C.S. POCHEE & SONS
Mumbai (Maharashtra)
✆ 28166135, 28726965
✉ ranjan@bom5.vsnl.net.in

C.S.I.R.
(Publications & Information Directorate)
Dr. K.S. Krishna Marg, New Delhi-110012
✆ 25746024, 25728385, Fax: 25731353, Telex: 031-77271 PID IN
✉ paid@sirnetd.ernet.in
Dir.: Dr. G.P. Phondke; **Bus.Intt.:** Collection and Dissemination of the information; **Spl.:** Sci. and Tech.

CADPLAN PUBLISHER AND DISTRIBUTORS
D-278/1, Okhla, Jamia Nagar, New Delhi-110025
✆ 26985103 ▮ 9811208332
Mailing Add.: Z-326/3, Okhla Main Rd., Jamia Nagar, Okhla, New Delhi-110025
Estd.: 1996; **Prop.:** Javed Khan; **Bus.Intt.:** Pub., L.S. & Rt.; **Spl.:** Acad., Soc.Sci., Sci., Pure & Applied, Tech. Books

CALCUTTA ASTROLOGICAL RESEARCH CENTRE
6A, Shyama Charan Dey St., Kolkata-700073 (West Bengal)

CALCUTTA BOOK HOUSE
1/1, Bankim Chaterjee St., Kolkata-700073 (West Bengal)
✆ (O) 22410965 (R) 24665946
Estd.: 1937; **Hd.Org.:** Chanchal Bhowal; **Bus.Intt.:** Pub.

CALCUTTA PUBLISHERS
14, Ramanath Majumder St., Kolkata-700009 (West Bengal)

CALENDAR MAKERS CORPN.
A-16, Naraina-II, New Delhi-110028
✆ 25704450, 25704451, 25704452, Fax: 25700644, Telex: 031-77122
Bus.Intt.: Exp.

CALICUT UNIVERSITY CENTRAL CO. STORES LTD.
No. 4347, Calicut University, Kozhikode-673635 (Kerala)
✆ 264075
Estd.: 1980; **Hd.Org.:** Co-Operative Society; **Bus.Intt.:** Pub. and B.S.

CAMBRIDGE BOOK DEPOT
3, Regal Building, Parliament St., New Delhi-110001
✆ 23363395, 23348805, Fax: 25546260
✉ cambridgebooks@hotmail.com
Ch.Exe.: Ms. Ranjana Bajaj; **Bus.Intt.:** WS & Rt.; **Spl.:** Collection of Books which are available with all the Leading Book Stores

CAMBRIDGE BOOK & STATIONERY CO.
20-D, Park St., Kolkata-700016 (West Bengal)
✆ 2299017

CAMBRIDGE PUBLISHING HOUSE
D-36, South Extension Part-I, New Delhi-110049
✆ 24619125, Fax: 24634935
✉ ragupta@ndb.vsnl.net.in, galgotia@ndf.vsnl.net.in
Estd.: 1965; **Prop.:** Arun Kumar Gupta; **Bus.Intt.:** Pub.; **Spl.:** Children Books

CAMBRIDGE UNIVERSITY PRESS INDIA PVT. LTD.
4381/4, Ansari Rd., Darya Ganj, New Delhi-110002
✆ 43543500, Fax: 91-11-23288534
✉ cup@cupind.com, cupdel@cupind.com
www.cambridgeindia.org
Estd.: 1534; **Country Man.:** Manas Saikia
Br.: 4764/2A, 23, Ansari Rd., Darya Ganj, New Delhi-110002 ✆ 23277332, 23285851, 23285852 ✉ cupdel@cupind.com
• C-22, C-Block Brigade MM, KR Rd. Jayanagar, Bangalore-560082 ✆ 26762764, Fax: 26761322, ✉ cupbang@cupind.com
• Plot No. 80, Service Industries, Shirvane Sector-1, Nerul Navi, Mumbai (Maharashtra) ✆ 27709172, Fax: 27709173,

cupmum@cupind.com
Bus.Intt.: Pub., WS, L.S. & Rt., Imp., Exp., Sub.Ag.; **Spl.:** Humanities & Soc.Sci., Sci. & Tech., Med., Law, Juvenile/Children, Gen. & Fiction etc.

CAMLIN LTD.
101, Satya Mansion, Ranjeet Nagar, Comp. Complex, New Delhi-110008

CAMPUS BOOK SHOP
P.O. Box 1254, Indian Institute of Sciences, Bangalore-12 (Karnataka)

CAMPUS BOOKS INTERNATIONAL
4831/24, Prahlad Street, Ansari Road, Darya Ganj, New Delhi-110002
✆ 23272541, Fax: 91-11-23257835
campusbooks@hotmail.com
Hd.Org.: Krishna Verma

CANDID MULTIMEDIA PVT. LTD.
C/o Mr. S. Mukherjee, H-157, Chittaranjan Park, New Delhi-110019

CANFED
Saksharatha Bhavan, Thiruvananthapuram (Kerala)

CAPITAL BOOK AGENCY
Pocket B-6, Flats No. 26-D, Mayur Vihar, Phase-III, Delhi-110091
✆ 35801198
Prop.: Mrs. Pratima Sharma; **Bus.Intt.:** Rt., L.S.; **Spl.:** Acad., Beh.Sci., Sci., Tech. Books

CAPITAL BOOK AGENCY
D-21, B, East Vinod Nagar, Delhi-110091

CAPITAL BOOK CENTRE
Shop No. 11, Narain Bazar, 10 Lalbagh, Lucknow-226001 (Uttar Pradesh)
✆ (O) 2231376 (R) 2627373 ▮ 3110212
Hd.Org.: A.A. Siddiqui; **Bus.Intt.:** B.S., General Order Suppliers; **Spl.:** Law (Indian & Foreign)

CAPITAL BOOK DEPOT
S.C.O. 3, Sector 17E, Chandigarh-160017
✆ 2702260, 2702594, Fax: 0712-2702594
ajayacbd@ch.1.vsnl.net.in
Estd.: 1952; **Man.:** Ajay Arora; **Bus.Intt.:** Rt., L.S., WS; **Spl.:** All types of Books/Publications in Indian and Foreign

CAPITAL FOUNDATION SOCIETY
A-43-D, Munirka Flats, New Delhi-110067

CAPITAL PUBLISHING COMPANY PVT. LTD.
7/28, Mahaveer St., Ansari Rd. Darya Ganj, New Delhi-110002
✆ 23284197, 23288719, Fax: 91-11-41562932
capitalb@capital-publishing.com
www.capital-publishing.com
Estd.: 1989; **Man.Dir.:** Raj D. Mirchandani
Br.: 5B, Chowringhee Lane, 1st Floor, Flat No.1H (Part), Kolkata-700016 (West Bengal)
✆ 033-22260745
capitalbookskol@yahoo.com
• 718/1, VI Main Hanumantha Nagar, Bangalore-560019 (Karnataka)
✆ 080-6676198, vadana69@yahoo.com
Bus.Intt.: Pub., WS, L.S. & Rt., Imp.; **Spl.:** Sci. & Tech., Med.

CAPITAL PUBLISHING HOUSE
358, Katra Sheikh Ranjha, Hauz Qazi, Delhi-110006

CAPITAL STUDENTS STORE
145, Ashok Nagar, Bhubaneshwar (Orissa)
✆ (O) 0764-2407813 (R) 255549
Estd.: 1975; **Prop.:** Bipin Charan Dash; **Bus.Intt.:** Rt.; **Spl.:** Books for Schools and Guides for competitive examinations in Oriya

CAPITAL TRADING COMPANY
Near Lalaji Bhavan, 294, Choura Rasta, Jaipur-302003 (Rajasthan)
✆ (O) 2566720 (R) 2520579
Hd.Org.: Kailash Gupt

CARE & CURE INTERNATIONAL LTD.
A-56/A, First Floor, Lajpat Nagar-II, New Delhi-110024
✆ 29844012, Fax: 29847741
carecure@nde.vsnl.net.in, care@carecure.com
Hd.Org.: M.D. Kanther; **Spl.:** Consultant for Providing Research, Training and Database Information on Alternative Therapies, etc.

CAREER PLAN
2nd Floor, 2514, Hudson Lines, Kingsway Camp, Delhi
✆ 27115656, 31012386
delhi@careerplanindia.com
Hd.Org.: Prashant Joshi; **Spl.:** Books for MBA Additional Test GRE and GMAT Tests

CAREER PUBLICATIONS
B-14, Vitthal Park, Samant Wadi, Nashik-422002 (Maharashtra)
✆ 2311422, Fax: 91-253-2318030
publications@careerandyou.com
www.careerandyou.com
Hd.Org.: Nishad R. Deshmukh

CAREERS DIGEST PUBLICATIONS
21, Shanker Market, New Delhi-110001
✆ 23314726
Estd.: 1992; **Hd.Org.:** Vikram Verma, Sammet, Rakheja

CARMEL BOOK STALL
Carmel Buildings, Banerji Rd., Kochi-682018 (Kerala)

✆ 2363590
Estd.: 1975; **Hd.Org.:** Sebastian Indanthuruthil; **Bus.Intt.:** B.S.

CARMEL BOOK STORES
Patna Women's College Campus, Bailey Rd., Patna-800001 (Bihar)
Bus.Intt.: Pub. and B.S.

CARMEL PUBLISHING CENTRE
St. Joseph's Press Buildings, Thiruvananthapuram-695014 (Kerala)
✆ 262888, 262956, 264404,
Telex: 0435-465 SJP IN
Estd.: 1980; **Hd.Org.:** Rockose Kolenchery; **Bus.Intt.:** Pub. and B.S.

CARTOON PRAKASHANEE
Kolkata (West Bengal)
✆ 24155744, 24152822, Fax: 4157443
✉ saras-cartoon@hotmail.com
Bus.Intt.: Pub. & B.S.

CASSETTES & BOOKS
37-A, Guru Nanak Marg, Kewal Park Extn., Azadpur, Delhi-110033
✆ 27242264

CASTLE BOOKS PVT. LTD.
IInd Floor, Jindal Trust Building, 1/8-B Asaf Ali Rd., New Delhi-110002

CAUSEWAY BOOK CENTRE
H. No. H/12, Jagatpuri, Delhi-110051
Prop.: S. Kayamraza; **Bus.Intt.:** Rt., L.S.

CAXTON PRINTERS
Hyderabad (Andhra Pradesh)
✉ caxton1@hd2.dot.net.in
Bus.Intt.: Printers & Pub.

CENGAGE LEARNING
56, Janpath, First Floor, Alps Building, New Delhi-110001
✆ 30484835, Fax: 91-11-30484834
✉ alok.srivastava@cengage.com
🌐 www.cengage.com
Hd.Org.: Alok Srivastava

CENTAX PUBLICATIONS PVT. LTD.
1522-B, Bisham Pitamah Marg, Opp. ICICI Bank, Defence Colony, New Delhi-110003
✆ 24693001, 24611224, Fax: 24635243
✉ centax@del2.vsnl.net.in
Hd.Org.: R.K. Jain; **Bus.Intt.:** Pub. & B.S.; **Spl.:** Excise and Customs

CENTRAL BOARD OF IRRIGATION AND POWER
Publication Department, Malcha Marg, Chanakyapuri, New Delhi-110021
✆ 26875017, 26870117, Fax: 26116347
✉ cbip@nda.vsnl.net.in
Bus.Intt.: Pub.; **Spl.:** Reports

CENTRAL BOOK AGENCY
Opposite Main Gate, Punjabi University, Patiala-147002 (Punjab)
✆ (O) 0175-2283292 (R) 2229642
Estd.: 1990; **Hd.Org.:** Vinod Kumar Madan; **Bus.Intt.:** B.S. and L.S.; **Spl.:** Adv. Books for Lib., Gen. Books and Tech.

CENTRAL BOOK HOUSE
Sadar Bazar, Raipur-492001 (Madhya Pradesh)
✆ 2534150
Hd.Org.: Anil Chawla

CENTRAL BOOK PUBLISHERS
8/1, Chintamoni Das Lane, Kolkata-9 (West Bengal)
Hd.Org.: Jamini Kanta Sen

CENTRAL BOOK STALL
Rani Jhansi Square, Sitabuldi, Nagpur-440012 (Maharashtra)
✆ 2526191, Fax: 0712-2555213
Estd.: 1963; **Hd.Org.:** S.G. Mangesh Mujumdar; **Bus.Intt.:** B.S. and L.S.; **Spl.:** Tech., Humanities, Sci.

CENTRAL BOOK STORES
Barh R.S., Patna-803214 (Bihar)
Bus.Intt.: Pub. and B.S.

CENTRAL CHINMAYA MISSION TRUST
Sandeepany Sadhanalaya, Saki Vihar Rd., Mumbai-400072 (Maharashtra)
✆ 28572367, 28575806, Fax: 28573065
✉ ccmt@vsnl.com
🌐 www.chinmayamission.com
Estd.: 1964; **Prop.:** Swami Tejomayananda; **Bus.Intt.:** Pub., WS, Exp.

CENTRAL COUNCIL FOR RESEARCH IN UNANI MEDICAL
61-65 Institutional Area, Janakpuri, New Delhi-110058
✆ 25611982

CENTRAL EDUCATIONAL ENTERPRISE
54B, Patuatola Lane, Kolkata-700009 (West Bengal)
Hd.Org.: Amitabha Sen

CENTRAL HINDI DIRECTORATE
West Block No. 7, R.K. Puram, New Delhi-110066
✆ 26105211, 26105212, 26109113, Fax: 26103160, 26100758
Hd.Org.: Pushpa Lata Taneja; **Bus.Intt.:** Pub.; **Spl.:** Bi-lingual and Multi-lingual Dictionaries

CENTRAL INLAND CAPTURE
Fisheries Research Institute, (Indian Council for Agricultural Research), Barrackpore-743101 (West Bengal)

CENTRAL INSTITUTE OF HIGHER TIBETAN STUDIES
Sarnath, Varanasi-221007 (Uttar Pradesh)

CENTRAL INSTITUTE OF HINDI
Hindi Sansthan Marg, Agra-282005 (Uttar Pradesh)
✆ 2530683-4, Fax: 91-562-2530684, 2530159
www.hindi.nic.in
Hd.Org.: Nityanand Pandey; **Bus.Intt.:** Pub.; **Spl.:** Hindi Books on Litt., Language and Linguistics, and also a Half-yearly Magazine, *Gaveshana*

CENTRAL INSTITUTE OF INDIAN LANGUAGES
Manasagangotri, Mysore-570006 (Karnataka)
✆ 2345040, Fax: 81-821-2515032
chandrashekar@ciil.stpmy.soft.net
www.ciil.org
Estd.: 1969; **Hd.Org.:** Udya Narayana Singh; **Bus.Intt.:** Pub.; **Spl.:** Textbooks, Research Monographs in Linguistics and Allied Disciplines in Indian Languages

CENTRAL LAW PUBLICATIONS
107, Darbhanga Colony, Allahabad-211002 (Uttar Pradesh)
Bus.Intt.: Pub.; **Spl.:** Law Books

CENTRAL LIBRARY
15/3, Shyama Charan Dey St., Kolkata-700073 (West Bengal)

CENTRAL NEWS AGENCY PVT. LTD.
P-23, Connaught Circus, New Delhi-110001
✆ (O) 23364448, 23364478, 23364508 (R) 26484703, Fax: 23626036
info@cna-india.com, nita@cna-india.com
www.cna-india.com
Estd.: 1933; **Chairman:** R.P. Puri; **Bus.Intt.:** B.S., Newspaper & Magazine Dist., Sub.Ag., Exp.; **Spl.:** Soc.Sci., Med. & Tech., Journals

CENTRAL PUBLISHERS
14, Ramanath Majumder St., Kolkata-700009 (West Bengal)

CENTRAL PUBLISHING CONCERN
8/1, Chintamoni Das Lane, Kolkata-700009 (West Bengal)

CENTRAL REFERENCE LIBRARY
Belvedere, Alipore, Kolkata-700027 (West Bengal)
✆ 24791721-22, Fax: 91-33-24791723
crlinb@cal.3.vsnl.net.in
www.crlindia.gov.in

CENTRAL WOMEN'S DEVELOPMENT STUDIES
25, Bhai Vir Singh Marg, Gole Market, New Delhi-110001

CENTRASIA PUBLISHING GROUP
B-C-48, Shalimar Bagh (West), Delhi-110052

CENTRE FOR AMBEDKAR AND DALIT LITERATURE
C-263-A, Chandan Sadan, Hardev Puri, Delhi-110093
✆ 22270380, Fax: 22270380
gautambookcentre@hotmail.com
Hd.Org.: Savitri Devi; **Bus.Intt.:** Pub.; **Spl.:** Sol., Hist., Ambedkar and Dalits

CENTRE FOR CULTURAL RESOURCES AND TRAINING
Plot No. 15-A, Sector-7, Pappankalan, Dwarka, New Delhi-110045
✆ 25074252/54/58, 25088630, Fax: 91-11-25088637
skdgccrt@del3.vsnl.net.in
Ch.Exe.: Mr. Surendra Kaul; **Bus.Intt.:** Pub.; **Spl.:** Arts and Crafts of India are being widely used for Cultural Edu. and Audio-visual Material

CENTRE FOR EDUCATION AND DOCUMENTATION
3, Suleman Chambers, 4 Battery St., Mumbai-400001 (Maharashtra)
✆ 22020019

CENTRE FOR ENTREPRENEURSHIP DEVP.
Bhopal (Madhya Pradesh)
✆ 2766461, 2766437, 2574772, Fax: 2763401
cedmap@vsnl.com
Bus.Intt.: Pub.

CENTRE FOR INDUSTRIAL & ECONOMIC RESEARCH
7, Community Centre, East of Kailash, New Delhi-110065
✆ (O) 26432335 (R) 26466824, Fax: 26440866
Exe.Dir.: S.R. Mohnot, **Bus.Intt.:** Research, Consultancy and Publication

CENTRE FOR RESEARCH IN RURAL & INDUSTRIAL DEVELOPMENT
2-A, Sector 19-A, Madhya Marg, Chandigarh-160019

CENTRE FOR RESEARCH PLANNING & ACTION (CERPA)
16, Dakshneshwar, 10, Hailey Rd., New Delhi-110001

CENTRE FOR SCIENCE AND ENVORONMENT
141, Institutional Area, Tughlakabad, New Delhi-110062
✆ 26981110, 26981124, Fax: 26985879
cse@cseindia.org
Bus.Intt.: Pub.

CENTRE FOR STUDIES IN CIVILIZATIONS
DD-24, Kalkaji, New Delhi-110019
✆ 26227831-36, Fax: 91-11-26227836
csc@del2.vsnl.net.in
Hd.Org.: D.P. Chattopadhyaya

CENTRE FOR STUDIES IN SCIENCE
A1-Homera Muzzammil, Manzil Complex, Dodhpur Rd., Aligarh-202002 (Uttar Pradesh)

CENTRE FOR THE DEVELOPMENT OF ENVIRONMENT AND RESOURCES
New Delhi
✆ 26804269
✉ suhasini@bol.net.in
Bus.Intt.: B.S.

CENTRE FOR YOUTH AND SOCIAL DEVELOPMENT
A-70, Sahib Nagar, Bhubaneshwar-751007 (Orissa)

CENTURY PUBLICATIONS
46, Masih Garh, New Friends Colony, Community Centre, New Delhi-110025
✆ 91-11-20281355
✉ centurypublications@hotmail.com
Hd.Org.: Smt. Jai Pali; **Bus.Intt.:** Pub.; **Spl.:** Med., Soc.Sci. and Humanities

CHAITANYA BHARATI
Barh R.S., Patna-803214 (Bihar)
Bus.Intt.: Pub. and B.S.

CHAITANYA BOOKS
32-A, Kamla Nagar, Delhi-110007
✆ 23840735, 232406469
Estd.: 2003; **Prop.:** Ms. Renu Mittal; **Bus.Intt.:** L.S.; **Spl.:** Acad., Beh.Sci., Soc.Sci., Comm., Sci., Med., Tech., Fiction, Juveniles, Rare, Journals & Magazines, Law

CHAITANYA PUBLISHING HOUSE
University Rd., Allahabad-221002 (Uttar Pradesh)

CHAKRABORTY & CO.
34, Prem Chand Boral St., Kolkata-12 (West Bengal)

CHAKRABORTY & CO.
8/C, Tamer Lane, Kolkata-700009 (West Bengal)

CHAKRABORTY & SONS
30/1B, College Row, Kolkata-700009 (West Bengal)

CHALANTIKA PRAKASHAK
4, College Row, Kolkata-700009 (West Bengal)
Hd.Org.: Sisir Bindu Chowdhury

CHALAVAT BOOK DEPOT
208, Khajuri Bazar, Indore-452002 (Madhya Pradesh)

CHAMPA LAL RANKA & CO.
1-GA-4, Jawahar Nagar, Jaipur-302004 (Rajasthan)
✆ 2654202, 2654155
✉ iranka@datainfosys.net
Estd.: 1964; **Prop.:** C.L. Ranka
Sh.: Dhamani Market, Chaura Rasta, Jaipur (Rajasthan) ✆ 2316241
Bus.Intt.: Pub.; **Spl.:** English, Hindi and Sanskrit in Rajasthani

CHANAKYA BOOK HOUSE
RZ-23B/335, Jagdamba Vihar, West Sagarpur, New Delhi-110046
✆ 25560039, 25506748
Estd.: 1992; **Hd.Org.:** Dilip Kumar Partner; **Bus.Intt.:** Pub., L.S. and Rt.

CHANAKYA CIVIL SERVICES TODAY
A/42-44, Manushree Building, Commercial Complex, Dr. Mukherjee Nagar, Delhi-110009
✆ 27653240, 27653242, Fax: 27652337
✉ ccst@chanakya-iasacademy.com
Hd.Org.: A.K. Mishra; **Bus.Intt.:** Pub.; **Spl.:** Journal for Competitive Examinations

CHAND BOOK DEPOT
Opp. Wheeler Senate Hall, Ashok Rajpath, Patna-800006 (Bihar)
Bus.Intt.: Pub. and B.S.

CHANDA BOOK DEPOT
Arya Kumar Rd., Machuatoli, Patna-800004 (Bihar)
Bus.Intt.: Pub. and B.S.

CHANDA MAMA INDIA LTD
JVL Plaza, Block A, 6th Floor, 626 (Old No. 501) Anna Salai Teynampet, Chennai-600018 (Tamil Nadu)
✆ 91-44-24322101
Hd.Org.: T.N. Ravi Shanker

CHANDAN BOOK STORE
Barh R.S., Patna-803214 (Bihar)
Bus.Intt.: Pub. and B.S.

CHANDAN PUSTAK BHANDAR
Gouripur, Jhandapur, Bhagalpur-853201 (Bihar)
Bus.Intt.: Pub. and B.S.

CHANDERMUKHI PRAKASHAN
E-578 Main Rd., Jagjit Nagar, Delhi-110053
✆ 22185874

CHANDI CHARAN BHOWMICK & BROS.
131, Raja S.C. Mallick Rd., Kolkata-47 (West Bengal)

CHANDNA BOOK HOUSE
Opp. Guru Teg Bahadur Complex, T.T. Nagar, Bhopal-462003 (Madhya Pradesh)
✆ 2554269, 3130992, Fax: 0755-2771828
✉ chandnabookhouse@hotmail.com

Estd.: 1976; **Prop.:** P.K. Chandna; **Bus.Intt.:** Rt. and L.S.; **Spl.:** Sci. & Tech.

CHANDRA PROKASH
Jasawanta Rd., Panbazar, Guwahati-781001 (Assam)

CHANDRA PRAKASHAN
A-166, Suraj Kund Colony, Gorakhpur-273015 (Uttar Pradesh)

CHANDRAKALA PUSTAK BHANDAR
Pirpainti, Bhagalpur-813209 (Bihar)
Bus.Intt.: Pub. and B.S.

CHANDRALOK PRAKASHAN
128/106, G. Block, Kidwai Nagar, Kanpur-208011 (Uttar Pradesh)
✆ 2616348
Estd.: 1991; **Bus.Intt.:** Pub.; **Spl.:** Hindi Gen. Books

CHANNEL PUBLICATIONS
Plot No. 45, Sector-29, Faridabad-121008
✆ 0129-25272022, Fax: 0129-25272284
✉ channelpub@hotmail.com
Estd.: 1999; **Prop.:** K.K. Lijhara; **Bus.Intt.:** Pub., Rt., L.S.; **Spl.:** Acad. Books

CHANSUN INTERNATIONAL
B-89, Malviya Nagar, New Delhi-110017
✆ 26417235
Estd.: 1991; **Ch.Exe.:** Rajinder Arora
Br.: Room 6, Hotel Asian Intel., Janpath Lane, New Delhi-110001
✆ 23713042, 23324690; Fax: 23323077

CHAPTER AND VERSE
200, Gera Plaza, First Floor No. 10, Boat Club Rd., Pune (Maharashtra)
✆ 26137870, Fax: 26137870
✉ candv@pn3.vsnl.net.in
Bus.Intt.: Pub., Rt. and Exp.

CHARNOCK'S COCKTAIL PUBLICATION
28/1, Shakespeare Sarani, 27-A, Ganga Jamuna Building, Kolkata-17 (West Bengal)

CHAROTAR PUBLISHING HOUSE
Opposite Amul Dairy, Civil Court Rd., P.B. No. 65, Anand, Kaira-388001 (Gujarat)
✆ (O) 02692-256237, 240089 (R) 244422, Fax: 02692-240089
✉ charotar@icenet.net, charotar@cphbooks.com
www.cphbooks.com
Estd.: 1944; **Prop.:** Ramanbhai C. Patel
Br.: Charotar Book Distributors, Opposite Amul Dairy, Court Rd., Anand, Kaira-388001 (Gujarat) ✆ 02692-256237, Fax: 240089
• Pradeep Publications, Civil Court Rd., Anand, Kaira-388001 ✆ 256237
• Rupalee Publications, Court Rd., Anand, Kaira-388001 ✆ 256237
• Charotar Associates, Court Rd., Anand, Kaira-388001 ✆ 256237
• Charotar Book Stall, Near Post Office, Vallabh Vidyanagar-388120 ✆ 232499
Bus.Intt.: Pub., WS, L.S. & Rt.; **Spl.:** Sci., Tech. & Med., Trade, Gen. (Incl. Lit. & Art)

CHARU PRAKASH
7A, College Row, Kolkata-700009 (West Bengal)

CHASVIK TRADES
2591, Hudson Lines, GTB Nagar, Delhi-110009
✆ 27132897, 27132902, Fax: 27137735
✉ chasvik@vsnl.com
Estd.: 1985; **Man.Prt.:** Kiran Kr. Arora; **Bus.Intt.:** Pub., B.S., L.S., WS and Exp.

CHATRA MAHAL
Arambag, Hooghly (West Bengal)

CHATTERJEE BOOK STALL
225/N, Sodepur Ist Lane, Thakurpukur, Haridevpur, Kolkata-700082 (West Bengal)

CHATTERJEE PUBLISHERS
15, Bankim Chatterjee St., Kolkata-700073 (West Bengal)

CHATTOPADHYAY BROTHERS
1/1/1A & B, Bankim Chatterjee St., Kolkata-700073 (West Bengal)

CHATURMUKH PRAKASHAN
23/1, College Row, Kolkata-700009 (West Bengal)

CHATWANI & SHAH PVT. LTD.
Zaver Baug, Rajarshi Shahu Maharaj Rd., Telli Galli, Andheri East, Mumbai-400069 (Maharashtra)
✆ 28343107, 28348739, 28343051, Fax: 022-28362974, Telex: 011-79172-RITA
Bus.Intt.: Exp.; **Spl.:** Books, Newspapers, Magazines, Journals etc.

CHAUKHAMBA ORIENTALIA
P.B. No. 2206, 9-UB, Bungalow Rd., Jawahar Nagar (Near Kirorimal College), Delhi-110007
✆ 91-11-23851617, 23858790
Estd.: 1892; **Hd.Org.:** Braj Pal Das Gupta; **Bus.Intt.:** Pub. and B.S.; **Spl.:** *Vedas, Puranas* and Books on Indology, Astrology, Ayurveda, etc. in Regional Languages

CHAUKHAMBA PUBLISHING HOUSE
4697/2, Street No. 21-A, Ansari Road, Darya Ganj, New Delhi-110002
✆ 32996391, Fax: 91-11-23286537
✉ chaukhamba@gmail.com
Hd.Org.: N.D. Gupta

CHAUKHAMBA SANSKRIT BHAWAN
P.B. No. 1160 Chowk,
(Bank of Baroda Building),
Varanasi-221001 (Uttar Pradesh)
✆ 91-542-2420414, 2404920
Estd.: 1915; **Hd.Org.:** Brajendra Kumar; **Bus.Intt.:** Pub.; **Spl.:** Sanskrit, Ayurveda, Indology

CHAUKHAMBA VIDYA BHAWAN
P.B. No. 69, Behind Banaras State Bank Building, Chowk, Varanasi-221001 (Uttar Pradesh)
✆ 2320404
@ cvbhawan@satyam.net.in
Bus.Intt.: B.S. and Pub.

CHAUKHAMBHA AMAR BHARATI
K-27/130, Gopal Mandir Lane, PB No. 138, Varanasi-221001 (Uttar Pradesh)

CHAUKHAMBHA PUBLICATIONS
4262/3, Ansari Rd., Darya Ganj,
New Delhi-110002
✆ 23268639, 23259050, Fax: 23268639
@ chaukhambha@mantraonline.com
Estd.: 1893; **Prt.:** Ritesh Gupta, Jitesh Gupta; **Bus.Intt.:** WS & Pub.; **Spl.:** Sanskrit, Ayurveda & Indo-logical Books

CHAUKHAMBHA SANSKRIT PRATISTHAN
38-UA, Bungalow Rd., Jawahar Nagar,
Delhi-110007
✆ 23856391, Fax: 91-11-41530902
@ csp_praveen@rediffmail.com
Estd.: 1984; **Hd.Org.:** J.D. Gupta; **Bus.Intt.:** Pub. and Dist.; **Spl.:** Ayurveda and Indology in English, Hindi and Sanskrit

CHAUKHAMBHA SANSKRIT SERIES OFFICE
K-37/99, Gopal Mandir Lane, Varanasi-121001 (Uttar Pradesh)
✆ 2333458
@ cssoffice@satyam.net.in
www.chowkhambaseries.com
Hd.Org.: Brajmohan Das Gupta;
Bus.Intt.: Pub.; **Spl.:** Indian Culture, Rel., Astrology etc.

CHAWALA BOOK DEPOT
Sector-3 Market, R.K. Puram,
New Delhi-110022
✆ 2674383, 2679400, 2674501, 26884849
Hd.Org.: Rakesh Kumar; **Bus.Intt.:** Pub. and B.S.; **Spl.:** School and Children Books in English and Hindi

CHAWLA PUBLICATIONS (P) LTD.
S.C.O. 4-5, 2nd Floor, Sector-17B
(Behind K.C. Theatre), Chandigarh-160017
✆ 0172-2705335, 2704445, 2715790
▮ 9815013186
Estd.: 1969; **Dir.:** Bhagat Jit Singh
Bus.Intt.: Pub; **Spl.:** Law Book and Law Journals for Advocates and Judiciary in English

CHAYAN PRAKASHAN
Dhobi Dhora, Hanuman Hattha,
Bikaner-334001 (Rajasthan)
✆ 2537099
Estd.: 1983; **Prop.:** Ram Kishan Chouhan; **Bus.Intt.:** Pub., B.S., L.S., WS, Dist.; **Spl.:** Sci. & Tech., Comp., Med., Mang., Law, Arts & Arch., Bio.Sci., Litt., Children & General

CHAYANIKA PRAKASHANI
16A, Tamer Lane, Kolkata-700009
(West Bengal)

CHEMTECH BOOKS (P.) LTD.
Mumbai (Maharashtra)
✆ 25912461
@ chemtech@bom3.vsnl.net.in

CHENNAI BOOKS
No. 6, Thayar Sahib II Lane,
Chennai-600002 (Tamil Nadu)
Prop.: S. Padmavathy; **Bus.Intt.:** Pub.; **Spl.:** Sci., Litt., Politics, Cinema

CHERAN BOOK HOUSE
137, Big Bazaar St., Coimbatore-641001 (Tamil Nadu)
✆ 2396623
Estd.: 1978

CHETAN EXPORTS
296/41, Samuel St., Mumbai-400003 (Maharashtra)
Bus.Intt.: Exp.

CHETANA BOOK HOUSE
Narayana Shastri Rd., Mysore-570024 (Karnataka)
Bus.Intt.: Pub.; **Spl.:** Fiction, Children's Books, Books for Litt., Textbooks, Collections, Books for Gen. Knowledge and Dictionaries in Kannada and English

CHETANA BOOKS & STATIONERY
Pirpainti, Bhagalpur-813209 (Bihar)
Bus.Intt.: Pub. and B.S.

CHETANA PRAKASH
Rajgarh Rd., Guwahati-781004 (Assam)

CHETANA PUBLICATIONS PVT. LTD.
263-C Khatauwad,
Goregaonkar Lane, Girgaon,
Mumbai-400004 (Maharashtra)
✆ 23857090, Fax: 91-22-23821910
@ cppl@chetanapublications.com
Hd.Org.: Anil J. Rambhia

CHETANA PUBLISHERS
Shastri Gali No. 3, Maujpur, Delhi-110053

CHETANA PVT. LTD.
34, K. Dubash Marg, Mumbai-400001 (Maharashtra)
✆ 22881159, 22824983, Fax: 022-22553412
karya@chetana.com
Estd.: 1946; **Man.Dir.:** Mrs. Chhaya Arya; **Bus.Intt.:** Pub., WS, L.S. and Rt. and Exp.

CHHATRA GYAN MANDIR
Bihta, Patna-801103 (Bihar)
Bus.Intt.: Pub. and B.S.

CHHATRA HITAISHI PUSTAK BHANDAR
Makhdumma, Bhagalpur-813102 (Bihar)
Bus.Intt.: Pub. and B.S.

CHHATRA PUSTAK BHANDAR
Khudwan, Aurangabad-824124 (Bihar)
Bus.Intt.: Pub. and B.S.

CHHATRA PUSTAK BHANDAR
Khiriawan, Madanpur, Aurangabad-824208 (Bihar)
Bus.Intt.: Pub. and B.S.

CHHATRA PUSTAK BHANDAR
OBRA, Aurangabad-824124 (Bihar)
Bus.Intt.: Pub. and B.S.

CHHATRA PUSTAK BHANDAR
Ballia, Begusarai-854208 (Bihar)
Bus.Intt.: Pub. and B.S.

CHHATRABANDHU
271, G.L.T. Rd., Kolkata-700036 (West Bengal)

CHHATRABANDHU PUSTAKALAYA
65, Kabi Sukanta Sarani, Kolkata-85 (West Bengal)

CHHATRAMAHAL
Arambag, Distt. Hooghly (West Bengal)
Prop.: Brajo Mohan Kundu

CHHATROPAYOGI PUBLICATIONS
Arya Kumar Rd., Machuatoli, Patna-800004 (Bihar)
✆ 50873, 52775, 52845, 57561
Bus.Intt.: Pub. and B.S.

CHHAYA BOOK CENTER
S.B. College Rd., Aurangpura, Aurangabad-431001 (Maharashtra)
✆ (O) 2333545 (R) 27336845, Fax: 0240-2351297
Prop.: Somnath Dongapure; **Bus.Intt.:** B.S.; **Spl.:** School and College Books

CHHAYA PRAKASHANI
32, College Row, Kolkata-700009 (West Bengal)

CHIEF EXECUTIVE OFFICER
West Bengal State Book Board, (A Government of West Bengal Organization), Arya Mansion (8th Floor), 6-A, Raja Subodh Mulick Square, Kolkata (West Bengal)

CHILDREN BOOK AGENCY
East Boring Canal Rd., Patna-800001 (Bihar)

CHILDREN BOOK CENTRE
Machuatoli, Patna-800004 (Bihar)
✆ 2670362
cbcravi@rediffmail.com
Bus.Intt.: Pub. and B.S.

CHILDREN BOOK DISTRIBUTORS
Arya Kumar Rd., Machuatoli, Patna-800001 (Bihar)
Bus.Intt.: Pub. and B.S.

CHILDREN BOOK HOUSE
Post Box No. 3854, A-4, Ring Rd., South Extension-I, New Delhi-110049
✆ 24636010/20/30, Fax: 24636011
neeta@giasdl01.vsnl.net.in
Estd.: 1954; **Prop.:** R.S. Gupta; **Bus.Intt.:** Pub., **Spl.:** Children's Books

CHILDREN CHOICE PUBLICATION PVT LTD
1st Floor, Sunil Complex, Western Kutchery Rd., Meerut-250002 (Uttar Pradesh)
✆ 2668092, Fax: 91-121-2668093
children.choice.123@yahoo.com
Hd.Org.: Arun Agarwal; **Bus.Intt.:** Pub.; **Spl.:** Children's Books in English and Hindi

CHILDREN LITERARY TRUST ASSAM
Publications Board Building, Bammunimaidan, Guwahati-781021 (Assam)

CHILDREN'S BOOK TRUST
Nehru House, 4, Bahadur Shah Zafar Marg, New Delhi-110002
✆ 23316970-74, Fax: 23721090
cbtnd@vsnl.com, cbt@vsnl.com
www.childrensbooktrust.com
Estd.: 1957; **Gen.Man.:** Ravi Shankar
Br.: 18C, Rayala Towers, 781, Anna Salai, Chennai-600002 ✆ 28521850
• G-14, Kamalalaya Centre, 156-A, Lenin Sarani, Kolkata-700013 ✆ 22365094; **Bus.Intt.:** Pub., Exp.; **Spl.:** Juvenile/Children

CHILDRENS' BOOKS DISTRIBUTORS
15, Ansari Rd., Darya Ganj, New Delhi-110002
✆ 23276118, 23284898, Fax: 51665736
rawatrajinder@rediffmail.com
Hd.Org.: Jai Saxena; **Bus.Intt.:** Dist.

CHILDREN'S WORLD
6, Poes Rd., M.M. Garden, Chennai-600018 (Tamil Nadu)
✆ 2451067
Hd.Org.: A.G.S. Mani; **Bus.Intt.:** Pub.;

Spl.: Nursery and Primary Schools Text Books, World Books, Stories, Gen. Books both in English and Tamil

CHILIKKUYIL BOOK VENTURE
20, P. Kothandapani St., Kumbakonam-612001 (Tamil Nadu)
✆ 0435-2430427
Estd.: 1980; **Secy.**: M. Gomathi; **Bus.Intt.**: Pub. and B.S.; **Spl.**: Litt., Politics, Soc.Sci.

CHIMANLAL KESHAVA LAL RANA
Sankoli Sheri, Manek Chowk, Ahmedabad-380001 (Gujarat)

CHINA BOOK CENTRE
C/o GBD Books, 16, Ansari Road, Near Mahavir Vatika, Darya Ganj, New Delhi-110002
✆ 23260022, Fax: 91-11-23911057
kaushalgoyal@yahoo.com
www.goyalbookshop.com
Hd.Org.: Kaushal Goyal

CHINAR BOOK CENTRE
922, Roohallah Khan St., Darya Ganj, New Delhi-110002
✆ 23281880, 2278243
Estd.: 1935; **Prop.**: Rajesh Didden; **Bus.Intt.**: Pub., L.S. and Rt.

CHINAR BOOKS & STATIONERS
F-1/4-29, Uttri Pitam Pura, Delhi-110088
✆ (R) 27346927 ▮ 9818623661
Hd.Org.: Rajiv Arora; **Bus.Intt.**: Dealers Books & Stationery; **Spl.**: Mang., Engg, Med., Comp., Sports etc.

CHINMAYA JNANPITH
74, Medha Apartments, Mayur Vihar, Phase-I, Delhi-110091
✆ 22759139
sudhirraman@yahoo.com, sudhir20@vsnl.net
Hd.Org.: Sudhir Sharma; **Bus.Intt.**: Pub.; **Spl.**: *Bhagwad Gita* and Books on Vedanta and its Phil. in Hindi

CHINMAY PRAKASHAN
153, Choura Rasta, Jaipur-302003 (Rajasthan)
✆ (O) 2316226 (R) 274087
Hd.Org.: Subhash Varma

CHINMAYA CENTRE OF WORLD UNDERSTANDING
89, Lodhi Rd., New Delhi-110003
✆ 24697848, 24623301, Fax: 24643290
ccwu@vsnl.com, chinmaya@bom2.vsnl.net.in
Hd.Org.: S.C. Vohra; **Bus.Intt.**: Pub.; **Spl.**: *Bhagwad Gita* and Books on Vedanta and its Phil.

CHINMAYA MISSION
No. 2, 13th Avenue, Harrington Rd., Chetpet, Chennai-600031 (Tamil Nadu)
✆ 28265641
Hd.Org.: M. Gomathi; **Bus.Intt.**: Pub.; **Spl.**: Swami Chinmayananda's Books on Hindu Rel.

CHINMAYA MISSION
Kolkata (West Bengal)
✆ 24665069, 24647076
chinmayakolkata@vsnl.net
Bus.Intt.: Pub.

CHINMAYA MISSION
89, Lodhi Road, New Delhi-110003
✆ 24697848, Fax: 91-11-24643290
ccwu@chinmayamissiondelhi.org
www.chinmayamissiondelhi.org
Hd.Org.: Col. S.C. Vohra

CHINTAMANI SAHITYA SAHYOG
'Ravi Varsha' Shramvihar Society, Savantvadi-416510 (Maharashtra)

CHINTHA PUBLISHERS
Manjalikulam Rd., Thiruvananthapuram-695001 (Kerala)
✆ 2330426
Estd.: 1973; **Bus.Intt.**: Pub.

CHINTHANA PRAKASHANA
681, "Anuradha Anuroopa", 12th Cross, 4th Main, MCR Extension, Bangalore-560040 (Karnataka)
✆ (O) 080-23354680 (R) 23387121
anupooja2000@yahoo.com
Estd.: 1970; **Hd.Org.**: H.R. Dasegowda; **Bus.Intt.**: Pub., L.S; **Spl.**: Humanities & Soc.Sci., Law, Children & General

CHIRAG BOOK DISTRIBUTORS
102, Kama Chambers, Opp. Shiyapura Police Chowki, Baroda-390001 (Gujarat)
✆ (O) 2410771 (R) 2489003 ▮ 9824080512, Fax: 2449003
dilchirag@yahoo.com
Estd.: 1987; **Prop.**: Dilipbhai V.; **Bus.Intt.**: L.S.; **Spl.**: Sci., Tech. and Soc.Sci.

CHIRANJIB PRAKASHANI
42, Beniatola Lane, Kolkata-700009 (West Bengal)
Hd.Org.: Chitta Singha Roy

CHIRATAN PRAKASHAN
A-57-58, Bahadur Apartments, Vikaspuri, New Delhi-110018
✆ 25516996, 25592113
Hd.Org.: Chandrasekhar Shastri

Bus. Intt.: Pub.; Regional Languages on Edu., Culture, *Vedas* and *Upanishads*, etc. in Hindi and Sanskrit

CHIRAYU PRAKASHAN
47, Charushree, Abhiman Shree Society, Pune-411008 (Maharashtra)

CHIRPI VELIYEEDU
46, Thaiyur, Chinnanma Nagar, Kelambakkam-603103, Chengai—Mang. Dist. (Tamil Nadu)

CHITHRA PRINTERS & PUBLISHERS
39/3006, Manikkath Rd., Kochi-682016 (Kerala)
✆ 2364005
Estd.: 1987; **Man.Prt.:** K. Nirmala; **Bus.Intt.:** Pub. and B.S.

CHITRA PRAKASHAN
312, Western Kutchery Rd., Meerut-250001 (Uttar Pradesh)
✆ (O) 91-121-2662271, 2663271, 2654217, 2644063 (R) 2642116, 2653587
9897036095, Fax: 2648704
rastogimayank@yahoo.com
Exe.: Mayank Rastogi; **Bus.Intt.:** Pub.

CHITRA PRESS
Thiruvalla-689101 (Kerala)
✆ 221232, 221332
Estd.: 1949; **Prop.:** Cyriac Mathew; **Bus.Intt.:** Pub.

CHITRAGUPTA KITAB GHAR
Chiraiyatand, Postal Park, Patna-800001 (Bihar)
Bus.Intt.: Pub. and B.S.

CHITRANGSU INSTITUTE OF ART & HANDICRAFT
2-B, Parasar Rd., Kolkata-700029 (West Bengal)
✆ 24663083, Fax: 91-33-24642494
chitrabhanucomp@vsnl.net
Hd.Org.: Atish Sinha; **Bus.Intt.:** Pub.; **Spl.:** Art, Design for Children

CHITRIKA PUBLICATIONS
4 KB-18, Jawaharnagar, Jaipur-302004 (Rajasthan)

CHOICE INTERNATIONAL
484, Double Storey, New Rajinder Nagar, New Delhi-110060
✆ 91-11-64163037
narkambooks@yahoo.com
Hd.Org.: Naresh Chowdhry; **Bus.Intt.:** Pub.; **Spl.:** Children's and Religious Books, Dictionaries, Pocket Books, etc. in English

CHOKHAMBA SURBHARATI PRAKASHAN
K-37/117, Gopal Mandir Lane, Varanasi-221001 (Uttar Pradesh)
✆ 257214, 263076, 2335263
Hd.Org.: Navneetdas Gupta

CHOTODER KOCHIPATA
17, Green Avenue, Kolkata-700075 (West Bengal)

CHOUBE GYAN JYOTI
Bihta, Patna-801103 (Bihar)
Bus.Intt.: Pub. and B.S.

CHOUKHAMBA VISHVA BHARATI
Opp. Chitra Cinema, Varanasi-221001 (Uttar Pradesh)

CHOURASIYA BOOK CENTRE
Pabhera, Patna-804455 (Bihar)
Bus.Intt.: Pub. and B.S.

CHOURASIYA PUSTAK BHANDAR
Ashok Rajpath, Patna-800006 (Bihar)
Bus.Intt.: Pub. and B.S.

CHOURASIYA PUSTAK BHANDAR
Kankerbagh, Lohianagar, Patna-800020 (Bihar)
Bus.Intt.: Pub. and B.S.

CHOWDHARY & CO. (PUBLISHERS) PVT. LTD.
Govind Mitra Rd., Patna-800004 (Bihar)
✆ 91-612-2681859
easternbooks@satyam.net.in
www.ccopc.com
Hd.Org.: Anil Chowdhary; **Bus.Intt.:** Pub.; **Spl.:** School textbooks in English and Hindi

CHOWDHARY BOOK STALL
Stall-21, Bankim Chatterjee St., Kolkata-73 (West Bengal)

CHOWDHARY GENERAL STORE
Rajaun, Bhagalpur-813107 (Bihar)
Bus.Intt.: Pub. and B.S.

CHOWDHARY PUBLISHERS
1, J.N. Tewary Rd., Dumdum, 24 Parganas (North) (West Bengal)
Hd.Org.: Makhan Sen Chowdhary

CHOWDHARY PUSTAK BHANDAR
Baunsi, Barhat, Bhagalpur-813206 (Bihar)
Bus.Intt.: Pub. and B.S.

CHOWDHRY EXPORT HOUSE
208, Rattan Jyoti, 18, Rajendra Place, New Delhi-110008
✆ 25755519, 25720209, Fax: 91-11-25755519
gphceh@del3.vsnl.net.in, goodwillbooksinternational@gmail.com
chowdhryexporthouse407_www.indiabizclub.com
Estd.: 1994; **Prt.:** A.S. Chowdhry, Rajneesh Chowdhry; **Bus.Intt.:** Dist., Exp.; **Spl.:** All Sub., Children, Text, Reference

CHOWKHAMBA KRISHNADAS ACADEMY
K-37/118, Gopal Mandir Lane, Near Golghar (Maidagin), P.B. No. 1118, Varanasi-221001 (Uttar Pradesh)
✆ (O) & (R) 2335020
✉ cssoffice@satyam.net.in
www.chowkhambaseries.com
Estd.: 1981; **Hd.Org.**: Kamalesh Kumar Gupta; **Bus.Intt.**: Pub., B.S., Exp.; **Spl.**: Humanities & Soc.Sci., Sci. & Tech., Med., Arts & Arch.

CHRISTIAN LITERATURE CENTRE
Panbazar, Guwahati-781001 (Assam)

CHRISTIAN LITERATURE SOCIETY (THE)
68, Evening Bazaar Rd., P.B. No. 501, Park Town, Chennai-600003 (Tamil Nadu)
✆ (O) 25354296/97 (R) 26414683
9840442847, Fax: 044-25354297
✉ jaivanth@yahoo.com
Estd.: 1858; **Hd.Org.**: Rev. Dr. Dayanandan Frances; **Gen.Sec.-in-Charge:** Joshua J. Singh; **Bus.Intt.**: Pub., B.S., L.S., Rt.; **Spl.**: Bookshops located all over South India, Publish Books in English and other Southern *Languages* and specialize in the fields of Church Hist., Mission, Theology, Phil., Interfaith Dialogue etc.

CHRONICLE PUBLICATIONS (P) LTD.
C-6-52, Safdarjung Development Area, New Delhi-110016
✆ 26519761, Fax: 26526443
✉ chronicl@ndf.vsnl.net.in

CHUCKERVERTTY CHATTERJEE & CO. LTD.
15, College Square, Kolkata-700073 (West Bengal)
✆ 2311425

CHUGH PUBLICATIONS
P.B. No. 101, 2, Starchay Rd., Civil Lines, Allahabad-221001 (Uttar Pradesh)
Prop.: Ramesh Chugh; **Bus.Intt.**: Pub.; **Spl.**: Humanities and Soc.Sci.

CINEMASS PUBLICATION
E-54-B, East Vinod Nagar, St. No. 2, Mayur Vihar Phase-II, Delhi-110091
✆ 22479951
Hd.Org.: Aman Chadha; **Bus.Intt.**: Pub.; **Spl.**: A Unique Film & T.V. Directory

CITY BOOK CENTRE
Gujari Bazar, Patna City, Patna-800008 (Bihar)
Bus.Intt.: Pub. and B.S.

CITY BOOK CENTRE
Budshah Chowk, Srinagar, Kashmir-190001 (Jammu & Kashmir)
✆ 2470158, 2478288, Fax: 2478266
✉ citybookcentre@rediff.com
Estd.: 1985; **Hd.Org.**: Javeed Ahmad
Br.: Basant Bagh Nai Sarak, Srinagar, Kashmir-190001 ✆ 2456395
✉ citybookcenter@yahoo.com
Bus.Intt.: Pub., WS, L.S. & Rt., Imp., Exp., Sub.Ag.; **Spl.**: Humanities & Soc.Sci., Sci. & Tech., Med., Law, Juvenile/Children Books, Gen. & Fiction etc.

CITY BOOK SHOP
Ruki Mahal, Calaba Causeway Colaba, Mumbai-400005 (Maharashtra)
Estd.: 1951

CITY BOOK SHOP
Shop No. 2, Anand Complex, Sector-17A, Chandigarh (Punjab)
✆ (O) 0172-2708612 (R) 2662541
09814017075, Fax: 2714376
✉ citybookshop123@yahoo.com
www.citybookkeeper.com
Estd.: 1996; **Prop.**: Rakesh Jain; **Bus.Intt.**: B.S., L.S., WS; **Spl.**: Sci. & Tech., Med., Bio.

CITY BOOKSELLERS
East Darwaza, Patna City, Patna-800008 (Bihar)
Bus.Intt.: Pub. and B.S.

CLARION BOOKS
18-9, Dilshad Garden, G.T. Rd., Delhi-110095
✆ (O) 22297792 (R) 24920063, Fax: 22282332
Estd.: 1976; **Prop.**: Shakhar Malhotra; **Bus.Intt.**: Pub.

CLARKE ASSOCIATES LTD.
P-5, Rohini Gardens Santhome High Rd., Chennai-600028 (Tamil Nadu)
✆ 24934667

CLASSIC BOOK HOUSE
550, D-Block, Rajajipuram, Lucknow-5 (Uttar Pradesh)

CLASSIC BOOK SERVICE
C-255, New Ashok Nagar, Delhi-110096
✆ 22712418 9818473946
Prop.: Arun Sharma; **Bus.Intt.**: L.S.; **Spl.**: Acad., Beh. Sci., Soc.Sci., Comm., Sci., Med., Tech., Law books

CLASSIC BOOKMAN PVT. LTD.
K-2104, Chittaranjan Park, New Delhi-110019

CLASSIC PUBLICATION
76E, Bandhab Nagar, Kolkata-28 (West Bengal)

CLASSIC PUBLISHING HOUSE
260-1, Chaura Rasta, Jaipur-302003 (Rajasthan)
Prop.: Mamata Gupta

CLASSIC PUBLISHING PVT. LTD.
Simmer Goltim Piodade, Divar, Ilhas (Goa)

CLASSICAL BOOK DISTRIBUTORS
B-202, Gali No. 12, Kamal Vihar,
Delhi-110084
✆ 26198169
Hd.Org.: Naresh Prasad, Mrs. Manju;
Bus.Intt.: L.S.; **Spl.:** Acad., Beh. Sci., Soc.Sci., Comm. & Law

CLASSICAL PUBLISHING COMPANY
28, Shopping Centre, Karampura,
New Delhi-110015
✆ (O) 25465978, 65903449 (R) 25572165
Estd.: 1976; **Prop.:** B.K. Taneja;
Bus.Intt.: Pub., B.S. and L.S.; **Spl.:** Sol., Mang., Phil., Hist., English, Pol.Sci.

CLASSIQUE BOOKS
9, Radha Nath Mallik Lane, Kolkata-700012
(West Bengal)
✆ (O) 2864-0300/2219-0255 (R) 2435-8263
▮ 9830014296, Fax: 22416983
✉ classiquein@yahoo.com
Hd.Org.: Biswajit Das; **Bus.Intt.:** Pub., Dist.

CLIFTON & CO. (P) LTD.
53/2, D.B. Gupta Rd., Karol Bagh,
New Delhi-110005
✆ 25726950

COCHIN LAW HOUSE
Kadvanthara, Cochin-682020 (Kerala)
✆ 2310523
Estd.: 1969; **Hd.Org.:** N.X. Varghese;
Bus.Intt.: B.S.

COFEE HOUSE
25B, Wilmoni Mitra Row, Kolkata-2
(West Bengal)

COLD SPRING HARBOR LAB. PRESS
New Delhi
✆ 26433992, 23243415, Fax: 23243225
✉ narosadl@nda.vsnl.net.in
Bus.Intt.: Pub. & Dist.

COLLEGE AGENCIES
Kumbhar Wad, Near Shahid Chowk,
Dudhia Talav Rd.,
Navsari-396445 (Gujarat)
✆ (O) 55277-248629 (R) 254025,
Tele-fax: 255277
Estd.: 1976; **Bus.Intt.:** WS

COLLEGE BOOK CENTRE
29/10, Ranganathan St., T. Nagar,
Chennai-600017 (Tamil Nadu)
✆ 24340358
Man.: V.S. Rajan; **Spl.:** Comp., Engg., Mang., Sci. and Humanities

COLLEGE BOOK DEPOT
83, Tripolia Bazar (Near Atish Gate)
Jaipur-302002 (Rajasthan)
✆ (O) 0141-2320827, 2312156 (R) 2564638,
Fax: 0141-2563256
✉ glp@satyam.net.in
Estd.: 1950; **Hd.Org.:** P.C. Jain
Br.: 601, Atlas, Lokhand Wala Complex, Andheri (West), Mumbai-400053 (Maharashtra) ✆ 26316131, 26317984
• 2/44, Ansari Rd., Darya Ganj,
New Delhi-110002 ✆ 23262528
Bus.Intt.: Pub. and B.S.; **Spl.:** Soc.Sci.

COLLEGE BOOK DEPOT
Khazanchi Rd., Patna-800004 (Bihar)
Bus.Intt.: Pub. and B.S.

COLLEGE BOOK HOUSE
P.O. Box 61720/2953 Single St., Karamana,
Thiruvananthapuram-695001 (Kerala)
✆ 279578
Estd.: 1970; **Prop.:** M. Eswaran;
Bus.Intt.: B.S.

COLLEGE BOOK STALL
B.N.R. Training College Campus, Gulzarbagh,
Patna-800007 (Bihar)
Bus.Intt.: Pub. and B.S.

COLLEGE BOOK STORE
1701-2, Nai Sarak, Delhi-110006
✆ 23279128, 23269426
Fax: 011-23269426
✉ cbspubs@del3.vsnl.net.in
🌐 www.cbspd.com
Hd.Org.: Sushil Kumar Jain; **Bus.Intt.:** Pub. and Dist.; **Spl.:** Med., Engg., Sci. & Tech., Agri., Earth Sci. etc.

COLLEGE BOOK STORES
Opp. B.N. College, Patna-800004 (Bihar)
Bus.Intt.: Pub. and B.S.

COLLEGE STORES
4, Garda College Shopping Centre, Sayaji Rd., Golwad, Navsari-396445 (Gujarat)
✆ (O) 02637-258642 (R) 251137
Estd.: 1969; **Hd.Org.:** Shanker Shamvani;
Bus.Intt.: B.S., Stationers and L.S.

COLLEGE STORES
1, Bankim Chatterjee St., Kolkata-700073
(West Bengal)

COLLEGE VIEW
Chouhatta, Patna-800004 (Bihar)
Bus.Intt.: Pub. and B.S.

COLLOQUIUM INDIA
14, Band Stand Apartment, B-J-Rd.,
Bandra (West) Mumbai-400050 (Maharashtra)

COLOUR PUBLICATIONS PVT. LTD.
Dhuruwadi, 126-A, A.V. Nagveka Marg, Prabhadevi, Mumbai-400025 (Maharashtra)
✆ 24306319, 24309318, 24309610, Fax: 91-22-2400601
Hd.Org.: Vijay Ragavan

COLOURFUL BOOKS INTERNATIONAL
69-A, Amrit Nagar, South Extn. Part-I, New Delhi-110049
9818263360
Hd.Org.: Akash Jain

COMDEX COMPUTER PUBLISHING
F-2/16, Ansari Rd., Darya Ganj, New Delhi-110002
✆ 23272783

COMET MEDIA FOUNDATION
Topiwala Lane School, Lamington Rd., Mumbai-400007 (Maharashtra)
✆ 23869052
comet_media@vsnl.com
Estd.: 1985; **Bus.Intt.:** Pub. and B.S.; **Spl.:** Sci. & Tech., Med.

COMIC WAY PUBLICATIONS
168, Desh Bandhu Apartments, Behind Desh Bandhu College, Kalkaji, New Delhi-110019

COMIC WORLD
257, Dariba Kalan, Delhi-110006
✆ 23266317, 23266232
Hd.Org.: Himanshu Verma; **Bus.Intt.:** Pub.; **Spl.:** Monthly Magazine, *Comic World* for Children in Hindi, English and Bengali

COMM. SEARCH (INDIA) PVT. LTD.
F-82/1, IInd St., Annanagar East, Chennai-600102 (Tamil Nadu)
✆ 26286164, Fax: 044-26286165
hpradeep@giasmd01.vsnl.net.in
Estd.: 1996; **Hd.Org.:** H. Pradeep; **Bus.Intt.:** Pub.; **Spl.:** Insurance and Health Care Books

COMMANDER FANCY STORE
Commander Complex, Kargil-Ladakh (Jammu and Kashmir)

COMMERCIAL AGENCIES
Riada Bhawan, Room No. 28-30, Ist Floor, Main Rd., Ranchi-834001 (Bihar)
✆ 2311453, 2313898, Fax: 0651-2313116
Estd.: 1974; **Hd.Org.:** Ashok Dutta
Br.: Opp. G.E.L. Church Complex, Main Rd., Ranchi-834001 (Bihar) ✆ 2311453, 2314365

COMMISSION FOR SCIENTIFIC & TECHNICAL TERMINOLOGY
West Block No. 7, R.K. Puram, New Delhi-110066
✆ 26102882, Fax: 91-11-26101220
Hd.Org.: K. Bijay Kumar; **Bus.Intt.:** Pub.; **Spl.:** Acad. Books, Dictionaries, Digests, Monographs and Journals

COMMISSIONER ARCHAEOLOGY
Direcorate of Archaeology Archives & Museums, Bhopal (Madhya Pradesh)
✆ 2553307, Fax: 91-755-2551478
Hd.Org.: Pankaj Roy; **Bus.Intt.:** Pub.; **Spl.:** Archaeological books, guide books, monographs, etc.

COMMONWEALTH HUMAN RIGHTS INITIATIVE
F1/12-A, Hauz Khas Enclave, Ground Floor, New Delhi-110016
✆ 26859823, 26864678, Fax: 26864688
chriall@nda.vsnl.net.in
Hd.Org.: Maja Daruwala; **Bus.Intt.:** Suppliers; **Spl.:** Material on Human Rights

COMMONWEALTH PUBLISHERS
4831/24, Prahlad St., Ansari Rd., Darya Ganj, New Delhi-110002
✆ 23272541, 23257835, Fax: 23257835
campusbooks@hotmail.com
Estd.: 1987; **Hd.Org.:** B.R. Verma; **Bus.Intt.:** Pub. & Dist.; **Spl.:** Humanities and Soc.Sci.

COMMUNICATION & MEDIA PEOPLE
15, Dehi Entally Rd., Kolkata-700014 (West Bengal)

COMP-POINT
A-28, Shivam Apartments, Block-D, Vikaspuri, New Delhi-110018
✆ 25505639, Fax: 25618305
comp_point21@yahoo.com
Hd.Org.: Veena Narang; **Bus.Intt.:** Pub.; **Spl.:** Textbooks for Children

COMP-POINT SYSTEMS (I) PVT LTD
B-2/13, Opp. Mira Model School, Janak Puri, New Delhi-110058
✆ 25501359, 25512028, Fax: 011-25549107
comppointsystems@gmail.com
www.techkidz.biz
Hd.Org.: Parveen Kumar Narang; **Bus.Intt.:** Dist.; **Spl.:** Developer and Distributor of educational softwares, CDs and audio-visual games.

COMPANY LAW JOURNAL
66/2230, Gurudwara Rd., P.B. No. 2693, Karol Bagh, New Delhi-110005
Bus.Intt.: Exp.

COMPETITION SUCCESS REVIEW PVT. LTD.
604, Prabhat Kiran Building, Rajendra Place, New Delhi-110008
✆ 25761086, 25712898

info@competitionreview.com
www.csr.in
Hd.Org.: S.K. Sachdeva
Br.: Competition Success Review, 18 Nawab Building, 327, Dr. D.N. Road, Mumbai-400001 (Maharashtra); ✆ 22833990, 22040987
• 606-A, Prabhat Kiran, Rajendra Place, New Delhi-110008
9810479149, ✆ 41523321
Bus.Intt.: Pub.; **Spl.:** Journals—*Competition Success Review* in English and Hindi, *General Knowledge Today* and *CSR Year Book* and books on current affairs and general knowledge

COMPETITION WIZARD
B-19, ALS House, Mukherjee Nagar, New Delhi-110009
✆ 91-11-27653714
competitionwizard@gmail.com
Hd.Org.: Jojot Mathew; **Bus.Intt.:** Pub.; **Spl.:** Educational Monthly *Magazine Competition Wizard* for IAS/PCS exams

COMPETITION WIZARD
H-16, Second Floor, Green Park Extn., New Delhi-110016
✆ 26164551, 26162979, 26106702, Fax: 26164551 Extn. 30
competition@vsnl.net
Hd.Org.: Shashank Atom; **Bus.Intt.:** Pub.; **Spl.:** Educational Magazine

COM-POINT PUBLISHERS & DISTRIBUTORS
8/21, West Patel Nagar, New Delhi-110008
✆ 25501359, 25512028, Fax: 25618305
comp_point21@yahoo.com
Prop.: Parveen Kamar; **Bus.Intt.:** Pub.; **Spl.:** Text Books on Comp. for Schools and Deals in Comp. Hardwares

COMPRINT INDIA
24-A, Sriram Rd., Near Hotel Oberoi Maidens, Delhi-110054

COMPUAID ENTERPRISES
E-107, LGF, Greater Kailash Part-II, New Delhi-110048
✆ 29225821, 29225836, Fax: 91-11-29223621
vijjip@compuaid-india.com
www.compuaid-india.com
Hd.Org.: Vijji Panangat; **Bus.Intt.:** Suppliers; **Spl.:** Broadcasting Equipment as an Aid to Education

COMPUTECH PUBLICATIONS LTD.
7/31, 1st Floor, Ansari Rd., Darya Ganj, New Delhi-110002
✆ (O) 23280163, 23280164 (R) 55192881, 22154457, Fax: 23280165
nap@newasianpub.com
www.computechpub.com
Estd.: 2002; **Dir.:** Anil Mehta; **Bus.Intt.:** Pub., B.S., WS, Exp.; **Spl.:** Sci. & Tech., Comp., Children & Gen.

COMPUTER & PRINTERS
46-A, Shastri Colony, G.T. Rd., Ambala Cantt.-133001 (Haryana)

COMPUTER BOOK CENTRE
12, Shrunagar Shopping Centre, M.G. Rd., Bangalore-560001 (Karnataka)
✆ 25587923, 25584641
Bus.Intt.: Rt., WS

COMPUTER BOOK MART
39/272, Pulleppadty Rd., Ernakulam, Kochi-682018 (Kerala)
✆ 0486-2368208
Estd.: 1993; **Prop.:** T.C. Alexander; **Bus.Intt.:** B.S.

COMPUTER BOOKSHOP (INDIA) (P) LTD.
2-B, Kitab Mahal, 190, Dr. D.N. Rd., Fort Mumbai-400001 (Maharashtra)
✆ 22070989, Fax: 22623551
cbs@vsnl.com
Hd.Org.: Amin Shroff; **Bus.Intt.:** B.S.; **Spl.:** Books on Comp.

COMPUTER BUSINESS MANAGEMENT (I) LTD.
2-C, Shakti Sadan, 'C' Block, 163, Lamington Rd., Mumbai-400007 (Maharashtra)
✆ 23096148, Fax: 23098587
Hd.Org.: Ajay Mehta; **Bus.Intt.:** Imp., Pub. Imparting Comp. Edu. and Publishing

COMPUTER CRAFT PUBLICATIONS
D-14, Om Vihar, Phase-V, Uttam Nagar, New Delhi-110059
✆ 25352770
Estd.: 1999; **Prop.:** V.K. Rajput; **Bus.Intt.:** Rt. & L.S.; **Spl.:** Acad., Soc.Sci., Comm., Tech., Fiction & Rare Books

COMPUTER DYNAMICS
9, Ashram Complex, Behind 56 Shops, 584, M.G. Rd., Indore-452001 (Madhya Pradesh)
✆ (O) 2534676, 2545494 (R) 2494108
9826014552
utidata@sancharnet.in
Hd.Org.: Krishna Dutt

COMPUTER HOUSE INFORMATION PUBLICATIONS
C-4/233, BDA Flats, Air Port Rd., Domlur, Bangalore-71 (Karnataka)

COMPUTER MART
Kashmir University Gate, Hazratbal, Srinagar, Kashmir-190006 (Jammu & Kashmir)
✆ 91-194-2428758, 2428526
abhamid@sancharnet.in
www.kashmironsale.com

Estd.: 1991; **Man.Prt.**: Altaf A. Bazaz; **Bus.Intt.**: Pub., L.S. & Rt., Imp., Exp., Sub.Ag.; **Spl.**: Humanities & Soc.Sci., Sci. & Tech., Law, Med., Gen. & Fiction etc.

COMPUTER ZONE
187-88, Sant Nagar, 101, Sai Plaza,
East of Kailash, New Delhi-110065
✆ (O) 26462065, 26227036/37 (R) 27257023, Fax: 26470740
computerzonedelhi@hotmail
www.czoneindia.com
Estd.: 1991; **Prop.**: Mrs. Sudarshan Verma; **Bus.Intt.**: Pub., WS, Rt., B.S.; **Spl.**: Tech., Comp. Sci. Books

COMPUTEX GRAPHICS
112, High Tech. Ind. Centre, Caves Rd.,
Jogeshwari East, Mumbai-400060
(Maharashtra)
✆ 28300092, 28363311
Estd.: 1984; **Bus.Intt.**: Exp.

CONCEPT BOOK CENTRE
108, Amarkunj Society, Ghodeod Rd., Surat
(Gujarat)

CONCEPT PUBLISHING COMPANY
A/15-16, Commercial Block, Mohan Garden,
New Delhi-110059
✆ 25351460, 25351794, Fax: 91-11-25357103
publishing@conceptpub.com
www.conceptpub.com
Estd.: 1974; **Prop.**: Ashok Kumar Mittal
Sh.: 4788/23, Ansari Rd., Darya Ganj,
New Delhi-110002 ✆ 23272187
Bus.Intt.: Pub.; **Spl.**: Humanities, Soc.Sci., Phil. & Rel., Agri., Anthropology, Eco., Geography, Hist., Sociology etc.

CONCORDE PRESS
4289/3, Ansari Rd., Darya Ganj,
New Delhi-110002

CONFLUENCE INTERNATIONAL
203/E 588, Greater Kailash-II,
New Delhi-110048
✆ 2926832, Fax: 91-11-29217095
confluence@connectgroup.in
Hd.Org.: Suresh Srivatsava;
Bus.Intt.: Pub.; **Spl.**: Translations of foreign language literautre into Hindi and literature of Hindi and English by Indian Writers

CONNEXIONS
W-122, IIIrd Avenue, Anna Nagar,
Chennai-600040 (Tamil Nadu)
✆ 044-26260429
Estd.: 1995; **Man.**: Albert Vincent;
Bus.Intt.: Rt. & L.S.; **Spl.**: Gen. & Trade, Professional, Electronic Products, Children Books, Greeting Cards & Toys (Indian & Foreign)

CONSCIOUS PUBLICATIONS
22B, DDA Flats,
New Friends Colony,
Jamoor Nagar, New Delhi-110065
✆ 26849682, 26561206
Estd.: 1995; **Bus.Intt.**: Pub. and B.S.;
Spl.: Sci. & Tech.

CONSORTIUM FOR EDUCATIONAL COMMUNICATIONS
IUAC Campus, Aruna Asaf Ali Marg,
New Delhi-110067
✆ 26896638, Fax: 91-11-26897416
cecugc@cec-ugc.org
www.cec-ugc.org
Hd.Org.: Director; **Spl.**: An inter-university centre under the University Grants Commission, promoting electronic media in higher education

CONSUL BOOK DEPOT
Bara Bazar, Nainital-263001 (Uttarakhand)
✆ 235219, 236164

CONSULTANTS CORPORATION OF INDUSTRIES
113-B, (Inside Mukat Pal Niwas), Chawri
Bazaar, Delhi-110006
✆ 23264792, 23273220, 23261030
Prop.: D.M. Aggarwal; **Bus.Intt.**: Pub.;
Spl.: Tech. Books, and All Industrial Consultants for Project Reports and Tech.

CONSUMER EDUCATION & RESEARCH CENTRE
Suraksha Sankool, Ahmedabad Gandhinagar
Highway, Thaltaj, Ahmedabad-380054
(Gujarat)

CONTEMPORARY TARGETT PRAFULL PVT. LTD.
203, Prakash House, 4379/B, Ansari Rd.,
Darya Ganj, New Delhi-110002
✆ 9810120001, Fax: 91-11-24355297
ctldel@vsnl.com
www.prafullgoradia.com
Hd.Org.: Lal Raisinghani; **Bus.Intt.**: Pub.;
Spl.: Hinduism in English

CONTINENTAL BOOK SELLERS
PD-109 B, Pitampura, New Delhi-110034
✆ 27222813
Prop.: K.R. Yadav; **Bus.Intt.**: L.S.

CONTINENTAL BOOK SUPPLIERS
Mumbai (Maharashtra)
cbsbooks@indiatimes.com
Bus.Intt.: B.S.

CONTINENTAL BOOKS
C-8/125-B, Lawrence Rd., Delhi-110035
✆ 27187110
Hd.Org.: Jagdeep Ahuja; **Bus.Intt.**: L.S.

CONTINENTAL PRAKASHAN
Vijayanagar Colony, Pune-411030
(Maharashtra)

CONTINENTAL PUBLISHERS
Plamoodu Pattom, Thiruvananthapuram-695004 (Kerala)
✆ 2446618, 2446638
Estd.: 1984; **Prop.:** P. Vijayamohan;
Bus.Intt.: Pub. and B.S.

CONTINENTAL PUBLISHING HOUSE
113, Munirka Vihar, New Delhi-110067

CONTROLLER OF PUBLICATIONS
(Union Ministry of Urban Development),
Civil Lines, Delhi-110054
✆ 22517800
Hd.Org.: S.K. Sopory; **Bus.Intt.:** Pub.;
Spl.: Ministries Departments of the Government of India including Periodicals, Gazettes, Acts, Reports etc.

CONVENT PUBLICATIONS
4229, Chatta Gossian, Jogiwada, Nai Sarak, Delhi-110006
✆ (O) 22922646 (R) 27224365
Estd.: 1980; **Hd.Org.:** Ravi Kumar;
Bus.Intt.: Pub.; **Spl.:** Edu. Books in Eng. & Hindi

CONWAY PRINTERS PVT. LTD.
Readymoney Terrace Annexe 167-C,
Dr. Annie Besant Rd., Worli, Mumbai-400018 (Maharashtra)
Bus.Intt.: Exp.

CORNER BOOKSTORE CO. PVT. LTD.
40/55, Chittranjan Park, Ground Floor,
New Delhi-110019
✆ 33163982, Fax: 26569167
✉ delhi@thecornerbookstore.com
www.thecornerbookstore.com
Hd.Org.: Aalok Wadhwa; **Bus.Intt.:** Pub.;
Spl.: Rel., Tourism, Edu., and also Fiction, and Non-fiction

CORONATION LITHO WORKS (THE)
Post Box No. 2, 38, Thiruthangal Rd.,
Sivakasi-626123 (Tamil Nadu)
✆ 222254-57, Fax: 04560-223231
✉ coronat@vsnl.com
Estd.: 1936; **Bus.Intt.:** Exp., B.S. and Rt.

CORPWORTH MARKETING PVT. LTD.
13, Institutional Area, Lodhi Rd.,
New Delhi-110003
✆ 24645132, 24603903, 24604407,
Fax: 91-11-24642435
✉ jaipal@manford.org
Ch.Exe.: Jaipal Anand; **Bus.Intt.:** Pub.;
Spl.: Mang. Books

CORRECT LIBRARY SERVICE
C-34, Sarvodaya Gali, Near Desu,
Plot West Karawal Nagar, Delhi-110094
✆ 22185970 ▮ 9810396373
Prop.: Ramesh Kumar Jha;
Bus.Intt.: L.S.; **Spl.:** Beh.Sci., Soc.Sci., Ficition, Juveniles

COSMO BOOKS
Round West Thrissur-680001 (Kerala)
✆ 2335292, 2335570, Fax: 2335642
✉ cosmoboo@md3vsnl.net.in
Estd.: 1992; **Prop.:** Mrs. Saramma Thomas
Br.: Cosmobooks, Al Ameen Building, Rly. Stn. Link Rd., Kozhikode-673002 (Kerala)
✆ 2703487, Fax: 2700049
✉ cosmoclt@sancharnet.in
• Cosmobooks, School Division, Taj Complex, PM Taj Rd., Kozhikode-673001 ✆ 2724622
• Cosmobooks, Pressclub Rd., Ernakulam, Kochi-682011 (Kerala) ✆ 2353818
Bus.Intt.: L.S. & Rt.; **Spl.:** Trade, Gen. (Incl. Lit. & Art), Juvenile/Children Books

COSMO PUBLICATIONS
24-B, Ansari Rd., Darya Ganj,
New Delhi-110002
✆ 23278779, 23280455, Fax: 23241200
✉ genesis@ndb.vsnl.net.in
Estd.: 1972; **Hd.Org.:** Rani Kapoor;
Bus.Intt.: Pub.; **Spl.:** Linguistics, Phil., Rel., Sol., Art and Culture in English

COSMO PUBLISHING HOUSE INDIA
17, Nishant Aprt. Thakker Nagar,
Sharanpur Rd., Nasik-2 (Maharashtra)
✆ 2314870, 2581081, Fax: 2314870
✉ cosmolog@bomb.vsnl.net.in
Bus.Intt.: Pub., L.S. & Exp.

COSMOPOLITAN BOOK HOUSE
24-B, Ansari Rd., Darya Ganj,
New Delhi-110002
✆ 23278779, 23280455, Fax: 23241200
✉ genesis@ndb.vsnl.net.in
Estd.: 1972; **Man.Dir.:** Subodh Kapoor;
Bus.Intt.: WS, Exp., L.S. and Rt., Sub.Ag.

COSMOS BOOK HIVE (P) LTD.
831, Phase-5, Udyog Vihar, Gurgaon (Haryana)
✆ (O) 91-348820 (R) 91-355790
Man.Dir.: Sanjay Nanda; **Bus.Intt.:** Pub.;
Spl.: Acad.

COSMOS BOOKS
E-70, Abul Fazl Enclave, P.O. Jamia Nagar, Okhla, New Delhi-110025
✆ 26950627, Fax: 26324566
Hd.Org.: Javed Ali; **Bus.Intt.:** B.S., Dist. and L.S.; **Spl.:** Soc.Sci., Rel., Culture, Sci. and Tech. in English, Hindi and Urdu

COSMOS PUBLICATIONS
Mettupalayam St., P.O. Box 56,
Palghat-678001 (Kerala)

✆ 227912
Estd.: 1989; **Prop.:** P.K. Vijayakumar; **Bus.Intt.:** Pub.

COVER TO COVER BOOKS (P) LTD.
Chennai (Tamil Nadu)
✆ 24830457, 24672665, Fax: 24881308
✉ naveens@md3.vsnl.net.in
Bus.Intt.: Dist. & B.S.

CRANBURY INTERNATIONAL INDIA
A-13, Green Park Extn., First Floor, Flat K-2, New Delhi-110016
✆ 26535929, 20042143, Fax: 26969159
✉ cranburyindia@bol.net.in, techtran@vsnl.com
Hd.Org.: D.K. Guna; **Bus.Intt.:** Dist.; **Spl.:** Foreign Litt. on Comp., Telecom, Soc.Sci., Professional Sub., etc.

CRANBURY INTERNATIONAL INDIA/DKG INFO SYSTEMS
C1A/115-B, Janak Puri,- New Delhi-110058
✆ 25531842, Fax: 91-11-25541258
✉ dkinfo@gmail.com
Hd.Org.: Ethan Atkin; **Bus.Intt.:** Dist.; **Spl.:** Foreign Litt. on Comp., Telecom, Soc.Sci., Professional Sub., etc.

CREATIVE BOOK CENTRE
"Sun Flower", 170, Llyods Rd., Gopalapuram, Chennai-600086 (Tamil Nadu)
✆ 28272726, 28272749, Fax: 28275039
✉ dynamic.maa@sm8springtrpg.ems.vsnl.net.in
Spl.: Comp. Books

CREATIVE BOOKS
'Shanti', CB-24, Naraina,
New Delhi-110028
✆ (O) 25698487, 25699518, 25775737 (R) 25775818
✉ creativebooks@hotmail.com
Estd.: 1989; **Hd.Org.:** Raj Tanwar, Tara Chand Tanwar; **Bus.Intt.:** Pub. and Dist.; **Spl.:** Litt. and Linguistics

CREATIVE BOOKS & PERIODICALS PVT. LTD.
Halima Building, 7 Nanabhai Lane, Mumbai-400001 (Maharashtra)
✆ 22043342, 22047895, Fax: 22833328
✉ creat@bom5.vsnl.net.in
Estd.: 1976; **Man.Dir.:** Padmakar Kotian; **Bus.Intt.:** Sub.Ag.; **Spl.:** Humanities & Soc.Sci., Sci. & Tech., Med.

CREATIVE CAREER PUBLICATIONS
A-54, Bapu Park, Kotla Mubarakpur, New Delhi-110003

CREATIVE EDUCATIONAL AIDS (P) LTD.
90, LGF World Trade, Centre Barakhamba Lane, Connaught Place, New Delhi-110001
✆ 23315483, 23720034, Fax: 23353365
✉ edutoys@del2.vsnl.net.in
Estd.: 1987; **Man.Dir.:** Raj Kumar
Br.: 410-A, Jaina Tower-I, District Centre, Janakpuri, New Delhi-110058;
Hd. Off.: 6, Toy City, Echotech-III, Greater Noida, Dist. G.B. Nagar-201306 (Uttar Pradesh)
• E-24, 1st Floor Sec. 3, Noida-201301 (Uttar Pradesh)
✆ 3066355, 3212355, Fax: 91-120-4355956
✉ edutoys@del2vsnl.net.in
🌐 www.creativeeduaids.com
Bus.Intt.: Pub., Manufacturer, Dist. and Exp.; **Spl.:** Pre-school Learning Games and Teaching Aids, Globes, etc.

CREATIVE ENTERPRISES
P.B. No. 7689, 143, Dahanukar Wadi, Kandivil (West), Mumbai-400067 (Maharashtra)

CREATIVE LEARNING
School of Creative Learning,
North Shastrinagar, Patna-800001 (Bihar)
✆ 2284662, Fax: 2597969
✉ vijoy_prakash@yahoo.com
🌐 www.creativelearningpatna.org
Hd.Org.: Vijoy Prakash; **Bus.Intt.:** Pub.; **Spl.:** Books and Educational Teaching aids related to Concentration, Memory, Imagination, Env. awareness and Creative Promotion as well as Audio Cassettes on *Yogic* visualisation and Devotional Prayers

CREATIVE PUBLICATION
93, Inside Mukat Rai Niwas, Chawri Bazar, Delhi-110006
✆ 23279417, 23985175, Fax: 23261030, 23279417
✉ vikas_aggarwal@vsnl.com
🌐 www.creativepublication.com
Hd.Org.: Vikas Gupta; **Bus.Intt.:** Pub. and B.S.; **Spl.:** Tech. Comp. and Gen. Books in Hindi

CREATIVE PUBLISHING HOUSE
70/1, Mahatma Gandhi Rd., Haridevpur, Kolkata-700082 (West Bengal)

CREATIVE TEACHING PRESS INDIA PVT. LTD.
RZ/12-B, Syndicate Enclave,
Opp. Dabri Chowk, New Delhi-110045
✆ 25381759, 25381813, Fax: 25381790
✉ edutoys@del2.vsnl.net.in
🌐 www.creativeeduaids.com
Hd.Org.: Raj Kumar; **Bus.Intt.:** Pub.; **Spl.:** Children's Books, Teacher Resource Books, Classroom Decoratives, Maps, Charts, Puzzles, etc.

CRESCENT PUBLICATIONS
109, B-Block, Sri Dattasai Commercial

Complex, RTC Cross Rd., Hyderabad-500020 (Andhra Pradesh)
✆ 55619277, Fax: 55619377
✉ info@computervignanam.net
Bus.Intt.: Pub.; **Spl.:** Comp. Vignanan

CREST PUBLISHING HOUSE
194, FIE, Patpar Ganj, Delhi-110092
✆ 22144204/5/7, Fax: 22144206
✉ sethidel@del6.vsnl.net.in
www.crestbooks.com
Estd.: 1992; **Prop. & Prt.:** Ashwin J. Shah, S.C. Sethi; **Bus.Intt.:** Pub.; **Spl.:** Phil., Rel., Classics, Library Sci., Dictionaries, etc.

CRITICAL QUEST
420, G Block Phase VI, Aya Nagar, New Delhi-110047
✆ 91-11-26502012
✉ criticalquest@hotmail.com
Hd.Org.: Josna T. Jacob; **Bus.Intt.:** Pub. & Dis.; **Spl.:** Books on social science written by eminent social reformists from across the globe

CROSS FORD
28-E, Nivedita Enclave, A-6, Paschim Vihar, New Delhi-110003
Bus.Intt.: Pub. and Dist.

CROSSWORD
Sohrab Hall, Ist Floor, Jn of RBN Connaught Rd., Behind Rly. Station, Pune-411001 (Maharashtra)
✆ 0212-6059600/1/2/3/4, Fax: 6059605
✉ crosswordpune@hotmail.com
Estd.: 1998; **Prt.:** Dinesh Gupta, Satish Gupta **Br.:** Books & More Enterprises Pvt. Ltd., ACR Towers, Ground Floor, 32, Residency Rd., Bangalore-560001 ✆ 080-5582411-6
✉ cwdblr@booksnmoreindia.com
Bus.Intt.: L.S. and Rt.; **Spl.:** Gen. and Trade, Acad., Professional, Children, Electronic, Products Books, Greeting Cards & Music cassettes

CROSSWORD
Basement Shri Krishna Shopping Centre, Mitha Khali, Ahmedabad-380009 (Gujarat)
✆ 079-2402238, 2408060, 2468176, Fax: 26444180
Hd.Org.: Gaurav Shah; **Bus.Intt.:** Rt.; **Spl.:** Gen. & Trade, Acad., Professional, Children, Electronic, Products Books, Greeting Cards, Toys & Music Cassettes

CROSSWORD
Ebony IInd Floor, D-4, South Extension-II, New Delhi-110049
✆ 26257645/46, 26256146, 26257645, Fax: 91-11-23715669

Estd.: 1994; **Man.:** Nand N. Jha; **Bus.Intt.:** Rt.; **Spl.:** Gen. & Trade, Children, Electronic Products Books, Toys & Gifts (Indian & Foreign)

CROSSWORD BOOKSHOP
Mahalakshmi Chambers, 22, Bhulabhai Desai Rd., Mumbai-400026 (Maharashtra)
✆ 022-24924882, 24938311, Fax: 24938406
✉ cwbrd@gdpl.com
Estd.: 1992; **Hd.Org.:** Eric Williams; **Bus.Intt.:** L.S. & Rt.; **Spl.:** Gen. & Trade, Professional, Children, Electronic Products Books, Toys & Other Merchandise (Indian & Foreign)

CRYSTAL PAGES PUBLICATIONS
New Delhi
✆ 25826880, 25826881, Fax: 25826882
✉ sanjay@crystalpages.net
Bus.Intt.: Pub.

CRYSTAL SHIP PUBLISHING
104, Skylark, 60, Nehru Place, New Delhi-110019

CSDS-SARAI PUBLICATIONS
29, Rajpur Road, Civil Lines, Delhi-110054
✆ 23942199, Fax: 91-11-23943450
✉ aftab@sarai.net
www.sarai.net
Hd.Org.: Ravi Sundaram; **Bus.Intt.:** Pub.; **Spl.:** Books and Magazines in English and Hindi on media, humanities and social issues

C-SOFT CONSULTANTS
C-464, Defence Colony, New Delhi-110024
✆ 91-11-41550249
✉ support@csoft.co.in
www.csoft-india.com
Hd.Org.: S.K. Jha; **Bus.Intt.:** Pub., Dist., B.S., Exp., Imp.; **Spl.:** Sci. and Tech., Software

CULTURAL BOOK DEPOT
331-A, Lamington Rd., Mumbai-400007 (Maharashtra)
✆ 23855172

CULTURAL PUBLICATIONS
Rajamian Marg, Aminabad, Lucknow-18 (Uttar Pradesh)
Prop.: S. Murti; **Bus.Intt.:** Litt.; **Spl.:** Dr. Ambedkar and Related Dalit Activities in Hindi

CULTURE HOUSE ISLAMIC REPUBLIC OF IRAN
18, Tilak Marg, New Delhi-110001
✆ 23383232-4, Fax: 23387547
✉ ichdelhi@yahoo.co.uk
www.iranhouseindia.com
Hd.Org.: Jalal Tamleh; **Bus.Intt.:** Promoter; **Spl.:** Publication from Iran on Art, Culture, Arch., Rel. etc.

CULTURE VISTAS MARKETING SERVICES PVT. LTD.
TC-4/19000(6) Pandit Colony, Kaudiar, Thiruvananthapuram-695003 (Kerala)
✆ 2311025, Fax: 91-471-2313170
✉ info@culturevistas.com
www.culturevistas.com
Hd.Org.: Sasi Kumar; **Bus.Intt.:** Pub.; **Spl.:** Digitalising and popularising information on arts, culture, technology, management and media

CURRENT BOOK DEPOT
18/53, Mall Rd. (Opp. Phool Bagh), Kanpur-208001 (Uttar Pradesh)
✆ 2367520, Fax: 0512-2311627
Estd.: 1952; **Man.:** Anil Khetan; **Bus.Intt.:** Gen. Books in Hindi

CURRENT BOOK HOUSE
White House, A-Wing, Flat No. 303, 3rd Floor, Naya Nagar Mira Rd. (E), Dist Thane-401107 (Maharashtra)
✆ 28554608
Estd.: 2002; **Bus.Intt.:** WS, L.S. & Rt.; **Spl.:** Humanities & Soc.Sci., Gen. & Fiction etc.

CURRENT BOOKS
Press Club Rd., Cochin-682011 (Kerala)
✆ 2351590, 2360933
Estd.: 1968; **Hd.Org.:** D.C. Kizakke Muri; **Bus.Intt.:** Rt., L.S.; **Spl.:** Gen. & Trade, Acad. Professional & Children Books (Indian & Foreign)

CURRENT BOOKS
D.C. Kizhakkemuri Edam, Good Shepherd St., Kottayam-686001 (Kerala)
✆ (O) 0481-2563114 (R) 2578214, Fax: 0481-2564758
✉ info@dcbooks.com
www.dcbooks.com
Estd.: 1952; **Man.Prt.:** Ravi Deecee; **Bus.Intt.:** Pub.; **Spl.:** Gen. Books and Encyclopaedias

CURRENT BOOKS
Round West, Thrissur-680001 (Kerala)
✆ (O) 2335570, 2335660 (R) 2335593, Fax: 91-487-2335642
✉ cosmobooks@asianetindia.com
Estd.: 1952; **Hd.Org.:** Peppin Thomas; **Bus.Intt.:** Pub. & B.S.; **Spl.:** Original Malayalam Literature as well as translations from other Indian languages

CURRENT BOOKS, TRICHUR
Round West, Thrissur-680001 (Kerala)

CURRENT INDIAN STATUTES
36, Sector 9-A, Chandigarh

CURRENT LEGAL PUBLICATIONS
28-B, Singar Nagar, Lucknow-226005 (Uttar Pradesh)
✆ 2455323, Fax: 2224328

CURRENT SUBSCRIPTION SERVICES
17-C, Citizen Enclave, Sector 14, Extension, Rohini, Delhi-110085
✆ 27863662, Fax: 91-11-27556242
✉ services@del2.vsnl.net.in
www.currentsubscription.com
Estd.: 1994, **Prop.:** S.K. Jain; **Bus.Intt.:** L.S. & Sub.Ag.; **Spl.:** Current year Foreign Journals Print & Online

CURRENT TECHNICAL BOOK DISTRIBUTORS
Delhi
✉ lbt@vsnl.net
✆ 27218194, Fax: 27234817 **Bus.Intt.:** L.S.

CURRENT TECHNICAL LITERATURE CO. (P) LTD.
Ist Floor, Opp. G.P.O., Malhotra House, Mumbai-400001 (Maharashtra)
✆ 22617616, 22611045, Fax: 22679786
✉ info@ctlmumbai.com
Estd.: 1950; **Dir.:** K. Viswanath
Br.: Jai Kumar Niketan, 6576, Ansari Rd., Darya Ganj, P.O. No. 7008, New Delhi-110002
✆ 23278737 ✉ ctldel@nda.vsnl.net.in
• 152, Thambu Chetty St., P.B. No. 128, Chennai-600001 ✆ 25342897
✉ chenctl@vsnl.com
• Opp. Blood Bank, Narayanguda, P.B. No. 1030, Hyderabad-500029
✆ 24752516
• 22, Chittaranjan Avenue, Kolkata-700072
✆ 22373138, Fax: 22373138,
✉ calcti@vsnl.com
Bus.Intt.: L.S. & Rt., WS, Imp.; **Spl.:** Sci. & Tech., Med.

CYBER BOOK SHOP
K-21, Navin Shahdara, Delhi-110032
✆ 22584239
Hd.Org.: Durga Rani; **Bus.Intt.:** Dist.; **Spl.:** Sci. and Tech.

CYBER BOOKS/BROWSE
1, Tilak Rd., Kolkata-700029 (West Bengal)
✆ 24640500, Fax: 033-24711841
Estd.: 1997; **Prop.:** Tuhin Chowdhury; **Bus.Intt.:** L.S. & Rt.; **Spl.:** Gen. & Trade, Acad., Professional (Indian and Foreign)

CYBER CD-ROM
K-21, Navin Shahdara, Delhi-110032
✆ 22584239
Ch.Exe.: Ms. Durga Rani

Bus.Intt.: Dealer and Dist.; **Spl.:** CD-ROM's on Edu., Infotainment Comp. Games, Clip Arts, Photos, Information and DTP

CYBER MULTIMEDIA (INDIA) LTD.
D-74, Panchsheel Enclave, New Delhi-110017
✆ 26491320, 26490019, Fax: 26496765
✉ neerajm@cmil.com, cybermm@cmil.com
Hd.Org.: Venayak Bhatnagar; **Bus.Intt.:** Pub., Imp. & Dist.

CYBER MULTIMEDIA (INDIA) LTD.
Cyber House, B-35, Sector-32, Institutional Area, Gurgaon (Haryana)
✆ 2491320, 2490019, Fax: 2496765
✉ dileshg@cmil.com
Ch.Exe.: Venayak Bhatnagar; **Bus.Intt.:** Dist. of CD-Rom

CYBER SPACE TECHNOLOGIES
65-D, Vikaspuri Extn. Pocket A, Outer Ring Rd., New Delhi-110018
✆ 25155339

CYBER TECH PUBLICATION
4264/3, Ansari Rd., Darya Ganj, New Delhi-110002
✆ (O) 23244078 (R) 25873694, Fax: 91-11-23280028
✉ cyberpublicationdelhi@yahoo.com
Man.Prt.: M.S. Rawat; **Bus.Intt.:** Pub.; **Spl.:** Acad., Comm., Sci., Tech., Sci., Engg. and Competition books

CYMIT INDIA
92/39C, Bose Pukar Rd., Kolkata-700009 (West Bengal)

■ ■ ■

D.B. CORP LTD. (MAGAZINE DIVISION)
105, INS Building, Rafi Marg,
New Delhi-110001
✆ 23710452, Fax: 91-11-23355867
vkgaur@bhaskarnet.com
www.bhaskarnet.com; **Hd.Org.:** Vinod Gaur
Br.: Plot No. 280, Sarkhej Gandhi Nagar Highway, Near YMCA Club, Makarba, Ahmedabad-380051 (Gujarat)
✆ 39888850, Fax: 91-79-5309501;
• 6, Dwarka Sadan, Press Complex, M.P. Nagar, Zone I, Bhopal-462011 (Madhya Pradesh)
✆ 39888840, Fax: 91-755-2675190
admin@mp.bhaskarnet.com;
Bus.Intt.: Pub.; **Spl.:** Monthly Hindi magazine, *Aha! Zindagi*, Children's magazine *Bal Bhaskar* (forthightly) and *Lakshya* (career oriented monthly) under the 'Dainik Bhaskar' group

D.B. PUBLISHING CO.
107, Keshab Chandra Sen St.,
Kolkata-700009 (West Bengal)
Gen.Secy.: Dulal Bhattashali

D.B. TARAPOREVALA & SONS (P) LTD.
210, Dr. D. Naroji Rd., Mumbai-400001 (Maharashtra)
✆ 022-220471433, 22071434
Estd.: 1864; **Hd.Org.:** Rusi Jal Taraporevala; **Bus.Intt.:** Pub. & Exp.; **Spl.:** Astrology, Palmistry, Yoga, Occult Sci., Hindu Phil.

D.C. BOOKS
Kurian Towers, Opp. Saritha Theatre,
Banerjee Rd., Cochin-18 (Kerala)
✆ 0484-2391295
Estd.: 1997; **Man.:** Premkumar T.R.; **Bus.Intt.:** L.S. and Rt.; **Spl.:** Gen. and Trade, Acad., Professional, Greeting cards, Magazines, Cassettes & Children Books, (Indian and Foreign Books)

D.C. BOOKS
D.C. Kizhakemuri Edam, Good Shepherd St.,
Kottayam-686001 (Kerala)
✆ 2563114, 2301614, Fax: 2564758
info@dcbooks.com, ravide@dcbooks.com, dcbooks@sanchar.net.com
www.dcbooks.com
Estd.: 1974; **Hd.Org.:** Ravi Deecee
Br.: Karimpanai Statue Avenue, Statue Jn., Thiruvananthapuram-695001
✆ 0471-2453379
Estd.: 1995; **Man.:** K.A. Tony Antoney
Bus.Intt.: Pub. and Dist.; **Spl.:** Fiction, L.S. and Rt., Gen. Books, Dictionaries, etc.

D.I. PUBLICATIONS PVT. LTD.
Mumbai (Maharashtra)
✆ 26327007, 26320239
dipublications@vsnl.com, dip@bom5.vsnl.net.in
Bus.Intt.: Pub. & B.S.

D.K. AGENCIES (P) LTD.
A/15-17, D.K. Avenue, Mohan Garden,
Najafgarh Rd., New Delhi-110059
✆ 25357104-5, Fax: 91-11-25357103
custserv@dkagencies.com, pubrel@dkagencies.com
www.dkagencies.com
Estd.: 1968 **Dir.:** Jaswant Rai Mittal
Br.: 4788-90/23, Ansari Rd., New Delhi-110002
✆ 23266890 pubrel@dkagencies.com
• D.K. Book Organisation,
A/18, Mohan Garden, New Delhi-110059
✆ 25357106, **Hd.Org.:** Surya P. Mittal
• D.K. Language Bookshop, A/15-17, Mohan Garden, New Delhi-110059 ✆ 25357107; **Hd.Org.:** Shalaj Mittal; **Bus.Intt.:** Pub., WS, L.S. & Rt., Exp., Sub.Ag.; **Spl.:** Humanities & Soc.Sci., Sci. & Tech., Med., Law, Gen. & Fiction etc.

D.K. FINE ART PRESS PVT. LTD.
A-6, Nimri Commercial Centre, Ashok Vihar, Phase-IV, Delhi-110052
✆ 91-11-27302451, 27302929
Hd.Org.: Parmod Mittal; **Bus.Intt.:** Exp.; **Spl.:** Engaged in offset printing and provides publishing services

D.K. PRINT WORLD (P) LTD.
Sri Kunj, F-52, Bali Nagar, New Delhi-110015
✆ 25453975, 25466019, Fax: 25465926
dkprintworld@vsnl.net
www.dkprintworld.com
Estd.: 1992; **Dir.:** Susheel Kr. Mittal, Mrs. Lata Mittal; **Bus.Intt.:** Pub., L.S.; **Spl.:** Culture, Archaeology Numismatics, Sanskrit Studies, Classical Litt., Aesthetic & Classical Arts, Theatre, Music and Dance, Reference and Guide Books, Social and Anthropological Studies, Traditional Phil., Tantra and Yoga, Hist., Ancient, Medieval and Modern, Rels., Hinduism, Buddhism and Islamic and other Indology-related Themes

D.K. PUBLISHERS DISTRIBUTORS PVT. LTD.
4834/24, Ansari Rd., Darya Ganj,
New Delhi-110002
✆ 23278368, 23261465, 23279215, 23278584, Fax: 23264368
dkpd@del3.vsnl.net.in
www.dkpd.com

Estd.: 1974; **Dir.:** Parmil Mittal, Pradeep Mittal, Praveen Mittal; **Bus.Intt.:** Pub. & Dist.; **Spl.:** Soc.Sci.

D.K. PUBLISHERS (INDIA)
31/12, B.S. Colony Vishwas Nagar, Shahdara, Delhi-110032
✆ 22231686

D.K. PUBLISHING HOUSE
11, Motia Market, Moti Masjid, Sultania Rd., Bhopal-462001 (Madhya Pradesh)
✆ 2543646, 2544883
Bus.Intt.: Pub. & L.S.

D.M. LIBRARY
Sardar Patel Marg, P.O. Box No. 1077, Allahabad-211001 (Uttar Pradesh)
Bus.Intt.: B.S. & Pub.

D.M. LIBRARY
42, Bidhan Sarani, Post Box No. 11453, Kolkata-700006 (West Bengal)
✆ 033-22413665, 23506385
Estd.: 1921; **Prt.:** Amulya Gopal Majumder, Ashish Gopal Mazumder; **Bus.Intt.:** Pub.; **Spl.:** Gen. Books, School and Colleges Text Books in Bengali

D.N. BOOK CORNER
Boring Canal Rd., Patna-800001 (Bihar)
Bus.Intt.: Pub. & B.S.

D.N. DAHAR AND SONS
15, B.C. Chaterjee St., Kolkata-700073 (West Bengal)

D.N. PUBLICATIONS
10/2, Ramanath Majumder St., Kolkata-700009 (West Bengal)

D.P. BOOK AGENCY
1-1609, Chittranjan Park, New Delhi-110019
✆ 26273801 ▮ 9810254121
Prop.: Devapriya Guha; **Bus.Intt.:** Pub., L.S.; **Spl.:** Acad., Sci., Soc.Sci., Reference

D.P.B. PUBLICATIONS
110, Chawri Bazar, Chowk Bulla, Delhi-110006
✆ (O) 23273220 (R) 22929819
Estd.: 1936; **Hd.Org.:** Balkrishan Gupta; **Bus.Intt.:** Pub.; **Spl.:** Rel., Tech. & Astrological

D.R. EXPORTS
New Delhi
✆ 24640153, Fax: 24640153
@ ragupta@ndb.vsnl.net.in
Bus.Intt.: Exp.

D.S. BOOKS INTERNATIONAL
Shop No. 202, N.P.A. Arcade, 23 M.G. Marg, Civil Lines, Allahabad-211011 (Uttar Pradesh)
✆ 2560866, Fax: 91-532-2560866
@ dsbooksinternational@indiatimes.com
Hd.Org.: K.P. Tiwari; **Bus.Intt.:** Exp.; **Spl.:** Importer and supplier of books and journals on legal, medical, scientific, technical, commercial, educational and professional subjects

D.S. PUBLISHERS (INDIA)
E-1/16, Darya Ganj, Near Kastle Guest House, New Delhi-110002
✆ 65253158, 41563757, Fax: 91-11-23244046
@ ds_bookmaster@yahoo.co.in
Hd.Org.: Vimal Sardana; **Bus.Intt.:** Pub.; **Spl.:** Children's Books including Educational Material and Gen. reference books

D.V.S. PUBLICATIONS
100, Tilak Khand, Giri Nagar, Kalkaji, New Delhi-110019
✆ 26225623
Prop.: D.V. Singh; **Bus.Intt.:** Pub., WS, L.S., Sub.Ag.; **Spl.:** Acad., Beh.Sci., Soc.Sci., Comm., Sci., Pure & Applied, Med., Tech., Rare Journals & Magazines

D.V.S. PUBLISHER
A.T. Road Gate No. 7, Guwahati-781009 (Assam)
✆ 2548965, 2525789, Fax: 2638295
@ dvs@gw1.dot.net.in, dvsgh@sancharnet.in
Estd.: 1992; **Prop.:** Vinay Sharma
Br.: H.B. Rd., Panbazar, Guwahati-781001
✆ 2638295, Fax: 2638295
@ dvs@gw1.dot.net.in
Bus.Intt.: Pub., WS, L.S. & Rt.; **Spl.:** Sci. & Tech., Humanities & Soc.Sci., Juvenile/Children

DAANISH BOOKS
26-B, Skylark Apartments, Gazipur, Delhi-110096
• C-502, Taj Apartments, Gazipur, Delhi-110096
✆ 91-11-22239812, ▮ 9868242343
@ daanishbooks@gmail.com
Rep.: Dhruv Narayan, Sunita Kumari

DADA CENTRE PUBLICATIONS
C/o Dr. L.N. Pandya, Flat No. 31, 6th Floor, Queens Lawn, S.V. Rd., Vile Parle (West), Mumbai-400056 (Maharashtra)

DAFFODILS PUBLICATIONS
H-3/112, Vardhaman Plaza Tower, Netaji Subhash Place, New Delhi-110034
✆ 47013394, Fax: 91-11-42470122
@ daffodilspub@yahoo.com
www.daffodilspub.com
Hd.Org.: Pooja Gupta; **Bus.Intt.:** Pub. & Dist.; **Spl.:** Books for Children

DAFFODILS TECHNOLOGIES
1, Dali Bagh, Butler Rd., Lucknow-226001 (Uttar Pradesh)
✆ 2208330, 2206852
✉ daffodilstechnologies@rediffmail.com
Estd.: 1997; **Prop.:** Amit Kumar; **Bus.Intt.:** L.S. & Rt.; **Spl.:** Sci. & Tech. (Comp.)

DAHIYA BOOK INTERNATIONAL
H. No. 377, G.T. Rd., Azadpur Village, Delhi-110033
✆ (O) 27222210, 27133464 (R) 0130-2573303
Fax: 011-27673844
Prop.: Raghbir Singh Dahiya; **Bus.Intt.:** WS, Dist., L.S.; **Spl.:** Mang., Arch., Acad., Beh.Sci., Comm., Sci. & Tech. Edu. etc.

DAKSHINA
C-5, St. Columbas Apartment, Plot 15, Sector 7, Dwarka, New Delhi-110075
✆ 91-11-25075116
✉ vayttadenvc@rediffmail.com
Hd.Org.: Grace Manuel; **Bus.Intt.:** Pub., Dist. & Spl.; **Spl.:** Malayalam language Books

DAKSHINA
14, Manocha Apartments, Vikas Puri, Delhi-110018
✆ 25593406, Fax: 25527689
Hd.Org.: V.C. Emmanual; **Bus.Intt.:** B.S.; **Spl.:** Malayalam Books

DALIT BAHUJAN INTELLECTUAL FORUM OF INDIA
387-A, J & K Pocket, Dilshad Garden, Delhi-110095
✆ 22298067 ▮ 9818385185
✉ dbifi777@hotmail.com
Hd.Org.: S.K. Biswas; **Bus.Intt.:** Pub. & Dist.; **Spl.:** Dalit Litt., Secular Media, Buddhist Litt. and Books on Indology

DALIT PRESS
BC/1-H, DDA Flats, Munirka, New Delhi-110067
✆ 26162892 ▮ 9810030126
Ch.Exe.: Mrs. Lovely George
Bus.Intt.: Pub.; **Spl.:** Books, Articles and Magazine for people interested in Dalits

DALIT SAHITYA RESEARCH FOUNDATION
C-263-A, 'Chandan Sadan', Hardevpuri, Delhi-110093
✆ 22570380, Fax: 22219239
✉ gautambookcentre@hotmail.com
www.geocities.com/gautambookcentre
Hd.Org.: S.S. Gautam; **Bus.Intt.:** Pub. and Dist.; **Spl.:** Ambedkar, Buddha and Dalits

DANAI BOOKS AND MUSIC STORE
Mangal Smruthi, 14th Khar Danda Rd., Khar, Mumbai-400052 (Maharashtra)
✆ 022-26487123
Estd.: 1992; **Hd.Org.:** Mrs. J. Mango; **Bus.Intt.:** Rt.; **Spl.:** Gen. & Trade, CD-ROMs, Magazines, Stationery, Audio & Video Cassettes & Games

DANAI BOOKSHOP
The Sindoorie Hotel, 24, Greams Rd., Chennai-600006 (Tamil Nadu)
✆ 044-2825019
Ch.Exe.: Prema Gopinath

DANAYAT BOOK DISTRIBUTORS
23, Farm Land, Central Bazar Rd., New Ramdaspeth Nagpur-440010 (Maharashtra)
✆ 2532015, 2557365,
Fax: 0712-2555213
Estd.: 1975; **Prt.:** Amit Mujumdar; **Bus.Intt.:** Dist.; **Spl.:** Mining, Electrical, Mechanical and Civil Engg.

DANIKA PUBLISHING COMPANY
4352/4C, Ansari Road, Darya Ganj, New Delhi-110002
✆ 91-11-30122482-83
✉ danikabooks@yahoo.com
Hd.Org.: Rajat Manocha; **Bus.Intt.:** Pub.; **Spl.:** Educational books and books for competitive exams

DARBARI OFFSET PVT. LTD.
Darbari Complex, Vill. & P.O. Ganaganagar, Distt. (N.) 24-Parganas-743250 (West Bengal)
Hd.Org.: Barin Mitra

DARBARI PROKASHAN
206, Bidhan Sarani, Kolkata-700006 (West Bengal)

DARBARI UDYOG
16/3E, Dixon Lane, Kolkata-700014 (West Bengal)

DARSAN BOOKS (P) LIMITED
Palayam, Thiruvananthapuram-695034 (Kerala)
✆ 276281
Estd.: 1982; **Man.Dir.:** Sebastian Mathew; **Bus.Intt.:** B.S.

DARSHAK EDUCATIONAL CONSULTANTS
6, Prabha Society, Harni Kishanwadi Rd., Vadodara-390022 (Gujarat)

DARSHAN BOOK STORE
Chowk Shikarpur, Patna City, Patna-800008 (Bihar)
Bus.Intt.: Pub. & B.S.

DARSHAN PEETH
177, Tagore Town, Allahabad-110002 (Uttar Pradesh)

DARSANA CULTURAL CENTRE
Sastri Rd., Kottayam-686001 (Kerala)
✆ 0481-2564755, 2564602
Estd.: 1984; **CMI Dir.:** George Edayadiyil; **Bus.Intt.:** Pub. & Organiser; **Spl.:** Kottayam Book Fair

DARSHANA INTERNATIONAL
Diwan Bazar, Moradabad (Uttar Pradesh)

DARSHITA PRAKASHAN
F-6, Shraddha Complex, Mehsana (Gujarat)

DARTEX INTERNATIONAL
A.H. 202, Sector-2, Salt Lake City, Kolkata-700091 (West Bengal)

DAR-UL-IAHAAT-KUTAB-ISLAMIA
Fatmahai Court, 4th Floor, 17 Maulana Azad Rd., Jacob Circus, Mumbai-400011 (Maharashtra)
Bus.Intt.: Pub. & Dist.

DAS BOOK HOUSE
14, Bankim Chatterjee St., Kolkata-700073 (West Bengal)

DAS (DUTTA) BOOK STALL
P.D.S. Corner, Stall-5, 7, Bankim, Kolkata-700073 (West Bengal)

DAS GUPTA & CO. (P) LTD.
54/3, College St., Kolkata-73 (West Bengal)
✆ 22414609, 22416531, Telex: BOIOLA, Fax: 22416479
✉ dgboiola@cal.vsnl.net.in
Estd.: 1886; **Bus.Intt.:** Pub., Imp., Exp.; **Spl.:** Humanities & Soc.Sci.

DAS GUPTA PRAKASHAN
C-15, College St. Market, Kolkata-700007 (West Bengal)

DAS MEDIA P. LTD.
No. 26, Poes Garden, Chennai-600086 (Tamil Nadu)
Bus.Intt.: Exp.

DAS PUBLISHERS
Baganda, Puraliapara, Howrah (West Bengal)

DAS PUBLISHING CONCERN
25/2, Bidhan Sarani, Kolkata-6 (West Bengal)

DAS PUSTAK BHANDAR
Bharkho, Amarpur, Bhagalpur-813126 (Bihar)
Bus.Intt.: Pub. & B.S.

DAS PUSTAK BHANDAR
Shambhuganj, Bhagalpur-813211 (Bihar)
Bus.Intt.: Pub. & B.S.

DAS TRADING COMPANY
35-A, Christopher Rd., Kolkata-700046 (West Bengal)

DASTAK PRAKASHAN
15, Preet Vihar, Tad, Pakhowal Road, Ludhiana (Punjab)
✆ 91-161-2807127 ▮ 989199332
✉ dastak_prakashan@gmail.com
Hd.Org.: Sukhvinder; **Bus.Intt.:** Pub., **Spl.:** Important literary works on socio-cultural issues by authors of Indian and foreign origin

DASTANE RAMCHANDRA & CO.
830, Sadashiv Peth, Chitrashala Chowk, Pune-411030 (Maharashtra)
✆ (O) 24478193, 24485950 (R) 25511964
Estd.: 1935; **Bus.Intt.:** Pub., **Spl.:** Humanities, Gen. Books, Childrens, Competition Sports

DATA BOOK DEPOT
2075, Nahar Khan Kucha Chelan, Darya Ganj, New Delhi-110002
✆ 91-11-23283494
Hd.Org.: Shaheen Parveen; **Bus.Intt.:** Pub., **Spl.:** Islamic literature in Urdu

DATANET INDIA PVT. LTD.
F-89/5, 1st Floor, Maa Anandamayi Marg, Okhla Industrial Area, Phase-I, New Delhi-110020
✆ 26810964-65-66, Fax: 011-26810968,
www.indiastat.com; **Hd.Org.:** R.K. Thukral; **Br.:** Sterling House, 7th Floor, 5/7, Sorabji Santuk Lane, Opp. Dr. Cowasji Hormasji Lane, Dhobi Talao, Mumbai-400002 (Maharashtra);
▮ 9323187101
✉ membership@datanetindia.com
Bus.Intt.: Pub., **Spl.:** Provide socio-economic statistical data on India and its states through Web portal www.indiastat.com Publisher of Indiastat e-year book.

DATTA BOOK CENTRE
15 UB, Kamla Nagar, New Delhi-110007
✆ 23975680
Estd.: 1969; **Ch.Exe.:** A.S. Datta; **Bus.Intt.:** Rt.

DATTSONS
J. Nehru Marg, Sadar, Nagpur-440001 (Maharashtra)
✆ (O) 2524659 (R) 2532544, Fax: 0712-2537896
✉ dattsons@hotmail.com
Estd.: 1954; **Hd.Org.:** Vinod Nangia; **Bus.Intt.:** Pub.; **Spl.:** Sci. & Tech., Comm. & Mang., Humanities

DAUGHTERS OF ST. PAL
143, Waterfield Rd., Bandra, Mumbai-400050 (Maharashtra)

DAWN PUBLISHERS
D-52, Jhandewalan, Factories Complex, Jhandewalan, New Delhi-110055

DAWOOD BOOK CENTRE
168/9, Angappa St., Chennai-600001 (Tamil Nadu)
✆ 91-44-25240079
Hd.Org.: S.N. Mohamed Mohideen

DAYA PUBLISHING HOUSE
1123/74 Deva Ram Park, Tri Nagar, Delhi-110035
✆ (O) 27383999, 27382765 (R) 23260116, Fax: 27382329
✉ dayabooks@vsnl.com
www.dayabooks.com
Estd.: 1986; **Prop.:** Anil Mittal
Br.: 4760-61/23, Ansari Rd., Darya Ganj, New Delhi-110002
✆ 23245578, 23244987, Fax: 27382329
✉ dayabooks@vsnl.com
Bus.Intt.: Pub., L.S.; **Spl.:** Acad. Biological, Sci., Env., Soc.Sci., Sci., Pure & Applied

DAYAL BOOK STORE
Sujaganj, Bhagalpur-812002 (Bihar)
Bus.Intt.: Pub. & B.S.

DAYAL PUSTAK BHANDAR
Kankerbagh, Patna-800020 (Bihar)
Bus.Intt.: Pub. & B.S.

DAYANAND PUSTAK BHANDAR
Belhar Sehebganj, Bhagalpur-813202 (Bihar)
Bus.Intt.: Pub. & B.S.

DAYANAND SANSTHAN
2286, Arya Samaj Rd., Karol Bagh, New Delhi-110005
✆ 28752741, 41004741, Fax: 91-11-23556005
Hd.Org.: Rakesh Rani; **Bus.Intt.:** Pub.; **Spl.:** Books on the *Vedas*, religion and writings of Maharshi Dayanand and monthly journal *Jangyan* in Hindi

DAYITVA BODH
55, UNI Apartment, Sector 11, Vasundhara, Ghaziabad-201010 (Uttar Pradesh)
▮ 9910462009
✉ dayitvabodh@rediffmail.com
Hd.Org.: Vishwanath Mishra
Bus.Intt.: Pub.; **Spl.:** Analytical material on various economic, political, social cultural and current issues

DAYSTAR PUBLICATIONS
3, Raisina Rd., 1 N.D.M.C. Market, New Delhi-110001
✆ 23352438, 22063201, Fax: 91-11-23736679
✉ daystar_publications@yahoo.co.uk
Estd.: 1978; **Hd.Org.:** Shailendra Kumar Mishra; **Bus.Intt.:** Pub., L.S. & Rt., Imp., Sub.Ag.; **Spl.:** Sci. & Tech., Med., Law

DAZZLE PUBLICATIONS PVT. LTD.
C-330, Vashi Plaza, Sector-17, Vashi, Navi Mumbai-400705 (Maharashtra)
Hd.Org.: Paul Parapilly

DEB BOOK AGENCY
116, Rafi Ahmed Kiwai Rd., Kolkata-55 (West Bengal)

DEB PRAKASHAN
22/A, College Row, Kolkata-700009 (West Bengal)

DEBARPITA PRAKASHANI
8B/1, Tamer Lane, Kolkata-700009 (West Bengal)

DEBE BOOK STALL
208, Khajuri Bazar, Indore-452002 (Madhya Pradesh)

DEBENDRA GRANTHALAYA
15, B.C. Chatterjee St., Kolkata-700073 (West Bengal)
Hd.Org.: Benu Chakraborty

DEBI PRAKASHAN
30, College Row, Kolkata-700009 (West Bengal)

DEBI STORES
Kandi, Murshidabad (West Bengal)
Hd.Org.: Shyamalesh Chatterjee

DEBLIPI
3, Ramanath Majumder St., Kolkata-9 (West Bengal)

DEEKSHA PRAKASHAN
1539, Ram Krishan Bhavan, Gali Mukesh Market, Gandhi Nagar, Delhi-110001

DEEP AND DEEP PUBLICATIONS (P) LTD.
F-159, Rajouri Garden, New Delhi-110027
✆ (O) 25435369, 25440916, 55479461 (R) 25440855, 32535220, 31075546, Fax: 91-11-25440916
✉ ddpubs@gmail.com, ddpbooks@yahoo.co.in
www.ddpbooks.com
Estd.: 1981; **Man.Dir.:** G.S. Bhatia
Sh.: 2/13, Ansari Rd., Darya Ganj, New Delhi-110002
✆ 23245122, 55479462, Fax: 91-11-23245122
✉ ddpubs@gmail.com, ddpbooks@yahoo.co.in
Bus.Intt.: Pub., B.S., Exp.; **Spl.:** Eco., Comm., Mang., Public Administration, Law, Pol.Sci., Edu., Military Sci.

DEEP BOOK CENTRE
Naroshankar Building (Basement),

Near Rajabahadur Hospital, Nasik-422001 (Maharashtra)
✆ (O) 0253-2594498 (R) 0253-2598120
✉ deepbooks2003@yahoo.com
Estd.: 1998; **Prop.:** Gothi Sandeep Tansukhlal; **Bus.Intt.:** B.S. and L.S.
Spl.: Humanities & Soc.Sci., Tech., Med., Mang., Arts & Arch., Gen., Comp.

DEEP CO-BOOK WORLD
69, Yashwant Place, New Delhi-110021
Sh.: Bookworld, 7, Palika Bazar, New Delhi-110001
Bookshop: Ashoka Hotel, New Delhi-110021
✆ (O) 24671645, 24104981, 23353223 (R) 26567491, 26856262
Prop.: Deep C. Jain; **Bus.Intt.:** Rt., L.S.; **Spl.:** Indology, Art, Arch., Travel & Phil. books

DEEP PRAKASHAN
6-A, Shyam Charan Dey St., Kolkata-700073 (West Bengal)

DEEP PUBLICATIONS
B-1/118, IInd Floor, Paschim Vihar, New Delhi-110063
✆ (O) 25259514 (R) 25264726
✉ deep_pub@hotmail.com
Estd.: 1989; **Prop.:** Vipul Jain
Bus.Intt.: Pub., L.S., Exp.; **Spl.:** Tech., Med.

DEEP PUBLISHING
Kanchan Market, Hospital Rd., Agra (Uttar Pradesh)
✆ 2261220, Fax: 2311012
✉ sumit8@sancharnet.in
Bus.Intt.: Pub.

DEEPA & COMPANY
2619-20, Ist Floor, New Market, Nai Sarak, Delhi-110006
✆ 22918382
Bus.Intt.: Rt. B.S.; **Spl.:** Text & Guide of School, College Level

DEEPA ENTERPRISES
J-392, New Rajender Nagar, New Delhi-110060
✆ 25850230
Hd.Org.: Ashok Saigal; **Bus.Intt.:** B.S.; **Spl.:** Gen., Sci. and Reference Books

DEEPA PRAKASHAN
146, Gyankhand-3, Indirapuram, Ghaziabad-201012 (Uttar Pradesh)
✆ 2900191, ▮ 9811271465, Fax: 91-11-23270889
✉ cbyash@yahoo.com
Hd.Org.: Chandra Bhushan
Bus.Intt.: Pub.; **Spl.:** Hindi Litt., Sci., Novels, Criticisms and Children's Books

DEEPA PREETHA PUBLICATIONS
C/o Devaki Hospital Limited, 148, Luz Church Rd., Mylapore, Chennai-600004 (Tamil Nadu)

DEEPAK BOOK DEPOT
Opp. Jalan School, Patna City, Patna-800008 (Bihar)
Bus.Intt.: Pub. & B.S.

DEEPAK BOOK STORE
Bawana Rd., Shahbad Daulatpur, Delhi
▮ 9818564834
✉ pradeepgrewal@redffmail.com
Hd.Org.: Pradeep Grewal; **Bus.Intt.:** Dealers; **Spl.:** All Stationery, Engg. Books, Civil Service Books & Engg. Service Books

DEEPAK ENTERPRISES
836, 28th A Main, 9th Block, Jayanagar, Bangalore-560004 (Karnataka)

DEEPAK PEN & BOOK STORE
Jhauganj, Patna City, Patna-800008 (Bihar)
Bus.Intt.: Pub. & B.S.

DEEPAK PRAKASHAN
D.P. House, 1 Durga Colony, 6 No. Chauraha, Kalpi Road, Morar, Gwalior-474006 (Madhya Pradesh)
✆ 4040200, Fax: 91-751-2368746
✉ deepakprakashan@hotmail.com
Estd.: 1981; **Prop.:** Deepak Gupta;
Bus.Intt.: Pub.; **Spl.:** Technical, management computer, environmental science, commerce, ITI and pharmacy books in Hindi and English

DEEPAK PUBLISHERS
Mai Hiran Gate, Jalandhar-147008 (Punjab)
✆ (O) 2281924, 2214196 (R) 2210996
Estd.: 1954; **Hd.Org.:** Charanjeet Lal; **Bus.Intt.:** Pub. and B.S., **Spl.:** Gen. Books

DEEPAK PUBLISHERS & DISTRIBUTORS
Gwalior (Madhya Pradesh)
✆ 325054, 330209
✉ anirudh110@sify.com
Bus.Intt.: L.S.

DEEPAK PUSTAK BHANDAR
Khalgaon (Colgong), Bhagalpur-813203 (Bihar)
Bus.Intt.: Pub. & B.S.

DEEPAK PUSTAK BHANDAR
Bakhtiarpur, Patna-803212 (Bihar)
Bus.Intt.: Pub. & B.S.

DEEPAK PUSTAKALAYA
Chiraiyatand, Patna-800001 (Bihar)
Bus.Intt.: Pub. & B.S.

DEEPALI GRAPHICS
Byculla Indl. Est., No. 407/A, D.K. Marg, Byculla, Mumbai-400027 (Maharashtra)

© 91-22-23724853/0153, Fax: 23720153
Hd.Org.: Jethalal Savla

DEEPAM BOOK CLUB
Griha Deepam, Vennikulam P.O., Pathanamthitta-689547 (Kerala)
Estd.: 1973; **Man.Prt.:** Mammen Philip; **Bus.Intt.:** Pub.

DEEPANALAM PUBLICATIONS
Palai, Kottayam-686575 (Kerala)
Estd.: 1968; **Man.Trustee:** James K. Zacharias; **Bus.Intt.:** Pub. & B.S.

DEEPAYAN
79, M.G. Rd., Kolkata-700009 (West Bengal)

DEEPIKA BOOK HOUSE
Sastri Rd., Kottayam-686001 (Kerala)
© 0481-2564547
Estd.: 1924; **Hd.Org.:** Lukose Parayaruthottom CMI, **Bus.Intt.:** Pub.

DEEPREKHA PRAKASHAN
17, Poornayan, Pt. D.D. Marg, Dombivli West, Distt. Thane (Maharashtra)

DEEPSHIKA PRAKASHAN
51/2, New Market, Near Liberty Cinema, Karol Bagh, New Delhi-110005

DEEPSHIKHA BOOKS & INFO SERVICES
A2/11A, Adarsh Apartments, Paschim Vihar, Delhi-110063
© 35340557, 32361740
✉ deepshikha_in2000@yahoo.com
Hd.Org.: Shradha Kaushal; **Bus.Intt.:** Pub.; **Spl.:** Educational Material for School Children

DEEPU PRAKASHAN
A-3/12, Satyawati Nagar, Ashok Vihar, Phase-III, Delhi-110052
© (O) 23258909, 23281911 (R) 27138165, Fax: 23258909
✉ tarunpub@yahoo.com
Estd.: 1980; **Prop.:** Deepak Arora; **Bus.Intt.:** Pub.; **Spl.:** School Text & Children Books in English & Hindi

DEHATI PUSTAK BHANDAR
4422, Nai Sadak, Delhi-110006
© 23279417, 23985175
Fax: 91-11-23261030
✉ hans@ndb.vsnl.net.in
Hd.Org.: Ramprakash Gupta; **Bus.Intt.:** Pub. and B.S.; **Spl.:** Ayurveda, Tech., Rel., Astrology, Comp., Gen. Books in Hindi

DEHATI PUSTAK BHANDAR
Khazanchi Rd., Patna-800004 (Bihar)
Bus.Intt.: Pub. & B.S.

DELHI ARYA PRATINIDHI SABHA
Arya Samaj Mandir, 15 Hanuman Rd., New Delhi-110001
© 23360150, 41500589, Fax: 91-11-23365959
✉ aryasabha@yahoo.com
Hd.Org.: Vinay Arya; **Bus.Intt.:** Pub.; **Spl.:** Regional Language, Rel., Culture and The *Vedas*

DELHI BIBLE INSTITUTE
50, Amrita Shergill Marg, Behind Khan Market, New Delhi-110003
© 24611311, Fax: 91-11-24638625
✉ dbi7bb@gmail.com
Hd.Org.: Isaac J. Shaw; **Bus.Intt.:** Pub. and Dist.; **Spl.:** *The Holy Bible* and children's books in various languages

DELHI BOOK COMPANY
M-12, Connaught Circus, New Delhi-110001
© 23416313, 23417268, Fax: 91-11-23625020
✉ mybooks@vishvbooks.com
www.vishvbook.com
Prt.: Rakesh Nath; **Bus.Intt.:** Pub., Rt. & Newspaper Dist.; **Spl.:** Fiction, Edu., Sci., Rel. Books in Hindi

DELHI BOOK HOUSE
77, Gokhale Market, Opposite New Courts, Tis Hazari, Delhi-110054

DELHI BOOK STORE
19, Ansari Rd., Opp. Fire Station, Darya Ganj, New Delhi-110002
© 23283333, 23281202, 23250909
9811084529, Fax: 91-11-23283781
✉ delhibooks@delnetworks.com, vjdelhibook@bol.net.in
www.delhibookstore.com
Estd.: 1957; **Prt.:** Jiwan Ahuja, Vijay Ahuja
Sh.: 1690, 1st Floor, Nai Sarak, Delhi-110006
© 23260070, 23267928, Fax: 23259595
Shop: 1696, Nai Sarak, Delhi-110006
© 23267928, Fax: 23259598
Bus.Intt.: Imp. American and British Books, WS, Dist., Pub. & Rt. of Med. Text & Reference Books; **Spl.:** Med., Tech., Comp., Agri., Geology, Mang. & Comm., Eco., Life Sci., Geo., Psych., Sol., Math., Biology, Physics, Chemistry and Gen. Books on all Sub.

DELHI BUREAU OF TEXT BOOKS
25/2, Institutional Area Pankha Rd., D-Block, Janakpuri, New Delhi-110058
© 25598049, 25504202, Fax: 91-11-25504901
Estd.: 1970; **Ch.Exe.:** Mr. Rajendra Kumar; **Bus.Intt.:** Pub. of Text Books from Class I to VIII in Hindi Medium

DELHI LAW HOUSE
77, Gokhale Market, Opp. Tis Hazari Courts, Delhi-110054

✆ (O) 23917627, 23963959 (R) 27241770, 27241716, Fax: 91-11-23941793
✉ sales@delhilawhouse.com, editorial@delhilawhouse.com
www.delhilawhouse.com
Man.Prt.: Mohan Sagar; **Bus.Intt.:** Pub. & B.S., Exp.; **Spl.:** Law Books & Reports (Indian & Foreign)

DELHI LIBRARY BOOK CENTRE
D-11/304, Nanda Devi Tower, Prashant Vihar, (Rohini) Delhi-110085
✆ (O) 27557680 (R) 27293793
✉ delhilibrary@yahoo.com
Estd.: 1994; **Prop.:** Anil Dhawan;
Bus.Intt.: Sub.Ag., L.S.; **Spl.:** Acad., Fiction, Journals & Magazines

DELHI LIBRARY NETWORK
40, Max Mueller Marg, New Delhi-110003

DELHI PRESS
E-3, Rani Jhansi Road, Jhandewalan, New Delhi-110055
✆ 41398888, 23529557, Fax: 011-23625020
www.delhipress.in
Estd.: 1939
Br.: M-12, Connaught Circus, New Delhi-110001; ✆ 23416313, 23417268
• 503, Narayan Chambers, Ashram Road, Ahmedabad-380009; ✆ 079-26577063, 26577845; • G-3, Ground Floor, HVS Court, 21 Cunningham Road, Bangalore-52
✆ 22268091; • 12-B, Maharana Pratap Nagar, Zone-I, Bhopal-462011; ✆ 2573057
• 79-A, Mittal Chambers, Nariman Point, Mumbai-400021; ✆ 022-22022409, 22025492
• Poddar Point, 3rd Floor, 113, Park Street, Kolkata-700016; ✆ 033-22298981, 22175315
• G-7, Pioneer Towers 1, Marine Drive, Kochi-682031; ✆ 0484-2371537
• B-G/3,4, Sapru Marg, Lucknow-226001
✆ 0522-2218856
• 14, Cison's Complex, Montieth Road, Chennai-600008; ✆ 044-28554448
• 111, Ashiana Towers, Exhibition Road, Patna-800001; ✆ 0612-2685286
• 122, Chenoy Trade Centre, 116 Park Lane, Secunderabad-500003
✆ 040-27896947, 27841596
• A-4, Shriram Wadala, Industrial Estate, Mumbai; ✆ 022-24101192
• Delhi Prakashan, Plot No. 18, Vivek Nagar, Near Sindh Camp Bus, Stand, Jaipur
✆ 3096580

DELHI PUNJABI PUBLISHER ASSOCIATION
51, Parda Bagh, Near Petrol Bagh, Darya Ganj, New Delhi-110002
✆ 23280657, 65966481
Fax: 91-11-23264342
Hd.Org.: Gurbachan Singh; **Bus.Intt.:** Pub.; **Spl.:** Punjabi Litt. and Religion

DELHI PUSTAK SADAN
30/36, Gali No. 9, Vishwas Nagar, Shahdara, Delhi-110032
✆ 22391120, 22912274, 22307340
✉ dpsbooks@mantraonline.com
Hd.Org.: Sanjeev Prashar; **Bus.Intt.:** Pub.; **Spl.:** Edu. Books and Study Materials in Hindi

DELHI SARASWAT SANGH
22-23, Hargovind Enclave, Chattarpur Rd., P.O. Maidan Garhi, New Delhi-110068
✆ 26302507, Fax: 26524541
✉ sangram32@yahoo.co.in
www.jayaguru.org
Hd.Org.: D.D. Pradhan; **Bus.Intt.:** L.S.; **Spl.:** Phil., Rel. and Spiritualism in English and Regional Languages

DELHI SIKH GURDWARA MANAGEMENT COMMITTEE
Guru Gobind Singh Bhawan, Gurdwara Rakab Ganj Sahib, New Delhi-110001
✆ 23712580-81, Fax: 91-11-23317511
✉ dsgmc@rediffmail.com
www.dsgpc.com
Hd.Org.: S. Paramjit Singh Sarna;
Bus.Intt.: B.S.; **Spl.:** Punjabi Books on Sikh Hist. and Rel.

DELHI WIRELESS INSTITUTE (REGD.)
5/74, W.E.A. Padam Singh Rd., Karol Bagh, New Delhi-110005
✆ (O) 25723659, 25723691 (R) 25103758, Fax: 25723691
✉ arvindm@vsnl.com
Estd.: 1947; **Prop.:** Arvind Malhotra;
Bus.Intt.: Rt.; **Spl.:** Tech., Journals & Magazines & Comp. Books

DELIGHT FORMS & BOOKS AGENCY
5/219, Lalita Park, Laxmi Nagar, Delhi-110092
✆ 91-11-22011761 ▮ 9868105925
Hd.Org.: Rajiv Kumar Gupta
Bus.Intt.: Retailer, L.S.

DELIP STORES
70/2, K.G. Bose Sarani, Kolkata-700085 (West Bengal)

DELUX PUBLICATIONS
Karl Marx Rd., Vijayawada-520002 (Andhra Pradesh)
✆ 0866-276636
Estd.: 1980; **Prop.:** P.V. Choudhary;
Bus.Intt.: Pub.; **Spl.:** Cookery, Language Usage and Grammar, Novels, Fictions and Children's books

DELUXE BOOK STORES
6-7, N.S.B. Shopping Centre, Opp. Stadium, Valsad-396001 (Gujarat)

DEO SAHITYA MANDIR
Amarpur, Bhagalpur-813101 (Bihar)
Bus.Intt.: Pub. and B.S.

DEPALI BOOK HOUSE
13/1B, Bankim Chatterjee St., Kolkata-700073 (West Bengal)

DEPARTMENT OF CULTURAL PUBLICATIONS
Ambujavilasam, Hospital Rd., Thycaud, Thiruvananthapuram-695014 (Kerala)
✆ 268193, 268351
Dir.: C. Gopinathan Nair; **Bus.Intt.:** Pub.; **Spl.:** Art, Culture and Litt. of Kerala and Biographies

DEPARTMENT OF LANGUAGE & CULTURE (H.P. GOVT.)
Shimla-171001 (Himachal Pradesh)
✆ 2258611, Fax: 0177-2258611
Dir.: Prem Sharma
Bus.Intt.: Deal in Printing; **Spl.:** Hindi, Hist., Archology, Arts

DEPARTMENT OF MALAYALAM LEXICON
University of Kerala, Thiruvanathapuram-695034 (Kerala)
✆ 2447329
Estd.: 1953; **Bus.Intt.:** Pub.

DEPARTMENT OF PRINTING & PUBLISHING
Mahatma Gandhi University, Hassan Manzil, Athirampuzha, Kottayam-686562 (Kerala)
Estd.: 1988; **Bus.Intt.:** Pub.

DEPARTMENT OF PUBLICATION
(Ministry of Urban Development & Poverty Alleviation), Civil Lines, Delhi-110054
✆ 23813764, Fax: 91-11-23817846
✉ acop.dep@nic.in
🌐 www.dept.pub.nic.in
Hd.Org.: Mohan Rao; **Bus.Intt.:** Stockist and Seller; **Spl.:** All Govt. of India Publications

DERASAL PRAKASHAN
447, Pili Kothi, Nai Basti, Kydgang, Allahabad-211003 (Uttar Pradesh)

DESABHIMANI BOOK HOUSE
Head Office, P.B. No. 172, Thiruvananthapuram-695001 (Kerala)

DESH RAJ LIBRARY & EDUCATIONAL BOOK SUPPLIER
A-62/63, Shakti Vihar, Near Kamal Model School, Mohan Garden, New Delhi-110059

DESHBANDHU PAPER HOUSE
28, Harish Neogi Rd., Kolkata-700067 (West Bengal)

DESHI VIDESHI BOOK TRADERS
JI/377, Kalkaji, DDA Flats, New Delhi-110019
✆ 26229790, 26221204
✉ deshivideshi@yahoo.com
Hd.Org.: Gagan Babbar
Bus.Intt.: Specialist and Stockist
Spl.: Archie Comics, Gen. Books, Cookery Books, Children's Books, etc.

DESHMUKH & CO.
473, Sadashiv, Tilak Rd., Pune-411030 (Maharashtra)

DESIGN POINT (THE)
Mumbai (Maharashtra)
✉ honesty@vsnl.com

DESTINATION WORLDWIDE
3/3465, 1st Floor, Regharpura, Karol Bagh, New Delhi-110005
✆ 25740525
✉ anju7@vsnl.com
Hd.Org.: Anju Jain; **Bus.Intt.:** Pub.; **Spl.:** Monthly Magazine *Destination Worldwide*

DEV DHARAM PRAKASHAN
Rangpuri, P.O. Mahipal Pur, New Delhi-110037
✆ 26897078

DEV LIBRARY
1, Sahama Charan Dey St., Kolkata-700073 (West Bengal)

DEV NAGARI PRAKASHAN
Chowra Rasta, Jaipur-302003 (Rajasthan)
Hd.Org.: Manmohan Rai Jain

DEV SAHITYA KUTHIR (P) LTD.
21, Jhamapukur Lane, Kolkata-700009 (West Bengal)
✆ 2350-24294/24295
Bus.Intt.: Pub., **Spl.:** Contemporary Children's Litt. in Bengali, English and Hindi

DEV SAMAJ PRAKASHAN
Dev Samaj Modern School, Sukhdev Vihar, New Delhi-110025
✆ 91-11-26911101
✉ mnj_1416@yahoo.com
Hd.Org.: Girwar Parsad Ji; **Bus.Intt.:** Pub.; **Spl.:** Socio-religious books and books on rational thinking and the philosophy of Bhagwan Dev Atma, founder of Dev Samaj

DEV SAMAJ PRAKASHAN
570, Double Storey, New Rajinder Nagar, New Delhi-110060

DEV SAMAJ PRAKASHAN
Dev Samaj Bhavan, Sector 36-B, Chandigarh
✆ 2624240, 2614213
Hd.Org.: Girwarprasad; **Bus.Intt.:** Pub.; **Spl.:** Socio-Rel. Books

DEVSANSKRITI VISHV VIDHYALAYA
Shantikunj, Haridwar (Uttarakhand)
✆ 261367, Fax: 91-334-260866
Hd.Org.: Harish Thakkar

DEVAVANI PARISHAD DELHI
R-6, Vani Vihar, New Delhi-110059

DEVELOPMENT ASSOCIATES
Flat No. 178-179, Pocket-7, Sector-2, Rohini, Delhi-110085
✆ 27524081
✉ da_india@hotmail.com
Hd.Org.: J.P. Malik; **Bus.Intt.:** Dist.;
Spl.: Books and Directories for NGOs on project formulation, Fundraising, etc.

DEVI BOOK STALL
Sringapuram, Kodungallur, Trissur-680001 (Kerala)
✆ 2602077, 2602177
Estd.: 1967; **Hd.Org.:** D.V. Devaraja Pai;
Bus.Intt.: Pub. and B.S.

DEVI PUBLISHERS & DISTRIBUTORS
Post Box No. 1066, Pattom P.O., Trivandrum-695004 (Kerala)

DEVKUMAR GANGOPADHYAY
221/N, Parui Paka Rd., Bakultola, Behala, Kolkata-700061 (West Bengal)

DEVNAGAR PRAKASHAN
250, Chaura Rasta, Jaipur-302003 (Rajasthan)
✆ (O) 2563171 (R) 2515328, 2606815
Hd.Org.: Manmohanraj Jain

DEWAN TRADING CORPORATION
156, Abdul Fazal Enclave, Jamia Nagar, New Delhi-110025
Bus.Intt.: Exp.

DEY BOOK CONCERN
14A, Tamer Lane, Kolkata-700009 (West Bengal)
Hd.Org.: Prasanta Dey

DEY BOOK STORE
13, Bankim Chatterjee St., Kolkata-700073 (West Bengal)

DEY BROTHERS
P-55, Ananda Palit Rd., Kolkata-700014 (West Bengal)

DEYS PUBLISHING
13, Bankim Chatterjee St., Kolkata-700073 (West Bengal)
✆ 22412330/9266, Fax: 91-33-22192041
Hd.Org.: Sudhangshu Dey; **Bus.Intt.:** Exp.;
Spl.: Manufacturers of Books

DHAKESWARY PUBLISHERS
93, Mahatma Gandhi Rd., Kolkata-700007 (West Bengal)

DHAKESWARY PUSTAKALAYA
10/2B, Ramanath Majumder St., Kolkata-700009 (West Bengal)

DHANAM PUBLICATION (P) LTD.
Cheruparambath Rd., Kadvanthara, Kochi-682020 (Kerala)
✆ 2315840, 2316494, Fax: 91-484-2317872
✉ dhanrubber@vsnl.net
Estd.: 1987; **Man.Dir.:** Kurian Abraham
Br.: Mumbai (Maharashtra) ✆ 26400829, 26400735, Fax: 26411894
✉ powath@bom3.vsnl.net.in
Bus.Intt.: Pub., B.S.

DHANISHTHA FOUNDATION
10-50-19, "Soudamani", Sirpuram, Visakhapatnam-530003 (Andhra Pradesh)
✆ 2571531, Fax: 2555834
Hd.Org.: K. Sivasankar

DHANLAL BROTHERS
70-5, Gandhi Marg, Mumbai-400002 (Maharashtra)
✆ 2317027, 2253716, Telex: 011-76061 Gala In
Hd.Org.: Kishor Gogri

DHANPAT RAI & CO. (P) LTD.
Educational & Technical Publishers, 1710, Nai Sarak, Delhi-110006
✆ 23265367, 23250251, Fax: 91-11-27233793
✉ dhanpatrai@gmail.com
🌐 www.dhanpatraico.com
Hd.Org.: Jagdish Kapur; **Bus.Intt.:** Pub.;
Spl.: Engg., Tech., Arch., Comp., etc. in English

DHANPAT RAI PUBLISHING CO. PVT. LTD.
4779/23, Ansari Rd., Darya Ganj, New Delhi-110002
✆ 23257526, 23257511, Fax: 99-11-23257525
✉ mail@dhanpatrai.in
🌐 www.dhanpatrai.in
Ed.Org.: Krishan Kapoor; **Bus.Intt.:** Pub.;
Spl.: Text and Reference Books for Schools, ITIs, Engg., Polytechnics and Colleges in English, Hindi and Punjabi

DHANPAT RAI PUBLICATIONS (P) LTD.
22, Ansari Rd., Darya Ganj, New Delhi-110002
✆ (O) 23246573, 23274073, 23246574
(R) 22152148, Fax: 22162852
✉ ishkapur@vsnl.com
🌐 www.dhanpatrai.com
Rgd.Off.: 67/4, 1st Floor, Madras House, Darya Ganj, New Delhi-110002

Estd.: 1997; Hd.Org.: Ish Kapur; Bus.Intt.: Pub. & Dist.; Spl.: Edu. Books on Engg. and Comp. in English

DHANRAJ BOOK HOUSE
528, Block-C, Sector 19, Rohini, Delhi-110085
✆ 27857044, Fax: 91-11-27857044
✉ dhanraj.books@gmail.com
Hd.Org.: Vinod Kumar Dhar; Bus.Intt.: Pub.; Spl.: Bookseller of Indian and foreign books on science subjects

DHANSIRI TRUST BOARD (REGD.)
Publication Division, Golaghat (Assam)

DHANWANTRA MED. & LAW BOOK HOUSE
592, Lajpat Rai Market, (Opp. Diwan Hall), Delhi-110006
✆ (O) 23866768, 23865746, 2621653 (R) 26416653, 26224372 ▮ 9810193330
✉ p.p.khanna@hotmail.com
Estd.: 1949; Man.Prt.: Suneel Khanna, P.P. Khanna; Bus.Intt.: Rt., L.S., Pub.'s Rep., WS, Imp. & Exp.; Spl.: Law Books & Law Journals on Civil Criminal, Services Taxation & Companies, Labour & Industrial Law, Govt. Books, Industry & Trade, Excise & Customs Agents, Govt. Pub., Pharmaceuticals & Med.

DHARMYATRA MAHASANGH
5070/1, Sant Nagar, D.B. Gupta Road, Karol Bagh, New Delhi-110005
✆ 28723934, Fax: 91-11-28724019
✉ dharm_parvah2007@yahoo.co.in
Hd.Org.: J.R. Garg; Bus.Intt.: Pub.; Spl.: Monthly newsletter based on pilgrimage centres in India

DHILLON GROUP OF PUBLICATIONS
E-71, First Floor, Main Rd., Kalkaji, New Delhi-110019
✆ (O) 26488448, (R) 26239536, 26439536, Fax: 91-11-26488748
✉ dhillongroup_publication@yahoo.co.in
Estd.: 1978; Prop.: Prof. Rajinder S. Dhillon; Bus.Intt.: Pub.; Spl.: Career and Competitive examinations. English Language-Practical Grammar, Word-Power, Composition, Intelligence, Reasoning, Mental Ability, Gen. Knowledge, Current Affairs, Humanities, Sci., Self-Improvement Courses, Hobbies, Health, Rel., Phil. and Psych.

DHINGRA BOOK HOUSE
F-171-B, Swarn House, Jagat Puri Main Rd., Delhi-110051
✆ 22021350, 22059251, 22426053, Telefax: 22059251
✉ mkdhingra@rediffmail.com
Hd.Org.: M.K. Dhingra, H.K. Dhingra; Bus.Intt.: Pub.; Spl.: Edu. and Gen. Books for Children

DHRUV & DEEP BOOKS
142-143, J.P. Nagar, 206, Ashiyana Andheri (W), Mumbai-400058 (Maharashtra)
Bus.Intt.: Dist. and Pub.

DHRUV BOOK CENTRE
3572, Jatwara, Near Sablok Clinic, Darya Ganj, New Delhi-110002
✆ 23255982 ▮ 9810188829
Hd.Org.: Omkar Gupta; Bus.Intt.: B.S.; Spl.: Furniture, Fashion, Graphic, Jewellery and Gen. Books

DIALOGUE PUBLICATIONS
Karimbam P.O. Via Thaliparamba, Kannur-2670142 (Kerala)
Estd.: 1986; Man.Dir.: K.C. Varghese; Bus.Intt.: Pub. and B.S.

DIAMOND BOOK AGENCY
3rd A, Rd., Sardarpura, Jodhpur-2342003 (Rajasthan)

DIAMOND BOOK CENTRE
Orchid Complex, Shop No. 110, 109, 1st Floor, 1367, Sadashiv Peth, Near Raja Kelkar Museum Chowk, Pune-411030 (Maharashtra)
✆ (O) 24486093, 4020281 (R) 25464752 Fax: 24486093
✉ diamond_books@hotmail.com
Estd.: 1986; Prop.: Mahesh D. Paste
Br.: Diamond Book Depot, 661, Narayan Peth, Pune-411030 (Maharashtra)
✆ (O) 24486093 (R) 25464752 Telefax: 24486093; • Star Book Service, 1367, Sadashiv Peth, Pune
Bus.Intt.: Pub., B.S., L.S., WS; Spl.: Humanities & Soc.Sci., Sci. & Tech., Mang., Law, Bio.Sci.

DIAMOND BOOK MANUFACTURERS
141, SDM Lane Sultanpet Cross, Bangalore-560053 (Karnataka)
✆ 22870012, Fax: 91-80-22870012
Hd.Org.: Shantilal Kothari; Bus.Intt.: Manufacturers; Spl.: Books, Stationery

DIAMOND COMICS (P) LTD.
257, Dariba Kalan, Delhi-110006
✆ (O) 23266232, 23266317, 2401093/94/95 (R) 0124-2354931 ▮ 9810003062, Fax: 91-11-24010393/94/95
✉ gulshanrai@diamondcomic.com
www.diamondcomic.com
Br.: A-22, Gobind Villa, Sector-63 Noida (Uttar Pradesh)

✆ 4238008, 4238009, Fax: 91-120-4238010
✉ info@diamondcomic.com, diamondcomicsindia@gmail.com, diamondcomicsindia@yahoo.com
• A-201, 'Royal Sands' (A-wing), New Link Road, Shastri Nagar Complex, Andheri (West), Mumbai-400053 (Maharashtra); ✆ 28935738, 26326039 ▮ 9820129206; • 178/30, Golmohar Avenue, Howrah-1, Kolkata (West Bengal) ✆ 033-6667159, ▮ 9830045756
• 13, Canara Bank Colony, Gandhi Nagar, Saligraman, Chennai-600093 (Tamil Nadu) ✆ 044-3624120, 3623624, ▮ 9840031079;
• 8/1, 1 Cross, 1st Floor, Main Road, Lingaihpalya, (Near Rama Krishna School), Ulsoor, Bangalore-560018 (Karnataka), ✆ 080-5561316, ▮ 9448462316;
• Flat No. 102, Vimla Vihar Apartment, Gautam Nagar, Dilshuk Nagar, Hyderabad-500016 (Andhra Pradesh) ✆ 040-24160571, ✉ raomedia@yahoo.com;
• B-314, Nandan Apartment, Ramdev Nagar, Ahmedabad-380015 (Uttar Pradesh) ✆ 079-2695606; • 215, Sholapur Bazar, Near Jain Temple, Pune-411001 (Maharastra) ✆ 4002061, Fax: 020-26361793, ▮ 9890035610,
✉ naren29@rediffmail.com
Estd.: 1951; **Man.Dir.:** Gulshan Rai; **Bus.Intt.:** Pub.; **Spl.:** Monthly Magazines *Manohar Kahaniyan*, *Satya Katha* and Popular Comic series like *Chacha Chowdhary*, *Billoo*, *Pinky*, etc. in English and Regional Languages

DIAMOND POCKET BOOKS (P) LTD.
X-30, Okhla Industrial Area, Phase-II, New Delhi-110020
✆ 41611861, Fax: 91-11-41611866
✉ sales@dpb.in
www.dpb.in
Hd.Org.: N.K. Verma; **Bus.Intt.:** Pub.; **Spl.:** Books on Fiction, Non-fiction, Religion, Culture, Health, Astrology, Sports, Literature and Children's books in Hindi, Urdu, Bangla, Marathi, Gujarati and Asamiya

DIAMOND POCKET BOOKS (P) LTD.
2715, Darya Ganj, New Delhi-110002

DIAMOND WORLD
A-95, Journal House, Janta Colony, Jaipur-302004 (Rajasthan)
Bus.Intt.: Exp.

DIANETICS AND SCIENTOLOGY
L-6, Hauz Khas Enclave, New Delhi-110016
✆ 41550913/34, Fax: 91-11-41550912
✉ horstt@airtelbroadband.in
www.scientologybooksindia.com
Hd.Org.: Horst Tubbesing; **Bus.Intt.:** Pub.; **Spl.:** Literature on self-development and on good living

DIGAMBAR JAIN TRILOKA SODHA SANSKRIT
Hastinapur, Meerut-250014 (Uttar Pradesh)

DIGANTHA SAHITYA
Industrial Area, Yey Yodi, Mangalore-575008 (Karnataka)

DIGVIJAY PUBLICATIONS
39, Sneh Wardhani, Tridake Colony, Nasik-422002 (Maharashtra)

DIGVIJAY VIDYAGURU PUBLISHING LTD.
First Floor, Nedumchalil Estate, Ammankovil Rd., Ernakulam, Cochin-682035 (Kerala)

DIKSHIT STORES
Degampur, Patna City, Patna-800011 (Bihar)
Bus.Intt.: Pub. and B.S.

DIKSOOCHI
Bangalore (Karnataka)
Fax: 23352696
✉ jeeva@blr.vsnl.net.in
Bus.Intt.: Pub.

DILLIPAHIPAGAM
A-280, Sidco Nagar, Villivakkam, Chennai-600049 (Tamil Nadhu)

DILIPRAJ PRAKASHAN PVT. LTD.
251C, Shaniwar Pet, Pune-411030 (Maharashtra)

DILPREET PUBLISHING HOUSE
F-198, Vishnu Garden, New Delhi-110018
✆ 25461409
Estd.: 1992; **Prop.:** H.S. Sethi; **Bus.Intt.:** Pub., L.S. & Rt.; **Spl.:** Humanities & Soc.Sci., Sci. & Tech.

DIMPLE PUBLISHING HOUSE
R-39, West Patel Nagar, New Delhi-110008
✆ (O) 25735410, 25744308 (R) 25735410
Estd.: 1993; **Prop.:** Sushma Mediratta; **Bus.Intt.:** Pub.; **Spl.:** Children Books in English and Hindi

DIN DUNIYA PUBLISHING CO.
Jama Masjid, Delhi-110006
✆ 23263450, 23280644
Estd.: 1921; **Hd.Org.:** Asif Fahmi

DINAPORE BOOK CENTRE
Sadar Bazar, Dinapore Cantt., Patna-801503 (Bihar)
Bus.Intt.: Pub. and B.S.

DINESH BOOK CENTRE
Station Rd., Vadnagar (Gujarat)

DINESH PRAKASHAN
364, Kar Kar Dooma, Delhi-110092

9868147869
Hd.Org.: Dinesh Kumar; **Bus.Intt.:** Pub. & Dist.; **Spl.:** Children's books in Hindi language

DINESH PUSTAK BHANDAR
Bakhtiarpur, Patna-803212 (Bihar)
Bus.Intt.: Pub. and B.S.

DINI BOOK DEPOT
4160, Urdu Bazar, Jama Masjid, Delhi-110006
Bus.Intt.: Exp.

DINMAN PRAKASHAN
3014, Charkhewalan, Delhi-110006
✆ 23947589
Hd.Org.: Anil Kumar; **Bus.Intt.:** Pub. and B.S.; **Spl.:** Litt. in Hindi

DIOCESAN BOOK DEPOT
Sastri Rd., Kottayam-686001 (Kerala)
✆ 2562575 **Estd.:** 1948

DIPIKA
16A, Tamer Lane, Kolkata-700006 (West Bengal)

DIRECTORATE GENERAL
Central Industrial Security Force, Block No. 13, GCO Comp., Lodhi Rd., New Delhi-110003

DIRECTORATE OF HINDI MEDIUM IMPLEMENTATION
Bag No. 2 & 4, Cavalry Lines, University of Delhi, Delhi-110007
✆ 91-11-27666939
Hd.Org.: Asha Gupta; **Bus.Intt.:** Pub.; **Spl.:** Books in Hindi on Soc.Sci. and Humanities for Graduates and Postgraduates

DISCOVERY PUBLISHING HOUSE
4831/24, Ansari Rd., Darya Ganj, New Delhi-110002
✆ (O) 23279245, 23253475 (R) 22414930, Fax: 23253475
✉ dphtemp@indiatimes.com
Estd.: 1983; **Prop.:** Tilak Wasan; **Bus.Intt.:** Pub.; **Spl.:** Encyclopaedias and Books on Edu., Travel, etc. in English

DISHA PRAKASHAN
138/16, Onkar Nagar-B, Tri Nagar, Delhi-110035
✆ 91-11-27385832, 27383646
Hd.Org.: Shakuntala Gupta
Bus.Intt.: Pub. and Dist.; **Spl.:** Creative Books in Hindi

DISHA PUBLICATIONS
B-32, Shivalik Main Road, Malviya Nagar, New Delhi-110017
✆ 91-11-26691021, 26691713
✉ aiets@rediffmail.com
www.dishapublication.com
Hd.Org.: Avinash Agarwal; **Bus.Intt.:** Pub.; **Spl.:** Books for schools and competitive examinations such as IIT, PMT, AIEEE, MBA

DISVAN ENTERPRISES
25, Mayfair Apartments, New Delhi-110016
✆ 2667118, Fax: 26966484

DIV SAHITYA CENTRE
Surajva Chowk, Div-362520 (Gujarat)

DIVI INTERNATIONAL
35-A, DDA Flats, Mansarovar Park, Shahdara, Delhi-110032
Hd.Org.: Atul Maheshwari; **Bus.Intt.:** Pub.; **Spl.:** Books in Hindi

DIVINE COMPUTERS PVT. LTD.
CP-8, NH-5, Railway Road, N.I.T. Faridabad-121001 (Haryana)
✆ 2412106, 2410764, 2370806, Fax: 0129-2413493
✉ mail@divinecd.com, garodia@satyam.net.in
Ch.Exe.: Vikas Garodia
Bus.Intt.: Develops, Produces, Publishes and Markets; **Spl.:** Edu. Software for Consumer and School Markets with a Primary focus on K-12 programs

DIVINE LIFE SOCIETY
P.O. Shivananda Nagar, Via Rishikesh-249192 (Uttar Pradesh)
✆ 135-2434780, 2430040, Fax: 135-2431190, Telex: Divinelife
Estd.: 1936; **Pres.:** Swami Chidananda Maharaj; **Bus.Intt.:** Pub., WS, L.S., Rt., Exp.

DIVINE SPARK
C-64/A, Janta Garden, Pandav Nagar, Delhi-110091
✆ 91-11-22755953
✉ shenoy_rajaram@hotmail.com
www.divinepark.org
Hd.Org.: A. Chandrashekar Udupa
Bus.Intt.: Pub.; **Spl.:** Books and Journals based on the teachings of Swami Vivekananda

DIVJOT PRAKASHAN
N-82, Shyamli, Ranchi-834002 (Jharkhand)

DIVYA BODHANAM
Orthodox Seminary, P.O. Box-98, Chungom, Kottayam-686001 (Kerala)
✆ 2566526
Estd.: 1984; **Hd.Org.:** C.C. Cherian; **Bus.Intt.:** Pub.

DIVYA CHANDRA PRAKASHANA
6th Main, 8th Cross, Phase II, K.H.B. Colony, Bangalore-560079 (Karnataka)

Hd.Org.: Smt. B.M. Kamala; **Bus.Intt.:** Pub., **Spl.:** Fictions, Collections, Gen. and Children's and Edu. Books in Kannada

DIVYA JYOTI PRAKASHAN
A-42, Shastri Nagar, Jodhpur-342003 (Rajasthan)

DIWA PRAKASHAN
3, Pustak Bazar, New Market, T.T. Nagar, Bhopal-462001 (Madhya Pradesh)
✆ 0755-2554138
Estd.: 1997; **Prop.:** Amitabh Jain; **Bus.Intt.:** Pub.; **Spl.:** M.P. State level Guides and I.A.S. Research Books

DIWAKAR STORES
Naubatpur, Patna-801109 (Bihar)
Bus.Intt.: Pub. & B.S.

DNYANOPASAK PRAKASHAN
C/o Dnyanopasak Shikshan Mandal's, College of Arts, Commerce & Science, PB No. 54, Near Zilla Parishad, Parbhani-431401 (Maharashtra)

DOABA HOUSE
1688, Nai Sarak, Delhi-110006
✆ 23274669, 55363037 ▮ 9811137322, Fax: 26968735
✉ amamikavivek@hotmail.com, doabahouse@hotmail.com
Estd.: 1924; **Prt.:** S.N. Malhotra, Vivek Malhotra; **Spl.:** Eng.Litt. and Edu. Books

DOCTORS LIBRARY (INDIA) PVT. LTD.
104, Jehangir Mansion, Behind Metro Cinema Rd., Mumbai-400020 (Maharashtra)
✆ 22058916, Fax: 91-22-22088291
✉ doctors@bom3.vsnl.net.in
Estd.: 1974; **Dir.:** S.J. Kulkarni; **Bus.Intt.:** Pub., L.S. & Rt., Imp., Sub.Ag.; **Spl.:** Med.

DOCTORS PUBLICATIONS (REGD.)
C-68, Gali No. 8, Basti Chivnot, Multani, Dhanda, Pahar Ganj, New Delhi-110055

DOCUMENTATION AND INFORMATION
Processing Syndicate, B/M-9, VSS Nagar, Bhubaneshwar-751004 (Orissa)

DOEACC SOCIETY
Electronics Niketan, 6, CGO Complex, New Delhi-110003
✆ 24362824, 24363330-32, Fax: 24363335
✉ doeacc@doe.ernet.in
Hd.Org.: P.N. Gupta; **Bus.Intt.:** Pub.; **Spl.:** Information Tech.

DOLPHIN BOOKS
4855-56/24, Harbans Street Ansari Road, Darya Ganj, New Delhi-110002
✆ 91-11-23271844
Hd.Org.: Rajeev Sharma; **Bus.Intt.:** Pub.; **Spl.:** Hindi language books on culture, biographies, general knowledge, self-improvement and books for children

DOLPHIN PRESS
B-17, Second Floor, Lajpat Nagar-II, New Delhi-110024
✆ 91-11-41720230
✉ israelrede@gmail.com
Hd.Org.: Raphael Israel; **Bus.Intt.:** Pub. and Imp.; **Spl.:** Books for children and young adults

DOLPHIN PUBLISHERS
57/4A, College St., Kolkata-700073 (West Bengal)

DOLPHIN PUBLICATIONS
M.G. Rd., 203, Shiv Darshan, Opp. Station, Santacruz (W), Mumbai-400054 (Maharashtra)
Bus.Intt.: Exp.

DOLPHIN PUBLICATIONS PVT LTD
Western India Art Litho Building, Plot No. 107, Marol Coop. Industrial Estate, Mumbai-400059 (Maharashtra)
✆ 40763000, Fax: 91-22-40763040
✉ dolphin3@mtnl.net.in
Hd.Org.: Vasant Kamat; **Bus.Intt.:** Pub. and Dist.

DOMINANT PUBLISHERS & DISTRIBUTORS
4378/4B, Murarilal St., Ansari Rd., Darya Ganj, New Delhi-110002
✆ 23281685, Fax: 91-11-23270680
✉ dominantbooks@post.com
🌐 www.dominantbooks.com
Estd.: 1998; **Dir.:** K.S. Saini; **Bus.Intt.:** Pub., and Dist.; **Spl.:** Textbooks, Dictionaries and Books on Information Technologies, Comp. Sci., Defence Studies, Soc.Sci. and also Books on Gen. Interest like Women Trafficking, Terrorism and other such fields

DOMINICAN PUBLICATIONS
St. Dominic's Ashram, Seminary Hill, Nagpur-440006 (Maharashtra)

DOMTOM PUBLICATIONS
Kottuppallil Buildings, Lakkattoor, Kottayam-686502 (Kerala)
Estd.: 1993; **Hd.Org.:** Dominic Thomas; **Bus.Intt.:** Pub. & B.S.

DOON VALLEY BOOK CENTRE
178/1, Saharanpur Rd., Dehradun-248001 (Uttarakhand)
✆ 2721470
Estd.: 1974; **Prop.:** S.K. Jain **Bus.Intt.:** L.S. and WS; **Spl.:** Edu. Books

DORLING KINDERSLEY INDIA (P) LTD.
14, Local Shopping Centre, DDA Market, Panchsheel Park, New Delhi-110017
✆ 26498851-4, Fax: 26498885
✉ saurabh.sri@dk.com
www.dk.com
Hd.Org.: P.M. Sukumar; **Bus.Intt.:** Pub.; **Spl.:** Books in Eng. Language

DORLING KINDERSLEY INDIA (P) LTD.
482, FIE, Patparganj, Delhi-110092
✆ 43030100, Fax: 91-11-22146071
✉ mail@pearsoned.co.in
www.pearsoned.con.in
Hd.Org.: Subroto Mozumdar
Bus.Intt.: Pub.; **Spl.:** Books in Eng. Language

DOVE MULTIMEDIA PVT. LTD.
270-A, Sant Nagar, 2nd Floor, East of Kailash, New Delhi-110065
✆ 91-11-32465319
✉ pebblesdove@gmail.com, dove@vsnl.com, info@pebbles-india.com
www.pebbles.in; **Hd.Org.:** D. Karthik; **Br.:** Flat No. 61, Marshalls Road, Egmore, Chennai-600008 (Tamil Nadu), ✆ 28546297; • No. 12, 3rd Floor Hind Services Ind., Bhagoji Kheer Marg, Shivaji Park, Dadar (W), Mumbai-28 (Maharashtra), ✆ 32566909; • 10-2-289/38, G-1 Pleasant Park Apartments, Shanti Nagar, Hyderabad-500028 (Andhra Pradesh), ✆ 32502527; • 198, 4th Main IInd Cross, Vivek Nagar, Further Extn., Bangalore-560047 (Karnataka), ✆ 32981150; • 44/217 1st Floor, Manapaati Parambu Lane, Off SRM Road, Near Jaisons Furniture, Ernakulam-682018 (Kerala), ✆ 0484-3200645; • 5/44, Rajendra Prasad Colony, 1st Floor (Lake Garden), Prince Mohammed Shah Road, Kolkatta-700095 (West Bengal) ✆ 32946369; **Bus.Intt.:** Book Seller; **Spl.:** Educational CDs such as rhymes, stories, etc. for children and adults in various Indian languages

DRAVADIAN LINGUISTICS ASSOCIATION
Publication Division Kerala, Panini Block, ISDL Complex, St. Xavier's College P.O., Thiruvanantapuram-695586 (Kerala)

DRAVIDA PUBLICATIONS
Delhi
✆ 22255165, Fax: 23368376
✉ keraladir@iname.com
Bus.Intt.: B.S. & Dist.

DREAM PALACE BOOK DISTRIBUTORS
484 D/S, New Rajinder Nagar, New Delhi-110060
✆ 91-11-64163037
✉ narkambooks@gmail.com
Hd.Org.: Kamal Chowdhry
Bus.Intt.: Pub. and supplier of Indian and foreign books

DREAM TEAM NETWORK SOLUTION (P) LTD.
C-97, Shastri Nagar, Jodhpur-342001 (Rajasthan)
✆ 91-291-2308074, 2308075
✉ info@lite-rom.com
Ch.Exe.: Mr. Ajay Sharma; **Bus.Intt.:** Exp.; **Spl.:** Web based Interachion/Automation Systems for Schools and Book Shops

DREAMLAND PUBLICATIONS
J-128, Kirti Nagar, Delhi-110015
✆ 25435657, 25106050, Fax: 25438283
✉ dreamland@vsnl.com
www.dreamlandpublications.com
Hd.Org.: Ved Prakash; **Bus.Intt.:** Pub.; **Spl.:** Children's Books, Edu. Charts, Maps and Atlases

DREAMTECH PRESS
19-A, Ansari Rd., Darya Ganj, New Delhi-110002
✆ 91-11-23284212
✉ sales@dreamtechbt.com dreamland@vsnl.com
www.dreamtechpress.com
Estd.: 2000; **Hd.Org.:** R.K. Gupta; **Bus.Intt.:** Pub.; **Spl.:** Information Tech. and Comp. in English

DRKRUNCH TECHNOLOGIES PVT. LTD.
Bangalore (Karnataka)
✆ 26681969, Fax: 26680320
✉ drkrunch@blr.vsnl.net.in
Bus.Intt.: Dist.

DUGAR BOOKS AND PRINTS
B-61, South Extension Part-I, New Delhi-110049
✆ 24621832, Fax: 24627755
✉ dugarbooks@yahoo.com
Estd. : 2003; **Hd.Org.:** Sharad K. Dugar; **Bus.Intt.:** Dealer; **Spl.:** Rare and Antique Books

DUGGAL PUBLISHERS & DISTRIBUTORS
50, Housing Board Colony, Kalka-133302 (Haryana)
✆ 01733-220360
✉ duggalpublishers@rediffmail.com
Estd.: 1991; **Prop.:** Ajay Duggal
Bus.Intt.: L.S. & Rt.; **Spl.:** Humanities & Soc.Sci., Sci. & Tech., Med., Law, Juvenile/ Children Books Gen. & Fiction etc.

DUNGARSI VIRJI BOOKSELLER
25/37, Divya Darshan, Jagdeeshnagar, Ghatkopar (West), Mumbai-400086 (Maharashtra)

DUNIYA PUBLICATIONS
J & K 309B, Dilshad Garden, Delhi-110095

DURGA BOOK CENTRE
Mahendru, Patna-801109 (Bihar)
Bus.Intt.: Pub. and B.S.

DURGA ENTERPRISES
WZ-200A, Gali No. 6, Lajwanti Garden, New Delhi-110046
✆ 91-11-28524316
✉ durgabooks10@yahoo.com
Hd.Org.: Harender Singh; **Bus.Intt.:** WS and Dist.; **Spl.:** Art, Children's Books, Cookery etc.

DURGA PUBLICATIONS
A-406/5, South Gaamdi, Delhi-110053
Hd.Org.: Yumna Shankar Tiwari

DURGA PUSTAK BHANDAR
Bharkho, Bhagalpur-813126 (Bihar)
Bus.Intt.: Pub. and B.S.

DURGA PUSTAK MANDIR
Khazanchi Rd., Patna-800004 (Bihar)
Bus.Intt.: Pub. and B.S.

DURGA TRADING CO.
Bakhri, Begusarai-848201 (Bihar)
Bus.Intt.: Pub. and B.S.

DURGA TRADING CORPORATION
Pacca Danga, Wadha, Versha, Jammu
✆ 2549919
Estd.: 1997; **Prop.:** Rami Gupta; **Bus.Intt.:** L.S., WS, Pub.; **Spl.:** Humanities & Soc.Sci., Sci., Mang. & Comm., Med.Sci., Law, Fiction & Gen.

DUTTA BARUAH & CO.
College Hostel Rd., Guwahati-781001 (Assam)
Hd.Org.: J.N. Dutta Baruah; **Bus.Intt.:** Pub.

DUTTA BOOK CORNER
9, Bankim Chatterjee St., Kolkata-73 (West Bengal)

DUTTA BOOK HOUSE
130-A, S.P. Mukherjee Rd., Kolkata-700026 (West Bengal)

DUTTA BOOK STORE
Bengikhowa, Guwahati-781001 (Assam)

DUTTA BOOK SUPPLY
Paschim Putiary, Samargarh, Kolkata-700041 (West Bengal)

DUTTA BROTHERS
Panbazar, Guwahati-781001 (Assam)

DUTTA PUBLISHERS
3/1, College Row, Kolkata-700009 (West Bengal)

DUTTSON BOOK MERCHANT
6, Old Post Office St., Opp. High Court & Assembly Hall, Kolkata-700001 (West Bengal)
Bus.Intt.: Pub. and B.S.

DWIVEDI PUSTAK BHANDAR
Goh, Aurangabad-824203 (Bihar)
Bus.Intt.: Pub. and B.S.

DYNAMIC PUBLICATIONS (I) LTD.
11, Shivaji Rd., Meerut-250001 (Uttar Pradesh)
✆ (O) & (R) 0121-2644766, 2642946, Fax: 0121-2645855
✉ sk_kpm@yahoo.com
www.dynamicpublication.com
Estd.: 2002; **Hd.Org.:** S.K. Rastogi; **Bus.Intt.:** Pub.; **Spl.:** Gen. Books, Vastu, Feng-Shui, Self-Improvement etc.

DYNAMIC SERVICES
Mumbai (Maharashtra)
✆ 22013123, 22019180, Fax: 22059539
✉ letterprint@vsnl.net
Bus.Intt.: Authorised Agents

DYUTI PRAKASHAN
Someshwar Bhawan, (Central Hotels), Station Rd., Patna-800001 (Bihar)

■ ■ ■

E.B.C. PUBLISHING PVT. LTD.
34, Lal Bagh, Lucknow-226001 (Uttar Pradesh)
✆ 2274901, 2224179, 2228359,
Fax: 2224328

E.B.S.C.O. BOOKSELLERS
Cutchery St., Erode-1 (Kerala)

E.D. GALGOTIA & SONS
17-B, Connaught Place, New Delhi-110001
✆ (O) 23322876, 23755150, 55304047
(R) 25788991 ▮ 9810561123
Estd.: 1930; **Prt.:** B.D. Galgotia, R.K. Galgotia, Ashok Galgotia, Ajay Galgotia; **Bus.Intt.:** Rt. and L.S.; **Spl.:** Arch., Mang., Soc.Sci., Children, Fiction, Art and Interior Decoration

E.D. GALGOTIA & SONS (TECHNICAL SECTION)
17-B, Connaught Place, P.O. Box 41,
New Delhi-110001
✆ (O) 23713227, 23713228 (R) 91-2353226, 2355271, Fax: 91-11-23327601
✉ galgotia@ndf.vsnl.net.in
Estd.: 1933; **Man.Prt.:** Suneel Galgotia; **Bus.Intt.:** Rt. and L.S.; **Spl.:** Country of Comp., Tech. and Med. Books

E-DIKSHA.COM
201, C.R.S. Bhawan, 1/28, Main Market,
Tilak Nagar, New Delhi-110018
✆ 25912191, 25912205, Fax: 25912205
✉ vitratra@bol.net.in
🌐 www.e-diksha.com
Hd.Org.: Harvinder Ratra; **Bus.Intt.:** Pub. & Dist.; **Spl.:** Sci. Project books, Working Sci. Models and Edu. CDs

EFY INTERPRISES PVT. LTD.
D-87/1, Okhla Industrial Area,
Phase-1, New Delhi-110020
✆ 26810601-02/03, Fax: 91-11-26817563, 26812312
✉ info@efyindia.com
🌐 www.efyindia.com
Hd.Org.: Ramesh Chopra;
Br.: A-001, Garden Mansions, Opp: Anjaneya Complex, Kodihalli, Airport Road, Bangalore-560008 (Karnataka)
✆ 25260023, 25260394, Fax: 080-25260394
✉ efyblr@efyindia.com; • 207, 'Shivsmruti, 49 Dr A.B. Road, Worli Naka, Opp. Central Bank, Mumbai-400018 (Maharashtra)
✆ 24950047, 24928520, 39514404,
Fax: 022-24954278,
✉ efymum@efyindia.com; • C/o. Roof & Services, Sawarkar Bhawan, Shivaji Nagar, Pune-411005 (Maharashtra), ▮ 9372407753,
✉ efypune@efyindia.com; • 61-A, Ground Floor, Ambassador Appt., Park Street, Kolkata-700016 (West Bengal),
✆ 22294788, Fax: 033-22650094
✉ efycal@efyindia.com; **Bus.Intt.:** Pub. and Dist.; **Spl.:** Databases in English as well as magazines on science and technology—*Electronics for you, LINUX For you, Electronics Bazaar and Facts for you*

E.M.A. TECHBOOK INTERNATIONAL
WZ-73 B, Todapur, P.O. Pusa,
New Delhi-110012
✆ 25713430, 25766709, Fax: 25789432
Hd.Org.: Anoop Datta Dewan

E-FRAME SOLUTIONS (P) LTD.
9, Darya Ganj, New Delhi-110002
✆ 41004022, Fax: 91-11-23245011
✉ info@eframes.in
🌐 www.eframes.in
Hd.Org.: Atul Gupta

E-FIRST SOLUTIONS INDIA P. LTD.
New Delhi
✆ 26933765, 23289578, Fax: 28611637
✉ tribhuwan.singh@efirstindia.com

EAGLE BOOK SERVICE
F-195, Mansarover Garden, (P.O. Ramesh Nagar), New Delhi-110015
✆ (O) 25939830, 25414391 (R) 25414391
▮ 9868183336
Estd.: 1974; **Prop.:** Joginder Singh Gill; **Bus.Intt.:** B.S. & Sub.Ag. & L.S.; **Spl.:** Law Books & Book Binders Authorised Agents for Govt. of India Publications

EARLYBIRD BOOKS PVT. LTD.
11115-B, Doriwalan, East Park Rd.,
Karol Bagh, New Delhi-110005
✆ 91-11-23518802, 23610700
✉ earlybirdbookspvtltd_1999@rediffmail.com
Hd.Org.: Madal Lal Gupta; **Bus.Intt.:** Pub.; **Spl.:** Edu. Books

EARTHEARE BOOKS
2, Anand, 17 Carmichael Rd., Anand Kamal Mahal Society, Mumbai-400026 (Maharashtra)

EARTHSCAN INDIA PVT. LTD.
New Delhi
✆ 23258325, 23270718, Fax: 23267224
✉ viva@mantraonline.com
Bus.Intt.: Pub.

EARTHWORM BOOKS PVT. LTD.
77/13, Corporation Shopping Complex,
CP Ramaswamy Rd., Alwarpet,
Chennai-600018 (Tamil Nadu)

© 26412314, Fax: 26427484
✉ ewb.maa@sml.sprintrpg.sprint.com
Bus.Intt.: Pub. and B.S.

EAST WEST BOOKS
C-69, Jitar Nagar, Delhi-110051
© 22504837
Prop.: Mrs. S.H. Naqvi; **Bus.Intt.:** Pub., WS, Rt., L.S.; **Spl.:** Acad., Beh.Sci., Soc.Sci., Comm., Sci., Pure & Applied, Tech. Rare

EAST WEST BOOKS (MADRAS) PVT. LTD.
571, Karmaveerar Kamaraj Bhavan, Poonamalle High Rd., Aminjikarai, Chennai-600029 (Tamil Nadu)
© 26602003, Fax: 26601974
✉ ewb@touchtelindia.net
Estd.: 1996; **Man.Dir.:** K.S. Padmanabhan
Br.: 3-5-1108, Maruthi Complex, Narayanaguda, Hyderabad-500029 (Andhra Pradesh); © 040-24750301, 24750304 ✉ ewbhyd@hd2.dot.net.in
• Praja Bhavan, 1st Floor, 53/2, Bulltemple Rd., Basavangudi, Bangalore-560019 (Karnataka); © 26606048, 26612243, Fax: 080-26679591 ✉ ewbblr@bgl.vsnl.net.in
Bus.Intt.: Pub., WS, Imp.; **Spl.:** Sci., Tech. & Med., Trade, Gen. (Incl. Lit. & Art), Humanities & Soc.Sci.

EASTERN BOOK COMPANY
34, Lal Bagh, Lucknow-226001 (Uttar Pradesh)
© 2223171, 2626517, 2274901, Fax: 91-522-2624328
✉ sales@ebc-india.com, sales@scconline.com, support@ebc-india.com
www.ebc.india.com
Estd.: 1946; **Prt.:** Prakash Lal Malik
Br.: Eastern Book Company, 5-B, Atma Ram House, 1, Tolstoy Marg, Connaught Place, Delhi-110001
© 23752321/22/23, Fax: 91-11-23752320;
• Eastern Book Company <Sales> 1267, Kashmere Gate, Old Hindu College Building, Near Corporation Office Main Gate, Delhi-110006
© 23917616, 23921656, Fax: 91-11-23752323;
• Manav Law House, 8/10, M.G. Marg, Opp. Bishop Johnson School, Allahabad-211001 (Uttar Pradesh)
© 2623551, 2560710, Fax: 0532-2623584, ▮ 9839052584, 9935254213 & 9415236484;
Bus.Intt.: Pub., WS, L.S. & Rt., Imp., Exp., Sub.Ag.; **Spl.:** Humanities & Soc.Sci., Law

EASTERN BOOK HOUSE
3rd Floor/136, M.L. Nehru Rd., Opp. Pan Bazar Girl's High School, Pan Bazar, Guwahati-781001 (Assam)
© (O) 2513876, 2519231 (R) 2636538, Fax: 2519231
✉ info@easternbookhouse.com
www.easternbookhouse.com
Estd.: 1995; **Prop.:** J.P. Sharma; **Bus.Intt.:** B.S., L.S., WS; **Spl.:** Humanities & Soc.Sci., Mang., Arts & Arch., Geo., Env.Sci., Children & Gen.

EASTERN BOOK LINKERS
5825, New Chandrawal, Jawahar Nagar, Delhi-110007
© 23850287, 32919869 ▮ 9811232913, Fax: 91-11-23970287
✉ ebl@vsnl.net
www.eblindology.com
Hd.Org.: Ravi Malhotra, Deepak Malhotra; **Bus.Intt.:** Pub., B.S. & L.S.; **Spl.:** Sanskrit, Music, Art, Rel., Phil. & Rare Books

EASTERN BOOK SELLERS
Near Hotel Samrat, A.T. Rd., Shantipur, Guwahati-9 (Assam)

EASTERN BOOKS (PUBLISHERS)
495, Ganesh Nagar Ext-II, Shakarpur, Madhuban Rd., Delhi-110092
© 91-11-22056652
✉ easternbooks@satyam.net.in
Ch.Exe.: Mr. Anil Chowdhary; **Bus.Intt.:** Pub.; **Spl.:** Children Books in English and Hindi

EASTERN EXPORTS
Chennai (Tamil Nadu)
© 28270975, Fax: 28255724
✉ eastern@satyem.net.in
Bus.Intt.: Exp.

EASTERN LAW HOUSE PVT. LTD.
54, Ganesh Chunder Avenue, Kolkata-700013 (West Bengal)
© 033-27-24989/2301, Cable: LAURIPORTS; Fax: 22150491
✉ elh@cal.vsnl.net.in
Estd.: 1918; **Dir.:** Asok De
Br.: 36, Netaji Subhash Marg, Darya Ganj, New Delhi-110002 © 011-2327-9982, Cable: LAURIPORTS, Telefax: 94-1111
Bus.Intt.: WS, L.S. & Rt., Imp., Exp., Sub.Ag.; **Spl.:** Law, Humanities & Soc.Sci.

EASTERN PUBLISHERS
G-59, Greater Kailash-2, New Delhi-110048
© 26437225, Fax: 26463676
Estd.: 1991; **Prop.:** Daljit Kaur; **Bus.Intt.:** Pub. and Exp.

EASTERN PUBLISHERS
Ramanath Majumder St., Kolkata-700009 (West Bengal)

EASTERN PUBLISHERS & DISTRIBUTORS
20, Gole Market, New Delhi-110001
© 23361097

ECONOMIC & POLITICAL WEEKLY
'Hitkari House' 6th Floor, 284, Shahid Bhagat Singh Rd., Mumbai-400038 (Maharashtra)
Bus.Intt.: Exp.

EDUCARE PUBLICATIONS
House No. 4, Flat No. 18, Third Floor, Gautam Nagar, (Behind Navjeevan Nursing Home)
New Delhi-110049
✆ 26602695, Fax: 91-11-26864126
✉ educare_publication@yahoo.co.in
Hd.Org.: Seema Mahendru
Bus.Intt.: Pub., B.S. & L.S.; **Spl.:** Sanskrit, Music, Art, Rel., Phil. & Rare Books

EDUCATION INTERNATIONAL INDIA
NSC Campus, Aruna Asaf Ali Rd.,
New Delhi-110067
✆ 26897418/19, Fax: 011-26897416
✉ cec@del2.vsnl.net.in
Bus.Intt.: University Video Lecture Courses

EDUCATION MATERIAL EXPORTS
Udyog Bhawan, 201, Sonawala Marg,
Goregaon (E), Mumbai-400063 (Maharashtra)
✆ 28756158/6563, 28717201/7202,
Fax: 28756068, 28728228
Hd.Org.: Vikram Joshi

EDUCATION PUBLISHING HOUSE
3108, Gali Aziz-Uddin Vakil, Kucha Pandit, Lal Kuan, Delhi-110006
✆ 2526162

EDUCATIONAL AIDS & CONSULTANCY SERVICES INDIA
373, Sector 37, Faridabad-121003 (Haryana)
✆/Fax: 2277253
✉ eacsi@mantraonline.com

EDUCATIONAL BOOK AGENCY
New Cinema Rd., Mahabirsthan,
Siliguri-734404 (West Bengal)
✆ (O) 2424956 (R) 2427499, Fax: 2431100
✉ ebagency@dte.vsnl.net.in
Estd.: 1980; **Prop.:** Surendra Rai;
Bus.Intt.: Pub.; **Spl.:** Edu.

EDUCATIONAL BOOK AGENCY
5-D, Kamla Nagar, Delhi-110007
✆ (O) 23844216, 23842077 (R) 25934928, 55150688, Fax: 91-11-23843447
✉ ebaindia2000@yahoo.co.in
🌐 www.indianpharmacopoeia.in
Hd.Org.: Adishwar K. Jain
Bus.Intt.: Dist. and Supplier; **Spl.:** Books on pure sciences, biological science, medicine, technology and reference books

EDUCATIONAL BOOK CENTRE
Vir Marg, Jammu-180001 (Jammu & Kashmir)
✆ (R) 2452040
Estd.: 1980; **Prop.:** S. Sital Singh;
Bus.Intt.: WS, L.S. & Rt.; **Spl.:** Humanities & Soc.Sci., Sci. & Tech., Med., Gen. & Fiction

EDUCATIONAL BOOK CENTRE
133, Gala Complex, Din Dayal Upadhyay Rd., Mulund, West Mumbai-400080 (Maharashtra)
✆ (O) 25603324, 25685341 (R) 25901148, Fax: 25685341
✉ ebc@vsnl.net
🌐 www.educationalbookcentre.com
Estd.: 1975; **Man.:** Mukesh H. Doshi
Br.: 33, Bhagwan Bhawan, 196, Samuel St., P.O. No. 5148, Mumbai-400080 (Maharashtra)
✆ 23757482, 23741954 ✉ ebc@vsnl.net
Bus.Intt.: WS, L.S. & Rt., Imp.; **Spl.:** Sci., Tech. & Med.

EDUCATIONAL BOOK CENTER
Oak Lodge, Lower Bharari Rd., Shimla-1 (Himachal Pradesh)
✆ 91-177-2650776, Tele Fax: 2656776
✉ educationalbookcenter@hotmail.com
Bus.Intt.: B.S. & L.S.; **Spl.:** Educational, General, Research & Carrier Oriented Books for all Level

EDUCATIONAL BOOK DISTRIBUTORS
XL/6813, G.S.S. Shopping Complex, Near Public Library, Convent Rd., Cochin-682035 (Kerala)
✆ 2355283, 2362675
Estd.: 1988; **Prop.:** Subeela Nanayana Pal

EDUCATIONAL BOOK ENTERPRISES
EC-161, Tagore Garden, New Delhi-110027
✆ (R) 2513124
Hd.Org.: Naresh Kohli; **Bus.Intt.:** Rt. WS, Pub.'s Rep., L.S.

EDUCATIONAL BOOK HOUSE
Muslim University Market, Aligarh-202001 (Uttar Pradesh)
✆ 0571-23768
Estd.: 1925; **Hd.Org.:** Asad Yar Khan

EDUCATIONAL BOOK SERVICES
M-6/60, M.I.G. Colony, D.N. Nagar, Andheri (W), Mumbai-400053 (Maharashtra)
✆ (O) 26368413 (R) 26252757
Estd.: 1993; **Hd.Org.:** Manish Kakker;
Bus.Intt.: L.S. and B.S.

EDUCATIONAL EMPORIUM
4, Housing Board Colony, Behind S.T. Depot, Amreli-365601 (Gujarat)

EDUCATIONAL ENTERPRISES
5/1, Ramanath Majumder St., Kolkata-9 (West Bengal)

EDUCATIONAL MEDIA CENTRE
P-19, Green Park Extension, New Delhi-110016
✆ 2234525

EDUCATIONAL PUBLISHERS
224, Shivaji Nagar, Madanganj,
Kishangarh-305080 (Rajasthan)

EDUCATIONAL PUBLISHERS
3191, Vakil St., Kucha Pandit, Lal Kuan,
Delhi-110006
✆ 23216162, 23214465, Fax: 23211540
✉ ephdelhi@yahoo.com, eph@onebox.com
Hd.Org.: Mohammad Mujtaba Khan;
Bus.Intt.: Pub.; **Supl.:** Urdu Litt., Islamic Litt., Gen. Reference Books, Dictionaries and Books on Islam

EDUCATIONAL PUBLISHERS & DISTRIBUTORS
Chittor-Amman Kovil Rd. JN., Behind
Shenoy's Theatre, Cochin,
Ernakulam Dist.-682035 (Kerala)
✆ 2372817, Fax: 2355283
✉ epd-pai@yahoo.com
Estd.: 1988; **Prop.:** Suseelanarayana Pai;
Bus.Intt.: Pub., WS, L.S. & Rt.; **Spl.:** Humanities & Soc.Sci., Sci. & Tech., Med., Law, Gen. & Fiction etc.

EDUCATIONAL PUBLISHERS & DISTRIBUTORS (INDIA) LTD.
Dr. Zakir Husain Institute Campus, Bailey Rd.,
Patna-800001 (Bihar)
✆ (O) 2220647 (R) 2263916, Telex: 022-406
Estd.: 1983; **Prop.:** B.K. Singh; **Bus.Intt.:** Pub.;
Spl.: Edu. Books in English and Hindi

EDUCATIONAL PUBLISHING HOUSE
3108, Gali Aziz-Uddin Vakil, Kucha Pandit,
Lal Kuan, Delhi-110006
✆ 23216162, 23214465, Fax: 91-11-23211540
✉ ephindia@gmail.com
🌐 www.ephbooks.com
Hd.Org.: Md. Mujtaba Khan
Bus.Intt.: Pub.; **Spl.:** Urdu literature, Islamic literature, general and reference books and dictionaries in English, Hindi and Urdu

EDUCATIONAL SUPPLIES
Block A-02, Ground Floor, Brigade MM
Industrial Complex, K.R. Rd., 400/1,
4th Cross, 7th Block, West Jayanagar,
P.B. No. 8204, Bangalore-560082
(Karnataka)
✆ 26769509, 26761289, Fax: 26769954
✉ jai@blr.vsnl.net.in
🌐 www.edu-supplies.com
Estd.: 1979; **Man.Prt.:** Jaiprakash M.S.
Br.: Book Paradise, #75, 8th "E", M.N. Rd., NIIT Towers, 4th Block, Jayanagar, Bangalore-560011 ✆ 26991070, 26637466, Fax: 26769954 ✉ bookparadise@satyam.net.in
🌐 www.book-paradise.com
Bus.Intt.: L.S. & Rt., Imp.; **Spl.:** Sci. & Tech.

EDUCATIONAL SUPPLIERS & TRADERS
Near Subzi Mandi, P.O.,
Kuchaman-341508
Distt. Nagaur (Rajasthan)

EDURITE TECHNOLOGIES PVT. LTD.
65-A, Ompro Towers,
III & IV Floor, Kalusarai,
New Delhi-110016
✆ 46068507, 46068508, Fax: 91-11-46068581
✉ subrotoroy@edurite.com,
marketingteam@edurite.com
🌐 www.edurite.com
Hd.Org.: Subroto Roy
Cor.Offi.: "TECH PARK", PESIT Campus, 100 Feet Ring Road, Banashankari III Stage, Bangalore-560085 (Karnataka)
✆ 26729298/3769/9263,
Fax: 91-80-26729301

EDUTECH INTERNATIONAL
405, ESI Colony, Basai Darapur,
New Delhi-110015
✆ 25171239
Hd.Org.: Rajesh Sharma; **Bus.Intt.:** Dealer;
Spl.: Edu. Book for Children

EFFICIENT BOOK DISTRIBUTORS
Flat No. 1294, Sector-A, Pocket-B,
Vasant Kunj, New Delhi-110070
✆ 26132262 ▮ 9811380682, Fax: 26132262
✉ effibook@satyam.net.in
🌐 www.efficientbooks.com
Hd.Org.: Sameer Kapoor; **Bus.Intt.:** Pub. and Dist.; **Spl.:** Indian and Foreign Books on Archaeology, Culture, Rel., etc.

EGMONT IMAGINATION (INDIA) LTD.
Dani Wolltex Compound, 158, Vidyanagri
Marg, Kalina, Santacruz (E),
Mumbai-400098 (Maharashtra)
✆ 56924700, Fax: 56924709
✉ ieegmont@bom4.vsnl.net.in
Ch.Exe.: Mr. Uday Mathur; **Bus.Intt.:** Pub.;
Spl.: Walt Disney and King Features in India for Children

EICHER GOODEARTH LIMITED
Eicher House, 12, Commercial Complex,
Greater Kailash-II, New Delhi-110048
✆ 41437600, Fax: 91-11-41437700
✉ maps@eicher.co.in
🌐 www.eichermaps.com
Hd.Org.: Girish Sidda; **Bus.Intt.:** Pub.;
Spl.: Maps, City Guides, Travel Guides etc.

EJAZ PUBLISHING HOUSE
2040, Kucha Chelan, Darya Ganj,
New Delhi-110002
✆ 23253268
Estd.: 1964; **Hd.Org.:** Syed Azhar Husain

EKANT BOOK CENTRE
BM 63, (West) Shalimar Bagh, Delhi-110058
✆ 27489083, 55152825
Hd.Org.: Anil Kumar; **Bus.Intt.:** Pub;
Spl.: Edu. Books in Hindi Language

EKLAVYA
E-10, Sankar Nagar, BDA Colony, Shivaji Nagar, Bhopal-462016 (Madhya Pradesh)
✆ 2463380, 6549033, Fax: 91-755-2461703
pitara@eklavya.in
www.eklaviya.in
Hd.Org.: C.N. Subramaniama
Bus.Intt.: Pub.; **Spl.:** Children and on Child Edu., Magazines: *Chakmak, Sandarbh* and *Strot*

EKTA BOOK COMPANY
Shop No. 2, New 54 Lawyers Chamber's Block, Delhi High Court, Shershah Rd., New Delhi-110003
✆ 23388588, 23383875, 23383334, Fax: 23383334
ektalaw@vsnl.com
www.lawbooseller.com
Estd.: 1976; **Prt.:** Y.P. Dudeja
Br.: Shop No. 5, Tis Hazari Court (Civil Side), Delhi-110054 ✆ 23934548, 23968383, Fax: 23934548
Bus.Intt.: Pub., WS, L.S. & Rt., Imp., Exp., Sub.Ag.; **Spl.:** Law, Trade, Gen. (Incl. Lit. Art)

EKTA BOOK COMPANY (SALES)
Shop No. 35, Local Shopping Centre, Gulmohar Park, New Delhi-110049
✆ 30621119, Fax: 91-11-26514798
ektabookcompany_s@yahoo.com
www.lawbooks.pel.net.in
Estd.: 1976; **Hd.Org.:** Dinesh K. Dudeja
Br.: Shop No. 5, Tis Hazari Court (Civil Side), Delhi-110054, ✆ 23934548, 23968383, Fax: 23934548
Bus.Intt.: Pub. and Dist.; **Spl.:** Books, magazines and reports on law

EKTA BOOK DISTRIBUTORS
R-37B, Vani Vihar, Uttam Nagar, New Delhi-110059
✆ (O) 56065579 (R) 25640621 ▮ 9811582579
ektabooks@yahoo.com
Estd.: 1998; **Prop.:** Usha Mishra; **Bus.Intt.:** Insti. and L.S.; **Spl.:** Acad., Humanities and Soc.Sci. Mang., Books on Woman Studies, Edu. and Tribal Studies, Med. Fiction, Acad. Soc.Sci., Comm.

EKTA LAW HOUSE
Shop No. 5, Civil Wing, Tis Hazari Courts, Delhi-110054
✆ 23968383, 23934548, 23388588
Prt.: Raj Pal Dudeja, Mrs. Manju Dudeja, Mrs. Geeta Dudeja
Br.: C-1, Panchsheel Enclave, New Delhi-110017 ✆ 26491875, 26499876
▮ 9811026696, 98110-48086, Telefax: 26499876
ektalaw@vsnl.com lawbookseller.com
Bus.Intt.: Rt., WS; **Spl.:** Law

EKUSHE
13/1, Bankim Chatterjee St., Kolkata-700073 (West Bengal)

ELEMENTOPATHY PRATISHAN
Nandgaoan Khandeshwar, Amravati-444708 (Maharashtra)
Estd.: 1964; **Bus.Intt.:** Pub. and B.S.;
Spl.: Med.

ELIC ENTERPRISES
7, Krishnaraj Apartment, Opp. Peoples Bank, Gole Colony, Nashik-422002 (Maharashtra)
✆ 0253-2580624
elicindia@yahoo.com
Hd.Org.: Rajesh Bang; **Spl.:** Comp./Elec. Books, CDs & Software

ELITE PUBLISHERS & DISTRIBUTORS
Shop No. 13, DDA Shopping Complex, Ber Sarai, (Opp. JNU Old Campus), New Delhi-110016
✆ (O) 26511961 (R) 26899239,
▮ 9811670046, Fax: 26511961
elitepublishers@vsnl.net
www.elitepublishers.org
Estd.: 1990; **Prop.:** Sharad Kapoor;
Bus.Intt.: Pub., L.S. & Rt., Imp.; **Spl.:** Humanities, Soc.Sci., Mang. & Reference Books, Acad., Beh.Sci., Sci., Law Books

ELITE PUBLISHING HOUSE PVT. LTD.
New Delhi
▮ 9810666503
rg_elite@yahoo.com
Bus.Intt.: Pub. & Dist.

ELSEVIER
(A Division of Reed Elsevier India Pvt Ltd.), Sri Pratap Udyog, 274 Capt. Gaur Marg, Srinivaspuri, New Delhi-110065
✆ 42890200, Fax: 91-11-42890201
infoindia@elsevier.com
www.elsevier.com
Hd.Org.: Sanjay Banerjee;
Bus.Intt.: Pub. and Dist.; **Spl.:** Books on Sci., Tech., Com. and Med. Sci.

ELSEVIER
Science & Tech. Books, 17-A/1, Main Ring Rd., Lajpat Nagar IV, New Delhi-110024
✆ 26447160, Fax: 26447156
esindia@vsnl.net, elservier@giasdol.insl.net.in
www.elsevierhealth.com
Gen.Man.(India): Robinder Bhakhri;

Bus.Intt.: Pub.; **Spl.:** Books and CD-ROMs on Sci. & Tech. and Med. Sci.

ELSEVIER SCIENCE
New Delhi
✆ 26464550, 26280848, Fax: 26475065
✉ harcourt@vsnl.com

ELTEK BOOK-N-KITS
No. 6, Ritchie St., Ist Floor, Mount Rd., Chennai-600002 (Tamil Nadu)
✆ 2835419, Fax: 9144-2835187
Estd.: 1983; **Prop.:** M. Suthanthiravel; **Bus.Intt.:** WS, L.S. and Rt., Imp.

EMBASSY BOOK DISTRIBUTORS
120, Great Western Building, Maharashtra Chamber of Commerce Lane, Fort, Mumbai-400023 (Maharashtra)
✆ 91-22-22819546
✉ embassy@vsnl.com
Estd.: 1992; **Prop.:** Sohin Lakhani; **Bus.Intt.:** Pub., Dist., Imp., L.S.; **Spl.:** Encyclopedia and Reference, Gen. Books

EMERALD PUBLISHERS
15-A, 1st Floor, Casa Major Rd., Egmore, Chennai-600008 (Tamil Nadu)
✆ 28193206, Fax: 28192380
✉ olivannang@yahoo.co.in
🌐 www.emeraldpublishers.com
Hd.Org.: G. Olivannan; **Bus.Intt.:** Pub.; **Spl.:** College and University level Textbooks in English Language

EMKAY PUBLICATIONS
B-19, East Krishna Nagar, Delhi-110051
✆ 22092191 ▮ 9891156083, Fax: 22046456
✉ emkay_pub@rediffmail.com
Estd.: 1975; **Hd.Org.:** M.K. Sood; **Bus.Intt.:** Pub.; **Spl.:** College and University-level Textbooks on Sci. and Tech.

EMMENEM PUBLICATIONS (P) LTD.
C/o Inter Pub. Pvt. Ltd., Ballard House, Ist Floor, Adi Marzhab Path, Fort, Mumbai-400038 (Maharashtra)

EMMOS BOOK STALL
Pathanamthitta-689001 (Kerala)

ENCYCLOPAEDIA BRITANNICA INDIA PVT. LTD.
114-116, Sushant Plaza, 'A' Block, Sushant Lok Phase-I, Gurgaon (Haryana)
✆ 5012150 ▮ 9810289145, Fax: 5012155
✉ corporate@ebindia.com, bcd@ebindia.com
🌐 www.britannicaindia.com
Hd.Org.: Aalok Wadhwa; **Bus.Intt.:** Pub.; **Spl.:** 32-volume *Encyclopaedia Britannica* in Electronic and Print form

ENCYCLOPAEDIA BRITANNICA (INDIA) PVT. LTD.
140, Zamrudpur Shopping Complex, N-Block Road, Greater Kailash-I, New Delhi-110048
✆ 46536450-53, Fax: 91-11-29245116
✉ bcd@ebindia.com
🌐 www.britannicaindia.com
Hd.Org.: K.M. Thomas; **Bus.Intt.:** Pub.; **Spl.:** 32-volume *Encyclopaedia Britannica* in Electronic and Print form

ENGINEERING COMPETITION TODAY
Oswal House, 1/11, Sahitya Kunj, M.G. Rd., Agra-282002 (Uttar Pradesh)
✆ 2156558, 2157671, 2154582, Fax: 2522141
✉ oswalbooks@vsnl.com, oswalbooks@indiatimes.com
🌐 www.bestsellersindia.com
Hd.Org.: Naresh Jain; **Bus.Intt.:** Pub.; **Spl.:** Magazines *Engineering Competition Today* and *Oswal Pratiyogita Vigyan* and Books for Competitive Exams

ENGINEERS INDIA RESEARCH INSTITUTE
4449, Nai Sarak, Main Rd., Delhi-110006
✆ (O) 23918117, 23916431, 23840361 (R) 31082370, Fax: 23916431
✉ eirisidi@bol.net.in
🌐 www.eiriindia.org
Estd.: 1978; **Hd.Org.:** Sudhir Kr. Gupta; **Bus.Intt.:** Pub.; **Spl.:** Industry, Sci. and Tech. as also Trade Directories

ENGINEERS TODAY
D-216A/1, Bhaskar Marg, Bani Park, Jaipur-302016 (Rajasthan)
✆ 2315392, 2201532
✉ engineerstoday@123india.com
Estd.: 1988; **Bus.Intt.:** Pub. and B.S.; **Spl.:** Sci. & Tech., Practical Books for Civil Engg. and Builders

ENGLISH BOOK & STATIONERY DEPOT (THE)
347, Sadar Bazar, Jhansi-284001 (Uttar Pradesh)
✆ (O) 2471241, 2470075 (R) 2471334
Estd.: 1935; **Prop.:** Sudhir Pal Arora; **Bus.Intt.:** L.S. & Rt.; **Spl.:** Humanities & Soc. Sci., Sci. & Tech., Comp., Med., Mang., Law, Arts & Arch., Bio., Children & Gen., Military Interests

ENGLISH BOOK DEPOT
Ferozpur (Punjab)

ENGLISH BOOK DEPOT (THE)
15, Rajpur Rd., Dehradun-248001 (Uttarakhand)
✆ 22655192, 2710958, Fax: 2658730
✉ sales@ebdbooks.com, sandeep@ebdbooks.com, ebdbooks@vsnl.com

www.ebdbooks.com
Estd.: 1923; **Prt.:** Sandeep Dutt
Br.: 31, Mohan Singh Place, New Delhi-110001
delhi@bookcafeco.com
Bus.Intt.: Pub., WS, L.S. & Rt., Imp., Exp., Sub.Ag.; **Spl.:** Sci. & Tech., Juvenile/ Children, Gen. & Fiction etc.

ENGLISH BOOK HOUSE
35B/B, IInd Extension, Gandhi Nagar, Jammu-180001 (Jammu & Kashmir)
✆ 22452040
Estd.: 1987; **Hd.Org.:** S. Harbinder Singh
Br.: Shop-8, Gurudwara Building, Nanak Nagar, Jammu; ✆ 22470195
Bus.Intt.: Pub., WS, L.S. & Rt., Imp, Sub.Ag.; **Spl.:** Humanities & Sco.Sci., Sci. & Tech., Gen. & Fiction etc.

ENGLISH BOOK STORE (THE)
17-L, Connaught Circus, New Delhi-110001
✆ 23417126, 23415031, 23417936, Fax: 23417731; ebs@vsnl.com
www.theenglishbookstore.com
Estd.: 1936; **Prop.:** Bhupinder Chowdhri;
Bus.Intt.: Pub., WS, L.S. & Rt., Imp., Exp., Sub.Ag.; **Spl.:** Aeronautics, Children Books, Culture, Ecology, Foreign Languages, Hunting, Himalayas, Mountaineering, Military, Rel., Shooting, Travels, Yoga

ENGLISH EDITION
5/10, 11, Jogani Industrial Complex, (Near ATI) V.N. Purav Marg, Chuna Bhatti, Mumbai-400022 (Maharashtra)
✆ (O) 25243531, 25274464, 55952261/62 (R) 25541853, Fax: 25233158
english_edition@hotmail.com
www.englishedition.net
Estd.: 1997; **Hd.Org.:** J.S. Sethi
Br.: 404, Ravi Building, Next to Central Camera, 189/191, DN. Rd., Fort, Mumbai-400001 ✆ 22618154, 22632504
english_edition@hotmail
• Churchgate, 35, Church St., Opp. Java City, Bangalore-560001 ✆ 5066121
english_edition@hotmail.com
Bus.Intt.: Pub., WS, Exp., Imp.; **Spl.:** Mang., Arts & Arch., Children & Gen.

ENKAY CORPORATION
Off.: Pocket B/2, CSC No. 6, Opp. Police Station, Lawrence Rd., Delhi-110035
✆ 91-011-27184398, 27180768, 56237493
9810282329, Fax: 91-011-27180768
jdis@del3.vsnl.net.in
Estd.: 2000; **Hd.Org.:** R.S. Bhatia
Rgd.: Delhi Consumer's Co-operative Wholesale Store Ltd., Karampura Road, Moti Nagar, New Delhi-110015
Bus.Intt.: Gen. Order Suppliers

ENKAY INTERNATIONAL
IX/1569, Gandhi Nagar, Delhi-110031
✆ (O) 22074782 (R) 22076113, Fax: 22076046
enkayi@eth.net
Estd.: 2000; **Hd.Org.:** Navneet Saggu;
Bus.Intt.: Pub., Exp.; **Spl.:** Humanities & Soc.Sci., Sci. & Tech.

ENKAY PUBLISHERS (P) LTD.
3-4, Malcha Marg Shopping Centre, Chanakyapuri, Delhi-110021
✆ (O) 23014777, 23014778, 23016994 (R) 24627947, 24631422, Fax: 23012314
Estd.: 1986; **Hd.Org.:** N.S. Kohli;
Bus.Intt.: Pub. and Exp.

ENN DEE
MR-18, Circular Rd., Nandini Layout, Bangalore-560096 (Karnataka)

ENTREPRENEURSHIP DEVELOPMENT
Institute of India, E.D.I. Campus Bhat, (Via Ahmedabad Airport & Indira Gandhi Bridge), P.O. Chandi Kheda-382424, Distt. Gandhi Nagar (Gujarat)

ENVIRONMENTALISTS
1/1286, H.I.G. Malviya Nagar, Jaipur-302107 (Rajasthan)

ERA BOOKS
52/47, Ramjas Rd., Karol Bagh, New Delhi-110005

ESS ESS PUBLICATIONS
4837/24, Govind Lane, Ansari Rd., Darya Ganj, New Delhi-110002
✆ 23260807, 23201533, 23274173, Fax: 23274173
essess@del3.vsnl.net.in
Hd.Org.: Sheel Sethi; **Bus.Intt.:** Pub.; **Spl.:** Lib. and Information Sci.

ESS ESS PUBLICATIONS/REFERENCE PRESS
4831/24, Govind Lane, Ansari Road, Darya Ganj, New Delhi-110002
✆ 23260807, 41563444, Fax: 91-11-41563334
info@essessreference.com
www.essessreference.com
Hd.Org.: Sumit Sethi; **Bus.Intt.:** Pub.; **Spl.:** Lib. and Information Sci.

ESS PEE KAY PUBLISHING HOUSE
4B, Jessan St., Ist Floor, Near LIC Anna Salai, Chennai-600002 (Tamil Nadu)

ESTEEM BOOK DISTRIBUTORS
166, Surinder Nagar, Nagpur (Maharashtra)
Estd.: 1996; **Prop.:** Prashant Podukhe

ESWAR PRESS
Archana Arcade, 27, Natesan St., T. Nagar, Chennai-600017 (Tamil Nadu)

✆ 52030431, Fax: 24339590
✉ gempeyes@md3.vsnl.net.in
Hd.Org.: M. Periyasamy; **Bus.Intt.:** Pub.; **Spl.:** Sci. & Tech.

ET4ALL ENTERPRISES
ETPO Art Gallery, 501/32, Nehru Place, New Delhi-110019
✆ 91-11-66603600
✉ ambdded@gmailcom
www.pranayamwatch.com
Hd.Org.: K.A. Agarwal; **Bus.Intt.:** Pub.; **Spl.:** Books on Indian culture in Hindi

ETTEKI BOOKS-N-KITS
No. 6, Ritchie St., Ist Floor, Mount Rd., Chennai-600002 (Tamil Nadu)

EURASIA PUBLISHING HOUSE PVT. LTD.
7361, Ram Nagar, Qutub Road, New Delhi-110055
✆ 23672080-82, ▮ 9899107446, 9911310888, Fax: 91-11-23677446
✉ schand@vsnl.com, info@schandgroup.com
www.schandgroup.com
Hd.Org.: Navin Joshi; **Bus.Intt.:** Pub.; **Spl.:** Sci. and Tech., Engg. and Math. for Schools and University Students

EUREKA MARKETING GROUP
B-12, Block III, Villa No. 55 (G.F.), Eros Garden, Suraj Kund Rd., Faridabad-121009 (Haryana)
✆ (O) & (R) 0129-2512067 ▮ 9818002483, Fax: 0129-25252222
✉ pandit@del3.vsnl.net.in
Prop.: Ms. Prem Pandit; **Bus.Intt.:** Pub.'s Rep.; **Spl.:** Applied Beh.Sci. Publications, Training Material & Games

EUROPEAN BUSINESS INFORMATION CENTRE
65, Golf Links, New Delhi-110003
✆ 24636675, Fax: 24633378
✉ Ebic@giasbm01.vsnl.net.in
ebic.india.com
Hd.Org.: S.K. Ghosh

EUROPEAN UNION
Delegation of the European Commission, 65, Golf Links, New Delhi-110003
✆ 24629237, Fax: 24629206
✉ eu@delind.cec.eu.int, delegation-india@cec.eu.int
www.delind.cec.eu.int
Hd.Org.: Michel Caillouet; **Bus.Intt.:** Promoter; **Spl.:** Large-scale Development Cooperation between European Union and India

EVANGELICAL LITERATURE SERVICE
Kesavadasapuram, Pattom, Thiruvananthapuram-695004 (Kerala)
✆ 2448916, Fax: 2442937
Estd.: 1954; **Gen.Secy.:** C. Benjamin; **Bus.Intt.:** Pub. and B.S.

EVANGELICAL LITERATURE SERVICE
95-A, Vepery High Rd., Chennai-600007 (Tamil Nadu)
✆ 25323231

EVELYN PUBLISHERS
Ella's College, B-108, Gulmohar Park, New Delhi-110049
✆ 26569703
Hd.Org.: Devi Prasanna; **Bus.Intt.:** Pub.; **Spl.:** Sci. and Tech.

EVEREST PUBLISHING HOUSE
"Everest Lane" Appa Balwant Chowk, Pune-411030 (Maharashtra)
✆ (O) 2459486, 2364469 (R) 2365790, Fax: 2459486
✉ everest@adnetindia.com
Br.: Everest Computer Book-Shop, Everest Lane, Opp. Prabhat Talkies, Pune-411030 (Maharashtra)
Estd.: 1987; **Bus.Intt.:** Pub.; **Spl.:** Tech., Comp. Books

EVERGREEN PUBLICATIONS (INDIA) LTD.
4738/23, Ansari Rd., Darya Ganj, New Delhi-110002
✆ (O) 23283372, 23264528, 23280337 (R) 22151265, Fax: 91-11-23289434, 23262183
✉ evergreen@del3.vsnl.net.in
www.evergreenpublications.com
Estd.: 1980; **Hd.Org.:** Nirmal Kumar Chopra; **Bus.Intt.:** Pub.; **Spl.:** Edu. books for Children

EVERGREEN SUPPLY AGENCY
Zaver Baug, Telli Galli, Rajarshi Shahu Maharaj Rd., Andheri (E), Mumbai-400069 (Maharashtra)
Bus.Intt.: Exp.

EXAMINER BOOK SHOP
35, Dalal St., Fort, Mumbai-400001 (Maharashtra)
✆ 2273690, 26400126

EXCEL BOOKS PRIVATE LIMITED
A-45, Naraina, Phase-I, New Delhi-110028
✆ 25795793/94, Fax: 25791701
✉ info@excelbooks.com
www.excelbooks.com
Estd.: 1993; **Hd.Org.:** Anurag Jain; **Br.:** 2/8, Ansari Road, Daryaganj, Delhi-110002
✆ 23247082-83, Fax: 91-11-25791701
✉ info@excelbooks.com
www.excelbooks.com

Bus.Intt.: Pub.; **Spl.:** Edu. Books on Mang. and Information Tech. in English

EXCEL MEDIA
4832/24, G-5, Govind Lane, Ansari Rd., Darya Ganj, New Delhi-110002
✆ 23251049, Fax: 91-11-23251049
excelmedia@vsnl.net
www.excelmedia.org
Hd.Org.: Rajat Kapoor; **Bus.Intt.:** WS, Dist.; **Spl.:** Books and Multi-media Products, Mang. Tech. books

EXECUTIVE BUSINESS CENTRE
K-1, Kailash Colony, New Delhi-110048

EXICOM (INDIA) PVT. LTD.
Mumbai (Maharashtra)
✆ 27634863 /4/5/6, Fax: 27680107
exipub@bom5.vsnl.net.in

EXPRESS BOOK SERVICE
2435, East St., Camp., Poona-411001 (Maharashtra)
✆ 2633666
Bus.Intt.: Dealers; **Spl.:** Sci., Tech., Edu., Encyclopedia, Reference Gen. Books & Magazines

EXPRESS BOOK SERVICE
Makhaniakuan, Patna-800004 (Bihar)
✆ 258024
Bus.Intt.: Pub. and B.S.

EXPRESS COLOUR SCAN PVT. LTD.
B-87, Naraina Indl. Area, Phase-II, New Delhi-110028
✆ 25703345 to 25703348, Fax: 25700111
castle@giasdl01.vsnl.net.in
Bus.Intt.: Exp.

EXPRESS PUBLICATIONS (MADURAI) LTD.
Express Estate, Chennai-600002 (Tamil Nadu)

EXPOSURE COMMUNICATIONS (P) LTD.
53, Veerabadran St., Nungambakkam, Chennai-600034 (Tamil Nadu)
✆ 28235453, 28215941-42, Fax: 28241799
exposure@eth.net
Ch.Exe.: Mr. S.M. Mohammed Ismail; **Spl.:** Frame, Mounted & Plain Posters, Table Tops

EZHILAGAM (PUBLISHERS AND BOOKSELLERS)
46, Selvavinayagar Koil St., Thiruvathipuram, (Cheyyar), T.S. District-604407 (Tamil Nadu)

F.E.B. ALLIANCE
FA-36, Vishal Enclave, New Delhi-110027
✆ 25442959, 25431178, 23320624
Hd.Org.: Gajinder Poul Singh Rana;
Bus.Intt.: Rt.

F.K. PUBLICATIONS
4323/3, Ansari Road, Darya Ganj,
New Delhi-110002
✆ 23250106, Fax: 91-11-23250141
www.future-kids.com
Hd.Org.: Rohit Jain, **Bus.Intt.:** Pub.;
Spl.: Edu. books for school and university levels

F.M.J. INTERNATIONAL PUBLICATIONS LTD.
B-13, 3rd Floor, A Block Shopping Complex,
Naraina Vihar, Ring Rd., New Delhi-110028

FABRO DYNAMICS
New MCH No. 541, St. No. 6, Vidyanagar,
Hyderabad-500044 (Andhra Pradesh)
✆ 27616512, 27610238, Fax: 27664144
fabrodynamics@yahoo.com

FACH PRESSE PUBLISHERS PVT. LTD.
1208, Regent Chamber, 208, Nariman Point,
Mumbai-400021 (Maharashtra)
✆ 24279183, Fax: 22825603
fach@boms.vsnl.net.in

FACTS AND FICTIONS
E/177, Krishna Market, Lajpat Nagar,
New Delhi-110024
✆ 29813598 ▮ 9891200855
Hd.Org.: Vijay Takeyar; **Bus.Intt.:** Pub.;
Spl.: Edu. books for Children in English

FAIR DEAL STATIONERS & BOOKSELLERS
Leh-Ladakh (Jammu and Kashmir)

FAIR TAIL
Leh (Jammu & Kashmir)
Bus.Intt.: B.S. and Newspaper Agents

FALCON BOOKS PVT. LTD.
B-2, Bhandari House, 91, Nehru Place,
New Delhi-110019
✆ 26432653, 26228514, Fax: 91-11-26448917
falconbpl@yahoo.co.in
www.falconbpl.com
Estd.: 1986; **Dir.:** Ashok K. Sharma,
Kishore Venkatesh
Br.: 139, Lower Ground Floor, Swapan Kunj,
Pocket A-8, Kalkaji Extension,
New Delhi-110019 ✆ 26091437
Bus.Intt.: WS, Pub., Sub.Ag., Pub.'s Rep., L.S.; **Spl.:** Acad., Sci., Pure and Applied, Tech., Rare, Journals and Magazines

FALCON GRAPHICS
F/1, Fismond Park, Datta Mandir Rd.,
Vakola Santa Cruz (East),
Mumbai-400055
(Maharashtra)

FALCON PRINTS & CONVERSIONS
268, Royapattah High Rd.,
Chennai-600014 (Tamil Nadu)
Bus.Intt.: Exp.

FAMILY BOOK SHOP
1A, Park St., Kolkata-700016
(West Bengal)
✆ 2293486
Estd.: 1979; **Hd.Org.:** Pramod Barman, Ashok;
Bus.Intt.: Rt. and Mail Order Service; **Spl.:** Gen., Children & Acad. Books (Indian & Foreign)

FAMILY WELFARE TRAINING & RESEARCH CENTRE
322, S.V.P. Rd., Mumbai-400004
(Maharashtra)

FAMOUS BOOK STORE
25, Janpath, New Delhi-110001
✆ 23311510

FAQIR CHAND & SONS
15-A, Khan Market, New Delhi-110003
✆ (O) 24618810 (R) 24618810,
Telefax: 24645540
Estd.: 1951; **Prop.:** Mrs. Uma Marwah;
Bus.Intt.: Rt. of Art Indology and Coffe Table Books and Order Suppliers; **Spl.:** Humanities, Fiction, Periodicals, Children Books and Books of Tourists' interest

FARID BOOK DEPOT (PVT.) LTD.
2159, M.P. St., Pataudi House,
Darya Ganj, New Delhi-110002
✆ 23289159, Fax: 91-11-23279998

FARID ENTERPRISES
422, Matia Mahal, Jama Masjid,
New Delhi-110006
✆ 23256590, Fax: 91-11-23279998

FARID EXPORTS
2158, M.P. St., Pataudi House, Darya Ganj,
New Delhi-110002
✆ 23289786, 23256590, Fax: 91-11-23279998
farid@ndf.vsnl.net.in
Bus.Intt.: Pub., Printers, B.S., Imp. & Leading Exp.; **Spl.:** Holy *Qur'an* and Islamic Books (Arabic, English, Hindi and Urdu)

FARM DIGEST PUBLICATIONS
5/32, Patel Gali, Vishwas Nagar,
Shahdara, Delhi-110032

✆ 22208405
Estd.: 1991; **Hd.Org.:** K.R. Nair; **Bus.Intt.:** Pub.; **Spl.:** Farm Digest Monthly in English and Agri. Books in English and Hindi

FARSIGHT PUBLISHERS AND DISTRIBUTORS
S-16, Naveen Shahdara, Delhi-110032

FASHION VISION
H-11, South Extn. Part-I, New Delhi-110049

FAXON INFORMATICS PVT. LTD.
P.B. No. 38087, 2nd Floor, 11th Cross, Malleswaram, Bangalore-560003 (Karnataka)
✆ 2367867, 2344598, Fax: 2344598, Telex: 08452041
Estd.: 1991; **Dir.:** N.V. Sathyanarayana; **Bus.Intt.:** Sub.Ag.

FAYAZ ENTERPRISES BOOK SELLERS
7, Iqbal Market, Sopore, (KMR)-193201 (Jammu and Kashmir)
✆ (O) 019524405 (R) 019524302
Estd.: 1988; **Dir.:** Col. Mohd. Syed; **Bus.Intt.:** L.S.; **Spl.:** Agri., Sci., Litt., Rel. Main Supply, Rt. for College Books, Magazines, Agri., English Med. Books and other Gen.

FEATURE PUBLICATIONS
2047/6, Chuna Mandi, Paharganj, New Delhi-110055
✆ 23555291, 23512785
Hd.Org.: Shanti Prasad Jain

FERTILISER DEVELOPMENT AND CONSULTATION ORGANISATION
204-204-A, Bhanot Corner, Pamposh Enclave, New Delhi-110048
✆ 26417801, 51633864, Cable: FERTUSE, Fax: 26862196, 26417801
✉ fdco@vsnl.net, hls_tandon@mantraonline.com
🌐 www.tandontech.8k.com
Estd.: 1984; **Dir.:** Dr. H.L.S. Tandon; **Bus.Intt.:** Pub., L.S. & Rt.; **Spl.:** Sci. & Tech.

FILEX SYSTEMS (P) LTD.
3/27, Roop Nagar, Delhi-110007
✆ 23925659, 23843404, Fax: 91-11-27781606
✉ filex@vsnl.com, filexsales@vsnl.net
Ch.Exe.: Mr. Amit Gupta; **Bus.Intt.:** Dealer; **Spl.:** Books, Files and Folders

FILHAAL
M-46/2, Second Floor, Shri Krishna Nagar, Patna-800001 (Bihar)
✆ 91-612-2525813
✉ filhaal_patna@yahoo.com
Hd.Org.: Preet Sinha, **Bus.Intt.:** Pub.; **Spl.:** Hindi Monthly Magazine, *Filhaal* and books on Social Sciences

FIREWALL MEDIA
22, Golden House, Darya Ganj, New Delhi-110002
✆ 23252574, Fax: 23252572
✉ colaxmi@hotmail.com
Hd.Org.: R.K. Gupta; **Bus.Intt.:** Pub.; **Spl.:** Sci. and Tech.

FIRMA KLM (P) LTD.
257B, BB Ganguly St., Kolkata-700012 (West Bengal)
✆ 22217294, 22374391, 24813198, Fax: 91-33-22256742
✉ fklm@satyam.net.in
Hd.Org.: S. Mukherjee; **Bus.Intt.:** Pub. and Dist.; **Spl.:** Indology, Soc.Sci. and Indigenous Therapy in Bengali. Also co-publish in Spanish, Japanese, Dutch, French and Italian

FIRST CHURCH OF CHRIST SCIENTIST
P.O. Box 3036, Lodhi Rd., New Delhi-110003
✆ 91-11-41826022
✉ juliasappenfield@hotmail.com
Hd.Org.: Julia Sappenfield
Bus.Intt.: Promoter; **Spl.:** Books on spiritual healing

FIRST EDITION
67 LGF, Kailash Hills, East of Kailash, New Delhi-110065
✆ 91-11-41621840
Hd.Org.: S. Kulbir Singh; **Bus.Intt.:** Pub.; **Spl.:** Books on religion, especially on Sikhism, gender issues and international topics

FIRST PUBLIC PROTECTION TRUST
11, (Old 4) Kandaswamy St., R.A. Puram, Chennai-600028 (Tamil Nadu)
✆ 24937008, 24950702, Fax: 91-44-24938488
✉ srinivasan@kmr.net
Bus.Intt.: Pub. and B.S.;
Spl.: Research and Public Education

FLAMINGO BOOKS (EXPORT)
11096, Doriwalan, East Park Road, Karol Bagh, New Delhi-110005
✆ 23535454, 23525867, Fax: 91-11-23612870
✉ sonipub@ndf.vsnl.net.in, sonipub@vsnl.com
🌐 www.sonibooks.com
Hd.Org.: G.D. Soni; **Bus.Intt.:** Pub. and Exp.; **Spl.:** Children's Books, Edu. and Gen. Books for School Children

FOCUS BOOK SHOP
(A division of Focus Press Pvt. Ltd.), 140/2, Lakshmi Nivas, 8th Cross (Lane Next to Titan Show Room), Maleswaram, Bangalore-560003 (Karnataka)
✆ 3346692, 33445402, Fax: 23424265

focus@mahiti.org, focusgroup@vsnl.net
Estd.: 1992; **Man.Dir.**: Ivo Rodrigues
Br.: 33/3, 8th Main, 12th Cross, Maleswaram, Bangalore-560003
Bus.Intt.: B.S., L.S.

FOCUS: THE BOOK SHOP
204, Mission St., Pondicherry (U.T.)
0413-2345513
m_anony@mailcity.com
Bus.Intt.: B.S. & Rt.

FOLKLORIST
B-41, Ganesh Marg, Babu Nagar, Jaipur-302105 (Rajasthan)
Bus.Intt.: Pub.

FOOD & AGRICULTURE ORGANIZATION OF THE UNITED NATIONS
C/o Oxford Book & Stationery Co., Scindia House, New Delhi-110001

FOREIGN LANGUAGE TEACHING AND RESEARCH PRESS
16, Ansari Road, Near Mahavir Vatika, Darya Ganj, New Delhi-110002
23263695, Fax: 91-11-23911057
kaushalgoyal@vsnl.com
www.goyalbookshop.com
Hd.Org.: Kaushal Goyal; **Bus.Intt.**: Dist.; **Spl.**: Books on foreign languages and dictionaries

FOREIGN PUBLISHERS' AGENCY
15/3, J.L. Nehru Rd., Kolkata-700013 (West Bengal)
22492255
Estd.: 1941; **Hd.Org.**: Mrs. N.R. Chatterjee; **Bus.Intt.**: Rt. and Mail Order Service; **Spl.**: Gen., Children & Academic Books (Indian and Foreign)

FORESIGHT BOOK DISTRIBUTORS
242, Kilpauk Garden Rd., Chennai-600010 (Tamil Nadu)
2619938, 26442836
Prop.: Amala George; **Bus.Intt.**: Imp. and Pub., Dist.; **Spl.**: Children's Interest, Photography, Advertising Jewellery

FORT BOOK STALL
Birya House, 113, Mody St., Ist Floor, Fort, Mumbai-400055 (Maharashtra)

FORTUNE BOOK COMPANY
177, Sultanpur Extn., Mehrauli, New Delhi-110030
26803975, 26803970, Fax: 26859212
Estd.: 1998; **Prop.**: Vijay Singh Rauthan; **Bus.Intt.**: Rt. & L.S.; **Spl.**: Tech. Books & Mang.

FORTUNE BOOKS
4374/4B, Ansari Rd., Darya Ganj, New Delhi-110002
23261597, 23255577, Fax: 23280289
anmilpublication@vsnl.com
www.anmolpublication.com
Hd.Org.: J.L. Kumar; **Bus.Intt.**: Pub.; **Spl.**: Children's books in English

FORUM BOOK HOUSE
Tank Bund Rd., Subhasnagar, Bangalore-560009 (Karnataka)
227673
Bus.Intt.: B.S., News Agents and Imp.

FORWARD PUBLISHERS
45B, Shyama Prasad Mukherjee Rd., Kolkata-700026 (West Bengal)

FOUNDATION BOOKS
4764/2A, 23, Ansari Rd., Darya Ganj, New Delhi-110002
23277332, 23285851-2, Fax: 23288534
cupdel@cupind.com
www.cambridge.org
Estd.: 1991; **Country Man.**: Manas Saikia
Br.: C-22, C-Block Brigade. M.M., K.R. Rd., Jayanagar, Bangalore-560082 (Karnataka)
26762764, Fax: 26761322
cupbang@cupind.com • Plot No. 80, Service Industries, Shirvane Sector-1, Nerul Navi Mumbai-400706 27709172, Fax: 27709173 cupmum@cupind.com
Resident Rep.: Ajit De, P.O. Agarpara Saktipur, (B.C. Sen Rd.), North 24 Parganas, West Bengal-743177
Fax: 25650669 9831087661
Bus.Intt.: Pub., WS, L.S. & Rt., Imp., Exp., Sub.Ag.; **Spl.**: Humanities & Soc.Sci., Sci. & Tech., Med., Law, Juvenile/Children, Gen. & Fiction etc.

FOUNDATION FOR ORGANISATIONAL
Adhitam Kendra, B-18, Institutional Area, New Delhi
Spl.: Research and Edu. Books

FOUNDATION MEDIA/FOUNDATION BOOKS
4764/2A, 23, Ansari Rd., Darya Ganj, New Delhi-110002
23277332, 23285851, 23285852, 23274196, 23288533, Fax: 23288534
cupdel@cupind.com
Prop.: Manas Pratim Saikia; **Spl.**: All Sub.

FOUNTAIN HEAD BOOK SHOP
No. 27, Laxmi Tower, Dr. Radhakrishnan Salai, Chennai-600004 (Tamil Nadu)
044-28280867
fhbooks@satyam.net.in
Estd.: 1993; **Man.**: G.K. Pillai; **Bus.Intt.**: Rt. and

L.S.; **Spl.:** Gen. & Trade, Acad., Professional, Children Books, Greeting Cards and Toys, Audio Cassettes, CD Multimedia, Stationery, Gifts and Magazines

FOUNTAINHEAD
(Showroom of India Book Dist., Mumbai), 41, Lavelle Rd., Bangalore-460001 (Karnataka)
✆ 2219777
✉ fhblore@satyam.net.in
Estd.: 1993; **Man.:** Anthony Louis; **Bus.Intt.:** Rt. and L.S.; **Spl.:** Gen. and Trade, Acad., Children Books, Greeting Cards and Stationery Toys (Indian and Foreign Books)

FRANK BROTHERS & CO. (PUB.) LTD.
4675-A, Ansari Rd., 21, Darya Ganj, New Delhi-110002
✆ 23263393, 23279936 (R) 26107579, Fax: 91-11-23269032
✉ connect@frankbros.com, frankbooks@vsnl.com
Estd.: 1930; **Chairman:** R.C. Govil
Sh.: IV/85, Chandni Chowk, Delhi-110006 ✆ 23276791, 23268884; **Br.:** 300, Shankaran Complex, Langford Rd., Bangalore-560025 ✆ 22278047, 22279497, Fax: 22245338 • 140/1, Shaktinagar, Bhopal-462024 ✆ 2782209; • 506-A, 5th Floor, Kamalaya Centre, 156-A, Lenin Sarani St., Kolkata-700013 ✆ 22375849, 22219779, Fax: 22219779; • 2/4, Kesarikuteeram, 27, West Cott. Rd. Royapettah, Chennai-600014 ✆ 28545795, 28527479, 24343214, Fax: 28527479; • 136, Moti Lal Nehru Rd., Opp. Pan Bazar Girls Higher Sec. School, Pan Bazar, Guwahati-781001 ✆ 2630150, 2593773, Fax: 2512093 • 4-1-938, 2nd Floor, Room No. 6, Krishna Complex, Tilak Rd. Abids, Hyderabad-500001; ✆ 24750305, 23220319, Fax: 24750305; • Edassery Building, Room No. 1, 3rd Floor, (Above Star Homes), Banerji Rd., High Court Junction, Kochi-682031 (Kerala) ✆ 2390610, 2397348, Fax: 0484-2397348 • 375/377, Babu Bldg., Room No. 24, Second Floor, Lamington Rd., Mumbai-400007 ✆ 23880678, 23866716, Fax: 022-23872250
Bus.Intt.: Pub., WS, L.S. & Rt., Exp.; **Spl.:** Juvenile/Children, Gen. & Fiction etc.

FRANK EDUCATIONAL AIDS (P) LTD.
A-34, Sector-4, Noida-201301 (Uttar Pradesh)
✆ 2537672-73, Fax: 91-120-2536500
✉ info@frankedu.com, frank@satyam.net.in
www.frankedu.com
Estd.: 1989; **Hd.Org.:** Rakesh Govil, Vijay Govil; • 4675-A, Ansari Road, 21 Darya Ganj, New Delhi-110002; **Bus.Intt.:** Pub.; **Spl.:** Children's Books, Jigsaw Puzzles, Board-games, etc.

FRANKSONS
G-2/16, Top Floor, Ansari Rd., Darya Ganj, New Delhi-110002
✆ 23276757, 23265160, 23260796, Fax: 23269032
✉ connect@frankbros.com
Estd.: 1989; **Hd.Org.:** Neeraj Govil; **Bus.Intt.:** Pub.; **Spl.:** School Textbooks

FREE ADS
Secunderabad (Andhra Pradesh)
✆ 27811025, 27811250, Fax: 27818568
✉ freeads@hd2.vsnl.net.in
Bus.Intt.: Pub.

FREE MITHRAM BOOK DEPOT & PUBLISHING HOUSE
Baker Rd., Kottayam-686001 (Kerala)
✆ (O) 2563965 (R) 263056
Estd.: 1948; **Prop.:** P.E. Varkey; **Bus.Intt.:** Pub. and B.S.

FRENCH BOOK CENTRE PVT. LTD.
A-3, D.D.A. Shopping Complex, Defence Colony, Ring Rd., New Delhi-110024
✆ 24699349, Telex: 31-272143, Fax: 24645917; Cable: Krip-in
✉ fbc@mantraonline.com
Estd.: 1980; **Dir.:** R. Kirpalani
Br.: French Book Shop, 38, BIS, Suffren St., Pondicherry-605001 ✆ 0413-238062
Bus.Intt.: Pub., WS, L.S. & Rt., Imp.; **Spl.:** Trade, Gen. (Incl. Lit. & Art)

FRENCH BOOK SHOP (THE)
C/o GPD Pvt. Ltd., Max Mueller Bhawan, 3, Kasturba Gandhi Marg, New Delhi-110001
✆ 23858362, Fax: 91-11-23850961
Hd.Org.: Ashwani Goyal
Bus.Intt.: B.S. & Rt.

FRIENDS BOOKS CENTRE
Bishanpur Rd., Begusarai-851101 (Bihar)
Bus.Intt.: Pub. and B.S.

FRIENDS BOOK DEPOT
12, University Rd., Allahabad (Uttar Pradesh)

FRIENDS BOOK STALL
Stall-59, 1, Bankim Chatterjee St., Kolkata-700073 (West Bengal)

FRIENDS BOOKS & STATIONERS
Kadamkuan, Patna-800003 (Bihar)
Bus.Intt.: Pub. and B.S.

FRIENDS DISTRIBUTORS
Govind Mitra Rd., Patna-800004 (Bihar)
Bus.Intt.: Pub. and B.S.

FRIENDS PUBLICATIONS (INDIA)
918, Dr. Mukerjee Nagar,
Near Batra Cinema, Delhi-110009
✆ (O) 27654826 (R) 27659446, Fax: 27654827
✉ frienpub@ndf.vsnl.net.in
Estd.: 1990; **Hd.Org.:** Sushil Gosain
Sh.: B/405 (Basement), Mukerjee Tower,
Opp. Batra Cinema, Commercial Complex,
Dr. Mukherjee Nagar, Delhi-110009
• 4787/23, Ansari Rd., Darya Ganj,
New Delhi-110002; ✆ 23246222, 23246333,
Fax: 91-11-27654827
✉ frienpub@yahoo.com
Bus.Intt.: Pub. and Dist.; **Spl.:** Physical Edu., Sports, Psych., Nutrition, etc.

FRIENDS' PUBLISHERS
Benodbehari, Cuttack-753002 (Orissa)
✆ (O) 0671-223278 (R) 221298
Estd.: 1957; **Prop.:** Sahadev Pradhan;
Bus.Intt.: Pub. and B.S. of Gen. Dictionaries, Children Literatures and Travelogues

FRONTLINE BOOKS
7, Palika Bazar, New Delhi-110001
✆ 23353223, 23320128,
Fax: 23721188, 23723366
✉ fln@del2.Vsnl.net.in
Estd.: 1992; **Man.:** D. Jain; **Bus.Intt.:** Pub.'s Rep.; **Spl.:** Foreign & Indian Book on Indians Fictions and Gen.

FULL CIRCLE PUBLISHING PVT. LTD.
J-40, Jorbagh Lane, New Delhi-110003
✆ 24620063, 24621011, 55654197-98,
Fax: 91-11-24645795
✉ gbp@del2.vsnl.net.in,
fullcircle@vsnl.com
🌐 www.atfullcircle.com
Hd.Org.: Shekher Malhotra
Br.: 173, Neb Sarai, New Delhi-110068
✆ 91-11-29532140
✉ gbp@del2.vsnl.net.in,
fullcircle@vsnl.com
• 5-B, Khan Market, New Delhi-110003
✆ 24655641, 24655643, Fax: 91-11-24645795
✉ fullcircle@vsnl.com;
• N-8, GK Part-I, N-Block Market,
New Delhi-110048
✆ 29245641-43, ✉ fullcircle@vsnl.com;
• Peach Tree, Sushant Lok, Phase 1, C-Block,
Gurgaon-122002 (Haryana),
✆ 4104168, Fax: 95-124-24645795,
✉ fullcircle@vsnl.com

Bus.Intt.: Pub.; **Spl.:** PB on Health, Self-improvement, Man., etc. in English and Hindi

FUSION BOOKS
X-30, Okhla Industrial Area,
Phase-II, Delhi-110020
✆ 91-11-41611862
✉ sales@diamondpublication.com
Hd.Org.: Narender Kumar; **Bus.Intt.:** Pub.; **Spl.:** Rel., Fiction, Non-fiction, Culture, Health, Yoga, Astrology, Sports, Litt. and Children's books in English, Urdu, Bengali, Marathi, Gujarati, Assamese and French

FUTURA BOOKS PONDICHERRY (P) LTD.
Pondicherry (U.T.)
✆ 0413-220992
✉ prpathi@rediffmail.com
Bus.Intt.: B.S. and L.S.

FUTURE ARTS
92-98, Modern Complex, Sai Road, Baddi Distt., Solan-173205 (Himachal Pradesh)
✆ 91-1795-320762
✉ info@futurearts.co.in
🌐 www.futurearts.co.in
Hd.Org.: Amit Sharma
Bus.Intt.: Pub. and Dist.; **Spl.:** Interactive educational aids and children's books

FUTURE LINKS
7-9, Shandidoot, Opp. Muktangan English School, Parvati Darshan, Pune-411009 (Maharashtra)

FUTURE POINT
H-1/A, Hauz Khas, New Delhi-110016
✆ 26569200-01, 26569800-01, 26850269,
26866000, Fax: 91-11-26569200-01
✉ mail@futurepointindia.com
Estd.: 1985; **Ch.Exe.:** Mr. Arun Bansal;
Bus.Intt.: Pub., **Spl.:** Astrological, Software, 'Leo Gold', Leo-Palm Comp. Horoscopes, Future Samachar (Astrological Magazine) & Yantras

FUTURE PUBLICATIONS PVT. LTD.
2049/6, Chuna Mandi, Pahar Ganj,
New Delhi-110055
✆ 23585043, Fax: 91-11-23587922
Hd.Org.: Rajeev Sharma; **Bus.Intt.:** Pub.; **Spl.:** Edu. Pub. in Hindi

FUTURE PUBLICATIONS (REGD.)
2047/6-Chuna Mandi, Pahar Ganj,
New Delhi-110055
✆ 23555291, 23512785, Fax: 23555291
Hd.Org.: Sidhartha Bahl; **Bus.Intt.:** Edu. Pub. in Hindi

■ ■ ■

G. PRINT (P) LTD.
317, Avanashi Rd., Coimbatore-641018 (Tamil Nadu)
✆ 233439
Hd.Org.: G.D. Gopal; **Bus.Intt.**: Pub.;
Spl.: Children's Books upto Hr. Sec. Level

G. RAM BOOKS PVT. LTD.
A-9, East Krishna Nagar, Delhi-110051
✆ 22531066, 22532912, Fax: 22012811
info@grambooks.com
www.grambooks.com
Hd.Org.: Sunil Kumar; **Bus.Intt.**: Pub.;
Spl.: Edu. Books for Children

G.A.E. PUBLISHERS
10, Raja Rajkrishan St., Suite 11, Post Box No. 11428, Kolkata-700050 (West Bengal)

G.B.D. BOOKS
16, Ansari Road, Near Mahavir Vatika, Darya Ganj, New Delhi-110002
✆ 41563695, Fax: 91-11-23911057
generalbookdepot@yahoo.com
www.generalbooks.com
Hd.Org.: Kaushal Goyal
Bus.Intt.: Pub. and Dist.; **Spl.**: Eng. and Fore. language books, dictionaries, fiction, management and self-development books

G.D.M.K. PUBLISHERS DISTRIBUTORS
WZ-430 E/1, Naraina, New Delhi-110028
✆ 25415043, 25014181, Fax: 25635908
sr_allbooks@vsnl.net
Hd.Org.: Mohindra K. Vashistha;
Bus.Intt.: Pub. and Dist.; **Spl.**: College Level Textbooks on all Sub.

G.I.N.N.
C/o Oxford University Press, 2/11, Ansari Rd., Darya Ganj, New Delhi-110002

G.K. BOOK WORLD
WZ-905-C, Ranibagh, Shakur Basti, Delhi-110034
✆ 27023670
Hd.Org.: Girish Bansal; **Bus.Intt.**: Dist.;
Spl.: Textbooks to Schools

G.K. ENTERPRISES
Popular Nursing Home Lane, Ashok Rajpath, Patna-800004 (Bihar)
Bus.Intt.: Pub. and B.S.

G.K. PUBLISHERS PVT. LTD.
H-205, Sector-63, Noida-201301 (Uttar Pradesh)
✆ 3250473, 4267181, 4267182, 4267184
Telefax: 0120-4267183
gkp@gkpublications.com, info@gkpublications.com
www.gkpublications.com
Estd.: 1993; **Hd.Org.**: Rakesh Mittal;
Bus.Intt.: Pub. and Dist.; **Spl.**: Tech. and Reference books for Competitions

G.N. BOOK STORE
Sharda Pd. Ghosh Lane, Govind Mitra Rd., Patna (Bihar)
Bus.Intt.: Pub. and B.S.

G.R. BATHLA & SONS PUB. & DIST.
654, Shiv Lok, Western Kutchery Road, Meerut-250001 (Uttar Pradesh)
✆ 2660709, 2660802, 4022486, Fax: 91-121-2664539
manojbathla@hotmail.com, grbathla@rediffmail.com
www.bathlabooks.com
Estd.: 1989; **Prop.**: Manoj Kumar Bathla
Br.: Boundry Road, Near Hotel Crystal Palace, Meerut (Uttar Pradesh); • Opp. Vikas Bhawan, Meerut Road, Muzaffarnagar (Uttar Pradesh);
✆ 2634060, 2433530, Fax: 91-131-2430676;
• Premises No. 101 & 102, 1st Floor, Municipal No. 3-6-108/1, Sanatna Building, 1st Floor, Main Road, Himayat Nagar, Hyderabad (Andhra Pradesh);
• 32, Patparganj Industrial Area, Delhi-110092
✆ 91-11-32917429
Bus.Intt.: Pub. and Dist.;
Spl.: School Text Books in English and Hindi

G.R. PUBLICATIONS
No. 39, Natesan, St., T. Nagar, Chennai-600017 (Tamil Nadu)
✆ 24341216, Fax: 044-24341164
Prop.: Sri V. Ganesh Ram; **Bus.Intt.**: Pub.;
Spl.: Gen. Books in Language Learning, Tech. Courses & Dictionaries, Guides, Workbooks and Map Drawing Books for Tamil Nadu State Board Syllabus

G.S. SALES CORPORATION
Kolkata (West Bengal)
✆ 24639930, 24644139
gsmacalcal3.vsnl.net.in

G.T. BOOK AGENCY
11/83, Punjabi Bagh, New Delhi-110026

GAAJ PRAKASHAN
Kedgaon (Shahurgar)-414005, Ahmednagar (Maharashtra)

GADOWDIA PUSTAK BHANDAR
Fed Bazar, Bikaner-334001 (Rajasthan)
Hd.Org.: Krishnalal Gadowdia

GAGAN PRINTERS AND PUBLISHERS
4782/2-23, 1st Floor, Darya Ganj,
New Delhi-110002
✆ 23279946
Prop.: Praveen Kumar Jain; **Bus.Intt.:** WS, Pub., Sub.Ag., Pub.'s Rep., L.S.; **Spl.:** Gen.

GAINSWELL CO.
7, Srirampur Rd., Garia, Kolkata-700084
(West Bengal)
Bus.Intt.: Exp.

GAJANAN PUSTAKALAYA
Tower Rd., Surat (Gujarat)
✆ 91-261-2424246, 2667419
✉ info@gajananbooks.com,
info@smartinfosys.net
Bus.Intt.: Rt.

GALA INTERNATIONAL
Bus-Stn-Aska-761110 (Orissa)
✆ 06822-273864
Estd.: 1990; **Prop.:** Rameswar Patro; **Bus.Intt.:** Pub. and B.S.; **Spl.:** Med., Humanities, Poems, GK and Homoeopathy

GALA PUBLISHERS
Behind Sukhramnagar, Gomtipur,
Ahmedabad-380022 (Gujarat)

GALAXY EXPORTS INC.
'Navneet Bhawan', Bhavani Shankar Rd.,
Dadar (West), Mumbai-400028 (Maharashtra)
Bus.Intt.: Exp.

GALAXY PUBLISHERS & DISTRIBUTORS
47, Iqbala Bad, Near Govt. Degree College,
Bemina, Srinagar, Kashmir-190001
(Jammu & Kashmir)
✆ 2491291
Estd.: 1985; **Hd.Org.:** Ejaz
Br.: Iqbala Bad Bemina, Srinagar Kashmir
Bus.Intt.: Pub., L.S. & Rt.; **Spl.:** Humanities & Soc.Sci., Sci. & Tech., Law, Juvenile/ Children, Gen. & Fiction etc.

GALAXY PUBLISHERS & DISTRIBUTORS
48/24, Meerapur, Allahabad-211003
(Uttar Pradesh)
✆ 2651534

GALAXY PUBLISHERS & DISTRIBUTORS
L-9, Kalkaji, New Delhi-110019

GALGOTIA BOOKSOURCE (P) LTD.
A6-21, Poorvi Marg, Vasant Vihar,
New Delhi-110057
✆ 26156455, Fax: 26156456
✉ mail@galgotia.com
Hd.Org.: Neeraj Galgotia; **Bus.Intt.:** Dist.; **Spl.:** All Kinds of Books

GALGOTIA PUBLICATIONS (P) LTD.
5, Ansari Rd., Darya Ganj, New Delhi-110002
✆ 23263334, 23288132, Fax: 23281909
✉ gppl@indiatimes.com
Estd.: 1984; **Man.Dir.:** Suneel Galgotia
Br.: E.D. Galgotia & Sons, 17-B, Connaught Place, New Delhi-110001 ✆ 23713227, 23321844, 23713228, Fax: 23713228
Bus.Intt.: Pub., WS, Imp., Exp.; **Spl.:** Sci., Tech. & Med.

GALGOTIA PUBLISHING COMPANY
6 A/4, W.E.A. Karol Bagh, New Delhi-110005
✆ (O) 25752918, 25751728 (R) 25751728, 25788991, Fax: 23755150
✉ galgotiabooks@rediffmail.com
www.galgotiabooks.com
Estd.: 1993; **Prt.:** R.K. Galgotia, Ashok Galgotia, Ajay Galgotia; **Bus.Intt.:** Pub., WS, L.S.; **Spl.:** Arch., Man. Health, Med. and Gen.

GAMABHANA PRAKASHAN
379, Shaniwar Peth, Pune-411030
(Maharashtra)
✆ (O) 0212-2458141 (R) 2456515
Estd.: 1979; **Prop.:** L.M. Kadu; **Bus.Intt.:** Deals; **Spl.:** Marathi Books of Childrens

GANAPATHI BOOK CENTRE
B-65, Mansa Ram Park, Near Uttam Nagar,
Najafgarh Rd., New Delhi-110059

GANASHAKTI
Kolkata (West Bengal)
✆ 22458950, Fax: 22448090
✉ mail@ganashkti.com
Bus.Intt.: Rt. & B.S.

GANDHARVA-VED PRAKASHAN (SHRI)
Pune (Maharashtra)
✆ 24493502
✉ gandharv_ved@hotmail.com
Bus.Intt.: Pub.

GANDHI BOOK DEPOT
Delhi Rd., Model Town, Rohtak-1 (Haryana)

GANDHI BOOK HOUSE
No. 1, Rajghat Colony, New Delhi-110002
✆ 23311714, Fax: 23236734
Hd.Org.: Anupam Mishra; **Bus.Intt.:** Pub. and B.S.; **Spl.:** Gandhian Thought and Sarvodaya in English and Hindi

GANDHI HINDUSTANI SAHITYA SABHA
1, Jawahar Lal Nehru Marg, Sannidhi,
Rajghat, New Delhi-110002
✆ 23318831
Hd.Org.: Kumari Kusamshah Mantri

GANDHI LITERATURE CENTRE
National Gandhi Mission, Rajghat, New Delhi-110002
✆ 23328310, 23310168, Fax: 23311793
✉ gandhimk@nda.vsnl.net.in
www.gandhimuseum.org
Bus.Intt.: Pub. and Dist.; **Spl.:** Litt. on Gandhi, Freedom Movement, Hist., Politics, Phil., Children's Books Nature Cure, Yoga and Allied Sub.

GANDHI PEACE FOUNDATION
221-23, Deen Dayal Upadhyay Marg, New Delhi-110002
✆ 23318314, Cable: SATYAGRAHA
Dir.: N. Krishna Swami; **Bus.Intt.:** Pub.; **Spl.:** Gandhi, Gandhian Thoughts, Sarvodaya, Ecology and Env.

GANDHI PRAKASHAN
Lakshmi Building, Lakshmi Ganj, Guna-473001 (Madhya Pradesh)
Hd.Org.: Shyam Narayan Vijaybargiya

GANDHI SAMARAK SANGRAHALAYA
Harijan Ashram, Ahmedabad-380027 (Gujarat)

GANDHI SHISHAK SANSTHAN
Maula, Begusarai (Bihar)
Bus.Intt.: Pub. and B.S.

GANDHI SMRITI AND DARSHAN SAMITI
5, Tees January Marg, New Delhi-1100011
✆ 23012843, 23011480, Fax: 011-23011480
✉ mkgandhi@del2.vsnl.net.in
www.gandhismriti.org
Ch.Exe.: Dr. Savita Singh; **Bus.Intt.:** Pub.; **Spl.:** Books and Photographs on Gandhiji, Bhajan Cassettes, Video Films on Gandhi

GANDHIYA ILAKKIYA SANGAM
Gandhi Museum, Madurai-625020 (Tamil Nadu)

GANDIV SAHITYA MANDIR
Lalgate, Chauta Pool, Surat-395003 (Gujarat)

GANESH BOOK HOUSE
Main Rd., Dinapore, Patna-810503 (Bihar)
Bus.Intt.: Pub. and B.S.

GANESH BROTHERS
Karpaga Vinayagar Nagar, Sekkalai P.O., Karaikudi-630002 (Tamil Nadu)

GANESH PUSTAK BHANDAR
Majhaul, Begusarai-851127 (Bihar)
Bus.Intt.: Pub. and B.S.

GANESH PUSTAK BHANDAR
Rajawar More, Bhagalpur-814159 (Bihar)
Bus.Intt.: Pub. and B.S.

GANGA DISTRIBUTORS
21-A, Ansari Road, Darya Ganj, New Delhi-110002
✆ 91-11-23275710
Hd.Org.: Arun Maheshwari
Bus.Intt.: Dist.; **Spl.:** Literary and other books in Hindi and English

GANGA KEVERI PUBLISHING HOUSE
D-35/77, Jangamawadimath, Varanasi-221001 (Uttar Pradesh)
✆ 0542-2327936
Estd.: 1992; **Hd.Org.:** Dr. K.G. Kendadamath; **Bus.Intt.:** Pub.; **Spl.:** Reference Books in English

GANGA KAUVERI
17, Kariangudi Chetty St., Velipalayam, Nagapattinam-611001 (Tamil Nadu)

GANGA PUSTAKALAYA
Muradpur, Patna-800004 (Bihar)
Bus.Intt.: Pub. and B.S.

GANGA SARAN & GRAND SONS
CK-3-B, 37/44, Bans Phatak, Varanasi-221001 (Uttar Pradesh)
✆ 2352425
Hd.Org.: Satish Bhargav

GANGADHAR PUBLICATIONS
Arundelpet, Vijayawada-520002 (Andhra Pradesh)

GANGAL PUBLICATIONS
10, Visanjee Park, Naigaon Cross Rd., Mumbai-400014 (Maharashtra)

GANGANATHA KENDRIYA SANSKRIT VIDYAPEETH
Motilal Nehru Park, Allahabad-390001 (Uttar Pradesh)

GANGARAMS
62-D, Clock Tower, Sarojini Devi Rd., Secunderabad-500003 (Andhra Pradesh)
✆ 040-27800691, 27805117
Estd.: 1992; **Man.:** G. Chatur Bhuj; **Bus.Intt.:** Rt. & L.S.; **Spl.:** Gen. & Trade, Acad., Professional, Greeting Cards & Children Books (Indian and Foreign Books)

GANGARAMS BOOK BUREAU
72, 4th Floor, Mahatma Gandhi Rd., Bangalore-560001 (Karnataka)
✆ 2551618, 25588015
✉ gangarams@vsnl.com
Estd.: 1977; **Hd.Org.:** N. Gangaram
Br.: Secunderabad (Andhra Pradesh)
✆ 27800691, 27805117
✉ ganga_rams@yahoo.com
Bus.Intt.: Pub. and Rt.; **Spl.:** Fiction, Tech., Children Books, Gen. Knowledge and Dictionary, Imp. of Foreign Books

GANGROMS INFOTECH
772, 4th Floor, M.G. Rd., Bangalore-560001 (Karnataka)
✆ 25586189, Fax: 91-80-25587540
Hd.Org.: N. Gangaram; **Spl.:** Software and Books

GANPATI PRAKASHAN
4/32, Subhas Gali, Vishwas Nagar, Shahdara, Delhi-110032
✆ 22424810

GARGI ENTERPRISES
C-2/186, Yamuna Vihar, Delhi-110053

GARGI PRAKASHAN
111, Sector-17A, Vasundara, Ghaziabad-201012 (Uttar Pradesh)
✆ 9868804857
✉ gargi_prakashan@yahoo.com
Hd.Org.: Buddhesh Mani; **Bus.Intt.:** Pub.; **Spl.:** Books in Hindi

GARGI PRAKASHAN
127, New Avas Vikas Colony, Saharanpur-247001 (Uttar Pradesh)
✆ 9837315676
✉ gargi_prakashan@yahoo.com
Hd.Org.: Buddheshmani; **Bus.Intt.:** Pub.; **Spl.:** Books in Hindi

GARIB NAWAJ
Bihta, Patna-801103 (Bihar)
Bus.Intt.: Pub. and B.S.

GARODIYA PUSTAK BHANDAR
Phad Bazar, Bikaner-334001 (Rajasthan)
✆ (O) 2520080 (R) 227930, 2524930
Hd.Org.: Kishanpal Garodiya

GATEWAY INDUSTRIES LIMITED
C-55, Wazirpur Industrial Area, Delhi-110052
✆ 27125736

GAURAV BOOK CENTRE
D-130, Sector-I, Avantika, Rohini, Delhi-110085
✆ 91-11-55763093 ▮ 9873096176
Hd.Org.: Sudhir Chaudhary
Bus.Intt.: B.S.; **Spl.:** General Library Books Supplier, Hindi & English Litt.

GAURAV INFORMATION SERVICES
321/2, Mehrauli Rd., Gurgaon-1 (Haryana)

GAURAV PUBLISHING HOUSE
L-11, Green Park Extn., New Delhi-110016

GAURAV PUBLISHING HOUSE
E-30, Jawahar Park, Near Vikas Marg, Laxmi Nagar, New Delhi-110092
✆ 22411949, Fax: 91-11-22411949
Prop.: Indra Vijay Singh; **Bus.Intt.:** Pub., L.S.; **Spl.:** Gen. and Fiction Books

GAURAV PUSTAK BHANDAR
Ist Pusta, A Block, (Near Gyan Builders), Sonia Vihar, Delhi-110094
✆ (O) & (R) 22178983
Prop.: Indra Vijay Singh; **Bus.Intt.:** Pub., B.S., L.S.; **Spl.:** Fiction Books

GAUREYA BOOKS INTERNATIONAL
WZ-574/A, Shiv Shakti Bhawan, Madipur, New Delhi-110063

GAUTAM BOOK CENTRE
C-263 A, Chandan Sadan, St. No. 9, Hardev Puri, Shahdara, Delhi-110093
✆ 22570380 ▮ 9810173667, Fax: 22119239
✉ gautambookcentre@hotmail.com
www.geocities.com/gautambookcentre
Estd.: 1994; **Prop.:** Anuj Kumar;
Bus.Intt.: Pub. and Dist.; **Spl.:** Litt. on Ambedkar, Buddha, Periyar, Phule and Dalits, Soc.Sci.

GAUTAM TRADERS & AGENCIES
2404, Chawri Bazar, Delhi-110006
Bus.Intt.: Exp.

GAUTAMA BROTHERS
39/18, Meston Rd., Kanpur-208001 (Uttar Pradesh)
✆ (O) 0512-2364601, 2224194 (R) 2544267, 2256026 ▮ 9838009946, Fax: 2311314
✉ gbrospub@sancharnet.net
Estd.:1929; **Hd.Org.:** Ashutosh Gautama, **Spl.:** School Book on all Sub. (High School, Inter & Middle Books of U.P. Boards)

GAYATHRI CLASSIC RELEASE
XIX/355, College Rd., Kottayam-686001 (Kerala)
✆ 2566850
Estd.: 1985; **Prop.:** Raja Sreekumar Varma; **Bus.Intt.:** Pub. and B.S.

GAYATRI PARIVAR
House No. H-608, Phase-I, Mohali, Chandigarh
✉ ajsansthan@awgp.org
Hd.Org.: Shriram Sharma Acharya
Br.: Gayatri Parivar Shakha, D-243, Indirapuram, Sipra Sun City, Ghaziabad (Uttar Pradesh)
✉ ajsansthan@awgp.org;
• Gayatri Pragya Mandan, HIG 522, Awas Vikas, Bulandshahar (Uttar Pradesh)
✉ ajsansthan@awgp.org, **Bus.Intt.:** Pub.; **Spl.:** Books in Hindi

GAYATRI PUBLICATIONS
133-S.F.S. Phase IV, Ashok Vihar, Delhi-110052
✆ 27142802, Fax: 27142802

mcpur@nda.vsnl.net.in
Estd.: 1993; **Man.**: Raj Kumar
Bus.Intt.: Pub.; **Spl.**: Soc.Sci.

GAYATRI PUSTAK BHANDAR
10-1828, Sonutaliya, Mahalaxmi Pole, Surat-395003 (Gujarat)

GAYATRI PUSTAK BHANDAR
Naugachia, Bhagalpur-853204 (Bihar)
Bus.Intt.: Pub. and B.S.

GAYEN BROTHERS
P.D.S. Corner, Stall No. 8, Bankim Ch. St., Kolkata-700025 (West Bengal)

GEETA AGENCIES
Belepet, Bangalore-560063 (Karnataka)
✆ 080-22874226
Estd.: 1960; **Bus.Intt.**: Pub.; **Spl.**: Fiction, Poem Collections and Dramas in Kannada

GEETA BOOK CENTRE
Shop No. 6, J.N.U. New Campus, New Delhi-110067
✆ 22669481

GEETA BOOK HOUSE
K.R. Circle, Mysore-570001 (Karnataka)
✆ 0821-233589
Hd.Org.: Gopalakrishna Rajamani; **Bus.Intt.**: Pub.; **Spl.**: Fiction, Collections, Edit Books, Belonging to Children, Texts, Sci. in Kannada, English and Sanskrit

GEETA GRAPHICS
J-436, Baljeet Nagar, (Prem Nagar Rd.), New Delhi-110008
✆ 25875330, 25871272
rphbooks@indiatimes.com, gitabooks@rediffmail.com
Estd.: 1994; **Prt.**: Manish Kr. Bhatia, Gita Saxena; **Bus.Intt.**: Dist., Printers, Software, DTP Data Processing; **Spl.**: Laser Printers, Designers, Consultants, Fiction

GEETA INTL. PUBLISHERS & DISTRIBUTORS
Delhi
✆ 22429715
dvmangla@hotmail.com
Bus.Intt.: Pub., Dist. & L.S.

GEETA PRESS
2609, Nai Sarak, Delhi-110006

GEETA PUBLICATION
Satti Bazar, Raipur-492001 (Madhya Pradesh)
✆ (O) 2537242 (R) 2539927

GEETA PVT. LTD. (THE)
Rgd.Off.: TC-35/555, Shornur Rd., Thiruvambady, Thrissur-680001 (Kerala)
✆ 0487-334306
Dir.: Amit Chaturvedi
Br.Off.: F-21/267, Laxmi Nagar, Delhi-110092
✆ 22442084 ▮ 9868020790
geeta_amrit123@yahoo.com
Bus.Intt.: Pub., B.S., L.S.; **Spl.**: Industrial, Tech., Music, Astrological and General Books

GEETANJALI
Samity Rd., Distt. Cooch Behar (West Bengal)
Hd.Org.: Banikanta Bhattacharya

GEETANJALI
19, College Row, Kolkata-700009 (West Bengal)

GEETANJALI BOOKSELLER
Khazanchi Rd., Patna-800004 (Bihar)
Bus.Intt.: Pub. and B.S.

GEETANJALI PUBLICATIONS
134, 8th Cross, 4th Main, Govindarajapuram Bangalore-560040 (Karnataka)
Hd.Org.: Smt. Susheela; **Bus.Intt.**: Pub.; **Spl.**: Fictions, Collections and Children's Books in Kannada

GEETH EXPORTS
Geetham Building, Royapuram, 102, East Mada Church Rd., Chennai-600013 (Tamil Nadu)
✆ 044-2511259, 2511169, Fax: 25226913
Estd.: 1991; **Bus.Intt.**: Exp.

GEETHA PUBLISHING HOUSE
T-565, Pragati Complex, Idgah Chowk, Delhi-110006
✆ 27775482, 27522668
Bus.Intt.: Pub. Rt.; **Spl.**: School & College Books and Dist. of N.C.E.R.T. Books

GEETIKA PRAKASHAN
Sahitya Vihar, Bijnor (Uttar Pradesh)
✆ 263232, Fax: 262375
giriraj3100@rediffmail.com
Hd.Org.: Meena Agarwal; **Bus.Intt.**: Pub.; **Spl.**: Hindi Litt.

GEM BOOK DISTRIBUTOR
A-294, DDA Flats, Kalkaji, Near Govindpuri Extn., New Delhi-110019
✆ 26023215
gbdo15@yahoo.com
Hd.Org.: Jyothi Lalwani; **Bus.Intt.**: Dist.

GEM BOOK DISTRIBUTOR
42-A, Nilgiri Apartment, Alaknanda, New Delhi-110019
✆ 42143438, Fax: 91-11-42143438
ramlalvani@yahoo.co.in

Hd.Org.: Jyothi Lalwani; **Bus.Intt.:** Dist.; **Spl.:** Indian art books and rare and old books

GEMANTAK BOOK SERVICE
115, Ramchandra Bldg., Mapusa,
Goa-403507

GENERAL BOOK AGENCY
Popular Nursing Home Lane, Ashok Rajpath,
Patna-800004 (Bihar)
Bus.Intt.: Pub. and B.S.

GENERAL BOOK DEPOT
1691, Nai Sarak, P.B. No. 1220, Delhi-110006
✆ (O) 23263695, 23250635 (R) 23938187, 55351643; Fax: 011-22940861, 23712710
▮ 9810229648
✉ contact@goyalbookshop.com
🌐 www.generalbooks.com
Estd.: 1933; **Prt.:** Kaushal Goyal, Ashwani Goyal
Br.: GBD Books, I-2/16, Ansari Road, 1st Floor, Opp. Saraswati School, Daryaganj, Delhi-110002; ✆ 23260022, 31086851
✉ kaushalgoyal@yahoo.com
🌐 www.goyalbookshop.com
Bus.Intt.: Pub. & Dist.; **Spl.:** Books on GMAT, GRE, TOEFL, SAT, English vocabulary Books by Normal Lewis, Man., Self-improvement, I.A.S. & Other Competition Exam Books, German & French Text Books & Ref. Books, Dictionaries etc.

GENERAL BOOK STORE
Rajun, Bhagalpur-813107 (Bihar)
Bus.Intt.: Pub. and B.S.

GENERAL BOOKS
A-66, College St. Market, Kolkata-700007
(West Bengal)

GENERAL KITAB GHAR
M.G. Rd., Katihar-854105 (Bihar)

GENERAL PRINTERS & PUBLISHERS
263/F, Raja Ram Mohan Roy Rd., Girgaon,
Mumbai-400004 (Maharashtra)
✆ (O) 022-23826854, 23873113 (R) 23642589, 23627547, Fax: 23827197
✉ thakker@bom3.vsnl.net.in
Estd.: 1952; **Exe.Dir.:** Vijay P. Thakker
Br.: E-56, DDA Flates, Saket,
New Delhi-110017 ✆ 26856399, 24992813
✉ ver_rak@hotmail.com
Bus.Intt.: Pub.

GENERAL VARIETIES STORES
Rafiganj, Aurangabad-824125 (Bihar)
Bus.Intt.: Pub. and B.S.

GENESIS MICRO-LINK PVT. LTD.
A-56, Naraina Industrial Area-I,
New Delhi-110028
✆ 25795245, Fax: 25792841
✉ gmlink@nda.vsnl.net.in
Estd.: 1996; **Ch.Exe.:** Vijay Kumar Aggarwal

GENIUS BOOKS & GAMES
59-A, Khan Market, New Delhi-110003
✆ 24646634
Estd.: 1994; **Bus.Intt.:** Rt. Bookshop

GENUINE PUBLICATIONS & MEDIA (P) LTD.
B-35, (Basement) Nizamuddin West,
New Delhi-110013
✆ 24352732, Fax: 91-11-24352048
✉ genuinepublications@yahoo.com
🌐 www.genuinepublications.com
Hd.Org.: Md. Manzoor Alam;
Bus.Intt.: Pub., Dist., Imp. and Exp.;
Spl.: Soc.Sci., Humanities, Rel., Law and Islamic studies in Eng., Hindi and Urdu

GEO-ENVIRON ACADEMIA
A-42, Shastri Nagar, Jaipur (Rajasthan)

GEOLOGICAL SOCIETY OF INDIA
P.B. 1922, Gavipura, Bangalore-560019
(Karnataka)

GEOLOGICAL SURVEY OF INDIA
Publication & Information Division,
29, Jawaharlal Nehru Rd., Kolkata-700016
(West Bengal)
✆ 22861698, Fax: 91-11-22521534
✉ dydgop4@cal3vsnl.gov.in
🌐 www.gsi.gov.in
Hd.Org.: P.M. Tejale; **Bus.Intt.:** Pub.;
Spl.: Geology, Mineral Resources and National Resources of the Country

GEOLOGISTICS LIMITED
A Centre, 4, L.S.C., Pocket-C, 6 & 7,
Vasant Kunj, New Delhi-110070
✆ 26130925, Fax: 26130930
✉ enquiries@geo-logistics.co.in
Hd.Org.: Andrew Birtley; **Bus.Intt.:** Provider;
Spl.: Freight and SCM Services and Integrated Logistics

GERMAN BOOK CENTRE
New No. 8 (Old No. 32), IInd Main Rd.,
CIT Nagar East, Chennai-600035
(Tamil Nadu)
✆ 24346244, 24346266, Telex: 23043,
Fax: 24346529
✉ germanbk@vsnl.com,
itpsesha@giasmd01.vsnl.net.in
🌐 www.germanbookcentre.com
Estd.: 1982; **Prop.:** S. Pattabiraman;
Bus.Intt.: Pub. & Dist.; **Spl.:** Reference Books in German Language

GERMAN BOOK SHOP
C/o GPD Pvt. Ltd., Max Mueller Bhawan, 3,
Kasturba Gandhi Marg, New Delhi-110001

✆ 23358534, Fax: 91-11-23850961
✉ goyal@vsnl.com
🌐 www.goyalsaab.com
Hd.Org.: Ashwani Goyal; **Spl.:** Foreign language publications, reference works, self-study language guides, dictionaries, etc.

GHALIB ACADEMY
Basti Hazrat Nizamuddin, New Delhi-110013
✆ 24351098, Fax: 91-11-24351098
✉ ghalibgaacademy05@yahoo.com
🌐 www.ghalibacademy.org
Hd.Org.: Aqil Ahmad; **Bus.Intt.:** Pub.; **Spl.:** Urdu Litt.

GHALIB INSTITUTE
Aiwan-e-Ghalib Marg, (Mata Sundri Lane), New Delhi-110002
✆ 23232583, Fax: 23236518
✉ ghalib@vsnl.net
Hd.Org.: Shahid Mahuli; **Bus.Intt.:** Pub.; **Spl.:** Ghalib and of Persian Litt. in Urdu, Hindi and Persian

GHAZALI BOOK DEPOT
Deoband-247554, Distt. Saharanpur (Uttar Pradesh)
Estd.: 1986; **Hd.Org.:** Wasif Ali

GHOSH & CHAKRABORTY
10, Shyama Charan Dey St., Kolkata-700073 (West Bengal)

GHOSH BROTHERS
148/2, Netaji Subhash Rd., Kolkata-700040 (West Bengal)

GHOSH BROTHERS
50, Sitaram Ghosh St., Kolkata-700009 (West Bengal)

GHOSH DASTIDAR PUBLISHING CONCERN
91, Tamer Lane, Kolkata-700009 (West Bengal)

GHOSH PUSTAK BHANDAR
Naugachia, Bhagalpur-853204 (Bihar)
Bus.Intt.: Pub. and B.S.

GIGGLES BOOK SHOP
Connemara Hotel, Binny Rd., Chennai-600002 (Tamil Nadu)
✆ 28520123

GIRDHARI LAL CHOPRA (AGENTS) P. LTD.
191/1, Gandhi Gate, P.O. Box-54, Amritsar-143001 (Punjab)
✆ 2292295, 2544338, Telex: 384225, Fax: 0091-0183-2553891
✉ jp@choprachess.com
🌐 www.choprachess.com
Estd.: 1920; **Man.Dir.:** J.P. Chopra; **Bus.Intt.:** WS, Imp., Exp., Sub.Ag.
Spl.: Art Craft, Books & Magazines

GIREESH PRAKASHAN
Langar Toli, Patna-800004 (Bihar)
✆ 256465
Hd.Org.: Nannelal Gupta

GIRI PUSTAK SADAN
Langertoli, Patna-800004 (Bihar)
Bus.Intt.: Pub. and B.S.

GIRI TRADING AGENCY
Sh.: No. 10, Kapaleeswarar Sannadhi St., Mylapore, Chennai-600004 (Tamil Nadu)
✆ 24940376, 24942530, 24953820, Fax: 91-44-24953821
✉ giritrading@vsnl.com
🌐 www.giritrading.com
Estd.: 1976; **Hd.Org.:** T.S. Srinivasan
Chennai Off.: No. 58/2, T.S.V. Koil St., Mylapore, Chennai-600004 (Tamil Nadu)
✆ 24953823, 24953817, 24643551, Fax: 24953821
✉ giritrading@vsnl.com
Mumbai Off.: Opp. P.O. Matunga, Mumbai-400019 (Maharashtra)
✆ 24141344, 24122316, Fax: 24143140
✉ giritradingagency@vsnl.com
Estd.: 1953; **Hd.Org.:** Ramanarayananan S.
Bus.Intt.: Pub., WS, Exp.

GIRIPRABHA BOOK HOUSE
P.O. Box 1, Idukki Central, Idukki Colony-685602 (Kerala)
✆ 04863-252277
Estd.: 1982; **Prop.:** Patathode Antony; **Bus.Intt.:** Pub. and B.S.

GIRJA BOOK CENTRE
C-133, Yamuna Vihar Rd., North Ghonda, Delhi-110053
✆ (R) 24602986
Res.: B-107, Khurana Enclave, Pavi Sadakpur, Loni, Ghaziabad (Uttar Pradesh)
Prop.: Girja Shankar Dubey; **Bus.Intt.:** L.S.

GITA BHAWAN
Swargashram Via Rishikesh, Paurigahwal-249304 (Uttarakhand)
✆ 2430122, Fax: 91-135-2440028
Hd.Org.: Vishnu Prasad Chandgothia
Bus.Intt.: Pub.; **Spl.:** Text and Comm. on *Gita*, *Ramayan*, *Puranas*, *Upanishads*, and character-building books in many languages; also publishes two monthly magazines—*Kalyan* in Hindi and *Kalyan-Kalpataru* in Eng.

GITA BOOK DEPOT
17, Raghuvir Society, Kalol (Mehsana) (Gujarat)

GITA ENTERPRISES
Rgd.Off.: 3026/7H, Ranjit Nagar, New Delhi-110008

© (O) 25847377, 25842605 (R) 25726250
✉ rphbooks@indiatimes.com,
gitabooks@rediffmail.com
Estd.: 1980; **Man.Prt.:** Manish K. Bhatia
Sales Off.: J-436, Baljit Nagar, (Prem Nagar Rd.), New Delhi-110008
© 25875330, 25871272
Bus.Intt.: Dist., Pub., Printers, Software; **Spl.:** Military, Library, Sci., Reference etc.

GITA PRESS
P.O. Gita Press, Gorakhpur-273005 (Uttar Pradesh)
© 2334721, Fax: 91-551-2336997
✉ booksales@gitapress.org
www.gitapress.org
Estd.: 1923; **Hd.Org.:** Vishnu Prasad Chandgothia, B.N. Agrawal;
Br.: Gita Press Gorakhpur Ki Pustak Dukan, 2609, Nayi Sarak, Delhi-110006,
© 23269678, Fax: 91-11-23259140
✉ gitapres@ndf.vsnl.net.in;
• Gobind Bhawan Karyalaya, 151, Mahatma Gandhi Road, Kolkata-700007 (West Bengal),
© 22686894, Fax: 91-33-22680251
• Gita Press Gorakhpur Ki Pustak Dukan, 282, Samaldas Gandhi Marg, (Princess Street), Near Marine Lines Station, Mumbai-400002 (Maharashtra), © 22030717
• Gita Press Gorakhpur Ki Pustak Dukan, 24/55, Birhana Road, Kanpur-208001 (Uttar Pradesh), © 2352351,
Fax: 91-512-2352351
• Gita Press Gorakhpur Ki Pustak Dukan, Ashok Rajpath, Opposite Women's Hospital, Patna-800004 (Bihar), © 91-612-2300325
• Gita Press Gorakhpur Ki Pustak Dukan, Court Sarai Road, Upper Bazar, Ranchi-834001 (Jharkhand), © 91-651-2210685
• Gita Press Gorakhpur Ki Pustak Dukan, Vaibhav Apartment, Opposite Nutan Niwas, Bhatar Road, Surat-395001 (Gujarat)
© 91-261-2237362, 2238065
• Gita Press Gorakhpur Ki Pustak Dukan, G-5, Shree Vardhan, 4 R.N.T. Marg, Indore-452001 (Madhya Pradesh)
© 91-731-2526516, 2511977
• Gita Press Gorakhpur Ki Pustak Dukan, 7, Bhim Singh Market, Near Railway Station, Jalgaon-425001 (Maharashtra)
© 91-257-2226393
• Gita Press Gorakhpur Ki Pustak Dukan, 41, 4-4-1, Dilshad Plaza, Sultan Bazar, Hyderabad-500096 (Andhra Pradesh)
© 91-40-24758311
• Gita Press Gorakhpur Ki Pustak Dukan, Shriji Kripa Complex, 851, New Etawari Road, Nagpur-440002 (Maharashtra)
© 91-712-2734354
• Gita Press Gorakhpur Ki Pustak Dukan, Bharatiya Towers, Badam Badi, Cuttack-753009 (Orissa)
© 91-671-2335481
• Gita Press Gorakhpur Ki Pustak Dukan, Mittal Complex, Ganjpara, Telghani Chowk Raipur-492009 (Chhattisgarh)
© 91-771-4034430
• Gita Press Gorakhpur Ki Pustak Dukan, 59/9, Nichibag, Varanasi-221001 (Uttar Pradesh)
© 91-542-2413551
• Gita Press Gorakhpur Ki Pustak Dukan, Sabjimandi, Motibazar, Haridwar-249401 (Uttarakhand)
© 91-1334-222657
• Gita Bhavan, P.O. Swargashram, Rishikesh-249304 (Uttarakhand)
© 91-135-2430122, 2432792
• Gita Press Mansion, 8/1 M, Racecourse-641018 (Tamil Nadu),
© 91-422-3202521
• Gita Press Gorakhpur Ki Pustak Dukan, 15, 4th 'E' Cross, K.S. Garden, Lalbagh Road, Bangalore-560027 (Karnataka)
© 91-80-22955190; **Bus.Intt.:** Pub.; **Spl.:** Rel. and Character-building Books, as also Monthlies *Kalyan* in Hindi and *Kalyan-Kalpataru* in English

GITANJALI BOOKSELLERS
Luz Ginza Complex, 140-Rayapettah High Rd., Chennai-600004 (Tamil Nadu)
© 28556944
Bus.Intt.: B.S. and Rt.

GITANJALI PUBLISHING HOUSE
2/12, Vikram Vihar, Lajpat Nagar-IV, New Delhi-110024

GITANJALI PUSTAK MAHAL
Kochas, Rohtas-821112 (Bihar)

GLOBAL BOOK & SUBSCRIPTION SERVICES
Rgd.Off.: I-22, West Patel Nagar, New Delhi-110008
© (R) 25723241, 25756029
Sales Off.: M-3, Ashoka Apartments, Commercial Complex, Ranjit Nagar, New Delhi-110008
© (O) 25709439, 25709440, 25709420, (R) 25723241, 25756029, Fax: 011-25756029
✉ rchandr-gegbss@axcess.net.in,
globale@ndf.vsnl.net.in,
globalex@bol.net.in
Prop.: P. Ramachandran; **Bus.Intt.:** L.S., Pub.'s Rep., Sub.Ag., Pub., WS & Exp.;

Spl.: Sci. & Med., Engg. & Tech., Comp., Comm. & Man., Soc.Sci., Language & Litt., Subscription Services, Children Books, Edu. Aids & Laboratory Apparatus & Chemicals etc.

GLOBAL BOOK HOUSE
Shri Ganesh Complex, (First Floor), Khajuri Bazar, Indore-452002 (Madhya Pradesh)
✆ 231196, 239457
Hd.Org.: R.M. Jain

GLOBAL BOOKS
University Rd., Molui Lane, Hazratbal, Srinagar-190006 (Jammu & Kashmir)
✆ 2410251
✉ globalbooks-sgr@yahoo.com
Estd.: 1999; **Hd.Org.:** Mehraj Uddin; **Bus.Intt.:** Pub., L.S. & Rt.; **Spl.:** Humanities & Soc.Sci., Sci. & Tech., Med., Law

GLOBAL BUSINESS PRESS
18-19, Dilshad Garden, G.T. Rd., Shahdara, Delhi-110095
Bus.Intt.: Pub.; **Spl.:** Indian and Foreign Titles

GLOBAL CHILDREN CARE & CURE FOUNDATION
New Delhi
✆ 26832036, 26925286, Fax: 26827137
✉ carecure@nde.vsnl.net.in
Bus.Intt.: Pub.

GLOBAL EXPORTS
I-22, West Patel Nagar, New Delhi-110008
✆ 25853241, Telefax: 25709441, 25756029
Prop.: P. Ramachandran; **Bus.Intt.:** Exp.; **Spl.:** Humanities & Soc.Sci., Sci. & Tech., Med., Juvenile/Children, Gen. & Fiction etc. Hotel Man.

GLOBAL INFORMATION SYSTEMS TECHNOLOGY PVT. LTD.
877, Phase V, Udyog Vihar, Gurgaon-122016 (Haryana)
✆ 4001410-13, Fax: 91-124-4052913
✉ gistdel@gist.com, gistdel@gist.in
🌐 www.gist.in
Estd.: 1980; **Hd.Org.:** Ashok Chawla
Br.: A-706, Sagar Tech Plaza, Andheri Kurla Road, Saki Naka Junction, Andheri, Mumbai-400072 (Maharashtra)
✆ 28506998, Fax: 91-22-28596747,
✉ gistmum@gist.in;
• Prestige Meridian-II, Unit No. S-306, Block 2, Level 3, M.G. Rd., Bangalore-560001 (Karnataka), ✆ 25595593, Fax: 91-80-25595564, ✉ gistban@gist.in
• Unit-B, 2nd Floor, Samilton Chambers, 181/1, A.J.C. Bose Rd., Kolkata-700014 (West Bengal), **Bus.Intt.:** L.S. & Rt., Imp., Sub. Ag.; **Spl.:** Sci. & Tech.

GLOBAL LEARNING SYSTEMS PVT. LTD.
First Floor, 169 Sai Enclave Bannargatta Road, L & T South City, Bangalore-560076 (Karnataka)
Hd.Org.: Vittal Bhandary
Bus.Intt.: Pub.; **Spl.:** Learning material and equipment for educational institutions

GLOBAL MEDIA PUBLICATIONS
J-51-A, 1st Floor, Abdul Fazal Enclave, Jamia Nagar, Okhla, New Delhi-110025
✆ 26323985 ▮ 9818327757, Fax: 26323985
✉ gmpublication@rediffmail,com
Hd.Org.: S. Ubaidur Rahman; **Bus.Intt.:** Pub. & Dist.; **Spl.:** Soc.Sci., Humanities, Current Affairs and Rel. in Urdu and English

GLOBAL VISION PUBLISHING HOUSE
F-4, 1st Floor, 'Hari Sadan', 20, Ansari Road, Daryaganj, (Near Delhi Book Store), New Delhi-110002
✆ 91-11-23261581, 23276291, 64694271, 43575199 ▮ 9810644769
✉ nsingh_2004@vsnl.net, globalvision.pub@gmail.com, gv.ph@hotmail.com
🌐 www.globalvisionpub.com
Estd.: 2000; **Hd.Org.:** N.K. Singh; **Bus.Intt.:** Pub.; **Spl.:** Soc.Sci. and Humanities, Sci. & Tech., Law, Juvenile/Children Books

GLOBAL VOLUNTEERS
Secunderabad (Andhra Pradesh)
✆ 25550193 ▮ 9861045164
✉ krajeshg@indiatimes.com

GLOBE DISTRIBUTORS
45/6, Civil Lines, Bhagwan Mahaveer Marg, Roorkee-247667 (Uttar Pradesh)
✆ 274836
Estd.: 1988; **Prop.:** Vipin Jain; **Bus.Intt.:** L.S. and Rt.

GLOBE PUBLICATIONS
C-62, Inderpuri, New Delhi-110012
✆ (O) 25727319, 25725130 (R) 25719333, Fax: 91-11-25737306
Hd.Org.: Mrs. Vinod Gurwara; **Bus.Intt.:** Pub., Sub.Ag.; **Spl.:** Subscription of Foreign Journals

GLOBE PUBLICATIONS PVT. LTD.
B-13, 'A' Block, Shopping Complex, Naraina Vihar, Ring Road, New Delhi-110028
✆ 45055555, 25770411, 25778875, 25770212, Fax: 91-11-25778876,
▮ 9810413740
✉ info@globepub.com
🌐 www.globepub.com
Man.Dir.: S.P. Gurwana
Br.: 703, Cauveri Block, National Game

Housing Complex, Koramangala,
Bangalore-560047 (Karnataka)
✆ 25711716, 30620122,
Fax: 91-80-25711136
✉ gpplblr@globepub.com
• 11/11, First Floor, Jeevarathnam Nagar, Adyar, Chennai-600020 (Tamil Nadu),
▮ 9382330333
✉ gpplchennai@globepub.com
• House No. 8-2-674/3, Raw House, A-1 Ground Floor Usha Arun Apartments, Road No. 13, Banjara Hills, Hyderabad-500034 (Andhra Pradesh)
✉ gpplhyd@globepub.com
• NPS Business Centre, 7A K.S. Roy Road, Kolkata-700001 (West Bengal)
✆ 22483749, 22488283, 224848872
Fax: 91-33-22430847
✉ gpplkol@globepub.com
• Flat No. 404, Sadiq Enclave, Near City Station, Lucknow-226003 (Uttar Pradesh)
▮ 9335555556, ✉ sshrivastav@globepub.com
• 106, Nirma Plaza, Makwana Road, Off Andheri Kurla Road Marol, Andheri (East), Mumbai-400059 (Maharashtra)
✆ 28596084, 28596086, 30914244,
Fax: 91-22-28596085
✉ gpplmumbai@globepub.com
Bus.Intt.: Pub., Sub.Ag: CD, Internet
Spl.: Sci., Tech., Med., Foreign Journals

GOAL PUBLICATION
151, Jor Bagh, New Delhi-110003
▮ 9868403166, Fax: 91-11-24621538
✉ scholarbooks@vsnl.com
Hd.Org.: Santosh Shekhar
Bus.Intt.: Pub.; **Spl.:** Books on religious epics, *Vedas*

GOBIND BALLABH PANT KRISHI EVAM PRADYOGIK VISHWAVIDYALAYA
Prakashan Nideshalaya, Pant Nagar, Dist. Udham Singh Nagar-263145 (Uttarakhand)
✆ 233579, Fax: 233473
✉ vc@gbpuat.ernet.in
Hd.Org.: S.P. Gupta; **Bus.Intt.:** Pub. and B.S.; **Spl.:** University Textbooks on Agri., Sci. and Tech. in Hindi

GOBIND SADAN
Flat 14, Gobind Sadan, Gadaipur, Mehrauli, New Delhi-110030
✆ 91-11-64517341
✉ ralph@gobindsadan.org
🌐 www.gobindsadan.org
Hd.Org.: Ralph Singh
Bus.Intt.: Pub.; **Spl.:** Books on meditation, healing, self-improvement and religion

GOEL BOOK AGENCY
Pune (Maharashtra)
✆ 020-24453267
✉ compuhut@pn2.vsnl.net.in

GOEL PRAKASHAN
359, Alam Gori Ganj, Bareilly (Uttar Pradesh)

GOEL PUBLISHING HOUSE
Meerut (Uttar Pradesh)
✆ 01210264476, Fax: 2645855
✉ sk_kpm@yahoo.com
Bus.Intt.: Pub. & B.S.

GOIL BROTHERS
Dhalpur, Kullu, Distt. Kullu (Himachal Pradesh)
✆ (O) 222464, 222233 (R) 224988, 224177
Estd.: 1959; **Prop.:** Davender Chand;
Bus.Intt.: Rt.; **Spl.:** Text Books, School and College Level Books

GOKUL MASIK PRAKASHAN
1194, Sadashiv Peth, Pune-411030 (Maharashtra)

GOLA PUBLISHERS
Near Shardashram, Bhavani Shankar Rd., Dadar, Mumbai-400028 (Maharashtra)

GOLAM MOSTAJA MONDAL
Negum Desh Bandhu Vidyamandir, P.O. Shimuliadanga, Distt. Burdwan (West Bengal)

GOLD BOOKS (INDIA)
4537, Daiwara, Nai Sarak, Delhi-110006
✆ 23918311, 22213772
✉ gold_pub@lycos.com
Hd.Org.: D.N. Sharma; **Bus.Intt.:** Pub. & Dist.;
Spl.: Comp., Med., Astrology, Self-improvement, Career, etc. in Hindi

GOLD COIN
2/28, Shefalee Building, 62, Phirozshah Rd., Santa Cruz (W), Mumbai-400054 (Maharashtra)
✆ 2327890, 2342625, 26124719
Estd.: 1986; **Prop.:** Rajesh Punambhai Patel

GOLDEN BOOK CENTRE
1096, A/70, Deva Ram Park, Tri-Nagar, Delhi-110035
✆ 27184418
Prop.: D.K. Verma; **Bus.Intt.:** Indological B.S., Library Order Suppliers and Sub.Ag.

GOLDEN BOOK HOUSE
79/1, Temple Rd., Near 11th Cross, Malleswaram, Bangalore-560003 (Karnataka)
Bus.Intt.: Composers Printers and Pub.

GOLDLINE PUBLISHERS
G-1, Vikas Chambers, Vikas Marg, U-136, Shakarpur, Delhi-110092

GONDWANA GEOLOGICAL SOCIETY
C/o University Dept. of Geology,

Law College Campus, Amravati Rd., Nagpur-440001 (Maharashtra)

GONU PUSTAK BHANDAR
Sanhola, Bhagalpur-813255 (Bihar)
Bus.Intt.: Pub. and B.S.

GOOD BOOK COMPANY
18/102, Sector 51, Dakshinpuri Ext., New Delhi-110062
✆ 26412594
Hd.Org.: M.C. Sharma; **Bus.Intt.:** L.S.

GOOD BOOK DISTRIBUTORS
31, Chowringee Rd., Kolkata-700016 (West Bengal)

GOOD BOOK TRUST ASSOCIATION PVT. LTD.
Main Rd., Ranchi-834001 (Bihar)
✆ 2205296
Estd.: 1964; **Hd.Org.:** P.M. Mathew

GOOD BOOKS
F-17/208, Harsha Complex, Dena Bank Building, Subhash Chowk, Laxmi Nagar, New Delhi-110092
✆ 22045655
Ch.Exe.: Mr. Sundeep Gulati; **Bus.Intt.:** Dist.; **Spl.:** Gen. and Children Books

GOOD BOOKS
Ashok Rajpath, Opp. Patna College, Patna-800006 (Bihar)
Bus.Intt.: Pub. and B.S.

GOOD COMPANIONS
Vododara (Gujarat)
✆ 2425433
girish@barodaview.com
Bus.Intt.: B.S. & Rt.

GOOD LUCK PUBLISHERS LTD.
415, Laxmi Deep Building, 9, Laxmi Nagar, District Centre, Delhi-110092
✆ (O) 22015110 (R) 22760953, Fax: 22727104
deepak3@nde.vsnl.net.in
Estd.: 2000; **Hd.Org.:** Deepak Aggarwal; **Bus.Intt.:** Pub.; **Spl.:** Textbooks and Gen. Books

GOOD NEWS PUBLICATION
Kanjikuzhy, Kottayam-686004 (Kerala)
✆ 2578201, 2562677
Estd.: 1983; **Man.Dir.:** V.M. Mathew; **Bus.Intt.:** Pub.

GOODPRINT
Mumbai (Maharashtra)
goodprint@vsnl.com
Bus.Intt.: Pub., Printers & B.S.

GOODWILL PUBLICATION
Longertoli, Patna-800004 (Bihar)

GOODWILL PUBLICATIONS
WZ-114, Sant Nagar, Tilak Nagar, New Delhi-110018

GOODWILL PUBLISHING HOUSE
B-3, Rattan Jyoti, 18, Rajendra Place, New Delhi-110008
✆ (O) 25750801, 25755519, 25820556 (R) 25851608, Fax: 91-11-25763428, Grams: GEEPEE
goodwillpub@vsnl.net
www.goodwillpublishinghouse.com
Estd.: 1991; **Prop.:** Rajneesh Chowdhry; **Bus.Intt.:** Pub. of PB; **Spl.:** PB in all Sub.

GOODWORD BOOKS
1, Nizamuddin West Market, New Delhi-110013
✆ 24355454, 24356666, Fax: 24357333
info@goodwordbooks.com
www.goodwordbooks.com
Hd.Org.: S. Khan; **Bus.Intt.:** Pub.; **Spl.:** Islam in Urdu and Hindi

GOPAL BHANDAR
East Makhaniakuan, Patna-800004 (Bihar)
Bus.Intt.: Pub. and B.S.

GOPAL PUSTAK BHANDAR
Amarpur, Bhagalpur-813101 (Bihar)
Bus.Intt.: Pub. and B.S.

GOPAL PUSTAK BHANDAR
Khazanchi Rd., Patna-800004 (Bihar)
Bus.Intt.: Pub. and B.S.

GOPAL STATIONERY STORE
Nathnagar, Bhagalpur-812006 (Bihar)
Bus.Intt.: Pub. and B.S.

GOPI RAM & SONS
4068, Nai Sarak, Delhi-110006
✆ 22923180
Estd.: 1948; **Spl.:** NCERT, CBSE, DBT, Central School, Open School, Med., Tech. Engg., College and Competition Books

GOPI RAM & SONS
2619/0, C-3, New Market, Nai Sarak, Delhi-110006
Estd.: 1961; **Bus.Intt.:** WS Agent; **Spl.:** NCERT Books

GOPICHAND PUBLICATIONS
Darariwari St., Suryarao Pet, Vijayawada-520002 (Andhra Pradesh)
Bus.Intt.: Pub. and B.S.

GOPSONS PAPERS LTD.
A-14 Sector 60, Noida (Uttar Pradesh)

gopsons@del3.vsnl.net.in
Bus.Intt.: B.S., Pub. & Paper Prod.

GORI KANNADA PRESS
Kasaragode-670121 (Kerala)

GOSPEL FOR KERALA
G.P.O. Box No. 202, Quilon-691003 (Kerala)

GOSPEL LITERATURE SERVICE
Udyog Bhavan, 250-D, Worli Rd.,
Mumbai-400030 (Maharashtra)
022-24930116, 56627243, Fax: 24935532
gls@bom2.vsnl.net.in, glsindia@vsnl.com
www.glsindia.com
Estd.: 1953; **Hd.Org.:** Joseph A.J.
Br.: GLS Press, Kanara Engg. Co.-Compound Pant Nagar, Ghatkopar (E), Mumbai-400075
• Gospel Literature Service, Opp. KSRTC MGN Towers, Pathanamthitta-689645
Bus.Intt.: Exp., Pub.

GOSWAMI PUSTAK BHANDAR
Sonaili, Katihar-854114 (Bihar)

GOUSIA BOOK DEPOT
Barbar Shah, Srinagar (Jammu & Kashmir)
2474589
Estd.: 1996; **Prop.:** Showkat Ahmad;
Bus.Intt.: Pub., WS, L.S. & Rt., Sub.Ag.;
Spl.: Humanities & Soc.Sci., Sci. & Tech., Law, Juvenile/Children Books, Gen. & Fiction etc.

GOUTAM BROTHERS
Mastan Rd., Kanpur-208001 (Uttar Pradesh)
2256026
Hd.Org.: Narain Goutam

GOUTAM PUSTAK BHANDAR
Mithapur, Patna-800001 (Bihar)
Bus.Intt.: Pub. and B.S.

GOVARDHANDAS G. SORATHIA
Sukhnath Chowk, Pitampura, Amreli-365601 (Gujarat)

GOVERNMENT OF INDIA STATIONERY OFFICE RECREATION WELFARE CLUB
3, Church Lane, Kolkata-700041 (West Bengal)

GOVERNMENT OF PUNJAB
Department of Languages, Patiala-142006 (Punjab)

GOVIND BALLABH PANT KRISHI EVAM PRODOGIK KENDRA
Pant Nagar-263145 (Uttarakhand)
233350, Fax: 91-5944-233473
Bus.Intt.: Pub.; **Spl.:** Research material on agriculture

GOVIND BOOK
No. 93, West Gate Manor, R.V. Rd., Bangalore-560004 (Karnataka)

GOVIND BOOK & MAGAZINE CORNER
Khazanchi Rd., Patna-800004 (Bihar)
Bus.Intt.: Pub. and B.S.

GOVIND BOOK DISTRIBUTORS
SO-12-6, Jyoti Nagar, Jaipur (Rajasthan)
Bus.Intt.: B.S.

GOVINDA BOOK HOUSE
59, Gautam Apartments, Gulmohar Park Rd., New Delhi-110049
(O) 26851413 (R) 26527481, Fax: 26527481
govindaberry@hotmail.com, govinda@ndf.vsnl.net.in
Estd.: 1978; **Prop.:** Deepak Berry; **Bus.Intt.:** L.S. & Rt.; **Spl.:** Humanities & Soc.Sci., Sci. & Tech., Med., Law

GOVINDRAM HASANAND
4408, Nai Sarak, Delhi-110006
23977216, 65360255, Fax: 91-11-23977216
ajayarya@vsnl.com, orders@vedicbooks.com
www.vedicbooks.com
Estd.: 1925; **Hd.Org.:** Ajay Kumar Arya;
Bus.Intt.: Pub., Dist. and Exp.; **Spl.:** Vedic Litt.

GOWARSONS PUBLISHERS (P) LTD.
A-143, Gulab House, Mayapuri Phase-I, New Delhi-110064
(O) 25403312/3 (R) 26961172/3787, Fax: 25403551
delaae07@giasdl01.vsnl.net.in
Estd.: 1972; **Hd.Org.:** Mohinder Kapur;
Bus.Intt.: Pub. and Exp.

GOYAL BOOK AGENCIES
31, Budhwar Peth, Pune-411002 (Maharashtra)

GOYAL BROTHERS PRAKASHAN/GOYAL BOOKS OVERSEAS PVT. LTD.
11/1903, Chuna Mandi, Pahar Ganj, P.B. No. 5720, New Delhi-110055
26107559, 23582812, 23584658
Estd.: 1960; **Hd.Org.:** Roshan Lal Goyal
Br.: F-75, Green Park Main, New Delhi-110016
26537772-3, Fax: 26963418
goyalgbp99@hotmail.com
Bus.Intt.: Pub. & Dist.; **Spl.:** Textbooks and Model Test Papers for CBSE and ICSE Examinations

GOYAL PUBLISHERS AND DISTRIBUTORS PVT. LTD.
86 UB, Jawahar Nagar, Delhi-110007
65157607, Fax: 91-11-23850961
goyal@goyalsaab.com
www.goyalsaab.com
Hd.Org.: Ashwani Goyal
Bus.Intt.: Pub. and Dist.; **Spl.:** Books on language-learning, word power, vocabulary, reference books and dictionaries

GOYAL OVERSEAS
B-5/200, Safdarjung Enclave,
New Delhi-110029
✆ 26160476, 26103710, Fax: 91-11-26183237
✉ goyaloverseas@hotmail.com
Bus.Intt.: Pub. and Exp.; **Spl.:** School Text and Reference Books

---

GOYAL PUBLISHERS & DISTRIBUTORS PVT. LTD.
86, U.B., Jawahar Nagar, Delhi-110007
✆ 23912186, 23918362, Fax: 23940861
✉ goyal@vsnl.com
www.goylsaab.com
Hd.Org.: Ashwani Goyal
Br.: Goyal Saab Publishers & Distributors, 86, U.B. Jawahar Nagar, Delhi-110007
✆ 23918362, 23981983, Fax: 23940861
✉ goyal@vsnl.com
Bus.Intt.: Pub. and Dist.; **Spl.:** Word Power and Vocabulary, and on French, German, Spanish and other Foreign Languages

---

GOYAL PUBLISHING HOUSE
5, Ansari Rd., Darya Ganj, New Delhi-110002
✆ (O) 23274375, 23274151, 23275092
(R) 23911583, 23964963, Fax: 23274151
✉ gph2004@yahoo.co.in
Estd.: 2003; **Prop.:** Harish Arora;
Bus.Intt.: Pub., B.S., WS

GRACE ENTERPRISES
E-13, New Madhupura Market,
Shahibaug Rd., Ahmedabad-380004 (Gujarat)
✆ 0272-2334008, 2339187, 2338112, Fax: 0272-2344405
Estd.: 1984; **Bus.Intt.:** Exp.

GRACE LITERATURE COMPANY (P) LTD.
241/5, Rohini Flats, 7th Avenue,
Annanagar West, Chennai-600101 (Tamil Nadu)
✆ 26282605, Fax: 28250226
Bus.Intt.: Dist.; **Spl.:** Multi-volume Sets, Encyclopeadias and Reference Books

---

GRAIL MESSAGE CENTRE
13, Bhagavati Nagar, Yousufguda,
Hyderabad-500045 (Andhra Pradesh)
✆ 91-40-23608484
✉ grailindia@gmail.com
www.grailmessage.org
Hd.Org.: Liess
Bus.Intt.: Pub. and Dist.;
Spl.: Books on philosophy and spirituality

GRAIL MESSAGE PUBLICATION CO.
C-153, Okhla Industrial Area, Phase-1,
New Delhi-110020
✆ 26372301-03
✉ am.stahl@arcor.de
Hd.Org.: Anna Stahl Venkat; **Bus.Intt.:** Pub. and Dist.; **Spl.:** Spiritual Knowledge, Questions Concerning Life & Death, Health, Youth & Phil. of life

---

GRAIL MESSAGE PUBLISHING COMPANY
Plot 10, Hylam Colony,
Hyderabad-500045 (Andhra Pradesh)
✆ 23608484
✉ grailind@hd2.dot.net.in
Hd.Org.: Jeyu Govindan; **Bus.Intt.:** Dist.;
Spl.: Foreign Books on God and Spiritualism

GRANADA LEARNING
3031, 13th Main, 5th Cross, HAL II Stage,
Indra Nagar, Bangalore-560008 (Karnataka)
✆ 56975950
✉ naveens@vsnl.com
Hd.Org.: Mal Hilton; **Bus.Intt.:** Pub.;
Spl.: Multimedia Edu. for Children

GRANTH ACADEMI
1659, Purana Darya Ganj, New Delhi-110002
✆ 23264676, Fax: 91-11-23253233
✉ info@prabhatbooks.com
Estd.: 1982; **Hd.Org.:** Pawan K. Agarwal;
Bus.Intt.: Pub.; **Spl.:** Novels, Fiction, Books on Lib.Sci., Gen. Knowledge, and Books for Children and Neo-literates in Hindi

---

GRANTH LOK
Third Floor, Near Model Town Cinema,
Ahmedabad-380001 (Gujarat)

GRANTH LOK
Khazanchi Rd., Patna-800004 (Bihar)
✆ 250716
Bus.Intt.: Pub. and B.S.

GRANTH LOK
1/11244-C, Near Kirti Mandir, Subhash Park,
Navin Shahdara, Delhi-110032
✆ 22827556
Hd.Org.: Tribhuvan Nath Sharma;
Bus.Intt.: Pub.; **Spl.:** Litt., Hist., Politics, Soc.Sci., etc. in Hindi

---

GRANTHLOK PRAKASHAK EVAM PUSTAK VIKRETA
10296, Lane No. 1, Gorakh Park,
Shahdara, Delhi-110032
✆ 91-65829441
Hd.Org.: Tribhuvan Nath Sharma
Bus.Intt.: Pub.; **Spl.:** Hindi Literature, children's books and translations in Hindi

---

GRANTH NIKETAN
Rajendra Kumar Rd., Patna-800016 (Bihar)

GRANTH NIKETAN
Naugachia, Bhagalpur-812006 (Bihar)
Bus.Intt.: Pub. and B.S.

GRANTH SAHAYOG SAHAKARI MANDALI LTD.
156/1, Taliani Pole, Sarangpur, Ahmedabad-380001 (Gujarat)

GRANTH SHILPI (INDIA) PVT. LTD.
Saraswati Complex, Subhash Chowk, Laxmi Nagar, Delhi-110092
✆ 22019320
Hd.Org.: Shyam Behari Rai; **Bus.Intt.:** Pub.; **Spl.:** Edu., Hist. and Eco. in Hindi

GRANTH VIKAS
C-37, Raja Park, Adarsh Nagar, Jaipur-302004 (Rajasthan) ✆ 2608180
Hd.Org.: Himanshu Varma

GRANTHA BHARATI
3A, College Row, Kolkata-700009 (West Bengal)
Hd.Org.: Vivekananda Ghosh

GRANTHA BHAWAN
Amareswari Niketan, Manbazar, Purulia-723101 (West Bengal)

GRANTHA BHAWAN
Bagmundi, Purulia (West Bengal)

GRANTHA CHAYAN
80E, Sarat Bose Rd., Kolkata-700025 (West Bengal)

GRANTHA-JAGAT
10/B, Fakir Chand Mitra St., Kolkata-700009 (West Bengal)
✆ 9830161039
Hd.Org.: Swapan Kumar Das; **Bus.Intt.:** Dist. and L.S.; **Spl.:** Books in Bengali Language

GRANTHA MANDIR
Binod Behari, Cuttack-753002 (Orissa)
✆ (O) 221133, 232984 (R) 231196, 234148
Estd.: 1955; **Prop.:** Abhiram Mohapatra

GRANTHA NIKETAN
18A, Shamacharan Dey St., Kolkata-700009 (West Bengal)
Hd.Org.: Sunil Bose; **Bus.Intt.:** Pub. and B.S.; **Spl.:** Gen. Books of all Categories

GRANTHA NILAYA
59/1B, Patuatola Lane, Kolkata-700009 (West Bengal)
Bus.Intt.: Pub. of Distinction in Bengali; **Spl.:** Collection of Best Short Stories of the World

GRANTHA PEETH
Panbazar, Guwahati-781001 (Assam)
Bus.Intt.: B.S. and Pub.

GRANTHA SAMABAYA
13C, College Row, Kolkata-700009 (West Bengal)

GRANTHA SAMABESH
Barisha Super Market, Shop No. B-29, Sakher Bazar, H.D. Rd., Kolkata-700008 (West Bengal)

GRANTHA TIRTHA
65/3A, College St., Kolkata-700073 (West Bengal)
✆ 23707602, Fax: 91-11-23630238
Estd.: 1978; **Hd.Org.:** S. Nayak
Bus.Intt.: Pub. and B.S.; **Spl.:** Bengali, English and Hindi School Text Books

GRANTHA VALI
Phule Kanyashala, 5th Floor, Babrekar Marg, Off. Gokhle Rd., Dadar (N), Mumbai-400028 (Maharashtra)

GRANTHAGAR
Post Box 4161, Dhaval Complex, Behind Navrangpura Post Office, Ahmedabad-380009 (Gujarat)
✆ 26408213
✉ granthagar@yahoo.com **Bus.Intt.:** Pub.

GRANTHAGAR
Amarpur, Bhagalpur-813101 (Bihar)
Bus.Intt.: Pub. and B.S.

GRANTHALAYA
308, Sarvodaya Nagar, Sasani Gate, Aligarh-202001 (Uttar Pradesh)
✆ 2410152
Hd.Org.: Abhey Kumar Gupta

GRANTHALAYA
Ramkrishnaganj, Mathchandipur Distt., Midnapore (East), (West Bengal)
Hd.Org.: Bimalendu Bhakta

GRANTHALAYA
Sujaganj, Bhagalpur-812002 (Bihar)
Bus.Intt.: Pub. and B.S.

GRANTHALAYA
Mirchaibari, Katihar-854105 (Bihar)

GRANTHALAYA PVT. LTD.
11A, Bankim Chatterjee St., Kolkata-700073 (West Bengal)
✆ 033-2312157, 2744614; **Bus.Intt.:** Pub.

GRANTHAMELA
Egra Bazar, Egra-721429, Distt. Midnapore (West Bengal)

GRANTHANA
8B, College Row, Kolkata-700009 (West Bengal)
Hd.Org.: Tushar Kanti Pandey

GRANTHAYAN
3988, Sarvodaya Nagar, Sasni Gate, Aligarh-202001 (Uttar Pradesh)
Hd.Org.: Abhay Kumar Gupta

GRAPHIC PUBLICATIONS (P) LTD.
2/13, Ansari Rd., Darya Ganj,
New Delhi-110002
✆ 91-11-23243520
✉ graphicpublication@yahoo.com
Estd.: 1993; **Hd.Org.:** Amit Jain;
Bus.Intt.: Pub. and Dist.; **Spl.:** Fine Arts, Comm. Arts, Child Arts, Advertising, Designing, Photography, etc.

GREEN CHANNEL PUBLICATIONS (I) PVT. LTD.
38, Swamipara, Bhudhana Gate, Meerut (Uttar Pradesh)
✆ 2402172, Fax: 91-121-2401289
Hd.Org.: Anil Kumar Agarwal
Bus.Intt.: Pub.; **Spl.:** Colourful books for children in Hindi and English

GREEN IDEOLOGICAL CENTRE
SCO 73, 3-B-II, S.A.S. Nagar, Chandigarh

GREEN SHILPI (INDIA) PVT. LTD.
B-7, Saraswati Complex, Subhash Chowk, Lakshmi Nagar, Delhi-110092
✆ 91-11-22025140
Hd.Org.: Shyam Bihari Rai
Bus.Intt.: Pub.; **Spl.:** Books on social Science, education, history, media and economics in Hindi

GREENLAND EXPORTS PVT. LTD.
14, Sir Thyagaraya Rd., T. Nagar, Chennai-600017 (Tamil Nadu)
Bus.Intt.: Exp.

GREENWOOD PUBLISHING
P 1/6, Ground Floor, DLF Phase-II,
Gurgaon-122002 (Haryana)
✆ 91-124-2576796
✉ overleaf@vsnl.net
www.greenword.com
Hd.Org.: Tony Sloggett
Bus.Intt.: Pub.; **Spl.:** Academic and general interest books and textbooks as well as books for librarians and other professionals

GREHLAXMI
X-30, Okhla Industrial Area, Phase-II,
New Delhi-110020
✆ 51611861-65, Fax: 51611866
✉ sulex@diamondpocketbooks.com
www.diamondpocketbooks.com
Hd.Org.: Manish Verma; **Bus.Intt.:** Pub.;
Spl.: Hindi Language Books and Journal *Grehlaxmi*

GRISH PRAKASHAN
Langar Toli, Patna-800004 (Bihar)
Hd.Org.: Nanhelal Gupt

GROLIER INTERNATIONAL PVT. LTD.
A-11, Kailash Colony,
New Delhi-110048
✆ 26281356, 26229088, Fax: 26281345
✉ agupta@in.grolier.aspac.com
Hd.Org.: Walter Lee; **Bus.Intt.:** Pub.;
Spl.: Children's Books, Encyclopaedias and Dictionaries

GROLIER INTERNATIONAL PVT. LTD.
Chintels Manor, First Floor, A-30,
Kailash Colony, New Delhi-110048
✆ 29239088, Fax: 91-11-29231345
✉ enquiry@grolier.co.in
www.grolier.co.in
Hd.Org.: H.S. Yeoh; **Bus.Intt.:** Pub.;
Spl.: Children's Books, Encyclopaedias and Dictionaries

GUDDU PUSTAK BHANDAR
Haripur, Begusarai (Bihar)
Bus.Intt.: Pub. and B.S.

GUIDANCE CENTRE
Pirbahore, Patna-800006 (Bihar)
Bus.Intt.: Pub. and B.S.

GUIDE PUBLICATIONS
J3/5, Rajouri Garden, New Delhi-110027
✆ (O) 25101947 (R) 25101304,
Fax: 25122524
✉ guidepub@del2.vsnl.net.in
Prop.: Vidya Sagar; **Bus.Intt.:** Pub.

GUJARAT BOOK FAIR
10, Walkeshwar, Ambawadi,
Ahmedabad-380015 (Gujarat)
✆ 26425808

GUJARAT GRANTHALAYA SEVA SANGH
4-A, Laxmi Nagar Society, Asha Rd.,
Ahmedabad-380013 (Gujarat)

GUJARAT PRAKASHAK MANDAL
C/o Adarsh Prakashan,
1760/1, Near Bala Hanuman,
Gandhi Road,
Ahmedabad-380001 (Gujarat)
✆ 91-79-22135560
Hd.Org.: Jitendra Desai; **Bus.Intt.:** Pub. and Booksellers

GUJARAT PUSTAKALAYA SAHAYAK SAHAKARI MANDAL LTD.
Sanstha Vasahat, Raopura, Vadodara-391014 (Gujarat)

GUJARAT SAHITYA AKADEMI
Abhikk Nagar Bhavan, Sector-17,
Gandhinagar-382017 (Gujarat)
✆ 91-79-23256797-98
Hd.Org.: V.V. Pandit; **Bus.Intt.:** Pub.;
Spl.: Regional Language books in Gujarati

GUJARAT SAHITYA PRAKASH
Post Box-70, Anand-388001 (Gujarat)

✆ 240161, Fax: 240178
✉ gsp@satyam.net.in
Bus.Intt.: Pub. and B.S.

GUJARATI SAHITYA PARISHAD
P.O. No. 4060, Ashram Rd. Riverside, Ahmedabad-380009 (Gujarat)

GUJRAT INSTITUTE OF DEVELOPMENT RESEARCH
Sarkheh Gandhi Nagar Higwaya, NR Gota Char Rasta, Distt. Ahmedabad, Gota-382481 (Gujarat)

GUJRAT LAW REPORTER OFFICE
57/2, Gandhi Rd., Opp. Jain Temple, Above Zandu Pharmacy, Ahemedabad-380001 (Gujarat)

GULATI BOOK'S SHOP
GH7/117, Meera Bagh, Paschim Vihar, New Delhi-110087
✆ 25288384, Fax: 25405758
Hd.Org.: Vinod Gulati; **Hd.Org.:** Pub.; **Spl.:** Cooking, Beauty, Health and Edu. books

GULSHAN BOOKS
Residency Road, Srinagar-190001
✆ 2477287, Fax: 91-194-2477287
✉ gulshanpub@rediffmail.com
🌐 www.gulshanbooks.com
Hd.Org.: Sheikh Ajaz; **Bus.Intt.:** Pub. and Dist.; **Spl.:** Books on the culture, lifestyle and folklore

GUNA INTERNATIONAL COMPANY
Madurai (Tamil Nadu)
✉ dolphin@md5.vsnl.net.in
Bus.Intt.: B.S. & Printers

GUNADA BOOK STALL
Sarupeta, Barpeta (Assam)
Bus.Intt.: B.S. and Rt.

GUPTA BOOK AGENCY
13-E, Bungalow Rd., Kamla Nagar, Delhi-110007
✆ 22515777, 22516377
Prop.: Prem Gupta; **Bus.Intt.:** L.S.

GUPTA BOOK MART
Dariyapur Gola, Near Radha Krishna Mandir, Patna (Bihar)
Bus.Intt.: B.S. and Pub.

GUPTA BROTHERS
Madan Gopal Marg, Kaiser Ganj, Ajmer (Rajasthan)
✆ (O) 2460919 (R) 2627870
✉ guptabrothersajmer@hotmail.com
Estd.: 1955; **Bus.Intt.:** Pub. and B.S.; **Spl.:** Edu., Hindi Litt., Sci., Maths, Sanskrit Litt.

GUPTA BROTHERS BOOKS
47-13-10/1, Dwaraka Nagar, Visakhapatnam-530016 (Andhra Pradesh)
✆ 2754454, 2748412, 2700899, Fax: 2747580
✉ guptabrothersbooks@hotmail.com
🌐 www.guptabrothers.com
Estd.: 1916; **Prop.:** V. Gopal Krishna Gupta (CEO)
Br.: Surya Bagh D. No. 28-1084, Opp. Chitralaya Theatre, Visakhapatnam-530020 ✆ 2502263 • Main Rd., D.No. 26-15-2, Opp. Hindu Reading Room, Visakhapatnam-530001 ✆ 2508020 • 43-17-30, T.N. Colony, Venkatarajunagar, Visakhapatnam-530016
✆ 2748412, 2728823, Fax: 2747580
✉ guptabrothersbooks@hotmail.com
Bus.Intt.: Pub., WS, L.S. & Rt.; **Spl.:** Juvenile/ Children, Gen. & Fiction etc.

GUPTA PRAKASHAN
D-35, South Extension, Part-I, New Delhi-110049
✆ 24616351, 24619125, Fax: 24634935
✉ ragupta@del2.vsnl.net.in
Estd.: 1956; **Hd.Org.:** Rameshwar Dass Gupta; **Bus.Intt.:** Pub.; **Spl.:** Edu. & Children's Books in English, Hindi & Urdu

GUPTA PRAKASHAN
Khajuri Bazar, Indore-452002 (Madhya Pradesh)
✆ 2454382

GUPTA PRAKASHAN
Nayatola, Patna-801105 (Bihar)
Bus.Intt.: Pub. and B.S.

GUPTA PUBLISHING HOUSE
623, M.G. Rd., Khajuri Bazar, Indore (Madhya Pradesh)
✆ (O) 2454921-22 (R) 2475113, Fax: 2431968, 2422201
Estd.: 1988; **Hd.Org.:** Dinesh Gupta; **Bus.Intt.:** Pub.; **Spl.:** Children Books from Nursery to VIII (Children Books Text Books, Guide and Note's Books)

GUPTA PUSTAK BHANDAR
Daudnagar, Aurangabad-824113 (Bihar)
Bus.Intt.: Pub. and B.S.

GUPTA PUSTAK BHANDAR
Chauriya Bariyarpur, Begusarai (Bihar)
Bus.Intt.: Pub. and B.S.

GUPTA PUSTAK BHANDAR
Mansoorchak, Begusarai-851128 (Bihar)
Bus.Intt.: Pub. and B.S.

GUPTA PUSTAKALAYA
Ramgarh Cantt., Hazaribagh-829122 (Bihar)

GURDAS KAPUR & SONS (P) LTD.
3623, Chawri Bazar, Delhi-110006
✆ (O) 22916942, 22916951 (R) 26436929
Estd.: 1939; **Hd.Org.:** Kamal Arora
Br.: Mai Hiran, Gate, Jalandhar City (Punjab) • 19-B, Cil Layout, Sanjay Nagar, R.M.V. Extn. II Stage, Bangalore-94 (Karnataka)
Bus.Intt.: Pub.; **Spl.:** Gen. Books for Children, Text Books for Primary Classes in Hindi, English and Punjabi

GURDIP SINGH & SONS
Clock Tower, Amritsar-143001 (Punjab)
Bus.Intt.: Exp.

GURJAR DESH CHARITABLE TRUST
Gujjar Colony, Bye-Pass, Jammu
✆ 462049, Fax: 463190
gurjarct@jla.vsnl.net.in
Estd.: 1990; **Hd.Org.:** S.M. Zafarali;
Bus.Intt.: Pub., L.S.; **Spl.:** Journals, Magazines & Periodicals

GURJAR GRANTH RATNA KARYALAYA
Near Ratanpole Naka, Gandhi Rd., Ahmedabad-380001 (Gujarat)
✆ (O) 22144663, 22149660 (R) 26446413, 26621539, Fax: 22149660
allbooks@sity.com
www.gurjarbiz
Estd.: 1927; **Prt.:** Manubhai G. Shah, Amar T. Shah
Br.: Gurjar Prakashan, 202, Tilak Raj Apt., Near Suryarath Bldg., Panchvati, Ahmedabad-380007 (Gujarat)
Bus.Intt.: Pub., B.S., L.S., WS, Exp.;
Spl.: Man., Children & General books in Gujarati

GURJAR PRAKASHAN
Ratanpole Naka, Gandhi Rd., Ahmedabad-380001 (Gujarat)

GURJAR SAHITYA BHAVAN
M.G. Rd., Opp. Ratanpole Naka, Ahmedabad-380001 (Gujarat)

GURDEV SIDDHA PEETH
P.O. Ganeshpuri, Distt., Thane-401206 (Maharashtra)

GURU MEDIA
Kurumullor Post, Kottayam-686632 (Kerala)

GURU NITYA CHAITANYA YATI
Narayana Gurukula, Fernhull P.O., Nilgiris-643004 (Tamil Nadu)
✆ 04323-23088
Hd.Org.: G.N. Chaitanya Yati; **Bus.Intt.:** Pub.;
Spl.: Indian Phil. and Rel.

GURU PRASAD BOOKS
Vaikom-686141 (Kerala)

GURU PUBLICATIONS
Kozhikode-673032 (Kerala)
Estd.: 1989; **Prop.:** A.S. Jeevan; **Bus.Intt.:** Pub. and B.S.

GURUKUL KANGRI VISHVAVIDYALAYA
Gurukul Kangri, Haridwar (Uttarakhand)
✆ 243037, Fax: 91-1334-246811
queries@gkvharidwar.org, mayank@gkvharidwar.org
www.gkvharidwar.org; **Estd.:** 1902
Hd.Org.: Jagdish Vidyalkar

GUWAHATI BOOK DEPOT
Panbazar, Guwahati-781001 (Assam)

GYAN BHANDAR
Guru Govind Singh Rd., Hazaribagh-825301 (Bihar)

GYAN BHARATI
4/14, Roop Nagar, Delhi-110007
✆ 23847128
Hd.Org.: Mohit Malik; **Bus.Intt.:** Pub.;
Spl.: Litt. and for Children in Hindi

GYAN BHARATI
Unit III, (Near Station), Bhubaneshwar (Orissa)
Bus.Intt.: B.S., L.S.; **Spl.:** School and College Text Books

GYAN BHARATI
Postal Park, Chiraiyatanad, Patna-800001 (Bihar)
Bus.Intt.: Pub. and B.S.

GYAN BHARATI BOOK DEPOT
Indrapuri Chowk, Hazaribagh-825301 (Bihar)

GYAN BHARATI NEWSPAPER STALL
Shahkund, Bhagalpur-813108 (Bihar)
Bus.Intt.: Pub. and B.S.

GYAN BOOKS PVT. LTD.
5, Ansari Rd., Darya Ganj, New Delhi-110002
✆ (O) 23282060, 23261060 (R) 27215974, 27459472, Fax: 011-23285914
books@gyanbooks.com
www.gyanbooks.com
Estd.: 1984; **Man.Dir.:** Amit Garg;
Bus.Intt.: Pub., Pub.'s Rep., L.S. and Exp.;
Spl.: Humanities and Soc.Sci.

GYAN DEEP
165-D, Kamala Nagar, New Delhi-110007
✆ 23842930 9810154549
gyandeep@mantraonline.com
Hd.Org.: V.K. Gupta; **Bus.Intt.:** Dealer;
Spl.: Edu. Books

GYAN DEEP
Daudnagar, Aurangabad-824113 (Bihar)
Bus.Intt.: Pub. and B.S.

GYAN DEEP PRAKASHAN
47-A, Kamala Nagar, Delhi-110007
✆ 22910064, Fax: 23557530
Bus.Intt.: Pub.; **Spl.:** School and Colleges Guides and Help Books

GYANDOOT PRAKASHAN
H-601, Friends Apartments, Delhi-110092
✆ 91-11-22242440
Hd.Org.: Meena Sharma; **Bus.Intt.:** Pub. and Dist.; **Spl.:** Litt. Books in Hindi

GYAN GANGA
205-C, Chawri Bazar, Delhi-110006
✆ 23257555, Fax: 23253233
✉ shubham@id.eth.net
Estd.: 1982; **Hd.Org.:** Piyush Kumar; **Bus.Intt.:** Pub. and B.S., **Spl.:** Hindi Novels, Fiction, Children's Litt., Dictionaries, Encyclopaedias, Biographies, etc.

GYAN GANGA
Sahi Complex, Boring Rd., Shrikrishnapuri, Patna-800013 (Bihar)
Bus.Intt.: Pub. and B.S.

GYAN KAILASH
Boring Rd., Chouraha, Patna-800001 (Bihar)
Bus.Intt.: Pub. and B.S.

GYAN KENDRA
Nayatola, Patna-800004 (Bihar)
✆ 250465
Bus.Intt.: Pub. and B.S.

GYAN LOK
Naugacha, Bhagalpur-813211 (Bihar)
Bus.Intt.: Pub. and B.S.

GYAN MANDIR
Patanker Bazar, Gwalior-1 (Madhya Pradesh)

GYAN MANDIR
Shambhuganj, Bhagalpur-813211 (Bihar)
Bus.Intt.: Pub. and B.S.

GYAN MANDIR
Goh, Aurangabad-824303 (Bihar)
Bus.Intt.: Pub. and B.S.

GYAN NIKETAN
Kachahary Rd., Begusarai-851101 (Bihar)
Bus.Intt.: Pub. and B.S.

GYAN NIKETAN
Goriamath Chowk, Mithapur, Patna-800001 (Bihar)
Bus.Intt.: Pub. and B.S.

GYAN PRAKASH
Rafiganj, Aurangabad-824125 (Bihar)
Bus.Intt.: Pub. and B.S.

GYAN PRAKASHAN MANDIR
Gouri Niwas, 2-B/5, Pawan Puri, Bikaner (Rajasthan)
✆ 0151-224359
Hd.Org.: Kuldip and Sandip Jansevi; **Bus.Intt.:** Pub.; **Spl.:** Hindi Litt. and Veterinary Sci.

GYAN PUSTAK KENDRA
Durganagari, Ichak, Hazaribagh-825402 (Bihar)

GYAN SAGAR PUBLICATIONS
C-143, Preet Vihar, Delhi-110092
✆ 23275594, 22528110 ▮ 9811625372, Fax: 23253832
✉ gyan@vsnl.net
Estd.: 1997; **Prop.:** Sushil Anand; **Bus.Intt.:** Insti. Pub.; **Spl.:** Humanities & Soc.Sci., Man. & Comm. Fiction & Gen.

GYAN SARITA
Hanuman Nagar, K. Jankerbagh, Patna-800020 (Bihar)
Bus.Intt.: Pub. and B.S.

GYAN SAROWAR
Near Commerce College, Kankerbagh Bye Pass Rd., Patna-800020 (Bihar)
Bus.Intt.: Pub. and B.S.

GYAN SAROWAR
Krishna Murari Market, Shastrinagar, Patna-800023 (Bihar)
Bus.Intt.: Pub. and B.S.

GYAN SHIKHA
Mahabir Sthan, Main Rd., Dinapore, Patna-801503 (Bihar)
Bus.Intt.: Pub. and B.S.

GYAN VIDYA MANDIR
Obra, Aurangabad-824124 (Bihar)
Bus.Intt.: Pub. and B.S.

GYAN VIGYAN
Gujari Bazar, Patna City, Patna-800008 (Bihar)
Bus.Intt.: Pub. and B.S.

GYAN VIGYAN PRAKASHAN
1-B, Netaji Subhash Marg, New Delhi-110002
✆ 23274443, 23288769
Hd.Org.: Aamod Maheshwari; **Bus.Intt.:** Pub.; **Spl.:** Sci. and Related Books in Hindi

GYAN VIGYAN RESEARCH INSTITUTE
1119, Abhinav Complex, J.P. Nagar, Adhartal Ward, Jabalpur-482004 (Madhya Pradesh)
✆ 2314697, Fax: 2516771
✉ divinesx@bom6.vsnl.net.in
Hd.Org.: Vijay Shankar Rai; **Bus.Intt.:** Pub.; **Spl.:** Research Works on Sci. and Phil.

GYAN VIGYAN SANSTHAN
60, Vrahanan St., Hapur-245101 (Uttar Pradesh)
Hd.Org.: Masroor Hasan

GYAN YAGYA PRAKASHAN
Plot No. 17 & 18, Indraprastha Bhawan, New Sabzi Mandi, Azadpur, Delhi-110033
✆ 27112592, 27242994
Fax: 91-11-27425700
ipcoldstorage@yahoo.com
www.ipcoldstorage.com
Hd.Org.: Sanjay Aggarwal
Bus.Intt.: Dist.; **Spl.:** Books on Spiritualism

GYANAGAR
M.G. Rd., Katihar-854105 (Bihar)

GYANALAYA
Bihpur, Bhagalpur-853201 (Bihar)
Bus.Intt.: Pub. and B.S.

GYANALOK
Malviya Marg, Hazaribagh-825301 (Bihar)

GYANAYAN
134-C, Mourya Lok, Patna-800001 (Bihar)
Bus.Intt.: Pub. and B.S.

GYANDA PRAKASHAN (P&D)
4837/24, Ansari Rd., Darya Ganj, New Delhi-110002
✆ 23272047
Hd.Org.: Smt. S. Choudhary

GYANDOOT PRAKASHAN
H-601, Friends Apartments, Delhi-110092
✆ 91-11-22242440
Hd.Org.: Meena Sharma; **Bus.Intt.:** Pub. and Dist.; **Spl.:** Litt. Books in Hindi

GYANESH PRAKASHAN
6, Nav Nariman Layout, Pratap Nagar, Nagpur-440022 (Maharashtra)

GYANODAY
17, M.I.G. Colony, Kankerbagh, Patna-800020 (Bihar)
Bus.Intt.: Pub. and B.S.

■ ■ ■

H & C PUBLISHING HOUSE
South Bazar, High Rd., Thrissur-680001 (Kerala)
✆ 2421462, 2421467
Estd.: 1947; **Hd.Org.:** T.I. Varghese; **Bus.Intt.:** Pub. and B.S.; **Spl.:** Gen. Books and Reference Books

H.C. NETH & BROTHERS
119, Ashutosh Mukherjee Rd., Kolkata-700025 (West Bengal)

H.F.Y. ENTERPRISES
D-56, Sector 55, Noida-201301 (Uttar Pradesh)
✆ 95120-2583702
hfy@homoeopathyforall.com
Hd.Org.: Anuj Arora; **Bus.Intt.:** B.S.

H.G. PUBLICATION
77, Madangir Village, (Near Pushpa Bhawan), New Delhi-110062
✆ (O) 29956981, 29052565, 26056076 (R) 26857452 9810563509, Fax: 26091643
Editor-in-Chief: Jag Mohan Balokhra; **Bus.Intt.:** Pub.; **Spl.:** Acad., Journals & Magazines

H.H. THE DALAI LAMAS CHARITABLE TRUST
Handicraft Exports, 16, Jor Bagh, Lodhi Rd., New Delhi-110003
Bus.Intt.: Exp.

H.J. BOOK AGENCY
D-68, Kamla Nagar, Delhi-110007
✆ 30919830, Fax: 91-11-23918777
hjbookag@yahoo.com
Hd.Org.: E. Agarwal; **Bus.Intt.:** Pub. & Dist.; **Spl.:** Journals on Sci. and Tech.

H.K. PUBLICATIONS
A-1/11, Shakti Nagar Extension, Delhi-110052
Bus.Intt.: Pub.; **Spl.:** Current Affairs, Humanities, Rel. and Soc.Sci.

H.L. SEGHAL CHARITABLE TRUST
1-1698, Malka Ganj Rd., Delhi-110054

H.M. DAMODAR
1194, Shanti Nagar, Ulhasnagar-421003 (Maharashtra)
✆ 2567401
damodar_mansharamani@hotmail.com
Bus.Intt.: Pub.; **Spl.:** Rel. Books

H.M. PUBLISHERS HOLDING LTD./PALGRAVE MACMILLAN
5A/4A, Ansari Road, Darya Ganj, New Delhi-110002
✆ 23272010, Fax: 91-11-23272010
palgrave@vsnl.com
www.palgrave.com
Hd.Org.: Kalpana Shukla; **Bus.Intt.:** Pub., **Spl.:** Books on soc. sciences, humanities, education, business management, engineering and reference as also journals in English

H.P.C. PUBLISHERS DISTRIBUTORS PVT. LTD.
4805/24, First Floor, Bharat Ram Rd., Darya Ganj, New Delhi-110002
✆ (O) 23254401, 23254402 (R) 26193544, Fax: 91-11-26193511, 23274405
hpc@vsnl.com
www.thebookservice.com
Estd.: 1994; **Hd.Org.:** Prabhat K. Jain; **Bus.Intt.:** Pub., B.S., Exp.

H.P.J. KAPOOR
3081, Pratap St., Netaji Subhash Marg, Darya Ganj (Behind Golcha), New Delhi-110002
✆ (O) 23273828 (R) 27184590, 26254325
Estd.: 1906; **Man.Prt.:** Prem Nath Kapoor; **Bus.Intt.:** Pub., WS, Rt.; **Spl.:** Interest Calculators, Ready Reckoners & Banking Books (Staff Awards & Settlements etc.) C.A.I.I.B. Exams and All India Directory of Banks' Branches, Law, Comm. & Banking books

H.R. PUBLISHERS
C/o Himalayn Res. Group, Post Bag No. 1, Tallital, Nainital-263002 (Uttarakhand)

HABITAT COMMUNICATIONS PVT. LTD.
2, First Floor, Devbhumi Apartments, Near Vijay Cross Rd., Navrangpura, Ahmedabad-380009
✆ 079-26467919, Fax: 26467919
habcom@yahoo.com
Estd.: 1999; **Hd.Org.:** Muktiraj Singh Ji Chauhan; **Spl.:** Human Habitat, Arch., Planning

HAJEE M.A. SHAHUL HAMEED & SONS
No. 21 (Old No. 10), Quaide Millath Rd., Chennai-600005 (Tamil Nadu)
✆ 91-44-28572535, 2842535, 2844061
Hd.Org.: Abdul Jaleel; **Bus.Intt.:** Pub.

HALDER PRAKASHANI
10/2B, Ramanath Majumder St., Kolkata-700009 (West Bengal)

HAMDAM BOOK DISTRIBUTORS
H-108, Babar St., Near Shahb Masjid, Batla House, Jamia Nagar, Okhla, New Delhi-110025
✆ 26986019
uzair_quddusi@rediffmail.com
Hd.Org.: Quddusi; **Bus.Intt.:** Dist. **Spl.:** Edu. Books in Urdu Language

HAMEEDIYA PUSTAK BHANDAR
Sanhola, Bhagalpur-813225 (Bihar)
Bus.Intt.: Pub. and B.S.

HAMESH TRADERS
58/2 FF, Opp. Jain Derasar Patasa Pole, Gandhi Rd., Ahmedabad-380001 (Gujarat)

HAMMERARTAG.COM
307, A Pocket C, Mayur Vihar, Phase II, Delhi-110091
9213310716
gayatry_070@yahoo.co.in
www.hammerartage.com
Hd.Org.: Gayatri Vashistha

HANISH & CO.
5, S.F.S. DDA Flat, Dr. Mukherjee Nagar, Delhi-110009
(O) & (R) 27654433
Estd.: 2001; **Prop.:** Hanish Sawhney; **Bus.Intt.:** Pub., WS, Pub.'s Rep.; **Spl.:** Fiction, Rare, Journals & Magazines

HANS AKSHAR PRAKASHAN PVT. LTD.
Ansari Rd., Darya Ganj, New Delhi-110002
23270377, 23250047
Hd.Org.: Rajendra Yadav; **Bus.Intt.:** Pub.; **Spl.:** Hindi Litt., Journal, *Hans*

HANS PRAKASHAN
18, Nyaya Marg, P.B. No. 103, Allahabad-211001 (Uttar Pradesh)
22623077
ar@nde.vsnl.net.in
Hd.Org.: Alok Rai; **Bus.Intt.:** Pub.; **Spl.:** Works by Premchand, Subhadra Kumari Chauhan, Amrit Rai, etc. in Hindi

HANSA PRAKASHAN
57, Natani Bhawan, Mishra Raja Ji Road, Chand Pole Bazar, Jaipur-302001 (Rajasthan)
2318365, Fax: 91-141-2318365
Hd.Org.: Puspa Devi Natani
Bus.Intt.: Pub. and Dist.; **Spl.:** Books on Sanskrit Language and Literature

HANSADHWANI PRAKASHANA
27, 1st Floor, Cottonpet Main Rd., Bangalore-560040 (Karnataka)
(O) 080-277750 (R) 23300918
Hd.Org.: S. Rangaswamy; **Bus.Intt.:** Pub.; **Spl.:** Fictions Collections, Gen. Books, Text Books, Children Books in Kannada

HANUMAN PUSTAK BHANDAR
Kursela, Katihar-854341 (Bihar)

HANUMAN PUSTAK BHANDAR
Jhanjharpur, Madhubani-847403 (Bihar)

HAPPY BOOK DEPOT
Model Town, Delhi Road, Near Durga Gas Agency, Rohtak-124001 (Haryana)
211615, Fax: 91-1262-210614
hbdrohtak@yahoo.com
www.happybookdepot.com
Estd.: 1952; **Dir.:** Gaurav Rakheja, Pawan Gulati; **Man.:** Neeta Rakheja; **Bus.Intt.:** WS, L.S. & Rt.; **Spl.:** Sci. & Tech.

HAPPY LOVING PEACEFUL BOOK PUBLISHING
C-9/9132, Vasant Kunj, New Delhi-110070

HAQUE BOOK STALL
Kacharigaon, N.T. Rd., Tezpur, Sonitpur-784001 (Assam)
03712-231129
Estd.: 1949; **Prop.:** Md. Reaj Haque
Br.: Gyan Bharati, Gorojmari, Tezpur Air Force, Tezpur (Assam); • Book Mart, Jaswanta Rd., Panbazar, Guwahati (Assam)
Bus.Intt.: Pub., B.S., L.S., WS;
Spl.: Humanities & Soc.Sci., Sci. & Tech., Comp., Law, Children & Gen.

HAR ANAND PUBLICATIONS PVT. LTD.
E-49/3, Okhla Industrial Area, Phase-II, New Delhi-110020
416303490, 416303491, 416303492
Fax: 91-11-41708607
haranand@rediffmail.com
www.haranandpublications.com
Estd.: 1988; **Hd.Org.:** Ashok Gosain, Ashish Gosain; **Bus.Intt.:** Pub., Printing; **Spl.:** Gen., Edu. and Children's Books

HAR PRASAD BHAGAVA
Educational Publication, 4/230, Kacheri Ghat, Agra-282004 (Uttar Pradesh)

HARAF PRAKASHANI
A-126, College St. Market, Kolkata-700007 (West Bengal)
Estd.: 1964; **Bus.Intt.:** Pub.; **Spl.:** Rel. and Classical in Bengali

HARBANS BOOK DEPOT
2619-20/11, New Market, Nai Sarak, Delhi-110006
23275451

HARCOURT EDUCATION, UK
B-5/47, Safdarjung Enclave, New Delhi-110029
26169147
overleaf@vsnl.net
Hd.Org.: Neil Morley; **Bus.Intt.:** Pub.; **Spl.:** Edu. Books

HARE KRISHAN TRUST
P.O. Box No. 123, Chandigarh-160017
2567009, 2702378
hktvibhu@yahoo.com, hktindia@sancharnet.in
Hd.Org.: Vineet Sharma; **Bus.Intt.:** Pub.; **Spl.:** Books, Audio/Video Cassettes, C.D's on Rel. and Indology

HARI BEHARI PRAKASHAN (P) LTD.
1203/81, Tri Nagar, Delhi-110035

HARI BOOK CENTRE
255, Rabindra Sarani, Kolkata-700007 (West Bengal)

HARI BOOK DISTRIBUTORS
WA-170, St. No. 6, Shakarpur, Delhi-110092
✆ 22503411
Hd.Org.: Harish Chandra Gupta; **Bus.Intt.:** Pub., L.S.; **Spl.:** Acad., Beh. Sci., Soc.Sci., Comm., Fiction, Juveniles

HARIDEVPUR BOOK HOUSE
88/7, M.G. Rd., Kolkata-6 (West Bengal)

HARIHAR PUSTAKALAYA
Tower Rd., Surat-395001 (Gujarat)

HARIMAN BOOK SELLERS
804, Mount Rd., Chennai-600002 (Tamil Nadu)
✆ 28520551
Estd.: 1971; **Bus.Intt.:** Pub., L.S. and Rt., Exp.

HARIOHM PUSTAK BHANDAR
Paschim Darwaza, Patna City, Patna-800008 (Bihar)
Bus.Intt.: Pub. and B.S.

HARIS PUBLICATION
Basti Hazrat Nizamuddin, New Delhi-110013
✆ 24350995
Fax: 91-11-26827731

HARISH BOOK SELLERS
Near Police Chokki, Ghanta Ghar, Jodhpur-342002 (Rajasthan)

HARISREE BOOKS
Vennikkulam, Pathanamthitta-689544 (Kerala)

HARISSREE BOOKS
P.O. Box No. 36, Punalur-691305 (Kerala)
✆ 0474-2743204
Estd.: 1985; **Prop.:** R. Radhakrishnan; **Bus.Intt.:** Pub. and B.S.

HARITHA PUSTAKA KENDRAM
Premier Building, Pattalam Rd., Thrissur-680001 (Kerala)
Estd.: 1993; **Hd.Org.:** I. Gopinath; **Bus.Intt.:** Pub. and B.S.

HARKRISHNAN BOOK COMPANY
F-4/68, Sector-15, Rohini, Delhi-110085
✆ 27884306 ▮ 9811373613
@ harkrishanbook@rediffmail.com
Hd.Org.: Vajinder Kr. Dhingra
Bus.Intt.: L.S.; **Spl.:** Beh.Sci., Comm., Med., Tech., Fiction, Rare & Law

HARLEQUIN MILLS AND BOON INDIA (P) LTD.
213, Raheja Chambers, Suite No. 206, Freepress Journal Road, Nariman Point, Mumbai-400021 (Maharashtra)
✆ 91-22-4050926
@ manish.singh@hmbindia.com
www.millsandboon.co.uk
Hd.Org.: Andrew J. Go
Bus.Intt.: Pub.; **Spl.:** World famous series of romance books

HARMAN PUBLISHING HOUSE
A-23, Naraina Industrial Area, Phase-II, New Delhi-110028
✆ 25895503, 25708193
@ harmanpublishing@yahoo.com
Estd.: 1987; **Hd.Org.:** Manjit Singh; **Bus.Intt.:** Pub.; **Spl.:** Art, Numismatics, Ancient Indian Hist., Music, etc. in English

HARNAM DASS & BROTHERS AGENCIES
Pacca Danga, Jammu Tawi-180001 (Jammu and Kashmir)
✆ (O) 2542175, 2574428 (R) 2470210, 2470209 ▮ 9419180999
@ rahul_nph@rediffmail.com
Estd.: 1910; **Prop.:** Narender Kumar Gupta; **Bus.Intt.:** Pub., WS, L.S. & Rt.; **Spl.:** Trade, Humanities & Soc.Sci., Gen. (Incl. Lit. & Art), Juvenile/Children Books

HARNANDI PUBLISHERS & DISTRIBUTORS (INDIA)
59/39, New Rohtak Rd., Karol Bagh, New Delhi-110005
✆ (O) 25718135 (R) 25813432-3,
Fax: 25764347
@ goelvkg@vsnl.com, geelvkg@vsnl.com
Estd.: 2000; **Prt.:** Krishan Kr. Goel, Vinod Goel; **Bus.Intt.:** Pub., WS

HARPER COLLINS PUBLISHERS INDIA LTD.
1A, Hamilton House, Connaught Place, New Delhi-110001
✆ 23352233, 23351736/38,
Fax: 91-11-23731402
@ ratna.joshi@harpercollins-india.com
www.harpercollins.co.in
Estd.: 1991; **Prop.:** Ms. Victoria Barnsley; **Br.:** A-53, Sector 57, Noida (Uttar Pradesh)
✆ 91-120-4044800
@ contact@harpercollins.co.in
Bus.Intt.: Pub., WS, L.S. & Rt., Imp., Exp.; **Spl.:** Humanities & Soc.Sci., Sci. & Tech., Med., Law, Juvenile/Children, Gen. & Fiction

HARSH BOOKS CORNER
B1/79, 1st Floor, Phase-2, Ashok Vihar, Delhi-110052
✆ 56218070

bhanu262@rediffmail.com
Estd.: 2003; **Prop.:** Dr. P.C. Bhanu; **Bus.Intt.:** B.S.; **Spl.:** Humanities & Soc.Sci., Sci. & Tech., Med., Mang.

HARSH PRAKASHAN
Kohinur Trilorsna Meda Upar, Ratanpole Naka, Gandhi Rd., Ahmedabad-380001 (Gujarat)

HARVARD BUSINESS SCHOOL PRESS
7, West Patel Nagar, New Delhi-110008
✆ 25819304-7, 25732841, 25732918, Fax: 25819302, 25819303
marketing_india@mcgraw-hill.com, xlderl/tmh/roystan@tmh.satyam.net.in
Hd.Org.: N. Subrahmanyam; **Bus.Intt.:** Pub.; **Spl.:** Textbooks on Engg., Comp. Sci., Business, Eco., Sci. and Soc.Sci. in English

HARYANA POLICE ACADEMY
Karnal, Haryana-132037
✆ 2350101, Fax: 91-184-2350101
dirhpambam@yahoo.co.in
www.haryanapoliceacademy.org
Hd.Org.: Vikas Narain Rai
Bus.Intt.: Pub.; **Spl.:** Books for general reader as well as for police personel, as part of 'Samvadi Police Programme' and 'Community Policing Interface'

HARYANA SAHITYA AKADEMI
Kothi No. 897, Sector-2, Panchkula-134112 (Haryana)
✆ 2565521, Fax: 2581807
Hd.Org.: Desh Nimrohi; **Bus.Intt.:** Pub.; **Spl.:** University-level Books on Anthropology, Sci., Language and Litt.

HARYANA SCIENTIFIC CORPORATION
Books & Publication Division, New Market, Gandhi Chowk, Hissar-125001 (Haryana)
✆ 235849, 235860, 236880, Fax: 236880
sursavi2001@yahoo.com
Hd.Org.: S.C. Jain; **Bus.Intt.:** Dist.; **Spl.:** Rice, Rice Production Skill and Agri.

HASMUKH STORES
52, Botad, Bhavnagar (Gujarat)

HASYA ACADEMY
C-III, New Rajender Nagar, New Delhi-110060
✆ (O) 26123636 (R) 25789717 ▮ 9810398662, Fax: 26121061
Estd.: 1990; **Hd.Org.:** Dr. Sarojini Pritam; **Bus.Intt.:** Pub.; **Spl.:** Children Litt.

HATHWAY INVESTMENTS PVT. LTD.
AB-10, Safdarjung Enclave, New Delhi-110029
✆ 26191421-24, Fax: 26191420
outlook@outlookindia.com
Hd.Org.: Maheshwar Peri; **Bus.Intt.:** Pub.; **Spl.:** Weekly Magazine *Outlook*

HAY HOUSE PUBLISHERS
Muskaan Complex, Plot No. 3, B-2, Vasant Kunj, New Delhi-110070
✆ 41761620, Fax: 91-11-41761630
contact@hayhouse.co.in
Hd.Org.: Ashok Chopra
Bus.Intt.: Pub.; **Spl.:** Books like fiction, non-fiction, management, philosophy, religion, self-help and children's books

HEALING BOOKS
887/5, Patel Nagar, PB No. 13, Gurgaon-122001 (Haryana)
✆ 2322779, 2322005, Fax: 91-2324782
ind-doc-ser@satyam.net.in
Bus.Intt.: Pub. and B.S.; **Spl.:** Popular/Alternative Health Books

HEALTH & SOCIAL SCIENCES SEMINAR COMMITTEE
Department of Med. Microbiology & Parasitology, Kolkata University, 244 B, Acharya J.C. Bose Rd., Kolkata-700020 (West Bengal)

HEALTH & WEALTH CARE CENTRE
WZ-14, 2nd Floor, Tihar Bus Stop, Subhash Nagar, New Delhi-110018
✆ 25121880 ▮ 9811482650
rk_suneja@rediffmail.com
Hd.Org.: Raj Kumar Suneja; **Spl.:** Books and Acupressure, Magnetotherapy and Feng Shui Products

HEALTH HARMONY
1920, St. No. 10, Chuna Mandi, Paharganj, Delhi-110055
✆ 23683100, Fax: 23610470
Bus.Intt.: Dist.; **Spl.:** Health

HEALTH INDIA
97, Sunder Block, Shakarpur, Delhi-110092
✆ 22240182, 22437823
Hd.Org.: Mrs. Saroj Ahoja

HEALTH PSYCHOLOGY
15/9, Yogadham, Lajpat Nagar Chowk, Lucknow-226003 (Uttar Pradesh)
✆ 91-522-2253011
Hd.Org.: D.N. Rai; **Bus.Intt.:** Pub.; **Spl.:** Quarterly magazine on health and yoga

HEALTH TIMES
A-13, Kamla Nehru Nagar, Jodhpur-342009 (Rajasthan)
✆ 2759042, Fax: 91-291-2759042
info@acupressure.com
www.acupressure.com

Hd.Org.: B.R. Chaudhury **Bus.Intt.:** Pub.; **Spl.:** Journal *Health Times* in Hindi

HEDUA BOOK STALL
183, Bidhan Sarani, Kolkata-700006 (West Bengal)

HEEMANSHU PUBLICATIONS
D-33, South Extension Part-I, New Delhi-110049
✆ (O) 24615544, 24693355 (R) 24694422, 24698807, Cable: "Booklovers", New Delhi
Estd.: 1965; **Hd.Org.:** K.A. Gupta; **Bus.Intt.:** Pub.; **Spl.:** School Textbooks and Children's Books in English, Hindi, Tamil, Kannada and Bengali

HELLO FRIEND BOOKS
A-81, Sector 5, Noida-201301 (Uttar Pradesh)
✆ 2423846/47/48, Fax: 091-120-2420324
✉ info@hellofriendbooks.com
www.hellofriendbooks.com
Bus.Intt.: Pub.; **Spl.:** Pub. and Manufacturer of Children & Art/Adult Books

HELPLINE PUBLICATIONS PVT. LTD.
RZ-C/24, Sitapuri Extension Part I, P.B. No. 45, New Delhi-110045
Bus.Intt.: Pub.; **Spl.:** Edu. books

HEMANTHA SAHITYA
972C, 4th Floor, E Block, Rajajinagar, Bangalore-560010 (Karnataka)
✆ 23354619

HEMCHANDRA GOSWAMI
Pathi, Golaghat-785004 (Assam)

HEMDIP AGENCIES
2nd Floor, Pushpa Bhavan, Madan Zanpa Rd., Vadodra-390001 (Gujarat)
✆ (O) 22422603, 22337503 (R) 22645502, Telefax: 0265-22422603
✉ hemdip@lawbooksagency.com
www.lawbooksagency.com
Estd.: 1973; **Hd.Org.:** Dipak Shah, Hetal Shah; **Bus.Intt.:** Pub. and B.S.; **Spl.:** Law books

HEMGANGA PRAKASHAN
27, Rajpur Road, Civil Lines, Delhi-110054
✆ 91-11-23954280
Hd.Org.: Udhay Vir
Bus.Intt.: Pub.; **Spl.:** Hindi Language books

HEMKOSH STATIONERS
Zoo-Norengi Rd., Guwahati-781004 (Assam)

HEMKUNT PUBLISHERS PVT. LTD.
A-78, Naraina Industrial Area Phase I, New Delhi-110028
✆ 25790032, 25792083, 25795079, Fax: 91-11-6113705
✉ info@hemkuntpublishers.com
www.hemkuntpublishers.com
Estd.: 1948; **Hd.Org.:** G.P. Singh
Bus.Intt.: Pub.; **Spl.:** Textbooks for Schools and Children's Books in English, Hindi and Punjabi

HEMPRA PUBLISHING HOUSE (P) LTD.
St. No. 3, Shiv Mandir Colony, Alipur, Delhi-110036
✆ 27196738
Hd.Org.: S.A. Jagannathan; **Bus.Intt.:** Pub.; **Spl.:** Edu. Books and Periodicals for Schools and Colleges

HERITAGE PUBLISHERS
C/o Book Circle, Ground Floor, Ravindra Mansion, 19-A Ansari Road, Darya Ganj, New Delhi-110002
✆ 23264444, 23266633, Fax: 91-11-23263050
✉ info@heritagepublishers.in
www.heritage@nda.nsnl.in
Estd.: 1973; **Prop.:** B.R. Chawla
Br.: 3-4-215E, 1st Floor, Kanchi Guda, Main Rd., Hyderabad-500027
✆ 27552322, 27552448;
• 89/1, Ahmol Gandhi Bazar, Main Rd. Basdvangudi, Bangalore-560004
✆ 26520413,
✉ heritage.blr@lycos.com
Bus.Intt.: Pub., WS, L.S. & Rt., Imp., Exp.; **Spl.:** Humanities & Soc.Sci., Sci. & Tech.

HI-TECH BOOK SERVICES
HR-87-A/4, Pul Pehlad Pur, Suraj Kund Rd., New Delhi-110044
▮ (O) & (R) 9811140844, Fax: 011-26362326
✉ htbooks@yahoo.com
Estd.: 1996; **Prop.:** Ajay Kumar; **Bus.Intt.:** L.S.; **Spl.:** Sci., Pure & Applied Med., Tech.

HIDERINA PRAKASHAN
993, Hosakerehalli, Layout, Banashankar Stage II, Bangalore-560085 (Karnataka)
✆ 080-2604175
Hd.Org.: C.H. Jacob Lobo; **Bus.Intt.:** Pub.; **Spl.:** Own Books in Kannada and English

HIGGINBOTHAMS LIMITED
116, Anna Salai, Chennai-600002 (Tamil Nadu)
✆ 28520640, 28521841-43, Fax: 28528101
✉ higginbothams@vsnl.com
Estd.: 1944; **Dir.:** S. Chandrasekhar
Br.: 68, Mahatama Gandhi Rd., Bangalore-560001 (Karnataka) ✆ 25325422, Fax: 25597674, **Hd.Org.:** Dominic Micheal
• Higginbothams Limited, Higginbotham Building, M.G. Rd., Trivandrum (Kerala)

✆ 0471-2331622, **Hd.Org.:** K. Bhaskaran **Bus.Intt.:** WS & Rt.; **Spl.:** Books, Stationery, Greeting Cards, CD ROMs and Multi-media Cassettes

HIGH COMMISSION OF CANADA
7/8, Shanti Path, Chanakya Puri, New Delhi-110021
✆ 41782312, Fax: 91-11-41782021
✉ malti.bhandari@international.gc.ca
www.india.gc.ca
Hd.Org.: David Malona

HIGH TEXT
316, Guru Nanak Pura, Adarsh Nagar, Jaipur-302004 (Rajasthan)
✆ 2621186
Hd.Org.: Kailash Jain; **Bus.Intt.:** Pub. and Dist.

HILAL PUBLICATIONS
2035, Qasimjan St., Delhi-110006
✆ 23288523, Fax: 23288234
✉ reyazul@giasdla.vsnl.net.in

HILLVIEW PUBLICATIONS PVT. LTD.
601, Mahima Classic, B-84 Tilak Nagar, Jaipur (Rajasthan)
✆ 2620340, Fax: 91-7452-223004
Hd.Org.: Rizwan Ejazi; **Bus.Intt.:** Pub.; **Spl.:** Hindi language books on national integration, personal development etc.

HIMACHAL ACADEMY OF ARTS, CULTURE AND LANGUAGES
Sangarmal Bhawan, Cliff-en-estate, Shimla-171001 (Himachal Pradesh)
✆ 2624330, Fax: 2623149
✉ hpstateacademy@gmail.com
Hd.Org.: Sudarshan Vashisth
Bus.Intt.: Pub.; **Spl.:** Art, Culture, Heritage and Litt. in Hindi

HIMACHAL PUSTAK BHANDAR
221, Saraswati Bhandar, Gandhi Nagar, Delhi-110031
✆ 22452602
Hd.Org.: Jiwan Sharma; **Bus.Intt.:** Pub.; **Spl.:** Novels, Poems and Books on Sci., Rel., Phil., etc.

HIMALA PUBLISHERS
New Delhi
✆ 26109397, 26107969
✉ himpub@nda.vsnl.net.in
Bus.Intt.: Pub.

HIMALAYA PUBLISHING HOUSE PVT. LTD.
4-B/4378, "Pooja Apartments", Murari Lal Street, Ansari Road, Darya Ganj, New Delhi-110002
✆ 23270392, Fax: 91-11-23256286
✉ himpub@vsnl.com
www.himpub.com
Estd.: 1977; **Prt.:** Mrs. Meena Pandey, Mr. S. Joshi; **Br.:** 'Ramdoot', Dr. Bhalerao Marg, Girgaon, Mumbai-400004 (Maharashtra)
✆ 23863863, 23860170, Fax: 91-22-23877178
✉ himpub@vsnl.com;
• Kundanlal Chandak Industrial Estate, Ghat Road, Nagpur-440018 (Maharashtra),
✆ 71227212-16, Fax : 91-712-71227212-15;
• No. 16/1 (Old 12/1), 1st Floor, Next to Hotel Highlands, Madhava Nagar, Race Course Road, Bangalore-560001 (Karnataka), ✆ 22281541, 22385461, Fax: 91-80-22286611;
• No. 2-2-1, 167/2H, 1st Floor, Near Railway Bridge, Tilak Nagar, Main Road, Hyderabad-500044 (Andhra Pradesh),
✆ 55501745, Fax: 91-40-27560041;
Bus.Intt.: Pub.; **Spl.:** Beh.Sci., Soc.Sci., Sci., Applied, Med. & Env., Law, Comm., Man., Eco., Comp. Sci., etc.

HIMALAYAN BOOKS
17-L, Connaught Place, New Delhi-110001
Bus.Intt.: Exp.

HIMALAYAN INSTITUTE HOSPITAL TRUST
Swami Rama Nagar, P.O. Doiwala, Distt. Dehradun-248140 (Uttarakhand)
✆ 2412068, Fax: 91-135-2412008
✉ hintsee@sancharnet.in
Hd.Org.: Vijay Dhasmana; **Spl.:** Books, CD's, Video

HIMALAYAN INSTITUTE PUBLICATIONS
425, Ground Floor, Sant Nagar, East of Kailash, New Delhi-110065
✆ 26405422, 26445422, 26446368, Fax: 26476432
✉ arun@himalayaninstitute.org, hidelhi@himalayaninstitute.org, hip34@hotmail.com
www.himalayaninstitute.org
Estd.: 1999; **Hd.Org.:** Rahul Agnihorti; **Bus.Intt.:** Pub., Exp.; **Spl.:** Yoga & Sprituality, General Books

HIMALAYAN INTERNATIONAL INSTITUTE OF YOGA, SCIENCE & PHILOSOPHY
24A, Malviya Nagar, New Delhi-110017
✆ 26469349
Estd.: 1972; **Hd.Org.:** Durga Prasad; **Bus.Intt.:** Pub.; **Spl.:** Yoga, Phil. etc. in English

HIMALAYAN PUBLISHERS
Legi Shopping Complex, Bank Tinali, Post Box 177, Itanagar-791111 (Arunachal Pradesh)
✆ 2218390, Fax: 2217066
Hd.Org.: B.B. Pandey; **Bus.Intt.:** Pub. & Dist.; **Spl.:** Soc.Sci., Mang., Litt.

HIMAKAR PRAKASHAN
80/17, Gulraj Qutr. III, Behind Parsi Temple, Nazeerabad Rd., Ajmer-305001 (Rajasthan)
Hd.Org.: Chandra Mohan Handa

HIMANSU BOOK DEPOT
10-1-20/A, Sisu Complex, Asilmetta Jn., Visakhapatnam (Andhra Pradesh)
✆ 2509838, 2508938
Estd.: 1997; **Hd.Org.:** M.L.N. Rao
Br.: A.G. Road, Vizianagaram (Andhra Pradesh) ✆ (O) 08922-225422, 231199 (R) 222134 ▮ 9440194455;
Hd.Org.: K.V.S.K. Prasad
Bus.Intt.: Rt.; **Spl.:** Gen. and Trade, Acad., Professional, Children Books and Greeting Cards (Indian and Foreign Books)

HIMANI PRAKASHAN (P) LTD.
11099, Doriwalan, East Park Rd., Karol Bagh, New Delhi-110005
✆ 23675821, 23635692; Fax: 91-11-23510045
Hd.Org.: Balraj Radhan

HIMANSHU BOOK COMPANY
7, Shri Jayendrapuri Bhavan, Near Sanyas Ashram, Ellisbridge, Ashram Rd., Ahmedabad-380006 (Gujarat)
✆ 079-26579685, 6583782
✉ hbc@icenet.net
Estd.: 1965; **Hd.Org.:** Vinit Shah; **Bus.Intt.:** Rt.; **Spl.:** Gen. and Trade, Acad., Professional and Children Books (Indian & Foreign Books)

HIMANSHU PUBLICATIONS
5K-51, Ram Singh Ki Badi, Sector-11, Udaipur-313001 (Rajasthan)
✆ 2583102

HIMKAR PRAKASHAN
80/17, Guljar Quarters No. 3, Behind Parsi Mandir, Nasirabad Rd., Ajmer-305001 (Rajasthan)
✆ 2425804
Hd.Org.: C.M. Handa

HIND BOOK DEPOT
Gandhi Market, Bankipore, Patna-800004 (Bihar)
Bus.Intt.: Pub. and B.S.

HIND BOOK HOUSE
A-29, New Friends Colony, New Delhi-110065
✆ (O) 26831827, 26843576 (R) 26843576, Fax: 26831827, 23725881
✉ hindbookhouse@vsnl.com, hindbookhouse@rediffmail.com
Prop.: Prithvi Raj, **Bus.Intt.:** WS & L.S.; **Spl.:** Humanities, Sci. & Tech.

HIND LAW HOUSE
28-A, Budhwar Peth, Appa Balwant Chowk, Pune-411002 (Maharashtra)
✆ (O) 2456535, 2453920 (R) 2464136, Fax: 2456535
Estd.: 1973; **Bus.Intt.:** Pub., Exp., Imp., L.S., Rt., WS, B.S.; **Spl.:** Law Sub.

HIND POCKET BOOKS (P) LTD.
18-19, Dilshad Garden, G.T. Road, Shahdara, New Delhi-110095
✆ 2297792, 2297793
Fax: 91-11-2282332

HIND PUSTAK BHANDAR
10-B, Netaji Subhash Marg, Darya Ganj, New Delhi-110002
✆ (O) 23268292-93 (R) 22917663, 22514581, Fax: 23280567
Estd.: 1976; **Hd.Org.:** Ramesh Kumar Gupta
Br.: J-2/16, Darya Ganj, Opp. Happy School, New Delhi-110002
✆ 23276539, 23272783/84, Fax: 23260518
✉ info@pustakmahal.com
Bus.Intt.: Pub.; **Spl.:** Self-improvement, health, Rel., Fitness, Comp., Mang., Alternative Med., Cookery, Children's Books

HIND PUSTAK BHANDAR
Gandhi Rd., Porbandar (Gujarat)

HIND-YUGM
1161, Sanjay Colony, Faridabad-121005 (Haryana)
▮ 98117416106
✉ hindyugm@gmail.com
www.hindyugm.com
Hd.Org.: Ajay Yadav
Spl.: Hindi language and literature

HINDI ACADEMY
Samudai Bhavan, Padam Nagar, Kishanganj, Delhi-110007
✆ 23693118, 23694562, Fax: 91-11-23696897
✉ hindiacademy_delhi@vsnl.net
Hd.Org.: Nanak Chand; **Bus.Intt.:** Pub.; **Spl.:** Hindi Language and Litt.

HINDI BOOK CENTRE
4/5-B, Asaf Ali Road, New Delhi-110002
✆ 23286757, 23258993, 23261696, 23268651, Fax: 91-11-23273335, 26481565
✉ info@hindibook.com, starpub@satyam.net.in
www.hindibook.com
Estd.: 1972; **Prt.:** Amar Nath, Anil K. Verma, Sunil Verma, Sanjay Verma; **Bus.Intt.:** B.S., Dist., Pub.; **Spl.:** Gen. & Acad. Books. Also stocking Punjabi, Urdu and other Indian Language Publications, Language Dictionaries

HINDI MADHYAM KARYANVAYA NIDESHALAYA
University of Delhi, Barrack Nos. 2 & 4, Cavalry Lines, Delhi-110007
✆ 27666839

Hd.Org.: Sujata Roy; **Bus.Intt.:** Provider; **Spl.:** Low-cost Hindi Textbooks and Reference Books to University Students on Soc.Sci. and Humanities

HINDI PRACHARAK PUBLICATIONS PVT. LTD.
C-21/30, Pishachmochan, Varanasi-221010 (Uttar Pradesh)
✆ (O) & (R) 2350425, 2356850, 2358470, Fax: 2350670
Estd.: 1905; **Hd.Org.:** Vijay Prakash Beri
Br.: 23, Kabir Rd., Kolkata-26 (West Bengal)
✆ 23225542, 2385852
Bus.Intt.: Pub.; **Spl.:** Hindi Litt., Children's Books and Monthly Journal *Hindi Pracharak Patrika*

HINDI PUSTAK BHAWAN
C-19, C.C. Colony, Opp. Rana Pratap Bagh, Delhi-110007

HINDI SAHITYA BHANDAR
55, Chopatiya Rd., Chowk, Lucknow-226001 (Uttar Pradesh)
Hd.Org.: Mahinder Kumar Mehra

HINDI SAHITYA NIKETAN
16, Sahitya Vihar, Bijnor-246701 (Uttar Pradesh)
✆ (O) 01342-262375 (R) 263232
✉ giriraj3100@rediffmail.com
🌐 www.hindisahityaniketan.com
Estd.: 1964; **Prop.:** Dr. Giri Raj Sharan Agarwal; **Bus.Intt.:** Pub.; **Spl.:** Hindi Litt.

HINDI SAHITYA SADAN
2, B.D. Chambers, 10/54, Deshbandhu Gupta Rd., Near Karol Bagh Police Station, New Delhi-110005
✆ 51545969, Fax: 23553624
✉ indiabooks@rediffmail.com
Hd.Org.: Padmesh Dutt; **Bus.Intt.:** Pub. and B.S.; **Spl.:** Novels, *Vedas* and Books on Phil. and Hist. in Hindi

HINDI SAHITYA SAMITI
Gurur Distt., Durg-491227 (Madhya Pradesh)

HINDI SAHITYA SAMMELAN
12, Sammelan Marg, Allahabad-211003 (Uttar Pradesh)
✆ 2404193, 2404191, Fax: 2404191
Estd.: 1910; **Hd.Org.:** Vibhuti Mishra; **Bus.Intt.:** Promoter; **Spl.:** Hindi Language through Publication of Literary, Rel. and Gen. Books

HINDI SAHITYA SANSAR UDYOG
1543, Nai Sarak, Delhi-110006
✆ (O) 23269443 (R) 22213191
Hd.Org.: Mahender Kumar Sharma

HINDI SEVA SADAN
Halan Ganj, Mathura-281001 (Uttar Pradesh)
✆ 2406633, 2409226
Hd.Org.: Dinesh Goyal

HINDU WRITERS FORUM
129-B, MIG Flats, Rajouri Garden, New Delhi-110027
✆ 91-11-25115281
Hd.Org.: K.V. Paliwal
Bus.Intt.: Pub., **Spl.:** Books on Hindi language, religion, philosophy, history and Indian culture in Hindi

HINDUSTAN BOOK AGENCY (INDIA)
F-19, Green Park Extension, New Delhi-110016
✆ 26163294-96, Telefax: 011-26193297
✉ hba@vsnl.com
Estd.: 1947; **Prt.:** Devendra K. Jain; **Bus.Intt.:** WS and L.S.; **Spl.:** Sci./Tech. Books and Microfiches

HINDUSTAN BOOK STORE
Raniganj, Gaya-824210 (Bihar)

HINDUSTAN LAW BOOK COMPANY
15/5, Jamir Lane, Ballygunge, Kolkata-700019 (West Bengal)
✆ 24405837, Fax: 24407669
✉ Jagadish@cal-vsnl.net.in, hlbc@cal2.vsnl.net.in
Atten-Hindustan Law Book Co.
Estd.: 1986; **Prop.:** D.P. Mukherjee
Br.: 8/2, K.S. Roy Rd., 1st Floor, Near High Court, Kolkata-700001 (West Bengal)
✆ 22484231, Fax: 24405837
Bus.Intt.: Pub., WS, L.S. and Rt. Exp., Sub.Ag.

HINDUSTAN LIBRARY
54/9, College St., Kolkata-700073 (West Bengal)

HINDUSTAN PUBLICATION
81, Angappan St., Chennai-600001 (Tamil Nadu)
✆ 2510450
Hd.Org.: Nafees; **Bus.Intt.:** Dist. and Pub.; **Spl.:** Islamic Litt. in English and Tamil

HINDUSTAN PUBLICATIONS
Mumtaz Building, Ballimaran, 2034-35, Qasimjan St., Delhi-110006
Bus.Intt.: Exp.

HINDUSTAN PUBLISHING CORPORATION
4805/24, First Floor, Bharat Ram Rd., Darya Ganj, New Delhi-110002
✆ (O) 23254401, 23254402 (R) 26193544, Fax: 91-11-26193511, 23274405
✉ hpc@vsnl.com, hpcpd@hpc.cc
🌐 www.hpc.cc, www.thebookservice.com

Estd.: 1959; Hd.Org.: Prabhat K. Jain; Bus.Intt.: Pub., Dist. and Global Exp.; Spl.: Acad. Journals and Books on Math., Soc. Sci., Fisheries, Man. and Indology

HINDUSTAN SUBSCRIPTION SERVICE
PMG Complex, 3rd Floor, 57, South Usman Rd., T. Nagar, Chennai-600017 (Tamil Nadu)
✆ 24342219, Fax: 24342219
hindsub@vsnl.com
Estd.: 1982; **Prop.:** S. Raghupathy; **Bus.Intt.:** Sub.Ag. & B.S.; **Spl.:** Sci. & Tech.

HINDUSTANI ACADEMY
12-D, Kamala Nehru Marg, Allahabad-211001 (Uttar Pradesh)
✆ 2600625
Hd.Org.: Harimohan Malviya; **Bus.Intt.:** Pub.; **Spl.:** Select Urdu and Hindi Litt., as also Quarterly Magazine *Hindustani*

HIRA BHAIYA PRAKASHAN
65, Patrakar Colony, Kanadia Rd., Indore-452001 (Madhya Pradesh)

HIRALAL PRINTING WORKS LTD.
Apt. No. 5, 3rd Floor, Readymoney Terrace, 167, Dr. A.B. Rd., Worli Naka, Mumbai-400018 (Maharashtra)
✆ 24936216, Fax: 24929204
Estd.: 1981; **Hd.Org.:** Rakesh Kumar Agrawal
Br.: Plot No. D-41/1, MIDC TTC Indl. Area, Opp. Turbhe Tele Exchange, Turbhe, New Mumbai-400613 (Maharashtra)
✆ 27672726, 27683013, Fax: 27682391
Bus.Intt.: Pub., WS, Exp., L.S. and Rt.

HITESH SAHITYA
C/o Popular Book Depot, Chaura Rasta, G015, S.S. Ravar Dhamani St., Jaipur (Rajasthan)
✆ 2325965
Hd.Org.: Satyadev Sharma; **Bus.Intt.:** Pub.; **Spl.:** Litt., Health, Astrology and Children's Books etc.

HOBBY PUBLISHERS
Ambika Market, Vaikom, Kottayam-686114 (Kerala)
Estd.: 1952; **Prop.:** N.K. Jose
Bus.Intt.: Pub.

HODDER ARNOLD INDIA
India Marketing Office, 4262-3, Ground Floor, Ansari Rd., Darya Ganj, New Delhi-110002
✆ 23270718, Fax: 23267224
arnoldindia@vivagroupindia.net
Hd.Org.: Vinod Vasishtha; **Bus.Intt.:** Pub.; **Spl.:** Textbooks for College-level Students on Sci., Self-improvement and Edu.

HOLYFAITH INTERNATIONAL
Gulab Bhawan, 6, Bahadur Shah Zafar Marg, New Delhi-110002
✆ 22518122, Fax: 91-11-22546557
holyfaith1@vsnl.net
www.mbdbooks.com
Hd.Org.: Ashok Kumar Malhotra
Bus.Intt.: Pub.; **Spl.:** School books from nursery to tenth standard

HOMEOPATHIC MEDICAL PUBLISHERS
20, Station Rd., Santacruz (West), Mumbai-400054 (Maharashtra)
Bus.Intt.: Exp.

HONESTY SUBSCRIPTION AGENCY
Bhiwandiwala Terrace, Shop No. 8, J.S.S. Rd., No. 618, Dhobi Talao, Mumbai-400002 (Maharashtra)
✆ 22088558, 22088568, Fax: 91-22-22086959

HONNA PRAKASHANA
102, 6th Cross Malleswaram, Bangalore-560003 (Karnataka)
✆ 23343253
Prop.: Dr. H. Sreenivasaiah
Bus.Intt.: Pub.; **Spl.:** Edu. Books, Gandhian Phil. Sci., Yoga and Travelogue in Kannada

HOPE INDIA PUBLICATIONS
85, Sector 23, Gurgaon-122017 (Haryana)
✆ 2367308, Fax: 91-11-26211396
9911402692
info@hopeindiapublications.com
www.hopeindiabookclub.com
Estd.: 2000; **Prop.:** Nitin Yadav; **Bus.Intt.:** Pub. & Dist.; **Spl.:** Soc.Sci., Humanities, Tech. and Reference Books

HORTICULTURE & ALLIED PUBLISHERS
27/3, Chakraberia Lane, Kolkata-700020 (West Bengal)

HORIZON: THE BOOK SHOP
Mumbai (Maharashtra)
✆ 26186278, 26188475
horizonbookshop@vsnl.com
Bus.Intt.: B.S.

HORIZON PUBLISHERS
44-B, Lowther Rd., Near Rising Sun Public School, Allahabad-211002 (Uttar Pradesh)
✆ 2461159, 2642780
horizonpub@hotmail.com
Estd.: 1986; **Prop.:** Raj Nayar
Bus.Intt.: Pub., WS, L.S. & Rt.; **Spl.:** Humanities & Soc.Sci., Sci. & Tech., Law, Med.

HOSANNA BOOKS
Hosanna Nagar, P.O. Box 31, Palai-686575 (Kerala)
Estd.: 1976; **Hd.Org.:** Joseph Pulikunnel; **Bus.Intt.:** B.S.

HOUSE PRIDE BOOKS
Goa
✆ 2515030, 2513429, Fax: 2513020
✉ manda_nana@hotmail.com
Bus.Intt.: B.S. & Dist.

HUMAN BIOLOGY PUBLICATIONS SOCIETY
Deptt. of Human Biology, Punjabi University, Patiala-147002 (Punjab)

HUMANA PRESS INC.
New No. 8, Old No. 32, Second Main Rd., CIT Nagar, East, Chennai-600035 (Tamil Nadu)
✆ 24346244, 24346266, Fax: 24346529
✉ itpsesha@giasmd01.vsnl.net.in
Hd.Org.: R. Seshadri; **Bus.Intt.:** Pub.; **Spl.:** Sci. and Med. in English

HUSAIN PUSTAK KENDRA
Asandapur, Gopalganj (Bihar)

HUSAINI BOOK DEPOT
Chaar Kaman, Pattarghatti, Hyderabad-500004 (Andhra Pradesh)

HYDARI BOOK DEPOT
Chhatta Bazar, Hyderabad (Andhra Pradesh)

HYDER & SONS
Gulzar Houz, Hyderabad (Andhra Pradesh)

HYDERABAD PUBLISHERS
10-2-5-8/1, A.C. Guards, Hyderabad-500004 (Andhra Pradesh)
Estd.: 1990; **Bus.Intt.:** Pub. and B.S.; **Spl.:** Adv. Books for Lib., Hist., Prehistory and Archaeology

■ ■ ■

I.A.B. PUBLISHERS AND DISTRIBUTORS PVT. LTD.
B-9, Ashoka Niketan (Behind Anand Vihar), Delhi-110092
✆ 22161701, 22161702, 23266480, 23266681, Fax: 011-22167103
Telefax: 031-79002 GITI-IN
✉ amit_iabpd@hotmail.com
Estd.: 1989; **Dir.:** Mrs. Kamlesh Jain, Amit Jain; **Bus.Intt.:** WS, Rt., L.S., Sub.Ag., Pub.'s Rep.; **Spl.:** Fiction, Journals & Magazines, Fine Arts, Travel/Tourism, Cooking, Cuisine, Children & Gen. Books

I.B. PUBLICATIONS & DISTRIBUTORS
1/9822, West Yorakh Park, St. No. 2, Shahdara, Delhi-110032
✆ 55298293 ▮ 9891190178, Fax: 22823839
✉ sanjeev-seth_in@yahoo.com
Hd.Org.: Dinesh Arora; **Bus.Intt.:** Pub., B.S., L.S., WS; **Spl.:** Humanities & Soc.Sci., Sci. & Tech., Comp., Med., Mang.

I.B.A. PUBLICATIONS
6269-P, Nicholson Rd., Ambala Cantt.-133001 (Haryana)
✆ 2630125, 2640126, Fax: 91-11-2601862
✉ ibapublications@rediffmail.com
Hd.Org.: S.B. Banerjee; **Bus.Intt.:** Pub.; **Spl.:** Gen. and Reference Books in English and Hindi

I.B.D. PUBLISHER AND DISTRIBUTORS
S-5, Akarshan Bhawan, 3rd Floor, Ansari Rd., Darya Ganj, New Delhi-110002
✆ 23251094, 23259102 ▮ 9811225032, Fax: 23259102
✉ piyush_gahlot@rediffmail.com
Estd.: 2001; **Prop.:** Amal Gahlot; **Bus.Intt.:** Rt., WS, Pub., L.S.; **Spl.:** Acad., Sci., Pure and Applied

I.B.I. DOTCOM PVT. LTD.
J-436, Baljeet Nagar, Prem Nagar Rd., New Delhi-110008
✆ 25875330, 25871272, Fax: 25786769
✉ ibicom@bol.net.in, ibicom@rediffmail.com
Estd.: 2000; **Man.Dir.:** Manish Bhatia; **Bus.Intt.:** Directories, Softwares; **Spl.:** Online Ref. Book on Book Trade

I.B.M. BOOK CENTRE
1st Floor, Tanibai Niwas, (Above Cleanex Laundry), Station Rd., Wadala, Mumbai-31 (Maharashtra)
✆ (O) 24150178 (R) 24149880, 24168220, Fax: 4162561
✉ ibm@bom3.vsnl.net.in
Estd.: 1960; **Bus.Intt.:** B.S.; Sci. & Tech., Med., (Industrial Med.), Comm. & Man., Humanities, Law (Industrial), Gen. Books, Professional like Insurance, Banking, Financial Services etc.

I.B.T. PUBLISHERS & DISTRIBUTORS
A-85, 2nd Floor, Derawal Nagar, Opp. Model Town-II, New Delhi-110009
✆ (O) 27143827, 27116769 (R) 27143827, Fax: 9-11-27234817
Estd.: 1977; **Prop.:** D.S. Chaudhary; **Bus.Intt.:** Rt., Pub., L.S.

ICFAI UNIVERSITY PRESS
1012-1013, Hemkunt Chambers, 89, Nehru Place, New Delhi-110019
✆ 66601854, Fax: 91-11-41617429
✉ srikar@icfaipress.org
🌐 www.icfaipress.org
Hd.Org.: N.J. Yasaswy; **Bus.Intt.:** Pub.; **Spl.** Books on mang., eco., insurance, finance, IT, training and general books. Also pub. magazines and journals

I.C.R.I.E.R.
40, Lodi Rd., New Delhi-110003

I.D.G. BOOKS INDIAN PVT. LTD.
4435/7, Ansari Rd., Darya Ganj, New Delhi-110002
✆ 23260877, 23270877, Fax: 23275895
✉ idgbooks@vsnl.com, idgbooks@bol.net.in
Hd.Org.: Vikas Gupta; **Bus.Intt.:** Pub. of Books on Comp.; Rep. for IDG Books Worldwide, U.S.A.

I.I.M.S. PUBLICATIONS
6/18, Jangpura Extension, Near Masjid Rd., (Double Story), New Delhi-110014
✆ 24329106, 24316915, 24311946, Fax: 24313503
✉ iimspub@nde.vsnl.net.in
Estd.: 1982; **Dir.:** Gopal K. Puri; **Bus.Intt.:** Pub.; **Spl.:** Humanities & Soc.Sci., Sci. & Tech., Gen. & Fiction etc.

I.I.T. SOFT (P) LTD.
A-1/308, Safdarjung Enclave, New Delhi-110029

I.J.C.P. GROUP OF PUBLICATIONS
New Delhi
✆ 26239415, 26239416, Fax: 26239411
✉ kkhcfl@giasd01.vsnl.net.in
Bus.Intt.: Pub.; **Spl.:** Med. Journals

I.K. INTERNATIONAL PVT. LTD.
S-25, Green Park Extension, Uphaar Cinema Market, New Delhi-110016

© 41755552-4, 26532251, ▮ 9810489922, Fax: 91-11-26532252
@ ik_in@vsnl.net
www.ikbooks.com
Hd.Org.: Krishan Makhijani
Retail Outlet: S-7 & 8, Green Park, Main Market, New Delhi-110016
© 26531279-80, Fax: 26532252
@ ik_in@vsnl.net
www.knowledgestoreonline.com
Hd.Org.: Krishan Makhijani
Br.: G-4 "Embassy Centre", 11 Crescent Rd., Kumara Park-East, Bangalore-560001
© 080-2350984/85, Fax: 080-2350991
@ ik_bang@vsnl.net
• A-6, Royal Industrial Estate, Naigaum Cross Rd., Wadala, Mumbai-400031 © 022-24173527-29, Fax: 022-24173526 @ ik_mumbai@vsnl.net
Bus.Intt.: Pub. and Dist.; **Spl.:** Books, Journals and CD-ROMs on Soc.Sci., Engg., Art and Craft, etc.

I.K.S. PUBLISHERS & DISTRIBUTORS
P.B. No. 76, Srinagar-190001 (Jammu and Kashmir)
@ ikssgr@del1.vsnl.net.in
Hd.Org.: G.M. Butt
Br.: 2002, Bul-buli Khana, Turkman Gate, Delhi-110006
© 23257706, Fax: 23279008
@ ikssgr@del2.vsnl.net.in, ikssgr@vsnl.com
Bus.Intt.: Pub.; **Spl.:** Hist., Politics, Geo. etc.

I.M.H.
A-48, Kailash Colony, New Delhi-110048
© 26433126
Hd.Org.: Badal Ray; **Bus.Intt.:** Pub. and Distributor of Bengali Books on all sub.

I.Q. TECH MEDIA PVT. LTD.
3rd Floor, Jhalawar, E.S. Patanwala Compound, L.B.S. Marg, Opp. Shreyas Cinema, Ghatkopar, Mumbai-400086
© 55969222, Fax: 91-22-55969739
@ janardhan@iqtechmedia.com, info@developeriq.com, raulojanardhan@hotmail.com
Ch.Exe.: Mr. Anoop Goyal; **Bus.Intt.:** Pub.; **Spl.:** Magazine, Software/Games and CDs

ISPCK (INDIAN SOCIETY FOR PROMOTING CHRISTIAN KNOWLEDGE)
Post Box 1585, 1654, Madarsa Road, Kashmere Gate, Delhi-110006
© 23866323, Fax: 91-11-23865490
@ ashish@ispck.org.in
www.ispck.org.in
Hd.Org.: Ashish Amos
Br.: ISPCK Book Shop, 51, Chowringhee Road, Kolkata-700071 (West Bengal)
© 91-33-22821804, @ sales@ispck.org.in;
• Opp. Liberty Cinema, Residency Road, Sadar, Nagpur-440001 (Maharastra)
© 91-71-22543425, @ sales@ispck.org.in
• ISPCK Chotanagpur Diocesan Bookshop (H.P.D. Center), P.O. Church Road, Ranchi-834001 (Bihar)
• ISPCK Jabalpur Diocesan Bookshop, Mission Boys Hostel, Jarbhata, Bilashpur-495001 (Madhya Pradesh);
• The Church of South India, C.S.I. Center, No. 5, White Road, Royapettah, Chennai-600014 (Tamil Nadu);
• Andhra Christian Theological College, Lower Tank Bund Road, Gandhi Nagar (P.O.), Hyderabad-500080 (Andhra Pradesh)
© 91-33-22421804, @ sales@ispck.org.in;
• Leonard Theological College, Post Box 36, Civil Lines, Jabalpur-482001 (Madhya Pradesh);
• ISPCK Christian Book Depot, Darjeeling, Diocese of Eastern Himilaya CNI, Diocesan Centre, Gandhi Road, Darjeeling (West Bengal)
© 91-33-4256389 ▮ 91113865490
@ ispck@nde.vsnl.net.in; **Bus.Intt.:** Pub.; **Spl.:** Books on philosophy, religion, sociology, indology and theology

I.S.R. PUBLICATION LTD.
10, Chowringhee Rd., Kolkata-700013 (West Bengal)
© 22805149, Fax: 91-33-22807370
Hd.Org.: S. Mahanti

IBADUSUK BOOKS AGENCY
Jackson Trace Rd., Laban, Shillong-793004 (Maghalaya)
© 2228357

ICHAMATI PRAKASHANI
A-134, College St. Market, Kolkata-7 (West Bengal)

ICON PUBLICATIONS PVT. LTD.
4331-3, Ansari Rd., Darya Ganj, New Delhi-110002
© (O) 23290091 (R) 22374923 ▮ 9818261853, Fax: 23290067
@ iconpub@eth.net
Hd.Org.: Rajiv Gupta; **Bus.Intt.:** Pub.; **Spl.:** Self-improvement, Phil., Rel., Health, Beauty, Astrology, Biographies, Current Affairs, Soc. Issues etc.

IDARA ADBIYAT-E-DILLI
Zayyed Barqui Press, Ballimaran, Delhi-110006

IDARA EXPORTS
168/2, Jha House, Hazrat Nizamuddin,
New Delhi-110013
✆ 26956832-33, Fax: 91-11-26942787
sales@idara.com
www.idara.com
Estd.: 1993; **Prt.:** Mohammad Anas;
Bus.Intt.: Pub., Dist., Exp.; **Spl.:** *Holy Quran*, Islam, Med., Engg., Comp. and Children Books

IDARA FIKRE JADEED
922, Kucha Rohella Khan, Tiraha Behram, Darya Ganj, New Delhi-110002
✆ 23281880, 2278243
Hd.Org.: Ajay Kumar Tindon; **Bus.Intt.:** Pub. and B.S.; **Spl.:** Urdu Fiction, Non-fiction, Children's and Islamic Litt.

IDARA KITAB UL SHIFA
2075, First Floor, Masjid Mazar Wali Naher Khan St., Kucha Chelan, Darya Ganj,
New Delhi-110002
✆ 23283494, Fax: 91-11-26987191
Hd.Org.: Syed Asad Hussain;
Bus.Intt.: Pub. and B.S.; **Spl.:** *Unani Tibbia* Books and Islamic Litt.

IDARA SHAHADAT-E-HAQUE
7/1, Jogabai, Jamia Nagar, Delhi-110025
Estd.: 1962; **Hd.Org.:** Khalid Hamidi

IDARA TABLEEGHE-E-DEEN
Deoband-247554, Distt. Saharanpur
(Uttar Pradesh)
Estd.: 1983; **Hd.Org.:** Waseem Ahmed Ghazi

IDEA INTERNATIONAL PUBLISHERS
4564, A/16, Ground Floor, Darya Ganj,
New Delhi-110002
✆ 23285054, 22777367
Fax: 91-11-23285055
Hd.Org.: Adarsh Pocali;
Bus.Intt.: Retailer, Pub. and L.S.;
Spl.: Academic, Commerce, Technical, Science Pure & Applied, Fiction, Soc.Sci. & Medical Books

IDEAL BOOK CENTRE
Chak Musallahpur, Patna (Bihar)
✆ (R) 0612-2663499

IDEAL BOOK CO.
Chabidas Rd., Dadar (West), Mumbai-400028
(Maharashtra)
✆ 24302126

IDEAL BOOK SELLER
WZ-88, Jwala Heri, Paschim Vihar,
New Delhi-110063
Estd.: 1999; **Prop.:** Rajesh Sharma;
Bus.Intt.: Rt., L.S., WS; **Spl.:** Humanities & Soc.Sci, Mang. & Comm., Engg. & Tech.

IDEAL BOOK SERVICE
I-Parvati Niwas, Khanapur Rd., Tilak Wadi,
Belgaum-6 (Karnataka)

IDEAL BOOK STALL
208/2, Rashbehari Avenue, Kolkata-700029
(West Bengal)

IDEAL PUBLISHERS
9/7B, Ramanath Majumder St.,
Kolkata-700009 (West Bengal)
Hd.Org.: Animesh Mandal

IDEAL PUBLISHING HOUSE PVT. LTD..
14, Veejay Towers, First Floor,
150 Ft. Bypass Road, Velacherry,
Chennai (Tamil Nadu)
✆ 91-44-42154259, 42154359
idealpublishinghouse@yahoo.co.in
Hd.Org.: K.S. Dhanasekar
Bus.Intt.: Pub.; **Spl.:** Maps, tourist guides and synthetic wall maps

IDEAL, 'THE DESIGNERS' BOOK SHOP
1st Floor, Doli Chamber, (Strand Cinema), Colaba,
Mumbai-400005 (Maharashtra)
✆ 22834452

IDEAS BOOKS
A-84, South Extension Part-II, New Delhi-110049
✆ 26251478, 26256466, Fax: 26256466
Hd.Org.: M.S. Lehri; **Bus.Intt.:** Dist.;
Spl.: Art, Arch., Interior Designing, Advt., Graphics, Photography, Fashion Designing, Jewellery, Digital Art, etc.

IDIOM BOOK SELLERS
Post Box No. 32, Cochin-682001 (Kerala)
✆ 91-484-2220432, 2224075
Hd.Org.: Shiva Kumar

IMAGE BOOKS
A3/10H, Sir William Jones Sarai,
Kolkata-700071 (West Bengal)

IMMAN FOUNDATION
Najafi House, 159, Nishanpara Rd.,
Mumbai-400009 (Maharashtra)
✆ 022-23720350, Fax: 23799559
Telefax: 11-73448 EMANIN
Hd.Org.: Moulana Alhaj Syed; **Bus.Intt.:** Pub.;
Spl.: Islam in Urdu, Hindi Gujarati and English

IMPERIAL BOOK HOUSE
56, College St., Kolkata-700073 (West Bengal)

IMPERIAL PUBLISHING HOUSE
T.C. No. 11/706, Jaya Sadan, PWD Division,
Office Rd., Trivandrum-695033 (Kerala)

IMPEX STATISTICS SERVICES
Mumbai (Maharashtra)

✆ 22080518, 22088151, Fax: 22055444
booksell@vsnl.net
Bus.Intt.: Imp., Exp. & Pub.

IMPRESSIONS
14, Saini Encalve, Vikas Marg Extn.,
Delhi-110092

IMPRINT
No. 112 AMSM Building, Beach Rd.,
Quilon-691001 (Kerala)

IMPRINT BOOKS
Boyce Pharmaceutical Building, Kadapakada,
Kollam-691008 (Kerala)
✆ 276809, 2741280
Estd.: 1990, **Prop.**: A. Rahiyanath Beevi; **Bus.Intt.**: Pub. and B.S.; **Spl.**: Gen. Books in Malayalam

IMRAN BOOK DEPOT
4/203, Lalita Park, Laxmi Nagar, Delhi-110092
✆ 22507486, 23287486, Fax: 22428786
imranbookdepot@vsnl.net
www.imranbookdepot.com
Hd.Org.: Abdul Rasheed Khan; **Bus.Intt.**: B.S.; **Spl.**: Islam in Urdu and English

INDCHEM RESEARCH AND DEVELOPMENT
Laboratory Plot No. 47, Developed Plots for Electrical & Electronics Industries, Seevaram Village Perungudi, Chennai-96 (Tamil Nadu)

INDEPENDENT BOOKS
135, Him Varsha Apartments,
103, I.P. Extension, Delhi-110092
✆ 22218624, 22411221
Hd.Org.: Vivek Sethi; **Bus.Intt.**: B.S. and Dist.; **Spl.**: Arch., Interior Design, Advertising, Man., Cooking, as also Children's Books

INDEPENDENT PUBLISHERS GROUP
C/o 'Tulika Books', 35-A/1, Shahpur Jat,
New Delhi-110049
✆ 26491448, 27666067 ▮ 9811692261
ipg.delhi@gmail.com
Hd.Org.: Mohd. Aslam
Bus.Intt.: Pub., Wholesaler, B.S.

INDEPENDENT PUBLISHING CO.
4774, Deputy Ganj, Sadar Bazar,
Delhi-110006

INDERPRASTH PRAKASHAN
K-71, Krishan Nagar, Delhi-110051
✆ 22214376, 22232274
Hd.Org.: Ashok Kumar Sharma

INDEX INTERNATIONAL
B-406, Vardhaman C.G.H.S.,
Mayur Vihar Phase-I Extn., New Delhi-110091
✆ 22714005, 22713475, Fax: 22714005
dorai@del3.vsnl.net.in

Dir.: S. Mahadevan; **Bus.Intt.**: WS, L.S.;
Spl.: Acad., Beh.Sci., Soc.Sci., Tech.

INDIA BIBLE PUBLISHERS
C-3/10, DDA Flats, East of Kailash,
New Delhi-110065
✆ 26849304

INDIA BOOK CENTRE
Ashok Rajpath, Chowhatta, Patna-800004 (Bihar)
✆ 2670681 (R) 2648345 ▮ 9835022986
ibcpatna@yahoo.com
Hd.Org.: K.K. Agrawal; **Bus.Intt.**: WS, Rt. & L.S.;
Spl.: Comp., Engg., Mang., Arts, Sci., Comm., C.A. CAIIB Competitive Books and School Books

INDIA BOOKS COMPANY
WZ-D14, Dayal Sir Colony,
Near Shri Nirankari Gurdwara, Uttam Nagar,
New Delhi-110059
✆ 91-11-25331361, 64527190
indiabookscompany@yahoo.co.in
Hd.Org.: Sanjay Kumar Gupta
Bus.Intt.: Pub., Dist. and library supplier

INDIA BOOK DISTRIBUTORS (BOMBAY) LTD.
1108, Arcadia, 195, Nariman Point,
Mumbai-400021 (Maharashtra)
✆ 40769200-01/15-16, 22825220, 22824646, 22872528, 22872532, 22824691,
Fax: 91-22-22872531
ibdho@ibd.co.in, websales@ibd.co.in
www.ibdwebstore.com
Estd.: 1980; **Man.Dir.**: Harkin Chatlani
Sales Sh.: India Book Distributors (Bombay) Ltd., New Majestic Shopping Centre, Basement 2, 19, & 20, Sir Jagannath Shankar Sheth Marg, Girgaum, Mumbai-400004 (Maharashtra),
✆ 23829508, 23879421, 23810142,
Fax: 91-22-23879421
booksales@ibd.co.in
Br.: Cindrella Apartments, 602,
Sachapir Street, Pune-411001 (Maharashtra)
✆ 91-20-26330636, 26359189
salespune@ibd.co.in; • 101-102, 106 Mota Chambers, 1st Floor, 9, Cunningham Road, (Millers Road), Bangalore-560052 (Karnataka),
✆ 22264544, 22208123,
Fax: 91-80-22254419,
salesbangalore@ibd.co.in; • 3-2-870/3/5, V.N.R. Commercial Complex, 1st Floor, Station Road, Opp: Tourist Hotel, Kachiguda, Hyderabad-500027 (Andhra Pradesh)
✆ 24734891, Fax: 91-40-24608576
saleshyderabad@ibd.co.in; • New No. 33, Old No. 15, Srinivas Perumal Sannathi, II Street, Royapettah, Chennai-600014 (Tamil Nadu),
✆ 39181214-15, 39181216-17,

Fax: 91-44-28353172,
✉ customerservicechennai@ibd.co.in;
• B-8, Classic House, 12-14 Doctor Lane, Gole Market, New Delhi-110001,
✆ 23360263, 23340515, Fax: 91-11-23340230
✉ salesdelhi@ibd.co.in; • 13, KYD Street, 1st Floor, Kolkata-700016 (West Bengal)
✆ 22165765, 32900910, 30284360-61, 30284362-64, Fax: 91-33-22165765,
✉ rajesh@ibd.co.in
Rt. Sh.: Fountainhead, 41, Lavelle Road, Bangalore-560001 (Karnataka)
✆ 91-80-22219777, 22229759
✉ fhblore@satyam.net.in
• 27, Laxmi Towers, 45, Dr. Radha Krishna, Salai, Mylapore, Chennai-600004 (Tamil Nadu), ✆ 91-44-28114087, 28112650
✉ fhbooks@satyam.net.in
Bus.Intt.: Pub., WS, L.S. & Rt.;
Spl.: Juvenile/Children, Gen. & Fiction etc.

INDIA BOOK FAIR
Delhi
✆ 27403422, 27213267, Fax: 27462079
✉ sales@indiabookfair.com

INDIA BOOK HOUSE
213, Radhadamodar Ki Gali, Loha Mandi, Choura Rasta, Jaipur (Rajasthan)
✆ 2314983

INDIA BOOK HOUSE
United India Life Insurance Building, F-20, Connaught Circus, (Middle Circle) New Delhi-110001
✆ 23313014, 23313015, Fax: 23351974
✉ magazines-delhi@ibhworld.com
www.ibhworld.com
Hd.Org.: Padmini G. Mirchandani; **Bus.Intt.:** Imp., Dist. and Sub.Ag.; **Spl.:** International Magazines, Weeklies and Dailies

INDIA BOOK HOUSE LTD.
412, Tulsiani Chambers, 212, Backbay Reclamation, Nariman Point, Mumbai-400021 (Maharashtra)
✆ 22840165, 22840626, Fax: 22835099
✉ info@ibhworld.com, indiabookhouse@vsnl.com
Estd.: 1952; **Man.Dir.:** Deepak Mirchandani
Br.: Lal Hiranandani, India Book House Ltd., Humayun Court, 20-A, Lindsay St., Kolkata-700087 ✆ 033-22498096, 22498097, 22496911, Fax: 22496911
✉ ibhkolkata@ibhworld.com;
• India Book House Ltd., I L Hira, Wellington Estate, 24 C-in-C Rd., Chennai-600105
✆ 044-28275217, 28273893, Fax: 28273893
• India Book House Ltd., Devaru Bhat, 5th Main Rd., Gandhi Nagar, Bangalore-560009
✆ 080-22261305, 22252385, Fax: 22258104
✉ ibhbangalore@ibhworld.com;
• India Book House Ltd., Manohar David, 3-4-424, Narayanguda, Hyderabad-500029
✆ 040-27564945, 27561140, Fax: 27567146
✉ ibhhyderabad@ibhworld.com;
• India Book House Ltd., Chiman Shah, S.N. Prabhakar, 8-A, Milap Bhavan, Bahadur Shah Zafar Marg, New Delhi-110002,
✆ 011-23328465, 23351729, 23351742, Fax: 51509423, 23351974
✉ books-delhi@ibhworld.com;
• India Book House, Saiva Prakasha Sabha Bldg., 1st Floor, M.G. Rd., Thiruvananthapuram-695001
✆ 22475443, ✉ ibhtvm@eth.net;
• Paramount Book Agency, Arch#29, Below Mahalaxmi Bridge, Mahalaxmi, Mumbai-400034 ✆ 24925651, Fax: 24950392
✉ paramount@ibhworld.com;
• Paramount Book Agency, H.K. House, 1st Floor, Ashram Rd., Ahmedabad-380009
✆ 26577068, Fax: 26577051
✉ pbaahememdabad@ibhworld.com
• Paramount Book Agency, 17, Mg Rd., 1st Floor, Pune Camp, Pune-411001
✆ 26131261
✉ pbapune@ibhworld.com
Estd.: 1952; **Bus.Intt.:** Pub., WS, Imp., Exp., Sub.Ag.; **Spl.:** Sci. & Tech., Juvenile/Children, Gen. & Fiction etc.

INDIA BOOK HOUSE LIMITED
Fleet Building Mathuradas, Vasanji Rd., Maral Naka, Andheri (East), Mumbai-400059 (Maharashtra)

INDIA BOOK HOUSE (P) LTD.
17, Eruchshaw Building, Third Floor 249, Dr. Dadbabhai Naoroji Road, Mumbai-400001 (Maharashtra)
✆ 66529500, Fax: 91-22-66529570
✉ info@ibhworld.com
www.marathitrakatha.com
Hd.Org.: Deepak G. Mirchandani
Bus.Intt.: Pub. and Dist.; **Spl.:** Indian general and technical books and magazines for children, *Amar Chitra Katha*

INDIA CLUB INC. (THE)
New Delhi
✆ 26851864
✉ bkbk@nda.vsnl.net.in
Bus.Intt.: B.S.

INDIA LAW HOUSE
40, Municipal Market, Connaught Place, New Delhi-110001

✆ (O) 23342300, 23742300 (R) 26838500, 26916700
Estd.: 1994; **Prop.:** R.C. Kataria;
Bus.Intt.: Pub., Dist.; **Spl.:** Law

INDIA LAW HOUSE
22, Sikh Mohalla, Near Friends Lodge,
Indore-452007 (Madhya Pradesh)
✆ 2530681

INDIA OFFSET PRESS
A-1, Mayapuri Industrial Area,
New Delhi-110064
Bus.Intt.: Exp.

INDIA RESEARCH PRESS
B-4/22, Safdarjung Enclave,
New Delhi-110029
✆ 24694610, 24694855, Fax: 24618637
✉ contact@indiaresearchpress.com
🌐 www.indiaresearchpress.com
Estd.: 1999; **Hd.Org.:** Anuj Bahri Malhotra;
Bus.Intt.: Pub.; **Spl.:** Soc.Sci., Eco. and Security Perspective of South Asia

INDIA RESEARCH PRESS/TARA PRESS
Flat No. 6, Khan Market,
New Delhi-110003
✆ 24694610, 24694855,
Fax: 91-11-24618637, 41757113
✉ contact@indiaresearchpress.com,
editor@indiaresearchpress.com
🌐 www.indiaresearchpress.com
Estd.: 1999; **Hd.Org.:** Anuj Bahri Malhotra;
Bus.Intt.: Pub. and exp.

INDIA TODAY BOOK CLUB
New Delhi
✉ bahrisons@vsnl.com
Bus.Intt.: B.S.

INDIALOG PUBLICATION PVT. LTD.
O-22, Lajpat Nagar-II, New Delhi-110024
✆ (O) 26320504, 26839936, 26935221
(R) 26913990, Fax: 26935221
✉ publishing@silicondocs.com,
gagan@silicondocs.com,
basant@oxdocs.net.au
🌐 www.indialogpublications.com
Estd.: 2000; **Dir.:** Basant Pandey,
Manisha Pandey; **Bus.Intt.:** Pub. and Dist.;
Spl.: Imported and Indian Gen. and Tech. Books and Magazines, Fiction, Non-Fiction-Film Studies, Diaspora Writing, Translations, Women Writing & Poetry

INDIAN BIBLOGRAPHIC CENTRE
76, Chandrika Colony, Sigra, Varanasi-221100
(Uttar Pradesh)
✆ 221337, Fax: 222337
✉ sullas80@hotmail.com
Bus.Intt.: Pub.

INDIAN BOOK CONCERN
3, Ramanath Majumder St., Kolkata-700009
(West Bengal)
Hd.Org.: P.C. Ghosh

INDIAN BOOK DEPOT (MAP HOUSE)
2937, Bahadurgarh Road,
Near Sadar Bazar, Delhi-110006
✆ 23673927, 23523635, Fax: 91-11-23552096
✉ ibdmaps@ndb.vsnl.net.in
Hd.Org.: Harish Chawla
Bus.Intt.: Pub. and B.S.; **Spl.:** Children's books, atlases, maps and educational charts

INDIAN BOOK DISTRIBUTING CO.
65/2, Mahatma Gandhi Rd., Kolkata-700009
(West Bengal)

INDIAN BOOK SHELF
25, Mega Mall, DLF-I, Quatab Enclave,
Gurgaon (Haryana)
✆ 91-124-459229
Hd.Org.: Babita Varma
Bus.Intt.: Dist.; **Spl.:** General books in various Indian languages

INDIAN BOOK STALL
15, Bankim Chatterjee St., Kolkata-700073
(West Bengal)

INDIAN BOOKS & PERIODICAL SYNDICATE
B-5/62, Dev Nagar, P.L. Rd., Karol Bagh,
New Delhi-110005
✆ 2572444, Fax: 25766699
✉ ibps@del3.vsnl.net.in
Bus.Intt.: Exp.

INDIAN BOOKS & PERIODICALS
2783 (1st Floor) Bhagat Singh Gali No. 6, Chuna Mandi, Pahar Ganj, New Delhi-110055
✆ 55354142 ▮ 9811393986
✉ ibp@ndf.vsnl.net.in
Estd.: 1980; **Prop.:** R.K. Mangal;
Bus.Intt.: Pub. & Dist.; **Spl.:** All Sub., Journals and Periodicals in English, Hindi and All Languages

INDIAN BOOKS CENTRE
40/5, Shakti Nagar, Delhi-110007
✆ (O) 27434930, 27126497 (R) 27130893, Fax: 27227336
✉ ibcindia@ibcindia.com, ibcindia@vsnl.com
🌐 www.indianbookscentre.com
Estd.: 1976; **Hd.Org.:** Sunil Gupta;
Bus.Intt.: Exp., Indological and Oriental Pub.
Spl.: Indology, Buddhist and Tibetan Studies and Journals in English, Sanskrit and Tibetan

INDIAN COMMITTEE FOR CULTURAL FREEDOM
Mumbai (Maharashtra)
✆ 22843416
✉ freedom@vsnl.com
Bus.Intt.: B.S.

INDIAN COUNCIL OF AGRICULTURAL RESEARCH
Krishi Bhavan, Dr. Rajendra Prasad Road,
New Delhi-110114
✆ 25843657, Fax: 91-11-25843567
bnicar@kab.delhi.nic.in
www.icar.org.in
Hd.Org.: A. Chaudhary; **Bus.Intt.:** Pub.;
Spl.: Handbooks, Gen. Books, Textbooks, Bulletins and Journals in English and Hindi on Research Findings in Agri. and Veterinary Sci.

INDIAN COUNCIL FOR CULTURAL RELATIONS
Azad Bhavan, New Delhi-110002
✆ 23370229, 23379158,
Fax: 233784441, 23378639
iccr@vsnl.com
Hd.Org.: Rakesh Kumar; **Bus.Intt.:** Pub.;
Spl.: Arabic quarterly, *Thaqafat-ul-Hind* and Books on Culture

INDIAN COUNCIL OF EDUCATION
A-2/59, Safdarjung Enclave, New Delhi-110029

INDIAN COUNCIL OF FORESTRY RESEARCH AND EDUCATION
P.O. New Forest, Dehradun-248006 (Uttarakhand)
✆ 223258, Fax: 0135-223258
Hd.Org.: D.N. Tiwari; **Bus.Intt.:** Pub.; **Spl.:** An Autonomous Body of the Ministry of Env. and Forests - Organises, Directs and Manages the Research and Edu. in the Field of Forestry and Allied Sci.

INDIAN COUNCIL OF HISTORICAL RESEARCH
35 Ferozeshah Road, New Delhi-110001
✆ 23382321, 23386973, Fax: 91-11-23383421
support@ichrindia.org
www.ichrindia.org
Hd.Org.: P.K. Shukla; **Bus.Intt.:** Pub.;
Spl.: Historical Findings and Books on Freedom Struggle, Soc.Sci. and Humanities

INDIAN COUNCIL OF MEDICAL RESEARCH
V. Ramalingaswami Bhawan, Ansari Nagar,
New Delhi-110029
✆ 26588895, 26588980, 26589794,
Fax: 91-11-26588662, 26588713
headquarters@icmr.org.in,
icmrhqds@sansad.nic.in
www.icmr.nic.in
Hd.Org.: N.K. Ganguly; **Bus.Intt.:** Pub.;
Spl.: Journals, Newsletters, Monographs, Tech. Reports and Periodicals and Non-periodicals on Health

INDIAN COUNCIL OF PHILOSOPHICAL RESEARCH
Darshan Bhavan, 36, Tughlakabad Institutional Area, Mehrauli Badarpur Rd. (Near Batra Hospital), New Delhi-110062
✆ 26094405, 26094403, Fax: 26092129
icpr@del2.vsnl.net.in
Hd.Org.: R.C. Pradhan, Kirit Joshi
Bus.Intt.: Pub.; **Spl.:** Research Papers in Phil. written by Eminent Philosophers

INDIAN COUNCIL OF SOCIAL SCIENCE RESEARCH
Aruna Asaf Ali Marg, New Delhi-110067
✆ 26192059, 23073438, 23383091,
Fax: 23381571, 26179834
rupa_chatterjee@hotmail.com
chna14@hotmail.com
www.icssr.org
Hd.Org.: Bhaskar Chatterjee; **Bus.Intt.:** Pub.; **Spl.:** Pamphlets, Monographs, Journals, etc. on Soc.Sci. Research

INDIAN DOCUMENTATION SERVICE
887/5, St. No. 6-A, Patel Nagar,
Post Box No. 13, Gurgaon-122001 (Haryana)
✆ (O) 2324782, 3093753 (R) 2322779,
Fax: 2324782
indoc@indiatimes.com
Estd.: 1970; **Ch.Exe.:** Satyaprakash; **Bus.Intt.:** Pub. and B.S.; **Spl.:** Soc.Sci. and Humanities, Alternative Health Systems and Occult Sci. in English

INDIAN EXPRESS EGMONT PUBLICATIONS LTD.
D-2, Maturas Mill Compound, Ideal Industrial Estate, SB Marg, Lower Parel,
Mumbai-400013 (Maharashtra)
Prop.: Uday Mathur

INDIAN EXPRESS NEWSPAPERS (B) P. LTD.
Mumbai (Maharashtra)
✆ 26411453, Fax: 26411455
ieegmont@bom4.vsnl.net.in
Bus.Intt.: Pub. & B.S.

INDIAN GEOPHYSICAL UNION
NGRI Campus, Uppal Rd., Hyderabad-500007 (Andhra Pradesh)

INDIAN HERITAGE TRUST
10, Kamaraj Bhavan, 573, Mount Rd., Chennai-600006 (Tamil Nadu)

INDIAN HYPNOSIS ACADEMY
Flat 179, Pocket-7, Sector-2, Rohini,
Delhi-110085
✆ 91-11-27524081
info@indianhypnosisacademy.com
www.developmentassociates.org
Hd.Org.: J.P. Malik

INDIAN INSTITUTE FOR NON-ALIGNED STUDIES
A-2/59, Safdarjung Enclave, New Delhi-110029

INDIAN INSTITUTE OF ADVANCED STUDY
Rashtrapati Nivas, Shimla-171005
(Himachal Pradesh)
✆2831390, Fax: 91-177-2831390
proiias@iias.org

www.iias.org
Hd.Org.: B.L. Mungekar; **Bus.Intt.:** Pub.;
Spl.: Monographs, Proceedings of Seminars, Journals and Books on Humanities and Soc.Sci.

INDIAN INSTITUTE OF APPLIED POLITICAL RESEARCH
(Publication Deptt.), H.S.-14, Kailash Colony (Mezzanine Floor), New Delhi-110048

INDIAN INSTITUTE OF FINANCE
Post Box 8488, Ashok Vihar, Delhi-110052
Spl.: Books and Journal Related to Finance, Banking, Comm. and Eco.

INDIAN INSTITUTE OF PUBLIC ADMINISTRATION
Indraprastha Estate, Ring Rd.,
New Delhi-110002
✆ 22372400/366, Fax: 23072440
iipaitc@nda.vsnl.net.in
www.iipaindia.org
Hd.Org.: Sanjeev Reddy; **Bus.Intt.:** Pub.;
Spl.: Public Administration

INDIAN INSTITUTE OF SINDHOLOGY
Post Box No. 10, Ward 4A, Adipur,
Kutch-370205 (Gujarat)
✆ 261569, 263851, Fax: 91-2836-260336
contact@sindhology.org
www.sindhology.org
Estd.: 1989; **Hd.Org.:** Moti Prakash;
Bus.Intt.: Pub.; **Spl.:** Books and Journals to Promote Sindhi Language, Litt., Art and Culture

INDIAN INSTITUTE OF SPIRITUALITY
Vinalaya, Malleswaram West P.O.,
Bangalore-560055 (Karnataka)

INDIAN JOURNAL OF APPLIED ECONOMICS
335, 3rd Cross, 2nd Block, 3rd Stage,
Basaneswara Nagar, Bangalore-560079
(Karnataka)
✆ 23303198, 23350484, Fax: 080-23303239
ijae.kps@axcess.net.in
Estd.: 1991; **Bus.Intt.:** Pub., WS

INDIAN LAW ACADEMY
C-1491, Rajaji Puram, Lucknow-226017
(Uttar Pradesh)

INDIAN LIBRARY ASSOCIATION
A/40-41, Flat No. 201, Ansal Bldg.,
Mukherjee Nagar, Delhi-110009
✆ 27117743
Hd.Org.: C.P. Vashishth; **Bus.Intt.:** L.S.;
Spl.: Organise Conferences, Seminars, Workshops, Lectures and Training Courses. It bring out Litt. including the ILA Bulletin, the ILA Newsletter, on the subject and has a Computerised Database for over 10,000 Lib.

INDIAN MANAGEMENT ACADEMY
C-1491, Rajaji Puram, Lucknow-226017
(Uttar Pradesh)

INDIAN MAP SERVICE
Pushkar Estate, 13/1-5, Light Industrial Area,
Sector G-Extn., Shastri Nagar,
Jodhpur-342003 (Rajasthan)
✆ 2740874, 2740574, Fax: 5102248
indianmap@satyam.net.in
Hd.Org.: R.P. Arya; **Bus.Intt.:** Cartographer and Pub.; **Spl.:** Maps

INDIAN MUSEUM
27, Jawaharlal Nehru Rd.,
Kolkata-700016 (West Bengal)
✆ 22861679, 22861702, Fax: 91-33-22861696
imbot@cal2.vsnl.net.in
www.indianmuseum-calcutta.org
Hd.Org.: C.R. Panda; **Bus.Intt.:** Pub.;
Spl.: Soc.Sci. and Humanities in English

INDIAN NATIONAL SCIENCE ACADEMY
Bahadur Shah Zafar Marg, New Delhi-110002
✆ 23221931-50, Fax: 23235648
insa@giasd101.vsnl.net.in
Hd.Org.: S.K. Sahni; **Bus.Intt.:** Pub.; **Spl.:** Hist. of Sci. and Journals on Math., Physical and Biological Sci. in English

INDIAN NAT. SCIENTIFIC DOCUMENTATION CENTRE
14, Satsang Vihar Marg, New Delhi-110067

INDIAN NEWS & BOOKS
(Pub., Dist. & Exp.), A-4C/173, Janakpuri, New Delhi-110058

INDIAN PETROLEUM PUBLISHERS
100/9, Nashuilk Rd., Dehradun-1 (Uttarakhand)
✆ 0135-2654074
ipp@garhwalhimalayas.com
Hd.Org.: Jripathi; **Bus.Intt.:** Pub. and B.S.

INDIAN PRESS PUBLICATION PVT. LTD.
36, Pannalal Rd., Allahabad-211002
(Uttar Pradesh)
✆ (O) 2600858 (R) 2600562
Hd.Org.: D.P. Ghosh

INDIAN PROGRESSIVE PUBL. CO. (P) LTD.
1, Rajendra Deb Rd., Kolkata-700009
(West Bengal)
Estd.: 1961; **Hd.Org.:** S.S. Bhattacharjee
Bus.Intt.: Pub.; **Spl.:** Comm. in Bengali and English

INDIAN PUBLISHERS DISTRIBUTORS
156-D, Kamla Nagar, New Delhi-110007
✆ 55354581, Fax: 91-11-23846233,
▮ 9312400620
info@indianpublishersdistributors.com,
sales@indianpublishersdistributors.com
www.indiapublish rsdistributors.com
Estd.: 1980; **Hd.Org.:** Satish Kumar Garg;
Bus.Intt.: Pub. and Dist.; **Spl.:** Human Rights,

Mass Communication, Rel., Edu., Hist., Politics, Sol. and Women's Studies

INDIAN PUBLISHING HOUSE
23, Darya Ganj, New Delhi-110002
✆ (O) 23274161, 23275267, 23242257
(R) 23842368
Dir.: K.L. Malik, S.K. Malik, M.M. Malik, B.B. Malik, N.K. Malik; **Bus.Intt.:** Pub. & WS; **Spl.:** Humanities & Soc.Sci.

INDIAN RED CROSS SOCIETY
1, Red Cross Rd., New Delhi-110001
✆ 23716441, Cable: INDCROSS, Telex: 66115

INDIAN SCHOLAR PUBLICATIONS
C-156, Sector-I, Devendra Nagar, Raipur-492009 (Madhya Pradesh)

INDIAN SOCIAL INSTITUTE
10, Institutional Area, Lodi Rd., New Delhi-110003
✆ 24611745, 24635096, 24694602, Fax: 91-11-24690660
isi@isidelhi.org.in
www.isidelhi.org.in
Estd.: 1951; **Asst.Tech.Off.:** K.A. Jacob; **Bus.Intt.:** Pub.; **Spl.:** Booklets on Law, Agri., Human Rights etc.

INDIAN SOCIETY FOR AFRO-ASIAN STUDIES
75, Defence Enclave, Vikas Marg, New Delhi-110092

INDIAN SOCIETY FOR PROMOTING CHRISTIAN KNOWLEDGE, THE
1654, Madarsa Rd., St. James Church, Compound P.O., 1585, Kashmere Gate Delhi-110006
✆ 22966323, 22966322, Fax: 011-22965490
ispck@nde.vsnl.net.in
www.ispck.org
Gen.Secy.: Rev. Ashish Amos
Asst.Gen.Secy.: K. Peterson
Br.: I.S.P.C.K., 51, Jawaharlal Nehru Rd., Kolkata-700071 (West Bengal) ✆ 033-22821804
• I.S.P.C.K., Opp. Liberty Cinema, Residency Rd., Sadar, Nagpur-440001 (Maharashtra)
• I.S.P.C.K. Chhotanagpur Diocesan, Bookshop (H.P.D. Centre), P.O. Church Rd., Ranchi-834001 (Bihar); • I.S.P.C.K. Jabalpur Diocesan Bookshop, Mission Boy's Hostel, Jarbhata, Bilaspur-495001 (Madhya Pradesh)
Spl.: Studies on Interfaith Dialogue, Rel., Theological, Biblical, Devotional Litt., Biographies, Communication and Development, Christian Life and Edu., Social and Pol.Sci., CNI Liturgical Pub. & Almanac & Lectionary

INDIAN SOCIETY FOR TRAINING & DEVELOPMENT
New Delhi
✆ 26867710, 26857157, Fax: 26867607

istd@ren02.nic.in
Bus.Intt.: B.S.

INDIAN SOCIETY OF ALLEOPATHY DEPTT. OF AGRONOMY
CCS, Haryana Agricultural University, Hissar-125004 (Haryana)

INDIAN SOCIETY OF AUTHORS
3265, Ranjit Nagar, New Delhi-110008
✆ 25723193
Estd.: 1982; **Hd.Org.:** Lt. Col. Gautam Sharma; **Bus.Intt.:** Promotion of Authors and their Interests

INDIAN SOCIETY OF DEVELOPMENT BIOLOGISTS
Department of Zoology, University of Pune, Pune-411007 (Maharashtra)

INDIAN SOCIETY OF ORIENTAL ART
15, Park St., (5th Floor), Kolkata-700016 (West Bengal)

INDIAN SOCIETY OF TREE SCIENTISTS COLLEGE OF FORESTRY
Dr. Y.S. Parmar University Forestry, Nauni (Solan)-173230 (Himachal Pradesh)

INDIAN STATISTICAL INSTITUTE
203, Barrackpore Trunk Rd., Kolkata-700035 (West Bengal)

INDIAN TAX INSTITUTE
34, Gujranwala Town, Part-II, Delhi-110033
✆ 27138192

INDIAN THOUGHT PUBLICATION
No. 23, Thanikachsalam Rd., T. Nagar, Chennai-600017 (Tamil Nadu)
✆ 24344529, Fax: 44-24342009
ksm@md2.vsnl.net.in
Prop.: R.K. Narayan; **Bus.Intt.:** Pub.
Spl.: Fiction and Children Books

INDIAN WRITING
(New Horizon Media Pvt. Ltd.)
33/15, Eldams Road, Alwarpet, Chennai-600018 (Tamil Nadu)
✆ 42009601, Fax: 91-44-43009701
support@nhm.in
www.nhm.in
Estd.: 2004; **Hd.Org.:** Badri Seshadri
Bus.Intt.: Pub.; **Spl.:** English fiction translations of the Indian language literature

INDIAN WRITERS PRESS
Division of Writers Club, C-23, Anna Nagar, Chennai-600102 (Tamil Nadu)

INDIANA
1488, Pataudi House, Darya Ganj, New Delhi-110002

✆ 24622827, Fax: 91-11-24623923
✉ indiana@nda.vsnl.net.in
Estd.: 1974; **Prop.:** Adish Chander;
Bus.Intt.: B.S., Exp.

INDIANA BOOKSHOP
2/1, Shyama Charan Dey St., Kolkata-700073 (West Bengal)
✆ 22417466, Fax: 033-22417032
Estd.: 1960; **Prop.:** R.K. Mangal; **Bus.Intt.:** Rt.;
Spl.: Gen., Children, Academic and Trade (Indian and Foreign Books)

INDIANE-BOOKS.COM
A-6, Nimri Commercial Centre,
Near Ashok Vihar Phase-IV, Delhi-110052
✆ 27452453, 27401672
✉ lpp@nde.vsnl.net.in
Hd.Org.: Pradeep Mittal; **Bus.Intt.:** Pub. and Promoter; **Spl.:** E-Books

INDICA BOOKS
D-40/18, Godowlia, Varanasi-221001 (Uttar Pradesh)
✆ 3294999, Fax: 91-542-2450818
✉ indicabooks@satyam.net.in, indicabs@nde.vsnl.net.in
www.indicabooks.com
Hd.Org.: Dilip Kumar Jaiswal; **Bus.Intt.:** Pub. and B.S.; **Spl.:** Indology, Phil., Rel. and Culture

INDICA PUBLISHERS & DISTRIBUTORS PVT. LTD.
7/31, Ansari Rd., Darya Ganj,
New Delhi-110002
✆ (O) 23243027, 23243028 (R) 27435512, Fax: 23243006
✉ ipdplbooks@yahoo.co.in
Estd.: 1997; **Hd.Org.:** Prashant Jain
Bus.Intt.: Pub., WS, L.S. & Rt., Imp., Exp., Sub.Ag.; **Spl.:** Humanities & Soc.Sci., Sci. & Tech., Med., Law, Bio.Sci., Agri. Engg., etc.

INDICUS ANALYTICS PVT. LTD.
B-17, Second Floor, G.K. Enclave-II,
New Delhi-110048
✆ 29222638, 29226711
✉ indic@indicus.net
www.indicus.net
Hd.Org.: Laveesh Bhandari;
Bus.Intt.: Organisation for Research;
Spl.: Eco. and Business

INDIRA GANDHI NATIONAL CENTRE FOR THE ARTS
Central Vista Mess Building,
(in front of National Archives) Janpath,
New Delhi-110001
✆ 23381303, Fax: 23388280
✉ kauladvait@rediffmail.com
Hd.Org.: N.R. Shetty; **Spl.:** Centre for Study of Critical Litt., Visual Arts like Arch., Sculpture, Graphics and also Performing Arts like Music, Dance, etc.

INDIRA GANDHI NATIONAL OPEN UNIVERSITY—ELECTRONIC MEDIA PRODUCTION CENTRE
Mktg. Cell, M.P.D.D., Maidan Garhi,
New Delhi-110068
✆ 26962450, Fax: 26855083
✉ ignoumkt@ignou.ac.in
Hd.Org.: Col. Rajive Kohli; **Bus.Intt.:** Provider of facilities for Higher Edu. through Distance Learning

INDIRA PATHIPPAKAM
60, First St., Dheenadayalu Nagar, Thiruverumbur, Tiruchi-620023 (Kerala)

INDIRA PRAKASHAN
A-11, Sector-D, Kunkar Bagh,
Patna-800020 (Bihar)

INDRIA PRAKASHANA
733, 5th Block, Rajajinagar, Bangalore-10 (Karnataka)
Hd.Org.: V. Indira; **Bus.Intt.:** Pub.
Spl.: Fiction and Collections in Kannada

INDIRA PRINTERS
C-63/5, Okhla Industrial Area, Phase-II,
New Delhi-110020
✆ 26829337, 26316876, 26830401,
Fax: 91-11-26830493, 26852280
✉ krishan@ned.vsnl.net.in
Hd.Org.: Krishan Makhijani; **Bus.Intt.:** Pub.

INDIRA PUBLISHERS
C/o Rekha Printers (P) Ltd., A-102/1 Okhla Industrial Area, New Delhi-110020
✆ 26834401

INDIRA PUBLISHING HOUSE
E-5/21, Arera Colony, Habibganj Thana Rd.,
Bhopal-462016 (Madhya Pradesh)
✆ 0755-2465238
✉ landmark_no1@satyam.net.in
Hd.Org.: Manish Gupta

INDMARK "OM GANESH"
16, Rest House Crescent,
Bangalore-560001
(Karnataka)

INDO-AMERICAN BOOKS
2261 G.F., Hudson Line, Kingsway Camp,
Delhi-110009
✆ 27138609, 27412409 ▮ 31058962,
Fax: 91-11-27122052
✉ vijay.sharma@iabooks.com, iab@iabooks.com
www.iabooks.com
Dir.: Vijay Sharma

INDO-BRITISH HISTORICAL
21, Rajaram Deehta Awnce, Chennai-600029 (Tamil Nadu)

INDO-EUROPEAN PUBLICATIONS
MG-91, Aliganj Scheme, Chetna Vihar, Sector-C, Lucknow-226020 (Uttar Pradesh)

INDO-US BOOKS CORPORATION
4402/5A, Ansari Road, (Opp. HDFC Bank), Darya Ganj, New Delhi-110002
✆ 23265523, 23260783, Fax: 23272766
manaspublication@vsnl.com
www.manaspublications.com
Hd.Org.: Prachi Garg; **Bus.Intt.:** Dist.

INDO-VISION (P) LTD.
II A-220, Nehru Nagar, Ghaziabad-201001 (Uttar Pradesh)
Hd.Org.: Dr. S.C. Bhartiya

INDOLOGICAL BOOK HOUSE
42-43, UB Jawahar Nagar, 1st Floor, Delhi-110007
✆ 30901148, Fax: 23922137
ioph@rediffmail.com
Hd.Org.: Gajendra Singh; **Bus.Intt.:** Pub., Dist. and L.S.; **Spl.:** Indology, Arch., Art Archaeology, Buddhism, Rel., Numismatic, Yoga and Phil.

INDOWORLD PRESS PUBLICATIONS
6-D, Mohan Mola, 622, Linking Rd., Mumbai-400052 (Maharashtra)

INDRAPRASTHA BOOKS & PERIODICALS
E-15/147, Rohini, Sector-8, Rohini, Delhi-110085
✆ 27112721 ▮ 9810340453
Estd.: 2002; **Hd.Org.:** Sanjay Vashishth; **Bus.Intt.:** L.S.; **Spl.:** Acad., Beh.Sci., Soc.Sci., Comm., Sci., Tech., Journals & Magazines

INDRAPRASTHA PRESS
Nehru House, New Delhi-110002

INDRAPRASTHA PRAKASHAN
K-71, Krishna Nagar, Delhi-110051
✆ 22099764, Fax: 91-11-22002274
indraprastha04@yahoo.com
Hd.Org.: Ashok Kumar Sharma;
Bus.Intt.: Pub. and Dist.; **Spl.:** Hindi Novels, Books on Sci., and for Children and Neo-literates

INDRAYANI SAHITYA
273, Shaniwar Peth, Pune-411030 (Maharashtra)
✆ 0212-2458598
Estd.: 1964; **Hd.Org.:** Shyam Dayarnav Khopardekar; **Bus.Intt.:** Dealear; **Spl.:** Marathi Books of Fine Art, Dramas, Poems, Novels, Cookery, Children's Litt., Small Industries, Math., Sci., Rel.s and Spiritual, Aesthetics and Modelling

INDU PRAKASHAN
29/2, Shakti Nagar, Delhi-110007
✆ 27451485
Estd.: 1967; **Prop.:** Diwakar Awasthi
Bus.Intt.: Indological Pub. and L.S.; **Spl.:** Hist., Pol.Sci., Sanskrit and Phil. Books

INDURAJA PRAKASHANA
902, 9th Cross, West of Chord Rd., Rajajinagar, Bangalore-560080 (Karnataka)
✆ 080-2350948
Bus.Intt.: Pub.; **Spl.:** Children Books

INDUS INTERNATIONAL
5-A (MIG), Rajouri Garden, New Delhi-110027
✆ 25151333, 25935289, Fax: 91-11-25115667
indus@indus-intl.com
www.indus-intl.com
Hd.Org. Lokesh Gidwani;
Bus.Intt.: B.S., Exp. and Pub.

INDUS PUBLISHING COMPANY
FS-5, Tagore Garden, New Delhi-110027
✆ 42133022, 42133622, 25151333, Fax: 91-11-42133985
indus@indus-publishing.com
www.indus-publishing.com
Estd.: 1987; **Prop.:** M.L. Gidwani, Lokesh Gidwani; **Bus.Intt.:** Pub.; **Spl.:** Soc.Sci., Himalayan Studies, Environment, Forestry and Wildlife

INFAR (INDIA) LTD.
7, Wood St., Kolkata-700016 (West Bengal)
Bus.Intt.: Exp.

INFINITEBOOKS.COM PVT. LTD.
100-Second Main Rd., Gandhi Nagar, Adyar, Chennai-600020 (Tamil Nadu)
✆ 91-44-24423744, 24423722, Fax: 24917441
books@bestcc.com, gopi@besl.cc.com
www.infinitebooks.com
Estd.: 1999; **Dir.:** S. Gopi; **Bus.Intt.:** L.S. & Rt., Sub.Ag.

INFINITY BOOKS
203, Shivam Tower, Community Centre, Paschim Vihar, New Delhi-110063
✆ 25264771, 25264782, Fax: 011-25255492
rsethi@vsnl.net
Estd.: 1997; **Prop.:** Rajeev Sethi;
Bus.Intt.: Pub.; **Spl.:** Man., Juvenile/Children, Gen. & Self-Improvement Books etc.

INFO BOOK DISTRIBUTORS
No. 22, 2nd Cross, Annaiah Reddy Layout, Ram Murthy Nagar, Dodda Banswadi, Bangalore-43 (Karnataka)
✆ 2206175, 5484300, Fax: 2206175

infob@vsnl.net
Bus.Intt.: Pub. and L.S.

INFO PLAS
Shop No. 32, (Gr. Floor), 3, Anna Nagar, Plaza, Anna Nagar, Chennai-600040 (Tamil Nadu)

INFO-RESOURCES MANAGEMENT SERVICE
22, Ashok Market, Near Old Subzi Mandi, Delhi-110007
✆ 27216150
Hd.Org.: Jotirmay Midhra; **Bus.Intt.**: L.S.
Spl.: Acad., Beh.Sci., Soc.Sci., Sci. - Pure and Applied, Tech., Law

INFOR SERVICE
C-14, Arnol, Gavanpada Rd., Mulund (East), Mumbai-400081 (Maharashtra)

INFORMATIC BOOKS
A-1/14, Krishna Nagar, Delhi-110051
✆ 55298293
ibd@rediffmail.com
Estd.: 2002; **Prop.**: P.K. Arora; **Bus.Intt.**: Pub., B.S., L.S., WS; **Spl.**: Humanities & Soc.Sci., Sci. & Tech., Comp., Med., Mang., Law, Arts & Arch., Bio.

INFORMATICS (INDIA) LTD.
337, 3rd Floor, Karuna Complex, Sampige Rd., Malleswaram, Bangalore-560003 (Karnataka)
✆ 23367867, 23365940, Fax: 23344598
info@informindia.co.in
www.informindia.co.in
Estd.: 1980; **Man.Dir.**: N.V. Sathyanarayna
Br.: #603.604, 1 Wing, Krishna Vasantha Sagar & Bldg. Thakur Village, Kano Viw (East), Mumbai-400101 ✆ 28878413
infomum@bom5.vsnl.net.in • 202, 1st Floor, Greater Kailash-I, New Delhi-110048
✆ 26467683, 26467698, Fax: 26467698,
infodel@vsnl.net.in • Flat No. 304, 3rd Floor, Brahmanand Co-Op. Society, Narangi, Baugh Lane, Pune-411001 ✆ 26119710
infopune@vsnl.com • CE-131, Ground Floor, Sector-1, Salt Lake City, Kolkata-700064, Fax: 23343583 infocal@cal.vsnl.net.in
• Flat No. 2, B-Block, Ground Floor, Shyams Apts. No. 12, Sriram Puram, 2nd St., Choolai Medu, Chennai-600094 ✆ 23615358
www.satishk@informindia.co.in
• No. 6-1-133/10, 1st Floor, Brook Bond Colony, Padmarao Nagar, Secunderabad-500025
✆ 27501342 infohyd@hd2.vsnl.in
Bus.Intt.: Pub.-CD ROM, L.S. & Rt.-CD ROM, Imp., Exp., Sub.Ag.; **Spl.**: Sci., Tech. & Med., Humanities & Soc.Sci., Trade, Gen. (Incl. Lit. & Art)

INFORMATION & EDUCATION SERVICES
30-B, Ber Sarai, Near IIT, Haus Khas, New Delhi-110016
✆ 26867005, Fax: 26885831
Estd.: 1990; **Hd.Org.**: Shivaji Bhattacharjee Pubrep; **Bus.Intt.**: Sub.Ag.

INFORMATION INDUSTRY PUBLISHERS
B-23, Inderpuri, New Delhi-110012

INFOSOURCE INDIA
1-1609, Chittaranjan Park Kalkaji, New Delhi-110019
✆ 26413801
Prop.: Biman Bhattacharya; **Bus.Intt.**: L.S.

INFOTECH STANDARDS INDIA (P) LTD.
Rgd.Off.: 1658, "Kartik House", Parsadi Gali Kotla Mubarakpur, New Delhi-110003
✆ (O) 56020164, 56020178, 55659120 (R) 26645636, 25509439 ▮ 9811224190, Fax: 011-51642947
standards@bol.net.in
Corp.Off.: G-17/C, GF "Ashirwad", South Extn. Part-II, New Delhi-110049 ✆ 26264946-7, Fax: 51642947 ▮ 9811224190
infostd@bol.net.in
www.standardsmedia.com
Estd.: 1993; **Dir.**: Ranbir Singh Kushvah, Virendra Singh Rawat, Kishore Kumar Teneja
Bus.Intt.: Pub., WS, Pub.'s Rep., L.S.;
Spl.: Authorised Suppliers for AIAG, API, ASQ, ASME, ASTM, AWS, BIS, DIN, IEE, IEEE, Industrial Press, Penwill, Springer Verlag, World Sci.

INFUSE INC
414, Osian Building, 12, Nehru Place, New Delhi-110019
✆ 26890365, Fax: 26893541
Estd.: 1990; **Bus.Intt.**: Pub.; **Spl.**: Man. and Organisational Books

INLAND PRINTERS PVT. LTD.
317, Raheja Chambers, FPJ Marg, Nariman Point, Mumbai-400021 (Maharashtra)
✆ 22852376, 22851032, 22851760, Fax: 022-22875464, Cable: QUALPRINT
Estd.: 1978; **Bus.Intt.**: Exp.

INNOSERV SYSTEMS PVT. LTD.
305, Bajaj House, 97, Nehru Place, New Delhi-110019
✆ 28619112, 28619113, 26855341, 26226680, Fax: 91-11-26286640, 26966911
rakesh@cdindia.com, sales@cdindia.com
Ch.Exe.: Mr. Rakesh Sarawgi; **Bus.Intt.**: Dealer; **Spl.**: CD Roms, Comp. Software and Multimedia CD Roms on a wide range of topics

INNOVATIVE BOOKS
321, Starshops, Vardhman Mall-Multiplex,

Badkhal Chowk, Mathura Road,
Faridabad-121002 (Haryana)
9999035066
innovativebooks4u@yahoo.co.in
www.innovativebooks4u.com
Hd.Org.: K. Rahman; **Bus.Intt.:** Pub.;
Spl.: Books for children

INNOVATIVE PUBLISHERS
D-16, Connaught Place, 1st Floor,
New Delhi-110001
23353951 Fax: 23713275
rajuprim@vsnl.com, oxford@vsnl.com
Estd.: 2002; **Prop.:** Mohan Primlani;
Bus.Intt.: Pub.; **Spl.:** Sci., Engg. & Tech.

INSAT BOOKS & PERIODICALS
'Onkar House', Basement No. 4, 4575/15,
Main Aggarwal Rd., Darya Ganj,
New Delhi-110002
23264151, 41562759, Fax: 91-11-23276109
insatbp@airtelbroadband.in
Hd.Org.: Suman Chaudhary; **Bus.Intt.:** Dist.;
Spl.: Sci. and Tech. Books by Foreign Pub.

INSHA PUBLICATIONS
6A, Kanal Seel St., Kolkata-700013
(West Bengal)

INSTANT PRINTERS
Lakshmi Complex, Ground Floor, New No. 8, (Old No. 52) North Boag Rd., T-nagar, Chennai-600017
(Tamil Nadu)
28251201, 28257898,
Fax: 91-44-28281843
Hd.Org.: Rajappa I.P.; **Bus.Intt.:** Printing and Publishing

INSTITUTE FOR RURAL ECO-DEVELOPMENT
234, Daudpur, Gorakhpur-273001
(Uttar Pradesh)

INSTITUTE FOR THE TRANSLATION OF HEBREW LITERATURE (THE)
C/o Embassy of Israel, 3, Aurangzeb Rd.,
New Delhi-110001
23013238

INSTITUTE FRANCIS DE PONDICHERRY
P.B. No. 151, 16, Rue Dumas,
Pondicherry-605001

INSTITUTE OF ASIAN STUDIES
Chemmancherry, Chennai-600019
(Tamil Nadu)

INSTITUTE OF ENCYCLOPAEDIC PUBLICATIONS
Government of Kerala,
Thiruvananthapuram-695001 (Kerala)

INSTITUTE OF HUMAN STUDY
2-2-4/1, University Rd., Hyderabad-500044
(Andhra Pradesh)

INSTITUTE OF KONGU STUDIES
74A, Line Rd., Gugai, Salem-636006
(Tamil Nadu)

INSTITUTE OF PROFESSIONAL PSYCHOLOGY
IPP Consilium Palachuvad,
Kakanad West Cochin-682030 (Kerala)
6517060, Fax: 91-984-6110021
kaliaden@gmail.com
www.e-psychologist.net
Hd.Org.: George J. Kaliaden,
Bus.Intt.: Pub.; **Spl.:** Books and journals on psychology, self-development, poetry, therapy, etc. Also pub. quarterly magazine on psychology, *Teens & Parents*

INSTITUTE OF SELF RELIANCE
103/B, HIG BDA, Duplex, Baramunda,
Bhubaneswar-751003 (Orissa)
2354662, Fax: 91-674-2354662
isrindia@sify.com
www.isrindia.com
Hd.Org.: S. Subudhi

INSTITUTE OF SKIN STUDIES
959/IV, SAS Nagar, Chandigarh-160059

INSTITUTE OF SOUTH INDIAN STUDIES
6, Nalla Thambi St., Off. Ellis Rd.,
Chennai-600002 (Tamil Nadu)
Hd.Org.: C.S. Subramanian

INSTITUTE OF STANDARD ENGINEERS
Madak Bhawan, 9, B.S.Z. Marg,
New Delhi-110002

INSTITUTE OF WOOD SCIENCE & TECHNOLOGY
Indian Council of Forestry Research & Edu.,
P.O. Malleswaram, Bangalore
(Karnataka)

INSTITUTION BHARATIYA VIDYA BHAVAN
Bharatiya Vidya Bhavan, Kasturba Gandhi Marg,
New Delhi-110001
23381369, Fax: 91-11-23382003
Ch.Exe.: Mr. Amrit Lal Jain; **Bus.Intt.:** Pub. and B.S.; **Spl.:** Indology Rel. Phil., Culture, Hist. and Astrology (English & Hindi)

INSTITUTION OF INFORMATION TECHNOLOGY
3/212, Ramappa Nagar, Perungudi,
Chennai-600096 (Tamil Nadu)

INSTITUTO CERVANTES
12, Prithviraj Road, New Delhi
41293013, Fax: 91-11-41293020
dirndel@cervantes.es
www.cervantes.es
Hd.Org.: Oscar Pujol

INTACH
71, Lodi Estate, New Delhi-110003

INTEGRAL BOOKS
Payyanur (Kerala)
booksintegral@yahoo.com
Bus.Intt.: B.S. & Dist.

INTEL BOOK DISTRIBUTORS PRIVATE LIMITED
240, Ground Floor, 13th Main, Banashankari 1st Stage, Bangalore-560050 (Karnataka)
26611448, 2601963, Fax: 26611448
ibd@satyam.net.in
Estd.: 1994; **Bus.Intt.:** WS, L.S., Consultant

INTELLECTUAL PUBLISHING HOUSE PVT. LTD.
23, Darya Ganj, Ansari Rd., New Delhi-110002
(O) 23275860 (R) 26473059, Fax: 23275860
Estd.: 1974; **Hd.Org.:** D.R. Chopra Deepak Rai Chopra; **Bus.Intt.:** WS and Pub.; **Spl.:** Politics, Sol., Rel. and Phil. Books

INTER BOOK COMPANY
20, M.G Marg, Civil Line, Allahabad (Uttar Pradesh)

INTER BOOK COMPANY
12, Nerode Behari, Mullick Rd., Kolkata-700006 (West Bengal)

INTER INDIA PUBLICATIONS
D-17, Raja Garden Extn., New Delhi-110015
25441120, 25467082
Estd.: 1977; **Prop.:** M.C. Mittal; **Bus.Intt.:** Pub.

INTER UNIVERSITY PRESS (P) LTD.
Educational Publishers, 30/7, Shakti Nagar, Delhi-110007
27134725, 27455876, Fax: 27431133
iup@iuppublisher.com
www.iuppublisher.com
Estd.: 1965; **Hd.Org.:** Brij Mohan Kaeley; **Bus.Intt.:** Pub.; **Spl.:** School Textbooks in English and Hindi

INTERADS ADVERTISING PVT. LTD.
4/24A, Asaf Ali Rd., New Delhi-110002

INTERCONTINENTAL BOOK AGENCY
106, Inderjit Singh Palace, X-320, Delhi Gate New Delhi-110002
23271108, 23254330, Fax: 91-11-23271108
iba@vsnl.net
Estd.: 1990; **Prop.:** Sunil Sachdeva; **Bus.Intt.:** L.S.; **Spl.:** Sci., Tech. and Comp.

INTERCULTURAL PUBLICATIONS (P) LTD.
15A/30, W.E.A. Karol Bagh, New Delhi-110005
Prop.: Ponnamma Chacko

INTEREST PUBLISHERS
Rajendra Mansion, 19A, Ansari Rd., Darya Ganj, New Delhi-110002

INTERLUDE TECHNOLOGIES
A5B/185B, First Floor, S.S. Mota Singh Road, Janakpuri, New Delhi-110058
91-11-25524087, 25506100, 25506200, 39583441
info@interludetech.com, sales@interludetech.com
www.interludetech.com
Estd.: 1998, **Hd.Org.:** Dilip Kumar Gupta; **Bus.Intt.:** Dist.; **Spl.:** Marketer of educational and entertainment CDs/DVDs, as well as stories, rhymes and games

INTERNATIONAL AGRICULTURAL RESEARCH CENTRES
Patancheru (Andhra Pradesh)
23296161, Fax: 2241239
icrisat@cgiar.org
Bus.Intt.: Pub.

INTERNATIONAL BIBLE SOCIETY INDIA
IBS India, 1204, Jubilee Hills, Rd.#60, Hyderabad-500033 (Andhra Pradesh)
23559322, Fax: 23559322
ibssasia@hdl.vsnl.net.in
www.biblesindia.com
Estd.: 1973; **Hd.Org.:** P.L.N. Murthy
Br.: IBS India-Publishing, 39/6822, Darragh Small, Chambers, MG Rd., Ravipuram, Cochin-682015
22383575, Fax: 22383810
tmmathew@bibleindia.com
• IBS India-Translations, #4 1st Cross BRR Layout, Dodda Banaswadi, Bangalore-560043 (Karnataka) 25454753, Fax: 25454915
edc@bgl.vsnl.net.in
• IBS India-North Region, 37, Cantonment Rd., Lucknow-226001
2222483, Fax: 2222061
lphlko@zyberwayavadh.com
• IBS India Hindi NIV Bible, Base 3 Consultancy P. Ltd., E-180, Greater Kailash-1, New Delhi-110048
28633021, Fax: 26417649
hindiniv@vsnl.net
Bus.Intt.: Pub. and Dist.; **Spl.:** The *Holy Bible* in all Indian Languages

INTERNATIONAL BIOGRAPHICAL RESEARCH FOUNDATION
'VEKUVA', 5-B, Corporation Colony, Hill Rd., Nagpur-440010 (Maharashtra)
(O)&(R) 0712-22231880, Fax: 22233454
Estd.: 1993; **Hd.Org.:** N.N. Murthy;
Spl.: Biography Biographical Books, Reference Books and Research oriented Publications

INTERNATIONAL BOOK AGENCY
Budsha Chowk, Srinagar (Jammu & Kashmir)
2436263, 2472206
Estd.: 1990; **Hd.Org.:** Shaikh Fayaz Ahmed; **Spl.:** Trade Gen., Litt. and Art, Sci. Tech. and Med.

INTERNATIONAL BOOK AGENCY
Flat No. 2, Nirala Market, Nirala Nagar, Lucknow-226020 (Uttar Pradesh)
✆ 2370506

INTERNATIONAL BOOK AGENCY
No. 45, Harikarishna Naidu St., Nardharajapuram P.O. Mabattur, Chennai-600053 (Tamil Nadu)
✆ 2653413 (PP)
Prop.: B.S. Purohit; **Bus.Intt.:** Dist. and Commission Agent; **Spl.:** International Standard Books on Reference, Litt., Crafts, etc.

INTERNATIONAL BOOK BUREAU
16, Hind Rajasthan Bldg., Ground Floor, Dada Saheb Phalke Rd., Dadar, Mumbai-400014 (Maharashtra)
✆ 24149995, 24147631, Fax: 24147631
✉ arjunibb@bom5.vsnl.net.in
Hd.Org.: Arjun H. Punjabi; **Bus.Intt.:** WS, L.S.; **Spl.:** Pharmacy, Chemistry, Chemical Engg., Mechanical Engg. and Man.

INTERNATIONAL BOOK CO.
12, Nerode Behari Mullick Rd., Kolkata-700006 (West Bengal)

INTERNATIONAL BOOK DISTRIBUTING CO.
Chaman Studio Building, 2nd Floor, Charbagh, Lucknow-226004 (Uttar Pradesh)
✆ 22450004, 22450007, 22459058, Fax: 22458629
✉ ibdco@sancharnet.in, sushil@1w1.vsnl.net.in
Estd.: 1977; **Man.Prt.:** Suneel Gomber; **Bus.Intt.:** Dist. and Stockist; **Spl.:** Agri., Veterinary, Biology, Sci. & Tech., Med. and Engg.

INTERNATIONAL BOOK DISTRIBUTING CO.
Khushnuma Complex Basement, 7 Meera Bai Marg, Behind Jawahar Bhawan, Lucknow-226001 (Uttar Pradesh)
✆ 2209542-45, Fax: 91-522-4045308
✉ ibdco@airtelbroadband.in
Estd.: 1977; **Man.Prt.:** Suneel Gomber; **Bus.Intt.:** Pub., Dist. and Stockist; **Spl.:** Agri., Vertinary, Biology, Sci. & Tech., Med. and Engg.

INTERNATIONAL BOOK DISTRIBUTORS
1st Floor, 4-Totlee Lane, Kolkata-700016 (West Bengal)

INTERNATIONAL BOOK DISTRIBUTORS
9/3, Rajpur Rd., (First Floor), P.B. No. 4, Dehradun-248001 (Uttarakhand)
✆ (O) 0135-2657497, 2656526 (R) 2650949, Fax: 2656554
✉ ibdbooks@sancharnet.in, rpsinghgahlot@yahoo.co.in
🌐 www.ibdbooks.com
Estd.: 1976; **Hd.Org.:** R.P. Singh; **Bus.Intt.:** Pub. and Dist.; **Spl.:** Agri., Botany, Forestry, Wildlife, etc.

INTERNATIONAL BOOK DISTRIBUTORS
Flat No. 17, Prakash Apartments, 5 Ansari Road, Darya Ganj, New Delhi-110002
✆ (O) 23271052 (R) 25888239, Fax: 23252951
✉ ibdnewdelhi@airtelbroadband.in
Prt.: Prem Chandra Lal; **Bus.Intt.:** Imp. and Dist.; **Spl.:** Soc.Sci. & Humanities

INTERNATIONAL BOOK DISTRIBUTORS, PUBLISHERS & LIBRARY SUPPLIERS
7/199, First Floor, Anand Baza, Swaroop Nagar, Kanpur (Uttar Pradesh)

INTERNATIONAL BOOK HOUSE
U-19, 20, Thadaram Complex, Zone-I, M.P. Nagar, Bhopal-462001 (Madhya Pradesh)
✆ 2578331, Fax: 0755-2710562
Bus.Intt.: B.S.; **Spl.:** Adv. Books for Lib., Gen. Books and Children Books

INTERNATIONAL BOOK HOUSE
C-115, Shakti Nagar Extension, Delhi-110052
✆ 27114245
Estd.: 1959; **Prop.:** Kuldip Singh Tulsi; **Bus.Intt.:** L.S.

INTERNATIONAL BOOK HOUSE PVT. LTD.
Indian Mercantile Mansions (Extn.), Madame Cama Rd., Mumbai-400001 (Maharashtra)
✆ 22021634, 22044859, 22021795-0765, Fax: 22851109
✉ ibh@vsnl.com, ibh@vsnl.in
🌐 www.intbh.com
Estd.: 1941; **Dir.:** Sanjeev Gupta
Br.: 5, Palace Court, 1 Kud St., Kolkata-700016 (West Bengal) ✆ 22294493, Fax: 22294493 • 13, S.N. Banerjee Rd., 2nd Floor, Kolkata-700016 (West Bengal) ✆ 22162678 • 97, Residency Rd., Bangalore-560025 (Karnataka) ✆ 22210193
Bus.Intt.: WS, L.S. & Rt., Imp., Sub.Ag.; **Spl.:** Humanities & Soc.Sci., Sci. & Tech., Med., Law, Juvenile/Children, Gen. & Fiction

INTERNATIONAL BOOK SUPPLIERS
529/420, Rahim Nagar, Nai Basti, Lucknow-226006 (Uttar Pradesh)

INTERNATIONAL BOOK TRADERS
A-85, Derawal Nagar, Opp., Model Town-II, Delhi-110009
✆ (O) 27143827, 27218194, 27234159 (R) 27233896, Fax: 91-11-27234817

ibt@vsnl.net
Prop.: D.S. Chowdhary; **Bus.Intt.:** Pub., WS and L.S.

INTERNATIONAL BOOKS
23, Nandhikoil St., Teppakulam,
Trichy-620002 (Tamil Nadu)
(O) 2703743, 2711599 (R) 2780447
try_intbook@sancharnet.in
Man.: R. Swaminathan; **Bus.Intt.:** B.S. & Dist.

INTERNATIONAL BOOKS & PERIODICALS SUPPLY SERVICES
38, Nishant Kunj, Pahari Dhiraj Enclave,
Pitam Pura, Delhi-110034
27107078, 27182217, Fax: 27020538
hkjain1975@yahoo.com
Estd.: 1983; **Prop.:** H.K. Jain; **Bus.Intt.:** Rt., WS, Pub., Sub.Ag.; **Spl.:** Botany, Zoology and Related Sub.

INTERNATIONAL BOOKS UPDATE
C/o Oscar Publications, C-558,
Lane No. 12, Majlis Park,
Adarsh Nagar, Delhi-110033
27130049, Fax: 91-11-27435724
buntyw@hotmail.com

INTERNATIONAL GAUDIYA VEDANT TRUST
Block B-3, Janakpuri, New Delhi-110058
91-11-25533568
krsnakauta@gmail.com
www.puribhakit.com
Hd.Org.: Raj Chand Das; **Bus.Intt.:** Pub.;
Spl.: Books on religion and spirituality

INTERNATIONAL GODIYA VEDANT TRUST
91-A, Amrit Puri, Garhi Sant Nagar,
East of Kailash, New Delhi-110065
26222542

INTERNATIONAL HUMAN PEACE HOME
Nangevalli-636454, Salem Distt. (Tamil Nadu)

INTERNATIONAL INSTITUTE OF TAMIL STUDIES
C.I.T. Campus. Adyar, T.T.T.I. Post,
Chennai-600113 (Tamil Nadu)
2350992, Fax: 2352781
Hd.Org.: Dr. Ramar Ilango; **Bus.Intt.:** Pub;
Spl.: Bi-lingual, Bi-annual, Journal 'Journal of Tamil Studies - Conducting Weekly, Monthly, Research Forum', National Seminars and Endowment Lectures

INTERNATIONAL ISLAMIC PUBLISHERS
437, Sarote St., Matia Mahal, Jama Masjid,
Delhi-110006

INTERNATIONAL LAW BOOK COMPANY
Delhi
23867810, 23864769
ilbco@vsnl.com
Bus.Intt.: Business & Dist.

INTERNATIONAL LIBRARY SERVICE
3/6, Alopibagh, Punjabi Colony,
Allahabad-211006 (Uttar Pradesh)
Bus.Intt.: Exp.

INTERNATIONAL MEDICAL BOOK DISTRIBUTORS
1-2 1st Floor, Trisandhya 'A' 97,
Dadasaheb, Phalke Rd., Dadar,
Mumbai-400014 (Maharashtra)
24147181, 24147142, Fax: 24144274
Estd.: 1977; **Hd.Org.:** Vinod S. Bhalani;
Bus.Intt.: Pub., WS, Imp., Exp.

INTERNATIONAL OBSERVER
D-55B, 2nd Floor, Pandav Nagar, Patparganj,
Delhi-110092
9810602915
internationalobserver@rediffmail.com
Hd.Org.: Jaswinder Singh Bhullar;
Bus.Intt.: Pub.; **Spl.** Punjabi Monthly News magazine

INTERNATIONAL PERIODICALS SUPPLIERS
268, Deepali Enclave, Pitampura,
Delhi-110034
(O) 27018098, 27018097 (R) 27021469
ips268@hotmail.com
Prop.: Mrs. Sunita Jain; **Bus.Intt.:** L.S.;
Spl.: Beh.Sci., Soc.Sci., Sci., Med., Tech. Journals and Magazines

INTERNATIONAL PUBLICATIONS
5820/42, Basti Harphool Singh,
Sadar Thana Rd., Delhi-110006
23557888, 23677888, 23357888,
Fax: 23557888
mappeople@liveindia.com,
maskpd@sify.com,
mail@mappeople.com
Hd.Org.: Shri Chand Jain; **Bus.Intt.:** Pub., Cartographer, Laminator and Exp.; **Spl.:** Maps, Charts Globes, etc.

INTERNATIONAL PUBLISHERS & DISTRIBUTORS
B-5/34, Safdarjung Enclave, New Delhi-110029
26108423, 26193187
Estd.: 1986; **Prop.:** C.L. Seghal
Br.: 102, Humayunpur, Safdarjung Enclave,
New Delhi-110029
Bus.Intt.: L.S. & Rt.; **Spl.:** Med.

INTERNATIONAL PUBLISHERS (INDIA)
82, Saakashara Apts, A-3, Paschim Vihar,
New Delhi-110063

INTERNATIONAL PUBLISHING HOUSE
College Road, Meerut (Uttar Pradesh)
4006365, Fax: 91-121-2664890
info@iph-india.com
www.iphindia.com
Hd.Org.: Rakesh Lal; **Bus.Intt.:** Pub.;
Spl.: Educational Books

INTERNATIONAL RANKA AND CO.
1-G-4, Jawahar Nagar, Jaipur-302004 (Rajasthan)
✆ 91-141-2654155, 2654202
✉ iranka@datainfosys.net
Hd.Org.: Savitri Rankha; **Bus.Intt.:** Pub. and Dist.; **Spl.:** Books on Rajasthan in English, Hindi, Sanskrit and Rajasthani

INTERNATIONAL SCIENTFIC PUBLISHING ACADEMY
4594/9, Ansari Road, Darya Ganj, New Delhi-110002
✆ 23250398, Fax: 91-11-25351521
✉ ispabooks@gmail.com
www.ispabooks.com
Hd.Org.: Saurabh Mittal; **Bus.Intt.:** Pub.; **Spl.:** Books on science & technology

INTERNATIONAL SOCIETY FOR KRISHNA CONSCIOUSNESS
Hare Krishna Hill, Sant Nagar, Main Rd., East of Kailash, New Delhi-110065
✆ 26280060, Fax: 91-11-26215421
✉ delhi@pamho.net
Estd.: 1966; **Ch.Exe.:** Mahamantra Das
Br.: Chennai (Tamil Nadu) ✆ 23343266
✉ nitai@md2.vsnl.net.in
Bus.Intt.: B.S., Pub.; **Spl.:** Religious Books

INTERNATIONAL SUBSCRIPTION AGENCY
Flat No. 2, Nirala Market, Nirala Nagar, Lucknow-226020 (Uttar Pradesh)
✆ 22789506, 2789103, 3110103
✉ intl@sancharnet.in
Estd.: 1991; **Prop.:** T.N. Malik
Br.: C-202, Sterling Apartments, 9, University Rd., Lucknow-226007 ✆ 22780653
✉ inter@zyberwayavadh.com • E-183, 3rd Floor, New Rajinder Nagar, New Delhi-110060
✆ 225762042
✉ inter@zhbarwayavadh.com
Bus.Intt.: Pub., WS, L.S. & Rt., Imp., Sub.Ag.; **Spl.:** Med. Humanities & Soc.Sci., Sci. & Tech.

INTERNATIONAL THOMSON PUBLISHING ASIAN
C/o R. Seshadri, 32, Second Main Rd., C.I.T. East, Chennai-600033 (Tamil Nadu)
✆ 24346529
✉ itpsesha@giasmd01.vsnl.net.in

INTERNATIONAL YOGA SOCIETY
Lal Bagh Colony, Loni, Ghaziabad-201102 (Uttar Pradesh)
✆ 0120-2600237, 2166237
✉ iys@vsnl.com, iys@ndf.vsnl.net.in
Estd.: 1974; **Hd.Org.:** Shashi Bhushan Mishra
Br.: Dumari Saran, Bihar • Barhi Gannaur, Sonipat (Haryana)
Bus.Intt.: Pub.; **Spl.:** Books and Magazines on Yoga, Vedanta, Spiritualism and Self-development

INTERNET BOOK CENTRE
13, Vakharia Bhavan, Joshi Lane Ghat, Kopar, (East) Mumbai-400077 (Maharashtra)

INTERPRINT
16-A, Naraina-II, New Delhi-110028
✆ 25704450/51/52, 25704234, 25707474
Fax: 91-11-2570644
Cable: CALMAKERS NEW DELHI
✉ mopl@del3.vsnl.net.in
Estd.: 1980; **Hd.Org.:** S.N. Metha;
Bus.Intt.: Pub., WS, L.S., Rt., Imp., Exp.

INTIME BOOKS SERVICES
85-86, Subhash Khand, Giri Nagar, Kalkaji, New Delhi-110019
✆ 26220958, 26426566, 35905898, 32035429, Fax: 26212122, 26288018
✉ itbookservices@yahoo.co.in
Estd.: 2003; **Hd.Org.:** Sameer Sikka
Bus.Intt.: Rt., Sub.Ag., Pub.'s Rep., L.S.
Spl.: Acad., Beh.Sci., Sci., Med., Tech., Fiction

INTL. PRINT-O-PAC-LTD.
B-204-205, Okhla Industrial Area, Phase-I, New Delhi-110020
✆ 26815199, 26817569, 26818199, 26815631, Fax: 91-11-26819439
Hd.Org.: Amila Singhvi; **Bus.Intt.:** Printing and Pub.

INVIS MULTIMEDIA
Pandit Colony, Kaudias, Thiruvananthapuram-695003 (Kerala)
✆ 2311832, 2319892, Fax: 0471-2313170
✉ infor@invismultimedia.com
Hd.Org.: M.R. Hari; **Spl.:** Coffee Table Book, Post Cards, Pictures CD-ROM's DVD, VCD's and Interactive CD-ROM's

IOS PRESS BV
B-13, A Block, LSC, 3rd Floor, Naraina Vihar, New Delhi-110028
✆ 45055540, Fax: 91-11-25778876
✉ p.sing@iospress.in
Hd.Org.: Praveen Singh Kuhad
Bus.Intt.: Pub. and Dist.; **Spl.:** Books on journals on science, medicine, electronics, etc.

IPD ALTERNATIVES
35A/1, Shahpur Jat, New Delhi-110049
✆ 91-11-26492040
✉ ipd.alternatives@gmail.com
Hd.Org.: Amrita Akhil; **Bus.Intt.:** Pub.; **Spl.:** Social science and humanities, women's studies, dalit studies and books for children

IQBAL BOOK DEPOT
Ashok Rajpath, Patna-800006 (Bihar)
Bus.Intt.: Pub. and B.S.

IQBAL PUBLISHING HOUSE
Khazanchi Rd., Patna-800006 (Bihar)
Bus.Intt.: Pub. and B.S.

IQRA INTERNATIONAL
422, Matia Mahal, Jama Masjid, Delhi-110006
✆ 23279392, Fax: 91-11-22427868
Bus.Intt.: Pub. and B.S.

IRRAWADDY PUBLICATIONS
C-482, Vikaspuri, New Delhi-110018
✆ 25504169, 25613636, Fax: 25614759
✉ mawthiri@hotmail.com
Hd.Org.: Chandra Prakash Prabhakar; **Bus.Intt.:** Dist.; **Spl.:** Regional Litt.

ISHAN BOOK HOUSE
297-A, Block South Gamsi Ext., Delhi-110053
✆ 22172844 (PP)
Prop.: Trilochan Joshi; **Bus.Intt.:** L.S.

ISHAAN PRAKASHAN
7/23, Ansari Road, Darya Ganj, New Delhi-110002 ✆ 91-11-23288769
Hd.Org.: Amod Maheswari; **Bus.Intt.:** Pub.

ISHWAR CHANDRA & CO.
Agarwal Bhawan, 1st Floor, 9983, Ram Behari Rd., Sarai Rohella, New Delhi-110005
✆ (O) 25716540, 23276843/44 (R) 27015091
Prop.: Ishwar Chandra; **Bus.Intt.:** L.S.;
Spl.: Specialise in Supplying Govt. Publications

ISKCON
Kolkata (West Bengal)
✆ 2476075, 2473757, Fax: 2478515
✉ calcutta@com.bbt.se
Bus.Intt.: Pub.

ISLAMI SAHITYA PRAKASHAN
1525, Sui Walan, New Delhi-110002
✆ 23283702

ISLAMI SAHITYA TRUST
1353, Chitli Qabar, Delhi-110006
✆ 91-11-23276741
Hd.Org.: Nasim Ahmad Ghazi Falahi
Bus.Intt.: Pub.; **Spl.:** Islamic books in Hindi

ISLAMIA LIBRARY
Marigaon, Naojan-785604 (Assam)

ISLAMIC BOOK HOUSE
2570, Churiwalan, Delhi-110006
✆ 23271717, Fax: 91-11-23265278
Bus.Intt.: Pub., Exp.; **Spl.:** Holy *Quran* & Other Islamic Litt. in English, Arabic, Urdu, French and Spanish

ISLAMIC BOOK SERVICE
2872/24, Kucha Chelan, Darya Ganj, New Delhi-110002
✆ (O) 23253514, 23265380, 23286551, 23272292 (R) 26941065, Fax: 011-23277913
✉ ibsdelhi@del2.vsnl.net.in, islamic@eth.net
🌐 www.islamic-india.com
Estd.: 1982; **Hd.Org.:** Abduls Sami;
Bus.Intt.: Pub., WS, L.S. & Rt., Exp.;
Spl.: Humanities & Soc.Sci., Juvenile/Children

ISLAMIC CENTRE
C-29, Nizamuddin West Market, Near DESU, New Delhi-110013

ISLAMIC FOUNDATION TRUST
138, Perambur High Rd., Chennai-600012 (Tamil Nadu)
✆ 26424401, 26426181, 26624401
Telefax: 044-24835120, Fax: 91-44-25365086
✉ iftchennai12@email.com

ISLAMIC PUBLISHING HOUSE
(Darul Kutubul Islamia) 4085, Urdu Bazar, Jama Masjid, Delhi-110006

ISLAMIC PUBLISHING HOUSE
10/529, M.P. Rd., Kozhikode-685001 (Kerala)
✆ 0495-276092, 2720092, Fax: 261752
Estd.: 1945; **Hd.Org.:** Islamic Service Trust;
Bus.Intt.: Pub. and B.S.; **Spl.:** Islamic Books

ISLAMIC PUBLISHING HOUSE
Fourland Building, Rajaji Road, Kozhikode, Calicut-673004 (Kerala)
✆ 91-495-2720072, 2724618
✉ iphcalicut@dataone.in
🌐 www.iphkerala.com
Hd.Org.: Sheikh Muhammed
Bus.Intt.: Pub.; **Spl.:** Books in Malayalam on history, Pol.science, fiction, Islam as well as children's books

ISLAMIC SERVICE TRUST
First Building, Silver Hills, Kozhikode-673012
✆ 91-495-27231305
Hd.Org.: Abdul Ahad Thangal
Bus.Intt.: Pub.; **Spl.:** Books in Malayalam on Islamic studies

ITALIAN EMBASSY CULTURAL CENTRE
New Delhi
✆ 26871901, 26871903, Fax: 26871902
✉ italcult@del3.vsnl.net.in
Bus.Intt.: Promoter

ITIHAS SHOODH SANSTHAN
Bulbhullian Rd., Mehrauli, New Delhi-110030
✆ 26963982
Estd.: 1980; **Hd.Org.:** Vijay Dev Jhari;
Bus.Intt.: Pub. and Dist.; **Spl.:** Hindi Litt.

ITHAS VIDYA PRAKASHAN
Aaramachine Gali, Dharam Colony, Nangloi,
Delhi-110047

IVY PUBLICATION HOUSE
25-C, Pocket A, Dilshad Garden,
Delhi-110095
✆ 23281029, 23244664
Fax: 91-11-23277098
www.sarupbooks.com
Hd.Org.: Smita Sharma; **Bus.Intt.:** Pub. and Dist.;
Spl.: Soc.Sci., Sci., Dictionaries and
Encyclopaedias

■ ■ ■

J

J.B. NANAK CHAND "CHAND"
Lower Dhalpur, Kullu-175101
(Himachal Pradesh)
✆ 224936
Estd.: 1961; **Hd.Org.:** Hitesh Kumar Sachdeva; **Bus.Intt.:** B.S. and Stationers; **Spl.:** School, College and Gen. Books

J.B.A. PUBLISHERS
5061, Sant Nagar, Karol Bagh,
New Delhi-110005
✆ 28726165, 91-11-41513850
sales@jba.in
www.jainbookagency.com
Hd.Org.: Vaishalik Jain
Bus.Intt.: Dist.; **Spl.:** Books on law, trade & industry, management, eco., computer, agric., soc.sciences, etc.

J.B.C. PUBLISHERS AND DISTRIBUTORS
2/39, Ansari Road, Darya Ganj,
New Delhi-110002
✆ 41564445, Fax: 91-11-41564440
jbcpd@airtelbroadband.in
www.jbcpd.com
Hd.Org.: Usha Rani Jain
Bus.Intt.: Pub. and Dist.; **Spl.:** Books on medicine, engineering, law, soc.science, management, bio-science and general books

J.B.D. BOOK DISTRIBUTOR
10149, Katra Chhajju Pandit, Model Basti,
Opp. Filmistan Cinema, New Delhi-110005
✆ (O) 36821450, 23629902 (R) 27420558
jbdbook@yahoo.com
Estd.: 1992; **Man.Exe.:** Mahesh Kumar Jain; **Bus.Intt.:** Pub., L.S. & Pub.'s Rep. and B.S.; **Spl.:** Sci. and Tech., Med., Comm. and Agri., Sci. Humanities, Soc.Sci., Man. and Engg. etc.

J.K. BOOK DISTRIBUTORS
H.S. Cox Business Centre,
52, Dr. V.B. Gandhi Marg, Kalaghoda,
Mumbai-400023 (Maharashtra)

J.K. BOOK STORES
Gujari Bazar, Patna City, Patna-800008 (Bihar)
Bus.Intt.: Pub. and B.S.

J.K. BOOK STORES
Rajapuri Pool, Patna-800001 (Bihar)
Bus.Intt.: Pub. and B.S.

J.K. JAIN BROTHERS
Motia Park, Sultania Rd., Bhopal-462001
(Madhya Pradesh)
✆ (O) 2242577 (R) 2748661
Estd.: 1964; **Prop.:** J.K. Jain; **Bus.Intt.:** L.S. and Rt.; **Spl.:** Bhopal Institutes only (Tech., Med., Comp. Books)

J.K. LAW HOUSE
Rasila Bhawan, F-40, Rehari Colony Rd.,
Jammu (Jammu & Kashmir)
✆ 2570061, Fax: 2573652
jklaw@sancharnet.in
Estd.: 1998; **Prop.:** Sunil Gupta; **Bus.Intt.:** Rt., L.S., Pub.; **Spl.:** Law

J.K. SUPPLIERS
No. 13/4, 4th Cross, Flower Garden,
Magodi Rd., Bangalore-23 (Karnataka)

J.M. JAINA & BROTHERS
3622, Mori Gate, Delhi-110006
✆ (O) 23966603, 23915064, 23950936
(R) 23964707, 23976292, Fax: 23986793
akalank@vsnl.com
Estd.: 1928; **Prop.:** Narendra Kumar Jain; **Bus.Intt.:** Pub., Dist.; **Spl.:** Govt. Pub., Gazettes, Law & Commercial Books BIS, CPWD, IRC, Civil Engg., Maps Dictionaries, Service Matters and Statutory Forms and Registers, Akalank Pub.

J.M.D. BOOKS
SU-162, Vishakha Enclave, Pitam Pura,
Delhi-110088
✆ 27341558 ▮ 9810816498
Prop.: D.K. Bhatheja; **Bus.Intt.:** L.S.

J.N. CHAKRABORTY & CO.
13, Bankim Chatterjee St., Kolkata-700073
(West Bengal)

J.N. GHOSH & SONS
6, Bankim Chatterjee St., Kolkata-700073
(West Bengal)

J.P. BOOK CORNER
Sector-8, Bokaro Steel City, Dhanbad-827008
(Bihar)

J.P. PRINT SYSTEMS (P.) LTD.
Hyderabad (Andhra Pradesh)
✆ 23732972, 23734117, Fax: 23750647
info@jpeamcet.com
Bus.Intt.: Printers

J.P. PUBLICATIONS
Opp. Ilapuram Hotel, Gandhinagar,
Vijayawada-520003 (Andhra Pradesh)
✆ 2627484
srinivasjp99@hotmail.com
Bus.Intt.: Pub. and B.S.; **Spl.:** School, Graduate, Adv. Books for Lib. and Gen. Books

J.P. PUBLISHING HOUSE
27/28, Shakti Nagar, Delhi-110007

✆ 27127209
Hd.Org.: Jagdish Prasad Yadav

J.P.H. ENTERPRISES
4095, Nai Sarak, Chawri Bazar, Delhi-110006
✆ 22914689, 22928615
Hd.Org.: Yash Pal

J.P.R. PUBLICATIONS
156-A9, Perumal Koil Noth, Car St., Vallicor-627117 (Tamil Nadu)

J.S. PRAKASHAN
2182, Sector 22-C, Chandigarh-160022
✆ 2714870
Hd.Org.: Jogiender Singh Vatas

JAFAR BOOK DEPOT
Rohtas-821311 (Bihar)

JAFEE PUBLISHING MANAGEMENT SERVICE
Kunnuparambil Buildings, Kurichy, Kottayam-686549 (Kerala)
✆ 04826-470, Fax: 0481-56822
Estd.: 1985; **Hd.Org.:** Santhamma Punnoose; **Bus.Intt.:** Publishing Consultants

JAGADHATRI PUBLISHERS
59/IB, Patuatola Lane, Kolkata-700009 (West Bengal)
✆ 033-2316315
Bus.Intt.: Pub.; **Spl.:** Bengali Fictions, Short Stories and Novels

JAGANMAL & SONS
Thungal Bazar, Imphal-I, Manipur

JAGANNATH RATHA
Binod Behari, Cuttack-753002 (Orissa)
✆ 0671-223669
Estd.: 1963; **Prop.:** Subhendu Sekhar Ratha; **Bus.Intt.:** Pub. and B.S.; **Spl.:** Gen. Litt. in Oriya

JAGAT PUSTAK MAHAL
Sheopuri, Patna-800023 (Bihar)

JAGATMATA PUBLISHERS
10/2B, Ramanath Majumder St., Kolkata-700009 (West Bengal)

JAGATRAM AND SONS
24/4855, Ansari Rd., Darya Ganj, New Delhi-110002
✆ 23271844, 22083206
Hd.Org.: Om Dutt Sharma; **Bus.Intt.:** Pub. and Dist.; **Spl.:** Moral Sci., Sci., Rel., Culture

JAGDAMBA PUBLISHING COMPANY
4771/23, 1st Floor, Mahavir Shree House, Opp. Choudhry Eye Centre, Ansari Rd., New Delhi-110002
✆ 23250048, 23258536 ▮ 9810576314
✉ jagdambhabc@yahoo.com
Estd.: 2000; **Prt.:** Kishana Nand Pujari, Narender Singh Bisht; **Bus.Intt.:** WS, Rt., L.S.; **Spl.:** Acad., Beh.Sci., Soc.Sci., Comm., Sci., Pure & Applied, Med., Tech., Law

JAGDISH SANSKRIT PUSTAKALAYA
Jhalaniyon Ka Rasta, Kishanpole Bazar, Jaipur-302001 (Rajasthan)
✆ 91-141-2312974
Hd.Org.: Om Prakash Sharma; **Bus.Intt.:** Pub.; **Spl.:** Books on *Vastushastra, Vedas,* Ayurveda, Phil., Astrology, Indian Culture and Sanskrit Litt.

JAGMANDER BOOK AGENCY
22-B/5, D.B. Gupta Rd., Dev Nagar, Karol Bagh, New Delhi-110005
✆ (O) 28713985, 28715483 (R) 28711147, 28711149, Fax: 28711147, 28714987
✉ jba@ndf.vsnl.net.in
Estd.: 1972; **Prop.:** Ajay Gupta; **Bus.Intt.:** L.S., Imp.; **Spl.:** Sci. & Tech., Med., Bio.Sci.

JAGRAN PRAKASHAN LTD.
F-21, 22, Sector-8, Gautam Budh Nagar, Noida-201301 (Uttar Pradesh)
✆ 2425961-62, Fax: 91-120-2425203
✉ delhi@nda.jagran.com
www.jagran.com
Hd.Org.: Sanjay Gupta; **Bus.Intt.:** Pub.; **Spl.:** Hindi daily *Dainik Jagran, Sakti India*, etc.

JAGRAN RESEARCH CENTRE
Jagran Building, 2, Sarvodaya Nagar, Kanpur-208005 (Uttar Pradesh)
✆ 2216161-64, Fax: 2216972, 2298040
✉ jrc@jagran.com
Bus.Intt.: Pub.; **Spl.:** Socio Eco., Statistical data Books of all the States, Distt. and U.Ts.

JAGRITY PRAKASHAN
F-109, Sector-27, Noida, Ghaziabad-201301 (Uttar Pradesh)
✆ 2538101
Hd.Org.: Krishnanand Sagar

JAI BHARATI PRAKASHAN
258/365 Muthiganj, Maya Press Rd., Allahabad-211003 (Uttar Pradesh)
✆ 2404409
Hd.Org.: Jhuggilal Gupta

JAI BHARATI PUBLISHING HOUSE
447, Peeli Koti, Nayi Basti, Keetganj, Allahabad-211003 (Uttar Pradesh)
Hd.Org.: Premadevi Gupta

JAI MANGALA GENERAL STORES
Chauriya Bariyarpur, Begusarai (Bihar)
Bus.Intt.: Pub. and B.S.

JAI PRAKASH NATH PUBLICATIONS
Nauchandi Crossing,
Gandhi Ashram Chowk, Garh Rd.,
Meerut (Uttar Pradesh)
✆ 2762403, 2762414, Fax: 2600013
✉ jpnpmrrt@rediffmail.com
Hd.Org.: V.N. Gupta; **Bus.Intt.:** Pub.;
Spl.: Engg., Med. Entrance, B. Tech, M.C.A., M.B.A., N.D.A. and Textbooks

JAICO PUBLISHING HOUSE
127, Mahatma Gandhi Rd., Mumbai-400023 (Maharashtra)
✆ 22676702, 22676802, 22672969,
Fax: 22656412
✉ jaicobom@bom5.vsnl.com,
jaicowbd@vsnl.com, jaicopub@vsnl.com
www.jaicobooks.com
Estd.: 1946; **Man.Dir.:** Ashwin J. Shah;
Exe.Dir.: S.C. Sethi; **Editor-in-Chief:** R.H. Sharma
Br.: Gen.Man.: D.M. Patel, Jaico's WS Book Distributors, 127, Mahatma Gandhi Rd., Mumbai-400023 (Maharashtra) ✆ 22676702, 22672969, 22676802, Fax: 22676802,
✉ jaicopub@vsnl.net.in • **Man.:** Sanjay Verma, Jaico Book Distributors, 194, FIE, Patpar Ganj, Delhi-110092 ✆ 22144204/5/7, Cable: JAICOBOOKS, Fax: 91-11-22144206
✉ sethidel@del6.vsnl.net.in, jaicobook@vsnl.net • Jaico Book Distributors, G-2, 16 Ansari Rd., Darya Ganj, New Delhi-110002 ✆ 23260651, 23260618, 23264748, Fax: 23278469 • **Man.:** M.K. Bal, Jaico Book Enterprises, 302, A.P.C. Roy Rd., Kolkata-700009 (West Bengal)
✆ 23600542, 23600543
✉ jaicocal@cal2.vsnl.net.in • **Man.:** Hemant Sharma, Jaico Book House, 41/1, Ist Main Rd., 6th Cross, Gandhinagar, Bangalore-560009 (Karnataka) ✆ 22267016, 22257083, Cable: JAICOBOOKS, Fax: 22257083
✉ jaicobgr@blr.vsnl.net.in • **Man.:** A.R. Sivaraman, Jaico Book Agency, No. 57, Dr. Giri Rd. T. Nagar, Chennai-600017 (Tamil Nadu),
✆ 28224582, 28222653,
✉ jaicoche@md3.vsnl.net.in • **Man.:** K.S. Anand, Jaico Book House, 3-4-494/1/2, Barakatpura, Hyderabad-500027 (Andhra Pradesh) ✆ 27551992, 27555699
✉ hyd1_jaicohyd@sancharnet.in
• Jaico Book House Pvt. Ltd., ELGI House, 2, Mill Office's Colony, Opp. Times of India, Ashram Rd., Ahmedabad-380009 (Gujarat)
✆ 26579865, 26578913
✉ jaicoahm@rediffmail.com
Bus.Intt.: Pub., WS, L.S., Rt., Imp.;
Spl.: Humanities & Soc.Sci., Sci. & Tech., Med., Juvenile/Children, Gen. & Fiction etc.

JAIDEEP PRAKASHAN
105, Naraina, Kabeerbage Samore, Pune-411030 (Maharashtra)

JAIHIND PRAKASHAN
Jhavabhachiwadi, Girgaon, Mumbai-400004 (Maharashtra)

JAIN ACHARYA DHARMASHRUT
Granthmala, Godhar Sadar, Alseesar House, S.C. Rd., Jaipur (Rajasthan)

JAIN BOOK AGENCY
C-9, Connaught Place,
New Delhi-110001
✆ (O) 23321663, 23320806, 23326728, 23416390-94, 51513851 (R) 25738897, Cable: GOVT. BOOKS, Fax: 23731117
✉ govtbooks@del3.vsnl.net.in,
sales@jainbookagency.com
www.jainbookagency.com
Estd.: 1935; **Prop.:** Vimal Vahan Jain, Vaishalik Jain & Nabhi Kumar Jain
Br.: Jain Book Agency (Southend), 1, Aurobindo Palace, Hauz Khas, New Delhi-110016 ✆ 26566113, 26567066 • JBA Book Agency, C-5, Connaught Place, New Delhi-110001
Bus.Intt.: WS, L.S. & Rt., Exp., Sub.Ag.;
Spl.: Law, Juvenile/Children, Gen., Comp. Books, Govt. Publications

JAIN BOOK DEPOT
Chadha Bhavan, 23/4, Shakti Nagar, Delhi-110007
✆ 31027550
✉ jainbookdepo@hotmail.com
Estd.: 1965; **Dir.:** Dr. Rajiv Kumar Jain
Bus.Intt.: Pub., WS, L.S. & Rt., Exp.;
Spl.: Humanities & Soc.Sci., Sci. & Tech., Law, Gen. & Fiction etc.

JAIN BOOK DEPOT
Delhi Rd., Opp. Med. College, Rohtak (Haryana)
✆ (O) 213355 (R) 211345
Estd.: 1966; **Prop.:** Atul Jain
Bus.Intt.: B.S., L.S.

JAIN BOOK HOUSE
S.C.O. No. 70-72 (2), Sector 17-D, Chandigarh
✆ 2702768
Bus.Intt.: B.S. and Pub.
Spl.: Law

JAIN BOOK STALL
Khajuri Bazar, Indore-452002 (Madhya Pradesh)

JAIN BOOKS & PERIODICALS
1586/113, Tri Nagar, Delhi-110035
✆ 27383728, Fax: 27182715
✉ jainbooks@vsnl.net, ibptn@hotmail.com
Estd.: 2002; **Prop.**: Mahesh Jain; **Bus.Intt.**: Sub.Ag., L.S., Pub.'s Rep.; **Spl.**: Tech., Sci.

JAIN BROTHERS
16/873, East Park Rd., Near Dr. Joshi Hospital, Karol Bagh, New Delhi-110005
✆ 23618426, 23619023, 27518426, Fax: 23638444
✉ jain_bros@hotmail.com
www.thejainbrothers.com
Estd.: 1952; **Prop.**: Sunil Kumar Jain; **Bus.Intt.**: Pub. & Dist.; **Spl.**: Engg., AMIE, Agri. & Sci. Pure & Applied Books

JAIN BROTHERS
4, Kalyan Bhavan, Ratanada Rd., Jodhpur-342001 (Rajasthan)
Bus.Intt.: Pub. and Tech. B.S.

JAIN BROTHERS
Lower Mall, Patiala
✆ 2218118, 2214118

JAIN INTERNATIONAL
21, Saumya Apartment, Ahmedabad-380014 (Gujarat)

JAIN PUSTAK MANDIR
Choura Rasta, Jaipur (Rajasthan)

JAIN PUSTAK MANDIR
Daudnagar, Aurangabad-824113 (Bihar)
Bus.Intt.: Pub. and B.S.

JAIN SULAB PATHAK MANCH
21-A, Darya Ganj, New Delhi-110002

JAIN VANI PRAKASHAN
10/33A, Gali No. 9, Vishwas Nagar, Shahdara, Delhi-110032

JAIN VISHWA BHARTI
Anuvrat Bhawan, 210, Deen Dayal Upadhyaya Marg, New Delhi-110002
✆ 23235576
Trustee: Lalit Garg; **Bus.Intt.**: The Centre is Engaged in the Research Activities and Publication; **Spl.**: Jain Litt.

JAINSON BOOK SHOP & STATIONERS
Indore (Madhya Pradesh)
✆ 2538787
✉ kitab2000@rediffmail.com
Bus.Intt.: B.S., L.S. & Rt.

JAIPUR BOOK HOUSE
389, Joshi Bhawan, Maniharon Ka Rasta, Tripolia Bazar, Jaipur-302003 (Rajasthan)
✆ 2305612, Fax: 2407260
Hd.Org.: Mohan Kumar Kashyap; **Bus.Intt.**: Pub.; **Spl.**: Health in Hindi

JAIPUR PUBLISHING HOUSE
S.M.S. Highway, Jaipur-302003 (Rajasthan)
✆ (O) 2319198, 2319124 (R) 2512152
Estd.: 1960; **Hd.Org.**: Ram Chander Agarwal

JAISHREE PRAKASHAN
4/115, Viswasnagar, Shahdara, Delhi-110032

JAISWAL BOOK STORE
Masaurhi, Patna-804452 (Bihar)
Bus.Intt.: Pub. and B.S.

JAISWAL PUSTAK BHANDAR
Kahalgaon (Colgong), Bhagalpur-813203 (Bihar)
Bus.Intt.: Pub. and B.S.

JAISWAL STORES
Bakhri, Begusarai-848201 (Bihar)
Bus.Intt.: Pub. and B.S.

JALALI ACADEMY
New Delhi
✆ 23265480, Fax: 23257189
✉ aakif@del3.vsnl.net.in
Bus.Intt.: Pub. & L.S.

JALEELA PUBLISHING HOUSE
21, West Car St., Tirunelveli-627006 (Tamil Nadu)

JAMA'AT AHMEDIYYA INTERNATIONAL
53, Institutional Area, M.G. Road, Tughlakabad, New Delhi-110062
✆ 26059094, Fax: 91-11-29958055
✉ dawood.ahmad@tcs.com
www.alislam.org
Hd.Org.: Dawood Ahmad; **Bus.Intt.**: Pub. and Dist.; **Spl.**: Hindi regional languages books on Islam

JAMBAWAN BOOK AGENCY
Fathima Nagar, Budalur Post, Thanjavur Distt.-613602 (Tamil Nadu)
✆ 04362-288840
✉ rajchristy@hotmail.com, jambawanbooks@hotmail.com
Estd.: 1997; Prop.: J. Christuraj; **Bus.Intt.**: L.S.

JAMMU BOOK STORE
Sh.: P.O. Surya Vihar Bhori, Patta (Talab Tillo), Jammu Tawi-180002 (Jammu and Kashmir)

Off.: Bushan Med. Hall Bld., Maesh Pura, Jammu Tawi-180002 (Jammu and Kashmir)
Estd.: 1988; **Prop.:** Balwinder Nirmohi

JAMWAL BOOK HOUSE
134A, Mohalah Maraina, Kacchi Chowani (Jammu and Kashmir)
Estd.: 1989; **Prop.:** Karan Singh Jamwal

JAN JAGRAN PRAKASHAN
30/13, Gardani Bagh, Patna-800002 (Bihar)

JAN SATHIYA PRAKASHAN
Tilak Chauk, Washim District Akola, Washim-444505 (Maharashtra)

JANA BOOK SHOP
71, Jatindra Mohan Avenue, Kolkata-5 (West Bengal)

JANA JAGRTHY PRASADHAKA SANGAM
Paravoor, Alappuzha-688004 (Kerala)
Estd.: 1991; **Hd.Org.:** Aloysious D. Fernandez; **Bus.Intt.:** Pub.

JANADA PRAKASHAN
Educational Publication, 24, Ansari Rd., Darya Ganj, New Delhi-110002
Prop.: S. Chowdhary

JANAK BOOK DISTRIBUTORS
C-203, Jhil Mil Colony, Shahdara, Delhi-110035
✆ 22162365
Estd.: 1994; **Prop.:** Pradeep Kumar Sehgal; **Bus.Intt.:** L.S.; **Spl.:** Acad., Beh.Sci., Soc.Sci., Comm., Sci., Pure & Applied, Tech., Fiction Juveniles, Rare & Law Books

JANAK PUBLISHERS
C-236, Vikas Puri, New Delhi-110018

JANAKI BOOK DEPOT
3/2, Shyama Charan Dey St., Kolkata-700073 (West Bengal)

JANAKI PRAKASHAN
Ashok Raj Path, Chauhatta, Patna-800004 (Bihar)

JANAM MARKETING
A-101, Shiv Dham, Sector-2, Airoli, Navi Mumbai-400078 (Maharashtra)
✆ 022-27691318, Fax: 022-27697788
@ janamark@vsnl.net.in
Estd.: 1997 **Prop.:** Ajay Malhotra; **Bus.Intt.:** WS, L.S. & Rt., Imp.; **Spl.:** Humanities & Soc.Sci., Sci. & Tech.

JANAPAD
68, Cossipore Rd., Kolkata-700036 (West Bengal)

JANAPRIYA PRAKASHAN
20/60, Gali No. 1, Vishwas Nagar, Delhi-110032

JANATA BOOK HOUSE
10/2B, Ramanath Majumder St., Kolkata-700009 (West Bengal)

JANATA PUBLISHERS
Navin, 7, Prahlad Plot, Rajkot (Gujarat)

JANATHA BOOK STALL
Thevara, Kochi-682013 (Kerala)
✆ (O) 2311341 (R) 2311225
Estd.: 1968; **Hd.Org.:** Thomas Palackal CMI; **Bus.Intt.:** Pub. and B.S.

JANATHA SERVICE CENTRE
Near New Church Basilicca, Thrissur-680001 (Kerala)
✆ (O) 223555 (R) 223560
Estd.: 1935; **Hd.Org.:** Chakko Avokkaran; **Bus.Intt.:** B.S.

JANBAAT DISTRIBUTORS
Second Floor, 34, Silver Park, Shiv Puri, Delhi-110051
▮ 9868078123
@ janbatt@yahoo.com
Spl.: Children's books in Hindi language

JANCHETNA
D-68, Nirala Nagar, Lucknow-226010 (Uttar Pradesh)
✆ 91-551-2241922
@ janchetna@rediffmail.com
Hd.Org.: Katyayani; **Bus.Intt.:** Pub. and Dist.

JANE'S INFORMATION GROUP
New Delhi
✆ 26516105, Fax: 26516105
@ janesindia@sify.com
Bus.Intt.: B.S.

JANEPA PUBLISHING HOUSE
10, Plaza Cinema Building, Connaught Place, New Delhi-110001

JANJATI VIKAS PARISHAD
P.O. Balipur, Dhanbad-828201 (Jharkhand)
Hd.Org.: Arti Mahto

JANKI PRASAD (BOOKSELLER)
Chitkohra Bazar, Patna-800002 (Bihar)
Bus.Intt.: Pub. and B.S.

JANKI PUSTAK SAAN
Gyanpeeth Compound, Khazanchi Rd., Patna-800004 (Bihar)
✆ 256704
Bus.Intt.: Pub. and B.S.

JANPRIYA PRAKASHAN
C-160, Lalbagh Colony, Loni,
Ghaziabad-201102 (Uttar Pradesh)
Hd.Org.: Premshankar Sharma

JANTA BOOK DEPOT
23, Shaheed Bhagat Singh Marg,
New Delhi-110001
✆ 23362985, 23369685, Fax: 23363685
Prop.: I.P. Gupta; **Bus.Intt.:** Rt. and B.S.;
Spl.: School, College Text and Gen. Books

JANTA BOOK DEPOT
1521/2, Wazir Nagar (Opp. Defence Colony, P.T. College), New Delhi-110003
✆ (O) 24692352, 24621791 (R) 26416656, Fax: 24604413
✉ mukkug@yahoo.com, milli@bol.net.in
Prop.: Harish Gupta; **Bus.Intt.:** WS, Dist.;
Spl.: Convent & Public Schools Books, Competition Books, College Books, Man. Books, Comp. Books, Stationery & Printing of all types

JANTA BOOK HOUSE
Sadar Bazar, Dinapore,
Patna-801503 (Bihar)
Bus.Intt.: Pub. and B.S.

JANTA BOOK STORE
Bihpur, Bhagalpur-853201 (Bihar)
Bus.Intt.: Pub. and B.S.

JANTA BOOK STORES
Gujari Bazar, Patna City, Patna-800008 (Bihar)
Bus.Intt.: Pub. and B.S.

JANTA BOOK STORES
Gandhi Chowk, Madhupur, Deoghar-815353 (Bihar)
Bus.Intt.: Pub. and B.S.

JANVADI SAHITYA SADAN
8, Gandhi Nagar, Agra-282003 (Uttar Pradesh)
✆ 0562-2527106
Estd.: 1980; **Prop.:** Alok Srivastava
Br.: 48-D, Shiv Mandir Marg, Gali No. 4, Maujpur, Delhi
Bus.Intt.: L.S.; **Spl.:** Humanities & Soc.Sci., Sci. & Tech., Med., Mang., Bio.Sci, Reference

JANVANI PRAKASHAN PVT. LTD.
30/35-36, Publishers St., (St. No. 9), Vishwas Nagar, Shahdara, Delhi-110032
✆ 22385935, 22382559
Hd.Org.: Arun Kumar; **Bus.Intt.:** Pub. and Dist.; **Spl.:** Hindi Litt. and Popular Sci., Edu. and Children's Books

JASMINE EXPORTS
32/34, Ambika Market, (Basement), 1st Old Hanuman Cross Lane, Kalbadevi, Mumbai-400002 (Maharashtra)
Bus.Intt.: Exp.

JASMINES EXEL
8-A, New Century Colony, Ambattur, Chennai-600056 (Tamil Nadu)
✆ 26255708

JASPAL PRAKASHAN
Khazanchi Rd., Patna-800004 (Bihar)
Bus.Intt.: Pub. and B.S.

JASPAL PUBLISHERS
East Makhania Kuan, Patna-800004 (Bihar)
Bus.Intt.: Pub. and B.S.

JATASTHAN SINDHI AKADEMI
J-7, Subhash Marg, 'C' Scheme, Jaipur-302001 (Rajasthan)

JATIYA PUSTAKALAYA
57-C, College St., Kolkata-73 (West Bengal)

JAVED BOOK DEPOT
Phulwarisharif, Patna-801505 (Bihar)
Bus.Intt.: Pub. and B.S.

JAWAHAR LIBRARIAN
Sadar Bazar, Mathura-281001 (Uttar Pradesh)
✆ (O) 2409630 (R) 2405110
Hd.Org.: Amarnath Pachuari

JAWAHAR PUBLISHERS AND DISTRIBUTORS
15, D.D.A. Market, Ber Sarai, Opp. J.N.U., New Delhi-110016
✆ (O) 26962973 (R) 27311367, 27315367
Prop.: Ravi Mazumdar; **Bus.Intt.:** Pub., WS, Rt., L.S., Pub.'s Rep.; **Spl.:** Acad., Soc.Sci.

JAWAHAR STORES & BOOK DEPOT
4, Sahajeevan, Shradhanand Rd., Vile Parle (East), Mumbai-400028 (Maharashtra)
✆ 24302126

JAY BOOK HOUSE
8, Jay Shiv Apartment, Near Vanvasi Kalayan Ashram, Nandivali Rd., Sunil Nagar, Dombivali (East), Thane (Maharashtra)
✉ jaybookhouseindia@rediffmail.com

JAY CEE PUBLICATIONS
AIMO House, Swamy Ram Tirath Nagar, 1E/11, Jhandewalan Extn., New Delhi-110055
✆ 23552591, 25382500, Fax: 91-11-25382100
✉ info@jaypeepublications.com
www.jaypeepublications.com
Estd.: 1984; **Hd.Org.:** Jagdish Chander Goyal; **Bus.Intt.:** Pub.; **Spl.:** School Textbooks in English and Hindi

JAY DEEP PRAKASHAN
B-2, Neel Sadan,
1426, Sadashiv Peth, Opp. Pune Vidya Peth,
Pune-411030 (Maharashtra)

JAY KAY BOOK HOUSE
Residency Rd., Jammu Tawi-180001
(Jammu & Kashmir)
✆ 2573560, 2470195
✉ jkbh@rediffmail.com
Estd.: 1969; **Prop.:** Kartar Singh
Br.: 40 Sector, 6A Extension, Trikuta Nagar,
Jammu Tawi-180004 ✆ (R) 2470195
Bus.Intt.: Pub., WS, L.S. & Rt., Sub.Ag.;
Spl.: Humanities & Soc.Sci., Sci. & Tech.,
Gen. & Fiction etc.

JAY KAY BOOK SHOP (REGD.)
Women's College Rd., Jamalatta Chowk,
Nawa Kadal, Srinagar, Kashmir-190002
(Jammu and Kashmir)
✆ (O) 0194-2421135 (R) 2425937,
Fax: 0194-2476686, 2426811
✉ jkbookshop@yahoo.com
🌐 www.youngpublishing.com
Estd.: 1973; **Prop.:** Sheikh Bashir Ahmed
Br.: Kitab Mahal, Botshah Mohalla, Lalbazar,
Srinagar-190011
Bus.Intt.: Pub., B.S., L.S., WS; **Spl.:** Sci. &
Tech., Med., Comm. & Man., Humanities,
Gen. Books

JAYA NIKETAN
359, Madhbapur, M.G. Rd., Allahabad
(Uttar Pradesh)
✆ 2441500
Hd.Org.: Akhilesh Shrivastab

JAYA SHREE TRUST
102, 16th Cross, Malleswaram,
Bangalore-560003 (Karnataka)
Bus.Intt.: Pub. and L.S.

JAYALAKSHMI INDOLOGICAL BOOK HOUSE
6, Appar Swami Koil St. (Upstairs), Mylapore,
Chennai-600004 (Tamil Nadu)
✆ 24990539, Fax: 044-24940066
Estd.: 1986; **Prop.:** S. Amirthavalli;
Bus.Intt.: B.S.; **Spl.:** Aesthetics, Ancient Hist.
& Culture, Ancient Math., Ancient Sci., Art,
Archaeology, Arch., Astrology, Astronomy,
Ayurveda, Dharmasastras, Dictionaries, Phil.
and Rel., Puranas, Reference Books

JAYANTI PUBLICATIONS
27-1-68, Karl Marx Rd., Vijayawada-520002
(Andhra Pradesh)
✆ 0866-267828
Estd.: 1955; **Prop.:** M. Perumallu;
Bus.Intt.: Pub.; **Spl.:** Fiction, Old Classics,
Sci., Life Histories, Reference, Children's
Books and Playlets in Telugu

JAYASWAL PUSTAK BHANDAR
Nagra Kothi, Baidyanath,
Deoghar-814112 (Bihar)
Bus.Intt.: Pub. and B.S.

JAYMECH SPARES AND SERVICES PVT. LTD.
Ismail Building, 27/A/B, 4h Floor, D.N. Rd.,
No. 381, Fountain, Mumbai-400001
(Maharashtra)
✆ 22023393, 22047629, Fax: 91-22-22047629
Hd.Org.: Jatin Mehta; **Bus.Intt.:** Exp.;
Spl.: Diaries, Journals Books, Calendars

JAYNA BOOK DISTRIBUTORS
1994-1995, Bank St., Chowk Chapparwala,
Karol Bagh, New Delhi-110005
✆ 25711741, 25752183
Estd.: 1949; **Prop.:** Rajinder Kumar Jain;
Bus.Intt.: Rt., WS, Pub., Sub.Ag., Pub.'s
Rep., L.S.; **Spl.:** Acad., Beh.Sci., Soc.Sci.,
Comm., Sci., Med., Tech., Fiction, Juveniles,
Rare, Journals and Magazines, Law

JAYPEE BROTHERS MEDICAL PUBLISHERS (P) LTD.
EMCA House, P.O. Box 7193, 23/23 B,
Ansari Rd., Darya Ganj, New Delhi-110002
✆ 23272143, 23282021, 23272703,
Fax: 23276490, 23281761
✉ jaypee@jaypeebrothers.com
🌐 www.jaypeebrothers.com
Estd.: 1988; **Hd.Org.:** Jitender Pal Vij;
Br.: Jaypee Journals & Periodicals,
Jaypee House, 4347-B, 4-C,
Madan Mohan St., Ansari Rd., Darya Ganj,
New Delhi-110002
✆ 23245672, Fax: 23276490
✉ jaypee@jaypeebrothers.com;
• Jaypee Pharma Customised Imprints (P)
Ltd., 16-G EMCA House, Ansari Rd.,
Darya Ganj, New Delhi-110002
✆ 23272143, Fax: 91-11-23245683
✉ tarun_jp@rediffmail.com
• **Man.:** Sandip Gupta, 1A, Indian Mirror St.,
Wellington Square, Kolkata-700013
(West Bengal) ✆ 22451926, Fax: 22456075,
✉ jpbcal@cal.vsnl.net.in
• **Man.:** R.N. Mandal, 202, Batavia Chambers,
8th Kumara Krupa Rd., Kumara Park East,
Bangalore-560001 (Karnataka)
✆ 22285971, 22382956, Fax: 22281761
✉ jaypeebc@bgl.vsnl.net.in
• **Regional Man.:** Uday Honne Madi, 106,
Amit Industrial Estate, 61, Dr. S.S. Rao Rd.,
Near M.G.M. Hospital Rd., Parel,
Mumbai-400012 (Maharashtra)
✆ 24124863, 24104532, Fax: 24160828
✉ jpmedpub@bom7.vsnl.net.in
• **Incharge**: Anil P. Pillai, 282, IIIrd Floor
Khaleel, Shirazi, Estate Fountain, Plaza
Pantheon Rd., Chennai-600008

✆ 28262665, 28259897, Fax: 28262331
✉ jpmedpub@md3.vsnl.net.in
• 4-2-1067/1-3, 1st Floor, Balaji Building, Ramkote Cross Rd., Hyderabad-500095 (Andhra Pradesh)
✆ 55610020, 24758498, Fax: 24758499
✉ jpmedpub@rediffmail.com
Bus.Intt.: Pub., WS, L.S. & Rt., Imp., Exp.; **Spl.**: Med., Sci., Tech.

JAYSHREE PRAKASHAN
4/115, Biswas Nagar, Shahdara, Delhi-110032
✆ 22146176

JEDIA ENTERPRISES
Shop No. 8, DDA Market, (Near Mahavira School), 31, G.T. Rd., Delhi-110033
✆ 27241029
Hd.Org.: Subhash Chand; **Bus.Intt.**: Dealer; **Spl.**: Fiction, Novels, Books for Children and Competitive Examinations

JEET PUBLICATIONS
7, Dimmani Sadan, Rani Ratan, Trivedi Rd., Mulund (W), Mumbai-400080 (Maharashtra)

JEEVAN BOOKS
Bharananganam, Kottayam-686578 (Kerala)
✆ 0482-218487
Estd.: 1985; **Hd.Org.**: Jose Vettickat; **Bus.Intt.**: Pub. and B.S.

JEEVAN DAN
30-A, Ramganj Bazar, Jaipur-302003 (Rajasthan)
✆ 0141-2562585, 2561715
Prop.: C.S. Agarwal; **Bus.Intt.**: Pub.; **Spl.**: Health and Med. Books Besides a Magazine *Jeevandan* in Hindi

JEEVAN PRABHAT PRAKASHAN
Jeevan Prabhat Press, Guru Govind Singh Industrial Estate, Goregaon, Mumbai-400063 (Maharashtra)
✆ 28746929, 26716587
Hd.Org.: Shri Satyanarayan Misher

JEEVAN PRATAP PRAKASHAN
Jeevan Pratap Press, 221, Guru Govind Singh Industrial Estate, Goregoan (East), Mumbai-400063 (Maharashtra)

JEEVAN SOFTECH LIMITED
Hyderabad (Andhra Pradesh)
✆ 23205739
✉ jeevan@hd2.vsnl.net.in

JEEVANSONS PUBLICATIONS
Delhi
✆ 23911358
✉ jpubin@yahoo.com.in
Bus.Intt.: Pub.

JEEVANVIDYA MISSION
A-2/5, Siddhartha Nagar, Building No. 5, Co. Op. Housing Society Ltd. Mumbai-400066 (Maharashtra)
✆ 28879015-16, Fax: 91-22-28845480
✉ wamanrao@jeevanvidya.org
🌐 www.jeevanvidya.org
Hd.Org.: P.R. Gore; **Bus.Intt.**: Pub.

JEFFSON PRINT MEDIA HOUSE
207, Garg Plaza, Plot No. 4 (Near Shakti Nagar) Railway Bridge, Delhi-110052
✆ (O) 20059037, 30931801 ▮ 9868286356 (R) 27226906, Fax: 27138119
✉ jeffry@ndf.vsnl.net.in
Estd.: 1991; **Prop.**: N. Jacob; **Bus.Intt.**: Pub.; **Spl.**: Text Books for Progressive Schools in English

JETLY & SONS
A-24, Krishna Park, Devli Rd., Khanpur, New Delhi-110062
✆ 91-11-29913614
Prop.: Sushil Kr. Jetly; **Bus.Intt.**: B.S.; **Spl.**: Art and Rare Books, Maps, Prints etc.

JHARISON (PUBLICATIONS DIVISION)
F-3/16, Ansari Rd., New Delhi-110002
✆ 23279853, Fax: 011-23280234
Estd.: 1982; **Hd.Org.**: Ravinder Dev Jhari; **Bus.Intt.**: Dist., Pub.; **Spl.**: Standard Eng.Litt.

JHARNA PUSTAKALAYA
Bandyoan, Purulia (West Bengal)

JIJNASA AGENCIES LTD.
1A, College Row, Kolkata-700009 (West Bengal)

JIJNASA PRAKASHAN
Suntankar Niwas, Sheri Gali, Belgaum (Karnataka)

JIL INFORMATION TECHNOLOGY LTD.
64/4, Site No, IX, Sahebabad Industrial Area, Dist. Ghaziabad-201001 (Uttar Pradesh)
✆ 24779569, 24779576, Fax: 91-120-24779582, 24775560, 24777972
Ch.Exe.: Alok Gaur; **Bus.Intt.**: Dealer; **Spl.**: Multimedia Teaching aid for School and College Students

JINA JYOTHI PRAKASHANA
23, Ratnatraya, Model House, IV St., Basavanagudi, Bangalore-560004 (Karnataka)
✆ 26767789
Estd.: 1974; **Bus.Intt.**: Pub.; **Spl.**: Rel., Phil. and Gen.

JINAY TRADERS
12, Maharaja Bldg., 135, J.S.S. Rd., Mumbai-400004 (Maharashtra)
✆ 23888987, 23888277, Fax: 22874236
Estd.: 1993; **Bus.Intt.**: Exp. and Imp.

JINDAL BOOK SERVICES
LG-4A, Ganpati Bhawan, 4675/21B,
Ansari Rd., Darya Ganj, New Delhi-110002
✆ (O) 23255012 (R) 23845862, Fax: 23282127
✉ sshjbs@yahoo.com
🌐 www.sshjbs/lockupindia.com
Estd.: 1995; **Prop.:** Sanjiv Kumar Jain;
Bus.Intt.: B.S., L.S., WS; **Spl.:** Humanities & Soc.Sci., Sci. & Tech., Comp., Mang., Law, Bio.Sci.

JINGLE ZONE ANIMATIONS (P) LTD.
302, Siddhartha Building, 96, Nehru Place,
New Delhi-110019
✆ 26224301, Fax: 91-11-26237785
✉ jinglezone@epaathshala.com
Hd.Org.: Sachin Jain

JITENDRA PUSTAK BHANDAR
Dhoria, Bhagalpur-813224 (Bihar)
Bus.Intt.: Pub. and B.S.

JITENDRA PUSTAK BHANDAR
Masaurhi, Patna-801505 (Bihar)
Bus.Intt.: Pub. and B.S.

JIWAN BOOKS INTERNATIONAL (P) LTD.
4809-11/24, Ansari Road, Darya Ganj,
New Delhi-110002
✆ 43541944, Fax: 91-11-43541900
✉ info@jiwanbooks.co
Hd.Org.: Bharat Mediratta
Bus.Intt.: Pub.

JIWAN PUBLISHING HOUSE (P) LTD.
24, Ansari Road, Darya Ganj,
New Delhi-110002
✆ 43541955/58, Fax: 91-11-43541911
Hd.Org.: Manoj Mediratta; **Bus.Intt.:** Pub.

JIWAN PUBLISHING HOUSE (P) LTD. INDIA
F-227, Mansarover Garden, New Delhi-110015
✆ 25462358, 25932219, 25937039
Fax: 25449314, 25453365
✉ info@jphbooks.com,
jphpltd@nde.vsnl.net.in
🌐 www.jphbooks.com
Estd.: 1970; **Hd.Org.:** U.R. Mediratta
Br.: Adda Hoshiarpur, Jalandhar City (Punjab) ✆ 259423 • Sector 20-D, Shop No. 58, Chandigarh ✆ 223008 • 57, PMG Complex, South Usman Rd., T Nagar, Chennai, (Tamil Nadu) ✆ 2447466
Bus.Intt.: Pub.; **Spl.:** Edu. Books for Children

JNAN ANNESAN
1/11, Paik Para, Row, Kolkata-700037
(West Bengal)

JNAN PRAKASHAN
23/1, College Row, Kolkata-700009
(West Bengal)
Hd.Org.: Jnanendra Kumar Roy

JNAN SANCHAYAN
5, Shyama Charan Dey St.,
Kolkata-700073 (West Bengal)

JNAN SANCHAYAN
16/3, Gariahat Rd., Kolkata-700019
(West Bengal)
✆ 2446372

JNANADA PRAKASHAN
4837/24, Ansari Rd., Darya Ganj,
New Delhi-110002
✆ 91-11-23272047
✉ jnanadabooksdelhi@yahoo.com
🌐 www.text.ind.in
Hd.Org.: S. Chowdhary; **Bus.Intt.:** Pub.;
Spl.: School and College Textbooks on Hist., Pol.Sci., Phil., etc.

JNANADA PUBLISHERS
Govind Mitra Rd., Patna-800004
(Bihar)
✆ 2689059
✉ jnanada@rediffmail.com
Estd.: 1948; **Bus.Intt.:** Pub.;
Spl.: Competitive & School Syllabus Based

JNANANJAN PRAKASHANI
31, College Row, Kolkata-700009
(West Bengal)

JNANDA PRAKASHAN AND DISTRIBUTORS
Govind Mitra Rd., Patna-800004 (Bihar)
Bus.Intt.: Pub. and B.S.

JNANMANDAL FOUNDATION
Barabit Stadium, Cuttack-753005
(Orissa)

JNANPITH PRATISHTHAN
18, Institutional Area, Lodhi Rd.,
New Delhi-110003
✆ 24656201, Fax: 91-11-24654197
✉ jnanpith@satyam.net.in
🌐 www.jnanpith.net
Hd.Org.: N.C. Jain; **Bus.Intt.:** Pub. & B.S.;
Spl.: Creative Litt., Rel., Monthly Journal *Naya Jnanodaya*

JNANPITH PUSTAK KENDRA /JNANPITH VIKRAI KENDRA
18, Institutional Area, Lodhi Rd.,
New Delhi-110003
✆ 24626467, 24698417, Fax: 24654197
✉ jnanpith@satyam.net.in
Hd.Org.: Prabhakar Shrotriya; **Bus.Intt.:** Pub. & B.S.; **Spl.:** Creative Litt., Rel., Monthly Journal *Naya Jnanodaya*

JODO GYAN EDUCATIONAL SERVICES/JODO UDYOG
E-12, Shakarpur, Britannia Chowk,
Delhi-110034
✆ 27102820 📱 9811949635, Fax: 27102820

jodogyandel@yahoo.com
www.jodogyan.org; **Hd.Org.:** E.K. Shaji

JOGEMAYA PRAKASHANI
60, Potuatola Lane, Kolkata-700009 (West Bengal)
Bus.Intt.: Pub.; **Spl.:** Children's Books in Bengali

JOHN'S GOOD BOOK
Bhati Charaya Ratanda, Jodhpur-342006 (Rajasthan)

JOHN WILEY & SONS
D-69, Hauz Khas, IInd Floor, New Delhi-110016
26518365, 26858760, 26969502, Fax: 26858760
aindia@wiley.com.sg
www.wiley.com
Represent: A.K. Bharti; **Bus.Intt.:** Pub., Pub.'s Rep.; **Spl.:** Acad., Beh.Sci., Soc.Sci., Comm., Sci. Pure & Applied, Med. Tech., Fiction, Rare, Journals and Magazines

JOSEPH THOMASONS & CO.
Nettikadan Block, Anand Bazar, South Railway Station Rd., Cochin-682016 (Kerala)
2355235, 2369784, Fax: 0484-2370031
Estd.: 1958; **Hd.Org.:** Andrew Nettikadan; **Bus.Intt.:** Pub. & B.S.

JOSHI BOOK DEPOT
Kotwali Bazar, Ambala City (Haryana)
Estd.: 1950; **Bus.Intt.:** Pub., B.S. and WS

JOSHI BOOK DISTRIBUTORS
20, Ansari Rd. Darya Ganj, New Delhi-110002
(O) 23263502, 23280058 (R) 22241822
Estd.: 1985; **Hd.Org.:** Nalin Joshi; **Bus.Intt.:** WS

JOSHI BROTHERS
Mira Datarno Tekro, Nava Bazar, Vadodara-390014 (Gujarat)

JOURNAL BOOK EMPORIUM
PNC Rd., Nalbari (Assam)

JOURNALS SUBSCRIPTION SERVICE
23, North West Avenue, West Punjabi Bagh, New Delhi-110026
25447609, 25447684
jssindia@hotmail.com
Prt.: Anil Arora, A.L. Arora, S. Mehra; **Bus.Intt.:** Sub.Ag.

JOY DURGA LIBRARY
8/A, College Row, Kolkata-700009 (West Bengal)

JOY MA TARA BOOK STALL
64, Mahatma Gandhi Rd., Kolkata-700009 (West Bengal)

JOYGURU PUSTAKALAYA
12/1/B, Bankim Chatterjee St., Kolkata-700073 (West Bengal)

JOYTI STORES
Near St. John the Baptist H School, Old Mumbai Rd., Thane-400601 (Maharashtra)
25352207

JUBILEE BOOK STORES
Jamadoba, Dhanbad-828112 (Bihar)

JUBILEE PRAKASHAN
Khazanchi Rd., Patna-800004 (Bihar)
Bus.Intt.: Pub. and B.S.

JUGA SAHITYA PRAKASHANI
77, Mahatama Gandhi Rd., Kolkata-700009 (West Bengal)

JUGAL KISHORE & CO.
23-C, Rajpur Rd., Dehradun-258001 (Uttarakhand)
2657782
Estd.: 1935; **Prop.:** V.K. Rastogi; **Bus.Intt.:** B.S. and Pub.; **Spl.:** Forestry, Env. and School Books in English and Hindi Languages

JUHI PRAKASHAN
4430, B-5-6 Vasant Kunj, New Delhi-110070

JUL'S PUBLISHING HOUSE
8635, East Park Rd., Karol Bagh, New Delhi-110005
(O) 2525466 (R) 2530910
Estd.: 1979; **Prop.:** Pradeep Bubna; **Bus.Intt.:** Pub.; **Spl.:** Children Edu. Books in English and Hindi

JULIE GENERAL STORES
Vijayhat, Bhagalpur (Bihar)
Bus.Intt.: Pub. and B.S.

JUNIOR GENIUS
A-369 C, New Ranjit Nagar, New Delhi-110008
25895379 9810086175, Fax: 25892456
Hd.Org.: Mathew George; **Bus.Intt.:** Manufacturers; **Spl.:** School Teaching Aids

JUPITER PUBLICATIONS
New Shakti Nagar, Ludhiana-141007 (Punjab)
2660921
Hd.Org.: L.D. Dewan; **Bus.Intt.:** Pub. and B.S.

JUPITOR PUBLISHERS
C-157, East of Kailash, New Delhi-110065

JUSTICE HOME
81/3, North Malaka, Allahabad (Uttar Pradesh)

JUTHIKA BOOK STALL
12, Bankim Chatterjee St., Kolkata-700073 (West Bengal)

JYANJYOTI
Mangaldoi, Darrang (Assam)

JYESTHA LITERARY TRUST
1, Arjun Apartments,
Gazetted Officers Colony,
Visakhapatnam-530002 (Andhra Pradesh)

JYOSTNA ENTERPRISE
Shop No. 60, College Sq., Kolkata-700073 (West Bengal)

JYOTHI BOOK HOUSE
K.K. Rd., Kottayam-686001 (Kerala)
✆ 2562448
Bus.Intt.: B.S.

JYOTHI PRAKASH
Golaghat-785621 (Assam)

JYOTHY BOOKS
Thrichur-680001 (Kerala)

JYOTI ASHRAM
Ananda Niketan Trust, 68, Lulla Nagar, Pune-411040 (Maharashtra)
✆ 91-20-26832632
@ jyotiashram@gmail.com
Hd.Org.: Prabhushri Swami Amar Jyoti; **Bus.Intt.:** Pub.; **Spl.:** Journals *Conscious Living* (English) and *Pratibuddha* (Hindi) and Religious Books

JYOTI BOOK DEPOT
Sagarmal Girdharilal Building, Shreejee Complex, Naya Sorak, Cuttack-2 (Orissa)
✆ 220648
Hd.Org.: Pradeep Kedia

JYOTI BOOK DEPOT
30-15-138, Dabagardens, Visakhapatnam-20 (Andhra Pradesh)
✆ (O) 0891-2746020, 2541201, 5566062-63 (R) 9849121001, Fax: 2541203
@ jbdvizag@yahoo.com, jbdindia@yahoo.com
www.jyotibookdepot.com
Estd.: 1986; **Man.:** Sunil Nevatia
Br.: 3-5-121/A-8, Sainath Complex, Ramkote, Hyderabad-500001 (Andhra Pradesh)
✆ 24758606, 24758703
@ jbdhyd2002@rediffmail.com
• Flat #105, 4787/23, Ansari Rd., Darya Ganj, New Delhi-110002
✆ 23268121, Fax: 23268122
Bus.Intt.: B.S. and Dist.; **Spl.:** School, Graduate, Adv. Books for Lib., Gen. Books and All Types

JYOTI BOOK DEPOT
Flat #105, 1 Floor, 4787/23, Ansari Rd., Darya Ganj, New Delhi-110002
✆ 23268121, Fax: 23268122
@ jbdindia@rediffmail.com
Hd.Org.: Sunil Nevatia; **Bus.Intt.:** Dist.; **Spl.:** Gen. Books and Encyclopaedias, Engg., Tech.

JYOTI ENTERPRISES
5825/7, New Chandrawal, Jawahar Nagar, Delhi-110007
✆ 91-11-23858405
@ jyoti_enterprises_1979@indiatimes.com
Hd.Org.: Rama Shankar Maheshwari
Bus.Intt.: Pub. and Dist.; **Spl.:** Books on all subjects

JYOTI PRAKASHAN
23rd Rd., TPS-III, P.B. 9814, Bandra, Mumbai-400050 (Maharashtra)

JYOTI PRAKASHAN
Panbazar, Guwahati-781001 (Assam)

JYOTI PRAKASHAN
32, Tiwari Ji Ka Hatha, Opp. Swagat Tourist Bungalow, Station Rd., Jaipur-6 (Rajasthan)
✆ (O) 276486 (R) 2516056, 2510211
Estd.: 1985; **Prop.:** Manohar Lal Agrawal; **Bus.Intt.:** Pub.; **Spl.:** Edu. Books in Hindi and English

JYOTI PUBLISHERS
New Delhi
✆ 25786163, 25737566, Fax: 25782601
@ jyotipub@yahoo.co.in

JYOTI PUBLISHERS AND DISTRIBUTORS
Dehradun (Uttarakhand)
@ jyotiannfor@hotmail.com

JYOTI PUSTAK BHANDAR
Kahalgaon, (Colgong), Bhagalpur-813203 (Bihar)
Bus.Intt.: Pub. and B.S.

JYOTI STORES
42, Main Rd., Nashik-422001 (Maharashtra)
✆ 2504026, 2597026, Fax: 2573630
@ joytistore@sify.com
Etd.: 1960; **Hd.Org.:** Khairnar Vasantdagdu
Br.: Jeevanchhaya Gangapur Rd., Murkute Colony, Nashik (Maharashtra)
✆ 2314558, 2578864, Fax: 2573630
• Mahatma Gandhi Rd., Nashik-422001 (Maharashtra)
Bus.Intt.: WS, L.S. & Rt.

JYOTISH VIMAL
G-31/8, Karunamoyee Estate, Sector-II, Salt Lake City, Kolkata-700091 (West Bengal)
✆ 23521779
Estd.: 1976; **Bus.Intt.:** Pub. and B.S.; **Spl.:** Adv. Books for Lib. and Astrology

JYOTSNA PRAKASHAN
Mohan Building, 162-B, J. Shankarsheth Marg, Girgaum, Mumbai-400004 (Maharashtra)
✆ 022-23877019, 23824071
✉ jyotsnaprakashan@vsnl.com, vlp@vsnl.net
Estd.: 1950; **Hd.Org.:** Milind L. Paranjape
Br.: 617, Nariana Lokhande, Talmeejaval, Pune-411030 (Maharashtra)
✆ 020-24451453
✉ jyotsnaprakashan@vsnl.com
Bus.Intt.: Pub.; **Spl.:** Art and Drawing Books

■ ■ ■

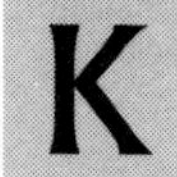

K. BHUSHAN BOOKSELLERS
625, Khajuri Bazar, Indore-452002 (Madhya Pradesh)
✆ 2431874

K. BOOK STALL
Sall KBS-49, 1, B.C. St., Near Sanskrit College Gate, Kolkata-700073 (West Bengal)

K. JAIN PUBLISHERS
Post Box 10, Post Ladnum-341306 (Rajasthan)

K. KRISHNAMURTHY
38, Thanikachalam Rd., T. Nagar, Chennai-600017 (Tamil Nadu)
✆ 24344519, Fax: 24342009
service@kkbooks.com, kkbooks@eth.net
www.kkbooks.com
Estd.: 1944; **Man.Prt.:** K. Krishnamurthy
Br.: Shop No. 31, Lal Bahadur Stadium, Hyderabad-500001 (Andhra Pradesh)
✆ 2231447
Bus.Intt.: Pub., WS, L.S. & Rt., Imp., Exp., Sub.Ag.; **Spl.:** Sci. & Tech., Mang.

K. SAGAR PUBLICATIONS
Shri Kripashri Society, R.P. Nagar, Nagpur-440012 (Maharashtra)

K.B. EDUCATIONAL TRADERS
S-3, West Patel Nagar, New Delhi-110008
✆ 25786408, 25873632, Fax: 25872197
Hd.Org.: Vinod Kumar Bansal; **Bus.Intt.:** Pub.; **Spl.:** Laminated Maps, Charts, Globes, Models and Edu. Books

K.B. ENTERPRISES
HX-99, E-7, Extension, Arera Colony, Bhopal-462016 (Madhya Pradesh)
✆ 0755-2465527, Fax: 2467472
Estd.: 2000; **Prop.:** K.B. Chakraborti;
Bus.Intt.: Pub., B.S., L.S.; **Spl.:** Humanities & Soc.Sci., Mang., Spiritual & Self-Astrology & Vastu Development

K.B. PRAKASHANI
114-D, Beliaghata Main Rd., Kolkata-700010 (West Bengal)

K.B. SATYANARAYANA (BOOK-LINKS)
84-Bima Nagar, (LIC Colony), Opp. Indira Park, Hyderabad-500080 (Andhra Pradesh)
✆ (O) 27567068 (R) 27611582
Hd.Org.: K.B. Satyanarayana

K.C. BOOK STALL
6, Shyama Charan Dey St., Kolkata-700073 (West Bengal)

K.C. SARCAR & CO.
Krishnanagar, Nadia (West Bengal)

K.G.'S. BOOK STALL
Municipal Bus Stand, Kottayam-686001 (Kerala)
✆ 2566893
Estd.: 1971; **Hd.Org.:** K.G. Sreedharan Nair;
Bus.Intt.: B.S.

K.I. BOOK BANK
62, Ashirwad Apartments, Plot No. 74, Patparganj, I.P. Extension, Delhi-110092

K.J. BOOK CENTRE
WZ-529, Madipur Village, New Delhi-110063
✆ 25446723, 25472752, 25478442
Prop.: Bal Ram Yadav; **Bus.Intt.:** Rt. L.S. and Pub.'s Rep.

K.K. MISHRA & CO.
Khatbin Sahi, Cuttack-753008 (Orissa)

K.K. PUBLICATIONS
109, 4855/24, Harbans Street, Ansari Road, Darya Ganj, New Delhi-110002
✆ 65185557, Fax: 91-11-30125577
9818020120
kkpdevinder@vsnl.net
Estd.: 1995; **Hd.Org.:** Kamal Kumar;
Bus.Intt.: Pub. and Dist.; **Spl.:** Soc.Sci. and Humanities in English and Hindi

K.K. PUBLICATIONS
B-1770, Jahangir Puri (Near SBI), Delhi-110033
✆ 27637048, 27636984, 27636835
9818020120
kkpdevinder@vsnl.net
Estd.: 1995; **Hd.Org.:** Devinder Kumar;
Bus.Intt.: Pub. and Dist.; **Spl.:** Soc.Sci. and Humanities in English and Hindi

K.L. MALIK & SONS PVT. LTD.
23, Darya Ganj, New Delhi-110002
✆ 23274161, Fax: 91-11-23254407
klmalik_23@yahoo.com
Hd.Org.: Mahendra Malik
Bus.Intt.: B.S., Pub. and WS to the Trade

K.L. PACHORI PRAKASHAN
8/D, Block-X, Indrapuri Loni, Ghaziabad-201102 (Uttar Pradesh)
✆ 2600651
Hd.Org.: Brahma Darshan Pachori;
Bus.Intt.: Pub.; **Spl.:** Hist., Pol.Sci., Phil., in Hindi and Sanskrit

K.L.M. BOOK HOUSE
Flat S, South Patel Nagar, P.B. No. 6037, New Delhi-110008

✆ (O) 25847913 (R) 25786720
Prop.: Lalit Malhotra; **Bus.Intt.:** L.S.; **Spl.:** Beh. Sci., Soc.Sci., Mang., Sci., Med., Tech. & Children Books

K.M. PUBLISHING
College Hostel Rd., Guwahati-781001 (Assam)

K.M. VARGHESE COMPANY
104-Hind (Rajasthan) Building, Dada Saheb, Phalke Rd., Dadar (East), Mumbai-400014 (Maharashtra)
✆ 24149074, 24144601, Cable: KEMVARG, Fax: 24146904
✉ km@varghese.net
www.varghese.net
Estd.: 1960; **Ch.Exe.:** K.M. Varghese
Br.: K.M. Varghese Company, Prakash House, 4379/4-B, Ansari Rd., New Delhi-110002
✆ 23287387, 23252612
Bus.Intt.: Pub., WS, L.S. & Rt., Imp.; **Spl.:** Sci. & Tech., Med.

K.N. BOOK HOUSE
WP-71, Wazir Pur Village, Ashok Vihar, Delhi-110052
✆ 27419375; **Hd.Org.:** Kedar Nath Gupta; **Bus.Intt.:** L.S.; **Spl.:** Acad. Beh. Sci., Soc.Sci., Comm., Sci., Med., Tech., Rare, Law

K.P. BAGCHI & COMPANY
286, B.B. Ganguli St., Kolkata-700012 (West Bengal)
✆ (O) 22367474 (R) 2236-9496, Fax: 033-22369496
✉ kpbagchi@hotmail.com
Estd.: 1972; **Prt.:** P.K. Bagchi; **Bus.Intt.:** Pub. and B.S.; **Spl.:** Humanities

K.P. BASU PUBLISHING CO.
42, Bidhan Sarani, Kolkata-700006 (West Bengal)

K.P. JAYASWAL RESEARCH INSTITUTE
Patna-800011 (Bihar)

K.P. PUBLISHERS & DISTRIBUTORS
H-68, LIG Flats, Ashok Vihar, Phase-I, Delhi-110052
✆ (O) 27240836 (R) 27138934
Estd.: 1978; **Prop.:** Kamal Prakash Gupta
Bus.Intt.: Pub., L.S.; **Spl.:** Sci., Tech. & Soc.Sci. & Med. Books

K.P.B. BOOKS PVT. LTD.
Kolkata (West Bengal)
✉ kpbbooks@hotmail.com

K.R. BROTHERS
Kozhikode-673001 (Kerala)
✆ 260565
Estd.: 1910; **Hd.Org.:** K. Rajeevan; **Bus.Intt.:** B.S. and Stationers

K.S.K. BOOK DISTRIBUTORS
171, Pocket Q, Dilshad Garden, Delhi-110095
✆ (O) 22593323 (R) 26188253
▮ 9810881414
✉ kskbooks@hotmail.com
Estd.: 2001; **Prop.:** K.S. Kunjuman; **Bus.Intt.:** L.S.; **Spl.:** Tech.

K.S.V. BOOK SUPPLIERS
212, Seemant Vihar, Kaushambhi, Ghaziabad-201001 (Uttar Pradesh)
✆ 95120-2771651
✉ ksvbooksuppliers@yahoo.co.in
Estd.: 2003; **Hd.Org.:** Mrs. Sonia Arora; **Bus.Intt.:** L.S., WS; **Spl.:** Engg. & Tech., Med.Sci., Law

KAANTHALAKAM
4, F/FL, Raheja Complex, 834, Anna Salai, Chennai-600002 (Tamil Nadu)
✆ 2834505, Fax: 2834728
✉ sachi@Giasmd01.vsnl.net.in
Prop.: K. Sachithananthan
Bus.Intt.: Pub., Imp., Exp.
Spl.: Tamil, Eng. Books from Srilanka and Stockists of Eelam Tamil Books

KABIR
D-59, IIIrd Floor, Pandav Nagar, Delhi-110092
✆ 22485139, Fax: 91-11-22485139
✉ neeraj.com@gmail.com
www.kabir.org.in
Hd.Org.: Manish Sisodia
Bus.Intt.: Pub., Dist. and Printer

KABIR PARAKH SANSATHAN
Sant Kabir Marg, Pritam Nagar, Allahabad-211011 (Uttar Pradesh)
✆ 2637520, 2436100
Hd.Org.: Dharmendra Das
Bus.Intt.: Promoter
Spl.: Teachings of Sant Kabir

KABIR PATH PRAKASHAN
2151/17/12A, New Patel Nagar, New Delhi-110008
✆ 25894637
✉ kabirpath@yahoo.co.in
Hd.Org.: Bhagwan Das Kabirpanthi; **Bus.Intt.:** Pub.; **Spl.:** Kabir and his Teachings, a Monthly Newsletter—*Kabir Path* and Organiser of Seminars on Kabir Litt.

KADAMBARI PRAKASHAN
5451, Shiv Market, New Chandrawal, Jawahar Nagar, Delhi-110007
✆ 91-11-65352060

kadambari_prakashan@yahoo.com
Hd.Org.: H.L. Aneja; **Bus.Intt.:** Pub.; **Spl.:** Hindi Litt., Criticisms and Textbooks

KADAMBI BOOKSELLERS
75, S.D. Rd., Secunderabad-500003 (Andhra Pradesh)
✆ 27705349
Estd.: 1951; **Hd.Org.:** Miss D.K. Rupa; **Bus.Intt.:** B.S. and L.S.; **Spl.:** Greeting Cards, Astrology Books and Magazines

KADHAMBINI PRAKASHANA
48, Kadhambi, Old Bangalore Rd., Chithradurga-577501 (Karnataka)
Hd.Org.: C.R. Parthasarathy
Bus.Intt.: Pub.; **Spl.:** Fiction Poems and Collection in Kannada

KAGZI HAND MADE PAPER IND.
Jaipur (Rajasthan)
✆ 730019, 730076, Fax: 732065
kagzi@jpl.dot.net.in
Bus.Intt.: Imp.

KAHAN PUBLICATIONS
15, Sureeji Complex, Near Ellis Bridge P.O., Ahmedabad-380006 (Gujarat)
✆ (O) 26576285, 26577054 (R) 26613359
Bus.Intt.: Pub.; **Spl.:** Ready Reckoners, Insurance Books

KAHKASHAN BOOK DEPOT
463 (Sami-Manzil), Chitla Gate, Chawri Bazar, Delhi-110006
✆ (O) & (R) 23286490 ▮ 9891026160
Estd.: 1980; **Prop.:** Jalaluddin;
Bus.Intt.: Pub., B.S.; **Spl.:** Children, General & Islamic Books in Urdu

KAILASH ASHRAM
New Delhi
✆ 23201505, 23256437
swbikash@hotmail.com, kailashmansarovar@usa.net
Bus.Intt.: Pub.

KAILASH LIBRARIES FRANCAISES
169, Lal Bahadur St., Pondicherry-605001

KAILASH PUBLICATIONS
Aurangpura, Aurangabad-431001 (Maharashtra)
✆ 0240-2353123
Estd.: 1976; **Hd.Org.:** Bishemver Kulkarni

KAILASH PUSTAK SADAN
30, Hamidia Rd., Shah Building, Bhopal-462001 (Madhya Pradesh)
✆ 2535366 ▮ 98270-53154
Estd.: 1960; **Hd.Org.:** Ravi Agarwal;
Bus.Intt.: WS and L.S.; **Spl.:** Pol.Sci., Eco.

KAILASH STORES
Kahalgaon (Colgong), Bhagalpur-3 (Bihar)
Bus.Intt.: Pub. & B.S.

KAILASO BOOKS
2/19, Ansari Rd., Darya Ganj, New Delhi-110002
✆ 30910969, 23445103, Fax: 2345103
kilaso@mantraonline.com
Estd.: 2002

KAIRALI BOOKS
New Bus Stand Shopping Complex, Tripunithura, Kochi (Kerala)
Estd.: 1991; **Prop.:** P. Santhakumar;
Bus.Intt.: B.S.

KAIRALI BOOKS
Temple Rd., Kottayam-686001 (Kerala)
✆ 2560018
Estd.: 1986; **Prop.:** P. Krishnakumar;
Bus.Intt.: Pub. and B.S.

KAIRALI CHILDREN'S BOOK TRUST
PB No. 624, DCB Complex, Good Shepherd St., Kottayam-686001 (Kerala)
✆ 0481-2564758
Estd.: 1980; **Chairman:** K.M. Mathew;
Bus.Intt.: Pub. and B.S.; **Spl.:** Biographical Encyclopaedia, Better in own as Mahatcharitamala for Children

KAIRALI MUDRALAYAM
D.C. Books Complex, Good Shepherd St., Kottayam-636001 (Kerala)
✆ 2563226
Estd.: 1978; **Man.Dir.:** D.C. Thara;
Bus.Intt.: Pub. and B.S.

KAITHAKKAL GRENDHALAYAM
XV/28 S. Naluvazhi, N. Parur, Kochi-683513 (Kerala)
Estd.: 1987; **Prop.:** Dr. K.R. Narayanan;
Bus.Intt.: Pub.

KALA PARAKASHAN
47-A, B.I.A. Block, Janakpuri, New Delhi-110058

KALA PRAKASHAN
P-10, Naveen Shahdara, Delhi-110032
✆ 22283744
Hd.Org.: Amarnath Shukal

KALABHARATI VITRAN
1712/1-B, Sadashiv Peth, Udyan Karyalaya Building, Pune-411030 (Maharashtra)
✆ 2477302
Bus.Intt.: Dist.; **Spl.:** Marathi Lalit and Edu.

KALACHINHA
Dakshin Gobondpur, 24-Parganas (S), West Bengal-743353
✆ 033-24779768

Estd.: 1989; Bus.Intt.: Pub.; Spl.: Med. Books in Bengali, English and Hindi

KALACHUVADU PATHIPPAGM
669, K.P. Rd., Nagercoil-629001 (Tamil Nadu)
✆ 2278525, Fax: 2231160
✉ kalachuvadu@sancharnet.in
www.kalachuvadu.com
Hd.Org.: S.R. Sundaram; **Bus.Intt.:** Pub.; **Spl.:** Novels, Poetry, Biography, Literary Criticisms, etc. in Tamil

KALAICHELVI BOOKSELLERS
185/5, IV Avenue, Kurinji Colony, Anna Nagar, Chennai-600040 (Tamil Nadu)
Hd.Org.: Ulaganathan Mani

KALAIVAANI PUTHAKALAYAM
No. 2, Sivagnanam Rd., Pondy Bazaar, Post Office St., T. Nagar, Chennai-600017 (Tamil Nadu)
✆ 24340356
Estd.: 1865; **Hd.Org.:** Seeni Thirunaavukkarasu; **Spl.:** Tamil Litt. Books only

KALAKSHETHRAM COMMERCIAL CORPORATION
IInd Floor, Kallakatta Building, Srirampet, Kasaragode-671121 (Kerala)
✆ 04995-221164
Estd.: 1991; **Man.Dir.:** P.V. Vimaladevi; **Bus.Intt.:** Pub. and B.S.

KALAKSHETRA PUBLICATIONS
Kalakshetra Rd., Thiruvanmiyur, Chennai-600041 (Tamil Nadu)
Bus.Intt.: Exp.

KALAM PRAKASHAN
148, Kasaba Peth, Pune-411011 (Maharashtra)
✆ 0212-2456515
Estd.: 1993; **Prop.:** Saraswati Pawar; **Bus.Intt.:** Dealers; **Spl.:** Marathi Books of Children's

KALASAVYA
A-G/3, M.S. Flats, Peshwa Rd., New Delhi-110001

KALASON PRAKASHAN
Kalyani Bhawan, Mal Godown Rd., Bikaner-334001 (Rajasthan)
✆ 2526890
Estd.: 1996; **Hd.Org.:** Smt. Kaladevi Kalayni; **Bus.Intt.:** Pub.; **Spl.:** Edu., Litt. and Poetry

KALI BOOK STALL
Bankim Chatterjee St. P.D.S., Kolkata-700073 (West Bengal)

KALI FOR WOMEN
K-36, Hauz Khas Enclave, 1st Floor, New Delhi-110016
✆ 26964947, 26524129, Fax: 26496597
✉ womenunltd@vsnl.net
www.kalibooks.com
Estd.: 1984; **Trustees:** Ritu Menon & Urvashi Butalia; **Bus.Intt.:** Pub., Exp.; **Spl.:** Third World Studies on Women which include books in the Soc.Sci. and Humanities, Gen. Non-fiction, Acad. Books, Fiction, Monographs and Pamphlets

KALIGANGA EXPORTS
44B, Kalikrishna Tagore St., Kolkata-700007 (West Bengal)
Bus.Intt.: Exp.

KALIGNAAN PATHIPAGAM
10, Kannadhasan Salai, T. Nagar, Chennai-600017 (Tamil Nadu)
✆ 24345641
Prop.: G. Masilamani; **Bus.Intt.:** Pub.; **Spl.:** Creative Litt., Religious Poetry, Self-Improvement, and Classics

KALIKATA PAPER MART
48, Bansdroni Place, Kolkata-700070 (West Bengal)

KALIMATA PUSTAKALAYA
57/2B, College St., Kolkata-700073 (West Bengal)

KALINGA PUBLICATIONS
10A, Pocket 1, Mayur Vihar, Delhi-110091
Hd.Org.: Mrs. Hem Lata; **Bus.Intt.:** Pub., L.S. (Exp. to South Africa)

KALINGA STUDENTS STORE
Bindo Behari, Cuttack-753002 (Orissa)
Estd.: 1962; **Prop.:** Kalicharan Tripathy; **Bus.Intt.:** Pub. and B.S.; **Spl.:** Gen. Litt. in Oriya Language

KALKAMI ENTERPRISES
10/10, Punjabi Market, Vishnu Garden, New Delhi-110018
Bus.Intt.: Exp.

KALPNA BOOK DISTRIBUTORS
B-1770, Jahangirpuri, New Delhi-110033
✆ 27637048, Fax: 91-11-30125577
✉ kkpdevinder@vsnl.net
Hd.Org.: Devendra Kumar; **Bus.Intt.:** Pub. and Dist.; **Spl.:** Books on Hindi literature and language

KALPANA BOOK HOUSE
56/1, Sitaram Ghosh St., Kolkata-700009 (West Bengal)

KALPANA PRAKASHAN
Near Kirana Bhavan, Hanumangarh Town, Sriganganagar-355513 (Rajasthan)
✆ 230017
Hd.Org.: Smt. Kamlesh Kaushik

KALPANA SHUKLA
Manager India, Macmillan Press Ltd., 5A/12, Ansari Rd., Darya Ganj, New Delhi-110002
✆ 23272010

KALPATARU
264, Diamond Harbour Rd., Kolkata-700034 (West Bengal)

KALPAVRIKSH
C/17A, Munirka, New Delhi-110067

KALPAZ PUBLICATIONS
C-30, Satyawati Nagar, Delhi-110052
▮ 9212729499
✉ kalpaz@hotmail.com
Hd.Org.: Shalini Garg
Bus.Intt.: Pub.; **Spl.:** Books on humanities and social sciences

KALRA PUBLICATIONS (P) LTD.
2619-20/11, New Market, Nai Sarak, New Delhi-110006
✆ 23256606, 23275451, Fax: 27654141
✉ kpplbooks@hotmail.com
Hd.Org.: Kamal Kalra; **Bus.Intt.:** Pub., **Spl.:** Sample Papers for CBSE Examinations, Dictionaries and Edu. Children's Books

KALYAN BOOK HOUSE
G.M. College Rd., Sambalpur-768001 (Orissa)
✆ (O) 2520121 (R) 2521121
Estd.: 1984; **Prop.:** B.K. Pandy; **Bus.Intt.:** Pub. and B.S.; **Spl.:** Gen. Books, Text Books

KALYANI EDUCATIONAL RHYTHMS
4697/3, 21, Ansari Rd., Darya Ganj, New Delhi-110002
✆ 23752610, ▮ 9811151099
Hd.Org.: Rajinder Gandhi; **Bus.Intt.:** Producer; **Spl.:** Edu. Cassettes for Children

KALYANI PUBLISHERS
B-1/1292, Rajinder Nagar, Ludhiana-141008
✆ 2760031, Fax: 91-11-2745872
Hd.Org.: Usha Raj Kumar
Bus.Intt.: Pub.; **Spl.:** Educational books on agriculture and allied topics, veterinary sciences, commerce, management etc. in English, Hindi and other Indian languages

KALYANI PUBLISHERS
1/1, Rajinder Nagar, Ludhiana-141008 (Punjab)
✆ 2400221, 2745756, Telefax: 0161-2403023, 2745872
Estd.: 1965; **Dir.:** Raj Kumar
Br.: 4779/23, Ansari Rd., Darya Ganj, New Delhi-110002 ✆ 23271469, 23274393, Fax: 23257234 • B-16, Sector 8, Noida (Uttar Pradesh) ✆ 229371 • No. 1, Mahalakshmi St., T. Nagar, Chennai-600017 (Tamil Nadu) ✆ 24344684 • 110/111, Bharatia Towers, Badambadi, Cuttack-753001 (Orissa)
✆ 2611391 • 3-5-1103, Narayanguda, Hyderabad-500002 (Andhra Pradesh)
✆ 2510368 • No. 10/2B, Ramnath Majumder St., Kolkata-700009 (West Bengal)
✆ 2316024
Bus.Intt.: Pub.

KAMAKHYA BOOK STALL
College Hostel Rd., Panbazar, Guwahati-781001 (Assam)

KAMAKHYA PRAKASHAN
D-228C, Murlidhar Shayam Colony, Bikaner-334004 (Rajasthan)
▮ 9414242891
Hd.Org.: Kirti Vardhan; **Bus.Intt.:** Pub. and Dist.; **Spl.:** Children's books in Hindi

KAMAKSHA
A-91, Ashok Vihar, Delhi-110052
✆ 27135288

KAMAL BOOK DEPOT
5, Gita Bhawan, Indore (Madhya Pradesh)

KAMAL BOOKS INTERNATIONAL
27, DDA Shopping Centre, Arjun Nagar, Safdarjung Enclave, New Delhi-110029
✆ 26101076, 26103896, 23270654
▮ 9810228919, Fax: 011-26185044, 26103896
✉ kamalbooks@yahoo.com
Sh.: I-1/16, Ansari Rd., Darya Ganj, New Delhi-110002 ✆ 23270654
✉ kbi@bol.net.in
Dir.: Harish Kumar, G.L. Verma; **Bus.Intt.:** Engg. Side of High Tech./Reports/Proceedings; **Spl.:** Petroleum, Chemical, Mechanical, Energy, Civil Environment, Electronics and Comp.

KAMAL LAW HOUSE
8/2, K.S. Roy Rd., Kolkata-700001 (West Bengal)
✆ 22101558, 22209841, Fax: 22202822
✉ lawpointcal@rediffmail.com
Bus.Intt.: Pub.; **Spl.:** Law Books

KAMAL PRAKASHAN
922, Kucha Rahilla Khan, Darya Ganj, New Delhi-110002
✆ 91-11-23245076
Hd.Org.: Anup Kumar
Bus.Intt.: Dist.; **Spl.:** English, Hindi and Sanskrit dictionaries

KAMAL PRAKASHAN
Khajuri Bazar, Indore-452002 (Madhya Pradesh)

KAMAL PRAKASHAN PUBLISHERS & DISTRIBUTORS
105, Mukundru Ganj Chowk, Pratapgarh-230001 (Uttar Pradesh)

KAMAL PUSTAK BHANDAR
Bihat, Begusarai-851135 (Bihar)
Bus.Intt.: Pub. and B.S.

KAMAL PUSTAK SADAN
10, DDA Shopping Centre,
Gulmohar Park, P.O. Box No. 3863,
New Delhi-110049
✆ 26414430
Hd.Org.: Satish Mehta; **Bus.Intt.:** L.S.

KAMALA BOOK STALL
P.D.S. Corner, Stall 26,
2, Ramanath Majumder St., Kolkata-700007
(West Bengal)

KAMALA PRAKASHANI
14, Beniatola Lane, Kolkata-700009
(West Bengal)

KAMALA PUSTAK BHAWAN
259A, Rabindra Sarani, Kolkata-700007
(West Bengal)

KAMBAN PATHIPPAM
1/19, Kuyarer St., Murungapakkam P.O.,
Pondicherry-605004

KAMESHWAR PRAKASHAN
Teliwara Chowk, Bikaner-334005 (Rajasthan)
✆ 2524330
Hd.Org.: Gayatri Devi Bissa; **Bus.Intt.:** Pub. and Dist.; **Spl.:** Hindi Books on *Vastushastra*, Astrology and Litt.

KAMGAR PRAKASHAN
548, Bhai Parmanand Colony,
Delhi-110009

KAMLA-RAJ ENTERPRISES
2273, Gali Bari Paharwali, Chawri Bazar,
Delhi-110006
✆ 091-011-23284126, 091-0124-4360430,
Fax: 091-0124-4361193;
▮ 9873186386, 9899513686
✉ kre@vsnl.com; kre@airtelmail.in
🌐 httpp://www.krepublishers.com
Estd.: 1989; **Prop.:** Ramesh Kumar Bhasin; **Bus.Intt.:** Pub.; **Spl.:** Humanities & Soc.Sci., Med., Life Sci.

KAMLESH SHAH PUBLISHERS & DISTRIBUTORS (P) LTD.
Mumbai (Maharashtra)
✆ 22181854, Fax: 22188007
Bus.Intt.: B.S., Pub. and Dist.

KAMLIYA BOOK DEPOT
Tatarpur, Bhagalpur-812002 (Bihar)
Bus.Intt.: Pub. and B.S.

KAMSA BOOKSELLERS
8, Rameswaram St., Chennai-600017
(Tamil Nadu)
✆ 044-24341305
Hd.Org.: K.A. Padmanabhan

KANAK PRAKASHANI
114-D, Beliaghata Main Rd., Kolkata-700010
(West Bengal)
✆ 033-23507602
Estd.: 1983; **Hd.Org.:** Smt. Juthika Nayak; **Bus.Intt.:** Pub. and B.S.; **Spl.:** Bengali School and College Textbooks in Bengali, English and Hindi

KANAK PUBLICATIONS
Gay House, 16F/3, Ansari Rd., Darya Ganj,
Delhi-110002

KANCHAN PUBLICATIONS
Ganesh Complex, Khajuri Bazar, Indore-452002
(Madhya Pradesh)
✆ 2451115

KANIKA PUBLICATIONS
R-40G, Dilshad Garden, Delhi-110095

KANISHKA BOOK CENTRE
18/78, St. No. 2, East Moti Bagh,
Sarai Rohilla, Delhi-110007
✆ 20038210, 20036278 ▮ 9810927808,
Fax: 23214634
✉ kanishka_book@yahoo.com
Estd.: 1999; **Hd.Org.:** Dinesh Singh; **Bus.Intt.:** L.S.; **Spl.:** Sci., Med., Tech. Books

KANISHKA PUBLISHERS AND DISTRIBUTORS
4697/5-21A, Ansari Rd., Darya Ganj,
New Delhi-110002
✆ 23270497, 23288285, Fax: 91-11-23288285
✉ kanisha_publishing@yahoo.co.in
Estd.: 1986; **Hd.Org.:** Madan Sachdeva
Br.: IX/2352, St. 12, Kailash Nagar,
Delhi-110031
Bus.Intt.: Pub.; **Spl.:** Comm., Pol.Sci., Public Administration, Sol., Tourism, Journalism

KANNADA PUSTAKA PRADHIKARA
Pampa Mahakavi Rd., Chamarajpet,
Bangalore-560018 (Karnataka)
✆ 080-2663812
Bus.Intt.: Pub.; **Spl.:** Gen. Books, Edu. Books of Neoliterates and Gen. Sci. in Kannada

KANNADA SAHITYA KARNATAKA PRAKASHANA SANSTHE
1507, Prasad Smaraka Kendra,
6th Cross, Irwin Rd.,
Mysore-570001 (Karnataka)
✆ 080-2602991, 26623584
Hd.Org.: H.K. Surendra; **Bus.Intt.:** Pub.; **Spl.:** Research, Edu. Books, Classics, Children's Books, Neoliterates, Editing of Old Litt., Translations, Editing of Dictionaries. One of the Oldest Publishing Establishment in Karnataka

KANNADA VIGNANA PARISHAD
"Vanasuma", 711, 10 'A' Main,
4th Block, Jaya Nagar, Bangalore-560011 (Karnataka)
✆ (O) 26633848 (R) 26548181
Estd.: 1976; **Bus.Intt.:** Pub. and B.S.; **Spl.:** Sci.

KANNADHASAN PATHIPPAGAM
23, Kannadhasan Salai, Thiyagaraya Nagar, Chennai-600017 (Tamil Nadu)
✆ 044-24332682, 24332681, Fax: 24338712
✉ kannadasan@vsnl.com, kanna@md2.vsnl.net.in
www.kannadasan.com
Estd.: 1976; **Prop.:** Gandhi Kannadhasan Babl
Br.: 1, Annai Complex, IIIrd St., Vasantha Nagar, Madurai-625003 ✆ 0452-2608793
✉ kannadasan@vsnl.com
Bus.Intt.: Pub., L.S. & Rt., Exp.; **Spl.:** Juvenile/ Children Books, Gen. & Fiction etc.

KANOON PRAKASHAK
Opp. Gurudwara, Anand Cinema, Jodhpur-342001 (Rajasthan)
✆ 2628979
✉ ncj@kanoonprakashak.com
Hd.Org.: N.C. Jain; **Bus.Intt.:** Pub.; **Spl.:** Hindi Books on Law and Dist. of Governmental Law

KANOON PRAKASHAN
A-191, Defence Colony, New Delhi-110024
✆ 24692616
✉ dk@kanoonprakashak.com
Hd.Org.: D.K. Mehdiratta; **Bus.Intt.:** Pub.; **Spl.:** Law Journals and Law Textbooks in Hindi

KANT PUBLICATIONS
1687, Multani Mohalla, Rani Bagh, Delhi-110034 ✆ 27186855

KANTA BOOK STALL
11-B, Bankim Chatterjee St., Kolkata-700073 (West Bengal)

KANTA SAHITYA PRAKASHAN
Maranda-176102 (Himachal Pradesh)

KANTI BOOK CENTRE
A-507/12, South Gamdi (Extn.), Kartar Nagar, Delhi-110053
✆ (O) & (R) 22941694 ▮ 9810869129
Prop.: Tahasil Dar Singh Raghav;
Bus.Intt.: Pub., L.S.; **Spl.:** Beh.Sci., Soc.Sci., Comm., Sci., Pure & Applied, Tech., Fiction

KANTI PUBLICATIONS
A-507/12, Kartar Nagar, Baba Shyam Giri Marg, South Gamdi (Extn.), Delhi-110053

KAPIL PUSTAK SADAN
Gwalior (Madhya Pradesh)
✆ 0751-3540717
✉ kapilsahni@mantrafreenet.com

KAPOOR BROTHERS
Lal Chowk, Srinagar (Jammu and Kashmir)
✆ 273503
Estd.: 1935; **Hd.Org.:** Raja Ram Kapoor

KAR KRIPA PUBLISHERS
Flat No. 8, Pocket No. 12, Block No. C2C, Janakpuri, New Delhi-110058

KARACHI STATIONERY MART
Shop No. 46, M.M. Janpath, New Delhi-110001
✆ (O) 23320950 (R) 2609311
Bus.Intt.: B.S. and Stationers

KARAKUSH PUBLISHERS & MEDIA PVT. LTD.
2035, Qasimjan St., Ballimaran, Delhi-110006

KARAMVIR BOOK DEPOT
Binzani Bhavan, Tilak Rd., Mahal, Nagpur-440002 (Maharashtra)
✆ 249444
Hd.Org.: M.S. Binzani

KARAN BOOK SHOP
GH 7/113, Meera Bagh, Paschim Vihar, New Delhi-110087
✆ 91-11-25288384
Hd.Org.: Karan Gulati
Bus.Intt.: B.S.; **Spl.:** Children's books and books on fashion, art, culture, cookery, etc.

KARAVALI PRAKASHANA
826, 5th Main Vijayanagar, Bangalore-560050 (Karnataka)
✆ 23302244, 23302245, 23353633
Hd.Org.: S.R. Hegde; **Bus.Intt.:** Pub.; **Spl.:** Fiction, Collections and Gen. Books in Kannada

KARMARKAR ENTERPRISES
Nanadeep, 153-A, Nappu Rd., Matunga, Mumbai-400019 (Maharashtra)

KARNA PUSTAK BHANDAR
Baunsi, Bhagalpur-813104 (Bihar)
Bus.Intt.: Pub. and B.S.

KARNATAKA BOOK AGENCY
No. 13, U. Kumara Park East, Bangalore-560001 (Karnataka)
✆ 2269448
Estd.: 1980; **Prop.:** Suresh C. Shah
Br.: Thunga Complex, Opp. Thribuvan Theater, Gandhinagar, Bangalore-560009
Bus.Intt.: Pub., L.S. & Rt.; **Spl.:** Humanities & Soc.Sci., Sci. & Tech., Juvenile/Children, Gen. & Fiction etc.

KARNATAKA GANDHI SMARAKA NIDHI
Gandhi Bhavan, Kumara Park East, Bangalore-560001 (Karnataka)
Bus.Intt.: Pub.

KARNATAKA LEKHAKIYARA SANGHA
No. 251, 2nd Cross, 3rd Main Chamarajpet, Bangalore-560018 (Karnataka)
Hd.Org.: Smt. Hemalatha Mahishi;
Bus.Intt.: Pub.; **Spl.:** All kinds of Books written by Women Writers Fiction, Collections, Poems/Dramas, Books Home Sci. and Gen. Books in Kannada

KARNATAKA MAKKALA SAHITYA PARISHAD
248, Hans Mansion, Between 16 & 17 Cross Sampige Rd., Malleswaram, Bangalore-560003 (Karnataka)
✆ 080-364488
Bus.Intt.: Pub.; **Spl.:** Children's Books and Translations in Kannada

KARNATAKA PUBLISHERS ASSOCIATION (R)
53, 'Ankita Pustaka', Gandhi Bazar Main Rd., Basavanagudi, Bangalore-560004 (Karnataka)
✆ 26617755, 91-80-26617100
ankitapustaka@rediffmail.com
Ch.Exe.: Mr. Prakash Kambathalli;
Bus.Intt.: Pub.; **Spl.:** Books in Kannada and English

KARNATAKA RAJYA VIGNANA PARISHAT
Bharathiya Vignana Mandira, Bangalore-560012 (Karnataka)
✆ 080-2340509
Bus.Intt.: Pub.; **Spl.:** Sci. Books in Kannada and English

KARPAGAM PATHAGALAYAM
18, Rajabather St., T. Nagar, Chennai-600017 (Tamil Nadu)

KARTIKEYA PUBLICATIONS
A-224, Defence Colony, Mawana Rd., Meerut-250001 (Uttar Pradesh)
✆ 0121-2620080, 2620219
Estd.: 1999; **Man.Prt.:** Lt. Gen. (Retd.) Mathew Thomas
Br.: 216, Sector 28, Noida - 31st, Distt. Ghaziabad-201303 (Uttar Pradesh)
✆ 85-255057, 85-231372
Bus.Intt.: Pub.; **Spl.:** Sci. & Tech. (Military Histories/Biographies)

KARUNA PRAKASHANI
18A, Tamer Lane, Kolkata-700009 (West Bengal)
✆ 033-22410256
Bus.Intt.: Pub.; **Spl.:** Rel. Books, Novels, Reference Books, Short Stories, Poems, Fictions by the Eminent Authors

KARUNAMAYEE PUSTAKALAYA
3, Durganagar Chakda, Nadia (West Bengal)

KASHISH BOOKS INTERNATIONAL
S-2/B-45, Dilshad Garden, Delhi
✆ 22113605
Estd.: 2002; **Prop.:** Anita Sharma;
Bus.Intt.: L.S.; **Spl.:** Humanities & Soc.Sci., Sci. & Tech., Comp., Mang., Law, Bio.Sci.

KASHMIR BOOK DEPOT
4, Maulana Azad Rd., Srinagar, Kashmir-191001 (Jammu & Kashmir)
✆ 2457968, Fax: 2457968
k_bookdepot@indiatimes.com
Estd.: 1960; **Hd.Org.:** Zahoor Ahamed
Br.: INDRK Complex, Budhah Chowk, Srinagar, Kashmir-190001 ✆ 2450262
Bus.Intt.: Pub., WS; **Spl.:** Humanities & Soc.Sci., Sci. & Tech., Med., Law

KASHMIR BOOK STORE
370, Bilal Colony, Near Hr. Sec. School (Boys), Soura, Srinagar-190011 (Jammu & Kashmir)
✆ 2425122 9419006365
Estd.: 2003; **Prop.:** Nazir Ahmad Banday;
Bus.Intt.: L.S.; **Spl.:** Humanities & Soc.Sci., Sci. & Tech., Mang., Bio.Sci.

KASHMIR KITAB GHAR
Residency Rd., Jammu-180001 (Jammu & Kashmir)
✆ 2573560
Estd.: 1989; **Hd.Org.:** Sundeep Singh
Br.: 81, Jawahar Nagar, Srinagar, Kashmir
Bus.Intt.: Pub., WS, L.S. & Rt.;
Spl.: Humanities & Soc.Sci., Sci. & Tech., Med., Law, Juvenile/Children Books, Gen. & Fiction, etc.

KASHMIR KITAB KHANA
P.T. Prem Nath, Dogra Marg, Jammu Tawi-180001 (Jammu and Kashmir)
Estd.: 1979; **Hd.Org.:** Parshotam Lal;
Bus.Intt.: Pub., L.S. and Rt., Sub.Ag.

KASHMIR LAW HOUSE
Kashmir University Rd., Hazartbal, Srinagar-190006 (Jammu & Kashmir)
✆ 2428758, Fax: 2428526
telehamid1@rediffmail.com
Estd.: 2002; **Hd.Org.:** A.B. Hamid;
Bus.Intt.: Pub., WS, L.S. & Rt., Imp., Exp., Sub.Ag.; **Spl.:** Law, Gen. & Fiction, etc.

KASHMIR VALLEY BOOK DEPOT
Basant Bagh, Nai Sarak, Srinagar, Kashmir-190001 (Jammu & Kashmir)
✆ 24701158, Fax: 2478288
Estd.: 1990; **Hd.Org.:** Mohd. Javeed;
Bus.Intt.: Pub., WS, L.S. & Rt., Imp., Exp., Sub.Ag., **Spl.:** Humanities & Soc.Sci., Sci. & Tech., Med., Law, Juvenile/Children Books Gen. & Fiction, etc.

KAT INDUSTRIAL CONSULTANTS PVT. LTD.
World Trade Centre, 38, Ground Floor,

Barakhamba Lane, Connaught Place, Babar Rd., New Delhi-110001
✆ 23411360, 51528137, 23849959,
▮ 9868182357, Fax: 23413183, 23842632
✉ katcon@del2.vsnl.net.in
🌐 www.katconsultants.com
Hd.Org.: Arun K. Gupta; **Bus.Intt.:** Pub.; **Spl.:** Industrial Books, Directories, Project Reports, Yellow Pages Loan/Detailed Techno-Eco. Feasibility Reports Market Survey Reports, CDs etc.

KATARIA BOOK STORES
1/2, Nandagar, Indore (Madhya Pradesh)

KATARIA-KATSON BOOK DISTRIBUTORS
2619-20, New Market, Nai Sarak, Delhi-110006
✆ 23286781
Bus.Intt.: B.S.; **Spl.:** School and College Text and Help Books

KATHA
A-3, Sarvodaya Enclave, Sri Aurobindo Marg, New Delhi-110017
✆ 26524350, 26524511, Fax: 91-11-26514373
✉ katha@katha.org, katha@vsnl.com, marketing@katha.org
🌐 www.katha.org
Exe.Dir.: Ms. Geeta Dharmarajan
Br.: Katha Khazana, MCD Demonstration Unit, Bhumiheen, Navjiwan, Jawahar Camps, Delhi-110019; • Katha Sreyas, 8, First Main Road, Karpagam Gardens, Adayar, Chennai-600020 (Tamil Nadu)
✆ 91-44-30904414;
• 48, Dhayan Devi Khanna Road, I Floor, Phool Bagan, Kolkata-700054 (West Bengal)
✆ 91-33-39502240; **Bus.Intt.:** Pub. & Dist.; **Spl.:** Fiction, Journals & Magazines

KATHA KAKINI
203/4D, Bidhan Sarani, Kolkata-700010 (West Bengal)

KATHA SANSAR
E-385C, Pratap Vihar, Near Gas Agency, Ghaziabad-201009 (Uttar Pradesh)
✆ 9818194985
Hd.Org.: Suranjan; **Bus.Intt.:** Pub.; **Spl.:** Magazine *Katha Sansar*

KATHAMALA
240, Vivekananda Rd., Kolkata-700006 (West Bengal)

KATHA-O-KAHINI (BOOKSELLERS PVT. LTD.)
13, Bankim Chatterjee St., Kolkata-700073 (West Bengal)

KATO KATHA
1/1, Ramanath Majumder St., Kolkata-700009 (West Bengal)

KATYAYANI PUBLISHERS AND BOOKSELLERS
C-1/184, Gali No. 22, Khajuri Khas, Delhi-110094
✆ 91-11-22967252
Hd.Org.: Balwant Singh Adhikari
Bus.Intt.: Pub., Dist. and B.S.; **Spl.:** All kinds of Library Books

KAUSIK BOOK AGENCY
4, Dhanalakshmi Avenue, 111, Cross St., Kasturba Nagar, Adyar, Chennai-600020 (Tamil Nadu)
✆ 2411460
Estd.: 1968-69; **Hd.Org.:** Mrs. V.R. Rajalakshmi

KAUSTHUB PRAKASHAN
29-A, Navanirman Society, Ranapratap Nagar, Nagpur-440022 (Maharashtra)

KAVERI BOOK SERVICES
4697/5-21A, Ansari Rd., New Delhi-110002
✆ 23288140, 23245799
✉ kaveri@del3.vsnl.net.in, kaveribooks@vsnl.com
Estd.: 1994; **Prop.:** Rakesh Goel; **Bus.Intt.:** Rt., WS, Pub., L.S.; **Spl.:** Acad., Soc.Sci.

KAVI PRAKASHAN
Lakhotiya Ka Chowk, Bikaner-334005 (Rajasthan)
Hd.Org.: Smt. Shashikala Bissa

KAVITA PRAKASHAN
Teliwara, Bikaner-334005 (Rajasthan)
✆ (R) 2529453
Estd.: 1978; **Hd.Org.:** Dinesh Ranga; **Bus.Intt.:** Pub. and B.S.; **Spl.:** Hindi Books

KAVITA PRAKASHAN
B-173, Gali No. 6, Subhash Vihar, North Ghonda, Delhi-110053
✆ 22268359

KAVITA PRAKASHANA
Kyatasandra, Tumkur Taluk (Karnataka)
Hd.Org.: Kavitha Krishna; **Bus.Intt.:** Pub.; **Spl.:** Fiction Poems, Dramas, Children's and Gen. Books in Kannada

KAVITHA PUBLICATION
Post Box No. 6123, No. 8 Muthu Krishnan St., T. Nagar, Chennai-600017 (Tamil Nadu)
✆ 28270980
Prop.: S. Chockalingam; **Bus.Intt.:** Pub.; **Spl.:** Novels, Books on Self-improvement Sports, Cookery, Rel., Jokes, Astrology, Neurology, Med. and Physical Edu., Osho Rajneesh and Children Books

KAYEM EXPORTERS
Mahnamel-130, Kurisummoodu, Changanacherry-686104 (Kerala)
Bus.Intt.: Exp.

KAZIRANGA PRAKASHAN
Anandram Baruah Rd., Guwahati-781001 (Assam)

KEDAR PRAKASHAN GRUHA
B-3, Vrushabha, Jaime Silveira Avenue, Altinho-Panaji, Goa-403001

KEDAR SUPPLIER (PRAKASHAN)
142, Shaniwarpeth, Pune-411030 (Maharashtra)
✆ 0212-2452658
Estd.: 1989; **Prop.:** A.S. Puranik;
Bus.Intt.: Dealers; **Spl.:** Marathi Books of School Library for 1st to 12th Std.

KEE PEE PUBLISHERS
A-1/2, Aditi Apartments, D-1, Block, Janakpuri, New Delhi-110058

KEEP BUSY PUBLISHERS (INDIA)
D-41/1, T.T.C. Industrial Area, Opp. Turbhe Tele. Exch. Midc., Navi Mumbai-400613 (Maharashtra)
✆ 27672726
Bus.Intt.: Pub.

KEERTHI PUBLISHING HOUSE PVT. LTD.
Manasa Train Bldg., Med. College P.O., Thiruvananthapuram-695011 (Kerala)

KEEZHI KATRU PUBLISHERS
10, Gowalia Sahib St., Fillis Rd., Chennai-600002 (Tamil Nadu)

KELADI MUSEUM & HISTORICAL
Research Bureau, Keladi, Sagar Talku, Distt. Shimoga-577401 (Karnataka)

KEN PUBLICATIONS
227, Pratap Kunj, Keshav Puram, Delhi-110035
Bus.Intt.: Pub. and L.S.

KENDRIYA HINDI NIDESHALAYA
Paschim Khand-VII, R.K. Puram, New Delhi-110066
✆ 2605211/33
Dir.: Ganga Prasad Vimal; **Spl.:** Beings out bi/tri-lingual Dictionaries of Indian Languages. It is also working on Multi-lingual Dictionary Project (13 languages), Lingua Records, Cassettes and Teach Yourself Books in Hindi

KENDRIYA HINDI SANSTHAN
Hindi Sansthan Marg, Agra-282005 (Uttar Pradesh)
✆ 2530684, 2530159, Fax: 91-11-2530684
✉ registrarkhs@yahoo.co.in
🌐 www.hindisansthan.org
Hd.Org.: Devendra K. Sharma; **Bus.Intt.:** Pub., **Spl.:** Hindi Books on Language and Linguistics, Litt., as also a Half-yearly Magazine *Gaveshana*

KENNEDY BOOK HOUSE
781, Mount Rd., Chennai-600002 (Tamil Nadu)
✆ 28521797
Prop.: V. Krishnan; **Bus.Intt.:** Rt.; **Spl.:** Gen. Books, Text Books all Sub. including Med.

KERALA BOOK MARKETING SOCIETY/BOOKMARK
Fort (P.O.), Punnapuram, Trivandrum-695023 (Kerala)
✆ 91-0471-2473921
✉ keralabookmark@yahoo.com
Hd.Org. A. Gokulendran

KERALA BOOK HOUSE
Kodungallur, Thrissur-680664 (Kerala)
Estd.: 1956; **Prop.:** K.K. Appu Menon;
Bus.Intt.: Pub. and B.S.

KERALA BOOKS & PUBLICATIONS SOCIETY
Kakkanad P.O., Kochi-682030 (Kerala)
✆ 2422223
Estd.: 1976; **Man.Dir.:** R.P.C. Nair

KERALA EXPORTERS & TRADERS
6, Aristo Apartments, Church Rd., Marol, Mumbai-400059 (Maharashtra)
✆ 28345112, 28214403, Fax: 28221497
✉ kerextra@vsnl.com
Bus.Intt.: Exp.

KERALA GANDHI SAMARK NIDHI
Gandhi Bhavan, Thychud, Trivandrum-695014 (Kerala)
✆ 2321786

KESARI PRAKASHAN
568, Narain Pet, Pune-411030 (Maharashtra)

KESHARI PUSTAK SADAN
Teghra, Begusarai-851133 (Bihar)
Bus.Intt.: Pub. and B.S.

KESHAV BHIKAIJEE DHAWLE
1st Batawadi, Girgaon, Mumbai-400004 (Maharashtra)

KHAAS KITAB FOUNDATION
D-307, Sarvodaya Enclave, Ground Floor, New Delhi-110017
✆ 26859641, Fax: 91-11-26859641
✉ vjafa@bol.net.in
🌐 www.geocities.com/khaskitab
Hd.Org.: Manorama Jafa; **Bus.Intt.:** Pub.

KHADI PRATISTHAN
15, College Square, Kolkata-700073 (West Bengal)

KHALSA BOOK HOUSE
25, Ashutosh Mukherjee Rd., Kolkata-700020 (West Bengal)

KHAMA PUBLISHER
B-7, Ajindra Market, 7255, Prem Nagar, Shakti Nagar, Delhi-110007

✆ 23945685, 23953626, Fax: 23945685
Hd.Org.: Anupam Banerjee; **Bus.Intt.:** Pub. and Dist.; **Spl.:** Humanities and English

KHANDELWAL BOOK DEPOT
Meston Ganj, Rampur (Uttar Pradesh)
✆ (O) 2324636, 2327963 (R) 2340906
khandelwal123@vsnl.com
Estd.: 1950; **Bus.Intt.:** B.S.; **Spl.:** School, Graduate, Adv. Books for Lib., Gen. Books on different topics

KHANI BOOKS
P.O. Box 87, P.R. Building, Tass Rd., Alwaye-683101 (Kerala)
Estd.: 1986; **Prop.:** M.G. Sasi Kumar; **Bus.Intt.:** Pub. and B.S.

KHANNA BANDHU
7, Tilak Rd., Dehradun-248005 (Uttarakhand)
✆ 2621485, 2621689, Fax: 2621689, 2760240
khannabandhu@vsnl.com, khannabandhu@sanchanet.in
Estd.: 1962; **Hd.Org.:** S. Khanna; **Bus.Intt.:** Pub. and Dist.; **Spl.:** Sci. and Tech., Forestry, Wildlife, etc.

KHANNA BOOK PUBLISHING CO. PVT. LTD.
1695, Nai Sarak, Delhi-110006
✆ 23283211, 23256658, Fax: 91-11-23256658
contact@khannaedu.com
www.khannaedu.com
Hd.Org.: Puneet Khanna; **Bus.Intt.:** Pub.; **Spl.:** Comp. and Engg.

KHANNA PUBLISHERS
2-B, Nath Market, Nai Sarak, Delhi-110006
✆ 22912380
Prop.: R.C. Khanna; **Bus.Intt.:** Pub.; **Spl.:** Engg. and Mang.

KHANNA TECHNICAL PUBLICATIONS
1694, Nai Sarak, Delhi-110006
✆ (O) 23256658 (R) 27134219
Prop.: Abinash C. Khanna; **Bus.Intt.:** Rt., WS

KHEDA ZILLA PUSTAKALAYA SAHAYAK MANDAL
C/o Dr. Ochhavlal H. Shah, 4, Jai Yamuna Society, Maninagar (E), Ahmedabad-380008 (Gujarat)

KHEL SAHITYA KENDRA/KSK PUBLISHERS AND DISTRIBUTORS
7/26-LGF, Ansari Road, Darya Ganj, New Delhi-110002
✆ 65190343 ▮ 9811088729, Fax: 91-11-42564726
khelsahitya1@rediffmail.com
www.khelsahitya.com
Estd.: 1985; **Hd.Org.:** Vivek Thani
Br.: WP-474, First Floor, Shiv Market, Ashok Vihar-I, New Delhi-110052
✆ 27233834, 27124378
Bus.Intt.: Pub.; **Spl.:** Sports and Physical Edu. in English

KHEMKAR PRAKASHAN
27, Gopala Park, Curenjkar Marg, Erandawane, Pune-411030 (Maharashtra)

KHEMRAJ SHRIKRISHNADASS
Shri Venkateshwar Press, Khemraj Shri Krishnadad Marg, 7th Khetwadi, Mumbai-400004 (Maharashtra)
✆/Fax: 23857456
khemraj@vsnl.com
Man.: D.S. Sharma; **Bus.Intt.:** Pub. **Spl.:** Old Sanskrit and Hindi Books

KHETRAPAL LAW HOUSE
70-71, M.G. Rd., Rampurawala Building, Indore-452007 (Madhya Pradesh)
✆ (O) 2531891 (R) 2557713
Estd.: 1997; **Prop.:** Amar Khetrapal; **Bus.Intt.:** L.S., B.S. and Pub.; **Spl.:** Law, Rel., Astrology and Ayurveda

KHETRAPAL PUBLICATIONS PVT. LTD.
27, M.G. Rd. (Rampurawala Building), Indore-452007 (Madhya Pradesh)
✆ 2540987, 2542437, Fax: 0731-2532796
Estd.: 1987; **Dir.:** B.S. Khetrapal; **Bus.Intt.:** Pub., B.S., L.S.; **Spl.:** Law Books, Govt. Offices and Library in English and Hindi

KHIDDERPORE BOOK DEPOT
1/2, Ramkamal St., Kolkata-700023 (West Bengal)

KHOMRAJ SHRIKRISHANDAS
91/109, Khomraj Shrikrishandas Marg, 7 Bee Khetbari Bank Rd. Corner, Mumbai-400004 (Maharashtra)
✆ 23857454
Hd.Org.: Shri Sanjay Murlidhar Bajaj

KHOSLA PUBLISHERS & DISTRIBUTORS
4380/4B, Ansari Rd., Darya Ganj, New Delhi-110002
✆ 23285376
Estd.: 1956; **Hd.Org.:** Harish Arora; **Bus.Intt.:** Pub. and Dist.; **Spl.:** Eng.Litt., Dictionaries and Books on Humanities, Sci.

KHUDA BAKHSH ORIENTAL PUBLIC LIBRARY
Ashok Rajpath, Patna-800004 (Bihar)
✆ 2301507, Fax: 91-612-2300315
pat_kbopl@dataone.in
www.kblibrary.nic.in
Hd.Org.: Mohammad Ziauddin; **Bus.Intt.:** Pub.; **Spl.:** Rare Manuscripts, Islamic Litt., Medieval Indian Hist., Oriental Studies, etc. in Urdu, Hindi and English

KHURANA PUBLISHING HOUSE
94, Manak Vihar, Delhi-110092
✆ 91-11-22386293, 22391292
✉ khuranapublishing@gmail.com
Hd.Org.: Parveen Khurana;
Bus.Intt.: Pub. and Dist.; **Spl.:** General books

KHURMI BOOKS
B-510, New Friends Colony, New Delhi-110065
✆ 26314690, 26323759, Fax: 26921585
✉ khurmieducation@yahoo.com
Estd.: 1995; **Hd.Org.:** N.S. Khurmi;
Bus.Intt.: Pub.; **Spl.:** Edu. and School-level Books on Sci.

KIDS EDUCATIONAL AIDS
F-31-A, Third Floor, Moti Nagar,
New Delhi-110015
✆ 91-11-64625512
Hd.Org.: Umesh Sachdeva
Bus.Intt.: Dist.; **Spl.:** Children's books

KILASO BOOKS
2/19, Ansari Rd., Darya Ganj,
New Delhi-110002
✆ 41562653, 41563798, Fax: 91-11-41562653
✉ kilasobooks@airtelbroadband.in
Estd.: 2002; **Hd.Org.:** Ashok Mehra;
Bus.Intt.: Pub., Dist. and Imp.;
Spl.: Research Based Books for Lib., Institutes & Colleges

KINDERSTON PUBLICATIONS
9, Gola Market, Darya Ganj,
New Delhi-110002
✆ 91-11-23272402
✉ inquiry@kp-ed.com
www.kp-ed.com
Hd.Org.: Vijay Raj Mittal **Bus.Intt.:** Pub.

KING BOOKS EDUCATIONAL PUBLISHERS
1684, Nai Sarak, Delhi-110006

KINSEY BROTHERS
New Delhi
✆ 23324446, Fax: 23328731
✉ kinse@del2.vsnl.net.in
Bus.Intt.: Pub.

KIRAN BOOKS INTERNATIONAL
DK-4-115, P.O. Domgarh,
Distt. Dhanbad-828107 (Jharkhand)
✆ 2252526, 2252644, Fax: 2251445
Estd.: 1997; **Prt.:** S.K. Jha; **Bus.Intt.:** WS, L.S. & Rt.; **Spl.:** Sci. & Tech.

KIRAN PRAKASHAN
RU-67, Pitampura, Delhi-110034
✆ 27072249

KIRAN PRAKASHAN
Khazanchi Rd., Patna-800004 (Bihar)
✆ (O) 2656682, 2653458 (R) 2656682
Estd.: 1965; **Hd.Org.:** S.N. Prasad;
Bus.Intt.: Pub.; **Spl.:** School Text Books for Competitive Examinations and Magazines in English and Hindi

KIRAN PUBLICATIONS
Old Mandi, Ajmer-305001 (Rajasthan)
✆ 2421984
Hd.Org.: Padamchand Jain; **Bus.Intt.:** Pub.;
Spl.: Gen. and Children's Books

KIRAN PUBLICATIONS
59, National Park, New Delhi
Hd.Org.: Devaraj Verma

KISALAYA PUBLICATIONS PVT. LTD.
C-2, Padma Apartment, 62/63,
New Manglapuri, Mehrauli, New Delhi-110030
✆ 26804169, 26800956
✉ suhasini@bol.net.in
Bus.Intt.: Pub.

KISHAN LAL & COMPANY
4050, Nai Sarak, Delhi-110006
✆ 22910301
Estd.: 1960; **Bus.Intt.:** B.S.; **Spl.:** School and College Books

KISHORE BOOK DEPOT
New Market, Begusarai-851101 (Bihar)
Bus.Intt.: Pub. and B.S.

KISHORE PUSTAK BHANDAR
Ashoka Market, Begusarai-851101 (Bihar)
Bus.Intt.: Pub. and B.S.

KISHORE PUSTAK BHANDAR
Ghogha, Bhagalpur-813110 (Bihar)
Bus.Intt.: Pub. and B.S.

KISHORE PUSTAK BHANDAR
Panjwara, Bhagalpur-813110 (Bihar)
Bus.Intt.: Pub. and B.S.

KITAB (THE BOOK PEOPLE)
3-A, Ellora Apartments, 25, Thirumurthy St.,
Thiagaraja Nagar, Chennai-600017
(Tamil Nadu)
✆ 28266075
Prop.: Nirmal Kamat; **Bus.Intt.:** B.S.;
Spl.: Art, Arch./Building Construction, Advertising, Graphic Arts, Animation, Photo Modern Writing in English and English Translations, Productivity Mang.

KITAB BHAVAN
1784, Kalan Mahal, Darya Ganj,
New Delhi-110002
✆ 23277392, 23277393, 23274686,
Fax: 23263383
✉ nasri@vsnl.com,
nasri@nda.vsnl.net.in
www.kitabbhavan.com

Estd.: 1962; **Prop.:** Nusrat Ali Nasri; **Bus.Intt.:** Pub., WS, Imp., Exp. **Spl.:** Islam & Islamic Studies in English, Urdu, Arabic & Persian, Holy Quran

KITAB GHAR
C-2, Chameliwala Market, M.I. Rd., Jaipur-302003 (Rajasthan)
✆ 91-141-2373363
Hd.Org.: Rampal
Bus.Intt.: Pub. and Dist.;
Spl.: Books in Hindi Language

KITAB GHAR
24/4855, Ansari Rd., Darya Ganj, New Delhi-110002
✆ 23271844, 23281844, Fax: 91-11-23281244
✉ kitabghar@hotmail.com
Hd.Org.: Devdatt Sharma; **Bus.Intt.:** Pub. and Dist.; **Spl.:** Hindi Litt., Autobiographies, Essays, Criticisms, Travelogues, Satires, Novels, etc.

KITAB GHAR
High Court Rd., Gwalior-474009 (Madhya Pradesh)
✆ (O) 2321019 (R) 2325989
Estd.: 1942; **Hd.Org.:** Rammohan Agarwal; **Bus.Intt.:** Pub. and B.S.; **Spl.:** Humanities

KITAB GHAR
Pan Bazar, Guwahati-781001 (Assam)
✆ 2544448
Hd.Org.: H. Bharali; **Bus.Intt.:** Pub.; **Spl.:** Edu. Books in English

KITAB GHAR
Barpeta (Assam)

KITAB GHAR
P.N.C. Rd., Nalbari (Assam)

KITAB GHAR
Main Rd., Gandhi Nagar, Delhi-110031

KITAB KENDRA
Sahitya Seva Sadan, Near Gujarat College, Cross Rd., Ahmedabad-380006 (Gujarat)
✆ 26422136
Estd.: 1977; **Man.Prt.:** R.D. Jani, K.R. Jani, B.R. Jani; **Bus.Intt.:** WS, L.S. & Rt.

KITAB MAHAL
College Square, Cuttack-753003 (Orissa)
✆ (O) 2648333 (R) 2613666, 2613999, Fax: 0674-2613301
✉ info@kitabmahal.net
www.kitabmahal.net
Estd.: 1951; **Prt.:** Jagadish Chandra Khandai
Br.: Kitab Mahal Agencies, Badam Bari, Cuttack-753102 ✆ 2312585
Bus.Intt.: Pub. and B.S.; **Spl.:** Sci. and Tech., Humanities, Gen. Books

KITAB MAHAL
22, Sarojini Naidu Marg, Allahabad-211001 (Uttar Pradesh)
✆ 2423466, Fax: 23289285
✉ kitab_mahal@hotmail.com
Hd.Org.: Raghvendra Agarwal
Bus.Intt.: Pub. and Dist.; **Spl.:** Educational books on commerce, management, sociology, public administration, etc.

KITAB MAHAL DISTRIBUTORS
28, Netaji Subhash Marg, Darya Ganj, New Delhi-110002
✆ 23273230, 23289285, Fax: 23289935
✉ kitab_mahal@hotmail.com
kmahal@del3.vsnl.net.in
Hd.Org.: Raghavendra Agarwal; **Bus.Intt.:** Pub. and Dist.; **Spl.:** Edu. Books on Comm., Mang., Sol., Public Administration, etc.

KITAB MAHAL (REGD.)
Botshah Mohalla, Near Safia Masjid, Lal Bazar, Srinagar (Jammu & Kashmir)
✆ 2421135
✉ kitabmahalpublishers@rediffmail.com
Estd.: 1989; **Hd.Org.:** Sheikh Sahid Bashir
Bus.Intt.: Pub., L.S., WS, Sub.Ag.
Spl.: Humanities & Soc.Sci., Mang. & Comm., Sci., Med.Sci.

KITAB MANJIL
Baruni, Begusarai-851112 (Bihar)
Bus.Intt.: Pub. and B.S.

KITAB MANJIL
Kurmahat, Bhagalpur-813224 (Bihar)
Bus.Intt.: Pub. and B.S.

KITAB MANZIL
Subzi Bagh, Patna-800004 (Bihar)

KITAB PUBLISHING HOUSE
D-52, Flatted Factories Complex, Jhandewalan, New Delhi-110055
✆ 2520124, 23543786 ▮ 9810049590, Fax: 27538699, Pager: 9628007661
✉ snchalta@giasdla.vsnl.net.in,
kitab@vsnl.com
Hd.Org.: Shamim Farooqi; **Bus.Intt.:** Pub., Dist. and L.S.; **Spl.:** Pol.Sci., Hist., Sol. etc.

KITABGHAR PRAKASHAN
24/4855, Ansari Road, Darya Ganj, New Delhi-110002
✆ 91-11-23271844, 23266207
✉ kitabghar_prd@yahoo.com
www.kitabgharprakashan.com
Hd.Org.: Satyavrat Sharma
Bus.Intt.: Pub.; **Spl.:** Hindi monthly magazine, *Samkaleen Sahitya Samachar* and Hindi literature, autobiographies, essays, etc.

KITABI DUNIYA
1955-Mohalla Qabristan,
(Opp. Anglo-Arabic School) Turkman Gate,
Delhi-110006
✆ 23288452, 35972589
✉ kitabiduniya@rediffmail.com
Hd.Org.: Iqbal Ali; **Bus.Intt.:** Pub.;
Sub.: Advanced Urdu Litt. and Urdu Poetry

KITABISTAN
Barauni, Begusarai-851112 (Bihar)
Bus.Intt.: Pub. and B.S.

KITAB SAMALYA
Anandaram Baruah Rd., Pan Bazar,
Guwahati-781001 (Assam)

KITAB WALA
2794, Gali Jhot Wali, Pahari Bhojila,
Delhi-110006
✆ 91-11-23240379, 23281499
Estd.: 1975; **Hd.Org.:** Syed Nayeem Hyder Naqvi; **Bus.Intt.:** Pub. and WS; **Spl.:** Urdu Literature, Fiction and Tech. Books

KITS & CONCEPTS (INDIA) PVT. LTD.
211/95, V.M. Street, T.V. Loganathan Towers,
Mylapore, Chennai-600004
✆ 24895335-36, Fax: 91-44-25910549
✉ kits_con@yahoo.com
www.kemathlab.com
Hd.Org.: G. Ramamoorthy

KIZHKKU PATHIPPAGAM
33/15, Eldams Road, Alwarpet,
Chennai-600018 (Tamil Nadu)
✆ 42009601, Fax: 91-44-43009701
✉ support@nhm.in
www.nhm.in
Hd.Org.: Badri Seshadri; **Bus.Intt.:** Pub.;
Sub.: Fiction, biographies, self-improvement, politics, history, business, religion, medical etc. in Tamil

KJANA JAGRTHY PRASADHAKA SANGAM
Paravoor, Alappuzha-688004 (Kerala)

KLING PUBLISHING HOUSE
12-B, Burla Market, Burla Sambalpur-768017
(Orissa)

KLUWER ACADEMIC PUBLISHERS
Sector 29, Plot No. 45, Faridabad-121008
(Haryana)
✆ 0129-2373639, Fax: 091-2273641
✉ kluwer@nde.vsnl.net.in
Estd.: 1987; **Hd.Org.:** Surinder Lijhara;
Bus.Intt.: Pub.; **Spl.:** Sci., Tech., Med., Law, Soc.Sci.

KNANAYA LAITY COUNCIL
Central Office, 13/155 Nattakaom,
Kottayam-686013 (Kerala)
Fax: 0481-2561822
Estd.: 1983; **Hd.Org.:** C. Markose;
Bus.Intt.: Pub.

KNOWLEDGE BOOKS INC.
D-136, Sector 36, Noida-201303
(Uttar Pradesh)
✆ 0120-2572246, 2574810, 2575981
▮ 9810191394
✉ komal@ndb.vsnl.net.in
Estd.: 2003; **Hd.Org.:** K.C. Agarwal;
Bus.Intt.: Pub.; **Spl.:** Electrical Engg.

KNOWLEDGE CITY BOOKS
501, Sanghvi Towers, Chulna Bhabola Rd.,
Vasai Rd., (West) Thane-401202
(Maharashtra)
✆ 2384718
✉ knowledgecity@rediffmail.com
Hd.Org.: Athar Hussain Rizvi; **Bus.Intt.:** Pub. & Dist.; **Spl.:** Rel., Ethics, Hist., and Litt.

KNOWLEDGE HOUSE
Exchange Rd., Near J & K Bank,
Srinagar-190001 (Jammu & Kashmir)
✆ 480052
Estd.: 1998; **Prop.:** Shabir Ahmed;
Bus.Intt.: L.S.; **Spl.:** Humanities & Soc.Sci., Sci., Engg. & Tech.

KNOWLEDGE PUBLISHERS
Kumarapuram, Med. College, P.O.,
Thiruvananthapuram-695011 (Kerala)
Estd.: 1988; **Prop.:** Nazeema Rasheed;
Bus.Intt.: Pub.

KNOWLEDGE STORE (THE)
New Delhi
✆ 26531279-80, Fax: 26532252
✉ ik_in@vsnl.net
Bus.Intt.: B.S. & Stationers

KNOWLEDGE WORLD
5A/4A, Ansari Rd., Darya Ganj,
New Delhi-110002
✆ 23263488 ▮ 9810483435, Fax: 23263498
✉ kwi@mantraonline.com
www.knowledgeworldonline.com
Estd.: 1986; **Prop.:** Kalpana Shukla;
Bus.Intt.: Pub., WS, L.S. & Rt., Imp., Sub.Ag.;
Spl.: Humanities & Soc.Sci., Sci. & Tech.

KOHINOOR BOOK CENTRE
Hyderabad (Andhra Pradesh)
✆ 23320602, Fax: 23309038
✉ kohinoorbookcentre1@rediffmail.com

KOHINOOR BOOK DISTRIBUTORS
No. 6/2, Railway Parallel Rd., Kumara Park
East, Bangalore-560001 (Karnataka)
✆ 22262691 (PP)
Estd.: 1993; **Bus.Intt.:** Rt., WS

KOHINOOR PUBLICATIONS
11099, Doriwalan, St. No. 2, East Park Rd., Karol Bagh, New Delhi-110005
✆ (O) 2736333, 23541852 (R) 27275580, 27273538
Estd.: 1992; **Hd.Org.:** Arun Ralhan; **Bus.Intt.:** Pub.; **Spl.:** School Text Books in English, Hindi and Punjabi

KOHLI PUBLISHERS & EXHIBITORS
40, Vaishali, Dadri Palam Rd., New Delhi-110045
✆ 25033377, 25391207, 25391008, Fax: 25036000
Hd.Org.: Gaurav Kohli; **Bus.Intt.:** Pub., Dist.; **Spl.:** Children's Books Encyclopaedia's and Edu. Teaching Aids

KOKATE PRAKASHAN
Kadambari Sahavas, Vasai Rd., Pune-401202 (Maharashtra)

KOMAL BOOK CENTRE
C/o Mahalaxmi Creations, Hira Compound, Opp. Navjeevan Society, Chembur Colony, Mumbai-400074 (Maharashtra)
✆ (O) 25575901 (R) 25574411
Estd.: 1996; **Prop.:** Ms. Sadhana Rao; **Bus.Intt.:** L.S., B.S.

KOMAL PRAKASHAN
1/5971, Kabool Nagar, Shahdara, Delhi-110032

KOMAL PUBLICATIONS
Kalol (NG), Nagaland
✆ 25344, Fax: 02764-24504
✉ bharatp200in@yahoo.com
Br.: Gandhinagar
✉ bharatp2000in@amulmail.com
Bus.Intt.: Pub. and Dist.

KONARK PUBLICATIONS
Museum Rd., Vijayawada-520002 (Andhra Pradesh)

KONARK PUBLISHERS
Binod Behari, Cuttack-753002 (Orissa)
✆ 0671-222879, 6000593
Prop.: Chandra Sekhara Patra; **Bus.Intt.:** Pub. and B.S.; **Spl.:** Gen. and Litt. in Oriya

KONARK PUBLISHERS PVT. LTD.
A-149, Main Vikas Marg, Shakarpur, Delhi-110092
✆ 22455731, 22504101, 22507103, 55244972, Fax: 22507103
✉ kpp123@eth.net, kprn@bol.net.in
Estd.: 1986; **Man.Dir.:** K.P.R. Nair
Br.: A38-A, Aruna Park, Shakarpur, Delhi-110092
• Care Blackie & Sons Pvt. Ltd., 93, Anna Salai, Chennai-600002 (Tamil Nadu)
✆ 28600225
• OM Sri Suryanarayana Plot 4, Astalakshminagar, First St., Alapakkam, Chennai-600116 (Tamil Nadu) ✆ 24769723
• A-150, Shakarpur, Delhi-110092
✆ 22504101, 22455731
Bus.Intt.: Pub., Exp.; **Spl.:** Humanities & Soc.Sci., Edu. Books for Schools/College & Comp. Books

KOSHAL BOOK DEPOT
3611/5, Narang Colony, Trinagar, Delhi-110035
✆ 91-11-65860877
✉ koshal.bookdepot@gmail.com
Hd.Org.: Rishi Pal Sharma
Bus.Intt.: Pub., Dist. and L.S.; **Spl.:** Hindi and English language books on art, archaeology, architecture, Indology, etc.

KOSHI BOOKS
Ram Mandir, Sector-I, Bokaro Steel City, Dhanbad-827009 (Bihar)

KOTAK BROS
B-337, Oshiwara Industrial Centre, New Link Road, Goregaon (W), Mumbai-400104 (Maharashtra)
✆ 28769572, Fax: 91-22-28769726
✉ kketan@bom5.vsnl.net.in
Hd.Org.: Ketan K. Kotak; **Bus.Intt.:** Pub., Dist. and Exp.; **Spl.:** Books on all subjects

KOTHARI PRAKASHAN GRAH
64, Fernandis Bridge, Gandhi Rd., Ahmedabad-380001 (Gujarat)

KOTTACKAL PUBLISHERS
Kottacakat, Manganam P.O., Kottayam-686018 (Kerala)
✆ 2578936
Estd.: 1960; **Prop.:** K.V. Mammen; **Bus.Intt.:** Pub.

KOUSHIK PRAKASHANI
107, Keshab Sen St., Kolkata-700009 (West Bengal)

KRANTIK PRAKASHANI
Stall 31, Block 5, B.C. Chatterjee St., Kolkata-700073 (West Bengal)

KRANTZ PUBLICATIONS
C-18, South Extension Part-II, New Delhi-110049
✆ 26252146, Fax: 91-11-26252146
✉ anilkrantz@vsnl.com
Hd.Org.: V.K. Sharma; **Bus.Intt.:** Pub.; **Spl.:** Self-Development Books

KRISHNA BOOK AGENCY
H. No. 101-102, Resham Ghar Colony, Jammu Tawi (Jammu and Kashmir)
✆ 2542361, 2543804, Fax: 2472906

Estd.: 1992; **Hd.Org.:** Harjeet Singh; **Bus.Intt.:** Pub., WS, L.S. & Rt.; **Spl.:** Humanities & Soc.Sci., Sci. & Tech., Law, Juvenile Children Books, Gen. & Fiction, etc.

KRISHNA BOOK DEPOT
Jalandhar Rd., Hoshiarpur (Punjab)

KRISHNA BOOK DISTRIBUTORS
Pocket-O, 18/B-3, Dilshad Garden, Delhi-110095
✆ 22116098 ▮ 9810834859, Fax: 22131719
✉ krishnabooks@yahoo.com
Estd.: 1995; **Prop.:** Ved Prakash; **Bus.Intt.:** Rt., L.S.; **Spl.:** Acad., Beh.Sci., Soc.Sci., Comm., Sci., Pure & Applied, Tech., Fiction Rare, Journals & Magazines, Law

KRISHNA BOOK STALL
1, Bankim Chatterjee St., P.D.S., Kolkata-700073 (West Bengal)

KRISHNA BOOKS INTERNATIONAL
2713, Kucha Chelan, Darya Ganj, New Delhi-110002
✆ 23276234
Estd.: 1985; **Prop.:** Mrs. Suksham Gupta

KRISHNA BOOKS SERVICE
935, Kucha Rohella Khan, Darya Ganj, New Delhi-110002
✆ 23281065 ▮ 9899345196
Hd.Org.: Manmohan; **Bus.Intt.:** B.S.; **Spl.:** Gen. Books

KRISHNA BOOKSELLER
Sujaganj, Bhagalpur-812002 (Bihar)
Bus.Intt.: Pub. and B.S.

KRISHNA BROTHERS
Mahatma Gandhi Marg, Ajmer-301001 (Rajasthan)
✆ 223577
Hd.Org.: Ashok Agarwal

KRISHNA FOUNDATION INDIA
Rajghat Fort, Varanasi-221001 (Uttar Pradesh)

KRISHNA PRAKASHAN MEDIA (P) LTD.
11, Shivaji Rd., Meerut-250001 (Uttar Pradesh)
✆ 0121-2644766, 2642946, Fax: 2645855
✉ sk_kpm@yahoo.com
🌐 www.krishnaprakashan.com
Estd.: 1960; **Hd.Org.:** S.K. Rastogi; **Bus.Intt.:** Pub.; **Spl.:** Edu., Competitive, Mang. and Engg. Books

KRISHNA PUSTAK BHANDAR
Godda-814133 (Bihar)

KRISHNA PUSTAK BHANDAR
Bhakharua More, Daudnagar, Aurangabad-824113 (Bihar)
Bus.Intt.: Pub. and B.S.

KRISHNA PUSTAK BHAWAN
Sangrampur, Monghyr-813212 (Bihar)

KRISHNA PUSTAK KENDRA
Dhaka, East Champaran-845418 (Bihar)

KRISHNA SAHITYA SADAN
263/2, Mehrauli, New Delhi-110030
Hd.Org.: Sanjay Kumar Gupta

KRISHNA TRADERS
285, Princess St., Mumbai-400002 (Maharashtra)
✆ 22011357, 22012103, Fax: 22083184
✉ k_tee@vsnl.com
Estd.: 1954; **Bus.Intt.:** Exp.

KRISHNADAS ACADEMY
Chowk (Chitra Cinema Building), PB No. 118, Varanasi-221001 (Uttar Pradesh)

KRISHNAMURTI FOUNDATION INDIA
Book Distribution Centre, C-15, Heramb Society, S.No. 115, Pashan Road, Pune-411021 (Maharashtra)
✆ 91-20-27284463
✉ kbooks2000@yahoo.com
🌐 www.jkrishnamurti.org
Hd.Org.: S. Manjani; **Bus.Intt.:** Promoter; **Spl.:** Krishnamurti's Teachings and Phil. through Books, Audios and Videos

KRISHNAMURTI FOUNDATION INDIA
Rajghat Edu. Centre, Rajghat Fort, Varanasi-221001 (Uttar Pradesh)
✆ 2331289, 2332536, Fax: 0542-2330218
✉ publications@kfionline.org
Hd.Org.: P. Krishna; **Bus.Intt.:** Pub.; **Spl.:** Works of the Philosopher of the Century J. Krishnamurti and his translated version in Hindi and other Languages

KRISHNAMURTI FOUNDATION INDIA
64/65, Greenways Rd., Raja Annamalaipuram, Chennai-600028 (Tamil Nadu)
✆ 24937803, 2332536
✉ publications@kfionline.org
🌐 www.kfionline.org
Hd.Org.: O.R. Rao; **Bus.Intt.:** Pub.; **Spl.:** Works of the Eminent Teacher and Philosopher J. Krishnamurti and materials relating to his life

KRISHNAMURTI PUBLICATIONS
F-21A, First Floor, Spencer Plaza, 769, Anna Rd., Chennai-600002 (Tamil Nadu)
✆ 91-44-2852646
Hd.Org.: Hariharan; **Bus.Intt.:** Pub.

KRISNA TRADERS
Princess St., 285, Mumbai-400002 (Maharashtra)
✆ 22012103, 22001357, Fax: 91-22-22060114
Hd.Org.: Piyush Gantha; **Bus.Intt.:** Exp.; **Spl.:** News Papers, Magazines

KRISTU JYOTI PUBLICATIONS
Kristu Jyoti College, Bangalore-560036 (Karnataka)

KRUKSHETRA PRAKASHAN PVT. LTD.
48/A-1/6, Rohini, New Delhi-110085
✆ 27056240
Hd.Org.: Devsharma Vedalankar; **Bus.Intt.:** Pub.; **Spl.:** Human Development and Children's Litt.

KULDEEP BOOK CENTRE
Dacca Danga Municipal Park, Jammu Tawi-180001 (Jammu and Kashmir)
Estd.: 1969; **Prop.:** Kuldeep Anand; **Bus.Intt.:** Pub's Rep., L.S. & Rt.

KUMAON SANSKRITI PARISHAD
Vaishnava Kunj, Nainital-263002 (Uttarakhand)

KUMAR & COMPANY
9, Hathroi, Ajmer Rd., Jaipur-302001 (Rajasthan)
Bus.Intt.: B.S. and Rt.

KUMAR BOOK CENTRE
Near Chalantika Cinema, Begusarai-851101 (Bihar)
Bus.Intt.: Pub. and B.S.

KUMAR BOOK DEPOT
208, Second Floor, V4 Plaza, Plot No. 16, KP Block Community Centre, Pitampura, New Delhi-110034
✆ 32411029, Fax: 91-11-27321743
✉ kumar_bookdepot@yahoo.co.in
Hd.Org.: Ashok Kumar
Bus.Intt.: Dist.; **Spl.:** Medical and nursing books published by Indian and foreign pub.

KUMAR BOOK STORE
Guman Pura, Kota (Rajasthan)
✆ 0744-220452
Estd.: 1993; **Prop.:** Choith Ram; **Bus.Intt.:** L.S., WS

KUMAR GALLERY (PVT.) LTD.
11, Sunder Nagar Market, New Delhi-110003
✆ 24611113, 24611133, 24618875, Fax: 24631195
Estd.: 1935; **Hd.Org.:** Virendra Kumar Jain; **Bus.Intt.:** Pub., WS, L.S., Rt., Imp., Exp.

KUMAR PRAKASHAN
E-1000, Saraswati Vihar, Delhi-110034
✆ 27020112
Hd.Org.: Baldev Das Kumar

KUMAR PUBLICATIONS
507, Vikram Tower, Rajendra Place, New Delhi-110008
✆ 25720718, 25760718, Fax: 25841718
✉ kumarpublications@rediffmail.com
Estd.: 1968; **Hd.Org.:** V. Kumar; **Bus.Intt.:** Pub. and Dist.; **Spl.:** Career Guides and Gen. Books in English

KUMAR PUSTAK BHANDAR
Panjwara, Bhagalpur-813110 (Bihar)
Bus.Intt.: Pub. and B.S.

KUMAR PUSTAK BHANDAR
Shamsher Nagar, Daudnagar, Aurangabad-824113 (Bihar)
Bus.Intt.: Pub. and B.S.

KUMAR PUSTAK BHANDAR
Devkund, Aurangabad-824202 (Bihar)
Bus.Intt.: Pub. and B.S.

KUMARAN PATHIPPAGAM
No. 2, Muthukrishnan St., P.B. No. 6124, T. Nagar, Chennai-600017 (Tamil Nadu)
✆ 28264046, 28241865, Fax: 91-44-28264046
✉ thambi@md2.vsnl.net.in
Hd.Org.: S. Vairavan; **Bus.Intt.:** Pub.; **Spl.:** Tamil Books on Reli., Self-Improvement, Tamil Med., Historical Novels, Astrology, Children Story Books and Various Sub. to Suit the Requirements of all Section of Society

KUMKUM PRAKASHAN
Opp. Model Cinema, Gandhi Rd., Ahmedabad-380001 (Gujarat)

KUMUD BOOK MARKETING SERVICES
B-2, Ambica-II, 119, Radheyshyam Park, Sector-5, Rajendra Nagar, Sahibabad-201005 (Uttar Pradesh)
✆ 95120-2639303 ▮ 9891371403
✉ come2_kbms@indiatimes.com
Estd.: 2002; **Hd.Org.:** Mohit Hastwala; **Bus.Intt.:** Rt., WS, Pub., L.S.; **Spl.:** Acad., Beh.Sci., Soc.Sci., Comm., Sci., Tech.

KUMUDAM
151, Purasavakkam High Rd., Chennai-600010 (Tamil Nadu)
Bus.Intt.: Exp.

KUNAL PUBLISHING HOUSE
12, Nath Building, Power House Rd., Kamal Park Extn., Azadpur, Delhi-110003
✆ 27143426
Prop.: Kunal Kapoor; **Bus.Intt.:** Pub.

KUNAL SUBSCRIPTION AGENCY
11, Mina Park Society, Near Kiran Park, Nava Wadaj, Ahmedabad-380013 (Gujarat)
✆ 7641553, 6563075
✉ pravinpnchal@jinpalonline.com
Estd.: 1976; **Prop.:** K.C. Panchal; **Bus.Intt.:** Pub., L.S. & Rt., Imp., Exp., Sub.Ag.; **Spl.:** Sci. & Tech.

KUNDALINI YOGA RESEARCH INSTITUTE
15/9, Yogadham, Lajpat Nagar Chowk, Lucknow-226003 (Uttar Pradesh)
✆ 2253011
Hd.Org.: Dinanatha Rai; **Bus.Intt.:** Pub.; **Spl.:** Books on Yoga, Naturopathy and Health

KUNDU BOOK HOUSE
Hura, Distt. Purulia-723130 (West Bengal)

KURAL NERI PATHIPPAGAM
12, Srini Vasulu Naidu St., Ayanavaram, Chennai-600023 (Tamil Nadu)

KURUKSHETHRA PRAKASHAN (P) LTD.
Kaloor Towers, Kaloor, Kochi, Ernakulam, Kerala-682017
✆ 2338324, Fax: 91-484-2338324
✉ kurukshethraprakasan@yahoo.co.in
Hd.Org.: E.N. Nandakumar
Bus.Intt.: Pub.; **Spl.:** Malayalam books

KURUKSHETRA UNIVERSITY BOOKS & STATIONERY SHOP
Shopping Centre, University Campus, Kurukshetra-136119 (Haryana)
✆ 01744-230073
Estd.: 1995; **Hd.Org.:** Vinit Arora; **Bus.Intt.:** Rt.

KUSHAL PUBLICATIONS & DISTRIBUTORS
Duyra Kitab Mahal Agency, A-3/4A, Trilochan Bazar, Mashodri, Varanasi-221001 (Uttar Pradesh)
Hd.Org.: Madanlal Mahrotra

KUSHWARA PUSTAK BHANDAR
Banka, Bhagalpur-813102 (Bihar)
Bus.Intt.: Pub. and B.S.

KUSUM PRAKASHAN
Navendu Sadan, Adarsh Colony Main Rd., Muzaffarnagar-251001 (Uttar Pradesh)
✆ 0131-2411636
Estd.: 1983; **Hd.Org.:** Smt. Kusam Kanta; **Bus.Intt.:** Pub.; **Spl.:** Adv. Books for Lib., Humanities, Linguistics Books

KUSUM PRAKASHAN
'Navchetan' Jaibhikhrao Rd., Narayan Nagar, Paldi, Ahmedabad-380001 (Gujarat)

KUSUM PUBLISHING SERVICES P. LTD.
New Delhi
✆ 26892495, 26892498, Fax: 26130069
✉ surit@vsnl.com
Hd.Org.: Surit Mitra; **Bus.Intt.:** Imp., Dist. & Pub.

KUTUB KHANA ANJUMAN E-TARAQQI-E-URDU
4181, Urdu Bazar, Jama Masjid, Delhi-110006
✆ 23282740, 23274339, Fax: 23263567
✉ sgagan@nde.vsnl.net.in
Estd.: 1939; **Bus.Intt.:** Pub. and Exp.; **Spl.:** Urdu Books

KUTUB KHANA AZIZIA
Urdu Bazar, Jama Masjid, Delhi-110006
✆ 23266422
Estd.: 1973; **Hd.Org.:** Abdul Hakeem; **Bus.Intt.:** Pub. of Urdu Books

KUTUB KHANA ISHYAT-UL-ISLAM (REGD.)
125-A, Sant Nagar, New Delhi-110065
✆ 26412015, 26291371, 51623889, Fax: 51623890
✉ sgagan@del5.vsnl.net.in
Estd.: 1977; **Prop.:** V.K. Sachdeva; **Bus.Intt.:** Pub., WS, Imp., Exp.; **Spl.:** Islamic Books

KUVAL PUBLICATIONS
143, Bells Rd., Chennai-600005 (Tamil Nadu)
Bus.Intt.: Exp.

KUWAIT EMBASSY INFORMATION OFFICE
5A, Shantipath, Chanakyapuri, New Delhi-110021
✆ 26884946, 24100791, Fax: 26881115
✉ kuinfo@kuwait-info.com
🌐 www.kuwait-into.com
Hd.Org.: Khaled Al-Razni; **Bus.Intt.:** Provider; **Spl.:** Litt. on Kuwait and Pub. of Newsletters: *Kuwait News* and *Kuwait Samachar*

KW PUBLISHERS PVT. LTD.
4676/21, First Floor, Ansari Road, Darya Ganj, New Delhi-110002
✆ 91-11-23263498, 43528107
✉ knowledgeworld@vsnl.net
🌐 www.kwpub.in
Hd.Org.: Kalpana Shukla
Bus.Intt.: Pub., Imp. and Exp.

KWALITY
Tilakmanjhi, Bhagalpur-812001 (Bihar)
Bus.Intt.: Pub. and B.S.

KWALITY BOOK COMPANY
31, Dharamtala St., Kolkata-700013 (West Bengal)
✆ 22446271, 22444746, 22446005, Fax: 24786854
Estd.: 1972; **Hd.Org.:** Harish Golani
Br.: Block 'A' New Alipore, Kolkata-700053 (West Bengal) ✆ 4780175

KWALITY STORE
National Highway, Gangtok (Sikkim)

L.B. ASSOCIATES
C-16, Sector 33, Noida (Uttar Pradesh)
✆ 4506666
hawkolba@satyam.net.in
Prop.: Linda Brady Hawke; **Bus.Intt.:** Pub., **Spl.:** Institutional Pub., Journals, Magazines & Periodicals

L.B. PUBLISHERS & DISTRIBUTORS PVT. LTD.
Indain Mercantile Mansions (Extn.), Madame Cama Rd., Mumbai-400039 (Maharashtra)
✆ 22024282, 22029397, Fax: 022-22875168
Estd.: 1979; **Ch.Exe.:** S.L. Lakshminarayanan
Br.: 90-91, M.G. Rd., Bangalore-560001 (Karnataka) ✆ 25587621, 25587302, Fax: 25586463
lbpdshp@bgl.vsnl.net.in
Bus.Intt.: L.S. & Rt., Imp., Sub.Ag.; **Spl.:** Sci. & Tech., Juvenile/Children, Gen. & Fiction etc.

L.B. PUBLISHERS & DISTRIBUTORS PVT. LTD.
M-55, G.K.-II, Commercial Complex, 2nd Floor, New Delhi-110048
✆ 26486816, 26217240, Fax: 91-11-26428684
delhi@timelifeindia.com
Estd.: 1979; **Ch.Exe.:** Mrs. Renu Khosla; **Bus.Intt.:** Dist.; **Spl.:** Time Life Books in India

L.B.S. PUBLICATIONS
4673/20 First Floor, Hari Sadan, Ansari Road, Darya Ganj, New Delhi-110002
bdbauruah@lbsbooks.com
www.lbsbooks.com
Hd.Org.: Bhaskar Dutta Baruah
Bus.Intt.: Pub.

L.B.S. PUBLICATIONS
Panbazar, Guwahati-781001 (Assam)
✆ 91-361-2543799
Prop.: Bhaskar Dutta Baruah
Lawyer's Book Stall is a Unit of LBS Publications

L.C.A. SOFT PVT. LTD.
B-15/7, Deepali Building, 92 Nehru Place, New Delhi-110048
✆ 91-11-66605878
lca4cd@yahoo.com
www.lca4cd.com
Hd.Org.: Manoj Kumar
Bus.Intt.: Pub. and Dist., **Spl.:** Children's books, reference books and educational aids

L.C.A. SOFTWARE
B-19/2, Deepali Building, 92 Nehru Place, New Delhi-110048
▮ 9212735340
mk5165620@yahoo.com
Hd.Org. Manoj Kumar

L.G. PUBLISHERS & DISTRIBUTORS
40, Shiv Mandir Lane, 1st Floor, Mayur Vihar, Phase-I, Delhi-110091
✆ 22795505 ▮ 9899202049, Fax: 22795641
Estd.: 2003; **Prop.:** Rahul; **Bus.Intt.:** B.S., L.S.; **Spl.:** Humanities & Soc.Sci., Sci. & Tech., Comp., Mang., Law, Arts & Arch.

L.I.P.S. PUBLICATIONS PVT. LTD.
Supreme Court Almanac, A-58, Bapu Pasu, Kotla Mubarakpur, New Delhi-110003

L.M. FURTADO & CO.
540-44, Kalbadevi Rd., Mumbai-400002 (Maharashtra)
✆ 22013105, 2756/3656, Fax: 22058750
furtados@vsnl.com
www.furtadosmusic.com
Estd.: 1865; **Prt.:** Ms. Nonabel Gomes; **Bus.Intt.:** B.S., WS, Imp.; **Spl.:** Music

L.R. BOOK DISTRIBUTORS
UB-4, Surya Kiran Building, 19, Kasturba Gandhi Marg, New Delhi-110001
✆ 23718081, 23725154, Fax: 23356444
lovdevandsons@w3c.com
Hd.Org.: Rajesh Kumar; **Bus.Intt.:** Dist.; **Spl.:** Books by Various Indian Pub.

LABDHI PRAKASHAN
Ahmedabad (Gujarat)
labdhiprakashan@hotmail.com
Bus.Intt.: B.S. & Dist.

LABOUR INDIA PUBLICATIONS
Marangattupally, P.O., Kottayam-686635 (Kerala)
✆ 0482-2251066
Estd.: 1983; **Prop.:** V.J. George; **Bus.Intt.:** Pub.

LAHARI BOOK DEPOT
C-25/1, Ramkatora Road, Varanasi-221001 (Uttar Pradesh)
▮ 9335755266
Estd.: 1888; **Hd.Org.:** Kamlapati Khatri; **Bus.Intt.:** Pub. and B.S.; **Spl.:** Hindi Books on Sci. and Magic, Especially *Chandrakanta Santati*

LAHORE BOOK HOUSE (THE)
Indore (Madhya Pradesh)
lahorebook@yahoo.com
✆ 2704435, Fax: 2554542
Bus.Intt.: B.S. & Dist.

LAHORE BOOK SHOP
2, Lajpat Rai Market,
Near Society Cinema,
Ludhiana-141004 (Punjab)

LAKHANI BOOK DEPOT
Shyam Sadan, Girgaum, Mumbai-400004 (Maharashtra)
✆ 23850016, 23854356, 23888594
Fax: 23865951
Hd.Org.: Sohin Lakhani; **Bus.Intt.:** Rt., Imp., Pub., L.S.; **Spl.:** All types of Gen. Books

LAKHETIYA BOOK STORES
Khajuri Bazar, Indore-452002 (Madhya Pradesh)
✆ 2450866

LAKSHITA BOOK DISTRIBUTORS
5/12, Ansari Road, Darya Ganj,
New Delhi-110002
✆ (O) 55842996 (R) 22822705
▮ 9818459861, 987115366
Prop.: Sat Prakash Katla; **Bus.Intt.:** B.S.; **Spl.:** Soc.Sci., Management, Eco., Reference Books, General Books, Commerce

LAKSHMI NILAYAM
53, Gowdia Mutt Rd., Royapettah,
Chennai-600014 (Tamil Nadu)
✆ (O) 28238698 (R) 28266283
Hd.Org.: V. Rajasekaran; **Spl.:** Books on Children, Devotional, Med., Cookery, Yoga, Jokes, Children Play, Novels, Listed Proverbs, Self-employment, Books Contain Baby Names

LAKSHMI PUBLICATIONS
Ramamandiram St., Governorpet,
Vijayawada-520002 (Andhra Pradesh)

LAKSHMI PUBLICATIONS
C-183/1, (HIG) Rajajipuram, Lucknow (Uttar Pradesh)

LAKSHMI PUSTAK BHANDAR
Kahalgaon, (Colong), Bhagalpur-813203 (Bihar)
Bus.Intt.: Pub. and B.S.

LAKSHMI PUSTAK BHANDAR
Deohara, Aurangabad-824114 (Bihar)
Bus.Intt.: Pub. and B.S.

LAKSHMI PUSTAK BHANDAR
Garhpura, Begusarai-848204 (Bihar)
Bus.Intt.: Pub. and B.S.

LAKSHMI PUSTAK BHANDAR
Majhaul, Begusarai-851127 (Bihar)
Bus.Intt.: Pub. and B.S.

LALAN PUSTAK BHANDAR
Rafiganj, Aurangabad-824125 (Bihar)
Bus.Intt.: Pub. and B.S.

LALIT CORPORATION
5, Mohamedi Manzil, 1st Floor,
70, Mohamedali Rd., Mumbai-400003 (Maharashtra)
✆ 23426523, 23442283, Fax: 23426523
Estd.: 1954; **Bus.Intt.:** Exp.

LALIT KALA AKADEMI
Rabindra Bhawan, 35, Ferozeshah Road,
New Delhi-110001
✆ 23387241, Fax: 91-11-23782485
✉ lka@lalithala.gov.in
🌐 www.lalitkala.org.in
Hd.Org.: Sudhakar Sharma
Spl.: Books and Journals on Art Catalogues, Monographs, Brochures and Multi-colour Reproductions

LALIT PRAKASHAN
29/59-A, Gali No. 11, Vishwas Nagar,
Shahdara, Delhi-110032
Hd.Org.: Pramodh Kumar Sharma;
Bus.Intt.: Pub.

LALITHA AND COMPANY
Ashok Nagar, Hyderabad-500020 (Andhra Pradesh)
✆ 91-40-27613164
Hd.Org.: Rama Rao

LALU BOOKS
Kottayam-686010 (Kerala)
Estd.: 1988; **Prop.:** N.N. Lalu; **Bus.Intt.:** Pub.

LAMBA BOOK DEPOT
Honeloo Complex (Basement), DA-8,
Vikas Marg, Shakarpur, Delhi-110092
✆ 22243958

LANCER BOOKS
P.B. No. 4236, 46, Ajit Arcade,
New Delhi-110048

LANCER INTERNATIONAL
P.B. No. 3802, New Delhi-110049
Bus.Intt.: Exp.

LANCER PUBLISHERS & DISTRIBUTORS
2/42(B), Sarvapriya Vihar, New Delhi-110016
✆ 26854691, Fax: 91-11-26960404
✉ lancer@lancerpublishers.com
🌐 www.lancerpublishers.com
Hd.Org.: Bharat Verma
Bus.Intt.: Pub.; **Spl.:** Books and Journals

LANCER PUBLISHERS PVT. LTD.
B-3, Gulmohar Park, New Delhi-110049

LAND MARK
E-5/21, Vivek Towers, Arera Colony,
Opp. Habibganj Police Station, Bhopal-462016 (Madhya Pradesh)
✆ 2565238, Fax: 2543624

Estd.: 1992; **Hd.Org.:** D.D. Verma; **Bus.Intt.:** L.S., Service Mail Order of Greeting Cards and Other Merchandise

LANDMARK
B, Apex Plaza, Nungambakkam High Rd., Chennai-600034 (Tamil Nadu)
✆ 28279637, 28259067, 28220147, Fax: 28259047
✉ landmark@md2.vsnl.net.in, landmark@vsnl.com
Estd.: 1987; **Hd.Org.:** Ms. Hemu Subrahmanyam
Br.: 1089, Lakshmi Plaza, Combines, Avanashi Rd., Coimbatore-37 (Tamil Nadu)
✆ 0422-2211168, Fax: 2210728; **Estd.:** 1992; **Hd.Org.:** Mrs. Shashikala
Bus.Intt.: Rt.; **Spl.:** Gen. and Trade, Acad., Professional, Greeting Cards and Toys, Music and Stationery and Children Books (Indian and Foreign Books)

LANDMARK
E-5/21, Arera Colony, Habibganj Thana Rd., Bhopal-16 (Madhya Pradesh)
✆ 2465238, Fax: 2411907
✉ landmark_no1@satyam.net.in
Estd.: 1993; **Hd.Org.:** Manish Gupta; **Bus.Intt.:** Rt., L.S.; **Spl.:** Humanities & Soc.Sci, Mang. & Comm., Engg. & Tech.

LARK BOOKS
Subarnarekha Chambers, A/9, Bhauma Nagar, Bhubaneshwar-751001 (Orissa)

LAST GENERATION PUBLICATION
South Janata Rd., 35/1759A, Palarivattom P.O., Cochin-682025 (Kerala)
Trustee: M.T. Abraham

LAVANYA EXPORTS
182, Lovely Home, 9, Cuffe Parade, Colaba, Mumbai-400005 (Maharashtra)
✆ 2241816, 22043761, Fax: 24933551
Estd.: 1989; **Bus.Intt.:** Exp.

LAW & COMMERCIAL PUBLISHERS
C-53, New Ranjit Nagar, New Delhi-110012

LAW BOOK COMPANY PVT. LTD. (THE)
18B, Sardar Patel Marg, Post Box No. 1004, Allahabad-211001 (Uttar Pradesh)
✆ 0532-2624905, 2624906, Fax: 2420852
Estd.: 1929; **Hd.Org.:** L.R. Bagga; **Bus.Intt.:** Pub., WS, L.S. and Rt., Imp., Exp., Sub.Ag.; **Spl.:** Law Books

LAW JOURNAL PUBLICATIONS
Jyendraganj, Gwalior-474009 (Madhya Pradesh)
✆ (O) 0751-2322-340, 2570591 (R) 2540118, 2369638
✉ lawjournal@mantramail.com
Estd.: 1952; **Bus.Intt.:** Pub.; **Spl.:** Law Books

LAW PUBLISHERS
8-C, Strachey Road, Civil Lines, Allahabad-211001 (Uttar Pradesh)
✆ 2660758, Fax: 91-532-2260781
✉ lawpub@sancharnet.in
🌐 www.law-publishers.com
Estd.: 1961; **Ch.Exe.:** Subhash Sagar; **Bus.Intt.:** Pub., L.S. & Rt., Imp., Exp., Sub.Ag.; **Spl.:** Law

LAW TIMES PRESS
56-C, Singar Nagar, Lucknow-226005 (Uttar Pradesh)
✆ 2456026, 2450652, Fax: 2623584

LAWMAN (INDIA) PVT. LTD.
119, Vinoba Puri, Lajpat Nagar-II, New Delhi-110024
✆ 41724129-30, Fax: 91-11-41724167
✉ abooks@vsnl.com
🌐 www.adityabooks.in
Hd.Org.: Bina Balani
Bus.Intt.: Pub. and Dist.; **Spl.:** Law Books

LAWYERS HOME (THE)
19, Sikh Mohalla, Near District Court, Indore-452007 (Madhya Pradesh)
✆ (O) 2544867, 2532252 (R) 2560978, 2563244
Estd.: 1961; **Hd.Org.:** Virendra Khetrapal; **Bus.Intt.:** Pub., B.S. and Court Suppliers; **Spl.:** Books in English and Hindi

LAWZ MEDIA PVT. LTD.
207, Essel House, 10 Asaf Ali Road, New Delhi-110002
✆ 23073522, Fax: 91-11-23073522
✉ lawzmagazine@gmail.com
🌐 www.lawzmagazine.com
Hd.Org.: Alok Krishna Agarwal
Bus.Intt.: Pub.; **Spl.:** Monthly journals *Lawz, statutez* and *key judgementz*

LAWZ MEDIA PVT. LTD.
1-64, Lajpat Nagar-I, 1st Floor, New Delhi
✆ 29811062, 26331062
✉ lawz@lawmagazine.com
Hd.Org.: Anuj Arora; **Bus.Intt.:** Pub. & Dist.

LAXMAN PUBLICATIONS
1871, Kucha Chelan, Khari Bauli, Delhi-110006

LAXMI BOOK DEPOT
Solanki Sadan, Shivaji Path, Thane-400601 (Maharashtra)
✆ 25367371

LAXMI BOOKS SUPPLIERS
22/11, Vishnupuri Colony, Aliganj, Lucknow (Uttar Pradesh)

✆ 0522-2382064
Prop.: S.K. Kar; **Bus.Intt.:** L.S.; **Spl.:** Humanities & Soc.Sci., Sci., Med. Sci., Engg. & Tech.

LAXMI PUBLICATIONS PVT. LTD.
113, Golden House, Darya Ganj, New Delhi-110002
✆ 43532500, 43532501
Fax: 91-11-23252572, 43532528
✉ info@laxmipublications.com, order@laxmipublications.com
🌐 www.laxmipublications.com
Estd.: 1974; **Dir.:** Saurabh Gupta
Br.: 129/1, 3rd Main Road, IX Cross, Chamrajpet, Bangalore-560018 (Karnataka)
✆/Fax: 080-26611561
✉ bangalore@laxmipublications.com
• 43/1394D, St. Benedict Road, Ernakulam North, Cochin-682018 (Kerala)
✆ 0484-2397004
✉ cochin@laxmipublications.com
• 104, Ist Floor, Madhiray Kaveri Tower, 3-2-19, Azam Jahi Road, Nimboliadda, Hyderabad-500027 (Andhra Pradesh)
✆ 040-24652333
✉ hyderabad@laxmipublications.com
• R.D.B. Chambers (Formerly Lotus Cinema), 106/A, 1st Floor, S.N. Banerjee Road, Kolkata-700014 (West Bengal)
✆ 22273773, 22275247, Fax: 033-22273773
✉ kolkata@laxmipublications.com
• ND-365, Adda Tanda Chowk, Jalandhar City-144001 (Punjab) ✆ 0181-2221272
✉ jalandhar@laxmipublications.com
• Radha Govind Street, Tharpagna, Ranchi-834001 (Jharkhand)
✆ 0651-2214764, 2204464
✉ ranchi@laxmipublications.com
• Pan Bazar, Rani Bari, Guwahati-781001 (Assam)
✆ 0361-2543669, 2513881, 2639740
✉ guwahati@laxmipublications.com
• 26, Damodaran Street, T. Nagar, Chennai-600017 (Tamil Nadu)
✆/Fax: 044-24344726
✉ chennai@laxmipublications.com
• 18, Madan Mohan Malviya Marg, Lucknow-226001 (Uttar Pradesh)
✆ 2209578, Fax: 0522-2204098
✉ lucknow@laxmipublications.com
• 142-C, Victor House, Ground Floor, N.M. Joshi Marg, Lower Parel (W), Mumbai-400013 (Maharashtra)
✆ 022-24915415, 24927869
✉ mumbai@laxmipublications.com
Bus.Intt.: Pub., **Spl.:** Books on higher education, Com. Sci., Engg., Information Tech., Humanities & Soc.Sci., Sci. & Tech., Juvenile/Children

LAXMI PUSTAK BHANDAR
Fernandis Bridge, Gandhi Rd., Ahmedabad-380007 (Gujarat)

LAZWAL PUBLISHERS & DISTRIBUTORS
A1, Homera Muzammil Manzil, Dodhpur, Aligarh-202001 (Uttar Pradesh)
✆ 0571-2405493, Fax: 0571-2401209
✉ maas@ndb.vsnl.net.in
Bus.Intt.: Pub. and B.S., **Spl.:** Islamic & Sci.

LEADERSHIP KNOWLEDGE CONSULTING
M1/12, DLF Phase II, Gurgaon-122002 (Haryana)
✆ 4103460-62, Fax: 91-124-4301464
✉ response@franklincoveyshouthasia.com
🌐 www.franklincovesouthasia.com
Hd.Org.: Lavleen Raheja

LEARNERS BOOK HOUSE
C.M.S., College Rd., Kottayam-686001 (Kerala)
✆ 2567438
Estd.: 1977; **Hd.Org.:** J. Thankamma; **Bus.Intt.:** Pub. and B.S.

LEARNERS PRESS (P) LTD.
L-11, Green Park Extension, New Delhi
✆ 6851023, Fax: 91-11-6851028
Bus.Intt.: Exporter, Manufacturer and Wholesale; **Spl.:** Publisher of Children's Books and Educational Aids for Children

LEELA PRAKASHAN
1/6590, East Rohtas Nagar, Shahdara, Delhi-110032
✆ 22118411, 22584998
✉ trimurtibooks@hotmail.com, trimurtibooks@yahoo.com
Estd.: 1980; **Hd.Org.:** Vikas Chadha
Spl.: Edu. Books

LEFTWORD BOOKS
12, Rajendra Prasad Rd., New Delhi-110001
✆ 23359456, 23356966, Fax: 23356966
✉ leftword@vsnl.com
🌐 www.leftword.com
Hd.Org.: Prakash Karat; **Bus.Intt.:** Pub.; **Spl.:** Marxism, Politics, Hist., Eco. and Phil.

LEGAL BOOK HOUSE
203, 'Legal Tower', Near District Court, Behind M.G. Rd. Gurudwara, Indore-452007 (Madhya Pradesh)
✆ 0731-2543506 ▮ 96101906, 9827033506, Fax: 0731-2540144
Estd.: 1985; **Prop.:** Raj Kumar Sehgal

LEGAL TIMES PUBLICATIONS (THE)
191, Yeswanthpur Circle Cross, Bangalore-560022 (Karnataka)

✆ 23371617
Estd.: 1970; **Bus.Intt.:** Pub.

LEHLING BOOK SHOP
Main Bazaar, Near Post Office, Leh Ladakh (Jammu & Kashmir)
✆ (O) 250792 (R) 250411
Estd.: 2002; **Prop.:** Sonam Yerphel; **Bus.Intt.:** Rt., L.S.; **Spl.:** Fiction, Rare, Journals and Magazines

LEKHAK SAMABAYA SAMITEE LTD.
E/92, College St. Market, Kolkata-700073 (West Bengal)

LEKHAN WACHAN PRAKASHAN
Viswanath Cooperative Housing Society, C-6, 'E' Ward, Third Floor, 5th Lane, Rajarampuri Extn., Takala, Kolhapur (Maharashtra)

LEKHANI PRAKASHAN
12/IB, Bankim Chatterjee St., Kolkata-700073 (West Bengal)

LEKHAPARA
18-B, Shyama Charan Dey St., Kolkata-700073 (West Bengal)

LEXICON BOOK DISTRIBUTOR
2652, Moti Mahal Street, Darya Ganj, New Delhi-110002
✆ 91-11-65937423
✉ lexicon.books@yahoo.co.in
Hd.Org.: Sufyan Khan
Bus.Intt.: Dist.; **Spl.:** General books

LIBCO BOOK DISTRIBUTORS
No. 1, Kiran Vihar, Vikas Marg Extn., Delhi-110092
✆ (O) & (R) 22371125 ▮ 9810274860
✉ libcobooks@email.com
Estd.: 1997; **Prop.:** Gurvinder Jeet Singh; **Bus.Intt.:** B.S., L.S.; **Spl.:** Acad., Beh.Sci., Soc.Sci., Pure & Applied, Tech., Med., Mang., Law, Arts & Arch. Books

LIBERTY INSTITUTE
C-4/8, Sahyadri Apartments, Plot 5, Sector 12, Dwarka, New Delhi-110045
✆ 25079215, Fax: 91-11-25079101
✉ info@libertyindia.org, liberty@nda.vsnl.net.in
www.libertyindia.org
Hd.Org.: Barun S. Mitra; **Bus.Intt.:** Pub.; **Spl.:** Litt. on Liberty and books on Pol. and Eco. Freedom, Globalisation, Free Trade, Phil.

LIBRARY BOOK CENTRE
1458, Malibara, Nai Sarak, Delhi-110006
✆ 23262043
✉ sudhir20@vsnl.net
Hd.Org.: Sudhir Sharma; **Bus.Intt.:** Pub. and B.S.; **Spl.:** Hindi Books on Hist., Sports, Culture

LIBRARY BOOK DISTRIBUTORS
4, Kiran Vihar, Opp. Karkar Dooma, Delhi-110092

LIBRARY BOOK SERVICE (INDIA)
11, Guru Angad Nagar Extension, Laxmi Nagar, Delhi-110092
✆ 22424522, Fax: 22224811
Hd.Org.: Amar Nath Sharma; **Bus.Intt.:** B.S., Pub., L.S.

LIBRARY INSTITUTE
96/10, Pushp Vihar, Sector-I, New Delhi-110017
✆ 26512441, 2651244, Fax: 26856992
Hd.Org.: Barun S. Mitra; **Bus.Intt.:** Rt., Pub.

LIBRARY OF TIBETAN WORKS & ARCHIVES
Gangohan Kyishong, Dharamsala-176215 (Himachal Pradesh)

LIBRARY REQUISITE
230, RPS Shaikh Sarai-I, New Delhi-110017

LIBRARY SERVICES UNLIMITED
22, Ashoka Market, Old Subzi Mandi, Delhi-110007
✆ (R) 27216750, 27476150
✉ tsut@rediffmail.com
Prop.: Narender Talreja; **Bus.Intt.:** L.S.

LIBSYS CORPORATION
D-7/A, Rockview Flats, Munirka, Delhi-110067
✆ 26171161-63, Fax: 26103661
Hd.Org.: A.K. Jain; **Bus.Intt.:** Software Pub. and Developer; **Spl.:** Library Automation

LIGHT OF LIFE SOCIETY OF INDIA
21, Y.M.C.A., Rd., Mumbai-400008 (Maharashtra)

LILI PUSTAK BHAWAN
Banka, Bhagalpur-813102 (Bihar)
Bus.Intt.: Pub. and B.S.

LIMCA BOOK OF RECORDS
D-1947, Palam Vihar, Gurgaon-122017 (Haryana)
✆ 2366907, Fax: 2366020
✉ vghose@abix.vsnl.net.in
Hd.Org.: Vijaya Ghose; **Bus.Intt.:** Pub.

LIMPID BOOK SERVICE
C-II, 28-K, New Ashok Nagar, Near G.C. Public School, Delhi-110096
✆ 22716459 ▮ 9818473964
Prop.: L.B. Shama; **Bus.Intt.:** Rt., L.S.; **Spl.:** Acad., Beh.Sci., Soc.Sci., Comm., Sci., Med., Tech., Fiction, Javeniles, Rare, Journals & Magazines

LINGUAPHONE
Pkt. 40/194, C.R. Park, Kalkaji,
New Delhi-110019
✆ 26239663
✉ sami2982002@yahoo.com
Hd.Org.: Sheela Das; **Bus.Intt.:** Pub. and Dist.; **Spl.:** Different types of Language Learning tools and Regional Language books

LINGUAPHONE HIGHLIGHTS
F-13, 1st Floor, East of Kailash,
New Delhi-110048
✆ 22371212 ▮ 9811346542
✉ deepikamago@hotmail.com
🌐 www.lotuslearning.com
Hd.Org.: Deepika Mago; **Bus.Intt.:** Dist. & Suppliers; **Spl.:** Language Learning products and Edu. Aids for Pre-primary Schools

LINK PUBLICATIONS
Gali Nawab, Mathura Gate, Bharatpur (Rajasthan) ✆ 91-5644-225023
Hd.Org.: Vijay Srivastava
Bus.Intt.: Pub.

LIPI PRAKASHAN
1, Ansari Rd., Darya Ganj, New Delhi-110002
✆ (O) 23288069 (R) 22259549
Hd.Org.: Shrikant Byas

LIPIKA
30/1A, College Row, Kolkata-700009 (West Bengal)

LIPINCOTT-RAVEN PUBLISHERS
4787/23, Ansari Rd., Darya Ganj,
New Delhi-110002
✆ 23256603
Bus.Intt.: B.S. and Pub.

LITERACY WORLD
1773, Sontha Liwalon Ka Rasta, Choura Rasta, Jaipur-302003 (Rajasthan)

LITERATURE HOUSE
14, Bahi Vir Singh Market, Putlighar, Amritsar (Punjab)

LITERATURE SYNDICATE
1/A, Rani Debendra Bala Rd.,
Kolkata-700002
(West Bengal)

LITRICO
1/7218, Shivaji Park, Shahdara,
Delhi-110032
✆ 22320635, Fax: 91-11-22320761
✉ litrico@vsnl.com
Estd.: 1984; **Prop.:** Jai Gopal Handa; **Bus.Intt.:** L.S. & Sub.Ag.; **Spl.:** Sci., Med., Tech. and Comp. Sci. and Back Volumes of Journals on all Sub.

LITTLE BOOKS
1/5971, Kabul Nagar, Shahdara,
Delhi-110032
✆ 91-11-65456828
Hd.Org.: Arun Maheshwari
Bus.Int.: Pub.

LITTLE DARLING EDUCATIONAL RHYTHMS
B-1A/40A, Janakpuri, New Delhi-110058
✆ (O) & (R) 25599327
✉ abishekpublications@hotmail.com
Prop.: Deepak Bajaj; **Bus.Intt.:** Pub., Dist., Producers; **Spl.:** Children's Books, as also Edu. Audio and Video Cassettes

LITTLE GENIUS
RG-Block, Pocket-B, Flat No. 446,
Raghubir Nagar, New Delhi-110027
✆ 25980771, Fax: 91-11-28114164
▮ 9868108195
✉ littlegeniusrk@yahoo.com
🌐 www.littlegeniusindia.net
Hd.Org.: Ravi Kumar

LITTLE FLOWER CO. (THE)
43, Ranganathan St., T. Nagar,
Chennai-600017 (Tamil Nadu)
✆ 24341538, 24336467, Fax: 24310659
✉ varadan@lifcobooks.com
Hd.Org.: T.N.C. Varadan; **Bus.Intt.:** Bringing out Pub., **Spl.:** Unique Literary and Cultural Significance and Priced very low

LITURGICAL BOOK CENTRE
Kalabhavan, Kochi-682018 (Kerala)
✆ 0484-2354222
Estd.: 1980; **Prop.:** Abel CMI; **Bus.Intt.:** Pub.

LIVING BIBLES INDIA
43, S.D. Rd., Secunderabad-500003 (Andhra Pradesh)
✆ 2831569, Fax: 2832269, Telex: 4256099
Estd.: 1973; **Hd.Org.:** P.L.N. Murthy
Br.: 42, Khan Market, Delhi-110003
✆ 24623455
• 4, Circus Market, Place, Kolkata-700017 (West Bengal)

LIVING LITERATURE CRUSADE
T-1433-A, Kumar Complex,
Wazir Nagar, Kotla Mubarakpur,
New Delhi-110003
✆ 24618818, 26670744
Fax: 24615121, 26420005
✉ loyall@ndf.vsnl.net.in
Hd.Org.: Rockwell Masih; **Bus.Intt.:** Pub., Dist.; **Spl.:** *Holy Bible* and other Christian Study, Audio-Video Tapes, etc. in Hindi and English

LIVING MEDIA INDIA LTD.
204, Competent House, F-14, Middle Circle, Connaught Place, New Delhi-110001
✆ 23325453, 23736970, Fax: 91-11-23327322
✉ ramarao@intoday.com
Estd.: 1975; **Ch.Exe.:** Mr. Aroon Purie; **Bus.Intt.:** Pub.; **Spl.:** The India Today Group

LOGOS PRESS
4788-90, Street No. 23, Ansari Road, Darya Ganj, New Delhi-110002
✆ 23272187, Fax: 91-11-26351794
✉ mail@logospressindia.com
www.logospressinadia.com
Hd.Org.: Dev Ashish Mittal
Bus.Intt.: Pub.; **Spl.:** Books on agriculture, anthropology, communication, religion, history, geography, etc. in English

LOGOS PRESS
A-81, Mohan Garden, New Delhi-110059

LOHIYA PRAKASHAN
'Kashitija' Kappagal Rd., Gandhinagar, Bellary-586103 (Karnataka)

LOK BHARTI PRAKASHAN
15-A, Mahatma Gandhi Marg, Allahabad-211001 (Uttar Pradesh)
✆ 2623665
Estd.: 1961; **Hd.Org.:** Dinesh Chandra Grover; **Bus.Intt.:** Pub.; **Spl.:** Hindi Litt. and Dictionaries

LOK HIT PRAKASHAN
D/53, Ram Nagar, Shastri Nagar, Jaipur-302016 (Rajasthan)

LOK PRAKASHAN
4693, Gali Umrao, Pahari Dhiraj, Delhi-110006
Bus.Intt.: Pub. and B.S.

LOK PRAKASHAN
3/118, Karan Gali, Vishwas Nagar, Shahdara, Delhi-110032
✆ 22433134, 22299908
Hd.Org.: Major Kumar Jain

LOK SABHA SECRETARIAT
186, Green Avenue, Amritsar-143001 (Punjab)
Bus.Intt.: Press and Public Relations

LOK SAHITYAGAR
Masjid Gali, Bhagalpur-812002 (Bihar)
Bus.Intt.: Pub. and B.S.

LOK SAHITYALAYA
SF, Asha Chambers, Baliya Kak Rd., Anand-388001 (Gujarat)

LOK SHIKSHA MANCH
1/11052-A, Subhas Park, Shahdara, Delhi-110032
✆ 91-11-65283371
Hd.Org.: Manoj Sharma; **Bus.Intt.:** Pub. & Dist.; **Spl.:** Hindi Litt.

LOK VANGAMAYA GRIHA
Bhupesh Gupta Bhawan, Leningrad Square, Prabhadevi, Mumbai-400025 (Maharashtra)

LOKA PRIYA PRAKASHAN
Keshav Bagh, 110, Princess St., Mumbai-400002 (Maharashtra)

LOKANEETHI ENTERPRISES
P.O. Box No. 2211, Edappally P.O., Kochi-682024 (Kerala)
✆ 2346219
Estd.: 1954; **Bus.Intt.:** Pub.; **Spl.:** Sci., Tech., Morals etc. in Malayalam & English

LOKAVANI-HALL MARK PRESS P. LTD.
Chennai (Tamil Nadu)
✉ lokavani@md2.vsnl.net.in
Bus.Intt.: Printers

LOKAYAT PRAKASHAN
883, Lodhan Ki Gali, M.D. Rd., Jaipur-302004 (Rajasthan)
✆ (O) 2600912 (R) 2547661
Estd.: 1991; **Hd.Org.:** Udai L. Sharma; **Bus.Intt.:** L.S. and Exhibiters; **Spl.:** Books at School and College

LOKBANI SANSTHAN
A-42, Ashok Nagar, Mandoli Rd., Shahdara, Delhi-110032
✆ 22287098
Hd.Org.: B.P. Singh

LOKBHARATI PRAKASHAN
Darbari Building, Mahatma Gandhi Marg, Allahabad-211001 (Uttar Pradesh)
✆ 91-532-2623314
✉ info@lokbhartiprakashan.com
Hd.Org.: Aamod Maheshwari
Bus.Intt.: Pub. & Dist.; **Spl.:** Hindi Litt.

LOKCHETNA PRAKASHAN
158/2, Lard Ganj, Shahid Smarak Path, Jabalpur-482002 (Madhya Pradesh)
✆ 2340543
Hd.Org.: Vikas Khare

LOKENATH SAHITYA MANDIR
12A, Bankim Chatterjee St., Kolkata-700073 (West Bengal)

LOKGEET PRAKASHAN
P.B. No. 29, Sirhind-140406 (Punjab)
Bus.Intt.: Pub. and Dist.

LOKMILAP TRUST
Sahjanand Swami Marg, Bhavnagar-364001 (Gujarat)

LOKRUCHI PRAKASHAN
Robertsganj, Sonbhadra (Uttar Pradesh)

LOKVADYAM GRAHA
Bhupesh Gupta Bhawan, Leningrad Square, Prabhadevi, Mumbai-400025 (Maharashtra)

LOKVANI
A-36, Chittaranjan Park, New Delhi-110019

LORDS BOOKS CENTRE
Dargah Hazrat-Bal, Opp. Kashmir University, PB No. 293, G.P.O. Srinagar-190001
✆ 2425152 (PP)
Estd.: 1996; **Prop.:** Niaz Shokh
Br.: Aali Masjid Eidgah, Srinagar-190002 ✆ 2426561 • Dabtal Zaina Kadal, Srinagar-190002 ✆ 2471052
Bus.Intt.: Pub., WS, L.S. & Rt., Imp.;
Spl.: Humanities & Soc.Sci., Sci. & Tech., Med., Law, Juvenile/Children, Gen. & Fiction

LORITA PATRA PRAKASHAN MANCH
Paran-Parvat, Mitan Ghat, Roy Jaikrishan Rd., Patna-800008 (Bihar)

LOTUS BOOKS
Main Rd., North Paravur, Kochi-683513 (Kerala)
✆ (O) 22125 (R) 22124
Estd.: 1966; **Hd.Org.:** A.K. Venugopal;
Bus.Intt.: B.S.

LOTUS EDUCATION NETWORK PVT. LTD.
New Delhi
✆ 26418944, 26963509, Fax: 26474646
✉ mystique_india@hotmail.com
Bus.Intt.: Dealer

LOTUS GROUP OF COMPANIES
825, New Pratap Chowk, Arjun Vihar, Delhi Cantt.-110010
✆ 25692831, 25699044
✉ usharma16@hotmail.com
Hd.Org.: Usha Sharma; **Bus.Intt.:** Dealer;
Spl.: Linguaphone for Learning Foreign Languages, English and Hindi

LOTUS LEARNING PVT. LTD.
516-B, Lotus House, S.V. Rd., Bandra (West), Mumbai-400050 (Maharashtra)
✆ 26400199, 26435052, 26441641, Fax: 2690458
✉ lotusmk@vsnl.com
www.thelotusgroup.com
Estd.: 1984; **Chairman:** Mina Krishnan
Br.: 97, 1st Floor, Mahalinga Puram, Main Rd., Nungabakkam, Chennai-600034
✆ 28213633, 28214467, Fax: 28230805
✉ lotusmds@md5.vsnl.net.in
• No. 57, 1st Floor, K.H. Rd., (Double Rd.), Opp. B.T.S. Depot, Near BPL Showroom, Bangalore-560027 ✆ 22213272, 22217772, Fax: 22242200 ✉ lotusbng@vsnl.com
• 3, Palm Place, Ground Floor, Kolkata-700019 ✆ 22400677, Fax: 22479163, ✉ lotuscal@vsnl.com • House No. 6-3-663/C/1, Officer's Colony, Punja Gutta, Hyderabad-500082 ✆ 23323713, 26503982, Fax: 23316837 ✉ lotushyd@hd2.dot.net.in
• F-13, East of Kailash, New Delhi-110048
✉ lotusdel@vsnl.com
Bus.Intt.: L.S. & Rt.; **Spl.:** Juvenile/Children, Gen. & Fiction etc.

LOTUS LEARNING PVT LTD
3rd Floor, Woodlands Buildings, D.H. Rd., Cochin (Kerala) ✆ 2369349
Estd.: 1984; **Hd.Org.:** K.G. Girish;
Bus.Intt.: Dist.; **Spl.:** World Book International

LOTUS PRESS (PUBLISHERS & DISTRIBUTORS)
4263/3, Ansari Rd., Darya Ganj, New Delhi-110002
✆ 91-11-32903912, 23280047
✉ lotus_press@sify.com
www.lotuspress.co.in
Estd.: 2003; **Prt.:** Amar Jeet Sehgal;
Bus.Intt.: Pub., WS; **Spl.:** Humanities & Soc.Sci., Children & Gen.

LOV DEV & SONS
B-II, Vandana Building, 11, Tolstoy Marg, New Delhi-110001
✆ 23311844, 31010029, Fax: 23356444
✉ lovdevandsons@w3c.com
Hd.Org.: Lov Dev Batheja; **Bus.Intt.:** Dist. and WS; **Spl.:** Indian and Foreign Books on Comp., as also Dictionaries Fiction, etc.

LOVEDALE EDUCATION PUBLISHERS
B-55, Derawal Nagar, Delhi
Bus.Intt.: Pub.; **Spl.:** Edu. books

LOVELY BOOK STALL
Changanacherry-686101 (Kerala)

LOVELY STORES
Stall-32, College Sqr. (Opp. C.U.)
Kolkata-700073 (West Bengal)

LOW COST TEACHING AIDS
18/3, Shakti Nagar, Delhi-110007
✆ 27130661, 27216115, Fax: 27435724
✉ lctas@oscarindia.com

LOW PRICE PUBLICATIONS
A-6, Nimri Commercial Center (Near Bharat Nagar), Ashok Vihar, Phase-IV, Delhi-110052
✆ 91-11-27302453

lpp@nde.vsnl.net.in
www.lppindia.com
Hd.Org.: Pradeep Mittal; **Bus.Intt.:** Pub.; **Spl.:** Indology, Soc.Sci. and Humanities in English

LOYAL BOOK DEPOT
College Rd., Meerut-250001 (Uttar Pradesh)
✆ 2663378, Fax: 91-121-4005329
Estd.: 1952; **Prop.:** Rakesh Lal;
Bus.Intt.: Dist.; **Spl.:** Sci., Humanities, Soc.Sci., Mang., Comp.

LUCKY BOOK SELLERS
Jalgaon (Maharashtra)
✆ 226750, Fax: 223399
luckybooksellers@rediffmail.com
Bus.Intt.: B.S.; **Spl.:** Business Directories

LUCKY EXPORTERS
50-A, Swami Nityanand Marg, Vile Parle (East), Mumbai-400057 (Maharashtra)
Bus.Intt.: Exp.

LUCKY PUBLISHERS
50, Sitaram Ghosh St., Kolkata-700007 (West Bengal)

LUCKY SPORTS CENTRE
Jhansi Rani Rd., Mandvi (Kutch) (Gujarat)

LUMIERE BOOKS
A-11/547, Kalyani-741235 (West Bengal)

LUXMI BHANDAR
Motor Stand Rd., Agartala-799001 (Tripura)

LYALL BOOK DEPOT
Chaura Bazar, Ludhiana-141008 (Punjab)
✆ 2745756, Fax: 2745872
Estd.: 1935; **Hd.Org.:** Raj Kumar
Br.: 4779/23, Darya Ganj, New Delhi-110002
✆ 23271469
• Motia Park, Sultania Rd., Bhopal-462001 (Madhya Pradesh)
✆ 2543624, 2545952, Fax: 0755-2736919
• Sector-1, University Market, Chandigarh-160014
✆ 2541150
Bus.Intt.: Pub., L.S. & Rt., Imp.; **Spl.:** Humanities & Soc.Sci., Sci. & Tech., Gen. & Fiction, etc.

M. BOOK STALL
1, Bankim Chatterjee St., Kolkata-700009 (West Bengal)

M. DUTTA
19B/1C, Tamer Lane, Kolkata-700009 (West Bengal)

M. KUMARASEN
94, Lloyds Rd., Chennai-600014 (Tamil Nadu)

M. LAKSHMAN BOOKSELLERS
1, Kilari Rd., Bangalore-560053 (Karnataka)
Hd.Org.: M. Lakshman; **Bus.Intt.:** Pub.; **Spl.:** Fiction, Colletions, Children's & Gen. Books

M.B. PUBLISHERS AND DISTRIBUTORS
G-1, Ganesh Plaza, Khajuri Bazar, Indore-452002 (Madhya Pradesh)
✆ (O) 0731-2451323 (R) 2556022
Prop.: Pankaj Agrawal; **Bus.Intt.:** Pub., WS; **Spl.:** Edu. Children Books and Other Books

M.B.D. ALCHEMIE PVT. LTD.
Gulab Bhawan, 6, Bahadur Shah Zafar Marg, New Delhi-110002
✆ 41509995, Fax: 91-11-41509996
✉ info@mbdalchemie.com
Hd.Org.: Ashok Kumar Malhotra

M.B.D. GROUP OF PUBLISHERS & PRINTERS
25, Motilal St., T. Nagar, Chennai-600017 (Tamil Nadu)
✆ 24343171
Bus.Intt.: Pub.; **Spl.:** Children's Nursery Books, Matriculation Books from I to X and CBSE - Guides from III to XII and ICSE, IX & X Text Book and Modern's Competitive books

M.C. BHANDARI FOUNDATION (MYSTIC INDIA MAGAZINE)
D-65, Ground Floor, Gulmohar Park, New Delhi-110011
✆ 23931393, 26521888, Fax: 23986100
✉ mysticindiamag@rediffmail.com
Hd.Org.: Suneel Babel; **Bus.Intt.:** Pub.; **Spl.:** *Mystic India* Magazine and Books on Indology, Yoga, Astrology, Occult Sci., etc.

M.C. BOOK HOUSE
Haripad-690514 (Maharashtra)

M.C. CHACKO
A1/270, Sector-IV, Rohini, New Delhi-110085
Estd.: 1978; **Hd.Org.:** Mrs. Ponnamma Chacko; **Bus.Intt.:** L.S. and Rt., Exp.

M.C. SARKAR & SONS PVT. LTD.
14, Bankim Chandra Chatterjee St., Kolkata-700073 (West Bengal)
Hd.Org.: Supriyo Sarkar; **Bus.Intt.:** Exp.

M.C.B. UNIVERSITY PRESS
B-13, 3rd Floor, A-Block Shopping Complex, Naraina Vihar, Ring Rd., New Delhi-110028

M.C.C. PUBLICATIONS
No. 3, 16th Cross, IIIrd Block, Jaya Nagar, Bangalore-560001 (Karnataka)
✆ 26549560, 26549561, Fax: 26656242
✉ mccpublications@vsnl.com
Estd.: 1979; **Man.Prt.:** G. Ramesh Kamath
Br.: Koppikar Rd., Hubli-580020 ✆ 2362506 • Narashima Krupa, Old Jewargi Rd., Gulbarga ✆ 422090 • 25, Devaraj Urs Rd., Mysore-570001 ✆ 2422142 • D-2, A Wing, IV Floor, Parsn Manere, 602, Anna Salai, Chennai-600006 ✆ 28277540
Bus.Intt.: Pub.; **Spl.:** Humanities & Soc.Sci., Sci. & Tech.

M.D. PUBLICATIONS (P) LTD.
M.D. House, 11, Darya Ganj, New Delhi-110002
✆ 41562846, Fax: 91-11-23275542
✉ contact@mdppl.com
www.mdppl.com
Dir.: Vijay Kumar Gupta, Mrs. Ranji Gupta; **Bus.Intt.:** Pub., WS, Rt.; **Spl.:** Acad., Beh.Sci., Soc.Sci., Botany, Journal and Magazines Law

M.G. PUBLISHERS & BOOK DISTRIBUTION AGENCY
34, Hirabagh Colony, Agra-282005 (Uttar Pradesh)

M.G.S. PUBLICATION
Kamalamandiram, S.S.K. Lau, Jawaharnagar P.O., Trivandrum-695041 (Kerala)

M.I. MALIK
H-1/131, Near Gurudwara, Opp. Metro Station, New Seelampur, Delhi-110053
✆ 22189493 ▮ 9810206631
Ch.Exe.: M.I. Malik; **Bus.Intt.:** Dealer; **Spl.:** Edu. Magic Items

M.I.T. ASSOCIATES (P) LTD.
Guru Krupa Mansion, 44, Nagappa St., Swastik Circle, Bangalore-560029 (Karnataka)
Hd.Org.: Mandhar Kamath V.

M. & J. SERVICES
Mohan Kunj (Ground Floor), 68, Jyotiba Fule Rd., Behind Gurudwara Naigaum Dadar (E), Mumbai-400014 (Maharashtra)
✆ 24134450, 24134216, 24110068, Fax: 91-22-24131476

M.J.P. PUBLISHERS
44 & 47, Nallathambi Street, Triplicane, Chennai-600005 (Tamil Nadu)

✆ 28441043, Fax: 91-44-28443347
✉ mjptnbh@rediffmail.com
mjppublishers.com
Hd.Org.: J. Chidambaram Pillai
Bus.Intt.: Pub.; **Spl.:** Textbooks and Reference books

M.K. BOOK DISTRIBUTORS
310, Shyamak Complex,
Opp. Sahajanand College, B/H,
Kamdhenu Complex, Ahmedabad-380015 (Gujarat)
✆ (O) 6306545 (R) 6305322,
Fax: (079) 6304097, 6421344
✉ mkbooks@egujarat.net
Estd.: 1982; **Prt.:** Mohan Kirpalani;
Bus.Intt.: Pub., Dist., L.S., Imp.; **Spl.:** Sci. and Tech., Research and IELTS

M.K. INTERNATIONAL
60, Abhaichand Gandhi Marg,
Mumbai-400003 (Maharashtra)
Bus.Intt.: Exp.

M.K.K. PUBLICATIONS
91-A, Ananda Palit Rd., Kolkata-700014 (West Bengal)

M.L. EXPORTS
4359/4, 1st Floor, Ansari Rd., Darya Ganj,
New Delhi-110002
✆ 23279396, Fax: 91-11-23277667
Hd.Org.: Himanshu Skekhar

M.L. & SONS
Gate No. 7-8, Near Clock Tower Restaurant,
Shivaji Stadium, Connaught Place,
New Delhi-110001
✆ 23362688, Fax: 91-11-23346219
Prop.: Sachin Gupta; **Bus.Intt.:** Dealer;
Spl.: Healthcare Mang. and Edu. Related Books and Magazine

M.M. BOOK PLAZA
Bangalore (Karnataka)
✆ 5486200 ▮ 9886029882
✉ mmbplaza@hotmail.com
Bus.Intt.: B.S. & Dist.

M.M. BROTHERS
22, Zakaria Shopping Centre,
Poison Rd., Anand-388001 (Gujarat)

M.M.C. DIGIPRESS PVT. LTD.
A-46, DSIDC Complex, Kirti Nagar,
New Delhi-110015
✆ 91-11-25927467, 25432580, 64530632
▮ 9212314134
✉ sales@mmcdigipress.com
www.mmcdigipress.com
Hd.Org.: Balkishan

M.M. ENTERPRISES
303, Karishma Mohant Rd. Extn., Ville Parle (E) Mumbai-400057 (Maharashtra)
Bus.Intt.: Exp.

M.M. NAINA EXPORTS (P) LTD.
99, Linghi Chetty St., Chennai-600001 (Tamil Nadu)
Bus.Intt.: Exp.

M.N. PUBLISHERS AND DISTRIBUTORS
W-112, Greater Kailash, Part-I,
New Delhi-110048
✆ 26484159, 26484190, Fax: 26484159
Hd.Org.: Neena Puri; **Bus.Intt.:** Pub.;
Spl.: Hindi Novels, Stories, Children's books and Sci., Palmistry, etc.

M.N.M. ASSOCIATES
C/o Hebbar Chemicals, 20, Shree Diamond Centre, LBS Marg, Vikroli, Mumbai-400078 (Maharashtra)

M.P. BOOK AGENCY
6, Meghdoot, 27 P.M. Rd., Vile Parle (East),
Mumbai-400057 (Maharashtra)

M.P.P. HOUSE
87, 1st Cross, Gandhi Nagar,
Bangalore-560009 (Karnataka)
✆ 22265901, 22260706, Fax: 22265901
✉ mphouse@vsnl.com
www.mpphouse.com
Estd.: 1926; **Prop.:** Gopinath C.A. & Anand C.G.
Br.: City Civil Court Complex,
Bangalore-560009 (Karnataka)
Bus.Intt.: Imp., Exp., Sub.Ag.; **Spl.:** Humanities & Soc.Sci., Law

M.R. BOOK CENTRE
Hyderabad (Andhra Pradesh)
✆ 23205684
✉ mrbookstall@usa.net
Bus.Intt.: B.S. & Dist.

M.R. BOOKS
Guwahati (Assam)
✆ 0361-2470746
✉ mrbooks2002@hotmail.com
Bus.Intt.: B.S.

M.R. DESAI PUBLICATIONS TRUST
G.K. Gokhale College, Kolhapur-416012 (Maharashtra)

M.R. PUBLICATIONS
2695, Kaley Khan Street, Kucha Chelan,
Darya Ganj, New Delhi-110002
▮ 9810784549
✉ abdus26@hotmail.com
Hd.Org.: Abdus Samad
Bus.Intt.: Pub.; **Spl.:** Books on Urdu

M.S. BHALLAS & CO. (P) LTD.
Flat No. 104, 1st Floor, 4262/3, Ansari Rd., Darya Ganj, New Delhi-110002
✆ 23257725, 23245609, Fax: 23256883
✉ info@msb.in
🌐 www.msb.in
Man.Dir.: M.S. Bhalla; **Bus.Intt.:** Pub.'s Rep.; **Spl.:** Med., Allied Health, Health Administration, Patient Care, Food Sci., Law & Business

M.S. BOOKS SERVICES
F-154/2, Lado Sarai, New Delhi-110030
✆ (O) 26528205, 26960433 (R) 26960433, 26528205 ▮ 9811103074
Prop.: Manish Sejwal; **Bus.Intt.:** L.S.; **Spl.:** Acad., Beh.Sci., Soc.Sci., Sci., Tech.

M.Y. PUBLICATIONS
P-137, Pillanji, Sarojini Nagar, New Delhi-110023
✆ 91-11-65860770, 65728240
✉ manjuli_prakashan@rediffmail.com
🌐 www.manjuliprakashan.in
Hd.Org.: Manjula Bhargava
Bus.Intt.: Pub.; **Spl.:** Eng. novels, stories, poetry, children's literature and books on military and social sciences

MAA PUSTAK BHANDAR
Kahalgaon (Colgong), Bhagalpur-813203 (Bihar)
Bus.Intt.: Pub. and B.S.

MAA TARA GENERAL STORES
Barari, Bhagalpur-812003 (Bihar)
Bus.Intt.: Pub. and B.S.

MAANSI BOOK DISTRIBUTORS
Delhi
✆ 23206479, 23276669
✉ mansibookdist@hotmail.com, sonutraders@yahoo.com
Bus.Intt.: B.S. & Dist.

MACMILLAN GLOBAL ACAMEDIC PUBLISHING
New Delhi
✆ 23271010
✉ jagat@del2.vsnl.net.in
Br.: Bangalore (Karnataka) ✆ 26792351,
✉ vvalli@bgl.vsnl.net.in
• Mumbai (Maharashtra) ✆ 26605844,
✉ palgravemum@vsnl.net

MACMILLAN INDIA LTD.
315-316, Raheja Chambers, 12, Museum Rd., Bangalore-560001 (Karnataka)
✆ 080-25586563, 25587878, Fax: 25588713
✉ rberi@bgl.vsnl.net.in
🌐 www.emacmillan.com
Estd.: 1883; **Man.Dir.:** Rajiv Beri
Br.: 21, Patullos Rd., Chennai-600002 (Tamil Nadu) ✆ 044-28520646, 28522448, Fax: 28523421 ✉ milmds@macmillan.co.in
• Mercantile House, Magazine, St., Reay Rd., Mumbai-400010 (Maharashtra)
✆ 022-23734401, 23726017, Fax: 23739802
✉ macray@bom3.vsnl.net.in
• 294, Bepin Behari, Ganguly St., Kolkata-700012 (West Bengal)
✆ 033-22379240, 22217359, Fax: 22258288
✉ milcal@macmillan.co.in
• 2/10, Ansari Rd., Darya Ganj, New Delhi-110002 ✆ 23273814, 23289443, 23273624, 23263969, Fax: 23272993
✉ mildel@macmillan.co.in,
🌐 www.macmillanindia.com
• Bhopal (Madhya Pradesh) ✆ 2553895
✉ milbpl@sancharnet.in
• Chandigarh ✆ 611561
✉ milchdbr@mantraonline.com
• Coimbatore (Tamil Nadu) ✆ 230940,
✉ milcbe@md3.vsnl.net.in
• Cuttack (Orissa) ✆ 311979
✉ ctk_macctk@sancharnet.in
• Guwahati (Assam) ✆ 516564
✉ macght@sancharnet.in
• Hubli ✆ 361944
✉ milhub@sancharnet.in
• Hyderabad (Andhra Pradesh) ✆ 23212867
✉ mcims@hd2.vsnl.net.in
• Jaipur (Rajasthan)
✆ 741308 ✉ miljpmp@sancharnet.in
• Lucknow (Uttar Pradesh) ✆ 208810
✉ macluck@sancharnet.in
• Madurai (Tamil Nadu) ✆ 530207
✉ mdu_milmdubr@sancharnet.in
• Nagpur (Maharashtra) ✆ 552595
✉ macnag@nagpur.dot.net.in
• Patna (Bihar) ✆ 232550
✉ macpat@sancharnet.in
• Pune (Maharashtra) ✆ 4329872
✉ macpune@pn2.vsnl.net.in
• Raipur (Madhya Pradesh) ✆ 432553
✉ macind@bom3.vsnl.net.in
• Thiruvanthapuram (Kerala) ✆ 2328314
✉ miltvmbr@md3.vsnl.net.in
• Visakhapatnam (Andhra Pradesh)
✆ 745384 ✉ milvizag@yahoo.com
Bus.Intt.: Pub., Exp.; **Spl.:** Humanities & Soc.Sci., Sci. & Tech.

MACMILLAN PRESS LTD.
5A/12, Ansari Rd., Darya Ganj, New Delhi-110002
✆ 23272010, 23257714, Fax: 23272010
✉ jagat@del2.vsnl.net.in
Prop.: Kalpana Shukla
Br.: Anita K. Kulkarni, 3-5/10, Talmakiwadi Tardeo Rd., Mumbai-400007 (Maharashtra)
✆ 022-23000458, Fax: 23000458

Bus.Intt.: Pub.; **Spl.:** Text and Reference Books on Humanities, Soc.Sci., Engg., Sci. Journals, etc. in English

MADAAN BOOK HOUSE
Punjabi University Campus, Patiala (Punjab)
✆ 0175-2283315
Estd.: 1980; **Prop.:** P.L. Madaan; **Bus.Intt.:** Pub., B.S., L.S., WS

MADADH PUSTAK BHANDAR
Nabinagar, Aurangabad-824113 (Bihar)
Bus.Intt.: Pub. and B.S.

MADAN BOOK DEPOT
Regal Building, 7, (Outside Kwality Restaurant), New Delhi-110001
Bus.Intt.: Rt. B.S.

MADAN PUBLISHERS
21, Municipal Building, Chowk Purani Kotwali, Patiala-147001 (Punjab)
✆ 260235
Estd.: 1983; **Bus.Intt.:** Pub., L.S., Rt.

MADEENA ISLAMIC BOOK CENTRE
Ramganj Bazar, Jaipur-302004 (Rajasthan)
Bus.Intt.: Pub.; **Spl.:** Urdu Books

MADHAV VIDYA BHAVAN
Shridham, 150, Old Gupta Colony, Delhi-110009
✆ 27249680 ▮ 9810563659, Fax: 27249680
✉ premacharyaji@yahoo.co.in
🌐 www.hindukyon.com
Hd.Org.: Premacharya Shastri; **Bus.Intt.:** Pub.; **Spl.:** Rel., *Vedic* and *Puranic* Litt. in Hindi

MADHU DEEP PUBLICATIONS
T-18, New Campus, Jawaharlal Nehru University, New Delhi-110067

MADHU LATHA PUBLICATION
Arundalpet, Vijayawada-520002 (Andhra Pradesh)
Estd.: 1982; **Prop.:** Smt. V. Rosamma; **Bus.Intt.:** Pub.; **Spl.:** Fiction and Gen. Books in Telugu

MADHU PRAKASH
Dergaon, Distt. Golaghat-785614 (Assam)

MADHU PRAKASHAN
42, Tashkand Marg, Allahabad-211001 (Uttar Pradesh)
Hd.Org.: Madhu Sehgal

MADHU RAJ PUBLICATIONS PVT. LTD.
909, Raviwar Peth, Pune-411002 (Maharashtra)
Hd.Org.: Madhu Seghal

MADHUBAN EDUCATIONAL BOOKS
A-22, Sector 4, Noida-201201 (Uttar Pradesh)
✆ 4078900, Fax: 91-120-4078999
✉ info@madhubanbooks.com
Hd.Org.: Sajili Shirodkar
Bus.Intt.: Pub., **Spl.:** Children's books

MADHUBAN EDUCATIONAL BOOKS
576, Masjid Rd., Jangpura, New Delhi-110014
✆ 24314605, 24315313, Fax: 24310879
✉ helpline@vikaspublishing.com
Hd.Org.: Piyush Chawla; **Bus.Intt.:** Pub.; **Spl.:** Textbooks on All Sub. and Gen. Reading Material for Children in English

MADHUR PRAKASHAN
2804, Gali Arya Samaj, Bazar Sitaram, Delhi-110006
✆ 23238631, 27513206
Hd.Org.: Rajpal Singh Shastri

MADHUR PRAKASHAN SANSTHAN
Satya & Sons, Railway Rd., Distt. Bulandshahar, Dibia-202393 (Uttar Pradesh)

MADHUR SAHITYA PRAKASHAN
94, Chandershekhar Marg, Gali No. 9, Salimar Village, Delhi-110052
✆ 27415084

MADHUR SANDESH SANGAM
E-20, Abul Fazal Enclave, Jamia Nagar, New Delhi-110025
✆ 26753327, Fax: 91-11-23276741
✉ madhursandeshsangam@yahoo.co.in
🌐 www.quranhindi.com
Hd.Org.: Parwaaz Rahmani; **Bus.Intt.:** Pub.; **Spl.:** Books on Islam in Hindi

MADHUSUDHAN BOOK STALL
14, Bankim Chatterjee St., Kolkata-700073 (West Bengal)

MADHYA PRADESH BOOK STALL
Khajuri Bazar, Indore-452002 (Madhya Pradesh)
✆ 2532732

MADHYA PRADESH HINDI GRANTH ACADEMY
Rabindranath Thakur Marg, Baan Ganga, Bhopal-462003 (Madhya Pradesh)
✆ 2553084, Fax: 2762123
Hd.Org.: Shiv Kumar Awasthi; **Bus.Intt.:** Pub.; **Spl.:** Sci., Tech., Arts, Music, Agri., Comp., etc. in Hindi

MADHYA PRADESH SAHITYA PARISHAD
Sanskriti Bhavan, Baanganga, Bhopal-462003 (Madhya Pradesh)
✆ 2554782, Fax: 2557942

Hd.Org.: Bhagwat Rawat; **Bus.Intt.:** Pub.; **Spl.:** Hindi Litt., Poetry, Plays, Criticisms, Essays etc. and Hindi Journal *Sakshatkar*

MADHYA PRADESH URDU ACADEMY
Mulla Ramuzi, Sanskriti Bhavan, Baanganga, Bhopal-462003 (Madhya Pradesh)
✆ 2551691
Hd.Org.: Aziz Qureshi; **Bus.Intt.:** Promoter; **Spl.:** Urdu Language, Litt. and Translations

MADHYAM BOOKS
142, Maitri Apartments, Plot No. 28, Patparganj, Delhi-110092
✆ 22521081, 22432054, Fax: 22524233
✉ kaval@nde.vsnl.net.in
Hd.Org.: Kavaljit Singh; **Bus.Intt.:** Pub.; **Spl.:** Soc.Sci. and Humanities in English

MADHYAMIK SHIKSHA NIDESHALAYA
Bikaner (Rajasthan)
✆ 2528875, Fax: 201861
✉ diredu@raj.nic.in
Bus.Intt.: Pub.

MADINA BOOK SHOP & STATIONERS
Qammarwari Chowk, Srinagar, Kashmir (Jammu & Kashmir)
✆ 0194-2478244, Fax: 2420154
Estd.: 1992; **Prop.:** Sheikh Mohammad Muzafar; **Bus.Intt.:** Pub., WS, L.S. & Rt.; **Spl.:** Humanities & Soc.Sci., Sci.: Pure & Applied Engg. & Tech. Mang. & Comm. Fiction & Gen.

MADRAS BOOK AGENCY
No. 2, First Cross St., South High Court Colony, Chennai-600049 (Tamil Nadu)
✆ 26260385, 25340962, 26289269
✉ mbamani@md3.vsnl.net.in
Estd.: 1956; **Bus.Intt.:** Pub. and B.S.; **Spl.:** Gen. Books and Law

MADRAS BOOK HOUSE
49, Ranganathan St., T. Nagar, Chennai-600017 (Tamil Nadu)
✆ 24341416, 24345304
Estd.: 1978; **Prop.:** W.H. Ashok Kumar Sole; **Bus.Intt.:** Pub., WS, L.S. & Rt.; **Spl.:** Sci. & Tech., Gen. & Fiction etc.

MAGADH PRAKASHAN
Sapna Apts., E-717A Pratap Vihar, Ghaziabad-201001 (Uttar Pradesh)
Prop.: Suranjan
Br.: 4649/123A, New Shahdara, Delhi-110032
✆ 28741502
Spl.: Litt. Books in Hindi

MAGIC TECH INDIAN PVT. LTD.
New Delhi
✆ 26423988, 26422149, Fax: 26482338
✉ bdewan@mtipl.com
Bus.Intt.: B.S.

MAGNA PUBLISHING CO. LTD.
Plot No. 1244, 100/E, Old Prabhadevi Rd., Prabhadevi, Mumbai-400025 (Maharashtra)
Bus.Intt.: Exp.

MAGNETIC POWER PUBLICATIONS
Hyderabad (Andhra Pradesh)
✆ 23221057, 56641057
✉ alpspprinter@uyahoo.com
Bus.Intt.: Pub.

MAGNOLIA BOOK AGENCY
C-1796, Jahangir Puri, Delhi-110033
✆ (R) 0120-2492657 ▮ 9811114398
Hd.Org.: R.A. Thakur; **Bus.Intt.:** L.S., Dist., WS & Rt.; **Spl.:** Academic Professional and Reference Books

MAGNUM BOOK DEAL
695, Kempamma Nilaya, Near Tab Pulveriser Jalahalli Cross, Bangalore-560057 (Karnataka)

MAGNUM BOOKS (P) LTD.
46-C, A-13, Fort View Apartments, Kalkaji Extension, New Delhi-110019
✆ 26090280, 31027384, Fax: 26090280
✉ arvindpassi@now-india.net.in
Hd.Org.: Arvind Passi; **Bus.Intt.:** Pub. and Dist.; **Spl.:** Text and Edu. Books and Audio Material for Children in English and Hindi

MAGNUM ENTERPRISES (REGD.)
46-C, Pocket A, 13, Fort View Apts., Kalkaji Extension, New Delhi-110019
✆ (O) & (R) 26990280, 26995986, Fax: 26995986
✉ magbooks@mantraonline.com
Bus.Intt.: Imp. and Dist.; **Spl.:** Edu. Reference Material, Rt. and Pub.

MAGOWA PRAKASHAN
759/97, Deccan Gymkhana, Shantibhavan, Pune-411004 (Maharashtra)

MAGRESS PRAKASHAN
41, Venkatesh Nagar, Khamala Rd., Nagpur-440025 (Maharashtra)

MAGUS MEDIA PVT. LTD.
C-153, Okhla Phase-I, New Delhi-110020
✆ 26327595/6/7, 26315108, 51616562, Fax: 91-11-26311243, 51616561
✉ india@lifepositive.com
Ch.Exe.: Mr. Parveen Chopra; **Bus.Intt.:** Pub.; **Spl.:** Magazine and Books

MAHABEER BOOK HOUSE
140, Bazar Gate St., Fort (Perin Narman), Mumbai-400001 (Maharashtra)

MAHABEER BOOK STALL
208, Khajuri Bazar, Indore-452002
(Madhya Pradesh)
✆ (R) 2485155

MAHABODHI BOOK AGENCY
4A, Bankim Chatterjee St., Kolkata-700073
(West Bengal)

MAHADEV BOOK STALL
12/1, Bankim Chatterjee St., Kolkata-700073
(West Bengal)

MAHADEV LIBRARY
Block-6, Stall-2, Kolkata-700073
(West Bengal)

MAHADEV RAMCHANDRA JAGUSTHE
Tran Darwaja, Ahmedabad-380001 (Gujarat)

MAHAJAN BOOK DEPOT
Near Central Bank, 5, Andhi Rd.,
Ahmedabad-380001 (Gujarat)
✆ 2356031
Estd.: 1988; **Prop.:** Jagdish K. Shah;
Bus.Intt.: L.S., Rt.

MAHAJAN BOOK HOUSE
25, Harzsiddth Chambers, Near Income Tax,
Ashram Rd., Ahmedabad-380014 (Gujarat)
✆ 2409799

MAHAJAN BROTHERS
Super Mkt. Basement, Near Natraj Cinema,
Ashram Rd., Ahmedabad-380008 (Gujarat)
✆ 2408537, Cable: PERIODICAL
Estd.: 1953; **Prop.:** Dinker Mahajan;
Bus.Intt.: Pub., WS, L.S. and Rt., Imp., Exp., Sub.Ag.

MAHAJATI PRAKASHAN
13, Bankim Chatterjee St., Kolkata-700073
(West Bengal)

MAHALAKSHMI MEDICAL PUBLISHERS
House No. 28, Rd. No. 1, Punjabi Bagh,
New Delhi-110026

MAHALAKSHMI PRAKASHAN
88, Mahajani Tola, Allahabad-211003
(Uttar Pradesh)
✆ (O) 2402007 (R) 2633074
Hd.Org.: Anup Kumar Mittal

MAHALAKSHMI PUBLICATIONS
Ambativeri St., Arundelpet, Vijayawada,
(Andhra Pradesh)

MAHALAXMI CHAMBERS
22, Bhulabhai Desai Rd., Mumbai-400026
(Maharashtra)
✆ 24920253

MAHALAXMI ENTERPRISES
P.B. No. 5617, No. 66, 57th A Cross,
6th Main Rd., Rajaji Nagar, 4th Block,
Bangalore-560010 (Karnataka)
✆ 23357433, 26742950, Fax: 23201967
✉ hrr@vsnl.com, hrr@bgl.vsnl.net.in
Estd.: 1984; **Prop.:** H.R. Ramu;
Bus.Intt.: Pub., WS, L.S. & Rt., Imp., Sub.Ag.;
Spl.: Sci. & Tech., Humanities & Soc.Sci., Med.

MAHAMAYA PUBLISHING HOUSE
12-H, Shanti Van Marg,
Opp. Traffic Kotwali, Darya Ganj,
New Delhi-110002
✆ 91-11-23275538
✉ mahamayaph@rediffmail.com
Hd.Org.: Ramesh Kapoor
Bus.Intt.: Pub.; **Spl.:** Books on soc.sciences and humanities

MAHANABHAW VISWABHARATI
Nandgaon Khandeshwar, Amravati-444708
(Maharashtra)

MAHARAJA FEATURES PVT. LTD.
5/226, Sion Rd., East, Mumbai-400022
(Maharashtra)
Bus.Intt.: Exp.

MAHARANI EDUCATIONAL PRODUCTS
T-61, West Patel Nagar, Near Khanna
Market, New Delhi-110008
✆ 25730051

MAHARASHTRA GRANTH BHANDAR
Mahadwar Rasta, Kolhapur-416001
(Maharashtra)

MAHARASHTRA RAJYA PATYAPUSTAK NIRMIT MANDAL
Balbharati, Senapati Bapat Marg,
Pune-411004 (Maharashtra)

MAHARASHTRA SAHITYA PARISHAD
Tilak Rd., Pune-411030 (Maharashtra)

MAHARASHTRA STATE BUREAU OF TEXT BOOK PRODUCTION AND CURRICULUM RESEARCH
Balbharati Senapati Bapat Rd., Pune-411004
(Maharashtra)

MAHARASHTRA VIDYAPEETH GRANTH NIRMITI MANDAL
Vidhi Mahavidhyalaya Parisar, M.G. Rd.,
Nagpur-440001 (Maharashtra)

MAHARISHI VED VIGYAN VIDYAPEETH PUBLICATION DIVISON
Maharishi Nagar, Noida-Dadari Rd.,
Ghaziabad-201304 (Uttar Pradesh)

MAHARSHI PUSTAK BHANDAR
Barauni, Begusarai-851112 (Bihar)
Bus.Intt.: Pub. and B.S.

MAHARSHI PUSTAK BHANDAR
Mirjanhat, Bhagalpur-812005 (Bihar)
Bus.Intt.: Pub. and B.S.

MAHASAPAN
51/12C, Sikdar Bagan St., Kolkata-700004 (West Bengal)
Bus.Intt.: Exp.

MAHATMA GANDHI ANTARRASHTRIYA HINDI VISHWAVIDYALAYA
16, Second Floor, Siri Fort Rd., New Delhi-110049
✆ 26254830, 26259308, Fax: 91-11-26263779
✉ hindiunv@nda.vsnl.net.in
Ch.Exe.: Ashok Vajpeyi; **Bus.Intt.:** Pub.; **Spl.:** Magazines, Books, Portfolios

MAHATMA GANDHI ANTARRASHTRIYA HINDI VISHWAVIDYALAYA
PB No. 16, Panchteela, Aarvi Road, Wardha-442001 (Maharashtra)
✆ 230904, 230912, Fax: 91-7152-230903
Hd.Org.: Hanuman Prasad Shukla

MAHATMA GANDHI UNVIERSITY
Athirampuzha P.O., Kottayam-686562 (Kerala)

MAHAVEER & SONS
3072/28, First Floor, Gola Market, New Golcha Champerkunj, Darya Ganj, New Delhi-110002
✆ 91-11-23287638
✉ mahaveersonspub@rediffmail.com
Hd.Org.: Joginder Singh
Bus.Intt.: Pub.; **Spl.:** Books on social science, humanities and education in Hindi and English

MA-HE NAZ
C/o Mr. Razi Uddin (Dy. S.P. Retd.), 474/9, Opposite Shia Degree College, Sitapur Rd., Daliganj, Lucknow-226020 (Uttar Pradesh)

MAHENDAR BOOKS
WZ 1598/F Nangal Raya, New Delhi-110046
✆ 28524169 ▮ 9811179058
Estd.: 1997; **Prop.:** Mahendar Kumar Sharma; **Bus.Intt.:** L.S.; **Spl.:** Soc.Sci.

MAHENDRA K. JOSHI
49, First Floor, Ellisbridge, Shopping Centre Opp. Townhall, Ashram Rd., Ahmedabad-380006 (Gujarat)

MAHESH BOOKS & STATIONERIES
213, Khajuri Bazar, Indore-452002 (Madhya Pradesh)
✆ 2546483

MAHESH LIBRARY PRAKASHAN SANSTHA
2/1, Shyama Charan Dey St., Kolkata-700073 (West Bengal)
✆ 033-2311479
Bus.Intt.: Pub. and L.S.; **Spl.:** Rel. Books in Bengali

MAHESHWARI PUBLICATIONS
G-4/120, Sector-15, Rohini, New Delhi-110085
Bus.Intt.: Pub.; **Spl.:** Hindi books

MAHI BOOK PALACE
Opp. Shanker Ashram, E.K. Rd., Vijay Nagar, Meerut-250001 (Uttar Pradesh)

MAHINDRA CAPITAL PUBLISHERS
276, Industrial Area, Phase-I, Panchkula, (Haryana)
✆ (R) 2564681 ▮ 098120-27990
Estd.: 1965; **Prop.:** Shailendra; **Bus.Intt.:** Pub.; **Spl.:** College, Help Books in English, Hindi and Punjabi

MAHTAB PUBLISHERS
T-485/1, Baljeet Nagar, Behind Thana Patel Nagar, New Delhi-110008

MAITHILI ACADEMY, PATNA
Shivpuri, Patna-800023
✆ 91-612-2280687
Hd.Org.: Raghuvir Mochi

MAITREY PUBLISHERS
1/11810, Panchsheel Garden, Naveen Shahdara, Delhi-110032
Hd.Org.: Kishore Sharma

MAITREYA PUBLICATION
4697/5, 21-A, Ansari Road, Darya Ganj, New Delhi-11002 ✆ 91-11-23275710
Hd.Org.: Arun Maheshwari
Bus.Intt.: Pub., **Spl.:** Literary books in Hindi

MAITY BOOK HOUSE
P.D.S. Corner Stall-7, Bankim Chatterjee St., Kolkata-700073 (West Bengal)

MAJESTIC AGENCIES
Vishnu Naka, Near Tilak Bridge, Mumbai-400028 (Maharashtra)
✆ 24305914

MAJESTIC BOOK STALL
Girgaon Naka, Near Tilak Bridge, Mumbai-400004 (Maharashtra)
✆ 23824083

MAKALI BOOK CENTRE
9, Bankim Chatterjee St., Kolkata-700073 (West Bengal)
Hd.Org.: Ashim Kumar Pyne

MAKKALA SAHITYA BHANDAR
Dhannure Niwas, 8-10-1/7, Akkamahadevi Colony, Bidar-585401 (Karnataka)

MAKKIA BOOKS PLC
D-277, Main Okhla Road, Jamia Nagar, New Delhi-110025
✆ 26841617, Fax: 91-11-26841618

▮ 9899228866
✉ info@makkiabooks.com
Hd.Org.: Naved Ansari
Bus.Intt.: Pub., **Spl.**: *Quran* in Urdu and Hindi

MAKTABA ABUL HASAN ALI
4182, Urdu Bazar, Jama Masjid, Delhi-110006
▮ 9810926346
Hd.Org.: Zain-ul-Abdin
Bus.Intt.: Pub. and Dist., **Spl.**: Urdu and Arabic books

MAKTABA-AI-FAISAL HAKIM
Shan Noor Faisal, Puranay Ganj (Chipian), Rampur-244901 (Uttar Pradesh)

MAKTABA-AL-HASANT
2241, Kucha Chelan, Darya Ganj, New Delhi-110002
✆ 91-11-41563256
✉ m_alhasanat@rediffmail.com, faisalfaheem@rediffmail.com
Estd.: 1947; **Hd.Org.**: A.M. Faheem
Bus.Intt.: Pub. and Dist.; **Spl.**: *Holy Quran*, Islamic Litt. and Books on Unani Med. in Hindi, Urdu and English

MAKTABA AL-RISALA
C-29, Nizamuddin West, New Delhi-110013
✆ 2611128, 2697333
Estd.: 1976; **Hd.Org.**: Samasnain

MAKTABA AL-SHIFA
2861, Kucha Chelan, Darya Ganj, Delhi-110002
✆ 91-11-23253268
Hd.Org.: Syed Aijaz Hussain
Bus.Intt.: Pub., **Spl.**: Urdu books

MAKTABA JAMIA LTD.
Shahid Alikhan, Jamia Nagar, New Delhi-110025
✆ 2630191
Bus.Intt.: Pub.; **Spl.**: Urdu Litt. and Children's Books

MAKTABA QASMI
435, Matia Mahal, Delhi-110006
✆ 23264969
Estd.: 1985; **Hd.Org.**: Ahmed Ali Qasmi

MAKTABA THANVI
Near Mohalia Diwan, Distt. Saharanpur, Deoband-247554 (Uttar Pradesh)
✆ 23287701
Estd.: 1990; **Hd.Org.**: Saeed Akhter

MAKTABA ZIKRA
421/2, Urdu Market, Matia Mahal, Jama Masjid, Delhi-110006

MALA PUBLICATION
51, Kalinath Munshi Lane, Kolkata-56 (West Bengal)

MALANKARA ORTHODOX CHURCH PUBLICATIONS
Devalokam P.O., Kottayam (Kerala)
✆ 2578499
Estd.: 1982; **Bus.Intt.**: Pub.

MALARIA RESEARCH CENTRE
20, Madhuvan, Vikas Marg, New Delhi-110092

MALAV SAHITYA MANDIR
213, Khajuri Bazar, Indore-452002 (Madhya Pradesh)
✆ (O) 2530284 (R) 254136

MALAYA PRINTING WORKS & BOOK STALL
Attingal, Thiruvananthapuram-695101 (Kerala)
✆ 04726-22839
Estd.: 1947; **Prop.**: R. Krishnan Nair;
Bus.Intt.: Pub. and B.S.

MALAYALA MANORAMA CO. LTD.
P.B. No. 26, K.K. Rd., Kottayam-1 (Kerala)
✆ 2563646, Fax: 2562479
✉ mmdelhi@mmkerala.com
Hd.Org.: Mammen Mathew
Br.: 68/6, Tolstoy Lane, Janpath, New Delhi-110001 ✆ 23752781, Fax: 23314670
Bus.Intt.: Pub.; **Spl.**: *Malayala Manorama Year Book*, English Magazine *The Week* and Hindi Magazine *Vanitha*

MALHOTRA BOOK DEPOT
6, Gulab Bhawan, Bahadur Shah Zafar Marg, New Delhi-110002
✆ 23317931, 23317787, 23318301, Fax: 011-23319471
✉ mgulab@del.2vsnl.net.in
Estd.: 1980; **Hd.Org.**: Ashok Kumar Malhotra;
Bus.Intt.: Pub., **Spl.**: Reference Material for Competitive Examinations, CBSE, ISCE and State Boards

MALHOTRA BROTHERS
Pacca Danga, Jammu Tawi-180001 (Jammu and Kashmir)
✆ 2572147, 2544617
Estd.: 1934; **Prop.**: Inder Malhotra;
Bus.Intt.: Pub., WS, L.S. & Rt.; **Spl.**: Sci. & Tech., Humanities & Soc.Sci., Law, Juvenile/Children

MALHOTRA PUBLICATION
11098-A, Dori Walan, East Park Rd., Karol Bagh, New Delhi-110005
✆ 23518789, 23517997
Hd.Org.: R.C. Malhotra;
Bus.Intt.: Manufacturers of Books, Publisher

MALHOTRA PUBLISHING HOUSE
B-6, DSIDC Complex, Kirti Nagar, New Delhi-110015

✆ (O) 25157006 (R) 25558788, 25610139, Fax: 91-11-25934597
✉ mph@vsnl.com
www.humlog.com
Estd.: 1985; **Prop.:** Vinay Malhotra; **Bus.Intt.:** Printers, Pub., Sub.Ag. & International B.S.; **Spl.:** Sci., Agri. and Horticulture, Journals & Magazines Books

MALIK & COMPANY
337, Chaura Rasta, Jaipur-302003 (Rajasthan)
✆ (O) 2575258, 2564858 (R) 2721417, 2721418, Fax: 0141-2396758
✉ sales@nationalpublishinghouse.com
Estd.: 1965; **Dir.:** Davendra Malik; **Bus.Intt.:** Pub., B.S., L.S., WS, Exp.; **Spl.:** Humanities & Soc.Sci., Comp., Mang., Children & General, Arts & Arch.

MALIK BOOK DEPOT
3212, Phatak Teliyan, Turkman Gate, Delhi-110006
▮ 9899711762
✉ aadilaseer@hotmail.com
Hd.Org.: Mhd. Adil Rashid
Bus.Intt.: Pub.; **Spl.:** Children's books Poetry, Stories, Novels etc. in Urdu

MALIK PUBLICATIONS
S-28, Greater Kailash, Part-I, New Delhi-110018

MALLICK BOOK HOUSE
57/1, College St., Kolkata-700073 (West Bengal)

MALLIGAI BOOK CENTRE
11, West Veli St., Madurai-625001 (Tamil Nadu)
✆ 2540534, 2341739
✉ malligaibc@eth.net
Hd.Org.: O.R. Suresh; **Bus.Intt.:** Even an Individual Order can be procured for a single title when the Customer Accepts our terms

MALLIKA BOOKS
348, Main Rd., Sant Nagar (Burari), Near Burari School, Delhi-110084
✆ (O) 27612927 (R) 27615096, Fax: 27617546
✉ mallikabooks@vsnl.net, mallika@now-india.net.in
Estd.: 1998; **Prop.:** D.K. Joshi; **Bus.Intt.:** Rt. & L.S.; **Spl.:** Acad., Beh.Sci., Soc.Sci. & Tech.

MALLIKA PUBLICATIONS (CEMI)
4324/59, Padamsing Rd., Karol Bagh, New Delhi-110005
Prop.: S.M.S. Tulsi

MAMTA BOOK DEPOT
(Sister Concern, Mamta Publications) Samandar Bagh, S.P. College Rd., Srinagar, Kashmir-190001 (Jammu & Kashmir)
✆ (O) 0194-2454788 (R) 2483579 ▮ 9419010695
Hd.Org.: Muhammad Shafi Lalla
Br.: Kaka Rd., Nai Sarak, Sri Nagar, Kashmir-190002 ✆ 2471135

MANA BOOKS INTERNATIONAL
86-B, Pocket-4, Mayur Vihar, Phase-I, Delhi-110091

MANAGEMENT & PRODUCTIVITY SERVICE
Care Conference Aids, SCO, 50-51, Sector 17-A, 1st Floor, Chandigarh-160017

MANAK PUBLICATIONS PVT. LTD.
B-7, 3rd Floor, Saraswati Complex, Subhash Chowk, Laxmi Nagar, Delhi-110092
✆ 22453894, 22042529, Fax: 011-22418599
✉ manak_publications@hotmail.com
info@manakpublications.com
www.manakpublications.com
Hd.Org.: M.P. Yadav; **Bus.Intt.:** Pub.; **Spl.:** Soc.Sci. and Humanities

MANAK PUBLISHERS & BOOK DISTRIBUTORS
B-162, Fateh Nagar, Jail Rd., New Delhi-110018
✆ (O) 25130991 (R) 25143734;
Hd.Org.: Tripat Singh; **Bus.Intt.:** Pub., WS

MANAS PUBLICATIONS
4402/5A, Main Ansari Road, Darya Ganj, New Delhi-110002
✆ (O) 23260783, 23265523 (R) 27131660, 27143052, Fax: 91-11-23272766
✉ manaspublications@vsnl.com
www.manaspublications.com
Estd.: 1971; **Prop.:** Mrs. Suman Lata, Vivek Kr. Garg
Br.: 29, Central Mkt., Ashok Vihar Phase-I, Delhi-110052;
• 4819, Mathur Lane, 24 Ansari Rd., Darya Ganj, New Delhi-110002
Bus.Intt.: Pub., Rt., L.S. & Dist., Exp.; **Spl.:** All Types of Indian & Foreign Acad., Comm., Soc.Sci., Juveniles & Law Books

MANASAYAN
Agarwal Complex, S-524, School Block, Shakarpur, Delhi-110092
✆ 22223919, Fax. 23271584
Estd.: 1955; **Prop.:** J.M. Ojha; **Bus.Intt.:** Pub., L.S. & Rt., Imp.; **Spl.:** Humanities & Soc.Sci.

MANASOLLASA PRAKASHANA
"Sneha" 3368, 13th Cross, R.R. Rd., Shastrinagar, Bangalore-560028 (Karnataka)
Hd.Org.: H.S. Parvathi; **Bus.Intt.:** Pub.; **Spl.:** Own Books

MANAV TIMES PRESS
8/10, M.G. Marg, Opp. Bishop, Jhonson School, Allahabad-211001 (Uttar Pradesh)
✆ 0532-2623551, Fax: 2623584

MANDAL & SONS
14, Bankim Chatterjee St., Kolkata-73 (West Bengal)

MANDIRA
16, Southern Ave, Kolkata-700006 (West Bengal)
✆ 033-2760812, Fax: 2744614
Estd.: 1984; **Hd.Org.:** Mandira Sen; **Bus.Intt.:** Pub. Exp.

MANGAADU KAMATCHI AMAN BUSINESS CORPORATION
9, Bapu St., Sambandanar Nagar Pammal, Chennai-600075 (Tamil Nadu)
✆ 2405444

MANGAI PATHIPPAGAM
700, MIG, Veettu Vasathi, Karriya Kudiyiruppu, Velachery Scheme, Chennai-600042 (Tamil Nadu)

MANGAL DEEP PUBLISHERS & DISTRIBUTORS
Duggar Building, M.I. Rd., Jaipur-302001 (Rajasthan)
✆ 0141-5102022, 2365086, Fax: 5102022
✉ mdpbk@sancharnet.in
Prop.: B.K. Mangal; **Bus.Intt.:** Pub. and Dist.; **Spl.:** Soc.Sci., Humanities, Sci. and Tech.

MANGALAM AGENCIES
Shop No. 19, 61, Mahatma Gandhi Rd., Kolkata-700009 (West Bengal)

MANHRMA GRANTH MALA
Laxmi Bhavan Subhash Rd., Dharwad-580001 (Karnataka)
✆ 241822

MANI MANIK PRAKASH
Panbazar, Guwahati-781001 (Assam)

MANIK BOOK SHOP
S.C.O. 70-72, Sector 17-D, Chandigarh-160017
✆ 2702936
Estd.: 1972; **Prop.:** J.M. Manik; **Bus.Intt.:** Rt. B.S. and WS; **Spl.:** Gen., Rel., Astrology and M.A. in English and Hindi

MANIKANT PUSTAK BHANDAR
Samukhiya More, Bhagalpur-814164 (Bihar)
Bus.Intt.: Pub. and B.S.

MANIMEKALAI PRASURAM
Post Box No. 1447, 4, Thanikachalam Rd., T. Nagar, Chennai-600017 (Tamil Nadu)
✆ 24342296, Fax: 044-24346082
Hd.Org.: Ravi Tamilvanan; **Bus.Intt.:** Pub.; **Spl.:** Astrology, Horoscopes, Comp., House Construction, Commercial, Plans etc.

MANIPAL POWER PRESS
Manipal-576119 (Karnataka)
Bus.Intt.: Exp.

MANIPAL PRINTERS & PUBLISHERS LTD.
Udayavani Building, Tile Factory Rd., Manipal-576119 (Karnataka)
✆ 270845, Fax: 08252-270563
✉ info@manipalpress.com
Estd.: 1948; **Bus.Intt.:** Printers and Pub.

MANIPURI SAHITYA PARISHAD
Poana Bazar, Imphal-795001 (Manipur)

MANISHA
Tilakmaidan Rd., Nutan Press Buildings, Muzaffarpur-832001 (Bihar)
✆ (O) 243993 (R) 242061
Estd.: 1964; **Man.Dir.:** D.P. Sharma
Br.: 93-B, Pocket-A, Phase-II, Ashok Vihar, Delhi-110052 ✆ 27418331
Bus.Intt.: Pub., B.S., Imp., L.S. & Rt.; **Spl.:** Humanities & Soc.Sci., Sci. & Tech.

MANISHA GRANTHALAYA (P) LTD.
4/3, Bankim Chatterjee St., Kolkata-700073 (West Bengal)
✆ 033-22415350
Prop.: Ranjit Sarker; **Bus.Intt.:** Exp.

MANITHAM PATHIPPAGAM
54, Rajaram Rd., Kalaignar Nagar, Tiruchi-600021 (Tamil Nadu)

MANIVASAGAR PATHIPPAGAM
31, Stringer St., Chennai-600108 (Tamil Nadu)
✆ (O) 25361039 (R) 24346955
Estd.: 1961; **Prop.:** M. Meenakshi Somasundaram
Br.: 12-B, West Sannathi St., Cuddalore Dist., Chidambaram-608001
Bus.Intt.: Pub.

MANJU PRAKASHAN
405/75, Chaupatian Rd., Lucknow-3 (Uttar Pradesh)

MANJUL PUBLISHING PVT. LTD.
10, Nishat Colony, 74 Bunglows, Bhopal-462003 (Madhya Pradesh)
✆ 4240340, 2545952, 2543624, Fax: 91-755-2736919
✉ manjul@manjulindia.com
www.manjulindia.com
Ch.Exe.: Mr. Vikas Rakheja; **Bus.Intt.:** Pub.; **Spl.:** Motivational Books and Hindi Books

MANJULI PRAKASHAN
P-4, Pillanji, Sarojini Nagar, New Delhi-110023
✆ 91-11-65728240, 65860770
✉ manjuli_prakashan@rediffmail.com
www.manjuliprakashan.in
Estd.: 1995; **Hd.Org.:** Manjula Bhargava; **Bus.Intt.:** Pub. and Dist.; **Spl.:** Hindi Litt., Children's Books and Books on Sci. and Military Sci.

MANMOHINI PRAKASHAN
1712/IB, Sadashiv Udyan Prasad, Pune-411030 (Maharashtra)

MANNA PRAKASHAN
20, Maharashi Debendra Rd., Kolkata-700007 (West Bengal)

MANNA PUBLICATIONS
30/1B, College Row, Kolkata-700073 (West Bengal)

MANNEYS BOOK SELLERS
7, Moledien Rd., Clover Centre, Pune-411001 (Maharashtra)
✆ 2651683, 2623214, Fax: 2634867
✉ manneys@vsnl.com
Estd.: 1948; **Prop.:** Manik V. Mani; **Bus.Intt.:** B.S. and L.S., Rt.; **Spl.:** Gen. Novel and Children Books (Indian and Foreign)

MANOHAR BOOK DEPOT
TBS Building, G.H. Rd., Kozhikode-673001 (Kerala)
✆ 260085, 260086, 264314
Estd.: 1951; **Prop.:** N.E. Manohar; **Bus.Intt.:** Pub.

MANOHAR GRANTHA MALA
Laxmi Bhavan, Subhas Road, Dharwad-580001 (Karnataka)
✆ 91-836-2441822
✉ ramakantjoshi@rediffmail.com
Hd.Org.: Ramakant G. Joshi
Bus.Intt.: Pub. **Spl.** Litt. Books in Kannada Language

MANOHAR PUBLISHERS & DISTRIBUTORS
4753/23, Ansari Road, Daryaganj, New Delhi-110002
✆ 23289100, 23262796, 23284848, 23260774, Fax: 91-11-23265162
✉ sales@manoharbooks.com
www.manoharbooks.com
Estd.: 1989; **Prop.:** Ajay Kumar Jain; **Bus.Intt.:** Pub., Dist., WS, L.S. & Rt., Imp., Exp., Sub.Ag.; **Spl.:** Humanities & Soc.Sci., Med.

MANOJ BOOKS DEPOT
Agnapur, Aurangabad (Bihar)
Bus.Intt.: Pub. and B.S.

MANOJ BOOKS DEPOT
761, Main Rd., Burari, Delhi-110084
✆ 27611116, 27611349, Fax: 91-11-27611546
Hd.Org.: Sawan Gupta; **Bus.Intt.:** Pub.; **Spl.:** Books of general interest in Hindi and English

MANOJ POCKET BOOKS
761, Main Rd., Burari, Delhi-110084
✆ 36303147-49 ▮ 56036444, Fax: 27616745
Hd.Org.: Sandeep Gupta; **Bus.Intt.:** Pub.; **Spl.:** Novels, Comics and Books on Self-improvement, Rel., Astrology, Health, etc. in Hindi

MANOJ PRAKASHAN
Publishers of Edu. Books,
Thiru Complex,
IInd Floor, 44, Pantheon Rd., Egmore, Chennai-600008 (Tamil Nadu)

MANOJ PUBLICATIONS
761, Main Rd., Burari, Delhi-110084
✆ 27611116, 27611349, 27611118, Fax: 27611546
✉ swan_gupta@mantraonline.com, manojpublication@mantraonline.com
Hd.Org.: Sawan Gupta; **Bus.Intt.:** Pub. and B.S.; **Spl.:** Rel. and Gen. Books

MANOJ PUSTAK BHANDAR
Jamhore, Aurangabad-824121 (Bihar)
Bus.Intt.: Pub. and B.S.

MANOJ PUSTAK BHANDAR
Rafiganj, Aurangabad-824125 (Bihar)
Bus.Intt.: Pub. and B.S.

MANOJ PUSTAK BHANDAR
Nawada Bazar, Bhagalpur-813101 (Bihar)
Bus.Intt.: Pub. and B.S.

MANOJ PUSTAKALAYA
Amba, Aurangabad-824111 (Bihar)

MANOJ SAHITYA SADAN
Khajuri Bazar, Indore-452002 (Madhya Pradesh)
✆ 2452405

MANORAMA BOOK STALL
Main Rd., Punalur-691305 (Kerala)
✆ (O) 0475-2223391 (R) 2222491
✉ josea@md5.vsnl.net.in
Estd.: 1960; **Prop.:** M.I. Abraham; **Bus.Intt.:** B.S.; **Spl.:** Graduate, Gen. Books, Ascent for various Magazines & Newspapers

MANORAMA PRAKASHAN
102C, Madhavadi, Khili No. 11, Nayagaon Cross Rd., Dadar, Mumbai-400014 (Maharashtra)

MANPREET PRAKASHAN
16/16, (1st Floor Backside), Geeta Colony, Delhi-110031
✆ 22451046, 31071252
Hd.Org.: Manpreet Singh; **Bus.Intt.:** Pub.; **Spl.:** Novels, Stories, Poetry, Plays, Criticisms and Children's Litt. in Punjabi Language

MANSEE BOOKS (P) LTD.
Flat No. 202, 2nd Floor, 4832/24, Ansari Rd., Darya Ganj, New Delhi-110002
✆ (O) 23283115 (R) 28126407, Fax: 23286610

mansibooks@vsnl.net
Dir.: Manoj Saxena; **Bus.Intt.:** WS, L.S., Pub.'s Rep.; **Spl.:** Acad., Beh.Sci., Soc.Sci., Comm., Sci., Tech., Journal & Magazines, Law

MANSI PRAKASHAN AUR VITRIK
39, Kailashpuri, Meerut (Uttar Pradesh)

MANU PRAKASHAN
Suwagpur, Guwahati-781008 (Assam)

MANUPATRA INFORMATION SOLUTIONS PVT. LTD.
B-37, Sector-1, Noida-201301 (Uttar Pradesh)
4014444, 4014515, Fax: 91-120-2443723
support@manupatra.com
contact@manupatra.com
www.manupatra.com
Hd.Org.: Deepak Kapor
Bus.Intt.: Pub. of law reports & legal database through print, online and CD mediums
Br.: 1, J.K. Business Centre, 3rd Floor, Nishka Avenue, Opp. Pizza Hut, Swastik Char Rasta, Navrangpura, Ahmedabad-380009
079-6512231, 9825434938
ahmedabad@manupatra.com
• 133K/11D, Beniganj, Near Law Collage, ADC, Allahabad-211003, 9889610048
allahabad@manupatra.com;
• No. 4807, 8th Floor, High Point IV, Palace Road, Bangalore-560001,
080-41138877, 41138866,
bangalore@manupatra.com;
• 26/320, Vijay Deep, Lokashah Nagar Near H.K. Plastic Factory, Out Side Mewari Gate, Distt. Ajmer, Beawar, Rajasthan-305901
9352574646, 9982674646
rajasthan@manupatra.com
• Cabin No. 42, SCO 92-93, (2nd Floor), Sector 17-C, Chandigarh-160017
0172-3054884, 9356067241
chandigarh@manupatra.com
• 2nd Floor, Flat No. 16A, Wellington Estate, No. 24, Ethiraj Salai, Chennai-600105
044-42028689,
chennai@manupatra.com
• Mahanadi Bihar, Backside of Ramadevi Appartments, P.O. Nayabazar, Cuttack-753004
9861016829, cuttack@manupatra.com
• Office No. 301, 3-6-365, Liberty Plaza, Himayat Nagar, Hyderabad-500029
040-65459600, 9391391711
hyderabad@manupatra.com
• G.D. Hasting Chambers, Ground Floor 7C, Kiran Shankar Roy Road, Kolkata-700001
033-32945322, 9836457013
kolkata@manupatra.com
• Global Trade Center Cabin No. 5, 1/1 Rambaug Colony, Lal Bahadur Shastri Road, Navi Peth, Pune-411030,
020-64000772
pune@manupatra.com;
• H.No. 1265, Near Gour Flour Mill, (Kalimath) Amanpur, Madan-Mahal, Jabalpur,
9826586386
jabalpur@manupatra.com;
• A-305, Gokul Arcade, Swami Nityanand Marg, Vile Parle (East), Mumbai-400057
022-28316114, 66954759
contactmumbai@manupatra.com

MANUEL INTERNATIONAL
42, Pedariar Koil St., Chennai-600001 (Tamil Nadu)
Bus.Intt.: Exp.

MANUSHAM PUBLICATIONS
Ruby Nagar, Changanachery, Kottayam-686103 (Kerala)
0481-2426550
manusham@md3.vsnl.net.in,
vattamattam@vsnl.com
Estd.: 1987; **Hd.Org.:** Mary Sebastian; **Bus.Intt.:** Pub. and B.S.; **Spl.:** Gen. Books, Humanities, Phil., Theology, Aesthetics

MANUSHI PRAKASHAN
C-174, Lajpat Nagar-I, New Delhi-110024
26839158, 26833022
Estd.: 1979; **Hd.Org.:** Madhu Kishwar; **Bus.Intt.:** Women and Society in English

MANVI PRAKASHAN
Manvi Prakashan Palace Rd., Panj Tirthi, Jammu (Jammu & Kashmir)
Prop.: Indu Bhushan; **Bus.Intt.:** L.S., Pub.

MAP AND AGENCIES
Chennai (Tamil Nadu)
22431941
mapsandagencies@mantraonline.com
Bus.Intt.: Cartographers & Map Digitisers

MAP EDUCATIONAL SERVICES PVT. LTD.
124, Sector-14, Gurgaon-122001 (Haryana)
26321669, 26325207, Fax: 26321865
mapintledu@sify.com
Hd.Org.: K. Pandya; **Bus.Intt.:** Pub.; **Spl.:** Edu.

MAP INDIA BUREAU
4110, Arya Pura, Subzi Mandi, Delhi-110007
22526812

MAPIN PUBLISHING (P) LTD.
10/B, Vidyanagar Society Part I, Usmanpura, Ahmedabad-380014 (Gujarat)
27545390-91, Fax: 91-79-27545592
mapin@mapinpub.com
www.mapinpub.com

Estd.: 1983; Hd.Org.: Mallika Sarabhai; Bus.Intt.: Pub.; Spl.: Indian Art, Arch., Archaeology, Crafts, Performing Arts, in English

MAQTABA BURHAN
Urdu Bazar, Delhi-110006

MAQTABA KHIZR-E-RAH
80A, Gaffar Manzil Extn., Jamia Nagar, New Delhi-110025

MARAR SAHITYA PRAKASAM
Sri Ramakrishna Ashrama, Sannidhi Panniyamkara, Kallai P.O., Kozhikode-673003 (Kerala)
Estd.: 1977; Hd.Org.: K.M. Sathya Narayanan; Bus.Intt.: Pub., B.S.

MARATHI PRAKASHAK PARISHAD
C/o Saraswati Book Co., 2A, Budhwar Peth, Balwant Chowk, Pune-411002 (Maharashtra)
✆ 24451219, Fax: 91-20-24454086
Hd.Org.: A.G. Kulkarni; Bus.Intt.: Pub.; Spl.: Tech. Marathi Books and Monthly Newsletter

MARATHI SAHITYA PARISHAD
Ismiya Bazar, Hyderabad-500027 (Andhra Pradesh)

MARATHI SANSHODHAN MANDAL
172, M.M.G.S. Marg, Dadar, Mumbai-400014 (Maharashtra)

MARATHWADA BOOK DISTRIBUTORS
Primal, Khadkeshwar, Aurangabad-431001 (Maharashtra)
✆ 223887

MARATHWADA SAHITYA PARISHAD
Aurangabad (Maharashtra)

MARG PUBLICATIONS
Army & Navy Building, 3rd Floor, 148, Mahatma Gandhi Rd., Mumbai-400001 (Maharashtra)
✆ 022-22842520, 22821151, Fax: 22047102
✉ margpub@tata.com
www.marg-art.org
Estd.: 1946; Chairman: J.J. Bhaba
Br.: C/o, Tata Services Ltd., Jeevan Bharati Tower 1, 10th Floor, 124, Connaught Circus, New Delhi-110001 ✆ 011-23327072-76, Fax: 011-23326265 ✉ rsrinath@tata.com
• C/o, The Tata Iron & Steel Co. Ltd., Tata Centre, 1st Floor, 43, Chowringhee Rd., Kolkata-700071 ✆ 033-22882174, 22248527, 22889251, Fax: 033-22885383
✉ margcal@vsnl.net.in
Bus.Intt.: Pub., L.S. & Rt., Exp., Sub.Ag.; Spl.: Indian & Related Art

MARGHAM PUBLICATIONS
8, Janaki Avenue, Abhiramapuram, Chennai-600018 (Tamil Nadu)
✆ 24995384, 24996759
Hd.Org.: M. Narayanan; Bus.Intt.: Pub.; Spl.: Text Books for U.G. and Professional Courses

MARIA BROTHERS
The Mall, Shimla (Himachal Pradesh)
✆ 25388
Bus.Intt.: B.S.

MARIE EXPORTS
49/7, Brandavan St., West Mambalam, Chennai-600003 (Tamil Nadu)
Bus.Intt.: Exp.

MARIGOLD BOOKS
13B, Raja Nagar, Neelankari, Chennai-600041 (Tamil Nadu)
✆ 24492307, 24491195, 24928209, Fax: 24491195, 24928209
✉ marigoldbks@satyam.net.in
Estd.: 1992; Hd.Org.: S.M. Mashure; Bus.Intt.: Pub.; Spl.: Children's Picture Books, Encyclopaedias, Arabian Tales, Fairy Tales, Activity Colouring Books and Nursery Rhymes

MARKAZI MAKTABA ISLAMI PUBLISHERS
D-307, Dawat Nagar, Abul Fazl Enclave, Jamia Nagar, New Delhi-110025
✆ 26971652, 26954341, Fax: 91-11-26947858
✉ mmipub@nda.vsnl.net.in
www.mmipublishers.net
Hd.Org.: Atiqur Rab
Br.: Markazi Maktaba Islami Publishers, Urdu Bazar, Jama Masjid, Delhi-110026
✆ 91-11-23253196
Bus.Intt.: Pub. and B.S.; Spl.: Islamic Litt. in Urdu, English and Hindi

MARKAZUL MA-ARIF EDUCATION AND RESEARCH CENTRE
F-15/7, Jogabai Extn., P.O. Box 9748, Jamia Nagar, New Delhi-110025
✆ 26916909
Hd.Org.: Mohd. Umar Gautam

MARUTI BHANDAR
Obra, Aurangabad-824124 (Bihar)
Bus.Intt.: Pub. and B.S.

MARY ANN LIEBERT INC
B-13, A Block, LSC 3rd Floor, Naraina Vihar, New Delhi-110028
✆ 45055555, Fax: 91-11-25778876
✉ varora@globe.pub.com
www.globepub.com
Hd.Org.: Tom Mulak
Bus.Intt.: Pub.; Spl.: Books and journals

MARY MARTIN BOOKSELLERS
123, 3rd St. Tatabad, Coimbatore-641012 (Tamil Nadu)

✆ (O) 0422-2499030 (R) 2495780,
Fax: 2495781
✉ mmbooks@vsnl.com
Estd.: 1960; **Prop.:** Sanchu Kesavamurthy; **Bus.Intt.:** B.S., L.S.; **Spl.:** Humanities & Soc.Sci., Mang., Law, Arts & Arch.

MASCOT'S BOOK SHOP
6, Sunder Nagar Market, New Delhi-110003
✆ 24618808
Estd.: 1973; **Prop.:** Chetan Shopra; **Bus.Intt.:** B.S.; **Spl.:** India and Indian Art Books

MASIHI SAHITYA SANSTHA
70, Janpath, New Delhi-110001
Hd.Org.: D. Selva Raj
Br.: 42, Khan Market, New Delhi-110003
✆ 24628043
Bus.Intt.: Rt. Bookshop; **Spl.:** Religious Books

MASOOMA & CO.
1590, Rodgran Chowk, Lal Kuan, Delhi-110006 ✆ 91-11-32407965
Hd.Org.: Sultanuddin Chaudhry
Bus.Intt.: Pub. and Dist.; **Spl.:** Islamic books in English, Hindi and Urdu

MASS EDUCATIONAL TECHNICAL TRAINING INSTITUTE
24 Parganas (South) (West Bengal)
✆ 24771447, 24772010, Fax: 24772010
✉ mass@cal.vsnl.net.in
Bus.Intt.: Pub.

MASS INTERNATIONAL
'Sankaralaya' 22A Melony Rd., T. Nagar, Chennai-600017 (Tamil Nadu)
Bus.Intt.: Exp.

MASTER COMPUTER
28, Iqbal Complex, Iqbal Park, Srinagar (Jammu & Kashmir)
✆ 2457846, 2431552, Fax: 245786
Prop.: Zahiel Imran; **Bus.Intt.:** Rt., L.S., WS; **Spl.:** Engg. & Tech., Mang. & Comm., Med. Sci., Law

MASTERMIND PUBLICATIONS (INDIA) PVT. LTD.
40, Jai Devi Nagar, Garh Rd., Meerut-250001 (Uttar Pradesh)
✆ 4020511, 4020519, Fax: 91-121-2760824
✉ rastoginischal@rediffmail.com
www.mastermindpublications.com
Hd.Org.: Nischal Rastogi; **Bus.Intt.:** Pub.; **Spl.:** Creative Children's Books in English and Hindi

MATA AMRITANANDAMAYI MISSION TRUST
Amritapuri P.O., Kollam-690525 (Kerala)
✆ 04756-221279, 2897578
Estd.: 1988; **Hd.Org.:** H.H. Mata; **Bus.Intt.:** Pub.

MATHRUBHUMI PRINTING AND PUBLISHING CO. LTD.
1/6, INS Building, Rafi Marg, New Delhi-110001
✆ 23733122, Fax: 91-11-23733124
✉ mbidelhi@gmail.com
Hd.Org.: M.D. Veerendra Kumar
Bus.Intt.: Pub.

MATHRUBHUMI PRINTING AND PUBLISHING CO. LTD.
K.P. Kesava Menon Rd., Kozhikode-673001 (Kerala)
✆ 256655, Fax: 256656, Telex: 0804-286
Estd.: 1923; **Hd.Org.:** M.P. Veerendra Kumar; **Bus.Intt.:** Pub.

MATRUSHRI
2-1-290/5/1, Lane Opp. Vijaya Bank, Nallakunta, Hyderabad-500044 (Andhra Pradesh)
✆ 27619469, 27669606
✉ matrushri@nettlinx.com
Hd.Org.: K.S. Arvind; **Bus.Intt.:** Pub.; **Spl.:** Edu. Books in Maths and Sci.

MAUJ PRAKASHAN GREH
Khetwadi, Girgaon, Mumbai-400004 (Maharashtra)

MAULIK SAHITYA PRAKASHAN
162-D, Kamla Nagar, Delhi-110007
✆ 23844450, 35380149, Fax: 23840251
Hd.Org.: Narain Dutt Mishra; **Bus.Intt.:** Pub.; **Spl.:** Books and Magazines on Moral Sci., Ancient India, etc. and Children's Books

MAXLATIVE TRADING CORPORATION
7/N, Ist Floor, Mohan Residency Building, 2nd Street, Kamraj Cross, Bangalore-560042 (Karnataka)
✆ 41124411, 91-80-41124411
✉ md@maxlative.com
www.maxlative.com
Hd.Org.: Ayesha Siddiqua

MAXMIN EDUCATION
40, Vaishali, Dabri Palam Rd., New Delhi-110045 ✆ 25033377
Hd.Org.: Jagdish Kohli; **Bus.Intt.:** Pub.; **Spl.:** Children's Books and Teaching Aids

MAXWELL MACMILLAN
International Publishing Group, Jai Saxena, E-11/10-1, Sector-1, Vashi, New Mumbai-400073 (Maharashtra)

MAXWELL MACMILLLAN PUBLISHING CO.
23, Prasad Nagar, DDA Flats, New Delhi-110005
Hd.Org.: Ben D. Johnston

MAYA BOOK CENTRE
Near Apsara Talkies, Aurangpura, Aurangabad-431001 (Maharashtra)

✆ 2335624
Estd.: 1989; **Prop.:** P.S. Dongapure; **Bus.Intt.:** Rt.; **Spl.:** School, College Text and Help Books of K.G. to P.G.

MAYA PUBLISHERS PVT. LTD.
Flat No. 35, Sector-A, Pocket-C, Vasant Kunj, New Delhi-110070
✆ 26892495, 26892498, Fax: 26130069
✉ surit@vsnl.com
Estd.: 1987; **Dir.:** Surit Mitra, Mrs. Kumkum Mitra; **Bus.Intt.:** Dist.; **Spl.:** Foreign Pub. on Soc.Sci., Humanities, Mang.

MAYANK PRAKASHAN
Misra Garden, Hanumanghari, Kankhal, Haridwar (Uttarakhand)

MAYUR BOOK DISTRIBUTORS
A/14, Unit-3, Kharvela Nagar, Bhubaneshswar-751001 (Orissa)
✆ 0674-2580377, 2402672,
Fax: 0674-2409304, 2440950
Hd.Org.: Susant Kumar Mohapatra

MAYUR PAPERBACKS
S-95, Sector 5, Noida-201301
✆ 4338365, Fax: 91-11-23254407
✉ sales@nationalpublishinghouse.com
Hd.Org.: S.K. Malik
Bus.Intt.: Pub.; **Spl.:** Books on humanities

MAYUR PRAKASHAN PVT. LTD.
372/18A, Civil Lines, Gwalior Rd., Jhansi-284001 (Madhya Pradesh)
✆ 2440682, 2441491
Hd.Org.: Satyadev Varma

MAYUR PUBLICATIONS
A-14, Unit 3, Kharavela Nagar, Bhubaneswar-751001 (Orissa)
✆ 2580377, Fax: 0674-2409304
Prop.: Rajeev Goel; **Bus.Intt.:** Pub.; **Spl.:** Children's Edu. Books in English, Hindi and Sanskrit

MAYUR PUBLICATIONS
14, Community Centre-II, Ashok Vihar, Phase-II, Delhi-110052
✆ (O) 27117350, 27132283 (R) 27114246, 27132312 **Estd.:** 1979; **Prop.:** Rajeev Goel

MAYUR PUBLICATIONS
1168/76, Deva Ram Park, Delhi-110035

MCGRAW-HILL BOOK CO.
7, West Patel Nagar, New Delhi-110008
✆ 25882743-46, 25882918, Fax: 25885154
✉ marketing_india@mcgraw-hill.com
🌐 www.tatamcgrawhill.com
Hd.Org.: N. Subrahmanyam; **Bus.Intt.:** Pub.; **Spl.:** Textbooks on Engg., Comp. Sci., Business, Eco., Sci. and Soc.Sci.

MCGRAW-HILL EDUCATION (INDIA) PVT. LTD.
B-4, Sector 63, Distt. Gautam Budh Nagar, Noida-201301 (Uttar Pradesh)
✆ 4383400, Fax: 91-120-4383401-03
✉ michael_cruz@mcgraw-hill.com, prakash_tiwari@mcgraw-hill.com
Br.: 444/1, Sri Ekambaranaicker Industrial Estate, Alapakkam, Porus, Chennai-600116
✆ 24769557-59, 24769560-62,
Fax: 044-24769564
✉ sigamani_johnson@mcgraw-hill.com
• 1st Floor, "Kala Nilayam", E-6, Vikarampuri Colony, Karkhana, Secunderabad-500009
✆ 27842412, Telefax: 91-40-27842436
✉ srivatsa_vijaya@mcgraw-hill.com
• AE-641, Sale Lake City, Sec.-1, (Near AE Market), Kolkata-700064
✆ 91-33-23372236
✉ sambrita_basu@mcgraw-hill.com
• 507, Powai Plaza, Central Avenue, Hiranandani Gardens, Powai, Mumbai-400076
✆ 91-22-65025723, 65025725
✉ kj_waghchhipawalla@mcgraw-hill.com
• 48-NOT Colony, Rajkamal Chowk, Vishwakarna Nagar, Nagpur-440027
✆ 91-712-2753399 ▮ 9960610502
✉ abhijit_bharne@mcgraw-hill.com
• 3A, Namdeo Smruti, 5 Shivprasad Society Panmala, Dattawadi, Pune-411030
✆ 91-20-24337604 ▮ 9822140696
✉ sharad_shinde@mcgraw-hill.com

MECRON PUBLISHERS (P) LTD.
5-2-15E, Sattur Rd., P.B. No. 23, Sivakasi, (Tamil Nadu)
✆ 04562-27423738, 221108,
Fax: 04562-272089, 226655
✉ mecron@md3.vsnl.net.in
Estd.: 1998; **Prop.:** Y.R. Ratnam;
Bus.Intt.: Pub.; **Spl.:** Gen. & Fiction

MEDHA BOOKS
X-11, Naveen Shahdara, Delhi-110032
✆ 22323672, Fax: 91-11-22321818
✉ medhabooks@gmail.com
🌐 www.medhabooks.com
Hd.Org.: Deepak Monga; **Bus.Intt.:** Pub. and B.S.; **Spl.:** Novels, Stories, Essays and Children's Litt.

MEDIA & PUBLISHING
84, Abul Fazal Enclave, Jamia Nagar, New Delhi-110025

MEDIA 2000
E-32-A, Amar Colony, Lajpat Nagar-IV, New Delhi-110024
✆ 26445191/2/3, Fax: 91-11-26217027
✉ info@media2k.com

Ch.Exe.: Baljeet Juneja; **Bus.Intt.:** Pub.; **Spl.:** Magazine for Kids & Parents, Media Sotcom the first Directory on Indian Websites

MEDIA BOOK SERVICE
5A, Zam Zam Colony, Ram Bagh,
Srinagar-190015 (Jammu & Kashmir)
✆ 0194-2435327
Estd.: 1999; **Hd.Org.:** Hilal Ahmad Dar; **Bus.Intt.:** WS, L.S. & Rt.; **Spl.:** Humanities & Soc.Sci.

MEDIA GRAPHICS
A-16, Sector-20, Noida-201301
(Uttar Pradesh)
✆ 28550421, Fax: 22258799
Prop.: P.I. Mamtani

MEDIA HOUSE
375-A, Pocket-2, Mayur Vihar, Phase-I,
Delhi-110091
✆ (O) 22750667 (R) 22751317
▮ 9810301010, Fax: 22757040
✉ books@indiancurrents.com,
mediabooks@hotmail.com
🌐 www.mediabooks.org
Estd.: 1994; **Prop.:** Dr. Xavier Vadakkekara; **Bus.Intt.:** Pub., B.S., L.S.; **Spl.:** Humanities & Soc.Sci., Fiction & Gen., Law, Insti. Pub.

MEDIA OVERSEAS
695, Loni Rd., Shahdara, Delhi-110032
✆ 22594752, 9868454103, 20535665,
Fax: 22119850
Estd.: 2003; **Prop.:** R.K. Mehra; **Bus.Intt.:** B.S., L.S., Exp., Imp.; **Spl.:** Humanities & Soc.Sci., Mang., Arts & Arch., Children & Gen.

MEDIA PROMOTERS & PUBLISHERS PVT. LTD.
20-G, Noshir Bharucha Marg, Mumbai-400007
(Maharashtra)

MEDIA STAR PVT. LTD.
7, Vaswani Mansion, 120, Dinshaw Vachha Road, Church Gate, Mumbai-400020
(Maharashtra)
✆ 22815538, Fax: 91-22-22839619
✉ ravi@mediastar.co.in
🌐 www.mediastar.co.in
Hd.Org.: Ravi Lalwai
Bus.Intt.: Dist.

MEDIA-CENTER/RUPOSHI BANGLA
261, Acharya Prafulla Chandra Rd.,
Ground Floor, Maniktola, Kolkata-700006
(West Bengal)
✆ 31069767, 23372549, Fax: 23336567
✉ hapipaul@rediffmail.com
Hd.Org.: Dibyadyuty Paul; **Bus.Intt.:** Pub., B.S. and Dist.; **Spl.:** Bengali Books and Magazines

MEDIA-CENTER/UJJAL BOOKS
261, Acharya Prafulla Chandra Rd.,
Ground Floor, Maniktola, Kolkata-700006
(West Bengal)
✆ 91-33-23607869
✉ hapipaul@rediffmail.com
Hd.Org.: Dibyadyuty Paul; **Bus.Intt.:** Pub., B.S. and Dist.; **Spl.:** Bengali Books and Magazines

MEDIAMATICS
C/o Prentice-Hall of India (P) Ltd.,
M-97, Connaught Circus,
New Delhi-110001
✆ 43031100, Fax: 91-11-43031144
✉ phi@phindia.com
🌐 www.phindia.com, www.mediamatics.com
Hd.Org.: Ashok K. Ghosh; **Bus.Intt.:** Imp. & Dist.

MEDIAMATICS
280, N.S.C. Bose Rd., P.O. Regent Park,
Kolkata-700040 (West Bengal)
✆ 24712721

MEDIASCOPE BOOK HOUSE
12, Gitanjali, Off. Arthur Bunder Rd.,
Culaba, Mumbai-400005
(Maharashtra)

MEDIAWARE SYSTEMS INDIA PVT. LTD.
10, Sir Thyagaraja Road, T. Nagar,
Chennai-600017 (Tamil Nadu)
✉ mediazmarket@yahoo.com
Hd.Org.: Balaji; **Bus.Intt.:** Dist.
Spl.: Children's Books

MEDICAL BOOK CORPORATION (THE)
446, Nanapeta Laxmi Rd., Pune-2
(Maharashtra)

MEDICAL HOUSE (DELHI)
3656, Kutub Road, Delhi-110006
✆ 65398987, 65675891, Fax: 91-11-23559348
✉ medicalhouse@airtelbroadband.in,
medicalhouse@hotmail.com,
medicalhouse@gmail.com
🌐 www.medicalhousedelhi.com
Hd.Org.: Davinder Lal Mehta
Br.: E-8, G.D.A. Market, Patel Nagar-II,
Ghaziabad-201001 (Uttar Pradesh)
✆ 95-120-2735551, 2835551 ▮ 9818647747
Bus.Intt.: Pub. and Dist.; **Spl.:** Books on Various Systems of Med. and Monthly Magazine: *Masik Chikitsak*

MEDICAL INDUSTRIES AROUND THE WORLD
FF-20, Palika Bazar, G.T. Rd.,
Ghaziabad-201009 (Uttar Pradesh)
✆ 24795783, 24716839
Fax: 91-120-24724818, 24716839
Hd.Org.: Vijay Sadana; **Bus.Intt.:** Exp.;

Spl.: Med. Related Products and Research Magazine Manufacturers of Med. Related Products and Research Magazine

MEDICO BOOKS
Medicobooks, Near S.M.S. Hospital, Jaipur-302004 (Rajasthan)
Estd.: 1965; **Bus.Intt.:** Pub., L.S. & Rt.; **Spl.:** Med.

MEDICO REFRESHER PUBLICATIONS
4807/24, Bharat Ram Road, Darya Ganj, New Delhi-110002
✆ 32019798, Fax: 91-562-2811145
✉ sumit8@sancharnet.in
Hd.Org.: Munna Lal Gupta
Bus.Intt.: Pub.; **Spl.:** •Medical books

MEDITECH BOOK DISTRIBUTORS
Bangalore (Karnataka)
✉ medibook@rediffmail.com
Bus.Intt.: B.S. & Dist.

MEENA ENTERPRISES
H-250, Ellis Nagar, Housing Board, Madurai-625010 (Tamil Nadu)
✆ (O) & (R) 0452-2602061 ▮ 9843260206
Estd.: 1987; **Prop.:** G. Santhana Krishnan; **Bus.Intt.:** L.S.; **Spl.:** All Books on All Sub.

MEENAKSHI ANMAL PUBLICATIONS
Samayittu Par House, 118, R.K. Mutt Rd., Chennai-600028 (Tamil Nadu)

MEENAKSHI PRAKASHAN
Mehra Building, Jaipur Rd., Ajmer-305001 (Rajasthan)
✆ 2621275
Estd.: 1977; **Hd.Org.:** Yogendra Kumar Mehra; **Bus.Intt.:** Pub. and B.S.;
Spl.: School, Graduate Text Books, Adv. Books for Lib. and Gen. Books

MEENAKSHI PRAKASHAN
4359/4, Ansari Rd., Darya Ganj, New Delhi-110002
✆ 23279396, Fax: 91-11-23279396
Hd.Org.: Himanshu Shekhar; **Bus.Intt.:** Exp.; **Spl.:** Manufacturers of Sci./Comp. Books

MEENU PRAKASHAN
H-33A, Kalkaji, New Delhi-110019
✆ 26425255
Hd.Org.: Smt. Shakun Joshi

MEER BROTHERS
Main Bazar, Sopore, Kashmir (Jammu & Kashmir)
✆ 2629
Estd.: 1947; **Prop.:** G.R. Meer

MEEZAN PUBLISHERS
Batmaloo, Opp. Fire Service Hqrs, Srinagar (Jammu & Kashmir)
✆ 470851, Fax: 457215

Bus.Intt.: Sole Dist. of National Council of Promotion of Urdu Language, Ministry of Human Resources Development, Govt. of India

MEGH PRAKASHAN
239, Gali Kunjas, Dariba Kalan, Delhi-110006
✆ 91-11-23278761, 65278761
✉ megh_prakashan@rediffmail.com
www.meghprakashan.com
Hd.Org.: Megh Raj Jain; **Bus.Intt.:** Pub. and Dist.; **Spl.:** Ancient Indian Sci. and Spiritualism, Rel., Phil., etc.

MEGHA BOOK DEPOT
CD-123C, Pitampura, Delhi-110088
✆ 27455172
✉ mehta7455172@rediffmail.com, mehta7455172yahoo.com
Estd.: 1985; **Hd.Org.:** R.K. Mehta
Bus.Intt.: L.S.; **Spl.:** Govt. Publications, Maps and Globes

MEGHA HILLS
10-96/1, Prem Vijay Nagar, Malkajgiri, Hyderabad-500047 (Andhra Pradesh)

MEGHALAYA BOOK STALL
Mamkhar Point, Bara Bazar, Shillong-793002 (Assam)
✆ (O) 2222350 (R) 2241891
Hd.Org.: Raj Narain

MEGHDOOT
4, Shyama Charan Dey St., Kolkata-700073 (West Bengal)

MEGNUM BOOKS
Saite 9, Ajanta Chheda Nagar, Mumbai-400089 (Maharashtra)

MEHARCHAND LACHHMANDAS PUBLICATIONS
4225-A, 1, Ansari Rd., Darya Ganj, New Delhi-110002
✆ (O) 23271568, 23281568
(R) 0124-5051104, Fax: 23271568
✉ atulnaahar@vsnl.com
Estd.: 1870; **Prop.:** Rajendra K. Naahar;
Bus.Intt.: Pub., B.S.; **Spl.:** Books in Sanskrit

MEHOOL PRAKASHAN
Lakshmanbagh, Dargagh Rd., Mulund Colony, Mumbai-400082 (Maharashtra)

MEHRAS
4767/23, 5, Ansari Road, Darya Ganj, New Delhi-110002
✆ 91-11-23273838
✉ mehras_delhi@vsnl.net
Hd.Org.: Chandra K. Mehra
Br.: G-1 & 2, Ghaswala Tower, P.G. Solanki Path, Near Minerva Cinema, Mumbai-400007
✆ 91-11-23082631, 23074966
✉ rupac@bom8.vsnl.net.in

• 15, Bankim Chatterjee Street, 2nd Floor, Kolkata-700073, ✆ 91-11-2196085, 2196087
✉ mehras_books@vsnl.net
Bus.Intt.: Wholesaler

MEHTA BOOK CENTRE
6/A, Moti Nagar, First Floor,
New Delhi-110015
✆ 25459817
Hd.Org.: Sunil Kumar; **Bus.Intt.:** L.S.

MEHTA BOOK SELLERS
322, Bhausingji Rd., Kolhapur-416012 (Maharashtra)
✆ (O) 0231-2542304, 2541881 (R) 2543260, Fax: 0231-2541881
✉ mehtabooks@eth.net
Estd.: 1989; **Prop.:** Anil D. Mehta; **Bus.Intt.:** Pub., WS, L.S. & Rt., **Spl.:** Sci., Tech. & Med., Law, Humanities & Soc.Sci., Trade, Gen. (Incl. Lit. & Art), Juvenile/Children Books

MEHTA PUBLISHERS
Mehta House, A-16, Naraina-II,
New Delhi-110028
✆ 25704450, 25707667, Fax: 25704234
✉ mopl@vsnl.com
Estd.: 1980; **Man.Dir.:** Gautam Mehta; **Bus.Intt.:** Pub., WS, L.S. & Rt., Imp., Exp.; **Spl.:** Med.

MEHUL BOOK SALES
Lokagutch Jain Building, 125-Walchand Hirachand Marg, Shop No. 1, Opp. V.T. Station, Mumbai-400001 (Maharashtra)
✆ (O) 22654657, 22694145, 22674944 (R) 24141216, 24184679, Fax: 22654657
✉ mehulbks@vsnl.com
Estd.: 1993; **Prop.:** Mehul Khandy, Rahul Khandy; **Bus.Intt.:** B.S.; **Spl.:** Adv. Books for Lib., Gen. Books and Tech. Books

MEMORY RETENTION WORKSHOP
93, Gujarat Vihar, Vikas Marg,
Delhi-110092
✆ 22542805, 22548006, Fax: 22248006
✉ gunjan-kapadia@rediffmail.com
Hd.Org.: Ramni Kapadia; **Bus.Intt.:** Dist.; **Spl.:** Books and Cassettes on Memory Improvement

MENAKA PRAKASHAN PVT. LTD.
2117, Sadashiv, Vijayanagar Colony,
Pune-411030 (Maharashtra)

MENTA BOOK DISTRIBUTORS PVT. LTD.
400/1, 4th Cross, 7th Block West,
P.O. Box No. 8225, Jay Nagar,
Bangalore-560082 (Karnataka)
✆ 26769509, 26761289, Fax: 26769954
✉ jai@blr.vsnl.net.in
Estd.: 1986; **Man.Dir.:** Venkatesh M.S.; **Bus.Intt.:** L.S. & Rt., Imp.

MENTOR BOOKS
Poornima Perumpoyil Kakkur, P.O.
Calicut-673019 (Kerala)

MENTOR PUBLISHERS
85, Gian Park, Chander Nagar, Delhi-110051
Hd.Org.: Neeraj Kumar

MERCURY SUBSCRIPTION SERVICE INTERNATIONAL
Magent House, No. 143, Infantry Rd.,
Bangalore-560001 (Karnataka)
Estd.: 1979; **Prop.:** K. Nagaraj;
Bus.Intt.: Sub.Ag.

MERIDIAN INTERNATIONAL
Tuticorn (Tamil Nadu)
✆ 328116, Fax: 327116
✉ sageer@vsnl.com
Bus.Intt.: B.S.

METHA PUBLISHING HOUSE
1216, Sadashiv Peth, Dhanasai Apartments,
Pune-411030 (Maharashtra)
✆ (O) 24476924 (R) 24476197 ▮ 9823015319, Fax: 0212-2475462
Estd.: 1976; **Prop.:** Sunil Mehta; **Bus.Intt.:** Pub.; **Spl.:** Books in Marathi, Hindi and English

METRO BOOKS PVT. LTD.
2/40, Ansari Road, Darya Ganj,
New Delhi-110002
91-11-43541022
✉ metrobooks@rediffmail.com
Hd.Org.: Mahesh Jain

METROPOLITAN BOOK CO. PVT. LTD.
1, Netaji Subash Marg, Darya Ganj, P.B. 7144,
New Delhi-110002
✆ 23271661, 23255914, Fax: 23272497
✉ metrobks@ndf.vsnl.net.in
Estd.: 1946; **Man.Dir.:** B.V. Gupta;
Jt. Man.Dir.: Vivek Gupta; **Bus.Intt.:** Pub., WS, L.S. & Rt., Imp., Exp.; **Spl.:** Humanities & Soc.Sci., Sci. & Tech., Law

METROPOLITAN BOOK CO.
93, Park St., Kolkata-700060
(West Bengal)

MICKY'S GALLERY
20, M.G. Marg, Civil Lines, Allahabad
(Uttar Pradesh)

MICRO E-COMMERCE LTD.
A-102, Sector 5, Noida (Uttar Pradesh)
✆ 2421544, 2421545, Fax: 95-120-2420330
✉ vipul@microecommerce.net,
mecom@microecommerce.net
Hd.Org.: Vipul Jain; **Bus.Intt.:** B.S.

MIDAS PUBLISHING HOUSE
A-11/134, Bhajanpura, Delhi-110053
✆ 22172380
Hd.Org.: D.B. Arora, Praveen Kumar; **Bus.Intt.:** Pub., Printer, B.S.

MIDLAND BOOK SHOP
Shop No. 20, Aurobindo Place Market, Hauz Khas, New Delhi-110016
✆ (O) 26867121 (R) 25266048, Fax: 26962718
@ midbook@bol.net.in
Estd.: 1983; **Prop.:** Mirza Yaseen Baig
Br.: G-8, Basement, South Extn. Part-I, New Delhi-110049 ✆ 24653880-81-82
Bus.Intt.: Rt.; **Spl.:** Fiction, Rare, Journals & Magazines

MIDNAPUR BOOK DEPOT
12, Bidhan Sarani, Kolkata-700006 (West Bengal)

MIGHTY MARKETERS
841, HAL II Stage, 7th, Main II Cross, Indira Nagar, Bangalore-560008 (Karnataka)

MILAN GENERAL STORES
Bakhri, Begusarai-851111 (Bihar)
Bus.Intt.: Pub. and B.S.

MILIND PRAKASHAN
H-3-178/2, K.S. Bagh, Hanuman Vyayam Shala Lane, Sultan Bazar, Hyderabad-500095 (Andhra Pradesh)
✆ (O) 24753737, 31052988 (R) 27562595
@ milindprakshan@rediffmail.com
Estd.: 1965; **Prop.:** Shrutikant Bharati; **Bus.Intt.:** Pub., Dist.; **Spl.:** Dravidian Litt., Translated into Hindi

MILINDER PRAKASHAN
267, Bararipur, Chhindwara-480001 (Madhya Pradesh)

MILLAT BOOK CENTRE
New Delhi
✆ 23274339, 23282740, Fax: 23263567
@ sgagan@vsnl.com
Bus.Intt.: Pub. & Exp.

MILLENNIUM BOOKS
Patna (Bihar)
✆ 220647, Fax: 229079
@ uks@vsnl.com
Bus.Intt.: Pub.

MILLENNIUM PUBLISHERS
New Delhi
✆ 24621791, 24692352, Fax: 24604413
@ milli@bol.net.in
Bus.Intt.: Pub.

MILTON BOOK COMPANY
17, New Survey Rd., Dehradun-248001 (Uttarakhand)
✆ 0135-2658692, 2659601
@ milton@ndb.vsnl.net.in
Estd.: 1982; **Bus.Intt.:** Pub. and B.S.; **Spl.:** Forestry and Wildlife

MINA BOOK AGENCY
No. 2, Mareet, Room No. 113, P.O. Kalyan, Distt. Nadia (West Bengal)

MINAR
16A, Tamer Lane, Kolkata-700009 (West Bengal)

MINAR BOOK STALL
Stall-28, Ramanath Majumder St., Kolkata-700009 (West Bengal)

MIND & BODY RESEARCH CENTRE
W-21, Greater Kailash Part-I, New Delhi-110048
✆ (O) 26412432, 26430337 (R) 516430337
@ dayanandverma@yahoo.com
www.instituteofpalmistry.com
Estd.: 1988; **Hd.Org.:** Dayanand Verma
Bus.Intt.: Pub.; **Spl.:** Books in Hindi on Psych., Spiritualism, Palmistry, Litt., Meditation, etc.

MIND POWER RESEARCH INSTITUTE
10, Mahaveer Colony, Sector-4, Udaipur-313001 (Rajasthan)

MINDSTORM COMPUTER INFORMATION PVT. LTD.
Gleneden Place, 813, Poonamalee High Rd., Chennai-600010 (Tamil Nadu)
✆ 26427633, 26427454, Fax: 25321076
@ info@compuserve.com
Hd.Org.: K. Jacob Thomas; **Bus.Intt.:** Rt.; **Spl.:** Comp., Professional Software Sales

MINERVA ASSOCIATED (PUBLICATIONS) PVT. LTD.
7-B, Lake Place, Kolkata-700029 (West Bengal)

MINERVA BOOK DISTRIBUTORS
6-A, Manik Complex, Near Chelipura High School, Station Rd., Aurangabad-5 (Maharashtra)
✆ 2320896
Estd.: 1982; **Prop.:** Dashrathe S.B.; **Bus.Intt.:** B.S. and L.S.

MINERVA BOOK HOUSE
46, The Mall, Shimla-171001 (Himachal Pradesh)
✆ 2203078, 2250523, Fax: 2254802
@ minerva@nde.vsnl.net.in, minerva_shimla@yahoo.com
Estd.: 1972; **Prop.:** Rajinder Aggarwal
Bus.Intt.: Pub., L.S. & Rt.
Spl.: Humanities & Soc.Sci., Law, Juvenile/ Children, Gen. & Fiction

MINERVA BOOK STALL
Post Box No. 27, Round West,
Thrissur-680001 (Kerala)
✆ (O) 2335478, 2335578 (R) 2383878, 2383879, Fax: 0487-2383878
minerva@md5.vsnl.net.in
Estd.: 1969; **Prop.:** T.I. George;
Bus.Intt.: B.S.; **Spl.:** School, Graduate, Adv. Books for Lib., Gen. Books and All Books

MINERVA PUBLICATIONS
6, 1st Floor, Pycrofts Rd., Triplicane,
Chennai-600005 (Tamil Nadu)
✆ 28445674, Fax: 28445674
minerva@hathway.com
www.minervaa.com
Hd.Org.: T. Nazibudeen; **Bus.Intt.:** Pub.;
Spl.: Children's Books and Dictionaries

MINHAS PRAKASHAN
R-2/114, Naya Rajnagar, Ghaziabad-201001
(Uttar Pradesh)

MINI BOOK STALL
9, Shyama Charan Dey St., Kolkata-700073
(West Bengal)

MINI MASTER
Post Office Rd., Savarkundala-363515
(Gujarat)

MINIKASHI PRAKASHAN
Mehar Building, Jeypur Rd., Ajmer-305001
(Rajasthan)
✆ 231275
Hd.Org.: Yogesh Kumar Mehra

MIRA ADITI CENTRE
Aspiration Aurovike, Kottakuppam-605104
(Tamil Nadu)

MIRA ADITI CENTRE
62, 'Sriranga' IInd Main, 1st Cross,
T.K. Layout, Saraswatipuram, Mysore-570009
(Karnataka)
✆ 0821-2330380
miraditi@hclinfinet.com,
miraditi@hotmail.com
www.ire-miraditi.org
Estd.: 1981; **Man.Trustee:** Patrice Marot;
Bus.Intt.: Pub., Exp., Imp., Dist.;
Spl.: Humanities & Soc.Sci., Phil., General

MIRAT PUBLICATIONS
Post Box. 4273, New Delhi-110048
Bus.Intt.: Exp.

MIRZA PUBLICATIONS
Hasanabad Rainawari, Srinagar,
Kashmir-190003 (Jammu & Kashmir)
✆ 272344
Estd.: 1974; **Prop.:** G.M. Mirza; **Bus.Intt.:** Pub., WS, L.S. & Rt.; **Spl.:** Humanities & Soc.Sci.

MITHU PRAKASHANI
18D, Tamer Lane, Kolkata-700009
(West Bengal)

MITRA & GHOSH PUBLISHERS PVT. LTD.
10, Shyama Charan Dey St., Kolkata-700073
(West Bengal)
✆ 033-22416420, 22419431
Estd.: 1934; **Prop.:** Sabitendranath Roy;
Bus.Intt.: Pub. and Exp.; **Spl.:** Bengali Novels, Fictions, Short Stories, Collections, Travelogues, for Juvenile Litt., Anthologies, Pioneer in Bengali Paperback, Bengali Journal Katha Sahitya and Popular Edition of Rachanavalis

MITRA LIBRARY
7, Chandi Ghosh Rd., Kolkata-700040
(West Bengal)

MITRA PRAKASHANI
206, Bidhan Sarani, Kolkata-700006
(West Bengal)

MITRATA OFFSET PRINT & PRAKASH PVT. LTD.
16/3E, Dixon Lane, Kolkata-700014
(West Bengal)

MITTAL BOOK DISTRIBUTORS
Delhi
✆ 23263913, 23257587, Fax: 23940285
dkm@ndb.vsnl.net.in
Bus.Intt.: WS, B.S. & Order Suppliers

MITTAL PUBLICATIONS
4594/9, Ansari Rd., Darya Ganj,
New Delhi-110002
✆ 25648725, 23250398, 25351493,
Fax: 25351521
mittalp@ndf.net.in, info@mittalbooks.com
mittalpublications.com
Hd.Org.: Naurang Rai
Br.: A-110, Mohan Garden, New Delhi-110059
✆ 25351493, 25351976, Fax: 91-11-25351521
mittalp@ndf.net.in
Bus.Intt.: Pub. and Dist.;
Spl.: Anthropology, Art, Culture, Eco., Sol., Phil.

MOBEL BOOK DISTRIBUTORS
H-43, Taksha Shila Apartments, Vastrapur,
Ahmedabad-380015 (Gujarat)
✆ 26756476, Fax: 079-6767618
mobelabad@yahoo.co.in
Estd.: 1980; **Bus.Intt.:** B.S.; **Spl.:** Graduate, Adv. Books for Lib., Gen. Books for All Sub. only Acad. Books

MOBEL BOOK DISTRIBUTORS
4, Samir Apartments, S.M. Rd., Near Amar Kunj Society, Nehru Nagar, Ambawadi,
Ahemdabad-380015 (Gujarat)

✆ 2407027
Estd.: 1980; **Prop.:** M.B. Mirchandani; **Bus.Intt.:** Imp.; **Spl.:** Humanities & Soc.Sci., Sci. & Tech., Law, Gen. & Fiction etc., Trade, Gen. (Incl. Lit. & Art)

MODEL PUBLICATION
Azhoor P.O., Thiruvananthapuram-695305 (Kerala)

MODEL PUBLISHING HOUSE
3, Shyama Charan Dey St., Kolkata-700073 (West Bengal)
✆ 033-22416130, Fax: 22412100
Estd.: 1955; **Prop.:** Jaideep Ghosh; **Bus.Intt.:** Pub.; **Spl.:** Novel, Poems, Stories, Translations, School Books etc.

MODERN BOOK AGENCY PVT. LTD.
10C, Bankim Chatterjee St.,
Kolkata-700073
(West Bengal)
✆ 241-249666, 2314025
Estd.: 1928; **Hd.Org.:** Debnarayan Bhattacharyya; **Bus.Intt.:** Pub.; **Spl.:** School, Colleges and Universities level Text Books and Reference Books in Different Sub. in Bengali, English and Hindi

MODERN BOOK CENTRE
G.P.O. Jn., M.G. Rd., Trivandrum-695001 (Kerala)
✆ 2331816, 2331826, 2333987, Fax: 2333186
modern@techpark.net
www.modernbookcentre.com
Estd.: 1979; **Man.Prt.:** Balakesavan N.E.; **Bus.Intt.:** L.S. & Rt.

MODERN BOOK DEPOT
LG-6, Akarshan Bhavan, 23, Ansari Rd.,
New Delhi-110002
✆ 23241471, 56022599,
Fax: 91-11-27241674
vinmedia@bol.net.in,
modbook@caltigen.com
Ch.Exe.: Mrs. Anita Kumar; **Bus.Intt.:** Dist.; **Spl.:** Books for NCERT, NOS, CBT/NBT

MODERN BOOK DEPOT
Unit-3, Station Square,
Bhubaneswar-751001 (Orissa)
✆ 0675-534374
modbooks@cal2.vsnl.net.in
Estd.: 1970; **Prop.:** Om Prakash; **Bus.Intt.:** Pub., L.S. and Rt., Sub.Ag.

MODERN BOOK DISTRIBUTORS
22A/1, Bholanath Nagar, Gali No. 2,
Shahdara, Delhi-110032
✆ 91-11-22307330
Hd.Org.: Vinod Kalia; **Bus.Intt.:** Pub.

MODERN BOOK HOUSE
18-20, Chandrika Towers,
Near Shastri Bridge, Jabalpur-482001 (Madhya Pradesh)
✆ 2315210
Estd.: 1945; **Prt.:** N.M. Surana & J.M. Surana; **Bus.Intt.:** WS, L.S. & Rt., Imp., Sub.Ag.; **Spl.:** Humanities & Soc.Sci., Sci. & Tech., Law, Gen. & Fiction etc.

MODERN BOOK HOUSE
Near Palayam Bus Stand, Kozhikode-673001 (Kerala)

MODERN BOOK HOUSE
S.C.O. No. 4-5, Sector-17B, IInd Floor,
Near K.C. Theatre, Chandigarh-160017
✆ 2772839
Estd.: 1997; **Prop.:** Jagtar Singh; **Bus.Intt.:** L.S.

MODERN BOOK HOUSE
Shivvilas Palace, Rajwada, Indore-452003 (Madhya Pradesh)
✆ 2543289
Estd.: 1962; **Hd.Org.:** Shobhit Nagar; **Bus.Intt.:** L.S.; **Spl.:** Pvt. Public Institutional Suppliers on Govt. Banking and Gen. Books

MODERN BOOK HOUSE
Doi Bhawan, Subhash Colony, Bhagat Ki Kothi, Jodhpur-342001 (Rajasthan)
✆ (O) 0291-2624850 (R) 0291-2548326
vikpankj@sancharnet.in
Estd.: 1997; **Prop.:** Pankaj Singh; **Bus.Intt.:** L.S. & Rt.; **Spl.:** Sci. & Tech., Bio., Agri.

MODERN BOOK HOUSE
Sagarampara Main Rd., Surat-395002 (Gujarat)

MODERN BOOK SHOP
Dhalpur Bazar, Kullu (Himachal Pradesh)
✆ 222555
Estd.: 1968; **Prop.:** Ravinder Kumar **Bus.Intt.:** L.S. in Distt. Kulu and Lohaul Spiti; **Spl.:** School and College Books

MODERN BOOKS
P.O. Box 1, Sulthanbathery,
Wayanad-673592 (Kerala)
✆ 220570
Estd.: 1972; **Hd.Org.:** P.U. Joy **Bus.Intt.:** Pub. and B.S.

MODERN BOOKS
High School Junction, Kollam-691009 (Kerala)
Estd.: 1970; **Prop.:** R. Radhakrishnan Nair **Bus.Intt.:** B.S.

MODERN COLUMN
10/2A, Tamer Lane, Kolkata-700009
(West Bengal)

MODERN INDIA PUBLISHERS
8A, College Row, Kolkata-700009
(West Bengal)

MODERN INTERNATIONAL PVT. LTD.
Delhi
@ mpml@ndf.vsnl.net.in
Bus.Intt.: Printers & Paper Product

MODERN LAW PUBLISHERS
Allahabad (Uttar Pradesh)
@ modernip@sancharnet.in
Bus.Intt.: Pub.; **Spl.:** Law Books

MODERN PUBLICATIONS EDUCATIONAL PUBLISHERS
1/35, Roop Nagar, New Delhi-110007
✆ 22520298, 22812803
Estd.: 1975; **Prop.:** Ashok Sharma;
Bus.Intt.: Pub., WS, L.S. and Rt.;
Spl.: Children Text Books in English and Hindi

MODERN PUBLISHERS
Gulab Bhawan, 6, Bahadurshah Zafar Marg,
New Delhi-110002
✆ 22518122, Fax: 91-11-22546557
@ holyfaith1@vsnl.net
Estd.: 1977; **Hd.Org.:** Ashok Kumar Malhotra
Br.: Kolkata (West Bengal)
✆ 22296863, 22161670
@ hficalbr@vsnl.net
Bus.Intt.: Pub.

MODERN PUBLISHING HOUSE
9, Gola Market, Darya Ganj,
New Delhi-110002
✆ 23278869
Estd.: 1980; **Prop.:** P.G. Mittal; **Bus.Intt.:** Pub.,
WS, L.S. & Rt.; **Spl.:** Gen. & Fiction etc.

MODERN STATIONERS
Sanawer Bazar, Srinagar
(Jammu and Kashmir)
Prop.: Gulam Mohd.; **Bus.Intt.:** B.S.

MODERN STATIONERS & PUBLISHERS
44/1, Beniatola Lane, Kolkata-700009
(West Bengal)

MODERN SUBSCRIPTION AGENCY
Delhi
✆ 27123293
@ modern_in@yahoo.com
Bus.Intt.: L.S.

MODI VANIJYA PVT. LTD.
2, Ganesh Chandra Avenue, 511,
Commerce House, Kolkata-700013
(West Bengal)
Bus.Intt.: Exp.

MOHAN PUSTAK BHANDAR
Nathnagar, Bhagalpur-812006 (Bihar)
Bus.Intt.: Pub. and B.S.

MOHAN LIBRARY
35A, Surya Sen St., Kolkata-700009
(West Bengal)

MOHENJADARO
29, Sunder Nagar Market,
New Delhi-110003

MOHIT ENTERPRISES
4675/21, Ganpati Bhawan, Ansari Rd.,
Darya Ganj, New Delhi-110002
✆ (O) 23255141, 23284136 (R) 22047044,
Fax: 23280611
Estd.: 1998; **Prop.:** Pawan Goel; **Bus.Intt.:** WS;
Spl.: Acad. Books

MOHIT PRAKASHAN
AA-166, Shalimar Bagh, New Delhi-110052
✆ (O) 27224337 (R) 27253552, Fax: 27486529
@ mohitpra@ndf.vsnl.net.in
Estd.: 1990; **Prop.:** Anil Gupta; **Bus.Intt.:** Pub.;
Spl.: Children Books in English, Hindi and
Punjabi

MOHIT PUBLISHERS AND EDUCATIONAL AIDS (INDIA)
B-4, Rajkamal Sadan, Community Centre,
Opp. C.B.S.E. Office, Preet Vihar,
Delhi-110092

MOHLA NEWS AGENCY
10, Outside Hall Gate, Amritsar-143001
(Punjab)
✆ (O) 533646 (R) 550043
Hd.Org.: K.P. Mohla; **Bus.Intt.:** B.S.;
Spl.: Fiction, Non Fiction, Children-Story
Books, Coluring Books, Encyclopedia,
Furniture, Foreign Books and Magazines

MONA ASSOCIATES
527, Thippasandra, J.B. Nagar,
Bangalore-560075 (Karnataka)
✆ 25285476
@ monassociates@yahoo.com,
ojaeyk@yahoo.com
Estd.: 1997; **Hd.Org.:** N. Balchandani;
Bus.Intt.: Pub.; **Spl.:** Self-Reliance Books on
Tech., Mkt., Self-help etc. and on Graphology

MONAN
3/1, College Row, Kolkata-700009
(West Bengal)

MONDAL & SONS
14, Bankim Chatterjee St., Kolkata-700073
(West Bengal)
Hd.Org.: Sudhir Kumar Mondal

MONDAL BOOK HOUSE
78/1, Mahatma Gandhi Rd., Kolkata-700073
(West Bengal)

© 033-22414141
Bus.Intt.: Pub.; **Spl.:** Novels, Childrens Books, Short Stories and Rel. Books etc.

MONDAL BROTHERS
A-20, College Steet Market, Kolkata-700007 (West Bengal)

MONIKA BOOK DISTRIBUTORS
4264/3, 1st Floor, Ansari Rd., Darya Ganj, New Delhi-110002
© 23243979 ▮ 9810562673, Fax: 23251437
✉ monika_books@hotmail.com
Prop.: Mrs. Laxmi Nautiyal; **Bus.Intt.:** Pub.'s Rep., L.S.; **Spl.:** Beh.Sci., Soc.Sci., Comm., Sci., Pure & Applied, Med., Tech. & Law

MONITOR INFORMATION SERVICES
Hyderabad (Andhra Pradesh)
© 55787065, Fax: 27552390
✉ emonitor@hd2.dot.net.in

MONTESSORI BAL SIKSHAN SAMITI
P.O. Rajaldesar, Churu-331802 (Rajasthan)
© 232006, 232668
Hd.Org.: Kundan Mal Baid; **Bus.Intt.:** Pub.; **Spl.:** Edu. Books and Guides for Schools

MOOLESHWARI TRADING BUREAU
Panchbhaya Danapith, Junagadh (Gujarat)

MORAYA PRAKASHAN
Anushree, 40/10, Erandwane, Pune-411030 (Maharashtra)

MORNING STAR (EDUCATIONAL PUBLISHERS)
4262/3, Gali Punjabian, Ansari Rd., Darya Ganj, New Delhi-110002
© 23244660, 23246113, Fax: 91-11-23244660
✉ pinto_anl@vsnl.com, latikap@ndy.vsnl.net.in
Hd.Org.: Nidhi Pinto; **Bus.Intt.:** Manufacturers of Edu. Publications

MOSAIC BOOKS
B-17, 2nd Floor, Lajpat Nagar-II, New Delhi-110024
© 51720230, Fax: 29813869
✉ israel4@vsnl.com
Estd.: 1989; **Hd.Org.:** Reuben Israel; **Bus.Intt.:** Pub.; **Spl.:** Soc.Sci., Mang., Fiction, Poetry, etc.

MOTHERLAND BOOK CENTRE
23, Nandhi Kovil St., Teppakulam, Tiruchi-2 (Tamil Nadu)
© 223743
Hd.Org.: R. Sridhar

MOTILAL BANARSIDASS PUBLISHERS PVT. LTD.
41, U.A. Bungalow Road, Jawahar Nagar, Delhi-110007
© 23858335, 23851985, 23852747, 23854826, Fax: 91-11-23850689
✉ mlbd@vsnl.com
www.mlbd.com
Estd.: 1903; **Prop.:** R.P. Jain
Br.: Chowk, Varanasi-221001
© 91-542-2412331, 3095108
✉ mlbdvns@sify.com;
• 8, Mahalakshmi Chambers, 22, Bhula Shai Desai Road, Mumbai-400026;
© 23513526, 23516583 30922105, Fax: 91-22-4963850
✉ mlbdmumbai@vsnl.net;
• Shop No. 11-13, Sanas Plaza, 1302 Baji Rao Road, Pune-411002;
© 24486190, 30902630, Fax: 91-212-660557
✉ mlbdpune@vsnl.net;
• 8, Camac Street, Kolkata-700017,
© 22824872, 30967029, Fax: 91-33-28350246
✉ mlbdkol@vsnl.net;
• Ashok Rajpath, Patna-800004,
© 2671442, 3096812, Fax: 91-612-2657641
✉ mlbdpatna@vsnl.net;
• 236, 9th Main, III Block Jayanagar, Bangalore-560011
© 91-80-26542591, 30611690
✉ mlbdbgl@vsnl.com;
• 203, Royapettah High Road, Mylapore, Chennai-600004
© 24982315, 30902598, Fax: 91-44-4940066
✉ mlbdbook@sancharnet.in;
• A-45, Phase-1, Naraina Industrial Area, New Delhi-110028,
© 25792734, 25795180, Fax: 91-11-25797221
✉ sjp@mlbd.com;
• A-44, Phase-1, Naraina Industrial Area, New Delhi-110028
© 25793423, Fax: 91-11-25797221
✉ warehouse@mlbd.com
Bus.Intt.: Pub., WS, L.S. & Rt., Imp., Exp.; **Spl.:** Humanities & Soc.Sci., Med.

MOTIRA PUBLICATIONS
61/4, Belgachia Rd., Kolkata-700026 (West Bengal)

MOTIVATE MARKETING INTERNATIONAL
Trade Centre No. 45, Dickenson Rd., Bangalore-560042 (Karnataka)

MOTIVE BOOKS
B-124, Jangpura-B, New Delhi-110014
© 65860009, 32436524
Fax: 91-11-65860009
▮ 9810338636, 9310338636
✉ info@motivebooks.com, sales@motivebooks.com,

editor@motivebooks.com, chairman@motivebooks.com
www.motivebooks.com
Estd.: 2006; **Hd.Org.**: Saji Maramon
Bus.Intt.: Pub.; **Spl.**: Children's books

MOU BOOK STALL
P.D.S. Corner Stall-25, Ramanath Majumder St., Kolkata-700009 (West Bengal)

MOUJ PRAKASHAN GRIHA
263-C, Khatan Wadi, Goregaonkar Lane, Girgaon, Mumbai-400004 (Maharashtra)
✆ 23871050, 23872426, Fax: 23808361
Estd.: 1951; **Spl.**: Litt.

MOUJI RAM SMRITI NYAS
A-4, Ring Road, South Extension I, New Delhi-110049
✆ 24636010/30, Fax: 91-11-24636011
neetabooks@vsnl.com
www.neetaprakashan.com
Hd.Org.: R.S. Gupta
Bus.Intt.: Pub.

MOULAVI BOOK DEPOT
P.O. Box 4, Kasargod-671121 (Kerala)
✆ 220216, 222216, Fax: 223338
Estd.: 1930; **Hd.Org.**: P.M. Abdul Khader; **Bus.Intt.**: B.S.

MOULIK LIBRARY
18B, Shyama Charan Dey St., Kolkata-700073 (West Bengal)

MOULIK SAHITYA PRAKASHAN
162-E, Kamla Nagar, Delhi-110007
✆ 22514550

MOUNAM BOOKS
Eravinalloor, Kottayam-686011 (Kerala)
Estd.: 1980; **Prop.**: Mariamma Thomas; **Bus.Intt.**: Pub. and B.S.

MOUSUMI BOOK STALL
14, Bankim Chatterjee St., Kolkata-700073 (West Bengal)

MOUSUMI PRAKASHNI
1A, College Row, Kolkata-700009 (West Bengal)

MUDDASIR BOOK DEPOT
The Bund Amera Kadal, Srinagar, Kashmir (Jammu & Kashmir)
Estd.: 1994; **Prop.**: Muddasir Akhtar; **Bus.Intt.**: L.S. & Rt.

MUDIT PRAKASHAN
101A, H-2/15, Bengali Colony, Mahavir Enclave, Palam Dabri Road, New Delhi-110045
✆ 45521005, Fax: 91-11-45521005
umesh1955@gmail.com
Hd.Org.: Umesh Sharma
Bus.Intt.: Pub.; **Spl.**: Hindi books on astrology, *Vasstu*, religion, etc.

MUDRA PRAKASHAN
4858 A/24, Darya Ganj, New Delhi-110002
✆ (O) 23277230, 23280711, 26564461, 2356743 (R) 22927668, 22911185, Fax: 23277230, 26963361
selina@vsnl.com, mudrit@hotmail.com
Estd.: 1984; **Prop.**: Hemant Gupta; **Bus.Intt.**: Pub.; **Spl.**: School Books in English and Hindi

MUDRAK PUBS. & DISTRIBUTORS
W-152, Greater Kailash-I, New Delhi-110048
Prop.: S.P. Kumaria
Br.: MB-15, Antriksh Bhavan, 22, Kasturba Gandhi Marg, New Delhi-110001
✆ (O) 23730818, 23738719 (R) 26416317
Bus.Intt.: Pub.

MUHIM PRAKASHAN
109, Rish Pal Puri, Ghaziabad-201001 (Uttar Pradesh)
Hd.Org.: Om Prakash Garg

MUKESH EDUCATIONAL STORE
J-3/60, D.D.A. Flats, Kalkaji, New Delhi-110019
✆ 26991910

MUKHERJEE PUBLISHING
8B/2, Tamer Lane, Kolkata-700009 (West Bengal)

MUKHTAR ENTERPRISES
Exchange Rd., Modina Chowk, Gow Kadal, Srinagar-190001 (Jammu & Kashmir)
Estd.: 2003; **Hd.Org.**: Mukhtar Ahmad Wani; **Bus.Intt.**: Pub., WS, L.S. & Rt.; **Spl.**: Law, Humanities & Soc.Sci, Gen. & Fiction etc.

MUKTA BOOK AGENCY
G-36, First Floor, Vijay Chowk, Laxmi Nagar, Delhi-110092
✆ 22445442
Hd.Org.: Hari Narain Ojha; **Bus.Intt.**: WS, Dist.; **Spl.**: Gen. Books

MUKTA PRAKASHAN
57/2F, College St., Kolkata-700073 (West Bengal)

MUKUL PRAKASHAN
J-2, Kailash Colony, New Delhi-110048

✆ 26432876
Estd.: 1971; **Prop.**: M.K. Lauria;
Bus.Intt.: Pub.

MULBERRY PUBLICATIONS
25, Arya Bhavan, S.M. St., Kozhikode-673001 (Kerala)
✆ 740746, 403603, Fax: 765531
@ shalvyd@com
Prop.: Daisy Jacquiline Periera; **Bus.Intt.**: Pub. and B.S.; **Spl.**: Gen. Books in Malayalam

MULLICK BROTHERS
55, College St., Kolkata-700009 (West Bengal)

MULTI MEDIA HRD (P) LTD.
National House, 6, Tulloch Rd., Apollo Bunder, Mumbai-400039 (Maharashtra)
✆ 22042281, 22826312, Fax: 22836478
@ info@multimediahrd.com
Hd.Org.: Ajay Aggarwal; **Bus.Intt.**: Imp. and Dist.; **Spl.**: Books, Activity Packs, CD-ROMs, Video Cassettes on Mang. and Human Resource Development, etc.

MULTI MEDIA INFORMATIONS
40, Nikhan LD Rd., Post Box No. 378 GPO, Srinagar-190001 (Jammu and Kashmir)
✆ 279034
Estd.: 1990; **Hd.Org.**: M. Din; **Bus.Intt.**: Pub., L.S., and Rt.

MULTINATIONAL BOOK SUPPLIERS
4/78, Juhu Tarang, New D.N. Nagar, Guru Nanak Rd., Extn., Andheri West, Mumbai-400053 (Maharashtra)

MULTIPLE ACTION RESEARCH GROUP
113-A, Shahpur Jat, Near Asiad Village, New Delhi-110016

MULTITECH PUBLISHING CO.
15, Yogesh Hingwala Lane, Ghatkopar East, Mumbai-400077 (Maharashtra)
✆ 25118820, 25130147
Prop.: Savinti Shah

MUMBAI MARATHI GRANTH SANGRAHALAY
172, MMGS Marg, Dadar, Mumbai-14 (Maharashtra)

MUNNA PUSTAK BHANDAR
Kharik Bazar, Naugachia, Bhagalpur-852202 (Bihar)
Bus.Intt.: Pub. and B.S.

MUNNA PUSTAK BHANDAR
Devkund, Aurangabad-824202 (Bihar)
Bus.Intt.: Pub. and B.S.

MUNSHIRAM MANOHARLAL PUBLISHERS PVT. LTD.
54, Rani Jhansi Road, New Delhi-110055
✆ 23671668, 23673650, 23636097, Fax: 91-11-23612745
@ mrml@mrmlbooks.com
🌐 www.mrmlbooks.com
Hd.Org.: Ashok Jain; **Bus.Intt.**: Pub.

MUNTIL
28, IInd Floor, Shanthi Complex, 26, Ranganathan St., T. Nagar, Chennai-600017 (Tamil Nadu)
✆ 24347983
Prop.: M.A. Aranganathan; **Bus.Intt.**: Pub. and B.S.; **Spl.**: Classic and Creative Literary Works including little Magazines

MURAHARI THEORIES TRAINING CENTRE
5/218, Sowkathali Rd., Paramudi-623707 (Tamil Nadu)
Hd.Org.: M.N.K. Nakanathan; **Bus.Intt.**: Pub. and B.S.; **Spl.**: Med. Books

MURARI LAL & SONS
4378/4B, Ansari Rd., Darya Ganj, New Delhi-110002
✆ (O) 23261839, 23254306 (R) 23232848
Estd.: 1993; **Prop.**: Rajeev Garg;
Bus.Intt.: Pub., B.S., L.S., WS

MUSIC BOOKS
(Delhi College of Music & Dance)
E-1009, Saraswati Vihar, Pitampura, Delhi-110034
✆ 91-11-27013346
@ music@musicbooks.in
🌐 www.musicbooks.in
Hd.Org.: Madan Mohan
Bus.Intt.: Pub. and Dist.; **Spl.**: Music books

MURUGAN MAGAZINE DISTRIBUTOR
12-13, Sakina Mansion, Parsiwada, Sahar Rd., Andheri (East), Mumbai-400099 (Maharashtra)
✆ 28310574, 28262118, Fax: 28381201
@ bombay@muruganmagazine.com, info@muruganmagazne.com
🌐 www.muruganmagazine.com
Estd.: 1987; **Ch.Exe.**: D. Murugan
Br.: 105, Keytuo Industrial Estate, Kondivitta, MIDC, Andheri (East), Mumbai-400059 (Maharashtra)
✆ 28350666, 28368716, 28257418, Fax: 28381201
@ info@murganmagazine.com
• 14, Buddha Vihar Rd., Coxtown, Bangalore-560005 (Karnataka)
✆ 080-25484748, 25481696, 25451586
@ bangalore@muruganmagazine.com
• F-3, Akshya Plaza, 55-56, Harris Rd., Opp. Egmore Court, Chennai-600002 (Tamil Nadu)

✆ 044-8589472, 8589308
✉ murugan@md4.vsnl.net.in
• 1882, Jagram Mandir Marg, 2nd Floor, Kotla Mubarakpur, New Delhi
✆ 51646278, 51646279
✉ delhimurugan@vsnl.net
• 1-7-321, Panchsheela Towers, 2nd Floor, Parklane Rd., Secunderabad-500003 (Uttar Pradesh)
✆ 040-27721029, Telex: 27722047
✉ murugan@hd2.dot.net.in
• 26, Kumar Place, 2409, East St., Camp, Pune-411001 (Maharashtra)
✆ 26353103, 26342456
✉ murugan@pn3.vsnl.net.in
Bus.Intt.: Imp., Exp., Sub.Ag.; **Spl.:** Sci., Tech. & Med., Humanities & Soc.Sci.

MYTEC PROCESS (P) LTD.
204, IV Cross, Lalbagh Rd., Bangalore-560027 (Karnataka) ✆ 22233328/3279,
Fax: 080-2233262 ✉ mytec@blr.vsnl.net.in
Estd.: 1970; **Hd.Org.:** S.P. Poddar;
Bus.Intt.: Pub.; **Spl.:** Children Books

MYTRAY PUBLICATION
4697/5, 21-A, Darya Ganj,
New Delhi-110002
✆ 23273167
Hd.Org.: Pradeep Saini
Bus.Intt.: Pub.; **Spl.:** Hindi Litt.

■ ■ ■

N. BHATTACHARYA & CO.
13, College Row, Kolkata-700009 (West Bengal)

N. MALLAPPA
2120, Someshwarapuram, Tumkur-560142 (Karnataka)
✆ 08167-28013; **Hd.Org.:** N. Mallappa;
Bus.Intt.: Pub.; **Spl.:** Biography in Kannada

N.A.V. SUBRAMANIAN BOOK AGENCY
2, Diwakar St., Bharani Colony, Saligramam P.O., Chennai-600093 (Tamil Nadu)
✆ 24724018, Fax: 24724018
✉ navsba@md3.vsnl.net.in
Estd.: 1968; **Prop.:** N.A.V. Subramanian;
Bus.Intt.: L.S. and Rt., Imp., Sub.Ag.

N.B. MODERN AGENCIES
Hill Cart Rd., Siliguri-734401 (West Bengal)
✆ 2521297, 2432349, Cable: ESSENTIALS, Fax: 2432349
✉ anand_prakash68@hotmail.com, sig_nbmodern@sancharnet.in
Estd.: 1962; **Prop.:** Jiwan Ram
Br.: Nehru Rd., Darjeeling
Bus.Intt.: Dist., L.S. & Rt.

N.C. KANSIL & SONS
Kansil Bhawan, 8606, Model Basti, New Delhi-110005
✆ 23550178, 23670178, Fax: 91-11-23550340
✉ nckmaps@gmail.com, mail@nckmaps.com
🌐 www.nckmaps.com
Estd.: 1932; **Hd.Org.:** L.D. Kansil;
Bus.Intt.: Pub. and Dealer; **Spl.:** Maps, Charts, Globes, Models and Teaching Aids

N.C.R.T. BOOK & STATIONERY
Sarai, Bhagalpur-812007 (Bihar)
Bus.Intt.: Pub. and B.S.

N.G.C. NETWORK (INDIA) PVT. LTD.
150, Infantry Road, 3rd Floor, Embassy Point Bangalore-560001 (Karnataka)
✆ 66947827, 91-80-66947902
✉ farhan@in.startv.com
🌐 www.nationalgrographic.co.in
Hd.Org.: Piyush Chakraborty

N.G.P.A. PUBLICATIONS
C-7/188, Sector 7, Rohini, New Delhi-110085
✆ 91-11-27043600
✉ ngpa@ngpacollege.com
🌐 www.ngpacollege.com
Hd.Org.: Sonu Gupta
Bus.Intt.: Pub., **Spl.:** Books on commerce and business

N.I.B. PUBLISHERS
13/22, W.C.A., Karol Bagh, New Delhi-110005

N.I.S. SPARTA LTD.
8, Balaji Estate, Sudharshan Munjal Marg, Kalkaji, New Delhi-110091
✆ 26203865, Fax: 26203851
Estd.: 1992; **Prt.:** Rajendra S. Pawar, Vijay K. Thadani, Sanjeev Duggal; **Bus.Intt.:** Insti. Pub., **Spl.:** Mang. & Comm. Journals, Magazines & Periodicals

N.I.T. PUBLISHERS
H-333, New Rajender Nagar, New Delhi-110060
✆ 25718115, 25782161, Fax: 25756560
Hd.Org.: T.R. Viz

N.J. SUPPLIERS
No. 13/4, 4th Cross, Flower Garden, Magodi Rd., Bangalore-23 (Karnataka)

N.L. PUBLICATIONS
Near Police Station, Kokrajhar (Assam)

N.M. TRIPATHI PVT. LTD.
164, Shamaldas Gandhi Marg, Mumbai-400002 (Maharashtra)
✆ 22013651, 22050048
Estd.: 1888; **Chairman:** D.M. Trivedi;
Bus.Intt.: Pub. and B.S.; **Spl.:** Gen. Books and Gujarati Litt.

N.P. MANEK EXPORTS (INDIA)
286, Jolly Centre, Tilak Rd., Santacruz (West) Mumbai-400054 (Maharashtra)
Bus.Intt.: Exp.

N.P.T. OFFSET PVT. LTD.
Chennai (Tamil Nadu)
✉ nptoffset@vsnl.com
Bus.Intt.: Printers & Pub.

N.R. BOOK DISTRIBUTORS
3923/18, Kanhaiya Nagar, Tri Nagar, Delhi-110035
✆ (O) 27383169 (R) 27187496 ▮ 9810047770
✉ nrbd@mantraonline.com, nrbd@vsnl.com
Prop.: Nirmal Jit Singh Ahluwalia;
Bus.Intt.: Dist.; **Spl.:** Foreign and Indian Books on Biological Sci., Phy., Chemistry, Comp., Sci., and also Encyclopaedias and Dictionaries

N.R. BOOK DISTRIBUTORS
1900, 1st Floor, Outram Lane, Kingsway Camp, Delhi-110009

✆ 91-11-27451900 ▮ 9810047770
Prop.: Avtar Walia
Bus.Intt.: L.S.; **Spl.:** Retailers, Applied & Pure Science, Agricultural and Bio.Sci.

N.R. BOOK SYNDICATE
129, Deepali Enclave, Pitampura, Delhi-110034
✆ (O) 27011652, 27196269 (R) 27018098, 27187496, Fax: 91-11-27276256, Telex: 31-79055 SRCH IN
✉ nrbooks@email.com
Prop.: Arvind Kumar Jain; **Bus.Intt.:** Suppliers; **Spl.:** Books and Periodicals on all Sci. and Tech. Sub.

N.R. BROTHERS
N.R. House, 46, Jaora Compound, M.Y.H. Rd., Indore 452001 (Madhya Pradesh)
✆ (O) 2701337, 2701640 (R) 2461821, 2462786, Fax: 0731-2701337
✉ nrbros@sancharnet.in, nrbros@bom4.vsnl.net.in
Estd.: 1954; **Hd.Org.:** Sunil Kumar;
Bus.Intt.: Pub. and B.S.; **Spl.:** Nursing & Medical Books

N.R.A.M.H. PRAKASHANA
Koteshwara, Dakshina Kannada-576222 (Karnataka)
Hd.Org.: Dr. Bhaskar Acharya; **Bus.Intt.:** Pub.; **Spl.:** Gen. Books in Kannada and English

N.S. BOOK TRADERS
M-1/26, Budh Vihar, Phase-I, New Delhi-110041
✆ 27918601
Prop.: Nagendra Kumar Sharma; **Bus.Intt.:** WS, Rt., L.S., Sub.Ag., Pub.'s Rep.; **Spl.:** Acad., Beh.Sci., Soc.Sci., Comm., Sci., Pure & Applied, Med., Tech., Fiction, Juveniles, Rare, Journals & Magazines, Law & Comp. Sci. & Information Tech. Books

N.S. PRINTERS AND PUBLISHERS
Delhi
✆ 23285932
✉ swanitee@hotmail.com
Bus.Intt.: Pub. & Printers

NAAZ BOOK DEPOT
Shop No. 1, Mohamed Ali Building, Mehemed Ali Rd., Mumbai-400003 (Maharashtra)
Fax: 23739805
Hd.Org.: Abdulla Aji Ali Mohammed;
Bus.Intt.: Exp. of Rel.; **Spl.:** Books, Greeting Cards

NAAZ KITAB GHAR
Shandar Kapda Market, Chitli Qabar, Delhi-110006
Hd.Org.: Md. Anwar

NABA BARNAMALA
2, Bankim Chatterjee St., Kolkata-700073 (West Bengal)

NABA BHARATI BHAWAN
31A, Patuatola Lane, Kolkata-700009 (West Bengal)

NABA BHARATI PRAKASHANI
5/2, Ramanath Majumder St., Kolkata-700009 (West Bengal)

NABA MUDRAN PVT. LTD.
Kolkata (West Bengal)
✆ 25555094, 25556558, Fax: 22511876
✉ santk@cal.vsnl.net.in
Bus.Intt.: B.S.

NABAJATAK PRAKASHAN
A-64, College St. Mkt., Kolkata-700007 (West Bengal)

NABAJUGA GRANTHALAYA
Bajrakabati Rd., Cuttack-753001 (Orissa)
✆ (R) 0671-2610277
Estd.: 1965; **Prop.:** Guru Charan Patnaik; **Bus.Intt.:** Pub. and B.S.; **Spl.:** Gen. and Pol. Litt.

NABANI BOOK STALL
72, B.C. Rd., Distt. Burdwan (West Bengal)
Hd.Org.: Golak Behari Dey

NABAPATRA PRAKASHAN
6, Bankim Chatterji St., Kolkata-700073 (West Bengal)
✆ 033-2314239, 22419239, 24406092
Estd.: 1978; **Prop.:** Prasoon Basu;
Bus.Intt.: Specialised in Indological Works and brings out Classical Bengali Litt., Hist. and Appealing Essays on Aesthetics, Literary Criticism etc.

NABARUN
A-128, College St. Mkt., Kolkata-700007 (West Bengal)

NABARUN BOOK HOUSE
554/B, New Alipur, Block-N, Kolkata-700053 (West Bengal)

NABHA CHALANTIKA
7, Nabha Kundu Lane, Kolkata-700009 (West Bengal)
✆ 2241-3314, 2413-0905, 2241-4375
Estd.: 1995; **Prop.:** Himanshu Bandyopadhyay; **Bus.Intt.:** Pub.; **Spl.:** Pub.

NABHI PUBLICATIONS
N-101A, 2nd Floor, Munshiram Bldg., Connaught Place, New Delhi-110001
✆ 23354823, 43640045

Fax: 91-11-23416103, 23731117
sales@nabhipublications.com
www.nabhipublications.com
Estd.: 1967; **Hd.Org.**: Nabhi Kumar Jain; **Bus.Intt.**: Pub., Imp., Exp.; **Spl.**: Taxation, Foreign Exchange, Labour Laws, Banking and Finance, etc. in English

NABIN PUSTAK BHANDAR
New Market, Dibrugarh (Assam)

NACHIKETA PRAKASHAN
62A, Vidya Vihar, Rana Pratap Nagar, Nagpur-440022 (Maharashtra)

NAFEEZ BOOK DEPOT
Shop No. 25, East St. Galkria, 2411, Pune-411001 (Maharashtra)
Bus.Intt.: B.S. and L.S.

NAG PUBLISHERS
11-A/UA Jawahar Nagar, Post Office Building, Delhi-110007
✆ 91-11-23857975, 23855883
nagpublishers@rediffmail.com
Estd.: 1975; **Prt.**: Surendra Pratap, Narendra Pratap, Smt. Amravati Devi; **Bus.Intt.**: Pub., B.S. and L.S.; **Spl.**: Puranic, Vedic, Indology, Religious etc.

NAGALAKSHMI PUBLICATIONS
8/2, Gangai Amman Koil St., Royapettah, Chennai-600014 (Tamil Nadu)

NAGARAJ & CO. (P) LTD.
153-A, Lattice Bridge Rd., Thiruvanmiyur, Chennai-600041 (Tamil Nadu)
✆ 24413133, 24911725, Fax: 28256982
amranagaraj@cyberwaveindia.com
Bus.Intt.: B.S. & Dist.

NAGARI PRACHARINI SABHA
Varanasi-221001 (Uttar Pradesh)
✆ 23286757, Fax: 2331277
Hd.Org.: Kusumakar Pandey
Res.Off.: Aruna Asaf Ali Rd., New Delhi
Bus.Intt.: Pub.; **Spl.**: Hindi Litt. and Encyclopaedias

NAGASRI BOOK HOUSE
No. 33, Shopping Complex, Jayanagar, Bangalore-560011 (Karnataka)
✆ 26630993
Estd.: 1976; **Bus.Intt.**: Rt.

NAGASRI EDUCATIONAL BOOKSELLERS
1/58, Ist Floor, Opp. Puttanna Chitra, Mandira, 4th Block Jayanagar, Bangalore-560011 (Karnataka)
✆ 2642381
Estd.: 1983

NAGEEN PRAKASHAN PVT. LTD.
310, Western Kutchery Rd., Meerut-250001 (Uttar Pradesh)
✆ (O) 2660099, 2663154, 2643154
(R) 2660098, 2663153, Fax: 2643153
nageenprakashan@yahoo.com, nageen@rediffmail.com
Estd.: 1966; **Hd.Org.**: Nageen Chand Jain; **Bus.Intt.**: Pub.; **Spl.**: ISC, ICSE, CBSE, U.P. Board and Competition Books

NAGESWARI PUBLICATIONS
Suryaraopet, Vijayawada-520002 (Andhra Pradesh)
✆ 0866-2434817
Estd.: 1972; **Prop.**: K. Venkateswara Rao; **Bus.Intt.**: Pub.; **Spl.**: Fiction and Non-Fiction in Telugu

NAGMANI PRAKASHAN
K-24, Hauz Khas, New Delhi-110016
Hd.Org.: Dr. Amrita Preetam

NAGPUR PRAKASHAN
Seetabardi Main Rd., Nagpur-440012 (Maharashtra)

NAGPUR POPULAR BOOK SHOP
Opp. Patwardhan High School, Sitabuldi, Nagpur-440012 (Maharashtra)
✆ 2524278
Estd.: 1975; **Hd.Org.**: Tendulkar; **Bus.Intt.**: L.S. and Rt.; **Spl.**: All Sub.

NAGRAJ NOVELTIES
112, 1st Floor, Dariba Kalan Delhi-110006
✆ 23251092, 23251109, Fax: 91-11-27611227
Hd.Org.: Sanjay Gupta; **Bus.Intt.**: Dist.; **Spl.**: Comics, Children's and Edu. Books

NAGRAJ NOVELTIES
330/2, Burari, Delhi-110084
✆ 27611838, 27613599
Hd.Org.: Raj Kumar Gupta; **Bus.Intt.**: Dist.; **Spl.**: Comics, Children's and Edu. Books

NAHAR BOOK STALL
623, Khajuri Bazar, Indore-452002 (Madhya Pradesh)
✆ (O) 2451876 (R) 2469304

NAISADAK COMPANY
Delhi
deepak2107@rediffmail.com

NAI SADI PRAKASHAN PVT. LTD.
A-7, Commercial Complex, Mukherjee Nagar, Delhi-110009
✆ 27658461-2, Fax: 27652700
naisadi@vsnl.com

Hd.Org.: Satish Verma; Bus.Intt.: Pub.; Spl.: Magazines

NALANDA BOOK & RECORD SHOP
Taj Mahal Hotel, Apollo Bunder Colaba, Mumbai-400001 (Maharashtra)
✆ 22022514
Estd.: 1973; Hd.Org.: R.V. Pandit; Bus.Intt.: Rt.; Spl.: Gen. and Trade Professional, Children Books and Greeting Cads (Indian and Foreign Books)

NALANDA BOOK CENTRE
City Centre Sector IV, Bokaro Steel City, Dhanbad-827004 (Jharkhand)

NALANDA BOOK STORE
37, Markham Rd., Bangalore-560025 (Karnataka)
✆ 25510307
✉ ikon_maya@hotmail.com, ikonmaya@bgl.vsnl.net.in
Hd.Org.: K.P. Chakravarti; Bus.Intt.: B.S.; Spl.: Rare Books on Phil., Rel., Litt., Hist., Fine Arts, etc.

NALANDA PRAKASHAN
29/502, East End Apartments, Mayur Vihar, Phase I, New Delhi-110096
✆ 22742291, Fax: 91-11-23279853
Estd.: 1980; Hd.Org.: Rudra Dev Jhari; Bus.Intt.: Pub. & Dist.; Spl.: Hindi Litt., Acad. and Edu. books and Reference Books for Libraries

NALINI PRAKASHAN
56/1B, Sitaram Ghosh St., Kolkata-700009 (West Bengal)

NALINI PRAKASHAN
178, Gayatri Apts., Umred Rd., Nagpur-440024 (Maharashtra)
✆ 2742881

NAMAN PRAKASHAN
4378/4B, Gali Murari Lal, Ansari Rd., Darya Ganj, New Delhi-110002
✆ 23254306
Hd.Org.: Nitin Garg; Bus.Intt.: Pub.; Spl.: Hindi Litt.

NAMDHARI DARBAR
K-17, Rajouri Garden, New Delhi-110027
✆ 25191122, 25156625, Fax: 25446060
✉ info@namdhariworld.com
Hd.Org.: H.S. Hanspal; Bus.Intt.: Pub.; Spl.: Punjabi Litt., Specially on Sikh Gurus, Spiritualism, Freedom Struggle, etc.

NANDA BOOK SERVICE
G-1, Raja House, Nehru Place, New Delhi-110019
✆ 91-11-26227279
Hd.Org.: Gurdeep Rai; Bus.Intt.: Dist.; Spl.: Books on computer, fiction, fashion and books for children

NANDA BOOK SERVICE
545, Gali No. 3, Guru Ram Dass Nagar, Laxmi Nagar, Delhi-110092
✆ 22530838, Fax: 22459177
✉ nandabook@hotmail.com
Hd.Org.: Gurdeep Rai; Bus.Intt.: Imp. and Dist.; Spl.: Books on Travel, Tourism, Furniture, Dictionaries and Encyclopaedias

NANDI BOOK HOUSE
8th Main Rd., Ganesha Blk, Mahalakshmi Layout, Bangalore-560086 (Karnataka)

NANDI BOOK SHOP
Hotel Varanasi-Ashoka, Varanasi (Uttar Pradesh)

NARAYAN BOOK AGENCY
Gandhi Gate, Mahal, Nagpur-440002 (Maharashtra)
✆ 2729571

NARAYAN KUTTI SANYAS ASHRAM
Matta Tekari Road, Dewas (Madhya Pradesh)
✆ 91-11-23381403
✉ urmil95@yahoo.co.in
Hd.Org.: U.K. Sharma
Bus.Intt.: Pub. and Dist.;
Spl.: Books on Spiritualism in Hindi

NARAYANA GURUKULAM
Sreenivasapuram, Varkala-695145 (Kerala)
✆ 0472-2602398
Estd.: 1953; Hd.Org.: Swami Muni Narayana Prasad; Bus.Intt.: Pub.; Spl.: Humanities

NARAYANA IIT ACADEMY
47-B, Kalu Sarai, Near IIT Flyover, New Delhi-110016
✆ 91-11-46080619
Bus.Intt.: Pub.

NARAYANA PRESS & BOOK STALL
Main Rd., Attingal, Thiruvananthapuram-695101 (Kerala)
Estd.: 1968; Prop.: N. Chellappan Pillai; Bus.Intt.: B.S.

NARAYANA PRINTING AND PUBLISHING
160, "Susheel", Ramnagar, Nagpur-440010 (Maharashtra)
✆ 91-712-2535913

NARAYANI STORES
Tarar, Bhagalpur-813226 (Bihar)
Bus.Intt.: Pub. and B.S.

NARBADA BOOK DEPOT
Andnerdeo, Jabalpur-482002 (Madhya Pradesh)
Prop.: S.K. Indirkhya

NARENDRA BOOK AGENCY & PUBLISHING HOUSE
1417, Gali Kishan Dutt, Maliwara,
Delhi-110006
✆ 23268470, 23259412, Fax: 23259412
✉ info@ebooksvision.com,
info@nph-india.com
www.ebooksvision.com, www.nph-india.com
Estd.: 1974; **Prop.:** N.K. Jain;
Bus.Intt.: Pub. & B.S.; **Spl.:** Books on Sci., Tech., Biological Sci. as also Acad. Journals and Magazines

NARESH PUBLISHERS
111, Shankar Rd. Market,
New Rajinder Nagar, New Delhi-110060
✆ 25723235, 25754442, 25746485,
Fax: 25746485
✉ narpubs@nda.vsnl.net.in
Estd.: 1972; **Hd.Org.:** Mohinder Chowdhary;
Bus.Intt.: Pub., WS; **Spl.:** Public and Convent School Books in English, Hindi, Urdu, Punjabi, Nepali

NARGIS INTERNATIONAL
69/2, Dakshinpura Rd., Kolkata-700028
(West Bengal)
Bus.Intt.: Exp.

NARIN PRAKASHAN
151-East Gobind Nagar, Sultanwind Rd.,
Amritsar (Punjab)

NARKAR PRAKASHAN
170/8, Purani Mandi, Ajmer-305001
(Rajasthan)

NARMADA NIKETAN BOOK DISTRIBUTORS
26/87, Shakti Nagar, New Delhi-110007
Prop.: Om Prakash; **Bus.Intt.:** L.S.

NARMADA PATHIPAGAM
16/7, Rajabethev St., T. Nagar,
Chennai-600017 (Tamil Nadu)
✆ 28280466, 28282237, Fax: 91-44-28253609
Hd.Org.: T.S. Ramalingam; **Bus.Intt.:** Pub., Exp., Manufacturers; **Spl.:** Tamil Book

NARNE PUBLICATIONS PVT. LTD.
8, Y.M.C.A. Complex, S.P. Rd.,
Secunderabad-500003 (Andhra Pradesh)
✆ 27800728, Fax: 27840246
✉ deepa@narne.com

NAROSA BOOK DISTRIBUTORS PVT. LTD.
22, Delhi Medical Association Rd.,
Darya Ganj, New Delhi-110002
✆ 23258579, 23259263, Fax: 91-11-23258934
✉ info@narosa.com
www.narosa.com
Estd.: 1977; **Hd.Org.:** Rosemarie Mehra
Br.: 35-36, Greams Rd., Thousand Lights,
Chennai-600006 (Tamil Nadu)
✆ 28295362, 28294592, Fax: 044-28290377
• 306, Shiv Centre, DBC Sector 17,
K.U. Bazar P.O., New Mumbai-400705
(Maharashtra)
✆ 27896907, 27892210, Fax: 27891930
• 2F-2G, Shivam Chambers, 53, Syed Amir Avenue, Kolkata-19 (West Bengal)
✆ 22814809, 22814834 Fax: 22814778
• Narosa Information Services & Narosa Publishing House, 22, Darya Ganj,
Delhi Medical Association Rd.,
New Delhi-110002
✆ 23243415-17, Fax: 23258934, 23243225
✉ narosa@ndc.vsnl.net.in,
narosad1@nda.vsnl.net.in
Bus.Intt.: Pub. and Dist.; **Spl.:** Indian and Foreign Sci., Engg., Tech. and Med. Books and Journals

NASIM BOOK DEPOT
25, G.B. Marg, Lucknow-225001
(Uttar Pradesh)

NASIR BOOK DEPOT (REGD.)
1, Aziza Building, Hazrat Nizamuddin,
New Delhi-110013
✆ 24350995, Fax: 91-11-26827731
Bus.Intt.: Pub., Printers, B.S., Exp.; **Spl.:** Holy *Qura'ans* and Islamic Books in (Urdu, Hindi, English and Arabic) and Islamic Items, etc.

NASU PUBLICATION INTERNATIONAL
20-B, Market St., Kolkata-87 (West Bengal)

NATAKA GRANDHA SALA
Vaikom P.O., Kottayam-686141 (Kerala)
Estd.: 1978; **Hd.Org.:** Vekkan Chairman;
Bus.Intt.: Pub. and B.S.; **Spl.:** Theatre Book

NATH PUBLISHING CO.
26B, Panditya Palace, Kolkata-700029
(West Bengal)
✆ 033-22410362, 2766946; **Hd.Org.:** Sumir Kumar Nath

NATH PUSTAK BHANDAR
194, Dariba Kalan, Delhi-110006
Hd.Org.: Kedarnath Agarwal; **Bus.Intt.:** Exp.;
Spl.: Books in Hindi

NATIONAL ACADEMY OF INDIA
164, K.B. Nagar, Fatehpur-212601
(Uttar Pradesh)

NATIONAL AHINSA FOUNDATION
446, First C. Rd., Jodhpur-342003 (Rajasthan)

NATIONAL ARCHIVES OF INDIA
Janpath, New Delhi-110001

NATIONAL ATLAS AND THEMATIC MAPPING ORGANISATION
CGO Complex, DF Block, 7th Floor, Salt Lake City, Kolkata-700064 (West Bengal)
✆ 033-23346460, Fax: 23346460

natmo@giascl01.vsnl.net.in
Hd.Org.: P. Nag; **Bus.Intt.:** Pub.; **Spl.:** Sci. and also Atlases and Maps

NATIONAL BOOK AGENCY
Opp. Setupati Higher Sc. School, 184, North Veli St., IInd Floor, Madurai-625001 (Tamil Nadu)
✆ 0452-2341304
nba_mduss@rediffmail.com
Bus.Intt.: B.S.

NATIONAL BOOK AGENCY FOR ISBN
Department of Higher Education, Ministry of Human Resource Development, New Delhi-110001
✆ 23394687, 91-11-23382436
Hd.Org.: Suresh Chand

NATIONAL BOOK AGENCY (P) LTD.
D.D. 42, Sector 1, Bidhan Nagar, Kolkata-700064 (West Bengal)
✆ (O) 033-2344530, 2343168 (R) 22411989
Estd.: 1939; **Hd.Org.:** Sunil Kumar Ganguli; **Bus.Intt.:** Pub.; **Spl.:** Pol.Sci., Litt., Popular Sci. and Med. etc. in Bengali, English, Hindi and Urdu

NATIONAL BOOK CENTRE
G-1, Prateek Apartments, 123, Vishnu Puri, Piplyarao, Indore-452001 (Madhya Pradesh)
✆ 269076
Estd.: 1965; **Hd.Org.:** Hardit Singh Daall; **Bus.Intt.:** L.S., Rt.

NATIONAL BOOK CENTRE
27-29, A.K. Gopalan Bhawan, Bhai Veer Singh Marg, New Delhi-110001
✆ 23344918, Fax: 23334165
Hd.Org.: Vandana Sharma; **Bus.Intt.:** Pub., Rt. B.S.

NATIONAL BOOK CENTRE
Nasik (Maharashtra)
✆ 2314821
nationalbooks@rediffmail.com
Bus.Intt.: B.S.

NATIONAL BOOK DEPOT
Sibandih, Bokaro Steel City, Dhanbad-827008 (Jharkhand)

NATIONAL BOOK DEPOT
Gorakhpur (Uttar Pradesh)
✆ 2339533, 2340342
national_book_depot@hotmail.com
Bus.Intt.: B.S.

NATIONAL BOOK DEPOT (THE)
Mumbai (Maharashtra)
✆ 24131362, 24165274, Fax: 24130877
prachint@bom7.vsnl.net.in
Bus.Intt.: Pub.

NATIONAL BOOK DISTRIBUTORS
J, 571/1, 3rd Cross, Ramakrishnapuram, S.C. Rd. (Behind Sudarshan Lodge), Bangalore-560009 (Karnataka)
✆ 22254517
Bus.Intt.: Rt., L.S. (Imp. and B.S.)

NATIONAL BOOK DISTRIBUTORS
8-B/20, Jawahar Society, Govindnagar, Borivali (West), Mumbai-400092 (Maharashtra)
✆ 28015163
Bus.Intt.: Stockists & Dealers; **Spl.:** Sci., Tech., Engg. and Higher Acad. Books

NATIONAL BOOK EMPORIUM
Nathnagar, Bhagalpur-812006 (Bihar)
Bus.Intt.: Pub. and B.S.

NATIONAL BOOK ENTERPRISES
3-4-874, Anuradha Apartments, Barkatpura, Hyderabad-500027 (Andhra Pradesh)
✆ 27561890, 27564442, Fax: 27560146
nbe77@rediffmail.com
Prop.: V. Sarda Devi; **Bus.Intt.:** L.S.

NATIONAL BOOK HOUSE
Dispensary Rd., Dehradun-248001 (Uttarakhand)
✆ 0135-2659430, Fax: 0135-2721470
Estd.: 1949; **Hd.Org.:** S.K. Jain; **Bus.Intt.:** WS (NCERT Sole Distr.) and L.S.; **Spl.:** School Book

NATIONAL BOOK HOUSE
Opp. High Court, Gwalior-474009 (Madhya Pradesh)
✆ 0751-2323640, 2364442
Prop.: M.L. Singhal; **Bus.Intt.:** Dist., WS, Rt., L.S.; **Spl.:** Tech., Edu. Books and Back Volumes of Journals

NATIONAL BOOK ORGANISATION (PUBLISHERS & DISTRIBUTORS)
H-39, Green Park Extension, New Delhi-110016
✆ 55652928 ▮ 9818341070
Prop.: Amarjeet Kaur Marwah
Br.Off.: 4378/4B, Murarilal St., 203, J.M.D. House, Ansari Rd., Darya Ganj, New Delhi-110002 ✆ 23271519
Bus.Intt.: Pub., Dist. and L.S.; **Spl.:** Agri., Eco., Geo., Hist., Library Sci., Litt., Pol.Sci., Public Administration, Books on Punjab, Rel., Sikhism and Sol.

NATIONAL BOOK SHOP
32-B, Pleasure Garden Market, Chandni Chowk, Delhi-110006
✆ 23278392, 23264342
nbs_books@sify.com
Hd.Org.: Rajinder Singh; **Bus.Intt.:** Pub.;

Spl.: Edu., Health, Astrology, Women Studies, Cookery as also Novels, Stories and Reference Books in Punjabi

NATIONAL BOOK STALL
Manorama Junction, Kottayam-686001 (Kerala)
Hd.Org.: Sahitya Pravarthaka Co-operative Societies Ltd., Kottayam

NATIONAL BOOK STALL
Koppikar Rd., Hubli-580020 (Maharashtra)
✆ (O) 0836-2367902 (R) 2353209
✉ nationalbook1@rediffmail.com
Estd.: 1952; **Prop.:** S.T. Viraktamath (Raju)
Br.: Aziz Mansion, Koppikar Rd., Hubli (Maharashtra)
✆ 0836-2260317
Bus.Intt.: WS, L.S.

NATIONAL BOOK STORE
Barahiya, Monghyr-811311 (Bihar)

NATIONAL BOOK STORE
Vidyapeeth Chowk, Lakhisarai, Monghyr-811311 (Bihar)

NATIONAL BOOK STORES
Ratanji Rd., Dhanbad-826001 (Jharkhand)

NATIONAL BOOK STORES
Kirkeno, Dhanbad-828147 (Jharkhand)

NATIONAL BOOK TRUST, INDIA
A-5, Green Park, New Delhi-110016
✆ 26569962, 26568052, 26561684, 26564020, Fax: 26851795
✉ nbtindia@ndb.vsnl.net.in
🌐 www.nbtindia.org.in
Hd.Org.: Shashi Shekhar Sharma
Br.: 5A, Bhawani Dutta East, Kolkata-700069 (West Bengal) ✆ 2413899
• Municipal Urdu Primary School, Babula Tank, Cross Lane, Opp. J.J. Hospital, Mumbai-400009 (Maharashtra) ✆ 23720442
• Bangalore (Karnataka) ✆ 6711994
✉ nbtindiasro@vsnl.net
• Bulandshahar (Uttar Pradesh)
✆ 05732-235199
✉ nbtb2@hotmail.com
Bus.Intt.: Pub.; **Spl.:** Gen. Readers and Children in English and Indian Languages

NATIONAL BUREAU OF SOIL
Survey & Land Use Planning, I.A.R.I. Campus, Pusa, New Delhi-110012

NATIONAL CENTRE FOR ORIENTAL STUDIES
A-19, Vijaya Nagar, (S.G.T.B. Nagar), Delhi-110009

NATIONAL COMPUTER LIBRARY (REGD.)
11/1, Prem Nagar, Behind Tilak Nagar Bus Stop, New Delhi-110058
✆ 25514223
Prop.: Ashok Arora; **Bus.Intt.:** Rt., WS, L.S.

NATIONAL COUNCIL FOR PROMOTION OF URDU LANGUAGE
Ministry of Human Resource Development, (Department of Secondary & Higher Education), Govt. of India West Block-1, Wing-6, R.K. Puram, New Delhi-110066
✆ 26103381, 26103938, 26179657, Fax: 91-11-26108159
✉ urducouncil@gmail.com, alijaved40@hotmail.com
🌐 www.urducouncil.nic.in
Hd.Org.: M. Hamidullah Bhat
Br.: Distant Education and Book Promotion, West Block-8, Wing-7, R.K. Puram, New Delhi-110066
✆ 26109746, 26169416, Fax: 91-11-26106425
• 22-7-110, III Floor, Sajid Yar Jung Complex, Block No. 1-5, Pathergatti, Hyderabad-500002
✆ 91-40-24415194
Bus.Intt.: Pub.; **Spl.:** Urdu Litt. for Promotion of Urdu Language

NATIONAL COUNCIL FOR SCIENCE & TECHNOLOGY COMMUNICATION
Tech. Bhavan, New Mehrauli Rd., New Delhi-110016

NATIONAL COUNCIL OF EDUCATION BENGAL
Jadavpur University, Kolkata-700007 (West Bengal)

NATIONAL COUNCIL OF EDUCATIONAL RESEARCH AND TRAINING
Sri Aurobindo Marg, New Delhi-110016
✆ 26560620, 26864811, Fax: 91-11-26868419
✉ proncert@yahoo.co.in
🌐 www.ncert.nic.in
Hd.Org.: Puran Chand
Br.: Chacha Nehru Bhawan (NCERT), Sri Aurobindo Marg, New Delhi-110016
✆ 26864801, 26864802, 26864803, Fax: 91-11-26864141
✉ proncert@yahoo.co.in
🌐 www.ciet.nic.in/welcome;
• Capt. D.P. Chaudhary Marg, Ajmer-305004
✆ 2643720, 2643864, 2643862, Fax: 91-145-2643871; • Shyamala Hills, Bhopal-462013, ✆ 2661300, 2661305, Fax: 91-755-2661668
✉ riebpl@sancharnet.in; • Sachivalaya Marg, Bhubaneswar-751022, ✆ 2540627, 2541625, 2541568, 2541620, 2542667, Fax: 91-674-2543782, ✉ riebbs@ori.nic.in
• Manasagangothri, Mysore-570006

© 2411830, 2411411, Fax: 91-821-2415665
www.mylibnet.org; • Jowai Road, Laitumukhrah, Shillong-793003, © 2226317, 2226359, 2229891, Fax: 91-364-2226359
• 131, Zone-II, M.P. Nagar, Bhopal-462011
© 2558160, 2556517, 2556504,
Fax: 91-755-2558128,
pssciv_bhopal@yahoo.co.in
www.psscive.nic.in
Bus.Intt.: Pub.; **Spl.:** School Textbooks, Workbooks, Supplementary Readers, Teachers' Guides, Research Monographs and Year Book on Edu.

NATIONAL EDUCATIONAL BOOKSELLERS
Tani Bai Nivas, Station Rd., Wadala, Mumbai-400031 (Maharashtra)

NATIONAL GANDHI MUSEUM
Rajghat, New Delhi-110002
© 23328310, 23310168, Fax: 23311793
gandhimk@nda.vsnl.net.in
Hd.Org.: Y.P. Anand; **Bus.Intt.:** Pub. and Dist.; **Spl.:** Litt. of Gandhi, Freedom Movement, Hist., Politics, Nature Cure, etc.

NATIONAL INFORMATION CENTRE FOR DRUGS AND PHARMACEUTICALS
Govt. of India Central Drug Research Instt., P.B. No. 173, Lucknow-226001 (Uttar Pradesh)

NATIONAL INFORMATION CENTRE FOR TEXTILES & ALLIED SUBJECTS
3rd Floor, Atira, P.O. Polytechnic, Ahmedabad-380015 (Gujarat)

NATIONAL INSTITUTE FOR THE VISUALLY HANDICAPPED LTD.
116, Rajpur Rd., Dehradun-248001 (Uttarakhand)
© 0135-224491
Hd.Org.: Col. A.K. Verma

NATIONAL INSTITUTE OF CONSTRUCTION MANAGEMENT & RESEARCH
Walchand Centre, Tardeo Rd., Mumbai-400034 (Maharashtra)
© 24952453, 24927847, Fax: 24961183
nicmarmb@giasbm01.vsnl.net.in, giasbm01.vsnl.net.in
www. nicmar.org
Estd.: 1983; **Hd.Org.:** Prof. K.N. Vaid; **Bus.Intt.:** Pub.; **Spl.:** Construction, Infrastructure and Mang. in English

NATIONAL INSTITUTE OF DESIGN
Paldi, Ahmedabad-380007 (Gujarat)
© 26639692-3-4, Fax: 26605242, 26621167, Cable: INSTITUTE, Telex: 1216322, N.D. IN
publication@nid.edu
www.nid.edu
Estd.: 1961; **Hd.Org.:** Darlie O. Koshy
Br.: C-141, Defence Colony, New Delhi-110024 © 2619634 • B-112, Rajaji Nagar, IND Estate, Bangalore-560044 (Karnataka) © 2359873
Bus.Intt.: Books on Design

NATIONAL INSTITUTE OF EDUCATIONAL PLANNING & ADMINISTRATION
17-B, Sri Aurobindo Marg, New Delhi-110016
© 26962120, 26962126, 2696780,
Fax: 26853041, 26865180
niepa@vsnl.com
Hd.Org.: B.P. Khandelwal; **Bus.Intt.:** Pub.; **Spl.:** Edu. Books

NATIONAL INSTITUTE OF INDUSTRIAL RESEARCH
106-E, Kamla Nagar, P.B. No. 2162, Delhi-110007
© 23823955, 23835654, 23845886,
Fax: 23841561
niir@vsnl.com
www.niir.org
Estd.: 1994; **Hd.Org.:** Ajay Kumar Gupta; **Bus.Intt.:** Pub.; **Spl.:** Books on Industry as also Directories, Project Reports, Market Survey Studies, etc.

NATIONAL INSTITUTE OF OCEANOGRAPHY
Publication Division, Dona Paula, Goa-403004

NATIONAL INSTITUTE OF OPEN SCHOOLING (NIOS)
B-31, B. Kailash Colony, New Delhi-110048
© 26452331, Fax: 26481569
bhdhyani@hotmail.com
www.nois.ac.in
Hd.Org.: Sunil Kaura; **Bus.Intt.:** Autonomous organisation under the Ministry of HRD, Govt. of India, Providing opportunities for continuing education

NATIONAL INSTITUTE OF PERSONAL MANAGEMENT
45, Jhowtala Rd., (Ist Floor), PB No. 10725, Kolkata-700019 (West Bengal)

NATIONAL INSTITUTE OF RURAL DEVELOPMENT
Rajendranagar, Hyderabad (Andhra Pradesh)

NATIONAL INSTITUTE OF SCIENCE COMMUNICATION
Dr. K.S. Krishnan Marg, Near Pusa Gate, New Delhi-110012
© 25843359, 25786301, Fax: 25843359
niscom@sirnetd.ernet.in, sales@niscom.res.in
www.niscair.res.in
Hd.Org.: V.K. Gupta; **Bus.Intt.:** Pub.; **Spl.:** Books and Journals on Sci. and Tech.

NATIONAL INSTITUTE OF SMALL INDUSTRY EXTENSION TRAINING
Yousufguda, Hyderabad-500045 (Andhra Pradesh)

NATIONAL LAW SCHOOL OF INDIA UNIVERSITY
Nagarbheri PB No. 7201, Bangalore-560072 (Karnataka)

NATIONAL LIBRARY
Sibmandir, Siliguri, P.O. Kadam, Tala-734433 (West Bengal)
✆ 2450907
Estd.: 1993; **Prop.:** Rathin Majumder
Br.: H.O. New Market, P.O. Dibrugarh-486001 (Assam)
Bus.Intt.: Rt., L.S., WS, Pub.

NATIONAL LIBRARY CENTRE
7-1, Chaitanyapuri, Malakpet, Hyderabad-500036 (Andhra Pradesh)

NATIONAL MUSEUM (PUBLICATION DIVISION)
Janpath, New Delhi-110001
Bus.Intt.: Publication Cell

NATIONAL PHYSICAL LABORATORY (CSIR) (Publication Division)
Pusa, New Delhi-110012

NATIONAL PRODUCTIVITY COUNCIL
5-6, Institutional Area, Lodhi Rd., New Delhi-110003
Hd.Org.: Mrs. Krishna Sahi

NATIONAL PSYCHOLOGICAL CORPORATION
4/230, Kacheri Ghat, Agra-282004 (Uttar Pradesh)

NATIONAL PUBLICATIONS
22, Anil Apartments Ist Floor, Jagdusha Nagar, Ghatkopar, West Mumbai-400086 (Maharashtra)

NATIONAL PUBLISHERS
206, Bidhan Sarani, Kolkata-700006 (West Bengal)
Hd.Org.: Ganendranath Banerjee

NATIONAL PUBLISHING HOUSE
2/35, Ansari Rd., Darya Ganj, New Delhi-110002
✆ 23274161, 23275267, Fax: 23254407
sales@nationalpublishinghouse.com
www.nphbooks.com
Estd.: 1952; **Hd.Org.:** S.K. Malik;
Bus.Intt.: Pub.; **Spl.:** Gen., Children, Reference and Career Books

NATIONAL PUBLISHING HOUSE
C-51, College St. Mkt., Kolkata-700007 (West Bengal)

NATIONAL RESEARCH DEVELOPMENT CORPORATION
20-22, Zamroodpur Community Centre, Kailash Colony Extn., New Delhi-110048

NATIONAL SCHOOL OF BANKING
Hyderabad (Andhra Pradesh)
✆ 23387715, Fax: 23387846
csvepa@yahoo.com
Bus.Intt.: B.S.

NATIONAL SCHOOL OF DRAMA
Bahawalpur House, 1 Bhagwandas Road, New Delhi-110001
✆ 23389402, 23387137, 23382821, Fax: 23384288
nsdr@rediffmail.com, info@nsd.gov.in
www.nsd.gov.in
Hd.Org.: Anuradha Kapur; **Bus.Intt.:** Pub.;
Spl.: Books on Plays and Dramas

NATIONAL SCIENCE WORKGROUP
A-91, Ashok Vihar Phase II, Delhi-110052
✆ 27135288
Hd.Org.: Dr. (Mrs.) Neeta; **Bus.Intt.:** Pub.;
Spl.: Projects and Models Construction for Schools (Sci., Geo.)

NATIONAL TRADERS
Opp. Apana Bazar, M.G. Rd., Valsad-396001 (Gujarat)

NATIONS LEAGUE OF PEN PALS
73, Surya Niketan Vikas Marg Extn., New Delhi-110092
✆ 22156117

NATPAGAM
140, Sami Naicken, St., Chintadripet, Chennai-600002 (Tamil Nadu)

NATPUR BOOK DEPOT
Mangalkot, Sant Bazar, Nadiad (Gujarat)

NATRAJ BOOK CENTRE
Natraj Cinema Compound, Ashram Rd., Ahmedabad-380009 (Gujarat)
✆ 26587930, 26588750, Fax: 079-26440767
natrajbooks@yahoo.com
Bus.Intt.: B.S.; **Spl.:** Adv. Books for Lib., Gen. Books and International Magazines

NATRAJ PRAKASHAN
A-98, Ashok Vihar, Phase-I, Delhi-110052
✆ 27219251, 27132906, Fax: 27148006
Hd.Org.: Smt. Kusum Goynka; **Bus.Intt.:** Exp.;
Spl.: Books in Hindi

NATRAJ PRAKASHAN
Rama Mukund Ranganath Maharaj, Prabhani, (Uttar Pradesh)

NATRAJ PUBLISHERS
17, Rajpur Rd., Dehradun-248001 (Uttarakhand)
✆ 2653382, 2654584, Fax: 2749914, 2651108
natrajbooks@vsnl.com
Estd.: 1965; **Prop.:** Upendra Arora;
Bus.Intt.: Pub., L.S. & Rt., Imp., Exp.;

Spl.: Humanities & Soc.Sci., Sci. & Tech., Gen. & Fiction etc.

NATUN ASOM MUDRON ARU PRAKASHAN
Panchabati Malow Ali, P.O. Box No. 78, Jorhat-785001 (Assam)
Bus.Intt.: Quality Printers, Pub. and International B.S.

NATURE CURE & YOGA HEALTH CENTRE
Lajpat Bhawan, Lajpat Nagar-IV, New Delhi-110024
✆ 26479601

NATURE CURE BOOKS
Kurumassery-683579 (Kerala)
Estd.: 1984; **Prop.:** Thomas Maliekal; **Spl.:** Books on Natural Therapy

NATURE PUBLISHING GROUP
3A, 4th Floor, DLF Corporate Park, Gurgaon-122002 (Haryana)
✆ 2881053-54, Fax: 91-124-2881052
j.srinivasan@nature.com
www.nature.com
Hd.Org.: Jaishree Srinivasan
Bus.Intt.: Pub.; **Spl.:** Journals

NATURE PUBLISHING GROUP
5A/12, Ansari Rd., Darya Ganj, New Delhi-110002
✆ 23244186, Fax: 23272010
harpal@nature.com
www.nature.com
Hd.Org.: Harpal Singh Gill; **Bus.Intt.:** Pub.; **Spl.:** Sci. Magazine, *Nature*

NATYA SAMPADA PRAKASHAN
5-6, Shivaji Temple, Dadar, Mumbai-400028 (Maharashtra)

NAV BHARAT BOOK HOUSE
D. No. 28-1-59/2, Karl Marx Rd., Vijayawada-520002 (Andhra Pradesh)
✆ (O) 0866-2430578 (R) 2435574; **Prop.:** P.S. Prakasa Rao; **Bus.Intt.:** Pub.; **Spl.:** Fiction and Health Sci. Series, Previously in Telugu

NAV BHARAT PRAKASHAN MANDIR
Pansari Bazar, Post Box No. 36, Saharanpur, (Uttar Pradesh)
✆ (O) 2744408 (R) 2745869
Estd.: 1965; **Hd.Org.:** Pramendra Bansal; **Bus.Intt.:** Pub.; **Spl.:** Edu. Books in English, Hindi and Urdu

NAV BHARAT PUBLICATIONS CO.
13/7, Gopalapuram First St., Chennai-600086 (Tamil Nadu)
✆ (O) 28114560 (R) 28111751, Fax: 044-28111554
navbharat@kmronline.com
Estd.: 1947; **Prop.:** Ishwarlal Sharma; **Bus.Intt.:** Pub., B.S., Exp.; **Spl.:** Juvenile/ Children, Gen. & Fiction etc.

NAV BHARAT PUBLICATIONS
33-15-6, Kadiyalavari St., Seetharampuram, Vijayawada-520004 (Andhra Pradesh)

NAV SAHITYA PRAKASHAN
15-UB, Bunglow Rd., Jawahar Nagar, Delhi-110007
✆ (O) 22912461 (R) 27139468
Estd.: 1957; **Hd.Org.:** O.P. Anand; **Bus.Intt.:** Pub.; **Spl.:** Edu. Books in English, Hindi and Urdu

NAV SAHITYA PRINTING & PUBLISHING COMPANY (P) LIMITED
5/E, Rani Jhansi Rd., New Delhi-110055
✆ 27524701, 27524924
Hd.Org.: Shameem Faizi; **Bus.Intt.:** Rt., WS, Pub., L.S.

NAV SAKCHHAR PRAKASHAN
21, Chetak Bridge, Maharana Pratap Nagar, Bhopal (Madhya Pradesh)

NAV SAKCHHAR PRAKASHAN
B-50, Sitaram Hida Ki Mori, Galta Rd., Jaipur-302003 (Rajasthan)
✆ 2601663
Hd.Org.: Bagbandas Jasoriya

NAV SUBRAMANIAN BOOK AGENCY
2, Diwakar St., Bharani Colony, Saligramam P.O., Chennai-600093 (Tamil Nadu)
✆ 2424018
Hd.Org.: N.A.V. Subramanian; **Bus.Intt.:** L.S., Sub.Ag.; **Spl.:** Sci., Tech. and Business Mang.

NAVA SAHITYA
Samadevi Rasta, Belgaum (Karnataka)

NAVABHARAT BOOK HOUSE
D. No. 28-1-59/2, Karl Marx Rd., Vijayawada-520002 (Andhra Pradesh)

NAVABHARAT BOOK STALL
Kirloskar Rd., Belgaum-590002 (Karnataka)

NAVAJIVAN PUBLISHING HOUSE
Navajivan Trust, P.O. Navajivan, Ahmedabad-380014 (Gujarat)
✆ (Press) 7542634 (O) 7540635 (R) 6442188
Estd.: 1929; **Hd.Org.:** Jitendra Desai; **Bus.Intt.:** Pub., WS, L.S., and Rt., Exp.

NAVAJIVAN TRUST
130, Princess St., Mumbai-400002 (Maharashtra)
✆ 2019756
Bus.Intt.: Pub.

Spl.: Famous "An Autobiography" by Mahatma Gandhi in Many Indian Languages

NAVAJOTHI BOOK HOUSE
20, Church St., Padmini Nagar, Pondicherry-605012
✆ 225320

NAVAJYOTHI PUBLICATIONS, PUBLISHERS & BOOK DISTRIBUTORS
Eluru Rd., Vijayawada-520062 (Andhra Pradesh)

NAVAKARNATAKA PUBLICATIONS (P) LTD.
Embassy Centre, 11, Crescent Rd., Kumara Part East, Post Box No. 5159, Bangalore-560001 (Karnataka)
✆ 22203580-81-82, Cable: BOOKCENTRE, Fax: 22203582
nkp@bgl.vsnl.net.in
www.navakarnatakabooks.com
Estd.: 1960; **Man.Dir.:** R.S. Rajaram
Br.: Navakarnataka Publications, Wholesale Division, 5th Floor, Main Gandhi Nagar, Bangalore-560009 ✆ 22251382
• Navakarnataka Publications, Kempegowda Circle, Bangalore-560009 ✆ 22872385
• Navakarnataka Publications, K.S. Rao Rd., Mangalore-575001 ✆ 2441016
• Navakarnataka Publications, Prestige Shopping Arcade, Ramaswamy Circle, Mysore-570024 ✆ 2424094
• Navakarnataka Publications, Station Rd., Gulbarga-585102 ✆ 224302
Bus.Intt.: Pub., WS, L.S. & Rt.; **Spl.:** Humanities & Soc.Sci., Sci. & Tech., Juvenile/Children, Gen. & Fiction etc.

NAVANEET PRAKASHAN
23, Hevait Rd., Allahabad-211003 (Uttar Pradesh)
✆ 2402517, Fax: 0532-2405386
Hd.Org.: Mrs. Shbeta Bansal

NAVARATNA BOOK HOUSE
28-2-20, Rahiman St., Arundolpet, Vijayawada-520002 (Andhra Pradesh)
✆ (R) 2432813
Estd.: 2001; **Bus.Intt.:** Pub.; **Spl.:** Children's Books in Telugu

NAVASAHITI BOOK HOUSE
Eluru Rd., Vijayawada-520002 (Andhra Pradesh)
✆ 0866-2432885
Estd.: 1975; **Prop.:** K. Prakasa Rao; **Bus.Intt.:** Pub.; **Spl.:** Fiction and Non-Fiction Books in Telugu

NAVAYUGA BOOK HOUSE
Hyderabad (Andhra Pradesh)
✆ 24754688
navayuga79@hotmail.com
Bus.Intt.: B.S.

NAVBHARAT SAHITYA MANDIR
134, Shamaldas Gandhi Marg, Princess St., P.B. No. 2835, Mumbai-400002 (Maharashtra)
✆ 22017213
Bus.Intt.: Exp.

NAVBHARAT SAHITYA MANDIR
Opp. Pataka Pole Bus-Stand, Gandhi Rd., Ahmedabad-380001 (Gujarat)
✆ 079-2380253

NAVCHETAN PRAKASHAN
G-5, Gali No. 16, Rajapuri, Uttam Nagar, New Delhi-110059
9810101036
Hd.Org.: Sarvesh Sharma; **Bus.Intt.:** Dist. and Pub.; **Spl.:** Hindi language books

NAVDEEP PUBLICATIONS
953, Nehru Road, Arjun Nagar, Kotla Mubarakpur, New Delhi-110003
✆ 24697006, 24697009, Fax: 91-11-24618474
info@navdeepublications.com
www.navdeepublications.com
Estd.: 1938; **Hd.Org.:** Navdeep Kapur
Br.: 19-B, CIL Layout, Sanjay Nagar, RMV. Extension Stage-II, Bangalore-94
✆ 91-80-23412409
info@navdeepublications.com
• Mai Hiran Gate, Jalandhar
✆ 91-181-280243, 281158
info@navdeepublications.com
Bus.Intt.: Pub.; **Spl.:** Edu. Books

NAVEEN BOOKS
Gram-Gamri, Gali No. 1, Chowdhri Ashok Ka Makan, Bhajanpura, Delhi-110053
✆ 22846599
Hd.Org.: Sangeeta Devi; **Bus.Intt.:** Pub.; **Spl.:** Palmistry, Astrology, *Vaastu*, Feng-shu, Yoga, Comp., Occult Sci., etc.

NAVEEN PRAKASHAN (REGD.)
85, Navyug Market, Ghaziabad-201001 (Uttar Pradesh)
✆ (O) 24790157, 24794554 (R) 0575-27523535, 2734698, Fax: 24790868
navpr@ndf.vsnl.net.in
Estd.: 1976; **Hd.Org.:** Sushil Kumar Jain; **Bus.Intt.:** Pub.; **Spl.:** Montessori Books in Hindi and English

NAVITA PUBLICATIONS
P.B. No. 6123, 8, Tyagaraj Nagar, Chennai-600017 (Tamil Nadu)

NAVJEEVAN BOOK CENTRE
248, Linking Rd., Bandra, Mumbai (Maharashtra) ✆ 26422157

NAVJIVAN PRAKASHAN
Navjivan Post Office, Ahmedabad-380014 (Gujarat)

NAVJOTI BROTHERS
Opp. Park, Modern School Building, Kaithal-132027 (Haryana)

NAVJYOTHI BOOK HOUSE
540, N/2 AR, C-Sector, Berkhera, B.H.E.L., Bhopal-21 (Madhya Pradesh)
✆ 0755-2754487 ▮ 9826088242
✉ pvanraj@yahoo.co.in, vanrajpaul@rediffmail.com
Man.Dir.: Vanraj Paul; **Bus.Intt.:** L.S. & B.S.; **Spl.:** Encyclopedia, Dictionaries, Children's Books, Fictions, Novels, Story, Personality Development, Phil. & Rel., Edu., Gen. School & College Books NCERT, CBSE, NBT, CBT, Comp., Engg., Competitive Books

NAVJYOTI PUBLICATIONS
Eluru Rd., Vijayawada-520002 (Andhra Pradesh)

NAVNEET EDUTAINMENT LIMITED
Mumbai (Maharashtra)
✆ 24989898, Fax: 24934343
✉ support@connectschool.com
Bus.Intt.: B.S.

NAVNEET PUBLICATIONS (INDIA) LTD.
Navneet Bhavan, Bhavani Shankar Road, Dadar (W), Mumbai-400007 (Maharashtra)
✆ 66626585, Fax: 91-22-66626470
✉ npil@navneet.com
🌐 www.navneet.com
Hd.Org.: Pradip Jhadhav
Br.: Navneet House, Gurukul Road, Memnagar, Ahmedabad-380052
✆ 66305000, Fax: 91-79-66305011
✉ npil.ahd@navneet.com
Bus.Intt.: Pub.; **Spl.:** Edu. Books for children

NAVODAYA BOOK DISTRIBUTORS
Opp. Arya Samaj, Badichamti, Hyderabad (Andhra Pradesh)

NAVODAYA PRAKASHAN
21-A, Ansari Road, Darya Ganj, New Delhi-110002
✆ 23273167, Fax: 91-11-23275710
Hd.Org.: Arun Maheshwari
Bus.Intt.: Dist.; **Spl.:** Literary and other books

NAVODAYA PUBLISHERS
Karl Marx Rd., Vijayawada-520002 (Andhra Pradesh)
✆ 0866-2573500, 2574500
✉ booklik@md4.vsnl.net.in
Estd.: 1957; **Prop.:** A. Rama Mohan Rao; **Bus.Intt.:** Pub., B.S., L.S.; **Spl.:** Humanities & Soc.Sci., Children & General

NAVODYA SALES
21-A, Darya Ganj, New Delhi-110002
✆ 23273167
Hd.Org.: Arun Maheshwari; **Bus.Intt.:** Pub. and Dist.; **Spl.:** Books in Hindi and English on All Sub.

NAVODAYA SUBSCRIPTION AGENCY
27-19-23, Durgiah St., Governorpet, Vijayawada-520002 (Andhra Pradesh)
✆ 2574022, 2473817
Estd.: 1973; **Prop.:** Ahalya Devi Vemulapalli B.Sc.; **Bus.Intt.:** Sub.Ag.

NAVRAJ PRAKASHAN
B-422/21, CB-Block, Gali No. 21, Main Market, Bhajanpura, Delhi-110053
✆ 9810589681, Fax: 22191341
Hd.Org.: Surya Prakash Srivastava;
Bus.Intt.: Pub. and Dist.; **Spl.:** Books in Hindi Litt., Geography, Pol.Sci., Hist., Eco., etc.

NAVRANG BOOKSELLERS & PUBLISHERS
RB-7, Inderpuri, New Delhi-110012
✆ 25835914, 25833803, Fax: 25833803
✉ navrang@navrangbooks.com
🌐 www.navrangbooks.com
Estd.: 1968; **Hd.Org.:** Nirmal Singal;
Bus.Intt.: Dist. and Exp.; **Spl.:** English and Sanskrit on Art, Archaeology, Hist., Indology

NAVRANG TRADERS
10, Ramnagar Near Prashant Nagar, Amravati-444606 (Maharashtra)
Prop.: A.Y. Bhurchandi

NAVSHEELA PRAKASHAN
A-75, Sriram Colony, Nilothi Extn. Nangloi, Delhi-110041
▮ 9213317238
Hd.Org.: Nandkumar Srivatsav
Bus.Intt.: Pub.; **Spl.:** Books in Hindi

NAVYUG BOOKS (INDIA)
H-2/23, First Floor, Mangal Bazar Road, Jahangirpuri, Delhi-110033
▮ 9910910967
✉ navyugbookindia@yahoo.com
Hd.Org.: N.A. Khan
Bus.Intt.: Pub. and Dist.; **Spl.:** Education

NAVYUG PRAKASHAN
39, U.A. Bungalow Rd., Jawahar Nagar, Delhi-110007
✆ 23966715
Hd.Org.: Vikas Kumar Kaura; **Bus.Intt.:** B.S.; **Spl.:** Rel. and Ayurvedic Books in Hindi

NAVYUG PUBLISHERS
K-24, Hauz Khas, New Delhi-110016
✆ 26518248, 26809942, 26802488

www.navyugpublishers.tripod.com
Estd.: 1954; **Hd.Org.:** S. Pritam Singh; **Bus.Intt.:** Pub. & B.S.; **Spl.:** Punjabi Litt.

NAVYUG PUBLISHERS
Pleasure Garden Market, Chandni Chowk, Delhi-110006

NAVYUG PUSTAK BHANDAR
Ist Floor, Navanaka Rd., Rajkot (Gujarat)

NAVYUG PUSTAK MANDIR
Bara Bazar, Main Rd., Baidyanath, Deoghar-814112 (Bihar)
Bus.Intt.: Pub. and B.S.

NAVYUG SAHITYA MANDIR
Tower Chowk, Baidyanath, Deoghar-814112 (Bihar)
Bus.Intt.: Pub. and B.S.

NAVYUG TRADERS
Desh Bandhu Gupta Rd., Dev Nagar, New Delhi-110005
✆ (O) & (R) 25722526
Prop.: B.N. Prakash; **Bus.Intt.:** L.S.; **Spl.:** Sci. and Tech.

NAYA GYANODAYA
18, Institutional Area, Post Box No. 3113, Lodhi Road, New Delhi-110003
✆ 24626467, 24654196, 24698417, 24656201, Fax: 91-11-24654197
sales@jnanpith.net, jnanpith@satyam.net.in
www.jnanpith.net
Hd.Org.: Ravindra Kalia
Bus.Intt.: Pub.; **Spl.:** Hindi literary magazine *Naya Gyanodaya*

NAYA PROKASH
206, Bidhan Sarani, Kolkata-700006 (West Bengal)
✆ (O) 033-23542130, 24110987 (R) 25387794 Fax: 25382897
npsales@cal2.vsnl.net.in
Estd.: 1960; **Hd.Org.:** Mrs. Bhubani Dhund

NAYA SAHITYA
1590, Madarsa Road, Kashmere Gate, Delhi-110006
✆ 23869812, Fax: 91-11-23867791
Hd.Org.: Meera Johri
Bus.Intt.: Pub.; **Spl.:** Children's books

NAYA UDYOG
206, Bidhan Sarani, Kolkata-700006 (West Bengal)
✆ 22414709, 22413540, 22190799
navudyog@vsnl.net
Estd.: 1960; **Hd.Org.:** P.S. Basu;
Bus.Intt.: Pub.; **Spl.:** Horticulture, Agri. and Allied Sub. in English

NAYA UDYOG
206, Bidhan Sarani, Kolkata-700006 (West Bengal)
✆ 2241-3540, 2219-0799
navudyog@vsnl.net
Estd.: 1992; **Prt.:** Partha Sankar Basu;
Bus.Intt.: Pub. and B.S.; **Spl.:** Sci. & Tech., Humanities, Gen. Books

NAYAN TARA
Baruah Bamun Gaon, Golaghat-785001 (Assam)

NAYANA
16, Bara Bazar, Nainital-263001 (Uttarakhand)
✆ 22887
Hd.Org.: Suresh Alsah; **Bus.Intt.:** L.S., Rt.

NAYANTORA PRAKASHAN
College Hostel Rd., Guwahati-781001 (Assam)

NAYYAR BOOK SERVICE
C-5/141, Lawrence Rd., Keshavpuram, New Delhi-110035
✆ 27180242
Hd.Org.: Mukesh Nayyar; **Bus.Intt.:** Pub.; **Spl.:** Gen. Books

NAZ PUBLISHING HOUSE
422, Matia Mahal, Jama Masjid, Delhi-110006
✆ 23246409, Fax: 91-11-23279392
nazp@del2.vsnl.net.in
www.nazpublishinghouse.com
Estd.: 1950; **Hd.Org.:** Abdul Samad;
Bus.Intt.: Pub.; **Spl.:** *Holy Quran* and Islamic Books in Urdu

NAZER PRAKASHAN
145-Verka, Amritsar (Punjab)

NECTAR PRINTS PVT. LTD.
A/127, Ghatkopar Indl. Estate, Off. L.B.S. Marg, Ghatkopar (W) Mumbai-400086 (Maharashtra)
✆ 25969633, 250007213, Fax: 91-22-25969634
Hd.Org.: Abid Ali Shaikh

NEEL KAMAL BOOK LINKS
Opp. Clock Tower, Ist Floor, Sultan Bazar, Hyderabad-500001 (Andhra Pradesh)
Bus.Intt.: WS, Rt. and L.S.

NEELABH PRAKASHAN
15A, M.G. Rd., Civil Lines, Allahabad-211003 (Uttar Pradesh)
Hd.Org.: Neelabh Ashq

NEELAM PRAKASHAN
Office of Uppar Shiksha Nideshak, Patna Magadh Pramandal, Meelar High School, Patna-1 (Bihar)

NEELAM PUBLISHERS (REGD.)
4451, Nai Sarak, Delhi-110006

✆ (O) 22918332, 2235275, 2238738
(R) 25701108
Estd.: 1972; **Prop.:** Shyam Bhambri;
Bus.Intt.: Pub.; **Spl.:** Edu. Books in English, Hindi and Punjabi

NEELAV PRAKASHAN
15-A, Mahatma Gandhi Marg, Civil Lines, Allahabad-211003 (Uttar Pradesh)
✆ 22623287, 22603023
Hd.Org.: Neelav Ashak

NEELESH PRAKASHAN
G-62, Gali V, Arjun Nagar, Delhi-110051
Hd.Org.: Neelesh Rajput

NEELKAMAL PUBLICATIONS PVT. LTD.
Educational Publishers (Exporters & Importers)
Sultan Bazar, Hyderabad-500095 (Andhra Pradesh)
✆ 24757140, 24757944, 24757197, Fax: 91-40-24757951
@ suresh@neelkamalpub.com
www.neelkamalpub.com
Hd.Org.: Suresh Chandra Sharma
Br.: BG-5/9B, Paschim Vihar, New Delhi-110063
✆ 91-11-25285894
@ sales@neelkamalpub.com
Bus.Intt.: Pub.; **Spl.:** Edu. Books on Various Disciplines in English

NEERAJ BOOK CENTRE
C-32, Arya Nagar Society, Flat No. 91, Patpar Ganj, Delhi-110092
▮ 9312869947
@ neerajmittal_2002@rediffmail.com
Hd.Org.: Neeraj Mittal
Bus.Intt.: Pub.; **Spl.:** Children's books

NEERAJ PUBLICATIONS
1507, 1st Floor, Nai Sarak, Delhi-110006
✆ 23260329, 65817881, Fax: 91-11-23285501
@ info@neerajbooks.com
www.neerajbooks.com
Hd.Org.: Neeraj Chopra; **Bus.Intt.:** Pub.;
Spl.: Edu. Books on Various Sub. and for Competitive Examinations

NEERAS BOOK DISTRIBUTORS
78-A, Gali No. 7, Ajay Park, Naya Bazaar, Najafgarh, New Delhi-110043
✆ 25324106
Hd.Org.: Tarakant Mishra; **Bus.Intt.:** Dist.;
Spl.: Hindi Litt.

NEETA PRAKASHAN
A-4, Ring Rd., South Extension Part-I, New Delhi-110049
✆ 24636010, 24636030, 24653600, Fax: 24636011
@ neetabooks@vsnl.com
www.neetaprakashan.com
Estd.: 1960; **Hd.Org.:** Shanti Devi Gupta;
Bus.Intt.: Pub.;
Spl.: Edu. Books on Various Sub. in English and Other Languages

NEHA BOOK SERVICE
C-56, Sangam Vihar, Near Tina Public School, New Delhi-110062
✆ 26087046, 26073910 ▮ 9811046881
Ch.Exe.: Mr. Umesh Sharma; **Bus.Intt.:** Dist.;
Spl.: Children's books, Audio Cassettes & CD-ROMs

NEHA PRAKASHAN
1415, Dr. Mukherjee Nagar, Near Batra Cinema, Delhi-110008
Bus.Intt.: Pub., Dist., B.S.

NELSON THORNES
P1/6, Ground Floor, DLF Phase-II, Gurgaon-122002 (Haryana)
✆ 91-124-2576796
@ overleaf@vsnl.net
www.nelsonthornes.com
Hd.Org.: Linden Harris
Bus.Intt.: Pub.

NEM CHAND & BROS.
Civil Lines, Roorkee-247667 (Uttarakhand)

NEO PUBLISHING COMPANY
226, Sant Nagar, East of Kailash, New Delhi-110065

NEOVISION PUBLISHERS (P) LTD.
E-58, IInd Floor, G.K.-I, New Delhi-110048
✆ 26241848, Fax: 26241559
@ neovisionpublishers@mail.com
www.agelessmindandspirit.com
Estd.: 2001; **Hd.Org.:** Vijay S. Jodha;
Bus.Intt.: Rt., WS, Pub., Pub.'s Rep., L.S.;
Spl.: Art & Photography

NETAJI RESEARCH BUREAU
Netaji Bhavan, 38/2, Lala Lajpat Rai Rd., Kolkata-700020 (West Bengal)
✆ 24756139
Estd.: 1957; **Bus.Intt.:** Pub.; **Spl.:** Hist., Pol., and International Affairs Housed in the Ancestral Bose family residence, Specialising in Netaji in Bengali, English, and Hindi

NETTIKADAN BOOKS (P) LTD.
Nettikadan Building, Karakkat Rd., Cochin-682016 (Kerala)
✆ 2366067, 2369784, Fax: 0484-2354695
@ mail@nettikadan.com
Estd.: 1988; **Hd.Org.:** Andrew Nettikkadan;
Bus.Intt.: B.S. and Exp.

NETWORK (INDIA) BOOK DISTRIBUTORS
C-273, Kidwai Nagar East, New Delhi-110023
✆ (R) 24631478 ▮ 9810398699,
Fax: 011-24635783
✉ kishor_megha@vsnl.net
Prop.: Kishore Kumar; **Bus.Intt.:** Rt., L.S.;
Spl.: Tech., Sci.

NETWORKS 18 PUBLICATIONS PVT. LTD.
Empire Complex First Floor,
414 Senapati Bapat Marg, Lower Parel,
Mumbai-400013
✆ 40019477, Fax: 91-22-66618985
✉ kannaniyer@network18online.com
Hd.Org.: Anusha Ramani

NEUROLOGICAL SOCIETY OF INDIA
Mansarovar, Book Rd., Baraitu,
Ranchi-834009 (Bihar)
Bus.Intt.: Pub.

NEW ACADEMIC PUBLISHERS
F-22, B/3, Laxmi Nagar, Delhi-110092
✆ 22413394, 22420827
✉ alsindia@sigmaonline.net
Prop.: Mrs. Vinay Puri
Br.: 3721/3, First Floor, Netaji Subhash Marg,
New Delhi-110002
✆ 23282663
✉ alsindia@hclinfinet.com
Bus.Intt.: Pub., L.S., Sub.Ag.; **Spl.:** Acad., Beh.Sci., Soc.Sci., Sci., Rare, Journals & Magazine

NEW AGE BOOKS
A-44, Naraina Industrial Area, Phase-I,
New Delhi-110028
✆ 25895218-19, 23922151, Fax: 25797221
✉ info@newagebooksindia.com,
nab@vsnl.net.in
www.newagebooksindia.com
Hd.Org.: Rajeev Parkash Jain; **Bus.Intt.:** Pub.;
Spl.: Rel., Phil., Spirituality, Hist. and Biographies and also Memoirs

NEW AGE INTERNATIONAL
23, Ansari Rd., Darya Ganj, New Delhi-110002
✆ 23252574, Fax: 23252572
✉ colaxmi@hotmail.com
Hd.Org.: R.K. Gupta; **Bus.Intt.:** Pub.;
Spl.: Engg., Med.Sci., Comp. etc.

NEW AGE INTERNATIONAL (P) LTD.
4835/24, Ansari Rd., Darya Ganj,
New Delhi-110002
✆ 23276802, 23258865, Fax: 91-11-23267437
✉ orders@newagepublishers.com,
info@newagepublishers.com,
sales@newagepublishers.com
Estd.: 1960; **Dir.:** K.K. Gupta
Br.: 36, Malikarjuna Temple Street,
Opp. ICWA, Bsavanagudi, Bangalore-560004
✆ 26677815, Fax: 91-80-26615247
✉ bangalore@newagepublishers.com
• 26, Damodaran Street, T. Nagar,
Chennai-600020; ✆ 24353401, 24359507,
Telefax: 91-44-24344726
✉ chennai@newagepublishers.com
• C/o. Laxmi Publications (P) Ltd.,
St. Benedict Road, Cochin-682018
✆ 91-484-2397004
✉ cochin@newagepublishers.com
• Hemsen Complex, Mohd. Shah Road,
Paltan Bazar, Near Starline Hotel,
Guwahati-781008;
✆ 91-361-2543669, 2513881,
✉ guwahati@newagepublishers.com
• No. 105, 1st Floor, Madhiray Kaveri Tower,
3-2-19, Azam Jahi Road, Nimboliadda,
Hyderabad-500027, ✆ 91-40-24652456
✉ hyderabad@newagepublishers.com
• C/o Laxmi Publications (P) Ltd., Adda Tanda
Chowk, Jalandhar,
✆ 91-181-2221272
• 106A, 1st Floor, S.N. Banerjee Road,
Kolkata-700014, ✆ 22275247,
Telefax: 91-33-22273773
✉ kolkata@newagepublishers.com
• 18, Madam Mohan Malviya Marg,
Lucknow-226001, ✆ 2209578,
Fax: 91-522-2204098
✉ lucknow@newagepublishers.com
• 142-C, Victor House, Ground Floor,
N.M. Joshi Marg, Lower Parel,
Mumbai-400013
✆ 91-22-24927869
✉ mumbai@newagepublishers.com
• C/o Laxmi Publications (P) Ltd.,
Radha Gobind Street, Tharpagma, Ranchi
✆ 91-651-2307764
Bus.Intt.: Pub., WS, L.S. & Rt., Imp., Exp., Sub.Ag.; **Spl.:** Humanities & Soc.Sci., Sci. & Tech., Med., Gen.

NEW AGE PUBLISHER (P) LTD.
12-B, Bankim Chatterjee St., Ground Floor,
Kolkata-700073 (West Bengal)
✆ 2418509
Hd.Org.: S. Sinha Ray; **Bus.Intt.:** Pub.;
Spl.: Humanities & Soc.Sci., Fiction & Gen.

NEW ALIPUR BOOK HOUSE
554/B, New Alipur, Block-N, Kolkata-700053
(West Bengal)

NEW ANIL BOOK CENTRE
Trunk Rd., Nellore-524001
(Andhra Pradesh)
Fax: 0861-231899

NEW ASIAN PUBLISHERS
7/31, Ansari Rd., Darya Ganj,
New Delhi-110002

✆ 23280163-65, Fax: 23280165
✉ mehta_anil@mailcity.com
www.newasianpub.com
Estd.: 1962; **Prop.:** Ravinder Kumar Mehta
Br.: 3911, Roshanpura, Nai Sarak, Delhi-110006 ✆ 23915650, 23941531
✉ mehta_anil@mailcity.com
Bus.Intt.: Pub., WS, L.S. & Rt., Imp., Exp.; **Spl.:** Sci. & Tech., Med., Comp.

NEW BABY BOOK STALL
10, Shyama Charan Dey St., Kolkata-700073 (West Bengal)

NEW BAIPATRA
2, Shyama Charan Dey St., Kolkata-700073 (West Bengal)

NEW BANI SHREE
9/4, Tamer Lane, Kolkata-700009 (West Bengal)

NEW BENGAL PRESS (P) LTD.
68, College St., Kolkata-700073 (West Bengal)
Bus.Intt.: Printers, Pub. & B.S.

NEW BHARATIYA BOOK CORPORATION
5824, New Chandrawal, Jawahar Nagar, Delhi-110007
✆ 91-11-23851294, 65195809
✉ newbbc@indiatimes.com
Hd.Org.: Subhash Chandra Jain; **Bus.Intt.:** Pub. and Dist.; **Spl.:** Indology, Sanskrit, Phil., Rel., Hist., Art, Arch. and Music

NEW BHARATIYA BOOK CORPORATION
Shop No. 18, Second Floor, 5574-A, Kashi Ram Market, New Chandrawal, Delhi-110007
✆ 23981294, Fax: 23956241
✉ deepak_nbbc@hotmail.com
Hd.Org.: Subhash Jain; **Bus.Intt.:** Pub. and Dist.; **Spl.:** Indology, Sanskrit, Phil., Rel., Hist., Art, Arch. and Music

NEW BISWAS BOOK STALL
Bankim Chatterjee St., Block-6, Stall-8A, Kolkata-700073 (West Bengal)

NEW BOOK COMPANY
Mai Hiran Gate, Jalandhar-147002 (Punjab)
Hd.Org.: S. Maheep Singh

NEW BOOK CO. (THE)
Shree Ram Arcade, 15A, J.L. Nehru Rd., Kolkata-700013 (West Bengal)
✆ 22493877
Estd.: 1947; **Hd.Org.:** Jagdish; **Bus.Intt.:** Rt. and Mail Order; **Spl.:** Children, Gen. and Trade Books (Indian and Foreign)

NEW BOOK CORNER (THE)
167/4, Lenin Sarani, IInd Floor, Kolkata-700072 (West Bengal)
✆ 23374872 / 0059, Fax: 24930043
✉ nbccal72@vsnl.net, anuttam@vsnl.net
Estd.: 1976; **Hd.Org.:** Anuttam Mallick; **Bus.Intt.:** Rt., L.S., WS

NEW BOOK CENTRE
Bharat Chambers, LG 14 Building No. 70-71, Scindia House, Connaught Place, New Delhi-110001
✆ 91-11-23356663
✉ newbookcentre@rediffmail.com
www.newbookcentre.com
Hd.Org.: Kishan Chand Rakheja
Bus.Intt.: Dist.

NEW BOOK DEPOT
18-B, Connaught Place, New Delhi-110001
✆ (O) 23320020, 23755124, 23318045 (R) 24697423, Fax: 91-11-23354027
✉ rakeshchandra@mantraonline.com
Estd.: 1925; **Man.Prt.:** Rakesh Chandra; **Bus.Intt.:** Rt.; **Spl.:** Med., Tech., Sci., Electronics, Reference, Art, Hist., Guides, Rel., Fiction & Largest Selection of Penguin Books in India

NEW BOOK DEPOT (THE)
Guwahati (Assam)
✆ 2517059, Fax: 2544719
✉ modbook@caltigen.com
Br.: Shillong ✆ 223476
✉ unipub@vsnl.com
Bus.Intt.: L.S. & Rt., Imp., and Sub.Ag.

NEW BOOK HOUSE
32, Tashkant Rd., Civil Lines, Allahabad-211001 (Uttar Pradesh)
✆ (O) & (R) 0532-2622879, 3150898
✉ sprakash@nde.vsnl.net.in
Estd.: 1962; **Prop.:** Suraj Prakash Agarwal; **Bus.Intt.:** WS, L.S. & Rt., Imp., Sub.Ag.; **Spl.:** Humanities & Soc.Sci., Sci. & Tech., Med., Law

NEW BOOK INTERNATIONAL
S.J.D.A. Market, Stall No. 81, Norge Tewing, Bus Terminal, Siliguri-734403 (West Bengal)

NEW BOOK SOCIETY OF INDIA
6A/53, W.E.A. Karol Bagh, New Delhi-110005
✆ (O) & (R) 25727886
Hd.Org.: Motia Devi; **Bus.Intt.:** Pub.

NEW BOOK STALL
Boarding Rd., Sibsagar (Assam)

NEW BOOK STALL
Dergaon, Golaghat (Assam)

NEW BOOK STALL
Pan Bazar, Guwahati-781001 (Assam)

NEW BOOK STALL (THE)
5/1, Ramanath Majumder St.,
P.B. No. 10836, Kolkata-700009
(West Bengal)
✆ (O) 033-2311433, 2313569 (R) 2314486
Estd.: 1922; **Prop.**: Mohendra Nath Paul;
Bus.Intt.: Pub.; **Spl.**: School and College Level Textbooks in Bengali and English

NEW BOOK SUPPLY AGENCY
18M, Tamer Lane, Kolkata-700009
(West Bengal)

NEW BOOK SYNDICATE
90/3, Mahatma Gandhi Rd.,
Kolkata-700007 (West Bengal)

NEW BOOK TRADERS
5-1-800, Osmania Medical College,
Opp. APCO Fabrics, Kothi,
Hyderabad-500095 (Andhra Pradesh)

NEW BOOK TRUST
4, Nabin Kundu Lane, Kolkata-700009
(West Bengal)

NEW BOOKS EMPORIUM
54/8, College St., Kolkata-700073
(West Bengal)

NEW CENTRAL BOOK AGENCY (P) LTD.
8/1, Chintamoni Das Lane,
Kolkata-700009 (West Bengal)
✆ 22418411, 22418537, 22419094,
Fax: 91-33-22413852, 22418537
✉ central@cal2.vsnl.net.in,
ncba@cal2.vsnl.net.in,
ncbapvtltd@eth.net
🌐 www.centralgroup.net
Estd.: 1991; **Hd.Org.**: S. Sinha Roy;
Bus.Intt.: Pub.; **Spl.**: College and University Level Textbooks on all Sub.

NEW CENTURY BOOK HOUSE (P) LTD.
8/5, Chintamani Das Lane, Kolkata-700009
(West Bengal)
✆ 22413411

NEW CENTURY BOOK HOUSE (P) LTD.
41-B, SIDCO, Industrial Estate,
Ambattur, Chennai-600098
(Tamil Nadu)
✆ 26258410, Fax: 91-44-26858410
✉ ncbhbook@yahoo.co.in
Estd.: 1950; **Hd.Org.**: Durai Raj
Bus.Intt.: Pub. and Exp.; **Spl.**: Edu. and Gen. Books in English, Hindi and Tamil

NEW CENTURY PUBLICATIONS
34, Gujranwala Town, Part-2, Delhi-110009
✆ 27247805, 27138192,
Fax: 091-011-27464774
✉ indiatax@del2.vsnl.net.in
Ch.Exe.: Sandeep Sury; **Bus.Intt.**: Pub., Dist., L.S.; **Spl.**: Eco., Comm., Mang., Taxation, Law, Pol.Sci., Advertising

NEW CENTURY PUBLICATIONS
4800/24, Bharat Ram Road, Ansari Road,
Darya Ganj, New Delhi-110002
✆ 23247798, 65396605, Fax: 91-11-41017798
▮ 9811266355
✉ indiatax@vsnl.com,
info@newcenturypublications.com
🌐 www.newcenturypublications.com
Hd.Org.: Sandeep Sury
Bus.Intt.: Pub.; **Spl.**: Eco., Comm., Mang., Taxation, Law, Pol.Sci. and Soc.Sci.

NEW COLLEGE BOOK STALL
Muvattupuzha-686661 (Kerala)
Estd.: 1968; **Prop.**: A.P. Thankappan Nair;
Bus.Intt.: B.S.

NEW COLLEGE STORE
7, Navsari High School Shopping Centre,
Opp. Shahi Masjid, Talav, Navsari-396445
(Gujarat)
✆ (O) 257917 (R) 244185
Fax: 02637-255277
Estd.: 1972; **Bus.Intt.**: Dist.; **Spl.**: Children's Books

NEW CONCEPTS
C-159, Naraina Industrial Area, Phase-I,
New Delhi-110028
✆ 56223494 ▮ 9868026219, Fax: 25587139
✉ newkconcepts@yahoo.com
Hd.Org.: Alok Mittal; **Bus.Intt.**: Pub.;
Spl.: Scholarly books in English

NEW CRESCENT PUBLISHING COMPANY
2035, Qasimjan St., Ballimaran,
Delhi-110006
✆ 23262545, Fax: 91-11-23282834
Hd.Org.: Muhammed Furqan

NEW DELHI BOOK SERVICES
4347/4C, Ansari Rd., Darya Ganj,
New Delhi-110002
✆ 23251834
Prop.: Gita Saxena

NEW DELHI PUBLISHING HOUSE
RZ-38/A, Vijay Enclave, Palam,
New Delhi-110045
Bus.Intt.: Quality Printers and Pub.

NEW EPOCK PUBLISHERS & DISTRIBUTORS
Dalgate, Opp. C.D. Hospital, Srinagar-190001
(Jammu & Kashmir)

Estd.: 1994; Hd.Org.: Mohammad Farooq Baba; Bus.Intt.: L.S., WS, Pub.

NEW ERA BOOK AGENCY
SCO 49-51, Basement, P.B. 52, Sector 17C, Chandigarh-160017
✆ 2702318, 2702189
✉ nebaaph@sancharnet.in, nebaaph@hotmail.com
🌐 www.newerainternational.com
Estd.: 1977; Hd.Org.: Anil Sharma, Nalin Sharma; Bus.Intt.: Pub., L.S., WS, Exp.; Spl.: Books on all Sub. in English and Hindi

NEW ERA BOOKS
No. 560/A, Madhu Complex, BSK 1st Stage, Bangalore-560050 (Karnataka)
✆ 080-26603244, 26420049, Fax: 26750079
✉ newera-rbs@hotmail.com, newrabooks@vsnl.net
Estd.: 1996-97; Bus.Intt.: B.S.; Spl.: Sci. & Tech. Books

NEW ERA PUBLICATIONS
Shah Faisal Market, Sopore-193201 (Jammu & Kashmir)
✆ (O) 01954-222588 (R) 222494, Fax: 222494
Estd.: 1984; Hd.Org.: Nisar Ahmad Bhat; Bus.Intt.: Pub., B.S., L.S.; Spl.: Humanities & Soc.Sci., Children & General, Bio.Sci. & Others

NEW ERA PUBLICATIONS PVT. LTD.
96, Gautam Nagar, New Delhi-110049
✆ 26601548
✉ tgoeldenite@gmx.net
Ch.Exe.: Thomas Goeldenite; Bus.Intt.: Pub.; Spl.: Edu. Books as well as on Non-fictional Books on Spiritual Topics

NEW INDIA BOOK COMPANY
P.O. Box 8807, 17, Kamal Phool Society, Collectors Colony, Chembur, Mumbai-400074 (Maharashtra)
✆ 25522240, 25528357
Hd.Org.: Mrs. Amrita Manchanda

NEW INDIA BOOKS
H-75, Mansarovar Park, Shahdara, Delhi-110032
✆ 22117119
Prop.: Sanjiv Kumar

NEW INDIA PUBLISHING AGENCY
101, Vikas Surya Plaza, CU Block, L.S.C. Mkt., Pitam Pura, New Delhi-110088
✆ 27341717, 27343030, Fax: 91-11-27341616
✉ newindiapublishingagency@gmail.com
🌐 www.bookfactoryindia.com
Hd.Org.: Sumit Pal Jain
Bus.Intt.: Pub. and Dist.; Spl.: Sci. and Tech., Agric., Biological, Horticultural and Geological Science

NEW INDIA PUBLISHING HOUSE
42, Mausam Vihar, Main Vikas Marg, Delhi-110051
✆ 22244711, 22418207
Estd.: 1978; Prop.: Prof. N.S. Kumar

NEW JACK PRINTING WORKS PVT. LTD.
Pandurang Budhkar Marg, Off. N.M. Joshi Marg, Lower Parel, Mumbai-400013 (Maharashtra)
✆ 24925481/82, 24925473
✉ newjack@vsnl.com
Estd.: 1943; Bus.Intt.: Exp.

NEW JANTA BOOK DEPOT
21A, Khan Market, New Delhi-110003
✆ 24611995
Estd.: 1997; Prop.: Rakesh K. Gupta; Bus.Intt.: B.S.; Spl.: Children, School and Gen. Books, Stationers and Printers

NEW KALIMATA BOOK STALL
6, S.C. Dey St., Kolkata-700073 (West Bengal)

NEW KITAB MAHAL
48, R.N. Tagore Rd., Dakshineswar, Kolkata-700076 (West Bengal)

NEW KITAB MANJIL
Tatarpur, Bhagalpur-812002 (Bihar)
Bus.Intt.: Pub. and B.S.

NEW LAKSHMI PUSTAK BHANDAR
Kahalgaon (Colgong), Bhagalpur-813203 (Bihar)
Bus.Intt.: Pub. and B.S.

NEW LAXMINARAYAN BOOK STALL
114-A, Lake Garden Super Mkt., Shop No. 72, Kolkata-700045 (West Bengal)

NEW LIFE BOOKS
25, Connaught Place, Dehradun-248001 (Uttarakhand)

NEW LIFE BOOKS
29/1362, Vyttila N.T.I. Jn., Kochi-682019 (Kerala)
✆ 2315595
Estd.: 1984; Prop.: Thomas T. Mathai

NEW LIGHT
10/2B, Ramanath Majumder St., Kolkata-700009 (West Bengal)

NEW LIGHT PUBLISHERS
B-8, Rattan Jyoti Building, 18, Rajendra Place, New Delhi-110008
✆ (O) 25737448, 25721761, 25712649 (R) 25764425, 25764479, 25711116

Fax: 25812385
newlight@vsnl.net, readwell@sify.com
Estd.: 1963; **Prt.:** Ramesh Chowdhary; **Bus.Intt.:** Pub., Exp.; **Spl.:** Gen. Knowledge, Competition Exam Guides, English Improvement, Self-Improvement, Astrology, Palmistry, Numerology, Dictionaries, Computer and Quiz Books

NEW LIGHT PUBLISHING CO. (P) LTD.
New Light House, P.B. No. 1066, Pattom Palace, Thiruvananthapuram-695015 (Kerala)

NEW LITTLE GENIUS
RG-Block, Pocket-B, Flat No. 446, Raghubir Nagar, (Behind Cement Godown), New Delhi-110027
✆ 51833110, 2591562, Fax: 25460771
Hd.Org.: Ravi Kumar; **Bus.Intt.:** Pub.; **Spl.:** Edu. Books and Tech. Aids

NEW MEDICAL HOUSE
Patel Nagar-II, Ghaziabad (Uttar Pradesh)

NEW MURJANI STORES
19, Yashwant Rd., Indore (Madhya Pradesh)
✆ 2475435

NEW OSCAR PUBLICATIONS PVT. LTD.
11071, St. No. 2, Doriwalan, Karol Bagh, New Delhi-110005
✆ 23682766, 23520716, Fax: 011-23520716
newoscarpub@yahoo.com
Estd.: 1989; **Bus.Intt.:** Pub.; **Spl.:** Children Books

NEW POPULAR BOOK SHOP
I.I.T. Campus Powai, Mumbai-400076 (Maharashtra)

NEW PUBLISHING CONCERN
30/1A, College Row, Kolkata-700009 (West Bengal)

NEW PUBLISHING HOUSE
27, Surya Sen St., Kolkata-700009 (West Bengal)

NEW RAMA BOOK HOUSE
Near Kunwar Cinema, Station Rd., Moradabad-244001 (Uttar Pradesh)
✆ (O) 2310175 (R) 2310201 ▮ 9837114005
Prop.: Deepak Aggarwal; **Bus.Intt.:** B.S. & Stationers

NEW READER'S PARADISE
18/B, Monohar Pukar, 2nd Lane, Kolkata-700029 (West Bengal)
✆ 24640431

NEW ROYAL BOOK COMPANY
First Floor, Shah Trade Centre, 32/16, Valmiki Marg, Lal Bagh, Hazrat Ganj, Lucknow-226001 (Uttar Pradesh)
✆ (O) 0522-2285607 (R) 2240644, 2248003, Fax: 2231569
nrbc@rediffmail.com
Estd.: 1985; **Hd.Org.:** Mirza Furqan Beg; **Bus.Intt.:** Pub., B.S., L.S.; **Spl.:** Humanities & Soc.Sci., Mang., Law

NEW SADHANA POCKET BOOKS
70, Roshanara Plaza, Roshanara Road, Delhi-110007
✆ 91-11-23830751, 32536004
Hd.Org.: Rajesh Sahni
Bus.Intt.: Pub.; **Spl.:** Books on religion, Ayurveda, Fiction, Yoga, Astrology, etc. in Hindi

NEW STAR BOOKSELLERS
Tehsil Rd., Sopore (Jammu & Kashmir)
Estd.: 1996; **Hd.Org.:** Irshad Ahmed Bhat; **Bus.Intt.:** L.S.

NEW STUDENTS BOOK CENTRE
Arundelpet Main Rd., Guntur-2 (Andhra Pradesh)
✆ (O) 2233332 (R) 2233335
nsbc74@yahoo.com
Estd.: 1985; **Bus.Intt.:** Pub. and B.S.; **Spl.:** Med.

NEW STUDENTS BOOK CENTRE
Karl Marx Rd., Vijayawada-520002 (Andhra Pradesh)
✆ 2572222, 2572211, Fax: 0866-2578333
babjee48@rediffmail.com, babjee48@yahoo.com
Vice Pres.: B. Babjee; **Bus.Intt.:** B.S.

NEW SUPRIYA BOOK STALL
12/1B, Bankim Chatterjee St., Kolkata-700073 (West Bengal)

NEW VIDYA MANDIR
Center Market, Sector III, B.S. City, Bokaro-827003 (Jharkhand)

NEW VIDYASREE
61, Mahatma Gandhi Rd., Kolkata-700009 (West Bengal)

NEWS & LITERATURE HOUSE
44-45, 1st Floor, Kalawati Paliwal Market, Gumanpura, Kota-324007 (Rajasthan)
✆ (O) 0744-2451339, 2364155, 2330779 (R) 0744-2422752, Fax: 0744-2330779, 2360275
nlh@kappa.net.in
Estd.: 1970; **Prop.:** Mrs. Kanta Jain; **Bus.Intt.:** Pub., WS, L.S. & Rt., Imp., Sup.Ag.; **Spl.:** Med.

NEWS PAPER AGENCY
Shivsagar (Assam)

NEWS SCRIPT
A-14, College St. Market,
Kolkata-700073 (West Bengal)

NEWSJOY PUBLICATIONS (PVT.) LTD.
67/4-A, Second Floor, Zamrudpur,
New Delhi-110048
✆ 26480505, 26448682, Fax: 26474646
✉ newsjoy@satyam.net.in,
editor@newsjoy.com
Hd.Org.: Nandini Oberoi; **Bus.Intt.:** Pub.; **Spl.:** Weekly Newspaper for Children and also Children's Books

NEWSPREAD
C/o Mr. L. Venkatraman, A3, Kartik,
113/114, Chhedanagar, Mumbai-400089
(Maharashtra)
Bus.Intt.: Exp.

NEXT DIMENSION MULTIMEDIA
303, Bajaj House, 97, Nehru Place,
New Delhi-110019
✆ 26237787, 51617787, Fax: 26237787
✉ nextd@vsnl.net
Hd.Org.: Mohd Imran Amin; **Bus.Intt.:** Dist. and Imp.

NEXUS INFORMATION SERVICES CO. (P) LTD.
Delhi
✆ 27001517, 22254625
Fax: 26859444
✉ nisc@vsnl.com, aiiebip@nisc.co.in
Bus.Intt.: Pub.

NIC MAR PUBLICATIONS
Walchand Centre, Tardeo,
Mumbai-400034 (Maharashtra)

NICE INTERNATIONAL PATTERN CO.
P.B. No. 130, F-118, Sector-27,
Noida-201301 (Uttar Pradesh)

NICE PUBLISHING SERVICES
19, Rashid Market Ext. Khureji, Delhi-110051

NICHOLAS BREALEY
(C/o Ajay Parmar & Co.), First Floor, 2/25,
Ansari Rd., Darya Ganj, New Delhi-110002
✆ 23284894

NIDHI PRAKASHAN
1590, Madrasa Rd., Kashmere Gate,
Delhi-110006
✆ 22965685, Fax: 22969377
Hd.Org.: Manoj Sharma

NIDHI PUBLISHERS (INDIA)
Bikaner (Rajasthan)
✆ 0151-543261
✉ nidhipub@rediffmail.com
Bus.Intt.: Pub.

NIHAL PUBLICATIONS
C-70, Gali No. 3, North Chajjupur,
Delhi-110094
✆ 35341930
Hd.Org.: Omkar Singh; **Bus.Intt.:** Pub.; **Spl.:** Hindi Litt.

NIHAR PRAKASHAN
14-A/65, WEA Karol Bagh, New Delhi-110005
✆ 25749240

NIIR PROJECT CONSULTANCY SERVICES
106-E, Kamla Nagar, P.B. No. 2162,
New Delhi-110007
✆ 23843955, 23845654, 23845886,
Fax: 91-11-23841561 ▮ 9811043595
✉ niir.india@gmail.com
www.niir.org
Hd.Org.: Ajay Kumar Gupta
Bus.Intt.: Pub.; **Spl.:** Technology books

NIKITA OVERSEAS PVT. LTD.
19-A, Ansari Rd., New Delhi-110002

NILESH PRAKASHAN
G-62/5, Arjun Nagar, Delhi-110051
✆ 22462676
Hd.Org.: Nilesh Rajput

NILOKANTHA BOOK HOUSE
Pan Bazar, Guwahati-781001 (Assam)

NIMEX TRADING CORPORATION
Abbas Manzil, Ist Floor, 11/13,
Bhandari St., Cross Lane, Mumbai-400003
(Maharashtra)
Bus.Intt.: Exp.

NIMITI PRAKASHAN
427, Mangalwar Peth, Narpatgir Chowk,
Pune-411011 (Maharashtra)
Spl.: Rel. and Phil. in Hindi

NINSACH TECHNOLOGIES
Hissar (Haryana)
✉ nitinrgoel@rediffmail.com
Bus.Intt.: B.S.

NIRALA PUBLICATIONS
2595, Kucha Chelan, Darya Ganj,
New Delhi-110002
✆ 23272505
Prop.: Srijana Sharma; **Bus.Intt.:** Pub.; **Spl.:** Indian Litt. and Himalayan Culture

NIRALA PUBLICATIONS
Guru Hari Bhavan, Sector III, E-313,
Bokaro Steel City, Dhanbad (Bihar)

NIRALA PUBLICATIONS
New Delhi
✆ 22453992
✉ nirala32@hotmail.com **Bus.Intt.:** Pub.

NIRALI PRAKASHAN
41, Budhwar Peth, Jogeshwari Mandir Lane, Pune-411002 (Maharashtra)
✆ 24450842, 24451512, Fax: 91-20-24495422
✉ pragatibooks@vsnl.net
🌐 www.pragationaline.com
Estd.: 1980; **Hd.Org.:** Jignesh C. Furia
Bus.Intt.: Pub.; **Spl.:** Books on pharmacy, engineering and general books

NIRMAL BOOK AGENCY
C-42, University Campus, Kurukshetra University, Kurukshetra-136119 (Haryana)
✆ 222938
Hd.Org.: Nirmal Goel; **Bus.Intt.:** Pub. and Dist.; **Spl.:** Soc.Sci., Edu., Hist., Eco. and Indology

NIRMAL BOOK AGENCY
89, Mahatma Gandhi Rd., Kolkata-700007 (West Bengal)
✆ 2415728, 2414003, Fax: 2419238
✉ pradip-saha@hotmail.com
Hd.Org.: Nirmal Kumar Saha

NIRMAL BOOKS
7/22, Ansari Rd., Darya Ganj, New Delhi-110002
✆ 23273880, 23275880
Estd.: 1993; **Prop.:** Smt. Nirmal Agarwal; **Bus.Intt.:** L.S.

NIRMAL PUBLICATIONS
A-139, Gali No 3, Kabir Nagar, Shahdara, Delhi-110032
✆ 22114193
Hd.Org.: Suresh Pal; **Bus.Intt.:** Pub., B.S. and Dist.; **Spl.:** Criticisms, Journalism, Music, etc.

NIRMAL PUSTAKALAYA
89, Mahatma Gandhi Rd., Kolkata-700007 (West Bengal)

NIRMALA PRAKASHANA
957, 'Santosh Sagara', Govinapura Extn., Tiptur-2572202 (Karnataka)
✆ (O) & (R) 08134-250507
Estd.: 1979; **Prop.:** Prof. T.S. Nirmala Nagaraj; **Bus.Intt.:** Pub.; **Spl.:** Children's Books, Functioning Specially to Promote Litt. for Children in Kannada

NIRMAN PRAKASHAN
1/3476-B, Ashok Marg, Ram Nagar Extension, Shahdara, Delhi-110032
✆ 2687204
Hd.Org.: Vinod Kumar Sharma;
Bus.Intt.: Pub.; **Spl.:** Gen. Books in Hindi, English, Sanskrit

NIRNAYASAGAR PRAKASHAN
23-28, Dr. Belkar St., Mumbai-400002 (Maharashtra)

NIROG SUKH
B-3, Mayur Complex, Shastri Nagar, Jaipur-302016 (Rajasthan)
✆ 2302995, 2233273, Fax: 2303558
✉ nirogsuk@datainfosys.net.in
Hd.Org.: Purushottam Vijayvargiya;
Bus.Intt.: Pub.; **Spl.:** Health Magazine *Nirog Sukh*

NISHA PRAKASHAN
B-198, Gali No. 11, Bhajanpura, Delhi-110053
✆ 27616237
Estd.: 1996; **Prop.:** Mrs. Santosh Saxena;
Bus.Intt.: L.S.; **Spl.:** Fiction

NISHANT PRAKASHAN
445, Sheri Galli, Belgaum-590002 (Karnataka)
✆ 228803
Estd.: 1993; **Prop.:** R.S. Lokapur;
Spl.: Presently Interested in Bringing out Books on Comparative Linguistics in Kannada, Marathi, English

NISHKAAM PEETH PRAKASHAN
R-12-A, (Basement) Hauz Khas, New Delhi-110016
✆ 26512504, 26512523
✉ editor@jyotirved.com
Prop.: Ms. Rajeshwari Shanker
Bus.Intt.: Pub. & Dist.

NITA MEHTA CULINARY ACADEMY PVT. LTD.
S-240, Greater Kailash Part-II, New Delhi-110048
✆ 65976202, Fax: 91-11-29225218
✉ nitamehta@email.com
🌐 www.nitamehta.com
Hd.Org.: Nita Mehta
Bus.Intt.: Dist. and B.S.; **Spl.:** Books on Cookery, Self-help, Feng-Shui, *Vaastu*, Reiki, Dog-Care, Home Remedies, etc.

NITA MEHTA PUBLICATION
E-159, Greater Kailash Part-II, New Delhi-110048
✆ (O) 29218574, 29218727, 23252948 (R) 29218727 📱 9810053070, 9810632282, Fax: 29225218, 23252948
✉ nitamehta@email.com
🌐 www.nitamehta.com
Estd.: 2001; **Prop.:** Anurag Mehta
Br.: Nita Mehta Publications, 3A/3, Asaf Ali Rd., New Delhi-110002 ✆ 23252948, 23250091, Fax: 26235218 ✉ nitamehtabooks@email.com
Bus.Intt.: Pub.; **Spl.:** Cookery, Self-help, Feng-Shui, *Vaastu*, Reiki, Dog-Care, Home Remedies, etc.

NITT LTD.
C-125, Okhla Phase-I, New Delhi-110020
✆ 26817341, 26817342

Fax: 26817344, Telefax: 031-75286
Estd.: 1981; **Hd.Org.**: Rajendra S. Pawar
Br.: M-14, NDSE-II, New Delhi-110049
✆ 26446740
Bus.Intt.: Exp.

NITHYANANDA DHYANAPEETAM
Nithyanandapuri, Kallugopahalli, Mysore Road, Bidadi, Bangalore-562109 (Karnataka)
✆ 91-80-65591844, 27202084
mail@nithyananda.org
www.nithyananda.org
Hd.Org.: Paramahamsa Nithyananda Swami
Bus.Intt.: Promoter and Pub.; **Spl.**: Books on meditation and spiritual healing

NITYA BHARATHI BOOKS
Chengannur-689121 (Kerala)
✆ 047812-22636
Estd.: 1986; **Hd.Org.**: Acharya Narendra Bhooshan; **Bus.Intt.**: Pub.

NITYANAND BOOK STORES
Mansoorchak, Begusarai-851128 (Bihar)
Bus.Intt.: Pub. and B.S.

NIYOGI OFFSET PRIVATE LIMITED
(Publishing Division) D-78, Okhla Industrial Area, Phase-I, New Delhi-110020
✆ 26826301, 26813350-52,
Fax: 91-11-26813830, 26810483
▮ 9810645410 bikash12@nda.vsnl.net.in
www.indiamart.com/niyogi
Prop.: Bikash D. Niyogi
Bus.Intt.: Pub.; **Spl.**: Books on Art & Culture, Heritage, Biography & Fiction in English Language

NOBEL BOOKS (P) LTD.
Thiruthiyad, Calicut, Kozhikode (Kerala)

NOBEL FOUNDATION
Flat No. 104-105, 28, Feroze Gandhi Rd., Lajpat Nagar-III, New Delhi-110024
✆ 26845477, 26845542, Fax: 26831814
webmaster@nobletfoundation.org

NOBEL PUBLISHERS (P) LTD.
542/16, Dr. Joshi Rd., Karol Bagh, New Delhi-110005
✆ (O) 27535576, 2730326 (R) 26893018
Estd.: 1989; **Hd.Org.**: Rajesh Ghai;
Bus.Intt.: Pub.; **Spl.**: Children's School Textbooks in English and Hindi

NOIDA NEWS (P) LTD.
48, Shardhanand Rd., Delhi-110006

NORMEN BETHUNE JANASWASTHYA
Andolan, 10-A, Parsibagan Lane, Kolkata-700009 (West Bengal)

NORTH INDIA PUBLISHERS & DISTRIBUTORS
E-343, Sonia Vihar, Delhi-110094
✆ 22179960
Hd.Org.: Tilak Raj Sharma; **Bus.Intt.**: Pub. and Dist.; **Spl.**: Hindi Books

NORTHERN BOOK CENTRE
4221/1, Ansari Rd., Darya Ganj, New Delhi-110002
✆ 23271626, 23280295, 23264519, 23280195, 23271626
Fax: 23252651
scs@del2.vsnl.net.in, nbcnd@ndb.vsnl.net.in
northernbook.com
Estd.: 1986; **Prop.**: Pratap Vaish;
Bus.Intt.: B.S.; **Spl.**: Pol.Sci., Hist., Geo., etc.

NOVA PUBLICATIONS
4743/23, Ansari Rd., Darya Ganj, New Delhi-110002
✆ 23283372, Fax: 23262183
evergreen@del3.vsnl.net.in
www.evergreenpublications.com
Hd.Org.: Nirmal Kumar Gupta;
Bus.Intt.: Pub., Exp.; **Spl.**: Children's Books and Edu. Books

NOVATECH SCIENTIFICS & INFORMATICS
Goyal Nagar, Manpur, Station Rd., Moradabad-244001 (Uttar Pradesh)
✆ 0591-2310723 ▮ 09412139878,
Fax: 2440070
sanjeev_seth_in@yahoo.com
Estd.: 2001; **Prt.**: Sanjeev Seth;
Bus.Intt.: B.S., L.S., WS; **Spl.**: Humanities & Soc.Sci., Sci. & Tech., Comp., Med., Mang.

NOVELTY & COMPANY
Tara Bhawan, Ashok Rajpath, PB No. 27, Patna-800004 (Bihar)
✆ (O) 2672775, 2687561 (R) 2650873, 2657183, Fax: 2687641
noveltyandco.@yahoo.com, noveltyandcompany@yahoo.com
Estd.: 1946; **Hd.Org.**: N.K. Jha;
Bus.Intt.: Pub., Rt. and L.S.;
Spl.: Statistics, Psych., Sol., Hist. and Phil. in Indian and Foreign

NOVELTY BOOK DISTRIBUTORS
7/28, Mahavir Lane, Ansari Rd., New Delhi-110002
✆ (O) 23242323 (R) 25798942
▮ 9811211264, Fax: 25422776
novelty@ndb.vsnl.net.in, noveltybook@vsnl.com
Prop.: Manohar Lal; **Bus.Intt.**: L.S.;
Spl.: Sci., Tech. and Mang. Books

NRITYALAL SEALS LIBRARY
202, Bidhan Sarani, Kolkata-700006 (West Bengal)

NUSRAT PUBLISHERS
Hyderi Market, Aminabad, Lucknow-226018 (Uttar Pradesh)
Prop.: Ani Nusrat; **Bus.Intt.:** Pub.; **Spl.:** Urdu Litt., Fiction, Criticism Poetry and Travelogues

NUTAN BOOK DEPOT
N.P. Shopping Centre, Shop No. 31, Opp. Bus-Stand, Lunawala (Panchmahal) (Gujarat)

NUTAN PUSTAKALAYA
Hariharganj, Aurangabad-824119 (Bihar)
Bus.Intt.: Pub. and B.S.

■ ■ ■

O.B.I. EXPORTS
4379/4B, Prakash House, Ansari Rd., Darya Ganj, New Delhi-110002
✆ 23263363, 23265303,
Fax: 91-11-23278091
✉ obi@del2.vsnl.net.in
Hd.Org.: Ajay Mago; **Bus.Intt.**: Pub.

O.B.S. BOOK DISTRIBUTORS
Oriental Apartments, B-44, Plot No. 50, Sector-9, Rohini, Delhi-110085
✆ (O) 23274303 (R) 27863510
Estd.: 1982; **Prop.**: Prodip Kumar Mago; **Bus.Intt.**: WS

OASIS EDUCATIONAL SERVICES PVT. LTD.
Oasis Bhawan, Opposite Jal Board, B-1, Vasant Kunj, New Delhi-110070
✆ 26124025-7, Fax: 26124028
✉ oescare@vsnl.net
www.oasiscare.com
Hd.Org.: D.P. Gupta; **Bus.Intt.**: Pub.; **Spl.**: Competitive books for Med. Examinations

OASIS BOOKS
17, Kutchery Rd., Mylapore, Chennai-600004 (Tamil Nadu)
✆ 24939276

OBEROI BOOK SERVICE
Shop No. 20, A1 North Block, Bahu Plaza Complex, Rail Head, Jammu-180001 (Jammu & Kashmir)
✆ 2471723, 2580017
Fax: 2472906
✉ obs@rediffmail.com
Estd.: 1992; **Prop.**: Inder Paul Singh; **Bus.Intt.**: L.S. & Rt.; **Spl.**: Humanities & Soc.Sci., Sci. & Tech., Law, Juvenile/Children, Gen. & Fiction etc.

OCCULT INDIA PUBLICATIONS
D-30, Okhla Industrial Area, Phase-I, New Delhi-110020

OCEAN BOOKS PVT. LTD.
4/19, Asaf Ali Rd., New Delhi-110002
✆ 23289555, 23289666, 23289777,
Fax: 91-11-23253233
✉ info@oceanbooks.in, prabhat1@vsnl.com
www.oceanbooks.in
Estd.: 1997; **Hd.Org.**: Pawan Kr. Agrawal; **Bus.Intt.**: Pub.; **Spl.**: Freedom Struggle, Yoga, Human Rights, Defence, etc. in English

OCTOPUS INDIA
2/25, Ansari Rd., New Delhi-110002
✆ 23284894, Fax: 23281819
✉ aparmar@vsnl.com
Hd.Org.: Ajay Parmar; **Bus.Intt.**: Dist.; **Spl.**: Books Published by Foreign Pub.

ODYSSEY BOOK SHOP
6, Ist Main Rd., Gandhi Nagar, Adyar, Chennai-600020 (Tamil Nadu)
✆ 044-24420393, 24908071
Estd.: 1995; **Hd.Org.**: D. Sudharshan; **Bus.Intt.**: Rt.; **Spl.**: Gen. and Trade, Acad., Professional, Electronic Products and Children Books

OFFICE OF THE REGISTRAR GENERAL, INDIA
2/A, Mansingh Rd., New Delhi-110011
✆ 23020629, Fax: 91-11-23383145
✉ rgoffice.rgi@nic.in
www.censusindia.gov.in
Hd.Org.: D.K. Sikri; **Bus.Intt.**: Pub.; **Spl.**: Reports, Monographs, CDs on 2001 Census

OFFICE OF THE STATE EDITOR
Kerala Gazetteers, Thiruvananthapuram-695010 (Kerala)

OFFICERS' ACADEMY
B-15, Harshita Complex, Faizabad Road, Lucknow-226016 (Uttar Pradesh)
✆ 91-522-652734
Bus.Intt.: Pub.; **Spl.**: Books on Social Science and Humanities

OJASAVI PUBLICATIONS
6, Bharati Artist Colony, Vinesh Marg, New Delhi-110092
✆ 22155169, 91-11-22144806
✉ ojasvipublication@yahoo.com
www.ojasvipublication.com
Hd.Org.: Purushottam Tyagi
Bus.Intt.: Pub.; **Spl.**: Books for children

OLD & NEW BOOKS
28, Panchdeep Apartments, Vikaspuri, New Delhi-110018
✆ 91-11-28538200
✉ coinbooks@rediffmail.com
www.coinbooks.esmartweb.com
Hd.Org.: R.D. Bhatt; **Bus.Intt.**: B.S.; **Spl.**: Old and New Books on Numismatics and Hist.

OLIVER PRESS
Nazarath Mansion, 189, Catholic Colony NR Church, Wadala, Mumbai-400031 (Maharashtra)

OLYMPUS BOOKS PVT. LTD.
57A, Park Street, Flat No. 16, Park Mansion, Kolkata-700016 (West Bengal)
Bus.Intt.: Exp.

OM BOOK SERVICE
1690, Ist Floor, Nai Sarak, Delhi-110006
✆ 23279323, 23274303, Fax: 23278091
✉ obl@del2.vsnl.net.in
🌐 www.ombooks.com
Estd.: 1960; **Prop.:** O.P. Mago
Br.: Om Books International, 4379, Parkash House, Ansari Rd., Darya Ganj, New Delhi-110002
✆ (O) 23265303, 23263363, 55350746 (R) 55453590, 55453591, 55453592, Fax: 23278091
✉ ombooks@eth.net, sales@ombooks.com
Bus.Intt.: Pub., WS, L.S. & Rt., Imp., Exp.; **Spl.:** Humanities & Soc.Sci., Sci. & Tech., Juvenile/Children, Gen. & Fiction etc.

OM BOOK SHOP
New Delhi
✆ 24653792, 24653793, Fax: 24653794
✉ sales@ombooks.com, leoamitvig@yahoo.com
Bus.Intt.: B.S.

OM BOOKS
Secunderabad (Andhra Pradesh)
✆ 2861282, Fax: 863956
✉ ombooks@omb.ind.com.org

OM BOOKS INTERNATIONAL
4379/4B, Ansari Road, Darya Ganj, New Delhi-110002
✆ 23265303, 91-11-23278091
✉ sales@ombooks.com
🌐 www.ombooks.com
Hd.Org.: Om Mago
Bus.Intt.: Pub. and Dist.; Spl.: Books on advertising, art, architecture, beauty, fiction, photography and travel

OM PRAKASH AGRAWAL BOOKSELLERS
Main Rd., P.B. No. 29, Near P.O., Jharsuguda-768201 (Orissa)
✆ 06645-263351
Prop.: Om Prakash Agrawal; **Bus.Intt.:** WS, B.S. and L.S.

OM PUBLICATIONS
1643A, Sector 29, Housing Board Colony, Faridabad-121008 (Haryana)
✆ 2272892, 3535574
✉ ipb@ndf.vsnl.net.in
Estd.: 1997; **Prop.:** Rakesh Kumar;
Bus.Intt.: Pub.; **Spl.:** Rel., Hist., Sol., Art and Pol.Sci. in English

OM PUSTAK BHANDAR
Afjuganj, Sultanganj, Bhagalpur-812213 (Bihar)
Bus.Intt.: Pub. and B.S.

OM SAI PUBLISHERS & DISTRIBUTORS
267/4, Govind Puri, Kalkaji, New Delhi-110019
✆ (O) 26232172 (R) 31061215
✉ bkumar_y&k@yahoo.com
Estd.: 1998; **Prop.:** Brijender Kumar;
Bus.Intt.: L.S., WS; **Spl.:** Humanities & Soc.Sci., Tech., Med., Mang.

OM SAKTHI BOOK HOUSE
Chennai (Tamil Nadu)
✆ 23811923, Fax: 23811923
✉ omsbh@rediffmail.com
Bus.Intt.: B.S.

OM SHANTI CANCER NIDAAN SANSTHAN
Chandan Mahal Apartments, Main Beli Rd., Jagdev Path, Bakri Bazaar, Patna-800014 (Bihar)
✆ 2598175 ▮ 9835086857
Hd.Org.: Chandra Madav Prasad;
Bus.Intt.: Pub.; **Spl.:** Edu., Books on Cancer Cure

OM VIGNESH PUBLISHERS
Plot No. 43, 24th Cross St., Padmavathy Nagar, Salaiyur, Chennai-600073 (Tamil Nadu)

OMAR ISLAMIC BOOKS EXPORTER
205, Thapar Chambers-II, Ring Rd., Opp. Kalindi Colony, New Delhi-110014
✆ 26919126, Fax: 91-11-26843787

OMEGA SCIENTIFIC PUBLISHERS
B-17, 2nd Floor, Lajpat Nagar Part-II, New Delhi-110024
✆ 26846071, 26918517, Fax: 26823869
✉ israel4@vsnl.com
Estd.: 1989; **Hd.Org.:** Reuben Israel;
Bus.Intt.: Pub.; **Spl.:** Sci., Tech. and Med.

OMKAR GYANDEEP PRAKASHAN
2875-A, Vangi Bol, Kolhapur-416012 (Maharashtra)

OMSONS PUBLICATIONS
T-7, Rajouri Garden, New Delhi-110027
✆ 25412452, Fax: 23289353
✉ omsons@hotmail.com, omsons@satyam.net.in
Bus.Intt.: Pub. and Dist.

ONKAR BOOK AGENCY
45-A, Humayunpur, Safdarjung Enclave, New Delhi-110029
✆ 26172096, 65691896, Fax: 91-11-41030456
✉ onkarbooks@hotmail.com
Estd.: 2000; **Prop.:** Kulbinder Singh;
Bus.Intt.: Rt., Sub.Ag., L.S.; **Spl.:** Acad., Sci., Pure and Applied, Med., Tech.

ONKAR BOOK AGENCY
61, Mahatma Gandhi Rd., Kolkata-700009 (West Bengal)

OORJA MUSIC
Pune (Maharashtra)

✆ 2630815, 2633880, Fax: 2622512
✉ sahil@pn2.vsnl.net.in

OPERATION MOBILISATION INDIA
Logos Bhawan Medchal Rd., Jeedimetla
Secunderabad-500855 (Andhra Pradesh)
✆ 2862578, 2863956, 2863188
Fax: 0842-2861457

OPPILLA AGENCY
No. 97, New Bus Stand, Complex I.T.I., Opp., Thiruverumber, Tiruchirapalli-600014 (Tamil Nadu)
Bus.Intt.: L.S.

OPTOMETRY TODAY
C4F/216, Janak Puri, New Delhi-110058
✆ (O) 25599839 (R) 25612301
✉ kumars@vsnl.com
Estd.: 1970; **Bus.Intt.:** Pub.; **Spl.:** Sci. Journals

ORBIT INTERNATIONAL
9/148, Khichri Pur Colony, Delhi-110096
✆ 22480042
Prop.: Zulfiquer Ali Khan; **Bus.Intt.:** L.S.; **Spl.:** Acad., Sci., Pure & Applied, Med., Tech., Journals & Magazines

ORIENT BOOK CORPORATION
P.O. Box 2858, New Delhi-110060

ORIENT BOOK CORPORATION
College St. Market, Kolkata-700073 (West Bengal)
Hd.Org.: Prahlad Pramanik; **Bus.Intt.:** Pub.

ORIENT EDUCATIONAL STORES
7/33, Ansari Rd., Darya Ganj,
New Delhi-110002
✆ 23264156, Fax: 91-11-23271065
✉ orientda@airtelbroadband.in
Hd.Org.: Deepak Agarwal; **Bus.Intt.:** Pub. and Manufacturer; **Spl.:** Laminated Maps, Charts, Globes, Models, Teaching Aids, etc.

ORIENT LAW HOUSE
A-37, Amar Colony, Lajpat Nagar-IV,
New Delhi-110024
✆ 26415150, 26483300
✉ orientlaw@now-india.net.in
Hd.Org.: G.D. Kataria; **Bus.Intt.:** Pub.; **Spl.:** Weekly Journal—*Supreme Court Journal* and Law Books

ORIENT BLACKSWAN LTD.
3-6-752, Himayatnagar, Hyderabad 500029 (Andhra Pradesh)
✆ 27662849/2850/5446/5447
Fax: 040-27645046
✉ centraloffice@orientblackswan.com
Br.: Tapovan, No. 46/47, Rama Rao Layout, Banashankari III Stage, Katriguppe, Bangalore-560085 (Karnataka)
✆ 26690258, Fax: 080-26691907
✉ bangalore@orientblackswan.com
• E-3 Senior MIG, Shankar Nagar, Near Bus Stop No. 6 1/2 Area Colony, Bhopal-462016 (Madhya Pradesh)
✆ 0755-2556173
✉ bhopal@orientblackswan.com
• Plot No. 120A, Satya Nagar, Bhubaneswar-751007 (Orissa)
✆ 0674-2543490
✉ info@orientblackswan.com
• Premises No. 1462, Sector 42/B, Chandigrah-160042 (U.T.)
✆ 0-931450917
✉ info@orientblackswan.com
• 160 Anna Salai, Chennai-600002 (Tamil Nadu)
✆ 28523346, 28523247, 28523358
Fax: 044-28522231
✉ chennai@orientblackswan.com
• 41/316 'Gour Mohan', Ambady Lane, Chittor Road, Ernakulam-682011 (Kerala)
✆ 0484-2374577, 2351372
✉ ernakulam@orientblackswan.com
• Col. J. Ali Road, Lakhotia, Guwahati-781001 (Assam)
✆ 0361-2514274, 2513057
✉ guwahati@orientblackswan.com
• 3-6-752 Himayatnagar, Hyderabad-500029 (Andhra Pradesh)
✆ 27662849, 2766850, Fax: 040-27645046
✉ hyderabad@orientblackswan.com
• 2 Krishna Vihar Colony, Ajmer Road, Jaipur-302006 (Rajasthan)
✆ 0141-2220203
✉ info@orientblackswan.com
• 17 Chittaranjan Avenue, Kolkata-700072 (West Bengal)
✆ 22128052, 22216284, Fax: 033-22129673
✉ kolkata@orientblackswan.com
• 27/1/C Gokhale Marg, Lucknow-226001 (Uttar Pradesh)
✆ 4021201, 3238489; Fax: 0522-2204345
✉ lucknow@orientblackswan.com
• Kamani Marg, Ballard Estate, Mumbai-400001 (Maharashtra)
✆ 22616918, 22695859, Fax: 022-22691278
✉ mumbai@orientblackswan.com
• 1/24 Asaf Ali Road, New Delhi-110002
✆ 23234957, 23237356, Fax: 011-23239172
✉ delhi@orientblackswan.com
• City Centre Ashok, Govind Mitra Road Patna-800004 (Bihar)
✆ 0612-2670838, 2663334
✉ patna@orientblackswan.com

ORIENT PAPERBACKS
5A/8, Ansari Road, First Floor, Darya Ganj, New Delhi-110002

✆ 23278877, Fax: 91-11-23278879
✉ orientpbk@vsnl.com,
sales@orientpaperbacks.com
www.orientpaperbacks.com
Estd.: 1975; **Hd.Org.**: Sudhir Malhotra
Br.: 'Vasant', Ground Floor, 3B Peddar Road, Mumbai-400026 (Maharashtra)
✆ 23510343, Fax: 91-22-23510229
• 3-6-280/A/5, Himayatnagar, Opp. Old MLA Qtrs., Hyderabad
✆ 91-40-23223252
Bus.Intt.: Pub.; **Spl.**: Eng. and Hindi PB on Self-improvement, Health and Fitness, Yoga, Palmistry, Astrology, Puzzles, Quizzes, etc.

ORIENT PUBLICATIONS
114, Surya Niketan, Opp. Anand Vihar, Delhi-110092
✆ (O) 22370737 (R) 22374753
▮ 9810693391
✉ orient_pub@rediffmail.com
Estd.: 1984; **Prop.**: Lalit Rajpal; **Bus.Intt.**: Pub., B.S., Dist., L.S. and Exp.; **Spl.**: Indology

ORIENT PUBLISHING HOUSE
Western Kutchery Rd., Meerut-250001 (Uttar Pradesh)

ORIENTAL BOOK CENTRE
Shop No. 18, 557-A, Ch. Kashi Ram Market, IInd Floor, New Chandramal, Delhi-110007
✆ 2704929

ORIENTAL BOOK CO.
Pan Bazar, Guwahati-781001 (Assam)

ORIENTAL BOOK CO. (P) LTD.
56, Surya Sen St., Kolkata-700009 (West Bengal)
✆ (O) 23504534, 23540728 (R) 23509563, 25128427
Estd.: 1945; **Hd.Org.**: Kripesh Bhattacherjee

ORIENTAL BOOK HOUSE
Ghasiyar Hawal, Srinagar-190011 (Jammu & Kashmir)
✆ 277382
Estd.: 1987; **Prop.**: Afaq Ahmad Mir; **Bus.Intt.**: Pub., WS, L.S. & Rt.; **Spl.**: Humanities & Soc.Sci., Sci. & Tech., Med., Law, Gen. & Fiction etc. Journals

ORIENTAL BOOK REPRINT CORPORATION
P.B. No. 5715, 54, Rani Jhansi Rd., New Delhi-110055

ORIENTAL BOOK SYNDICATE
44/1, Beniatola Lane, Kolkata-700009 (West Bengal)

ORIENTAL DISTRIBUTORS
18/C, Tamer Lane, Kolkata-700009 (West Bengal)

ORIENTAL EDUCATIONAL STORES
7/33, Ansari Rd., Darya Ganj, New Delhi-110002
✆ 23264156

ORIENTAL ENTERPRISES
31-B (IInd Floor), Rajpur Rd., Dehradun (Uttarakhand)
✆ 0135-2654218, Fax: 2652111
✉ oriental@samcharet.in
Resi.: 25A, Kalidas Rd., Dehradun-248001
Estd.: 1980; **Prop.**: Devender Singh; **Bus.Intt.**: Pub., B.S., L.S.; **Spl.**: Sci. & Tech., Agri., Forestry & Botany

ORIENTAL INSTITUTE OF RELIGIOUS STUDIES INDIA PUBLICATIONS
Vadavathoor P.O., Kottayam-686010 (Kerala)
✆ 2578319, 2578525
Estd.: 1976; **Hd.Org.**: Xavier Koodapuzha; **Bus.Intt.**: Pub.

ORIENTAL RESEARCH INSTITUTE
Sri Venkateswara University, Tirupati-517502 (Andhra Pradesh)
Bus.Intt.: Pub. and B.S.

ORIENTAL WATCHMAN PUBLISHING HOUSE
Salisbury Park, P.B. No. 1417, Pune-411037 (Maharashtra)
✆ 020-4261441, 4273017, Cable: WATCHMAN, Telex: 145-735 SUD IN, Fax: 020-4261638
✉ owph@pn2.vsnl.net.in
Estd.: 1898; **Gen.Man.**: G.S. Robert Clive; **Bus.Intt.**: Pub. and B.S.; **Spl.**: Health, Edu. & Religious Books

ORIGINALS
A-6, Nimri Commercial Centre, Near Ashok Vihar, Phase-IV, Delhi-110052
✆ 27452453, 27401672
✉ lpp@nde.vsnl.net.in
www.lippindia.com
Hd.Org.: Pradeep Mittal; **Bus.Intt.**: Pub.; **Spl.**: Acad. books on Humanities and Soc.Sci.

ORION BOOKS
387-A J&K Pocket, Dilshad Garden, Delhi-110095
✆ 22298067
✉ orionbooks74@hotmail.com
Bus.Intt.: Pub. and Dist.

ORISSA ENVIRONMENTAL SOCIETY
D-39, Block 7, Javaydev Vihar, Near R.R.L., Bhubaneswar-751013 (Orissa)

ORISSA PUBLISHERS & BOOKSELLERS' ASSOCIATION
Binod Behari, Cuttack-753002 (Orissa)
✆ 2612855
Hd.Org.: Subhendu Sekhar Ratha
Bus.Intt.: Promoter; **Spl.**: Oriya Language and Litt.

OSA BOOKS & PERIODICALS PVT. LTD.
7/28, Lower Ground Floor, Vardaan House, Mahavir Lane, Ansari Rd., Darya Ganj, New Delhi-110002
✆ 23259171, 26460705, Fax: 23259161
✉ osabooks@hotmail.com
Hd.Org.: Rakesh Sagar; **Bus.Intt.:** Pub. and Dist.; **Spl.:** Comp., Mang., Sci. and Tech., Published by Indian and Foreign Pub.

OSCAR PUBLICATIONS
Ganderpora Idgah, Srinagar (Jammu & Kashmir)
✆ (O) 271140 (R) 273642
Estd.: 1989; **Prop.:** Shakeel Ahmed Hafiz; **Bus.Intt.:** Pub.; **Spl.:** School Text Books, Art Books, Books on Gen. Knowledge, I.Q. Test Series in English and Urdu

OSCAR PUBLICATIONS
Delhi
✆ 27130449, 27435724, Fax: 27435724
✉ info@oscarindia.com, oscar@del2.vsnl.net.in
Bus.Intt.: Pub. & B.S.

OSHAN PUBLICATIONS
922, Kucha Rohella, Tihara Behram Khan, Darya Ganj, New Delhi-110002

OSHO DHARMTEERTHA SANNYAS ASHRAM
51, Jaffershaw St., Tiruchirappalli-620008 (Tamil Nadu)
✆ 043-228408, 2700408
Hd.Org.: Swami Mohan Bharti; **Bus.Intt.:** B.S., Pub.; **Spl.:** Books of Osho Translated in Tamil Language, Selling English and Hindi Books of Osho Published by Osho Commune International, Poona, Selling English and Hindi Video and Audio Cassetts of Osho's Discourses

OSHO LOVE AFFAIR
2/69, Roop Nagar, Delhi-110007
✆ 23967450, 23981989, Fax: 23935532
✉ osholoveaffair@vsnl.com
Hd.Org.: Pradeep Wadhwa; **Bus.Intt.:** Pub.; **Spl.:** Books and Audio Tapes on Osho's Discourses and Meditation

OSHO MEVLANA MEDITATION CENTER
Hyderabad (Andhra Pradesh)
✆ 55629311
✉ mahacon@hd1.vsnl.net.in
Bus.Intt.: B.S.

OSHO PUBLICATIONS, PUNE
17, Koregaon Park, Pune-411001
✆ 4019999, Fax: 4019900
✉ distrib@osho.net
🌐 www.osho.com
Hd.Org.: Mukesh Sarda; **Bus.Intt.:** Pub. & Dist.; **Spl.:** Books and Audio-Video tapes of Osho

OSHO VISION
Tao Publishing (P) Ltd., 50, Koregaon Park, Pune-411001 (Maharashtra)
Spl.: Books on Meditation, Phil. etc. by Rajneesh 'OSHO'

OSHO WORLD FOUNDATION
C-5/44, Safdarjung Development Area, New Delhi-110016
✆ 65694869, Fax: 91-11-26691074
✉ contact@oshoworld.com
🌐 www.oshoworld.com
Hd.Org.: Swami Atul Anand; **Bus.Intt.:** Promoter, Pub. & Dist.; **Spl.:** Books and CDs on Osho Litt.

OSWAAL BOOKS
Oswaal House, 1/11, Sahitya Kunj, M.G. Road, Agra-282002 (Uttar Pradesh)
✆ 2856558, 2857671, Fax: 91-562-2854582
✉ contact@oswaalbooks.com
🌐 www.oswaalbooks.com
Estd.: 1950; **Hd.Org.:** Naresh Jain **Bus.Intt.:** Pub.

OSWAL BOOK AGENCIES
Oswal House 1/11, Sahitya Kunj, M.G. Rd., Agra-282002 (Uttar Pradesh)

OSWAL COMPETITION BOOKS
Agra (Uttar Pradesh)
✆ 0562-215655-8, Fax: 2522141
✉ oswalbooks@indiatimes.com
Bus.Intt.: Pub.

OSWAL PRINTERS & PUBLISHERS (P) LTD.
14/131, Hospital Rd., Agra-282003 (Uttar Pradesh)
✆ 275686, 261713
Hd.Org.: Naresh Jain; **Bus.Intt.:** Pub.; **Spl.:** ICSE, Children Textbooks in Eng. and Hindi

OTHER BOOKS
79, Mahatma Gandhi Rd., Kolkata-700009 (West Bengal)

OUTLOOK PUBLISHING (INDIA) PVT. LTD.
AB/10, Safdarjung Enclave, New Delhi-110029
✆ 26191421-24, Fax: 91-11-26191420
✉ yourhelpline@outlookindia.com
🌐 www.outlookindia.com
Ch.Exe.: Maheshwer Peri; **Bus.Intt.:** Pub.; **Spl.:** Weekly Magazine

OVERLEAF
P1/6, Ground Floor, DLF Phase-II, Gurgaon-122002 (Haryana)
✆ 95-124-2576796

overleaf@vsnl.net
Hd.Org.: S. Seshadri
Bus.Intt.: Dist.; **Spl.:** Children's books published by foreign pub. from USA & UK

OVERSEAS BOOKS
B-1-A, DDA Flats, Nr. Central School, Tagore Garden Extension, New Delhi-110027
✆ 25463308, 55394449, Fax: 91-11-25114297
overseas_bks@yahoo.co.in
Prop.: Mrs. M. Gupta
Bus.Intt.: Dist., B.S. and L.S.;
Spl.: Science, Technology, Soc.Sci. and Management etc.

OVERSEAS PRESS (INDIA) PVT. LTD.
2/15, Ansari Rd., Daryaganj, New Delhi-110002
✆ 23269503, Fax: 91-11-23250262
info@overseaspub.com
www.overseaspub.com
Prop.: Narinder Kumar Nijhara;
Bus.Intt.: Pub., Dist. Imp. and Stockist;
Spl.: Books on science and technology, social sciences, marketing, etc.

OVERSEAS PUBLICATIONS SERVICES
14, Hare Street (1st Floor), Kolkata-700001 (West Bengal)
✆ 22484007
Estd.: 1970; **Hd.Org.:** Mrs. Minoti Chandra;
Bus.Intt.: Pub., Imp., Exp., Sub.Ag.

OXBRIDGE BOOKS (INDIA)
11090, Doriwalan, East Park Rd., Karol Bagh, New Delhi-110005
✆ 23516869, 23515954, 27173984
Hd.Org.: Satyapal Punjhi; **Bus.Intt.:** Pub.;
Spl.: Edu. Books on Computer, Soc.Sci., Math., Pure Sci., etc.

OXFORD & IBH PUBLISHING CO. PVT. LTD.
66, Janpath, New Delhi-110001
✆ (O) 23415896, 23416951, 23324578, 23320518 (R) 26862327, 26967714, Fax: 51517559
oxford@vsnl.com
Estd.: 1962; **Man.Dir.:** Mohan Primlani
Br.: D-16, Connaught Place, New Delhi-110001 ✆ 23415896, 23416951, Fax: 51517559, 23710090
• 22, Park Mansion, 57, Park St., Kolkata-700016 (West Bengal)
✆ 2291389, Cable: SCHOLAR
Bus.Intt.: Pub.; **Spl.:** Humanities and Soc.Sci., Mang. and Comm., Sci., Engg. and Tech., Med. Sci.

OXFORD BOOK & STATIONERY CO.
Darjeeling (West Bengal)
✆ 254325

OXFORD BOOK & STATIONERY CO.
Scindia House, Connaught Place, New Delhi-110001
✆ (O) 23315896, 23315308 (R) 24623066, Fax: 91-11-23713275
oxford.pubs.@axcess.net.in;
Hd.Org.: H.T. Primlani; **Bus.Intt.:** Sub.Ag.;
Spl.: Books and Periodicals

OXFORD BOOK COMPANY
B-46, Natraj Nagar, Imliwala Phatak, Jaipur-302015 (Rajasthan)
✆ 2762072, 2594705, Pager: 9698 260052, Fax: 0141-2593892
abdpublishers@rediffmail.com
Hd.Org.: G.K. Agrawal; **Bus.Intt.:** L.S.;
Spl.: University and College Lib. of Jaipur

OXFORD BOOK DEPOT
Main Street, Mhow (Madhya Pradesh)

OXFORD BOOK DEPOT
Opp. Railway Station, Moradabad (Uttar Pradesh)

OXFORD BOOK STORE GALLERY
17, Park Street, Kolkata-700016 (West Bengal)
✆ 2298509, 2297662, Fax: 22499250
oxfordbooksstore@hotmail.com, a-jairam@hotmail.com
Estd.: 1920; **Hd.Org.:** Ms. Priti Paul;
Bus.Intt.: Rt., L.S., Mail Order Service (Indian and Foreign) Exp.; **Spl.:** All Types of Books, Greeting Cards, Toys and Children Books

OXFORD EXPORT HOUSE
66, Janpath, New Delhi-110001
✆ 23324578, 23320518, Fax: 23710090
oxford@vsnl.com
Man.Dir.: Mohan Primlani

OXFORD PUBLISHING HOUSE
39, M.G. Rd., Haridevpur, Kolkata-700082 (West Bengal)

OXFORD SUBSCRIPTION COMPANY
68, Shakespeare Sarani, 2nd Floor, Post Box No. 16154, Kolkata-700004 (West Bengal)
✆ 22473345, 22409308, 22409728

OXFORD UNIVERSITY PRESS
1st Floor, YMCA Library Building, 1, Jai Singh Road, Post Box 43, New Delhi-110001
✆ 43600300, Fax: 91-11-23360897
admin.in@oup.com
www.oup.com
Estd.: 1912; **Man.Dir.:** Manzar Khan
Br.: C-3 & C-38, Block-C, Sector-59, Dist. Gautam Budh Nagar, Noida
✆ 2587738, 2587742-45,

Fax: 91-120-2587741
✉ customerservice.in@oup.com
Sales Off.: 2/11, Ansari Road, Daryaganj, P.O. Box 7035, New Delhi
✆ 23273841-12, 23253647
Fax: 91-11-23277812
✉ delhi.in@oup.com
• 167, C.S.T. Road, Vidyanagari P.O., Kalina Santacruz (East), Mumbai-400098
✆ 26521034-35, 66973891-92
Fax: 91-22-26521133
✉ mumbai.in@oup.com
• Plot No. A1-5, Block GP, Sector V, Salt Lake Electronics Complex, Kolkata-700091
✆ 23573739/40/41, 23573947/8
Fax: 91-33-23573738
✉ kolkata.in@oup.com
• 289, Anna Salai, Chennai-600006
✆ 28112107, Fax: 91-44-28110962
✉ chennai.in@oup.com
Sh.: Ground Floor, Lilavati Chambers, Behind Handloom House, Ashram Road, Ahmedabad-380009, ✆ 26574291, 26575137, Fax: 91-79-26575291
✉ oupahd@dataone.in
• 94, Industrial Area, 4th 'B' Cross, 5th Block, Koramangala, Bangalore-560095
✆ 41216287, 41216288
Fax: 91-80-25538736
✉ bangalore.in@oup.com
• Plot No. 2B & 2C, Unit-3, Kharavela Nagar, Behind Ram Mandir, Bhubaneswar-751001
✆ 2530116, 3262888, Fax: 91-674-2530117
✉ oupbbsr@bsnl.in
• SCO 45 & 46, 1st Floor Sector 8C, Madhya Marg, Chandigarh-160009
✆ 91-172-2545794, 2547117
✉ oup_chd@dataone.in
• 2/11, Ansari Road, Daryaganj, P.O. Box 7035, New Delhi, ✆ 23273841/2
Fax: 91-11-23277812
✉ csdel.in@oup.com;
• Kadavil Building, G-132, Door No. 28/8, Panampilly Nagar, Ernakulam, Cochin-682036
✆ 2322425, Fax: 91-484-2322428
✉ ernakulam.in@oup.com
• Pragjyotish Apartment (First Floor), M. Tayabullah Road, Dighali Pukhuri (East), Guwahati-781001 ✆ 2131349/2543050,
Fax: 91-361-2513310
✉ oxfordguw@dataone.in
• First Floor, H.No. 8-2-577, Road No. 7, Banjara Hills, Hyderabad-500034
✆ 23356425/65769685, Fax: 91-40-23356424
✉ hyderabad.in@oup.com
• A-19, Main Sahakar Path, Near Nehru Sahakar Bhavan, Jaipur
✆ 91-141-5124989/2743816
✉ oupjaipur@yahoo.co.uk
• B-7/18, Sector K, Aliganj, Lucknow-226024
✆ 4024120, Fax: 91-522-2762472
✉ ouplko@airtelbroadband.in
• Emarat-Al-Harmain, Near Punjab National Bank, Bank Road, Patna-800001
✆ 2230971, Fax: 91-612-2200845
✉ oup_patna@sify.com
Bus.Intt.: Pub., Imp. and Exp.;
Spl.: Humanities & Soc.Sci, Sci. & Tech., Med., Law, Juvenile/Children

OXONIAN PRESS PVT. LTD.
N-56, Brigade Rd.,
Post Box No. 2587,
Bangalore-560025 (Karnataka)

P. ANDREW VALSAN
Tamil Nadu Postgraduate Teachers, Association, 12, Annie Niwas Koiladivilai, Nagarcoil-629001 (Tamil Nadu)

P. AHSMUKHLANI CO.
Opp. Central Bank, Surendranagar (Gujarat)

P. CHAND AND CO. PUBLISHERS
2603, Nai Sarak, New Delhi-110006
✆ (O) 23263386, 27430823, 22910242 (R) 27215834
Estd.: 1977; **Hd.Org.:** Prem Chand Gupta; **Bus.Intt.:** Pub.; **Spl.:** National Income, Accounting, Rashtriya Aay Lekhanken, Evaluation of Indian Economy +2, Elementary Statistics

P.A.D.U. PUBLICATIONS
8, Shiva Market II, Madhuban Chowk, Pitampura, Delhi-110034
✆ 27026218
Estd.: 1991

P.A.V. AUDIO VISUAL
Delhi
✆ 22112976, 22286071, Fax: 22112976
pavaudiovisual@yahoomail.com
Spl.: Maps & Charts

P.B. INTERNATIONAL
14, Raja Rammohan Ray Sarani (Second Floor), Kolkata-700009 (West Bengal)
✆ 033-23541386 ▮ 9831143468, Fax: 033-25520278
pbinternational@rediffmail.com
Hd.Org.: G.C. Biswas; **Bus.Intt.:** Pub., Dist., B.S.

P.B. PUBLICATIONS (P) LTD.
Sector 16/2120, Faridabad (Haryana)

P.B.D. PUBLISHERS & DISTRIBUTORS (REGD.)
1507, Nai Sarak, Delhi-110006
✆ 23285501, 23260329, Fax: 23285501
info@neerajbooks.com
Estd.: 1990; **Prop.:** Neeraj Chopra; **Bus.Intt.:** Pub. and Dist.; **Spl.:** Edu. Books

P.C. CHAKRABORTY & CO.
74, Bechu Chatterjee St., Kolkata-700009 (West Bengal)

P.C. JAIN & COMPANY
Imphal (Manipur)
✆ 0385-221756, 225004
newsagency1@rediffmail.com
Bus.Intt.: B.S. & Dist.

P.C.M. BOOK SHOP
1st Floor, Sundaram Complex, (Near Shiv Vishnu Temple), 91, Usman Road, T. Nagar, Chennai-600017 (Tamil Nadu)
✆ 044-24337329
mdspcm@yahoo.com
Hd.Org.: Sajan, K.A.; **Bus.Intt.:** B.S.; **Spl.:** NCERT, CBSE & MATRIC Reference Books, Children's Books & Guides, Comp., Engg., Med., Mang., Entrance Exams Competitive Books, Litt. Stories, Fictions, Dictionaries etc.

P.G. DEPARTMENT (SANSKRIT) UTKAL UNIVERSITY
Vani Vihar, Bhubaneswar-751004 (Orissa)

P.G.T. BOOKS INTERNATIONAL
270-F, Arjun Nagar, Safdarjung Enclave, New Delhi-110029
✆ (O) 26167998 (R) 25500143, Fax: 011-26196409
pgtbooks@indiatimes.com
Estd.: 1987; **Prt.:** P.C. Ramanathan, M.N. Vijayakumar; **Bus.Intt.:** Rt. and L.S.; **Spl.:** Sci., Pure & Applied, Sci., Tech. and Man.

P.J. MEHTA (DR.)
64, Poddar Rd., Hari Bhawan, Mumbai-400026 (Maharashtra)

P.K. BROTHERS
S.M. St., Kozhikode-673001 (Kerala)
✆ (O) 0495-264993 (R) 275752
Hd.Org.: P. Bhuvenesh; **Bus.Intt.:** Pub. and B.S.; **Spl.:** Gen. Books

P.K. ENTERPRISES
Block-77, Opp. St. Patrick's Junior College, Agra-282002 (Uttar Pradesh)
✆ (O) 2353506 (R) 2260384, 2261091
Estd.: 1990; **Hd.Org.:** P.K. Jain; **Bus.Intt.:** B.S.; **Spl.:** All Subject and Specialised in School Books (English)

P.K. ENTERPRISES
Hyderabad (Andhra Pradesh)
✆ 23308329
rahulchoudhary18@hotmail.com
Bus.Intt.: B.S.

P.M. BAGCHI & CO. PVT. LTD.
19, Gulu Ostagar Lane, Kolkata-700006 (West Bengal)
✆ 22554-9806, 2543-0063
Hd.Org.: Jayana Bagchi

P.N. PUSTAK BHANDAR
Ghogha, Bhagalpur-813205 (Bihar)
Bus.Intt.: Pub. and B.S.

P.S. MULTIMEDIA
1/4222, Ansari Rd., Darya Ganj, New Delhi-110002

✆ 23278368, 23261465, Fax: 91-11-23264368
✉ psm@dkpd.com, dkpd@del3.vsnl.net.in
Ch.Exe.: Parmil Mittal; **Bus.Intt.:** Dist.;
Spl.: CD's

P.S.R. COMPUTERS AND GRAPHIX ARTS
13/1, Ali Asber Rd., Bangalore-560052 (Karnataka)

P.T. BOOK INTERNATIONAL
B-45, Gali No. 10, Gagan Vihar, (Near Molar Band School), Badarpur, New Delhi-110044
✆ 26662006 ▮ 9810726769
Hd.Org.: Pramod Tiwari; **Bus.Intt.:** L.S.;
Spl.: Beh.Sci., Soc.Sci., Sci., Tech. & Rare

P.V. SUBHA RAO
Jawaharlal Nehru Centenary Library, I Pingidi-534342, Korvur Mandal, West Godawari Distt. (Andhra Pradesh)

PAARI NILAYAM
184, Broadway, Chennai-600018 (Tamil Nadu)
✆ 2515561
Hd.Org.: K.A. Chellappan; **Bus.Intt.:** Pub. and Dist.; **Spl.:** Tamil Books on Litt., Phil., Rel. and Tailoring, Annamalai University Publications, Kasi Madam, International Institute of Tamil Studies and Sahitya Academy

PACE ELCOT AUTOMATION LTD.
IInd Floor Khlleli Khalleli Centre, 149, Montieth Rd., Egmore, Chennai-600008 (Tamil Nadu)

PACIFIC PRESS
A1/2, Lok Vihar, Pitampura, Delhi-110034
✆ 27108207, 32324154
✉ pacificpress@red.com
Hd.Org.: Vidya Mahrotri; **Bus.Intt.:** Dist.;
Spl.: Advt., Arch., Art, Photography, Graphics, Interior Design, Cookery, Web Design

PADMA BOOK HOUSE
49/649, Palakkad-678012 (Kerala)
✆ (O) 2530399 (R) 2501018
Estd.: 1994; **Hd.Org.:** Krishnakumar C.;
Bus.Intt.: B.S.; **Spl.:** School, Graduate, Adv. Books for Lib., Gen. Books of All Types

PADMA BOOK STALL
27, Alexandra Press Rd., Nagerocoil, Kanya Kumari Distt.-629001 (Tamil Nadu)
Estd.: 1986; **Bus.Intt.:** L.S. and Rt.

PAHI PRAKASH
Pan Bazar, Guwahati-781001 (Assam)

PAI & COMPANY
Paico Buildings, Jew St., Ernakulam, Cochin-682035 (Kerala)
✆ 2382068, 2381515, Cable: PAICO
Fax: 0484-2353163
✉ paico@paicoindia.com
www.paicoindia.com
Estd.: 1955; **Ch.Exe.:** Manoj V. Pai
Br.: Pai & Company, Broadway, Ernakulam, Cochin-682031 (Kerala)
✆ 2361020, Fax: 0484-2353163
• Pai & Company, M.G. Rd., Ernakulam, Cochin-682035 (Kerala)
✆ 2355835, Fax: 0484-353163
• Pai & Company, M.G. Rd., Opp. Ayurveda College, Thiruvananthapuram-605001 (Kerala)
✆ 0471-2330116; • Pai & Company, K.K. Rd., Kottayam-686002 (Kerala)
✆ 0481-2562391; • Pai & Company, Kallai Rd., Calicut-673002 (Kerala)
✆ 0495-2302851
• Pai & Company, Paico Buildings, Press Rd., Thiruvananthapuram-695001 (Kerala)
✆ 0471-2330813
Bus.Intt.: Pub., WS, L.S. & Rt., Imp., Exp., Sub.Ag.; **Spl.:** Humanities & Soc.Sci., Sci. & Tech., Med., Juvenile/Children, Gen. & Fiction

PAI & SONS
190, Big Bazaar St., Coimbatore-641001 (Tamil Nadu)
✆ 2393024, 5586050
✉ paisons@md3.vsnl.net.in
Estd.: 1952; **Hd.Org.:** N. Anand Pai;
Bus.Intt.: L.S. and Rt.

PAI BROTHERS
"Madhavam", Thirumal Bhagam P.O., Kerala-688540

PAKSHIKKOOTTAM BOOKS
Near Adhyapaka Bhavan Statue, Thiruvananthapuram-695001 (Kerala)
Estd.: 1993; **Hd.Org.:** C.S. Sanal Kumar;
Bus.Intt.: Pub. and B.S.

PAL BOOK DISTRIBUTORS
Shop No. 4, A.C. Market, Surya Kiran Building, Mall Rd., Ludhiana (Punjab)
✆ (O) 0161-2446858 (R) 2459923
✉ book-pal@yahoo.com
Estd.: 1993; **Prop.:** Gurdev Singh;
Bus.Intt.: B.S., L.S., **Spl.:** Humanities & Soc.Sci., Sci. & Tech., Comp., Mang., Children & General, Arts & Arch.

PALAKA PRAKASHAN
1714-B, Pili Kothi, S.P. Mukherjee Marg, Delhi-110006

PALANI PARAMOUNT PUBLICATIONS
69-D, Anna Nagar, Palani-624602 (Tamil Nadu)
✆ 04545-242332, 243212, Fax: 244316
✉ spalani1@md4.vsnl.net.in
Prop.: P. Sarojini; **Bus.Intt.:** Pub.; **Spl.:** College Textbooks, Gen. and Reference Books in English

PALANIAPPA BROTHERS
25 (Old no. 14), Peters Rd., Royapettah, Chennai-600014 (Tamil Nadu)
✆ (O) 044-28132863 (R) 28275685
Fax: 28133350
✉ sales@palbrothers.com
Estd.: 1942; **Hd.Org.:** S.M. Palaniappa Chettiar; **Bus.Intt.:** Pub., **Spl.:** Gen. Books Text Books and Guides

PALANIAPPA BROTHERS LTD.
P.B. No. 312, Teppakulam, Tiruchirapalli-687002 (Tamil Nadu)

PALGRAVE MACMILLAN
5A/12, Ansari Rd., Darya Ganj, New Delhi-110002
✆ 23272010, 23259643, Fax: 23272010
✉ jagat@del2.vsnl.net.in
www.palgrave.com
Hd.Org.: Kalpna Shukla
Br.: Pan Macmillan Ltd., 5A/12, Ansari Rd., Darya Ganj, New Delhi-110002
✆ 23272010, 23259643, Fax: 23272010
✉ panmacmillan@vsnl.com
www.panmacmillan.com
Bus.Intt.: Pub., **Spl.:** Soc.Sci., Humanities, Edu., Engg., Sci., Journals etc. in English

PALJOR PUBLICATION
H-9, (Basement) Jangpura Extn., New Delhi-110014
✆ (O) 24325643, 24325644, 25312952 (R) 24312416, Fax: 011-24325643
✉ palpub@vsnl.com, palpub@tibet.net
www.paljorpublications.com
Estd.: 1993; **Prop.:** Tsewang Gyalpo, CEO, **Exe.:** Ngawang Gyltsen; **Spl.:** Books on Tibetan Studies, *i.e.* Tibetan Buddhism, Hist., Culture, Language, Pechas & Fiction etc.

PALLAV PRAKASHAN
1458, Malibada, Nai Sarak, Delhi-110006
✆ 22250627
Hd.Org.: Yashpal Sharma

PALLAVI PRAKASHAN
A-35, Nirman Vihar, Delhi-110092
Hd.Org.: Pallavi Sood
Br.: X-6, Hauz Khas, 1st and 2nd Floor, New Delhi-110016

PAN PUBLISHERS
203/4D, Bidhan Sarani, Kolkata-700006 (West Bengal)
Hd.Org.: Prasanta Pan

PANAI PATHIPPAGAM
C-227, Kamarajar Rd., Thirunagar, Madurai-625016 (Tamil Nadu)

PANCHARATAN FIRM
Howly, Barpeta (Assam)
Bus.Intt.: Pub.

PANCHSHEEL PRAKASHAN
Film Colony, Jaipur-302003 (Rajasthan)
✆ 2315072, Fax: 2326554
✉ panchsheel_j@sify.com
Estd.: 1968; **Prop.:** Moolchand Gupta; **Bus.Intt.:** Pub., WS, L.S. & Rt.; **Spl.:** Humanities & Soc.Sci., Tech. & Med., Juvenile/Children, Gen. & Fiction etc.

PANDEY BAL VIKASH PUSTAK BHANDAR
Risiup, Aurangabad-524111 (Bihar)
Bus.Intt.: Pub. and B.S.

PANDEY BOOK HOUSE
39A, Sector-17A, Anand Theatre Complex, Chandigarh-160017
✆ 2713010, 2711093
Estd.: 1994; **Prop.:** A.K. Pandey; **Bus.Intt.:** B.S. and L.S. on Computer, 1st to B.A., Competition Books and Guides in English

PANDEY PUSTAK KENDRA
Amba, Aurangabad-824111 (Bihar)
Bus.Intt.: Pub. and B.S.

PANDEY PUSTAKALAYA
Radha Market, Hariharganj, Aurangabad-824119 (Bihar)
Bus.Intt.: Pub. and B.S.

PANDEY PUSTAKALAYA
Nabinagar, Aurangabad-834301 (Bihar)
Bus.Intt.: Pub. and B.S.

PANDULIPI
16, Shyama Charan Dey St., Kolkata-700073 (West Bengal)
Bus.Intt.: Pub.; **Spl.:** Fiction, Poetry Collection, Children's Litt., Rel. Books in Bengali and Hindi

PANDULIPI PRAKASHAN
77/1, East Azad Nagar, Delhi-110051
✆ 22090064, 22094275
Hd.Org.: Hari Ram Dwivedi; **Bus.Intt.:** Pub. and B.S.; **Spl.:** Hindi Litt.

PANIMA BOOK DISTRIBUTORS
16, Prakash Apartments, 5, Ansari Rd., Darya Ganj, New Delhi-110002
✆ 23264039, 23282623, Fax: 23264039
✉ panimabooks@satyam.net.in
Hd.Org.: Jasjit Singh Gujral; **Bus.Intt.:** Dist.; **Spl.:** Life Sci., Agri., Bio., Physical Sci., Comp. and Med.Sci.

PANIMA EDUCATIONAL BOOK AGENCY/ PANIMA PUBLISHING CORPORATION
C-8, Safdarjung, Development Area, Opp. IIT, Gate, Hauz Khas, New Delhi-110016
✆ 23264039, 23282623, 26866488

Fax: 26863145
panimabooks@satyam.net.in
Estd.: 1967; **Prop.**: Inderjit Singh Gujral
Br.: Panima Subscription Agency, 16, Prakash Apartments, 5, Ansari Rd., New Delhi-110002 (O) 23264039, 23282623 (R) 26219027, Fax: 26863145
• 33-35, Sriji Apartments, Gandhi Nagar 5th Cross, Bangalore-560009
080-22256718, 22282684, Fax: 22282684
panima@blr.vsnl.net.in
Bus.Intt.: Pub., Dist., WS, L.S. & Rt., Imp., Sub.Ag.; **Spl.**: Journals on Agri. Biological Sci., Med., Life Sci., Engg., Physical, Sci. & Tech.

PANJAB BOOK DEPOT
1503, Nai Sarak, Delhi-110006
23260329, 23266788, 23285501
Estd.: 1948; **Hd.Org.**: Chander Chopra

PANJAB PRAKASHAK
J-6/85, Rajouri Garden, New Delhi-110027
25410410

PANJAB UNIVERSITY
Publication Bureau, Panjab University, Chandigarh-160014
(O) 0172-2541782, 2694273 (R) 2694273
Estd.: 1948; **Hd.Org.**: H.R. Grover;
Bus.Intt.: Pub. and Dist.; **Spl.**: College Level Books, Gen. Books and Doctoral Dissertations, Specially on Sikh Rel. and Phil. in English and Regional Languages

PANKAJ BOOK CENTRE
Khajuri Bazar, Indore-452002 (Madhya Pradesh)
2535986

PANKAJ PRAKASHAN
G-7/96, Sector-15, Rohini, Delhi-110085
27893988
Estd.: 1978; **Hd.Org.**: Smt. Usha Malhotra;
Bus.Intt.: Pub.; **Spl.**: Gen. Books, Story, Novel in Hindi

PANKAJ PUBLICATION
M-114, Vikas Puri, New Delhi-110018
Sales Off.: 3, Regal Building, Sansad Marg, New Delhi-110001
30955771, 23363395, 23348805, Fax: 23363395
vikas@pankajbooks.com, book@vsnl.com
www.pankajbooks.com
Hd.Org.: Vikas Bajaj; **Bus.Intt.**: Pub. & Exp.;
Spl.: Indology, Indian Art, Music and Culture

PANKAJ PUBLICATIONS INTERNATIONAL
69, Kishan Ganj Market, Delhi-110007
33100770
support@pankajpublicationint.com, pankaj_arora@sandesh.com
www.pankajpublication.com
Estd.: 1992; **Prop.**: Pankaj Arora
Bus.Intt.: L.S.; **Spl.**: Acad., Beh.Sci., Soc.Sci., Comm., Rare, Fashion, Design, Textile Design, Art, Interior & Edu. Books etc.

PANKAJ PUSTAKALAYA
Madanpur, Aurangabad-824208 (Bihar)
Bus.Intt.: Pub. and B.S.

PANSY BOOKS
RZ-66A, Somesh Vihar, Chhawla Village, New Delhi
25317355 9868272107
Estd.: 2003; **Prop.**: Rakesh Gautam;
Bus.Intt.: L.S.; **Spl.**: All Sub.

PANTHER PUBLISHERS PVT. LTD.
No. 33, First Main, Koramangala First Block, Bangalore-560034 (Karnataka)
5505836, 5505837, 5537145, Fax: 5505981
panther_publishers@vsnl.com
www.pantherpublishers.com
Estd.: 1987; **Man.Dir.**: P.T. Rajasekharan
Br.: 222, Imain, I Block, Jakkasandra, Extension Koramangla, Bangalore-560034
25522869, 25539640, Fax: 25537145
• 5, Vijay Banjara, 1-10-84, Mayur Marg Begumpet, Hyderabad-500016
27764127, 27760947, Fax: 27760947
panther@sol.net.in
Bus.Intt.: Pub., WS; **Spl.**: Sci. & Tech., Med.

PAPPAM INDIA
R-Block, 9-C, Dilshad Garden, New Delhi-110095
22286286

PAPYRUS PVT. LTD.
DSIDC No. 5, (Scheme-I), Phase 2, Okhla Industrial Area, New Delhi-110020
Bus.Intt.: Exp.

PARADISE BOOK COMPANY
19, College St., Kolkata-700012 (West Bengal)

PARAG PRAKASHAN
1-2/16 Main Ansari Rd., Darya Ganj, New Delhi-110002
23280234, Fax: 23280234
Hd.Org.: Neetu Jhari; **Bus.Intt.**: Pub.;
Spl.: Hindi Language, Litt. and Children's Books

PARAGATI LIBRARY
8B/1, Tamer Lane, Kolkata-700009 (West Bengal)

PARAGON ENTERPRISE
Kolkata (West Bengal)

✆ 2808924, 2808925, Fax: 2801620
✉ southest@cal2.vsnl.net.in
Bus.Intt.: Exp. & Imp.

PARAKASHAK
82/1, M.G. Rd., Kolkata-700009 (West Bengal)

PARAMAMITRA PRAKASHAN
D-Pocket 214, Dilshad Garden, Delhi-110095
✆ 23917538, 22295900
Hd.Org.: Madhuri Pandey; **Bus.Intt.**: Pub.; **Spl.**: Indology and Litt. in Hindi, Sanskrit, Pali and Prakrit Languages

PARAMANI
Station Rd., Sibsagar (Assam)
Bus.Intt.: Pub.

PARAMESWARI PRAKASHAN
B-109, Preet Vihar, Delhi-110092
Hd.Org.: Rajeev Sharma

PARAMITA PUBLICATION
3, Shyama Charan Dey St., Kolkata-700073 (West Bengal)

PARAMOUNT INTERNATIONAL (BOOK DISTRIBUTORS)
16/90D, Faiz Rd., Karol Bagh, New Delhi-110005
✆ (O) 27776821 (R) 27772484, Fax: 23550107
Hd.Org.: Mohd. Abdullah Qureshi;
Bus.Intt.: Rt., WS, Pub.'s Rep. and L.S.

PARAMOUNT PRAKASHAN
245, Naraina Pet Lakshmi Rd., Pune-411030 (Maharashtra)

PARAMOUNT SALES (I) PVT. LTD.
484, Double Storey, New Rajender Nagar, New Delhi-110060

PARAMVIR ENTERPRISES
Jalandhar (Punjab)
✆ 236248, 241248, Fax: 241248
✉ parament@jla.vsnl.net.in
Bus.Intt.: WS, B.S. & Suppliers

PARANESH S. SIRAVARA
No. 47, 11th 'A' Cross, III Phase, J.P. Nagar, Bangalore-560078 (Karnataka)
✆ 26633701
Bus.Intt.: Consultant

PARAS AGENCIES
Delhi
✆ 22391636
✉ paras_agencies@rediffmail.com
Bus.Intt.: B.S.

PARAS MEDICAL BOOKS PVT. LTD.
Opp. Vivek Vardhini College, Jambagh Road, Putlibowli, Hyderabad-500095 (Andhra Pradesh)
✆ 66821071, 91-40-24731903
✉ parasmedicalbooks@gmail.com
Hd.Org.: Atul Kothari, Hitesh Kothari
Bus.Intt.: Pub. and Dist.; **Spl.**: Books on medicine and related fields of study

PARAS MEDICAL PUBLISHERS
5-1-473, Jambagh Rd., P.B. No. 544, Hyderabad-500095 (Andhra Pradesh)
✆ 24742239, Fax: 91-40-66366642
✉ parasmedpub@hotmail.com, parasmedicalbooks@indiainfo.com
Estd.: 1995; **Hd.Org.**: Divyesh A. Kothari;
Bus.Intt.: Pub. and Dist.; **Spl.**: Books and Electronic Media Products on Med. Sci.

PARAS NEWS AGENCY
Joli Bunglow, S.T. Stand Rd., Jamnagar (Gujarat)

PARAS PUBLICATIONS
C-7, Vasant Kunj, North Avenue, Santacruz (West), Mumbai-400054 (Maharashtra)
Bus.Intt.: Exp.

PARAVIDYA RESEARCH FOUNDATION
Vivekanand Yogashram Hospital, Patparganj Rd., Khureji, New Delhi-110051
✆ 22202142, 22210663, 22424057, Fax: 22424057
✉ healing@bol.net.in
Hd.Org.: Acharya Keshav Dev; **Bus.Intt.**: Pub.;
Spl.: Books on Occult Sci. in Regional Languages

PARBATI PRAKASHAN
College Hostel Rd., Pan Bazar, Guwahati-781001 (Assam)
Bus.Intt.: Pub.

PARCHURE PRAKASHAN
Mehta Bhavan, 311, Raja Ramamohan Roy Marg, 44, Girgaon, Mumbai-400004 (Maharashtra)

PARENTS BOOK STALL
Bankim Chatterjee St., Stall-64, Kolkata-700073 (West Bengal)

PARESH PUBLICATIONS
115, New Chinch Bunder Rd., Mumbai-400009 (Maharashtra)
Bus.Intt.: Exp.

PARIBESHAN
18, Diamond Harbour Rd., Barisha, Kolkata-700008 (West Bengal)

PARIBUS PUBLISHERS & DISTRIBUTORS
14, Nizamuddin Market (West), New Delhi-110013

PARICHAY OVERSEAS
8E, Jhandewalan Extn., New Delhi-100055

✆ (O) 27519819 (R) 27775163
Hd.Org.: Harish Malhotra; **Bus.Intt.:** Pub.

PARIDRISHYA PRAKASHAN
6, Dadi Santok Lane, Dhobi Talab, Marine Lines, Mumbai-400002 (Maharashtra)
✆ 22019268, 38918055, Fax: 22019268
✉ hindikitaben@rediffmail.com
Hd.Org.: Raman Mishra; **Bus.Intt.:** Pub. and B.S.; **Spl.:** Art, Cinema, Theatre and Litt. in Hindi

PARIJAT PRAKASHAN
Kamta Sadan, East Boring Canal Rd., Patna-800001 (Bihar)
✆ 9910170711
✉ parijat.publication@gmail.com
Hd.Org.: Ranjan Kumar Singh
Bus.Intt.: Pub.; **Spl.:** General Books

PARIKALPANA PRAKASHAN
C/o Janchetana, D-68, Nirala Nagar, Lucknow-226010 (Uttar Pradesh)
✆ 91-522-2786782, 3096414
✉ parikalpana@gmail.com
Hd.Org.: Arvind Singh; **Bus.Intt.:** Pub.; **Spl.:** Fiction, Poetry, Literary Criticism, Hist., Politics, Soc.Sci., Phil., Translations of World Literary Classics in Hindi

PARIMAL BOOK STALL
15, College Square, Kolkata-700073 (West Bengal)

PARIMAL PRAKASHAN DISTRIBUTORS
Parimal Building, Khadkeshwar, Aurangabad-431001 (Maharashtra)
✆ 2323887
Estd.: 1970; **Prop.:** Anant B. Dashrathe
Br.: 159/2, Shanimar Peth, Pune-30 (Maharashtra) ✆ 2481039
Bus.Intt.: Pub. and L.S.; **Spl.:** Maharashtra Institutions in Marathi, Hindi and Eng. Language

PARIMAL PUBLICATION
27/28, Shakti Nagar, Delhi-110007
✆ 91-11-23845456, 47015168, 65441516
✉ parimal@ndf.vsnl.net.in
🌐 www.parimalpublication.com
Estd.: 1982; **Hd.Org.:** K.L. Joshi;
Bus.Intt.: Pub.; **Spl.:** Ancient Indian Litt.—the *Vedas*, *Puranas*, Indian Phil., Ayurveda, etc. in Sanskrit

PARIMALA PARKASHAN
17, MIG Baghambari, Abas Yojana, Allapur, Allahabad-211006 (Uttar Pradesh)
✆ 2501771
Hd.Org.: Shivkumar Sahay

PARIVARTAN PUBLICATION
112/B, DDA Flats, Mansarover Park, Shahdara, Delhi
✆ 9873383398
✉ parivartanpublication@yahoo.co.in
Bus.Intt.: Pub.; **Spl.:** Books in English

PARLE BOOK CENTRE
'Seva Sadan' 22-D J Rd., Vile Parle (West), Mumbai-400056 (Maharashtra)
✆ 26140981

PARMAMITRA PRAKASHAN
A&B Pocket, 10/C, Group III, Dilshad Garden, Delhi-110095

PARMAN PRAKASHAN
86, Mohan Singh Place, New Delhi-110001

PARMESHWARI PRAKASHAN
B-109, Preet Vihar, Delhi-110092
✆ 22050766
Hd.Org.: Manoj Sharma; **Bus.Intt.:** Pub. and B.S.; **Spl.:** Novels, Poetry, Travelogues, Essays, Criticisms, etc. in Hindi

PARNASREE
6/1, Dum Dum Rd., Kolkata-700030 (West Bengal)

PARRAGON PUBLISHING INDIA PVT. LTD.
101-C, 2nd Floor, Kundan House, Ashram, New Delhi-110014
✆ 42828750, Fax: 91-11-42828756
✉ sales@parragonpublishing.co.in
🌐 www.parragonpublishing.in
Hd.Org.: Vineet Sharma; **Bus.Intt.:** Pub.

PARROT READS PUBLISHERS
14-Dakshinapuram, Jawaharlal Nehru University, New Delhi-110067
✆ 26492710-11, Fax: 91-11-26742382
✉ rajivjha@parrotreads.com
Hd.Org.: Rajiv Jha; **Bus.Intt.:** Pub. & Rep.; **Spl.:** Foreign Publishers on Soc.Sci., Humanities, Mang., Art Craft, etc.

PARSHVA PARKASHAN
Nisha Pole Zaveriwad, Relief Rd., Ahmedabad (Gujarat)

PARUL PRAKASHAN
889/58, Tri Nagar, Delhi-110035
✆ 27198995
Hd.Org.: Kumar Narender

PARYAVARAN GYAN YAGYA SAMITI
5/16, Vinay Khand, Gomti Nagar, Lucknow (Uttar Pradesh)
✆ 2342730, 2391479
Hd.Org.: Radhekrishan Dube; **Bus.Intt.:** Dist.; **Spl.:** Litt. on Env. and Ecology in Hindi

PASCHIM BENGAL PUSTAK BIKRATA SAMITY (KANDI UNIT)
18D, Tamer Lane, Kolkata-700009 (West Bengal)

PASCHIMANCHAL PRAKASHAN
26, Mansukh Nagar Society, Bhavsagar, Hostel, Nababadez, Ahmedabad-380013 (Gujarat)
Hd.Org.: Yogesh Abasthi

PASCHIMBANGA PRAKASHAK SABHA
206, Bidhan Sarani 1st Floor, Kolkata-700006 (West Bengal)
✆ 23506720, Fax: 2413852
✉ asen.central@axcess.net.in
Hd.Org.: Tapas Saha; **Bus.Intt.:** Promoter of books by Pub. of West Bengal in Bengali

PASHI ENTERPRISE
199C, S. Mukherjee St., Konnagar Hooghly (West Bengal)

PASIDI PRACHURANALU
6-3-23/2, New Banguda, Secunderabad-500380 (Andhra Pradesh)

PASSI PUBLICATION (P) LTD.
1054, Tiraha Behram Khan, Darya Ganj, New Delhi-110002
Br.: 303-304, Virat Bhawan, Dr. Mukherjee Nagar, New Delhi-110009
✆ 27652341, 27652369
Bus.Intt.: Pub.

PATEL BOOK CENTRE
Sector IX-A Rd., Bokaro Steel City, Dhanbad-827009 (Bihar)

PATEL PUSTAK BHAWAN
Gaini, Aurangabad-824124 (Bihar)
Bus.Intt.: Pub. and B.S.

PATHAK PUBLISHER & DISTRIBUTOR
E-6134, Sangam Vihar, New Delhi-110062
✆ 26098013 ▮ 9818085794
Estd.: 1997; **Prop.:** Mr. Suman Pathak; **Bus.Intt.:** Pub., Dist. & L.S.; **Spl.:** Acad. and Soc.Sci.

PATIL ENTERPRISES
434, Narayan Peth, Umashankar Apartment, Near Patrya Maruit, Pune-411030 (Maharashtra)
✆ 2487629, 2483223
Estd.: 1992; **Hd.Org.:** Uday Patil; **Bus.Intt.:** L.S.; **Spl.:** Books to College Lib. (Marathi and English)

PATRA BHARATI
3/1, College Row, Kolkata-700009 (West Bengal)
✆ 2241-1175, Fax: 22354-0462

PATRA'S PUBLICATIONS
2, Shyama Charan Dey St., Kolkata-700073 (West Bengal)

PATRIKA BOOKING CENTRE
7A/47, W.E.A., (Channa Market), Karol Bagh, New Delhi-110005
✆ 25761619, 30932031, Fax: 25720390
✉ patrika@vsnl.com
Hd.Org.: Sandeep Dhingra; **Bus.Intt.:** Imp. and Dist.; **Spl.:** Advertising, Designing, Photographic, Graphic Comp. Sci., Fashion and Interior Decoration Books

PATRIKA PRAKASHANA
9, East Anjanaeya Temple Rd., Basavangudi, Bangalore-560004 (Karnataka)
Hd.Org.: P. Lankesh; **Bus.Intt.:** Pub.; **Spl.:** Fiction, Poems, Dramas and Gen. Books in Kannada

PATRIKA SYNDICATE
9/10, Agarchand Mansion, 150, Anna Salai, Chennai-600002 (Tamil Nadu)

PATRIKA SYNDICATE PVT. LTD.
13, Darya Ganj, New Delhi-110002
✆ 23274443, 23259353, 23255118, Fax: 23261290
✉ bidel@ndb.vsnl.net.in
Regional Man.: Anil Taneja; **Bus.Intt.:** Imp., Dist.; **Spl.:** Tech., Med. Books

PATWAL BOOK DISTRIBUTORS
B-222, Ch. Shishram Complex, Near Royal Homeo Pharmacy, Main Market, Badar Pur, New Delhi-110044
▮ 9811040794
Prop.: S.S. Patwal
Bus.Intt.: L.S.; **Spl.:** Technical & Soc.Sci.

PAUL MEDICO
45, Manicktola Main Rd., Kolkata-54 (West Bengal)
Bus.Intt.: Exp.

PAULINE BOOK & MEDIA CENTRE
13/5, W.E.A. Padam Singh Rd., Karol Bagh, New Delhi-110005
✆ 25851260, 25785465
✉ paulinedel@mantraonline
Ch.Exe.: Liza Louis; **Bus.Intt.:** Pub.; **Spl.:** Books and Audiovisuals

PAULINE BOOK & MEDIA CENTRE
Residency Rd. Sadar, Nagpur-440001 (Maharashtra)
✆ 2555047
Estd.: 1990; **Bus.Intt.:** Rt. B.S.

PAULSON PRESS PVT. LTD.
Yogmaya Bldg., 2nd, 3rd and 4th Floors, Street No. 13, M.D. Rd., Paharganj, New Delhi-110055
✆ 23547532, 55379214, Fax: 91-11-23545182

paulson@nde.vsnl.net.in,
paulson_press_ltd@vsnl.net.in
www.asiatodaygroup.com
Estd.: 1995; **Hd.Org.:** R.K. Gupta;
Bus.Intt.: Pub., Imp. and Exp.;
Spl.: Directories, News Magazines, Books, Journals and CDs

PAVAI PUBLICATIONS
17/42, Jani Jan Khan Rd., Royapettah, Chennai-600014 (Tamil Nadu)
28482441, Fax: 91-11-28482973
pavai123@yahoo.com
Hd.Org. A. Sivalingam; **Bus.Intt.:** Pub.

PAVALAR PANNAI
62, Maraimalaiadigal Rd., Pondicherry-605001

PAWAN BOOK SHOP
L-33, Sector XI, Noida-201301 (Uttar Pradesh)

PAWAN SALES AGENCY
F-17/208, Harsha Complex, Dena Bank Building, Subhash Chowk, Laxmi Nagar, New Delhi-110092
22045655
Ch.Exe.: Mr. Sundeep Gulati;
Bus.Intt.: Dist.; **Spl.:** Renowed Gen. & Children Books

PAYRUS PUBLISHING HOUSE
E-8, Kalkaji, New Delhi-110019

PAZHANI PARAMOUNT PATHIPPAGAM
69-D, Anna Nagar, Palani-624602 (Tamil Nadu)

PEACOCK BOOKS
7/22, Ansari Rd., Darya Ganj, New Delhi-110002
(O) 23273880, 23285873 (R) 25413460, Fax: 23285873
info@atlanticbooks.com
atlanticbooks.com
Prop.: K.R. Gupta; **Bus.Intt.:** Pub., B.S., L.S., WS; **Spl.:** World Classics

PEARL BOOKS
3834/XI, Shanti Niketan Building, IInd Floor, Pataudi House Road, Darya Ganj, New Delhi-110002
23258245, 23258254, Fax: 91-11-23280028
pearlbooks.delhi@gmail.com
Hd.Org.: Meenu Talan
Bus.Intt.: Pub. and Dist.; **Spl.:** Books in Eng.

PEARL (INDIA) PUBLISHING HOUSE PVT. LTD.
24-B/9, Desh Bandhu Gupta Rd., Dev Nagar, Karol Bagh, New Delhi-110005
25812253, 25815254, Fax: 25754739
info@sumanprakashan.com,
info@pearl-india.com
www.pearl-India.com
Estd.: 1982; **Hd.Org.:** Nitin Malhotra;
Bus.Intt.: Pub.; **Spl.:** Children's Textbooks upto Middle School in Hindi

PEARL PUBLISHERS
206, Bidhan Sarani, Kolkata-700006 (West Bengal)
033-22410176, 24737071
Estd.: 1978; **Hd.Org.:** Madan Bhattacherjee;
Bus.Intt.: Pub.; **Spl.:** Soc.Sci., Marxism, Hist. and Edu. Books of Children in Bengali

PEARSON EDUCATION (SINGAPORE) PVT. LTD.
482, F.I.E. Patparganj, Delhi-110092
22146067-70, Fax: 22146071
mail@personed.co.in
www.pearsoned.co.in
Estd.: 2000; **Gen.Man.:** Subroto Muzumdar;
Bus.Intt.: Pub.; **Spl.:** Computer Sci., Engg., Humanities & Soc.Sci., Sci., Math. & Statistics, Business & Eco., ELT & School

PEEKAY TREE CROPS
Development Foundations, M.I.G. 141, Gandhi Nagar, Cochin-682020 (Kerala)

PEEPEE PUBLISHERS AND DISTRIBUTORS (P) LTD.
160, Shakti Vihar, Pitam Pura, Delhi-110034
91-11-55195868 9811156083
pawan_vij@peepeepub.com,
anupam_vij@peepeepub.com,
peepee160@yahoo.com,
peepee160@rediffmail.com
www.peepeepub.com
Hd.Org.: Pawaninder P. Vij
Corporate Off.: 7/31, Ansari Road, Darya Ganj, Post Box: 7243, New Delhi-110002
Bus.Intt.: Pub. and Dist.; **Spl.:** Medical, Dental and Nursing Books

PEHEL-BFC
C-88, South Extension-II, New Delhi-110049
51640571-6
kirans@pehel-bfc.org
www.pehel-bfc.org
Hd.Org.: Kiran Shaheen; **Bus.Intt.:** Pub.;
Spl.: Right to Information for the Poor, in Hindi and other Indian Languages

PEN-TIMES PUBLISHERS AND DISTRIBUTORS
C-176, St. No. 7, Bhajanpura, New 11, Delhi-110053
33336030 9891460555, Fax: 22561933
pentimes@yahoo.com
Hd.Org. Vishal Bhasin; **Bus.Intt.:** Pub. and Dist.; **Spl.:** Acad. and Ency.

PEN BOOKS PVT. LTD.
P.B. No. 143, Palace Rd., Aluva, Cochin-683001 (Kerala)

✆ (O) 0484-2621668, 2620377, 2625414 (R) 2620668, Fax: 2620668
✉ penbooks@md3.vsnl.net.in
Estd.: 1993; **Hd.Org.:** Poly K. Ayyampilly; **Spl.:** Gen. & Acad. (Fiction, Non-fiction)

PENCRAFT INTERNATIONAL
B-1/41, Ashok Vihar, Phase-II,
New Delhi-110052
✆ 27120156, 23277084, Fax: 27443784
✉ pencraft@nda.vsnl.net.in
Estd.: 1991; **Prop.:** Mrs. Saraswati Jain; **Bus.Intt.:** Pub., WS, L.S. & Rt.; **Spl.:** Humanities & Soc.Sci., Gen. & Fiction etc.

PENGUIN BOOKS INDIA PVT. LTD.
#11, Community Centre, Panchsheel Park, New Delhi-110017
✆ 26494401, 26494405/02, Fax: 26494403
✉ penguin@del2.vsnl.net.in
www.penguinbooksindia.com
Estd.: 1985; **Ch.Exe.:** David Davidar
Br.: Harish Shenoy, Syndicate Bank Staff, Anand Co-Op. Hsg. Society, B/4, Opp. Mini Nagar, S.N. Dubey Rd., Rawal Pada, Dahisar (East), Mumbai-400068 ✆ 28966019
✉ shenoyharish77@hotmail.com
• Nirmalaya Roy Choudhury, Penguin Books India Pvt. Ltd., 258/4 A.P.C. Rd., Ground Floor, (C.E.S.C. Cash Office Building), Kolkata-700009
✆ 033-23545466, Telefax: 033-23545211
✉ nirmalya@hotmail.com
• Philip Koshy, 63, Devrajnagar, Selaiyur P.O., (Near Bharat Engineering College), Tambaram, Chennai-600073
✆ 044-22292457
✉ philipsusan@chequemail.com
Bus.Intt.: Pub., Imp., Exp.; **Spl.:** Humanities & Soc.Sci., Juvenile/Children Books, Gen. & Fiction etc.

PENMAN PUBLISHERS
7308, Prem Nagar, Shakti Nagar, Delhi-110007
✆ 27112806, Fax: 2398642
✉ penman_bks@hotmail.com
Hd.Org.: J.L. Gupta; **Bus.Intt.:** Pub.; **Spl.:** Indology, Oriental Litt., Vedas, Rel. and Phil. in Hindi and Sanskrit

PENPALS CIRCLE
A House of Friendship, PB 101, Gandhi Mkt., Chaura Bazar, Ludhiana-141008 (Punjab)
✆ 0161-2702054, Fax: 0161-2708615
Estd.: 1980; **Hd.Org.:** Mrs. Suman Bhagotra; **Bus.Intt.:** Pub.

PENRAM INTERNATIONAL PUBLISHING (INDIA)
313, Bussa Ugyog Bhavan, T.J. Rd., Sewree, Mumbai-400015 (Maharashtra)
✆ 22-24602247, Fax: 91-22-24160604
Hd.Org.: Mangesh Sawant; **Bus.Intt.:** Manufacturers of Book Publishing

PENTA BOOK DISTRIBUTORS
1st Floor, Darussalam Complex, Mavoor Rd., Calicut-673004 (Kerala)
✆ 0495-2725746
✉ pentabooks@yahoo.com
Br.: T.C. 51/3181, Sunitha Bhavan, Koliyacode, Industrial Estate P.O., Thiruvananthapuram-19 ✆ 04712-490323
Bus.Intt.: L.S., WS, & Rt.; **Spl.:** Acad., Professional & Reference Book

PENTAGON PRESS
101, AVG Bhawan, M-3, Middle Circle, Connaught Place, New Delhi-110001
✆ (O) 23415198, 23415205 (R) 25137459, Fax: 51517091
✉ rajanarya@vsnl.com
Prop.: Rajan Arya; **Bus.Intt.:** Pub.; **Spl.:** Mang., IT, Ency. Illustrated Storybooks, Biographies, PB etc.

PENTAGON PRESS
BE-276, St. No. 5, Hari Nagar, New Delhi-110064
✆ 25490455, 25491263, Fax: 25403549
✉ rajanarya@vsnl.com
Hd.Org.: Rajan Arya; **Bus.Intt.:** Pub.; **Spl.:** Edu. Books on Man., Information Tech., Litt. for Children and Adults in English

PENTAGON PRESS
206, Peacock Lane, Shahpur Jat, New Delhi-110049
✆ 26491568, 64706243, Fax: 91-11-26490600
✉ rajan@pentagon-press.com, pentagon_press@yahoo.com
www.pentagon-press.com
Estd.: 1994; **Prop.:** Rajan Arya
Bus.Intt.: Pub.; **Spl.:** Mang., IT, Ency. Illustrated Storybooks, Biographies, PB etc.

PEOPLE'S LITERARY AND CULTURAL
Federation-A.P. Nagaram (P.O.), Via Tenali (R.M.S.), Guntur Distt.-522268 (Andhra Pradesh)

PEOPLE'S PUBLISHERS HOUSE P. LTD.
5-E, Rani Jhansi Rd., New Delhi-110055
✆ 91-11-23523349, 23529823
Estd.: 1940; **Hd.Org.:** K.S. Negi
Br.: 2, Marina Arcade, C.P., New Delhi-110001
✆ 23324064
• Near SSS-I Auditorium, Jawaharlal Nehru University, Delhi-87
Bus.Intt.: Pub. and Dist.; **Spl.:** Books in English and Hindi

PEOPLES BOOK HOUSE
Mahar House, 15 Cowasji Patel St., Fort, Mumbai (Maharashtra)
✆ 22873768

PEOPLES BOOK SOCIETY
72, Bankim Chandra Chatterjee St., Kolkata-700073 (West Bengal)
Bus.Intt.: Pub. and Dist.; **Spl.:** Progressive Books and Journals

PEOPLES CORNER
10, Shyama Charan Dey St., Kolkata-700073 (West Bengal)

PEOPLES PUBLISHING HOUSE
23, Raj Bagh, Srinagar (Jammu & Kashmir)
✆ 274820
Hd.Org.: W.M. Bhatt; **Bus.Intt.:** L.S. and Pub.'s Rep.

PEPPIN THOMAS
Thrissur (Kerala)
✆ 235292, 27033487, 2335593
✉ cosmobooks@sancharnet.in
Bus.Intt.: B.S.

PERFECT BOOK AGENCY
E-5, Krishna Nagar, Delhi-110051

PERFECT POOJAS
21-A, Sector-IV, Bhagat Singh Marg, New Delhi-110001
▮ 9868114853
Hd.Org.: U.K. Sharma; **Bus.Intt.:** Dist.; **Spl.:** Rel. Books, Especially on Worship, in Hindi

PERIODICAL EXPERT BOOK AGENCY
D-42, Vivek Vihar, Delhi-110032
✆ 22215045, 22200534
Estd.: 1974; **Prop.:** M.P. Singh Gahlot
Br.: G-56, IInd Floor, Vikas Marg, Laxmi Nagar, Delhi-110092
Bus.Intt.: Pub., WS, L.S. and Rt., Imp., Exp.

PERIYAR SELF-RESPECT PROPAGANDA INSTITUTION
No. 50, E.V.K. Sampath Rd., Periyar Thidal, Vepery, Chennai-600007 (Tamil Nadu)
✆ 2586555, Fax: 044-2584109
Hd.Org.: K. Veeramani; **Bus.Intt.:** Pub.; **Spl.:** Books to Propagate Periyars thoughts and works, Book on Rationalism Self-respect and as well as Politico, Socio-economic, Cultural issues of Tamil Nadu in Particular

PERSONAL BOOKSHOP (THE)
10, Congress Building, 573, Mount Rd., Chennai-600006 (Tamil Nadu)
✆ 24349216
Prop.: V. Vijayalakshmi; **Bus.Intt.:** Dist., L.S., Rt. and Pub.; **Spl.:** Phil., Indology and Sanskrit

PERSONELL BOOK/GORAKHNATH TEMPLE, GHORAKHPUR
C/o Ashok Tiwari, A-1/28, Janakpuri, New Delhi-110058
▮ 9818068025
www.gorakhnath.com
Hd.Org.: Yogiraj Shivender Nath
Bus.Intt.: Pub.; **Spl.:** Books on Yoga, History and Culture

PETER LANG PUBLISHING GROUP
125-B, 1st Floor, Shahpur Jat, New Delhi-110049
✆ 64613894, 91-11-26742382
✉ info@parrotreads.com
www.petertang.com
Hd.Org.: Rajiv Jha
Bus.Intt.: Pub.; **Spl.:** Books and Journals

PHADKE PRAKASHAN
Phadke Bhavan, Harmandir Jawal, Dudhali, Kolhapur-416012 (Maharashtra)

PHARMA BOOK SYNDICATE
4-3-375, Ansuya Bhavan, Opp. Central Bank, Hydrabad-500095 (Andhra Pradesh)
✆ 23445666, Fax: 91-40-23445611
✉ info@pharmabooksyndicate.com
www.pharmabooksyndicate.com
Hd.Org.: Anil Shah
Bus.Intt.: Pub. and Dist.; **Spl.:** Text-books and reference books on science subjects, medicine and pharmacy

PHAROS MEDIA & PUBLISHING PVT. LTD.
Pharos House, D-84, Abul Fazal Enclave-I, Jamia Nagar, New Delhi-110025
✆ 26927483, 26932825, 26822883
Fax: 26835825, 24697333
✉ zik.pharos@axcess.net.in

PHILHAL
M-46/2, (Second Floor), Shrikrishna Nagar, Patna-800001 (Bihar)
✆ 2500476
✉ filhal@rediffmail.com
Hd.Org.: Preeti Sinha; **Bus.Intt.:** Pub.; **Spl.:** Soc.Sci. in Hindi Besides the Hindi Journal *Philhal*

PHOENIX PUBLISHING HOUSE PVT. LTD.
21, Prakash Apartments, 5, Ansari Rd., Darya Ganj, New Delhi-110002
✆ 23276688, 23276611, 23276625, 23259222, 23270743, Fax: 23283141
✉ ouseph@del3.vsnl.net.in
www.phoenixpub.bizland.com

Estd.: 1994; **Man.Dir.:** P.V. Ouseph; **Bus.Intt.:** Pub.

PICCADAILLY BOOK SHOP
64, Shanker Market, Connaught Place, New Delhi-110001
✆ 23313993
Estd.: 1947; **Hd.Org.:** S.P. Choudary; **Bus.Intt.:** Rt. and Mail Order Suppliers; **Spl.:** Occult Sci., Rel., Phil., Hist. and Indology

PICTAK BOOKS
Post Box No. 6087, 15/12, 2nd Floor, East Patel Nagar, New Delhi-110008

PIE EDUCATION
44-A/2, Jassum House, Kalu Sarai, Sarvapriya Vihar, New Delhi-110016
✆ 26527444, 26568545, Fax: 26962662
info@pieeducation.com
Hd.Org.: Anil Umre; **Bus.Intt.:** Pub.; **Spl.:** Learning Material for Competitive Examinations

PILGRIMS BOOK HOUSE
B-27/98, A-8, Nawabganj Road, Durga Kund, Varanasi-221010 (Uttar Pradesh)
✆ 2314060, 2312496, 2312456, Fax: 91-542-2312456 ▮ 9811300970
pilgrimsbooks@sify.com, pilgrims@satyam.net.in
www.pilgrimsbooks.com
Hd.Org.: Rama Nand Tiwari
Br.: Shop No. 1626, Raj Guru Road, Chuna Mandi, Pahar Ganj, Metro Polish Building, Opp. Imperial Cinema, New Delhi-110055
✆ 23584015, Fax: 91-11-23285081
pilgrimsinde@gmail.com
Bus.Intt.: Pub. and Dist.; **Spl.:** Books on travel, religion, health and traditional Indian medicine system, etc.

PILLAI BOOK SUPPLIERS
C-1/117A, Lawrence Rd., Delhi-110035
✆ 27180826, 27100081
Estd.: 1993; **Prop.:** G.V. Pillai; **Bus.Intt.:** B.S., Dist. and L.S.

PIMPLAPURE BOOK DISTRIBUTORS
Ogle Wada Near Hindu Girls School, Mahal, Nagpur-440032 (Maharashtra)
✆ (O) 2724318, 2773552 (R) 2752667
Estd.: 1991; **Prop.:** Ashok P. Pimplapure; **Bus.Intt.:** Pub., B.S., L.S., WS; **Spl.:** Humanities & Soc.Sci., Tech., Mang.

PINK CITY BOOK HOUSE
154, Janak Puri-II, Imli Wala Phatak, Near New Vidhan Sabha Bhawan, Jaipur-302005 (Rajasthan)
✆ 0141-2594768 ▮ 9414079477
Hd.Org.: Mahendra Kumar

PINKA AGENCIES
2645/1, Sant Nagar, Delhi-110034

PINKY BOOK DISTRIBUTORS
4759/XI, Pratap St. 23, Ansari Rd., Darya Ganj, Delhi-110002
✆ 23246089, 23246362, Fax: 23246535
ouseph@del13.vsnl.net, pinky@ndb.vsnl.net.in
Estd.: 1979; **Hd.Org.:** J.L. Dua; **Bus.Intt.:** Dist., Imp.; **Spl.:** Dictionaries & Journals Titles, Children Reference Books & Encyclopaedia

PINNACLES BOOKS PVT. LTD.
4271/3, Ansari Rd., Darya Ganj, New Delhi-110002
✆ 23290162, Fax: 23290162
Estd.: 1996; **Hd.Org.:** Sanjib Bose
Br.: Thakurbari Rd., Kadam Kuan, Patna-800003 ✆ (O) 2671356, 2689717 (R) 2674079, Fax: 2670010
bbpdpat@gisclol.vsnl.net.in
Bus.Intt.: Pub. & Dist.; **Spl.:** Textbooks, References

PINTER PUBLISHERS
1-GHA-22, Jawahar Nagar, Jaipur-302004 (Rajasthan)

PIONEER AGENCY
8/LA, Shyama Charan De St., Kolkata-700073 (West Bengal)
Bus.Intt.: Exp.

PIONEER BOOK CO. PVT. LTD.
160, D.N. Rd., Fort, Mumbai-400001 (Maharashtra)
✆ (O) 22046759, 22043883 (R) 26484434
Hd.Org.: Rajiv Pahwa; **Bus.Intt.:** Pub.; **Spl.:** Meri Saheli and Hi Fashion

PIONEER BOOK HOUSE
120-C, Indirapuri Colony, Indore-1 (Madhya Pradesh)

PIONEER BOOK SERVICES
47, Nallathamby St., Triplicane, Chennai-600005 (Tamil Nadu)

PIONEER BOOKS
1559, Outram Lines, Near Kingsway Camp, Delhi-110009
✆ 27220965, 27463827 ▮ 9810020918, Fax: 011-27463827
Prop.: Dheeraj Narula; **Bus.Intt.:** Law Pub., B.S. & Dist.; **Spl.:** Law Books for Students Lawyers

PIONEER PRINTERS
2/27, Seth Gali, Agra-282003 (Uttar Pradesh)

✆ (O) 264909 (R) 265176
Prop.: R.K. Agarwal

PIPING & ENERGY PRODUCTS (P) LTD.
Z-18, Okhla Industrial Area, Phase II,
New Delhi-110020
Bus.Intt.: Exp.

PITAMBAR PUBLISHING COMPANY PVT. LTD.
888, East Park Road, Karol Bagh,
New Delhi-110005
✆ (O) 23670067, 23625528, (R) 25883437
Fax: 91-11-25883427 ▮ 9811080291
pitambar@bol.net.in
Prop.: Anand Bhushan
Bus.Intt.: Pub.

PITARA-EKLAVYA
Eklavya, E-10, Sankar Nagar, BDA Colony,
Shivaji Nagar, Bhopal-462016 (Madhya Pradesh)
✆ 2463380, Fax: 91-755-2461703
pitara@eklavya.in
www.eklaviya.in
Hd.Org.: C.N. Subramaniam
Bus.Intt.: Pub.; **Spl.:** Children Books

PITMAN S.S. PUBLICATIONS
51/3, D.B. Gupta Rd., Karol Bagh,
New Delhi-110005

PIXIE PUBLICATIONS INDIA (P) LIMITED
Karnal (Haryana)
✆ 2242174, 2242175, Fax: 2204619
info@poultrytimesofindia.com
Bus.Intt.: Pub.

PIYUSH PRINTERS PUBLISHERS PVT. LTD.
G-12, Udyog Nagar, Rohtak Rd.,
Industrial Area, New Delhi-110041

PIYUSH PRINTERS PUBLISHERS PVT. LTD.
B-161, Gujranwala Town, Part-I, Delhi-110033
✆ 27242115, 23261804
Prop.: Manju Dhawan; **Bus.Intt.:** Pub. and L.S.

PIYUSH SALES CORPORATION
C/o Gayatri Book Store, Zilla Panchayat Rd.,
Amreli-365604 (Gujarat)

PLANET MULTI MEDIA
New Delhi
✆ 25740588, 25730546
sales@cdrom-india.com
Bus.Intt.: B.S.

PLANMAN MEDIA PVT. LTD.
IIPM Corporate Office, Unit 9 & 10, Level-2,
Southern Park, D-2 Saket, New Delhi-110017
✆ 41799616, Fax: 91-11-41799555
bhupinn@yahoo.co.in
www.planmanmedia.com
Hd.Org.: Abhimanyu Bhose
Bus.Intt.: Pub.; **Spl.:** Business Manazine—*Business & Economy, Business & Marketing, The Sunday, Indian* and *The Indian PC Magazine*

POCKET BOOK CENTRE
Opp. Jyoti Sangh, Relief Rd.,
Ahmedabad-380001 (Gujarat)
✆ 2360732
Estd.: 1960; **Hd.Org.:** H.K. Doshi;
Bus.Intt.: Pub., WS, L.S. and Rt., Sub.Ag.

POCKET BOOKS DISTRIBUTING CO.
Examiner Press Building, 2nd Floor,
35, Dalal St., Fort, Mumbai-400023
(Maharashtra)
✆ 22671801, Fax: 22671367
Estd.: 1956; **Prop.:** Tulsi Shah
Br.: 16, State Bank St., 2nd Floor,
(Mount Rd.) Chennai-600002 (Tamil Nadu)
✆ 28570594; • Vishal Rohan Apartments,
Flat No. 6,699, Narayan Peth, Laxmi Rd.,
Pune-411030 (Maharashtra) ✆ 24455172
Bus.Intt.: WS, Imp.; **Spl.:** Humanities &
Soc.Sci., Juvenile/Children, Gen. & Fiction

PODDAR PUSTAK BHANDAR
Banka, Bhagalpur-813205 (Bihar)
Bus.Intt.: Pub. and B.S.

POET INDIA PUBLICATIONS
20, Alangudi Rd., Pundukottai-622001
(Tamil Nadu)

POETS INTERNATIONAL
360, 11th Cross, IInd Block, Jawanagar,
Bangalore-560011 (Karnataka)

POINTER PUBLISHERS
807, Vyas Building, S.M.S. Highway,
Jaipur-302003 (Rajasthan)
✆ 2568159, 2518286, Fax: 2568159, 2562000
pointerpub@hotmail.com
Hd.Org.: Shashi Jain; **Bus.Intt.:** Pub.;
Spl.: Gen. and Reference Books on Arts,
Sci., Env. Sci., etc. in English

POLYMER RESEARCH CENTRE
Bangalore (Karnataka)
✆ 5289359
pcenterbangalore@usa.net
Bus.Intt.: B.S.

PONDICHERRY INSTITUTE OF LINGUISTICS & CULTURE
101-C, Savarirayalu St.,
Pondicherry-605001

PONNA PUBLICATIONS
T.C. 37/723, South St. Fort,
Thiruvananthapuram (Kerala)
Estd.: 1985; **Prop.:** P. Rajalekshmi;
Bus.Intt.: Pub. and B.S.

POOJA BOOK SERVICE
57, Yashoda Housing Society, Gokhale Rd., Pune-411016 (Maharashtra)
✆ 2373450 ▮ 98230-54285
Bus.Intt.: L.S.; **Spl.:** All Subject

POOJA BOOK SPACE
Pacca Danga, Wadha Verha, Jammu (Jammu & Kashmir)
✆ 549919, Fax: 547862
Estd.: 1999; **Prop.:** Ms. Banti Jad; **Bus.Intt.:** L.S., WS, Pub.; **Spl.:** Humanities & Soc.Sci., Sci., Engg. & Tech., Mang. & Comm., Med.Sci., Journals, Magazines & Periodicals

POOJA PRAKASHAN
B-33, Floted Factory Complex, Jhandewalan, New Delhi-110055
✆ 23533737 ▮ 98112-49405
poojaprakashan@yahoo.com, surendersharmadel@hotmail.com
Hd.Org.: Surender Sharma; **Bus.Intt.:** Pub. & Dist.

POOJA PRAKASHAN
Anand Bhavan, Bhadurpur, Samastipur (Bihar)
Hd.Org.: Haribansh Tarun

POOMKAVANAM PUBLICATIONS (PVT) LTD.
17/500, G.22-Ruby Building, Rajaji Rd., Kozhikode-673004 (Kerala)
✆ 275130
Estd.: 1986; **Prop.:** Husain Randanthan; **Bus.Intt.:** Pub.

POONAM BOOK SERVICE CENTRE
4564-A/16, Darya Ganj, New Delhi-110002
✆ (O) 30908197, 23285054 (R) 22777367, Fax: 23285055
pbsco2@yahoo.com, poonam02@rediffmail.com
Estd.: 1975; **Prop.:** R.R. Mukherji; **Bus.Intt.:** Dist. & L.S.; **Spl.:** Sci., Tech., Industrial, Chemistry and Bio., Reference Books

POONAM PRAKASHAN
6-B, Kaushik Puri Gali No. 1, Old Seelampur (E), Delhi-110031
✆ 22203781; **Hd.Org.:** P.K. Punam

POONAM PUSTAK BHANDAR
Bihpur, Bhagalpur-853201 (Bihar)
Bus.Intt.: Pub. and B.S.

POONGODI PATHIPAGAM
14, Sithiraikulam West St., Mylapore, Chennai-600004 (Tamil Nadu)
✆ 24943074
Prop.: V. Subbaiah; **Bus.Intt.:** Pub. and B.S.

POORNA PUBLICATIONS
TBS Building, G.H. Rd., Kozhikode-673001 (Kerala)
✆ 0495-2720085-6, Fax: 0495-2721414
tbsbook@vsnl.com
www.tbsbooks.com
Estd.: 1945; **Hd.Org.:** N.E. Manohar; **Bus.Intt.:** Pub.; **Spl.:** Literary books in Malayalam

POORNIMA PRINTERS
204, Parvati Industrial Estate, Sun Mill Compound, Lower Parel, Mumbai-400013 (Maharashtra)
✆ 24921421, Fax: 24602210
Bus.Intt.: Pub., **Spl.:** Books in Hindi language

POORVA PRAKASHAN
X/3897, Gali No. 13, Shanti Mohalla, Gandhi Nagar, Delhi-110031
✆ 91-11-22447039
Hd.Org.: Surendra Kumar Shukla
Bus.Intt.: Pub. and Dist.; **Spl.:** Textbooks for schools and colleges

POORVANCHAL PRAKASHAN
1180, A-Block, Sonia Vihar, Delhi-110094
✆ 22178983
poorvanchalprakashan@yahoo.com
Hd.Org.: Indravijay Singh; **Bus.Intt.:** Pub. and Dist.; **Spl.:** Literary Books in Hindi

POORVODAY PRAKASHAN
68, Kaushikpuri, Old Seelampur, Delhi-110031
Hd.Org.: Pradeep Kumar

POOVAZHAKI PATHIPAGAM
29/2, Srinivasa Perumal Sannathi St., Royapettah, Chennai-600014 (Tamil Nadu)
✆ 24800325, 24833180, Fax: 24811755
aruram@md2.vsnl.net.in
Hd.Org.: T. Logambal; **Bus.Intt.:** Pub.; **Spl.:** Gen. Book in Tamil

POPULAR BOOK DEPOT
31-32, Jawahar Bhawan, Roshan Pura, New Market, Bhopal-462003 (Madhya Pradesh)
✆ 220951
Estd.: 1998; **Prop.:** Motilal Singhal; **Bus.Intt.:** L.S., Rt. & WS; **Spl.:** Med. and Tech.

POPULAR BOOK DEPOT
217, Raja Ram Mohan Roy Marg, Girgaon, Mumbai-400004 (Maharashtra)
✆ 23829401
Estd.: 1924; **Hd.Org.:** Manmohan Bhatkal; **Bus.Intt.:** Pub. L.S. and Rt., Exp., Sub.Ag.

POPULAR BOOK DEPOT
G-15, S.S. Towers, Dhamani St., Chaura Rasta, Jaipur-302003 (Rajasthan)
✆ 2325965, 298290, 289555
Hd.Org.: P.N. Agarwal; **Bus.Intt.**: Pub. and Dist.; **Spl.**: Naturopathy and School and College-level Textbooks

POPULAR BOOK HOUSE
75, Deccan Gymkhana, Pune-411004 (Maharashtra)
✆ 5671737, 5673315, Fax: 2375600
✉ pop@pn2.vsnl.net.in
Estd.: 1954; **Hd.Org.**: Sunil Gadgil; **Bus.Intt.**: Imp., L.S., Rt., WS, B.S.; **Spl.**: Gen. and Trade, Acad., Professional, Children, Electronic Products Books, Greeting Cards, Toys, CDs

POPULAR BOOK SERINI
B-30/21, BHV Gate, Lanka, Varanasi-221005 (Uttar Pradesh)

POPULAR BOOK STALL
Petal Chowk, Sector IX, Bokaro Steel City, Dhanbad-827009 (Bihar)

POPULAR BOOK STORE
Opposite Patna College, Patna-800004 (Bihar)

POPULAR BOOK STORE
Nallh Mar Rd., Nawa Kadal, Srinagar, Kashmir-190009 (Jammu & Kashmir)
Estd.: 1988; **Hd.Org.**: Mohd. Abdullah Hani
Br.: 95, Behind Neelam Theatre, Srinagar, Kashmir (Jammu & Kashmir)
Bus.Intt.: L.S. of Rt.

POPULAR BOOK STORES
Raikhand Near Bhadra, Ahmedabad-380001 (Gujarat)

POPULAR LIBRARY
13/1, Bankim Chatterjee St., Kolkata-700073 (West Bengal)

POPULAR PRAKASHAN (P) LTD.
301, Mahalaximi Chambers, 22 Bhucabhai Desai Road, Mumbai-400026 (Maharashtra)
✆ 23530303, Fax: 91-22-23535294
✉ sales@popularprakashan.com
www.popularprakashan.com
Estd.: 1924; **Hd.Org.**: Harsha Bhatkal
Br.: 4648/1, Ansari Rd., 21, Darya Ganj, New Delhi-110002 ✆ 23265245, 23280068
Fax: 091-011-23279203
✉ populardel@mantraonline.com
• Bangalore (Karnataka)
✆ 25598215, 25588101
✉ blrvans@blr.vsnl.net.in
• Kolkata (West Bengal) ✆ 24660812
Fax: 24644614 ✉ stree@cal2.vsnl.net.in
Bus.Intt.: Pub., WS, Rt., L.S.;
Spl.: Soc.Sci., Humanities, Med., Computer Sci., Music, Eco, Litt., Phil. Rel., Politics, Biography and Current Affairs, Focus Books for High Quality PB, in English Belles Lettre in Marathi Co-publishing activity with Encyclopedia Britannica

POSTAL HISTORY SOCIETY
CH 17-1-18, Atul Grove Rd., New Delhi-110001

POTHUVIJNANAM PUBLICATIONS
Kayamgulam-690502 (Kerala)

POWER & PROCESS TECHNOLOGIES PUBLICATION DIVISION
1305, Rohit House 3, Tolstoy Marg, New Delhi-110001

PRABAHA PRAKASHAN
22A, College Row, Kolkata-700009 (West Bengal)

PRABEEN PRAKASHAN
1/1079 E, Mehrauli, New Delhi-110030
✆ 26511833, 26516773
Hd.Org.: Shrikishan Gupta

PRABEER KUMAR LAHA
C/o No. Basak, 8-B, Madhu Gupta Lane, Kolkata-700012 (West Bengal)

PRABHA PUBLICATIONS
2/12 B, (Backside) Jangpura 'A', New Delhi-110017
✆ 24313463

PRABHA SONI
7, Karmayog Flats, Sardar Patel Nagar, Ahmedabad-380006 (Gujarat)

PRABHAT BOOK CENTRE
High Court Rd., Gwalior-9 (Madhya Pradesh)
✆ 322879, 334108
✉ anirudh110@sify.com
Bus.Intt.: Pub. and B.S.

PRABHAT BOOK DISTRIBUTORS
Delhi
✆ 22436362, 22427066
✉ exposofttech@rediffmail.com
Bus.Intt.: B.S. and Dist.

PRABHAT BOOK HOUSE
Vanchiyur, Thiruvananthapuram-695035 (Kerala)
✆ 0471-271533, 270688
Hd.Org.: P. Ravindran; **Bus.Intt.**: Pub. and B.S.; **Spl.**: Gen. and Textbooks

PRABHAT PRAKASHAN
4/19, Asaf Ali Rd., New Delhi-110002

✆ (O) 23289555, 23289666, 23289777, 23264676 (R) 22540400, Fax: 23253233
✉ prabhat@indianabooks.com, prabhat@vsnl.com
🌐 www.indianabooks.com
Estd.: 1959; **Prop.**: Shyam Sunder
Br.: 205, Chawri Bazar, Delhi-110006
Bus.Intt.: Pub.; **Spl.**: Book in Hindi on Litt., GK, etc. as also Children's Books and Dictionaries

PRABHODHAN PRAKASHAN
'Ayee' Shivnagar, Soot Giranee Marg, Latoor-431512 (Maharashtra)

PRABHU BOOK HOUSE
Kochi (Kerala)
✆ 0484-354012
✉ skrpai@stayam.net.in
Bus.Intt.: B.S. & Dist.

PRABHU BOOK SERVICE
P.O. Box 21, Sadar Bazar, Subzi Mandi Crossing, Gurgaon-122001 (Haryana)
✆ (O) 26320588 (R) 26306778, Fax: 26329805
✉ prabook@del3.vsnl.net.in
Estd.: 1962; **Prop.**: Vijay Kumar Jain
Br.: 30, Hauz Khas Village, Near Power House Health Club, 1st Floor, New Delhi-110016
✆ 26561284
Bus.Intt.: L.S. & Rt., Imp., Exp., Sub.Ag.; **Spl.**: Humanities & Soc.Sci.

PRABHUDDHA PRAKASHANA
93, "Vishwa Ranga" Ist Cross, K.G. Extension, Bangalore-560009 (Karnataka)
✆ 080-2267216
Hd.Org.: Gandasi Vishweshwara
Bus.Intt.: Pub.; **Spl.**: Fiction, Collections, Mythological, Humour and Gen. Books in Kannada

PRABHUS BOOKS
Ayurveda College Junction, Old Sreekanteswaram Rd., Thiruvananthapuram-695001 (Kerala)
✆ (O) 0471-2478397, 2473496 (R) 2478393, Fax: 91-471-2473496
✉ books@prabhusbooks.com
Estd.: 1987, **Hd.Org.**: K. Venugopal; **Bus.Intt.**: B.S., L.S., WS

PRABTHA PRINTING WORKS
Kondotty, Malappuram-673638 (Kerala)

PRACHEE PRAKASHAN
303, Sadachar Raiyani Gram, Shimpoli Rasta, Borivli West, Mumbai-400092 (Maharashtra)

PRACHEE PUBLICATIONS
1-2-212/6/F, Gaganmahal St. 12, Domalguda, Hyderabad-500029 (Andhra Pradesh)
✆ 27630703
Estd.: 1993; **Prop.**: P.P.C. Joshi; **Bus.Intt.**: Pub.; **Spl.**: Rare Old Books in Telugu

PRACHI (INDIA) PVT. LTD.
309, Allied House, Inder Lok, Delhi-110035
✆ 23656678, 23659695, Fax: 23659209
✉ info@prachipublications.com
🌐 www.prachipublications.com
Hd.Org.: Dinesh Tyagi; **Bus.Intt.**: Pub.; **Spl.**: School Textbooks and Edu. Books

PRACHI PRAKASHAN
22, Suryakiran Market, Sahid Nagar, Bhubneswar-751007 (Orissa)
✆ (O) 0674-2541621 (R) 2442896
Estd.: 1977; **Bus.Intt.**: Pub. and B.S.; **Spl.**: Reference Litt., School and Graduate Level Text & Children Litt. in English & Oriya

PRACHI PRAKASHAN PUBLISHERS & DISTRIBUTORS
B-224, Avantika Rohini, Sector 4, New Delhi-110085
✆ 27278732
Estd.: 1990; **Prop.**: Ved Prakash Mishra
Br.: 69688, Begumganj Makbra, Faizabad (Uttar Pradesh)
Bus.Intt.: Pub., WS, L.S. and Rt.

PRACHI PUBLICATIONS (INDIA) PVT. LTD.
309, Allied House, Inder Lok, Delhi-110035
✆ 23653191, Fax: 91-11-23659209
✉ info@prachipublications.com
🌐 www.prachipublications.com
Hd.Org.: Mukesh Tyagi; **Bus.Intt.**: Pub.; **Spl.**: School Textbooks and Edu. Books

PRACHI SAHITYA PRATISTHAN
Binod Behari, Cuttack-753002 (Orissa)
Estd.: 1986; **Bus.Intt.**: Pub. and B.S.; **Spl.**: Varieties of Books, Novels, Short Stories, Poems, Criticisms, and above all the Litt. for Children Handbooks and Gen. Knowledge for School and College Students in Oriya

PRACHYA PRAKASHALAY
56, Surya Sen St., Kolkata-700009 (West Bengal)
Hd.Org.: Hitendu Bhattacherjee

PRADEEP PRAKASHAN
C2/88, Yamuna Vihar, Delhi-110053
Hd.Org.: Pradeep Kumar

PRADEEP PRAKASHAN
246, Kar Kar Dooma, Delhi-110030
✆ 91-11-22372604
Hd.Org.: Sandeep Kumar Gautam
Bus.Intt.: Pub., **Spl.**: Children's Books and General Books

PRADEEP PUBLICATIONS
Couri Rd., Anand Kaira-388001 (Gujarat)
✆ 225627, 226237

PRADEEP PUSTAK BHANDAR
Charan, Aurangabad-824301 (Bihar)
Bus.Intt.: Pub. and B.S.

PRADHAN BOOK STALL
Bankim Chatterjee St., P.D.S. Corner, Kolkata-73 (West Bengal)

PRADIP PRAKASHAN
C-2/88, Yamuna Vihar, Delhi-110053
✆ 22260763
Hd.Org.: Shripradip

PRAGATI BOOK HOUSE
1676-A, 14th Main Rd., 1st Cross, Prakashnagar, Bangalore-560021 (Karnataka)
✆ 80-23324037, 23324437,
Fax: 91-80-23324848
Hd.Org.: Bharat Salva; **Spl.:** Edu. Books

PRAGATI BOOK HOUSE
Museum Rd., Vijayawada-520002 (Andhra Pradesh)

PRAGATI BOOKS PVT. LTD.
Pragati House, 119, Budhwar Peth, Jogeshwari Mandir Lane, Pune-411002 (Maharashtra)
✆ (O) 020-24450842, 24451512, 4022708
(R) 25430133, Fax: 24495422
✉ pragatibooks@vsnl.net
🌐 www.pragationline.com
Man.Dir.: Jignesh Furia; **Bus.Intt.:** Pub.; **Spl.:** Sci. & Tech., Comp., Mang.

PRAGATI PERIODICALS SUBSCRIPTION AGENCY
Block-B, House-788, 1st Floor, Avantika, Rohini, Sector-1, Delhi-110085
✆ 27521237 ▮ 9810202312, Fax: 27521237
✉ ppsa@vsnl.net, ppsa@mantraonline.com
Estd.: 2001; **Prt.:** Prahlad Dhasmana, Satyendra Kumar
Br.: 6MF/235-Block-7, Sector-6, Near Agam Kuan Thana, Bahadurpur Housing Colony, Karnkarbagh, Patna-20
Bus.Intt.: L.S., Rt., Sub.Ag.; **Spl.:** Humanities & Soc.Sci., Sci. & Tech., Med.

PRAGATI PRAKASHAN
Post Box 62, New Market, Begum Bridge, Meerut-250001 (Uttar Pradesh)
✆ (O) 2661657, 2640642, 2651907
(R) 2663838, 2654661, Fax: 2663838
✉ pragatiprakashan@yahoo.com
🌐 www.pragatiprakashan.com
Estd.: 1955; **Hd.Org.:** K.K. Mittal; **Bus.Intt.:** Pub.; **Spl.:** Acad. Books on Physical Sci., Life Sci., Man. and for Med. and Engg. Examinations

PRAGATI PUBLICATIONS
4382/4B, Ansari Rd., Darya Ganj, New Delhi-110002
✆ 23280585
✉ pragati1@ndf.vsnl.net.in
Estd.: 1978; **Prop.:** Vinod Kapoor
Br.: 4263/3, Ansari Rd., Darya Ganj, New Delhi-110002 ✆ 23290174, 23290217
✉ pragati1@ndf.vsnl.net.in
Bus.Intt.: Pub., L.S. & Rt., Imp.;
Spl.: Humanities & Soc.Sci.

PRAGATI SANSTHAN
H-601, Friends Apartments, Patparganj, Vikas Marg, Delhi-110092
✆ 91-11-22242440
Hd.Org.: Meena Sharma; **Bus.Intt.:** Pub. & Dist.; **Spl.:** Litt. Classics in Hindi

PRAGATISHIL PUSTAK BHANDAR
Court Compound, Aurangabad-824101 (Bihar)
Bus.Intt.: Pub. and B.S.

PRAGYA PRAKASHAN MANCH
C-54, Shivaji Park, New Delhi-110026
✆ 25431046
Hd.Org.: Mrs. Indira Sawapan

PRAGYA PUBLICATIONS
D-50, South Extension, Part I, New Delhi-110049

PRAHARIDURG PRAKASHAN SOCIETY
H-58, Old Khandala Rd., Pune Dist., Lonavla-410404 (Maharashtra)
✆ 273721/71041
Estd.: 1986; **Secy.:** Richard Gabriel;
Bus.Intt.: Pub., WS, L.S. & Rt., Imp., Exp., Sub.Ag.; **Spl.:** Humanities & Soc.Sci.

PRAJA PRINTERS (P) LTD.
Praja Bhawan, 53/2, Bull Temple Rd., Bangalore-560019 (Karnataka)

PRAJAHITA PUBLISHERS
1-1-1/18/1, Golconda, 'X' Rd.s, Adjacent to Musheerabad, Telephone Exchange, Hyderabad-500020 (Andhra Pradesh)
✆ 27631001, 23317271, 2222169
▮ 98480-56789, Pager: 9622531234,
Fax: 23322046
Estd.: 1987; **Hd.Org.:** Gouru Tirupati Reddy; **Bus.Intt.:** Pub.; **Spl.:** Books on Vaastu Shastra

PRAJASAKTI BOOK HOUSE
Hyderabad (Andhra Pradesh)
✆ 23660013, 27635136, Fax: 27639921

pbhhyd@yahoo.co.in
Bus.Intt.: B.S. & Dist.

PRAJASHAKTHI BOOK HOUSE
Karl Marx Rd., Vijayawada-520002 (Andhra Pradesh)
(O) 0866-2432792 (R) 266277, 261424
Estd.: 1966; **Hd.Org.:** Mortoru Hanumantha Rao; **Bus.Intt.:** Pub.; **Spl.:** Contemporary Books, Pol.Sci., Marxist Litt. and Criticism

PRAJESH PRAKASHAN
Opp. Model Cinema, Gandhi Rd., Ahmedabad-380001 (Gujarat)

PRAJNA PRAKASHAN
34, Kailash Mandir, Kanpur-248001 (Uttar Pradesh)

PRAJNA PUBLICATIONS
Hospital Rd., Duillya, Howrah-711302 (West Bengal)

PRAKASH AND COMPANY
406, Gali No. 8, Phool Bagh Colony, Meerut City-250002 (Uttar Pradesh)
2771049
jaiprakash_co@rediffmail.com
Estd.: 1990; **Dir.:** Jai Prakash;
Bus.Intt.: Pub., WS, L.S. & Rt., Imp.;
Spl.: Sci. & Tech., Med.

PRAKASH BHAWAN
15, Bankim Chatterjee St., Kolkata-700073 (West Bengal)
033-2313266
Hd.Org.: S. Mukherjee

PRAKASH BOOK DEPOT
Bara Bazar, Bareilly-243003 (Uttar Pradesh)
(O) 0581-2470217 (R) 2476499
Estd.: 1936; **Hd.Org.:** Prem Prakash Shinghal; **Bus.Intt.:** Pub. and B.S.; **Spl.:** Litt., English, American, Indo-English, Hindi, Defence Studies, Sanskrit, Humanties

PRAKASH BOOK DEPOT
M-86, Connaught Place, New Delhi-110001
23416566, 23416897, Fax: 23246975
accounts@prakashbooks.com
www.prakashbooks.com
Estd.: 1948; **Ch.Exe.:** Ashwani Sabharwal
Br.: 4223/1, Ansari Rd., Darya Ganj, New Delhi-110002 23243051-2, Fax: 23246975 sales@prakashbooks.com
• H.No.-129, Sunder Path Marg, Bani Park, Jaipur-320006 (Rajasthan) 2203174
jaipursales@prakashbooks.com
• No. 4, 3rd Cross, 4th Main, Gandhi Nagar, Bangalore-560009 (Karnataka)
bangaloresales@prakashbooks.com
Bus.Intt.: Pub., WS, Imp., Exp.; **Spl.:** Sci. & Tech., Juvenile/Children, Gen. & Fiction

PRAKASH BOOK DISTRIBUTORS
D-6/23, Dayalpur, P.O. Gokulpuri, Delhi-110094
Hd.Org.: Ved Prakash
Br.: O-18/B-3, Dilshad Garden, Delhi
Bus.Intt.: Rt., L.S.

PRAKASH BOOK DISTRIBUTORS
490, DDA Flats, GTB Enclave, Nand Vihar, Delhi-110093
22118400, 22138251, 22181230, Fax: 22118400
prakashbooksd@rediffmail.com
Hd.Org.: Manju Joshi; **Bus.Intt.:** Pub. and B.S.; **Spl.:** College-level Books on Sci., Math., Hist., Geo., Man. in English and Hindi

PRAKASH BOOKS INDIA PVT. LTD.
4223/1, Ansari Road, Darya Ganj, New Delhi-110002
23247062-65, Fax: 91-11-23246975
sales@prakashbooks.com, info@prakashbooks.com
www.prakashbooks.com
Estd.: 1948; **Hd.Org.:** Ashwani Sabharwal
Bus.Intt.: Pub. and Dist., Spl.: Books on Travel, Science & Technology, Computer, Fiction, Children's Books etc.
Br.: 4th Main, 4th Cross Gandhi Nagar, Bangalore, 91-80-22201411/24
bangaloresales@prakashbooks.com
• House No. 129, Sunder Path Marg, Badodiya, Basti Bani Park, Jaipur
91-141-2203174
jaipursales@prakashbooks.com
• Old No. 104, New No. 23, Nelson Manickam Road, Aminjikarai, Chennai-600029
91-44-30914382, 52112526, 23742574
chennaisales@prakashbooks.com

PRAKASH BROTHERS
46, Bhagat Singh Market, Near Gole Mkt., New Delhi-110001
23362615, 23362616
Bus.Intt.: B.S., Stationers and Gen. Order Suppliers

PRAKASH PUBLICATIONS
46, Zila Parishad Bagar, Muzaffarnagar-251001 (Uttar Pradesh)
(O) 0131-2403263, 2433530 (R) 2406562, 2403354, Fax: 2430676
manojbathla@hotmail.com
www.bathlabooks.com
Estd.: 1967; **Hd.Org.:** Prakash Chand Bathla; **Bus.Intt.:** Pub.; **Spl.:** Sci. & Tech.

PRAKASH PUBLICATIONS
No. 6-38, Kalamma St., Chamarajanagar-571313 (Karnataka)

© 91-08226-22824, Fax: 91-8226-22824
Estd.: 1989; **Bus.Intt.:** Pub. and B.S. (Mail Order); **Spl.:** Higher Studies/Scholarships Opportunities in Foreign Countries, 'Studies in U.S.A.', 'Study Abroad', 'U.S. Scholarships Directory', 'Indian Scholarships Handbook', 'International Scholarships Handbook'

PRAKASH PUSTAK BHANDAR
Sabour, Bhagalpur-813210 (Bihar)
Bus.Intt.: Pub. and B.S.

PRAKASH SALES CORPN.
Near Geman Bakery, Main Bazar, Leh-Ladakh (Jammu & Kashmir)
© 252328, 252894
Prop.: Om Prakash Rajput; **Bus.Intt.:** B.S. & Rt.

PRAKASHAN HOUSE
10, Pan Dreeba, Lucknow-226004 (Uttar Pradesh)
© 2452696
Hd.Org.: Rohit Bhargav

PRAKASHAN SANSTHAN
4715/21, Dayanand Marg, Darya Ganj, New Delhi-110002
© 23253234, 65283371, Fax: 91-11-23287713
Hd.Org.: Harish Chandra Sharma;
Bus.Intt.: Pub. & Dist.; **Spl.:** Books in Hindi on Litt., Edu., Hist., Soc.Sci., etc.

PRAKHAR PRAKASHAN
11486/A, Subhash Park Extn., Naveen Shahdara, Delhi-110032
Hd.Org.: Ajay Kumar

PRAMBH PRAKASHAN
R-64, Sector-12, Pratap Vihar, Ghaziabad-201009 (Uttar Pradesh)
© 2722464
Hd.Org.: Mrs. Savrinima Tushar

PRAMCO (INDIA) PVT. LTD.
New Delhi
© 26922072, 26934735, Fax: 26934734
✉ pramcolearning@vsnl.net, pramco@usa.net
Bus.Intt.: Dist.

PRAMILA BOOK AGENCY
Bankim Chatterjee St., Stall-4, Block-6, Kolkata-700073 (West Bengal)

PRAMOD PUSTAK BHANDAR
Shivanarayanpur, Bhagalpur-813203 (Bihar)
Bus.Intt.: Pub. and B.S.

PRANAB BOOK AGENCY
15, College Square, Kolkata-700012 (West Bengal)

PRANIC HEALING FOUNDATION OF DELHI
3/23, Shanti Niketan, New Delhi-110021
© 28660565/66/67, Fax: 91-11-28660567
✉ phfd@vsnl.com
Estd.: 1995; **Ch.Exe.:** Capt. K.V. Kunhi Krishnan; **Bus.Intt.:** Pub.; **Spl.:** Books on Pranic Healing and Related Topics written by Grand master Choa Kok Sui

PRANJAL ART PUBLISHERS
69, Baba Ka Purva, Nishatganj, Lucknow-226006 (Uttar Pradesh)
▮ 9935799066
✉ pranjal_art@gmail.com
Hd.Org.: Rambabu
Bus.Intt. Pub.; **Spl.:** Hindi language publisher of posters, calendars and greeting cards, etc.

PRANTIK
73, Mahatma Gandhi Rd., Kolkata-700009 (West Bengal)

PRARAMBHA PRAKASHAN
R-64, Sector-12, Pratap Vihar, Ghaziabad-201009 (Uttar Pradesh)
© 2742464
Hd.Org.: Swarnima Tushar; **Bus.Intt.:** Pub.;
Spl.: Books on Hindi Litt. and Poetry

PRASAD LIBRARY
College Hostel Rd., Pan Bazar, Guwahati-781001 (Assam)

PRASAD PUBLISHING CO.
College Hotel Rd., Pan Bazar, Guwahati-781001 (Assam)

PRASANNA TRUST
51, Ground Floor, 6th and 8th Main, 16th Cross, Malleswaram, Bangalore-560055
© 41535832, Fax: 91-80-23444112
✉ prasannatrust@vsnl.com
🌐 www.swamisukhabodhananda.org
Hd.Org.: P.R. Madhav
Bus.Intt.: Pub.

PRASAR BOOKSELLERS
1888, Atabhai Avenue, Bhavnagar-364002 (Gujarat)
© 0278-568452
✉ prasaradl@sancharnet.in

PRASHANT BOOK AGENCY
4263, A/3, 1st Floor, Ansari Rd., Darya Ganj, New Delhi-110002
© 65398961, Fax: 91-11-23251390
✉ prashantbooks@hotmail.com
Estd.: 2004; **Prop.:** Karanvir Singh Sisodia;
Bus.Intt.: B.S., L.S.; **Spl.:** Sci. & Tech.

PRASHANT BOOK DISTRIBUTORS
G-38, Aruna Nagar, Civil Lines, Delhi-110054
▮ 9811734184
Estd.: 2001; **Prop.:** Durga Prasad;
Bus.Intt.: WS, L.S.; **Spl.:** Acad., Soc.Sci.,

Sci., Pure and Applied, Tech., Fiction, Journals and Magazines

PRASHANT BOOK DISTRIBUTORS
Shakti Building, 1st Floor, 2 Netaji Subhash Marg, Darya Ganj, New Delhi-110002

PRASHANT BOOK ENTERPRISES
1/6499, East Rohtas Nagar, Shahdara, Delhi-110032

PRASHANT BOOK HOUSE & PUBLICATIONS
17, Stadium Shopping Centre, Opp. State Bank of India, Jalgaon-425001 (Maharashtra)
✆ (O) 0257-2227231 (R) 0257-2252374
✉ prashantbook@yahoo.com
Estd.: 1990; **Hd.Org.:** Rangrao A. Patil
Br.: "Dnyudeep" Plot No. 2, Chaitany Nagar, Opp. Progressive English School, Jalgaon-425001
Bus.Intt.: Pub., B.S., Rt. and L.S.; **Spl.:** Text, Acad. and Research Books in North Maharashtra

PRASHANT PUBLICATIONS
Regency House, BM-12, (West) Shalimar Bagh, Delhi-110088
✆ (O) 27480144, 27482403 (R) 27481259
Fax: 27480144, 27482403
✉ prashantbooks@indiatimes.com, prashantbooks@yahoo.co.in
Estd.: 1999; **Ch.Exe.:** R.K. Gupta;
Bus.Intt.: Pub.; **Spl.:** Child Psy., Home Mang., Home Therapy as well as books for Children

PRASHANTH PRAKASHANA
15, Shivananda Nilaya, Yadavagiri, Mysore-570020 (Karnataka)
Hd.Org.: Naguvanahalli Ratna; **Bus.Intt.:** Pub.; **Spl.:** Fiction, Poems, Collection, Gen. Books and Own Books in Kannada

PRASUN KR. CHAKRABORTY
162/165, Lake Gardens, Kolkata-700045 (West Bengal)

PRATAP HOMOEO PHARMACY & CLINIC
944/A, Nehru Rd., Arjun Nagar, Kotla Mubarakpur, New Delhi-110003
✆ 24623859, 24645728, 24623856,
Fax: 24647774
✉ kpsdhama@bol.net.in
Hd.Org.: Suman Dhama
Br.: 945/1 Nehru Rd., Arjun Nagar, Kotla Mubarakpur, New Delhi-110003
Bus.Intt.: Pub. and Dist.; **Spl.:** Homoeopathic Books and Monthly Journal: *The Homoeopathic Prestige*

PRATAP PUSTAK BHANDAR
Parvashripathar, Bhagalpur-813115 (Bihar)
Bus.Intt.: Pub. and B.S.

PRATAYA PRAKASHANI
61, Mahatma Gandhi Rd., Kolkata-700009 (West Bengal)

PRATHAM BOOKS
A-1/7, Safdarjang Enclave (Basement), New Delhi-110029
✆ 65684113, Fax: 91-11-26716083
✉ info@prathambooks.org
www.prathambooks.org
Hd.Org.: Ashok Kamath
Bus.Intt.: Pub.; **Spl.:** Children's Books

PRATHMIC & MADHYAMIC SHIKSHA
Department of Education, Bikaner (Rajasthan)

PRATHUSHA BOOKS
Taliparamba-670141 (Kerala)

PRATIBHA BOOKS
5/2525, Bank Rd., Calicut-673001 (Kerala)

PRATIBHA PRAKASHAN
29/5, Shakti Nagar, Delhi-110007
✆ 91-11-23848485, 23840390
9350884227, 9350906327
✉ info@pratibhabooks.com
www.pratibhabooks.com
Hd.Org.: Radhey Shyam Shukla;
Bus.Intt.: Pub. & B.S.; **Spl.:** Sanskrit, *Vedas*, Rel., Indian Phil., Ancient Indian Hist., Art, Indian Music, Archaeology, Indology, etc.

PRATIBHA PRAKASHANA
2625, 8th A Main Banashankari, Phase II, Bangalore-560070 (Karnataka)
Hd.Org.: H.V. Krishnaswamy; **Bus.Intt.:** Pub.; **Spl.:** All Kinds of Books in Kannada

PRATIBHA PRAKASHANI
1/63A, Vidyasagar Colony, Kolkata-700047 (West Bengal)

PRATIBHA PRATISHTHAN
1661, Dakhni Rai St., Netaji Subhash Marg, New Delhi-110002
✆ 23257555, Fax: 23253233
✉ prabhat@indianabooks.com
Estd.: 1982; **Prop.:** Prabhat Kumar;
Bus.Intt.: Pub. and Dist.; **Spl.:** Novels, Stories and Books for Children and Neo-literates in Hindi

PRATIKSHA PUBLICATIONS
Kashi Nath Ji Ki Gali, Gopal Ji Ka Rasta, Kaopir-301001 (Rajasthan)

PRATIMAAN PRAKASHAN
UC-13, Usha Park, Hari Nagar, New Delhi-110064
Prop.: Raghubir Singh; **Bus.Intt.:** Pub. and L.S.; **Spl.:** English and Hindi

PRATIMAAN PRAKASHAN
30, Kuncharoy Ganga Prasad, Allahabad-211003 (Uttar Pradesh)
Hd.Org.: Smt. Rajani Malhotra

PRATISABDA PRAKASHANI
1/63 A, Vidyasagar Colony, Kolkata-700047 (West Bengal)
Estd.: 1981; **Hd.Org.:** Souvikn Chauroborls

PRATYAYA PRAKASHANI
61, Mahatma Gandhi Rd., Kolkata-700009 (West Bengal)
✆ 033-22413357
Estd.: 1983; **Prop.:** Banshidhar Singha; **Bus.Intt.:** Pub.; **Spl.:** Textbooks and Literary Works Books in English, Hindi and Associated Languages

PRATIYOGITA DARPAN
2/11A, Swadeshi Bima Nagar, Agra-282002 (Uttar Pradesh)
✆ 2531101, 2602653, Fax: 2531940
✉ upkarl@sancharnet.in
Hd.Org.: Mahendra S. Jain; **Bus.Intt.:** Pub.; **Spl.:** Magazines *Pratiyogita Darpan* and *Samanya Gyan Darpan* in Hindi, and *Competition Science Vision* in English

PRATIYOGITA SAHITYA SERIES
Agra (Uttar Pradesh)
✆ 351665, 353400, Fax: 351568
✉ kanhaiya@ndb.vsnl.net.in
Bus.Intt.: Pub.

PRATYUSH BOOK SERVICE
J-96, Kartar Nagar, Delhi-110053
✆ 22941498
Prop.: Rajesh Kumar Dubbet; **Bus.Intt.:** L.S.; **Spl.:** Acad., Beh.Sci., Soc.Sci., Comm., Med. & Fiction

PRAVEEN PRAKASHAN
246, Kar Kar Dooma, Delhi-110092
▮ 9312492269
✉ praveenbooksdist@rediffmail.com
Hd.Org.: Praveen Kumar Gautam
Bus.Intt.: Pub. and Dist.; **Spl.:** Children's Books, General Books and CDs

PRAVEEN PRAKASHAN
4760-61, Second Floor, 23, Ansari Road, Darya Ganj, New Delhi-110002
✆ 91-11-65651098
✉ info@praveenbooks.com
www.praveenbooks.com
Hd.Org.: Kishan Gupta
Bus.Intt.: Pub; **Spl.:** Children's Literature, Novels, Stories, Poetry and Books on Science in Hindi

PRAVEEN PUSTAK BHANDAR
Rajaun, Bhagalpur-813107 (Bihar)
Bus.Intt.: Pub. and B.S.

PRAVIN PRAKASHAN (P) LTD.
Opp. Municipal Corporation, Labh Chambers, Dhebar Rd., Rajkot-360001 (Gujarat)
✆ 2232460, 2234602
Hd.Org.: Gopal M. Patel; **Spl.:** Rel., Litt., Poems, Children Books

PRAVIN PUSTAK BHANDAR
Labh Chambers, Ist Floor, Opp. Municipal Corporation, Near Bus Stand, Rajkot-360001 (Gujarat)
✆ 2234602, 2232460
Bus.Intt.: B.S. and L.S.

PRAYAG PRAKASHAN
164-A, Tripathi Colony, Sohbatiya Bagh, Allahabad-211006 (Uttar Pradesh)
Hd.Org.: Akhilesh Kumar Mishra

PRAYAG PUSTAK BHAVAN
20-A, University Rd., Allahabad-211002 (Uttar Pradesh)
✆ 2461505, 2460028, Fax: 2503295
Hd.Org.: Radhey Shyam Jaiswal; **Bus.Intt.:** Pub.; **Spl.:** University-level Textbooks and Books for Competitive Examination

PRAYAGRAJ PUBLICATION
56/13, Motilal Nehru Rd., Allahabad-211002 (Uttar Pradesh)
✆ 2600592
Hd.Org.: Punit Agarwal

PRAYAS PUBLISHERS & BOOKSELLERS
Kolkata (West Bengal)
✆ 2241-0176, Fax: 25124630
✉ prayasbook2@hotmail.com
Bus.Intt.: Pub. & Dist.

PRECISE COMPUTER TOOLING CO.
DDA Shed, A-121, Okhla Industrial Area, Phase-II, New Delhi-110020
✆ 26836173, Fax: 26813896
✉ elcon@del2.vsnl.net.in
Hd.Org.: Vinod Gupta; **Bus.Intt.:** Dist.; **Spl.:** Children's Books and Edu. Teaching Aids

PREDRISHYA PRAKASHAN
6, Dadi Santuk Lane, Dhobi Talaab, Mumbai-400002 (Maharashtra)
✆ 22019268

PREET LADI PRAKASHAN
Preet Nagar, Amritsar-143004 (Punjab)
Hd.Org.: Ms. Poonam Shammi

PREETI MANDIR PRAKASHAN
1/6816, Rohtas Nagar East, Babarpur, Delhi-110032
Hd.Org.: Supavitra Bhasin

PREETI PUBLISHING HOUSE
EC-132, Inder Puri, New Delhi-110012
✆ 25739025, 25759802, 25759824, 25759303
Estd.: 1990; **Prop.:** Gurjeet Kaur Sethi
Br.: 741-A, Lastmor, Gandhi Nagar, Jammu (Jammu and Kashmir)
Bus.Intt.: Pub., WS, L.S. and Rt.

PREETI PUBLICATIONS
C-1/2, Pandara Park, New Delhi-110003

PREFACE BOOKS
Shivali Apts, Plot No. 1, S.No. 25/4, Chintamani Society, Karvey Nagar, Pune-411052 (Maharashtra)
✆ 2349491
Estd.: 1998; **Hd.Org.:** Anshul Chawla

PREFACE BOOKS
Mumbai (Maharashtra)
✆ 24988054, Fax: 24988048
✉ preface@vsnl.com

PREFECT PRESS (P) LTD.
30/1, East Patel Nagar, New Delhi-110008

PREM BOOK DEPOT
Vings Way, Sadarbazar, Jabalpur-482001 (Madhya Pradesh)
✆ 2320840
Hd.Org.: Prashant Dubey; **Bus.Intt.:** B.S., L.S., Magazine's Agents

PREM CHAND PUBLICATIONS
39-3-51, Mazid St., Opp. S.B.I. Labbipet, Vijayawada-520010 (Andhra Pradesh)

PREM NATH & SONS
30/35, Publisher's Street, Gali No. 9, Vishwas Nagar, Shahdara, Delhi-110032
✆ 91-11-22382559
Hd.Org.: Arun Kumar Sharma
Bus.Intt.: Pub. and Dist.; **Spl.:** Hindi Litt. and Populár Science, Educational and Children's Books

PREM PRAKASHAN MANDIR
3012, Ballimaran, Delhi-110006
✆ 22918110, 22947589, 22266235
Hd.Org.: Prem Chand Sharma; **Bus.Intt.:** Pub. and B.S.; **Spl.:** English and Hindi

PREMA PIRASURAM
35, Arcot Rd., Kodambakkam, Chennai-600024 (Tamil Nadu)
✆ 24800325, 24833180, Fax: 044-24811755
✉ aruramdmd2.vsnl.net.in
Estd.: 1952; **Ch.Exe.:** R.M. Ravi; **Bus.Intt.:** Pub. and B.S.; **Spl.:** Mythology, Astrology, Soc., Historical Novels and Gen. Books

PREMA SAI PRAKASHANA
"Sree Guruprasad" 845, 4th Main Rd., Vijyanagar, Bangalore-560040 (Karnataka)
✆ 080-2301822
Estd.: 1973; **Hd.Org.:** A.S. Bhat; **Bus.Intt.:** Pub.; **Spl.:** Fiction and Gen. Books in Kannada

PREMCHAND SAHITYA SANSTHAN
Premchand Park, Batiyathatha, Gorakhpur-273001 (Uttar Pradesh)
✆ 2312708

PREMIER BOOK SHOP
46/1, Church St., Bangalore-560001 (Karnataka)
✆ 25588570
Estd.: 1971; **Prop.:** T.S. Shanbhag

PREMIER BOOK STALL
Up-Hill, Malappuram-676505 (Kerala)
Estd.: 1977; **Prop.:** P. Hamza; **Bus.Intt.:** B.S.

PREMIER PUBLISHING PVT. LTD.
47, Noor Veerasamy St., Nungambakkam, Chennai-600034 (Tamil Nadu)
✉ premierbooks@hotmail.com, manahabi2002@hotmail.com
www.sambooks.com
Hd.Org.: S. Habibullah; **Bus.Intt.:** Pub.; **Spl.:** Business & Mang., Health, Rel. Culture, etc. in Tamil and English

PREMSHEEL PRAKASHAN
289, Bank Wali Gali, Azadpur, Delhi-110033
✆ 27253503, 27242100
Hd.Org.: Apoorva Sharma; **Bus.Intt.:** Pub. and B.S.; **Spl.:** Literary and Gen. Books in Hindi

PRENTICE-HALL OF INDIA PRIVATE LIMITED
M-97, Connaught Circus, New Delhi-110001
✆ 23411779, 23418078, 23415326, Fax: 91-11-23417179
✉ phi@phindia.com
www.phindia.com
Estd.: 1963; **Hd.Org.:** Ashok K. Ghosh
Br.: 'Rimjhim House', 111, Patparganj Industrial Estate, Delhi-110092
✆ 43031100, 22143344, Fax: 91-11-43031144, 22141144
Bus.Intt.: Leading Pub.; **Spl.:** University Level Text and Reference Books

PREPRINT INTERNATIONAL
B-12 A, Arundathi Apartments, 110, C.P. Ramasamy Rd., Alwarpet, Chennai-18 (Tamil Nadu)

PRESCHOOL LEARNERS.COM
K-63, Jangpura Extn., New Delhi-110014
✆ 24311060
✉ sireeshbhatnagar@hotmail.com
Hd.Org.: Sireesh Bhatnagar; **Bus.Intt.:** Dealer; **Spl.:** Edu. Products for Pre-school Children

PRESENTATION BOOKS
9-B, 1st Floor, Auqaf Complex, Kashmir University Rd., Hazratbal, Srinagar-190006 (Jammu & Kashmir)
✉ presentbooks@yahoo.com
✆ (R) 0194-2424744
Estd.: 2001; **Prop.:** Bilal Ahmad Khan; **Bus.Intt.:** L.S. & Rt.; **Spl.:** Humanities & Soc.Sci., Sci. & Tech., Med., Law, Gen. & Fiction etc.

PRESIDENCY LIBRARY
15, Bankim Chatterjee St., Kolkata-700073 (West Bengal)

PRESS & PUBLICATIONS
Guru Nanak Dev University, Amritsar-143005 (Punjab)
✆ 2258837
Bus.Intt.: Pub. Research Journals in Different Sub.; **Spl.:** Rel., Hist., Pol.Sci.

PRESS & PUBLICATIONS SYNDICATE OF INDIA
15, Abubekar Mansion, 2nd Floor, Shahid Bhagat Singh Rd., Colaba, Mumbai-400039 (Maharashtra)

PRESS TRUST INDIA LTD.
4, Parliament St., New Delhi-110001

PRESTIGE BOOKS
3/25, East Patel Nagar, New Delhi-110008
✆ 25507139, 25737849, Fax: 25507139
Prop.: Ms. D. Renu; **Bus.Intt.:** Pub.; **Spl.:** Litt., Women's Studies and Feminism

PRESTIGE PUBLISHERS
A-1B/96B, Krishna Apartments, Paschim Vihar, New Delhi-110063
✆ 25261798, 25278090
▮ 9811047234, 9811130697
Prop.: C.L. Bhatia; **Bus.Intt.:** Pub., WS, Rt., L.S.; **Spl.:** All Types of Books except Engg., Med. & Psychological

PRESTIGE TUTORIAL SAMITHI
Publications Division, Prestige Tutorial Samiti, Devriya (Uttar Pradesh)
✆ 91-5568-222005, 248180
✉ prestigetutorial@mail.com
Hd.Org.: Kanhaiya Singh
Bus.Intt.: Pub.; **Spl.:** Books on Education in Hindi

PRIDE PUBLICATIONS
D-5/24, Krishna Nagar, Delhi-110051
Prop.: B.M. Anand; **Bus.Intt.:** Pub.; **Spl.:** Children Edu. Books in English, Hindi and Urdu

PRIMAL PUBLISHERS
C-007, Yamuna Apartments, Alaknanda, New Delhi-110019

PRIME BOOK SHOP
J. Nehru Marg, Sadar, Nagpur-440001 (Maharashtra)
✆ (O) 2524659 (R) 2532544, Fax: 0712-2537896
✉ primebookshop@hotmail.com
Estd.: 1979; **Bus.Intt.:** B.S.; **Spl.:** Graduate, Adv. Books for Lib. and Gen. Books

PRIME MAG. SUBSCRIPTION SERVICES PVT. LTD.
Rgd.Off.: K-20, Model Town, Delhi-110009
✆ 27441746, Fax: 27210420
✉ primemag@mantraonline.com
Corporate Off.: B-114, G.T.K. Rd., Industrial Area, Delhi-110033; ✆ 27430239
▮ 9891088702 ✉ primemag@dishnetdsl.net
Estd.: 2003; **Hd.Org.:** Akhil Bhatia;
Bus.Intt.: Sub.Ag.; **Spl.:** Journals, Magazines & Periodicals

PRIME PUBLISHING HOUSE
127, Niti Khand-III, Indirapuram, Ghaziabad-201012 (Uttar Pradesh)
✆ 95120-2900076 ▮ 9818478547
✉ primehouse@rediffmail.com
Estd.: 2003; **Prt.:** Harish Rawat;
Bus.Intt.: Pub., L.S.; **Spl.:** Humanities & Soc.Sci., Sci. & Tech., Mang., Bio.Sci.

PRIME TIME PUBLICATIONS (P) LTD.
New Delhi
✆ 25713032, 25820554
Fax: 91-11-25741149
✉ hitads@ndb.vsnl.net.in
Bus.Intt.: Pub., Dist., & Printers

PRIMEROSE STATIONERS & BOOKSELLERS
Main Bazar, Sopore, Kashmir-193201 (Jammu & Kashmir)
✆ 221384, Fax: 220400
Estd.: 2002; **Hd.Org.:** E.R. Hami Dullah Changal; **Bus.Intt.:** WS, L.S. & Rt., **Spl.:** Sci. & Tech.

PRIMULACEAE BOOKS
Abhijit Villa, BPO Ecchey, Kalimpong, Darjeeling-734301 (Assam)
Bus.Intt.: Exp.

PRINCE BOOK DEPOT
3C/27, New Rohtak Rd., New Delhi-110005
✆ 25718880, 27116968
Estd.: 1972; **Prop.:** Raj Prakash;
Bus.Intt.: Pub., WS, L.S. and Rt., Exp.

PRINT & BLOCK CONCERN (KOLKATA)
Kolkata (West Bengal)
✆ 22339207, 22392696, Fax: 22392696
✉ kishorebinani@vsnl.net

PRINT AND BUDIA ASSOCIATES 'PRACHAR'
11, Community Centre, East of Kailash, New Delhi-110065

PRINT HOUSE (INDIA)
5, T.B. Sapru Marg, Lucknow-226001 (Uttar Pradesh)
✆ 2231333, 2219495, Fax: 2228586
Estd.: 1981; **Prop.**: Raj Prakash;
Bus.Intt.: Pub., WS, L.S. and Rt., Exp.

PRINT INN (HOUSE OF BOOKS)
Pune (Maharashtra)
✉ print.inn@netkracker.com
Bus.Intt.: Pub. and Dist.

PRINT LINE BOOKS
235, Jagriti Enclave, Vikas Marg, Delhi-110092
✆ 22163582, 43023727, Fax: 91-11-22143023
✉ tinytotpub@hotmail.com
Hd.Org.: Shyam Dua
Bus.Intt.: Pub.; **Spl.**: Biographies, Children's Books, Classics and Books on General Knowledge, etc.

PRINT MEDIA PUBLISHERS & PRINTERS
109, New Deopuri, Meerut (Uttar Pradesh)

PRINT PUBLISHING
406, Sant Nagar, East of Kailash, New Delhi-110065
✆ 26405715, Fax: 26405716
✉ khuranas@del2.vsnl.net.in
Hd.Org.: T.G. Krishna

PRINTFORT BOOK HOUSE
B-55, Nehru Ground, NIT, Faridabad-121001 (Haryana)

PRINTLINE BOOKS
235, Jagriti Enclave, Vikas Marg, Delhi-110092
✆ 22167314, 22163582, Fax: 22143023
Hd.Org.: Shyam Dua; **Bus.Intt.**: Pub.;
Spl.: Gen. Books and Eng. Litt.

PRINTMAAN
8, Adhyaru Industrial Estate, Sunmill, Compound, Lowerparel, Mumbai-400013 (Maharashtra)
✆ 24944119, 24944156, Fax: 24922226
Estd.: 1985; **Bus.Intt.**: Exp.

PRINTS INDIA
11, Darya Ganj, New Delhi-110002
✆ 23268645, 23271378, 23257864
Cable: INDOLOGY, Fax: 23275542, 6475450
✉ printsin@nde.vsnl.net.in
Estd.: 1966; **Prt.**: Chandu Lal Gupta;
Bus.Intt.: Pub., L.S. & Rt., Exp.;
Spl.: Soc.Sci., & Humanities, Sci. & Tech., Med., Law, Juvenile/Children, Gen. & Fiction etc.

PRINTWELL PUBLISHERS AND DISTRIBUTORS
S-12, Shopping Centre, Tilak Nagar, Jaipur-302004 (Rajasthan)
✆ 2623753, 2620359, Fax: 0141-2623015
Hd.Org.: Smt. Kiran Gupta

PRISM BOOK PVT. LTD.
1865, 32 Cross BSK, 1 Stage, Bangalore-560070 (Karnataka)
✆ 26713991, 26714108, 26714060, Fax: 26713979
✉ pranesh@prismbooks.com, prism@vsnl.com
🌐 www.praneshs@prismbooks.com
Estd.: 1991; **Dir.**: Pranesh Siravara
Br.: 3-6-502/C St. No. 6, Lane 2, Himayatnagar, Hyderabad-500029
✆ 27660308, Fax: 040-27605939
✉ prismhyd@pol.net.in
• N. Rajendra Ghare, Ransur At Post Manda (W), TAL, Kalyan Station, Titwala-421605
✆ 25378760, Fax: 022-25378760
• 281630A K.P. Valluvan Rd., Kadavanthra, Cochin-682020 ▮ 9847080034
✉ mahesh_prism@yahoo.com
Bus.Intt.: Pub., WS, L.S. & Rt., Imp., Sub.Ag.; **Spl.**: Humanities & Soc.Sci., Sci. & Tech., Med.

PRISM PUBLICATIONS
1-Minaxi, Swastick Park, Sion, Trombay Rd., Chambur, Mumbai-400071 (Maharashtra)

PRISON FELLOWSHIP INDIA (JUBILEE BOOKS)
P.O. Box 189, Kottayam-686001 (Kerala)
✆ 2578528, 2578376
Hd.Org.: Kunjumon Chacko; **Bus.Intt.**: Pub.

PRITHVI BOOK AGENCY
Sri Krishnarajendra Rd., Opp. Vanivilas Hospital, Fort, Bangalore-560002 (Karnataka)
✆ 6703939, 6701060
✉ prithvibooks@hotmail.com
Estd.: 1956; **Bus.Intt.**: Rt., WS, L.S., Pub.

PRITIBHA PRATISTAHAN
1685, Daknirai St., Netaji Subhash Marg, New Delhi-110002
✆ 23289666

PRITIMAN PRAKASHAN PVT. LTD.
Bhopal (Madhya Pradesh)
✆ 550291, 555442, Fax: 555449
✉ rajonas@vsnl.com
Bus.Intt.: Pub. & Dist.

PRIYA BOOK DISTRIBUTORS
Z-60 (Old No. B-40), Narain Vihar, Prem Nagar-II, Near Kirari Nahar, Delhi-110041
✆ (R) 35902598 ▮ 9811167944
✉ priyabook_prompt@yahoo.com.sg
Estd.: 2003; **Prop.**: Kailash C. Saemwal
Br.: 2096, Sector-8, Faridabad-121006
Bus.Intt.: Pub., B.S., L.S.;
Spl.: Humanities & Soc.Sci., Children & General, Arts & Arch., Insti. Pub.

PRIYA BOOK HOUSE
A-19, Vijay Nagar (S.G.T.B. Nagar), Delhi-110009
✆ 27332127
Hd.Org.: Naresh Sachdeva; **Bus.Intt.**: Pub., Rt., L.S. and Journal's Suppliers

PRIYA BOOKS PVT. LTD.
Aurangpura, Aurangabad-431001 (Maharashtra)
✆ 2336945
Estd.: 1997; **Hd.Org.**: Somnath Dongapare; **Bus.Intt.**: WS; **Spl.**: Trade of Aurangabad and Surrounding Area (School, College Text, Help Books)

PRIYA PRAKASHANA
"Shubha" 286, 26th Cross, Banashankari II Stage, Bangalore-560070 (Karnataka)
✆ 080-2608614
Hd.Org.: Padma Gururaj; **Bus.Intt.**: Pub.; **Spl.**: Fiction Collections in Kannada

PRIYA SAHITYA SADAN
2226-B Block, Gali No. 33, Pehla Pusta, Sonia Vihar, Delhi-110094
✆ 91-11-22968185
Hd.Org.: Pawan K. Srivastava
Bus.Intt.: Pub. & Dist.; **Spl.**: Books in Hindi

PRIYADARSINI PUBLICATIONS
Museum Rd., Governorpet, Vijayawada-520002 (Andhra Pradesh)

PRIYAM BOOK DEPOT
R-6, Vani Vihar, Uttam Nagar, New Delhi-110059
✆ 91-11-25639146
✉ priyambookdepot@rediffmail.com
Hd.Org.: Priyamvada
Bus.Intt.: Pub.; **Spl.**: Books on Indian Culture, Religion, etc. in Hindi and Sanskrit

PRIYANK BOOK & STATIONERY CENTRE
2, Marwari Rd., Bhopal-462001 (Madhya Pradesh)
✆ 2544079, 2540365, Fax: 2533955
Estd.: 1987; **Hd.Org.**: Manish Jain; **Bus.Intt.**: WS; **Spl.**: Trade and Suppliers to Public Schools of School and College Books

PRODUCTIVITY PRESS (I) (P) LTD.
23, Thanikachalam Rd., T. Nagar, Chennai-600017 (Tamil Nadu)
✆ 24344519, Fax: 044-24342009
✉ k.k.cheenu@ppl.sprintrgp.ems.vsnl.net.in
ksm@md2.vsnl.net.ins
Hd.Org.: K. Krishnamurthy; **Bus.Intt.**: Pub; **Spl.**: Books Relating to Productivity and Quality, Spirituality and Yoga under Ganesh & Co.

PROFESSIONAL BOOK HOUSE
8, Parijat, 5th Lane, Pandurang Wadi, Goregaon (E), Mumbai-400063 (Maharashtra)
✆ 28728072 ▮ 9821226410
✉ professionalbkhouse.com.india Times
Estd.: 1998; **Hd.Org.**: U.A. Kutty; **Bus.Intt.**: B.S., Dist., L.S.; **Spl.**: Sci. & Tech., Med., Comm. & Man., Humanities, Law, Gen. Books, Children Books

PROFESSIONAL BOOK SERVICE
Hyderabad (Andhra Pradesh)
✆ 27664180, 55595618
✉ huk2bux_pbs@yaboo.com.in,
pbs_prob@tatanova.com
Bus.Intt.: B.S.

PROFESSIONAL BOOKS
140, V.O.C. St., Soorambatti, Erode-638009 (Kerala)

PROFESSIONAL BOOKS TRADER
5-A, J.K. Towers, 3/2, Zackaria Colony Second St., Choolaimedu, Chennai-600094 (Tamil Nadu)
✆ 044-24723998
✉ pbtvijay@eth.net
Estd.: 1982; **Hd.Org.**: S. Vijayaraghavan; **Bus.Intt.**: Dealer and Supplier; **Spl.**: Med. and Tech. Books in English

PROFESSIONAL CHINTAMANI SHUKLE
58, Krishnapuri, Mathura-281001 (Uttar Pradesh)

PROFESSIONAL NETWORK ENTERPRISES
19, Gurudwara Rd., Lucknow-226004 (Uttar Pradesh)
✆ 2245929
Estd.: 1989; **Prop.**: Dr. Mrs. Renu Gupta; **Bus.Intt.**: WS, L.S. and Rt.

PROF. S.N. TRIPATTI
Memorial Foundation, 71, Krishna Bagh, Nagwa, Varanasi-221005 (Uttar Pradesh)

PROGNYA PRAKASHAN
20A, Sukia St., Kolkata-700009 (West Bengal)
✆ 330-2350-9560
Bus.Intt.: Pub.; **Spl.**: Socio-cultural,

Historical Books on the Eminent Personalities. Besides the Novels, Short Stories, Poems and Children's Litt.

PROGRESS PUBLISHERS
Post Box No. 9423, D-5/24, Krishna Nagar, Delhi-110051
✆ (O) 22243463 (R) 22212513, Fax: 22211791
@ progress.india@vsnl.com
Estd.: 1976; **Hd.Org.**: K.P. Gupta;
Bus.Intt.: Pub.; **Spl.**: Textbooks for Mission Schools in English and Hindi

PROGRESSIVE BOOK CENTRE
Lanka, P.O. B.H.U., Varanasi-221005 (Uttar Pradesh)

PROGRESSIVE BOOK DEPOT
5, Narain Nagar, Opp. Bhopal University, Bhopal-462026 (Madhya Pradesh)
✆ 2787983; Fax: 0755-2555347
Estd.: 1970; **Bus.Intt.**: Pub. and B.S.;
Spl.: Comm. & Man., Humanities, Gen. Books

PROGRESSIVE BOOK DISTRIBUTORS
4997, Bara Ram Dwana, Pahar Ganj, New Delhi-110055

PROGRESSIVE BOOK FORUM
33, College Row, Kolkata-700009 (West Bengal)

PROGRESSIVE CORPORATION P. LTD.
Jehangir Wadia Building, 3rd Floor, 51, Mahatma Gandhi Rd., Fort Fountain, Mumbai-400023 (Maharashtra)
✆ 22044813, 22041634, 22875818
Estd.: 1932; **Hd.Org.**: Rustom S. Davar;
Bus.Intt.: Pub., WS, L.S. and Rt.

PROGRESSIVE CURRICULUM MANAGEMENT PVT. LTD.
Ammankovil Rd., P.O. Box 3610, Ernakulam, Kochi-682016 (Kerala)
✆ 2354047, 2352778, 2333604, Fax: 2339823
@ ekmpcm@sancharnet.in
Estd.: 1986; **Hd.Org.**: T.I. Semry; **Bus.Intt.**: B.S.

PROGRESSIVE PUBLISHERS
37-A, College St., Kolkata-700073 (West Bengal)
✆ 22191595
Ch.Exe.: Mr. Suprokash Basu;
Bus.Intt.: Pub.; **Spl.**: High Quality Textbooks for Higher Studies in Pol.Sci., Hist., Edu. & Allied Reference Books

PROKASIKA
Pan Bazar, Guwahati-781001 (Assam)

PROMILLA & CO., PUBLISHERS
C-127, Sarvodaya Enclave, New Delhi-110017
✆ 26864124, 33335186
@ ashok@ashokbutani.com, abutani@biblioasia.com
Hd.Org.: Ashok Butani
Br.: Biblio South Asia, C-127, Sarvodaya Enclave, New Delhi-110017
Bus.Intt.: Pub., Exp.; **Spl.**: Human Right, Soc.Sci., Pol.Sci., Rel. & Phil., General

PROMINENT PUBLISHERS DISTRIBUTORS
18, Vigyan Lok, Vikas Marg Extn., Delhi-110092
✆ 22158906, 22150526, Fax: 011-22140454
@ vipinm48@hotmail.com, prominent_publishers@hotmail.com
Estd.: 1992; **Exe.Dir.**: Surendar Mohan;
Bus.Intt.: Pub., WS, L.S., Pub.'s Rep.;
Spl.: Acad., Comm., Tech., Rare, Beh.Sci., Sci., Pure & Applied, Fiction, Soc.Sci., Med., Juveniles & Law Books

PROMOD BATRA VIJAY BATRA & ASSOCIATES
G-44, Nizamuddin West, New Delhi-110013
✆ 24359898, 24356038, Fax: 91-11-24357980
@ thinkinc@vsnl.com, thinkinc@successcorners.com
www.successcorners.com
Hd.Org.: Promod Batra
Bus.Intt.: Pub. and B.S.; **Spl.**: Books on Management, Attitude, Family Relationships, Stress, etc.

PROUTIST UNIVERSAL PUBLISHERS
209, Khirki Main Rd., Malviya Nagar, New Delhi-110017

PROVA PRAKASHNI
Nona Chandpara Pukur, 24-Pgs(N), Mathpara, (West Bengal)

PSC & SCHMIDT PERIODICALS
Flat No. 2, Nirala Market, First Floor, Nirala Nagar, Lucknow-226020
✆ 2789506, 91-522-4012302
@ sanjay@periodicals.com
www.periodicals.com
Hd.Org.: Gerhard Schmidt
Bus.Intt.: Supplier and Reprinter;
Spl.: Academic Journals

PSYCHI BOOK PUBLISHING HOUSE
C-9/9132, Vasant Kunj, New Delhi-110070
Prop.: Ashirvatham V. Ross

PUBLIC BOOK DEPOT
Iqbal Market, Opp. Townhall Lane, Sopore-193201 (Jammu & Kashmir)
✆ (O) 01954-222582 (R) 222494
▮ 9419032184, Fax: 222494
Estd.: 1980; **Prop.**: Abdur Rashid Bhat;
Bus.Intt.: B.S., L.S.; **Spl.**: Humanities & Soc.Sci., Sci. & Tech., Med., Law, Juvenile/ Children, Gen. & Fiction etc.

PUBLICATION & INFORMATION DIRECTORATE
CSIR Hillside Rd., New Delhi-110002

PUBLICATION BOARD ASSAM
Bamuni Maidan, Guwahati-781021 (Assam)
✆ 0361-2550742
Prop.: Kumud Goswami; **Bus.Intt.:** Pub.; **Spl.:** Litt., Sci., Classics and Children's Books in Assamese

PUBLICATION BUREAU
E-162, Shastri Nagar, Delhi-110052
✆ 23676503, 23656950 ▮ 9811647980, Fax: 23656950
✉ pubbureau@now-india.net.in, sales@publicationbureau.com
Estd.: 1995; **Prop.:** Vivek Sehgal;
Bus.Intt.: Stockist of Books, Indian & Foreign Standards, Software, CC-Roms; **Spl.:** Books on Civil Electrical, Mechanical, Instrumentation, Quality Systems, Man., Comp. Sci. & Law etc.

PUBLICATION SCHEME
C-12, 13, First Floor, Ganga Mandir, Opp. Khandelwal Girls' College, Sansar Chandra Rd., Jaipur-302001 (Rajasthan)
✆ 5104038, 2601801, 2320680, Fax: 2376922
✉ parampsj@datainfosys.net
www.pubscheme.con
Hd.Org.: Siya Sharan Natani
Bus.Intt.: Pub.; **Spl.:** Soc.Sci. and Humanities, Particularly on Ayurveda and Indology in English

PUBLICATIONS DIVISION
8, Esplanade East, Kolkata-700069 (West Bengal)
✆ 22488030

PUBLICATIONS DIVISION
Anna University, Anna Nagar, Chennai-600025 (Tamil Nadu)

PUBLICATIONS DIVISION
Madras University, Triplicane, Chennai-600001 (Tamil Nadu)

PUBLICATIONS DIVISION
Madurai Kamaraj University, Palkalal Nagar, Madurai-625021 (Tamil Nadu)

PUBLICATIONS DIVISION
Govt. of India Press Rd., Thiruvananthapuram-695001 (Kerala)
✆ 2330650
Estd.: 1979; **Hd.Org.:** G. Shyam Nadh;
Bus.Intt.: Pub.

PUBLICATIONS DIVISION
Ministry of Information and Broadcasting, Government of India, Soochna Bhawan, CGO Complex, Lodhi Road, New Delhi-110003
✆ 24365610, 24367260, Fax: 91-11-24365609
✉ dpd@sb.nic.in
www.publicationsdivision.nic.in
Estd.: 1941; **Hd.Org.:** Veena Jain
Br.: Sales Emporium, "A" Wing F&G Block Ground Floor, Rajaji Bhavan, Besant Nagar, Chennai-600090 (Maharashtra) ✆ 24917673
Bus.Intt.: Pub. and B.S.; **Spl.:** Art, Culture, Biography, Hist., Reference Works, etc.

PUBLICATIONS INDIA
4/5B, Asaf Ali Rd., New Delhi-110002

PUBLICATIONS SCHEME
57, Missra Rajaji Ka Rasta, Jaipur-302001 (Rajasthan)
✆ (O) 244105 (R) 2320680
Hd.Org.: S.S. Natani; **Bus.Intt.:** Printers, Pub. & Dist.; **Spl.:** English & Hindi

PUBLISHERS & ADVERTISERS
J-6, Krishan Nagar, Delhi-110051
✆ 22247619, 22437702
Estd.: 1970; **Hd.Org.:** Nand Kishore Vikram;
Bus.Intt.: Pub.

PUBLISHERS & BOOKSELLERS GUILD
Guild House, 2B, Jhama Pukur Lane, Kolkata-700009 (West Bengal)
✆ 23604588, 23544417, 23577717, Fax: 23604566
✉ guild@cal2.vsnl.net.in
www.kolkatafaironline.com
Ch.Exe.: Kalyan Shah;
Bus.Intt.: Organiser of the Kolkata Book Fair and Promoter of Books and Bengali Language

PUBLISHERS' AND BOOKSELLERS' ASSOCIATION OF BENGAL
93, Mahatma Gandhi Rd., Kolkata-700007 (West Bengal)
✆ 22411993
Hd.Org.: Dulal Bhattashali; **Bus.Intt.:** Promoter; **Spl.:** Bangla Books

PUBLISHING HOUSE
14, Ramanath Majumder St., Kolkata-700009 (West Bengal)

PUBLISHING ORBIT
61, Mahatma Gandhi Rd., Kolkata-700009 (West Bengal)

PUBLISHING SYNDICATE
44A, Beniatola Lane, Kolkata-700009 (West Bengal)

PULIANI AND PULIANI
Ground Floor, Sujatha Complex, 1st Cross, Gandhinagar, Bangalore-560009 (Karnataka)
✆ 2254052, Fax: 91-80-2872881
Hd.Org.: Ved Prakash; **Bus.Intt.:** Exp. of Books

PULIKESHI PRAKASHANA
2nd Main, Yeshawanthapura, Bangalore-560022 (Karnataka)
✆ 2364758
Hd.Org.: Raghusutha; **Bus.Intt.:** Pub.; **Spl.:** Fiction, Collections, Dramas, Historical and Mythological Books in Kannada

PULIKKOTTIL PUBLISHERS
Kandanassery P.O., Thrissur-680102 (Kerala)
✆ 2556408
Estd.: 1993; **Prop.:** P.J. Pious; **Bus.Intt.:** Pub.

PUNAM PRAKASHAN
6-B, Koshikpuri, Old Silampur (East), Delhi-110031
✆ 22203781
Hd.Org.: P.K. Punam

PUNASCHA
9A, Nabin Kundu Lane, Kolkata-700010 (West Bengal)
✆ 22413572, Fax: 91-33-23732427
✉ pnbooks@sify.com
Estd.: 1988; **Hd.Org.:** Sandip Nayak; **Bus.Intt.:** Pub. and Exp.; **Spl.:** Children's Books and Research Work on Biography, Litt., Hist., etc. in Bengali

PUNCHA BOOK STALL
Puncha, Purulia (West Bengal)

PUNE SAHITYA VITARAN
273, Shaniwarpet, Pune-411030 (Maharashtra)
✆ 0212-2458598
Estd.: 1989; **Bus.Intt.:** Deals; **Spl.:** Marathi Books of Fine Art, Novels, Dramas, Poems, Sci., Cooking, Children's Litt., Small Industries, Math., Spiritual, Religious, Aesthetics and Modeling

PUNE VIDYARTHI GRIHA PRAKASHAN
1786, Sadashiv Peth, Pune-411030 (Maharashtra)

PUNEET BOOKS
Jaipur (Rajasthan)
✆ 9414035174
✉ vikal_goyal@yahoo.com
Bus.Intt.: B.S.

PUNEET PRASHANT PRAKASHAN
Books & Stationery Market, Kach Beri Rd., Rohtak (Haryana)

PUNJAB BOOK CENTRE
S.C.O. 1126-27, Sector 22B, Chandigarh-160022
✆ 232052, 2701952, Fax: 2601304
✉ punjabbookcentre@usa.net
Estd.: 1962; **Hd.Org.:** Tulsi Ram; **Bus.Intt.:** Pub., WS, Library, Suppliers and Rt. in Punjabi

PUNJAB STATE UNIVERSITY TEXT-BOOK SHOP
S.C.O. 289-91, Sector 32D, Chandigarh-160032
✆ 0172-601983, 614564, 601658
Hd.Org.: S. Bhupinder Singh; **Bus.Intt.:** Pub.; **Spl.:** School and College Textbooks in Punjabi besides English-Punjabi Dictionary

PUNJABI ACADEMY
DDA Community Centre, Sadar Thana Rd., Motia Khan, Paharganj, New Delhi-110055
✆ 23616265, 23615979, 23616243, Fax: 23615979
✉ punjabiacademydelhi@rediffmail.com
Hd.Org.: S. Rawail Singh; **Bus.Intt.:** Pub. of Research and Reference Books and Books for Children in Punjabi

PUNJABI PUBLISHERS ASSOCIATION
Bazar Mai Sewan, Amritsar-143006
✆ 2545787, Fax: 2543965
Hd.Org.: Kulwant Singh Suri; **Bus.Intt.:** Pub. & Promoter; **Spl.:** Books on Culture of Punjab

PUNJABI PUSTAK BHANDAR
257, Dariba Kalan, Delhi-110006
✆ (O) 23266317, 23266232, 23273493, (R) 24697952, 24624352
Hd.Org.: Gulshan Rai Verma; **Bus.Intt.:** WS and Exp.; **Spl.:** Hindi, English and Punjabi

PUNJABI SAHIT SABHA
10, Vishnu Digambar Marg, New Delhi-110002
✆ 23221486, 23238142
Hd.Org.: Kartar Singh Duggal; **Bus.Intt.:** Promoter; **Spl.:** Punjabi Litt., Language and Culture

PUNJABI WRITERS' COOPERATIVE SOCIETY LTD.
H-108, Shivaji Park (Punjabi Bagh), New Delhi-110026
✆ 25932888, Fax: 25191287
Hd.Org.: Maheep Singh; **Bus.Intt.:** Pub.; **Spl.:** Punjabi Litt. and Books on Rel., Phil.

PUNTHI PUSTAK
136/4-B, Bidhan Sarani, 2nd Floor, Kolkata-700004 (West Bengal)
Bus.Intt.: Exp.

PURANDARE PRAKASHAN
1228, Sadashiv, Perugetajawal, Pune-411030 (Maharashtra)

PURBANCHAL PRAKASH
Ambari, Guwahati-781018 (Assam)

PURBANCHAL PRAKASH
G.N. Bardoloi Rd., P.B. 1585, Kashmere Gate, Delhi-110006

PURBASHREE PRAKASHAN
A.T. Rd., Jorhat (Assam)
Bus.Intt.: Pub.

PURE TECH. CORPORATION
264, IInd Floor, Rauzapillai St., Pondicherry-605001
Bus.Intt.: Exp.

PURNA PRAKASHAN
8A, Tamer Lane, Kolkata-700009 (West Bengal)

PURNANANDA PUBLICATIONS
1288, "Purnananda" MIG House, Magadi Rd., Bangalore-560078 (Karnataka)
✆ 080-2350204, 2352976
Bus.Intt.: Pub.; **Spl.:** Edu. and Gen. Books

PURNEKAR COMPETITION BOOK HOUSE
208, Khajuri Bazar, Indore-452002 (Madhya Pradesh)
✆ (O) 2540704 (R) 2485637

PURNIMA BOOK CENTRE
Narottam Niwas, Nehru Rd., Vile Parle (East), Mumbai-400057 (Maharashtra)
✆ 26125872

PURNIMA BOOK HOUSE
Congress Office Rd., Governorpet, Vijayawada-520002 (Andhra Pradesh)

PURNIMA PUBLISHERS
Mahotra Clinic, Main Bazar, Near Gandhi Chowk, Pathankot-145001 (Punjab)

PUROGAMI PRAKATANALAYA
10th Cross, Malleswaram, Bangalore-560003 (Karnataka)
Hd.Org.: Mavinakere Ranganathan;
Spl.: Fiction, Collections, Edu., Gen. and Text Books in Kannada

PURULIA BOOK AGENCY
Barakar Rd., Purulia (West Bengal)

PURULIA BOOK DEPOT
Hat-tala, Distt. Purulia (West Bengal)

PURVODAYA PRAKASHAN
7/8, Darya Ganj, New Delhi-110002
✆ 23274956, Fax: 91-11-43541934
✉ purvodaya1950@yahoo.com
Hd.Org.: Pradeep Kumar; **Bus.Intt.:** Pub.; **Spl.:** Litt., Culture, Hist. and for Children in Hindi

PURWANCHAL PRAKASHAN
Brij Bihan Sadan (Near Karbala), Jagadishpur, Bodhia (Uttar Pradesh)

PURWANCHAL PRAKASHAN
1180, A Block, Soniya Vihar, Near Gyan Builders, Delhi-110094
✆ 22178983
Estd.: 1995; **Hd.Org.:** Inder Vijay Singh;
Bus.Intt.: Dist. and L.S.; **Spl.:** Hindi Books

PUSHPAK SALES AGENCY
Ganpati Bhawan, 4675-B/21, Ansari Rd., Darya Ganj, New Delhi-110002
✆ 23257939, 23258184, Fax: 23258184
✉ pushpakbooks@yahoo.com
Bus.Intt.: WS & Dist.; **Spl.:** Fiction, Gen., Children Books, Dictionary, Ency. etc.

PUSTAK BAZAR COM
New Delhi
✆ 26410316, 26951188, Fax: 25816394
✉ corpris@vsnl.com
Bus.Intt.: B.S.

PUSTAK BHANDAR
A-17, College St. Mkt., Kolkata-700007 (West Bengal)

PUSTAK BHANDAR
Govind Mitra Rd., Patna-800004 (Bihar)

PUSTAK BHANDAR
Bhakharua More, Daudnagar, Aurangabad-824101 (Bihar)
Bus.Intt.: Pub. and B.S.

PUSTAK BHANDAR
Rafiganj, Aurangabad-824125 (Bihar)
Bus.Intt.: Pub. and B.S.

PUSTAK BHANDAR
Pachrakhua Sihari, Aurangabad-824115 (Bihar)
Bus.Intt.: Pub. and B.S.

PUSTAK BHANDAR
Lower Dhalpur, Kullu-175101 (Himachal Pradesh)
✆ 01902-224470
Estd.: 1961; **Prop.:** Vinay Sood;
Bus.Intt.: Rt.; **Spl.:** Text Books School and College Level Books

PUSTAK BHAWAN
625, Khajuri Bazar, Indore-452002 (Madhya Pradesh)
✆ (O) 2452256 (R) 2411515

PUSTAK BHAWAN
Opp. Khudabaksh, Ashok Raj Path, Patna-800004 (Bihar)

PUSTAK BHAWAN
Deo, Aurangabad-824202 (Bihar)
Bus.Intt.: Pub. and B.S.

PUSTAK BHAWAN
Kanpur (Uttar Pradesh)
✆ 2365223

[@] pustakbhawan@yahoo.com
Bus.Intt.: Pub., B.S. & Dist.

PUSTAK BIPANI
27, Beniatola Lane, Kolkata-700009 (West Bengal)
Bus.Intt.: Quality Pub., Dist. and B.S.

PUSTAK GHAR
Naugachia, Bhagalpur-853204 (Bihar)
Bus.Intt.: Pub. and B.S.

PUSTAK KENDRA
Ishipur, Barahat, Bhagalpur-813206 (Bihar)
Bus.Intt.: Pub. and B.S.

PUSTAK MAHAL
Saraju Prasad Rd., Distt. Maldah (West Bengal)
Hd.Org.: Madan Mohan Bhutra

PUSTAK MAHAL
Bhakharua, Daudnagar, Aurangabad-824301 (Bihar)
Bus.Intt.: Pub. and B.S.

PUSTAK MAHAL
J-3/16 (Opp. Happy School), Darya Ganj, New Delhi-110002
✆ 23272783-84, 23276539, Fax: 91-11-23260518
[@] pustakmahal@vsnl.net.in
info@pustakmahal.com
www.pustakmahal.com
Estd.: 1974; **Hd.Org.:** Ram Avtar Gupta
Sal. Cent.: 10-B, Netaji Subhash Marg, Daryaganj, New Delhi-110002
✆ 23268292, 23279900, Fax: 91-11-23280567
[@] rapidexdelhi@indiatimes.com
• 6686, Khari Baoli, Delhi- 110006
✆ 91-11-23944314, 23911979
Br.: 22/2, Mission Road, (Shama Rao's Compound), Bangalore-560027
✆ 2234025, Fax: 91-80-2240209
[@] pustak@sancharnet.in
• 23-25, Zaoba Wadi, (Opp. V.I.P. Showroom), Thakurdwar, Mumbai-400002
✆ 22010941, Fax: 91-22-22053387
[@] rapidex@bom5.vsnl.net.in
• 5-1-707/1, Brij Bhawan, (Beside Central Bank of India Lane), Bank Street, Koti, Hyderabad-500095
✆ 24737530, Fax: 91-40-24737290
[@] pustakmahalhyd@yahoo.co.in
• Khemka House, 1st Floor, (Opp. Women's Hospital), Ashok Rajpath, Patna-800004 ✆ 91-612-2673644
[@] rapidexptn@rediffmail.com
Bus.Intt.: Pub.; **Spl.:** Children's Books and on Popular Sci., Language Learning, Self-improvement, Health, etc.

PUSTAK MAHAL PUBLISHERS BOOKSELLERS
10-B, Netaji Subhas Marg, Darya Ganj, New Delhi-110002
✆ 23268292
Bus.Intt.: Order Suppliers of Books

PUSTAK MANDIR
4, Market Complex, Sector-18, Rourkela-769003 (Orissa)
✆ 2692759
Hd.Org.: Sudhansu Kumar Bhool
Br.: 7483, Tel Mill Marg, Ram Nagar, Pahar Ganj, New Delhi-110055
Hd.Org.: Kamla Lata; **Bus.Intt.:** Pub.; **Spl.:** Children's Edu. Books in English, Hindi and Oriya

PUSTAK NIKETAN
Nabinagar, Aurangabad-824301 (Bihar)
Bus.Intt.: Pub. and B.S.

PUSTAK PETH VITRAN
Aurangabad (Maharashtra)
✆ 347271
[@] pustakpeth@yahoo.com
Bus.Intt.: L.S.

PUSTAK PRATISHTHAN
4715/21, Second Floor, Dayanand Marg, Darya Ganj, New Delhi-110002
✆ 65283371, Fax: 91-11-23287713
Hd.Org.: Jai Prakash Sharma
Bus.Intt.: Pub. and Dist.; **Spl.:** Books on Hindi Litt. as well as Children's Books

PUSTAK PRAKASHANI
82/1, Mahatma Gandhi Rd., Kolkata-700009 (West Bengal)

PUSTAK SADAN
Siris, Aurangabad-824101 (Bihar)
Bus.Intt.: Pub. and B.S.

PUSTAK SADAN
D.N. Singh Rd., Bhagalpur-812002 (Bihar)
Bus.Intt.: Pub. and B.S.

PUSTAK SADAN
Kharik Bazar, Naugachia, Bhagalpur-853202 (Bihar)
Bus.Intt.: Pub. and B.S.

PUSTAK SADAN
Sabour, Bhagalpur-813210 (Bihar)
Bus.Intt.: Pub. and B.S.

PUSTAK SADAN
Pachrakhua, Sihari, Aurangabad-824115 (Bihar)
Bus.Intt.: Pub. and B.S.

PUSTAK SAMABESH
1, Bankim Chatterjee St.,
Kolkata-700073
(West Bengal)

PUSTAKALATO SNEHAM
Secunderabad (Uttar Pradesh)
✆ 27015295
✉ sureshkosaraju@yahoo.co.in

PUSTAKALAYA
170/1, Madhupur, Baharampur,
Murshidabad (West Bengal)

PUSTAKYAN
2/4240-A, Ansari Rd.,
New Delhi-110002
✆ 23274513, 23278858
✉ subodhbooks@vsnl.net
Hd.Org.: Anil Kumar;
Bus.Intt.: Pub.;
Spl.: Litt., Astrology, etc. in Hindi

PUSTHAKA CHANDANA
278/8, 20th Main Vijayanagar,
Bangalore-560040 (Karnataka)
Bus.Intt.: Pub.; **Spl.:** Fiction and Gen. Books in Kannada

PUTHI PRAKASH
Harabala Market, G.M.C.H. Rd., Bhagagarh,
Guwahati-781005 (Assam)

PUTHIPATRA (CALCUTTA) P. LTD.
9, Anthony Bagan Lane, Kolkata-700009
(West Bengal)
✆ (O) 23506720, 23505722 (R) 23441771
Estd.: 1964; **Hd.Org.:** Tapsa Saha

PUTHITIRTHA PRAKASHAN
Hemchandra, Goswami Path,
Golaghat Distt.-785621 (Assam)
Bus.Intt.: Pub. and B.S.

PUTUL PUSTAK BHANDAR
Amarpur, Bhagalpur-812002 (Bihar)
Bus.Intt.: Pub. and B.S.

■ ■ ■

Q-PROD PUBLISHERS
40/21-A, Manohar Kunj, Gautam Nagar, New Delhi-110049
Prop.: Rakesh Pandey

QASMI KUTUB KHANA
Jama Masjid, Talab Khatikan, Jammu Tawi (Jammu & Kashmir)
✆ (O) 2545388 (R) 2564049
Estd.: 1965; **Prop.:** Atta-Ur-Rahman; **Bus.Intt.:** Pub., WS, L.S. & Rt., Imp., Sub.Ag.; **Spl.:** Med., Gen. & Fiction etc.

QAZI PUBLISHERS & DISTRIBUTORS
B-35, Nizammudin West, Basement, New Delhi-110013
✆ 24352732, 23259526, Fax: 24352048
✉ qazipublishers@yahoo.com
www.genuinepublications.com
Estd.: 1987; **Hd.Org.:** Mohd. Ali; **Bus.Intt.:** Pub., Dist. & Exp.; **Spl.:** *Holy Quran* and Islamic Litt.

QUALITY BOOK SERVICE
Plot No. 422/3, Laxmi Vihar, Burari, Delhi-110084
✆ 91-11-27613806 ▮ 9810229692
Prop.: Mrs. Kumari Sabita
Bus.Intt.: Retailer, L.S.

QUALITY PUBLISHERS
Ramamandiram St., Vijayawada-520002 (Andhra Pradesh)
✆ 0866-2433261
Estd.: 1957; **Prop.:** K. Murali Krishna; **Bus.Intt.:** Pub.; **Spl.:** Fiction and Non-Fiction Books, Children Books, Epics, Prabandhams, Text Books etc. in Telugu

QUALITY PUBLISHERS
3, Ramnath Majumder St., Kolkata-700009 (West Bengal)

QUALITY SALES & SERVICES
Thiruvananthapuram (Kerala)
✆ 2326789, 2332158, Fax: 2491491
✉ qssbooks@rediffmail.com
Bus.Intt.: B.S.

QUAMAR BOOK DEPOT
Garari Bazar, Via Jogiara, Darbhanga-847303 (Bihar)

QUARK
A-45, Phase VIII-B, Industrial Area, Mohali (Punjab)
✆ 2254412, Fax: 2254413
✉ sales@quarkindia.com
Prop.: Fred Ebrahimi; **Bus.Intt.:** Developer of Tools and Technologies for Pub.

QUARTETTE BOOK DISTRIBUTORS PVT. LTD.
116, Budhwar Peth, Flat No. 7 & 8, Shri Vidya Apartment, 3rd Floor, Jogeshwari Lane, Pune-411002 (Maharashtra)
✆ 2481289, 2487271
Bus.Intt.: WS Dist. and L.S.

QUARTETTE BOOKS DISTRIBUTORS P. LTD.
Mumbai (Maharashtra)
✆ 24965864, 24965865, Fax: 24965866
✉ qartett@bom3.vsnl.net.in
Bus.Intt.: WS Dist. and L.S.

QUARTETTE BOOK HOUSE (P) LTD.
E-1/16 (Basement), Ansari Rd. Darya Ganj, New Delhi-110002
✆ (O) 23276843, 23276844 (R) 27011631
Hd.Org.: Sunil Saxena; **Bus.Intt.:** WS, Pub.

QUEST BOOKS COMPANY
Hd.Off.: 1658, "Kartik House", Parsadi Gali, Kotla Mubarakpur, New Delhi-110003
✆ (O) 24692671, 24622451, 55659120 (R) 26645636, 25509439, Fax: 24617654
Sales Off.: G-17/C, GF "Ashirwad", South Extn. Part-II, New Delhi-110049
✆ 56020164, 56020178, 26264946, 26264947 ▮ 9811224190, Fax: 51642947
✉ qbc@bol.net.in
www.gqcpl.com
Estd.: 1998; **Prt.:** Ranbir Singh, V.S. Rawat, K.K. Taneja; **Bus.Intt.:** Stockists, Dist., L.S.; **Spl.:** Books on quality Man. Systems ISO 9000, ISO 14000 - QS 9000, TPM, SPC, TQM, Six Sigma, Benchmar King, Env., Engg. & Sci. Tech.

QUEST EDUCATIONAL SERVICE LTD.
H-24, Green Park Extension, New Delhi-110016

QUIXOT MULTIMEDIA PVT. LTD.
D-25, 2nd Floor, Manohar Park, East Punjabi Bagh, New Delhi-110026
✆ 28313048, Fax: 91-11-28313048
✉ sales@quixotmultimedia.com
Hd.Org.: Ashish Kapoor
Bus.Intt.: Pub. and Dist.; **Spl.:** Educational Software, CD's and Video Games

QURAISHI & SONS PUBLICATIONS
Moti Masjid, Lar-Deoria-274502 (Uttar Pradesh)

QURAN-O-SUNNAT ACADEMY
Sharief Cottage, Armoor-503224 (Andhra Pradesh)

■ ■ ■

R. CAMRRAY & CO. PVT. LTD.
9-33, Mission Row Extension, Kolkata-700013 (West Bengal)
✆ 33-22379709, Fax: 91-33-22156680
Hd.Org.: Sujit Kumar Kerr; **Bus.Intt.:** Exp.; **Spl.:** Indian Books, Periodicals Manufacturers of Printing of Law Books

R. CHAND & COMPANY
1, Ansari Rd., Darya Ganj, New Delhi-110002
✆ 23273566, 23257796, Fax: 23268760
✉ rchand-co@rediffmail.com
Estd.: 1964; **Prop.:** Gauri Shanker Sharma; **Bus.Intt.:** Pub.; **Spl.:** School and College Textbooks in Sci., Math., Comm., Eco., Pol.Sci., etc.

R. LALL BOOK DEPOT
Near Government Inter College, Begum Bridge Rd., Meerut-250001 (Uttar Pradesh)
✆ 2643623, 2666235, Fax: 2530505
Hd.Org.: Vinay Rakheja; **Bus.Intt.:** Pub. & Dist.; **Spl.:** College-level Edu. and Competition, B.Ed., M.Ed., Home Sci.

R.A. BOOK AGENCY
B-98, 1st Floor, Mangal Bazaar Rd., Laxmi Nagar, Delhi-110092
✆ (O) & (R) 22430805, 22513962 ▮ 9810158917, Fax: 91-11-22430805
✉ raba1@sify.com, raba@del2vsnl.net.in
Estd.: 1994; **Prop.:** Vijay Prakash
Br.: 3328, Sector 21D, 2nd Floor, Chandigarh-160022 **Br.Man.:** Ankur Sharma ▮ 9815221610
Bus.Intt.: WS, Rt., L.S.; **Spl.:** Acad., Comm., Tech., Rare & Sci., Pure & Applied Books

R.B.S.A. PUBLISHERS
340, Chaura Rasta, Jaipur-302003 (Rajasthan)
✆ 2575826, Fax: 91-141-2575826
✉ info@rbsapublishers.com
🌐 www.rbsapublishers.com
Estd.: 1985; **Prt.:** Surendra Parnami
Bus.Intt.: Pub. and Dist.; **Spl.:** Books on Commerce, Science, Humanities & Soc.Sci.

R.D.I. PRINT & PUBLISHING P. LTD.
Orient House, ADI Marzban Path, Ballard Estate, Mumbai-400038 (Maharashtra)
✆ 22617291, 22611459, Fax: 22613347, Telefax: 01183406
Estd.: 1978; **Hd.Org.:** S. Johri; **Bus.Intt.:** Pub.

R.G. BROTHERS
2/1, Shyama Charan Dey St., Kolkata-700073 (West Bengal)

R.J. TECH PUBLISHERS
XXXIX/5615, Ravipuram Rd., Ernakulam, Cochin-682016 (Kerala)
✆ 0484-2383448, 2507007
Hd.Org.: V.K. Jayachandran; **Bus.Intt.:** Pub., Dist., L.S.

R.K. BOOK DISTRIBUTORS
4/2, Mitra Kua Ki Gali, Loha Kham, Police Lane, Ajmer-305001 (Rajasthan)
✆ 2420637
Hd.Org.: Raj Kumar Garg; **Bus.Intt.:** Soc.Sci., Gen. Books and L.S.

R.K. BOOKS
4215/1, Ansari Road, Darya Ganj, New Delhi-110002
✆ (O) 23278337, 23261774 (R) 22048678 Fax: 91-11-51562798 ▮ 9312654192
✉ rkbooks@vsnl.net
Hd.Org.: Ramakant Khandelwal
Bus.Intt.: B.S.; **Spl.:** Geography, Environment and Soc.Sci.

R.K. BOOKS & DISTRIBUTORS
1539, Ram Krishan Bhavan, Gali Mukesh Market, Gandhi Nagar, Delhi-110031

R.K. BOOKS AGENCIES
Nanded (Gujarat)
✆ 02462-33655, Fax: 51955
✉ ek_patil2001@yahoo.com
Bus.Intt.: B.S.

R.K. ENTERPRISES
Shop No. 16, Jawahar Nagar, Jaipur-302004 (Rajasthan)
✆ 2652042, 2077619
Hd.Org.: Raj Kumar Sharma; **Bus.Intt.:** Dist.; **Spl.:** Hist. and Culture of Rajasthan State in English, Hindi and Sanskrit Languages

R.K. INTERNATIONAL
Naseem Bagh, Suderbal, Srinagar-190006 (Jammu & Kashmir)
✆ 0194-2425000
Estd.: 1990; **Bus.Intt.:** Pub., B.S. and L.S.; **Spl.:** Med., Engg. and Gen. Books

R.K. STORES
11-B, Bankim Chatterjee St., Kolkata-700073 (West Bengal)

R.K. TECHNO SCIENCE AGENCY
G-7, Sidharth Chambers, 55-A, Kalu Sarai, (Hauz Khas Bus Terminal) New Delhi-110016

✆ (O) 26524341 (R) 26969531,
Fax: 91-11-26524769
✉ rktsa@ndf.vsnl.net.in
Prop.: S.L. Kanojia; **Bus.Intt.:** Rt., L.S.

R.K. PUBLISHERS & DISTRIBUTORS
2/36, Ansari Road, Darya Ganj,
New Delhi-110002
✆ 23272868 ▮ 9810828952
✉ rkpddelhi@yahoo
Hd.Org.: Rajat Khanna
Bus.Intt.: B.S.

R.K.V. MEDIA PVT. LTD.
B-6/91, 1st Floor, Safdarjung Enclave,
New Delhi-110029
✆ 51651841, Fax: 51651843
Hd.Org.: Vipin Arora; **Bus.Intt.:** Pub.;
Spl.: Magazine *The Eternal Solutions*

R.K.V. MEDIA PVT. LTD.
S-1A, Arjun Nagar, Safdarjung Enclave,
New Delhi-110029
✆ 41651841-2, Fax: 91-11-41651843
✉ wecare@eternall.org.in
🌐 www.eternall.org.in
Hd.Org.: Umesh Sharma; **Bus.Intt.:** Pub.;
Spl.: Magazine *The Eternal Solutions*

R.M. ASSOCIATES
5, Nav Neelam, Sea Face Rd., Worli,
Mumbai-400018 (Maharashtra)
Bus.Intt.: Exp.

R.N. PUBLISHERS
57-58, Gulastan Carmicheal Rd.,
Mumbai-400026 (Maharashtra)

R.N.B. MERCHANTILE PVT. LTD./ R.N.B. OVERSEAS PVT. LTD.
AE-17, Tagore Garden, 2nd Floor,
New Delhi-110027
✆ 25166761, Fax: 25447253
✉ info@rambajaj.com
🌐 www.rambajaj.com
Estd.: 1999; **Prt.:** Radhey Shyam
Br.: Bajaj House, Rani Bazar, Bikaner-334001 (Rajasthan) ✆ 0151-2547874, Fax: 2521844
Hd.Org.: Vikram Bajaj; **Bus.Intt.:** Pub.;
Spl.: Humanities & Soc.Sci., Mang., Children & General

R.P. BIBLE BOOK HOUSE
T-481/3G, Baljeet Nagar, New Delhi-110008
✆ 25819463
Hd.Org.: Ram Prashad; **Bus.Intt.:** B.S.;
Spl.: The *Bible*, Posters and Children's Books

R.P. DISTRIBUTORS
9662/65, Islam Ganj, Library Rd.,
Azad Market, Delhi-110006
✆ (O) 27514886, 27777366 (R) 26193163,
Fax: 26167194, 27777366
Estd.: 1986; **Prop.:** Ajay Arora;
Bus.Intt.: Merchant Imp., Exp.

R.P. GUPTA & SONS
P.B. No. 9417, B-6/13, Krishna Nagar,
Delhi-110051
✆ (O) 22243463 (R) 22212513
Estd.: 1989; **Hd.Org.:** Smt. Kanta Gupta

R.R. BOOK CENTRE
Dayaband, Bilaspur-495001 (Madhya Pradesh)
Prop.: Dinesh Bharat; **Bus.Intt.:** L.S.

R.R. PUBLISHERS
B-9/6273, Vasant Kunj, New Delhi-110070
✆ 91-11-26898183
Hd.Org.: Rani Sehgal
Bus.Intt.: Pub.; **Spl.:** Children Books

R.R. SHETH & CO.
'Dwarkesh' 1st Floor, Near Royal Apartments,
Khanpur, Ahmedabad-380001 (Gujarat)
✆ (O) 25356573 (R) 26589508,
Fax: 25321732
✉ sales@rrsheth.com
🌐 www.rrsheth.com
Estd.: 1926; **Prop.:** Bhagatbhai B. Sheth,
Man.Dir: Chintan Sheth
Br.: 110-112, Princes St., Keshav Baug,
Mumbai-400002 (Maharashtra)
✆ (O) 022-22013441 (R) 26183182
▮ 9820019823
✉ rrsheth_co@hotmail.com,
chintan@rrsheth.com
Bus.Intt.: Pub., B.S., L.S., WS, Exp.;
Spl.: Children & General books in Gujarati

R.S. BOOK & PRINTS
A-40, South Extension Part-II,
New Delhi-110049
✆ 26257095, Fax: 26253011
✉ rsbooks@spectranet.com
Hd.Org.: Sanjiv Jain; **Bus.Intt.:** Dealer;
Spl.: Antique and Rare books on Travel, Hist., Lithographs, Engravings, etc.

R.S. PUBLISHERS & DISTRIBUTORS
Plot No. 55, Kukreja Plaza,
Shop No. 57 & 58, Sector-11,
CBD Belapur (E),
Navi Mumbai-400614 (Maharashtra)
✆ 27579974/75
✉ rspdbooks@hotmail.com
Estd.: 2003; **Prop.:** Rohit Agarwal;
Bus.Intt.: B.S., L.S., WS; **Spl.:** Humanities & Soc.Sci., Mang., Arts & Arch.

R.T. BOOK COMPANY
H.No. 1178, Govt. Housing Colony, Ompora,
Badgam-191111 (Jammu & Kashmir)
Estd.: 1980; **Hd.Org.:** Mohd. Yousuf Bhat;
Bus.Intt.: L.S. and Rt.

R.V. PUBLISHERS
Faridabad (Haryana)
✆ 3315310, Fax: 3710090
✉ rajuprim@vsnl.com
Bus.Intt.: B.S.

RAAJ PRAKASHAN
10, Dayanand Vihar, Vikas Marg Extn., Delhi-110092
Hd.Org.: S.K. Gupta; **Bus.Intt.:** Pub.; **Spl.:** Edu. Books

RAAJHAS BOOK SHOP
S-69C, 2nd Floor, 2nd Phase, Spencer Plaza, Chennai-600002 (Tamil Nadu)
✆ 91-44-9841017069
Hd.Org.: Raja; **Bus.Intt.:** Pub.; **Spl.:** Numerology

RABINDRA LIBRARY
Bankim Chatterjee St., Kolkata-700073 (West Bengal)
Hd.Org.: Rabindranath Biswas

RACE MEDIA GREEN PAGES
A-1, Abul Fazal Enclave, Okhla, Jamia Nagar, New Delhi-110025

RACHANA BOOKS
P.R. Buildings, Tass Rd., Alwaye-683101 (Kerala)
Estd.: 1993; **Hd.Org.:** Madhu Kunnathully; **Bus.Intt.:** Pub. and B.S.

RACHANA PRAKASHAN
57, Natani Bhawan, Mishra Rajaji Ka Rasta, Chand Pole Bazaar, Jaipur-302001 (Rajasthan)
✆ (O) 0141-2318365 (R) 2311916
▮ 9414067580
Estd.: 1972; **Man.Dir.:** Vinod Kumar Natani; **Bus.Intt.:** Pub., B.S., L.S., WS; **Spl.:** Sanskrit and Hindi Litt.

RACHANA PRAKASHAN (P) LTD.
79, Ambedkar Rd., Ghaziabad (Uttar Pradesh)
✆ (O) 0575-2755131 (R) 0575-2732295
Estd.: 1995; **Hd.Org.:** Satish Gupta

RACHANA PUBLICATIONS
Pushpanjali Complex, Rajpur (Palampur)-176016 (Himachal Pradesh)

RACHEL PRAKASHAN
11/250, Old Municipal Quarters, Mani Nagar (East), Ahmedabad-8 (Gujarat)

RACHNA BOOK CENTRE
A-761, Shastri Nagar, Delhi-110052
✆ 27771539
Prop.: Narendra Kumar Kapoor; **Bus.Intt.:** Rt.

RACHNA BOOKS & PERIODICALS
Gangtok (Sikkim) ✆ 03592-24336
✉ rachna_books@yahoo.co.in
Bus.Intt.: B.S.

RACHNA PRAKASHAN PVT. LTD.
79, Ambedkar Rd., P.B. No. 36, Ghaziabad (Uttar Pradesh)
✆ 32980, Fax: 32982
✉ rachnaprakashan@mantraonline.com
Bus.Intt.: Pub. and Dist.

RACHNA SAGAR (P) LTD.
79, 1st Floor, Kedar Nath Marg, Opp. Ansari Market, Darya Ganj, New Delhi-110002
✆ (O) 23285568-69, 23246027, 23201691 (R) 27459316, 27418469, Fax: 23243519
✉ rachnasagar@hotmail.com
Hd.Org.: Ankur Gupta, Neeraj Gupta
Br.: No. 48, 1st Floor, 5th Main Rd., Chamrajpet, Bangalore
• 28, Natesan St., T. Nagar, Chennai
Bus.Intt.: Pub.; **Spl.:** Edu. Books for Children and Sample Papers

RACHNAKAR PRAKASHAN
Gurudwara Marg, Purniya-854301 (Bihar)
✆ 91-6454-244688
Hd.Org.: Priyamvad Kumar; **Bus.Intt.:** Pub.; **Spl.:** Hindi Litt.

RADHA KRISHNA ANAND & CO.
Pacca Danga, Jammu-180001 (Jammu & Kashmir)
✆ (O) 2546691 (R) 248357, Fax: 2578357
✉ radhakrishananand2000@rediffmail.com
Estd.: 1948; **Founder:** Late Sh. Radha Krishnan Anand; **Prt.:** Om Prakash Kohil, Kuldeep Anand; **Bus.Intt.:** L.S. & Rt.; **Spl.:** Humanities & Soc.Sci., Sci. & Tech., Juvenile/Children

RADHA POCKET BOOKS
33, Hari Nagar, Meerut-250002 (Uttar Pradesh)
✆ 2518734

RADHA PUBLICATIONS
4231/1, Ansari Rd., Darya Ganj, New Delhi-110002
✆ 91-11-23254306
✉ radhapublications@yahoo.com
Hd.Org.: Radha Rani, Rajeev Garg; **Bus.Intt.:** Pub.; **Spl.:** Eco., Pol.Sci., Hist., Sol., Litt., and Music

RADHA PUSTAKALAYA
8, Shyama Charen Dey St., Kolkata-700073 (West Bengal)

RADHAKRISHNA PRAKASHAN PVT. LTD.
7/31, Ansari Rd., Darya Ganj, New Delhi-110002
✆ 23266498, 23276379, Fax: 91-11-23278144
✉ info@radhakrishanprakashan.com
🌐 www.radhakrishanprakashan.com
Ch.Exe.: Ashok Kumar Maheshwari; **Bus.Intt.:** Pub.; **Spl.:** Hindi Litt. and Books

on Hist., Politics, Phil., Sol., Biography, Autobiography, Fiction etc.

RADHIKA PUBLICATION
Museum Rd., Governorpet, Vijayawada-520002 (Andhra Pradesh)
Bus.Intt.: Pub. and B.S.

RADHU GOSWAMI
68, Nabarum Palli, S.P. Mukherjee Rd., P.O. Sodepur, Distt. 24 Parganas (N)-743178 (West Bengal)

RADIANT ENTERPRISE
81/1, Nimchand Moitra St., Kolkata-700035 (West Bengal)

RADIANT PUBLISHERS
K-4/4, Model Town-II, Delhi-110009
✆ 9818300870, 9891070005
Hd.Org.: Nidhi Kaura; **Bus.Intt.:** Pub. & Dist.; **Spl.:** Dictionaries for Children, also Cookery and Gen. Books

RADIANT PUBLICATIONS PVT. LTD.
No. 537, 5th Floor, Chanderalok Complex, S.D. Rd., Secunderabad-500003 (Andhra Pradesh)

RADICA INFORMATICS
C-6/129, Yamuna Vihar, New Delhi-110053
✆ 22196636
✉ gku_1@yahoo.com
Estd.: 2002; **Prop.:** Girish Kumar Upadhyay; **Bus.Intt.:** L.S.; **Spl.:** Humanities, Soc.Sci., Mang. & Comm., Sci., Engg. & Tech.

RADICAL BOOKS PVT. LTD.
S-8, IIIrd Floor, Akarshan Bhawan, 23 Ansari Road, Darya Ganj, New Delhi-110002
✆ 23283639, Fax: 91-121-2521607
✉ ck@radicalbooks.co.in
www.radicalbooks.co.in
Bus.Intt.: Pub.; **Spl.:** School textbooks, picture books, coffee table books, encyclopaedia, fiction, etc.

RADICAL IMPRESSION
43, Baniatola Lane, Kolkata-700009 (West Bengal)

RAGHAVA PRAKASHANA
54, 3rd Cross, Gavipuram, Bangalore-560019 (Karnataka)
✆ 080-2608374
Hd.Org.: Prof. M.V. Seetaramaiah; **Spl.:** Fiction, Collections, Research Works and Own Books in Kannada

RAHI KITAB GHAR
C-20, Jyoti Colony, Gali No. 5, Loni Rd., Shahdara, Delhi-110032
✆ 91-11-23240379
Hd.Org.: Fareha Jawahar Naqvi; **Bus.Intt.:** Pub.; **Spl.:** Islamic Art, Arch. and Rel. in Urdu

RAHUL BOOKS
A-136, New Seelampur, Delhi-110053
✆ 22562985 ▮ 9811445334
Estd.: 1990; **Prop.:** Kanwar Pal; **Bus.Intt.:** L.S.; **Spl.:** Acad., Behavioural Sci., Soc.Sci., Comm., Sci., Pure and Applied Tech., Law

RAHUL FOUNDATION
C/o O.P. Sinha, 69, Baba Ka Purva Papermill Rd., Nishatganj, Lucknow-226006 (Uttar Pradesh)
✆ 2383928
✉ rahulfoundation@rediffmail.com
Hd.Org.: Mukul Srivastava; **Bus.Intt.:** Pub.; **Spl.:** Books in Hindi on Hist., Politics, Soc.Sci., Phil., Socialism and Marxism, Indian and Foreign Classics

RAHUL FOUNDATION
Sanskrit Kutir, Kalyanpur, Gorakhpur-273001
✆ 2241922, Fax: 3096414
✉ rahulfoundation@rediffmail.com
Hd.Org.: Mukul Srivastava; **Bus.Intt.:** Pub.; **Spl.:** Book in Hindi on Hist., Pol., Soc.Sci., Phil., Socialism and on Marxism

RAHUL PRAKASHAN
30/64, Gali No. 8, Vishwas Nagar, Shahdara, New Delhi-110032
✆ 22056715
Hd.Org.: Parmod Gautam; **Bus.Intt.:** Pub. and B.S.; **Spl.:** Hindi Novels, Criticisms, Dalit Litt.

RAHUL PUBLICATIONS
Subash Bazar, Meerut-250002 (Uttar Pradesh)

RAHUL PUBLISHING HOUSE
34, Central Market, Ashok Vihar, Delhi-110052

RAINA TRANSCONTINENTAL LTD.
B-29, Vishal Tower, Janakpuri Distt. Centre, New Delhi-110058

RAINBOW BOOK CO.
New Height Publishers, 1367/21, Hari Singh Nalwa, Karol Bagh, New Delhi-110005
✆ 25721211, 25717821
Estd.: 1938; **Hd.Org.:** R.D. Taneja
Br.: 1685, Nai Sarak, Delhi-110016
✆ 23263658
Bus.Intt.: Pub., WS, Subscription New Heights

RAINBOW BOOK PUBLISHERS
Central Bank Building, Kallissery P.O., Chengannur-689124 (Kerala)
✆ 2426427

nomarainbow@sify.com
www.rainbow-books.com
Hd.Org.: N. Rajesh Kumar; **Bus.Intt.:** Pub. and Promoter; **Spl.:** Litt. in Malayalam Language

RAINBOW PUBLISHERS LTD.
A-19, Sector-56, Noida-201301 (Uttar Pradesh)
✆ 91-24584977, 011-22724314, 23951378
▮ 9810579302, Fax: 23940154
rainbow_p@vsnl.net,
yaten@nda.vsnl.net.in
Hd.Org.: Dhruva Narayan; **Bus.Intt.:** Pub. and Dist.; **Spl.:** Soc.Sci. and Humanities

RAINBOW PUBLISHING HOUSE
1901, Lehswa St., Bazar Sita Ram, Delhi-110006

RAJ BHASHA PRAKASHAN
158A, FF, Nanak Malhotra, Kesavpuram, Delhi-110051
Hd.Org.: Subhash Chandra Malhotra

RAJ BOOK CENTRE
329, Indra Vihar, Delhi-110009
✆ 27454933, 27652926, Fax: 27444926
jatin159@yahoo.com,
jain159@rediffmail.com
Hd.Org.: Jitender Kalra; **Bus.Intt.:** Dist.; **Spl.:** Books on *Vaastushastra*, feng shi, Osho, Sports, Health, Cookery, etc.

RAJ COMICS
708, Burari, Delhi-110084
✆ 27612037, 27611038, Fax: 27611227
www.rajcomics.com
Hd.Org.: Manoj Gupta; **Bus.Intt.:** Pub.; **Spl.:** Comics of Characters like Nagraj, Doga, Parmanu, etc.

RAJ ENTERPRISES, BOOK DISTRIBUTORS
Flat No. 407, Vyankatesh Darshan, Pt. Deen Dayal Rd., Vishnunagar, Dombivali (West), Mumbai-421202 (Maharashtra)
✆ (O) 2481534 (R) 2485595
Estd.: 1984; **Prop.:** Prafull Dighe; **Bus.Intt.:** Dist., L.S.; **Spl.:** Humanities & Soc.Sci., Mang., Bio.Sci., Reference Books

RAJ KAMAL PRAKASHAN PVT. LTD.
1-B, Netaji Subhash Marg, New Delhi-110002
✆ 23274463, 23288769, Fax: 23278144
rajkamalprakashan@email.com
Estd.: 1976; **Dir.:** Ashok Maheshwari; **Bus.Intt.:** Pub.; **Spl.:** Tech., Fiction & Soc.Sci.

RAJKIRAN BOOK AGENCY
14/11, Kaushik Enclave, Nathu Pura Road, Delhi-110084
✆ 91-11-27613386
rajkiranbooks@yahoo.co.uk
Estd.: 1970, **Hd.Org.:** Kiran Sharma **Bus.Intt.:** B.S. and L.S.; **Spl.:** Books on Engineering, Science & Technology, etc.

RAJ KRISHNA PUSTAKALAYA
206, Bidhan Sarani, Room No. 9, Kolkata-700006 (West Bengal)

RAJ POCKET BOOKS
330/2, Burari, Delhi-110084
✆ 91-11-27612037/39
Hd.Org.: Manoj Gupta
Bus.Intt.: Pub.; **Spl:** Books on Astrology, *Vaastu-shastra*, Health, Yoga, etc.

RAJ POCKET BOOKS
112, Dariba Kalan, Delhi-110006
✆ 23251109, 23251092
Hd.Org.: Sanjay Gupta; **Bus.Intt.:** Pub.; **Spl.:** Astrology, *Vaastushastra*, Health, Yoga

RAJ PRAKASHAN (PUBLISHERS)
10, Dayanand Vihar, Vikas Marg, Extn., Delhi-110092
✆ (O) 22150555, 22141098 (PP)
Estd.: 1970; **Prop.:** S.K. Gupta

RAJ PUBLICATIONS
R-115/2, Model Town, Delhi-110009

RAJ PUBLICATIONS
Kedar Complex, Delhi Gate, Meerut City-250002 (Uttar Pradesh)
✆ 0121-227859, Fax: 2513756
Prop.: Rajesh Agarwal; **Spl.:** Books on Electronics in English and Hindi

RAJ PUBLISHERS
15-B, Zion (West) St., Nagercoil-629001 (Tamil Nadu)

RAJ PUBLISHERS & DISTRIBUTORS
119/426, Darshanpurwa, Kanpur-208012
✆ 0512-2234537
Hd.Org.: Raju Gupta; **Bus.Intt.:** B.S., L.S.

RAJ PUBLISHING HOUSE
9/5123, Old Seelampur (East), Gali No. 1, Delhi-110031
✆ (O) & (R) 22503781
Estd.: 1970; **Hd.Org.:** Rajesh Rani; **Bus.Intt.:** Pub. & Dist.; **Spl.:** Hindi Litt.

RAJ PUBLISHING HOUSE
43, Parnami Mandir, Govind Marg, Jaipur-302004 (Rajasthan)
✆ 2622141, 2650410
rajpublishing@satyam.net.in
Hd.Org.: Kiran Parnami; **Bus.Intt.:** Pub. and Dist.; **Spl.:** Lib.Sci., Mang., Comm., Physics, and Gen. books

RAJ PUSTAK BHANDAR
Naugachia, Bhagalpur-813211 (Bihar)
Bus.Intt.: B.S. and Pub.

RAJA LAXMI BOOK HOUSE
Hyderabad (Andhra Pradesh)
✆ 23402835, 55585883, Fax: 55363209
✉ rlbhpra2002@yahoo.com
Bus.Intt.: B.S.

RAJA NAACHCHU PUBLICATIONS
C/359, 80 Fort Rd., IInd Floor,
Bharthiyar Apts., Anna Nagar,
Madurai-625020
(Tamil Nadu)

RAJA POCKET BOOKS
330/1, Burari, Delhi-110084
✆ 27611410, 27612036, 23251092, 23251109, Fax: 27611227
✉ sales@rajcomics.com
www.rajcomics.com
Estd.: 1986; **Hd.Org.:** Manoj Gupta; **Bus.Intt.:** Pub.; **Spl.:** Health, Astrology, Occult Sci., Hindi Litt.

RAJANI PRAKASHAN
5/288, Kanti Nagar, Gali V, Delhi-110051
Hd.Org.: Sanjeev Kumar

RAJASREE TRADERS
P.P. Rd., Perumbavoor-683542 (Kerala)
Estd.: 1967; **Prop.:** K. Saji;
Bus.Intt.: B.S.

RAJASTHAN ADULT EDUCATION ASSOCIATION
7-A, Jhalana Institutional Area, Jaipur-302004 (Rajasthan)
✆ 2517464, 2510912, Fax: 2517464
✉ rajadult@jp1.dot.net.in
Hd.Org.: Nand Kishore Acharya;
Bus.Intt.: Pub.; **Spl.:** Neo-literates, Rural Adults and Children Books in Hindi

RAJASTHAN EDUCATIONAL STORE
Dawooji Mandir Rd., Bikaner-334001 (Rajasthan)
Hd.Org.: Gopal Acharya

RAJASTHAN HINDI GRANTH AKADEMI
Plot No. 1, Jhalana Sansthanik Kshetra, Jaipur-302004 (Rajasthan)
✆ 2711129, Fax: 91-11-2710341
✉ hindgranth@indiatimes.com
www.rajhg.com
Hd.Org.: Vasudev Devnani
Bus.Intt.: Pub.; **Spl.:** Hindi Text and Reference Books on Engg., Agri., Sci., Soc.Sci., Law, Journalism

RAJASTHAN PATRIKA PVT. LTD.
'Kesargarh', J.L.N. Marg, Jaipur-302004 (Rajasthan)
✆ 39404142, Fax: 91-141-2566011
✉ info@rajasthanpatrika.com
www.rajasthanpatrika.com
Hd.Org.: Gulab Kothari; **Bus.Intt.:** Pub.;
Spl.: *Vedic* Litt., Mang., Art, Indology, etc.

RAJASTHAN PEOPLE'S PUBLISHING HOUSE (P) LTD.
Chameliwala Market M.I. Rd., Jaipur-302002 (Rajasthan)
✆ (O) 2372704, 2373363 (R) 2521574
Prop.: Rampal
Br.: 101/148, Ravi Marg, Patel Marg, Agarwal Farm, Mansarovar, Jaipur-20
✆ 781282
Bus.Intt.: Pub. and Dist.; **Spl.:** Sci., Engg., Med. and Chiljdren besides Soc.Sci. in English and Hindi

RAJASTHAN PRAKASHAN
28-29, Tripolia Bazar, Jaipur-302002 (Rajasthan)
✆ (O) 2322443 (R) 2204597
Estd.: 1952; **Prop.:** Rajendra Jasoria;
Bus.Intt.: Pub., B.S., L.S., WS; **Spl.:** Edu. books for Children

RAJASTHAN PRAKASHAN HOUSE
40, Elaji Ka Chowk, Ganesh Ghati, Udaipur-313001 (Rajasthan)
✆ 227693
Hd.Org.: Kailashprakash Joshi

RAJASTHAN PUSTAK VYAVASAYEE SANGH
251, Khatetno Ka Rasta, Jaipur-302001 (Rajasthan)
✆ (O) 2319198, 2319094 (R) 2592052

RAJASTHAN URDU ACADEMY
J-3, Subhash Marg, 'C' Scheme, Jaipur-302001 (Rajasthan)
✆ 2382664, 2381945
Hd.Org.: Moazzam Ali; **Bus.Intt.:** Pub. and Promoter; **Spl.:** Books in Urdu Language

RAJASTHANI BOOK DISTRIBUTORS
149, Pratap Nagar, Mayur Vihar, Phase-I, Delhi-110091
✆ 22255774

RAJASTHANI GRANTHAGAR
Sojti Gate, Jodhpur-342001 (Rajasthan)
✆ (O) 2623933 (R) 2432567, Fax: 2611555
✉ rgranthagar@satyam.net.in
Estd.: 1980; **Hd.Org.:** Rajendra Singhvi;
Bus.Intt.: Pub. and Dist.; **Spl.:** Books on Rajasthan's Hist., Culture, Language, etc.

RAJAT BOOK CORNER
Opp. Medical College, Circular Rd., Amritsar-143001 (Punjab)
✆ (O) 2223055 (R) 2212747
✉ happyrajan@rediffmail.com
Estd.: 1952; **Prop.:** Rajat Batra, Rajan Arora

Br.: 8, Narain Singh Rd., Near Trimurti Circle, Jaipur-302004
✆ (O) 2568833 (R) 2352555
Fax: 0141-2563344
✉ rajatbooks@satyam.net.in
Bus.Intt.: L.S. & Rt.; **Spl.:** Med., Juvenile/ Children, Gen. & Fiction etc.

RAJAT PUBLICATIONS
4/31-32, Geeta Colony, Delhi-110031
✆ (O) 22207277 (R) 22438482
Prop.: Seema Wajan; **Bus.Intt.:** Pub.; **Spl.:** Soc.Sci.

RAJAT PUBLICATIONS
4675/21, Ansari Rd., Darya Ganj, New Delhi-110002
✆ 23267924, 22507277
Estd.: 1998; **Hd.Org.:** Seema Wasan; **Bus.Intt.:** Pub.; **Spl.:** Man., Sci. and Humanities in English

RAJATHI EXPORTERS
13, Kamaraj Rd., Sivakasi-626123 (Tamil Nadu)
✆ 22519104, 22523904, Fax: 04560-221365
Estd.: 1991; **Bus.Intt.:** Exp.

RAJBHASHA PRAKASHAN
Flat No. 96, Pocket G-7, Sector-15, Rohini, Delhi-110085
✆ 27893988
Estd.: 1988; **Hd.Org.:** Subhash Chand Malhotra; **Bus.Intt.:** Pub.; **Spl.:** Gen. Books

RAJBHASHA PUSTAK PRATISHTHAN
L-45, Gali No. 5, Shivaji Marg, Kartar Nagar, Delhi-110053
▮ 9868109002
Hd.Org.: Rajendra Kumar Yadav
Bus.Intt.: Pub.; **Spl.:** Books on Litt. and Children's Books in Hindi

RAJBHASHA VIBHAG
Ministry of Home Affairs, Loknayak Bhavan, Khan Market, New Delhi-110003
✆ 24617695, 24698054, 24617807,
Fax: 91-11-24611031
✉ nicdol@alpha.nic.in
Hd.Org.: Vijay P. Goyal; **Bus.Intt.:** Pub.; **Spl.:** Government Publications Journals

RAJDHANI GRANTHAGAR
59, H-IV, Lajpat Nagar, New Delhi-110024

RAJEEV PUSTAK BHANDAR
Shambhuganj, Bhagalpur-813211 (Bihar)
Bus.Intt.: Pub. and B.S.

RAJENDRA PUBLISHING HOUSE PVT. LTD.
202, Patel Estate, B-40, New Link Rd., Andheri (W), Mumbai-400053 (Maharashtra)
✆ 26301930, 26300741; 26300742,
Fax: 26301940
Estd.: 1988; **Chairman:** R.K. Tandon; **Bus.Intt.:** Pub., WS, L.S. & Rt., Imp., Exp., Mail Order Dist.; **Spl.:** Humanities & Soc.Sci., Med., Gen. & Fiction etc.

RAJENDRA PUSTAK BHANDAR
Siris, Aurangabad-824101 (Bihar)
Bus.Intt.: Pub. and B.S.

RAJENDRA PUSTAK BHAWAN
Rafiganj, Aurangabad-824125 (Bihar)
Bus.Intt.: Pub. and B.S.

RAJESH BOOK AGENCY
WA-67B, Shakarpur, Laxmi Nagar, Delhi-110092
✆ 91-11-22445442
Hd.Org.: Rajesh; **Bus.Intt.:** Dist. and Supplier; **Spl.:** General Books

RAJESH BOOKSELLERS
12-B, Kartik Swami Society, Outside Shahpur Gate, Ahmedabad-380001 (Gujarat)

RAJESH JAIN & CO.
1936, First Floor, Fountain, Near Hamraj Clinic, Chandni Chowk, Delhi-110006
✆ 91-11-23868005
✉ rajeshjain@india.com
🌐 www.numismaticindia.com
Hd.Org.: Rajesh Jain

RAJESH PRAKASHAN
G-5/62, Arjun Nagar, Delhi-110051
▮ 9891793339
Hd.Org.: Inderesh Rajput
Bus.Int.: Pub., **Spl.:** Hindi Litt.

RAJESH PUBLICATIONS
4226/A1, Ansari Road, Darya Ganj, New Delhi-110002 ✆ 91-11-23274550
✉ rajeshpublications@rediffmail.com
🌐 www.rajeshpublications.com
Hd.Org.: Mohan Lal Gupta
Bus.Intt.: S.B.; **Spl.:** Books on Life Sciences, Business & Management, Social Sciences and Humanities etc.

RAJESH PUSTAK BHANDAR
Naugachia, Bhagalpur-853202 (Bihar)
Bus.Intt.: Pub. and B.S.

RAJESH PUSTAK BHANDAR
Kahalgaon (Colgong), Bhagalpur-8463203 (Bihar) **Bus.Intt.:** Pub. and B.S.

RAJESH PUSTAK BHAWAN
Old G.T. Rd., (Near Post Office), Aurangabad-824101 (Bihar)
Bus.Intt.: Pub. and B.S.

RAJESHWAR BOOKS PVT. LTD.
B-2/211 (Basement), Safdarjung Enclave, New Delhi-110029
✆ 26177569, Fax: 91-11-26183871
✉ rajeshwarbooks@gmail.com
Prt.: Miss. Niru Mathur, Miss. Sanjana; **Bus.Intt.:** Dist.; **Spl.:** Edu., Psy., Sol., Criminology, etc.

RAJESHWARI PUTHAGER NILAYAM
4, Muthi Krishnan St., T-Nagar, Chennai-600017 (Tamil Nadu)
✆ 44-28202073, Fax: 91-44-28202073
Hd.Org.: N. Balakrishnan; **Bus.Intt.:** Manufacturers of Book Pub.

RAJHANS PRAKASHAN
1025, Sadashivpet, Near Nagnath Par, Pune-411030 (Maharashtra)
✆ (O) 022-24473459, 24465063 (R) 25435113, 25442113, Fax: 24473459
✉ rajhans1@pn2.vsnl.net.in
Estd.: 1955; **Hd.Org.:** Dileep G. Majgaonkar; **Bus.Intt.:** Pub.; **Spl.:** Pol., Socio-Eco., Sci.Env., Biography, Autobiography, Edu. and Med. etc.

RAJHANS PRAKASHAN MANDIR
Ram Nagar, Meerut (Uttar Pradesh)
Hd.Org.: Mahendra Prasad Goel; **Bus.Intt.:** Pub.

RAJHAUNS VITARAN
1, Meenakshi Building, Panaji, Goa-403001
✆ 2220320, 2232177
✉ rdbhide@goacom.com
Estd.: 1976; **Bus.Intt.:** Pub.; **Spl.:** Edu., Children Litt. etc.

RAJIV BOOK HOUSE
30, Palika Bazar, New Delhi-110001
✆ 23323692
Bus.Intt.: Rt.; **Spl.:** Books on Travel, Art, Indian Culture, Photography

RAJIV PRAKASHAN
189-A/1, Alopi Bagh Colony, Allahabad-211006 (Uttar Pradesh)
Hd.Org.: Rajiv Ranjan Roy

RAJIV PUBLISHERS
4442, Nai Sarak, Delhi-110006
✆ 22911143 ▮ 9810069520
Estd.: 1964; **Hd.Org.:** Sandeep Khanna; **Spl.:** Geo., Hist. and Sci.

RAJKAMAL PRAKASHAN (P) LTD.
1-B, Netaji Subhash Marg, New Delhi-110002
✆ 23274463, 23288769, Fax: 23278144, 23251803
✉ info@rajkamalprakashan.com
🌐 www.rajkamalprakashan.com
Estd.: 1947; **Hd.Org.:** Ashok Maheshwari; **Bus.Intt.:** Pub.; **Spl.:** Litt., Hist., Pol., Sol., Phil., Biography as also the Quarterly magazine, *Alochana* in Hindi

RAJNI PRAKASHAN
5/288, Gali No. 5, West Kranti Nagar, Delhi-110051
Hd.Org.: Sanjeev Kumar Maheshwari

RAJPAL & SONS
1590, Madarsa Rd., Kashmere Gate, Delhi-110006
✆ 23865483, 23869812, Fax: 91-11-23867791
✉ mail@rajpalsons.com
🌐 www.rajpalsons.com
Estd.: 1947; **Hd.Org.:** Vishwanath, Meera Johri; **Bus.Intt.:** Pub. and B.S.; **Spl.:** Dictionaries, Encyclopaedias, Novels, Stories, Biographies, Children's Books, etc.

RAJPUROHIT PRAKASHAN
Champakheri Rajpurohit Kutir, Chouteena Khan, Bikaner (Rajasthan)

RAJSHRI PRAKASHAN
C-12/460, Yamuna Vihar, Delhi-110053
Hd.Org.: Manoj Tomar

RAJSHRI PRODUCTIONS (P) LTD.
(Publishing House Division), Bhavana Ist Floor Opp. Kismet Cinema, 422, Veer Savarkar Rd., P.B. No. 9103, Prabhadevi, Mumbai-400025 (Maharashtra)

RAJSURYA PRAKASHAN
D-Block, 2/41-A, Ganwari Vistaar, Bhajanpura, Delhi-110053
✆ 23209736
Estd.: 1996; **Hd.Org.:** Rajkumar Srivastava; **Bus.Intt.:** Pub.; **Spl.:** Hindi Novels, Stories, Criticisms, etc.

RAJU PUSTAK BHANDAR
Shahpur, Aurangabad (Bihar)
Bus.Intt.: Pub. and B.S.

RAJU PUSTAKALAYA
Dumari Deo, Aurangabad-824202 (Bihar)
Bus.Intt.: Pub. and B.S.

RAJUSHA PUBLICATION
A-30/10-K, Mata Mandir Marg, Gali No. 1, East Maujpur, Behind Seth Bhagwan Das School, Shahdara, Delhi-110053
✆ 22175255, 31049485, Fax: 22968809
✉ rajushapublication@msn.com
Hd.Org.: Usha Sharma; **Bus.Intt.:** Pub.; **Spl.:** Reference Material for NGOs and Registered Societies Engaged in Soc. Welfare

RAJYA PARIKRAMA PRESS SERVICE
Sanjay Gandhi Market, (Photo Copy Centre), Opp. Revenue Building, Birchand Patel Path, Patna-800001 (Bihar)

RAJYA SABHA SECRETARIAT
Room No. 2, Parliament House Annexe, New Delhi-110001
✆ 23034160, Fax: 91-11-23013917
rssa@sansad.nic.in
www.rajyasabha.nic.in
Hd.Org.: P.D. Mehre; **Bus.Intt.:** Pub.; **Spl.:** Parliamentary Publications

RAKA PRAKASHAN
40-A, Motilal Nehru Rd., Allahabad-211002 (Uttar Pradesh)
✆ 2466791
Hd.Org.: Rakesh Tiwari; **Bus.Intt.:** Pub.; **Spl.:** Books in Hindi on Phil., Hist., Art, Culture, etc.

RAKESH BOOK AGENCY
WA-67B, Shakarpur, Delhi-110092
✆ 91-11-65476479
Hd.Org.: Rakesh
Bus.Intt.: Dist.; **Spl.:** General Books

RAKESH BOOK SERVICE
277/17, Shiv Mandir, Wazirabad (Behind Bengali Clinic), Delhi-110054
9811131636
Prop.: Budhu Ram Pal; **Bus.Intt.:** L.S.; **Spl.:** Acad., Beh.Sci., Soc.Sci., Comm., Sci., Pure & Applied, Tech., Fiction, Juveniles, Law

RAKESH PUSTAK BHANDAR
G.T. Rd., Aurangabad-824101 (Bihar)
Bus.Intt.: Pub. and B.S.

RAKTAKARABEE
10/2B, Ramanath Majumder St., Kolkata-700009 (West Bengal)

RAM & CO. BOOK DEPOT
P.B. No. 242, P.J. Extension, Davangere-577002 (Karnataka)
✆ 228094
Hd.Org.: K.J. Srinevas

RAM ADVANI BOOKSELLERS
Mayfair, Building, GPO Box 154, Lucknow-226001 (Uttar Pradesh)
✆ 0522-2224057, Fax: 0522-2223511
radvani@sancharnet.in
Hd.Org.: Ram Advani; **Bus.Intt.:** Rt., Library Order Service and Mail Order Suppliers; **Spl.:** Fiction, Politics and Social Issues Spltn, in Serving Civil Servants by Mailing Indian and Foreign Books

RAM CHANDER & SONS
New Delhi
✆ 23412065, 23416276,
Fax: 23411484
sundra@mantraonline.com
Bus.Intt.: B.S. & Dist.

RAM KISHORE MISHRA
Head of the Sanskrit Deptt., M.M. Degree College, Khekhra-201101, Meerut (Uttar Pradesh)

RAM KRISHNA PRAKASHAN
Chitrangada Complex, Vidisha-464001 (Madhya Pradesh)
✆ 237100, 250200, Fax: 91-7592-250200
Hd.Org.: Girjesh Silakari; **Bus.Intt.:** Pub. and Dist.; **Spl.:** Hindi Litt.

RAM LAL KAPUR TRUST
P.O. Bahal Garh, Sonepat-131021 (Haryana)
Hd.Org.: Swami Vidyanand Saraswati
Spl.: Vedic Litt. Books in Hindi

RAM NATH KAUL LIBRARY OF PHILOSOPHY
(Publication Division), Philosophy Department University of Allahabad, Allahabad-211002 (Uttar Pradesh)

RAM PRASAD & SONS
1, Balvihar, Hamidia Rd., Bhopal-462003 (Madhya Pradesh)
✆ 2533389, 2534718
Estd.: 1960; **Hd.Org.:** B.N. Agarwal
Bus.Intt.: Pub.; **Spl.:** Text Books of College Level—All Sub.

RAMA BROTHERS INDIA PVT. LTD.
2629, Bank St., Karol Bagh, New Delhi-110005
✆ (O) 25727313, 25815936 (R) 25875288
9811026021, Fax: 25815936
ramabrothers@mantraonline.com, naval_passi@mantraonline.com
Hd.Org.: K.K. Pasi, **Dir.:** Naval Passi; **Bus.Intt.:** Pub. and Dist.; **Spl.:** Eng.Litt. and Notes for University Students

RAMA PUBLISHING HOUSE
Bhagwan Mahavir Marg, Barot, Meerut-250611 (Uttar Pradesh)
✆ 01234-262560
Bus.Intt.: Pub.; **Spl.:** Agricultural and Dairy Sci. in Hindi

RAMAKRISHNA MATH
Hyderabad (Andhra Pradesh)
✆ 27633937, Fax: 27633936
rkmath@hd2.dot.net.in
Bus.Intt.: B.S.

RAMAKRISHNA MISSION
Ramakrishna Ashrama Marg, Paharganj, New Delhi-110055
✆ 23587110, 23583023, Fax: 91-11-23580848
✉ rkndlh@ndf.vsnl.net.in, ashram@rkmissiondel.org, rkmissiondelhi@vsnl.com
www.rkmissiondel.org
Hd.Org.: Swami Gokulananda;
Bus.Intt.: Dist.; **Spl.:** Books on Ramakrishna, Vivekananda, Vedanta, Yoga, Psych. and Meditation in English and other Languages

RAMAKRISHNA NEWS AGENCIES
Hyderabad (Andhra Pradesh)
✆ 24614641, 24602491, Fax: 24614346
✉ rknewsagencies@rediffmail.com
Bus.Intt.: News Agency

RAMAN BOOKS
259, IV Main Rd., Indiranagar, Chennai-600020 (Tamil Nadu)

RAMAN MEDIA NETWORK
463, DPS Apartments, Plot No. 16, Sector-4, Dwarka, Phase-I, New Delhi-110045
✆ 26975809 ▮ 9810319059
✉ rmnindia@yahoo.com
Estd.: 2002; **Prop.:** Rakesh Raman;
Spl.: Knowledge Story Books for Childrens

RAMANA MAHARASHI CENTRE FOR LEARNING
40/4-II Cross, Lower Palace Orchards, Bangalore-560003 (Karnataka)

RAMANAND VIDYA BHAVAN
J-3/227, DDA Kalkaji, New Delhi-110019

RAMANUJAN MATHEMATICAL SOCIETY
National College, Tiruchi-620001 (Karnataka)

RAMARUN PRAKASHAN
A-2, Ring Rd., NDSE-I, New Delhi-110049
✆ (O) & (R) 24619126
Estd.: 1959; **Prop.:** Ram Avtar Gupta;
Bus.Intt.: Pub.; **Spl.:** Children's Books in English and Hindi

RAMASHRAYA BOOK DEPOT
Subhas Rd., Dharwar-580001 (Karnataka)
✆ (O) 2442487 (R) 2740515, 2740998
✉ ramashraya_pub@yahoo.com
Estd.: 1927; **Prt.:** Raju, Vasant; **Bus.Intt.:** B.S., L.S., WS; **Spl.:** Sci. & Tech., Comp., Med., Mang., Law, Children & Gen.

RAMAUTAR BOOKS
Semapur, Katihar-854115 (Bihar)

RAMBHA JYOTI
Post Box No. 508, Chandigarh-160018

RAMDASS BOOKSELLER
Khiriawan, Madanpur, Aurangabad-824208 (Bihar)
Bus.Intt.: Pub. and B.S.

RAMESH BOOK DEPOT
65, Shivaji Nagar, Civil Lines, Jaipur-302006 (Rajasthan)
✆ 2220742, Fax: 91-141-2220742
✉ sumeetchandok@hotmail.com
Hd.Org.: Sumeet Chandak
Bus.Intt.: Pub.; **Spl.:** Educational Books

RAMESH BOOK DEPOT
S-255, Greater Kailash Part-II, New Delhi-110048
✆ 51637730-2, Fax: 51637730
✉ sumeetchandak@hotmail.com
Hd.Org.: S.N. Chandak; **Bus.Intt.:** Pub.;
Spl.: Books for Graduates and Postgraduate Level and other Professional courses

RAMESH PUBLISHING HOUSE
12-H, New Darya Ganj Road, Opp. Traffic Kotwali, New Delhi-110002
✆ 23275124, Fax: 91-11-23275224
✉ rphbooks@nda.vsnl.net.in
www.rameshpublishinghouse.com
Hd.Org.: O.P. Gupta, **Bus.Intt.:** Pub.

RAMKRISHNA BOOK STALL
12/1B, Bankim Chatterjee St., Kolkata-700073 (West Bengal)

RAMKRISHNA PUSTAK BHAWAN
15, Bankim Chatterjee St., Kolkata-700073 (West Bengal)

RAMNARAYAN LAL BENI PRASAD
4, Katra Rd., Allahabad-211002 (Uttar Pradesh)
✆ 2641701, 2641446
Hd.Org.: Sanjay and Anand Agarwal

RAMNIKA FOUNDATION
A-221, Defence Colony, New Delhi-110024
✆ 24658368
✉ shilpayan@mantramail.com
Hd.Org.: Ramnika Gupta; **Bus.Intt.:** Pub.;
Spl.: Hindi Litt.

RAMPUR RAZA LIBRARY
Hamid Manzil, Rampur-244901 (Uttar Pradesh)
✆ 2325045, 2327244, Fax: 91-595-2340548
✉ whsiddiqui@rediffmail.com
www.razalibrary.gov.in
Hd.Org.: W.H. Siddiqi

RAMSWAROOP GAUR
Mokhampura, Post Office Bichoon, Jaipur (Rajasthan)

RANDHIR BOOK SALES
Railway Rd., Haridwar-249401 (Uttarakhand)

RANDOM HOUSE GROUP
I-4, Ground Floor, Lajpat Nagar-I,
New Delhi-110024
✆ 29818663, Fax: 29818663
✉ randomhouse@vsnl.net
🌐 www.randomhouse.com
Hd.Org.: Rahul Srivastava, Nandan Jha; **Bus.Intt.:** Pub.; **Spl.:** Fiction, Non-fiction, Books on Man., Self-help, etc.

RANDOM HOUSE INTERNATIONAL
2/25, Ansari Rd., Darya Ganj,
New Delhi-110002
✆ 23284894

RANDOOM HOUSE (THE)
Delhi
✆ 2405416
✉ nandanjha@vsnl.com
Bus.Intt.: B.S. & Dist.

RANDOM HOUSE PUBLISHERS INDIA PVT. LTD.
301, World Trade Tower, Barakhamba Lane,
New Delhi-110001
✆ 41528305-06, Fax: 91-11-41528307
✉ nskrishna@randomhouse.co.in
🌐 www.randomhouse.co.in
Hd.Org.: N.S. Krishna
Bus.Intt.: Pub. and Dist.; **Spl.:** Fiction, non-fiction, self-help and business management as also Children's books, reference books, dictionaries, etc.

RANEE PUBLICATIONS
P.B. No. 7154, 12H, New Darya Ganj Rd.,
New Delhi-110002
✆ 23251502, Fax: 23276025
✉ raneepublications@vsnl.com
Hd.Org.: Ram Nath Gupta; **Bus.Intt.:** Pub.; **Spl.:** Gen. Books, Journals, Comp. Magazine

RANGADWAR PRAKASHAN
A-6, Purnheshwar, Gulabi Tekra,
Ahmedabad-380015 (Gujarat)

RANG PRAKASHAN/JAINSON BOOK SHOP
33, Bakshi Gali, Rajbada, Indore-452004
(Madhya Pradesh)
✆ 2538787, Fax: 91-731-2469627
✉ info@jainsonbookworld.com
🌐 www.jainsonbookworld.com
Hd.Org.: Manish Jain
Bus.Intt.: Pub. and Dist.; **Spl.:** Books and Journals on Science & Technology, Engineering, Computers, Management, Medicine, Hindi Litt., Children's Litt. etc.

RANI PRAKASHAN
K-21, Naveen Shahdara, Delhi-110032
✆ (O) & (R) 22284239
Estd.: 1958; **Prop.:** Mrs. Durga Rani; **Bus.Intt.:** B.S., Pub. & L.S.; **Spl.:** Fashion, Textile, Psych., Child Development, Encyclopedias & Reference Books

RANI PUBLICATIONS
533-A, Poonamalle High Rd., Vapery,
Chennai-600007 (Tamil Nadu)
✆ 25324771
✉ rani.chen@gems.vsnl.net.in
Estd.: 1969; **Bus.Intt.:** Exp.

RANI PUSTAK BHANDAR
Jagdishpur, Bhagalpur-813105 (Bihar)
Bus.Intt.: Pub. and B.S.

RANJAN PRAKASHAN
8/1A, Shyama Charan Dey St.,
Kolkata-700073 (West Bengal)

RANJAN PUBLICATIONS
16, Ansari Rd., Darya Ganj,
New Delhi-110002
✆ 23278835, 23282998, Fax: 23275124
✉ ranjanpublications@rediffmail.com
Hd.Org.: Atul Goyal; **Bus.Intt.:** Pub. and Dist.; **Spl.:** Astrology, Palmistry and Occult Sci.

RANJEET PUSTAK BHANDAR
Amarpur, Bhagalpur-813101 (Bihar)
Bus.Intt.: Pub. and B.S.

RANJIMA PUBLICATIONS
Mammoodu P.O., Changanacherry-686553
(Kerala)
Estd.: 1984; **Hd.Org.:** Usha Nampoorhiri; **Bus.Intt.:** Pub.

RANJIT BOOK STALL
1723/7, E. Ward, City Bus Rd., Rajarampuri,
Kolhapur-416608 (Maharashtra)

RANJIT PUBLISHERS
Apt. 31 Mayfair Garden, Hauz Khas,
New Delhi-110016
✆ 26867592, Fax: 26866635; **Bus.Intt.:** Pub.; **Spl.:** Humanities and Litt. Books

RANJIT PUSTAK BHANDAR
Majhaul, Begusarai-851127 (Bihar)
Bus.Intt.: Pub. and B.S.

RANNADE PRAKASHAN
2345, Mahalaxinipole, Raipur, Ahmedabad
(Gujarat)

RARE PUBLICATIONS
6/486-A, P.G. Complex, Bank Rd.,
Kozhikode-673001 (Kerala)
✆ (R) 265030
Estd.: 1991; **Prop.:** K. Sarath Chandran; **Bus.Intt.:** Pub. and B.S.

RAS-RANG
P-12, Narmada Marg, Sector-11,
Noida-201301 (Uttar Pradesh)

✆ 2546308
Hd.Org.: Vinay Krishna Chaturvedi; **Bus.Intt.:** Pub.; **Spl.:** Books on Hindi Poetry, Urdu Verse, etc.

RASHMI JYOTI PUSTAK BHANDAR
Majhaul, Begusarai-851127 (Bihar)
Bus.Intt.: Pub. and B.S.

RASHMIC BANSAL
New Delhi
✆ 26928653, 26928658, Fax: 26919528
✉ bansal@vastushastri.com
Bus.Intt.: B.S.

RASHTRA BHASHA PRAKASHAN
518/6-B, Vishwas Nagar, Shahdara, Delhi-110032
✆ 22204524
Hd.Org.: Rajkumar Sharma

RASHTRAWADI TIMES
12-H, Opp. Traffic Kotwali, Darya Ganj, New Delhi-110002
✆ 91-11-22321377
Hd.Org.: T.S. Tiwari; **Bus.Intt.:** Pub. & Dist.; **Spl.:** Edu. books in Hindi, English & Sanskrit

RASHTRIYA EKTA PRAKASHAN
Plot No. 133, Deepak Marg, Adarsh Nagar, Jaipur-302004 (Rajasthan)

RASHTRIYA PRAKASHAN MANDIR
Motia Park, (Near Water Tenki), Bhopal-462003 (Madhya Pradesh)
✆ 2530375
Hd.Org.: Jayshankar Dixit

RASHTRIYA SAHITYA
G-17, Fourth Floor, Jagatpuri, Delhi-110051 ✆ 91-11-22505852
Hd.Org.: Meena Sharma
Bus.Intt.: Pub.; **Spl.:** Books on culture, Litt, History, etc. in Hindi

RASHTRIYA SALES AGENCIES
9-B, Sehkar Nagar (C), Shilp Colony, Jhotbara, Jaipur (Rajasthan)
Hd.Org.: Mahaveer Gupta

RASHTRIYA SANSKRIT SANSTHAN
56-57, Institutional Area, Janakpuri, New Delhi-110058
✆ 28524993, 28524995, 28520976, 28520977, Fax: 91-11-28521948
✉ rsks@nda.vsnl.net.in
🌐 www.sanskrit.nic.in
Estd.: 1970; **Hd.Org.:** V. Kutumba Sastry; **Bus.Intt.:** Pub.; **Spl.:** Rare Out-of-print Books in Sanskrit and Research Journal *Sanskrit Vimarsha*

RASHTRIYA SANSKRIT SANSTHAN
Campus Ganganjali Jha, Chandra Shekhar Park, Allahabad
✆ 91-11-25540976
✉ rsks@nda.vsnl.net.in
🌐 www.sanskrit.nic.in
Estd.: 1970; **Hd.Org.:** V. Kutumba Sastry
Bus.Intt.: Pub.; **Spl.:** Books in Sanskrit and Research Journal, *Sanskrit Vimarsha*

RASHTRIYA SANSKRIT VIDYAPEETH
Tirupathi-517507 (Andhra Pradesh)
✆ 2286799, Fax: 91-877-2287809
✉ registrar_rsvp@yahoo.co.in
🌐 www.rsivdyapeetha.ac.in
Hd.Org.: H.K. Satapathy
Bus.Intt.: Pub.; **Spl.:** Books on Sanskrit as well as *Sastras* and Indology

RASHTROTHANA PARISHAT
93/1, Keshav Shilpa, Kempegowda Nagara, Bangalore-560019 (Karnataka)
✆ 080-26612731, 22210932, 26612730
Hd.Org.: M.C. Jayadev; **Bus.Intt.:** Pub.; **Spl.:** Biographies, Philosophical, Mythological Books, Rel. and Culture in Kannada and Eng.

RASIK ANTARBHARATI
484/90, Swaroop Mitra Mandal Society, Parrati, Pune-411009 (Maharashtra)
✆ 91-20-24440730
✉ rasikantarbharati@vsnl.net
Hd.Org.: Yogesh Nandurkar
Bus.Intt.: Pub., Dist. and L.S.; **Spl.:** Books on all subjects, Mainly in Marathi

RASIK SAHITYA BHANDAR
Shamlaji, Tq-Bhiloda, (Sabarkantha) (Gujarat)

RASTOGI PUBLICATIONS
Shivaji Rd., Meerut-250002 (Uttar Pradesh)
✆ 2510688, 2516080, Fax: 22521545
✉ info@rastogipublications.com
🌐 www.rastogipublications.com
Estd.: 1966; **Hd.Org.:** H.K. Rastogi; **Bus.Intt.:** Pub.; **Spl.:** Text and Edu. Books for Children

RATAN BOOK STALL
Peary Charan Sarkar St., Stall-85, Kolkata-700073 (West Bengal)

RATAN PRAKASHAN MANDIR
1/185-C, Professor's Colony, Delhi Gate, Agra (Uttar Pradesh)
✆ 2520019, 2527465, Fax: 91-562-2527463
✉ sales@ratanprakashan.com
🌐 www.ratanprakashan.com
Hd.Org.: Atul Jain; **Bus.Intt.:** Pub.; **Spl.:** Edu. books for Children, including Textbooks

RATAN SUBSCRIPTION SERVICES
5A, Citizen Enclave, Sector 14, Extn., Rohini, New Delhi-110085
✆ 30125002, Fax: 91-11-23240195
ratansubscription@hotmail.com
Hd.Org.: Ashish Gupta

RATIONAL BUSINESS CORPORATION
New Delhi
✆ 27462300, 27462700, Fax: 22915357
ashish@desmat.com
Bus.Intt.: B.S.

RATIONAL LIFE PUBLICATIONS
Post Box No. 13, Gurgaon-122001 (Haryana)

RATIONALIST SOCIETY OF INDIA
Guru Nanak St., Barnala-148101 (Punjab)

RATNA BOOK HOUSE
7, Shyama Charan Dey St., Kolkata-700073 (West Bengal)

RATNA BOOK STORES
36, Akhil Mistry Lane, Kolkata-700009 (West Bengal)

RATNA PRAKASHAN
2/73, Viveknagar, Jadavpur, Kolkata-700075 (West Bengal)

RATNA SAGAR PVT. LTD.
Virat Bhavan, Mukherjee Nagar, Commercial Complex, Delhi-110009
✆ 27654095-99, 47038000,
Fax: 91-11-27650787, 47038099
rsagar@nda.vsnl.net.in
www.ratnasagar.com
Estd.: 1982; **Man.Dir.:** Dhanesh Kumar Jain
Br.: 39/18, Circular Road, United India Colony, Kodambakkam, Chennai-600024
✆ 23727550, 24800065, 24804009,
Fax: 91-44-42322050
rsagar.chn@ratnasagar.com
• 1-1-287/31/1, Bapu Nagar, Municipal Market Road, Chikkadpally, Hyderabad-500020
✆ 66611100, 27662275, 64592220,
Fax: 91-40-27662275
rsagar.hyd@ratnasagar.com
• 60, Ist Floor, Dr Sundari Mohan Avenue, Kolkata-700014 ✆ 22846321, 22866086,
Fax: 91-33022845807
rsagar.kol@ratnasagar.com
• D-150-C, Gautam Marg, Nirman Nagar, Jaipur-302019 ✆ 3101725,
Fax: 91-141-3101725
rsagar.jaipur@ratnasagar.com
• A-1539, Indira Nagar, Lucknow-226016
✆ 2310276, Fax: 91-522-2310161
rsagar.lko@ratnasagar.com
• 50/935-E, Bank Junction Edappally, Kochi-682024 ✆ 6577993,
Fax: 91-484-4055972
rsagar.kochi@ratnasagar.com
• No. 116, 1st Floor, 1st Main Road, M.L.A. Layout, R.T. Nagar, Bangalore-560032
✆ 23637479, Fax: 91-80-23637479
rsagar.blr@ratnasagar.com
• Ground Floor (Eastern Side), 29/1, Chandragandhi Nagar, Bypass Road, Madurai-625016 ✆ 91-452-6462888
rsagar.madurai@ratnasagar.com
• 11, Hem Kunj, Vijay Park, Opp. IMA Blood Bank, Dehradun (Uttarakhand)
✆ 91-135-3245795
rsagar.ddn@ratnasagar.com
• 205, Mewad, E.S. Patan, Wala Compound, L.B.S. Marg, Opp. Shreyas Cinema, Ghatkopar (W), Mumbai-400086
rsagar.mumbai@ratnasagar.com
• 59, F.C. Road, Uzan Bazar, Guwahati-780001 ✆ 91-361-2731762
rsagar.guw@ratnasagar.com
• Flat No. 101, Karpuras Asha Apartment, Kavi Raman Path, Nageswar Colony, Patna-800001
✆ 2526026, Fax: 91-612- 2526026
rsagar.patna@ratnasagar.com
• 128/41, Block-D, Kidwai Nagar, Kanpur ✆ 91-512-3022144, 3046495
rsagar.kanpur@ratnasagar.com
Bus.Intt.: Pub., WS, L.S. & Rt.;
Spl.: Juvenile/Children, Gen. & Fiction etc.

RATNAKAR BOOKSELLERS
High School Rd., Near Deval Talkies, Miraj-416410 (Maharashtra)
✆ (O) 2222564, 2220107 (R) 2224285,
Fax: 2227574
Estd.: 1999; **Prop.:** Prakash Shaha;
Bus.Intt.: WS, L.S. & Rt.

RATTAN PRAKASHAN MANDIR
4715/16, 21, Darya Ganj, Dayanand Marg, New Delhi-110002
✆ (O) 23264905 (R) 0562-350366
Prt.: Prem Chand Jain, Ravi Jain, Atul Jain
Bus.Intt.: Pub., Rt., L.S.; **Spl.:** Beh.Sci., Soc.Sci., Mang., Tech.

RAVANI BANDHU BOOKSELLERS
Noti Bazar, Near Post Office, Vallabh Vidyanagar-388120 (Gujarat)
✆ 230158
Estd.: 1959; **Hd.Org.:** Ravani Anjantray Jamnadas

RAVE MEDIA
22-C, Pocket E, Siddhartha Extn., New Delhi-110014

✆ 26340503, Fax: 91-11-26349902
✉ niha@ravemedia.in
www.ravemedia.in
Hd.Org.: Rahul Srivastava

RAVI BOOK HOUSE
2/469, Jyoti, 14th Rd., Chembur, Mumbai-400071 (Maharashtra)
✆ 25518925

RAVI BOOKS
C-9/39, Yamuna Vihar, Delhi-110053
✆ 22914588 ▮ 9810554502
✉ ravibooksdelhi@rediffmail.com
Prop.: Ravi Verma; **Bus.Intt.:** Rt., Pub.; **Spl.:** Acad., Beh.Sci., Soc.Sci.

RAVI KIRAN PRAKASHAN
C/o Ravikiran Mhalas, 8/B, Vanavihar Colony, Near Bhosala Military School, Nasik-422005 (Maharashtra)

RAVI POCKET BOOKS
33, Hari Nagar, Meerut City (Uttar Pradesh)
✆ 91-121-2531011, 2521067
✉ a2zcomputerbooks@yahoo.co.in
Hd.Org.: Manesh Jain
Bus.Intt.: Pub.; **Spl.:** Books on Computer, Electronics as well as dictionaries in Hindi

RAVI SAHITYA PRAKASHAN
Hall Bazar, Amritsar-143006 (Punjab)

RAVINDER PRAKASHAN
2/8A, Jangpura A, New Delhi-110014
✆ 24633784
Prop.: Vinod Kumar; **Spl.:** Books for Children and Gen. Books

RAVINDER PRAKASHAN
3/1, Batuk Krishan Banerjee Marg, New Katra, Allahabad-211002 (Uttar Pradesh)
✆ 26640948, 2641594
Hd.Org.: Anuj Bhargav

RAVINDER SINGH & SONS
410, Model Town Market, Near Greater Junction, Jalandhar-144003 (Punjab)
✆ 91-181-2461681
✉ arundhi99@hotmail.com
Hd.Org.: Ravinder Singh
Bus.Intt.: Pub.; **Spl.:** Educational and Reference Books

RAVINDRA BOOK HOUSE
202, Sangita Flats, Chandranagar Society, Waghodia Rd., Opp. Water Tank, Vadodara-390019 (Gujarat)
Hd.Org.: Vinod Parikh

RAVINDRA BOOK SHOP
46/1, Church St., Bangalore-560001 (Gujarat)

RAVINDRA PRESS
1590, Madarsa Road, Kashmere Gate, Delhi-110006
✆ 23869812, Fax: 91-11-23867791
Hd.Org.: Vishwanath
Bus.Intt.: Pub.; **Spl.:** Children's Books, Encyclopaedias, Biographies, Science Books, etc. in Hindi

RAVIRAJ PRAKASHAN
458/2, Sadashiv, Tilak Rd., Pune-411030 (Maharashtra)

RAVISH PUBLISHERS
B-1, 101, Anusuya Enclave, Near Shinde Chhatri, Wanowari, Pune-411004 (Maharashtra) ✆ 2670510

RAWAT BOOKSELLERS
3-NA-20, Jawahar Nagar, Jaipur-302004 (Rajasthan)
✆ 2651748, 2657006, Fax: 2651748
✉ rawatbooks@pinkline.net, rawatpublication@hotmail.com
Prop.: K.C. Rawat

RAWAT PUBLICATIONS
Satyam Apartments, Sector-3, Jain Temple Rd., Jawahar Nagar, Jaipur-302004 (Rajasthan)
✆ 2651748, 2657006, Fax: 2651748
✉ info@rawatbooks.com
www.rawatbooks.com
Hd.Org.: Pranit Rawat; **Bus.Intt.:** Pub. and Dist.; **Spl.:** Sol., Anthropology, Geo., Env. Sci., Man. and Litt.

RAY'S PUBLISHING HOUSE
17-A, Jadu Mitra Lane, Kolkata-700004 (West Bengal)
✆ 255594837

READ BOOKS
G-31, Commercial Complex, Sheikh Sarai Phase-I, New Delhi-110017
✆ 40529050, Fax: 91-11-40529050
✉ readbooks@gmail.com
Hd.Org.: Asha Gilotra
Bus.Intt.: Pub. and Supplier; **Spl.:** Books on Soc.Sci., Humanities, Management, Science & Technology, Fiction and Reference Books

READER'S CHANNEL
E2/506, Bharat Nagar, 5th Floor, 342 Grant Rd., Mumbai-400007 (Maharashtra)
✆ 23079026

READERS CORNER
Fraser Rd., Patna-800001 (Bihar)
✆ 0612-2225958, Fax: 2221099
✉ readerscorner1969@rediffmail.com
Estd.: 1969; **Prop.:** Bijoy Kumar Sinha;

Bus.Intt.: L.S. and Rt.; **Spl.:** Gen. and Trade, Acad., Professional and Children Indian and Foreign Books

READERS PARADISE
63, Warden Rd., Breach Candy,
Mumbai-400026 (Maharashtra)

READERS PUBLICATIONS
P. Box No. 75, Thiruvalla-689101 (Kerala)
✆ (O) 0473-2636395 (R) 2619416,
Fax: 0473-2631308
✉ readers@md4.vsnl.net.in
Estd.: 1988; **Dir.:** Raju George; **Bus.Intt.:** Pub. and B.S.; **Spl.:** Religious Christian Books and Gen. Books

READERS SERVICE
59/5A, Garfa Main Road, Kolkata-700075 (West Bengal)
✆ 91-33-24180158
Hd.Org.: Tandrita Chandra
Bus.Intt.: Pub.; **Spl.:** Books on Soc.Sci. and Environment in Bangla

READERS VISION
210, IInd Floor, Jaina Tower IIIrd,
A-1, Janak Puri, New Delhi-110058
✆ 25618864

READWELL PUBLICATIONS
B-8, Rattan Jyoti Building,
18, Rajendra Place, New Delhi-110008
✆ 25712649, Fax: 91-11-25812385
✉ readwell@sify.com
Hd.Org.: Amit Chowdhary
Bus.Intt.: Pub.; **Spl.:** Books on Learing Indian & Foreign Languages, Dictionaries, etc. as well as Children's Books and Textbooks

READWORTHY PUBLICATIONS PVT. LTD.
A/18, Mohan Garden, Near Nawada Metro Station, New Delhi-110059
✆ 25371324, Fax: 91-11-25371323
✉ info@readworthypub.com
🌐 www.readworthypub.com
Hd.Org.: Shalaj Mittal; **Bus.Intt.:** Pub.; **Spl.:** Academic, Reference and Scholarly Books on Humanities, Soc.Sci., Medicine, Environment, Science & Technology, etc.

REBUS PUBLISHING HOUSE
Shri Bhat, Post Box-577 GPO, Srinagar, Kashmir-190011 (Jammu & Kashmir)
✆ 252005
Estd.: 1990; **Hd.Org.:** M.G. Ahmed; **Bus.Intt.:** Pub., WS, L.S. and Rt.

RED INK LITERARY AGENCY
Flat No. 6, Khan Market,
New Delhi-110003
✆ 24694610, Fax: 91-11-24618637
✉ anuj.redink@gmail.com
🌐 www.redinkliteraryagency.com
Hd.Org.: Anuj B. Malhotra
Bus.Intt.: Pub.; **Spl.:** South Asian Litt. in Eng. and a Literary Agency showcasing Indian Litt.

REFLECT PUBLICATIONS
30, Mahatma Gandhi Rd., Kolkata-700009 (West Bengal)
✆ 033-23500013

REGAL BOOK DEPOT
2607-A, Nai Sarak, Delhi-110006
✆ (O) 23283743 (R) 23253743,
Fax: 011-23276198
Prop.: Madan Mohan Gupta
Br.: Kamal Pushap Prakashan, 2607, Nai Sarak, Delhi-110006
✆ (R) 23284125
Spl.: Hindi Litt.

REGENCY BOOK SHOP
Hotel Hyatt Regency, R.K. Puram,
New Delhi-110066

REGENCY PUBLICATIONS
20/36-G, Old Market, West Patel Nagar,
New Delhi-110008
✆ 25883539, 25884571 ▮ 9811011264,
Telefax: 25783571
✉ regency@satyam.net.in
🌐 www.regency-books.com
Sh.: 4772/23, Bharat Ram Rd., Darya Ganj, New Delhi-110002 ✆ 23251405, 24060485
Estd.: 1972; **Prop.:** Arun Verma;
Bus.Intt.: Pub.; **Spl.:** Soc.Sci., Humanities, Women/Child Studies, Law, Botany, Agri., Edu., Art and Archaeology, Rel., Studies in North-East India and Topical

REGENERATIONS
Pooja Apartment, 4B, Ansari Road,
Darya Ganj, New Delhi-110002
✆ 23255799, 23287589, Fax: 91-11-23270385
✉ aryanbooks@vsnl.com
🌐 www.aryanbooks.com
Hd.Org.: Vikas Arya; **Bus.Intt.:** Pub.

REGIONAL CANCER CENTRE
P.O. Box 2417, Medical College Campus,
Trivandrum-695011 (Kerala)

REHBAR CORNER
2936, Kalan Masjid, Turkman Gate,
Delhi-110006
Bus.Intt.: Exp.

REKHA BOOK DISTRIBUTORS
Chennai (Tamil Nadu)
✆ 28141665
✉ rekhabhs@md5.vsnl.net.in

REKHA-O-LIPI
23-B, Ghosh Lane, Kolkata-700006
(West Bengal)

REKHA PRAKASHAN
16, Darya Ganj, New Delhi-110002
✆ (O) 23279904, 23279907 (R) 26321783, Fax: 91-11-2321783
✉ bnaryan@satyam.net.in
🌐 www.museumoffolkandtribalart.org
Hd.Org.: B.N. Aryan; **Bus.Intt.:** Pub.; **Spl.:** Art & Indology, especially Folk and Tribal Art of Indian in English

REKHA PRINTERS PVT. LTD.
A-102/1, Okhla, Industrial Estate, Phase-II, Delhi-110020
✆ 26830401, 26829337, Fax: 26852280
✉ krishan@nde.vsnl.net.in
Bus.Intt.: Exp., Pub. and Printers

REKHA PUBLISHING HOUSE
A-406/7, South Gamri, Delhi-110053

RELIABLE BOOK SERVICE
Shreyans Building, 46, Ada Bazar, (Opp Triwedi Sadan), Indore-452004 (Madhya Pradesh)
✆ 2763269, Fax: 2532298
Estd.: 1992; **Hd.Org.:** Dharmendra Jains; **Bus.Intt.:** L.S.; **Spl.:** Sci., Tech. and Man.

RELIANCE DISTRIBUTORS
89/2, Gali No. 1, Radhey Puri Extn. II, Trans Yamuna, Delhi-110051
Hd.Org.: Rajesh Kumar; **Bus.Intt.:** L.S.; **Spl.:** Comm., Med. Tech.

RELIANCE PUBLISHING HOUSE
3026/7H, Shiv Chowk, Ranjit Nagar, South Patel Nagar, New Delhi-110008
✆ 25842605, 25842748, 25847377, Fax: 25842605
✉ reliance@indianbooksindustry.com, rphbooks@indiatimes.com
🌐 www.ibicom.com
Estd.: 1985; **Prop.:** Dr. S.K. Bhatia
Br.: J/436, Baljit Nagar, New Delhi-110008
✆ 25786769
✉ info@indianbookindustry.com
Bus.Intt.: Pub., WS, L.S. & Rt., Imp., Exp.; **Spl.:** Trade Directories

REM DISTRIBUTORS INDIA
A-13, Green Park Extension, Flat F2, Ist Floor, New Delhi-110016
✆ 26535929, 25500998, Fax: 26969159, 26117058
✉ dkginfo@bol.net.in
Hd.Org.: Christopher Vaughan
Bus.Intt.: Dist.; **Spl.:** Books and Magazines from Abroad

REMADHAV PUBLICATIONS PVT. LTD.
C-22, R.D.C., 3rd Floor, Raj Nagar, Ghaziabad-201001 (Uttar Pradesh)
✆ 2754228, Fax: 91-120-2702672
✉ contact@remadhav.com
🌐 www.remadav.com
Hd.Org.: Atul Garg; **Bus.Intt.:** Pub.; **Spl.:** Litt. from all Indian Languages

RENAISSANCE PUBLISHING HOUSE
C-69, Sitar Nagar, Parmara Rd., New Delhi-110051

RENOMMEE HOUSE OF PUBLICATIONS
D-33, South Extension Part-I, New Delhi-110049
✆ (O) 24615544, 24693355 (R) 24694422, 24698807
Estd.: 1981; **Hd.Org.:** Neeraj Gupta

RENUKA PRAKASHAN
"Sobat" 24 Swatantrya Sainik Colony, Wageshwarwadi, Aurangabad-431001 (Maharashtra)
✆ 2337506

REPLIKA PRESS PVT. LTD.
A-229, DSIDC, Narela Industrial Park, Narela, Delhi-110040
✆ 27781158, 27781709, 27781610, Fax: 91-11-27781254
Hd.Org.: Bhuvnesh Seth; **Bus.Intt.:** Exp., Manufacturers

REPRO SALES INDIA PVT. LTD.
34/2, Beadon St., Kolkata-700006 (West Bengal) **Bus.Intt.:** Exp.

REPUBLIC BOOK HOUSE
M.G. Rd., Katihar-854105 (Bihar)

RESEARCH & INFORMATION SYSTEM
40-B, Lodhi Estate, New Delhi-110003

RESEARCH BOOK CENTRE
4348/4C, Madan Mohan St., Ansari Rd., New Delhi-110002

RESEARCH BOOK CENTRE
1-29, Bhuta Niwas, Dr. Ambedkar Rd., Matunga, Mumbai-560041 (Maharashtra)

RESEARCH FOUNDATION
Mumbai (Maharashtra)
✉ resfaxexports@indiatimes.com
Bus.Intt.: B.S.

RESEARCH FOUNDATION FOR SCIENCE TECHNOLOGY AND ECOLOGY
A-60, Hauz Khas, New Delhi-110016
✆ 26968077, 26863772, Fax: 91-11-26856795
✉ vshiva@vsnl.com
Ch.Exe.: Mrs. Radha Holla;
Bus.Intt.: Dealer; **Spl.:** Books and Posters

RESEARCH INDIA PRESS
E-6/34, Sangam Vihar, New Delhi-110062
✆ 91-11-26047013
✉ researchindiapress@yahoo.co.in
Hd.Org.: Suman Kumar Pathak
Bus.Intt.: Pub. and Dist.; **Spl.**: Books on Soc.Sci., Archaeology, Numismatics, Buddhism, etc.

RESEARCH INDIA PUBLICATIONS
D1/71, Top Floor, Sector-16,
Rohini, Delhi-110089
✆ 65394240, Fax: 91-11-27297815
✉ info@ripublication.com,
subscription@ripublication.com,
services@ripublication.com
www.ripublication.com
Estd.: 1998; **Hd.Org.**: M.K. Jha
Br.: B-2/84, Ground Floor, Rohini, Sector-16, Delhi-110089
Bus.Intt.: Pub. and Dist.; **Spl.**: Research Journals on Science and Technology, Mathematics, Mechanics, Oceanography, Environment etc.

RESEARCH PRESS
1st Floor, Arun House, 2/25, Ansari Rd.,
New Delhi-110002
✆ 23284894, 23281819, Fax: 91-11-23281819
✉ researchpress@vsnl.com
www.researchpress.co.in
Prop.: Ajay Parmar; **Bus.Intt.**: Dist. & Pub.'s Rep.; **Spl.**: Comm./Man., Fiction/Gen., Soc.Sci.

RESEARCH PUBLICATIONS
89, Tripolia Bazar, Jaipur-300002
(Rajasthan)
✆ (O) 0141-2318415 (R) 0141-2570320
Fax: 0141-2563256
Bus.Intt.: Pub. and Suppliers; **Spl.**: Comm. & Man., Humanities, Law, Gen. and Other Books

RESEARCH PUBLISHERS
Inside Merti Gate, Jodhpur-342001
(Rajasthan)

RESEARCH TRENDS
Council of Scientific Research, Integration,
T.C. 29/1121, Sreekanteswaram,
Trivandrum-695023 (Kerala)
✆ 344424, Fax: 344423
✉ rtrends@md2.vsnl.net.in

RESEARCHCO
1865, Tri Nagar, Delhi-110035
✆ 27233889, 27128547
Hd.Org.: Naresh Kumar Jain; **Bus.Intt.**: Rt., Exp. and L.S.

RESEARCHCO BOOK CENTRE
4735/22, 2nd Floor, Prakash Deep Building,
Ansari Road, Darya Ganj, New Delhi-110002
✆ 23240257, Fax: 91-11-23240273
✉ akjain@del2.vsnl.net.in
Hd.Org.: Arvind Kumar Jain, H.K. Lakhiani;
Bus.Intt.: Stockist and Dist.; **Spl.**: Sci. and Tech. Research Books, Annual and Serial Publications and Back Volume Journals

RESOURCE CENTRE FOR ADULT AND CONTINUING EDUCATION
E-8/195, Thilanga, Bhopal-39
(Madhya Pradesh)
✆ 4277911, Fax: 91-755-2562647
Hd.Org.: Swati Chandorkar
Bus.Intt.: Pub.; **Spl.**: Books in Hindi Language for Rural Folk, the Underprivileged and Neo-Litt.

RESPONSE BOOKS
B-1/11, Mohan Cooperative,
Industrial Area, Mathura Road,
New Delhi-110044
✆ 40539222, Fax: 91-11-40539234
✉ info@sagepub.in
www.sagepub.in
Hd.Org.: Vivek Mehra; **Bus.Intt.**: Pub.;
Spl.: Books for Indian Business Community

RESPONSE BOOKS
B-42, Panchsheel Enclave, New Delhi-110017
✆ 26491290, Fax: 26491290
✉ responsebooks@indiasage.com
www.indiasage.com
Estd.: 1995; **Hd.Org.**: Tejeshwar Singh;
Spl.: Business and Mang.

REWA BOOK DISTRIBUTORS CO.
33, Tansen Complex, Sirmaour Complex,
Rewa-486001 (Madhya Pradesh)
✆ 222093

RGTI BOOK DIVISION
Rgti Technology Solutions (P) Ltd., 1E, 44, Eldams Rd., Teynampet, Chennai-600018
(Tamil Nadu)
✆ 91-44-24335238, 24335272, 32660278
✉ vijay.k@rgtitech.com
www.anthempress.com
Man.: Vijay K. Janardanan

RICHA (INDIA) PUBLISHERS
Bisson Ka Chowk, Bikaner-334001
(Rajasthan)

RICHA PRAKASHAN
New Delhi
✆ 24640153, Fax: 24634935
✉ ragupta@ndb.vsnl.net.in
Bus.Intt.: Pub.

RICHA PRAKASHAN
11, Chandan Apartment, Almora Rd.,
Pachpakhadi, Thane-421190 (Maharashtra)

RICHA PUSTAK BHANDAR
Rajaun, Bhagalpur-813107 (Bihar)
Bus.Intt.: Pub. and B.S.

RICHARDCARSWELL.COM
16, Ansari Road, Near Mahavir Vatika, Darya Ganj, Delhi-110002
9310260022, Fax: 91-11-23911057
kaushalgoyal@yahoo.com
www.richardcarswell.com
Hd.Org.: Kaushal Goyal; **Bus.Intt.:** Pub. and Dist.; **Spl.:** Richard Carswell's Books on Word Power, Self-improvement, etc.

RIFCON SAT SAHATIYA KENDRA
Jodhpur (Rajasthan)
308155
rathisuresh@hotmal.com, suresh@sureshrathiindia.com

RIHA ENTERPRISES
AM-172, Shalimar Bagh, Delhi-110056
Bus.Intt.: Exp.

RIMA PUBLISHING HOUSE
EA-33, Inderpuri, New Delhi-110012
25834855 9810438091
Hd.Org.: Surinder Singh Sethi; **Bus.Intt.:** Pub. and Dist.; **Spl.:** Encyclopaedias, Edu. Books on Jammu and Kashmir in English

RINKI BOOK STALL
1, Bankim Chatterjee St. (front of 75 No. Stall), Kolkata-700073 (West Bengal)

RISHAB & COMPANY
122-B, Ahinsa Vihar, Sector-9, Rohini, Delhi-110085
27863380, 27860147 9810493153
Hd.Org.: Rishabh Nand Jain;
Bus.Intt.: L.S.; **Spl.:** Text Books

RISHBHCHARAN JAIN AND SANTTI
4697/5-21A, Darya Ganj, New Delhi-110002
23264168
Hd.Org.: Digdarshancharan Jain

RISHI EXPORTS
Arch No. 29, Malakshmi Bridge, West Approach, Mumbai-400034 (Maharashtra)
24925651, 24927383, 24942538
Fax: 022-24950392, 22048163
Telefax: 011-86297 DANI IN
ibhpba@vsnl.com
Bus.Intt.: Exp.

RISHI PUBLICATIONS
G.P.O. Box 1130, Varanasi-221001 (Uttar Pradesh)
2221337, Fax: 0542-2221337
Prop.: Ullas Sharma; **Spl.:** Soc.Sci., Humanities, Industry

RISING PUBLISHERS
K-4/4, Model Town-II, Delhi-110009
55496808, 27415504 9818300870
www.sadhnapublications.com
Hd.Org.: Nidhi Kaura
Bus.Intt.: Pub.; **Spl.:** Children's Books and General Books in English

RISING SUN TRADERS
F-141, Mast Garh, Jammu-Tawi-180001 (Jammu & Kashmir)
2543126
Hd.Org.: Sunil Sharma; **Bus.Intt.:** Pub., WS, L.S. & Rt.; **Spl.:** Humanities & Soc.Sci., Sci. & Tech., Med.

RITANA BOOKS
81, Defence Colony, Flyover Market, New Delhi-110024
24617278, Fax: 24636063
ritana@vsnl.com
www.ritanabooks.com
Estd.: 1984; **Ch.Exe.:** Rock Furtado;
Bus.Intt.: Pub., WS, L.S. & Rt., Imp., Exp.;
Spl.: Humanities & Soc.Sci., Gen. & Fiction

RITIKA BOOK HOUSE
503, Skyline House, 85, Nehru Place, New Delhi-110019

RITU PRAKASHAN
Khajuri Bazar, Indore-452002 (Madhya Pradesh)
2451567

RITWIK PRAKASHAN
24, Vitthalbhai Patel Bhavan, Rafi Marg, New Delhi-110001
23725470, 23514862, Fax: 23558613, 23542142
tarunvijay@vsnl.com
www.panchjanya.com
Hd.Org.: Rajrani; **Bus.Intt.:** Pub.;
Spl.: Books on Travel and Culture, Especially on Kailash Mansarovar, in Indian Languages

RIVERSTONE PRESS
44, Maheshwari Apartments, Sector-14, Plot No. 6, Rohini, Delhi-110085
55151448, Fax: 27345935
riverstonepress@vsnl.net
Hd.Org.: Richie Maheshwary;
Bus.Intt.: Printing, Copyediting, Typesetting, Design, etc.

RIYAZ IMPEX
10/11, Kusumbhai Building, 2/6, Ismail Curstay St., Mumbai-400003 (Maharashtra)
23460577, 23473257, Fax: 23471803
riyazimp@vsnl.com
Bus.Intt.: Exp., B.S.

ROHAN BOOK COMPANY
G-22, Indraprastha Apartments,
Plot No. 114, Patpar Ganj,
Delhi-110092
✆ 22303898, Fax: 91-11-22309396
rohanbooks@gmail.com
www.rohanbooks.net
Prop.: Arun Jain, Vinod Kalia
Bus.Intt.: Pub.; **Spl.:** Children's Journal and Edu. Books

ROLI BOOKS (P) LTD.
M-75, Greater Kailash, Part-II Market,
New Delhi-110048
✆ 29212271, 29212782, 40682000
Fax: 91-11-29217185
info@rolibooks.com,
editorial@rolibooks.com
www.rolibooks.com
Estd.: 1978; **Dir.:** Pramod Kapoor
Br.: 80/275, Near Patel Marg, Mansarovar, Jaipur-302020 (Rajasthan)
✆ 0141-2781015
• 59/103, D-1, Sigra, Varanasi-221001 (Uttar Pradesh)
✆ 0542-2221940, 2221941
Bus.Intt.: Pub.; **Spl.:** Humanities & Soc.Sci.

ROMIL PUBLISHERS (P) LTD.
A-18, Gali No. 10, East Azad Nagar,
Delhi-110051
✆ (O) 22211154, 22436849 (R) 22421652, 22217558, Fax: 011-22212435, 22048017
romilpub@ndf.vsnl.net.in
Estd.: 1992; **Hd.Org.:** I.P. Gupta

ROOPA BOOKS PVT. LTD.
S-12, Shopping Complex, Tilak Nagar,
Jaipur-302004 (Rajasthan)
Hd.Org.: Mahendra Gupta; **Bus.Intt.:** Pub., L.S.; **Spl.:** Soc.Sci.

ROOPAL BOOK STALL
14, Chanakya Complex, Vania Vad College Rd., Nadiad (Distt. Kheda) (Gujarat)
✆ 02692-235353
and_roopalbook@rediffmail.com

ROSHAN BOOK SERVICE
544, Jheel Khuranja, Delhi-110051
9990213714
Hd.Org.: Roshanlal

ROSHAN-DI-HATTI
4424, Nai Sarak, Delhi-110006
✆ 22524809
Estd.: 1990; **Bus.Intt.:** B.S. and Rt.

ROSHANI PRAKASHAN
212, CL/A, Ashok Mitra Road, Kanchrapara, North 24 Parganas-743145 (West Bengal)
✆ 91-33-25850249
roshnaiprakashan@sify.com
Hd.Org.: Prashant Bharati; **Bus.Intt.:** Dist. and Organizer

ROSS MASOOD HALL
Aligarh Muslim University, Aligarh-202002 (Uttar Pradesh)

ROUTLEDGE (TAYLOR AND FRANCIS GROUP)
512, Mercantile House,
15, Kasturba Gandhi Marg,
New Delhi-110001
✆ 23712131, 23351453, Fax: 23712123
routledg@satyam.net.in
www.tandf-co.uk
Hd.Org.: Prabir Bhambal; **Bus.Intt.:** Pub.; **Spl.:** Sci., Humanities, Soc.Sci., Med., Engg., Psy., Asian Studies, etc.

ROY & ASSOCIATES
2, Guru Prasad Chowdhury Lane,
Kolkata-700009 (West Bengal)

ROY BOOK CONCERN
2, Shyama Charan Dey St.,
Kolkata-700073 (West Bengal)

ROY BOOK PLACE
10, Shyama Charan Dey St., Kolkata-700073 (West Bengal)

ROY PUBLICATIONS
Block-14, Flat-119, Rajendra Nagar,
Patna-16 (Bihar)
Sh: Arya Kumar Rd. (Bihar)
✆ 2672544, 2663343, Fax: 2669954
roy60@sify.com
Estd.: 1982; **Prop.:** Ashok Kumar Roy
Br.: Arun Kr. Roy, 5/1425/1, Mohan Nagar, Karmchari Sahkari Awaas Samiti Ltd., Vasundhra, Sector-5, Ghaziabad (Uttar Pradesh) ✆ 2883485
Bus.Intt.: WS, L.S., Rt.; **Spl.:** Sci. & Tech., Med.

ROY PUBLISHER
Kalibari Rd., Siliguri, Darjeeling (West Bengal)

ROYAL BOOK DEPOT
College Rd., Kottayam-686001 (Kerala)
✆ 0481-2566648, 2567023
Estd.: 1970; **Prop.:** M.V. Thomas;
Bus.Intt.: Pub. and B.S. of Gen. Books

ROYAL BIBLIOMAN
D.V.G. Rd., Basavanagudi, Bangalore-560004 (Karnataka)
✆ 080-6615209, 6694074, Fax: 6615209
bkdas@pacific.net.in
welcom.to/royalbibiloman
Ch.Exe.: Bipin Kumar; **Bus.Intt.:** B.S., L.S. & Imp.; **Spl.:** Sci., Tech, Med.

ROYAL BOOK DEPOT
Bhilai (Madhya Pradesh)
✆ 431093, Fax: 0788-392386
royalboosks@rediff.com

ROYAL BOOK SERVICE
2652, Khajoor St., Behind Moti Mahal Restaurant, Darya Ganj, New Delhi-110002
✆ 26986238
Hd.Org.: Farman U. Khan; **Bus.Intt.:** Dist.; **Spl.:** Fashion, Furniture

ROYAL BOOK TRADERS
Central Administrative Tribunal, Faridkot House, Copernicus Marg, New Delhi-110001
✆ 23385540, 23385904, Fax: 25169542
Hd.Off.: 18/18A, Moti Nagar, New Delhi-110015
✆ 25433599, 25168022
Prt.: Rajiv Sachar, Sunjiv Sachar; **Bus.Intt.:** Rt., L.S., Imp. & Dist.; **Spl.:** Law Books & Law Journals

ROYAL EDUCATIONAL BOOK DEPOT
KC-35A, Ashok Vihar Phase-I, Delhi-110052
✆ 27244399
Estd.: 1948; **Hd.Org.:** Amit Anand; **Bus.Intt.:** Dist.; **Spl.:** Books on Law

ROYAL EDUCATIONAL STORES
Old No. B-53, New No. A-117, Shop No. 6, Capt. Satish Marg, Rishi Nagar, Rani Bagh, New Delhi-110034
✆ 27034400, Fax: 91-11-27034832
info@royaleducationbooks.com
www.royaleducationalstores.com
Hd.Org.: Vishal Sabharwal
Bus.Intt.: Pub.; **Spl.:** Educational Books for Children and Manufacturer of Educational aids

ROYAL PUBLISHERS
57/2E, College St., Kolkata-700073 (West Bengal)

ROYAL PUBLISHERS (PVT.) LTD.
G-6/4832, Ansari Rd., Darya Ganj, New Delhi-110002
✆ (O) 23253648, 23244667 (R) 22821397, Fax: 91-11-23250591
royalpublishers2002@yahoo.co.in
Estd.: 1998; **Man.Dir.:** Rajender Kumar, K.K. Gupta; **Bus.Intt.:** Pub.

RUBY BOOK CONCERN
15, Bankim Chatterjee St., Kolkata-700073 (West Bengal)

RUBY PUBLISHERS
42/1, Beniatola Lane, Kolkata-700073 (West Bengal)

RUDRA INTERNATIONAL HOUSE (P) LTD.
25-B/2, New Rohtak Rd., Near Liberty Cinema New Delhi-110005
✆ 25781565, 25781566, 25781567, Fax: 91-11-25781561
Hd.Org.: Rajesh Gupta
Bus.Intt.: Manufacturers of Book Publication

RUMA PUBLICATIONS
15A, Tamer Lane, Kolkata-700009 (West Bengal)

RUMI RUPAK
New Market, Naojan-785604 (Assam)
Bus.Intt.: Pub.

RUNA BOOK STORES
5, Bidhan Sarani, Kolkata-700006 (West Bengal)

RUNNER
13C, College Row, Kolkata-700009 (West Bengal)

RUNWAL PAPER STORES
Chaumukhi Pul, Ratlam (Madhya Pradesh)

RUPA & CO.
Post Box No. 12333, 15, Bankim Chatterjee St., Kolkata-700073 (West Bengal)
✆ 22416597, 22410691, Fax: 22410691
info@rupabooks.com
www.rupapublications.com
Estd.: 1936; **Prt.:** Raju Barman
Br.: P.B. No. 7017, 7/16, Ansari Rd., Darya Ganj, New Delhi-110002
✆ 23278586, 23272161, 23266759, 23270260
9810118431, Fax: 23277294
info@rupabooks.com
• 135, South Malaka, Allahabad-211001 (Uttar Pradesh)
✆ 2606833, Fax: 2611020
• G-1 & 2, Ghaswalla Tower, P.G. Solanki Path, Lamington Rd., Mumbai-400007 (Maharashtra)
✆ 23082631, Fax: 23088212
rupa@hom8.vsnl.net.in
• Bangalore (Karnataka)
✆ 6679127-30
rupadakshinblr@yahoo.co.in
• Chennai (Tamil Nadu)
✆ 28218301-02
rupadakshinche@vsnl.net
• Hyderabad (Andhra Pradesh)
✆ 23222360, 23222370
rupaandcohyd@hotmail.com
Bus.Intt.: Pub., WS, L.S. & Rt., Imp., Exp.; **Spl.:** Humanities & Soc.Sci., Sci. & Tech., Med., Law, Juvenile/Children, General & Fiction etc.

RUPA & CO. (DAKSHIN)
F-1/11, Model Town, Delhi-110009
✆ 27129101, Fax: 27436867
Hd.Org.: R.K. Mehra; **Bus.Intt.:** Dist.; **Spl.:** Gen., Trade and Acad. Books

RUPA PRAKASHANI
37/5, Beniatola Lane, Kolkata-700009 (West Bengal)

RUPAL AGENCY
10-B, Sattar Taluka Society, Opp. High Court, Ahmedabad-380014 (Gujarat)
Bus.Intt.: Pub. and Dist.

RUPALEE PUBLICATIONS
Couri Rd., Anand Kaira-388001 (Gujarat)
✆ 225627, 226237

RUPALI BOOK STALL
14, Bankim Chatterjee St., Kolkata-700073 (West Bengal)

RUPAYANA
27, M.G. Rd., Rampurawala Building, Indore-452007 (Madhya Pradesh)
✆ 2531720 ▮ 9826031720
Fax: 2557593
Estd.: 1949; **Prop.:** S.N. Rupayana; **Bus.Intt.:** Rt. and B.S.; **Spl.:** Gen. and Paperback Books on All Sub. in English and Hindi

RUPY PUBLISHERS
C-11, Sagar Apartment, 6, Tilak Marg, New Delhi

■ ■ ■

S. BANERJEE & CO.
6, Ramanath Majumder St., Kolkata-700009 (West Bengal)

S. BOOK SHOP
E-72, Ground Floor, South Extension, Part-I, New Delhi-110049
✆ 24649294, 24690653, Fax: 91-11-26854131
Estd.: 1995; **Ch.Exe.:** S.M. Zafar;
Bus.Intt.: B.S. of Arch., Graphics, Health & Care, Art & Crafts, Cooking, Gardening, Fashion Design, Fiction & Non-Fiction, Autobiography, Rel., Business Mang. and Children Books etc.

S. CHAND & COMPANY LTD.
7361, Ram Nagar, Qutab Rd., New Delhi-110055
✆ 23672080-81-82, Cable: ESCHAND, Fax: 91-11-23677446
✉ schand@vsnl.com
www.schandgroup.com
Estd.: 1937; **Man.Dir.:** Ravindra Kumar Gupta
Br.: No. 6, Ahuja Chambers, 1st Cross, Kumara Krupa Rd., Bangalore-560001
✆/Fax: 080-22268048
✉ bangalore@schandgroup.com
• 285-J, Bipin Bihari, Ganguli St., Kolkata-700012
✆ 033-22367459, Telefax: 22373914
✉ kolkata@schandgroup.com, clschand@del6.vsnl.net.in
• S.C.O. 6, 7 & 8 Sector-9D, Chandigarh-160017 ✆ 0172-2749376-77
✉ chandigarh@schandgroup.com
• 152, Anna Salai, Chennai-600002
✆ 28460026, Telefax: 044-28460026
✉ chennai@schandgroup.com
• Dilip Commercial (1st Floor), M.N. Rd., Pan Bazar, Guwahati-781001 ✆ 0361-2522155
✉ guwahati@schandgroup.com
• Sultan Bazar, Hyderabad-500195
✆ 040-24651135, 24744815, Telefax: 24651135
✉ hyderabad@schandgroup.com
• Mai Hiran Gate, Jalandhar-144008
✆ 0181-2401630
✉ jalandhar@schandgroup.com
• 613-7, M.G. Rd., Ernakulam, Kochi-682035 Telefax: 0484-2381740
✉ kochi@schandgroup.com
• Mahabeer Market, 25, Gwynne Rd., Lucknow-226018
✆ 0522-2284815, Telefax: 2226801
✉ lucknow@schandgroup.com
• Blacki House, 103/5, Wal Chand Hira Chand Marg, Opp. G.P.O., Mumbai-400001
✆ 022-22690881, Telefax: 22610885
✉ mumbai@schandgroup.com
• 3, Gandhi Sagar East, Nagpur-440002
✆ 2723901 Telefax: 0712-2723901
✉ nagpur@schandgroup.com
• 104, Citicentre, Ashok Govind Mitra Rd., Patna-800004, Telefax: 0612-2671366, 2302100
✉ patna@schandgroup.com
• 1st Floor, Bhartia Tower, Badambadi, Cuttack-753009 (Orissa)
✆ 2332580-81 ▮ 9437023695
• Heritage Nagar, Gujarat Vidyapeeth, Ashram Rd., Usmanpure, Ahmedabad
✆ 27541965, 27542369
• 1st Floor, 52-A, Rajpur Rd., Dehradun-248011
Bus.Intt.: Pub., WS, L.S. & Rt., Imp., Exp.;
Spl.: Humanities & Soc.Sci., Sci. & Tech., Med.

S. CHAND TECHNOLOGIES PVT. LTD.
48, Community Centre, New Friends Colony, New Delhi-110065
✆ 26326022-23, Fax: 26326024
✉ sctech@vsnl.net
Hd.Org.: Himanshu Gupta; **Spl.:** Edu. CD-ROMs and Magazines

S. DINESH & CO.
Post Box No. 813, Near Sitla Mandir, Circular Rd., Jalandhar-144008 (Punjab)
✆ 2280208, 2892393, 250979, Fax: 91-181-2281980
✉ dinesh97@jha.vsnl.net.in
Ch.Exe.: Paul Jain; **Bus.Intt.:** Pub., B.S., Exp.; **Spl.:** Edu. Books & Gen. Books

S. DINESH & COMPANY
3728, First Floor, Netaji Subhash Marg, Darya Ganj, New Delhi-110002
✆ 23250628, 2328260-76, Fax: 0181-2281980
✉ dinesh97@jla.vsnl.net.in
www.sdinesh&co.com
Hd.Org.: Shri Paul Jain, Dinesh Jain;
Bus.Intt.: Pub. and Exp.; **Spl.:** Edu. Books of College and Professional Level

S.K. KATARIA & SONS
4760/23, Ansari Road, Darya Ganj, New Delhi-110002
✆ 91-11-23243489
✉ katariabooks@yahoo.com
Hd.Org.: Sanjeev Kataria
Bus.Intt.: Pub.; **Spl.:** Engineering Books and Books on Computers

S. KARGER (INDIA)
B-5/132, Safdarjung Enclave, New Delhi-110029

✆ 26109931, Fax: 2606504
✉ fmunshi_unixl@yahoo.co.uk
Hd.Org.: K.K. Ghosh; **Bus.Intt.:** Rt., WS, Pub.'s Rep., L.S.

S. PAUL & CO.
2457, Nalwa St., Pahar Ganj, New Delhi-110055
✆ (O) 2527840 (R) 2601937
Estd.: 1958; **Bus.Intt.:** Pub.; **Spl.:** Children's School Textbooks in English and Hindi

S. SARCAR & CO.
14A, Nasiruddin Rd., Kolkata-700017 (West Bengal)

S. VISWANATHAN (PRINTERS & PUBLISHERS) PVT. LTD.
"Acton Lodge", 38, McNichols Rd., Chetput, Chennai-600031 (Tamil Nadu)
✆ (O) 28265623, 28265633 (R) 28263359, Fax: 28256002
✉ svprint@md2.vsnl.net.in
Estd.: 1971; **Hd.Org.:** V. Subramaneian
Br.: Pondicherry
✆ 334980, 223328, Fax: 334836
✉ sahmat@auroville.org.in
Bus.Intt.: Printing, Pub. and Exp.; **Spl.:** College Text Books

S.A. PUBLICATIONS
3185, Gali Azizuddin Wakeel, Kucha Pandit, Lal Kuan, Delhi-110006
✆ 26925606

S.B. BOOK STALL
M.C. Rd., Adoor, Pathanamthitta (Kerala)
Estd.: 1974, **Prop.:** P. Chellappan; **Bus.Intt.:** B.S.

S.B. MAKHIJA AND BROTHERS
39, Khurshid Market, Sadar Bazar, Delhi-110006
✆ 27770443, Fax: 25749195
Prop.: S.B. Makhija; **Bus.Intt.:** WS, Pub.'s Rep.; **Spl.:** Imported Children Books

S.B. PUBLICATIONS
Binod Behari, Cuttack-753002 (Orissa)
✆ 0671-2610739
Estd.: 1981; **Prop.:** Ch. N.K. Nanda; **Bus.Intt.:** Pub. and B.S.; **Spl.:** College Level Text and Reference Books as well as Oriya Literary and Works in English and Oriya

S.B.A. PUBLICATIONS
11, Merdith St., Kolkata-700072 (West Bengal)

S.B.C. PUBLISHERS
10980, East Park Rd., New Delhi-110005
✆ (O) 27522975 (R) 23544692
Estd.: 1989; **Prop.:** Tej Ram

S.B.D. SUBSCRIPTION SERVICES (SUDARSHAN BOOK DISTRIBUTORS)
51/1, New Market, Near Liberty Cinema, Karol Bagh, New Delhi-110005
✆ 25723138, 55450350, Fax: 91-11-25817268
✉ spdbooks@gmail.com
Ch.Exe.: Sudarshan Dhingra; **Bus.Intt.:** Dist.; **Spl.:** Books on Advertising, Graphics, Photography, Interior Fashion and Other type of Design Books & CD-ROMs

S.B.H. PRAKASHANA
42, Manjushri Nilaya, 2nd Stage, 2nd Cross, Vinobanagar, Shimoga-577204 (Karnataka)
✆ (R) 08182-249790
Estd.: 1975; **Hd.Org.:** Dr. S.B. Hosaman; **Bus.Intt.:** Pub.; **Spl.:** Own Books in Kannada

S.B.P. CONSULTANTS & ENGINEERS PVT. LTD.
19-A, Ansari Rd., Darya Ganj, New Delhi-110002
✆ 23243075, 23284212, Fax: 23243078
✉ sbpcon@ndf.vsnl.net.in, salls@sbpprojectfinder.com, sbpindia@hotmail.com
🌐 www.sbpprojectfinder.com
Estd.: 1971; **Man.Dir.:** Rajendra Kumar Gupta
Br.: G-2/16, Ansari Rd., Darya Ganj, New Delhi-110002
Bus.Intt.: Pub., WS, L.S. & Rt., Imp., Exp.; **Spl.:** Sci. & Tech.

S.B.S. PUBLISHERS DISTRIBUTORS
Railway Parallel Rd., Kumara Park East, Bangalore-560001 (Karnataka)
✆ 2262815, 2266088, Fax: 2269648, Cable: BOOKSLAND
✉ sales@sbpprojectfinder.com, sapua@giasbg1.vsnl.net.in
Estd.: 1983; **Ch.Exe.:** Deepak S. Shah; **Bus.Intt.:** Pub., WS, L.S. & Rt.; **Spl.:** Sci. & Tech., Humanities & Soc.Sci., Med., Law, Juvenile/Children Books Gen. & Fiction etc.

S.C. SARKAR AND SONS PVT. LTD.
1/C, Bankim Chatterjee St., Kolkata-700073 (West Bengal)
✆ 91-33-2416305, Fax: 91-33-2192424
Hd.Org.: Ajoy De; **Spl.:** Law Books

S.D. BOOK STALL
14, Bankim Chatterjee St., Kolkata-700073 (West Bengal)

S.E.I. TECHNOLOGIES PVT. LTD.
1211, Padma Tower-I, 5, Rajendra Place, New Delhi-110008
✆ 25755920, 25762725, 25762726, Fax: 011-25766775, 25755000
✉ seitech@pobox.com
Estd.: 1997; **Hd.Org.:** Shantanu Prakash

Br.: 1021, Ist Main, 4th Block, Dr. Rajkumar Rd., Rajaji Nagar, Bangalore-560010 (Karnataka)
✆ 3406113
Bus.Intt.: Rt., Imp. and Dist.; **Spl.:** Edu. CD's and Books

S.F.S. PUBLISHING HOUSE
Vinalaya, Malleswaram West, Bangalore-560056 (Karnataka)

S.G. UNHALE BOOKSELLERS
Tilak Rd., Mahal, Nagpur-400002 (Maharashtra)
✆ 2721082

S.H. BOOK DEPOT
Kavala, Changanacherry-686101 (Kerala)
✆ 222125
Estd.: 1939; **Prop.:** Scaria Aabraham;
Bus.Intt.: B.S.

S.I. & CO.
Paona Bazar, Imphal-795001 (Manipur)

S.I.B. IMPEX
AE-17, 2nd Floor, Tagore Garden, New Delhi-110027
Bus.Intt.: Pub. & Promoter

S.J. EDUCATIONAL ENTERPRISE
Egra, Midnapore (Bihar)

S.K. BOOK TRADERS
15, Bankim Chatterjee St., Kolkata-700073 (West Bengal)

S.K. EDUCATIONALS PVT. LTD.
P.P. Towers, 3rd Floor, Netaji Subhash Place, Main Rd., New Delhi-110034
✆ 27158461-63, Fax: 91-11-27158460
✉ heights@bol.net.in
Estd.: 1999; **Ch.Exe.:** Ajay Gupta

S.K. ENTERPRISES (PUBLISHERS AND DISTRIBUTORS)
Kamal Chowk, Near Prabhakar Yewle House, Nagpur-440017 (Maharashtra)
✆ 2644758

S.K. KATARIA & SONS
4424/6, Guru Nanak Market, Nai Sarak, Delhi-110006
✆ 22937396

S.K. KATARIA & SONS
First Floor, Kataria Building, Opp. Clock Tower, Ludhiana-141008 (Punjab)

S.K. KOCHHAR
1/A, Janta Hospital, Bolath, Distt. Kapurthala-144622 (Punjab)

S.K. MEDICAL DISTRIBUTORS
L-9, Surender Singh Bldg., Red Light Crossing, Mahipalpur, New Delhi-110037

✆ 26897048, 23761727, Fax: 26895391,
Telefax: 03173086
Estd.: 1992; **Prop.:** S.K. Shah;
Bus.Intt.: Pub., WS, L.S. and Rt., Imp., Exp., Sub.Ag.

S.K. PUBLISHERS
A-47, Amar Colony, New Delhi-110024
✆ 26486161, 22204524
Hd.Org.: Subhash Chander

S.K. PUBLISHERS
660/10, Krishna Colony, Gurgaon-122001 (Haryana)
✆ 91-2320495
Hd.Org.: Manmohan

S.K.B. BOOK SHOP
137, 137A, Cherry Rd., Salem-636001 (Tamil Nadu)
✆ 2414579, 2267059
Estd.: 1980; **Bus.Intt.:** Pub. and B.S.;
Spl.: Sci. & Tech.

S.K.W. ENTERPRISES
E-11/A, East of Kailash, New Delhi-110048
✆ (O) 26462068, 26461632 (R) 22914789
Prop.: Sudarshan Varma; **Bus.Intt.:** Rt., WS, L.S. and Pub.

S.M. BOOK DISTRIBUTORS
T-2321, Faiz Rd., Karol Bagh, New Delhi-110005
✆ (O) & (R) 25751562 ▮ 9810154719,
Fax: 25854388, Pager: 9632-125335
✉ vipian@rediffmail.com
Estd.: 1984; **Prop.:** Vipan Mehta;
Bus.Intt.: Dist. & L.S., **Spl.:** Acad., Tech., Pure & Applied Sci., Law, Comp., Mang., Agri., and Swamy Pub.

S.M. JAGANNATHAM BOOK HOUSE
35, Nandhikoil St., Tiruchirapalli-620002 (Tamil Nadu)
✆ 226817
Estd.: 1919; **Prop.:** J.S. Selvaraj

S.M. PUBLISHERS
Maheshwari Market, Sadar Bazar, Gurgaon-122001 (Haryana)

S.P. & SONS
Khajuri Bazar, Indore-452002 (Madhya Pradesh)
✆ (O) 2451933 (R) 2471530

S.P. PUBLICATIONS
622/111, Indradeep Market, 1st Floor, Khajuri Bazar, Indore-452002
✆ 2451933, 2617741
Bus.Intt.: Pub. and Dist.; **Spl.:** School, Graduate, Adv. Books for Lib., Gen. Books, Engg., Comp. Books

S.P. PUBLISHERS
2/7, Atul Krishna Market, Maldah (West Bengal)

S.R. TECHNICO (BOOK HOUSE)
4435-36, 7 Ansari Rd., Darya Ganj, New Delhi-110002
✆ 23241021, Fax: 91-11-23242621

S.R.C. PUBLISHERS (PVT.) LTD.
Rahim Khatoon Precincts, Hyderguda, Hyderabad-500029 (Andhra Pradesh)
✆ 23241033, Fax: 23249722
✉ srcpublishers@hotmail.com
Estd.: 1992; **Bus.Intt.:** Pub.; **Spl.:** Humanities and Gen. Books

S & S BOOK SERVICES
12/59, Subhash Nagar, New Delhi-110027

S.S. BAGAI
G-14, Masjid Moth, G.K. Part-III, New Delhi-110048

S.S. BOOKSELLERS PUBLISHERS DISTRIBUTORS
2237, Shora Kothi, Sabzi Mandi, Near Ghantaghar, Delhi-110007
✆ 23980434
Estd.: 1982; **Prop.:** Satnam Singh Talwar; **Bus.Intt.:** L.S.

S.S. EDUCATIONAL (AIDS) STORES
B-9/295, Sector-5, Rohini, Delhi-110085
✆ 27053526, 55455851
Hd.Org.: Anju Dhawan, Girish Malhotra
Br.: S.S. Educational Aids, C-5/89, Sector-5, Rohini, Delhi-110085
✆ 27053526, 27056395
✉ s.seducationalaids@hotmail.com
www.s.seducationalaids.20m.com
Bus.Intt.: Manufacturer and Supplier; **Spl.:** Edu. Aids and School Decorations

S.S. PUBLISHERS
IX/5572, West Seelam Pur, Near Gandhi Nagar, Delhi-110031
✆ 22433202
Prop.: J.L. Uppal; **Bus.Intt.:** L.S.; **Spl.:** Soc.Sci.

S.S. PUBLISHING CO. PVT. LTD.
65, Sunder Nagar, New Delhi-110003
✆ 24618700
Estd.: 1964; **Hd.Org.:** Mrs. Kamla Sachdev; **Bus.Intt.:** L.S. and Rt., Imp., Sub.Ag.

S.S.A. BOOK SERVICE
32, Bhargave Lane, Boulevard Rd., Civil Lines, Delhi-110054 ✆ (O) & (R) 23963029
Estd.: 1984; **Prop.:** Jai Chand Dogra; **Bus.Intt.:** Rt., L.S.; **Spl.:** All Subjects

S.T. REDDIAR & SONS (QUILON) PVT. LTD.
S.T.R. Building, Main Rd., Quilon-691001 (Kerala)
✆ 278778, 275140, 277921
✉ estiar@md4.vsnl.net.in
Estd.: 1886; **Hd.Org.:** B. Multhukrishnan; **Bus.Intt.:** Pub. and B.S.

S.V. BROTHERS
No. 8, Plot No. 124, Ganesh Nagar, Basti Nau, Jalandhar-144001 (Punjab)
Bus.Intt.: Exp.

S.V. PRESS & LASER PRINT
Neyyattinkara, Thiruvananthapuram (Kerala)
✆ 0471-2222259
Estd.: 1956; **Hd.Org.:** A.J. Jacob; **Bus.Intt.:** Pub. and B.S.

S.V.S. BOOKS DISTRIBUTORS
PB No. 5004, 20, Vinayakanagar, Banashankari Ist Stage, Bangalore-560050 (Karnataka)
✆ 26696039, Fax: 26696039
✉ svsbooks@gjiasbga.vsnl.net.in
Estd.: 1983; **Prop.:** S.M. Subramanyam; **Bus.Intt.:** L.S. and Rt.

S.V.U. ORIENTAL RESEARCH INSTITUTE
Sri Venkateswara University, Tirupati-517502 (Andhra Pradesh)

SAAKSHRTA PRATISTHAN
489, Hanuman Ji Ka Rasta, Jaipur-302003 (Rajasthan)
✆ (O) 2560113 (R) 2515375, 2511446
Hd.Org.: Surya Prakash Goyal

SAAROL HEALTH AND RESEARCH FOUNDATION
14/84, Vikram Vihar, Lajpat Nagar-IV, New Delhi-110024
✆ 26235168, Fax: 26212016
✉ info@saaol.com
www.saaol.com
Hd.Org.: Bimal Chajjer; **Bus.Intt.:** Pub.; **Spl.:** Books, Magazines, and VCDs on Heart Care and Proper Cooking Methods, in English and Hindi

SABARIMALAIAN BOOK DISTRIBUTORS
No. 3, Sanjeevappa Lane, Avenue Rd. Cross, Bangalore-560002 (Karnataka)
✆ 22270314
Estd.: 1993; **Bus.Intt.:** Rt., L.S.

SABAR MAJHE AAMI
45A, Block-C, New Alipur, Kolkata-700053 (West Bengal)

SABDA
Sri Aurobindo Ashram, Pondicherry-605002
✆ (O) 2334980, 2223328 (R) 2223367, 2334958, Fax: 2223328
✉ sabda@sriaurobindoashram.org
www.sabda.sriaurobindoashram.org
Estd.: 1952; **Hd.Org.:** Mira Gupta

Bus.Intt.: Pub. and Dist.; **Spl.:** Books on The Mother's Phil., Yoga, Spiritualism, Sol., Indology, etc.

SABDA LOKA
Ranihat, Cuttack-753001 (Orissa)
Estd.: 1989
✆ (O) 0671-2613619/729 (R) 2612922
Bus.Intt.: Pub. and B.S.; **Spl.:** English and Oriya

SABDASILPA
C/o Chayanika, Bangchatta Rd., P.O. & Dte., Cooch-Behar-736101 (West Bengal)

SABHARWAL BOOK WHOLESELLERS
7/9A, Ansari Rd., Darya Ganj, New Delhi-110002
✆ 23255747, Fax: 23279603
Estd.: 1970; **Prt.:** K.L. Sabharwal
Br.: 4831/24, Prahlad St., Ansari Rd., Darya Ganj, New Delhi-110002 ✆ (O) 55390704, 23250586 (R) 25764304 ▮ 9811220876, Fax: 23279603 ✉ varun.book@yahoo.co.in
Bus.Intt.: WS, Imp.; **Spl.:** Beh.Sci., Comp., Soc.Sci., Mang., Sci.—Pure & Applied, Tech. and Encyclopaedias and Dictionaries

SABSON BOOK STALL
Changanacherry-686101 (Kerala)

SACHI PRAKASHAN
21, UNI Apartments, Sector-11, Vasundhara, Ghaziabad-201012 (Uttar Pradesh)
✆ 2880329, Fax: 91-120-2880324
✉ screenindia@gmail.com
Hd.Org.: Vinod Kumar
Bus.Intt.: Pub.

SADANA PUBLISHERS & DISTRIBUTORS
FF-20, Palika Bazar, G.T. Rd., Ghaziabad-201009 (Uttar Pradesh)
✆ 2750356 ▮ 9810130829, Fax: 2750356
✉ vijaysadana@hotmail.com
Estd.: 1992; **Hd.Org.:** Vijay Sadana;
Bus.Intt.: Pub., B.S.; **Spl.:** Directories of All Trades

SADBHAVNA PRAKASHAN
A-139, Gali No. 3, 100 Ft. Rd., Kabeer Nagar, Delhi-110094
Hd.Org.: Rajbhadur Singh

SADGRANTHA BHANDAR
Sri Jagannath Complex, Sabara Srikhetra, Koraput-764020 (Orissa)

SADHANA BOOK EMPORIUM
B-2/125-A-2, Bhadaini, P.O. Shivala, Varanasi-221001 (Uttar Pradesh)
✆ 0542-2313591
Estd.: 1996; **Hd.Org.:** Vijay Kumar Gupta;
Bus.Intt.: Dist.; **Spl.:** Art, Archeology, Ancient Hist. Books in English and Hindi and Bengali

SADHANA BOOK PLACE
H.No. 2118, Sector-16, Faridabad-121002 (Haryana)

SADHANA FOUNDATION
17, Koregaon Park, Pune-411001 (Maharashtra)
✆ 2628562, Fax: 2624181
Estd.: 1986; **Prop.:** Mukesh Sharma
Br.: 31, Israil Mohalla, Bhagwan Bhuvan Masjid, Bunder Rd., Mumbai-400002 (Maharashtra)
✆ 23757275, 23757618
Bus.Intt.: L.S. & Rt., Imp.

SADHANA PRAKASHAN
A/2, New Asmita Apartments, Near Commerce College Site, Stadium Rd., Navrangpura, Ahmedabad-380009 (Gujarat)
✆ 079-2462345

SADHANA POCKET BOOKS
39, UA Bungalow Rd., Jawahar Nagar, Delhi-110007
✆ 23966715, 23914161
Hd.Org.: B.R. Sahni; **Bus.Intt.:** Pub. and Dist.; **Spl.:** Rel., Ayurveda, Will Power, Sex Edu., Sports, etc.

SADHANA PUBLICATIONS
106, 1st Floor, Usha Kiran Commercial Complex, Nani Wala Bagh, Azadpur, Delhi-110033
▮ 9891070005
Hd.Org.: Nidhi Kaura; **Bus.Intt.:** Pub. & B.S.; **Spl.:** Rel., Cookery, Inspiration and Children's Books in Hindi

SADHNA BOOK DEPOT
Vir Marg, Jammu (Jammu and Kashmir)
✆ 0191-2578432, 2450272
Estd.: 1997; **Prop.:** Sardar Parminder Singh; **Bus.Intt.:** Rt., L.S.

SADHNA PRAKASHAN
A-136, Vikas Puri, New Delhi-110018

SADHNA PUBLICATIONS
K-4/4, Model Town II, Delhi-110009
✆ 91-11-27415504, 55496808
www.sadhnapublications.com
Hd.Org.: Nidhi Kaura; **Bus.Intt.:** Pub.; **Spl.:** General Books and Books on Yoga, Ayurveda, Religion, Astrology, Numerology, etc. in Hindi and English

SADHU VASWANI MISSION
IInd Floor, Shanti Niketan, New Delhi-110021
✆ 26871385

SAEED INTERNATIONAL (REGD.)
E-9, Jungpura Extension, New Delhi-110014
Bus.Intt.: Exp.

SAFDAR HASHMI MEMORIAL TRUST (SAHMAT)
8, Vithal Bhai Patel House, Rafi Marg, New Delhi-110001
✆ 23711276, 23323077, Fax: 23351424
✉ sahmat@nde.vsnl.net.in
Hd.Org.: Bhishm Sahni; **Spl.:** Children's Litt., Collection of St. Plays, Books on Secular and Plural Tradition, Etiquettes and Thos, Posters, Audio and Video Cassettes are Part of its Media Drive

SAGAR PRAKASHANA
1679, 14th Main, 5th 'A' Cross, Banashankari, Stage II, Bangalore-560050 (Karnataka)
Hd.Org.: R. Janardhan; **Bus.Intt.:** Pub.; **Spl.:** Novels, Collections and Gen. Books in Kannada

SAGAR PUBLICATIONS
72, Ved Mansion, Janpath, New Delhi-110001
✆ 23320648, 23328245, Fax: 24632222
✉ sagarpub@vsnl.net.in
Estd.: 1974; **Hd.Org.:** Narender Sagar; **Bus.Intt.:** Pub.; **Spl.:** Med., Indian Art, Arch., Astrology, Archaeology, Occult Sci. and Vedic Litt.

SAGAR PUBLISHERS & DISTRIBUTORS
Nagpur (Maharashtra)
✆ 527134, 452735, Fax: 544093
✉ tcraft@ipindia.com
Bus.Intt.: Pub. & Dist.

SAGE PUBLICATIONS INDIA (P) LTD.
B1/I-1, Mohan Cooperative, Industrial Area, Mathura Road, New Delhi-110044
✆ 40539222, Fax: 91-11-40529234
✉ info@sagepub.in
www.sagepub.in
Hd.Org.: Vivek Mehra; **Bus.Intt.:** Pub.; **Spl.:** Books and Journals on Soc.Sci., Development studies, and Business Management

SAGE PUBLICATIONS INDIA (P) LTD.
32, M-Block Market, Greater Kailash-I, New Delhi-110048
✆ 26485884, 26444958, 26453915, Fax: 26472426
✉ sageind@nda.vsnl.net.in
www.indiasage.com
Estd.: 1981; **Man.Dir.:** Tejeshwar Singh
Br.: B-42, Panchsheel Enclave, New Delhi-110017 ✆ 26491290, 26491293, 26491294, Fax: 26491290
✉ marketing@indiasage.com, sage@vsnl.com
• 59/5, Prince Baktiar Shah Rd. (Ground Floor) Tollygunje, Kolkata-700033
✆ 24172642, 24220611
✉ sageind@md4.vsnl.net.in
• 11, Saravana St., T. Nagar, Chennai-600017 ✆ 24345822, 24348132
✉ sageind@md4.vsnl.net.in
• 31, Lal Bahadur Stadium, Post Box-131, Hyderabad-500001 ✆ 23231447, 23230674
✉ sageindia@vsnl.net • 1187/37, Ameya, Shaji Nagar Off Ghole Rd., Pune-411005
✆ 5513407, 5513408
✉ sageindia@vsnl.net
Bus.Intt.: Pub. of Business Books, Scholarly and Professional Books and Journals; also Distribute the Books and Journals of its American and British Affiliates; **Spl.:** Soc.Sci. (scholarly and professional) and Business Mang.

SAGHAI EXPORTERS
Raj Buildings, P.O. Box No. 1231, 162, Linght Chetty St., Chennai-600 001 (Tamil Nadu)
✆ 25341711, 25340731, 25340751, Fax: 25342323, Telex: 41-6575
Estd.: 1965; **Hd.Org.:** N.E. Fernando; **Bus.Intt.:** Exp.

SAGNIK
37-A, College Row, Kolkata-700009 (West Bengal)
Bus.Intt.: Pub.; **Spl.:** Religious, Books for Children, Novel, Bengali Reference Books and Tourism Books

SAHA BOOK STALL
19, Shyama Charan Dey St., Kolkata-700073 (West Bengal)

SAHA PUBLICATIONS
A-127, B.D. Chambers, 10/54, D.B. Gupta Rd., Karol Bagh, Delhi-110005
Estd.: 1969; **Prop.:** B.P. Saha

SAHAJA EXPORTS INTERNATIONAL
24B, College Row, Kolkata-700009 (West Bengal)
✆ 2190466, 2414003, Fax: 033-24192338
✉ sahityam@cal2.vsnl.net.in
Estd.: 1989; **Prop.:** Pradip Kumar Saha
Br.: 89, M.G. Rd., Kolkata-700007 (West Bengal)
✆ 2241003
Bus.Intt.: Exp.

SAHAJA YOGA
C-17, Institutional Area, Behind Qutab Hotel, New Delhi-110016

SAHARAYU MHARTRE (DR.)
5, 2nd Floor, 372-A, Cadell Rd., Dadar, Mumbai (Maharashtra)

SAHASRARA PUBLICATIONS
1143, Sector 37, Aum Vihar, Noida-201303 (Uttar Pradesh)
✆ 011-91-574902
Estd.: 1995; **Prop.:** Opender Nath Karir; **Bus.Intt.:** Pub.

SAHITI NAVJEEVAN BOOK LINKS
Museum Rd., Vijayawada-520002 (Andhra Pradesh)
✆ (O) 0866-2434118 (R) 2474597
Estd.: 1967; **Prop.:** P. Rama Koteswara Rao; **Bus.Intt.:** Pub.; **Spl.:** Litt., Sci. and Fiction Books in Telugu

SAHITYA AKADEMI
Rabindra Bhavan, 35, Ferozeshah Road, New Delhi-110001
✆ 23386626-28, Fax: 91-11-23382428
✉ ecy@ndn.vsnl.net.in, sahityaakademisales@vsnl.net
Hd.Org.: K. Satchidanandan
Br.: 'Swati', Mandir Marg, New Delhi-110001
✆ 23364207, 23745297, 23364204, Fax: 91-11-23364207
✉ sahityaakademisales@vsnl.net
• Central College Campus, University Library Building, Dr. B.R. Ambedkar Veedhi, Bangalore-560001 ✆ 22245152, Fax: 91-80-22121932;
• Jeevan Tara Building, 23-A/44X, Diamond Harbour Road, Kolkata-700053,
✆ 24787405, 24781806, Fax: 91-33-24789375
✉ regsecy@vsnl.net;
• 172, Mumbai Marathi Granth, Sangrahalaya Marg, Dadar, Mumbai-400014,
✆ 4135744, 4078302, Fax: 91-22-4147650;
• Guna Buildings, IInd Floor, No. 443 (304), Anna Salai, Teynampet, Chennai-600018
✆ 91-44-24311741
✉ sahityaakademi@yahoo.co.uk
Bus.Intt.: Pub.; **Spl.:** Indian Litt. by Eminent and Award-winning Authors in twenty-two Indian Languages

SAHITYA AKADEMI/M.P. SANSKRITI PARISHAD
Sanskriti Bhavan, Baan Ganga Chauraha, Bhopal-462003 (Madhya Pradesh)
✆ 2554782, Fax: 91-755-2557942
Rep.: Devendra Deepar
Bus.Intt.: Pub.; **Spl.:** Novels, Poetry, Plays, Story, Essays etc. in Hindi

SAHITYA AMRIT
4/19, Asaf Ali Rd., New Delhi-110002
✆ 23289555, Fax: 91-11-23289666
✉ info@prabhatbooks.com
Hd.Org.: Shyam Sundar; **Bus.Intt.:** Pub.; **Spl.:** Hindi Magazine *Sahitya Amrit*

SAHITYA BELA PRAKASHAN
T-127, Shukar Bazar, St. No. 4, Om Vihar, Uttam Nagar, Delhi-110059
Hd.Org.: Naresh Sharma

SAHITYA BHANDAR
50, Chahchand Zero Rd., Allahabad-211003 (Uttar Pradesh)
✆ 2400787, 2402072, 2622711
Hd.Org.: Satish Chandra Aggrawal; **Bus.Intt.:** Pub.; **Spl.:** Hindi Litt.

SAHITYA BHANDAR
Jangama Bhandar, Jangama Maestri Galli 1, Balepet, Bangalore-560053 (Karnataka)
Bus.Intt.: Pub.; **Spl.:** Fiction, Poems, Dramas, Edu., Gen., Children's Books Biographies in Kannada

SAHITYA BHANI
28, Old Allapur, Allahabad-211006 (Uttar Pradesh)
✆ 2500255
Hd.Org.: Narender Shukal

SAHITYA BHARTI
K-71, Krishna Nagar, Delhi-110051
✆ 22002274, Fax: 91-11-22099764
✉ sahityabharti@yahoo.com
Hd.Org.: Poonam Sharma
Bus.Intt.: Pub. and Dist.; **Spl.:** Hindi Books on Litt., Art, Culture, Sci., Tech. for Children and Neo-literates

SAHITYA BHARATI PUBLICATIONS PVT. LTD.
C-21/30, A-B, Pishachmochan, Varanasi-221010 (Uttar Pradesh)
✆ 2421168, Fax: 2359222
Hd.Org.: Ganesh Vishwakarama; **Bus.Intt.:** Pub.; **Spl.:** Edu. Books for Children in Hindi, Bengali and English

SAHITYA BHARATI PUBLICATIONS (PVT.) LTD.
211/1, Bidhan Sarani, Kolkata-700006 (West Bengal)
Hd.Org.: Rajendra Prasad Berry

SAHITYA BHARTI
K-71, Krishna Nagar, Delhi-110051
✆ 22002274, Fax: 22054604
✉ sb@mailz.net
Hd.Org.: Poonam Sharma; **Bus.Intt.:** Pub. and Dist.; **Spl.:** Hindi Books on Litt., Art, Culture, Sci., Tech. for Children and Neo-literates

SAHITYA BHAWAN
Gora Nakhas Rd., Bhopal-462001 (Madhya Pradesh)
✆ (R) 2530832

SAHITYA BHAWAN PUBLICATIONS
Hospital Rd., Agra-282003 (Uttar Pradesh)
✆ 2531013, Fax: 91-562-2531351

rsvbansal@hotmail.com
Estd.: 1961; **Hd.Org.:** K.L. Bansal; **Bus.Intt.:** Pub.; **Spl.:** Edu. Books on Soc.Sci. and Humanities for College and Competitive Exams

SAHITYA BHAWAN PUBLISHERS & DISTRIBUTORS PVT. LTD.
34, Lajpat Kunj, Civil Lines, Agra-282002 (Uttar Pradesh)
2523369 9412258080, 9412258081, Fax: 91-562-2858183
sahityabhawan@dataone.in
www.sahityabhawan.com
Hd.Org.: Rajeev Bansal, Sanjay Bansal; **Bus.Intt.:** Pub.; **Spl.:** Edu. Books for Schools, Colleges and Competitive Examinations

SAHITYA BHAWAN PVT. LTD.
93, K.P. Kakad Rd., Allahabad-401077 (Uttar Pradesh)
2401077
Hd.Org.: Grish Tandan

SAHITYA BISTAR PATAL
Shantikunj, Haridwar (Uttarakhand)
260602, Fax: 91-334-260866
Hd.Org.: Kailash Mahajan

SAHITYA MANDIR
2619-20, New Market, Nai Sarak, Delhi-110006
(O) 23286781 (R) 27211659
Hd.Org.: Anil Kumar Gupta

SAHITYA MANDIR
Opp. Ancholi Sheri, Bawasidi, Gopipara, Surat-395004 (Gujarat)

SAHITYA MUDRANALAYA
City Mill Compound, Kankaria Rd., Ahmedabad-380022 (Gujarat)
Bus.Intt.: Exp.

SAHITYA NIDHI
29/59, Gali No. 11, Vishwas Nagar, Shahdara, Delhi-110032
22463429
Hd.Org.: Kesavdev Sharma

SAHITYA NIKATEN
E-87/3, College St. Mkt., Kolkata-700007 (West Bengal)

SAHITYA NIKETAN
37/50, Gilis Bazar, Shivala Rd., Kanpur-208001 (Uttar Pradesh)
2311678
Hd.Org.: Manoj Kapoor; **Bus.Intt.:** Pub. and B.S.; **Spl.:** Sci. & Tech., Humanities, Gen. Books

SAHITYA PRACHARAK
3011, Ballimaran, Delhi-110006
22918110 (PP)
Hd.Org.: Omprakash Sharma

SAHITYA PRAKASH
5/1, Ramanath Majumder St., Kolkata-700009 (West Bengal)

SAHITYA PRAKASHAN
9, Apka Bazar, Hospital Rd., Agra-282003 (Uttar Pradesh)
2360920, 2157379
Estd.: 1977; **Hd.Org.:** Satish Kumar Agarwal; **Bus.Intt.:** Pub. and B.S.; **Spl.:** Humanities, Edu., Psych. and Home Sci.

SAHITYA PRAKASHAN
101, Pratap Nagar, Mayur Vihar Phase-I, Delhi-110091
22790165
yogendrapalsahitya@yahoo.com
www.bookglacier.com
Hd.Org.: Yogendra Pal; **Bus.Intt.:** Pub. and B.S.; **Spl.:** Hindi Litt. and Books on Culture, Hist., Sci., Sports, etc.

SAHITYA PRASAR & LOK HITKARI SAMITI
11109, Doriwalan, East Park Rd., Karol Bagh, New Delhi-110005
23552350, Fax: 35394228
Hd.Org.: Ved Prakash Punshi; **Bus.Intt.:** Pub.; **Spl.:** Edu. Books and Indian Culture

SAHITYA PRASAR KENDRA
Opp. Patwardhan High School, Sitabuldi, Nagpur-440012 (Maharashtra)
2523702; **Estd.:** 1965; **Hd.Org.:** Laxman Kulkarni; **Spl.:** Litt., Novels and Stories etc. in Marathi Language

SAHITYA PRASAR KENDRA
9, Dr. Deshmukh Lane, V.P. Rd., Mumbai-400004 (Maharashtra)

SAHITYA PRAVARTHAKA CO-OPERATIVE SOCIETY LTD.
P.O. Box 95, Kottayam-686001 (Kerala)
2564111, 2564112, 2564114, 2560452
Estd.: 1945; **Hd.Org.:** P. Gopinath; **Bus.Intt.:** Pub. and B.S.; **Spl.:** Gen. Books

SAHITYA SADAN
Laheria Tola, Law Rd., Gaya-823001 (Bihar)
2220500, Fax: 2220600
sahityasadan@rediffmail.com
Estd.: 1951; **Prop.:** Radhey Raman Prasad **Bus.Intt.:** WS, L.S. & Rt.; **Spl.:** Humanities & Soc.Sci., Sci. & Tech., Juvenile/Children

SAHITYA SADAN
124/15, E Block, Govind Nagar, Kanpur-208006 (Uttar Pradesh)
249593, 244469
Estd.: 1960; **Hd.Org.:** Om Prakash Gupta; **Bus.Intt.:** WS, L.S., Rt., Imp.

SAHITYA SADAN
R.S.S. Rest House Compound, Naipier Rd., Kanpur-208004 (Uttar Pradesh)
Hd.Org.: Sanjay Kakad; **Bus.Intt.:** Pub. and Dist.

SAHITYA SADANA
134, Near Doddammathaji Temple, Kevempunagar, Mysore-570023 (Karnataka)
Hd.Org.: Smt. Sharada; **Bus.Intt.:** Pub.;
Spl.: Fiction and Collections

SAHITYA SAGAR (THE BOOK SHOP)
Shop No. 18, F-Block Market, Sector-12, (Near Water Tank), Noida
✆ 2551399 ▮ 9811499063
Hd.Org.: Sudhansh; **Bus.Intt.:** B.S.;
Spl.: NCERT, School & College, Open School, Competitive, Novels & Poetry, Cookery & Beauty, Nature Cure & Yoga Books

SAHITYA SAHAKAR
E-10/4, Krishna Nagar, Delhi-110051
Hd.Org.: Mishrilal Sharma; **Bus.Intt.:** Pub.;
Spl.: Books in Hindi

SAHITYA SAHAKAR
29/62-B, Gali No. 11, Vishwas Nagar, Delhi-110032
✆ 22385703
Hd.Org.: Madanlal Sharma, Ramesh Sharma
Bus.Intt.: Pub.; **Spl.:** Hindi Litt., Dictionaries and Vedas in Sanskrit

SAHITYA SAMBHAR
82, Mahatma Gandhi Rd., (1st Floor), Kolkata-700009 (West Bengal)

SAHITYA SAMSHODHAN PRAKASHAN
C/o Girishbhai S. Jesalpoura, 13, Tejpal Society, Fatehnagar, Paldi, Ahmedabad-380007 (Gujarat)

SAHITYA SANGAM
New 100, Lookerganj, Allahabad-211001 (Uttar Pradesh)
✆ 2615449, 2623385
Hd.Org.: Alok Chaturvedi; **Bus.Intt.:** Pub. and Dist.; **Spl.:** Hindi Litt. and Books on Painting, Sculpture, Contemporary Hist., Pol.Sci., etc.

SAHITYA SANGAM
Bava Sidi, Opp. Pancholi Sheri, Gopalpura, Surat-395001 (Gujarat)
✆ (O) 02610-2427882, 2432563 (R) 2423878
Br.: Sahitya Sankool, Chaura Bazar, Surat-395003 (Gujarat) ✆ 0261-2431449
Bus.Intt.: Pub. and B.S.

SAHITYA SANGAM
Kachi Chhowni, Jammu Tawi-180001 (Jammu and Kashmir)
✆ 249593, 244469, Cable: SS JAM
Estd.: 1960; **Man.Prt.:** Om Parkash Gupta
Br.: Globe Traders, Shop No. 4, Bus Stand, Jammu-Tawi-180001 (Jammu & Kashmir)
✆ 2549049, Cable: SS JAM
Bus.Intt.: WS, L.S. & Rt., Imp.

SAHITYA SANGAM
Bhakharua More Daundnagar, Aurangabad-824113 (Bihar)
Bus.Intt.: Pub. and B.S.

SAHITYA SANSAD
R.Z. 35-B, St. No. 1-A, Kailashpuri X, New Delhi
Hd.Org.: R. Shyam

SAHITYA SEVA PRAKASHAN
117, Bhavanipet, Satara (Maharashtra)

SAHITYA SHODH SANSTHAN
8A/141, W.E.A., Karol Bagh, New Delhi-110005
✆ 25726216
Hd.Org.: R.K. Seth; **Bus.Intt.:** Pub.;
Spl.: Tamil Litt. and Books on Indian Culture in Hindi and Tamil

SAHITYA SINDHU PRAKASHANA
Nrupathunga Rd., K.R. Circle, Bangalore-560001 (Karnataka)

SAHITYA UPKRAM
Basha Pustakalaya, Police Line, Madhuban, Karnal-132037 (Haryana)
▮ 9354762343
✉ sahitya_upkram@yahoo.co.in
Hd.Org.: Vikas Narayan; **Bus.Intt.:** Pub.

SAHITYA VANI
28, Purana Allapur, Allahabad-211006 (Uttar Pradesh)

SAHITYA VIHAR
IB, Mahendra Srimani St., Kolkata-9 (West Bengal)
✆ 033-23509563

SAHITYA VISTAR PATAL
Q-2, Sector-12, Gautam Budh Nagar, Ghaziabad (Uttar Pradesh)
▮ 9312026563
Hd.Org.: Kailash Mahajan

SAHITYA VITHI PRAKASHAN
27/111, Gali No. 7, Vishwas Nagar, Shahdara, Delhi-110032
▮ 9811280634
✉ drpradeep@mantraonline.com
Hd.Org.: Sudesh; **Bus.Intt.:** Pub., **Spl.:** Hindi Novels, Poetry and Children's Books

SAHITYAGAR
Dhamani Market Ki Gali, Choura Rasta, Jaipur-302003 (Rajasthan)

✆ 2310785, 2322382
Hd.Org.: Ramesh Verma; **Bus.Intt.**: Pub. & Dist.; **Spl.**: Hindi Litt.

SAHITYAM
18-B, Shyama Charan Dey St., Kolkata-700073 (West Bengal)

SAHITYASAR
Dhamani Market Ki Gali, Choura Rasta, S.M.S. Highway, Jaipur-302003 (Rajasthan)
✆ 2310785

SAHITYIKA
161/2/1, Rash Behari Avenue, Kolkata-700029 (West Bengal)
✆ 28700222, Fax: 24642494
chitrabhanucomp@vsnl.net
Hd.Org.: Santosh Adhikary; **Bus.Intt.**: Pub.; **Spl.**: Books in Bangla Language

SAHNI BROTHERS
16, Aap Ka Bazar, Hospital Rd., Agra-282003 (Uttar Pradesh)
✆ 2263483, 2360913, Fax: 2263483
Estd.: 1978; **Hd.Org.**: Basant Sahni; **Bus.Intt.**: Pub. and Exp.; **Spl.**: Dictionaries and Children's Books

SAHNI PUBLICATION
E-4/26, Model Town, Delhi-110009

SAHNI PUBLICATIONS
4777, Dr. Mitra Gali, Roshanara Rd., Delhi-110007
✆ 23822006, 23820751, Fax: 91-11-23914283
sahni@sahnipublications.com
www.sahnipublications.com
Estd.: 1987; **Hd.Org.**: Rajesh Sahni; **Bus.Intt.**: Pub.; **Spl.**: Gen. Sci., Med., Cookery, Legends, Stories, Will Power, etc.

SAHNI PUBLISHERS & DISTRIBUTORS
Gwalior (Madhya Pradesh)
✆ 0751-540717
kapilpustaksadan@rediffmail.com

SAHODARA KALA VRANDA
Prakashana, Mannagudda, Mangalore-575003 (Karnataka)

SAHODARAN PATANA SAMGHOM
Sarigame, Moolavattom P.O., Kottayam-686026 (Kerala)
✆ 2560036
Estd.: 1989; **Hd.Org.**: Kurichy Sadan; **Bus.Intt.**: Pub.

SAHYOG AGENCIES
35-D, Haripark Flats, Opp. Ankur Bus-Stop, Naranpura, Ahmedabad-380013 (Gujarat)
✆ (O) 27498458 (R) 27475179
9825032641, 9426010165
Estd.: 1987; **Prop.**: S.R. Sanghavi
Br.: St. Xavier's Book Stall, Ahmedabad • St. Xavier's Agencies, Ahmedabad
Bus.Intt.: B.S., WS; **Spl.**: Comp., Children & General, English Med. School Books

SAHYOG PRAKASHAN
41, Sahyog Apartment, Mayur Vihar, Phase I, Delhi-110091 ✆ 22259371
Estd.: 1986; **Bus.Intt.**: Pub. and Dist.; **Spl.**: Hindi Books

SAHYOG PUSTAK BHANDAR
Khesar, Bhagalpur-813207 (Bihar)
Bus.Intt.: Pub. and B.S.

SAI BABA EDUCATIONAL AIDS
U-31, Shakar Pur, Delhi-110092
✆ 22041749, 31054660 9810883413
saibabaeducationalaids@yahoo.co.in
www.saibabaeducationalaids.com
Hd.Org.: Manish Gupta
Bus.Intt.: Manufacturer and Supplier; **Spl.**: Edu. Goods and Teaching Aids

SAI BOOK HOUSE
Inder Place Market Shop No.1, Sanjoli, Shimla-170006 (Himachal Pradesh)

SAI BOOK INTERNATIONAL
D-500A, Gali No. 62, Mahaveer Enclave, Part-III, New Delhi-110045
✆ 25556834
Prop.: Sh. Ghanshyam Singh; **Bus.Intt.**: L.S.; **Spl.**: Acad., Beh.Sci., Soc.Sci., Comm., Sci., Pure & Applied, Tech. Books

SAI BOOKS
2/8-A, Jangpura-A, New Delhi-110014
✆ 24315110
Hd.Org.: Vinod Kumar; **Bus.Intt.**: Pub.; **Spl.**: Books for Children in English

SAI EARLY LEARNERS PVT. LTD.
A-59, Okhla Industrial Area, Phase-II, New Delhi-110020
✆ 26386165, 26387070, Fax: 26383788
ghai@nde.vsnl.net.in, sterlin.gpvb@axcess.net.in
www.sterlingpublishers.com
Hd.Org.: Vikas Ghai; **Bus.Intt.**: Pub.; **Spl.**: Wall Charts, Wipeclean Picture Books and Playmats for Children in English

SAI EDUCATION INTERNATIONAL PUBLISHING CENTRE
58-B, SDF, Sector-15A, Noida-201301 (Uttar Pradesh)
✆ 120-2512116, Fax: 2513226
humilityseries@rediffmail.com, humilityseries@indiatimes.com
Estd.: 2001; **Hd.Org.**: Meenal Gupta

Spl.: Inspirational, Edu. in Human Values, Spirituality, Phil., Multicultural

SAI ENTERPRISES
4/54-55, Katra Resham Tajganj, Agra-282001 (Uttar Pradesh)
✆ 2331325, 2330270, 2232021, Fax: 91-562-2310433, 2330270
✉ rdaultani@hotmail.com
Ch.Exe.: Mr. Rajesh Daultani; **Bus.Intt.:** Pub. of their first book will be a Tribute to Dheru Bhai Ambani

SAI SYAM PUBLICATIONS
332, Prasanth Nagar, Med. College P.O., Trivandrum-695011 (Kerala)

SAI TOWERS PUBLISHING
23/1142, Vijayalakshmi Colony, Kadugudi, Bangalore-67 (Karnataka)
✆ 28455758, 28451648, Fax: 28451649
✉ bangalore@saitower@vsnl.com
www. saitowers.com
Bus.Intt.: Pub.

SAIBYA PRAKASHAN BIBHAG
86/1, Mahatma Gandhi Rd., Kolkata-700009 (West Bengal)
Hd.Org.: Rabin Pal; **Bus.Intt.:** Pub. and Dist.

SAIFEE BOOK AGENCY
11, Ameen Bldg. E.R. Rd., Mumbai-400003 (Maharashtra)
✆ 022-2863690
Estd.: 1982; **Hd.Org.:** Yusuf Sharaf Ali Golwala; **Bus.Intt.:** Pub. and B.S.

SAINATH BOOK CENTRE
206, Mumbai Market, Tardeo Rd., Mumbai-400034 (Maharashtra)
✆ 24949708, 24928203
Estd.: 1968; **Hd.Org.:** B.G. Borde
Br.: G-11, Mahendra Chambers, V.T. Magazine Market, D.N. Rd., Mumbai-400001
Bus.Intt.: WS

SAKET PRAKASHAN
215/5, W Rly. Junction, Bandra (West), Mumbai-400050 (Maharashtra)

SAKET PRAKASHAN PVT. LTD.
115, M.G. Nagar, Station Rd., Aurangabad-380002 (Bihar)

SAKET PROJECTS LTD.
Saket House, Panscheel, Usmanpura, Ahmedabad-380013 (Gujarat)
✆ 79-27551931, Fax: 91-79-27550452
Bus.Intt.: Industrial Journals and Publications

SAKHI PRAKASHAN
Gota Wala Kothi, Sadabad Gate, Hathras-204101 (Uttar Pradesh)

SAKSHARA PRAKASHAN
35-A, DDA Flats, Mansarovar Park, Shahdara, Delhi-110032
Hd.Org.: Rajesh Kumar; **Bus.Intt.:** Pub. and Dist.; **Spl.:** Children's Litt. and Books on Other Sub. in Hindi

SAKSHI PRAKASHAN
S-16, Naveen Shahdara, Delhi-110032
✆ 22324833, Fax: 91-11-22324833
✉ goelbooks@rediffmail.com
Hd.Org.: Sakshi Goel; **Bus.Intt.:** Pub.; **Spl.:** Books on All Sub. in Hindi and English

SALAMSONS
79-3B, Fanoonswala Building, Sankli St., Mumbai-400008 (Maharashtra)
Bus.Intt.: Exp.

SALES OVERSEAS
D-20, Green Park, New Delhi-110016

SALONI PUBLISHING HOUSE
Ganpati Bhawan, 4675/21, Ansari Rd., Darya Ganj, New Delhi-110002
✆ (O) 30912396, 33059560 (R) 30915583
▮ 9811142321, Fax: 23280611
✉ salonipublishinghouse@yahoo.com
Estd.: 2001; **Prop.:** Praveen Jain; **Bus.Intt.:** Pub.; **Spl.:** Humanities & Soc.Sci., Mang., Children & Gen.

SALT LAKE BOOK CONSORTIUM
AE-286, Salt Lake City, Kolkata-700064 (West Bengal)

SALT PUBLICATIONS
Legal Aid Programme Office, Nagampadam, Kottayam (Kerala)
✆ 2562514
Estd.: 1986; **Hd.Org.:** Francis Vallopma CMI Director; **Bus.Intt.:** Pub.

SAMAH ENTERPRISES
153, Angappa Naicken St., Chennai-600001 (Tamil Nadu)
Bus.Intt.: Exp.

SAMAJ SHIKSHA PRAKASHAN
1590, Madarsa Rd., Kashmere Gate, Delhi-110006
✆ 23869812, 23865483, Fax: 23867791
Hd.Org.: Vishwanath, Meera Johri; **Bus.Intt.:** Pub.; **Spl.:** Biographies and Children's Litt. in Hindi

SAMAJA PUSTAKALAYA
Shivaji Rd., Dharwad (Karnataka)
✆ 0836-28616
Hd.Org.: Manohar Ravindra; **Bus.Intt.:** Pub.; **Spl.:** Fiction, Collections, Children's Books, Biographies, Travelogues and Edu. Books in Kannada and English

SAMANTA BOOK STALL
C.B.S. Stall-9, Kolkata-700073
(West Bengal)

SAMARTH SUBSCRIPTION AGENCY
1170/27, Shivaji Nagar, Pune-411005
(Maharashtra)
✆ 25534073, 24012796
Estd.: 1954; **Man.**: Shrikant Pratinidhi
Br.: 1329 Jangali Maharaj Rd., Shivajinagar, Pune-411005 (Maharashtra)
Bus.Intt.: Pub., L.S. & Rt., Imp., Sub.Ag.;
Spl.: Sci. & Tech., Med.

SAMAY PRAKASHAN
I-1/16, Shanti Mohan House, Ansari Rd., Darya Ganj, New Delhi-110002
✆ 23272145, 23270889, Fax: 23270889
✉ samayprakashan@yahoo.co.in
www.samayprakashan.com
Estd.: 1996; **Hd.Org.**: Kalpana Bhushan;
Bus.Intt.: Pub.; **Spl.**: Hindi Litt., Sports, Cinema, Hist., Sci., Novels, Criticisms, Plays, Journalism and for Children

SAMAYANTAR PRAKASHAN
79-A, Dilshad Garden, Delhi-110095
✆ 91-11-22744598
✉ samayantar@yahoo.com
Hd.Org.: T.P. Chaubay
Bus.Intt.: Pub.; **Spl.**: Monthly Magazine, *Samayantar* and Books on Soc.Sci. and Eco., etc. in Hindi

SAMAYIK PRAKASHAN
3320-21, Jatwara, Netaji Subhash Marg Darya Ganj, Delhi-110002
✆ (O) 23282733, 23270715, 23270716 (R) 22175472, 22262499, Fax: 23270715
✉ samayikprakashan@rediffmail.com
Estd.: 1968; **Hd.Org.**: Mahesh Bharadwaj;
Bus.Intt.: Pub.; **Spl.**: Hindi Novels, Stories, Satires, Books on Journalism, Sci. and for Children

SAMBAD
57/2D, College St., Kolkata-700073
(West Bengal)

SAMBA PUBLISHING COMPANY PVT. LTD.
152, Peters Rd., Chennai-600086
(Tamil Nadu)
✆ (O) 28523222, 28522532 (R) 28278493, 28522532
Estd.: 1956; **Hd.Org.**: R. Thirupathi Swami

SAMEER PRAKASHAN
395, Sector 37-D, Chandigarh-160023

SAMGAM BOOK STALL
Municipal Bus Stand, Kannur-670594 (Kerala)
✆ 2700008, 2721008, 2721808,
Fax: 0497-2700008
Estd.: 1980; **Bus.Intt.**: Pub. and B.S.;
Spl.: Humanities, Gen. Books

SAMI PUBLICATIONS PVT. LTD.
2241, Kucha Chelan, Darya Ganj, New Delhi-110002
✆ 23253514, 23277913,
Fax: 23277913
✉ ibsdelhi@del2.vsnl.net.in
Bus.Intt.: Pub., WS, L.S. & Rt., and Exp.

SAMIR PUSTAKALAYA
61, Mahatma Gandhi Rd., Kolkata-700009
(West Bengal)

SAMIRAN BOOK HOUSE
15, B.C. St., Kolkata-700073
(West Bengal)

SAMKALEEN PRAKASHAN
2762, Rajguru Marg, Paharganj, New Delhi-110055
Hd.Org.: Krishan Khullar

SAMMAT PRAKASHAN
374, Sind Housing Society, Aundh, Pune-411007 (Maharashtra)

SAMPARK PRAKASHAN
7/101, R.H.B., Hanumangarh, Sangam-335512 (Rajasthan)
Hd.Org.: Smt. Kamlesh Sharma

SAMPARK PRAKASHAN
B-14, Dayanand Colony, Lajpat Nagar, New Delhi-110024

SAMRAT PUBLISHERS
Pallikulam Rd., Thrissur-680001
(Kerala)

SAMSARA BOOK STALL
Al-Ameen Shopping Complex, Tana, Irinjalakuda-680125 (Kerala)
Estd.: 1992; **Hd.Org.**: A.G. Sivasankaran;
Bus.Intt.: Pub. and B.S.

SAMSKAR
18, Chitra Vihar, Delhi-110092
✆ 22541930, Fax: 22512980
✉ madhulika-ag@hotmail.
Estd.: 1981; **Man.Dir.**: Mrs. Hem Bhatnagar; **Bus.Intt.**: Pub., B.S.;
Spl.: Humanities & Soc.Sci., Neo-Litt., Music, Flok Art, Edu. Books for Children in Hindi

SAMSKRITI
C-9020, Vasant Vihar, New Delhi-110057
✆ 26137390, 26473482, Fax: 26473482
✉ samskriti@vsnl.com
Estd.: 1998; **Prt.**: M. Sengupta, H. Das, Ms. Amrita Sengupta; **Bus.Intt.**: Pub. & Dist.;
Spl.: Soc.Sci., Humanities, Mang. and Entrepreneurship, etc.

SAMTA BOOKS PERSONAL BOOK SHOP
10, Congress Building, 575, Mount Rd., Chennai-600006 (Tamil Nadu)
✆ 2459572, 2454216
Estd.: 1953; **Hd.Org.:** V. Vijaya Lakshmi; **Bus.Intt.:** Pub., WS, L.S. and Rt., Exp.

SAMTA PRAKASHAN
30/64, Gali No. 8, Vishwas Nagar, Shahdara, Delhi-110032
✆ 22386715
Hd.Org.: Ramphal Gautam; **Bus.Intt.:** Pub. and Dist.; **Spl.:** Hindi Novels, Criticisms, Plays, Dalit and Buddhist Litt. and Books for Children

SAMTA SAHITYA SADAN
40, Meena Colony, Imli Wala Phatak, Jaipur-302005 (Rajasthan)

SAMVAD SAHITYA PRASAR
I-501, Shastri Nagar, Meerut-250004 (Uttar Pradesh)
✆ 91-121-2764866
✉ samvadindia@vsnl.net
Hd.Org.: Ramendra Nath
Bus.Intt.: Pub.; **Spl.:** Hindi Translations of World Litt., Biographies, Autobiographies, Fiction and Books on Cinema and Contemporary Hindi Litt.

SAMYAK PRAKASHAN
32/3, Club Rd., Paschim Puri, New Delhi-110063
✆ 65706888, 25216147 ▮ 9810161823, 9810249452
✉ budhdharam@bol.net.in
www.samyakprakashan.com
Hd.Org.: Sundeep Shant; **Bus.Intt.:** Pub.; **Spl.:** Buddhist Litt. for Children and Adults in Hindi

SANATAN SANSTHA
S/571, Greater Kailash Part II, New Delhi-110048
✆ 91-11-65174562
Hd.Org.: Sudarshan Prasad Gupta
Bus.Intt.: Promoter; **Spl.:** Books on Health, Religion and Spirituality

SANCHAR PUBLISHING HOUSE
H-9/2, Malviya Nagar, New Delhi-110017
Estd.: 1990; **Prop.:** Jagdish Malhotra; **Bus.Intt.:** Pub.

SANCHAYAN
New Town, Alupurduar, Distt. Jalpaiguri (West Bengal)
Hd.Org.: Nikhilesh Chatterjee

SANDEEP
11, Nabin Kundu Lane, Kolkata-700009 (West Bengal)
✆ 033-22413572
Estd.: 1984; **Prop.:** Swapna Nayak; **Bus.Intt.:** Pub.; **Spl.:** House of School Textbooks in Bengali, English and Hindi

SANDEEP BOOK CENTRE
15, Bankim Chatterjee St., Kolkata-700073 (West Bengal)

SANDEEP PRAKASHAN
Town & P.O., Talode-425413, District Dhule (Maharashtra)

SANDEEP PUBLISHERS AND DISTRIBUTORS
B-31, Gharoli Dairy Form, Mayur Vihar Phase-III, Delhi-110096
▮ 9868853420
✉ sandeep_publishers_distributors@yahoo.com
Hd.Org.: Sandeep Kumar Gautam
Bus.Intt.: Pub and Dist.; **Spl.:** General Books, Children's Books and CDs

SANDHAN
B-2/51, Sector-16, Rohini, Delhi-110085
✆ 27296030
✉ subhanjali@rediffmail.com
Hd.Org.: Lal Bahadur Verma;
Bus.Intt.: Promoter; **Spl.:** Social and Cultural Upliftment of Society

SANDHANI
54/3, College St., Kolkata-700073 (West Bengal)

SANDHU SCIENTIFIC EDUCATIONAL AID
WZ-57 Plot No. 111, Vishnu Garden, New Delhi-110018
Bus.Intt.: Dealer; **Spl.:** Hindi Books

SANDHYA LIBRARY
22, Bidhan Sarani, Kolkata-700006 (West Bengal)

SANDHYA PRAKASHANI
4G/IB, Seals Garden Lane, Kolkata-700002 (West Bengal)

SANGAM BOOK DEPOT
4754/23, Akarshan Bhavan, Ansari Rd., Darya Ganj, New Delhi-110002
✆ 23272106, 23289417, Fax: 23289417
✉ sbd@bol.net.in
Hd.Org.: Rajesh Khurana; **Bus.Intt.:** Dist.; **Spl.:** Government of India Books and Journals

SANGAM PRAKASHAN
Sangam Chowk, Muzaffarnagar-251001 (Uttar Pradesh)
✆ (O) 0131-2406428 (R) 2404900
Prop.: G.D. Gupta

SANGAM PRAKASHAN
8/39, Aasa Jagan Nivas,
Bhogipura, Shahganj, Agra-282010
(Uttar Pradesh)

SANGAM PUBLISHERS & DISTRIBUTORS
11115-B, Doriwalan, East Park Road,
Karol Bagh, New Delhi-110005
✆ 23518802, Fax: 23610700
✉ sangampublishers@rediffmail.com
Hd.Org.: Madan Lal Gupta
Bus.Intt.: Pub. & Dist.; **Spl.:** Hindi Books on Various Sub.

SANGAT PRINTERS PVT. LTD.
C-105, Naraina Industrial Area,
Phase I, New Delhi-110028
✆ 41411217, Fax: 41412032
✉ tulipchildrenbooks@gmail.com
www.tulipchildrenbooks.com
Hd.Org.: Sarbjit Singh
Bus.Intt.: Pub. & Exp.; **Spl.:** Nursery Rhymes, Story Books, Colouring and Activity Books, etc. under 'Tulip' Banner

SANGEET KARYALAYA
Banki Bhawan, Hathras-204101
(Uttar Pradesh)
✆ 05722-233933, 231111, 230123,
Fax: 07522-230123
Estd.: 1935; **Hd.Org.:** Laxmi Narayan Garg;
Bus.Intt.: Pub., B.S., L.S., WS, Rt.;
Spl.: Music and Dance as also Monthly Magazine *Sangeet*

SANGEET NATAK ADKADEMI
Rabindra Bhawan, Feroze Shah Road,
New Delhi-110001
✆ 23387246, Fax: 23385715
✉ sangeetnatak@bol.net.in
www.sangeetnatak.org
Hd.Org.: Jayant P. Kastuar
Bus.Intt.: Pub.; **Spl.:** National Academy of Music, Dance and Drama Functions as the Apex Body for the Performing arts and also Pub. Litt. on Relevant Subjects

SANGEET PRESS
Gali Gangadhar, Mursan Gate,
Hathras-204101 (Uttar Pradesh)
✆ 05722-233933, 231111,
Fax: 05722-230123
Hd.Org.: Rita Garg; **Bus.Intt.:** Pub. and Dist.; **Spl.:** Music and Dance

SANGEETA BOOKS
Village Gamari, Gali No. 1,
Near Ration Office, Bhajanpura,
Delhi-110053
✆ 22866599, 65246795
Hd.Org.: Sangeeta Devi; **Bus.Intt.:** Dist.;
Spl.: Indian and Foreign Books and Journals on All Sub.

SANGEETA PRAKASHAN
Bhaya Rosada, Samastipur, Eroth-848210
(Bihar)
▮ 9431692189
Hd.Org.: Narayan Mehta; **Bus.Intt.:** Pub.;
Spl.: Hindi Language Books on Equality and Promotion of Humanitarian Values

SANGEETA SCIENTIFIC HOUSE
LG-4A, Ganpati Bhawan, 4675/21B,
Ansari Road, Darya Ganj, New Delhi-110002
✆ (O) 23255012 (R) 52351024,
Fax: 91-11-23282127 ▮ 9810050340
✉ sshjbs@yahoo.com
Hd.Org.: Narender Kumar Jain
Bus.Intt.: Wholesaler; **Spl.:** Humanities, Soc.Sci., Sci. & Tech., Computer Science, Management, Law, Bio-Sciences, Journals on Agricultural Science

SANGHI PRAKASHAN
1587, Sanghiji Ka Rasta, Chaura Rasta,
Jaipur (Rajasthan)
✆ (O) 2317568 (R) 2523155
Hd.Org.: Vijender Kumar Sanghi

SANGHMITRA PRAKASHAN
Gautam Nagar (Bouddha Vihar)
Nagpur-440001 (Maharashtra)

SANGHVI PRAKASHAN
564, M.G. Rd. Sanghvi Market, Indore-452002
(Madhya Pradesh)
✆ 2451073 ▮ 9826067005, Fax: 2450430
Estd.: 1967; **Hd.Org.:** Pankaj Sanghvi;
Bus.Intt.: Pub., **Spl.:** School Help Books from K.G. to XII

SANGITA PUBLICATION (PVT) LTD.
B-137, Karampura, New Delhi-110015
✆ (O) 31027550 (R) 32350690
Estd.: 2003; **Man.Dir.:** Mrs. Seema Jain
Br.: Sole Distributors: Jain Book Depot,
4737A/23, Ansari Rd., Darya Ganj,
New Delhi-110002
• 23/4, Shakti Nagar, Delhi-110006
Bus.Intt.: Pub., L.S.; **Spl.:** Humanities & Soc.Sci., Sci. & Tech., Comp., Mang., Arts & Arch., Bio.Sci.

SANGUIDE PUBLISHERS CONCERN
3, Ramanath Majumder St., Kolkata-700009
(West Bengal)

SANJAY & COMPANY
A-1/353, Shah & Nahar Indl. Estate,
Dhanraj Mill Compound, Lower Parel,
Mumbai-400013 (Maharashtra)
✆ 020-24968068/69, Fax: 24965876

sanjay@tarladalal.com
www.tarladalal.com
Estd.: 1987; **Hd.Org.:** Sanjay Dalal; **Bus.Intt.:** Pub.; **Spl.:** Cookery Books in English, Hindi & Gujarati

SANJAY BOOK CENTRE
K-38/6, Golehouse, Varanasi-221001 (Uttar Pradesh)
✆ 2333504
Hd.Org.: Sanjay Agarwal

SANJAY BOOK STORE
Uphara, Aurangabad (Bihar)
Bus.Intt.: Pub. and B.S.

SANJAY BOOK STORE
Rajendra Prasad Rd., Bhagalpur-812002 (Bihar)
Bus.Intt.: Pub. and B.S.

SANJAY ENTERPRISES
New Delhi
✆ 25727696, 26663600
sundaram@bom2.vsnl.net.in
Bus.Intt.: Dist.

SANJAY K. MOHANTY
Barabati Stadium, Cuttack-753005 (Orissa)

SANJAY PRAKASHAN
1/6281, Gali No. 3, East Rohtas Nagar, Shahdara, Delhi-110032
✆ 27420386
Hd.Org.: Sanjay Sharma; **Bus.Intt.:** Pub., L.S. & Dist.; **Spl.:** Humanities, G.K., and Encyclopaedias

SANJAY PRAKASHAN
4378/4B, 209, JMD House, Ansari Rd., Darya Ganj, New Delhi-110002
✆ 23245808, 51045808
sanjay-prakashan@yahoo.com
Hd.Org.: Somnath Dhall; **Bus.Intt.:** Pub. & Dist.; **Spl.:** Hindi Litt., Music and Sanskrit

SANJAY PUSTAK BHANDAR
Khesar, Bhagalpur-813207 (Bihar)
Bus.Intt.: Pub. and B.S.

SANJAY SUPPLIERS (PUBLISHERS)
Plot 23B, Senadattapeth, Pune-411030 (Maharashtra)
Estd.: 1991; **Prop.:** Jyoti Sanjay Puranik; **Bus.Intt.:** Deals; **Spl.:** Marathi Books for School Lib.

SANJEEVA PRAKASHAN
Chhota Bazar, Lal Kurti, Meerut Cantt. (Uttar Pradesh)
✆ (O) 0121-2642913, 2646343 (R) 2769694, 2765496
Hd.Org.: Rajiv Rastogi; **Bus.Intt.:** Pub.; **Spl.:** Edu. Books

SANJIV PRAKASHAN
14, Ramanath Majumder St., Kolkata-700009 (West Bengal)

SANJIV PRAKASHAN
3613, Subhash Marg, Darya Ganj, New Delhi-110002
✆ (O) 23276551, 23252909 (R) 22160229
Hd.Org.: Satyendra Gupta

SANJNA BOOKS
434, Narayan Peth, Shop No. 2, Near Patrya Maruti, Uma Shankar Apts., Pune-411030 (Maharashtra)
✆ 2483223
Hd.Org.: Sunil L. Kulkarni; **Bus.Intt.:** Dist. & L.S.

SANKAR BHATTACHARYA & CO.
10, B.T. Rd., Sintheemore, Kolkata-700005 (West Bengal)

SANKAR BOOK STALL
117, B.K. Paul Avenue, Kolkata-700005 (West Bengal)

SANKAR PUSTAKALAYA
23/1, College Row, Kolkata-700009 (West Bengal)

SANKEERTHANAM PUBLICATIONS
Kadappakkada P.O., Kollam-691008 (Kerala)
✆ 0474-3207700
sankeerthanamklm@yahoo.co.in
Hd.Org.: Asramam Bhasi; **Bus.Intt.:** Pub.; **Spl.:** Malayalam Books

SANKHLA PRINTERS
Sugan Nivas, Chandansagar, Bikaner-334001 (Rajasthan)
✆ 2200955, Fax: 2204100
vagdevi_jpi@sancharnet.in
www.vagdevi.biz
Hd.Org.: Deepchand Sankhla
Br.: Sarjana, Jaal Gatta, Phad Bazaar, Bikaner-334001 ✆ 9414136999, Fax: 2204100
Bus.Intt.: Pub.; **Spl.:** Books in Hindi and Rajasthani

SANMARG PRAKASHAN
16, U.B. Bungalow Rd., Jawahar Nagar, Delhi-110007
✆ (O) 23851772 (R) 27866245
Prop.: Arun Kumar Sharma; **Bus.Intt.:** Pub. & Dist.; **Spl.:** Edu. Books in Hindi

SANMITRA PRAKASHAN
690-B, Ravuvaram Nidajwada, Kolhapur-416012 (Maharashtra)

SANNCHI SANDESH
32, Dr. Ambedkar Colony, Subhash Nagar, Bhopal-462023 (Madhya Pradesh)

SANSKAR
18, Chitra Vihar, Delhi-110092
✆ 22541930
✉ samskar_culp@hotmail.com
Hd.Org.: Hem Bhatnagar; **Bus.Intt.:** Pub.; **Spl.:** Educational Books and Children's Books in Hindi

SANSKAR BHARTI PRAKASHAN
11109, Doriwalan, East Park Rd., Karol Bagh, New Delhi-110005
✆ 23552350, 23628160, 23512733, Fax: 23628160, 23552350
✉ sbharti@vsnl.com, vishalarora@mantraonline.com
Estd.: 1978; **Hd.Org.:** Vishal Arora; **Bus.Intt.:** Pub.; **Spl.:** Edu. Books for Children in English and Hindi

SANSKAR SAHITYA KENDRA
12, Padmagiri Apartment, Mirambica Rd., Naranpura, Ahmedabad-380013 (Gujarat)

SANSKARS BOOKSELLERS
393, Ist 'D' Main Rd., Domlur Layout, Bangalore-560071 (Karnataka)
✆ 2567899, 2561356, Fax: 080-23345014
Estd.: 1964; **Bus.Intt.:** Rt.

SANSKRIT BOOK (PVT.) LTD.
Indological Pub. & B.S., 28/1, Bidhan Sarani, Kolkata-700006 (West Bengal)

SANSKRIT GRANTHAGAAR
109, Aggarwal Plaza, Sector 14, Rohini, New Delhi-110085
✆ 65441516
Hd.Org.: Himanshu Joshi; **Bus.Intt.:** Pub.; **Spl.:** Sanskrit Litt.

SANSKRIT PARISHAD
University of Saugar, Sagar-470003 (Madhya Pradesh)

SANSKRIT PUSTAK MANDIR
38, Bidhan Sarani, Kolkata-700006 (West Bengal)

SANSKRITI BHARTI
Mata Mandir Gali, Jhandewalan, New Delhi-110055
Bus.Intt.: Pub. & Dist.

SANSKRITI PRAKASHAN
A-304, Deivik Apartments, Evershine City, Wasai (Maharashtra)
✆ 0250-2462469
✉ samvadindia@vsnl.net
Hd.Org.: Harishchandra; **Bus.Intt.:** Pub.; **Spl.:** Hindi Translations of World Litt., Biographies, Auto-Biographies, Fiction and Books on Cinema and Contemporary Hindi Litt.

SANSKRITI PUBLICATIONS
58, Ist Avenue, Vettuvankanni, East Coast Rd., Chennai-600041 (Tamil Nadu)

SANSKRITI SANSTHAN
143, Khwaja Kutub, Bareilly (Uttar Pradesh)
✆ 0581-2474242
Hd.Org.: Arvind Suri; **Bus.Intt.:** Pub.; **Spl.:** *Vedas, Upanishads, Gita, Puranas,* Yoga, Astrology, etc.

SANT ISHER SINGH RAREWALA
Education Trust, 179-Model Gram, Ludhiana (Punjab)

SANT KRIPA PRAKASHAN
1035, Sadashiv Peth, Gyaneswari Niwas, Pune-411030 (Maharashtra)

SANT NIRANKARI MANDAL PUBLICATIONS
Sant Nirankari Colony, Sant Nirankari Satsang Bhavan, Delhi-110009

SANTHA BOOK STALL
CCSB, Alappuzha-688001 (Kerala)

SANTHA BOOK STALL
Guruvahyoor-680101 (Kerala)

SANTHA BOOK STALL
Palghat-678001 (Kerala)

SANTHAM BOOK (P.) LTD.
Chennai (Tamil Nadu)
✆ 24354622, 24354655
✉ santhambooks@mantramail.com

SANTHOSH BOOK ENTERPRISES
3-5-1107, First Floor, Narayanguda, Hyderabad-500029 (Maharashtra)
✆ 24753804, 24752107, Fax: 24752107

SANTHYAM PUBLICATIONS
Shah Bhavan, Kottanmukal Junction, Addor P.O., Pathanamthitta (Kerala)
✆ 04734-22365
Estd.: 1991; **Prop.:** Badsha; **Bus.Intt.:** Pub.

SANTOSH BOOK & GIFT SHOP
Le Meridien Hotel, 4, Shopping Arcade, Windsor Place, New Delhi-110001
✆ 2383960, 2383864

SANTOSH PRAKASHAN
Tikuriya (Near Old Hospital), Panna-488001 (Madhya Pradesh)
Hd.Org.: Rajaram Tripathi

SANTOSH PUSTAK BHANDAR
Ramdiri, Begusarai-851138 (Bihar)
Bus.Intt.: Pub. and B.S.

SANU SREE
1/1, Harekrishna Seth Lane, Kolkata-700050 (West Bengal)

SANYAL & CO.
1/1A, Bankim Chatterjee St., Kolkata-700073 (West Bengal)

SANYALS
26, Main Rd., Jamshedpur-831001 (Jharkhand)
✆ 2423768, 2425639
Estd.: 1947; **Hd.Org.:** B.N. Sanyal

SAPNA BOOK HOUSE
Thunga Complex, Opp. Tribhuvan Theatre, Gandhi Nagar, Bangalore-560009 (Karnataka)
✆ 22266088, 22261871, 22262815, 22269448, Fax: 91-80-22269648
sapnabooks@vsnl.com, sapna@giasbgrl.vsnl.net.in
www.sapnaonline.com
Estd.: 1967; **Prop.:** Nitin S. Shah
Br.: Book Mark, Near Bashyam Circle, Sadashi Vanagar, Bangalore-560003
✆ 3446444, 3446445
Bus.Intt.: Pub., WS, L.S. & Rt.; **Spl.:** Text Books, Biographies and Motivational Books in Kannada

SAPPHIRE (INDIA) PUBLISHERS PVT. LTD.
B-33, Mayapuri Industrial Area, Phase-I, New Delhi-110064
✆ 45567067, 28114044, Fax: 28114045
schoolbks@yahoo.co.in
Hd.Org.: Nitin Malhotra; **Bus.Intt.:** Pub.; **Spl.:** School Textbooks for Children

SAPRA & SAPRA PUBLISHERS DISTRIBUTORS PVT. LTD.
51, Ring Rd., Lajpat Nagar-III, New Delhi-110024
✆ 26837040, Fax: 26322498
psapra@ndf.vsnl.net.in
Hd.Org.: P. Sapra; **Bus.Intt.:** Pub. and Dist.; **Spl.:** Reference, Homoeopathy and Gen. Books as also *Directory of Periodicals Published in India*

SAQI BOOK DEPOT
4157-A, Urdu Bazar, Delhi-110006
✆ 22180638
Estd.: 1988; **Hd.Org.:** Abdul Ghani; **Bus.Intt.:** Printer, Pub. and B.S.; **Spl.:** Fiction and Non-fiction in Urdu

SARA BOOKS PVT. LTD.
4832/24, Ansari Rd., Darya Ganj, New Delhi-110002
✆ 23266107, Fax: 23266102
sarabooks@eth.net
Hd.Org.: Ravindra K. Saxena; **Bus.Intt.:** Dist.; **Spl.:** Foreign and Indian Books on Engg., Tech., Med., Law, Soc.Sci., and Mang.

SARADA BHAWAN
Balu Bazar, Cuttack-753002 (Orissa)
✆ 0671-223602
Estd.: 1962; **Prop.:** Bhikaricharan Mohapatra; **Spl.:** Gen. Litt. in Oriya

SARADA PUBLICATIONS
6-7-19-C Sakkerivani Upstairs, Koti St., Srikakulam-532001 (Andhra Pradesh)

SARADHI BOOK DEALERS
P.O. Rd., Kottayam-686001 (Kerala)
✆ 2564934
Estd.: 1976; **Prop.:** S.P. Nampoothiri; **Bus.Intt.:** Pub. and B.S.

SARALA BOOK DEPOT
Kunnamkulam, Thrissur-680503 (Kerala)
Estd.: 1952; **Prop.:** Peter Cheruvathur; **Bus.Intt.:** Pub. and B.S.

SARANSH PRAKASHAN (P) LTD.
142-E, Pocket-4, Mayur Vihar, Phase-I, Delhi-110091
✆ 22713253
Hd.Org.: Mohan Gupta; **Bus.Intt.:** Pub.; **Spl.:** Hindi Originals and Translations of Indian and World Litt. and Books on Soc.Sci.

SARAS BOOKS
2/31, Ansari Rd., Darya Ganj, New Delhi-110002
✆ (O) 23283800, 23256861 (R) 25812682
9810124244, Fax: 011-23264765
cuckoo@ndf.vsnl.net.in
Estd.: 1993; **Prop.:** Satish Malik; **Bus.Intt.:** WS, Pub.'s Rep., Imp., Stockists & Dist.; **Spl.:** Sci., Engg. Tech., Mang. & Soc.Sci.

SARASWAT PUSTAK BHANDAR
Gole Bazar, Sambalpur (Orissa)

SARASWATHA PRAKASHANA
Hayagreeva Nagar, Udupi, D.K.-576102 (Karnataka)
✆ 08252-229139
Hd.Org.: Smt. Jaya V. Shenoy; **Bus.Intt.:** Pub.; **Spl.:** Own Books in Kannada and English

SARASWATI BOOK AGENCY
94, Sitaram Ghosh St., Kolkata-700009 (West Bengal)

SARASWATI BOOK CENTRE
A-1/4, Guru Nanak Nagar, Bhagirathi Vihar, Phase-II, Karawal Ngr. Rd., Delhi-110094
✆ 22187231
Estd.: 1996; **Prop.:** Raja Ram Chauhan; **Bus.Intt.:** L.S.; **Spl.:** Soc.Sci.

SARASWATI BOOK CO. (INDIA)
C/o O.C. Tandon, 20 Vakil Lane, New Delhi-110001

SARASWATI BOOK DEPOT
209, Jawahar Marg, Rajmohalla, Indore (Madhya Pradesh)
✆ 266420

SARASWATI BOOK STALL
12/1/1A, Bankim Chatterjee St., Kolkata-700073 (West Bengal)

SARASWATI BOOK STALL
Numaligarh, Golaghat-785632 (Assam)
Bus.Intt.: Pub.

SARASWATI BOOKS
B-206, Tajram Gali No. 1, Gamri Rd., Ghonda, Delhi-110053
✆ 22197739 ▮ 9810284558
Prt.: Mukesh Kumar, D.N. Roy; **Bus.Intt.:** L.S.; **Spl.:** Acad., Soc.Sci., Sci., Tech.

SARASWATI HOUSE (P) LTD.
9, Daryaganj, Near Telephone Office, New Delhi-110002
✆ 23281022, 23283022, 23243022, 23244022, Fax: 23245011, 23243519
✉ delhi@saraswatihouse.com
🌐 www.saraswatihouse.com
Ch.Exe.: Atul Gupta
Br.: No. 48, Ist Floor, V Main Road, Chamrajpet, Bangalore-560018
✆ 26619880, 26672813
✉ bangalore@saraswatihouse.com
• SCO 262, Ist Floor, Sector 32-D, Chandigarh-160030
✆ 2624882, 9316114344
✉ chandigarh@saraswatihouse.com
• 28, Natesan Street, T. Nagar, Chennai-600017
✆ 24343740, 24346531, Fax: 24333508
✉ chennai@saraswatihouse.com
• Room No. 41/2796/B-6, North Square, Paramara Road, Ernakulam North, Kochi-682018
✆ 9895730119, Fax: 24333508
✉ kochi@saraswatihouse.com

Bus.Intt.: Pub.; **Spl.:** Edu. Books for Secondary & Sr. Secondary Classes and College Level Text books

SARASWATI LIBRARY
206, Bidhan Sarani, Kolkata-700006 (West Bengal)
✆ 033-22414845
Hd.Org.: Bibhas Bhattacherjee; **Spl.:** Hist., Phil., Rel., Art, Anthropology, Eng.Litt. and Works of Poet Sukanta Bhattacharya

SARASWATI NIKUNJ
D.N. Singh Rd., Bhagalpur-812002 (Bihar)
Bus.Intt.: Pub. and B.S.

SARASWATI OFFSET PRINTERS PVT. LTD.
Saraswati House, A-5/II, N.I.A., New Delhi-110028
✆ 25701311, 25894647, Fax: 91-11-25709519
Hd.Org.: Arun K. Agarwal; **Bus.Intt.:** Pub.

SARASWATI PRAKASHAN
"Saraswatichhaya", 20, New Samarthnagar, Opp. Nirala Bazar, Aurangabad-431001 (Maharashtra)
✆ (O) 2336445 (R) 2336845, Fax: 0240-2351297
Hd.Org.: Kumar Indure; **Bus.Intt.:** Pub.; **Spl.:** Help Books, Gen. Books and Hard Books

SARASWATI PRAKASHAN
Baidyanath Press Lane, Baidyanath, Deoghar-814112 (Bihar)
Bus.Intt.: Pub. and B.S.

SARASWATI PRAKASHAN MANDIR
83A/69A, New Bairhena, Allahabad-211003 (Uttar Pradesh)
✆ 2605573
Hd.Org.: Vyas Narayan Bhat

SARASWATI PUBLISHERS & DISTRIBUTORS
494, Avadh Bihari Ki Gali, Govind Raoji Ka Rasta, Chandpole Bazar, Jaipur-302001 (Rajasthan)
✆ 2325125
Prop.: Onkar Nath Tripathi; **Bus.Intt.:** B.S., L.S.; **Spl.:** Humanities & Soc.Sci., Sci. & Tech., Mang., Law, Bio.Sci.

SARASWATI PUBLISHERS DISTRIBUTORS
2503, Jai Lal Munshi Ka Rasta, Behind Kamani Centre, Jaipur-302001 (Rajasthan)

SARASWATI PUSTAKALAYA
Barisha, Bagnabarh, Distt. Midnapore (West) (Bihar)
Hd.Org.: Rabindranath Hazra

SARASWATI PUSTAK BHANDAR
48C, Circular Garden Reach Rd.,
Kolkata-700023 (West Bengal)

SARASWATI PUSTAK BHANDAR
Amarpur, Bhagalpur-813101 (Bihar)
Bus.Intt.: Pub. and B.S.

SARASWATI PUSTAK BHANDAR
Ishipur, Barahat, Bhagalpur-813206 (Bihar)
Bus.Intt.: Pub. and B.S.

SARASWATI PUSTAK BHANDAR
Bharkho, Bhagalpur-813126 (Bihar)
Bus.Intt.: Pub. and B.S.

SARASWATI PUSTAK BHANDAR
Panjwara, Bhagalpur-813110 (Bihar)
Bus.Intt.: Pub. and B.S.

SARASWATI PUSTAK BHANDAR
Shivanarayanpur, Bhagalpur-813203 (Bihar)
Bus.Intt.: Pub. and B.S.

SARASWATI PUSTAK BHANDAR
Hathikhana, Ratan Pole, Ahmedabad-380001 (Gujarat)

SARASWATI PUSTAK BHANDAR
Akbarnagar, Bhagalpur-812002 (Bihar)
Bus.Intt.: Pub. and B.S.

SARASWATI PUSTAK BHANDAR
Bhakharua More, Daudnagar,
Aurangabad-824113 (Bihar)
Bus.Intt.: Pub. and B.S.

SARSAWATI PUSTAK BHANDAR
Haspura, Aurangabad-824216 (Bihar)
Bus.Intt.: Pub. and B.S.

SARASWATI PUSTAK BHANDAR
Ketaki, Aurangabad-824216 (Bihar)
Bus.Intt.: Pub. and B.S.

SARASWATI PUSTAK BHANDAR
Obra, Aurangabad-824124 (Bihar)
Bus.Intt.: Pub. and B.S.

SARASWATI PUSTAK BHANDAR
Majhaul, Begusarai-851127 (Bihar)
Bus.Intt.: Pub. and B.S.

SARASWATI PUSTAK BHANDAR
Matihani, Begusarai-851139 (Bihar)
Bus.Intt.: Pub. and B.S.

SARASWATI SADAN
Haspura, Aurangabad-824120 (Bihar)
Bus.Intt.: Pub. and B.S.

SARASWATI SADAN
Katoria, Bhagalpur-813106 (Bihar)
Bus.Intt.: Pub. and B.S.

SARASWATI SADAN
Rajaun, Bhagalpur-813107 (Bihar)
Bus.Intt.: Pub. and B.S.

SARASWATI SAHITYA SADAN
Victoria Hall, Baidyanath, Deoghar-814112 (Bihar)
Bus.Intt.: Pub. and B.S.

SARASWATI VIHAR
J-40, Jorbagh Lane, New Delhi-110003
✆ 24620063, Fax: 24645795
✉ fullcircle@vsnl.com
Hd.Org.: Shekhar Malhotra
Bus.Intt.: Pub.; **Spl.:** Books on General Interest in Hindi

SARAT BOOK HOUSE
18-B, Shyama Charan Dey St.,
Kolkata-700073 (West Bengal)
✆ (O) 033-22418389, 22418060, 22413700
(R) 22461059, 22468069, Fax: 033-22418060
✉ sarat@cal2.vsnl.net.in
www.saratbookhouse.com
Estd.: 1954; **Prt.:** Amar Chand Dey;
Bus.Intt.: Pub. & Dist.; **Spl.:** Academic Books Ranging from Pure Sci., Life Sci., to Soc.Sci. & Humanities

SARAT PUBLISHING HOUSE
9/4, Tamer Lane, Kolkata-700009
(West Bengal)

SARBHUN SAMPARK BHASHA SIMITI
Vishno Kunj, Nainital-263002 (Uttarakhand)
✆ 235038

SARDANA'S ART CENTER
87, Mohan Singh Place, Connaught Circus,
New Delhi-110001
Hd.Org.: Vivek Sardana

SARITA PRAKASHAN
397/1, Varada, Senapati Bapat Marg, Traffic Signal Square, Pune-411016 (Maharashtra)

SARJANA
Sanghala Printers Parisar, Shivbadi Road,
Bikaner-334003 (Rajasthan)
✆ 2260830
✉ vagdevibooks@gmail
Hd.Org.: Deepchand Sankhla
Bus.Intt.: Pub.; **Spl.:** Children and General Books in Hindi

SARKAR & CO.
2582, Nai Sarak, Delhi-110006
✆ 27135288, Pager: 9267038166
Estd.: 1942; **Prop.:** Sarkar; **Bus.Intt.:** Pub., Dist., B.S.; **Spl.:** Text Books for School and College

SARKAR PRAKASHAN
B-4, College St. Market, Kolkata-110007 (West Bengal)

SAROJ PRAKASHAN
955, DDA Flats, GTB Enclave, Nand Vihar, Delhi-110093
Prop.: Saroj Joshi; **Spl.:** Hindi Litt., Books for Children and Music Lovers

SAROJ PRAKASHAN
646-47, Katra, Allahabad-211002 (Uttar Pradesh)
✆ (O) 0532-2608334 (R) 2641566
✉ sarojprakashan@rediffmail.com
Estd.: 1955; **Hd.Org.:** Ramcharan Das Agrawal; **Bus.Intt.:** Pub., L.S.; **Spl.:** Soc.Sci., Sci. & Tech., Med., Bio.Sci., Agri., Engg., General

SAROJA PUBLICATIONS
6-A, Mayfair Apts., Rd. No. 2, Banjara Hills, Hyderabad-500034 (Andhra Pradesh)

SARTHAK PRAKASHAN
100-A, Gautam Nagar, New Delhi-110049
✆ 26567317, Fax: 26866683
Hd.Org.: Piyush Pandit; **Bus.Intt.:** Pub. and Dist.; **Spl.:** Hindi Litt. and Reference Books

SARUP & SONS
4740/23, Ansari Rd., Darya Ganj, New Delhi-110002
✆ 23281029, 23244664, Fax: 23277098
✉ sarupandsonsin@hotmail.com
www.sarupbooks.com
Hd.Org.: Prabhat Kumar Sharma; **Bus.Intt.:** Pub.; **Spl.:** Reference and Textbooks on Soc.Sci., Life Sci., Rel. and Indology

SARVESH PRAKASHAN
Plot No. 40, Patia, Brij Enclave Extension, P.O. Bajardiha, Varanasi-221109 (Uttar Pradesh)

SARVODAYA ILAKKIYA PANNAI
32/1, West Veli St., Madurai-1 (Tamil Nadu)
✆ 2541746
Hd.Org.: S. Thirunavukkarasu; **Bus.Intt.:** Pub. House to spread the Ideas of Gandhi, Vinoba and Sarvodaya Movement and Selling Latest Books on all Sub. from all Countries of the World

SARVODAYA SAHITYA PRAKASHAN
K-61/99-100 Bulanala, Varanasi-221007 (Uttar Pradesh)
Hd.Org.: Tarun Bhai

SARYESH PUBLICATIONS
Shripad Karve Rd., 64/14, Erandwane, Pune-4 (Maharashtra)

SASADHAR PRAKASHANI
10/2B, Ramanath Majumder St., Kolkata-700009 (West Bengal)

SASTA SAHITYA MANDAL
N-77, Connaught Circus, New Delhi-110001
✆ 23310505, 41523565, Fax: 41523565
✉ manager@sastasahityamandal.org
www.sastasahityamandal.org
Hd.Org.: Indra Nath Chowdhury; **Bus.Intt.:** Pub. & Dist.; **Spl.:** Books by Gandhi, Nehru, Tolstoy, Khalil Gibran and on Health

SASTRA SAHITYA PARISHAD
Pulimoodu Jn., Kottayam-686001 (Kerala)

SAT PRAKASH SANCHAR KENDRA
Bhanwarkua Chowraha, Indore-1 (Madhya Pradesh)

SAT SAHITYA BHANDAR
57-B, Pocket A, Ashok Vihar, Part-II, Delhi-110052
✆ 27420386
Hd.Org.: L.N. Sharma

SAT SAHITYA PRAKASHAN
205-B, Chawri Bazar, Delhi-110006
✆ 23257555, Fax: 91-11-23276316
Prop.: Shyam Sunder; **Bus.Intt.:** Pub.; **Spl.:** Sci., Math., Litt., Dictionaries and books for Children and Neo-Literates

SAT SAI BOOKS
C-6/8, D.D.A. Flat, Sector-15, Rohini, New Delhi-110085
✆ 25160765
Estd.: 1998; **Prop.:** Desh Raj Lama; **Bus.Intt.:** L.S.; **Spl.:** Beh.Sci., Soc.Sci., Sci., Pure & Applied and Law Books

SAT VICHAR DARSHAN
Mumbai (Maharashtra)
✆ 23864919, 23866986, Fax: 23866435
✉ ddsat@giasbm01.vsnl.net.in

SATENDER PRAKASHAN
30, Old Allapur, Allahabad-211006 (Uttar Pradesh)
✆ 2500255
Hd.Org.: Satender Shukal

SATHI MAHAL
Binod Behari, Cuttack-753002 (Orissa)
✆ 0671-225383
Prop.: Radeshyam Mohanty; **Bus.Intt.:** Pub. and B.S.

SATHIAPRAKASHINI BIBLE PUBLISHING COMPANY
Angamalli-683572 (Kerala)
✆ 452499, 453083
✉ daniel@giasmd01.vsnl.net.in

Estd.: 1944; **Prop.**: A.P. Daniel;
Bus.Intt.: Pub.

SATHWIKA PRAKASHANA
345, "Samrudha" Lakshmi Rd., 7th Cross, Shantinagar, Bangalore-560027 (Karnataka)
✆ 080-22233729
Hd.Org.: K. Usha; **Bus.Intt.**: Pub.;
Spl.: Fiction and Collection

SATHYAM LITERATURE SERVICE
Eraviperoor P.O. (Pathanamthitta Distt.), Thiruvalla-689542 (Kerala)
✆ 0437-26286
Estd.: 1988; **Hd.Org.**: C.V. Vadavana;
Bus.Intt.: Pub. and B.S.; **Spl.**: Christian Litt. in Malayalam

SATISAR PUBLISHERS
B-30, 2nd Floor, Chandergupt Complex, Subhash Chowk, Laxmi Nagar, New Delhi-110092
✆ 22415948, 22416673
Estd.: 1989; **Prop.**: Kanwal Krishan Handoo;
Bus.Intt.: Pub., WS, L.S., Rt., Exp.

SATHVANE PRAKASHAN
C/o Magnetic Health Centre, Hingna Rd., Indira Gandhi Nagar, Nagpur (Maharashtra)

SATISFY
115, 2nd Floor, Adchini, Mehrauli Rd., New Delhi-110017
✆ (O) 26514859 (R) 26192018
Estd.: 1994; **Prt.**: Mrs. Monika Kumara, Mrs. Saroj Saxena; **Bus.Intt.**: Rt.; **Spl.**: Tech. Books

SATISH AGENCIES
673, 10th Cross, 2nd Stage, West of Chord Rd., Bangalore-560086 (Karnataka)
✆ 23329697, Fax: 23329697
Estd.: 1983; **Bus.Intt.**: WS L.S.; **Spl.**: School, College and Library, Representing over 100 Pub. in India for ICSE, CBSE and State Board Books

SATISH BOOK ENTERPRISE
135, Ashok Nagar, Agra-282002 (Uttar Pradesh)
✆ 2263557
Estd.: 1969; **Hd.Org.**: Satish Jain;
Bus.Intt.: WS, L.S. and Rt., Sub.Ag.

SATISH PRINTERS & PUBLISHERS
209/1, Kajari Bazar, M.G. Rd., Indore-452002 (Madhya Pradesh)
✆ 2537214, 2454376
Estd.: 1971; **Prop.**: Satish Agrawal;
Bus.Intt.: Pub.; **Spl.**: Comm. and Edu. Help and Text/Series Books

SATISH SERIAL PUBLICATIONS
115, Express Tower, Commercial Complex, Azadpur, Delhi-110033
✆ 27672852, 27672469, Fax: 27672046
✉ info@satishserial.com
www.satishserial.com
Estd.: 1970; **Prop.**: Satish Kumar Jain;
Bus.Intt.: Pub. & Dist.; **Spl.**: Books and Journals on Agril., Veterinary Sci., Geo., Sci., Math. Subscription Agent for Foreign Journals

SATLUJ PRAKASHAN
SCF 267, Sector 16, Panchkula-134113 (Haryana)
✆ 5048541, Fax: 0172-2570725
Hd.Org.: Desh Nirmohi; **Bus.Intt.**: Pub. & Dist.; **Spl.**: Books in Hindi on Litt.

SATNAM ENTERPRISES
2/9, Ground Floor, Ansari Road, Darya Ganj, New Delhi-110002
✆ 41563911, 23289119
✉ mail@sbspublishers.com, satnamenterprises@indiatimes.com
Hd.Org.: Ishpreet S. Bhasin
Br.: S.B.S. Publishers & Distributors Pvt. Ltd., 30/19-19A, Ist Floor, West Patel Nagar, New Delhi-110008
✆ 2587434, Fax: 25874314
✉ mail@sbspublishers.com
Bus.Intt.: Dist., Imp. & Exp.; **Spl.**: Art, Arch., Islam, Sci. & Tech., and books from Iran and around the world

SATYA DHARMA BODH MISSION
236/1, 22 Civil Lines, Roorkee, Distt., Hardwar-247667 (Uttarakhand)
✆ 01332-27100
✉ arorafmc@utr.ernet.in
Hd.Org.: Ashok Rochlani; **Bus.Intt.**: Pub.;
Spl.: Books on Human Values, Spiritualism, Positive thinking, Self-development, etc.

SATYA DHARMA BODH MISSION
501, Prayag Flats, Parle Point, Surat (Gujarat)
✆ 2322639
✉ satyadharm2002@yahoo.co.in
Hd.Org.: Ashok Rochlani; **Bus.Intt.**: Pub.;
Spl.: Books in Hindi on Sci., Phil., etc. as well as Promoter of Vegetarianism

SATYA MANDIR
B-116/2 Indira Nagar, Lucknow-226016 (Uttar Pradesh)

SATYA PRAKASHAN
16/7698, New Market, New Rohtak Rd., New Delhi-110005
✆ 25720653, 25725679, 25753594
Estd.: 1954; **Hd.Org.**: Smt. Sumitra Handa;
Bus.Intt.: Pub., WS, L.S. and Rt., Exp.

SATYAM BOOK SYNDICATE
1/6499, East Park, Rohtas Nagar, Shahdara, Delhi-110032
✆ 22137877 ▮ 32005204
Prop.: Ashok Kr. Sharma; **Bus.Intt.:** Rt., Pub.'s Rep., L.S.; **Spl.:** Acad., Soc.Sci., Comm., Sci., Pure & Applied

SATYAM BOOKS
2/13, Ansari Rd., Darya Ganj, New Delhi-110002
✆ (O) 23245698, 23242686 (R) 22459334, Fax: 23267131
✉ satyambooks@hotmail.com
Estd.: 1996; **Prop.:** Satish Upadhyay; **Bus.Intt.:** Pub.; **Spl.:** Law, Mang., Sci. & Tech., Soc.Sci. (All kinds of Indian & Foreign Books)

SATYAM PUBLISHING HOUSE
N-3/25, Mohan Garden, New Delhi-110059
✆ 25358640
✉ satyampub_2006@yahoo.com
Hd.Org.: R.D. Pandey; **Bus.Intt.:** Pub.; **Spl.:** Religious & Edu. books in Hindi and Sanskrit

SATYAM SHIVAM
A.T. Rd., Jorhat (Assam)
Bus.Intt.: Pub.

SATYANARAYAN GENERAL STORES
Main Bazar, Debhari-388001 (Gujarat)

SATYAVIR GOEL
H.No. 1 Deepali, Pitampura, New Delhi-110085
✆ 27021789, Fax: 23521027
✉ infor@battingperfectsix.com
🌐 www.battingperfectsix.com
Hd.Org.: Satyavir Goel; **Bus.Intt.:** Pub.; **Spl.:** Book *Perfect Six* which is about assessing one's Batting ability and is meant for Players and General Readers

SATYENDRA PRAKASHAN
30, Purana Allahpur, Allahabad-211006 (Uttar Pradesh)
Hd.Org.: Satyendra Shukla

SAUHARDA BOOK STORE
1683, Hanumantha Rd. St., 2nd Main, Mysore-570001 (Karnataka)
✆ 424394
✉ yajiv@bgl.vsnl.net.in, rajiv@dgl.vsnl.net.in
Estd.: 1976; **Prop.:** K.R. Seshadri; **Bus.Intt.:** L.S. & Rt.; **Spl.:** Humanities & Soc.Sci., Sci. & Tech., Law

SAUJANYA BOOKS
165-E, Kamala Nagar, Delhi-110007
✆ 22923541, Fax: 22919007
✉ saujanya@del3.vsnl.net.in
Estd.: 1992; **Bus.Intt.:** Exp.; **Spl.:** Books, Newspapers, Magazines, Journals etc.

SAURABH BOOKS & EDUCATIONAL SERVICE
Delhi
✆ 27471067, 27477867, Fax: 27471067
✉ anoop_sareen@rediffmail.com
Bus.Intt.: B.S. & Dist.

SAURABH PRINT-O-PACK
A-64, Defence Colony, New Delhi-110024
✆ 45239621, Fax: 91-118-4620476
Hd.Org.: Vikrant Gulati; **Bus.Intt.:** Exp. and Manufacturers

SAURABH PUBLISHING (P) LTD.
B-3, Ground Floor, New Krishna Park, Vikaspuri, New Delhi-110018
✆ 25509668
✉ deepak_saurabh@yahoo.com
Hd.Org.: Deepak Aggarwal
Bus.Intt.: Pub.; **Spl.:** Books in Hindi

SAURABH PUSTAK BHANDAR
Opp. Padshahni Pole, Relief Rd., Ahmedabad-380001 (Gujarat)

SAURABH: THE READERS BOOK SHOP
Rajendra Prasad Rd., Bhagalpur-812002 (Bihar)
✆ 421108
✉ shreeman8@yahoo.com
Hd.Org.: Shreeman Narayan; **Bus.Intt.:** Pub. and B.S.

SAVAN BOOKS
P.O. Box No. 8649, "Shivani" Block II-F4 (4th Floor), 40, East Coast Rd., Thiruvanmiyur, Chennai-600041 (Tamil Nadu)
✆ (O) 24454500, 24421229 (R) 24413792, Fax: 91-044-24910910
✉ asis56@md3.vsnl.net.in, assisbi@md3.vsnl.net.in
Estd.: 1991; **Prop.:** N. Lakxmikanth
Br.: 75/95, 4th Main Rd., CITB, Bapuji Nagar, Bangalore ✆ 080-26747006
Bus.Intt.: L.S. & Rt., Imp., Sub.Ag.
Spl.: Sci. & Tech., Med.

SAVEN SEAS
D-10/5, Okhla Industrial Area, Phase-II, New Delhi-110020

SAVERA BOOK DISTRIBUTORS
88-G, Gandhi Ashram Chowk, Garh Rd., Meerut-250002 (Uttar Pradesh)
✆ (O) 0121-2700304, 2700637 (R) 2704717, 2701862 ▮ 9836000901, Fax: 2704244
Estd.: 1993; **Prop.:** Amrish Kumar Sharma; **Bus.Intt.:** Pub., B.S., L.S., WS; **Spl.:** Mang. Comp., Tech., Engg. and College Books

SAVI KANNADA BALAGHA
101, Second Floor, 4th Main Chamarajapet, Bangalore-560018 (Karnataka)
Hd.Org.: Rajkumar; **Bus.Intt.:** Pub.; **Spl.:** Own Books

SAVITA PRAKASHAN
1/3 H, East Azad Nagar, Delhi-110051
✆ 22241937
Hd.Org.: Vivek Gupta

SAVITA SAHITYA SADAN
6-1-630/5, Khairatabad, Hyderabad-500004 (Andhra Pradesh)
✆ 2235960
Estd.: 1985; **Prop.:** Yogesh Kumar Chandak; **Bus.Intt.:** B.S. and L.S.

SAVITHA PRAKASHANA
25, 'Balligava' Dattatreya Nagar, Banashankari Stage III, Bangalore-560085 (Karnataka)
Hd.Org.: Venugopal Soraba; **Bus.Intt.:** Pub.; **Spl.:** Fiction and Poem Collections in Kannada

SAVITRI ENTERPRISES
Capt. Hitesh Mehta Marg Market, Opp. S.B.I., Malviya Nagar, New Delhi-110017
Estd.: 1987; **Prop.:** R.S. Khanna

SAWAN KIRPAL PUBLICATIONS
Spiritual Society, H-11, Vijay Nagar, Delhi-110009
✆ 27210722

SAWAN PUBLICATIONS
Sawan Cottage, F-239, Pandav Nagar, Patpar Ganj, Delhi-110092

SCHOLAR PUBLISHING HOUSE (P) LTD.
85, Model Basti, New Delhi-110005
✆ 23541299, 2362303, Fax: 23676565
✉ scholar@vsnl.com, scholar@del2.vsnl.net.in
🌐 www.scholargroup.com
Estd.: 1968; **Hd.Org.:** Y.P. Ranade
Bus.Intt.: Pub.; **Spl.:** Children's Books and School Textbooks

SCHOLARS HUB
P/10B, F.F. Jangpura Extn., New Delhi-110014
✆ 24310049, 41720543 📱 9811170218
✉ vipinscholarshub@yahoo.co.in
Prop.: Vipin Bajaj; **Bus.Intt.:** Pub. & Imp.; **Spl.:** Edu. Books, Audio and CDs

SCHOLARS PUBLISHING FORUM
A-13, Green Park Extension, New Delhi-110029

SCHOLARS PUBLICATIONS
171, Bankers St., Meerut Cantt.-250001 (Uttar Pradesh)

SCHOLASTIC INDIA (P) LTD.
Golf View Corporate Tower-A, Third Floor, DLF Phase-V, Gurgaon-122002 (Haryana)
✆ 0124-4068940 (6 Lines), Fax: 0124-4068946
✉ clubs.del@scholastic.co.in
🌐 www.scholasticindia.com
Estd.: 1996; **Hd.Org.:** Neeraj Jain
Br.: Door No. 14, 29th Cross Street, Indira Nagar, Adyar, Chennai-600020
✆ 044-24450546, 24450548, Fax: 044-24450547
✉ clubs.chn@scholastic.co.in
• 351 Jodhpur Park, Kolkata-700068
✆ 033-24143525, 24144221, Telefax: 033-24143474
✉ clubs.kol@scholastic.co.in
• 105, Sears Tower, Opposite IIPM, Gulbai Tekra, Ahmedabad-380015
✆ 079-65450725
✉ clubs.ahm@scholastic.co.in
• SCO-22, First Floor, Swastic Vihar, Sec-5, Mansa Devi Complex, Panchkula-134109 ✆ 0172-4643590
• Udhyog Bhavan, Office No-67, Opp. Brijwasi Sweets, Sonawala Road, Goregaon East, Mumbai-400063
✆ 022-6711223
✉ clubs.mum@scholastic.co.in
• No.1, Ground Floor, Manali Building, Orion Complex, Aundh Road, Pune-411003
✆ 0212-25820355, Telefax: 0212-25815301
✉ clubs.pne@scholastic.co.in
• 5/BC-106, First Floor, 5th B-Cross, HRBR Layout, 3rd Block, Kalyan Nagar, Bangalore-560043 ✆ 080-25446445, Telefax: 080-25446419
✉ clubs.blr@scholastic.co.in
• H.No. 5-8-369/1/C, Clock House 2002, Chirag Ali Lane, Abids, Hyderabad-500001
✆ 040-65966268, 23202775
✉ clubs.hyd@scholastic.co.in
• RZ-158, Kishangarh, Vasant Kunj, New Delhi-110070 ✆ 011-26139535
Bus.Intt.: Pub.; **Spl.:** Children's Books in English and Hindi and Organiser of Book Clubs and Book Fairs of Books from All over the World

SCHOOL-FELLOW
B/L-51, Anand Vihar, Jail Rd., New Delhi-110064
✆ 55692662
✉ schoolfellow@sify.com
Hd.Org.: Usha Seth; **Bus.Intt.:** Pub.; **Spl.:** Bimonthly Edu. Magazine *School-Fellow* for Schools and Students

SCI-TECH MEDIA
18-H, Pocket-4, Phase I, Mayur Vihar, Delhi-110091

© 22719192, 22715313, 35349254
✉ scitech_media@yahoo.com,
bookjunction@hotmail.com
Estd.: 1997; **Prop.**: Rahul Arora; **Bus.Intt.**: L.S., WS; **Spl.**: Sci. & Tech., Comp., Mang. books

SCIENCE DIRECT
17-A/1, Main Ring Rd., Lajpat Nagar-IV,
New Delhi-110024
© & Fax: 26447164
✉ esindia@vsnl.net
www.sciencedirect.com
Hd.Org.: Pradeep Kumar; **Bus.Intt.**: Pub.; **Spl.**: Journals and Online Databases

SCIENCE PRESS
C/o Narosa Publishing House Pvt. Ltd., 22, Darya Ganj, Delhi Medical Association Rd., New Delhi-110002
© 23258579, 23259263, Fax: 23258934, 23243225
✉ narosa@ndc.vsnl.net.in
Hd.Org.: Wang Jixiang; **Bus.Intt.**: Pub.; **Spl.**: Med. and Sci. and Tech. in China

SCIENTIFIC AND TECHNICAL BOOKS
U-3, MIG Flats, Prasad Nagar,
New Delhi-110005
© 25713604 ▮ 9810234957, Fax: 25819143
✉ stb@vsnl.net
Estd.: 1977; **Prop.**: Suresh Kumar Ajbaney; **Bus.Intt.**: L.S.; **Spl.**: Beh.Sci., Mang., TQM, Quality Control and Comp.Sci.

SCIENTIFIC BOOK CENTRE
Hengrabari Housing Rd., Dispur,
Guwahati-781006 (Assam)
© (O) 0361-2266846 (R) 0361-2221273
✉ sbcbook@sify.com
Estd.: 1999; **Prop.**: R.V. Pillai; **Bus.Intt.**: Pub., L.S.; **Spl.**: Tech.

SCIENTIFIC BOOK DEPOT
Cuttack (Orissa)
© 0671-614183
✉ ctk_scbkdpt@sancharnet.in
Bus.Intt.: B.S.

SCIENTIFIC BOOK DISTRIBUTORS
A/252, Sector 19, Noida-201301 (Uttar Pradesh)
© 915-2531238
Prop.: Vijay Laxmi Aggarwal; **Bus.Intt.**: Rt. and L.S.; **Spl.**: Soc.Sci., Sci. Pure and Applied Med., Tech. and Law

SCIENTIFIC BOOK DISTRIBUTORS
C-3/327, First Floor, Yamuna Vihar,
Delhi-110053
© 91-11-22265762
Prop.: Mrs. Radha Rani; **Bus.Intt.**: Rt. and L.S.

SCIENTIFIC BOOK MART
Sarkar Building (First Floor), Sakchi,
Jamshedpur-831001 (Bihar)

SCIENTIFIC BOOKS & PERIODICALS
10, Hornby Bldg., 2nd Floor, 172-174 DN Rd., Fort, Mumbai-400001 (Maharashtra)
© 22071227, 2582287, Fax: 22070396
✉ scpdcals@vsnl.com
Estd.: 1987; **Prop.**: A.M. Navlekar; **Bus.Intt.**: Sub.Ag.; **Spl.**: Sci. & Tech., Med.

SCIENTIFIC BOOKS SUPPLIERS
102, Vikas Surya Plaza, C.U. Block,
L.S.C. Market, Pitampura, Delhi-110088
© & Fax: 27341616
✉ sciencebooks@rediffmail.com,
jlejain@satyam.net.in,
jb_jain@satyam.net.in
Estd.: 1987; **Hd.Org.**: J.B. Jain; **Bus.Intt.**: B.S.; **Spl.**: Pure and Applied Sci., Back Volumes of Journals, etc.

SCIENTIFIC DATA BANK SERVICES PVT. LTD.
21, Patullos Rd., Chennai-600002
(Tamil Nadu)
© 28524124, Fax: 044-28524124
Bus.Intt.: Photo-typesetting, Data Capture, Printing, Typography, Printing and Publishing Activities

SCIENTIFIC INSTRUMENTS STORES
J-355, New Rajinder Nagar,
New Delhi-110060
© 25751501, 25745527, Cable: "SIS NEW DELHI"
Estd.: 1944; **Prop.**: Mrs. Avinash Thakore; **Bus.Intt.**: Deals; **Spl.**: Geographicals Books, Maps Atlasses, Charts, Globes

SCIENTIFIC INTERNATIONAL PVT. LTD.
4850/24, Ansari Road, Darya Ganj,
New Delhi-110002
© (O) 23287580 (R) 22461388
▮ 9811016553, Fax: 23286096
✉ sipldlhi@vsnl.net
www.cbspd.com
Man.Dir.: Satish Kumar Jain
Bus.Intt.: Dist.; **Spl.**: Med., Tech., Mang, Life Sci., Art & Arch., Engg.

SCIENTIFIC LITERATURE CO.
"Barjatya Chambers", 44, Jaora Compound, Indore-452001 (Maharashtra)
© (O) 2701041, 2701879 (R) 2496284
Fax: 2702088
Estd.: 1986; **Hd.Org.**: Dr. H.S. Bhargava; **Bus.Intt.**: B.S.; **Spl.**: Graduate, Adv. Books for Lib., Gen. Books and Med.

SCIENTIFIC MINING PUBLISHERS
Quarter No. 14, Type V, CMRS Colony, Barwa Rd., Dhanbad-826001 (Jharkhand)

SCIENTIFIC PUBLISHERS (INDIA)
5-A, New Pali Rd., P.B. No. 91, Jodhpur-342001 (Rajasthan)
✆ 2433323, 2624154, Fax: 2512580, 2512712
info@scientificpub.com, amrish@jpl.vsnl.net.in, atrans@jp1.dot.net.in
www.scientificpub.com
Estd.: 1976; **Hd.Org.:** Pawan Kumar Sharma; **Bus.Intt.:** B.S., Pub. and Dist.; **Spl.:** Sci. and Tech. Books and Journals

SCIENTIFIC SERVICES
1-1-180/15, RTC Cross Rd., Hyderabad-500020 (Andhra Pradesh)
✆ 27611708, 26501483
scientific_services@rediffmail.com
Estd.: 1970; **Prop.:** S. Gopala Rao; **Bus.Intt.:** L.S. & Rt., Sub.Ag.; **Spl.:** Humanities & Soc.Sci., Sci. & Tech., Gen. & Fiction etc.

SCIENTIFIC TECHNICAL EDUCATIONAL PUBLISHING CO-OPERATIVE SOCIETY
Opp. AG's Office, Thiruvananthapuram-695001 (Kerala)

SCITECH PUBLICATIONS (INDIA) PVT. LTD.
4 Anna St., Chitalapakkam, Chennai-600064 (Tamil Nadu)
✆ 044-22238403
scitechcorp@yahoo.co.in
www.scitechpublications.com
Estd.: 1998; **Prop.:** M.R. Purushothaman; **Bus.Intt.:** Pub.; **Spl.:** Sci. & Tech., Mang. and Reference

SCORPIO BOOKS
35-D, Basti Kabir, Malka Ganj, Delhi-110007
✆ 22524801
Hd.Org.: Satish Kumar; **Bus.Intt.:** L.S.; **Spl.:** Sci. and Tech.

SCORPIO BOOKS
44-R, Model Town, Rohtak-124001 (Haryana)

SCREEN WORLD PUBLICATION
Prakash Photo, Studio, 295, N.C. Kelkar Rd., Dadar, Mumbai-400028 (Maharashtra)
✆ (O) 28908039 (R) 28692244
swpub@bom3.vsnl.net.in, screenworldndia.com
Estd.: 1980; **Bus.Intt.:** Pub. and B.S.; **Spl.:** Film Directories, Filmography, etc.

SEAGULL BOOKS
26, Circus Avenue (1st Floor), Kolkata-700017 (West Bengal)
✆ 033-22873737, 22877942
Fax: 033-22805143
seagullfoundation@vsnl.com
www.seagullindia.com
Br.: A-27, Defence Colony, Basement, New Delhi-110024 ✆ 51552571/72
seagulldelhi@touchtelindia.net
Estd.: 1997; **Hd.Org.:** Naveen Kishore; **Bus.Intt.:** Pub., Dist. and Imp.; **Spl.:** Art, Cinema, Theatre, Beh. & Soc.Sci.

SEAKING MARINE COMPANY
New No. 39 (Old No. 18), Moore St., 1st Floor, Chennai-600001
✆ 25227651, 25220547, Fax: 91-44-25230044
Hd.Org.: S. Manivannan; **Bus.Intt.:** Exp.; **Spl.:** Perishables, Apparels, Books

SEASONS PUBLISHING
38, Arcot Rd., Chennai-600026 (Tamil Nadu)
✆ 2422475, Fax: 24837037
Prop.: M. Karthik Meiyappan; **Bus.Intt.:** Pub. and Exp.; **Spl.:** Children Books

SEE SATHYA PUBLICATIONS
32, Janata Flats, Konti Sikhara, Punjagutta, Hyderabad-504082 (Andhra Pradesh)

SEEK FOUNDATION
586, IInd Cross, V. Main, Hanumantha Nagar, Bangalore-560019 (Karnataka)

SEEMA PRAKASHAN
11, Usha Society Nr., Head Post Office, Anand-388001 (Gujarat)
✆ (O) 259315 (R) 234740
Estd.: 2003; **Bus.Intt.:** Pub., B.S., L.S.; **Spl.:** Soc.Sci., Mang., Arts & Arch.

SEEMA SAHITYA BHAWAN
283 G, New Loyalpur, Delhi-110051

SEEMANT PRAKASHAN
922, Kucha Rohella Khan, Tiraha Behram Khan, Darya Ganj, New Delhi-110002
✆ (O) 23270284, 23281880 (R) 28278243
Estd.: 1976; **Prop.:** Narinder Nath; **Bus.Intt.:** Pub., WS, L.S. and Exp.; **Spl.:** Hist., Library Sci., Litt., Ficition and Children Books in Hindi, Urdu & English Language

SEETA PRAKASHAN
Moti Bazar, Distt. Aligarh, Hathras-204101 (Uttar Pradesh)
Hd.Org.: Seetaram Gupta

SEGMENT BOOK DISTRIBUTORS
22, Prakash Deep DMA Road, Darya Ganj, New Delhi-110002
✆ 41631191, Fax: 41563498
segment@vsnl.net
www.segmentbooks.com

Estd.: 1979; **Prop.**: Sanjog Kapoor; **Bus.Intt.**: Stockist, Dist., Imp.; **Spl.**: Sci. & Tech., Humanities & Soc.Sci., Mang., Information Tech., Reference Books and Encyclopeadias

SEHAN PRAKASHAN
C-12, Kesar Apartments, Jog Hospital Marg, Pound Rd., Pune-411038 (Maharashtra)

SEHGAL BOOK DEPOT
4454, Nai Sarak (Near Roshan Pura), Delhi-110006
✆ 22915332, 23950746
Estd.: 1950; **Prop.**: Swarn Sehgal

SEHGAL BOOK DISTRIBUTORS
6 'N' Block Market, Greater Kailash-I, New Delhi-110048
✆ (O) 26246522, 26453295 (R) 26473477
Hd.Org.: Harjit Singh Sehgal; **Bus.Intt.**: Rt., L.S. and Pub.'s Rep.

SEHGAL BROS. BOOKSELLERS
South Extension Market-I, New Delhi-110049
✆ 24602273
Bus.Intt.: Rt. and WS; **Spl.**: Gen. Imported Books

SEHGAL PUBLISHERS SERVICE
C/o Super Tri Star Shop No. 4, 1800-A/9, Govind Puri Extn., Kalkaji, New Delhi-110019

SEKAL EKAL
8B/1, Tamer Lane, Kolkata-700009 (West Bengal)

SELECT BOOK POINT
3-5-944, Flat No. 211, 2nd Floor, Kubera Towers, Narayanaguda, Hyderabad-500029 (Andhra Pradesh)
✆ (O) 040-55628895, 55628896, 55730858 (R) 24330931, Fax: 55730858
✉ sbp_book@yahoo.com
Estd.: 1994; **Prop.**: P. Seetharam Reddy; **Bus.Intt.**: L.S.; **Spl.**: Humanities & Soc.Sci., Mang.

SELECT BOOK SERVICE SYNDICATE
2/41, Sant Vihar Lane, Darya Ganj, New Delhi-110002
✆ 23247795, 33102624, Fax: 23278271
✉ sbs.sushil@airtelbroadband.in
Estd.: 1968; **Prt.**: Manmohan Kapoor, Sushil Kapoor, Manoj Kapoor; **Bus.Intt.**: Pub. & Imp.; **Spl.**: Soc.Sci., Humanities, Env., Comp.Sci., and Math.

SELECT BOOK SHOP
71, Brigade Rd. (Cross), Bangalore-560001 (Karnataka)
✆ 080-23386880, 5580770; Fax: 080-25711129
✉ selectobookshop@hotmail.com
www.selectbookshop.com
Estd.: 1945; **Prop.**: K.K.S. Murthy; **Bus.Intt.**: Pub. & B.S.; **Spl.**: Rare and Antique Books

SELECTION
148/4, N.S.C. Bose Rd., Ranikuthi Regent Park, Kolkata-700040 (West Bengal)

SELECTION BOOK SERVICE
B-42, Christian Colony, Near Patel Chest, Delhi University, Delhi-110007
Hd.Org.: Swati Thaker

SELECTIVE & SCIENTIFIC BOOKS
C-73/B, (Ground Floor), Pandav Nagar, Patparganj, Delhi-110092
✆ 22484131, 23352438 ▮ 9810766022, Fax: 23736679
✉ ssbooks@rediffmail.com
Prop.: Shailendra Mishra
Br.: 3/4, Raisina Rd., Near 1 No. NDMC Market, Opp. Chelmsford Club, New Delhi-110001
✆ 23352438 ▮ 9810002715
✉ ssbook@usa.net, ssbooks@rediffmail.com
Bus.Intt.: Pub. & L.S.; **Spl.**: Forensic Sci., Criminology, Security, Sci. & Library Books

SELF-DEVELOPMENT PUBLICATIONS
Mehta 18, Sujata, Opp. Police Station, Juhu Rd., Santacruz, West, Mumbai-400054 (Maharashtra)

SELF-DEVELOPMENT STUDY CENTRE
Temple Rd., Idukki Distt., Thodupuzha-685584 (Kerala)

SELINA PUBLISHERS
4725/21A, Dayanand Marg, Darya Ganj, New Delhi-110002
✆ (O) 23280711, 23277230, 23927688 (R) 23911185, Fax: 23277230
✉ selina@vsnl.com
Hd.Off.: 2, Goela Lane, Under Hill Rd., Civil Lines, Delhi-110054
✆ 23947699
Prop.: H.L. Gupta; **Bus.Intt.**: Pub.; **Spl.**: ICSE School Text Books

SELVI BOOK SHOP
Madurai (Tamil Nadu)
✆ 0452-345169, 343510
✉ selvibooks_mdu@sify.com

SEN BOOK STALL
1, Bankim Chatterjee St., Kolkata-700073 (West Bengal)

SEN ROY & CO. PVT. LTD.
15, Bankim Chatterjee St., Kolkata-700073 (West Bengal)

SENGUPTA BOOK STALL
Stall-54, 1, Bankim Chatterjee St.,
Kolkata-700073 (West Bengal)

SERIALS PUBLICATIONS
4830/24, Ansari Rd., Darya Ganj,
New Delhi-110002
✆ 23245225, Fax: 23272135
✉ serials@satyam.net.in
www.serialspublications.com
Hd.Org.: S.K. Jha; **Bus.Intt.:** Pub. and Dist.; **Spl.:** Journals on Law, Comp.Sci. & Soc.Sci.

SERV SEVA SANGH PRAKASHAN
Rajghat, Varanasi-221001 (Uttar Pradesh)
✆ 2331285
Hd.Org.: Hemdev Sharma

SERVANTS OF PEOPLE SOCIETY
Lajpat Bhavan, Lajpat Nagar-IV,
New Delhi-110024
Presi.: Mannubhai Patel

SERVICES PUBLISHING HOUSE
86, Hamidia Rd., Bhopal-462001
(Madhya Pradesh)
Bus.Intt.: B.S. and Pub.

SERVODAY SAHITYA PRAKASHAN
K-61/99-100, Bulanath, Varanasi-221001
(Uttar Pradesh)
✆ 2333867
Hd.Org.: Ramji Singh

SETH & COMPANY
Shop No. 5 & 6, New 54,
Lawyer's Chamber Block, Next to UCO Bank,
Delhi High Court, Sher Shah Rd.,
New Delhi-110003
Rgd.Off.: S-148, Greater Kailash-I,
New Delhi-110048
✆ (O) 23387578, 23387579, 23387479, 23956081 (R) 26221555, Fax: 26221555, 23387479
✉ sethair60@hotmail
Estd.: 1980; **Man.Dir.:** Rohit Seth; **Bus.Intt.:** Pub., WS, Rt., Pub.'s Rep., L.S.; **Spl.:** Journals & Magazines, Law (Dist.—All India Reporter Ltd.)

SETH GOVIND DAS TRUST
Raja Gokuldas Place, 191, Kotbali Bard,
Jabalpur-482002 (Madhya Pradesh)
✆ 2340800
Trustee: Smt. Ratan Kumar

SETHI BOOK HOUSE
C-6/124, Yamuna Vihar, Delhi-110006
✆ 22921153
Estd.: 1989; **Hd.Org.:** Vir Bhan Sethi; **Bus.Intt.:** Rt. and L.S.; **Spl.:** Acad., Beh.Sci., Soc.Sci., Comm., Sci., Med., Fiction, Rare, Law

SEVAK PUBLICATIONS
306, Sri Hanuman Industrial Estate, GD.
Ambedkar Rd., Wadala, Mumbai-400031
(Maharashtra)
✆ 24120747, 24131198, Fax: 24168612
✉ sevak@bom2.vsnl.net.in
Bus.Intt.: Pub. and Exp.

SHABD AUR SHABD
D-118, Ashok Vihar, Phase-I, Delhi-110052
✆ 27253503, 27242100
Hd.Org.: Praveen Sharma
Bus.Intt.: Pub. and B.S.; **Spl.:** Hindi Novels, Stories, Biographies, Plays, Poetry, Children's Books, etc.

SHABD PEETH
743, Motilal Nehru Nagar, Allahabad-211002
(Uttar Pradesh)
✆ (O) & (R) 2501771
Hd.Org.: Smt. Madhury Sahay

SHABDA VAIPHAV PRAKASHAN
755, Sadashiv Peth, Pune-411030
(Maharashtra)
Bus.Intt.: B.S. and Pub.

SHABDH KALASH
M-55, Pratap Nagar, Delhi-110007
✆ 20215005, Fax: 22825582
Hd.Org.: Sunita; **Bus.Intt.:** Pub.
Spl.: Litt., & Literary Personalities in Hindi

SHABDALOK PRAKASHAN
1760/1, Near Bala Hanuman,
Gandhi Rd., Ahmedabad-380001
(Gujarat)

SHABDASANDHAN PRAKASHAN
107, Sakshara Apartments,
A-3, Paschim Vihar, New Delhi-110063
✆ 25268341, Fax: 25268341
✉ shabdasandhan@yahoo.com
Hd.Org.: Sudha Upadhyaya
Bus.Intt.: Pub.; **Spl.:** Original Litt., Culture, Edu. Soc.Sci., etc. in Hindi

SHABDSRISHTI PRAKASHAN
C-5/S-2, East Jyoti Nagar, Durgapuri Chowk,
Shahdara, Delhi-110032
✆ 22110789
Hd.Org.: Arun Maheshwari; **Bus.Intt.:** Pub. & Dist.; **Spl.:** Hindi & English Books

SHAFFI & COMPANY
Near Bus Stand, Main Bazar, Sopore,
Kashmir (Jammu & Kashmir)
✆ (O) 01954-222071 (R) 01954-222514
Estd.: 1975; **Prop.:** Mohmad Shaffi Yousufi; **Bus.Intt.:** Pub., B.S., L.S., Stationeries;

Spl.: Sci. & Tech., Med., Mang., Law, Bio.Sci.

SHAFIK PUSTAK BHANDAR
Narayanpur, Bhagalpur-853203 (Bihar)
Bus.Intt.: B.S. and Pub.

SHAH BOOK DEPOT
No. 48, G.H. Rd., Opp. Chennai Medical College, Chennai-600003 (Tamil Nadu)
✆ (O) 25342875 (R) 24846693
Prop.: A.K. Ghosh; **Bus.Intt.:** Dealers; **Spl.:** Med. Dental, Nursing, Pharmacy and Veterinary Books

SHAH LALIT KUMAR & CO.
Main Bazar, Div.-362520 (Gujarat)

SHAH STORES
Kapadia Bazar, Near V.S. Hospital, Ellis Bridge, Ahmedabad-380006 (Gujarat)

SHAHEED BHAGAT SINGH YADGARI PRAKASHAN
154, Shaheed Karnail Singh Nagar, Phase 3, Opp. Om Bakery, Pakhowal Road, Ludhiana-141002 (Punjab)
▮ 9888025102
✉ sbyp@gmail.com
Hd.Org.: Sukhvinder; **Bus.Intt.:** Pub. & Promoter; **Spl.:** Life and Ideology of Shaheed Bhagat Singh in Punjabi

SHAIBYA GRATHAN BIBHAG
8/1A, Shyama Charan Dey St., Kolkata-700073 (West Bengal)

SHAIBYA PRAKASHAN BIBHAG
86/1, Mahatma Gandhi Rd., Kolkata-700009 (West Bengal)
✆ 224121748
Hd.Org.: Rabin Bal

SHAILAJA PRAKASHAN
1/6281, Gali No. 3, East Rohtash Nagar, Shahdara, Delhi-110032
✆ 22320798
✉ shailjaprakashan@rediffmail.com
Prop.: Vijay Kumar Sharma; **Bus.Intt.:** Dist., L.S.; **Spl.:** Indian and Foreign books for Children as well as Ency. and Reference Books

SHAILI PRAKASHANA
SRA Printers, 66-3, K.R. Rd., Opp. Post Office, Bangalore-560004 (Karnataka)
Estd.: 1969; **Hd.Org.:** G. Apprameya; **Bus.Intt.:** Pub.; **Spl.:** Novels, Dramas, Poems, Film Stories

SHAILMA.COM PVT. LTD.
B-217, Sector-26, Noida-201301
D-4, Pamosh Enclave, Greater Kailash, New Delhi-110048
✆ 24441818 ▮ 9810423528, Fax: 24441818
✉ shailma@vsnl.com
Ch.Exe.: Mr. Vipul Verma; **Bus.Intt.:** Pub.; **Spl.:** Magazines related to Comp., Business & Economy

SHAIVA BHARATI SHODH PRATISHTHANAM
D-35/77, Jangamawadimath, Varanasi-221001 (Uttar Pradesh)

SHAKIR BOOK HOUSE
Barahpura, Bhagalpur-812001 (Bihar)
Bus.Intt.: B.S. and Pub.

SHAKSHARA PRAKASHAN
C-4/S-2, East Jyoti Nagar, Durgapuri Chowk, Shahdara, Delhi-110032
✆ 22110789
Hd.Org.: Arun Maheshwari; **Bus.Intt.:** Pub. & B.S.; **Spl.:** Books in Hindi and English

SHAKTI BOOK DEPOT
39/40, Devi Ahilya Marg, Indore (Madhya Pradesh)

SHAKTI BOOK HOUSE
3B, DDA, Flat, Mansarover Park, Shahdara, Delhi-110032 ✆ 22291202
Prop.: Mrs. Sunita Sharma; **Bus.Intt.:** L.S.; **Spl.:** Acad., Beh.Sci., Soc.Sci., Comm., Sci., Pure & Applied, Tech., Fiction Law

SHAKTI STORES
259, Rabindra Sarani, Kolkata-700066 (West Bengal)

SHAKUN PRAKASHAN
3625, Netaji Subhash Marg, Darya Ganj, New Delhi-110002
✆ (O) 23271818 (R) 23274378, 23255745, Fax: 22927500
Estd.: 1961; **Hd.Org.:** Subhash Jain

SHAKUNTALA KALA NIKETAN
A-3, C.C. Colony, Opp. R.P. Bagh, Delhi-110007
✆ 27113945, 27117366
✉ shakuntlakalaniketan@yahoo.com
Hd.Org.: Smt. Punam Bajaj; **Bus.Intt.:** Pub.; **Spl.:** *Mehndi*, Embroidery, Knitting, Tailoring, Crochet, etc.

SHALABH PUBLISHING HOUSE
249/5, Nai Sarak, Shastri Nagar, Meerut-250001 (Uttar Pradesh)
✆ 0121-2761797, 2769939 ▮ 941220183
Estd.: 1976; **Prop.:** Shalabh Kumar; **Bus.Intt.:** Pub., B.S., L.S.; **Spl.:** Humanities & Soc.Sci.

SHALAKA PRAKASHAN
4/32, M.I.G. Colony, D.N. Nagar, J.P. Rd., Andheri (W), Mumbai-400058 (Maharashtra)

SHALIMAR PUBLISHING HOUSE
27, Prafull Nagar, Lanka Crossing Lanka, Varanasi-221005 (Uttar Pradesh)

SHANKAR DAYAL PUSTAKALAYA
Dihra, Aurangabad-824130 (Bihar)
Bus.Intt.: Pub. and B.S.

SHANKAR PUBLICATION
C-325, St. No. 14, Bhajanpura, Delhi-110053
✆ 22567452 ▮ 9818587915
Hd.Org.: Sanjay Dhall; **Bus.Intt.:** L.S., Stockist; **Spl.:** Indian and Foreign Books

SHANKAR PUSTAK BHANDAR
Tandwa, Aurangabad-824302 (Bihar)
Bus.Intt.: Pub. and B.S.

SHANKAR PUSTAK BHANDAR
Panjwara, Bhagalpur-813110 (Bihar)
Bus.Intt.: B.S. and Pub.

SHANKAR PUSTAK BHANDAR
Vijayhat, Bhagalpur (Bihar)
Bus.Intt.: B.S. and Pub.

SHANKAR'S BOOK AGENCY PVT. LTD.
103, Munish Plaza, 20, Ansari Rd., P.O. Box-7031, New Delhi-110002
✆ 23279967, 23257771, 65381560, Fax: 11-23285534
sbapld@vsnl.com, sbapld@gmail.com
www.shankarsbook.com
Estd.: 1963; **Man.Dir.:** S.D. Ahuja
Br.: 133-E, Lenin Sarani, P.O. Box No. 8889, Kolkata-700013 (West Bengal)
✆ 033-22463257, 65253997, Fax: 91-33-22463257, 2440947
davinder@vsnl.com, sbaplkol@gmail.com
Bus.Intt.: Imp., Dist. & Stockist; **Spl.:** Sci. & Tech., Edu. Litt.

SHANTALA ARTS ACADEMY
Pulikeshi Rd., First Main, Yashwantpur, Bangalore-560022 (Karnataka)

SHANTHA PUBLISHERS
Muthuvizha Illam, No. 13/5, Sripuram, 2nd St., Royapettah, Chennai-600014 (Tamil Nadu)
✆ 28115618, 28265618, 28266018, Fax: 28116018, 28266018
admin@shanthapublishers.com
www.shanthapublishers.com
Hd.Org.: R. Rajmohan; **Bus.Intt.:** Pub.; **Spl.:** Tamil Books on Edu., Psych. and Methods of Teaching at College Level

SHANTHAM BOOK HOUSE
89/B-I, S.P. Koil St., Chidambaram-608001 (Tamil Nadu)
✆ 04144-20263, Fax: 22265
Prop.: M. Muralidharan; **Bus.Intt.:** Rt. and L.S.; **Spl.:** Reference and Text books

SHANTI BOOKS & SHANTI PUBLICATIONS
27, Anna Salai, Mount Rd., Chennai-600002 (Tamil Nadu)
✆ 28546719, 28440060
Estd.: 1976; **Prop.:** Janakiraman; **Bus.Intt.:** Pub. and B.S.; **Spl.:** Humanities & Soc.Sci., Sci. & Tech., Comp., Mang., Law, Children & General, Arts & Arch. in English and Tamil

SHANTI PRAKASHAN
528, Pooth Khurd, Delhi-110039
✆ 27753568, 27753200 ▮ 910553674
shantisarwar@eth.net
Hd.Org.: Tejpal Singh; **Bus.Intt.:** Pub. and Dist.; **Spl.:** Art, Communication and Sci.

SHANTI PRAKASHAN
84/1, Old Bahrena, Allahabad-211003 (Uttar Pradesh)
✆ 2608496
Hd.Org.: Mrs. Krishnadevi Misher

SHANTI PRAKASHAN
M-3, Punjabi Basti, Aruna Nagar, Majnu Ka Tila, Delhi-110054
✆ 22910456
Hd.Org.: Tejpal Singh

SHANTI PRAKASHAN
Shop No. 1, Tawa Complex Atera Colony, Bhopal-420016 (Madhya Pradesh)

SHANTI PRAKASHAN
Sahitik Pustakon Ke Prakashak Aur Vitrik, 39, Kailashpuri, Meerut (Uttar Pradesh)

SHANTI PUBLICATIONS
492E/5A, Mahaveer Block, St. No. 5, Bholanath Nagar, Shahdara, Delhi-110032
✆ 22307950
info@shantipublications.com
www.shantipublications.com
Hd.Org.: Rakesh Sharma; **Bus.Intt.:** Pub.; **Spl.:** Children's Books and Edu. Books

SHANTI PUSTAK MANDIR
K-71, Krishna Nagar, Delhi-110051
✆ 22214376
Hd.Org.: Smt. Shanti Devi

SHANTI PUSTAK SADAN
Kharik Bazar, Naugachia, Bhagalpur-853202 (Bihar)
Bus.Intt.: B.S. and Pub.

SHARADA BOOKS & STATIONERY
Katoria, Bhagalpur-813106 (Bihar)
Bus.Intt.: B.S. and Pub.

SHARADA PRAKASHAN
542, K.L. Keedganj, Allahabad-211003 (Uttar Pradesh)
✆ 2602779
Hd.Org.: Santosh Kumar Sonkar

SHARADA PRAKASHAN
M.G. Rd., Jalgaon (Madhya Pradesh)

SHARADA PUBLISHERS' DISTRIBUTORS
D-33, Radhey Puri, P.O. Krishna Nagar, Delhi-110051
✆ 22245206
Estd.: 1992; **Hd.Org.:** Bijay Samajdar, Swapan Samajdar; **Bus.Intt.:** Dealers; **Spl.:** Books from Russia, U.S.A., U.K., Japan, China and All Leading Indian Pub.

SHARADA PUBLISHING HOUSE
111, Vidya Vihar Apartment, Sector 9, Rohini, Delhi-110085
✆ 32921560, 27552102
✉ bansal-sph@rediffmail.com
Hd.Org.: Anjana Bansal; **Bus.Intt.:** Pub.; **Spl.:** Art, Archaeology, Arch., Hist., Cul. Rel., Phil., Music, etc. in Eng. as well as Sanskrit Litt., and Dictionaries

SHARADA PUBLISHING HOUSE
40, Anand Nagar, Inderlok, Delhi-110035
✆ 30921560, 27552102
Hd.Org.: B.L. Bansal; **Bus.Intt.:** Pub.; **Spl.:** Art, Hist., Culture, Music, Dance, Rel., Phil., etc. as also Sanskrit Litt.

SHARADA SADAN
96, Zero Rd., Allahabad-211010 (Uttar Pradesh)
✆ 2401440, 2402612
Hd.Org.: Sureshchandra Agarwal

SHARADABEHN
Chimanbhai Edu. Research Centre, "Darshan", Opp. Ranakpur Society Shahibag, Ahmedabad-380004 (Gujarat)

SHARAN BOOK DEPOT
Jaipur (Rajasthan)
✆ 601801, 320680
✉ parampsj@detainfosys.net
Bus.Intt.: B.S. and Pub.

SHARDA BOOK DEPOT
P.O. Motinagar, Dhanbad-828120 (Jharkhand)
✆ 0326-2253950, Fax: 0326-2251445
✉ shardabookssin@yahoo.com
Estd.: 2001; **Hd.Org.:** S.K. Sinha; **Bus.Intt.:** B.S., L.S.; **Spl.:** Sci. & Tech., Comp., Mang., Bio.Sci.

SHARDA PRAKASHAN
16/F, 3 Gay House, Ansari Rd., Darya Ganj, New Delhi-110002
✆ 23279853, 23280234
Fax: 23280234, 23279853
✉ jhari@ndb.vsnl.net.in
Estd.: 1978; **Prt.:** Vijay Dev Jhari, Rudra Dev Jhari, Ravinder Dev Jhari
Bus.Intt.: Pub., Dist. & L.S.; **Spl.:** Hindi Language & Litt. & Children Books, Pioneer Pub. of Indian Classics

SHARDA PUSTAK BHANDAR
Court Rd., Baidyanath, Deoghar-814112 (Bihar)
Bus.Intt.: B.S. and Pub.

SHARDA PUSTAK BHANDAR
Bihat, Begusarai-851135 (Bihar)
Bus.Intt.: B.S. and Pub.

SHARDA PUSTAK BHANDAR
D.N. Singh Rd., Bhagalpur-812002 (Bihar)
Bus.Intt.: B.S. and Pub.

SHARDA PUSTAK BHANDAR
Kahalgaon (Colgong), Bhagalpur-812203 (Bihar)
Bus.Intt.: B.S. and Pub.

SHARDA PUSTAK BHANDAR
Sultanganj, Bhagalpur-813213 (Bihar)
Bus.Intt.: B.S. and Pub.

SHARDA PUSTAK BHAWAN
11/12, University Rd., Allahabad-211002 (Uttar Pradesh)
✆ 2461162, 2644643
Hd.Org.: Dashrath Prasad Jaiswal; **Bus.Intt.:** Pub. and Dist.; **Spl.:** University Level and Competitive Examination Books in Hindi

SHARIPAD PRAKASHAN
2791A, Ward, Varunteerth, Kolhapur-416012 (Maharashtra)

SHARMA BOOK AGENCY
3374, Govind Raijika Rasta, Purani Basti, Jaipur-302001 (Rajasthan)
✆ 0141-2311204
Estd.: 1994; **Bus.Intt.:** B.S.; **Spl.:** Chemistry Books

SHARMA BOOK COMPANY
E-210, St. No. 5, Subash Vihar, North Ghonda, Delhi-110053
✆ 22194496 ▮ 9811574058
Hd.Org.: Madan Singh; **Bus.Intt.:** Dist. & L.S.; **Spl.:** Books on All Sub in English and Hindi

SHARMA BOOK COMPANY
K-16/22, St. No. 15, West Ghonda, Delhi-110053
✆ 22194496 ▮ 9811574058
Hd.Org.: M.P. Sharma; **Bus.Intt.:** Dist.; **Spl.:** Books on All Sub in English and Hindi

SHARMA BOOK DEPOT
Pustak Path, Ranchi-834001 (Bihar)

SHARMA BOOK DISTRIBUTORS
4761/23, Ansari Rd., New Delhi-110002
✆ (O) 23267686, 22415871 (R) 22187534
Hd.Org.: Mahesh Chand Sharma;
Bus.Intt.: L.S.

SHARMA FINE ARTS
Haroon Building, Room No. 8/B, 1st Floor, Princess St., No. 190, Opp. Bank of Baroda, Mumbai-400002 (Maharashtra)
✆ 22-22057012, Fax: 91-22-22003482
Hd.Org.: R.G. Sharma; **Bus.Intt.:** Pub. of Poster's

SHARMA PUSTAK BHANDAR
Shermari Bazar, Bhagalpur-813209 (Bihar)
Bus.Intt.: B.S. and Pub.

SHATAXI INDIA
C-406, Mahalaxmi Appartments, Plot No. 4, Sector-2, Dwarka, New Delhi-110075
✆ (O) 25095186 (R) 30961766
Hd.Org.: P. Ranjan; **Bus.Intt.:** L.S.;
Spl.: Commerce, Technical, Sciences, Pure & Applied, Journals & Magazines, Soc.Sciences and Medical Books

SHAYAMAL BOOK STORE
Pripainti, Bhagalpur-813105 (Bihar)
Bus.Intt.: B.S. and Pub.

SHAYAM PRAKASHAN
104/435, P. Rd., Kanpur-208012 (Uttar Pradesh)
✆ 2545453

SHAYAM SUNDER PUSTAK BHANDAR
Jagdishpur, Bhagalpur-813105 (Bihar)
Bus.Intt.: B.S. and Pub.

SHEEL PRAKASHAN
A-35, Sonari West, Jamshedpur-831011 (Jharkhand)
Hd.Org.: Dr. Kumad

SHEELA PRAKASHAN
B-4/214, Safdarjung Enclave, New Delhi-110029
✆ 24613206
Hd.Org.: Sheel Singh; **Bus.Intt.:** Pub.;
Spl.: Compilations of Poems, *Ghazals*, Stories as well as Educational Books for Children

SHEETAL BOOK HOUSE
A-31-34, Jaina Building, Commercial Complex, Dr. Mukerjee Nagar, New Delhi-110009
✆ (O) 27654539, 27652565 (R) 27652892, 27655493
Prop.: Surinder Kumar; **Bus.Intt.:** L.S.

SHEIKH GHULAM MOHD. & SONS
Maisuma Bazar, Srinagar, Kashmir-190001 (Jummu & Kashmir)
✆ 2472206
Estd.: 1959; **Hd.Org.:** Sheikh Mohamad Fayaz
Br.: Shaheen Book Stall, Budshah Chowk Amira Kodal, Srinagar, Kashmir-190001 (Jummu & Kashmir) ✆ 2472206
• Inter National Book Agency; Budshah Chowk, Srinagar, Kashmir-190001
✆ 2436263
Bus.Intt.: L.S. & Rt., Imp., Exp.

SHEIKH JAVEED AHMAD
Budshah Chowk, Srinagar, Kashmir-190001 (Jammu & Kashmir)
✆ 2478288, Fax: 2470158
✉ citybookcener@yahoo.com
Estd.: 2003; **Hd.Org.:** Sheikh Javeed Ahmad; **Bus.Intt.:** Pub., WS, L.S. & Rt., Imp., Exp., Sub.Ag.; **Spl.:** Humanities & Soc.Sci., Sci. & Tech., Med., Law, Juvenile/ Children Books, Gen. & Fiction etc.

SHEIKH MOHD USMAN AND SONS (REGD.)
Fairdeal Market, Residency Rd., Srinagar, Kashmir-190001 (Jammu & Kashmir)
✆ (O) 2491291 (R) 2477287, Fax: 2477287
✉ sh_usman@rediffmail.com
www.gulshanbookskashmir.com
Estd.: 1950; **Prop.:** Sheikh Mohd Usman
Br.: Exchange Rd., Gow Kadal Chowk, Srinagar, Kashmir-190001
✆ 0194-2472081, Fax: 2479238
Bus.Intt.: Pub., WS, L.S. & Rt.;
Spl.: Humanities & Soc.Sci., Sci. & Tech., Law, Juvenile/Children, Gen. & Fiction etc.

SHEKHAR PUSTAK BHANDAR
Saidpur, Bhagalpur-853205 (Bihar)
Bus.Intt.: B.S. and Pub.

SHEKHER PRAKASHAN
108, Chack Joro Rd., Allahabad-211003 (Uttar Pradesh)
✆ 2402832
Hd.Org.: D.P. Agarwal

SHEO SHAKTI PUSTAKALAYA
Rafiganj, Aurangabad-824125 (Bihar)
Bus.Intt.: B.S. and Pub.

SHERIDEN BOOK COMPANY
12-H, Shanti Van Marg, Opp. Delhi Police Officers Mess, Darya Ganj, New Delhi-110002
✆ 23260511, 23287423, 23281705, Cable: TRANSWORLD, Fax: 23287423
✉ contact@sheridenbooks.com
www.indiamart.com/sheridenbooks.com
Estd.: 1986; **Prop.:** R.K. Jain

Br.: 208, Navratan Premises, 69, P.O. Mellow Rd., Carnac Bunder, Mumbai-400009
✆ 23426134, 23425649
✉ kailaji@bom5.vsnl.net.in
Bus.Intt.: Pub., WS, L.S. & Rt., Imp., Exp.; **Spl.:** Humanities & Soc.Sci., Sci. & Tech., Med.

SHETH PUBLISHING HOUSE
G-12, Suyog Industrial Estate, Opp. Vitrum Glass Factory, L.B.S. Marg, Near Powai-Vikhroli Junction, Vikhroli (West) Mumbai-400089 (Maharashtra)
✆ 25774200, 25773707-08, Fax: 25774200
✉ sph@bom5.vsnl.net.in
Hd.Org.: Harin M. Sheth
Br.: Delhi Fax: 28211174
✉ shilpayan@mantramail.com
Bus.Intt.: Pub., Imp., & Dist.; **Spl.:** Edu. Books for Children

SHIKHA PUSTAK BHANDAR
Rajendra Prasad Rd., Bhagalpur-812002 (Bihar)
Bus.Intt.: B.S. and Pub.

SHIKHAR MERCHANDISE CORPORATION
604, Prabhat Kiran Rajendra Place, New Delhi-110008
✆ 25761086, Fax: 91-11-25736317
Hd.Org.: Ram Malhotra; **Bus.Intt.:** Pub.

SHIKSHA BHARATI
1590, Madarsa Rd., Kashmere Gate, Delhi-110006
✆ 23869812, 23865483, Fax: 23867791
Hd.Org.: Vishwanath, Meera Johri
Bus.Intt.: Pub.; **Spl.:** Children's Books, Encyclopaedias, Biographies, Sci., etc. in Hindi.

SHIKSHA BHARTI PUBLICATIONS PVT. LTD., SIDDHARTHA PRAKASHAN, SUMIT PRAKASHAN
2450, Hudson Lines, Kingsway Camp, Delhi-110009
✆ 27213196, 27122053, Fax: 27122053
Hd.Org.: Harish Kalra; **Bus.Intt.:** Pub.; **Spl.:** School Textbooks on all Sub.

SHIKSHA VIBHAG, RAJASTHAN
Madhyamik Shiksha Nideshalaya, Bikaner-334001 (Rajasthan)
✆ 2528875, Fax: 2201861
✉ diridu@raj.raj.nic.in
Hd.Org.: P.K. Goel; **Bus.Intt.:** Pub.; **Spl.:** Hindi Monthlies *Shivira Patrika* and *Naya Shikshak/ Teaching Today*

SHILALEKH PUBLISHERS
4/32 Subhash Gali, Vishwas Nagar, Shahdara, Delhi-110032
✆ 22303184 ▮ 9868049123
Fax: 22155926
✉ shilalekhbooks@rediffmail.com, info@shilalekhbooks.com
www.shilalekhbooks.com
Estd.: 1988; **Hd.Org.:** Satish Sharma; **Bus.Intt.:** Pub.; **Spl.:** Novels and Stories, Children's Litt., Books on Adult Edu., Astrology, etc. in Punjabi, Hindi and Urdu

SHILPAYAN
10295, Lane No. 1, West Gorakh Park, Shahdara, Delhi-110032
✆ 22821174, 22827190, Fax: 22821174, 22827190
✉ shilpayan2005@yahoo.co.in
Hd.Org.: Sarvesh Sharma; **Bus.Intt.:** Pub.; **Spl.:** Literary and Edu. Books in Hindi

SHILPI PRAKASHAN
117, C/7, Meerapur, Allahabad (Uttar Pradesh)
✆ 2653632
Hd.Org.: Santosh Chaturvedi

SHILPI PRAKASHAN
68, Ramkrishan Park, Aminabad, Lucknow-226002 (Uttar Pradesh)
✆ 2213222, 2224695
Hd.Org.: Beena Kanodia

SHIPRA LIBRARY SERVICES & SHIPRA PUBLICATIONS
115-A, 3rd Floor, Vikas Marg, Shakarpur, Delhi-110092
✆ (O) 65277210, 22500954, 22458662 (R) 22017531, Fax: 22458662
✉ info@shiprapublications.com
www.shiprapublications.com
Estd.: 1990; **Prop.:** D. Kumar; **Bus.Intt.:** B.S., L.S. & Pub.; **Spl.:** Acad. and Research Books in Soc.Sci., Humanities and in Sci. and Tech.

SHIR DESAI & SONS
441-C, Bhawsingh Rd., Gujari Corner, Kolhapur-2 (Maharashtra)

SHISHU SAHITYA SAMSAD (P) LTD.
32-A, Acharya Prafulla Chandra Rd., Kolkata-700009 (West Bengal)
✆ (O) 23507669, 23503195 (R) 24644864, 24642929, Fax: 23603508
✉ samsad@cal3.vsnl.net.in
Estd.: 1951; **Man.Dir.:** Debajyoti Datta; **Bus.Intt.:** Pub., Exp.; **Spl.:** Juvenile/Children

SHITTE PRAKASHAN VIBHAG
Guru Gobind Singh Study Circle, Model Town Extension, Ludhiana-141002 (Punjab)
✆ 0161-2450352
Hd.Org.: Sarabjeet Singh

SHIV BOOKS DISTRIBUTORS
D-85, Om Vihar Phase-V, Uttam Nagar, New Delhi-110059
✆ (O) & (R) 25352105
Prop.: Manoj Goswami; **Bus.Intt.:** L.S.; **Spl.:** Med., Mang., Children & General, Defence Terrorism

SHIV DAS & SONS
9665, Islam Ganj, Library Rd., Azad Market, Delhi-110006

SHIV KHERA
C-6/4 Vasant Vihar, New Delhi-110057
✆ 26148804, Fax: 26145626
shivkhera@shivkhera.com
www.shivkhera.com
Hd.Org.: Shiv Khera; **Bus.Intt.:** Pub. & Author; **Spl.:** Books on Positive Thinking and Healthy Living

SHIV MARUTI ENTERPRISES
MB-5, Antriksh Bhavan, 22, K.G. Marg, New Delhi-110001

SHIV MARUTI ENTERPRISES
2393/218, 2nd Floor, Vidya Market, Chatta Shahji, Chawri Bazar, Delhi-110006
✆ 22535082
Prop.: Mrs. Murti Devi; **Bus.Intt.:** WS, Rt., L.S.

SHIV OM WORLD
D-114, Sarita Vihar, New Delhi
✆ 29941296
urmil95@yahoo.co.in
www.forensicbooksworld.com
Prop.: Urmil Sharma; **Bus.Intt.:** Pub. & Dist.; **Spl.:** Spiritualism in Hindi

SHIV SHAKTI BOOK CENTRE
624, M.G. Rd., Khajuri Bazar, Indore-452002 (Madhya Pradesh)
✆ (O) 2450234 (R) 2538455, Fax: 2538455
Estd.: 1966; **Hd.Org.:** Ramesh Murarka/ Deepesh Agrawal; **Bus.Intt.:** B.S.; **Spl.:** Comp., Med., Engg., Mang., Law & Competition

SHIV SHAKTI BOOK DISTRIBUTOR
C-293, Gali No. 10, Prem Vihar (Shiv Vihar), Karawal Nagar, Delhi-110094
✆ 91-11-22933897
Hd.Org.: Daleep Kumar; **Bus.Intt.:** B.S. and L.S.

SHIV SHAKTI BOOKS TRADERS
WZ-574/A Shiv Shakti Bhavan, (Near Masjid) Madipur, New Delhi-110063
✆ 25215082, 25935082, Fax: 011-25211682
ssbt@forensicbooksworld.com
www.forensicbooksworld.com
Estd.: 1989; **Prop.:** Mrs. Murti Devi; **Bus.Intt.:** Pub. & Dist.; **Spl.:** Forensic Sci., Cri., Police Studies, Criminal Law, etc.

SHIV SHAKTI ENTERPRISES
8, Shiva Market-II, Madhuban Chowk, Pitampura, Delhi-110034

SHIV SHAKTI TRADERS
797, Shanti Nagar, Gopal Pura Bypass, Tank Rd., Jaipur-18 (Rajasthan)
✆ 5140608, 2074092
Hd.Org.: Sunil K. Jain; **Bus.Intt.:** Pub. & Dist.; **Spl.:** College and University Level books on Soc.Sci.

SHIV TRADERS
113, Pach Danga, Jammu-Tawi (Jammu & Kashmir)
✆ 249257
Estd.: 1990; **Bus.Intt.:** Pub., WS, L.S. and Rt.

SHIV TRADERS
Shiv Smriti, Maliwada Rd., Junagadh-362004 (Gujarat)

SHIVA LAL AGARWALA & COMPANY
Hospital Rd., Agra-282003 (Uttar Pradesh)
✆ 2365999, 2360134, Fax: 2365974
Estd.: 1930; **Hd.Org.:** Chandra Mohan Agarwal; **Spl.:** Edu. Text books, Hist., Pol.Sci. and Geography

SHIVA NANDA MATH AND YOGASHRAM SANGHA
471, Netaji, Colony, Kolkata-700019 (West Bengal)

SHIVA PRAKASHAN
Khajuri Bazar, Indore-452002 (Madhya Pradesh)
✆ 2454172

SHIVA PUBLISHERS DISTRIBUTORS
1-DA-2, Sector-4, Hiranmagari, Udaipur-313001 (Rajasthan)
✆ (O) 2583051 (S) 2415516 (R) 2460051
Hd.Org.: Smt. Durga Taldar; **Spl.:** All Types of Library Books

SHIVALAYA ENTERPRISES
42, Ekta Apartments, Geeta Colony, Delhi-110031
✆ (O) & (R) 22445526 ▮ 9811892244
books@indianacademicpublisher.com
www.shivalayabooks.com
Estd.: 1995; **Prop.:** Rajkumar Gupta; **Bus.Intt.:** Pub. & Dist.; **Spl.:** Soc.Sci. & Humanities in English & Hindi

SHIVALIK BOOK CENTRE
S.C.O. 61, Sector-17-D, Chandigarh-160017
✆ 2704768, Fax: 2773155
Hd.Org.: Ashutosh, Navneet Vermani;

Bus.Intt.: Rt. and L.S.; **Spl.:** Competition, Comp., Engg., Gen., College & Department Books

SHIVALIK PRAKASHAN
27/16, Shakti Nagar, Delhi-110007
✆ 42351161, Fax: 23842641
✉ shivalikprakashan@yahoo.com
Estd.: 1998; **Hd.Org.:** Virendra Nath Tiwari; **Bus.Intt.:** Pub., Dist.; **Spl.:** Phil., Indology, Ancient Hist., in Hindi and Sanskrit

SHIVAM BOOK DISTRIBUTOR
86-B, East Laxmi Market,
East Guru Angad Nagar, Laxmi Nagar,
Delhi-110092
✆ 22017177
Hd.Org.: Dharam Vir Sharma;
Bus.Intt.: Pub. & B.S.; **Spl.:** Children's Story Books, Dictionaries, Ency., etc.

SHIVAM ENTERPRISE
Opp. Vanita Vishram, Dawn Rd., Crescent, Bhavnagar-364001 (Gujarat)
✆ (O) 2514365 (R) 2433413
Estd.: 1982; **Bus.Intt.:** B.S. and Stationers

SHIVAM INTERNATIONAL BOOK SERVICE
C-7/201, Dispensary Rd., Bhajan Pura, Delhi-110053
✆ 22187534
Estd.: 1997; **Prop.:** K.S. Sharma;
Bus.Intt.: L.S.; **Spl.:** Foreign, Indian Book and Globe Maps

SHIVAM PRAKASHAN
190-B/10, Rajroop Pur, Allahabad (Uttar Pradesh)
✆ 2432041
Hd.Org.: Rakesh Kumar Shukla, Rakesh Tiwari;
Bus.Intt.: B.S.; **Spl.:** Hindi and Children's Litt. as also Books on Sci., Hist., Art, etc.

SHIVANI BOOK DISTRIBUTORS
ZF-18, Shiva Enclave, A-4, Paschim Vihar, New Delhi-110063
✆ (O) & (R) 25267568 ▮ 9818436910
Fax: 011-25251557
✉ shiv_distributors@yahoo.co.in
Prop.: Shiv Chaudhary; **Bus.Intt.:** L.S.
Spl.: Humanities & Soc.Sc., Sc. & Tech. Mang.

SHIVANI BOOKS
4855/24, Harbans Singh St., Darya Ganj, New Delhi-110002
▮ 9350870414, Fax: 011-23281244
✉ shivanibooks@hotmail.com
Hd.Org.: Shivani Sharma
Bus.Intt.: Pub. & Dist.; **Spl.:** Children's Books and Hindi Language

SHIVARANI PRAKASHANI
8B/2, Tamer Lane, Kolkata-700009 (West Bengal)

SHIVNERI PUBLISHERS & DISTRIBUTORS
Mama Londhe Plots, Gadge Nagar, Amravati-444603 (Maharashtra)
✆ 0721-2660860 ▮ 9422856777
✉ ujjwaladeshmukh@rediffmail.com
Man.Dir.: Dr. Ujjwala S. Deshmukh;
Bus.Intt.: Pub. & Dist.

SHONA BOOK STALL
Edepal-679576 (Kerala)

SHORTHAND HOUSE
(Vishist Prakashan) C4B/66, Janakpuri, New Delhi-110058
✆ 25553702
Hd.Org.: G.D. Bist; **Bus.Intt.:** Pub. and Dist.; **Spl.:** Edu. Books, Audio Cassettes on Shorthand, Typewriting and Office Work

SHREE ALMORA BOOK DEPOT
Mall Rd., Almora-263601 (Uttarakhand)
✆ (O) 230148, 22113, 23561 (R) 233043, 234113, Fax: 234113
✉ shyam2@nde.vsnl.net.in
Estd.: 1960; **Hd.Org.:** Vinod Prasad Agrawal
Br.: A-2, 7/B-Lawrence Rd., New Delhi-110052
Bus.Intt.: Pub. and B.S.; **Spl.:** Sci. & Tech., Med., Comm. & Mang., Humanities, Law, Gen. Books, Hindi & English

SHREE BAIDYANATH AYURVED BHAVAN
D-28, First Floor, Greater Kailash Part-I, New Delhi-110048
✆ 26229910

SHREE BOOKS
Capital Centre, M.G. Road, Trivanandapuram-695001 (Kerala)
✆ 0471-2466169
✉ nomarainbow@sify.com
Hd.Org.: Rajesh Kumar; **Bus.Intt.:** Pub.;
Spl.: Fiction and General Books in Malayalam

SHREE BOOK CENTRE
Gala No. 8, Kakad Industrial Estate, S. Keer Marg (Off. L.J. Road), Matunga, Mumbai-400016 (Maharashtra)
✆ 022-24377516, 022-24309183
Hd.Org.: Jayesh Dungarshi Baua
Bus.Intt.: Pub., Imp. & Dist.; **Spl.:** Children's Books as well as Gen. Books

SHREE BOOK SQUARE
Hyderabad (Andhra Pradesh)
✆ 27566820
✉ shreebooksquare@yahoo.com
Bus.Intt.: B.S.

SHREE EXPORTS
3980/2, Chawri Bazar, Delhi-110006
Bus.Intt.: Exp.

SHREE GANGA PUSTAKALAYA
Trilochan, Varanasi-221001
(Uttar Pradesh)

SHREE GREEN BOOK HOUSE
MIG-149-B, Indirapuram, GMS Rd.,
P.O. Majra, Dehradun-248171 (Uttarakhand)
✆ 0135-2621932, Fax: 0135-22621141
✉ sgbhdon@yahoo.co.in
Mkt.Man.: Ravindra Sharma; **Bus.Intt.:** B.S.

SHREE INDORE BOOK DEPOT
504, M.G. Rd., Indore-452007
(Madhya Pradesh)
✆ 2432479, 2544316
Estd.: 1939; **Hd.Org.:** Sunil K. Agarwal; **Bus.Intt.:** B.S., Pub. and L.S.; **Spl.:** Comp. and Mang. Sci.

SHREE KABIR GYAN PRAKASHAN KENDRA
Sant Kabir Gyan Marg, Sirodhi,
Sirsiya, Giridih (Jharkhand)
✆ 06532-223393
✉ kabirgyanmandir@yahoo.com
Bus.Intt.: Pub.; **Spl.:** Hindi Language

SHREE MAHAVIR BOOK DEPOT
2603, Nai Sarak, New Delhi-110006
✆ (O) 23262993, 23270792, 23263386
(R) 27430823, 27215834
Estd.: 1948; **Man.Dir.:** Ramkanwar Gupta; **Bus.Intt.:** Pub.; **Spl.:** Textbooks

SHREE NATRAJ PRAKASHAN
A-507/12, Kartar Nagar,
South Gamri Extension, Delhi-110053
✆ 22941694
Hd.Org.: S. Raghav; **Bus.Intt.:** Pub.; **Spl.:** General Books in Hindi Language

SHREE NAV JEEVAN AGENCY
1808, Sadashiv Peth, Deshmukhwadi,
Near Pune Vidyarthi Griha, Nav Jeevan
Mangal Karyalaya Premises, Pune-411030
(Maharashtra)
✆ 91-20-4020662, Telefax: 91-20-4477804
✉ snja9@hotmail.com
Hd.Org.: K.K. Nehra; **Bus.Intt.:** B.S.

SHREE NAVJIVAN BOOK MFG. CO.
110, Zaveri Bazar, Mumbai-400002
(Maharashtra)
✆ 22-2412102, Fax: 91-22-2402021
Hd.Org.: Nitin Kumar;
Bus.Intt.: Manufacturers;
Spl.: All Types of Accounts Books

SHREE NIWAS PUBLICATIONS
F-300, 2nd Floor, Vaishali Nagar,
Jaipur (Rajasthan)
✆ 0141-2353254, Fax: 91-175-2353254
✉ shreniwas300800@gmail.com
Hd.Org.: Narendra Kumar Khandelwal; **Bus.Intt.:** Pub.; **Spl.:** Comm., Mang. & Hum. in English & Hindi

SHREE PARAMHANS SWAMI ADGADANANDJI ASHRAM TRUST
29-A, French Rd., 1st Floor,
Opp. Merchant Club, Chowpatty,
Mumbai-400007
(Maharashtra)
✆ 56303811, 56349000, Fax: 23643109
✉ suneja@bom7.vsnl.net.in,
contact@yatharthgeeta.com
Hd.Org.: Jiten Sushil Choksey; **Bus.Intt.:** Pub.; **Spl.:** Books and Cassettes on Gita and on Discourses by Swamiji

SHREE PRABHA EDUCATIONAL AIDS
WZ-350 A/7, Sri Nagar, Street No. 2,
Rani Bagh, Delhi-110034
✆ 27106652
✉ shreeprabhaeducationalaids@gmail.com
Hd.Org.: Harish Kumar Gupta; **Bus.Intt.:** Pub. & B.S., **Spl.:** Edu. Materials for Schools such as Wooden Blocks, Models, Maps and Charts

SHREE PRAKASHAN
69, Roshan Plaza, Roshan Ara Road,
Delhi-110007
✆ 23822006
Hd.Org.: Vijay Sharma; **Bus.Intt.:** Pub. & B.S.; **Spl.:** Hindi Books

SHREE PRAKASHAN
4/32, Subhash Gali, Vishwas Nagar,
Shahdara, Delhi-110032
✆ 22303184, 22424810, Fax: 22155926
Hd.Org.: Satish Sharma; **Bus.Intt.:** Pub.; **Spl.:** Litt. Books, Children's Books, Hist. and Religious Books in Punjabi

SHREE PRINTING PRESS
16/1, Justice Manmatha Mukherjee Row,
Kolkata-700009 (West Bengal)
Bus.Intt.: Exp.

SHREE PUBLISHERS & DISTRIBUTORS
20, Ansari Rd., Darya Ganj,
New Delhi-110002
✆ 23273027 ▮ 9212015603
✉ shreebook@yahoo.co.in
🌐 www.shreepublishers.com
Estd.: 2003; **Prop.:** Mohit Jain; **Bus.Intt.:** Pub., B.S., L.S., WS; **Spl.:** Humanities & Soc.Sci., Sci.

& Tech., Comp., Med., Mang., Arts & Arch., Bio.Sci.

SHREE RAVISHREE NIDHI
B-7-8-Shreepal Apartments, Aradhana Talkies, Parehpakhadi, Thane Mumbai-400002 (Maharashtra)

SHREE SAHITYIK SANSTHAN
E-10/666, Uttaranchal Colony, Near Sangam Cinema, Loni Border, Ghaziabad (Uttar Pradesh)
✆ 24603892
Hd.Org.: Fateh Chand; **Bus.Intt.:** Pub.; **Spl.:** Hindi Books

SHREE SAI PRAKASHAN
24 Roshan Plaza, Roshan Ara Road, Delhi-110007
✆ 23820751
Hd.Org.: B.D. Gaur; **Bus.Intt.:** Pub. **Spl.:** Hindi and Regional Language Books

SHREE SARSWATI SADAN
A-1/32, Safdarjung Enclave, New Delhi-110029
✆ 26101539, 26183864
Hd.Org.: Amitabh Ranjan; **Bus.Intt.:** Pub.; **Spl.:** Hindi Books on Hist. and Pol.Sci.

SHREE SHREE ANANDAMAYEE SANGH
Shree Ma Anandamayee Ashram, Kalkaji, New Delhi-110019
✆ 26826813
Hd.Org.: D. Mukhopadhyaya; **Bus.Intt.:** Pub.; **Spl.:** Books in English, Bengali, Gujarati and Hindi on the Life and Teachings of Shree Shree Anandamayee Ma

SHREE SUNEETA BOOK CENTRE
81, Khajuri Bazar, G-2, Ganesh Plaza, Indore-452002 (Madhya Pradesh)
✆ 2451009, 2542267, 2481813
Estd.: 1972; **Hd.Org.:** Lalchand Paryani; **Bus.Intt.:** Pub., B.S., Order Supplier; **Spl.:** Library and Govt. Institutions of Hist., Pol.Sci. and Sol. Books

SHREE SUNITA PRAKASHAN
23, Kunmar Mandil, Khajuri Bazar, Indore-452002 (Madhya Pradesh)

SHREE VINAYAK BOOKS
297-A, Block South Gamri Extn., Delhi-110053
✆ (O) 22946689, 20524542, Fax: 23250435
Prop.: Mukesh Joshi; **Bus.Intt.:** L.S.; **Spl.:** Acad., Beh.Sci., Soc.Sci., Comm., Sci., Pure & Applied, Med., Tech., Fiction, Rare, Journals & Magazines, Special Stock: Library Sci., Mang., Comp. Edu., Sports

SHREEMA BOOK AGENCY
A-72, JR. MIG Machna Colony, Bhopal-462016 (Madhya Pradesh)
✆ 2555142
Estd.: 1991; **Hd.Org.:** Mrs. Tripti Guha Thakurta, T. Kimar Dey Partners
Br.: 14/2, MIG Anjali Complex, Jain Mandir, Bhopal-462003 (Madhya Pradesh)
✆ 2762846
Bus.Intt.: Pub., L.S. and Rt.; **Spl.:** Text Books

SHREENATH DOCUMENT SERVICE
C-2/5-C, Lawrence Rd., Delhi-110035
Bus.Intt.: B.S., Pub., Sub.Ag.

SHREYA PUBLICATIONS
2B/2, Picnic Garden, 3rd Lane, Kolkata-700039 (West Bengal)
✆ 033-23439310, Fax: 033-22465756
✉ shreyapublications@yahoo.co.in
Hd.Org.: Saroj Kanti Das; **Bus.Intt.:** Pub. & Dist.; **Spl.:** Sol., Eco., Litt., etc. in Bangla

SHRI AADINATH BOOK CENTRE
G-25, Super Bazar, Opp. HDFC, State Bank Chowk, Yawatmal-444501 (Maharashtra)
✆ 240682; **Estd.:** 1996; **Prop.:** Dilip C. Lodha; **Bus.Intt.:** Rt. Bookshop for Text and Gen. Books; **Spl.:** Med., Engg., Polytechnic/ITI/ D.Pharma

SHRI ANADAMAYEE MA SANGH
Anandamayee Ashram, Kalkaji, New Delhi-110019

SHRI ASHAPURA AGENCY
Opp. Indrabai Girls High School, Shop No. 1, FF, Bhuj-370001 (Gujarat)

SHRI GOPAL PUBLICATIONS
H.No. 3-3-860, Kutabi Guda, Opp. Arya Samaj Mandir, Kachiguda, Hyderabad (Andhra Pradesh)

SHRI JAINENDRA PRESS
A-45, Naraina Industrial Area, Phase-I, New Delhi-110028
✆ 25795180, Fax: 011-25797221
✉ sjp@mlbd.com
www.mlbd.com
Hd.Org.: J.P. Jain; **Bus.Intt.:** Pub.; **Spl.:** Travel, Hinduism, Buddhism, History, Art, Culture, Litt., Psy., Soc.Sci., etc. in Hindi

SHRI JAYA STORE
Rajendra Prasad Rd., Bhagalpur-813105 (Bihar)
Bus.Intt.: Pub. and B.S.

SHRI KRISHNA KRUPA STORES
Near S.T. Stand, Distt. Mehsana, Kheralu-380025 (Gujarat)

SHRI KRISHNA PUSTAK BHANDAR
Beside Alka Cinema, Begusarai-851101 (Bihar)
Bus.Intt.: Pub. and B.S.

SHRI KRISHNA SAHITYA SADAN
2135/36, Shora Kothi, Subzi Mandi,
Clock Tower, Delhi-110007
✆ 9899671737
Hd.Org.: Shailendra Kumar; **Bus.Intt.:** Pub. & B.S.; **Spl.:** Phil., and History in Hindi and Sanskrit

SHRI KRISHNA SAIKSHANIK SADHAN KENDRA
Dabhan Bhagol, Sherkand Talav,
Nadiad-387001 (Gujarat)
✆ (O) 0268-2565198 (R) 2529019
Estd.: 1985; **Prop.:** Sudhirbhai Shah; **Bus.Intt.:** Pub., L.S., WS; **Spl.:** Children & General

SHRI LAL BAHADUR SHASTRI RASHTRIYA SANSKRIT VIDYAPEETH
Katwaria Sarai, Qutab Institutional Area,
New Delhi-110016
✆ 46060555, 46060502, Fax: 46060633
www.slbsrsv.ac.in
Hd.Org.: Vachaspati Upadhyaya; **Bus.Intt.:** Pub.; **Spl.:** *Shodhprabha* Magazine and Books on Law, Grammar, Phil., Criticism and Litt. in Sanskrit

SHRI PRAKASHAN MANDIR
C/o Dr. G.M. Parikh,
19, Atmajyoti Society, Subhanpura,
Vadodara-380013 (Gujarat)
Bus.Intt.: B.S. and Pub.

SHRI PRAKASHAN
H-24/7, Civil Lines, Qasari Deeh, Durg-491001 (Madhya Pradesh)
✆ 2326234
Hd.Org.: Smt. Santosh Agarwal;
Bus.Intt.: B.S. and Pub.

SHRI PRAKASHAN
4/32, Subhash Gali, Vishwas Nagar,
Shahdara, Delhi-110032
Bus.Intt.: Pub.; **Spl.:** Hindi Books

SHRI PRAMHANS SWAMI ADGADANANDJI ASHRAM TRUST
Bldg No. 29, First Floor, French Road,
Opp. Merchant's Club Chowpatty,
Mumbai-400007 (Maharashtra)
✆ 022-66555300, Fax: 022-23643109
contact@yatharthgeeta.com
www.yatharthgeeta.com
Hd.Org.: Jiten Sushil Choksey;
Bus.Intt.: Pub.; **Spl.:** Translations and Cassettes of *Bhagwad Gita* and on Discourses by Swami Adgadanandji Maharaj

SHRI PRANNATH MISSION
Shree Krishna Pranami Mandir, Hakikat Nagar, G.T.B. Nagar, Delhi-110009
✆ 27658111, Fax: 011-27658111
prannathmission@gmail.com
www.pranami.org
Hd.Org.: Mohan Priya Charya;
Bus.Intt.: Pub. and Promoter; **Spl.:** Books on the Ideas and Teachings of Sant Prannath

SHRI RAGHAVENDRA GLOBAL BOOKS
6, (New No. 11) Chandrasekaran St.,
Mandaveli, Chennai-600028 (Tamil Nadu)
✆ 24956971
Hd.Org.: V. Narayanan; **Bus.Intt.:** B.S.;
Spl.: Engg., Comp. & Mang.

SHRI RAGHAVENDRA PRAKASHANA
Ambarkodla, Ankola-581314 (Karnataka)
✆ (O) 08388-633076 (R) 630370,
Fax: 633076
Estd.: 1973; **Prop.:** Vishnu Naik;
Bus.Intt.: Pub.; **Spl.:** Fiction, Edu., Sci. and Children's Books in Kannada

SHRI RAMAKRISHNA
Basavanagudi Rd., Bangalore-560004 (Karnataka)
Bus.Intt.: Pub.; **Spl.:** Rel. Books, Biographies and Mythological Books in Kannada, English, Telugu and Tamil

SHRI RAM CHANDRA MISSION
'Chennai Centre', Gayathri, 19, North St.,
Sriram Nagar, Chennai-600018 (Tamil Nadu)

SHRI RAM CHANDRA MISSION
2, Institutional Area, Sector IV, R.K. Puram,
New Delhi-110022
✆ 26192797

SHRI SAI PRINTORGRAPHERS
B-6 (Basement), Mukerjee Tower, Opp. Batra Cinema, Commercial Complex, Dr. Mukherjee Nagar, Delhi-110009
Sh.: 101 FF, 4787/23, Ansari Rd., Darya Ganj, New Delhi-110002
✆ (O) 27654826 (R) 27659446, Fax: 27654827
frienpub@ndf.vsnl.net.in
Estd.: 1994; **Hd.Org.:** Jagdish C. Gosain;
Spl.: Edu. Publishers of Books on Sci. and Soc.Sci.

SHRI SAMARTH BOOK DEPOT
Tilak Rd., Aurangpura, Aurangabad-431001 (Maharashtra)
✆ 2335535, 2265535, Fax: 2335535
Estd.: 1960; **Prop.:** R.D. Borde;
Bus.Intt.: L.S.; **Spl.:** All subs. of Colleges/ Universities

SHRI SAMARTH VASTU BHANDAR
Gandhi Chowk, Chandrapur-442401 (Maharashtra)
✆ 253125
Estd.: 1956; **Prop.:** Vijay R. Tambekar;

Bus.Intt.: B.S.; **Spl.:** Engg. Polytechnic, Law, Mang., Comp. Books

SHRI SAWARTH BOOK DEPOT
Tilak Rd., Aurangpura, Aurangabad-431001 (Maharashtra)

SHRI TRADING & MARKETING CO.
Shrivitthal Chambers, Laxminagar Square, Nagpur-440022 (Maharashtra)
Hd.Org.: Prashant Redine

SHRI VEDMATA GAYATRI TRUST
Shanti Kunj, Haridwar-249411 (Uttarakhand)

SHRI VIDYA PRAKASHAN
250, Shaniwarpet, Ashtaphuja Rasta, Pune-411030 (Maharashtra)

SHRI VISHWA PRAKASHAN
Pustak Bazar, 71, New Market, T.T. Nagar, Bhopal-462003 (Madhya Pradesh)
✆ 2554138, 2661119

SHRI YOG VEDANT SEVA SAMITI
Sant Shri Asaramji Ashram, Upper Ridge Rd., Opp. Rabindra Rangashala, New Delhi-110060

SHRIJEE'S BOOK INTERNATIONAL
F-38, South Extension, Part-1, New Delhi-110049
✆ 24601418, 51646263, 51646355
▮ 9818263360
Estd.: 2002; **Hd.Org.:** Mukul Jain; **Bus.Intt.:** Pub., Dist. & B.S.; **Spl.:** Cookery, Interior Design, Furniture, Business, etc. and books for Children

SHRIJI STORE
Main Bazar, Div-362520 (Gujarat)

SHRIJI TRADERS
Near Jain Dharmashala, Naroda, Ahmedabad-380009 (Gujarat)

SHRIKRISHNA PUBLISHING HOUSE
24, Sreshtha Vihar, Delhi-110092
✆ 22167508

SHRIRAM BOOK AGENCY
727, D. Sadashiv, B. Gadgil Rasta, Pune-411030 (Maharashtra)

SHRIRAM BOOK DEPOT
Shrikrishna Niwas, Gokhale Rd., Naupada, Thane-400602 (Maharashtra)
✆ 25391745

SHRIYANS PUBLICATIONS LTD.
22, Bhagwandass Market, Second Floor, Chaura Rasta, Jaipur-302003 (Rajasthan)
✆ 2325795, 2320713, Fax: 2323606
✉ preeti78@datainfosys.net
Hd.Org.: Abhay Mehta; **Bus.Intt.:** Pub.; **Spl.:** Books for Children based on CBSE Syllabus

SHROFF PUBLISHERS & DISTRIBUTORS (PVT.) LTD.
C-103, M.I.D.C., Pawane, TTC, Industrial Area, Navi Mumbai-400705 (Maharashtra)
✆ 022-27634290, 27689126, Fax: 022-27683337
✉ spdorders@shroffpublishers.com, spdinfo@shroffpublishers.com
www.shroffpublishers.com
Hd.Org.: Aziz Shroff
Br.: Basement, 2/11 Ansari Road, Daryaganj, New Delhi-110002 ✆ 011-23243337, 23243338, Fax: 011-23243339
✉ spddel@shroffpublishers.com
• 23, Damodharan St., (Old No. 12), T. Nagar, Chennai-600017 ✆ 044-24315343, 24315340, Fax: 044-24315342
✉ spdchennai@shroffpublishers.com
• Gujrat Colony, Kothrud, Pune-400029
▮ 9823953174
✉ devendra@shroffpublishers.com
• H.No. 2-123, Street No. 2, Vani Nagar, Malkaj Giri, Hyderabad-500047
▮ 9885059050, 9908573692
✉ jayashanker@shroffpublishers.com
• 7B Haati Bagan Road, First Floor, Kolkata-700014 ✆ 033-22849329, 22847954, Fax: 033-22406109
✉ spdkol@shroffpublishers.com
• 7, Sharada Colony, Basaveshwar Nagar, 8th Main, Bangalore-560079
✆ 080-41287393, 41287394, Fax: 080-41287392
✉ spdblr@shroffpublishers.com
• 13-A, Krishnapuram, Second Cross Street, Kamarajarsalai, Madurai-625009
▮ 9360653881
✉ jothikumar@shroffpublishers.com
Bus.Intt.: Pub. and Dist.; **Spl.:** Books on Comp. and Allied Sub.

SHUBH BOOK HOUSE
GH7/117, Meera Bagh, Paschim Vihar, New Delhi
✆ 25288384, Fax: 25251688
Hd.Org.: Vinod Gulati; **Bus.Intt.:** Pub.; **Spl.:** Edu. and Children's books as well as Cookery

SHUBHA BOOK CENTRE
105-D, Aram Bagh, New Delhi-110055
✆ 23632679
Hd.Org.: S.K. Das; **Bus.Intt.:** Dist. & B.S.; **Spl.:** Ramakrishna and Vivekananda Litt.

SHUBHDA PRAKASHAN
1/11052 A, Subhash Park, Shahdara, Delhi-110032

✆ 22822586
Hd.Org.: Rahul Sharma; **Bus.Intt.:** Pub.; **Spl.:** Hindi Litt., Poetry, Criticisms, etc.

SHUBHI PUBLICATIONS
232, City Centre, M.G. Road, Gurgaon-122002 (Haryana)
✆ 0124-4088499, Fax: 0124-4375200
✉ shubhipublications@yahoo.co.in
www.shubhi-india.com
Hd.Org.: Sanjay Arya; **Bus.Intt.:** Pub., Imp. & Exp.; **Spl.:** Reference books on Soc.Sci., Rel., Phil., Litt., Edu., Pol., International Affairs, Humanities, Self-help, Edu., Art and Arch., etc.

SHUBKAMNA PRAKASHAN
P-10, Naveen Shahdara, Delhi-110032
✆ 22283744
Hd.Org.: Smt. Sadhna Shukal

SHUCHITA PRAKASHAN
7/1, Jawahar Lal Nehru Rd., Allahabad-211002 (Uttar Pradesh)

SHUKLA BOOK DEPOT
Munadpur, Patna-800004 (Bihar)

SHYAM BOOK DEPOT
680-81, Nai Sarak, Delhi-110006
✆ 23253351
Estd.: 1996; **Spl.:** N.C.E.R.T., C.B.S.E. School and Colleges and Competition Level Books

SHYAM BOOK DISTRIBUTORS
A-752, Gadoli Dairy Colony, Mayur Vihar Phase-III, Delhi-110096
✆ 22616562
Hd.Org.: Vinod K. Sharma; **Bus.Intt.:** Dist.; **Spl.:** Hindi Litt.

SHYAM BOOK DISTRIBUTORS
25, Ganesh Nagar, Nivaru Bypass Road, Jhotwara, Jaipur-302012 (Rajasthan)
✆ 0141-2469209
Hd.Org.: V.K. Sharma; **Bus.Intt.:** Dist.; **Spl.:** General Books in Hindi

SHYAM BROTHERS
2619-20/18, New Market, Nai Sarak, Delhi-110006
✆ 23253351, 23150632
Hd.Org.: Shyam Sunder Sharma; **Bus.Intt.:** Pub., B.S. & Stockist; **Spl.:** Textbooks and Edu. books

SHYAM PRAKASHAN
104/435 P. Rd., Kanpur-208012 (Uttar Pradesh)
✆ 2545453, 2256623, Fax: 0512-2316242
Estd.: 1974; **Hd.Org.:** Satyakam Pahariya; **Bus.Intt.:** Dealers; **Spl.:** Children Books in Hindi and English Language

SHYAM PRAKASHAN
Geetanjali Apartment, 1926, Nataniyon ka Rasta, Jaipur-302003 (Rajasthan)
✆ 0141-2317659, Fax: 0141-5113854
Estd.: 1985; **Hd.Org.:** Om Prakash Agarwal; **Bus.Intt.:** Pub.; **Spl.:** Indian Art and Culture, Children's Litt., Edu., Hindi Litt., etc. in Hindi and Sanskrit

SHYAM PUSTAK BHANDAR
G.T. Rd., Aurangabad-824101 (Bihar)
Bus.Intt.: Pub. and B.S.

SHYAM PUSTAK BHANDAR
Meston Ganj, Rampur (Uttar Pradesh)
✆ (O) 2324671 (R) 2351515
✉ 98371-80333@escotel mobile.com
Estd.: 1960; **Bus.Intt.:** B.S.; **Spl.:** School, Graduate, Adv. Books for Lib. and Gen. Books

SHYAMA CHARAN BOOK HOUSE
267, B.B. Chatterjee Rd., Kolkata-700042 (West Bengal)

SHYAMCO BOOK DISTRIBUTORS
Kochappilly Building, Veekshanam Rd., Ernakulam, Cochin-682018 (Kerala)
Prop.: M.S.R. Babu

SIBA EXIM (PVT.) LTD.
1/11760 A, Panchsheel Gardens, Naveen Shahdara, Delhi-110032

SIBASHISH BASU
4/1, Fakir Para Rd., Kolkata-700034 (West Bengal)

SIDDHARATHA PUBLISHERS
194, Guru Nanak Market, Karol Bagh, New Delhi-110005

SIDDHARTH BROTHERS
Hyderabad (Andhra Pradesh)
✆ 24412408
✉ siddharthchalksnboards@rediffmail.com
Bus.Intt.: B.S. and Dist.

SIDDHARTH INTERNATIONAL
Babu Genu Rd., No. 65, Opp. P.N. Bank, Mumbai-400002 (Maharashtra)
✆ 91-22-22065989, 22080476, Fax: 22003130
Hd.Org.: Parvind Jain; **Bus.Intt.:** Exp.; **Spl.:** Books, Periodicals, Magazines

SIDDHARTH PUBLICATIONS
1026/13, Urban Estate, Karnal-132001 (Haryana)

SIDDHARTH PUBLICATIONS
10, DSIDC Scheme II, Phase-II, Okhla Industrial Area, New Delhi-110020
✆ 26915718, 26838568, Fax: 22208551
Estd.: 1985; **Prop.:** Arun Raj Malhotra

SIDDHARTHA SOFT SERVICES
Secunderabad (Andhra Pradesh)
✆ 27806308, 27806466
✉ softservices@rediffmail.com

SIDDHARTH TRADERS
25-C, Rajpur Rd., Dehradun-248001 (Uttarakhand)
✆ 2652031
Estd.: 1992; **Hd.Org.:** Pradeep Kumar Rastogi
Bus.Intt.: B.S.; **Spl.:** Gen. and Text Books

SIDDIQUI BOOK CENTRE
Karbala Bazar, Siwan-841226 (Bihar)

SIDHANSHU PUBLICATIONS
4696/79, Regharpura, Karol Bagh, New Delhi-110005
✆ (O) 25728376, 25723874, 25745765 (R) 25743875
Estd.: 1975; **Hd.Org.:** Naresh Kumar Gupta

SIDHARTH PUBLICATIONS
New Delhi
✆ 51613753/54, Fax: 2638805/06
✉ arpl@id.eth.net
Bus.Intt.: Pub. & Printers

SIDRAH PUBLISHERS
Niamatullah Building, Niamatullah Rd., Aminabad, Lucknow-226018 (Uttar Pradesh)

SIGMA ENTERPRISES
C/o Sri Aurobindo Circle "Auroshrine" 'T' Point, J.N. Marg, Sitabuldi, Nagpur-440012 (Maharashtra)
✆ (O) 2545532 ▮ 9422114770, 9422131370, Fax: 0712779303
Estd.: 1996; **Prt.:** Awaak Shekhar Baantee, Prafulla Ram Lanjewar; **But.Intt.:** B.S., Suppliers; **Spl.:** Sci. & Tech., Mang., Arts & Arch., Bio.Sci., Engg.

SIKANDER BOOKS & STATIONERY
S.M. College Compound, Khanjarpur, Bhagalpur-812001 (Bihar)
Bus.Intt.: Pub. and B.S.

SIKH BOOKS
Amritsar (Punjab)
✉ sukhdev_2000@yahoo.com
Bus.Intt.: B.S.

SIKKAS GROUP
N-28 & 67, Connaught Circus, New Delhi-110001
✆ 25654257-59, Fax: 25654256
✉ sales@sikkas.com
Hd.Org.: Sanjeev Sikka; **Bus.Intt.:** Provider of Freight Services to Pub.

SIKSHA DIKSHA
160, Beliaghata Main Rd., Kolkata-700073 (West Bengal)

SIKSHA PRASAR-O-JANAKALYAN SAMSAD
60/1/1, Suren Sarkar Rd., Kolkata-700010 (West Bengal)

SIKSHA SANGHA
14, Ramanath Mazumder St., Kolkata-700009 (West Bengal)
✆ 22190526, 22417396
✉ siksha@vsnl.net
Estd.: 1957; **Prt.:** Birendra Nath Som
Br.: Aditi Pustak Bhawan, 27-B, Sree Gopal Mullick Lane, Kolkata-700012 ✆ 22417396
Spl.: Juvenile/Children

SIKSHAK PUSTAKALAYA
A-130, College St. Mkt., Kolkata-700007 (West Bengal)

SILIKUYIL
20, Kothandapani St., Kumbakonam-612201 (Tamil Nadu)

SIMON & SCHUSTER INTERNATIONAL
C/o Prentice-Hall of India (P) Ltd., M-97, Connaught Circus, New Delhi-110001

SIMRO BOOK AGENCY
14/214, New Moti Nagar, Near Karam Pura Terminal, New Delhi-110015
✆ 25167495 ▮ 9868344917
✉ nd-simro@rediffmail.com
Estd.: 2003; **Prop.:** Praveen Lata;
Bus.Intt.: L.S., Imp.; **Spl.:** Sci. & Tech., Mang., Law

SINDHI ACADEMY, DELHI
C.P.O. Building, Kashmere Gate, Delhi-110006
✆ 23862848, Fax: 23862992
Hd.Org.: Sindhu Bhagia Mishra;
Bus.Intt.: Pub.; **Spl.:** Edu. and Children Litt. in Sindhi Language, Sindhi Art

SINDHI ACADEMY, DELHI
D.D.A. Community Centre, Sadar Thana Rd., Pahar Ganj, New Delhi-110055
✆ 23553392, 23670319, Fax: 23682710
Estd.: 1994; **Ch.Exe.:** Dr. Jetho Lalwani;
Bus.Intt.: Pub.; **Spl.:** Edu. and Children Litt. in Sindhi Language

SINGA ROHINI TRADING COMPANY
15/1, South Street, Singarohini Illam, Tambaram (W), Chennai-600045 (Tamil Nadu)

✆ 044-22266117
✉ singarohini@yahoo.co.in
Bus.Intt.: Developer & Seller; **Spl.:** Edu. Software, CDs and Games

SINGH BROTHERS
Bazar Mai Sewan, Amritsar-143006 (Punjab)
✆ 2545787, 2550739, Fax: 2543965
✉ info@singhbrothers.com, singhbro@vsnl.com
www.singhbrothers.com
Hd.Org.: S. Satnam Singh; **Bus.Intt.:** Pub., B.S. and Exp.; **Spl.:** Punjabi Books on Sikh Rel. and Hist.

SINGH ENTERPRISES
23, Ajit Nagar, Amirtsar-143006 (Punjab)
✆ 0183-2230555
Prop.: Gursagar Singh; **Bus.Intt.:** Pub. and Exp.; **Spl.:** Books on Punjabi Litt. and Sikhism

SINGHAL PUBLICATION
H.No. 157, A-2, block (West) Sant Nagar, Burari, Delhi-110084
✆ 91-11-27616474
Hd.Org.: Parmod Kumar Singhal
Bus.Intt.: Pub. and L.S.; **Spl.:** Law Books

SINGLA LAW AGENCY
S.C.O. 4-5, Sector-17-B, Chandigarh-160017
✆ (O) 0172-2772015, 2703736 (R) 2569103, Fax: 0172-2710937
Estd.: 1981; **Prop.:** M.G. Singla;
Bus.Intt.: Pub.; **Spl.:** Law Books, Text Books and Law Periodicals (Only Lawyers Edition) in English

SINHA BOOK DEPOT
Ballia, Begusarai-854208 (Bihar)
Bus.Intt.: Pub. and B.S.

SINHAND PUBLICATIONS
Nagpur (Maharashtra)
✆ 642003, 646474, Fax: 643994
✉ nagaloka@nagpur.dot.net.in
Bus.Intt.: Pub.

SIRAJ PUBLICATIONS
422, Matia Mahal, Jama Masjid, Delhi-110006
✆ 23254518, 23286506, Fax: 91-11-22429803
Hd.Org.: Siraj Ahmed;
Bus.Intt.: Manufacturers of Printed;
Spl.: Islamic Books

SIRI SUDHINDRA PUBLISHING HOUSE
No. 92-94, 8th Cross Malleswaram, Bangalore-560003 (Karnataka)

SISHU BHARATI INTERNATIONAL
22/1, Ghose's Lane (North), Post Belurmath, Distt. Howarh-711202 (West Bengal)

SISHU SAHITYA SAMSAD PVT. LTD.
32, Acharya Prafulla Chandra Rd., Kolkata-700009 (West Bengal)

SISHU SAHITYA PRAKASHANI
3, Ramanath Majumder St., Kolkata-700009 (West Bengal)

SISUSATHI BOOK STALL
15, College Square, Kolkata-700073 (West Bengal)

SITA BOOK HOUSE
303-D, 1st Floor, Kunil Centre, G.H.S. Rd., Hampankatta, Mangalore-575001 (Karnataka)
✆ (O) 2442122 (R) 2439244

SITA BOOKS & PERIODICALS PVT. LTD.
308, Arjun Centre, Govandi Station Rd., Mumbai-400088 (Maharashtra)
✆ 55973281, 55973282, 55973283, Fax: 55973284
✉ ssrao@bom5.vsnl.net.in, sitabook@bom7.vsnl.net.in
www.sitabooks.com
Estd.: 1991; **Dir.:** Suresh S. Rao, Pushpa S. Rao, Sandesh S. Rao
Br.: Sita Book House, 303 D, 1st Floor, Kunil Centre, G.H.S. Rd., Harmpankatta, Mangalore-575001 ✆ 442122
Bus.Intt.: Pub., WS, L.S. & Rt., Imp., Exp., Sub.Ag.; **Spl.:** Humanities & Soc.Sci., Sci. & Tech.

SITA PRAKASHAN
Moti Bazar, Hathras-204101 (Uttar Pradesh)
Estd.: 1980; **Hd.Org.:** Dr. Sita Ram Gupta;
Bus.Intt.: Pub.; **Spl.:** Gen. Books

SIVA EXPORTS
51, Apparaswamy Koil St., Mylapore, Chennai-600004 (Tamil Nadu)
Bus.Intt.: Exp.

SIVASIDHANTA PUBLICATIONS
Broadway, Chennai-600001 (Tamil Nadu)

SIXTH DIMENSION MULTIMEDIA PVT. LTD.
302, Siddhartha Building, 96, Nehru Place, New Delhi-110019
✆ 26224301, 26237785, 26547785, Fax: 91-11-26237785
✉ sixthdimension@vsnl.com
Ch.Exe.: Mr. Sachin Jain; **Bus.Intt.:** Pub.;
Spl.: Game CD for Kids, Software

SKELETON ARTS
8/9, Kamanwala Chambers, 4th Floor, Sir P.M. Rd., Mumbai-400001 (Maharashtra)
Bus.Intt.: Exp.

SMALL INDUSTRY RESEARCH INSTITUTE
4/43, Roop Nagar, New Delhi-110007

✆ 22521895, 22910805, 22916804, Cable: SIRINDCONS, Telefax: 31-6108 SIRI IN, Fax: 91-11-22910805
Estd.: 1972; **Man.Dir.:** Diwan Chand Gupta; **Bus.Intt.:** Pub., WS, L.S., Rt., Exp., Sub.Ag.

SMART BOOK HOUSE
Exchange Rd., Near J & K, Srinagar-190001 (Jammu & Kashmir)
✆ 480052
Estd.: 2002; **Hd.Org.:** Shabir Ahmad; **Bus.Intt.:** L.S.; **Spl.:** Humanities & Soc.Sci., Mang. & Comm., Engg. & Tech.

SMITA PUBLISHING HOUSE
1150-B, Unit-9, Bhubaneswar (Orissa)

SMRITI BOOKS
New Delhi
✆ 26816142, 26844615, Fax: 24458269
✉ sunitapb@hotmail.com, sunitapb@usa.net
Bus.Intt.: Pub.

SMRUTHI PRAKASHANA
37, Chikkanna Building, Mysore Rd., Bangalore-560026 (Karnataka)
Hd.Org.: K.V. Chandranna Gowda; **Spl.:** Gen. and Edu. Books in Kannada

SNAB PUBLISHERS PVT. LTD.
3A/3, Asaf Ali Rd., New Delhi-110002
✆ (O) 23250091, 29214011, 30921147 (R) 26214011, 26238727, Fax: 23252948
✉ nitamehta@nitamehta.com
www.snabindia.com, www.nitamehta.com
Estd.: 1994; **Hd.Org.:** Subhash Mehta
Br.: E-159, GK.-II, Editorial & Marketing Office, New Delhi-110048
Bus.Intt.: Pub.; **Spl.:** Cookery, Comp., Beauty, Health Care, Home Remedies, etc.

SNEHVARDHAN PRAKASHNAN
4, Swarda, Plot No. 3, Pashan Rd., Abhimenshri, So Smor, Pune-411008 (Maharashtra)

SOBHAGYA DEEP PRAKASHAN
Flat No. 45, First Floor, Central Market, Lajpat Nagar, New Delhi-110024
✆ 29840051
✉ sobhagyadep@yahoo.co.in
Ch.Exe.: R.P. Dhamija; **Bus.Intt.:** Pub.; **Spl.:** Hindi Magazine & Astrological Books, *Sobhagya Deep*

SOBHAGYA DEEP PRAKASHAN
74, Ring Rd. Market, Sarojini Nagar, New Delhi-110023
✆ 26262699, 26262605, Fax: 26264534
✉ sobhagya@vsnl.net
www.astrohelper.com
Ch.Exe.: R.P. Dhamija; **Bus.Intt.:** Pub.; **Spl.:** Hindi Magazine & Astrological Books

SOCIAL CHANGE PAPERS
C-27, Raksha Kunj, Paschim Vihar, New Delhi-110063
✆ 23255303
Hd.Org.: Bharat Dogra; **Bus.Intt.:** Pub.; **Spl.:** Books in Hindi and English on Human Rights, Hist., Rel., Env., Health, Communal Harmony, People's Movement, etc.

SOCIETY FOR CREATIVE INTELLIGENCE
Plot 310-P, Sector-39, Adjacent to Sector-32, Gurgaon-122001 (Haryana)
✆ 26580220, 26138805
✉ cosmicbeam@vsnl.com
Hd.Org.: S.L. Sharma; **Bus.Intt.:** Pub.; **Spl.:** Metaphysical and Occult Sci. and Manufacturer of Learning and Teaching Aids

SOCIETY FOR FOREST & ENVIRONMENTAL MANAGEMENT
C-81, East End Apartments, New Ashok Nagar, Mayur Vihar, Phase-I, New Delhi-110096
✆ 22714257
Hd.Org.: H.N. Mathur; **Bus.Intt.:** Pub.; **Spl.:** Env., Forestry, Wildlife to Create Env. Awareness

SOCIETY FOR INTEGRATED DEVELOPMENT OF HIMALAYAS
Mussorie (Uttarakhand)
✆ 2631304, 2632904
✉ sidhsri@sancharnet.in
Bus.Intt.: Pub.

SOCIETY FOR POLICY ANALYSIS & DEVELOPMENT
8-2-695/A, Rd. No. 12, Banjara Hills, Hyderabad-500034 (Andhra Pradesh)

SOCIETY FOR SCIENCE & ENVIRONMENT
61, Bhagwan Nagar, New Delhi-110014

SOCIETY FOR THE PROMOTION OF AMATEUR RADIO
P.B. No. 2437, Mezzanine Floor, Kannanthanam Chambers, Cochin-682016 (Kerala)

SOCIETY OF BIOSCIENCES
25/4, Ram Bagh Rd., Muzaffarnagar-251001 (Uttar Pradesh)

SOCIETY OF SERVANTS OF GOD
Yashwant Place, Satya Marg, Chankyapuri, New Delhi-110021

SOFTMAX SOFTWARE SOLUTION
A-17, Preet Vihar, Ground Floor, Delhi-110092
✆ 65250328, 42444652
✉ softmax_education@yahoo.com

www.softmaxeducation.com
Estd.: 2000; **Hd.Org.**: Inder Malik
Bus.Intt.: Developer; **Spl.**: Edu. Softwares, Edu. CDs, 3D Rhymes and Stories, Interactive VCDs, etc.

SOGANI BOOK HOUSE
Shop No. 3, Rajani Bhavan, M.G. Rd., Indore-452001 (Madhya Pradesh)
✆ 2545130, 2546928, Fax: 2544597
✉ sbh@bom4.vsnl.net.in

SOHAN LALL MADAAN
21, Municipal Market, Chowk Purani Kotwali, Patiala-147001 (Punjab)
✆ (O) 2224235 (R) 2219683,
Fax: 0175-2217592
Estd.: 1990; **Bus.Intt.**: Pub., B.S., L.S.; **Spl.**: Soc.Sci., Comm. & Mang., Humanities, General Books

SOLOTOY
16/39, Subash Nagar, New Delhi-110027
✆ 25145549
Bus.Intt.: Dealers; **Spl.**: Edu. Toys and Games

SOM RAJ PURI
4-5, Lawrence Plaza, 9A, Lawrence Rd., Amritsar-143001 (Punjab)
✆ 2227759, 2210884, Fax: 183-2221744,
Cable: AKSHAY
Estd.: 1959; **Hd.Org.**: Nirmal Puri

SOM SUDHA PRAKASHAN
Plot No. 5, Pocket-11, Sector-5, Rohini, New Delhi-110085
✆ 27057070, 27058080, Fax: 27041515
✉ somsudha@eth.net
Estd.: 1978; **Prop.**: Rupendra Kashyap;
Bus.Intt.: Pub.; **Spl.**: Edu. books in English, Hindi and Sanskrit

SOMA BOOK AGENCY
42/1, Beniatola Lane, Kolkata-700009 (West Bengal)
Hd.Org.: Amarendra Chakraborty

SOMA BOOK SUPPLY
Stall-64/2, 1, Bankim Chatterjee St., Kolkata-700073 (West Bengal)

SOMA PRAKASHANI
P-3A, Nilgopal Park, Kolkata-700084 (West Bengal)

SOMAIYA PUBLICATIONS (P) LTD.
Fazalbhoy Building 45-47, Mahatma Gandhi Road, Post Box No.384, Fort, Mumbai-400014 (Maharashtra)
✆ 022-22858430/40/50,
Fax: 91-22-22047297
www.somaiya.com
Estd.: 1962; **Hd.Org.**: K.G. Nair
Mkt.Off.: Warden House 3rd Floor, PM Road, Fort, Mumbai-400001
✆ 91-22-22884635/5631/4294
Br.: Bank of Baroda Building, 6th Floor, Parliament St., New Delhi-110001
✆ 23723351, 23324929, Fax: 23723351
✉ somaiya@ndf.vsnl.net.in
• Utility Buildings, Tower Block, 4th Floor, J.C. Road, Bangalore 560002
✆ 91-80-2236479, Fax: 91-80-2219103
Bus.Intt.: Pub.; **Spl.**: Indology, Phil., Edu., Eco., Politics, Rel., Hist., Sol.

SOMENATH PRAKASHAN
Block-5, Stall-3, Bankim Chatterjee St., Kolkata-700073 (West Bengal)

SOMI PUBLICATIONS (P) LTD.
11099, Doriwalan, East Park Rd., Karol Bagh, New Delhi-110005
✆ 27828831

SONA BOOKS PRIVATE LTD.
F1/11, Model Town, Delhi-110033
✆ 27221175, 27218029, Fax: 27436867
Estd.: 1980; **Ch.Exe.**: Mrs. K. Mehra;
Bus.Intt.: Dist.; **Spl.**: Acad. and Gen. Trade

SONA PRODUCTS PVT. LTD.
B-180, Okhla Industrial Area-I, New Delhi-110020
✆ 26811313-21, Fax: 26811317
✉ business@sonaproducts.com
Hd.Org.: Kishore K. Mittal; **Bus.Intt.**: Pub.; **Spl.**: Children's Books, Specially Exercise and Drawing Books

SONA OVERSEAS
New Delhi
✉ overseas@sonaproducts.com
Bus.Intt.: Printers

SONA PRODUCTS PRIVATE LTD.
New Delhi
✉ business@sonaproducts.com
Bus.Intt.: Printers

SONAL BOOK ENTERPRISES
Bethandi Morh, Sunjwan Rd., Bye Pass, Jammu-180001 (Jammu & Kashmir)
✆ (O) 2463522 (R) 09419195660,
Fax: 0191-2454119
✉ ranjeev81@rediffmail.com
Estd.: 1996-97; **Prop.**: P.S. Jasrotia;
Bus.Intt.: L.S.; **Spl.**: Beh.Sci., Soc.Sci., Comm., Sci., Pure & Applied, Med., Tech., Fiction, Law

SONALI PUBLICATIONS
4831/24, Ansari Rd., Darya Ganj, New Delhi-110002

✆ (O) 23279245, 23253475 (R) 22414930
✉ dphtemt@indiatimes.com
Prop.: S.N. Katyal; **Bus.Intt.:** Pub.;
Spl.: Reference Books

SONGHATI
102, Satyen Roy Rd., Behela, Kolkata-700034 (West Bengal)
Bus.Intt.: Dist. and Pub.

SONI BOOK DEPOT
Nawadih Rd., Aurangabad-824101 (Bihar)
Bus.Intt.: Pub. and B.S.

SONI PUBLICATIONS (P) LTD.
11096, East Park Rd., Doriwalan, Karol Bagh, New Delhi-110005
✆ 23628831, 23535454, Fax: 23612870
✉ sonipub@ndf.vsnl.net.in
Estd.: 1980; **Hd.Org.:** G.D. Soni;
Bus.Intt.: Pub.; **Spl.:** Primary-level Textbooks on All Sub.

SONIA ART'S COMBINE
8/357, Punjabi Colony, G.T.B. Nagar, Mumbai-400037 (Maharashtra)
Bus.Intt.: B.S. and Pub.

SONIK ENTERPRISES
AG-206, Shalimar Bagh, Delhi-110088
✆ 27470419 ▮ 9811616990
Hd.Org.: Deepak Malhotra;
Bus.Intt.: Manufacturer; **Spl.:** Edu. Teaching Aids and School Equipment

SONKA PUBLICATIONS (INDIA) PVT. LTD.
7526, Tel Mill Marg, Ram Nagar, New Delhi-110055
✆ (O) 23637669, 23623653, 23533349 (R) 27266091, 26163206, Fax: 23546669
Estd.: 1987; **Man.Dir.:** Rajiv Gupta;
Bus.Intt.: Pub.; **Spl.:** Edu. books upto high school level

SOORIYA COMPUTER CENTRE & DESHTOP PUBLISHER
4/328, Ashokapuram, Coimbatore-641022 (Tamil Nadu)

SOURCE PUBLISHERS (P) LTD.
Tara Mahal, Plot 756, 5th Rd., Khar, West Mumbai-400052 (Maharashtra)
✆ 26465741, 26001558, Fax: 26002060
✉ source@bom2.vsnl.net.in
Hd.Org.: Shoaib S. Ranalvi
Br.: H 2, Sector 39, Noida-201301
✆ 0120-4319501
✉ sourcedel@airtelbroadband.in
Bus.Intt.: Pub., L.S. & Rt., Imp.; **Spl.:** Arch., Interior, Cosmetology, Cookery, Health and Wellness

SOUTH ASIA DISTRIBUTORS & PUBLISHERS
N-163, Panchshila Park, New Delhi-110017
✆ 26494077, 26490267,
Fax: 91-11-26491482, 29955643
✉ sadp@nda.vsnl.net.in
Man.Dir.: B.S. Dhiman; **Bus.Intt.:** Pub., L.S. and Sub.Ag.; **Spl.:** Foreign Journals in all Sub.

SOUTH ASIAN PUBLISHERS (P) LTD.
50, Siddharth Enclave, P.O. Jangpura, New Delhi-110014
✆ 26345315, 26345713
✉ sapub@ndb.net.in
Hd.Org.: Vinod; **Bus.Intt.:** Pub.;
Spl.: Sci., Pol.Sci., Engg.

SOUTH INDIA SAIVA SIDDHANTHA WORKS PUBLISHING SOCIETY TIN LTD. (THE)
154, T.T.K. Rd., Alwarpet, Chennai-600018 (Tamil Nadu)
✆ 2454157, 2455299
Hd.Org.: R. Muthukumaraswamy
Br.: Publishing Society, Tinnevelly Ltd., 91, East Car St., Tirunelveli-6 (Tamil Nadu)
Bus.Intt.: Tamil Languages Litt., Hist., Culture, Rel., Phil. and Books in English on the above mentioned Subjects

SOUTH INDIA SALISIAN SOCIETY
The Citadel, 18, Londons Rd., Chennai-600010 (Tamil Nadu)

SOUTH POINT BOOK SHOP
16/M, Mandivila Garden, Kolkata-700029 (West Bengal)

SOUTHERN BOOK STALL
149, Anand Nagar, Inder Lok, New Delhi-110035
✆ (O) 25465808 (R) 27100081
Hd.Org.: K.G.K. Kurup; **Bus.Intt.:** L.S.

SOUTHERN BOOK STALL
Near K.S.R.T.C., M.C. Rd., Thiruvalla (Kerala)
Estd.: 1955; **Prop.:** Eapen Jacob;
Bus.Intt.: B.S.

SOUTHERN BOOK STAR
A-2/13-A, Lawrence Rd., Delhi-110035
✆ (O) 27100223, 27381363 (R) 27109260
✉ sbookstar@satyam.net.in
Estd.: 1989; **Prop.:** K.G.K. Kurup
Rgd.Off.: TC-13/1212, Kumarapuram, Near CSI Church, Medical College P.O., Thiruvananthapuram-695011 (Kerala)
✆ (O) 0471-2554132 (R) 2442316,
Fax: 2557299
✉ sbookstar@satyam.net.in
Bus.Intt.: Pub., B.S., L.S.; **Spl.:** Sci., Pure

& Applied, Tech., Journal & Magazines, Agri., Animal Sci., Botany, Ecology, Entomology, Env., Fisheries, Forestry, Horticulture, Zoology

SOUVENIR PUBLISHERS
11263, Kela Kothi, Gaushala Rd., Doriwalan, Delhi-110005
✆ (O) 23515437, 55155020, 23681500
(R) 23627138, Fax: 91-11-23670004
✉ souvenir@hotmail.com,
sovenirpublishers@hotmail.com
Estd.: 1973; **Prop.:** O.P. Shastri, Gopal Krishan

SOWBAGYA PUBLICATIONS
94, Dasaralhan St., Baskar Colony, Chennai-600092 (Tamil Nadu)

SPANTECH PUBLISHERS PVT. LTD.
708, Pragati Tower, 26, Rajendra Place, New Delhi-110008

SPARDHA PRAKASHAN
2A Kush Bhawan, Gurunanak Nagar, Sakchi, Jamshedpur-1 (Jharkhand)
✆ 0657-2487423, Fax: 0657-2487423
✉ priya_spardha@sify.com
Hd.Org.: Priyanka Verma
Bus.Intt.: Pub., **Spl.:** Competitive Exams as well as Monthly Journal *Spardha* in Hindi

SPECTRUM BOOKS INTERNATIONAL
13/1, 1st Cross, Shankarapuram, Bangalore-560004 (Karnataka)
✆ 26600262, 26618602
Estd.: 1995; **Bus.Intt.:** L.S., Rt.

SPECTRUM BOOKS PVT. LTD.
116 T.C. Jaina Tower III, Ist Floor, Local Shopping Centre, A-1 Block, Janak Puri, New Delhi-110058
✆ 25623501, 25507922, Fax: 25611640
✉ spectrumindia@vsnl.com
www.spectrum-ind.com
Estd.: 2001; **Hd.Org.:** Kalpana Rajaram, K.K. Padmanabhan; **Bus.Intt.:** Pub.;
Spl.: Books on Gen. Knowledge and Current Affairs for Competitive Exams as also Monthly Magazine *Competition & Career Spectrum*

SPECTRUM COMMUNICATIONS (P) LTD.
9/1, Institutional Area, Aruna Asaf Ali Marg, Vasant Kunj, New Delhi-110067
✆ 26857211, 26857225, 26965572, Fax: 26868506
Estd.: 1986; **Hd.Org.:** Anil Metre, Mrs. Reena Metre; **Bus.Intt.:** Pub.

SPECTRUM MAGAZINE LTD.
Prospect Chambers, 4th Floor, D.N. Rd., Fort, Mumbai-400001 (Maharashtra)
✆ 22043149, 22835724, 22047662, Fax: 91-22-22045921
Hd.Org.: Anil Metre; **Bus.Intt.:** Exp. and Manufacturers; **Spl.:** Magazines

SPECTRUM PUBLICATIONS
Pan Bazar, Main Rd., Guwahati-781001 (Assam)
✆ (O) 0361-2638435 (R) 0361-2546244, 2520361, Fax: 0361-2638434
✉ unipub@bsnl.in
www.spectrumpublications.in
Estd.: 1976
Br.: 298-B, Tagore Park Extn., Model Town-1, Delhi-110009
✆ 27241674, 27135299, Fax: 23241471
✉ unipub@sancharnet.in
Bus.Intt.: Pub.; **Spl.:** School, Adv. Books for Lib., Gen. Books and Children Books

SPHATIK PRAKASHAN
3, Museum Rd., Jaipur-302004 (Rajasthan)
Hd.Org.: Rajendra Shankar Bhat;
Bus.Intt.: Pub. and Dist.

SPIC & SPAN PUBLISHERS
1439/23, Hari Singh Nalwa St., Karol Bagh, New Delhi-110005

SPIDER BOOKS
A4-73/1, Seventh Main Road, Shanthi Colony, Anna Nagar Chennai-600040 (Tamil Nadu)
✆ 91-44-42171048
✉ spider@spiderbooks.net
Hd.Org.: Mubarak; **Bus.Intt.:** Pub.;
Spl.: Children's Books such as Fiction, Activity Books, Folktales and books on Mythology, Quiz, General Knowledge, etc.

SPIRE MEDIA PVT. LTD.
E-6, Greater Kailash-I, New Delhi-110048
✆ 26282025, Fax: 91-11-26282026
✉ injoespire.co.in, contact@spire.co.in
Hd.Org.: Rajiv Tawakley; **Bus.Intt.:** Pub.

SPIRITUAL QUEST
P-11, New Howrah Bridge Approach Rd., Kolkata-700001 (West Bengal)
✆ 22355366, Fax: 22351386
✉ ranjit@8877.com
Hd.Org.: Ranjit Dugar; **Bus.Intt.:** Pub.;
Spl.: Teachings of Acharya Maha Pragya and Gen. books on Spiritualism

SPIRITUAL SCIENCES SERIES
41/2, Amod Kunj, University Campus, Roorkee-247664 (Uttarakhand)

SPORTS PUBLICATIONS
7/26, Ansari Road, Darya Ganj, New Delhi-110085
✆ 65749511, Fax: 23240261
✉ lakshythani@hotmail.com

www.sportspublication.trade-india.com
Hd.Org.: Lokesh Thani; **Bus.Intt.:** Pub. and Stockist; **Spl.:** Sports and Physical Edu.

SPRING TIME SOFTWARE
M-2, Harsha House, Karampura Commercial Complex, New Delhi-110015
✆ 45091750, Fax: 91-11-45091750
info@springtimesoftware.net
www.springtimesoftware.net
Hd.Org.: Chander Shekhar; **Bus.Intt.:** Dist.; **Spl.:** Books, Office Automation Saftwares and Web-based solutions for Book trade

SPRINGER BOOKS (INDIA) PVT. LTD.
6, Community Centre, Panchsheel Park, New Delhi-110017
✆ 26412765, 26436423, Fax: 26468717, Cable: NAROSA, Telex: 31-71298
Estd.: 1980; **Hd.Org.:** Sunil Paul
Br.: 35-36, Greams Rd., Thousand Lights, Chennai-600006 (Tamil Nadu)
✆ 28275362, Fax: 044-28240377
Bus.Intt.: WS, L.S. and Rt., Imp.

SPRINGER-VERLAG GMBH & CO. KG
906-907, Akash Deep Building, Barakhamba Rd., New Delhi-110001
✆ 23358590, Fax: 23358716
svdel@nde.vsnl.net.in
www.springeronline.com
Hd.Org.: Sanjiv Goswami; **Bus.Intt.:** Pub.; **Spl.:** Med., Math., Physics, Life Sci., Comp. Sci. and Engg. in English

SQUARE PRINT SERVICES
55 A, Pocket A-3, Everest Apartment, Kalkaji Extension, New Delhi-110019
✆ 40511986
sps-ajay@rediffmail.com
Hd.Org.: Ajay Chaudhry
Bus.Intt.: Promoter; **Spl.:** Children's books and Edu. Aids

SREE BANASHANKARI PRAKASHANA
Kodlipete, Kodagu-571231 (Karnataka)
Hd.Org.: Chandrashekhar; **Bus.Intt.:** Pub.; **Spl.:** Fiction, Gen. and Own Books in Kannada

SREE BHARATI PUBLISHERS
5, Shyama Charan Dey St., Kolkata-700073 (West Bengal)

SREE GANESH BOOK CENTRE
S.V. Rd., Borivili (West), Mumbai-400092 (Maharashtra)
✆ 28051257

SREE GAYATHREE PUBLICATIONS
3/55, Ajith Singh Nagar, Vijayawada-520015 (Andhra Pradesh)

SREE GOVINDA PUBLISHERS
18, Netaji Subhas Rd., Kolkata-700001 (West Bengal)

SREE GURU LIBRARY
204, Bidhan Sarani, Kolkata-700006 (West Bengal)

SREE INDU PUBLICATIONS
2, Muthu Krishnan St., Pondy Bazaar, P.B. No. 1040, T. Nagar, Chennai-600017 (Tamil Nadu)
✆ 28281902
Prop.: V.K.R. Ramanathan;
Bus.Intt.: Pub.; **Spl.:** Tamil Best Sellers, Gen. & Children Books

SREE JANAINDRA PRESS
X-45, Naraina Industrial Area, Phase-I, New Delhi-110027
✆ 25795180

SREE MA PRAKASHANI
4, Shyama Charan Dey St., Kolkata-700073 (West Bengal)

SREE NATH LIBRARY
127/2, Diamond Harbour Rd., Kolkata-700063 (West Bengal)

SREE PRASANTHI PUBLICATION TRUST
3-5-941, Susheelwadi, Himayatnagar, Hyderabad (Andhra Pradesh)

SREE RAGHAVENDA PRAKASHANA
799, K.R. Pet, Shimoga-577202 (Karnataka)
Hd.Org.: H.M. Raghavendrachar;
Bus.Intt.: Pub.; **Spl.:** Novels and Own Books in Kannada

SREE RAJA RAM BOOK DEPOT
1/6, Kushal Shopping Mayur Complex, Apids, Hyderabad-500001 (Andhra Pradesh)

SREE RAMA PUBLISHERS
Hyderabad (Andhra Pradesh)
✆ 24743514, 55825299
sreeramapublishers@yahoo.com

SREE SARASWATI PRESS LTD.
11, B.T. Prasanthinilayam, Anantpur-515134 (Karnataka)
Bus.Intt.: Exp.

SREE SOWMYA PRAKASHANA
93, 3rd Main, Bhuvaneshwarinagar, Kenjapura Agrahara, Magadi Rd., Bangalore-560023 (Karnataka)
Hd.Org.: Smt. Rajeswari;
Bus.Intt.: Pub.; **Spl.:** Fiction and Collections in Kannada and English

SREENARAYANA DHARMASANGOM TRUST
(Sree Narayana Press & Book Stall),
Sivagiri Mutt, Varkala-695141 (Kerala)
Bus.Intt.: B.S.

SREENIVASA PRAKASHANA
Hanakere, Mandya-571428 (Karnataka)
Hd.Org.: Smt. Sharada Thimmappa;
Bus.Intt.: Pub.; **Spl.:** Gen. and Own Books in Kannada

SRI ARAVIND CHETANA SAMAJ
6562/1, Chamelian Rd., Delhi-110006
▮ 9310052647, Fax: 23556005
satm@satm.net
www.satm.net
Hd.Org.: Gyanchandra
Bus.Intt.: B.S.; **Spl.:** Litt., Guide Papers for Self-development and Books of Sri Aurobindo and the *Vedas*

SRI ARAVIND CHETANA SAMAJ
6562/9, Chamelian Rd., Delhi-110006
✆ 23674147, 33044906 Fax: 30904335
sachetas@satm.net
Hd.Org.: Sukhbir Arya, Arvind Mohan Devsheersh
Br.: "Abhigyaan Shaakuntalam", M-21, South City, Gurugram-122001 (Haryana)
✆ 91-124-1581335 satm@satm.net
Bus.Intt.: B.S.; **Spl.:** Books on Sri Aurobindo and *Vedas*

SRI AUROBINDO BOOKS DISTRIBUTION AGENCY
Sri Aurobindo Ashram, Pondicherry-605002
✆ 2333154, 2334458, Fax: 2330682,
Cable: SABDA, Telefax: 0469221 SAS IN
saapress@auroville.org.in
Estd.: 1952
Br.: Sahakar B. Rd., Church Gate, Mumbai-20 (Maharashtra) ✆ 22043076
• 8, Shakespeare Sarani, Kolkata-700071 (West Bengal)
Bus.Intt.: Pub., WS

SRI BALAJI PUBLICATIONS
6-3-347/2 Dwarkapuri Colony,
Hyderabad-500482 (Andhra Pradesh)

SRI BHUMI PUBLISHING CO.
79, Mahatma Gandhi Rd., Kolkata-700006 (West Bengal)
✆ 22410591, 24407784
Estd.: 1941; **Hd.Org.:** Arun Purkayastha;
Bus.Intt.: Pub.

SRI BIJOY KRISHNA PRAKASHANI
66, College St. Mkt., Kolkata-700073 (West Bengal)

SRI DURGA PRAKASHANI
23/1, College Row, Kolkata-700009 (West Bengal)

SRI DURGAI PUBLICATION
21, Madurai Veeran Koil St., T. Nagar, Chennai-600017 (Tamil Nadu)
✆ 24346849
Prop.: R. Rameshbabu; **Bus.Intt.:** Printers, Pub. and B.S.; **Spl.:** Best Tamil Books

SRI ESWAR ENTERPRISES
'Archana Arcade', No. 27, Natesan St., T. Nagar, Chennai-600017 (Tamil Nadu)
✆ (O) 24345902, 24323659, 24339591
(R) 22244431, Fax: 24339590
yempeges@md3.vsnl.net.in
www.eswar.com
Estd.: 1985; **Prop.:** M. Periyasamy;
Bus.Intt.: B.S. and Dist.; **Spl.:** Sci., Tech., Mang. and Comp. Floppies and Consumables. Books on Comp. and Tech. of the following Foreign Pub.

SRI GANESH AGENCY
132-H, Pocket-4, Mayur Vihar Phase-I, Delhi-110091
✆ 22717685, 22716669
Fax: 22716669
gopalun@yahoo.com
www.numerounopanditsethuraman.com
Hd.Org.: V.S. Guruswami; **Bus.Intt.:** Dist.;
Spl.: Numerology in Hindi, English and Tamil

SRI GAYATRI PRINTOGRAPHS
New Delhi
✆ 23286757, 23274874, Fax: 23273335
info@hindibook.com
Bus.Intt.: Printers & Pub.

SRI GIRI TRADING AGENCY
58/2, T.S.V. Koil St., Mylapore, Chennai-600004 (Tamil Nadu)
✆ 24943551, Fax: 044-24953821
akshayaa@md2.vsnl.net.in
www.webindia.com/giri
Hd.Org.: T.S. Aiyappan
Sh.: 10, Kapaleewarar Sannadhi, South St., Mylapore, Chennai-600004 (Tamil Nadu)
✆ 24940376, 24942530
Bus.Intt.: Pub., B.S., Exp.

SRI GIRIJA PRACURANALU
B-31, Vidyalankar, Srinivasanagar Colony, Guntur-2522006 (Andhra Pradesh)

SRI GOURANGA PRAKASHANI
16-A, Tamer Lane, Kolkata-700009 (West Bengal)

SRI GRANTHALAYA
Sultanganj, Bhagalpur-812001 (Bihar)
Bus.Intt.: Pub. and B.S.

SRI HARSAPUSHPAMRITAM JAIN GRANTHAMALA LAKHABAVAL
C/o Srutagyan Bhavan, 45, Digvijaya Plot, Jamnagar, Saurashtra (Gujarat)

SRI JAGANNATH RESEARCH CENTRE
Puri (Orissa)
✉ sjrcpuri@hotmoil.com
Bus.Intt.: Pub., B.S. and L.S.

SRI KALI PRAKASHANI
206, Bidhan Sarani, Kolkata-700006 (West Bengal)

SRI KATHIA BABA CHARITABLE TRUST
B-227, Chittaranjan Park, New Delhi-110019
✆ 26276182
www.kathibaba.com
Hd.Org.: S.P. Paul; **Bus.Intt.:** Pub.; **Spl.:** Rel., Humanity, Phil., etc.

SRI M.V. PATHIPPAGAM
163, Netaji Rd., Madurai-625001 (Tamil Nadu)

SRI MAHALAXMI BOOK ENTERPRISES
Museum Rd., Eluru Rd. Corner, Governorpet, Vijayawada (Andhra Pradesh)
✆ 0866-2433322, 2430448
Estd.: 1978; **Hd.Org.:** U.K. Vishwa Mohan; **Bus.Intt.:** Pub.; **Spl.:** Fiction and Non-Fiction

SRI MARIAMMAN STORES
439, Main Bazaar, Virudhunagar-626001 (Tamil Nadu)
✆ (O) 245417 (R) 280793 Fax: 245417
✉ sunder@virudhunagaronline.com
Estd.: 1947; **Prop.:** J. Sundara Moorthy; **Bus.Intt.:** B.S., L.S., WS; **Spl.:** Graduate, Adv. Books for Lib., Sci. & Tech., Comm. & Mang., Humanities

SRI MIRA TRUST
Flat No. C-2, Skyline, 29, Roman Rolland Rd., Pondicherry-605001

SRI MITHRA PUBLICATIONS
Museum Rd., Government, Vijayawada-520002 (Andhra Pradesh)
✆ 0866-277526, 2434711
Estd.: 1987; **Prop.:** U. Murali Krishna; **Bus.Intt.:** Pub.; **Spl.:** Fiction and Non-Fiction Books in Telugu

SRI NAGAR LAW JOURNAL PUBLICATIONS
29, Goggi Bagh, Srinagar-190008 (Jammu and Kashmir)

SRI PADMALAY PUBLICATIONS
Ramendrayan St., Eluru Rd., Vijayawada-520002 (Andhra Pradesh)
✆ 0866-267498
Estd.: 1987; **Prop.:** D. Balamurali Krishna; **Bus.Intt.:** Pub.; **Spl.:** Novels, Sci. and Gen. Books in Telugu

SRI PRAKASHANA
248, Hans House, 16/17th Cross, Sampinge Rd., Bangalore-560003 (Karnataka)
Hd.Org.: Smt. Nirupama; **Bus.Intt.:** Pub.; **Spl.:** Fiction, Collections and Children's Books in Kannada

SRI PRAKASHANI
7, Nabin Kundu Lane, Kolkata-700009 (West Bengal)

SRI RAM TRUST PUBLICATIONS
A-7, Second Avenue, East Anna Nagar, Chennai-600102 (Tamil Nadu)

SRI RAMA PUBLISHERS
15-1-513 Siddiamber Bazar, Hyderabad-500012 (Andhra Pradesh)

SRI RAMAKRISHNA MATH
P.B. No. 635, 16, Ramakrishna Math Rd., Mylapore, Chennai-600004 (Tamil Nadu)
✆ 24941231, 24941959, Fax: 24943955
✉ srkmath@giasmd01.vsnl.net.in
Estd.: 1897; **Hd.Org.:** Swami Gautamanands; **Bus.Intt.:** Pub., B.S. and L.S. Exp.; **Spl.:** Ramakrishna, Vivekananda and Vedanta Litt.

SRI RAMKRISHANA BOOK STALL
Kozhikode-673001 (Kerala)

SRI RAMKRISHANA BOOK STALL
Thrissur-680001 (Kerala)

SRI RAMKRISHANA MATH PUBLICATION DEPT.
Puranattukara P.O., Thrissur-680651 (Kerala)
✆ 223719
Estd.: 1958; **Hd.Org.:** Swami Mridananda; **Bus.Intt.:** Pub.

SRI RAMKRISHNA SRI MA
Prakashan Trust, 579, 18-B, Chandigarh-160018

SRI SAI BOOKLINKS
Hyderabad (Andhra Pradesh)
✆ 27564391
✉ allani@safy.com
Bus.Intt.: B.S.

SRI SAI BOOKS
No. 110/6, 2nd Main, P.P. Layout, B.S.K. 3rd Stage, P.B. No. 8520, Bangalore-560085 (Karnataka)
✆ 26695133
Estd.: 1996; **Bus.Intt.:** L.S.

SRI SANGEETHA VANI
No. 91, V.M. St. Mylapore, Chennai-600004 (Tamil Nadu)

✆ 24981196
✉ tambi@md2.vsnl.net.in
Prop.: M. Natarajan; **Bus.Intt.:** Pub. and B.S.; **Spl.:** Gen. Books

SRI SARASWATI SADAN
A-1/32, Safdarjung Enclave, New Delhi-110029
Hd.Org.: Amittabh Ranjan

SRI SATGURU PUBLICATIONS
1st Floor, 40/5, Shakti Nagar, Delhi-110007
Bus.Intt.: Pub.; **Spl.:** Indology and Hist. Books

SRI SATHYA SAI RAM EDUCATIONAL BOOKS
PG-Block, 30, 2nd Floor (Possangipur), Janak Puri, New Delhi-110058
✆ 25507375 ▮ 9810900937
✉ sssreb@yahoo.co.in
Estd.: 2003; **Prop.:** G. Venkateshwaran; **Bus.Intt.:** L.S.; **Spl.:** Humanities & Soc.Sci., Sci. & Tech., Mang., Children & General

SRI SATHYA SAI TOWERS HOTELS PVT. LTD.
3/604, Main Rd., Post Box No. 2, Prasanthi Nilayam-515134 (Andhra Pradesh)
✆ 08555-287270, 287327, Fax: 287302
✉ prasanthi@saitowers.com
www.saitowers.com
Estd.: 1992; **Man.Dir.:** R. Padmanabhan
Br.: Sai Towers Publishing, 23/1142, Vijaya Lakshmi Colony, Kadugodi, Bangalore-560067
✆ 080-28451648, 28455758, Fax: 28451649
✉ kishore@saitowers.com
Dir.: Kishore B. Venkat
Bus.Intt.: Pub., WS, Exp.; **Spl.:** Spiritual & Phil.

SRI SELVA NILAYAM
107/1, Gowdia Mutt Rd., P.B. No. 5571, Royapettah, Chennai-600014 (Tamil Nadu)
✆ 28263184
Prop.: P.L. Muthukaruppan; **Bus.Intt.:** L.S., Rt., B.S. and Pub.; **Spl.:** Novels, Children Books Cookery, Sci., Gen. Knowledge Books in Tamil Languages

SRI SIDDHESWARI LIBRARY
27, Shibdas Bhaduri St., Shyambazar, Kolkata-700004 (West Bengal)

SRI SIDHALINGA PRAKASHANA
19, IX-A, 38th Cross, V Block, Jayanagar, Bangalore-560041 (Karnataka)

SRI SRI RADHA PARTHASARATHY TRUST
Sant Nagar, East of Kailash, New Delhi-110065
✆ 26235133-37, Fax: 26215421
✉ mahamantra.gkg@pambo.net
Hd.Org.: Mahamantra Das; **Bus.Intt.:** Dist. & B.S.; **Spl.:** *Vedas* and Rel. Litt. in various Indian Languages

SRI SRI RAMAKRISHNA PRAKASHANI
51, Netaji Subhash Rd., P.O. New Barrackpore, North 24 Parganas-743276 (West Bengal)
✆ 033-25512078
Estd.: 1989; **Hd.Org.:** Kanailal Datta; **Bus.Intt.:** Pub.; **Spl.:** Religious and Cultural Books, Collection of Poems in Bengali

SRI SRINIVASA PUBLICATIONS
A.T. Agraharam, Guntur-522004 (Andhra Pradesh)

SRI SUDHANSHU KUMAR MUKHOPADHYAY
Old Mission Rd., Bankura-722101 (West Bengal)

SRI SWAMI PATHIK SEWA SAMITI
28, Vidhan Sabha Marg, Lucknow (Uttar Pradesh)

SRI TARA PRAKASHANI
206, Bidhan Sarani, Kolkata-700006 (West Bengal)

SRI VANI STORES
13-683, R.F. Rd., Anantpur-515001 (Andhra Pradesh)
✆ (O) 08554-240114 (R) 08554-232114
✉ srivani38@hotmail.com
Estd.: 1962; **Bus.Intt.:** B.S.; **Spl.:** School, Graduate, Adv. Books for Lib. and Gen. Books

SRI VENKATESHWARA STEAM PRESS
Dhemraj Shri Krishendass Marg, P.O. Bldg., Mumbai-400004 (Maharashtra)
✆ 022-23857456
Prop.: Muralidhar S. Bajaj; **Bus.Intt.:** Indian Phil., Culture and Litt. in English and Sanskrit

SRI VIDYA PRAKASHANI
9/2B, Tamer Lane, Kolkata-700009 (West Bengal)

SRI VIDYADHIRAJA PUBLICATIONS
Geethanjally, Perumon, Kollam-691601 (Kerala)
Estd.: 1988; **Hd.Org.:** K.R.C. Pillai; **Bus.Intt.:** Pub. and B.S.

SRI VIJAYALAKSHMI PUBLICATIONS
Eluru Rd., Opp. Rahman Park, Vijayawada-520002 (Andhra Pradesh)

SRI VINAYAKA PUBLICATIONS
B-17, Prashant Vihar, New Delhi-110085

SRIDHAR PRAKASHANI
203/4D, Bidhan Sarani, Kolkata-700006 (West Bengal)

SRIJAN PUBLISHERS PVT. LTD.
206, Roots Tower, Laxmi Nagar District Centre, Delhi-110092
✆ 22444147, Fax: 42448400

Hd.Org.: Narendra Khanna
Bus.Intt.: Pub.; Spl.: Edu. and School Textbooks

SRIJAN SOLUTIONS PVT. LTD.
New Delhi
✆ 25727253, 25727254, Fax: 25721592
✉ info@srijansolutions.com
Bus.Intt.: Pub.

SRIKANTA MOHANTY (DR.)
Elite Publications, P.O. Rasulgarh, Bhubaneswar-751010 (Orissa)

SRIKANTHA PRAKASHANA
7/61/2, "Mandhara" 1st Main Rd., Padmanabhanga, Bangalore-560070 (Karnataka)
Hd.Org.: C.K. Nagaraj Rao; Bus.Intt.: Pub.; Spl.: Fictions, Travelogue, Collections and Gen. Books in Kannada

SRIKUNJ SADBHAVANA MANCH
'Sri Kunj', F-52, Bali Nagar, New Delhi-110015
✆ 25466019, 25453975, Fax: 25465926
✉ contact@srikunj.com
www.srikunj.com
Hd.Org.: Susheel Kumar Mittal; Bus.Intt.: Pub.; Spl.: Rel., Phil. and Soc. Welfare in Hindi

SRIMUKHA PUBLICATIONS
Flat 101: Kanchi Residency, H.No. 11-19, P&T Colony Mall Rd., Dilsukh Nagar, Hyderabad-500060 (Andhra Pradesh)
Estd.: 1963; Prop.: K.R.K. Mohan; Bus.Intt.: Pub.; Spl.: Research and Gen. Books

SRINGARA PRAKASHANA
Brahmin's Rd., Chiknayakanahali-572214 Tumkur Distt. (Karnataka)
✆ 08133-227116, 227416
Estd.: 1987; Bus.Intt.: Pub.; Spl.: School Text Book, Gen. Book and Children Litt.

SRINIVAS FINE ARTS
35-A, Velayutham Rd., Post Box No. 193, Sivakasi-626123 (Tamil Nadu)
✆ 221588, 220813, Fax: 04560-220058, Cable: GRAPHPRINT, Telex: 0448-206 SFA IN
Estd.: 1967; Bus.Intt.: Exp.

SRINIVAS STATIONERY STORE
Nawada Bazar, Bhagalpur-853204 (Bihar)
Bus.Intt.: Pub. and B.S.

SRIPAL NAGAR JAINA SHVETTAMBAR MUNI
12, Jamanada Mehta Marg, Balkeshwar, Mumbai-400066 (Maharashtra)

SRIRAM NIRUVANANGAL
10, Kasturi Estate, Chennai-600086 (Tamil Nadu)

SRISHTI
A-94, Neeti Bagh, New Delhi-110049

SRISHTI BOOK DISTRIBUTORS
4378/4-B, 202 IInd Floor, J.M.D. House, Ansari Rd., Darya Ganj, New Delhi-110002
✆ 51012315, 31109420
Estd.: 2002; Prop.: M.S. Chauhan; Bus.Intt.: Pub., L.S., WS; Spl.: Humanities & Soc.Sci., Sci. & Tech., Bio.Sci.

SRISHTI PRAKASHAN
106, Adharshila Commercial Complex, South Gandhi Maidan, Patna-800001 (Bihar)

SRISHTI PUBLISHERS & DISTRIBUTORS
A-79, Chittaranjan Park, New Delhi-110019

SRIVIDYA SANSKRITI SANSTHAN
D-117, Museum Flats, Bhubaneswar-751014 (Orissa)

ST. JOSEPH'S BOOK STALL
Convent Square, Alappuzha-688010 (Kerala)

ST. JOSEPHS ORPHANAGE BOOK STALL
Changanacherry, Kottayam-686101 (Kerala)
✆ 220040, Fax: 225540
Estd.: 1968; Hd.Org.: Joseph Panakkezham
Bus.Intt.: Pub. and B.S.

ST. MARY'S PRESS & BOOK DEPOT
Changanacherry, Kottayam-686101 (Kerala)
✆ 2366589
Estd.: 1975; Bus.Intt.: Pub. and B.S.

ST. PAUL BOOK CENTRE
Broadway, Kochi-682031 (Kerala)

ST. PAUL INTERNATIONAL BOOK CENTRE
H-30/33, Connaught Circus, New Delhi-110001
✆ 23320381, 51513127
✉ spi6@debol.net.in
Estd.: 1964; Hd.Org.: F.R. Francis Maniamkerry; Bus.Intt.: Pub., WS, L.S. & Rt.; Spl.: Juvenile/Children Books

ST. PAUL PUBLICATIONS
58/23rd Rd., T.P.S. III, P.B. No. 9814, Bandra, Mumbai-400050 (Maharashtra)
✆ 26510023, 26400126, Fax: 26454425
✉ stpauls@vsnl.com
Bus.Intt.: Pub. and Dist.

ST. THOMAS BOOK STALL
Chengannur-689121 (Kerala)

ST. THOMAS PRESS & BOOK DEPOT
Kozhencherry, Pathanamthitta-689641 (Kerala)

✆ 04731-22347
Estd.: 1943; **Prop.:** M.A. Paul;
Bus.Intt.: Pub. and B.S.

STAMP AIDS
D-57, N.D.S.E.-I, New Delhi-110049

STANDARD BOOK AGENCY
11, Darya Ganj, New Delhi-110002
✆ 23279440, Fax: 23252583
✉ stanbook@vsnl.net
Estd.: 1982; **Prop.:** Chakresh Kumar Jain; **Bus.Intt.:** Dist. & B.S.; **Spl.:** Fine Arts, Arch., Textile, Fashion, Interior, Med., Tech. Books & Journals

STANDARD BOOK COMPANY
125, Municipal Market, (Super Bazar Compound), Connaught Place, New Delhi-110001
✆ 23414447, 23413899, Fax: 23413828
✉ sales@sbcindia.com
Hd.Org.: S.L. Jain, R.K. Jain; **Bus.Intt.:** Rt., WS, Pub.

STANDARD BOOK COMPANY (THE)
142, Chaura Rasta, Jaipur-302003 (Rajasthan)
✆ (O) 2311455 (R) 2314087
Hd.Org.: Tarachand Varma

STANDARD BOOK HOUSE
(Tirumurthi Bhawan) 48/10G/1, Argara, Behind Bata Co., Hussainganj, Lucknow (Uttar Pradesh)
✆ 2235808
Estd.: 1974; **Hd.Org.:** Ramesh Singh; **Bus.Intt.:** L.S.

STANDARD BOOK TRUST
15A, Tamer Lane, Kolkata-700009 (West Bengal)

STANDARD LIBRARY SERVICE
4/9, Asaf Ali Rd., New Delhi-110002
✆ 23276334
Estd.: 1957; **Hd.Org.:** R.P. Puri; **Bus.Intt.:** Library Equipments

STANDARD LITERATURE CO. PVT. LTD. (THE)
UG-42, Som Datt Chambers-II, 9 Bhikaji Cama Place, New Delhi-110066
✆ 26176546, 41656254, Fax: 41656019
✉ standlit@airtalbroadband.in, newdelhi@standlitbooks.com
www.standlitbooks.com
Estd.: 1924; **Dir.:** Subrata Basu
Regd.Off.: 76, Acharya Jagadish Chandra Bose Road, Kolkata-700014
✉ thestandard@dataone.in, info@standlitbooks.com
Br.: Bharath Bhavan, Room No-12, (1st Floor), No. 34 Central Street, Bangalore-5600001
✆ 080-22868976, Fax: 41130793
✉ standlit@rediffmail.com, bangalore@standlitbooks.com
• Plot No. 538, Saheed Nagar, Bhubaneswar-751007 (Orissa)
✆ 0674-2540931
✉ standlitbbsr@yahoo.com, bhubaneswar@standlitbooks.com
• 16, Ritchie Street, Anna Road, Post Box No. 3728, Chennai-600002
Telegram: STANLITCO
✆ 044-28411431, 28413932, Fax: 044-28415171
✉ litstand@yahoo.com, chennai@standlitbooks.com
• Building No. XL/7254 (1st Floor), Gopala Prabhu Road, Ernakulam, Cochin-682035 (Kerala)
✆ 0484-2350987
✉ cochin@standlitbooks.com
• Ruplal Dutta Path, Central Chowkidinghee, Dibrugarh-781007
✆ 0373-2324510, Fax: 2323385
✉ dibrugarh@standlitbooks.com
• B.K. Kakati Road, Ulubari (Next to D.G.P. Office) Guwahati-781007
✆ 0361-2451015, Fax: 2459105
✉ standard_ghy@yahoo.co.in, guwahati@standlitbooks.com
• A-18, Everest Building, Tardeo Road, Mumbai-400034 ✆ 022-23515571
✉ mumbai@standlitbooks.com
• Himalaya Apartment, Ground Floor, Flat No. 2, Plot No. 19, Ravi Nagar, Nagpur-440033 ✆ 0712-2558548
✉ nagpur@standlitbooks.com
• Jylli Shop, Nongthymmai Main Road, Shillong-793014 ✆ 0364-2232381
✉ global@neline.com, shillong@standlitbooks.com
Bus.Intt.: Pub., WS, Rt., L.S. & Imp., Exp.; **Spl.:** Soc.Sci., Sci., Pure & Applied, Med., Juvenile, Fiction, Gen. & Fiction, Reference Books & Encyclopedias

STANDARD NETWORK SERVICES
1808, Prasadi Gali, Kotla Mubarakpur, New Delhi-110003
✆ 24601325, 31082327 ▮ 9891158484
✉ infostd@bol.net.in, sns1@bol.net.in
Prop.: C.S. Rawat; **Bus.Intt.:** Rt., L.S.; **Spl.:** Tech.

STANDARD PRESS (INDIA) PVT. LTD.
34-G, Satya Nagar, Near YRTV School, Sivakasi-626123
✆ 91-4562-421108
Bus.Intt.: Manufacturer; **Spl.:** Quality Diaries, Calendars, Books, Children Books

STANDARD PUBLISHERS DISTRIBUTORS
1705-B, Nai Sarak, P.B. No. 1066,
Delhi-110006
✆ 23262700, 23285798, 23257220,
Fax: 23243180, 23273335
✉ stpub@vsnl.com
www.standardpublishers.com
Hd.Org.: A.K. Jain; **Bus.Intt.:** Pub. and Dist.; **Spl.:** Textbooks on Engg., Sci. and Tech.

STANDARD PUBLISHERS (INDIA)
H.O.: 225, Gupta Palace, A-2/42,
Rajouri Garden, New Delhi-110027
✆ (O) 25415043, 25435043 (R) 25014181,
Fax: 25374397
✉ srallbooks3@bol.net.in
Hd.Org.: Kamlesh Sharma
Bus.Intt.: Pub., Printers, Dist., Govt. Suppliers; **Spl.:** University Level Books

STANDARDS BOOK INDIA
1808, Second Floor, Prasadi Gali,
Kotla Mubarak Pur, New Delhi-110003
✆ 24601325
Estd.: 1999; **Prop.:** P.S. Rawat; **Bus.Intt.:** Rt.; **Spl.:** Sci., Pure & Applied, Med., Tech.

STAR BOOK SERVICE
Pune (Maharashtra)
✆ 4486093, Fax: 4024752
✉ mahesh_pashte@yahoo.com
Bus.Intt.: B.S.

STAR BOOKS DISTRIBUTOR
24/4800, Bharat Ram Road,
Darya Ganj, New Delhi-110002
✆ 41562819, 23264462, Fax: 23264451
✉ sales@star-bk.com
www.star-bk.com
Hd.Org.: Ekagra Aggarwal
Bus.Intt.: Dist. & Stockist; **Spl.:** Sci., Tech., Academic and Research Books and Journals

STAR BOOKS INTERNATIONAL
Praikara, Mavelikara-690101 (Kerala)
✆ 0479-2300638
Estd.: 1980; **Bus.Intt.:** B.S.; **Spl.:** Books on All Topics

STAR PUBLICATIONS
11, Roadways Colony, Loha Mandi,
Agra-282002 (Uttar Pradesh)
✆ 2111805, 2512173
Hd.Org.: Anil Agarwal; **Bus.Intt.:** Pub.; **Spl.:** Home Sci. in Hindi

STAR PUBLICATIONS
72, Big St., Triplicane, Chennai-600005
(Tamil Nadu)
✆ 28544740
Hd.Org.: R.M. Kannappan; **Bus.Intt.:** Pub. and B.S.; **Spl.:** Sci. and Children Books, Novels, Devotional and Fish Culture Books

STAR PUBLICATIONS PVT. LTD.
4/5B, Asaf Ali Rd., New Delhi-110002
✆ (O) 23261696, 23286757, 23257220, 23274874 (R) 26410363, 26427181
Fax: 23273335, 26481565
✉ starpub@satyam.net.in,
hbc@satyam.net.in
www.starpublic.com
Estd.: 1969; **Hd.Org.:** Amarnath Varma
Br.: Export-Department, N-33, Greater Kailash Part-I, New Delhi-110048
✆ 26468427, Fax: 26481565
Bus.Intt.: Pub. and Exp.; **Spl.:** Bilingual and Trilingual Dictionaries

STAR PUBLISHERS
50, Sitaram Ghosh St., Kolkata-700009
(West Bengal)

STARAND BOOK STALL
"Dhannur" Sir P.M. Rd., Fort, Mumbai-400001
(Maharashtra)
✆ 22660994, 22661719, Fax: 022-22088071
Estd.: 1952; **Hd.Org.:** T.N. Shanbhag; **Bus.Intt.:** B.S. and Pub.

STATE INSTITUTE OF CHILDREN'S LITERATURE
University P.O., Thiruvananthapuram-695034
(Kerala)
✆ 262276, 268549
Estd.: 1981; **Hd.Org.:** Dr. Kurias Kumbalakuzhy; **Bus.Intt.:** Pub.

STATE INSTITUTE OF ENCYCLOPAEDIC PUBLICATIONS
Thycaud, Thiruvananthapuram-695014
(Kerala)
✆ 263567, 263692
Estd.: 1962; **Hd.Org.:** Prof. M. Achuthan; **Bus.Intt.:** Pub.

STATE INSTITUTE OF LANGUAGES NALANDA
Thiruvananthapuram-695003 (Kerala)
✆ 2437238, 2436306
Estd.: 1968; **Hd.Org.:** K.P. Sasidharan; **Bus.Intt.:** Pub.; **Spl.:** Textbooks on all Sub. for Schools and Colleges in Malayalam besides Three Periodicals

STATE RESOURCE CENTRE
Jamia Milla, Jamia Nagar,
New Delhi-110025

STATESMAN LTD. (THE)
148, Barakhamba Rd., New Delhi-110001
✆ 23315911, Fax: 23353055, 23315295
✉ sman@nde.vsnl.net.in
Hd.Org.: C.R. Irani; **Bus.Intt.:** Pub.; **Spl.:** The daily *The Statesman* as also books on Pol. and Edu. Sub.

STELLAR INDUSTIRES PVT. LTD.
New Delhi
✆ 26833520, 26828769, Fax: 26316201
✉ stellarpp@vsnl.com
Bus.Intt.: B.S.

STERLING BOOK HOUSE
181, D.N. Rd., Fort, Mumbai-400001 (Maharashtra)
✆ 22612521, 22659599, Fax: 22623551
✉ sbh@vsnl.com, sterling@bom5.vsnl.net.in
www.sterlingbookhome.com
Estd.: 1956; **Prop.:** Abdul Sultan Shroff; **Bus.Intt.:** Pub., WS, L.S. & Rt., Imp., Exp.; **Spl.:** Sci. & Tech., Med., Law

STERLING PUBLISHERS PRIVATE LIMITED
Hd.Off.: Sterling House, A-59, Okhla Industrial Area, Phase-II, New Delhi-110020
✆ (O) 26387070, 26386209, 26386165, 26385677 (R) 26162422, 26162426, Fax: 26383788
✉ mail@sterlingpulishers.com, info@sterlingpublishers.com
www.sterlingpublishers.com
Delhi Sales Off.: 4806, Mezzanine Floor, Bharat Ram Rd., 24, Darya Ganj, New Delhi-110002
Hd.Org.: S.K. Ghai; **Bus.Intt.:** Pub., Dist., Exp.; **Spl.:** Children's Books, Edu., PB, School and University level Textbooks on all Sub.

STONE HILL FOUNDATION PUBLISHING PVT. LTD.
G-309, Panampilly Avenue, Panampilly Nagar, Kochi-682036 (Kerala)
✆ 0484-2321513, 4012517, Fax: 91-484-2321778
✉ editionindia@asianetindia.com
Hd.Org.: Mohan G. Nair
Bus.Intt.: Pub.; **Spl.:** Malayalam Language Books on Self-improvement, Env., Sci., and Spiritualism

STONE TECHNOLOGY CENTRE
'Rastogi House', B-9, Vivekanand Marg, Jaipur-302001 (Rajasthan)
✆ 0141-2376171, 2379653, Fax: 2365232
✉ stonetec@sancharnet.in, vikram97@hotmail.com
Hd.Org.: K. Vikram; **Bus.Intt.:** Pub.

STORY OF LIFE (THE)
Muzaffarnagar (Uttar Pradesh)
✉ pksharma@nda.vsnl.net.in
✆ 403987, 402456, Fax: 402870
Br.: New Delhi ✆ 23254454, Fax: 23254454
✉ mukeshin@giasd101.vsnl.net.in
Bus.Intt.: Pub.

STORYTELLERS
13-B, 3rd Floor, N.S. Marg, Darya Ganj, New Delhi-110002
✆ 23254454, Fax: 91-11-23254454
Hd.Org.: H.P. Rao; **Bus.Intt.:** Manufacturers; **Spl.:** Books and Periodicals

STRAND BOOK STALL
"Dhannur", Sir P.M. Rd., Fort, Mumbai-400001 (Maharashtra)
✆ 22661994, 22661719, 22614613, Fax: 022-22051754, 22630154
✉ strandbookstall@vsnl.com
strandbookstall.com
Estd.: 1952; **Ch.Exe.:** T.N. Shanbhag
Br.: S-113/114, Manipal Centre, 47, Dickenson Rd., Bangalore-560042 (Karnataka)
✆ 25580000, Telefax: 080-25582222
Bus.Intt.: L.S. & Rt., Imp., Sub.Ag.; **Spl.:** Humanities & Soc.Sci., Sci. & Tech., Juvenile/Children Books, Gen. & Fiction etc.

STRAWBERRY STOP/S.S. EDUCATIONAL (AIDS) STORES
B-9/295, Sector 5, Rohini, Delhi-110085
✆ 27053526, 27056395
▮ 9811059403, 9810021148
✉ sseducationalaids@hotmail.com
www.sseducationalaids.com
Hd.Org.: Ritu Malhotra
Br.: S.S. Educational Aids, C-5/89, Sector-5, Rohini, Delhi-110085
✆ 27053526, 27056395
Bus.Intt.: Manufacturer and Supplier; **Spl.:** Edu. Aids and School Decorations

STREE
16, Southern Avenue, Kolkata-700026 (West Bengal)
✆ 24660812, Fax: 24664614, 24666677
✉ stree@cal2.vsnl.net.in
www.streebooks.com
Hd.Org.: Mandira Sen; **Bus.Intt.:** Pub.; **Spl.:** Soc.Sci. and Humanities in Bangla and English

STREE LEKHA
15/55, Cambridge Rd., Jeevan Kendra Layout Bangalore-560008 (Karnataka)
✆ 25278628, 25269307
Bus.Intt.: Rt. B.S. and L.S.

STRUCTURAL DESIGNERS & CONSULTANTS (P) LTD.
Raiker Bhawan, 4th Floor, Plot No. 9, Sector-17, Vashi, Mumbai-400003 (Maharashtra)

STUDENT AID PUBLICATIONS
235, RG Complex II, Sector 14, Prashant Vihar, Rohini, Delhi-110085

✆ 27557146, Telefax: 27557146
✉ stuaid@nda.vsnl.net.in,
editoral@studentaidpublications.in
🌐 www.studentaidpublications.in
Hd.Org.: S.C. Soni; **Bus.Intt.:** Pub.;
Spl.: Career Directories and Career-oriented Litt. in English

STUDENT BOOK CENTRE
Z-19, Main Market, West Patel Nagar, New Delhi-110008
✆ 25880695
Hd.Org.: Sunil Wadhwa **Bus.Intt.:** B.S.;
Spl.: Children's Books, Classics, Litt., School and College-level Textbooks

STUDENT BOOK DEPOT
4481, Nai Sarak, Delhi-110006
✆ 23931172, 23965618
Hd.Org.: Surender Mohan Gupta;
Bus.Intt.: Pub.; **Spl.:** Dictionaries and Med. Guides

STUDENT BOOK DEPOT
Below Masjid, Main Bazar, Leh (Jammu & Kashmir)

STUDENT BOOK DEPOT
Upper Bazar, Ranchi (Jharkhand)
✆ 2203048, 2200123, Fax: 2220642
Estd.: 1958; **Prop.:** Nand Kishor Lal;
Bus.Intt.: L.S. & Rt.; **Spl.:** Sci. & Tech.

STUDENT BOOK HOUSE
Char Minar, Hyderabad-500002 (Andhra Pradesh)
Estd.: 1952; **Hd.Org.:** Syed Fakhruddin Husain

STUDENT CORNER
Ishipur, Barahat, Bhagalpur-813206 (Bihar)
Bus.Intt.: Pub. and B.S.

STUDENT CORNER
Ashananpur, Bhagalpur-853205 (Bihar)
Bus.Intt.: Pub. and B.S.

STUDENT CORNER
Naugachia, Bhagalpur-853204 (Bihar)
Bus.Intt.: Pub. and B.S.

STUDENT EMPORIUM
New Market, Dibrugarh (Assam)
Bus.Intt.: Pub.

STUDENT FRIENDS
Lailakh Bhagalpur-813205 (Bihar)
Bus.Intt.: Pub. and B.S.

STUDENT STORES
Brances Bamung Gaon, Golaghat (Assam)
Bus.Intt.: Pub.

STUDENTS' AGENCIES (I) PVT. LTD.
102, Konark Shram, Behind Everest Building, 156, Tardeo Rd., Mumbai-400034 (Maharashtra)
✆ 022-23513334/5/6/7, Fax: 23514212
✉ students@vsnl.com,
students@bom3.vsnl.net.in
🌐 www.books-n-all.com
Estd.: 1968; **Man.Prt.:** K.K. Shah
Br.: Books-N-All, 101, Konark Shram, 156, Tardeo Rd., Mumbai-400034
✆ 23526457, 23513334, Fax: 23514212
✉ inquiry@books-n-all.com
Bus.Intt.: WS, Imp., Exp.;
Spl.: Humanities & Soc.Sci., Sci. & Tech., Juvenile/Children, Gen. & Fiction etc.

STUDENTS BOOK CENTRE
Haspura, Aurangabad-824120 (Bihar)
Bus.Intt.: Pub. and B.S.

STUDENTS BOOK STALL
300, Gopal Lal Thakur Rd., Kolkata-700030 (West Bengal)

STUDENTS BOOK STALL
117, B.K. Paul Avenue, Kolkata-700005 (West Bengal)

STUDENTS BOOK STALL
Sub Jail Rd., Alwaye (Kerala)
✆ 223165
Estd.: 1944; **Prop.:** Rosily George;
Bus.Intt.: B.S.

STUDENTS CORNER
Motinagar, Dhanbad-828120 (Jharkhand)
✆ 0326-251516, Fax: 0326-251445
✉ scbooks@rediffmail.com,
studentscorner@libraryservicemail.com
Estd.: 1986; **Prop.:** Mrs. Prabha Jha;
Bus.Intt.: L.S.; **Spl.:** Sci.: Pure & Applied Engg. & Tech., Mang. & Comm., Med. Sci.

STUDENTS EMPORIUM
24-B, Noor Mohammed Lane, Kolkata-700009 (West Bengal)

STUDENTS FRIENDS
Bhakharua More, Daudnagar, Aurangabad-824101 (Bihar)
Bus.Intt.: Pub. and B.S.

STUDENTS FRIENDS
Patna (Bihar)
✉ shiv frinds@yahoo.com
✆ 673291, Fax: 669158 **Bus.Intt.:** Pub.

STUDENTS GUIDE CENTRE
9, Bankim Chatterjee St., Kolkata-700073 (West Bengal)

STUDENTS STORES
K.S. Raj Rd., Kolkata-700032 (West Bengal)

STUDENTS STORES PVT. LTD.
Students House, Post Box 1511,
Kashmere Gate, Delhi-110006
✆ 23928377, 23965726, 23951867,
Fax: 23936758
devra@vsnl.com
www.devrabooks.com
Estd.: 1951; **Man.Dir.:** Shalindra Sharma
Br.: House No. B-20, Yulzar Bagh,
Patna-800007 ✆ 0612-2311166
Bhupinder Chaturvedi, 51-Kabir Nagar,
Dayalbagh, Agra-282005 ✆ 0562-2570656
• Atulya Srivastava ✆ 0612-2681966
• Jobi Thomas, Abra Distributors, No. 28,
Kh. Rd., Ayanavaram, Chennai-600023
✆ 044-26474747, 26449663, 2660710
abba-doo@yahoo.com
Bus.Intt.: Pub., WS, Exp.; **Spl.:** Juvenile/
Children/School Text

STUDENTS VARIETY
72/A, Raja Dinendra St., Kolkata-700006
(West Bengal)

STUDIO 2000 (P) LTD.
P-11, Patropolis Colaba Rd., Mumbai-400005
(Maharashtra)
✆ 22186618

STUFUN DOT COM. PVT. LTD.
Mumbai (Maharashtra)
✆ 28862529, Fax: 28541370
info@stufun.com

SUBALIKA PUBLICATIONS
4, Banker's Colony, Kumaran Nagar,
Tiruchirappalli-620017 (Kerala)

SUBARNAREKHA
73, M.G. Rd., Kolkata-700009
(West Bengal)

SUBHA BOOK CENTRE
105-D, Aram Bagh, New Delhi-110055
✆ 23632679
subha_books@rediffmail.com
Prop.: S.K. Das
Bus.Intt.: Dist., B.S.; **Spl.:** Children's Books
and Litt. on Vivekananda and Ramakrishna

SUBHAS LIBRARY
12, Simla St., Kolkata-700006
(West Bengal)

SUBHAS STORES (REGD.)
Books Paradise, 72, Avenue Rd.,
Bangalore-560002 (Karnataka)
✆ 22216624
Estd.: 1948; **Hd.Org.:** S. Prakash

SUBHASH BOOK AGENCIES/SUBHASH PUBLISHING HOUSE
No. 116, 5th Main 6th Cross,
(Near Ram Mandir Stop) Chamarajpet,
Bangalore-560018 (Karnataka)
Prop.: A.S. Gupta, A. Satish

SUBHASH BROTHERS
2606, Nai Sarak, Delhi-110006
✆ (O) 23261011, 23283733 (R) 25748440
9810004034, Fax: 23261011
info@subhashbrothers.com
Estd.: 1965; **Hd.Org.:** S.C. Bajaj

SUBHASH PUSTAK BHANDAR
Ghogha, Bhagalpur-813205 (Bihar)
Bus.Intt.: Pub. and B.S.

SUBHEKSHANA
27, Park Avenue, Kolkata-700075
(West Bengal)

SUBLIME PUBLICATIONS
18, Jain Bhawan, Opp. N.B.C., Shanti Nagar,
Jaipur-302006 (Rajasthan)
✆ 2220590
Estd.: 1988; **Bus.Intt.:** Pub.; **Spl.:** Comm. &
Mang., Humanities, Gen. Books

SUBODH GRANTHMALA KARYALAY
Pustak Path, Ranchi-834001 (Bihar)
✆ 0651-202858, 200819
suboh12@dte.vsnl.net.in

SUBODH POCKET BOOKS
2/4240-A, Ansari Rd., New Delhi-110002
✆ 23274513, 23278858
anilkumar@subodhbooks.com,
subodhbooks@vsnl.net
Hd.Org.: Anil Kumar; **Bus.Intt.:** Pub.;
Spl.: Astrology, Health, Yoga, Biography,
Litt., Poetry and Women-related Issues in
Hindi

SUBRATA BOOK STALL
Kulpi, Distt. 24-Parganas (South)
(West Bengal)
Hd.Org.: Mrinmoy Naskar

SUBROOP & BROTHERS
601, Khajuri Bazar, Indore-452002
(Madhya Pradesh)
✆ (O) 2452330 (R) 2451652

SUCCESS BOOK SERVICE
A-516/9, South Gamari, New Delhi-110053
✆ 22180227
Estd.: 2001; **Prop.:** S.N. Sharma;
Bus.Intt.: L.S.; **Spl.:** Soc.Sci., Comm.,
Sci.

SUCCESS PUBLISHING HOUSE
1, Bidhan Sarani, Kolkata-700073
(West Bengal)

SUCCESS SYSTEMS INFOTECH
Delhi

✆ 27187227, 27105555
✉ vaid@giasd01.vsnl.net.in

SUCHINTAN PRAKASHAN
3146, 1st Floor, Sector 27-D, Chandigarh-160019
✆ 2570031
Prop.: Jagjit Gagan; **Spl.:** Indian Litt., Soc.Sci., Humanities, Ecology, Med. and Sci.

SUCHVARDHAN PUBLISHING HOUSE
4, Sharda, Plot No. 3, Pashan Rd., Opp. Abhimanshree, Pune-411008 (Maharashtra)

SUDAMA PRAKASHAN
Kamta Sadan, Boring Rd., Patna-800001 (Bihar)

SUDARSHAN BOOK DISTRIBUTORS
51/1, New Market, Near Liberty Cinema, Karol Bagh, New Delhi-110005
✆ 25723138, 55450350, Fax: 91-11-25817268
✉ spds@bol.net.in
Ch.Exe.: Sudarshan Dhingra; **Bus.Intt.:** Dist.; **Spl.:** Books on Advertising, Graphics, Photography, Interior Fashion and Other type of Design Books & CD-ROMs

SUDARSHAN PUBLICATIONS (P) LTD.
1105, Ambadeep Building, 14, Kasturba Gandhi Marg, Connaught Place, New Delhi-110001
✆ 51520717, 51520718, Fax: 51520718
✉ sudarshanpublication@hotmail.com
Estd.: 2003; **Hd.Org.:** B.K. Sudarshan; **Bus.Intt.:** Pub., WS, L.S. & Rt., Imp., Exp., Sub.Ag.; **Spl.:** Humanities & Soc.Sci., Sci. & Tech., Juvenile/Children Books, Gen. & Fiction etc.

SUDERSHAN BOOKSELLERS AND PUBLISHERS
156-D, Kamla Nagar, Delhi-110007
✆ 22916233
Prop.: S.K. Garg; **Bus.Intt.:** Rt. and L.S.

SUDHA PUBLICATIONS
23/380, Punkunam, Thrissur-680002 (Kerala)
✆ 223361
Estd.: 1968; **Prop.:** Sudha Chaturvedi; **Bus.Intt.:** Pub. and B.S.

SUDHA PUBLICATIONS PVT. LTD.
B-5, Prabhat Kiran, Rajendra Place, New Delhi-110008
✆ 25718495, 25712898, Fax: 25754647
✉ csrindia@mantraonline.com
www.competitionsuccessreview.com
Estd.: 1960; **Man.Dir.:** S.K. Sachdeva; **Bus.Intt.:** Pub.; **Spl.:** Gen. Books and Books for Competitive Examinations

SUDHANSHU BANDHU
E-9/23, Vasant Vihar, New Delhi-110057
✆ 26142085, 26148152
Hd.Org.: Haribabu Kansal

SUGAR TECHNOLOGISTS ASSOCIATION
21, Community Centre, East of Kailash, New Delhi-110065

SUGAT BOOK DEPOT
Dr. Ambedkar Rd., Nagpur-440017 (Maharashtra)
✆ (O) 2640413 (R) 2640142
✉ sugatbookdepot@sify.com
Hd.Org.: Tulsi Pagare

SUGAVA PRAKASHAN
861/1, Sadashiv Peth, Pune-411030 (Maharashtra)

SUJAN PUBLICATIONS
7-B, Lake Place, Kolkata-700029 (West Bengal)

SUJAYA PATHIPPAGAM
42, Kamakoti Nagar, 4th Cross St., Valasaravakkam, Chennai-600087 (Tamil Nadu)

SULABH PRAKASHAN
17, Ashok Marg, Lucknow-226001 (Uttar Pradesh)
✆ 2280378, 2280381
Hd.Org.: Veerendra Kumar

SULABHA BOOKS
Triveni Gardens, Poot Hole, Thrissur-680004 (Kerala)
✆ (R) 2334133
Estd.: 1992; **Bus.Intt.:** Pub.

SULEKHA ADVERTSING PVT. LTD.
Patna (Bihar)
✆ 220648, 220647, Fax: 230347
✉ poppycool@hotmail.com
Br.: New Delhi ✆ 23260075, 23260980, Fax: 23289074
✉ sulekha@nde.vsnl.net.in
Bus.Intt.: B.S., Rt.

SULEMAN PUSTAK BHANDAR
Bakhri, Begusarai-848201 (Bihar)
Bus.Intt.: Pub. and B.S.

SULTAN CHAND & SONS
4792/23, Darya Ganj, New Delhi-110002
✆ 23247051, 23243183
Fax: 23266357
Estd.: 1950; **Prop.:** S.C. Aggarwal; **Bus.Intt.:** Pub., L.S. & Rt., Imp., Exp.; **Spl.:** Humanities & Soc.Sci., Sci. & Tech., Law, Juvenile/Children

SULTAN CHAND & SONS (P) LTD.
4859/24, Opp. Geeta Bhawan Mandir, Darya Ganj, New Delhi-110002
✆ 23251727, 23272532, 23243939
Fax: 011-23254295
✉ scs@del2.vsnl.net.in, nbcnd@mdb.vsnl.net.in
www.sultan-chand.com
Estd.: 1981; **Prop.**: Vivek Agarwal, Satish Agarwal; **Bus.Intt.**: Pub.; **Spl.**: Humanities & Soc.Sci., Mang. & Comm., Sci.: Pure & Applied, Institutional Publications

SUMAIYAH DISTRIBUTORS PVT. LTD.
4228/1, Ansari Rd., Darya Ganj, New Delhi-110002
✆ 23244148, 23285674, Fax: 23244133
✉ sumaiyah@vsnl.net, sumaiyahbook@yahoo.com
Estd.: 2002; **Man.Dir.**: Mrs. Firoza Khanam; **Bus.Intt.**: Pub. and Dist. **Spl.**: Sci. Books

SUMAN BOOK CENTRE
88, Princess St., Anand Bhuvan, Mumbai-400002 (Maharashtra)
✆ 22056305, 22010765
Estd.: 1960; **Bus.Intt.**: Pub. and B.S.; **Spl.**: Fiction, Health, Cookery, Astrology and Gen. Books

SUMAN PRAKASHAN
28/2A, Bidhan Sarani, Kolkata-700073 (West Bengal)

SUMAN PRAKASHAN
A-42, Ashok Nagar, Mandavili Rd., Shahdara, Delhi-110093
Hd.Org.: Brihmapal Singh

SUMAN PRAKASHAN
98, Mansur Building, Princes St., Mumbai-400002 (Maharashtra)
✆ 22611972

SUMAN PRAKASHAN
24-B/9, Desh Bandhu Gupta Rd., Dev Nagar, New Delhi-110005
✆ 25760759, 51596090, Fax: 25754739
✉ info@sumanprakashan.com
www.sumanprakashan.com
Estd.: 1970; **Hd.Org.**: Nitin Malhotra; **Bus.Intt.**: Pub.; **Spl.**: Children's Textbooks from Nursery to Class 8th in English

SUMAN PUSTAK BHANDAR
Pawai, Bhagalpur-813125 (Bihar)
Bus.Intt.: Pub. and B.S.

SUMANGAL ENTERPRISES
13, Mogra Pada, Off. Nagardas Rd., Mumbai-400069 (Maharashtra)
Bus.Intt.: Exp.

SUMEE BOOKS
B-4/291, Sector-7, Rohini, Delhi-110085
✆ (O) 27048568 (R) 27278568
Prop.: Sushil Malhotra; **Bus.Intt.**: B.S., L.S.

SUMEET PUBLICATIONS
1680, Nai Sarak, Delhi-110006
✆ 23281704
✉ ca.sumeetgupta@yahoo.com
Hd.Org.: Surya Kant Gupta; **Bus.Intt.**: Pub.; **Spl.**: Children's and Edu. books as also Textbooks for Schools and Colleges

SUMIT ENTERPRISES
4675/21, Ganpati Bhawan, Ansari Rd., Darya Ganj, New Delhi-110002
✆ (O) 23255141, 23284136 (R) 30916277
Fax: 23280611
Estd.: 2003; **Prop.**: Lokesh Kumar; **Bus.Intt.**: Pub.

SUMIT PRAKASHAN (REGD.)
2450, Ground Floor, Hudson Lines, Kingsway Camp, Delhi-110009
✆ 27213196, 27122053,
Fax: 91-11-27415581
Hd.Org.: Harish Kumar Kalra; **Bus.Intt.**: Pub.; **Spl.**: School Textbooks on all Subjects

SUMIT PUBLICATIONS
2619-20/19, 1st Floor, New Market, Nai Sarak, Delhi-110006
✆ (O) 23269963 (R) 27213196
Estd.: 1989; **Hd.Org.**: Harish Kalra; **Bus.Intt.**: Pub.; **Spl.**: Children Story & Text Books in English and Hindi

SUMIT PUBLICATIONS
113-B, Inside Mukat Rai Niwas, Chawri Bazar, Delhi-110006
✆ 23264792

SUMITRA DEVI
7, Kallappa Block, Bangalore-560004 (Karnataka)
Bus.Intt.: Pub.; **Spl.**: Fiction and Poems Collections in Kannada

SUMITRA PRAKASHAN
(A Unit of Lokbharti Prakashan), 15A, M.G. Road, Allahabad-211001 (Uttar Pradesh)
✆ 91-532-2623314
Hd.Org.: Amod Maheshwari; **Bus.Intt.**: Pub.; **Spl.**: Children's books Especially on the Nation, its Flora & Fauna and Env., etc.

SUMITRA PRAKASHAN
16/4, Hastings Rd., (Opp. Bahuguna Market), Allahabad-211001 (Uttar Pradesh)

© 2623665
Hd.Org.: Vachna Grover; **Bus.Intt.:** Pub.; **Spl.:** Novels by Eminent Indian Authors—Premchand, Jai Shankar Prasad, Bankim Chandra Chatterjee, Sharat Chandra, etc. in Hindi

SUMITRA PUSTAK BHANDAR
Mansoorchak, Begusarai-851128 (Bihar)
Bus.Intt.: Pub. and B.S.

SUMSAC INTERNATIONAL & GYAN DEEP
S-34, Palika Bazar, Mini Market, Connaught Place, New Delhi-110001
© 23358398, 23842930, 23328669
9810154549, 9312352191
sumsac@satyam.net.in, gyandeep@mantraonline.com
www.sumsacbooks.com
Hd.Org.: Vinod Kumar Gupta;
Bus.Intt.: Dist.; **Spl.:** Arch., Interior Designing, Furniture, Fashion, Art, Gardening, etc.

SUN FLOWER BOOK AGENCY
B/13, Cherry Blossom D'monte Lane, Orlem Malad (West), Mumbai-400064 (Maharashtra)
© (O) & (R) 28833168
Estd.: 1987; **Prop.:** Mr. & Mrs. Pardeshi;
Bus.Intt.: L.S.

SUN PUBLICATIONS
515, M.G. Rd. (Near Distt. Court), Indore-452007 (Madhya Pradesh)
© 2551853
Estd.: 1980; **Bus.Intt.:** B.S. Supplies in Indore and Bhopal; **Spl.:** Law

SUN PUBLISHING CO.
C-36, Way Fair Gardens, New Delhi

SUNDARA PUSTAKA PRAKASHANA
1st Cross, Sapthapura, Dharwad-580001 (Karnataka)
Hd.Org.: Dr. Shivananda Gali;
Bus.Intt.: Pub.; **Spl.:** Research Works, Gen., Children's, Edu. and Edited Works in Kannada

SUNDEEP PRAKASHAN
3916/16, Kanhaiya Nagar, Tri Nagar, Delhi-110035
© 27382430, 27382530
Fax: 91-11-27382430
info@sundeepbooks.com, books@vsnl.com
www.sundeepbooks.com
Hd.Org.: Sundeep Singhal
Bus.Intt.: Pub.; **Spl.:** Indology, Art Archaeology, Arch., Rel., Phil., Music, Hist., Culture

SUNDER BOOK DEPOT
Mai Hiran Gate, Jalandhar (Punjab)

SUNDER PUSTAK BHANDAR
4059/1, Nai Sarak, Delhi-110006
© 23954118 9868752507, 9416758674
Estd.: 1992; **Hd.Org.:** Kawal Preet Singh

SUNDER SAHITYA SADAN
882, St. Beri Bali, Bazar Sitaram, Delhi-110006
© (O) 23252909 (R) 22160229
Hd.Org.: Pankaj Kumar

SUNDERDAS GIANCHAND
644, J.S.S. Rd., Dhobi Talao, Mumbai-400002 (Maharashtra)
© 22080518, 22088151, Fax: 22055444
ramshe@bom5.vsnl.net.in

SUNEEL SAHITYA SADAN
A-101, Gali No. 1, U. Ghonda, Delhi-110053
Hd.Org.: Mahesh Kumar Bharadwaj

SUNIL BOOK SERVICE
16/873, East Park Road, Near Dr. N.C. Joshi Hospital, Karol Bagh, New Delhi-110005
© 23618426, Fax: 91-11-23638444
9818568722, 9871078971
jain_bros@hotmail.com
Hd.Org.: Sunil Kumar Jain
Bus.Intt.: Wholesaler and B.S.;
Spl.: Engineering, Agricultural, Sciences Pure and Applied Books

SUNIL CHAKRABORTY
56, Surya Sen St., Depti Books, Kolkata-700099 (West Bengal)

SUNIL PUBLISHERS & DISTRIBUTORS
Lalwani Press Rd., Bhopal-462001 (Madhya Pradesh)
© (O) 2543476 (R) 2547298
Estd.: 1976; **Hd.Org.:** Rajendra Kumar Jain; **Bus.Intt.:** WS; **Spl.:** Trade for Text and Help Books (School and Colleges)

SUNIL PUSTAK BHANDAR
Baunsi, Bhagalpur-813104 (Bihar)
Bus.Intt.: Pub. and B.S.

SUNIL SAHITYA SADAN
3320-21, Jatwara, Darya Ganj, New Delhi-110002
© 23270715-6, 23282733, Fax: 23270715
Hd.Org.: Mahesh Bharadwaj;
Bus.Intt.: Pub.; **Spl.:** Hindi Novels, Stories Children's Litt. and Books on Journalism, Sci., etc.

SUNITA PRAKASHANI
49/70, Prince Golam Md. Saha Rd., Kolkata-700033 (West Bengal)

SUNNY & SABU PUBLICATIONS
Shalimar Chambers, College P.O.,
Kochi-682035 (Kerala)
✆ 2350788, 2355144
Estd.: 1992; **Prop.:** Sunny K. Paramunda; **Bus.Intt.:** Pub.

SUNNY BOOK SHOP
Lower Dhalpur, Kullu-175101
(Himachal Pradesh)
✆ (R) 224898
Estd.: 1990; **Hd.Org.:** Sanjiv Dogra; **Bus.Intt.:** B.S., Stationers, Sports Goods Dealer Gen. Order Supplier

SUNRISE PUBLICATIONS
B-7, 3rd Floor, Saraswati Complex,
Subash Chowk, Laxmi Nagar, Delhi-110092
✆ 22025199
sunprisepublication@front.ru
www.sunrisepublications.in
Hd.Org.: Raman Gaur; **Bus.Intt.:** Pub.; **Spl.:** Eco., Hist., Sol., Panchayati Raj, Women Studies, Edu., Child Labour, Home Sci., Jainism, Psy., Geo.

SUNRISE PUBLISHERS
E-22C, Jawahar Park, Laxmi Nagar,
Delhi-110092
✆ & Fax: 22469733
sunrisepub@rediffmail.com
www.sunrisepublisher.com
Hd.Org.: Sushil Gupta; **Bus.Intt.:** Pub.; **Spl.:** Children's Books in English

SUNRISE PUBLISHERS
32/33A, Street No. 9, Bhikam Singh Colony,
Vishwas Nagar, Shahdara,
Delhi-110032
✆ 22307415, Fax: 91-11-22307414
9810237091
sunrisepub@rediffmail.com
www.sunrisepublisher.com
Hd.Org.: Sushil Gupta; **Bus.Intt.:** Pub., Exp.; **Spl.:** Children's Books Edu. books, Puzzles and Rhymes

SUNRISE PUBLISHING HOUSE
198/40, Ramesh Market, East of Kailash,
New Delhi-110065
✆ 26286781 9818442310, Fax: 51620812
m_c_sharma@yahoo.com
www.sunrisedelhi.com
Hd.Org.: Manjul Sharma; **Bus.Intt.:** Pub.; **Spl.:** School Textbooks and Question Banks in Business Studies, Accounting Theory and Eco.

SUNSHINE BOOKS
1075/1-2, No.1, 1st Floor, Old Post Office
Building, Mehrauli, New Delhi-110030
✆ 26646773, 26641833, 26640619,
Fax: 26641833
info@sunshine-books.com
www.sunshine-books.com
Contact Person: Mr. Krishan Gupta; **Bus.Intt.:** Pub. of Edu. Books

SUNSHINE BOOKS
4760-61, 2nd Floor, 23 Ansari Road,
Darya Ganj, New Delhi-110002
✆ 41564077 9312229307,
Fax: 011-41564077
info@sunshine-books.com
www.sunshine-books.com
Hd.Org.: Vibha Gupta
Bus.Intt.: Pub.; **Spl.:** Litt., Rel., Sci., Children's Litt., etc. in Hindi

SUNVIN BOOK DISTRIBUTORS
612, Sector 29, Arun Vihar, Noida-201303
(Uttar Pradesh)
✆ 915-2550795
Hd.Org.: Vinay Kumar Khanna, Vinish Kumar Khanna; **Bus.Intt.:** Rt., L.S.

SUPER BOOK DISTRIBUTORS
F-1/16 (Basement), Ansari Rd., Darya Ganj,
New Delhi-110002
✆ (O) 23258106, 23277876 (R) 26838340, 26232806, Telefax: 23277876
Prt.: K.R. Gupta, Arun Malhotra;
Bus.Intt.: WS, Dist.; **Spl.:** Env. Sci., Military Sci., Sports, Gardening Books, on India Fashion Tech., Arch., Interiordesign + Decoration, Cooking, Children & Gen. Books

SUPER BOOK HOUSE
Sind Chambers, Shahid Bhagat Singh Rd.,
Colaba, Mumbai-400005
(Maharashtra)
✆ 22830446, 22020106, Fax: 228330751
superbh@vsnl.com
Hd.Org.: M.S. Lehri; **Bus.Intt.:** Dist.; **Spl.:** Art, Arch., Interior Design, Landscaping, Furniture, Advt., Graphics, Photography, Textile, Fashion, Jewellery, Digital Art

SUPER BOOK HOUSE
S.C.O. 50-51, First Floor, Sector-17A,
Chandigarh-160017
✆ 2708091
Prop.: Ravinder Kumar; **Bus.Intt.:** B.S. and L.S.

SUPER DISTRIBUTORS
New Delhi
✆ 25727696, Fax: 25854747
sundaram@bom2.vsnl.net.in
Bus.Intt.: B.S. & Dist.

SUPER SALES CORPORATION
23, Lal Mohammed St., Chepauk, Chennai-600005 (Tamil Nadu)

SUPERNOVA PUBLISHERS & DISTRIBUTORS PVT. LTD.
Basement N-34, Greater Kailash, Part-I, New Delhi-110048
✆ 29239349, 29238285, Fax: 91-11-29239249
✉ info@supernovapublishers.com, snpd_india@yahoo.co.in
www.supernovapublishers.com
Hd.Org.: Udayan Singh
Br.: 34-35, A.R.D. Complex, R.K. Puram, Sector-13, New Delhi-110066 ✆ 26870299
• First Floor, 59, Patua Tola Lane, Kolkata-700009 (West Bengal)
✆ 033-65142455, Telefax: 033-22571646
Bus.Intt.: Pub. and Dist.; **Spl.:** Eng. Language books from Penguin, Harper, Britannica, Parragon, etc.

SUPRAKASHANI
8B, College Row, Kolkata-700009 (West Bengal)
✆ (R) 033-2523519
Estd.: 1946; **Prop.:** Udhindra Ch. Maitra; **Bus.Intt.:** Pub.

SUPREME BOOKS (REGD.)
13/8, Indra Vikas Colony, Mukherjee Nagar, Delhi-110009
✆ 27605404, 27650514, 23256606, 23275451, Fax: 27650514, 27654141
✉ supremebooksr@hotmail.com
Hd.Org.: Ripan Kalra; **Bus.Intt.:** Pub., B.S.; **Spl.:** Children's Books, Crayons, Colouring Material, etc.

SURA BOOKS (P) LTD.
1620, 'J' Block, 16th Main Road, Anna Nagar, Chennai-600040 (Tamil Nadu)
✆ 26162173, 26161090, 26161099, Fax: 26162173
✉ surabooks@eth.net, enquiry@surabooks.com
Estd.: 1991; **Hd.Org.:** V.K. Subburaj; **Bus.Intt.:** Pub.; **Spl.:** Gen./Paperback Books in English, Tamil, Bengali and Malayalam

SURA COLLEGE OF COMPETITION
(Publication Division), Plot No. 1620, 16th Main Rd., Anna Nagar, West Chennai-600040 (Tamil Nadu)
✆ 26266524, Fax: 26266173
Prop.: V.K. Subburaj; **Bus.Intt.:** Book Pub.

SURABHI PRINTERS & PUBLISHERS
C-10, Tagore Garden, New Delhi-110027

SURAJ ART PRESS
45, Pandhreeba, Allahabad-211003 (Uttar Pradesh)
✆ 2401392
Hd.Org.: Baburam Agarwal

SURBHI BOOK DISTRIBUTOR
FU-04A, First Floor, G-13, Pratibha Tower, Community Centre, Vikaspuri, New Delhi-110018
✆ 25525999, Fax: 25525999
✉ soodanil@yahoo.com
Estd.: 1989; **Hd.Org.:** Anil Sood; **Bus.Intt.:** Dist.; **Spl.:** Indian and Foreign Books on Mang., Industry and Engg.

SURBHI ENTERPRISES
Delhi
✆ 25257319
✉ surabhis@bol.net.in
Bus.Intt.: Pub.

SURBHI PUBLICATIONS
S.M.S. Highway, Jaipur-302003 (Rajasthan)
✆ 2311204
Hd.Org.: Smt. Indu Bhatia

SURENDRA BOOK SERVICE
3501, Kucha Lalman, Near Police Station, Darya Ganj, New Delhi-110002
✆ 23273984, 55159385 ▮ 9811068537
Prop.: S.L. Paul; **Bus.Intt.:** Rt., B.S.; **Spl.:** All Sub.

SURENDRA RAY & CO.
18/20, Kazi Sayed St., Mumbai-400009 (Maharashtra)

SURESH & COMPANY
4140, Aryapura, Subzi Mandi, Delhi-110007
✆ 23828315, 23826812
✉ mapchart@now-india.net.in
Hd.Org.: S.C. Jain; **Bus.Intt.:** Pub. and Dist.; **Spl.:** Maps, Atlases, Globes, Tourist Guides as also Children's Books

SURESH AND COMPANY
54, 4th Cross, Hanumanthanagar, Bangalore-560019 (Karnataka)
Hd.Org.: G. Kallaiah; **Bus.Intt.:** Printer, Pub. and Dist.; **Spl.:** Gen., Edu., Text

SURESH BOOK CENTRE
Hospital Rd., Udaipur-313001 (Rajasthan)

SURESH BROTHERS
Khajuri Bazar, Indore-452002 (Madhya Pradesh)
✆ (O) 2454388 (R) 2471829

SURESH PUSTAK BHANDAR
Rafiganj, Aurangabad-824125 (Bihar)
Bus.Intt.: Pub. and B.S.

SURINDER KUMAR & SONS
30/21A-22A, Gali No. 9, Vishwas Nagar, Delhi-110032
✆ & Fax: 22381709 (R) 22391263 ▮ 9868152951
Prop.: Sandeep Kumar; **Bus.Intt.:** Pub., WS, L.S.; **Spl.:** Hindi Litt. and its translations in Regional Languages

SURJAN SINGH FARYADI
113-B, J&K Pocket, Dilshad Garden, Delhi-110032

SURJEET BOOK DEPOT (S) REGD.
Satnam Group, 4075, Nai Sarak, Delhi-110006
✆ (O) 23915967, 23942124 (R) 23911825, 23923108
Estd.: 1950; **Prop.:** Satnam Singh; **Bus.Intt.:** Pub., Rt., B.S.; **Spl.:** Acad. and Competition Books of all sorts under one roof, Comm., Beh.Sci., Sci., Pure & Applied, Soc.Sci. & Law Books

SURJEET PUBLICATIONS
7-K, Kolhapur Rd., Kamala Nagar, Delhi-110007
✆ (O) 23914746, 23914174, 23982395 (R) 27453842, Fax: 23918475
✉ surpub@del3.vsnl.net.in
Estd.: 1976; **Hd.Org.:** Surjeet Singh; **Bus.Intt.:** Pub.; **Spl.:** Textbooks and Reference Books on English Language and Litt., Hist., Pol.Sci., Eco., Mang., etc.

SURJEET PUSTAK BHANDAR
Nawadih Rd., Aurangabad-824101 (Bihar)
Bus.Intt.: Pub. and B.S.

SURJYA HAZARIKA EDUCATIONAL TRUST
Chandrakanta Press Building, Chandrakanta Hazarika Path, Tarun Nagar, Guwahati-781005 (Assam)
✆ 91-361-2458807, Fax: 91-361-2529094
✉ surjyahazarika@rediffmail.com
Hd.Org.: Surjya Kanta Hazarika; **Bus.Intt.:** Pub.; **Spl.:** Asamiya and English Language Books on Various Subjects and Producer of Documentary Telefilms, etc.

SURUCHI PRAKASHAN
Keshav Kunj Jhandewalan, New Delhi-110055
✆ 23514672, 23679996, Fax: 23679914
✉ suruchiprakashan@vsnl.net
Hd.Org.: Raj Pal Vasan; **Bus.Intt.:** Pub.; **Spl.:** Children's Litt. as well as books on Socialism, Rel., Hist., etc.

SURVEY OF INDIA PERIODICALS
"Euro Mall CP", B-1, Palika Bazar Extn., Connaught Place, New Delhi-110001
✆ 30919843, 32325775
Fax: 91-11-23722122
✉ sipsurvey@rediffmail.com, sipsurvey@indiatimes.com
Hd.Org.: Sushma Sawhney; **Bus.Intt.:** Pub.; **Spl.:** Books in Punjabi

SURYA BHARATI PRAKASHAN
2596, Nai Sarak, Delhi-110006
✆ 23266412
Hd.Org.: Tansukhram Gupta; **Bus.Intt.:** Pub. and B.S.; **Spl.:** Literary, Political Edu. and Religious Books in Hindi

SURYA (INTERNATIONAL) BOOK SERVICES
S-5, Kaladeep Mansion, B-23/25, Kailash Colony, New Delhi-110048
✆ 26460799, 28631082
Estd.: 1982; **Prop.:** Anil Kapoor; **Bus.Intt.:** L.S.; **Spl.:** Mang., Tech. and Soc.Sci.

SURYA INTERNATIONAL PUBLICATIONS
4-B, Nashville Rd., Dehradun-248001 (Uttarakhand)
✆ 2650172, Fax: 0135-2654173
Estd.: 1987; **Hd.Org.:** P.K. Rastogi; **Bus.Intt.:** Pub.; **Spl.:** Agri., Botany, Forestry, Zoology, Chemistry & Gen. School and College Text Books

SURYA PRABHA PRAKASHAN
2/9, Ansari Rd., Darya Ganj, New Delhi-110002
✆ 23285915, 25477805 ▮ 9871814577
✉ suryaprabhap@yahoo.co.in
🌐 www.suryaprabhaprakashan.com
Estd.: 1981; **Hd.Org.:** M.K. Sharma; **Bus.Intt.:** Pub. and Dist.; **Spl.:** Academic books, Fiction and Books on Comm., Mang., Env., Litt., etc.

SURYA PRAKASHAN
624, Khajuri Bazar, Indore-452002 (Madhya Pradesh)
✆ (O) 2451876 (R) 2414168
Estd.: 1986; **Prop.:** Banarsi Das Agrawal; **Bus.Intt.:** Pub.; **Spl.:** Notes and Guides of Soc.Sci. for Devi Ahilya University in Hindi

SURYA PRAKASHAN MANDIR
Dauji Rd. (Nehru Marg), Bikaner-334005 (Rajasthan)
✆ (O) 0151-2541501 (R) 2526292, 2547151
▮ 01513106824
Estd.: 1964; **Man.Dir.:** Dr. Prashant Bissa
Br.: Bisson Ka Chowk, Bikaner-334005 (Rajashtan)
• 42, Sainik Basti, Nagaur (Rajasthan)
Bus.Intt.: Pub., B.S., L.S., WS, Dist.; **Spl.:** Humanities & Soc.Sci., Sci. & Tech., Med., Law, Children & General, Arts & Arch., Bio.Sci., Litt. (English/Hindi)

SURYA PRINT PROCESS PVT. LTD.
9/54, Kirti Nagar, Industrial Area,
New Delhi-110015
Bus.Intt.: Exp.

SURYA PUBLICATIONS
G-6/4832, 24, Ansari Rd., Darya Ganj,
New Delhi-110002
✆ (O) 23553648 (R) 22276531
Estd.: 1993; **Hd.Org.:** Vijay Kamal;
Spl.: Agri., Forestry, Env., Zoology, Wildlife and Textbooks for Schools

SURYA PUBLICATIONS
4-B, Nashville Rd., Dehradun-248001
(Uttarakhand)
Prop.: Rekha Rastogi

SURYAM SCIENTIFIC SURGICO (REGD.)
Delhi
✆ 23911254, 23974378, Fax: 23923568
shivscientific@vsnl.net
Spl.: Sci. Instruments

SURYAMOHAN PUSTAK BHANDAR
Shahkund, Bhagalpur-813108 (Bihar)
Bus.Intt.: Pub. and B.S.

SURYASTRA COMMUNICATIONS PVT. LTD.
C-43, First Floor, Green Park Main,
New Delhi-110016
✆ 26520479
infor@suryastra.com
www.suryastra.com
Hd.Org.: Anuj Agarwal; **Bus.Intt.:** Pub.;
Spl.: Originals and Translations both within India and Abroad, on Litt. & Med.

SUSHIL PRAKASHAN
212, Khajuri Bazar, Indore-452002
(Madhya Pradesh)
✆ 2535892 ▮ 98260-21001, Fax: 2530007
Estd.: 1974; **Hd.Org.:** Pradip Khandelwal;
Bus.Intt.: WS and Traders; **Spl.:** School and College Books

SUVARTHA BHAVAN
T.K. Rd., Thiruvalla-689101 (Kerala)
✆ (O) 2640334 (R) 2604016,
Fax: 0473-2630503
jins@giasmd01.vsnl.net.in,
suvarthabhava@rediffmail.com
Estd.: 1987; **Hd.Org.:** Sunny Abraham;
Bus.Intt.: Pub. and B.S.; **Spl.:** Christian Spiritual, Religious, Phil., Counselling and Gen. Books

SUVIDHA DISCOUNT MART PVT. LTD.
New Delhi
✆ 23350335
database@satyam.net.in
Bus.Intt.: Mail Order Supplier

SUVIDHA LAW HOUSE PVT. LTD.
28, Malviya Nagar, Roshanpura,
Bhopal-462003 (Madhya Pradesh)
✆ 2551597, 2559586, Fax: 2559586
law@satyam.net.in
www.suvidhalawhouse.com
Estd.: 1985; **Prt.:** Vijay Bangia
Br.: 8, Hotel Amit Moti Bagh Chowk,
Raipur-497001 ✆ 2228583, 5050400
• 71, Tilak Path, Indore ✆ 5073323
Bus.Intt.: Pub. & B.S.; **Spl.:** Law Books in Hindi and English

SUVIDYA BOOK AGENCY
149, Shaniwar Peth, Pune-411030
(Maharashtra)
✆ (O) 0212-2454893 (R) 2452658
Estd.: 1994; **Prop.:** Anant Sitaram Puranik;
Bus.Intt.: Pub. and B.S.; **Spl.:** School Library Books in Marathi

SUYOGYA PRAKASHAN
W-116, Greater Kailash-I,
New Delhi-110048
✆ 26465652
Hd.Org.: Sudhir Puri; **Bus.Intt.:** Pub. and B.S.; **Spl.:** Hindi Novels, Stories, Plays, Poetry, etc.

SUYOGYA PRAKASHAN
W-112, Greater Kailash, Part-I,
New Delhi-110048
✆ 29234190, 29244159
Fax: 91-11-23973082
atmaram_books@hotmail.com
Hd.Org.: Yogeshwar Puri; **Bus.Intt.:** Pub. and B.S.; **Spl.:** Hindi Novels, Stories, Plays, Poetry, etc.

SWADESH PRAKASHAN PVT. LTD.
11090, Doriwalan, East Park Rd., Karol Bagh,
New Delhi-110005
✆ 23516869, 23624858, Fax: 23551489
sppl@yahoo.com
Hd.Org.: Satya Pal Punshi;
Bus.Intt.: Pub.; **Spl.:** Edu., Comp. Books for Children in English, Hindi and Sanskrit

SWAMI JAYDEV
Tat Baba Anand Foundation, Gopeshwar,
Venderban-281121 (Uttar Pradesh)
✆ 244252

SWAMI JYOTIRMAYANANDA ASHRAM
Lal Bagh, Loni, Ghaziabad-201102
(Uttar Pradesh)
✆ 91-120-2600237
iys@vsnl.com, iys@ndf.vsnl.net.in
www.iys-loni.org
Estd.: 1984; **Hd.Org.:** Swami Jyotirmayanand;

Bus.Intt.: Pub.; **Spl.:** Books and Magazines on Yoga, Vedanta, Spiritualism and Self-development in Hindi and English

SWAMI NARAYAN BOOK DEPOT
20, Sarvamangal Society, Naranpura, Ahmedabad-380013 (Gujarat)

SWAMI RAMA CENTRE
Dehradun (Uttarakhand)
✆ 2412068, Fax: 2412008
✉ hitsrc@sancharnet.in; **Bus.Intt.:** B.S.

SWAMI RAMA TIRTHA MISSION
1-E/16, Swami Rama Tirtha Nagar (Jhandewalan Extn.), New Delhi-110055
✆ 23528302, 23559350
✉ sstmissiondelhi@yahoo.co.in
Hd.Org.: Sunita Malhotra; **Bus.Intt.:** Pub.; **Spl.:** Books and Magazines on Yoga, Vedanta, Spiritualism and Self-development in Hindi

SWAMI SANTDAS INSTITUTE OF CALCUTTA
101, Southern Avenue, Kolkata-700029 (West Bengal)

SWAMI VIVEKANANDA SEVASHRAMN
Kanakkam Palayam, Kallipatti Via-638505 (Tamil Nadu)

SWAMY LAW HOUSE
Doraiswamy Iyer Rd., Ernakulam-682035 (Kerala)
✆ (O) 2361341, 2366285 (R) 2431236, Fax: 2366285
✉ swamylawhouse@spectrum.net.in
Estd.: 1985; **Prop.:** N.V. Yegnaraman; **Bus.Intt.:** Pub. and B.S.; **Spl.:** Law Books

SWAMY PUBLICATIONS
Sandhya Mansions, 164, R.K. Mutt Rd., R.A. Puram, Chennai-600020 (Tamil Nadu)

SWANTHIKA PRAKASHANA
Kavya, Kanthamangala, Ajjawara, Sulya-574246 [D.K.] (Karnataka)
Hd.Org.: Prabhakar Sheela;
Bus.Intt.: Pub.; **Spl.:** Fiction, Collections and Own Books in Kannada

SWAPANDEEP PUBLISHERS & BOOKSELLERS
7-E, Sitala Lane, Kolkata-700005 (West Bengal)
Bus.Intt.: Pub.; **Spl.:** Bengali Language

SWAPNA PRINTING WORKS PVT. LTD.
52, Raja Rammohan Sarani, Kolkata-700009 (West Bengal)
Bus.Intt.: Exp.

SWARAJ PRAKASHAN
7/14, Gupta Lane, Ansari Rd., Darya Ganj, New Delhi-110002
✆ 23289915 ▮ 9350544790
✉ swaraj_prakashan@yahoo.co.in
Hd.Org.: Ajay Mishra
Bus.Intt.: Pub.; **Spl.:** Humanities & Soc. Science (Eng. & Hindi)

SWARN JAYANTI
1/5971, Kabool Nagar, Shahdara, Delhi-110032
✆ 65456828, 22281640
Hd.Org.: Arun Maheshwari;
Bus.Intt.: Pub. & Dist.; **Spl.:** Hindi Litt. as also Reprints of Magazines, etc. of Post-Independence Era

SWARUP SAHITYA SADAN
213, Khajuri Bazar, M.G. Rd., Indore-452002 (Madhya Pradesh)
✆ (O) 2531686 (R) 2543764
Estd.: 1991; **Prop.:** Dinesh Jain;
Bus.Intt.: Pub. and L.S.; Children Books and All Sub. except Med.

SWATANTRA PRAKASHAN SANSTHAN
32, Shanti Nagar, Saudagar Vihar, Kanpur Rd., Lucknow (Uttar Pradesh)
✆ 2431996
Hd.Org.: Swami Aatmanand;
Bus.Intt.: Pub.; **Spl.:** *Vedas*, Rel., Meditation, *Gita*, Phil., etc.

SWATANTRA PRAKASHAN SANSTHAN
Korhari Barhalganj, Ghorakpur (Uttar Pradesh)
✆ 2431926
Hd.Org.: Swami Aatmanandji;
Bus.Intt.: Pub.; **Spl.:** *Vedas*, Rel., Meditation, *Gita*, Phil., etc.

SWATHI BOOKS BUREAU (P) LTD.
Vijaya Shanthi Complex, 16, Rameswaram Rd., T. Nagar, Chennai-600017 (Tamil Nadu)
✆ 24341424
Hd.Org.: S.S. Ragunathan;
Bus.Intt.: L.S. and Imp.

SWATI ENTERPRISES
1, Church Rd., Aliganj, Lucknow-226002 (Uttar Pradesh)
✆ 2268129

SWATI N. PATEL
31, Barsh Apts., Pritam Nagar, Ellisbridge, Ahmedabad-380006 (Gujarat)

SWATI PUBLICATIONS
34, Central Market, Ashok Vihar, Delhi-110052

SWATI PUBLICATIONS
Anil Bldg., Suryarao Pet,

P.B. No. 339, Vijayawada-520002 (Andhra Pradesh)

SYNDICATE BOOKS
1/2729, Ram Nagar, Loni Rd., Shahdara, Delhi-110032
✆ 22124822; **Hd.Org.:** Shyam Gupta; **Bus.Intt.:** L.S.

SYNDICATE PUBLICATIONS
2nd Floor, Med. Market, Ashok Rajpath, Patna-800004 (Bihar)

SYSCON MARKETING
Vaibhav Chambers, 1st Floor, 7/1, Ushaganj, Indore-452001 (Madhya Pradesh)
✆/Fax: 466933

SYSTEMS SALES BOOK DISTRIBUTORS
F-1, Panacea, Opp. Ayodhya Hospital, Wanowrie, Pune-411040 (Maharashtra)
✆ 2612469
Bus.Intt.: L.S.; **Spl.:** Mang., Engg., Comm., Eco., Comp., Tech., Humanity, Soc.Sci.

■ ■ ■

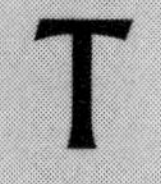

T.B.H. PUBLISHERS & DISTRIBUTORS
7A, Sunkurama St., Chennai-600001 (Tamil Nadu)
✆ 25390150, 25387156, 25362305, 2852457, 28663168, Fax: 044-25392754, 28587710
tbhpd@md4.vsnl.net.in
Estd.: 1994; **Prop.**: T. Dhanasekar;
Bus.Intt.: Dist. and WS, B.S.; **Spl.**: Graduate, Adv. Books for Lib. and Gen. Books

T.B.I. PUBLISHERS DISTRIBUTORS
46, Housing Society, South Extension-I, New Delhi-110049
✆ 24632903, 24690513, 24693257, Fax: 24610576, 23325247
tbi@del3.vsnl.net.in, tbidelhi@dartmail.dart.net.com
www.timelessartbooks.com
Estd.: 1984; **Prt.**: Ravi Sabharwal;
Bus.Intt.: Pub., WS, L.S. & Rt., Imp., Exp.;
Spl.: Trade, Gen. (Incl. Lit. & Art), Juvenile/ Children Books

T.B.S. PUBLISHERS & DISTRIBUTORS
T.B.S. Building, G.H. Rd., Calicut-673001 (Kerala)
✆ (O) 0495-2720085/86, 2720086, (R) 2721160, Fax: 0495-2721414
tbsbook@vsnl.com
www.tbsbooks.com
Estd.: 1958; **Hd.Org.**: Nebalakrishanmarar, N.E. Manohar
Br.: Poorna Publications Calicut-1, Manohar Book Depot, Calicut (Kerala)
Bus.Intt.: Pub., B.S., L.S., WS, Exp.;
Spl.: Humanities & Sco.Sci., Tech., Med., Mang., Law, Arts & Arch., Children & Gen. books

T.F.Y. TECHNICAL PUBLICATIONS
20-F, Kamala Nagar, Delhi-110007
✆ 23919914, 27211146, Fax: 27137530
mukat@vsnl.com

T.K.L. RAO PUBLICATIONS
723/A, III Block, Rajajinagar, Bangalore-560010 (Karnataka)
Hd.Org.: T.K. Lakshman Rao; **Bus.Intt.**: Pub.;
Spl.: Own Books in Kannada

T.L.C. SERVICES
133, Varun Apartment, 58/28, Sector 62, Noida (Uttar Pradesh)
✆ 24584379 ▮ 98113122697
Estd.: 1999; **Prop.**: Hirel K. Singha;
Bus.Intt.: L.S., WS; **Spl.**: Humanities & Soc.Sci., Mang. & Comm., Engg. & Tech., Fiction & Gen.

T.M. PUBLISHING CO.
32/3, Bantra East Lane, Kadamtala, Howrah-711101 (Assam)

T.M. RAMANUJAN (DR.)
No. 2, 7th Cross St., West Shenoy Nagar, Chennai-600030 (Tamil Nadu)

T.M.A. PAI HUMAN RESOURCE DEVELOPMENT (DR.)
Kunjibettu, Udupi-576102 (Karnataka)

T.N. KRISHNIAH & SONS
Chickpet, Bangalore-560053 (Karnataka)
Estd.: 1960; **Bus.Intt.**: Pub.; **Spl.**: Mythological, Religious and Astrological Books Predictions in Kannada

T.N.M. SAMARKA GRANTHAMALE
'Mahadevasri', 3rd Cross, Vin Vinobanagar, Tumkur (Karnataka)

T.R. PUBLICATIONS PRIVATE LTD.
PMG Complex, 2nd Floor, 8 (Old 57), South Usman Rd., T. Nagar, Chennai-600017 (Tamil Nadu)
✆ 24340765, 24322920, Fax.: 2348837
trpubs@md5.vsnl.net.in
www.trpubs.com
Estd.: 1973; **Man.Dir.**: T. Ramanujam
Bus.Intt.: Pub., WS, L.S. & Rt., Imp.;
Spl.: Humanities & Soc.Sci., Sci. & Tech.

T.T. MAPS & PUBLICATIONS LTD.
(Maps Division), Regd. Office No. 328, G.S.T. Rd., Coromepet, Chennai-600044 (Tamil Nadu)
✆ 22368824, 22368565, 22368923, Fax: 044-2404525,
Telefax: 041-26154 TTKP IN
Hd.Org.: A.R. Krishna; **Bus.Intt.**: Pub.;
Spl.: Cartography Based Publications for the Tourism and Edu. purpose. Self Publications like TTK Modern School Atlas in various Indian Languages, Outline Map for Schools, Wall Map, Rd. Atlas and Tourist Oriented Maps.

T.T.K. PHARMA PRINTING DIVISION
328, G.S.T. Rd., Chromepet, Chennai-600044 (Tamil Nadu)
✆ 2401824, 2401865, 2401923, Fax: 044-22367535, Cable: MAPSLIT, Telefax: 041-26154
Estd.: 1965; **Hd.Org.**: A.R. Krishna;
Bus.Intt.: Pub. and Exp.

TAGORE BOOK HOUSE
Near Bus Stand, Kanhangad, Kasaragode-671315 (Kerala)
Estd.: 1990; **Prop.**: P.V. Radhakrishnan;
Bus.Intt.: B.S.

TAGORE PUBLISHERS
33, Vishal Nagar, Pakhowal Rd., Ludhiana-141002 (Punjab)

TAJ COMPANY
3151, Turkman Gate, Delhi-110006
✆ (O) 23230630 (R) 23222128, Fax: 23237241
✉ taj@ndf.vsnl.net.in
Estd.: 1982; **Bus.Intt.:** Pub.; **Spl.:** Rel. Books and Islamic Litt.

TAJ OFFICE
Mohamed Ali Rd., Mumbai-400003 (Maharashtra)
Bus.Intt.: Exp.

TAJ PUBLISHERS
7166, Beriwala Bagh, Delhi-110006
✆ 27516989
Prop.: Kausar Ahmad

TAJ PUBLISHERS AND PERFUMERS
Mohamedali Rd., No. 36, Mumbai-400003 (Maharashtra)
✆ 23424806, Fax: 91-22-23094149
Hd.Org.: Suhail Saifi

TAKBEER PUBLICATIONS (P) LTD.
1st Floor, Khan Complex, Madeena Chowk, Gawkadal, Srinagar-190001 (Jammu & Kashmir)
✆ (O) 0194-2473818 (R) 01933-213354, Fax: 0194-2473818
✉ ehsan04@sancharnet.in
Estd.: 1987; **Man.Dir.:** A.E. Quddusi
Br.: College Rd., Opp. Distt. Hospital, Pulwama-192301 (Jammu & Kashmir)
Bus.Intt.: Pub., B.S., L.S., WS;
Spl.: Humanities & Soc.Sci., Comp., Children & General, Litt.

TAKHLEEQKAR PUBLISHERS
104/B, Yawar Manzil, I-Block, Laxmi Nagar, Delhi-110092
✆ 22442572
✉ qissey@rediffmail.com
Hd.Org.: Anees Amrohvi; **Bus.Intt.:** Pub. and Dist.; **Spl.:** Contemporary Urdu Fiction, Novels, Poetry, Criticism, Travelogues and Auto-biographies

TAKHLEEQKAR PUBLISHERS
1779, Kucha Dakhni Rai, Darya Ganj, New Delhi-110002
✆ 22442572

TAKSHASHILA PRAKASHAN
23/4761, Darya Ganj, New Delhi-110002
✆ 23258802, 22513959, Fax: 23258767
✉ takshila_prakashan@indiatimes.com
Hd.Org.: Tej Singh, P.S. Bisht; **Bus.Intt.:** Pub. & Dist.; **Spl.:** University and College level in Hindi Language

TALENT BOOK SELLERS
Muslim High School Campus, Tatar Pur, Bhagalpur-812002 (Bihar)
✆ (O) 2404460 (R) 2404461
Estd.: 1988; **Bus.Intt.:** B.S.;
Spl.: School, Graduate, Adv. Books for Lib. and Gen. Books

TAMIL NADU BOOK HOUSE
47, Nallathambi St., Triplicane, Chennai-600005 (Tamil Nadu)
✆ 2832984, 28441043, 28443381
✉ pillai12@vsnl.net
Hd.Org.: J.C. Pillay
Br.: Perumal North Car St., Tirunelveli Junction, Tirunelveli-627001 (Tamil Nadu) ✆ 223110
Bus.Intt.: L.S., Pub. and WS
Spl.: Indian Reference Books

TAMIL NADU BOOKSELLERS & DISTRIBUTORS ASSOCIATION
C/o Amudha Nilayam Ltd., 17, Sripuram Second St., Royapettah, Chennai-600014 (Tamil Nadu)
✆ 28111790, Fax: 28111806
✉ tamilnadubooksellers@gmail.com
Hd.Org.: A.G. Subramaniam;
Bus.Intt.: Promoter and Dist.
Spl.: Books in Tamil on Language and Litt., Arts, Culture, Linguistics, Translations, etc.

TAMIL NADU TEXTBOOK SOCIETY
E.V.K. Sampath Mansion, College Rd., Chennai-600006 (Tamil Nadu)

TAMIL PUTHAKALAYAM
11, Sivaprakasam St., P.B. No. 5193, Pondy Bazar, T. Nagar, Chennai-600017 (Tamil Nadu)
✆ 24345904
Hd.Org.: Akilankannan
Bus.Intt.: Pub.
Spl.: Modern Tamil Litt., Award Winning Books in Fiction, Non-fiction, Short Stories, Plays, Criticism, Sci., Humanities, Rel. and Self-improvement Books

TAMILARASI PATHIPPAGAM
18/1, Rajabather St., T. Nagar, Chennai-600017 (Tamil Nadu)
✆ 28241865, 28264046
✉ thambi@md2.vsnl.net.in
Hd.Org.: M. Selvarajan
Bus.Intt.: L.S., Rt. and Pub.
Spl.: Sci. Novels and Children Books in Tamil Languages

TAMILLAND PRINTERS & TRADERS PVT. LTD.
328, G.S.T. Rd., Chromepet, Chennai-600044 (Tamil Nadu)

TAMIZH PUTHAKALAYAM
11, Sivapragasam St., T. Nagar,
Chennai-600017 (Tamil Nadu)

TANITHTHANISH PATHIPPAGAM
64, Thattanchavadi, Pondicherry-605009

TANVIR BOOK DEPOT
Rafiganj, Aurangabad-824125 (Bihar)
Bus.Intt.: Pub. and B.S.

TAPAN BOOK STALL
15, Bankim Chatterjee St., Kolkata-700073
(West Bengal)
Bus.Intt.: Rt. Book Shop

TAPAN BOOK STALL
54/6, College St., Kolkata-700073
(West Bengal)

TAPAS BOOK HOUSE
27, Kabi Sukanta Sarani, Kolkata-700085
(West Bengal)

TARA BOOK AGENCY
Kamacha, Varanasi-221010 (Uttar Pradesh)

TARA MA STORES
1/2, Baroaritola Rd., Beliaghata,
Kolkata-700010 (West Bengal)

TARA PUBLISHING
38/GA Shoreham, 5th Avenue Besant Nagar,
Chennai-600090 (Tamil Nadu)
✆ 24401696, Fax: 91-44-24453658
✉ mail@tarabooks.com
www.tarabooks.com
Hd.Org.: Gita Wolf; **Bus.Intt.**: Pub.;
Spl.: Children's Books and Art Books

TARAKNATH STORES
College Square, (West), Stall-41,
Opp. Cal. University, Kolkata-73 (West Bengal)

TARAKSHEEL SOCIETY BHARAT
C/o Tarakbharti Parkashan, St. No. 8,
K.C. Rd., Barnala-148101 (Punjab)
✆ 233244, 241744, Fax: 241744
✉ taraksheel@yahoo.com,
amitter@ch1.dot.net.in
Hd.Org.: Megh Raj Mitter; **Bus.Intt.**: Pub.;
Spl.: Books on Sci. in Punjabi and Hindi

TARAN COMMUNICATIONS
Basu Dham, Kadamkuan, Patna-3 (Bihar)
✆ 91-612-2691666, 310205,
Fax: 91-612-2691777
Hd.Org.: Coomar Arunodaya; **Bus.Intt.**: Pub.;
Spl.: Self-improvement, Spiritualism and the Teachings of Acharya Sudarshanji Maharaj

TARIT PROKASHANI
18J, Tamer Lane, Kolkata-700009
(West Bengal)
Hd.Org.: Bihuti Bhusan Majumder

TARU-BOOKS & JOURNALS
G-159, Paschim Vihar, New Delhi-110063
✆ 25580534, 25575166, Fax: 25585397
✉ taru@POBoxes.com
Estd.: 1976; **Hd.Org.**: Harish Gupta;
Bus.Intt.: Exp.; **Spl.**: Publications and Journals

TARUN BOOK DISTRIBUTORS
C-8/74-A, Lawrence Rd., Delhi-110035
✆ 27103844
Hd.Org.: Tarun Ahuja; **Bus.Intt.**: Dist.;
Spl.: Med., Nursing, Pharmacy, Sci., etc.

TARUN BOOK TRADERS
Rd. No. 7, Kothi No. 27, East Punjabi Bagh,
New Delhi-110026
✆ 25119776, 25419165
Estd.: 2000; **Prop.**: Tarun Bhutani;
Bus.Intt.: Rt.; **Spl.**: Journals and Magazines, Law

TARUN OFFSET PRINTERS
A-1, Mayapuri Industrial Area,
New Delhi-110064
Bus.Intt.: Exp. of Books

TARUN PRAKASHAN
Shanti Niketan, H-218, Shastri Nagar, Meerut
(Uttar Pradesh)
✆ 2250004
Hd.Org.: Tarachand Pal "Baical"

TAT-BABA FOUNDATION
G-1/1165-A, Mansarovar Park, Shahdara,
Delhi-110032
✆ 64614501, Fax: 23254006
Estd.: 1979; **Hd.Org.**: Anand Dev Tat Baba;
Bus.Intt.: Pub.; **Spl.**: Self-improvement,
Meditation and Rel. in Hindi

TATA ENERGY RESEARCH INSTITUTE
Darbari Seth Block, India Habital Centre,
Lodhi Rd., New Delhi-110003
✆ 24682100, 24682111, Fax: 4682144, 4682145
✉ mailbox@teri.res.in
www.teriin.org
Estd.: 1974; **Prop.**: R.K. Pachauri;
Bus.Intt.: Pub.; **Spl.**: Energy, Env. and Sustainable Development

TATA INFOMEDIA LIMITED
401-409, Prakashdeep Building, 7, Tolstoy
Marg, New Delhi-110001
✆ 23327880-82, 23730037-39, 55303278-80,
Fax: 23327884
✉ tildelhi@vsnl.net
Hd.Org.: Mandeep Singh; **Bus.Intt.**: Pub.;
Spl.: Children's Books

TATA INFOMEDIA LIMITED
414, Veer Savarkar Marg, Mumbai-400025
(Maharashtra)

✆ 24300941, Fax: 022-24302707,
Telefax: 011-71093 TPL IN
✉ brightsparks@tatainfomedia.com
Estd.: 1955
Br.: Ahmedabad (Gujarat)
✆ 7544242, 7544244
✉ tdl@adl.vsnl.net.in
• Bangalore (Karnataka)
✆ 5597282, 5597284
✉ tilbang@vsnl.com
• Kolkata (West Bengal)
✆ 2462965, 2462967, Fax: 2462964
✉ tilcal@giascl01.vsnl.net.in
• 401-409, Prakash Deep Building, 7, Tolstoy Marg, New Delhi-110001
✆ 23310842, 55303278, Fax: 23327884
✉ brightsparks_del@rediffmail.com
www.tatainfomedia.com
• Hyderabad (Andhra Pradesh)
✆ 23392226, Fax: 23393488
✉ tatadonl@hd2.vsnl.net.in
• Pune (Maharashtra) ✆ 5820446, 5820448, Fax: 4008287 ✉ tilpune@vsnl.com
• Indore (Madhya Pradesh)
✆ 526090 to 526093, Fax: 526094
✉ tilindor@bom6.vsnl.net.in
Bus.Intt.: Pub. and Exp.

TATA INSTITUTE OF SOCIAL SCIENCES
P.B. No. 8313, Sion, Trombay Rd., Deonar, Mumbai-400088 (Maharashtra)

TATA MCGRAW-HILL PUBLISHING CO. LTD.
7, West Patel Nagar, New Delhi-110008
✆ (O) 25882743-6, 25882918 (R) 26444797, Fax: 25885154, 25883902
✉ XLDEL/TMH/TMH@tmh.satyam.net.in, info_india@mcgraw-hill.com, marketing_india@mcgraw-hill.com
www.tatamcgrawhill.com
Estd.: 1970; **Man.Dir.**: N. Subrahmanyam
Br.: 1st Floor, Sucra Mansion, 158, Arcot Rd., Vadapalani, Chennai-600026
✆ 23726041-42, 24843630, Fax: 24845906
✉ chandra-sekhar@mcgraw-hill.com
• 3310, 1st Floor, 8th Cross HalL II Stage, Indira Nagar, Bangalore-560038
✆ 5263097, Fax: 5272797
✉ girish-blr@tatamcgraw-hill.com
• 1st Floor, Kalanilayam, E-6, Vikram Puri Colony, Karkhana, Secunderabad-500009
✆ 27842412, 27814303, Fax: 27842436
✉ mjc-hyd@tatamcgraw-hill.com
• 696, Lake Town, Block-A, Kolkata-700089
✆ 25212235, 25213252
✉ tmhcal@tatamcgraw-hill.com
• 3A, Namdeo Smruti, 5, Shivprasad Society, Panmala Dattawadi, Pune-411030
✆ 24337604
✉ uday-pune@tatamcgraw-hill.com
Bus.Intt.: Pub., Imp., Exp.;
Spl.: Humanities & Soc.Sci., Sci. & Tech., Med.

TATA PUBLISHERS (REGD.)
1/9185, St. No. 5, West Rohtas Nagar, Shahdara, Delhi-110032
✆ 22290254, 22115544
Hd.Org.: B.S. Kohli; **Bus.Intt.**: Engg.;
Spl.: Competitive Examination Books

TAUSCO BOOK DISTRIBUTORS
160, Sector-A, Pocket-C, Vasant Kunj, New Delhi-110070
✆ (O) 26890397 (R) & Fax: 26136821
✉ tausco@nde.vsnl.net.in
Estd.: 1992; **Hd.Org.**: Muneesh Saggar;
Bus.Intt.: Dist.; **Spl.**: Sci. & Tech., Soc.Sci., Mang.

TAXMANN PUBLICATIONS PVT. LTD.
59/32, New Rohtak Rd., Karol Bagh, New Delhi-110005
✆ (O) 28712352, 25743662, 25743692 (R) 25195502, 25435691, Fax: 28715041
✉ mitra_pal@taxmann.com
www.taxmann.com
Estd.: 1972; **Man.Dir.**: Amit Bhargava;
Bus.Intt.: Imp., Exp., Sub.Ag.; **Spl.**: Law, Mang. & Accounts

---

TAXSHILA PRAKASHAN
98-A Hindi Park, Darya Ganj, New Delhi-110002
✆ 30128802, 23258802, Fax: 23258802
✉ taxshila_prakashan@indiatimes.com
Hd.Org.: Tej Singh Bisht; **Bus.Intt.**: Pub. and Dist.; **Spl.**: Dictionaries, Novels, Folk Litt., and Books on Tourism, Journalism, Env., Art, Drama, etc. in Hindi

---

TAYLOR & FRANCIS BOOKS INDIA PVT. LTD.
912 Tolstoy House, 15-17 Tolstoy Marg, New Delhi-110001
✆ 23712131, Fax: 91-11-23712132
✉ tandfindia@airtelbroadband.in
www.taylorfrancis.co.uk.in
Hd.Org.: Prabir Bhambal; **Bus.Intt.**: Pub.;
Spl.: Sci., Humanities, Soc.Sci., Edu., Med., Engg., Psy., Reference, Asian Studies, etc.

TEACHERS BOOK AGENCY
13C, College Row, Kolkata-700009 (West Bengal)

TEACHERS BOOK CONCERN
22D, College Row, Kolkata-700009 (West Bengal)

TECHMEDIA
202, Munish Plaza, 20, Ansari Rd., New Delhi-110002

✆ (O) 23267741, 23272329, 23254990, 23254991 (R) 23969355, Fax: 23262008
✉ tm@vsnl.com
🌐 www.bpbonline.com
Estd.: 1998; **Hd.Org.**: Rajiv Jain; **Bus.Intt.**: Pub., Comp.; **Spl.**: Comp. Books

TECHNICAL & COMMERCIAL BOOK COMPANY
75, Gokhale Market, Opp. New Courts, Tis Hazari, Delhi-110054
✆ (O) 23920956 (R) 25267900
Estd.: 1913; **Prop.**: Dwarka Nath Mehra; **Bus.Intt.**: WS, Rt., Pub. & L.S.;
Spl.: Tech., Architecutre, Comp., Mang. Law, Reference & Rare Books

TECHNICAL BOOK BUREAU (INDIA)
192, Badarpur, Near Badi Chopal, Badarpur, New Delhi-110044
✆ 26955317 ▮ 9810990700
✉ tech_book_bureau_india@yahoo.com
Prop.: G.S. Rawat; **Bus.Intt.**: L.S.;
Spl.: Acad., Tech., Comp. & Mang. Books

TECHNICAL BOOK HOUSE
Satellite Colony, Surjwan Rd., Jammu (Jammu & Kashmir)
✆ (O) 2462175, 2463522 (R) 09419195660, Fax: 2454119
Estd.: 2000; **Prop.**: Punjab Singh; **Bus.Intt.**: Pub., L.S. & Rt., WS; **Spl.**: Comp., Mang., Arts & Arch.

TECHNICAL BOOK SERVICES
844, Dastur Meher Rd., Pune-411001 (Maharashtra)
✆ (O) 2633468, 2630281, 2638319 (R) 2641884, 2648076, Fax: 0212-2638319
Prop.: J. Borges; **Bus.Intt.**: B.S.; **Spl.**: Comp., Engg. and Mang. Books

TECHNICAL BOOKSHOP
G-5, South Extension-I, New Delhi-110049
✆ 24617030, Fax: 24617235
Hd.Org.: Mrs. Subhadra Devi, Subhash Arora; **Bus.Intt.**: Rt. and WS

TECHNICAL BOOK SOURCE
202, Onkar House, 15 Aggarwal Rd., Darya Ganj, New Delhi-110002
✆ 23289038 ▮ 9891324324, Fax: 23275357
✉ technicalbook2000@yahoo.co.in
Hd.Org.: Rakesh Chaudhary; **Bus.Intt.**: Imp., Dist.; **Spl.**: Sci., Tech., Engg., Arch. & Textiles Books

TECHNICAL BOOK SUPPLIERS
2A/2, Jia Sarai, Near I.I.T. Hauz Khas, New Delhi-110016
✆ 26523543 ▮ 9818055076
Estd.: 1995; **Prop.**: Girish Chandar Sharma; **Bus.Intt.**: Rt., L.S.; **Spl.**: Acad., Comm., Tech., Beh.Sci., Sci., Pure & Applied, Soc.Sci. & Med. Books

TECHNICAL BUREAU INDIA (P) LTD.
E/261, Shastri Nagar, Post Ashok Vihar, Delhi-110052
✆ 23649501, 23648477 ▮ 9811589130, Fax: 011-23648477
✉ ahuja_gaurav@satyam.net.in, technical_bureau@yahoo.com, techbureau@safy.com
Prop.: Mrs. Nirmal Ahuja; **Bus.Intt.**: Imp., Stockists and Dist., Sub.Ag., Order Suppliers; **Spl.**: Books, Journals, Standards, Software, CD Roms, Liaison Work & Gen.

TECHNICAL PUBLISHERS
Main Rd., Guntur-522003 (Andhra Pradesh)
✆ (O) 224211 (R) 224209
Estd.: 1970; **Prop.**: P. Narasimha Rao

TECHNICAL PUBLICATIONS
Office No. 1, Amit Residency, 412 Shaniwar Peth, Pune-411030 (Maharashtra)
✆ 91-20-24495496, Fax: 91-20-24495497
✉ technical@vtubooks.com
🌐 www.vtubooks.com
Hd.Org.: Ravindra Wani; **Bus.Intt.**: Pub.; **Spl.**: Engg., Electonics, Electrical, Mechanical, Comp., Information Tech.

TECHNIZ BOOKS INTERNATIONAL
4/12 (Basement), Kalkaji Extension, Opp. Nehru Place, New Delhi-110019
✆ 26284790, 26284791, 26486911, 26414791 ▮ 9810510602, 931107238
Fax: 26473611, 26472188
✉ info@technizbooks.com, abitechbooks@vsnl.net
🌐 www.technobooks.com
Estd.: 2001; **Hd.Org.**: A.K. Parwanda; **Bus.Intt.**: Imp., Dist., Pub., Rt. & L.S.;
Spl.: Engg. & Tech., Technical Codes & Standards, Journals & Magazines

TECHNO ECONOMIC RESEARCH INSTITUTION
J-7, Saket, New Delhi-110017

TECHNOBOOKS.COM
G-8, C-D-E, Eros Apartment, 56, Nehru Place, New Delhi-110019
✆ 51606573, 26281273, Fax: 26473611
✉ info@technobooks.com
🌐 www.technobooks.com
Hd.Org.: Ashok Kumar Parwanda; **Bus.Intt.**: Dist.; **Spl.**: Textbooks on Engg. & Tech., Comp.Sci., Med.Sci. and Mang.

TECHNOLOGY INFORMATION FORECASTING AND ASSESSMENT COUNCIL (TIFAC)
Technology Bhawan, New Mehrauli Rd., New Delhi-110016
✆ 26862331, Fax: 26863866
✉ publication@tifac.org.in, ghosh@tifac.ernet.in
Hd.Org.: Y.S. Rajan; **Bus.Intt.:** Pub.; Sci. and Tech.

TECHNOMECH BOOKS INTERNATIONAL
65, Chandu Park, Krishna Nagar, Delhi-110051
✆ 22513724 ▮ 9891652475, Fax: 011-51642947
✉ tbibooks@indiatimes.com
🌐 www.gbcp.com
Estd.: 2003; **Prop.:** Saurabh Sharma
Br.: G-17C, 1st Floor, Aashirwad, South Extension Part-II, New Delhi-110049
Bus.Intt.: Pub., B.S., L.S., Imp.; **Spl.:** Sci. & Tech., Mang.

TECHKNOW BOOK DISTRIBUTORS
460, Auto Commercial House, 4th Floor, Kennedy Bridge, Mumbai-400007 (Maharashtra)

TEJ GROUP OF PUBLICATIONS
Sun Publications, 8-B, Bahadurshah Zafar Marg, New Delhi-110002
✆ 23316722, Fax: 91-011-23317947, Cable: TEJ IN
Hd.Org.: M.R.S. Mani

TEJ PRAKASHAN
98-A, Hindi Park, Darya Ganj, New Delhi-110002
✆ 30128802, 23258802, Fax: 23258802
Hd.Org.: Tej Singh Bisht; **Bus.Intt.:** Pub.; **Spl.:** Travel, Journalism Linguistics, Env., Uttarakhand Lit., etc. in Hindi

TEJAS STORES
Near Mitha Chowk, Zalod-381970 (Gujarat)

TEKSONS BOOK SHOP
G-4, 1st Floor, South Ext. Market Part-I, New Delhi-110049
✆ 24617030, 24640649, Fax: 24617238
✉ taksons@del3.vsnl.net.in
Estd.: 1972; **Prop.:** Subhash Arora
Br.: M-7, Greater Kailash, Part-I, New Delhi-110048 ✆ 26483587, 51632155, Fax: 011-24617238 • 13, Community Centre, Near PVR, Saket, New Delhi-110017 ✆ 51664245, 51664246 • G-24, Sector-18, Noida ✆ 2513131, 2511363
Bus.Intt.: Pub., WS, L.S. & Rt. Imp., Exp.; **Spl.:** Fiction and Children Books

TELEDIRECT (INFORMATION) INDIA PVT. LTD.
S-351, Panchsheel Park, New Delhi-110017
✆ 23324751, Fax: 23311573
Estd.: 1990; **Hd.Org.:** Ahmed Ali

TELUGU VIDYARTHI
P.B. No.1, Fort Rd., Machalipatnam-521001 (Andhra Pradesh)

TEX-MEDIA
1014, Mantolla, Pahar Ganj, New Delhi-110055
✆ 23623778, Fax: 23518290
Hd.Org.: Vijay Kumar; **Bus.Intt.:** Dist.; **Spl.:** Mang., Comp., Textiles, Fashion, etc.

TEXT BOOK CENTRE
Teghra, Begusarai-851133 (Bihar)
Bus.Intt.: Pub. and B.S.

THAKKAR STATIONERS
Doctor St., Vasi Talav, Mitha Kuva Gali Chowk, "Ashirvad" P.B. No. 30, Mahuva-364290 (Gujarat)
✆ 02844-222141, 225141 ▮ 9426272294
✉ thakkarstat@yahoo.co.in
Hd.Org.: Mayank Thakkar; **Bus.Intt.:** B.S. & Stationers; **Spl.:** Library Books, A/C Books, Sports & Games

THAMARAI NOOLAGAM
No. 7, NGO Colony, IIIrd St., Vadapalani, Chennai-600026 (Tamil Nadu)
✆ 23620249
Estd.: 1979; **Prop.:** R.C. Mohan;
Bus.Intt.: Pub.; **Spl.:** Siddha Litt. in Tamil

THANU FOUNDATION
Post Box No. 7162, E-32, Anna Nagar (East), Chennai-600102 (Tamil Nadu)
✆ 26260882, Telex: Thanufound, Fax: 044-26214494
✉ thanufound@mailcity.com
Estd.: 1968; **Hd.Org.:** Dr. S. Chidambrarathanu Pillai; **Spl.:** Siddha Med. Litt. Research Centre, Conducting Diploma in Siddha Med. in Tamil and English

THAR BLISS PUBLISHING HOUSE
29, Bhagat-Ki-Kothi, Jodhpur-342001 (Rajasthan)

THE AATMIC SCIENCE FOUNDATION
26D/1, Pannalal Road, Allahabad-211002 (Uttar Pradesh)
✆ 91-532-2461303
✉ editor.sos@gmail.com
🌐 www.scienceofsoul.com
Hd.Org.: Dinesh Singh; **Bus.Intt.:** Pub.; **Spl.:** Sci., Rel., Spirituality, Phil., Journal *Science of Soul*

THE ACADEMIC OF SANSKRIT RESEARCH
Melkote-571431 (Karnataka)

THE ACADEMY OF COMPARATIVE PHILOSOPHY & RELIGION
Belgaum, Gurudeo Mandir, Hindwadi, Belgaum-590011 (Karnataka)

THE ALLIANCE COMPANY
244, R.K. Math Rd., Mylapore, Chennai-600004 (Tamil Nadu)
✆ 24941314
Hd.Org.: K.V.S. Mani and V. Srinivasan; **Bus.Intt.:** Pub.; **Spl.:** Quality Books for over 100 years

THE ASIASTIC SOCIETY
1, Park St., Kolkata-700016 (West Bengal)
✆ 22290779, 22297251, 22497250, Fax: 22172355
aslibcal@vsnl.net.in
www.asiaticsocietycal.com
Hd.Org.: Ramakanta Chakrabarty; **Bus.Intt.:** Pub.; **Spl.:** Books on Indology and Oriental Studies

THE ASSOCIATION OF CHRISTIAN PUBLISHERS & BOOKSELLERS IN INDIA
C/o ISPCK, 1654, Madarsa Rd., Delhi-110006

THE BEST BOOK SHOP
K-138 & K-139, Gupta Apartments, Kalkaji (Near Govindpuri), New Delhi-110019
✆ 51601086
bestbooks@india.com
Hd.Org.: Dhiraj Bakshi; **Bus.Intt.:** Dist.

THE BIBLE SOCIETY OF INDIA
The Bible House, P.B. No. 114, Kottayam (Kerala)
✆ 2562103
Estd.: 1956; **Bus.Intt.:** Pub.

THE BOMBAY SUBSCRIPTION AGENCY
Mahavir Apt., Near Bhatia Hospital, Tardeo Rd., Mumbai-400004 (Maharashtra)
✆ 23801729, 22307147, Fax: 91-22-23812229
Hd.Org.: S.P. Jain; **Bus.Intt.:** Exp. of Books

THE BOOK CANVASSERS
38-A, MIG, Katwaria Sarai, Qutab Enclave, Opp. Qutab Hotel, New Delhi-110016
✆ 25684742, 25587469
Prop.: M. Goel; **Bus.Intt.:** L.S.

THE BOOK FACTORY
231, Sector-15A, Noida (Uttar Pradesh)
✆ 9810044500
Hd.Org.: Ankur Verma; **Bus.Intt.:** Pub.; **Spl.:** Children's books, Books on Rel., Self-help, Culture, Health, Yoga, Sports and Lit. in Hindi, Bangla, Marathi, Gujarati and Asamiya

THE BOOK GALLERY
25-A, Khan Market, New Delhi-110003
✆ 24625066 **Bus.Intt.:** Retail B.S.

THE BOOK HOUSE
Shop No. 97, Gandhi Market, Piplani Bhel, Bhopal-21 (Madhya Pradesh)
Hd.Org.: A.S. Shailesh

THE BOOK MARK
A-2, Mahatma Gandhi Rd., Part-II, New Delhi-110049
✆ 24693216, 24644071, Fax: 24634935
ragupta@del2.vsnl.net.in
Estd.: 1998; **Prop.:** Suparn Vaidik; **Bus.Intt.:** Retail of Children, Hist., Art Culture and Fiction, Non Fiction Books (Indian and Foreign)

THE BOOK POINT (INDIA) LTD.
3-5-820, Hyderguda, Hyderabad-500029 (Andhra Pradesh)

THE BOOK SELLER
F-37, Street No. 5, West Chander Nagar, Delhi-110051
✆ 91-11-22373161 ▮ 9810039279
Prop.: Vinay Khanna; **Bus.Intt.:** L.S.; **Spl.:** Academic, Behavioural Sci, Soc.Sci., Commerce, Sciences-Pure & Applied, Technical Law

THE BOOK SHOPPE
407/1, 7th Block, Opp. Raheja, Arcade, Koramangala, Bangalore-560095 (Karnataka)
✆ (0) 25084623, 25716993, Fax: 91-80-25716993, 25533022
bcipub@blr.vsnl.net.in
Estd.: 1998; **Bus.Intt.:** B.S., **Spl.:** Graduate, Adv. Books for Lib., Gen. Books and Periodicals

THE BOOK WORLD
1st Floor, Ansal Plaza, Khel Gaon Rd., New Delhi-110049
✆ 51754032 ▮ 9811352932
Hd.Org.: Mahendra Kumar; **Bus.Intt.:** Dist.; **Spl.:** Art, Arch., Fashion Designing, etc.

THE BRIGHT LAW HOUSE
Pratap Cloth Market, Bhiwani Stand, Near Punjab & Sind Bank, Rohtak-124001 (Haryana)
Bus.Intt.: Pub. and B.S.; **Spl.:** Law Books

THE CENTRAL BOOK
Stall-50, 1, Bankim Chatterjee St., Kolkata-700073 (West Bengal)
Bus.Intt.: B.S. and Pub.

THE CHILDREN'S KNOWLEDGE CENTRE
H.No. 44, Sector-30, Faridabad-121001 (Haryana)
✆ 91-129-2273712
libresource@gmail.com

www.ckcbooks.com
Hd.Org.: Meenu Arora; **Bus.Intt.:** Dist.; **Spl.:** Reference Books, Ency. Teacher Resource Books, Self-help and Activity books for Children and Libraries

THE COUNCIL EDUCATION CHAMBER OF COMMERCE IN INDIA
3rd Floor, Y.B. Chavan Centre, Gen. J. Bhosle Marg, Nariman Point, Mumbai (Maharashtra)

THE DACCA STUDENTS LIBRARY
5, Shyama Charan Dey St., Kolkata-700009 (West Bengal)

THE ENERGY AND RESOURCES INSTITUTE
Darbari Sethi Block, India Habitat Centre Complex, Lodhi Road, New Delhi-110003
✆ 24682100, 41504900,
Fax: 91-11-24682144-45
teripress@teri.res.in
www.teriin.org
Hd.Org.: R.K. Pachauri; **Bus.Intt.:** Pub.; **Spl.:** Scholarly Titles on issues related to Energy, Env. and Sustainable Development, as well as books for children on Env.

THE ERABHOOMI BOOK STALL
East Nadu, Guruvayoor-680101 (Kerala)
✆ 2556757
Estd.: 1981; **Prop.:** Puthur Ramesh Kumar; **Bus.Intt.:** Pub. and B.S.

THE ETHOS
Books & Publications Division, Oasis Complex, Thrissur-680018 (Kerala)
Bus.Intt.: B.S. and Pub.

THE FAMILY INDIA
F-41, South Extension Part-I,
U & I Building, Second Floor,
New Delhi-110049
✆ 9810188578
contact@thefamilyindia.org
www.thefamilyindia.org
Hd.Org.: S. Pillai; **Bus.Intt.:** Dist.; **Spl.:** Books on Chatacter Building, Personality Development as well as books for children

THE FEDERATION OF EDUCATIONAL PUBLISHERS IN INDIA
X-39, Karkardooma Institutional Area, Delhi-110092
✆ 22376175, 22377017
Hd.Org.: R.K. Gupta; **Bus.Intt.:** Pub.; **Spl.:** School and College-level Textbooks and Engaged in Co-publishing and Co-authorship with Asia and Africa

THE FOUNDATION FOR RESEARCH IN COMMUNITY HEALTH
3-4, Trimiti-B Apartments, 85, Anand Park, Aundh, Pune-411007 (Maharashtra)
✆ 25887020, Fax: 25881308
frchpune@giaspn01.vsnl.net.in
Hd.Org.: N.H. Antia; **Bus.Intt.:** Promoter; **Spl.:** Litt. on Health Related Sub.

THE GEETA PRIVATE LIMITED
32/85, Thiruvambadi, Thrissur-680001 (Kerala)
✆ 2334306
Estd.: 1951; **Hd.Org.:** Sudha Chaturvedi; **Bus.Intt.:** Pub. and B.S.

THE GLOBE BOOK DEPOT
130, Palika Bazar, New Delhi-110001
✆ (O) 23329377 (R) 95120-2573686,
Fax: 91-11-26465678
Prop.: R.C. Arora and P.K. Arora; **Bus.Intt.:** B.S. and L.S.; **Spl.:** Military Sci. and General Books

THE HARITAGE
G-14, Akhilesh Tower, Hari Parvat,
M.G. Rd., Agra-282002
(Uttar Pradesh)
✆ 0562-2353524

THE HINDU
859 & 860, Anna Salai, Chennai-600002 (Tamil Nadu)
✆ 91-44-28589060,
Fax: 91-44-28545703
marketing@thehindu.co.in
www.thehindu.com
Hd.Org.: N. Murali; **Bus.Intt.:** Pub.; **Spl.:** English Newspaper *The Hindu* and magazine—*Business Line, The Sportstar, Frontline*, etc.

THE HINDUSTAN TIMES
18-20, Kasturba Gandhi Marg,
New Delhi-110001
Bus.Intt.: Pub.; **Spl.:** Newspaper

THE HOUSE OF LETTERS
202, Magnum House, Opp. Milan Cinema, Karampura, New Delhi

THE INDIAN NATIONAL TRUST FOR ART AND CULTURAL HERITAGE
71, Lodi Estate, New Delhi-110003

THE INFOWARE HOUSE
21, Ishwar Park, Opp. Prashant Society, Hindu Colony Ishwar Bhuwan Rd., Navrangpura, Ahmedabad-380014 (Gujarat)
✆ 6460896, 31015889, Fax: 91-78-2133292
is@vsnl.com,
infowarehouse_2000@yahoo.com
www.hindicdrom.com
Ch.Exe.: Prabhakar S. Agarwal; **Bus.Intt.:** Pub. & Dist.; **Spl.:** Comp., Gen. books in English, Hindi, Gujarati and Marathi

THE INTERNATIONAL BOOK SERVICE
Deccan Gymkhana, Pune-41004 (Maharashtra)
✆ (0) 25677405 (R) 25678060
✉ interbhs@pn3.vsnl.net.in
Estd.: 1931; **Prop.:** U.V. Dixit; **Bus.Intt.:** B.S.; **Spl.:** Graduate, Adv. Books for Lib. and Gen. Books

THE JANAPRIYA PUBLISHERS
42A, Shib Narayan Das Lane, Kolkata-700006 (West Bengal)

THE KARNATIC MUSIC BOOK CENTRE
No. 14, Sripuram, First St., (Near Ajanta Hotel), Royapettah, Chennai-600014 (Tamil Nadu)
Bus.Intt.: L.S.; **Spl.:** Music Books

THE KASHMIR BOOK SHOP
Sharwani Rd., Srinagar-190001 (Jammu and Kashmir)

THE KUPUSWAMI SASTRI
Research Institute, 84, Royapettah High Rd., Mylapore, Chennai-600004 (Tamil Nadu)

THE LIFE ETERNAL TRUST
C-17, Institutional Area, Behind Qutab Hotel, New Delhi-110017
✆ 26178156, Fax: 26866801
✉ kalrajesh@rediffmail.com
www.sahajayoga.org.in
Hd.Org.: K. Natraj; **Bus.Intt.:** Promoter; **Spl.:** Litt. on the Teachings of Mataji Shri Nirmala Devi

THE LIVING TREASURE (REGD.)
9/101, Subhash Nagar, New Delhi-110027
✆ 32950633 ▮ 9811655321, Fax: 91-11-25440685
✉ contact@thelivingtreasure.com
www.thelivingtreasure.org
Hd.Org.: Mohinder Pal Singh; **Bus.Intt.:** A Registered NGO engaged in Personality Development and Voluntary Service for the needy

THE LOTUS GROUP
6-3-663/C1, Officers Colony, Punjagutta, Hyderabad-500082 (Andhra Pradesh)
✆ 91-40-23413713, 26613982
Hd.Org.: Samiksha Thakur; **Spl.:** Books and Periodicals

THE MALABAR PRINTERS
Payyannur-670307 (Kerala)

THE MEDICAL TIMES
325/10, 1st Floor, T.H. Rd., Chennai-600005 (Tamil Nadu)
✆ 28510282, Fax: 91-44-28550455
Hd.Org.: Ravi; **Bus.Intt.:** Pub.

THE MILLION RESEARCH CENTRE
Ambagan, Benoyapalli, Santiniketan, Bolpur-731235 (West Bengal)

THE MODERN BOOK DEPOT
Pan Bazar, Main Rd., Post Box No. 45, Guwahati-781001 (Assam)
✆ 0361-2517059, Cable: UNIPUB, Fax: 0361-2544791
✉ unipub@sancharnet.in
Sales Off.: Hotel Monsoon Building, Utirot Singh Rd., Shillong-743001
✆ 0364-2223476 ✉ unipub@vsnl.com
Estd.: 1953 (in Shillong); **Prop.:** Mrs. Anita Kumar; **Bus.Intt.:** L.S. & Rt., Imp., Sub.Ag.; **Spl.:** Humanities & Soc.Sci., Law, Juvenile/ Children, Gen. & Fiction, Maps & Charts etc.

THE MODERN BOOK DEPOT
15-A, J.L. Nehru Rd., Opp. Light House Cinema, Kolkata-700013 (West Bengal)
✆ 22490933, Fax: 22493102
✉ modca@vsnl.com
Estd.: 1949; **Prop.:** Prem Prakash; **Bus.Intt.:** Pub., WS, L.S. & Rt., Imp.; **Spl.:** Humanities & Soc.Sci., Juvenile/ Children, Gen. & Fiction etc.

THE NATIONAL MEDICAL JOURNAL OF INDIA
All India Institute of Medical Science, Ansari Nagar, New Delhi-110029

THE NEW CHAYANIKA
269, B.B. Chatterjee Rd., Kolkata-700042 (West Bengal)

THE NEW ORDER BOOK CO.
Opp. Town Hall, Ellis Bridge, Ahmedabad-380006 (Gujarat)
✆ 26579065
Hd.Org.: Sarojben Dinkerbhai Trivedi; **Bus.Intt.:** B.S.; **Spl.:** Antiquarian Research-Oriented Books and on Islam Hist., Art, Persia

THE OTHER INDIA BOOK STORE
Above Mapusa Clinic, Mapusa-403507 (Goa)
✆/Fax: 2263305
Bus.Intt.: Rt. and L.S.

THE REBEL PUBLISHING HOUSE PVT. LTD.
50, Koregaon Park, Pune-411001 (Maharashtra)

THE REGISTRAR PRINTING & PUBLICATION DIVISION
Warehouse, Indira Gandhi National Open University, Maidan Garhi, New Delhi-110068

THE SCHOOL LIBRARY
60, Patuatola Lane, Kolkata-700009 (West Bengal)

THE SELF-EMPLOYMENT BUREAU (PUBLICATION)
24/2/19, Mondal Para Lane, Kolkata-700050 (West Bengal)
✆ 91-33-25460304
✉ scbpcal@vsnl.net
Hd.Org.: Chhaya Ganguly; **Bus.Intt.**: Pub.; **Spl.**: Books on Cultural Hist., Links between the people of India, America, Australia and other Asian Countries

THE SOBANA OFFSET PRINTERS
35, 3rd Main Rd., Industrial Town, Raja Nagar, Bangalore-560044 (Karnataka)

THE STANDARD BOOK COMPANY
4/18, Morzaria Indl. Estate, Bannerghatta Rd., Bangalore-560029 (Karnataka)
✆ 25535522, 25535544, 25535588, Fax: 25536323
✉ standard@vsnl.com
www.standardbookcompany.com
Estd.: 1935; **Man.Prt.**: H. Kamalanath; **Bus.Intt.**: L.S. & Rt., Imp., Sub.Ag.; **Spl.**: Humanities & Soc.Sci., Sci. & Tech., Med.

THE STATE TELUGU PUBLISHERS ASSOCIATION
C.V.R.G.M. High School Campus, Vijayawada-520001
Bus.Intt.: Promoter of Telugu Publications

THE STUDENTS LIBRARY
56, Central Rd., Jadavpore, Kolkata-32 (West Bengal)

THE STUDENTS STORE
Paona Bazar, Imphal-795001 (Manipur)
✆ (O) 2223077, 2220407 (R) 2220441
Estd.: 1995; **Prop.**: S. Nishikanta Singh

THE THEOSOPHICAL PUBLISHING HOUSE
C/o The Theosophical Society, Adyar, Chennai-600020 (Tamil Nadu)
✆ 24911338, 24466613, Fax: 91-44-24901399
✉ tphindia@vsnl.com, theos.soc@gems.vsnl.net.in
www.ts-adyar.org
Hd.Org.: Dr. Govindaraj; **Bus.Intt.**: Pub.; **Spl.**: Theosophym, Rel., Phil. and Sci.

THE TIMES OF INDIA
Hyderabad (Andhra Pradesh)
✆ 23355335, Fax: 23355302
✉ rajesh.kondru@timesgroup.com
Bus.Intt.: News Agency

THE UNIQUE BOOK CENTRE
6, Bankim Chatterjee St., Kolkata-700073 (West Bengal)

THE UNITED BOOK HOUSE
6, Nashvilla Rd., Dehradun-248001 (Uttarakhand)
✆ (O) 0135-2656100 (R) 2655724
Estd.: 1974; **Hd.Org.**: K.C. Sharma; **Bus.Intt.**: B.S. and L.S.; **Spl.**: All Sub. in English and Hindi Language

THE UNITED BOOK HOUSE
WP-105C, Pitam Pura, New Delhi-110088
✆ 91-11-27323798 ▮ 9811211139
✉ rajiv_ubh_delhi2000@yahoo.com
Prop.: Rajiv Sharma; **Bus.Intt.**: B.S.; **Spl.**: Institutions, Library, Schools, Colleges, Veterinary Books

THE UNITED THEOLOGICAL COLLEGE
Post Box No. 4613, 63 (Old No. 17), Miller's Rd., Benson Town, Bangalore-560046 (Karnataka)

THE UNIVERSITY BOOK AGENCY
15-3, Elgin Rd., Allahabad-211001 (Uttar Pradesh) ✆ (O) 2420906 (R) 2622392
Estd.: 1923; **Bus.Intt.**: Pub.; **Spl.**: Comm., Mang., Law and Humanities

THE VARIETY BOOK DEPOT
AVG Bhavan, M-3, Connaught Circus, P.O. Box-505, New Delhi-110001
✆ (O) 23417175, 23412567, 23415030 (R) 24602032, 24624028, Fax: 91-11-23415335, 51517201
✉ varietybookdepot@rediffmail.com
Prop.: Om Arora; **Bus.Intt.**: Pub.; **Spl.**: Magazines on Fashion, Embroidery, Interiors, Children Books & Travel Books

THE VARIETY BOOK HOUSE
12, Padamdev Complex, Ridges, Shimla-171001 (Himachal Pradesh)

THE VIVEKA FOUNDATION
25-C, DDA Flats, Shahpurjat, New Delhi-110049
✆ 26492473
✉ viveka4@vsnl.com
Hd.Org.: Rukmini Sekhar; **Bus.Intt.**: Pub.; **Spl.**: Soc.Sci. & Humanities

THE WALT DISNEY CO. (INDIA) PVT. LTD.
4th Floor, Peninsula Tower 1, Peninsula Corporate Park, GK Market, Lower Parel, Mumbai-400013 (Maharashtra)
✆ 91-22-66516618, 56637752, Fax: 91-33-66541709
✉ naveen.chopra@disney.com
www.disney.in
Hd.Org.: Naveen Chopra; **Bus.Intt.**: Pub.; **Spl.**: Books for Children on Various Topics

THE WESTERN INDIAN MANUFACTURER'S AGENCY PRIVATE LIMITED
Peerbhai Mansion, 456, Sardar V.P. Rd., Mumbai-400004 (Maharashtra)

THE WISE OWL
I-85B LGF, Lajpat Nagar-II, New Delhi-110024
✆ 41721050, 29813206,
Fax: 91-11-41721050
✉ thewiseowl@bol.net.in
Hd.Org.: Jatin Mehta, Ashish Gupta
Bus.Intt.: Representation Agency for International Publishers

THE WORD BOOKSHOP
899, Bootee St., Next to Railway Reservation Centre, Pune-411001 (Maharashtra)
✆ 0212-2633118, Fax: 2630522
Estd.: 1990; **Prop.:** Ajay Sain; **Bus.Intt.:** Rt.; **Spl.:** Gen. Trade Acad., Professional Children Books (Indian and Foreign Books)

THE WORLD BANK
70, Lodhi Estate, New Delhi-110003
✆ 41479465, 24617241
Fax: 91-11-24619393
✉ balasubramanian@worldbank.org
www.worldbank.org
Hd.Org.: Isabel M. Guerrero;
Bus.Intt.: Promoter of Investments;
Spl.: Health, Edu., Env., and Rural Development Sectors

THE WRITE CHOICE
'Sheela Heights' 257/258, Karve Rd., Near Butte Patil Complex, Paud Patna, Pune-411038 (Maharashtra)
✆ 2344234

THEATRE FOUNDATION
Garage Studio Theatre, 5/57 Nav Nirman Nagar, Ahmedabad-380013 (Gujarat)

THEMA
46, Satish Mukherjee Rd., Kolkata-700026 (West Bengal)
✆ 033-2743111
Estd.: 1987; **Prop.:** Ms. Kalyani Ghosh; **Bus.Intt.:** Pub.; **Spl.:** Litt., Sci., Soc.Sci. and Cinema in Bengali and English

THENMAZHAI PATHIPPAGAM
34, Kothaval St., Alandur Rd., Chennai-600016 (Tamil Nadu)
✆ (O) 22342101 (R) 22340383
Prop.: S.P. Vellaiyappan

THEOLOGICAL PUBLICATIONS IN INDIA
P.B. No. 5553, Malleswaram West P.O., Bangalore-560055 (Karnataka)
✆ 23340504
Estd.: 1969; **Bus.Intt.:** Pub. and Exp.

THEOSOPHY CO. (INDIA) PVT. LTD.
Theosophy Hall, 40, New Marine Lines, Mumbai-400020 (Maharashtra)

THIEME MEDICAL AND SCIENTIFIC PUBLISHERS (P) LTD.
2/15, Ansari Raod, Darya Ganj, New Delhi-110002
✆ 23263522, Fax: 91-11-23263522
✉ thieme-santosh@gmail.com
www.thieme.com
Hd.Org.: Santosh Kumar Verma;
Bus.Intt.: Pub., **Spl.:** Books on Neurosurgery, Radiology, Orthopaedics, Audiology, Speech and Hearing, Complementary Medicine, etc. Also Publish CDs, DVDs and online Journals for Medical Community

THILAKAM PUBLICATIONS
Devia S Complex, 5-A, Venkatesa Chowdhry St., Tambaram, Chennai-600045 (Tamil Nadu)

THINK/GOODWORD BOOKS
New Delhi
✆ 24697971, Fax: 24697333
✉ skhan@vsnl.com
Bus.Intt.: Pub.

THINK INCORPORATED
G-42, Nizamuddin West, New Delhi-110013
✆ 24356464, 24359898, 24354253,
Fax: 24357980
✉ thinkinc@vsnl.com
www.successcorners.com
Estd.: 1996; **Pres.:** Pramod Batra
Br.: Think Inc + Father Son and Co., F-8, Nizamuddin (W), New Delhi-110013
✆ (O) 24359898, 24352453 (R) 24356464,
Fax: 24357980 ✉ thinkinc@vsnl.com
Bus.Intt.: B.S.; **Spl.:** Mang. and Islam

THIRD EYE
Foundation of India,
33, New Colony, Kurukshetra (Haryana)

THIRD WORLD NETWORK
A-60, Hauz Khas (2nd Floor), New Delhi-110016

THIRRUKKUMARAN PATHIPPAGAM
66, Sabapathipuram St., Thiruehendur-628215 (Kerala)

THIRUMAGAL NILAYAM
No. 55, Venkatnarayana Rd., T. Nagar, Chennai-600017 (Tamil Nadu)
✆ 24342899, 24327696, 24337428,
Fax: 44-24341559
✉ thirumagal@intamm.com
Estd.: 1979; **Hd.Org.:** A. Ramanathan;
Bus.Intt.: Pub., B.S. and Exp.; **Spl.:** Gen. Books

THIRUMALI BOOK HOUSE
No. 2 Sunkarma St., Y.M.C.A. Building, Chennai-600001 (Tamil Nadu)
✆ 2562305, 2582956
Prop.: G. Thirumalai; **Bus.Intt.:** Dist., Rt. and Pub.; **Spl.:** Sci. and Tech., Soc.Sci. and Gen.

THIRUSA DASSU
Vaikom P.O., Kottayam-686141 (Kerala)
Estd.: 1990; **Hd.Org.:** Vekkam; **Bus.Intt.:** Pub. and B.S.

THOMAS INTERNATIONAL PUBLISHING COMPANY INDIA PVT. LTD.
New Delhi
✆ 23359130, 23359167, Fax: 23359170
trim@vsnl.com

THOMAS NELSON & SONS LTD.
C/o. R. Seshadri, 32, Second Main Rd., C.I.T. East, Chennai-600033 (Tamil Nadu)

THOMAS NELSON & SONS LTD.
New Delhi
✆ 24346244, 24346266
germanbk@vsnl.com
Bus.Intt.: Rt., B.S. & Dist.

THOMSON ASIA (PTE) LTD. INDIA
2, Geetanjali, Opp. Indus Ind Bank, 234, S.V. Rd., Bandra (W), Mumbai-400050 (Maharashtra)
✆ 26453960, Fax: 26453907
sunil.patki@thomsonlearning.com.sg
www.thomsonlearningasia.com
Prop.: Sunil Patki
Br.: Thomson Learning, 2, Geetanjali, Opp. Indusind Bank, 234, S.V. Rd., Bandra (W), Mumbai-400050 ✆ 26453960, Fax: 26453907
tlindia@vsnl.com, sspatki@vsnl.com
Bus.Intt.: Pub.; **Spl.:** Print and Electronic Materials for the Edu. Professional and Reference Markets

THOMSON INFORMATION SOUTH ASIA PVT. LTD.
(Thomson International Legal & Regulatory)
GESCO Corporate Center, The Great Eastern Center, 70 Nehru Place, New Delhi-110019
✆ 26209428, 26209419, Fax: 91-11-26209422
ambika.nair@thomson.com
www.geniuseschool.com
Hd.Org.: Ambika Nair; **Bus.Intt.:** Provider of Integrated Information Solutions on Legal, Tax, Accounting and Intellectual Property in English

THOMSON INTERNATIONAL PUBLISHING
32, 11 Main Rd., CIT East, Chennai-600035 (Tamil Nadu)
✆ 044-2456246, Fax: 2459295
Hd.Org.: R. Seshadri

THOMSON PRESS (INDIA) LTD.
C-35, Phase-II, Noida-201305 (Uttar Pradesh)
✆ 24562925, 24562949, 24562049, Fax: 24562969
amanocha@thomsonpress.com
Hd.Org.: Vinod Kumar; **Bus.Intt.:** Printer; **Spl.:** All Kinds of Reading Material by State-of-the-art Printing Tech.

THOMSON PRESS (INDIA) LTD.
18/35, Milestone, Delhi Mathura Rd., Faridabad-121007 (Haryana)
✆ 91-129-2285520-1, 91-11-51616080, Fax: 91-129-2284511, 91-11-26818670-5
kraina@thomsonpress.com
www.thomsonpress.com
Estd.: 1967; **Hd.Org.:** Vinod Kumar
Br.: New Delhi ✆ 26814425, 26818915, Fax: 26818670 rpiplani@thomsonpress.com

THREE STAR PUBLICATIONS (P) LTD.
1484-87, Arya Samaj St., Bazar Sita Ram, Delhi-110006
✆ 23236758, 23237209, Fax: 91-11-23235438
tspbooks@bol.net.in
www.tspbooks.com
Hd.Org.: Vijay Sharma; **Bus.Intt.:** Pub.; **Spl.:** Edu. Books for Children in Hindi Language

TIBBI DIGEST AL-SHIFA
2075, Kucha Chelan, Darya Ganj, New Delhi-110002
✆ 23253268
Hd.Org.: Syed Aijaz Hussain
Bus.Intt.: Pub.; **Spl.:** Urdu Monthly Magazine Covering Health, Hygiene, etc.

TIFFANY DESIGNS
C-47, Okhla Industrial Area, Phase-I, Delhi-110020
Bus.Intt.: Exp.

TILAK BOOK STORE
5/2, Beniapukur Rd., Kolkata-700014 (West Bengal)

TILAK MAHARASHTRA VIDYAPEET
Gultekadi, Pune-411037 (Maharashtra)

TIME BOOKS
Mumbai (Maharashtra)
✆ 23885563, 23887801
bombay@readnbuy.net
Bus.Intt.: B.S.

TIMELY BOOKS CENTRE
30, Chittaranjan Avenue, 2nd Floor, Kolkata-700012 (West Bengal)
✆ 22376794, 22366794, Fax: 22374149
timely@vsnl.net

Estd.: 1976; Prop.: Jayant D. Tanna;
Bus.Intt.: WS, L.S. and Rt., Imp., Exp.

TIMES BOOK AGENCY
C-587, Sushant Lok, Phase-I,
Gurgaon-122001 (Haryana)
✆ 2385918, 2385035, Fax: 2385035
Estd.: 1998; **Prop.:** P.D. Jain; **Bus.Intt.:** Mail Order Suppliers; **Spl.:** Law, Acct. Tech. Books

TIMES BOOK GALLERY
25-A, Khan Market, New Delhi-110003
✆ 24625066, Fax: 23225247
Estd.: 1989; **Hd.Org.:** Mrs. Anju Sabharwal; **Bus.Intt.:** Rt. and L.S.; **Spl.:** Gen. and Trade, Acad. and Children Books (Indian and Foreign)

TIMES MIRROR INTERNATIONAL PUBLISHERS
C/o Viva Marketing, 4327/3,
Ansari Rd., Darya Ganj,
New Delhi-110002

TIMES PAPERBACK CO.
P.B. No. 121, Mahatma Gandhi Rd.,
35, Partappura, Agra-282001
(Uttar Pradesh)

TINY BOOK CENTRE
College Square (West), Kolkata-700073
(West Bengal)

TINY TOT PUBLICATIONS
235, Jagriti Enclave, Vikas Marg,
Delhi-110092
✆ 22163582, 22167314, Fax: 22143023
✉ tinytotpub@hotmail.com
Hd.Org.: Shyam Dua; **Bus.Intt.:** Pub.; **Spl.:** Children's Picture Books on Colouring, Stories, Activity, Puzzles, Quiz, etc.

TIRUMALA SOFTWARE
807 Manjusha, 57 Nehru Place,
New Delhi-110019
✆ 26444341, Fax: 91-11-26473611
✉ tirumala@email.com
www.geniuseschool.com
Hd.Org.: Rakesh Gupta; **Bus.Intt.:** Developer of CDs, VCDs and inter-active multimedia packages on education for children

TIRURANGADI BOOK STALL
Korambayil Arcade, Pandikad Rd., Manjeri,
Malappuram (Kerala)
Estd.: 1990; **Prop.:** K. Musthafa; **Bus.Intt.:** Pub. and B.S.

TIWARI PUBLICATIONS
C-2098, Indira Nagar, Lucknow-226016
(Uttar Pradesh)

TIWARI PUBLICATIONS
B-622, Arvind Nagar, Ghonda,
Delhi-110053
Hd.Org.: Rameshwar Prasad Tiwari

TIWARI PUSTAK SADAN
Bijaipur, Gopalganj-841508 (Bihar)

TODAY TOMORROWS PRINTERS & PUBLISHERS
4435-36/7, Ansari Rd., Darya Ganj,
New Delhi-110002
✆ 23241021, 23242621, Fax: 23242621
✉ ttpp@vsnl.com
Estd.: 1975; **Prop.:** Ramesh K. Jain; **Bus.Intt.:** Pub., WS, L.S. & Rt., Imp., Exp., Sub.Ag.; **Spl.:** Agri., Bio-Sci., Geol., Humanities & Soc.Sci., Sci. & Tech.

TOOBA FORWARDING AGENCIES
Habba Kadal Chowk, Srinagar
(Jammu & Kashmir)
✆ (O) & (R) 0194-2456153
Estd.: 2002; **Man.:** Irfan; **Bus.Intt.:** L.S.; **Spl.:** Humanities & Soc.Sci., Sci. & Tech., Comp., Med.

TOP JOURNALS & TRADE SERVICE
97-A, Pocket A, Sukhdev Vihar,
New Delhi-110025
✆ (O) 26832913 (R) 26832913,
Fax: 91-11-26832913
✉ mmseigell@yahoo.com
Estd.: 1987; **Prop.:** M.M. Seigell
Bus.Intt.: B.S.; **Spl.:** Magazines on Fashion Designs, Textiles, Colours, Forecasts, Pantone

TOP PUBLICATIONS (REGD.)
4093, Nai Sarak, Chawri Bazar, Delhi-110006
✆ 22923280
Estd.: 1992; **Prop.:** Rajiv Rastogi; **Spl.:** Eco., Mang., Edu. Books (B.A. & Com.)

TOTAL LIBRARY SOLUTION (I) PVT. LTD.
WZ-248, 2nd Floor, Inder Puri,
New Delhi-110012
✆ 25832289, 25836593, 25833253
Fax: 25831179
✉ tls@del3.vsnl.net.in, tls@vsnl.com
www.tllindia.com
Estd.: 1998; **Ch.Exe.:** Rajiv Kumar Mishra
Rgd.Off.: F-7, D Saket, New Delhi-110017
✆ (R) 26859444
Br.: Om Niwas, Ground Floor, CTS 470, Shipoli Village, Shimpoli Rd., Borivili (W), Mumbai-92 ✆ 09821520261
• 18, Jay Enclave, New Bowenpally, Secunderabad ✆ 37952711 ▮ 9848098186
• N-67, Dum Dum Estate, Kolkata-700028
• No. 97, 1st Block, 2nd Main, 8th Cross, B.E.L. Layout, Vidyaranyapura, Bangalore-560097 ✆ 09845287259
Bus.Intt.: Subscription Services

TOUHA ENTERPRISES
Shamaswari, K.K. Mouhlla, Srinagar-190002
(Jammu & Kashmir)

© 2453417
tahapub.2003@yahoo.com
Man.Prt.: Asif & Riyaz; **Bus.Intt.:** Pub., B.S., Dist. & Stationeries

TOWARDS FREEDOM
AH-202, Sector-2, Saltlake, Kolkata-700091 (West Bengal)
© 91-33-23212902, 23591529, 31030579
towardsfreedom@vsnl.net
Bus.Intt.: Pub. & B.S.

TOWER PERIODICAL SUBSCRIPTION AGENCY
194, Dr. Natesan Rd., Triplicane, Chennai-600005 (Tamil Nadu)
© 8472305
prhpn@yahoo.com
Estd.: 2000; **Hd.Org.:** P.S. Parthipan; **Bus.Intt.:** Sub.Ag.

TRADE LINK
G-1/461/A, Behind Dal Mill, Uttam Nagar, New Delhi-110059

TRAFFICO ENGINEERS
New Delhi
© 26831100, 26921100
traffico@ndf.vsnl.net.in
Bus.Intt.: Pub. & Dist.

TRANS ASIA PUBLICATIONS
62/6, Ber Sarai, Opp. J.N.U., New Delhi-110016

TRANS-INDIA BOOK DISTRIBUTORS
A-148, Harnam Singh Market, Ismailpur Rd., Jaitpur, Badarpur, New Delhi-110044
9899214093
transindiabooks@indiatimes.com
Estd.: 2003; **Prop.:** Santosh Kr. Singh; **Bus.Intt.:** L.S.; **Spl.:** Beh.Sci., Soc.Sci., Sci., Tech.

TRANSWORLD BOOK SERVICES
134, Khanna Market, Lodhi Rd., New Delhi-110003
© (O) 24624055, 24652250 (R) 24535043
9810004985, Fax: 28535043
twbs@del3.vsnl.net.in
Estd.: 1971; **Prop.:** T.A. Ramanathan
Br.: 643, Prashanth Nagar, Medical College P.O., Thriuvananthapuram
Bus.Intt.: L.S. & Rt., Imp., Exp.; **Spl.:** Sci. & Tech., Med.

TRANSWORLD MEDIA INC.
90/85B, Top Floor, Malviya Nagar, New Delhi-110017
© 26893233
Hd.Org.: K. Sidharath; **Bus.Intt.:** Pub. and Writer

TRANSWORLD SUBSCRIPTION AGENCY
12-11-1396, Boudhanagar, Seethaphal Mandi P.O., Secunderabad-61 (Andhra Pradesh)
© 270772216, Fax: 27075614
transhyd@hd1.vsnl.net.in
Estd.: 1985; **Prop.:** P.V.K. Sastry; **Bus.Intt.:** Sub.Ag.; **Spl.:** Journals, Magazines & Periodicals

TRAVANCORE LAW HOUSE
Congress House, M.G. Rd., Kochi-682011 (Kerala)
© 2353766
Estd.: 1934; **Prop.:** Susan Joseph; **Bus.Intt.:** Pub. and B.S.; **Spl.:** Law Books

TRAVANCORE PUBLICATIONS
P.O. Box 5812, Manacaud, Thiruvananthapuram-695009 (Kerala)
© 276363, 277063
Estd.: 1983; **Prop.:** M.S. Navas; **Bus.Intt.:** Pub. and B.S.; **Spl.:** Children's Books and Reference Books in Malayalam

TRAYAEE PRAKASH
62-A, College St., Kolkata-700073 (West Bengal)

TREASURE ISLAND
464/1, Nandnam, Annasalai, Chennai-600035 (Tamil Nadu)
© 2452477
Estd.: 1995; **Prop.:** G.K. Pillai; **Bus.Intt.:** WS, L.S., Rt.

TREECRAFT COMMUNICATIONS
Jaipur (Rajasthan)
© 0141-2340333
treecrft@jp1.dot.in
Br.: Bhopal (Madhya Pradesh)
© 2573138, 2556672
tripathga@vsnl.com
Bus.Intt.: Pub. and B.S.

TRICEL BOOK SHOP
Fraser Rd., Patna-800001 (Bihar)
© 0612-2221412
Estd.: 1967; **Prop.:** R. Banka; **Bus.Intt.:** Rt.; **Spl.:** Gen. and Trade, Acad., Professional Indian and Foreign Books and Greeting Cards

TRICOLOUR BOOKS
9662-B, Islam Ganj, Azad Market, Delhi-110006

TRIDEEP PRAKASHANI
10, Nabin Kundu Lane, Kolkata-700009 (West Bengal)

TRIKAL JYOTI
Panchang Karyala, Balotra-344022 (Rajasthan)

TRIMANI PUSTAK BHANDAR
Kahalgaon (Colgong), Bhagalpur-813203 (Bihar)
Bus.Intt.: Pub. and B.S.

TRIMURTHY ENTERPRISES
G-17-A, Lane No. 4, Malook Singh Marg,
Arun Nagar (West), Delhi-110051
✆ 22059382
Prop.: Arvind Kumar; **Bus.Intt.:** L.S.

TRIMURTI SALES AGENCY
S.T. Rd., Near Railway Crossing,
Junagadh-362001 (Gujarat)

TRIO ENTERPRISE
8/1, Bhabani Dutta Lane, Kolkata-700073
(West Bengal)
✆ 22198749, 31030780
Prt.: A.K. Dey

TRIPATHGA
G-204, Sarita Vihar, New Delhi-110003
✆ (O) & (R) 26473123
Hd.Org.: Vandan Kumar; **Bus.Intt.:** Pub., L.S.; **Spl.:** English and Hindi

TRIPATHGA PRAKASHAN (P) LTD.
D-2, Dayanand Block, Shakarpur,
Delhi-110092
✆ 91-11-22026541
✉ tripathga@hotmail.com
🌐 www.tripathga.com
Hd.Org.: Mohini Devi; **Bus.Intt.:** Pub.; **Spl.:** Hindi Litt. including Poetry, Fiction, Language and Grammar, Children's Litt., Art, Hist., etc.

TRIPATHGA PRAKASHAN (P) LTD.
4, Indus Park Phase-I, Ayodhya Nagar,
Bypass Rd., Bhopal-462021 (Madhya Pradesh)
✆ 91-755-5283460, 91-11-22026541
✉ tripathga@hotmail.com
Hd.Org.: Vandita; **Bus.Intt.:** Pub.; **Spl.:** Hindi Language, Litt. and Grammar, Hist., Art and Culture, etc.

TRIPATHI BOOK DISTRIBUTORS
NPA-Arcade, Shop No. 212,
23, M.G. Marg, Civil Lines,
Allahabad-211001 (Uttar Pradesh)
✆ 91-532-2561162, Fax: 91-532-2560866
✉ tbxalld@sancharnet.in
Estd.: 1986; **Prop.:** Harihar Tripathi; **Bus.Intt.:** L.S. & Rt.; **Spl.:** Sci. & Tech., Med., Law, Comp. and other Professional books

TRIRATNA GRANTHMALA
Dhammachakra Pravartan,
Mahavihar Dapodi, Pune-411012
(Maharashtra)

TRIRATNA GRANTHAMALYA
44, Meshram Building, Dr. Ambedkar Rd.,
Nagpur-440017 (Maharashtra)
✆ 642003, 646474
✉ nagaloka@nagpr.dot.net.in

TRISEA PUBLICATIONS (P) LTD.
Bhagat Singh Marg, Saharanpur-247001
(Uttar Pradesh)
✆ 2726724, Fax: 0132-2727104
Prop.: Deepak Aggarwal

TRISHUL PUBLICATIONS
216, Sector 28, Noida-201303
(Uttar Pradesh)
✆ (O) 011-33338285 (R) 3097662
✉ integral@del3.vsnl.net.in
Estd.: 1985; **Prop.:** Brigadier Man Mohan Sharma; **Bus.Intt.:** Pub.; **Spl.:** Military Affairs

TRISHUL PUBLICATIONS
37/3, Nehru Rd., Dehradun-248001
(Uttarakhand)
✆ 2658407
Estd.: 1982; **Prop.:** Major D.S. Bisht (Retd.); **Bus.Intt.:** Pub.; **Spl.:** Welfare, Security, Administrative Reform & Development and Gen. Books

TRUEMAN BOOK COMPANY
4353/4C, Ansari Rd., Darya Ganj,
New Delhi-110002
✆ 23242482, 23242483
Fax: 91-11-23242483
✉ trueman@satyam.net.in
Hd.Org.: Rajat Manocha; **Bus.Intt.:** Pub. & B.S.; **Spl.:** Textbooks for Schools, Colleges and Books for Competitive Exams

TRUEWAN BOOK CO.
Adda Hoshiarpur, Jalandhar (Punjab)
✆ 2223519

TRUMP & GATES
2nd Floor, 65, Regal Building,
Connaught Place, New Delhi-110001
✆ 23367497, 23367498,
Fax: 91-11-23367687
✉ info@trumpandgates.com
Ch.Exe.: Arvind Bamhi; **Bus.Intt.:** Pub.; **Spl.:** Books/Aids for MBA Entrance Exams

TSR BOOK CLUB
23, Vasant Enclave,
New Delhi-110057
✆ 26142031, 26144805

TUHINA PUSTAKALAYA
Kachari Rd., Purulia
(West Bengal)

TULIKA BOOKS
35-A/1, 3rd Floor, Shahpur Jat,
New Delhi-110049
✆ 26491448, 26491625, Fax: 26497999
✉ tulika@ndf.vsnl.net.in
Hd.Org.: Indira Chandrasekhar;
Bus.Intt.: Pub.; **Spl.:** Acad. Books on Soc.Sci. and Humanities in English

TULIKA PUBLISHERS
No. 13, Prithvi Avenue,
Abhiramapuram, Chennai-600018
(Tamil Nadu)
✆ (O) 24981639, 24671117 (R) 24991176,
Fax: 24671113
✉ kaka@tulikabooks.com,
tulbooks@md4.vsnl.net.in
www.tulikabooks.com
Estd.: 1996; **Prop.:** Radhika Menon;
Spl.: Children Books

TULI-QALAM
1, College Row, Kolkata-700009
(West Bengal)

TULSI BOOK CENTRE
Madurai (Tamil Nadu)
✆ 0452-749928
✉ tulsibookmdu@yahoo.com
Bus.Intt.: B.S.

TULSI PRAKASHAN
C/2098, Indira Nagar, Lucknow-220016
(Uttar Pradesh)
✆ 2383501
Hd.Org.: Trilochan Bhatt

TURNING POINT: A BOOK SHOP
75, Town Hall Rd., (Opp.) College House,
Madurai-625001 (Tamil Nadu)
✆ (O) 0452-2347398, 5370937 (R) 5377558,
Fax: 738382 ✉ bookplaza@rediffmail.com
Estd.: 2002; **Prop.:** A.K. Kuppu Ram;
Bus.Intt.: B.S., L.S., WS; **Spl.:** Humanities & Soc.Sci., Tech., Mang., Ars & Arch., Children & Gen. books

TUSHAR PUBLICATIONS
C-21, Jhandewalan, F.F. Complex,
Rani Jhansi Rd., New Delhi-110055
✆ (O) 23671520, 23556407 (R) 26145330,
26148870, Fax: 23610394
✉ subhashgoel_13@sify.com
Estd.: 1990; **Prop.:** Subhash Goel

TWENTIETH CENTURY PUBLICATIONS
N-1, BMC House, Middle Circle,
Connaught Place, New Delhi-110001
✆ 23312187, Telex: 23310417
Estd.: 1977; **Prop.:** Neeru Kaungar;
Bus.Intt.: L.S. and Rt.

■ ■ ■

U.B.S. PUBLISHERS' DISTRIBUTORS LTD.
5, Ansari Rd., Darya Ganj, New Delhi-110002
✆ 23273601, 23266645-46, Cable: ALLBOOKS, Fax: 91-11-23276593, 23274261
✉ ubspd@gobookshopping.com, ubspd@ubspd.com
🌐 www.ubspd.com
Estd.: 1963; **Chairman:** C.M. Chawla
Br.: 10, 1st Main Rd., Gandhi Nagar, Bangalore-560009 (Karnataka) ✆ 22263901, 22253903, 22263902, Fax: 2263904
✉ ubspdbng@eth.net • 60, Nelson, Manickam, Aminji Karai, Chennai-600029 (Tamil Nadu) ✆ 23746272, 23746251, 23746252, Fax: 23746287
✉ ubspd@che.ubspd.com, vijayan@che.ubspd.com • 8-1/B, Chowringhee Lane, Kolkata-700016 (West Bengal) ✆ 22521821, 22522910, 22529437, Fax: 22523027
✉ ubspdcal@cal.vsnl.net.in • 5A, Rajendra Nagar, Patna-800016 (Bihar) ✆ 2672856, 2673973, 2686170, Fax: 2686169
✉ ubspdpat@sancharnet.in • 80, Noronha Rd., Cantonment, Kanpur-208004 (Uttar Pradesh) ✆ 2369124, 2362665, Fax: 2315122 ✉ ubskup@lw1.vsnl.net.in • 143, Maharana Pratap Nagar, Zone-1, Bhopal ✆ 25203183, 25203193, Fax: 2555285
✉ ubspdbhp@sancharnet.in
Bus.Intt.: Pub., WS, L.S. & Rt., Imp., Exp., Sub.Ag.; **Spl.:** Humanities & Soc.Sci., Sci. & Tech., Juvenile/Children, Gen. & Fiction etc.

U.D.H. PUBLISHERS AND DISTRIBUTORS (P) LTD.
4762-63/23, Ansari Rd., Darya Ganj, New Delhi-110002
✆ 23258449, 23246533, 41562623, 41562603, 65499654, Fax: 23258474
✉ udhpd@vsnl.net, udhpd@airtelbroadband.net.in
🌐 www.udhpd.com
Estd.: 1981; **Prop.:** K.K. Thukral;
Br.: 4078, 1st Floor, Nai Sarak, Delhi-110006
✆ 23918642, 23934494, 65499655
Bus.Intt.: Pub. & Dist.; **Spl.:** Text and Reference Books on Comp., Mang., Engg. & Tech.

U.N. BOOK DISTRIBUTORS
S/U-162, Vishakha Enclave, Pitampura, Delhi-110034
✆ 27071558, 27229558
Estd.: 1991; **Hd.Org.:** D.K. Bhatheja; **Bus.Intt.:** L.S.; **Spl.:** Sci., Tech., Mang. and Comp.

U.N. DHRIR & SONS PVT. LTD.
15, Bankim Chatterjee St., Kolkata-700073 (West Bengal)
✆ 22416255, Fax: 91-33-22416255
Hd.Org.: P. Dhar; **Bus.Intt.:** Exp. and Manufacturers of Books

---

U.N. GHOSH & CO.
39/A, Nirmal Chandra St., Kolkata-700012 (West Bengal)

U.P. HINDI SANSTHAN
Hindi Bhavan, M.G. Rd., Hazratganj, Lucknow-226001 (Uttar Pradesh)
Hd.Org.: Rajarshi P.D. Tandon

U.P. SANGEET NATAK AKADEMI
Kesarbagh, Lucknow-226001 (Uttar Pradesh)
Hd.Org.: Viswanath V. Srikande

U.S. PUBLISHERS
CK-37/44B, Bansphatak, Varanasi-221001 (Uttar Pradesh)
✆ 2352240, 2331576
Hd.Org.: Umeshchandra Bhargav

U.S.A. BOOK AGENCIES
Post Box No. 1114, Nanganallur, Chennai-600061 (Tamil Nadu)
✆ 044-22329773
Estd.: 1989; **Bus.Intt.:** B.S.; **Spl.:** Sci. & Tech.

U.S.G. PUBLISHERS & DISTRIBUTORS
Shop No. 11, I-Block Market, Durga Mandir, Sarabha Nagar, Ludhiana-141001 (Punjab)
✆ 2457072, 2460327
Estd.: 1982; **Prop.:** Mrs. Daljit Ghai;
Bus.Intt.: Pub., WS, L.S. and Rt.

UDAI PUSTAK BHANDAR
Gandhi Path, Sasaram, Rohtas-821115 (Bihar)

UDAYA BOOK CENTRE
6, Sivaprakasam St., Mount Rd., Chennai-600002 (Tamil Nadu)
✆ 044-2834401
Hd.Org.: U.M. Husain

UDAYACHAL
Rashtrakavi Dinkar Path, Rajendra Nagar, Patna-800016 (Bihar)

UDAYAN PRAKASANI
7, Ramanath Majumder St., Kolkata-700009 (West Bengal)

UDBODHAN OFFICE
1, Udbodhani Lane, Baghbazar, Kolkata-700003 (West Bengal)
✆ 033-2542248
Spl.: Ramakrishna, Vivekananda Litt. and Vedanta Litt.

UJJAL BOOK STORES
Kolkata (West Bengal)
✆ 23515515, 22416258
✉ itbpc@gems.vsnl.net.in
Bus.Intt.: Pub. and B.S.

UJJAL SAHITYA MANDIR
K-2/1, Marcus Square, Barnaparichya, Kolkata-700007 (West Bengal)
✆ 9433131948
Estd.: 1956; **Hd.Org.**: Snigddya Jyoty Paul; **Bus.Intt.**: Pub. and B.S.; **Spl.**: Bengali Litt.

UMA PUBLISHING
1, Ramanath Majumder St., Kolkata-700009 (West Bengal)

UMA PUSTAK BHANDAR
Mahadeopur, Bhagalpur-554116 (Bihar)
Bus.Intt.: Pub. and B.S.

UMANG BOOKS
37-A, Guru Nanak Marg, Kewal Park Extension, Azadpur, Delhi-110033

UMANG STATIONERIES MART
3, Jayrampur Colony, Indore (Madhya Pradesh)
✆ 266124

UMAR COLLEGE BOOKSHOP
Kupwara, Kashmir-193222 (Jammu & Kashmir)
Estd.: 1991; **Prop.**: Mohamad Umar Baba
Bus.Intt.: Pub., L.S. and Rt.

UMESH PRAKASHAN
100 Luker Ganj, Allahabad-211001 (Uttar Pradesh)
✆ 9335845720
Hd.Org.: Onkar Swaroop Chaturvedi; **Bus.Intt.**: Pub.; **Spl.**: Books on Hindi Lit.

UMESH PRAKASHAN
5, Nath Market, Nai Sarak, Delhi-110006
✆ 22915961, 27114117
Hd.Org.: Shiv Sant

UMESH PUSTAK BHANDAR
Durgawati, Rohtas-821105 (Bihar)

UNICATE PUBLISHERS & DISTRIBUTORS
'Unicate House', 72, Viman Nagar, Pune-411014 (Maharashtra)
✆ 6631067, 6631894, Fax: 6631067
✉ unicate@vsnl.com
🌐 www.unicatepublications.com
Estd.: 1992; **Hd.Org.**: S.D. Sharma; **Bus.Intt.**: Pub. & Dist.; **Spl.**: Books for Children

UNICORN BOOK SERVICE
F-270, Saraswati Kunj Apts., 25, I.P. Extension, Patpar Ganj, Delhi-110092
✆ 22720284, 22724183, 22723713
Fax: 91-11-22720284
✉ unicornbooks@yahoo.com
Estd.: 1993; **Prt.**: Rajeev Kumar, M.L. Kaushal; **Bus.Intt.**: L.S.; **Spl.**: Acad., Comm., Tech., Beh.Sci., Sci., Pure & Applied Books

UNICORN BOOKS PVT. LTD.
J-3/16, Ansari Rd., Darya Ganj, New Delhi-110002
✆ (O) 23272783-84, 23276539 (R) 23969846, Fax: 23257790, 23260518
✉ unicornbooks@vsnl.com
Hd.Org.: Ashok Gupta; **Bus.Intt.**: Pub.; **Spl.**: Edu. Books on Comp., Mang., Business and of Gen. Interest

UNILIB BOOK DISTRIBUTORS
D-5, 1031/21, Khajurikhas, Delhi-110094
✆ (O) & (R) 22172104 ▮ 9811338695, 9811385231
Prop.: Sanjay Sharma; **Bus.Intt.**: L.S.; **Spl.**: Acad., Beh.Sci., Sci., Tech.

UNIMO PUBLICATIONS/UNIVERSAL MEDIA ORGANISATION
3/13, Ground Floor, West Patel Nagar, New Delhi-110008
✆ 25884680
✉ unimo@unito-world.org
🌐 www.unito-world.org
Hd.Org.: Amit Paul; **Bus.Intt.**: Pub. & Exp.; **Spl.**: Indology, Art, Culture, Phil., Edu., etc.

UNIQUE BOOK AGENCY
L.J. College Building, Vastrapur, Ahmedabad-380015 (Gujarat)
✆ 079-6747453, 6742878, Fax: 079-6750417
✉ ljbca@wilnetonline.net, ljcc@wilnetonline.net

UNIQUE BOOK MEDIA
17, Shri Chander Chinnar Complex, Opp. Women College, Maulana Azad Rd., Srinagar-190001 (Jammu & Kashmir)
✆ 2481364
Estd.: 1995; **Hd.Org.**: Mrs. Nighat Ara; **Bus.Intt.**: WS, L.S., & Rt.

UNIQUE BOOK MEDIA
Media Mahal, Friends Colony, Barzulla, Srinagar (Jammu & Kashmir)
✆ (O) 0194-2458436 (R) 2430133
Estd.: 1997; **Man.**: Billal; **Bus.Intt.**: L.S.; **Spl.**: Humanities & Soc.Sci., Sci. & Tech., Comp., Mang., Law

UNIQUE BOOK SERVICE
16/47, Tilak Nagar, New Delhi-110018
Prop.: R.C. Mullick; **Bus.Intt.**: L.S.

UNIQUE BOOKSELLERS
3/79, New M.I.G. Colony, Bandra (E), Mumbai-400051 (Maharashtra)

© 26407833, 26429568
Prop.: Rachana Adsale; **Bus.Intt.:** B.S., Pub. and L.S.

UNIQUE PUBLISHERS
M-51, Lajpat Nagar-II, New Delhi-110024
© 41564400-11, Fax: 91-11-41564422
uniquepublishersindia@gmail.com
www.uniquepublishersindia.com
Estd.: 1979; **Hd.Org.:** Amarjeet Singh Chopra; **Bus.Intt.:** Pub.; **Spl.:** Educational books for various Competitive Exams such as UPSC, SSC, Railway, Banking, American and Anglo-Indian Lit.

UNIQUE SELLERS
G-4, Akarshan Bhawan, 23, Main Ansari Rd., Darya Ganj, New Delhi-110002
© 23245444, 23245111, Fax: 23245111
uniqueselr@hotmail.com
www.uniquesellers.com
Estd.: 1988; **Prop.:** Gurmeet Singh Pooji; **Bus.Intt.:** Pub. & B.S.; **Spl.:** Sci. & Tech.

UNIQUES BOOKS
46, APC Rd., (Opp. U.B.I.), New Barrackpore, Kolkata (West Bengal)
© 25522881

UNISTAR BOOKS PVT. LTD.
SCO 26-27, Sector 34-A, Chandigarh-160022
© 5077427-8, Fax: 5089761
pcis@rediffmail.com
Hd.Org.: Rohit Jain; **Bus.Intt.:** Pub.; **Spl.:** Fiction, Non-fiction, Translations, Books on Sci., Phil., Edu., Med., Self-help, Comp., etc. in English, Hindi, and Punjabi

UNITED BOOK AGENCY
A-762, G.D. Colony, Mayur Vihar, Phase-III, New Delhi-110096
© 22610942
Hd.Org.: Umesh Chandra; **Bus.Intt.:** Dist.; **Spl.:** All Kinds of Books

UNITED BOOK AGENCY
31, College Row, Kolkata-700009 (West Bengal)

UNITED BOOK HOUSE
72-C, Mahatma Gandhi Rd., Kolkata-700009 (West Bengal)

UNITED BOOK HOUSE
C-1/184, Gali No. 22, Khajuri Khas, Delhi-110094
© 22171252
Hd.Org.: M.C. Gupta; **Bus.Intt.:** L.S.; **Spl.:** Fiction and All type of Books

UNITED BOOK TRADERS (THE)
5, Bhagat-Ki-Kothi, New Pali Rd., Jodhpur-342001 (Rajasthan)
© 0291-2624154
scienti@sancharnet.in
www.scentificpub.com
Estd.: 1986; **Prop.:** Mrs. Asha Sharma; **Bus.Intt.:** L.S.; **Spl.:** Humanities & Soc.Sci., Comm., Law, Sci. (Pure & Applied) Engg. & Tech.

UNITED BOOKS & PERIODICALS
7, Vishwadham, Prabhat Colony Rd., Santacruz (West), Mumbai-400055 (Maharashtra)
© 26116909, 26105852
Fax: 91-22-26105852
gavakar@bom4.vsnl.net.in, unitedbooks@vsnl.com
Bus.Intt.: B.S. and Dist.

UNITED CHILDREN'S MOVEMENT REGD.
12A/39, WEA, Karol Bagh, New Delhi-110005
© (O)&(R) 25722830 ▮ 9899435248, Fax: 25781744
darshan@unitedchild.org
www.unitedchildren.org
Estd.: 1979; **Hd.Org.:** Darshan Singh; **Bus.Intt.:** Pub., **Spl.:** Humanities & Soc.Sci., Children & Gen. books

UNITED MAP CO. (DELHI)
L-4, Shastri Nagar, Delhi-110052
© 23657395, 23650165, Fax: 23650165
unimapco@bharatconnect.com
Bus.Intt.: Maps

UNITED NATIONAL UNIV. PUBLICATIONS
A-45, Parayavaram Complex, Maidan Garhi Rd., New Delhi-110063
© (O) 26865084 (R) 26967637
Hd.Org.: Shobha Singh; **Bus.Intt.:** Rt., WS, Pub., Rep., L.S.

UNITED NATIONS EDUCATIONAL, SCIENTIFIC AND CULTURAL ORGANIZATION
UNESCO House, B-5/29, Safdarjung Enclave, New Delhi-110029
© 26713000, Fax: 26713001-2
newdelhi@unesco.org, unesco.delhi@unesco.org
www.unesco.org/newdelhi
Hd.Org.: Minja Yang; **Bus.Intt.:** Pub.; **Spl.:** Books on Higher Edu., Development of Human Resources, Sustainable Development, Evaluation of Sci. and Tech., Safeguarding and Enrichment of Cultural Identities etc. in English

UNITED PERIODICALS SERVICES
A-503/3, Shastri Nagar, Delhi-110052
▮ 9811128028
Estd.: 2002; **Prop.:** Ashok Kumar Jain; **Bus.Intt.:** L.S.; **Spl.:** Journals and Magazines

UNITED PUBLICATION
L-4, Shastri Nagar, Delhi-110052
✆ 23657395, 23650165, Fax: 23650165
✉ unimapco@bharatconnect.com
Hd.Org.: Rajesh Sood; **Bus.Intt.:** Pub.; **Spl.:** Children's Primary Books, Maps, Charts and Globes in all Indian Languages

UNITED PUBLISHERS
Post Box No. 82, Pan Bazar, Main Rd., Guwahati-781001 (Assam)
✆ 2517059, Fax: 2544791
✉ unipub@sancharnet.in
Br.: New Delhi ✆ 23241471, 27241674, Fax: 56022599 ✉ vinmedia@bol.net.in
Bus.Intt.: Pub. and Dist.

UNITED PUBLISHING HOUSE
B-1/12, Safdarjung Enclave, New Delhi-110029
Hd.Org.: Suresh Goyal; **Bus.Intt.:** Pub.; **Spl.:** Children's Textbooks in English and Hindi

UNITED WRITERS
Flat No. 10, 3 Middleton Row, Kolkata-700071 (West Bengal)

UNIVERSAL BOOK AGENCY
G.B. Rd., Gaya-823001 (Bihar)
✆ 221116

UNIVERSAL BOOK COMPANY
20-4-1052, Mahabood Chowk, Hyderabad-500002 (Andhra Pradesh)

UNIVERSAL BOOK COMPANY
20, Mahatma Gandhi Marg, Allahabad-211001 (Uttar Pradesh)
✆ (O) 2623467 (R) 2624953, Fax: 0532-2624383
Estd.: 1948; **Bus.Intt.:** B.S.; **Spl.:** School, Graduate, Adv. Books for Lib., Gen., Humanities, Sci., Med. and Comp. Books

UNIVERSAL BOOK CORPORATION
546, Kalbadevi Rd., Dhobitalao, PB No. 2540, Mumbai-400002 (Maharashtra)
✆ 22061159, 22016122, 22050629, 22078096, Fax: 22014080, 22062404
✉ unibooks@vsnl.com
Estd.: 1928; **Prop.:** Shamim Shroff; **Bus.Intt.:** Pub., WS, L.S. and Rt., Imp., Exp. and Sub.Ag.

UNIVERSAL BOOK DEALS
C-40, Shanker Nagar, Shivaji Rd., Bhopal-6 (Madhya Pradesh)

UNIVERSAL BOOK DEPOT
Khazanchi Rd., Patna-800004 (Bihar)

UNIVERSAL BOOK DEPOT
Mai Hiran Gate, Jalandhar City-144008
✆ 2400396
Estd.: 1970; **Hd.Org.:** Subhash C. Rakheja; **Bus.Intt.:** L.S. & Rt.; **Spl.:** Humanities & Soc.Sci., Sci. & Tech., Juvenile/Children Books, Gen. & Fiction etc.

UNIVERSAL BOOK DISTRIBUTING CO.
First Floor, Arif Chambers I, Kapoorthala Complex, Lucknow-226020 (Uttar Pradesh)
✆ 2374909, 2333401, Fax: 2374909
✉ ubdco@sancharnel.in, ubdco@lw1.vsnl.net.in
Estd.: 1974; **Man.:** R.C. Lal
Br.: M-14-B, Gole Market, Mahanagar, Lucknow ✆ 2387180 • A-1, Arif Chamber I, Kapoorthala Complex, Lucknow ✆ 2329641 • Near Bhootnath Temple, Shivani Market, Lucknow ✆ 2352387 • 2/300, Vivek Khand Gomti Nagar, Lucknow ✆ 2392720
Bus.Intt.: L.S. & Rt., Imp.; **Spl.:** Humanities & Soc.Sci., Sci. & Tech., Juvenile/Children, Gen. & Fiction etc.

UNIVERSAL BOOK DISTRIBUTORS (P) LTD.
5, Ansari Rd., Post Box-7081, New Delhi-110002
✆ 23273601, 23266647, 23280292
Cable: ALLBOOKS, Fax: 91-11-23267593
Estd.: 1977; **Dir.:** C.M. Chawla; **Bus.Intt.:** Imp.; **Spl.:** Humanities & Soc.Sci., Sci. & Tech., Med., Law, Juvenile/ Children, Gen. & Fiction etc.

UNIVERSAL BOOK HOUSE
A-31, Jal Jawalaji Building, Vijayanagar, Pragatinagar Rd., Naranpura, Ahmedabad-600013 (Gujarat)
✆ 27472685, Fax: 079-27436053
Prop.: R.K. Sharma; **Bus.Intt.:** WS, L.S. and Rt.; **Spl.:** Humanities and Soc.Sci., Mang. & Comm., Sci.: Pure and Applied Engg. & Tech.

UNIVERSAL BOOKSELLERS
82, Hazratganj, Post Box No. 20, Lucknow-226001 (Uttar Pradesh)
✆ 2225894, 2224135, 2238398, Fax: 2218547
✉ universal@lwl.vsnl.net.in
Estd.: 1974; **Hd.Org.:** Chander Prakash
Bus.Intt.: Pub., WS, L.S. and Rt., Imp.; **Spl.:** Gen. and Trade, Acad., Professional, Children, Electronic Products (CD-ROMS) (Indian and Foreign Books)

UNIVERSAL BOOK SERVICE
7/15, Marhatal, Jabalpur-482002 (Madhya Pradesh)
✆ 2310591, 2314961, Fax: 2313843
✉ manish_batheja@yahoo.com
Hd.Org.: Anoop Chand; **Bus.Intt.:** B.S.

UNIVERSAL BOOK SERVICE
28, Budhwar Peth, Pune-411002 (Maharashtra)

✆ 4455188
✉ universalbooks@eth.net
Bus.Intt.: B.S. and Dist.

UNIVERSAL BOOK SHOP
27, DDA Shopping Centre, Arjun Nagar, Safdarjung Enclave, New Delhi-110029
✆ (O) 26101076, 26103896 (R) 26186743, 26185044 ▮ 9810228919, Fax: 26103896, 26185044
✉ ubsbookshop@yahoo.com
Estd.: 1997; **Prop.:** K. Kishore Verma
Br.: I-1/16, Ansari Rd., Darya Ganj, New Delhi-110002 ✆ 23270654
Bus.Intt.: Rt., L.S.; **Spl.:** Med., Tech., Fiction

UNIVERSAL BOOK STALL
1697, Nai Sarak, Delhi-110006
✆ (O) 23261903, 23250653, 23273601 (R) 25787112, Fax: 011-23272595, 23250653
✉ ubsns@bol.net.in
Prt.: Puran Lal Arora, Vjay Kumar Arora, Hari Saran Arora; **Bus.Intt.:** WS, Rt., L.S.; **Spl.:** Med., Dental, Pharmacy, Nursing, Comp. Engg., Sci.—Pure & Applied, Mang., Beh. & Soc.Sci.

UNIVERSAL BOOK STALL
5, Ansari Rd., New Delhi-110002
✆ 23273601, 23266646
Fax: 91-11-23274261, 23276593
✉ ubspd@upspd.com
🌐 www.upspd.com
Hd.Org.: C.M. Chawla; **Bus.Intt.:** Dist.; **Spl.:** Textbooks on Mang., Self-improvement, English Language, Litt. and Humanities by Indian and Foreign Pub.

UNIVERSAL BOOK STORE
1, Sanjeve Naik Lane, Avenue Rd. Cross, Bangalore-560002 (Karnataka)
✆ (O) 22270074 (R) 23412375
Estd.: 1993; **Hd.Org.:** Raj and Shyam Kapoor; **Bus.Intt.:** Rt. and WS; **Spl.:** Med., Dental, Nursing, Pharmacy, Comp. Sci., Mang.

UNIVERSAL BOOK STORE
Med. Market, Ashok Rajpath, Patna-800004 (Bihar)
✆ 2666310
Estd.: 1982; **Prop.:** Kamal Kapoor; **Bus.Intt.:** Rt. and WS

UNIVERSAL BOOK STORE
S.C.O. 68, Sector-17D, Chandigarh-160017
✆ 0712-2702558
Estd.: 1949; **Hd.Org.:** Bupesh Batheja; **Bus.Intt.:** Rt. B.S. and L.S.; **Spl.:** Gen., Comp. and All text Books (Foreign and Indian)

UNIVERSAL BOOK TRADERS
80, Gokhale Market, Opp. Tis Hazari Courts, Delhi-110054
✆ 23911966, 23990487, 23961288, Fax: 23924152
✉ unilaw@vsnl.com
🌐 www.unilawbooks.com
Estd.: 1956; **Man.Prt.:** M.G. Arora
Br.: C-27, Connaught Place, (Between Odeon & Plaza Cinema), New Delhi-110001
✆ (O) 23416277, 23418671 (R) 27434438, 27234101, Fax: 23418014
✉ unilaw@vsnl.com
Bus.Intt.: WS, L.S. & Rt., Imp., Exp.; **Spl.:** Law

UNIVERSAL BOOKSELLERS & PUBLISHERS DISTRIBUTORS
Pacca Danga, Jammu Tawi-180001 (Jammu & Kashmir)
✆ 2573574
Estd.: 1997; **Prop.:** Om Prakash Kohli; **Bus.Intt.:** Pub., WS, L.S. & Rt.; **Spl.:** Humanities & Soc.Sci., Sci. & Tech., Med., Law

UNIVERSAL JOURNAL SERVICES
769/1, Lake Town, Block-A, Kolkata-700089 (West Bengal)

UNIVERSAL LAW PUBLISHING CO. PVT. LTD.
C-FF-IA, Ansal's Dilkhus Industrial Estate, G.T. Karnal Rd., Delhi-110033
✆ (O) 27215334, 27438103, 27458529 (R) 27459020, 27234101, 27459023, Fax: 27459022
✉ unilaw@vsnl.com
🌐 www.unilawbooks.com
Estd.: 1995; **Chairman.:** M.G. Arora, **Dir.:** Pradeep Arora, Sajeev Arora, Manish Arora; **Bus.Intt.:** Pub.; **Spl.:** Law

UNIVERSAL PUBLICATION
401, Ganesh Complex, Khajuri Bazar, Indore-452002 (Madhya Pradesh)
✆ 2453094
Hd.Org.: C.S. Sharma

UNIVERSAL PUBLISHERS DISTRIBUTORS
B-10, South Ganesh Nagar, Patparganj Rd., Delhi-110092
Bus.Intt.: Pub. and Dist.

UNIVERSAL PUBLISHING CORPORATION
534, Kalbadevi Rd., Dhobitalao, PB No. 2540, Mumbai-400001 (Maharashtra)
✆ 22061159, 22016122
Estd.: 1985; **Prop.:** S.A. Shroff; **Bus.Intt.:** Pub., WS, L.S. and Rt., Imp., Exp.

UNIVERSAL SUBSCRIPTION AGENCY (P) LTD.
Plot No. 877, Phase-V, Udyog Vihar,
Gurgaon-122016 (Haryana)
✆ 0124-5001410-13, Fax: 5052913
✉ gistdel@gistglobal.com
www.gistglobal.com
Estd.: 1980; **Man.Dir.:** A.K. Chawla
Br.: 18-19, Community Centre, Saket, New Delhi-110017 ✆ 26519579, Cable: WORLDMAGS • 119-A, A-5 Bldg, 1st Floor, Lok Bharti, Marol Maroshi Rd., Andheri-East, Mumbai-400059
9820430866
✉ gistmum@gistglobal.com
• Unit-B, 2nd Floor, Samilton, Chambers, 181/1, A.T.C. Bose Rd., Kolkata-700014
✆ 033-22842111, 22841127, Fax: 22849773
✉ gistcal@gistglobal.com
• Prestige Meredian-II, Unit No. S-306, Block-2, Level-3, M.G. Rd., Bangalore-560001
✆ 080-25595564, 25595593, Fax: 25595564
✉ gistban@gistglobal.com
Bus.Intt.: L.S. & Rt., Imp., Sub.Ag.; **Spl.:** Sci. & Tech., Med.

UNIVERSITIES PRESS (INDIA) LTD.
3-6-752, Himayat Nagar, Hyderabad-500029 (Andhra Pradesh)
✆ 27662849/50, Fax: 27645046
✉ hyd2_upilco@sancharnet.in, upilcoend@dot.net.in
www.universitiespress.com
Hd.Org.: Madhu Reddy; **Bus.Intt.:** Pub.; **Spl.:** Acad. and Edu. Books on Sci., Tech. and Mang.

UNIVERSITIES PRESS (INDIA) PVT. LTD.
Indian Mercantile Chambers, Kamani Marg, Ballard Estate, Mumbai-400038 (Maharashtra)
✆ 22616918, 22616919, Cable: LONGMANS, Telefax: 011-84934
Bus.Intt.: Exp.

UNIVERSITY BOOK CENTRE
Opp. Medical Crossing, Delhi Rd., Rohtak-124001 (Haryana)
✆ 212041
Estd.: 1978; **Prop.:** Radhe Shyam Sharma; **Bus.Intt.:** Dist.; **Spl.:** Indian and Foreign Books

---

UNIVERSITY BOOK DEPOT
S.C.O. 49-51, Sector-17C, Chandigarh-160017
✆ (O) 2703273 (R) 2564681
Estd.: 1971; **Hd.Org.:** Narinder Pahuja; **Bus.Intt.:** Rt. B.S.; **Spl.:** Eng., Hindi and Punjabi

---

UNIVERSITY BOOK HOUSE
15-UB, Bangalow Rd., Jawahar Nagar, Delhi-110007
✆ (O) 23919154 (R) 27259272
Telefax: 23977542
Prop.: S.M. Katial, Sanjay M. Katial, Sajal M. Katial; **Bus.Intt.:** Pub., Rt., L.S.; **Spl.:** Beh.Sci., Soc.Sci., Mang. & Law

---

UNIVERSITY BOOK HOUSE
Prakasham Rd., Tirupati-517506 (Andhra Pradesh)

UNIVERSITY BOOK HOUSE PVT. LTD.
79, Chaura Rasta, Jaipur-302003 (Rajasthan)
✆ 2311466, 2313382, Fax: 91-141-4013697
✉ uni_bookhouse@yahoo.com
Estd.: 1991; **Hd.Org.:** C.K. Jain; **Bus.Intt.:** Pub., Dist. & L.S.; **Spl.:** Comm., Mang., Home Sci., Hist., Pol.Sci., Public Administration, etc.

UNIVERSITY OF KASHMIR, SRINAGAR
University Campus, Hazratbal, Srinagar-190006 (Jammu & Kashmir)
✆ 91-194-2427448, Fax: 91-194-2427448
✉ rufai@kashmiruniversity.net
www.kashmiruniversity.net
Hd.Org.: Abdul Wahid Qureshi; **Bus.Intt.:** Promoter; **Spl.:** Books and Journals on Various Disciplines

---

UNIVERSITY PUBLICATION
7/31, Ansari Rd., Darya Ganj, New Delhi-110002
✆ 23243006
Estd.: 1995; **Bus.Intt.:** Pub. and Dist.; **Spl.:** Hindi Gen. Books for Library Supplies

---

UNIVERSITY PUBLICATIONS
Vishalakshi Bhawan, Chowk, Varanasi-221001 (Uttar Pradesh)
Hd.Org.: Anuraj Modi

UNMESH PRAKASHAN
26, Parvati, Pune-411001 (Maharashtra)

UPADHYAY BOOK SERVICE
B/2, C/5, Janak Puri, New Delhi-110058
Prop.: Padma Dutt Upadhyay; **Bus.Intt.:** L.S.

UPKAR PRAKASHAN
A-1/279, Lawrence Rd., Delhi-110035
Hd.Org.: Krishan Kumar

UPKAR PRAKASHAN
2/11A, Swadeshi Bima Nagar, Agra-282002 (Uttar Pradesh)
✆ (O) 91-562-2530966, 3208693
9837050002 (R) 2531313, 2530390, Fax: 91-562-2531940
✉ info@upkarprakashan.com
www.upkarprakashan.com
Estd.: 1972; **Hd.Org.:** Mahendra S. Jain; **Bus.Intt.:** Pub.; **Spl.:** Books in English and Hindi on Competitive Exams and Sub. of Gen.

Interest, and Hindi Magazines *Pratiyogita Darpan* and *Samanya Gyan Darpan*

UPPAL PUBLISHING HOUSE/ UPPAL BOOK STORE
3, Ansari Rd., Darya Ganj,
New Delhi-110002
✆ (O) 23273756, 23286571 (R) 22083884
Fax: 23286571
✉ uph@mantraonline.com
Estd.: 1967; **Prt.**: Bhim Sen Uppal, Shadi Lal Uppal, Rakesh Uppal, Sunil Uppal
Bus.Intt.: Pub., Dist., L.S.; **Spl.**: Soc.Sci., Humanities, Mang., Library Sci., Beh.Sci. and Gen. Books

UPPANI PUBLICATIONS
St. Vincent Monastery, Pala,
Kottayam-686575 (Kerala)
✆ 22493
Estd.: 1990; **Prop.**: Mathew Edamana;
Bus.Intt.: Pub.

UPPER INDIA TECHNOLOGIES (E-DIKSHA.COM)
201, C.R.S. Bhawan, 1/28, Main Market,
Tilak Nagar, New Delhi-110018
✆ 25993861, 25912191, 25912205
▮ 9810475590, Fax: 91-11-25993861
✉ ediksha@bol.net.in
www.ediksha.com
Hd.Org.: Inder Ratra; **Bus.Intt.**: Pub. & Dist.;
Spl.: Edu. Books, CDs and Other Edu. Aids

UPVAN GRANTHALAYA
Sonamukhi Nagar, Sangaria Fanta,
Salawas Rd., Jodhpur-342005 (Rajasthan)
✆ 2748488, 2747931, Fax: 5120509
✉ upvangranthalaya@sify.com
Hd.Org.: Sanjeev Prajapati; **Bus.Intt.**: Pub. & Dist.; **Spl.**: Med. Plants, Gardening, Farming, Fertilisers, Pesticides, Horticulture, etc.

URDU ACADEMY, DELHI
CPO Building, Kashmere Gate, Delhi-110006
✆ 23863697, 23830635/36/37/38,
Fax: 91-11-23863773
✉ urduacademydelhi@yahoo.co.in
Hd.Org.: M.H. Abidi; **Bus.Intt.**: Pub.;
Spl.: Urdu Litt. on Soc., Cultural and Language Issues

URDU BOOK REVIEW
1739/3 Basement, New Kohinoor Hotel,
Pataudi House, Darya Ganj,
New Delhi-110002
✆ 23266347
✉ artifiqbalubr@yahoo.co.in
www.urdubookreview.com
Hd.Org.: M. Arif Iqbal; **Bus.Intt.**: Pub.;
Spl.: Urdu Journal on Books carrying Book Reviews on all subjects and index of Urdu research papers, Magazines, Journals, etc.

URDU MARKAR
Azeemabad, Patna-800001 (Bihar)

URDU SAHITYA AKADEMI
Old Vidhan Sabha Building, Sector-17,
Gandhinagar-382017 (Gujarat)
✆ 3226897
Hd.Org.: V.V. Pandit; **Bus.Intt.**: Pub.;
Spl.: Books on Urdu Litt.

URDU SCIENCE
665/12, Zakir Nagar, New Delhi-110025
✆ 26924366, Fax: 26924366
✉ parvaiz@ndf.vsnl.net.in
Hd.Org.: M. Aslam Parvaiz; **Bus.Intt.**: Pub., Dist.; **Spl.**: Urdu Sci. Monthly, Sci. Litt. in Urdu

URMILA ENTERPRISES
Naugachia, Bhagalpur-853204 (Bihar)
Bus.Intt.: Pub. and B.S.

URVISH BOOK STORES
7, Triveni Apartment, Timaliyawad,
Surat-395001 (Gujarat)
✆ (O) 2475102, 2470405 (R) 2473302
✉ urvishstores@yahoo.com
Estd.: 1975; **Bus.Intt.**: Pub. and B.S.;
Spl.: School, Adv. Books for Lib. and Gen.

USBORNE PUBLISHING
B-5/47, Safdarjung Enclave,
New Delhi-110029
✆ 26169147
✉ overleaf@vsnl.net
Hd.Org.: Yvonne Riddell; **Bus.Intt.**: Pub.;
Spl.: Edu. books for Children in English

USEFUL BOOK SERVICE
S-3/21-23, Shastri Market, Near 'B' Block Crossing, Indira Nagar, Lucknow-226016 (Uttar Pradesh)
✆ 2380063, 2346805, 2769345, Fax: 2388535
✉ useful@id.eth.net, useful@satyam.net.in
Estd.: 1988; **Man.Dir.**: Alok K. Gupta;
Bus.Intt.: L.S. & Rt., Imp.; **Spl.**: Humanities & Soc.Sci., Sci. & Tech.

USHA BOOKS INTERNATIONAL
7, Rajendra Nagar, Patna-800016 (Bihar)
✆ 2665701, 2687149
Estd.: 1995; **Prop.**: H.L. Gulati;
Bus.Intt.: Pub., WS; **Spl.**: Humanities & Soc.Sci.

USHA PUBLICATIONS
1, Ansari Rd., Darya Ganj, New Delhi-110002

USHA PUBLICATIONS
Neem St., Veer Mohalla, Jodhpur-342001 (Rajasthan)
Estd.: 1974; **Hd.Org.**: Ms. Usha Thanvi;
Bus.Intt.: Pub.; **Spl.**: English Books and Periodicals

USHA PUBLISHING HOUSE
13/1, B.C. Chatterjee St., Kolkata-700073 (West Bengal)

USHA UPADHYAY
617, 38th Main, Rajender Nagar, Bangalore (Karnataka)

UTKARSH BOOK SERVICE
701, Deccan Gymkhana, Pune-411001 (Maharashtra)
✆ (O) 2322479, 2327958 (R) 2372389, 2367836
Estd.: 1965; **Prop.:** S.V. Joshi; **Bus.Intt.:** Pub., Dist., L.S., Rt., WS, B.S.

UTKARSH BOOKS DISTRIBUTORS
New Delhi
✆ 26496964
✉ utkarshbd@rediffmail.com
Bus.Intt.: B.S. and Dist.

UTKARSH PRAKASHAN
H-19/60, Sector-7, Rohini, Delhi-110085

UTKARSH PUBLICATIONS
RZ-B-72, Pratap Garden, Uttam Nagar, New Delhi-110059
✆ 25533689, Fax: 25533897
✉ kokchalovebug@rediffmail.com
Hd.Org.: Rekha Kokcha; **Bus.Intt.:** Pub.; **Spl.:** Stories and Novels on Soc. Aspects in Hindi

UTPAL PUBLICATIONS
R-22, Khaneja Complex, 2nd Floor, Shakarpur, Delhi-110092
✆ (O) 22464458 (R) 26493456
▮ 9818447636
✉ utpalbooks@rediffmail.com
Prop.: Utpal Kaul; **Bus.Intt.:** Pub., L.S.; **Spl.:** Kashmir Litt.

UTSAB PUBLICATIONS
C/o Prekshan Newspaper, Sudarsanpur, Raiganj-733134 (West Bengal)

UTTAM PRAKASHAN
1/5971, Kabul Nagar, Shahdara, Delhi-110032
✆ 65458628
Hd.Org.: Arun Maheshwari; **Bus.Intt.:** Pub. & Dist.; **Spl.:** Books in Hindi and English

UTTAM PRAKASHANI
23/2, Chatterjee Para Lane, Kadamtala Howrah-711101 (West Bengal)

UTTAM PUSTAK BHANDAR
Natwar, Rohtas-802218 (Bihar)

UTTAR BIHAR ARYA SABHA
Arya Samaj, Ghimipokhar, Muzaffarpur-842001 (Bihar)

UTTAR PRADESH HINDI SANSTHAN
Rajarshi P.D. Tandon Hindi Bhavan, 6, Mahatma Gandhi Marg, Lucknow-226001 (Uttar Pradesh)
✆ 3048205-06, Fax: 91-522-3048205
✉ director@hindisansthan.in
🌐 www.hindisansthan.in
Estd.: 1976; **Hd.Org.:** Sunil Kumar Saxena **Bus.Intt.:** Pub.; **Spl.:** Sci., Tech. and Reference Books in Hindi

UTTAR PRADESH SANGEET NATAK ACADEMI
Kesar Bagh, Lucknow-226001 (Uttar Pradesh)
✆ 246872, 2458244, 234933
Hd.Org.: Vishavnath B. Shrikhandey; **Bus.Intt.:** Pub.; **Spl.:** Theatre and Drama

UTTAR PRADESH URDU AKADEMI
Vibhuti Khand, Gomti Nagar, Lucknow-226010 (Uttar Pradesh)
✆ 2720683, Fax: 2720683
✉ upuacc@avadh.net
Hd.Org.: Mohammad Shahidullah Khan; **Bus.Intt.:** Pub.; **Spl.:** Literary, Acad., Reference and Children's Books in Urdu

■ ■ ■

V. PUBLICATION BOOK STALL
College Rd., Kottayam-686001 (Kerala)
✆ 0481-2567470/71, 2302980
✉ info@vpublishers.com
Estd.: 1986; **Prop.:** P.R. Samiyath;
Bus.Intt.: B.S. and Rt.

V. PUBLISHERS
P.O. Box 31, College Rd., Kottayam-686001 (Kerala)
✆ 0481-2567470, 2567471
Estd.: 1972; **Prop.:** V.K. Moosakutty;
Bus.Intt.: Pub., L.S.; **Spl.:** Low Priced V. Dictionaries

V. VALLIAPPAN
8, Second Cross, Vivekananda Colony, Kanakapura Rd., J.P. Nagar, Bangalore-560078 (Karnataka)
✆ 2643250, Fax: 26633706
Bus.Intt.: Consultant

V.B. ANUSANDHAN PARISHAD
Shantiniketan Professors Colony, Jnanpur, Varanasi-221304 (Uttar Pradesh)
Hd.Org.: Kapil Dev Dwivedi

V.B.D. PUBLICATIONS
First Floor, Surana Chambers, Gandhi Chowk, Sadar, Nagpur-440001 (Maharashtra)
✆ 253684, Fax: 0712-2555092
Estd.: 1987; **Hd.Org.:** S.K. Banerjee;
Bus.Intt.: Pub.; **Spl.:** Help Books Diploma and Degree Level for Engg. and Pharmacy Students

V.K. BOOK EXHIBITORS
G-31, Vishnu Garden, New Delhi-110018
✆ (O) & (R) 25103714
Prop.: Vijay Kumar Kharwal; **Bus.Intt.:** Dealers;
Spl.: All Kinds of Children Books, Gen., Reference Books, L.S.

V.K. (INDIA) ENTERPRISES
4323/3, Ansari Rd., Darya Ganj, New Delhi-110002
✆ 23250105, 23250106, Fax: 23250141
✉ trjain@vsnl.com, delhi@vkpublications.com
🌐 www.vkpublication.com
Estd.: 1985; **Prop.:** Rahul Jain
Br.: Bazar Radha Kishan, Ambala City
✆ 91-171-2519130, 2519448
✉ ambala@vkpublications.com
• 83, Marudhar Nagar, Jaipur
✆ 91-982915541
✉ jaipur@vkpublications.com
• Bangalore, Contact Person: Mr. B Manjunath
✆ 91-9986167032
✉ banglore@vkpublications.com
Bus.Intt.: Pub., WS, L.S.; **Spl.:** Soc.Sci., Comm. & Eco.

V.K. PUBLICATIONS
5, Ansari Rd., Darya Ganj, New Delhi-110002
✆ 23290105, Fax: 91-11-23290141
✉ trijain@vsnl.com
Prop.: Mrs. Vimla Kumari Jain
Bus.Intt.: Pub., L.S. and Wholesaler;
Spl.: Soc.Sci., Commerce & Eco.

V.K. PUBLISHERS
380, V, Block, Rajajinagar, Bangalore-560010 (Karnataka)

V.K. PUBLISHING HOUSE
10, Subhash Market, Bareilly (Uttar Pradesh)

V.K.G. BOOKS INTERNATIONAL
New Delhi
✆ 26480970, 26421114, Fax: 26486287
✉ vkgboks@ndb.vsnl.net.in
Bus.Intt.: B.S.

V.P.H. SUBSCRIPTION SERVICES
106, Vivekananda Rd., Kolkata-700006 (West Bengal)
Telex: 2413389, Fax: 23588297
✉ vijoyaph@cal2.vsnl.net.in
Estd.: 1999; **Bus.Intt.:** Sub.Ag.; **Spl.:** Med., Humanities & Soc.Sci., Sci. & Tech.

V.R. ENTERPRISES
D-11, Delhi Citizen Society, Sector-13, Rohini, Delhi-110085
✆ 27565562, Fax: 27865139
✉ vrenterprises@mantraonline.com
Ch.Exe.: Vipul Kumar; **Bus.Intt.:** Supplier;
Spl.: Edu. Teaching Aids, Maps, Charts, Globes and Display Systems

V.R.P. PUBLISHERS
203A, Sukh Sagar, N.S. Patkar Marg, Opera House, Mumbai-400007 (Maharashtra)

V.S.N. & CO.
Maruthy Nagar, 1st Line, Vijayawada-520004 (Andhra Pradesh)

V.S.P. BOOKS INTERNATIONAL
E-66, Kalkaji, New Delhi-110019
Prop.: Ashok Kumar
Br.: B-7/88, Skipper House, 88, Nehru Place, New Delhi-110019
✆ 26438812, Telefax: 031-66608
Spl.: Sci. and Tech. Books and L.S.

VAARAANTARI RANI (RANI WEEKLY)
1091, Periyar Ever High Rd., Chennai-600007 (Tamil Nadu)
✆ 25324771, Cable: VARARANI
✉ rani.chen@gems.vsnl.net.in
Estd.: 1962; **Hd.Org.:** Rani Syndicate; **Bus.Intt.:** Exp.

VAASTU-FENGSHUI-HOME DECORS
New Delhi
✆ 25701836
✉ wondervision@hotmail.com

VADYAR & SONS
Palghat-678001 (Kerala)

VADYARAMBHAM PUBLISHERS
Maithanam, Varkala-695141 (Kerala)
✆ 22871, 23773
Estd.: 1984; **Prop.:** S. Viswanath; **Bus.Intt.:** Pub. and B.S.

VAGDEVI BOOKSELLERS
Gur Banga Complex, 47-15-4, Dwaraka Nagar, Visakhapatnam-16 (Andhra Pradesh)
✆ 0891-2547264
Estd.: 1996; **Hd.Org.:** M. Narasimha Murthy; **Bus.Intt.:** B.S., Rt. and L.S.; **Spl.:** Gen. and Trade, Acad., Professional, Children Books Greeting Cards and Toys (Indian and Foreign)

VAGDEVI PRAKASHAN
Sugan Nivas, Chandan Sagar, Bikaner-334001 (Rajasthan)
✆ (O)&(R) 2200955, 2521200, Fax: 2204100
✉ vagdevi_jp1@sancharnet.in
www.vagdevi.biz
Estd.: 1986; **Hd.Org.:** Mahima Sankhla; **Bus.Intt.:** Pub.; **Spl.:** Books in Hindi on Litt., Art, Culture, Phil., Pol.Sci., Hist., etc.

VAGYOGA CHETANA PUBLICATION
Yogic Voice Consciousness Institute, B-3/131-A, Shivala, Varanasi-221001 (Uttar Pradesh)
✆ 2311706, Fax: 0542-2314615
✉ Vagyoga@hotmail.com
Estd.: 1981; **Hd.Org.:** Vachaspati Tripathi

VAIBHAV BOOK CENTRE
688, Narayan Peth, Appa Balawant Chowk, Pune-400030 (Maharashtra)
✆ 2456951

VAIBHAV ENTERPRISES
30-G, Pocket-IV, Mayur Vihar, Phase-I Delhi-110091
✆ 22713593 ▮ 9811389367
Estd.: 1996; **Prop.:** Neeraj Kumar Sharma; **Bus.Intt.:** L.S.; **Spl.:** Beh.Sci., Comm., Sci., Tech., Comp., Mang., Arts & Arch. Books

VAIBHAV LITCO
90-C, D.D.A. Colony, Gulabi Bagh, Delhi-110007
✆ 38108989, 20043308 ▮ 9810425755, Telefax: 23646564
✉ vaibhavlitco@rediffmail.com
Hd.Org.: Balraj Sharma; **Bus.Intt.:** Rt., WS, L.S.; **Spl.:** Beh.Sci., Med., Tech.

VAIBHAV PRAKASHAN
755, Sadashiv Peth, Fadtara Chowk, Pune-411030 (Maharashtra)

VAIBHAVSHALI
10607-A, Mohan Park, Naveen Shahdara, Delhi-110032
✆ 22825580, Fax: 91-11-22825582
Hd.Org.: Sunita; **Bus.Intt.:** Pub.; **Spl.:** Children books

VAICHARIKI SANKALAN
334-A, Mayur Vihar-I, Pocket-II, Delhi-110091
Hd.Org.: Smt. Monika Mohini

VAICHARIKI SANKALAN
B-65, Mayur Vihar, Phase-I, Delhi-110091
✆ 22492676
Hd.Org.: Mohini Chopra

VAIDYANATH AYURVED BHAVAN LTD.
Great Nag Rd., Nagpur-440009 (Maharashtra)
✆ 2741867, 2742325

VAK (THE SPIRITUAL BOOKSHOP)
P.O. Sri Aurobindo Ashram, 16, J.N. St., Pondicherry-605002
✆ 234908, 234542
✉ himatsingka@auroville.org.in
Estd.: 1982; **Bus.Intt.:** Exp.

VAK-SAHITYA (P) LTD.
33, College Row, Kolkata-700009 (West Bengal)

VAKILS FEFFER AND SUMENS LTD.
Haque Building, 9, Spratt Rd., Ballard Estate, Mumbai-400001 (Maharashtra)
✆ (O) 22619121, 22611221 (R) 22631977, Fax: 22610432
✉ bimal@vakilsonline.com
www.vakilsonline.com, www.vakilspublications.com
Estd.: 1960; **Hd.Org.:** Bimal A. Mehta; **Spl.:** Art, Cookery, Rel., and Mythology, Child Care and Gen. Non-fiction

VALARUNNA PRAKASHAN
Vazhode, Karumom P.O., Thiruvananthapuram-695002 (Kerala)

VALLABH PRAKASHAN
C/o S.V.-221, Pitampura, Delhi-110034

VALLEY BOOK HOUSE
Kashmir University Rd., Srinagar-190006 (Jammu & Kashmir)
✆ 2428526, Fax: 2427537
✉ telehamid1@rediffmail.com

Estd.: 1994; Prt.: Ab. Hamid, Altaf Ahamed; Bus.Intt.: Pub., WS, L.S. & Rt., Sub.Ag.; Spl.: Humanities & Soc.Sci., Sci. & Tech., Med., Law, Gen. & Fiction etc.

VALLI PATHIPPAGAM
4/6, New Kancheepuram Rd., Cheyyaru-604407 (Tamil Nadu)

VALLI PUTHAGA NILAYAM
8A, Sundareswara Koil St., Royapettah, Chennai-600014 (Tamil Nadu)
Prop.: M.R.M. Karuppaiah; **Bus.Intt.:** Pub.; **Spl.:** Novels, Short Stories, Essays, Children Books, Self-Improvement Books, Rel. Books

VALLUVAR PANNAI
22, Second Main Rd., C.I.T. Nagar, Chennai-600035 (Tamil Nadu)
✆ 24330511
Prop.: N. Palanniyappan

VALNES ART FOUNDATION
9, Bishop Wallers Avenue, Chennai (Tamil Nadu)

VALUE BOOKS PVT. LTD.
15-A/55, W.E.A., Saraswati Marg, Karol Bagh, New Delhi-110005
✆ 98105-07555, 98115-28900, Fax: 91-11-25860888
✉ galoswal@yahoo.com
Hd.Org.: Gurbachan Singh; **Bus.Intt.:** Imp. and Dist.

VANASHREE PRAKASHAN
Ujire-574240 (Karnataka)

VANATHI PATHIPPAGAM
13, Deevidayala St., T. Nagar, Chennai-600017 (Tamil Nadu)
✆ 24342810
Prop.: Y. Thirunavukkarasu; **Bus.Intt.:** Pub. and B.S.; **Spl.:** Quality Tamil Books

VANDNA BOOK AGENCY
109-B Block, Ground Floor, Preet Vihar, Delhi-110092
✆ 22050766
Hd.Org.: Vandna Sharma; **Bus.Intt.:** Pub.; **Spl.:** Hindi language books on culture, general knowledge, self-improvement and books for children

VANI PRAKASHAN
4695-21-A, Ansari Rd., Darya Ganj, New Delhi-110002
✆ (O) 23273167, 23275710 (R) 22286292, 22110879, Fax: 23275710
✉ vaniprakashan@gmail.com, vani_prakashan@mantraonline.com
Prop.: Arun Maheshwari; **Bus.Intt.:** Pub.; **Spl.:** Books on Hindi Lit.

VANITY BOOKS INTERNATIONAL
A-38/2, Maya Puri, New Delhi-110064

VANJIKKO PATHIPPAGAM
9, Kurai Nagar, Madurai-18 (Tamil Nadu)

VANS INFORMATION AND INVESTOR SERVICES LTD.
New Delhi
✆ 23279201, 23279202, Fax: 23279203
✉ vansdel@nda.vsnl.net.in
Bus.Intt.: WS, Rt. and L.S., Pub. and Dist.

VANSHA BOOKS INTERNATIONAL
3722 (First Floor) N.S. Marg, Darya Ganj, New Delhi-110002
✆ 23273561, 27211827, 23201598
Fax: 91-11-27211827
Estd.: 2000; **Prop.:** Ms. Vandana Kochhar **Bus.Intt.:** WS, Pub.'s Rep.; **Spl.:** Acad., Beh.Sci., Soc.Sci., Sci., Pure & Applied, Tech., Law, Juveniles & Fiction

VANYA PRAKASHAN
Rajiv Gandhi Bhavan, 35, Shyamala Hills, Bhopal-462002 (Madhya Pradesh)

VARADA PRAKASHAN PVT. LTD.
397/1, S. Bapat Rd., Traffic Signal Sq., Pune-411006 (Maharashtra)
✆ (O) 25651877 (R) 25655654
Estd.: 1998; **Bus.Intt.:** Pub.; **Spl.:** Gen. Books

VARANASI PUSTAK VYAVASAYEE PARISHAT
C/o Gupta Gen. Trading Co., Kamaghanta, Bulanala, Varanasi-222010 (Uttar Pradesh)

VARDHMAN BOOKS
C-1/146, Yamuna Vihar, Delhi-110053
▮ (O) 9811287652 (R) 32367515
✉ vardhmanbooks@indiatimes.com
Estd.: 2003; **Prop.:** Gaurav Jain; **Bus.Intt.:** B.S., L.S.; **Spl.:** Humanities & Soc. Sci., Tech., Med., Mang.

VARDHMAN PUBLICATIONS
139-C, DDA Flats, Jhilmil Colony, Delhi-110095
✆ 22141122, 35201206
✉ vardhmanmaps@yahoo.com
Hd.Org.: Pramod K. Jain; **Bus.Intt.:** Pub.; **Spl.:** Road Atlases, Tourist Guides and also Books for Children and Neo-Literatures

VARIETY BOOK HOUSE
35, New Market, T.T. Nagar, Bhopal (Madhya Pradesh)
✆ 0755-2554057
Estd.: 1980; **Hd.Org.:** S.P. Wadhwa; **Bus.Intt.:** Rt. and L.S.; **Spl.:** Gen., Trade and Children Books (Indian and Foreign Books)

VARIETY BOOK STORE
S.C.O. No. 69, Sector-17-D, Chandigarh-160017

© 2702241, Fax: 0172-2710894
vbs_69@yahoo.com
Estd.: 1949; **Hd.Org.**: Ratan Lal, Mohinder Paul, Pankaj; **Bus.Intt.**: B.S., L.S., Rt.;
Spl.: Children Gen. and Ref. Books on all Sub. in English and Hindi (Indian and Foreign)

VARMA BOOK DISTRIBUTORS
649, Narayan Peth, Appa Balwant Chowk, Pune-411030 (Maharashtra)
© 24450595, 24456525, Fax: 24450148
guest@biointu.ernet.in, varma@vsnl.com
Estd.: 1983; **Hd.Org.**: Sudha Vishwanth Joshi, R.V. Joshi; **Bus.Intt.**: Dist., L.S. B.S.

VARSHA BOOK DISTRIBUTORS
3-6-584/2B, St. No. 8, Himayatnagar, Hyderabad-500029 (Andhra Pradesh)
© 27632126
varshabooks@usa.net
Estd.: 1993; **Prop.**: P. Dwaraka Nath;
Bus.Intt.: L.S.; **Spl.**: Soc.Sci., Sci. and Tech.

VARSHNEY PRAKASHAN
250/21, Sant Tukaram Rd., Mumbai-400009 (Maharashtra)
© 23430355/0443/4718
Estd.: 1977; **Hd.Org.**: Chandra Pal Gupta;
Bus.Intt.: Rt., Pub.

VARTAMAN PRAKASHAN
22/83, West Patel Nagar, New Delhi-110008
Hd.Org.: Amarjit Singh

VARTIKA PRAKASHAN
W-127-A, Greater Kailash-I, New Delhi-110048
© 29230181
anil@bol.net.in
Hd.Org.: Amarnath; **Bus.Intt.**: Pub. and B.S.;
Spl.: Children's Litt. and Gen. Books in Hindi

VARUN BOOKS INTERNATIONAL
4831/24, Prahalad St., Ansari Rd., Darya Ganj, New Delhi-110002
© 23250586, 23255747, 55390704
9811220876, Telefax: 23279603
varunbooks@rediffmail.com, varunbooks@yahoo.co.in
Estd.: 1997; **Prop.**: Manish Sabharwal;
Bus.Intt.: WS to the Trade; **Spl.**: Beh.Sci., Comp., Soc.Sci., Mang. Sci., Pure & Applied Tech., Encyclopedias & Dictionaries

VARUN EXPORTS
4819/XI, Prahlad Street, 24 Ansari Road, Darya Ganj, New Delhi-110002
© 23289259, 23271632, 23286096, Fax: 91-11-23286096
varunex@vsnl.net
www.cbspd.com
Hd.Org.: Seema Jain; **Bus.Intt.**: Exp.;
Spl.: Med., Engg., Sci. and Tech., Gen., Art and Agri., Mang., Comp., Life Sci., Food Sci., Maths.

VARUN TOYS
182, Rehmat Ali Ka Ahatha, Ghaziabad (Uttar Pradesh)
© 95-120-2735398
Bus.Intt.: Dist.; **Spl.**: Educational Toys

VASAN BOOK COMPANY
4637/20, F-12, Hari Sadan, Ansari Road, Darya Ganj, Opp. Fire Station, New Delhi-110002
© 23245666, 23283078, Fax: 91-11-41563666
info@harisai.com, vasan@harisai.com
www.harisai.com
Showroom: Harisai, LG-31, Parsvnath City Centre Mall, Sector-12, Faridabad (Haryana)
© 91-11-0129-4011566, 2299633
info@harisai.com
Hd.Org.: Pritam Singh; **Bus.Intt.**: Dist.;
Spl.: Maps as well as Books and CDs for Children

VASAN BOOK DEPOT
Vinayaka Towers, 1st Cross, Gandhi Nagar, Bangalore-560009 (Karnataka)
© 6705679, 2264709, Fax: 6705107
vasanbks@bgl.vsnl.net.in
Estd.: 1981; **Bus.Intt.**: Rt., WS, Pub.;
Spl.: Cookery and Gen. Books

VASAN PUBLICATIONS
No. 25, Vasan Towers, Dr. T.C.M. Royan Rd., (Goods Shed Road), Bangalore-560053 (Karnataka)
© 26705679, 26705107, Fax: 080-26705107
info@mastermindbooks.com
www.mastermindbooks.com
Estd.: 1981; **Hd.Org.**: K.T. Raghunathan;
Bus.Intt.: Pub. & Dist.; **Spl.**: Children's Books, Tourist Maps and Guides, etc.

VASANTHA BOOK STALL
Kollam (Kerala)
© 2748572, Fax: 2743311
vasanthabooks@rediffmail.com

VASANTHA PATHIPPAGAM
Plot No. 9, Door No. 26, Joseph Colony, Adambakkam, Chennai-600088 (Tamil Nadu)
© 22530954, 22533667
Estd.: 1968; **Man.Dir.**: Dr. Alandur KO. Moganarangan; **Bus.Intt.**: Pub.;
Spl.: Books for Children, Litt. in Tamil

VASHA BHAVAN
Halan Ganj, Mathura-281001 (Uttar Pradesh)
© 2406633, 2409226
Hd.Org.: K.L. Goyal

VASUNDHARA PRAKASHAN
Palika Bazar, Near Relief Cinema, Salapas Rd., Ahmedabad-380001 (Gujarat)

VASUNDHARA PRAKASHAN PVT. LTD.
602, Gateway Plaza, Hiranandani Gardens, Powai, Mumbai-400076 (Maharashtra)
✆ 56960587, 25705857, Fax: 25705291
envirotekindia@vsnl.net
www.vasundharabooks.com
Hd.Org.: Sudha Arora; **Bus.Intt.:** Pub. and Dist.; **Spl.:** Indian Litt. in various Indian Languages

VASUNDHARA PUBLICATIONS
Eonadu Compound, Somajiguda, Hyderabad-500482 (Andhra Pradesh)

VATAYAN PRAKASHAN
73, Banarsidass State, Timarpur, Lucknow Rd., Delhi-110007
✆ 22928085
Hd.Org.: Smt. Bala Sharma

VATSAL PRAKASHAN
Near Blind School, Bikaner-334003 (Rajasthan)
✆ 91-151-2206452
vagdevibooks@gmail.com
Hd.Org.: D.C. Sankhla; **Bus.Intt.:** Pub.; **Spl.:** Adolescents and Children's books in Hindi and English

VAYU BOOK SHOPPING.COM
2/25, Ansari Raod, Darya Ganj, New Delhi-110002
✆ 65235268, Fax: 91-11-41564445
vayubookshopping@yahoo.com
Hd.Org.: Rajiv Kumar Jain; **Bus.Intt.:** Pub. & L.S.; **Spl.:** Books on Med., Engg., Law, Soc.Sci., Mang., Bio-Sci. and General Books

VED PUSHAP PUBLISHER
14-C Extension, Gandhi Nagar, Jammu (Jammu & Kashmir) **Hd.Org.:** Ved Prakash

VEDA-SANSTHANA
C-22, Rajouri Garden, New Delhi-110027
✆ 25102316
vedic_science@yahoo.co.in
www.veda-sansthan.org
Hd.Org.: Abhaydev Sharma; **Bus.Intt.:** Pub.; **Spl.:** Books in Hindi on *Vedas*, *Samhitas*, Sanskrit Language and Spirituality and allied subjects

VEDANTA PUBLICATIONS
No. 11, South Mada St., Srinagar Colony, Saidapet, Chennai-600015 (Tamil Nadu)

VEDARASA PRAKASHANA
Railway Station Rd., Kasaragode-560021 (Karnataka)
Hd.Org.: H.J. Bolegaonkar; **Bus.Intt.:** Pub.; **Spl.:** Poems in Kannada

VEDIC ANUSANDHAN SAMITI
11-E-31, Lajpat Nagar, New Delhi-110024

VEDMATA GAYATRI TRUST
Shanti Kunj, Haridwar-249411 (Uttarakhand)
✆ 0133-2424309, 2426403, Fax: 2423866
Estd.: 1929; **Spl.:** Books on Yoga, Spiritual Sci. by Pandit Shriram Sharma Acharya in Hindi only

VEDPAL LAW HOUSE
27, M.G. Rd., Rampurawal Building, Indore-452007 (Madhya Pradesh)
✆ 2543493 ▮ 9622580453
Estd.: 1975; **Hd.Org.:** Vedpal Wadhwa, Sanjay Wadhwa; **Bus.Intt.:** Pub. and Dist. and L.S.; **Spl.:** Law Books only

VEE KUMAR PUBLICATIONS PVT. LTD.
507, Vikram Tower, Rajendra Place, New Delhi-110008
✆ 25720718, 25760718, Fax: 25711718
kumarpublications@rediffmail.com
Hd.Org.: V. Kumar; **Bus.Intt.:** Pub.; **Spl.:** Career Guides, Gen. and Children's books

VEENA BOOK CENTRE
426, 2nd Floor, Alankar Pearl Plaza, Kempegowda Rd., Bangalore-560009 (Karnataka)
✆ 23469183, 2876706, 2265077, Fax: 23469359, 2261132
vbc@bgl.vsnl.net.in
Estd.: 1979; **Bus.Intt.:** L.S. & Rt., Imp., Sub.Ag.; **Spl.:** Sci. & Tech., Med.

VEENA PUSTAK BHANDAR
Devkund, Aurangabad-824202 (Bihar)
Bus.Intt.: Pub. & B.S.

VEENA PUSTAK BHANDAR
Babhangama, Bhagalpur-813123 (Bihar)
Bus.Intt.: Pub. and B.S.

VEENA PUSTAK BHANDAR
Haspura, Aurangabad-824120 (Bihar)
Bus.Intt.: Pub. and B.S.

VEENA PUSTAK BHAWAN
Khazanchi Rd., Patna-800004 (Bihar)
✆ 2652023, 2653122, 2654648
Estd.: 1959; **Hd.Org.:** Rajesh Mishra

VENDRAME INSTITUTE PUBLICATIONS
Sacred Heart College, Shillong-793008 (Meghalaya)
✆ (O) 0364-2250141 (R) 2250577
mathias@sancharnet.in
Estd.: 1976; **Bus.Intt.:** Pub. and B.S.; **Spl.:** Rel., Culture Books

VENUS EDUCATIONAL TRADERS AND PUBLICATIONS
Gajanan Nagar, Plot No. 35, Electronic Zone, SQ. Hingna Road, Nagpur-440016
✆ 91-7104-235724
Hd.Org.: Vijay; **Bus.Intt.:** Pub. and Dist.; **Spl.:** Educational charts in Hindi and Regional Languages

VENUS ENTERPRISES
B-2/85, Ashok Vihar, Phase-II, Delhi-110052
✆ 27119367
Hd.Org.: Pyarelal Kaul, R.K. Khodhar; **Bus.Intt.:** Pub., L.S., Sub.Ag.; **Spl.:** All Govt. Publications, Retailing of Rare Books

VENUS PRAKASHAN
Tapscharya, 381C, Shaniwarpet Pune-411030 (Maharashtra)

VENUS PRESS & BOOK DEPOT
Koni, Pathanamthitta-689691 (Kerala)
✆ 2342216, 04751-216, 04751-246
Estd.: 1946; **Prop.:** Suseela Sekhar; **Bus.Intt.:** Pub. and B.S.; **Spl.:** Gen. Books

VENUS PUBLICATIONS
286, Delhi Gate Bazar, New Delhi-110002

VERMA BOOK DISTRIBUTORS
649, Narayan Peth, Pune-30 (Maharashtra)
✆ 91-020-2450595, Fax: 91-020-2450148
Estd.: 1983; **Prt.:** Ravivarma V. Joshi; **Bus.Intt.:** L.S.; **Spl.:** Humanities & Soc.Sci., Mang. & Comm., Sci.: Pure & Applied, Engg. & Tech., Journals, Magazines and Periodicals, Law, Fiction and Gen.

VERMA PUSTAK BHANDAR
Goh, Aurangabad-824203 (Bihar)
Bus.Intt.: Pub. and B.S.

VERMA PUSTAK BHANDAR
Haspura, Aurangabad-824120 (Bihar)
Bus.Intt.: Pub. and B.S.

VERMA PUSTAK BHANDAR
Tandwa, Nabinagar, Aurangabad-824302 (Bihar)
Bus.Intt.: Pub. and B.S.

VESPARTEK PUBLISHERS DISTRIBUTORS
4-A, Jessan St. (1st Floor), Off. Wood Rd., Mount Rd., Chennai-600002 (Tamil Nadu)
✆ 28540079
Hd.Org.: P.T. Kasturi Rangan

VETHA PUBLICATIONS
8, Narasimhapuram, Mylapore, Chennai-600004 (Tamil Nadu)

VIBHA BOOKS INTERNATIONAL
11-A, Hauz Rani, Ved Saini Niwas, Malviya Nagar, New Delhi-110017
9868525200
vibhabooks@hotmail.com
Hd.Org.: Ravindra K. Chauhan; **Bus.Intt.:** Dist.; **Spl.:** Books on Soc.Sci., Mang., Sci. & Tech., and Comp.Sci.

VIBHA PRAKASHAN
50, Chachand, Allahabad-211003 (Uttar Pradesh)
Hd.Org.: Jagdish Prasad Agrawal

VIBHA PRAKASHAN HOUSE
986, Kalyani Devi, Allahabad-211003 (Uttar Pradesh)
Hd.Org.: Ramprakash Agarwal

VICTORY BOOK HOUSE
Muvattupuzha-686661 (Kerala)
✆ 232943
Estd.: 1979; **Prop.:** K.J. Cherian; **Bus.Intt.:** Pub. and B.S.

VICTORY GRAPHIK
H.No. 5-3-654/1/A, Topkhana Road, Adj. Lane to Begam Bazar Police Station, Hyderabad-500012 (Andhra Pradesh)
✆ 91-40-24613753, Fax: 91-49-24613731
victorygraphik@yahoo.co.in
www.victorygraphik.com
Hd.Org.: Jitender Jain; **Bus.Intt.:** Pub.; **Spl.:** Edu. Charts in English language

VIDARBHA BOOK DISTRIBUTORS
Salpekar Building, Jhansi Rani Square, Sitabuldi, Nagpur-440012 (Maharashtra)
✆ 2524747
Estd.: 1967; **Hd.Org.:** Prabhakar Keshaorao Salpekar; **Bus.Intt.:** B.S., L.S., Dealing; **Spl.:** School Gen. Books

VIDARBHA SAMSHODHAN MANDAL
W-High Court Rd., Civil Lines, Nagpur-440001 (Maharashtra)

VIDHARBHA SAHITYA SANGH
Vani, Dist. Yawatmal (Maharashtra)

VIDHI SAHITYA PRAKASHAN
Bharatiya Vidhi Sansthan Bhavan, Bhagwan Das Rd., New Delhi-110001
✆ 23385259, Fax: 23387589
Hd.Org.: S.R. Daleta; **Bus.Intt.:** Pub. and B.S.; **Spl.:** Books and Journals on Law and Books on Central Government Rules and Regulations in Hindi

VIDHI SAHITYA PRAKASHAN
Vibhagiy Prakashan Bikri Kender, Vikas Bhawan, Secretariat, Patna-800015 (Bihar)

VIDHI SEVA
Choudhary Kuteer, E-31, Mansarovar Garden, New Delhi-110015
Hd.Org.: Pankaj Choudhary

VIDHYARAMBHAM PUBLISHERS
Mullakkal, Alappuzha-688011 (Kerala)
✆ 0477-261151, 261111, 261182, 261867
Estd.: 1915; **Prop.:** N. Chellappan Chettiar; **Bus.Intt.:** Pub.

VIDHYARATHI PRAKASHAN
K-71, Krishan Nagar, Delhi-110051
Hd.Org.: Divender Kumar Sharma

VIDYA BHARATI
40-F, Nimtala Ghat St., Kolkata-700006 (West Bengal)

VIDYA BHAWAN
Chaura Rasta, Jaipur-3 (Rajasthan)
✆ 2313972 ▮ 9828014807
Estd.: 1949; **Prop.:** N.K. Arun; **Bus.Intt.:** Pub.; **Spl.:** School and College Text Books and Gen. Books of Vastugyan, Cookery, Acupressure in Hindi and English Language

VIDYA BHAWAN
620, M.G. Rd., Khajuri Bazar, Indore-452002 (Madhya Pradesh)
✆ 2454464, 2541903
Estd.: 1960; **Hd.Org.:** Anil Agrawal, R. Agrawal; **Spl.:** Guides of College Level in all Sub. for M.P. Universities in English and Hindi

VIDYA BOOKS
C-53, New Ranjit Nagar, New Delhi-110008
✆ 25707396 ▮ 9811387853, Fax: 25707396
✉ vidyabooks97@rediffmail.com
Estd.: 1983; **Prop.:** Mrs. Shoba Nayar
Br.: 1, Padikkal House, Pallikunnu (Ambika Rd.) Kannur-670004 (Kerala)
Bus.Intt.: Pub., B.S., L.S.; **Spl.:** Humanities & Soc.Sci., Sci. & Tech., Comp., Mang., Law, Children & General

VIDYA BOOKS PUBLISHERS
Aurangpura, Aurangabad-431001 (Maharashtra)

VIDYA CHITR PRAKASHAN
4226-B/1, Ansari Rd., Darya Ganj, New Delhi-110002
✆ 23262667, 23271400, Fax: 23271400
✉ vidyachitr@indiatimes.com, vcp@vsnl.com
Hd.Org.: Subhash C. Jain; **Bus.Intt.:** Digital Cartographer, Pub., Laminator, Exp. and Printer; **Spl.:** School and Tourist Maps, Charts and Globes in Indian Languages

VIDYA MANDIR
8, Shyama Charan Dey St., Kolkata-700073 (West Bengal)
Bus.Intt.: Pub.

VIDYA MANDIR
Tiwari Bigha, Rafiganj, Aurangabad-824125 (Bihar); **Bus.Intt.:** Pub. & B.S.

VIDYA MANDIR
Centre Market, Sector-III, Bokaro Steel City, Dhanbad-827003 (Jharkhand)

VIDYA NIKETAN
Narayanpur, Bhagalpur-853203 (Bihar)
Bus.Intt.: Pub. and B.S.

VIDYA PRAKASHAN
125/64, K (NTC), Govind Lane, Kanpur-208006 (Uttar Pradesh)
Hd.Org.: Veerendra Shukla

VIDYA PRAKASHAN
Ruikar Rd., Nagpur-440002 (Maharashtra)
✆ 2760581

VIDYA PRAKASHAN HOUSE
986, Kalyani Devi, Allahabad-211003 (Uttar Pradesh)
Hd.Org.: Ramprakash Agarwal

VIDYA PRAKASHAN MANDIR
19, Swami Para, Budhana Gate, Meerut-250001 (Uttar Pradesh)
✆ (O) 2516012, 2510830 (R) 2511192, 2513783, Fax: 2512755
✉ info@vidyaprakashan.com
Estd.: 1979; **Hd.Org.:** Vinay Kumar Jain
Br.: Cuttack (Orissa) ✆ 2620637, 2617260
✉ ctk_vpuri@sancharnet.in

VIDYA PRAKASHAN MANDIR
4262/3, Ansari Rd., Darya Ganj, New Delhi-110002
✆ 23282453, 23277104
Fax: 91-11-23258737
Hd.Org.: Jagdish Kumar Shukla; **Bus.Intt.:** Pub. & B.S.; **Spl.:** Stage Plays, Fiction, Children's books in Hindi

VIDYA PRAKASHAN MANDIR LTD.
Vidya Lok, T.P. Nagar, Meerut-250002 (Uttar Pradesh)
✆ 2510830, 2513845, Fax: 2512755
✉ info@vidyaprak.com
Hd.Org.: Pradeep Kumar Jain; **Bus.Intt.:** Pub.; **Spl.:** School-level Books in English, Hindi, Punjabi, Urdu and Sanskrit

VIDYA PUSTAK BHANDAR
Baarun, Aurangabad-824112 (Bihar)
Bus.Intt.: Pub. and B.S.

VIDYA VIHAR
1660, Kucha Dakshnirai St., Darya Ganj, New Delhi-110002
✆ 23257555, Fax: 91-11-23253233
✉ prabhatbooks@id.eth.net
Estd.: 1988; **Hd.Org.:** Saroj Agarwal; **Bus.Intt.:** Pub.; **Spl.:** World Classics and Books on Health, Yoga, Library Sci. in Hindi

VIDYANIDHI
1/5971, Kabul Nagar, Shahdara, Delhi-110032
✆ 65456828
Hd.Org.: Arun Maheshwari; **Bus.Intt.:** Pub. and B.S.; **Spl.:** Hindi and English books

VIDYANIDHI PRAKASHAN
D-10/1061, (Near Sri Mahagauri Mandir), Khajuri Khas, Delhi-110094
✆ 22175638
Hd.Org.: Badri Nath Tiwari; **Bus.Intt.:** Pub. & B.S.; **Spl.:** Books on Grammar, Phil., *Vedas, Puranas* in Sanskrit

VIDYAPURI
Balu Bazar, Cuttack-753002 (Orissa)
✆ (O) 2620637 (R) 2617260
ctk-vpuri@sancharnet.in
www.vidyapuri.com
Estd.: 1961; **Hd.Org.:** Pitamber Misra; **Bus.Intt.:** Pub., B.S., L.S., WS; **Spl.:** Gen. Books in Oriya & English Languages, College Text Books on Arts, Sci. & Comm.

VIDYARAMBHAM PUBLISHERS
PB No. 4410, Mullakkal, Alappuzha-688011 (Kerala)
✆ 0477-2251259, 2261151, Fax: 2254658
vidyarambham@sancharnet.in
www.vidyarambham.net
Estd.: 1919; **Prop.:** N. Chellappan Chettiar; **Bus.Intt.:** Pub. and B.S.; **Spl.:** School, Graduate, Gen. Books, Ayurveda, Devotional, Astrology, Palmistry etc. in Malayalam only

VIDYARTHI BOOK DEPOT
Palace Rd., Radhanpur (Banaskantha), (Gujarat)

VIDYARTHI KENDRA
College Gate, Bareilly-243001 (Uttar Pradesh)

VIDYARTHI KENDRA
D-45/3, Luxa Rd., Varanasi (Uttar Pradesh)
✆ 2329888, 2320730, Fax: 2391322
vidyarti@nde_vsnl.net.in
Bus.Intt.: B.S. & Pub.

VIDYARTHI MITRAM PRESS AND BOOK DEPOT
Baker Rd., Kottayam-686001 (Kerala)
✆ (O) 0481-2563281 (R) 0481-2562616
Hd.Org.: Koshy P. John; **Bus.Intt.:** Pub. and Dist.; **Spl.:** Gen. and Edu. Books

VIDYARTHI PRAKASHAN
K-71, Krishna Nagar, Delhi-110051
✆ 22214376
Hd.Org.: Devinder Kumar Sharma

VIDYARTHI PRAKASHAN (P) LTD.
Bhagat Singh Marg, Post Box No. 161, Saharanpur-247001 (Uttar Pradesh)
✆ (O) 2726724, 2726298 (R) 2725179, 2726245, Fax: 0132-2727104
vidyarthipark@rediffmail.com
Estd.: 1985; **Hd.Org.:** Deepak Aggarwal; **Bus.Intt.:** Pub.; **Spl.:** School Textbooks and Gen. books

VIDYARTHI PUSTAK BHANDAR
Khudwan, Aurangabad-824124 (Bihar)
Bus.Intt.: Pub. and B.S.

VIDYARTHI PUSTAK BHANDAR
Akbarnagar, Bhagalpur-813223 (Bihar)
Bus.Intt.: Pub. and B.S.

VIDYARTHI PUSTAK BHANDAR
Banka, Bhagalpur-813102 (Bihar)
Bus.Intt.: Pub. and B.S.

VIDYARTHI PUSTAK BHANDAR
Nabinagar, Aurangabad-824301 (Bihar)
Bus.Intt.: Pub. and B.S.

VIDYARTHI PUSTAK BHANDAR
Baunsi, Bhagalpur-813104 (Bihar)
Bus.Intt.: Pub. and B.S.

VIDYARTHI PUSTAK BHANDAR
D.N. Singh Rd., Bhagalpur-853204 (Bihar)
Bus.Intt.: Pub. and B.S.

VIDYARTHI PUSTAK BHANDAR
Panjwara, Bhagalpur-813110 (Bihar)
Bus.Intt.: Pub. and B.S.

VIDYARTHI PUSTAK BHANDAR
Punsia, Bhagalpur-813109 (Bihar)
Bus.Intt.: Pub. and B.S.

VIDYARTHI PUSTAK BHANDAR
Shahkund, Bhagalpur-813213 (Bihar)
Bus.Intt.: Pub. and B.S.

VIDYARTHI PUSTAK BHANDAR
Belhar, Bhagalpur-813202 (Bihar)
Bus.Intt.: Pub. and B.S.

VIDYARTHI PUSTAK BHANDAR
War, Aurangabad-824103 (Bihar)
Bus.Intt.: Pub. and B.S.

VIDYARATHI PUSTAK BHANDAR
Terhi Nath Mandir Chowk, Begusarai-851101 (Bihar)
Bus.Intt.: Pub. and B.S.

VIDYARTHI PUSTAK BHANDAR
Bihat, Begusarai-851135 (Bihar)
Bus.Intt.: Pub. and B.S.

VIDYARTHI PUSTAK BHANDAR
Majhaul, Begusarai-851127 (Bihar)
Bus.Intt.: Pub. and B.S.

VIDYARTHI PUSTAK BHANDAR
Jodhadih More, Chas. Bokaro Steel City, Dhanbad-827103 (Jharkhand)

VIDYARTHI SALES AGENCIES
Shop No. 5, Hendre Mansion, Khotachiwadi, 157/159, J.S.S. Rd., Girgaon, Mumbai-400004 (Maharashtra)
✆ 23829330, 23867279, 23851416
▮ 9821770062, Fax: 23895661
✉ vidyarthi@rolta.net
Hd.Org.: Bharat Shah

VIDYASAGAR BOOK AND PAPER HOUSE
Hattola, Purulia (West Bengal)

VIDYASAGAR PUSTAK MANDIR
7B, College Row, Kolkata-700009 (West Bengal)
Hd.Org.: Sukumar Das

VIDYODAYA LIBRARY (P) LTD.
72, Mahatma Gandhi Rd., Kolkata-700009 (West Bengal)
Hd.Org.: Bankim Chattopadhyay

VIDYUT HARSHIT & CO.
Mohan Kunj, Ground Floor, 68, Jyotida Rd., Behind Gurudwara, Naigun Dadar, Mumbai-400014 (Maharashtra)
✆ 24134216, 24134450, Fax: 24131476
Estd.: 1987; **Hd.Org.:** N.L. Shah; **Bus.Intt.:** Rt.

VIGYAN BHARATI
B-78, Surya Nagar, Ghaziabad (Uttar Pradesh)
▮ 9868246202
Hd.Org.: Saurabh Sharma; **Bus.Intt.:** Pub. and Dist.; **Spl.:** Books on all subjects in Hindi

VIGYAN PRACHAR PRAKASHAN
1/41, Singh Sabha Rd., Delhi-110032

VIGYAN PRASAR
A-50, Institutional Area, NCMRWF Building Sector-62, Phase-II, Noida-201307 (Uttar Pradesh)
✆ 0120-2404430/31/35/36 (R) 26175242, Fax: 91-120-2404437
✉ vigyan@hub.nic.in
🌐 www.vigyanprasar.gov.in
Estd.: 1989; **Hd.Org.:** V.B. Kamble; **Bus.Intt.:** Pub. and Populariser; **Spl.:** Sci. through Books, Activity Kits, Posters, Charts, Audio-video Cassettes, CD-ROMs, etc.

VIJ BOOK STORE
4675-A (Back Side), 21 Ansari Road, Darya Ganj, New Delhi-110002
✆ 011-43596460, 65449971
Telefax: 011-43596460
✉ vijbooks@rediffmail.com
🌐 www.vijbooksonline.com
Estd.: 2005; **Hd.Org.:** Rohan Vij
Bus.Intt.: Pub., Dist., L.S.; **Spl.:** Defence Books, Military Studies/Hist., Fiction, Non-Fiction, Comp., Mang., Coffee Table Books, Children & General (Eng. & Hindi)

VIJAY BOOK AGENCY
Post Office Rd., Begusarai-851101 (Bihar)
Bus.Intt.: Pub. and B.S.

VIJAY BOOK SERVICE
CD-123-C Pitampura, Delhi-110034
✆ 27316172
✉ mehta-76@hotmail.com
Hd.Org.: R.K. Mehta; **Bus.Intt.:** B.S. & L.S.; **Spl.:** Govt. Publications, Gen. and Law Books, Maps and Globes

VIJAY GOEL
S-16, Naveen Shahdara, Delhi-110032
✆ 22324833, Fax: 91-11-22324833
✉ goelbooks@rediffmail.com
Hd.Org.: Vijay Goel; **Bus.Intt.:** Pub.; **Spl.:** Books to Phil., Indology, Rel. Hist. Culture, etc.

VIJAY PRAKASHAN
New Delhi
✆ 25462580, 25422580, Fax: 25422580
✉ galaxy10@vsnl.com
Bus.Intt.: Maps & Charts

VIJAY PRAKASHAN MANDIR
B-21/76, Kamasha, Varanasi-221001 (Uttar Pradesh)
Hd.Org.: Vijay Kumar Agarwal

VIJAY PUBLICATIONS
47/4, Old Rajinder Nagar, Dada Chellaram Marg, New Delhi-110060
✆ 25745433, 25737173
Hd.Org.: Mrs. Vijay Kohli; **Bus.Intt.:** Pub.; **Spl.:** Sikh Religious Books in Hindi, English and Punjabi

VIJAY PUBLISHERS
5, Gola Market, Darya Ganj, New Delhi-110002
✆ 23272402, Fax: 23288748
Hd.Org.: Vijay Raj Mittal; **Bus.Intt.:** Pub.; **Spl.** Hindi Books on Litt., and Neo-Literates and Children

VIJAY PUSTAK BHANDAR
Bakhri, Begusarai-848201 (Bihar)
Bus.Intt.: Pub. and B.S.

VIJAY PUSTAK BHANDAR
Barahat, Bhagalpur-813103 (Bihar)
Bus.Intt.: Pub. and B.S.

VIJAY STORES (AHMEDABAD)
Vijay Magazine World, 62, Kalyan Bhuvan,

2nd Floor, N.R. Rupam Cinema, Relief Rd., Ahmedabad-380001 (Gujarat)
✆ 079-25356479, 25331321
Fax: 2403492, 25356479
✉ vijay_magazine@indiatimes.com, pkamdarad1@sancharnet.in
Estd.: 1953; **Prop.**: Prakash Kamdar; **Bus.Intt.**: L.S. & Rt., Sub.Ag.; **Spl.**: Sci. & Tech., Med.

VIJAYA BOOK DEPOT
Mullakkal, Alappuzha-688011 (Kerala)
✆ 2261121
Hd.Org.: Rajendran N.C.; **Bus.Intt.**: Pub.; **Spl.**: Books in Malayalam on Astrology, Ayurveda, *Tantra*, Rel., Devotion, etc.

VIJAYA PATHIPPAGAM
P.B. No. 338, 20, Raja St., Coimbatore-641001 (Tamil Nadu)
✆ (O) 2394614 (R) 2807489
Estd.: 1977; **Bus.Intt.**: Pub. and B.S.; **Spl.**: Gen. Books

VIJAYA PRAKASHAN
118, Someshwara Complex II, Satellite Rd., Ahmedabad-380015 (Gujarat)
✆ 6924003 Fax: 26764765
✉ shevadepd@yahoo.co.uk, vijpr@yahoo.com
Estd.: 1965; **Prop.**: Pratap D. Shevade; **Bus.Intt.**: L.S. & Rt., Imp., Sub.Ag.; **Spl.**: Sci. & Tech.

VIJAYA PRAKASHAN MANDIR
B-21/76, Kamachcha, Varanasi-222003 (Uttar Pradesh)
Hd.Org.: Vijay Kumar Agarwal

VIJAYA SAHITHYA PRAKASHANA
547, 3rd Cross, Banashankari, 1st Stage, 2nd Block, Bangalore-560050 (Karnataka)
Hd.Org.: K. Vijaya; **Bus.Intt.**: Pub.; **Spl.**: Novels and Collections

VIJAYA STORES
Chennai (Tamil Nadu)
✆ 2494007, 24954932
✉ vijayastores@vsnl.net.in

VIJAYA TRADERS
8C, Pycrofts Rd., Triplicane, Chennai-600005 (Tamil Nadu)

VIJAYA VAHINI PRAKASHANA
22/A, Gramadevatha Rd. 104, Malvalli, Bangalore-560004 (Karnataka)
Hd.Org.: Shamsunder K.; **Bus.Intt.**: Pub.; **Spl.**: Fiction, Collections and Gen. Books in Kannada

VIJAYA VIHAARAM
Secunderabad (Andhra Pradesh)
✆ 27007053, Fax: 27002240
✉ vijayavihaaram@rediffmail.com
Bus.Intt.: B.S.

VIJAYAWADA BOOK FESTIVAL SOCIETY
Anjanam Buildings, CVRGM High School Campus, Gopala Reddy Rd., Governorpet, Vijayawada-520002 (Andhra Pradesh)
✆ 0866-2570843, 2573354
✉ bookfestvj@sancharnet.in
Hd.Org.: R. Ramaswamy; **Bus.Intt.**: Organiser of Book Fairs in Vijayawada

VIJAYKUMAR GOVINDRAM HASANAND
Delhi
✆ 23914945, 23977216, Fax: 23911057
✉ ajayarya@vsnl.com
Bus.Intt.: B.S. & Dist.

VIJOY BOOK HOUSE
142-B, SFS DDA Gulabi Bagh, Delhi-110007
✆ 23651219
Estd.: 1998; **Prop.**: G. Ajit Kumar; **Bus.Intt.**: L.S.

VIKALP PRAKASHAN
3314-15, Bank St., Karol Bagh, New Delhi-110005
✆ 25723321

VIKAS BOOK DISTRIBUTORS
71/3, St. No. 11, East Azad Nagar, Krishna Nagar, Delhi-110051
✆ 22098340
✉ vikas_book@yahoo.com
Hd.Org.: Vikas Sharma; **Bus.Intt.**: Dist.; **Spl.**: Children's Books as well as Edu. Charts and Maps

VIKAS BOOK HOUSE
Chathannoor, Kollam-691572 (Kerala)

VIKAS BOOKS (BOOKSELLERS)
Pacca Danga, Jammu Tawi-180001 (Jammu & Kashmir)

VIKAS BOOKS LTD.
306, II Floor, EMCA Chambers, 51, Darya Ganj, New Delhi-110002
✆ 32445202, 23287224,
Fax: 91-565-2601537
✉ atuljain@vikasbooksltd.com
www.vikasbookslimited.com
Hd.Org.: Atul Jain; **Crop.Off.**: 1/185-C, Professors Colony, Delhi Gate, Agra-282002 ▮ 9719004902
✆ 91-562-2520019, 2527465, 3290206
Fax: 91-562-2527463; **Br.**: No. 46, IInd Floor, K.H. Road, Bangalore-560027

✆ 51144625 ▮ 9844064715
• 18, Pratibha Complex, Jublee Road, Bakshipur, Gorakhpur ✆ 2337178
• 3-4-771/C, IInd Floor, Thakur Residency, Opp. C.C. Shroff Hospital, Barkatpur, Hyderabad ✆ 55685535, 32972893
• 504, M.G. Road, Opp. Kothari Market, Indore ✆ 2432479, Fax: 2548114
• 677, Bichoon Market Kishan Pole Bazar, Jaipur ✆ 2314256
• Tilak Hall Lane, Meston Road, Kanpur ✆ 2363549 ▮ 9336106323
• 129 A, Mukta Ram Babu Street, Kolkata ▮ 9331993306 ✆ 22193306
• Western Kutchery Road, Meerut ✆ 2641622
• Sagar Industries, 41/3/2, Mozes Wadi, Vadgaon Sheri, Pune ▮ 9226113414, 9373335252
• G-66-C, Amrapali Shopping Arcade, Vasant Vihar, Pokhran Road No. 2, Thane (West)-400610, Mumbai ✆ 022-32929650 ▮ 9323806004
Bus.Intt.: Pub. and Dist.; **Spl.:** Dealer in Books for Children

VIKAS LAW HOUSE
712, Church Rd., Jwala Nagar, Shahdara, Delhi-110032
✆ 22410091, 22230491
✉ vikas_law@rediffmail.com
Estd.: 1993; **Prop.:** Vikas Gupta; **Bus.Intt.:** Rt., L.S.; **Spl.:** Tech., Med. & Law Books

VIKAS PAPERBACKS
IX/221 Main Road, Gandhi Nagar, Delhi-110031
✆ 32932084, Fax: 91-11-23281244
✉ vikaspaperbacks@yahoo.com
Hd.Org.: Kiran Sharma; **Bus.Intt.:** Pub. and Dist.; **Spl.:** Children's Books including Stories, Poetry, Fiction and Plays

VIKAS PRAKASHAN
(A Division of Navneet Publications), Navneet Bhavan, Bhavani Shanker Rd., Dadar, Mumbai-400028 (Maharashtra)

VIKAS PRAKASHAN
4064, Nai Sarak, Delhi-110006
✆ 22919027
Spl.: Hindi, Map Books, Social Study

VIKAS PRAKASHAN
Rambagh Rd., Ganeshpeth, Nagpur-18 (Maharashtra)
✆ 2724411, 2721461

VIKAS PRAKASHAN
127/145, W-1, Saket Nagar, Kanpur-208006 (Uttar Pradesh)
Hd.Org.: Keshav Kumar Vajpayee

VIKAS PUBLISHING HOUSE PVT. LTD.
First and Second Floor, A-22, Sector-4, Noida-201301 (Uttar Pradesh)
✆ 0120-4078900, Fax: 0120-4078999
✉ helpline@vikaspublishing.com
Estd.: 1969; **Hd.Org.:** C.M. Chawla
Regd.Off.: 576, Masjid Road, Jangpura, New Delhi-110014 **Br.:** First Floor, N.S. Bhawan, 4th Cross, 4th Main, Gandhi Nagar, Bangalore-560009
✆ 22204639, Fax: 080-22281254
• Damodhar Centre, New No. 62, Old No. 59, Nelson Manickam Road, Aminjikarai, Chennai-600029
✆ 044-23744547, 23743891
• 35, Palm Avenue, Kolkata-700019
✆ 22833494, Fax: 033-22817049
• F-16 & F-20, Nand Dham Industrial Estate, Marol, Andheri (East), Mumbai-400059
✆ 29204345, 29202324, 29201931, Fax: 022-29201931; **Bus.Intt.:** Pub.; **Spl.:** Edu., Acad. and Professional Textbooks on Mang., Comm., Engg. and Comp.

VIKAS VARTUL TRUST
Above Dr. Dhanak's Dispensary, Pirchhalla Sheri, Bhavnagar-364001 (Gujarat)

VIKHYAT BOOK DEPOT
192-A, Sarat Bose Rd., Kolkata-700029 (West Bengal)
✆ 2265169

VIKMANS MULTIMEDIA (INDIA) PVT. LTD.
104, Red Rose Building, 50, Nehru Place, New Delhi-110019
✆ 26429547, 26212325, Fax: 11-26429547
✉ skaur@del12.net.in
www.vikmans.com
Hd.Org.: Manish Chhabra, Surinder Kaur Bhutani, **Bus.Intt.:** Wholesellers, Rt. and Pub.

VIKRAM BOOK DEPOT
111-A/410, Ashok Nagar, Kanpur-208112 (Uttar Pradesh)

VIKRAM BOOK LINKS
Kothuri Srirama Murthy St., Durga Agraharam, Vijayawada-520002 (Andhra Pradesh)
✆ 0866-2432515, 2434326
Estd.: 1979; **Prop.:** R. Ramaswamy; **Bus.Intt.:** Pub. and Dist.

VIKRAM PRAKASHAN
E-11/5, Krishan Nagar, Delhi-110051
✆ 22244275
Hd.Org.: Pankaj Diwedi; **Bus.Intt.:** B.S. & Pub.

VIKRAM PUBLISHERS
P.B. No. 454, K.S. Murthy St.,

Durga Agraharam, Vijayawada-520002 (Andhra Pradesh)
✆ 0866-2435137, 2434819
Estd.: 1974; **Prop.:** G. Narayana Rao;
Bus.Intt.: Pub.

VIKRAMSHILA PUSTAK BHANDAR
Kahalgaon (Colgong), Bhagalpur-813203 (Bihar)
Bus.Intt.: Pub. and B.S.

VIKRAV BOOK DISTRIBUTOR
House No. 123, Block CPA, New Seelampur, Delhi-110053 ✆ (O) 22187607 (R) 22915762
Estd.: 2000; **Prop.:** Vikas Agarwal;
Bus.Intt.: B.S., L.S.; **Spl.:** Humanities & Sco. Sci., Tech., Med., Mang. and Gen. books

VIMAL PRAKASHAN
Manorima House, Rd. No. 10H, Rajendra Nagar, Patna-800016 (Bihar)
Bus.Intt.: Pub. and B.S.

VIMALA BOOK CENTRE
Amalapuri, Kozhikode-673001 (Kerala)
Estd.: 1970; **Prop.:** Joseph Muklel CMI;
Bus.Intt.: B.S.

VINAKA BOOK CENTRE
Obra, Aurangabad-824124 (Bihar)
Bus.Intt.: Pub. and B.S.

VINAYAKA AGENCIES
Bangalore (Karnataka)
✆ 23307022, 23303142, Fax: 23381559
✉ kpn_pacemaker@usa.net
Bus.Intt.: B.S.

VINAYAKA BOOK DISTRIBUTORS
13-K, Kamaraj Rd., Bangalore-560042 (Karnataka) ✆ 25589920
Estd.: 1981; **Prop.:** K.G. Nayak; **Bus.Intt.:** WS; **Spl.:** Fiction, Non-Fiction, Furnitures, Cookery, Fashion, Children and Gen. Books

VINAYAKA BOOK STALL
Pazhavangadi Fort, Thiruvananthapuram-695023 (Kerala)
✆ 274358; **Estd.:** 1960; **Hd.Org.:** Sankara Raman; **Bus.Intt.:** B.S.

VINE PRESS
9/2-B, Hayes Rd., Bangalore-560025 (Karnataka)

VINOD BOOK DEPOT
Post Box No. 130, Pacca Danga, Jammu Tawi-180001 (Jammu & Kashmir)
✆ 248909, Fax: 247885
Estd.: 1960; **Hd.Org.:** P.L. Gupta;
Bus.Intt.: Pub., L.S. and Rt., Exp., Sub.Ag.

VINOD PRAKASHAN
Rajendra Market, Bank More, Dhanbad-826001 (Bihar)

VINOD PUBLISHERS & DISTRIBUTORS
Pacca Danga, Wadha Verha, Jammu (Jammu & Kashmir)
Hd.Org.: Rajiv Gupta

VINOD PUSTAK BHANDAR
Sabour, Bhagalpur-813210 (Bihar)
Bus.Intt.: Pub. and B.S.

VINOD PUSTAK BHANDAR
Rafiganj, Aurangabad-824125 (Bihar)
Bus.Intt.: Pub. and B.S.

VINOD PUSTAK MANDIR
11/6, Dr. Rangeya Raghav Marg, Agra-282002 (Uttar Pradesh)
✆ (O) 2155179, 2155187 (R) 2524532,
Fax: 0562-2519090
✉ vpm@agr.dot.net.in, vpm@sancharnet.in
Estd.: 1947; **Prt.:** Rajeev Agarwal;
Bus.Intt.: Pub., B.S., L.S., WS; **Spl.:** Gen. Books, Edu., Nursery, Psych. and Home Sci.

VINOD PUSTAKALAYA
Bhakharua More, Daudnagar, Aurangabad-824113 (Bihar)
Bus.Intt.: Pub. and B.S.

VINTAGE BOOKS
Shop No. 4, 30, Hauz Khas Village, First Floor, New Delhi-110016
✆ 26867595, 26567709
✉ vinbooks@bol.net.in, vintage_books@yahoo.com
Hd.Org.: Vipin Jain; **Bus.Intt.:** Dist. of Antique Books, Lithographs, Photographs, etc.

VINTAGE HERITAGE
71, New Vellala St., Kodambakkam, Chennai-600024 (Tamil Nadu)

VINTAGE MEDIA
Delhi ✆ 27241674, 27135299
✉ vinmedia@vsnl.net.in
Br.: Guwahati (Assam)
✆ 2517059, Fax: 2544791
✉ unipub@gw1.dot.net.in
Bus.Intt.: B.S.

VIPRAJARA PRAKASHANA
144, Reservoir St., Basavangudi, Bangalore-560004 (Karnataka)
Hd.Org.: Sumathi Anand Murthy;
Bus.Intt.: Pub.; **Spl.:** Fiction and Collections in Kannada

VIRENDRA BOOK DEPOT
Agnapur, Aurangabad (Bihar)
Bus.Intt.: Pub. and B.S.

VIRGO PUBLICATIONS
L-67A, Malviya Nagar, New Delhi-110017
Bus.Intt.: Pub. and Dist.

VISA PUBLICATIONS
55, Venkatanarayan Salai, T. Nagar, Chennai-600017 (Tamil Nadu)
✆ 24343207, Fax: 044-24341559
Prop.: T. Visalakshmi; **Bus.Intt.:** Pub. and B.S., WS and Rt.; **Spl.:** English and Tamil

VISALA ANDHRA PUBLISHING HOUSE
Vignana Bhavan Bank St., Hyderabad-500001 (Andhra Pradesh)
✆ 24744580, 24735905, 24602946, Fax: 91-40-24735905
✉ visalaandhraph@yahoo.com
Hd.Org.: P. Rajeswara Rao; **Bus.Intt.:** Pub., Dist. and B.S.

VISHAL BOOK CENTRE
4, Totte Lane, Kolkata-700016 (West Bengal)
✆ 033-22527816, 22523709, Fax: 033-22523564
✉ vishal@cal.vsnl.net.in
Estd.: 1985; **Prop.:** S.C. Jain; **Bus.Intt.:** WS

VISHAL PRAKASHAN MANDIR
Ashirwad Bhawan, 189 New Mohanpuri, Meerut-250001 (Uttar Pradesh)
✆ 0121-2648776, 2642596, 2519897, Fax: 91-121-2668118
✉ info@vishalprakashanmandir.com
www.vishalprakashanmandir.com
Hd.Org.: Vijay Rastogi; **Bus.Intt.:** Pub.; **Spl.:** Books to Promote Literacy and Education

VISHAL PUBLICATION CO.
Books Market, Old Railway Road, Jalandhar-144008 (Punjab)
✆ 0181-2232294, Fax: 91-181-5005403
✉ vishalpubco@rediffmail.com
Hd.Org.: Dinesh Jain; **Bus.Intt.:** Pub. and Dist.; **Spl.:** Educational Books and Arts, Sci. Engg., Mang., etc.

VISHAL PUBLICATIONS
Kailash Market, Dariyapur, Patna (Bihar)
933438683
Hd.Org.: Deepak Vishal; **Bus.Intt.:** Pub. & B.S.; **Spl.:** Books in Hindi

VISHAL PUBLISHERS
P.O. Box No. 1221, Sector 14, Panjab University Campus, Chandigarh-160014
✆ (O) 2541150 (R) 2695123
Estd.: 1999; **Prop.:** Vishal Arora
Spl.: Edu. & Gen.

VISHAL PUSTAK BHANDAR
Incorp Industrial Consultants of India, 4449, Nai Sarak (Near Roshanpura), PB No. 1764, Delhi-110006

VISHAL SAHITYA MANDIR
10-A, Gitanjali Society, Tithal Rd., Valsad (Gujarat)

VISHALANDHRA BOOK HOUSE
Karl Marx Rd., Vijayawada-520002 (Andhra Pradesh)
✆ 0866-274949, 275764
Estd.: 1966; **Bus.Intt.:** Pub.; **Spl.:** Novels, Sci. and Gen. Books in Telugu

VISHAVNATH PRAKASHAN
Navapura (Baraganesh), Varanasi-221001 (Uttar Pradesh)
Hd.Org.: Umashanker

VISHNUCHAND & SONS
5751, Jogiwara, Nai Sarak, Delhi-110006
Hd.Org.: Vishunchandra Sharma

VISHV GRANTH MALA
A-4 Eaden Road, Vrindawan Complex, Evershine City, Vasai Road, Thane-401208 (Maharashtra)
✆ 9970016684
✉ samvadindia@vsnl.net
Hd.Org.: Vikram Kumar; **Bus.Intt.:** Pub.; **Spl.:** Hindi Translation of World Lit., Biographies, Auto-Biographies, Fiction and Books on Cinema and Contemporary Hindi Lit.

VISHV VIJAY PVT. LTD.
M-12, Connaught Circus, Opp. Fire Brigade, New Delhi-110001
✆ 23321313, Fax: 51540714, 23625020
✉ mybooks@vishvbooks.com
www.vishvbooks.com
Estd.: 1940; **Man.Dir.:** Rakesh Nath
Br.: 12-B, Maharana Pratap Nagar, Zone-1, Bhopal-462001 ✆ 2573057 • 79-A, Mittal Chamber Nariman Point, Mumbai-400021 ✆ 22022409 • 14, First Floor, Cisons Complex, Montieth Rd., Chennai-600008 ✆ 28554448 • Poddar Point, Third Floor, 113, Park St., Kolkata-700016 ✆ 22298981 • 111, Ashiana Towers, Exhibition Rd., Patna-800001 ✆ 2685286 • B-93, 4, Sapru Marg, Lucknow-226001 ✆ 2218856 • 503, Narayan Chambers, Ashram Rd., Ahmedabad-380009 ✆ 2657763 • A/4, Shri Ram Industrial Estate, P.D. Ambedkar Marg, Wadala-400031 ✆ 22022409
Bus.Intt.: Pub.; **Spl.:** Hindi Language books on GK, Soc.Sci. as well as Litt.

VISHVA BHARATI RESEARCH INSTITUTE/VISHVA BHARATI BOOK AGENCY
Shanti Niketan, Professors Colony, Gyanpur, Bhadohi-221304 (Uttar Pradesh)
✆ 05414-251045, Fax: 91-5414-251045
✉ drbdvivedi@hotmail.com
Estd.: 1972; **Hd.Org.:** Dr. K.D. Dvivedi; **Bus.Intt.:** Pub. and Dist.; **Spl.:** Hindi Books on Indian and Vedic Culture and Related Litt., Sanskrit, Vedic

VISHVAS PUBLICATIONS PVT. LTD.
167, Industrial Area, Phase-II, Chandigarh
✆ 2653139, 2641778, 2385649, Fax: 2641778
✉ vishvas@glide.net.in
Hd.Org.: H.S. Sachar; **Bus.Intt.:** Pub.; **Spl.:** Textbooks, Practical Note Books and Books on Comp., English and Hindi Grammar

VISHVESHWARAN AND BOOK AGENCY
P.O. Sadhu Ashram, Hoshiarpur-146021 (Punjab)

VISHVNATH PRAKASHAN
Navpura (Badaganesh), Varanasi-221001 (Uttar Pradesh)
✆ 2331889, 2344969, 2334769
Hd.Org.: Umashanker; **Bus.Intt.:** Pub. and B.S.

VISHWA BHARATI YOGA SANSTHAN
A-138, Priyadarshini Vihar, Delhi-110092
✆ 22525818, Fax: 22547253
✉ prembhatia_vbys@yahoo.com
www.yogacareandcure.org
Hd.Org.: Acharya Prem Bhatia; **Bus.Intt.:** Pub.; **Spl.:** Yoga and Health in Hindi

VISHWA INTERNATIONAL PUBLICATIONS
H.No. 10-3/79, N.V. Layout, Gulbarga-585103 (Karnataka)

VISHWA KALYAN PRAKASHAN TRUST
Near Kambojnagar, Mehsana-384002 (Gujarat)

VISHWA PUBLISHERS & DISTRIBUTORS
Abhankar Wada, Kothari Bhavan, Jawal Mahal, Nagpur-440002 (Maharashtra)
✆ 2726592
Bus.Intt.: Pub. and Dist.; **Spl.:** Hindi and Marathi Textbooks for College and University Students

VISHWA VIDYALAYA PRAKASHAN
Ck. 56/35, Vishalakshi Building, Chowk, Varanasi-221001 (Uttar Pradesh)
✆ (O) 2413741, 2413082 (R) 2436349, 2311423, Fax: 0542-2413082
✉ sales@vvpbooks.com
www.vvpbooks.com
Estd.: 1950; **Prt.:** Anurag Modi
Br.: Manas Granthagar, 25, Ramapuri Colony Sankatmochan, Varanasi-221005
✆ 0542-2311423 ✉ vvp@vsnl.com
Bus.Intt.: Pub., L.S. & Rt.; **Spl.:** Litt., Indology, Spirituality, Hist., Journalism, and Mass Communication in Hindi and Sanskrit

VISHWAKARMA PUSTAK BHANDAR
Ismailpur, Naugachia, Bhagalpur-853204 (Bihar)
Bus.Intt.: Pub. and B.S.

VISHWANATH PRAKASHAN
Nawapura (Baraganesh), Lohatia, Varanasi-221001 (Uttar Pradesh)
✆ (O) 2441769, 2441311, 3092724 (R) 3092724, Fax: 2441311
Estd.: 1962; **Prop.:** Uma Shankar Singh; **Bus.Intt.:** Pub.; **Spl.:** Children & General

VISHWANATH PUSTAK BHANDAR
Naugacha, Bhagalpur-853204 (Bihar)
Bus.Intt.: Pub. and B.S.

VISHWANATH PUSTAK BHANDAR
Punsia, Bhagalpur-813109 (Bihar)
Bus.Intt.: Pub. and B.S.

VISHWANI PUBLICATIONS
830, Sadashiv Peth, Chitrashala Chowk, Pune-411030 (Maharashtra)
Bus.Intt.: Pub. and B.S.

VISION BOOKS
1590, Madarsa Rd., Kashmere Gate, Delhi-110006
✆ 23867791
Hd.Org.: Vishwanath, Meera Johri; **Bus.Intt.:** Pub.; **Spl.:** Books for Children in Hindi

VISION BOOKS PVT. LTD.
5A/8, Ansari Road, First Floor, Darya Ganj, New Delhi-110002
✆ (O) 23278877 (R) 23972062, Fax: 91-11-23278879
✉ mail@orientpaperbacks
www.visionbooksindia.com
Estd.: 1977; **Hd.Org.:** Sudhir Malhotra; **Bus.Intt.:** Pub. and Dist.; **Spl.:** Books on Business Mang., Quality, Mkt., Finance, etc. in English

VISION WORLD WIDE
New Delhi
✆ 25767207, 25729468, Fax: 25767205
✉ gbajaj@hotmail.com
Bus.Intt.: B.S. and Dist.

VISISHTADVAITA PRACHARINI SABHA
Sri Desika Vidya Bhavanam, 27, Venkatesa Agraharam, Mylapore, Chennai-600004 (Tamil Nadu)

VISTA INTERNATIONAL PUBLISHING HOUSE
V-196, Near Shiv Sadhana Mandir, C-11, Yamuna Vihar, Delhi-110053
✆ 22921212, 65126093
✉ viph-vista@hotmail.com
Hd.Org.: Satya Vir Sharma; **Bus.Intt.:** Pub.; **Spl.:** Books on Edu., Pol.Sci., Women and Child Studies, Rel., Sol., etc.

VISTAAR PUBLICATIONS
M-32, Greater Kailash, Market Part-I,
New Delhi-110048
Bus.Intt.: Pub. and Dist.

VISVABHARATI
6, Acharya Jagadish Bose Rd.,
Kolkata-700017 (West Bengal)
✆ 033-22479868/69
Bus.Intt.: Pub.

VISWA VIJAY PRAKASHAN (P) LTD.
M-12, Connaught Circus,
New Delhi-110001
✆ 23321313
Hd.Org.: Rakesh Nath

VISWAKOS PARISHAD
73A, Amherst Row, Kolkata-700017
(West Bengal)
✆ (R) 033-23509670
Estd.: 1987; **Hd.Org.:** Dilip Kumar Sinha; **Bus.Intt.:** Pub.; **Spl.:** Encyclopaedia, Anthologies of Articles on Different Topics Biographies and Translation works in Bengali and English

VISWANATH PRAKASHAN
K-57/177A, Navapura-Badaganesh,
Varanasi-221001 (Uttar Pradesh)
Hd.Org.: Umashankar Simha

VITASTA PUBLISHING PRIVATE LIMITED
2/15, Ansari Road, Daryaganj,
New Delhi-110002
✆ 23283024, Fax: 91-11-23263522
✉ renu@vitastapublishing.com
www.vitastapublishing.com
Estd.: 2004; **Hd.Org.:** Renu Kaul Verma; **Bus.Intt.:** Pub.; **Spl.:** Books with Specialisation in Sci. & Tech., Health Sci. as well as Soc.Sci.

VITHAYATHIL PUBLICATIONS
Broadway, Ernakulam, Kochi-682031
(Kerala)
✆ (R) 2364642, Fax: 91-484-2361309
Estd.: 1987; **Prop.:** Paul Vithayathil; **Bus.Intt.:** Pub., Dist., Exp.

VITHI CHETAN
Raj Vilas, Rathkhana, Bikaner-334001
(Rajasthan)

VITTAL PRAKASHAN
1457, Shukrawar Peth, Bhau Maharaja Bol,
Pune-411002 (Maharashtra)
✆ 0212-24541515, 2451833
Estd.: 1990; **Hd.Org.:** Vitthal R. Patil; **Bus.Intt.:** Dealer; **Spl.:** Marathi Books or Children's

VIVA BOOKS PVT. LTD./VIVA MARKETING
4737/23, Ansari Rd., Darya Ganj,
New Delhi-110002
✆ 42242200, 42242214,
Fax: 91-11-23267224
✉ viva@mantraonline.com,
viva@vivagroupindia.net,
vivamarketing@vivagroupindia.net
www.vivagroupindia.com
Estd.: 1991; **Man.Dir.:** Vinod Vasishtha
Br.: 7, Sovereign Park Apartments, 56-58 K.R. Road, Basavanagudi, Bangalore-560004 (Karnataka) ✆ 26607409, Fax: 26607410
✉ vivabangalore@vivagroupindia.net
• Jamals Fazal Chambers, 26 Greams Road, Chennai-600006 (Tamil Nadu)
✆ 28290304, 28294241, Fax: 28292993
✉ vivachennai@vivagroupindia.net
• 101 & 102 , 3-4-637 to 641, Moghal Marc Apartments, Narayanguda, Hyderabad (Andhra Pradesh)
✆ 27564481, Telefax: 27564482
✉ vivahyderabad@vivagroupindia.net
• B-103, Jindal Towers, 21/1A/3 Darga Road, Kolkata-700017 (West Bengal)
✆ 22816713, Telefax: 22836381
✉ vivakolkata@vivagroupindia.net
• Plot No 76, Service Industries, Sector 1, Nerul, Navi Mumbai-400706 (Maharashtra)
✆ 27721273, 27721274
✉ vivamumbai@vivagroupindia.net
• Viva Books Inc, 11169 Maryland Manor Ct., Germantown, MD 20876, USA
✆ 3015281136 ✉ info@vivabooksus.com
Bus.Intt.: Pub., WS, L.S. & Rt., Imp., Exp.; **Spl.:** Humanities & Soc.Sci., Sci. & Tech., Juvenile/Children, Med., Law, Mang., Gen. & Fiction etc.

VIVA PRAKASHAN
50, Chachand, Allahabad-211003
(Uttar Pradesh)
✆ (O) 2402072, 2400787 (R) 2622711
Hd.Org.: Viva Agarwal; **Bus.Intt.:** B.S. and Dist.

VIVEK PRAKASHAN
7-UA, Jawahar Nagar, Delhi-110007
✆ (O) 23854014, 23944465 (R) 26948198, 27651104, Fax: 23944014
✉ vivek.prakashan@rediffmail.com
Estd.: 1980; **Hd.Org.:** Asha Rani; **Bus.Intt.:** Pub. and Dist.; **Spl.:** Text and Reference Books on Sol., Pol.Sci., Eco., Hist., and Anthropology in Hindi

VIVEK PUBLISHERS
285, Ram Nagar, Ambala City-134002
(Haryana)

VIVEK PUBLISHING HOUSE
Dhamani Market, Chaura Rasta,
Jaipur-302003 (Rajasthan)
✆ 2314214
Hd.Org.: N.K. Bahri; **Bus.Intt.:** B.S. and Dist.

VIVEKA PUBLICATIONS
3/39, Samad Rd., Aligarh-202001
(Uttar Pradesh) ✆ 2505581
Estd.: 1974; **Bus.Intt.:** Pub. and B.S.; **Spl.:** Humanities and Gen. Books

VIVEKANAND NIDHI
149/1E, Rashbehari Avenue, Kolkata-700014
(West Bengal)

VIVEKANAND YOGASHRAM
Patparganj Rd., Khureji, Delhi-110051
✆ 22502142, Fax: 22424057
healing@bol.net.in
www.mudrasforhealing.com
Hd.Org.: Acharya Keshav Dev;
Bus.Intt.: Pub.; **Spl.:** Yoga, Astrology and the Occult Sci.

VIVIDH BHARATI PRAKASHAN
Near Kali Bari, 131-A/1,
Rajrooppur, Allahabad-211011
(Uttar Pradesh)
✆ (O) & (R) 2430437
Estd.: 1962; **Hd.Org.:** Radheshyam Agarwal; **Bus.Intt.:** Pub.; **Spl.:** Vedic and Tantra-Mantra Litt. and Gen. Books

VIVU PRAKASHAN
C-11, Shyam Enclave, Sahivabad,
Ghaziabad-201005 (Uttar Pradesh)
✆ 2868186
Hd.Org.: Vidyabhushan Bhardwaj

VIYAN PRASAR
C-24, Qutab Institutional Area,
New Delhi-110016 ✆ 26864157

VOHRA & CO. PUBLISHERS PVT. LTD.
3, Round Building, Kalbadevi Rd.,
Mumbai-400002 (Maharashtra)

VOHRA PRAKASHAN
Chaura Rasta, Jaipur-302003 (Rajasthan)
Hd.Org.: Susheela Kumar Jain

VOHRA PUBLISHERS & DISTRIBUTORS
36, M.G. Rd. (Behind Kalpana Talkies),
Civil Lines, Allahabad-211001 (Uttar Pradesh)
✆ 2607468
Hd.Org.: P.P. Vohra; **Bus.Intt.:** Pub. and B.S.

VOICE OF INDIA
2/18, Ansari Rd., New Delhi-110002

VOLUNTARY HEALTH ASSOCIATION OF INDIA
Tong Swasthya Bhawan, 40,
Institutional Area Behind Qutab Hotel,
New Delhi-110016
✆ 26518071-72, 26515018, Fax: 26853708
vhai@vsnl.com, vhai@del2.vsnl.net.in
www.vhai.org
Hd.Org.: Alok Mukhopadhyay; **Bus.Intt.:** Pub.; **Spl.:** Low-cost, Health-Care, Material for Health Edu.

VORA BOOK CENTRE
6, Princes Building, E.R. Rd., Near J.J. Hospital,
Traffic Signal, Mumbai-400003 (Maharashtra)
✆ 23754161, Fax: 23778079
Estd.: 1968; **Prop.:** Ratilal Kunverji Vora;
Spl.: All Types of Med., Dental, Pharmacy and Nursing Books

VORA MEDICAL PUBLICATIONS
6, Princess Building, E.R. Rd.,
Near J.J. Hospital Traffic Signal,
Mumbai-400003 (Maharashtra)
✆ 23754161, 23704053, Fax: 23704053
voramedpub@yahoo.co.in
Hd.Org.: Kaushik K. Gada; **Bus.Intt.:** Pub.;
Spl.: Med., Dental, Nursing

VRINDA PUBLICATIONS (P) LTD.
B-5, Ashish Complex, Opp. Ahlcon Public
School, Mayur Vihar, Phase-I, Delhi-110091
✆ 22755315-16, Fax: 22757220, 22795949
vrinda@ndf.vsnl.net.in
www.vrindaindia.com
Estd.: 1997; **Hd.Org.:** Dinesh Kant;
Bus.Intt.: Pub.; **Spl.:** Eco., Comm., Mang., Eng.Litt. and Soc.Sci.

VRISHABCHARAN JAIN & TRUST
4697/5-21, Darya Ganj, New Delhi-110002
Hd.Org.: Digdarshan Charan Jain

VRITTI STORE
Rafiganj, Aurangabad-824125 (Bihar)
Bus.Intt.: Pub. and B.S.

VRUNDAVAN BOOK HOUSE
Thalayolaparambu P.O., Kottayam-686605
(Kerala)
Estd.: 1984; **Prop.:** N. Krishnan Nair;
Bus.Intt.: B.S.

■ ■ ■

W. NEWMAN & CO. LTD.
3, Old Court House St., Kolkata-700009 (West Bengal)
✆ 22489436
Estd.: 1864; **Hd.Org.:** B.B. Patra; **Bus.Intt.:** B.S. and L.S., Rt.; **Spl.:** Acad., Children, Trade and Professional Books, Indian and Foreign

W.P. PUBLISHERS & DISTRIBUTORS PVT. LTD.
109, Second Floor, Kasturi Nagar, East of NGEF, Bangalore-560043 (Karnataka)
✆ 32721980, 5273536, 5273207, Fax: 91-80-41642688
✉ murali@wppublishers.com, mail@wpublishers.com
🌐 www.wppublishers.com
Hd.Org.: Murali Ramaswamy
Br.: Chennai (Tamil Nadu) ✆ 24328327, Fax: 24328327 ✉ wpch@satyam.net.in
Bus.Intt.: Pub. and Dist.; **Spl.:** Sci. and Tech. in English

W.R. GOYAL PUBLISHERS & DISTRIBUTORS
86, UB Jawahar Nagar, Delhi-110007
✆ 23852986, Fax: 91-11-23850961
✉ goyal@vsnl.com
🌐 www.goyalsaab.com
Hd.Org.: Ashwani Goyal; **Bus.Intt.:** Pub. and Dist.; **Spl.:** Books on Foreign Languages, Self-improvement as also Dictionaries and Reference Books

WWW.E-DIKSHA.COM
201, CRS Bhawan, 1/28, Tilak Nagar, New Delhi-110018
✆ 25912191, 25912205, Fax: 25912205
✉ uitratra@bol.net.in
Hd.Org.: Inder Ratra; **Bus.Intt.:** Pub. and Dist.; **Spl.:** Books and CD-ROMs on Sci. and Tech. in English

WWW.QUR'AN HINDI.COM
E/20, Abul Fazal Enclave, Jamia Nagar, New Delhi-110025
✆ 23276741, Fax: 91-11-23276741
Hd.Org.: Javed Iqbal; **Bus.Intt.:** Pub. and Dist.; **Spl.:** *Quran* and Books on Islam in Hindi

WADHWA & COMPANY
DD-13, Kalkaji Extn., Near Kalkaji P.O., New Delhi-110019
✆ 26482756, 26232344, Fax: 26228898
✉ wadhwa@wadhwain.com
🌐 www.wadhwain.com
Estd.: 1950; **Prt:** O.P. Wadhwa, K.K. Wadhwa, V.K. Wadhwa & S.K. Wadhwa
Br.: Mehadia Square Dhantoli, Nagpur-440012 (Maharashtra)
✆ 0712-523819, 525679
Bus.Intt.: Pub.; **Spl.:** Law

WADHWA & COMPANY
Rampurawala Building 27, M.G. Rd., Indore (Madhya Pradesh)
✆ (O) 2541868 (R) 2537519, Fax: 0731-2537519
Hd.Org.: Hans Raj Wadhwa; **Bus.Intt.:** B.S. and Pub.; **Spl.:** Law

WADHWA AND COMPANY
J-2/5, Khirki Extension, Malviya Nagar, New Delhi-110017
✆ 26285370 ▮ 9810190604
Prop.: Sanjeev Wadhwa; **Bus.Intt.:** Pub., Rt.; **Spl.:** Law

WADHWA BOOK COMPANY
H-Block, Flat No. 8, Neel Kamal Apartment, Vikaspuri, New Delhi-110018
Prop.: Sanjeev Wadhwa
Br.: 109, Sector-10, Faridabad (Haryana)
✆ (O) 91-2287731 (R) 2262063
Bus.Intt.: Pub. Rt.; **Spl.:** Law Books

WADHWA PUBLICATIONS
19/68, Punjabi Bagh, New Delhi-110026
✆ 25930562
Prt.: Mrs. Varendra Wadhwa; **Bus.Intt.:** Rt., B.S., WS, Pub., Pub.'s Rep., L.S.; **Spl.:** Acad., Beh.Sci., Soc.Sci., Comm., Sci. — Pure & Applied, Med., Chemical, Fiction, Juveniles, Rare, Journals Magazines & Law Books

WALDEN BOOKS
6-3-871, Greenlands, Begumpet, Hyderabad-500016 (Andhra Pradesh)
✆ 23313434, Fax: 23393344
✉ walden@hd1.vsnl.net.in
Estd.: 1990; **Hd.Org.:** V. Ram Prasad; **Bus.Intt.:** Rt.; **Spl.:** Gen. and Trade, Acad., Professional, Electronic Products, Greeting Cards and Toy, Stationery, Gift, Music and Children Books, Indian and Foreign Books

WARDA BOOKS
Warda, Senapati Bapat Marg, Pune-411016 (Maharashtra)
Bus.Intt.: B.S. and Pub.

WARRIERS BOOK HOUSE
Near K.S.R.T.C., Kayamkulam, Alappuzha (Kerala)
✆ 22684
Estd.: 1979; **Prop.:** K. Thrivikkrama Warrier; **Bus.Intt.:** Pub. and B.S.

WATTAN PUBLICATIONS
17, Shri Chander Chinar Complex, M.A. Rd., Opp. Govt. Women's College, Srinagar-190001 (Jammu and Kashmir)
✆ (O) 0194-2458436, 2458794 (R) 2451722
✉ wattan_publications@yahoo.com
Estd.: 1990; **Man.Dir.**: Manzoor-Ul-Haque; **Bus.Intt.**: Pub., WS, L.S. and Rt.; **Spl.**: Humanities & Soc.Sci., Sci. & Tech., Juvenile/Children, Gen. & Fiction etc.

WEBNOTIONS BOOKS INDIA PVT. LTD.
(Brand Name: a1books.co.in)
H-30, Sarita Vihar, New Delhi-110076
✆ 91-9899868109
✉ shinug@a1bookd.com
www.a1books.co.in
Hd.Org.: Shinu Gupta; **Bus.Intt.**: Dist.; **Spl.**: English languages books

WELLWISH PUBLISHERS
P/P-5, Maurya Enclave, Delhi-110034

WELLWORTH BOOKS INTERNATIONAL
106C, AG-1, Vikaspuri, New Delhi-110018
✆ 25521743, Fax: 91-11-25524078
✉ wellworthbooks@yahoo.co.in
Hd.Org.: Mukesh Sharma; **Bus.Intt.**: Pub. and Dist.; **Spl.**: Books on Art, Archaeology, Architecture, Indology, History, Culture, Management as also Dictionaries and Encyclopaedias

WEST BENGAL PUBLISHERS
4, College Row, Kolkata-700009 (West Bengal)
Bus.Intt.: B.S. and Pub.

WEST BENGAL STATE BOOK BOARD
Arya Mansion, 8th Floor, 6A, Raja Subodh Mullick Square, Kolkata-700013 (West Bengal)
✆ 22367854
Estd.: 1971; **Hd.Org.**: Gunendranath Majumdar; **Bus.Intt.**; Pub.; **Spl.**: University Level Books in Bengali on Humanities, Comm., Comp., Sci., Agri. etc.

WESTERN BOOK DEPOT
Residency Rd., Sadar, Nagpur-440001 (Maharashtra)
✆ (O) 2524659 (R) 2532544, Fax: 0712-2537896
✉ westernbookdejul@hotmail.com
Estd.: 1935; **Hd.Org.**: Vinod Nangia; **Bus.Intt.**: B.S.; **Spl.**: School, Graduate, Adv. Books for Lib. and Gen. Books

WESTERN BOOK DEPOT
Pan Bazar, Guwahati-781001 (Assam)
✆ (O) 2543228 (R) 2547016
Estd.: 1964; **Hd.Org.**: Ramesh Kumar; **Bus.Intt.**: Pub., WS, L.S. and Rt.; **Spl.**: Med., Humanities & Soc.Sci., Comp., Mang., Children and Gen. Books

WESTLAND BOOK PVT. LTD.
Bangalore (Karnataka)
✆ 26606048, 26612243
✉ ewbbir@dg1.vsnl.net.in
Hd.Org.: Hemu Ramiah
Br.: 571, Poonamalle High Rd., Aminjikarai, Chennai-600029 (Tamil Nadu)
✆ 42080417-18, Fax: 91-44-26642794
✉ ewb@airtelbroadband.in
Bus.Intt.: Pub., Dist., Imp.; **Spl.**: Foreign publishers including *Random House* and *Orion*

WESTERN GHAT PUBLICATIONS
27/3, IATM, Girinagari, Pune-411025 (Maharashtra)

WESTERN INDIA BOOK CORPORATION
Daruwala Building, Athwa Lines, Surat-395001 (Gujarat)

WESTVILLE PUBLISHING HOUSE
47, B-5, Paschim Vihar, New Delhi-110063
✆ 25284742, 25267469, Fax: 25267469
✉ westville_2002@yahoo.co.in
Estd.: 1994; **Hd.Org.**: Mrinal Goel; **Bus.Intt.**: Pub.; **Spl.**: Agri., Eco. and Mang. and L.S.

WILCO INTERNATIONAL/WILCO PUBLISHING HOUSE
33, Sri Saibaba Marg, I.T.T.S. House, Off Rampart Row, Mumbai-400001 (Maharashtra)
✆ 22842574, 22041420, Fax: 91-22-22041429
✉ wilco@bom2.vsnl.net.in, wilcos@vsnl.com, wexports@bom5.vsnl.net.in
www.wilcobooks.com
Hd.Org.: Ajai Shah; **Bus.Intt.**: Pub. and Dist.; **Spl.**: Books and Magazines including Children's books, Fiction, Interior & Graphic Design, Art & Arch., General & Reference, etc.

WILD LIFE INSTITUTE OF INDIA
New Forest, Dehradun-248006 (Uttarakhand)

WILEY-DREANTECH INDIA (P) LTD.
4435/7, Ansari Rd., Darya Ganj, New Delhi-110002
✆ 23260877, 23270877, Fax: 23275895
✉ ldgbooks@vsnl.com, wdt@vsnl.net
www.wileydreamtech.com
Ch.Exe.: Vikas Gupta; **Bus.Intt.**: Pub. & Dist.; **Spl.**: Sci. & Tech. as well as Informative Journals

WILEY INDIA (P) LTD.
4435/7, Ansari Rd., Darya Ganj, New Delhi-110002
✆ 43630000, 23260877, 23270877, Fax: 91-11-23275895

csupport@wileyindia.com, wdt@vsnl.net
www.wileyindia.com
Ch.Exe.: Vikas Gupta; **Br.:** 14, Dr. Raj Kumar Road, 4th N Block, Rajaji Nagar, Bangalore-560010
080-23132383, 9341262124, Telefax: 080-23124319
wdtblr@bgl.vsnl.net.in
• 7/2, First Floor, Chandrodhaya Co-op Housing Society, opp. Swastik Chambers, C.S.T Road Chembur, Mumbai-400071
25240934, 25240978, 9322293884. Telefax: 022-25240934
wdtmumbai@vsnl.net
Bus.Intt.: Pub. & Dist.; **Spl.:** Journals on Sci. & Tech. Medicine, Trade, Ency., Training Materials, online products and services

WINDOM PUBLISHING PVT. LTD.
A-25, 4th Floor, Nelson Chambers, 115, Nelson Manickam Rd., Chennai-600029 (Tamil Nadu)
23743062, 23745826
pkmadhu@md3.vsnl.net.in
Estd.: 1998; **Hd.Org.:** P.K. Madhavan; **Bus.Intt.:** Pub. & B.S.

WINGS PUBLICATIONS
17, Gupta Layout, South End, Basavangudi, Bangalore-560004 (Karnataka)
(O) 26637244, 2649002 (R) 26722861
wings@theoffice.net
Bus.Intt.: Pub.; **Spl.:** Ready Reconers on Insurance Industry

WINLAND BOOKS
Shop No. 331, P.H.C. Rd., Arookutty P.O., Cherthala, Alappuzha (Dist.)-688535 (Kerala)
0478-2872886 9846192611
nishadebrahim@hotmail.com
Hd.Org.: Nishad E.; **Bus.Intt.:** Dist.; **Spl.:** Law Books, Children Books, Foreign Books

WINNERZ TRACK
141-A, Pocket-A2, Mayur Vihar Phase-III, Delhi-110096
22619775
winnerztrack@gmail.com
Hd.Org.: Aarti Paul; **Bus.Intt.:** Pub.; **Spl.:** Books on Hindi Language and Literature

WINSAR PUBLISHING CO.
Off.: 56/5D, Canal Road, Shop: 4 Dispensary Road, Jakhan, Dehradun-248001 (Uttarakhand)
91-135-3294463
info@uttarakhandyearbook.com
www.uttarakhandyearbook.com
Hd.Org.: Kirti Nawani; **Bus.Intt.:** Pub. & Dist.; **Spl.:** Books on Uttarakhand's History, Literary, Geo., Env., etc.

WINSOME BOOKS INDIA
209, F-17 Harsha Complex, Subhash Chowk, Laxmi Nagar, Delhi-110092
43026937, Fax: 91-11-65845445
windsomebooks@rediffmail.com
www.windsomebooks.com
Hd.Org.: Narender Verma; **Bus.Intt.:** Pub. & Dist.; **Spl.:** Books on Buddhism, Religion and Spirituality.

WISDOM BOOKS PVT. LTD.
11/B, Earle St., Kolkata-700026 (West Bengal)
(O) 33-24764311/4313, Fax: 24764313
admin@wisdombooks.com
Estd.: 1994; **Man.Dir.:** Angelo Pugliese; **Bus.Intt.:** B.S.; **Spl.:** Sci. & Tech., Med., Humanities, Law, Gen. Books, Indological, Hist., Rel.s, Phil., Ethics, etc.

WISDOM PUBLICATIONS
24, Masih Garh (Okhla), New Delhi
Bus.Intt.: Pub. & B.S.

WISDOM PUBLICATIONS
C-14 DSIDC Work Centre, Jhilmil Colony, Delhi-110095
65289229, Fax: 91-11-22157646
wisdompublications@rediffmail.com
Hd.Org.: Pradeep Sehgal; **Bus.Intt.:** Pub. & Dist.; **Spl.:** Books on Comm., Mang., Env., etc.

WISDOM TREE
4779/23, Ansari Road, Darya Ganj, New Delhi-110002
23247966-7, Fax: 91-11-23247966
wisdomtree@vsnl.com
www.wisdomtreeindia.com
Hd.Org.: Shobit Arya; **Bus.Intt.:** Pub. & Dist.; **Spl.:** Art, Spiritualism, Self-help, Mang., Yoga, etc. in English and Hindi

WISHWA PRAKASHAN PUBLISHERS & EXPORTS LTD.
(A Unit of New Age International), 4835/24, Ansari Rd., Darya Ganj, New Delhi-110002
23288149

WITNESS BOOKS
S-1, B-17, La Campala Colony, Miramar, Panaji, Goa-403001
0832-2463050 9823026348, Fax: 2463050
witnessbooks@rediffmail.com
Estd.: 2002; **Hd.Org.:** Arun Sinha

WIZARD BOOK DISTRIBUTORS & PUBLISHERS
C-19/Z-2, Dilshad Garden, Delhi-110092
22597126 9810064598
Estd.: 1998; **Prop.:** Dinesh Kumar; **Bus.Intt.:** Rt., WS & Pub.; **Spl.:** Acad., Beh.Sci., Soc.Sci., Comm., Sci. — Pure & Applied, Med., Tech., Fiction & Law Books

WOLTERS KLUWER ACADEMIC PUBLISHERS
C-14, Qutab Institutional Area, PB No. 4612, Hauz Khas, New Delhi-110016
✆ 26520175, Fax: 26520176
✉ kluwer@nde.vsnl.net.in
Hd.Org.: Surinder Kumar Lijhara
Br.: Faridabad (Haryana)
✆ 273639
Fax: 273641
✉ kluwer@nde.vsnl.net.in
Bus.Intt.: Pub.; **Spl.:** Books and Journals on Sci. and Tech., Med., Law, etc.

WOLTERS KLUWER ACADEMIC PUBLISHERS
202, IInd Floor, Unit No. 4, Plot No. 7 & 8, Vardman Centre, Nehru Place, New Delhi-110019
✆ 46530300, Fax: 91-11-46530399
✉ vinay.singh@wolterskluwer.com
🌐 www.cchindia.co.in
Hd.Org.: M.S. Mani
Spl.: Global content Provider for Healthcare Professionals, Pharmacists, Academicians, etc.

WONDERLAND PUBLISHERS
668/4, Shree Nagar, Gali No. 2, Shakur Basti, Delhi-110034
✆ 27102745
✉ wonderlands@mantraonline.com
Estd.: 2000; **Hd.Org.:** Rajesh Bhanot;
Bus.Intt.: Pub.; **Spl.:** Books and Charts for Children in English, Hindi and Urdu

WONDERVISION
A-43, Mohan Garden, New Delhi-110059
📱 9810094519
✉ wondervision@rediffmail.com
Ch.Exe.: Mr. Jagdeep Mendiratta;
Bus.Intt.: Printing and Production;
Spl.: Meditation Frames, Cards and Books

WORDSPEAK INC.
Pooja Apartment, 4B Ansari Road, Darya Ganj, New Delhi-110002
✆ 23255799, 23287589,
Fax: 91-11-23270385
✉ aryanbooks@vsnl.com
🌐 www.aryanbooks.com
Hd.Org.: Vikas Arya
Bus.Intt.: Pub.; **Spl.:** Books on Self-help, Spirituality, Rel., Phil., Hist., and traditional wisdom

WORLD AHLUL-BAYT (A.S.)
Islamic League, Najafi House, 159, Nishanpara Rd., Mumbai-400009 (Maharashtra)

WORLD ASSEMBLY OF MUSLIM YOUTH
New Delhi
✆ 26929354, Fax: 23282834
✉ wamy@satyam.net.in
Bus.Intt.: Dist.

WORLD BOOK
Kolkata (West Bengal)
✆ 2192328
✉ worldbook@sify.com
Bus.Intt.: B.S. & Serial Pub.

WORLD BOOK ENTERPRISES
12-H, Shanti Van Marg, Opp. Traffic Kotwali, Darya Ganj, New Delhi-110002
✆ 23273025
✉ worldbook@mantraonline.com
Estd.: 1985; **Prop.:** Ramesh Kapoor;
Bus.Intt.: B.S.; **Spl.:** Graduate, Adv. Books for Lib. and Gen. Books

WORLD BOOK HOUSE
7/333A, Jawala Nagar, Shahdara, Delhi-110032
Hd.Org.: Suresh Kumar Sharma

WORLD BOOK HOUSE
Guwahati (Assam)
✉ tnsatyal@yahoo.co.in
Bus.Intt.: L.S.

WORLD BOOK INC. INDIGO
Indian Mercantile Mansions Extn., Madame Cama Road, Colaba, Mumbai-400001 (Maharashtra)
✆ 22040477
✉ indigoedu.vsnl.net
🌐 www.worldbook.com
Bus.Intt.: Pub. & Dist.; **Spl.:** Educational books in English

WORLD BOOK SERVICE
Plot No. 34, Ramanujam Nagar, P.T.C. Colony, Chennai-600041 (Tamil Nadu)

WORLD BOOK SERVICE
6, Lav Kush Bunglows, Sindhi Society, Chembur, Mumbai-400071 (Maharashtra)
✆ 25222240, Fax: 25294971
✉ hsk@giasbm01.vsnl.net.in
Estd.: 1972; **Prop.:** H.S. Khanna;
Bus.Intt.: L.S., Imp.; **Spl.:** Odd Pub.

WORLD BOOKS
322/6, Baba Lane, Durgah Mohalla, Near K.R. Puram Railway Station, Old Madras Rd., Bangalore-560016 (Karnataka)
✆ (O) 56996472 (R) 9845698062
✉ pmjoyworlds@yahoo.com.in
Estd.: 1983; **Bus.Intt.:** B.S., L.S.; **Spl.:** Sci. & Tech., Humanities & Soc.Sci., Mang., Arts & Arch., Bio.Sci., Children and Gen. books

WORLD GAMES & PUZZLES
A-6, Pandara Rd., New Delhi-110003

WORLD HEALTH ORGANIZATION
World Health House, Indraprastha Estate, Ring Rd., New Delhi-110002
✆ 23370804, 23318607, Fax: 91-11-23370809
publications@searo.who.int
www.searo.who.int/publications-sales
Hd.Org.: Samlee Plianbangchang; **Bus.Intt.**: Pub.; **Spl.**: Med. and Health Related Journals

WORLD ISLAMIC PUBLICATIONS
18, Matia Mahal, Jama Masjid, Delhi-110006
✆ 23279874
Estd.: 1975; **Hd.Org.**: Shamsur Rehman Agwani

WORLD KNOWLEDGE CENTRE
13/H/2, Raja Manindra Rd., Kolkata-700037 (West Bengal)

WORLD LITERATURE
Chugh House, Lal Bahadur Shastri Marg, P.B. No. 7305, Bhundup, Mumbai-400078 (Maharashtra)
✆ 25650606, Cable: SAHAYOG, Mumbai
Estd.: 1966; **Prop.**: T.S. Krishnan

WORLD PRESS PVT. LTD. (THE)
37A, College St., Kolkata-700073 (West Bengal)
✆ 231-1074, 231-3288
Estd.: 1947; **Hd.Org.**: S. Bhattacharjee, L.C. Bhattacharjee

WORLD SCIENTIFIC PUBLISHING CO. PTE. LTD.
No. 10, Royal Park, 34, Park Rd., Tasker Town, Bangalore-560051 (Karnataka)
✆ 22863744, 22865189, 22229351, Fax: 22863744, 23344593
wspcind@blr.vsnl.net.in
www.worldscientific.com
Hd.Org.: R. Sankaran; **Bus.Intt.**: Pub. and Dist.; **Spl.**: Sci., Tech., Med., Life Sci., Mang.

WORLD SCIENTIFIC PUBLISHING CO. PVT. LTD.
16A, South West Boag Road, T. Nagar, Chennai-600017 (Tamil Nadu)
✆ 22773551
jnangia@wspc.com
www.wspc.com
Hd.Org.: K.K. Phua
Bus.Intt.: Pub.; **Spl.**: Books and Journals on Sci. & Tech., Med. and Business

WORLD WIDE FUND FOR NATURE INDIA (WWF-INDIA) BOOK SHOP
B-172, Max Muller Marg, Lodhi Estate, New Delhi-110003
✆ 41504802, Fax: 91-11-41504779
marketing@wwfindia.net
www.wwfindia.org
Hd.Org.: Ravi Singh;
Bus.Intt.: Pub.;
Spl.: Promoter of Env. Consciousness for conservation of Wildlife. Publications include issues on Wildlife, Global Warming, etc.

WORLDVIEW PUBLICATIONS
58, U.B. Bungalow Rd., Jawahar Nagar, Delhi-110007
✆ 23918974, Fax: 23919045
worldview@vsnl.com
Hd.Org.: Sachin Rastogi; **Bus.Intt.**: Pub.; **Spl.**: Textbooks in Litt., Hist., Pol.Sci. and Eco. in English

WORLDWIDE BOOK TRADERS
H.No. 19, Gali No. 2, Radhay Puri Extension, Part-II, Delhi-110051
✆ (O) 22448456 (R) 22485269
33186318, 33189529
diwan-96@hotmail.com
Estd.: 2003; **Prop.**: Madan Singh & N. Sharma; **Bus.Intt.**: L.S.; **Spl.**: Humanities & Soc.Sci., Sci. & Tech., Comp., Mang., Children & General, Arts & Arch., Bio.Sci.

WRITERS' CO-OPERATIVE SOCIETY
H-108, Shivaji Park, New Delhi-110026
Hd.Org.: Dr. Maheep Singh

WRITERS HOUSE IMPRINT
27, Hemkunt Colony, New Delhi-110048
✆ (O) 26221584 (R) 26434018
Prop.: A.P.S. Wasu; **Bus.Intt.**: Pub. & Dist.; **Spl.**: Acad., Beh.Sci., Comm., Fiction

WRITER'S PUBLISHING HOUSE
Shop No. 5, Commercial Complex, Surendra Place, Opp. Barkatulla University, Bhopal-462026 (Madhya Pradesh)
✆ 2485444, 2481101
wphbhopal@yahoo.co.in
Estd.: 2003; **Bus.Intt.**: Pub., L.S. & Rt.; **Spl.**: Humanities & Soc.Sci., Sci. & Tech., Gen. & Fiction etc.

WRITER'S WORKSHOP
162/92, Lake Gardens, Kolkata-700045 (West Bengal)

WROX INDIA PVT. LTD.
Mumbai (Maharashtra)
✆ 28251811, 28252563, Fax: 28309533
support@wrox.co.in
Bus.Intt.: Rt. & B.S.

XACT GROUP
Modi Complex, Building No. 2,
Ashok Vihar Phase-II, Delhi-110052
✆ 91-11-27228802, 27442268,
Fax: 91-11-47091120
✉ info@xactstudio.com
www.xactstudio.com
Hd.Org.: Rahul Singhal; **Bus.Intt.:** Pub.;
Spl.: Ency., Children's books, Coffee-table Books, Pictorial Dictionaries, Activity Books and other Edu. Material in English and regional languages

Y.K. PUBLISHERS
Block-77, Opp. St. Patrick's Junior College,
Sanjay Place, Agra-282002 (Uttar Pradesh)
✆ (O) 91-562-2853506, 3121141 (R) 2211091
Estd.: 1984; **Prop.:** Y.K. Jain; **Bus.Intt.:** Pub., B.S. and Dist.; **Spl.:** Indian and Foreign Text, Gen. and Reference Books on Mang., Humanities, Sci., etc. in English

Y.R. PUBLICATIONS
7694, G.T. Rd., Delhi-110007

Y.S. SHASTRY HOROSCOPE BANK
D.No. 7-4-9, Rama Rao Peta, Kakinada East,
Godavari Distt. (Andhra Pradesh)

YADAV LAW AGENCY
S.C.O. 4-5, Sector 17-B, Chandigarh-160017
✆ 2702814
Prop.: B.R. Yadav; **Bus.Intt.:** WS, Pub. and L.S.; **Spl.:** Law Books in English

YADGAR BOOK DEPOT
Main Rd., Bhutahi, Sitamarhi-843317 (Bihar)

YAHYA BOOK DEPOT
3122, Gali Sushila, Turkman Gate,
Delhi-110006
✆ 23222128, Fax: 91-11-23237241
Hd.Org.: Rafiq Ahmad; **Bus.Intt.:** Printed and Exp.; **Spl.:** Islamic Books

YAK BOOK CHANNEL
Post Box No. 130, Pacca Danga,
Jammu Tawi-180001 (Jammu & Kashmir)
✆ 0191-248909, 2549919, 2578909,
Fax: 247885, 2547862
✉ rajiv1@nde.vsnl.net.in
Estd.: 1972; **Man.Dir.:** Rajiv K. Gupta;
Bus.Intt.: Pub., WS, L.S. & Rt., Exp., Sub.Ag.
Spl.: Humanities & Soc.Sci., Sci. & Tech., Med., Law, Juvenile/Children, Gen. & Fiction

YAQOOB BROTHERS
Kashmir University Rd., Hazratbal,
Srinagar-190006 (Jammu & Kashmir)
✆ (O) 0091-194-2425880 (R) 2421578,
Fax: 2427537
✉ yaqoob@nde.vsnl.net.in
Br.: Sudrabal University Town
✆ 2426808
Estd.: 1998; **Man.Dir.:** M. Yaqoob;
Bus.Intt.: Pub. & Dist.; **Spl.:** Books & Journals

YARLUNG PUBLICATIONS
Dolker House, D-10, Kalkaji,
New Delhi-110019

YASH PUBLISHING HOUSE
14, Pawanpuri, Bikaner (Rajasthan)
✆ 0151-2207587
✉ yash_pub@yahoo.com
Bus.Intt.: Pub.

YASHDEEP PRAKASHAN
1349 Sector-16, Faridabad-121002 (Haryana)
✆ 91-129-4074957, Fax: 91-129-4074957
✉ vikeshbeniwal@yahoo.com
Hd.Org.: Vikesh Beniwal; **Bus.Intt.:** Pub.;
Spl.: Hindi language books on various subjects

YASHOMATI PUSTAKALAYA
Pachrakhua, Sihari, Aurangabad-824115
(Bihar)
Bus.Intt.: Pub. and B.S.

YASIR GOLDEN PUBLISHING HOUSE
Near Id-Gah Rd., Doda City-182202
(Jammu and Kashmir)
Estd.: 1993; **Prop.:** Yasir Ahmed Zargar;
Bus.Intt.: Pub., L.S. and Rt.

YATAN PUBLICATIONS
208, Defence Colony, Flyover Mkt.,
New Delhi-110024

YATIN PUBLICATIONS (REGD.)
Delhi
✆ 23285501, 23260329, Fax: 23285501
✉ info@brilliantbooksindia.com
Bus.Intt.: Pub.; **Spl.:** Comp. Books

YATRA PUBLICATIONS
Kodungallur (Kerala)

YATRI PRAKASHAN
B-131, Sadatpur, Gali No. 2, Delhi-110094
✆ 91-11-22969962

Hd.Org.: Shrikant Mishra; **Bus.Intt.:** Pub. and Dist.; **Spl.:** Hindi Litt. & Soc. issues

YESHWANT RAO CHAUHAN PRATISTHAN
Plot No. 7 & 9, Gen. J. Bhosle Marg, Mumbai-400021 (Maharashtra)

YODA PRESS
G-93, Connaught Circus, New Delhi-110001
✆ 43582770, 23324096
✉ parul@yodapress.com
www.yodapress.com
Hd.Org.: Arpita Das, Parul Nayyar; **Bus.Intt.:** Pub.; **Spl.:** Dynamic non-fiction titles on gender and sexuality, urban studies and architecture, Indian history, film studies, etc.

YOGA CONSCIOUSNESS TRUST
Yoga Chaitanyaramam, Vijinigiri, Jami Mandal, Vizianagaram Distt.-535250 (Andhra Pradesh)
✆ 91-8966-278680
✉ kiranvsr@yahoo.com
www.yogachaitanya.org
Hd.Org.: P. Ravindranadh; **Bus.Intt.:** Pub.; **Spl.:** Books on Yoga, self-improvment, spirituality, etc. in English and Telugu

YOGA PUBLISHING HOUSE
264, 2nd Floor, Dayanand Vihar, Delhi-110092
✆ 91-11-22376155
✉ girikripa@vsnl.com
Estd.: 1996; **Prop.:** A.R. Balakrishanan
Head Off.: 'Girikripa', 462, Crosscut Road, Coimbatore-641012
✆ (O) 0422-2235588, 2235537 (R) 0422-5378494, 0297-537-8494
9443023633
Bus.Intt.: Pub. and Wholesaler; **Spl.:** Yoga Books, Health & Spiritual

YOGA PUBLICATIONS TRUST
Munger (Bihar)
✆ 06344-222430, Fax: 220169
✉ ypt@yogavision.net
Bus.Intt.: Pub.

YOGA SOCIETY
Ghaziabad (Uttar Pradesh)
✆ 4600237
✉ iys@ndf.vsnl.net.in **Bus.Intt.:** Pub.

YOGADA SATSANG DHYANA KENDRA
No. 6, Murari Avenue, Landers Rd., Kilpauk, Chennai-600010 (Tamil Nadu)
✆ 23362948

YOGANDER PRAKASHAN
Bhikhna Pahari, Patna-800004 (Bihar)

YOGESH PRAKASHAN
16/8, Indira Nagar, Pune-411037 (Maharashtra)
Estd.: 1992; **Prop.:** Anant M. Burte; **Bus.Intt.:** Deals in Marathi Books of Children

YOGESH PRAKASHAN
Ishipur, Barahat, Bhagalpur-813206 (Bihar)
Bus.Intt.: Pub. and B.S.

YOGI BOOK CENTRE
70/70A, Zaveri Bazar, Mumbai-400002 (Maharashtra)
✆ (O) 22053493 (R) 28017161
Bus.Intt.: B.S.; **Spl.:** Tech., Sci., Industrial and College Books

YOGIRAM PRAKASHANA
1180, 11A Cross, 9A, Main Rd., Mahalakshmipuram, Bangalore-560086 (Karnataka)
✆ 080-23323205
Hd.Org.: M.P. Ramiah; **Bus.Intt.:** Pub.; **Spl.:** Fiction, Gen. and Children's Books, Biographies in Kannada

YOGODA SATSANGA DHYANA KENDRA
Hyderabad (Andhra Pradesh)
✆ 27767261, 23358331, Fax: 23746671
✉ ipshah@nomus.net.in
Bus.Intt.: Pub.

YOGODA SATSANGA SAKHA KENDRA, DELHI
11-12, Bhai Vir Singh Marg, Near Gole Market, New Delhi-110001
✆ 91-11-23346271, 23362948, Fax: 91-11-23362948
✉ yssdelhikendra@gmail.com
Hd.Org.: G.R. Sethi; **Bus.Intt.:** Pub.; **Spl.:** Books on Yoga, Meditation and Spiritualism

YOGODA SATSANGA SOCIETY OF INDIA
Paramahansa Yoganda Pith, Ranchi-834001 (Jharkhand)
✆ 91-651-2460071
✉ info@yogoda.in
www.yssofindia.org
Hd.Org.: Smaranananda; **Bus.Intt.:** Pub.; **Spl.:** Founded by Sri Paramahansa Yogananda, the Satsanga Society is publishing his writings and teachings and also books on yoga, meditation and spiritualism.

YOGSON INTERNATIONAL
New Delhi
✆ 23541299, 23628303, Fax: 23676565
✉ scholar@vsnl.com
Bus.Intt.: Pub. & Exp.; **Spl.:** Edu.

YOUNG ANGELS
C-75, Kirti Nagar, New Delhi-110015

✆ 91-11-45044727
✉ youngangels01@gmail.com
Hd.Org.: Vani Mehra; **Bus.Intt.:** Pub.; **Spl.:** Magazine for children based on value education

YOUNG BROTHERS
100, Model Basti, Near Filmistan Cinema, New Delhi-110005
✆ (O) 23673244 (R) 23514259, Fax: 011-23673244
Estd.: 1943; **Prop.:** Naresh Kumar Aron; **Bus.Intt.:** WS, Rt., L.S., Dist.; **Spl.:** Exclusive Med. & Nursing Books Stockist

YOUNG MAN & COMPANY
888, Nai Sarak, New Delhi-110006
✆ 23263298, 23274593, Cable: ADITYAM, Delhi
Estd.: 1925; **Hd.Org.:** Rajendra Kumar Arun

YOUTH CENTRE
Municipality Chowk, Dumka-814101 (Bihar)

YUG KALYAN
Gita Press, P.O. Gita Press, Gorakhpur-273005 (Uttar Pradesh)
✆ 2333030, Fax: 91-551-2336997
✉ manager@gitapress.org
www.gitapress.org
Hd.Org.: Vishnu Prasad Chandgothia
Bus.Intt.: Pub.; **Spl.:** House Magazine of Gita Press, provides information about latest releases, price-list changes, and announcements of the Press

YUG NIRMAN YOJNA
Gayatri Tapobhumi, Jaisinghpura, Mathura-281003 (Uttar Pradesh)
✆ 2530128, Fax: 91-565-2530200
✉ ajsansthan@awgp.org
www.awgp.org
Hd.Org.: Mrityunjay Sharma
Bus.Intt.: Pub.; **Spl.:** Books on personal, family and general development, spirituality, religion, *Vedas* and *Upanishads*, history, culture, etc. in English, Hindi and regional languages

YUGAL BOOK DEPOT
Ballia, Begusarai-854208 (Bihar)
Bus.Intt.: Pub. and B.S.

YUGBODH SAHITYA
518/6B, Vishwas Nagar, Karkari Rd., Delhi-110032
✆ 22393227, Fax: 22381709
Hd.Org.: Gaurav Sharma; **Bus.Intt.:** Pub. & Dist.; **Spl.:** Children's books on Hindi Litt.

YUVA PRAKASHANI
206, Bidhan Sarani, Kolkata-700006 (West Bengal)

YUVANTAR PUBLICATIONS
PB No. 759, 64, Raja Bazar, Bangla Sahib Marg, New Delhi-110001
✆ 23365920
Hd.Org.: Usha Kiran
Bus.Intt.: Pub. and Dist.; **Spl.:** Books and Career Guides on Med., Health, Sci. and Humanities

YUVATHA BOOK HOUSE
P.O. Box 524, Kozhikode-673002 (Kerala)
✆ 76412, Fax: 77121
Hd.Org.: Aboobacker Karakkunnu
Bus.Intt.: Pub.

■ ■ ■

ZAFFAR BOOK DEPOT
Kutcherry Rd., Gaya-823001 (Bihar)

ZAKIR HUSAIN INSTITUTE FOR NON-FORMALS CONTINUING EDUCATION (DR.)
Bariley Rd., Patna-800001 (Bihar)

ZAMIER BOOKS
Hospital Rd., Mandar, Ranchi-835214 (Jharkhand)

ZAMIR KHAN & BROS.
Chowk, Faizabad (Uttar Pradesh)
✆ 225993
Estd.: 1956; **Bus.Intt.:** B.S.; **Spl.:** School, Graduate, Adv. Books for Lib., Gen. Books and Competition's Book

ZARANU PRAKASHAN
5, Adivasi Shopping Centre, Opp. Post Office, Distt. Baroda, Chhotandepur-391165 (Gujarat)

ZEALOT BOOK AGENCY
607, Ganga Jangid Complex, Mira Rd., Mumbai-401107 (Andhra Pradesh)
✆ 28118025
Hd.Org.: Avinash Balan

ZENITH GLOBAL CONSULTANT LTD.
102-C, Mittal Court, 224, Nariman Point, Mumbai-400021 (Maharashtra)
✆ 22046094-95, Fax: 22041844
zenglobe@bom3.vsnl.net.in
Hd.Org.: Hiru Bijlani; **Bus.Intt.:** Consultant; **Spl.:** Developing Business Skill and E-learning via CD-ROMs, Intranet, etc.

ZIA PUBLISHER & DISTRIBUTOR
K-119, Abul Fazl Enclave, Jamia Nagar, Okhla, New Delhi-110025
✆ 26326560
Hd.Org.: Zafar Ahmad; **Bus.Intt.:** Pub. and Dist.; **Spl.:** Books on Islam, *Holy Quran*, Islamic Hist., Law, etc.

ZILLA SAHAKARI MUDRANALAYA LTD.
Manilal Kothari Marg, Surendranagar (Gujarat)

ZOOLOGICAL SURVEY OF INDIA
234/4 A.J.C. Bose Rd., 13th Floor, Nizam Palace, Kolkata-700020 (West Bengal)
✆ 22875463, Fax: 24006893
rrr-ppozsi@yahoo.com
www.enviszsi.org
Hd.Org.: Ramakrishna; **Bus.Intt.:** Pub.; **Spl.:** Books and Research Papers on Zoology in English

ZOOLOGICAL SURVEY OF INDIA
M-Block, New Alipore, Kolkata-700053 (West Bengal)
✆ 22475463, Fax: 24008595
ratis-raj@hotmail.com, dirzsi@wb.nic.in
Ch.Exe.: Dr. J.R.B. Alfred; **Bus.Intt.:** Pub.; **Spl.:** Books and Research Reports on Zoology

ZORBA PUBLICATIONS
1620, Karimpura Bazar, Ludhiana-141008 (Punjab)
Prop.: Vipan Nayyar; **Bus.Intt.:** Pub.; **Spl.:** Osho Litt. in Punjabi

ZUBAAN
128 B, Ist Floor Shahpur Jat, New Delhi-110049
✆ 26494617, 26494618, Telefex: 26494613
zubaanwbooks@vsnl.net, zubaan@gmail.com
www.zubaanbooks.com
Estd.: 2003; **Hd.Org.:** Urvashi Butalia; **Bus.Intt.:** Pub.; **Spl.:** Soc.Sci., Humanities written on and by women

■ ■ ■